PENGUIN REFERENC

Penguin Pocke

The name *Puzzler* is synonymous with enjoyable puzzles. *Puzzler* is the oldest and best known of all puzzle magazines, and the company is renowned for its puzzle expertise. As the largest puzzle publisher in the UK, and probably the world, Puzzler Media now publishes sixty titles in more than twenty countries.

PENGUIN POCKET CROSSWORD FINISHER

PENGUIN BOOKS

PENGUIN BOOKS

Published by the Penguin Group
Penguin Books Ltd, 80 Strand, London WC2R 0RL, England
Penguin Group (USA) Inc., 375 Hudson Street, New York, New York 10014, USA
Penguin Group (Canada), 90 Eglinton Avenue East, Suite 700, Toronto,
Ontario, Canada M4P 2Y3 (a division of Pearson Penguin Canada Inc.)
Penguin Ireland, 25 St Stephen's Green, Dublin 2, Ireland (a division of Penguin Books Ltd)
Penguin Group (Australia), 250 Camberwell Road, Camberwell,
Victoria 3124, Australia (a division of Pearson Australia Group Pty Ltd)
Penguin Books India Pvt Ltd, 11 Community Centre,
Panchsheel Park, New Delhi – 110 017, India
Penguin Group (NZ), cnr Airborne and Rosedale Roads, Albany,
Auckland 1310, New Zealand (a division of Pearson New Zealand Ltd)
Penguin Books (South Africa) (Pty) Ltd, 24 Sturdee Avenue,
Rosebank, Johannesburg 2196, South Africa

Penguin Books Ltd, Registered Offices: 80 Strand, London WC2R 0RL, England

www.penguin.com

First published 2006
1

ISBN-13: 978–0–141–02074–7
ISBN-10: 0–141–02074–1

Introduction

Crosswords are great fun but, at times, can also be very frustrating. There is nothing more exasperating than being unable to finish a puzzle.

Help is at hand. *Penguin Pocket Crossword Finisher* is a reference book specially designed to bring to light any missing word when, as is usual in crossword solving, every other letter is known. The dictionary is in two sections – the first half lists words that can be completed with even letters missing; the second half has those words with odd letters missing. Both halves contain words from four to nine letters in length. So, for example, if _A_C_N (clue: Bird of prey) is the vexing word, turn to the second section, within six-letter words, and the word FALCON will soon reveal itself. Think of it not as cheating, but necessary research!

Regular solvers will know that crossword dictionaries traditionally include many thousands of words that would never appear in a published puzzle: never mind the quality, feel the width! As puzzle experts, we take a different view. This book is unusual because it focuses only on words that you can expect to find in crosswords, including common phrases and proper nouns.

PART ONE

Odd-letter Intersections

ACAS	AGED	AVID	ANON	ARVO	BODS	BRIN	BIND	BARR
ADAM	AGES	AVIS	ATOM	ANYA	BODY	BRIO	BING	BARS
AFAR	AHEM	AVIV	ATOP	ADZE	BUDD	BRIT	BINS	BART
AGAR	ALEC	AXIL	AVON	BAAL	BUDE	BAJA	BOND	BERG
AGAS	ALED	AXIS	AVOW	BEAD	BUDS	BAKE	BONE	BERT
AHAB	ALEE	AZIZ	AWOL	BEAK	BAEZ	BAKU	BONG	BIRD
AJAR	ALES	ANKA	AZOV	BEAM	BEEB	BIKE	BONN	BIRO
AJAX	ALEX	ANKH	ALPH	BEAN	BEEF	BIKO	BONO	BORE
ALAN	AMEN	AOKI	ALPS	BEAR	BEEN	BALA	BONY	BORG
ALAS	AMEX	ASKS	AMPS	BEAT	BEEP	BALD	BRNO	BORN
AMAH	ANEW	AUKS	ASPS	BEAU	BEER	BALE	BUNG	BURL
ARAB	APED	ABLE	ACRE	BIAS	BEES	BALI	BUNK	BURN
ARAL	APES	ABLY	AERO	BLAB	BEET	BALL	BUNS	BURP
ARAN	APEX	AILS	AFRO	BLAG	BIER	BALM	BYNG	BURR
ASAP	AREA	ALLY	AGRA	BLAH	BLED	BELA	BLOB	BURT
AWAY	ARES	ARLO	AIRD	BOAR	BLEU	BELL	BLOC	BURY
ABBA	AVER	AULD	AIRE	BOAS	BLEW	BELS	BLOG	BYRD
ABBE	AWED	AWLS	AIRS	BOAT	BOER	BELT	BLOT	BYRE
ALBA	AWES	AXLE	AIRY	BRAD	BRED	BILE	BLOW	BASE
AMBO	AXED	ACME	AURA	BRAE	BREE	BILK	BOOB	BASH
ASBO	AXEL	AIMS	AWRY	BRAG	BREN	BILL	BOOK	BASK
ARCH	AXES	ALMA	ALSO	BRAM	BRER	BOLD	BOOM	BASS
ARCS	AYES	ALMS	APSE	BRAN	BREW	BOLE	BOON	BAST
ACDC	ALGA	AMMO	ABTA	BRAS	BYES	BOLL	BOOP	BESS
ADDS	ARGO	ARMS	ACTS	BRAT	BIFF	BOLT	BOOR	BEST
ADDY	ACHE	ARMY	ALTO	BRAY	BUFF	BULB	BOOS	BISE
AIDA	ACHY	ACNE	ANTE	BABA	BAGS	BULK	BOOT	BOSH
AIDE	ASHE	AINT	ANTI	BABE	BEGS	BULL	BRON	BOSS
AIDS	ACID	ANNA	ANTS	BABS	BOGS	BOMB	BROS	BUSH
ALDA	ADIE	ANNE	ANTZ	BABY	BUGS	BUMF	BROW	BUSK
ALDO	ADIT	ANNO	ARTS	BIBS	BAHT	BUMP	BUOY	BUST
ANDI	AGIN	ARNE	ARTY	BOBS	BEHN	BAND	BAPS	BUSY
ANDY	AKIN	ARNO	ASTI	BACH	BEHR	BANE	BOPS	BATH
ASDA	ALIG	AUNT	AUTO	BACK	BOHT	BANG	BUPA	BATS
AUDI	AMID	ACOL	ABUT	BECK	BAIL	BANK	BARA	BATT
ABED	AMIN	AEON	ADUR	BUCK	BAIO	BANN	BARB	BETA
ABEL	AMIS	AGOG	AGUE	BADE	BAIT	BANS	BARD	BETE
ABET	ANIL	AHOY	ALUM	BEDE	BLIP	BAHT	BARE	BETH
ACED	APIA	ALOE	ALUN	BEDS	BOIL	BEND	BARI	BETS
ACER	ARIA	AMOK	AQUA	BIDE	BRIE	BENN	BARK	BITE
ACES	ARID	AMOS	ARUM	BIDS	BRIG	BENT	BARM	BITS
ADEN	ASIA	AMOY	ARUN	BODE	BRIM	BENZ	BARN	BOTH

BOTT	COAT	CAIN	CONE	CORK	CAVE	DIDO	DYKE	DONT
BUTE	COAX	CEIL	CONK	CORM	CAVY	DODD	DALE	DRNO
BUTS	CRAB	CHIC	CONS	CORN	COVE	DODO	DALI	DUNE
BUTT	CRAG	CHIN	CONY	CORR	CAWS	DUDE	DALY	DUNG
BYTE	CRAM	CHIP	CHOO	CURB	COWL	DUDS	DELI	DUNK
BAUM	CRAN	CHIT	CHOP	CURD	COWS	DEED	DELL	DUNN
BLUB	CRAW	CLIO	CHOW	CURE	DDAY	DEEK	DILL	DYNE
BLUE	CYAN	CLIP	CLOD	CURL	DEAD	DEEM	DOLE	DHOW
BLUR	CABS	COIF	CLOG	CURS	DEAF	DEEP	DOLL	DION
BOUT	COBB	COIL	CLOP	CURT	DEAL	DEER	DOLT	DIOR
BRUT	COBH	COIN	CLOT	CASE	DEAN	DEES	DULL	DOOM
BEVY	COBS	COIR	CLOY	CASH	DEAR	DIED	DULY	DOOR
BAWD	CUBA	CRIB	COOK	CASK	DHAL	DIES	DAME	DROP
BAWL	CUBE	CUJO	COOL	CASS	DIAL	DIET	DAMN	DUOS
BOWL	CUBS	CAKE	COOP	CAST	DIAZ	DOER	DAMP	DAPS
BOWS	COCA	COKE	COOS	COSH	DRAB	DOES	DAMS	DEPP
BOXY	COCK	CALF	COOT	COST	DRAG	DREW	DEMI	DIPS
BAYS	COCO	CALL	CROP	COSY	DRAM	DREY	DEMO	DOPE
BEYS	CADE	CALM	CROW	CUSH	DRAT	DUEL	DIME	DUPE
BOYD	CADI	CALX	CAPE	CUSP	DRAW	DUES	DIMS	DARA
BOYO	CADS	CELL	CAPO	CUSS	DRAY	DUET	DOME	DARE
BOYS	CEDE	CELT	CAPP	CYST	DUAL	DYED	DUMA	DARK
BRYN	CEDI	COLA	CAPS	CATE	DYAN	DYER	DUMB	DARN
BUYS	CODA	COLD	CEPS	CATO	DABS	DYES	DUMP	DART
BUZZ	CODE	COLE	COPE	CATS	DEBS	DAFT	DANA	DERG
CAAN	CODY	COLL	COPS	CCTV	DEBT	DEFT	DANE	DERN
CHAD	CAEN	COLS	COPT	CETE	DIBS	DEFY	DANI	DERV
CHAN	CHEF	COLT	COPY	CITE	DUBS	DENE	DANK	DIRE
CHAP	CHER	CULL	CUPS	CITY	DACE	DUFF	DENE	DIRK
CHAR	CHEW	CULP	CARD	COTE	DECK	DUFY	DENI	DIRT
CHAS	CHEZ	CULT	CARE	COTS	DECO	DIGS	DENS	DORA
CHAT	CLEF	CAME	CARL	CUTE	DICE	DOGE	DENT	DORM
CHAV	CLEO	CAMP	CARP	CUTS	DICK	DOGS	DENY	DORS
CHAY	COED	CAMS	CARR	CAUL	DOCK	DAHL	DINA	DORY
CIAO	CREE	COMA	CARS	CHUB	DUCE	DOHA	DINE	DURY
CLAD	CREW	COMB	CART	CHUG	DUCK	DAIL	DING	DASH
CLAM	CUED	COME	CARY	CHUM	DUCT	DAIS	DINK	DESI
CLAN	CUES	COMO	CERE	CLUB	DYCE	DOIN	DINO	DESK
CLAP	CAFE	CANE	CERT	CLUE	DYCK	DRIP	DINT	DISC
CLAW	CUFF	CANS	CIRE	COUP	DADA	DOJO	DONE	DISH
CLAY	CAGE	CANT	CORD	CRUX	DADO	DAKS	DONG	DISK
COAL	COGS	CENT	CORE	CRUZ	DADS	DUKE	DONS	DISS

DOSE	EVAN	ERIC	EIRE	FRAY	FELL	FIRE	GLAM	GOGO
DOSH	EWAN	ERIE	ERRS	FIBS	FELT	FIRM	GNAT	GAIA
DOSS	EXAM	ERIK	EURO	FOBS	FILE	FIRS	GNAW	GAIL
DUSK	EYAM	ERIN	EYRE	FACE	FILL	FORD	GOAD	GAIN
DUST	EYAS	EVIE	EZRA	FACT	FILM	FORE	GOAL	GAIT
DATA	EBBS	EVIL	EASE	FOCH	FILO	FORK	GOAT	GLIB
DATE	ELBA	EXIT	EAST	FADE	FOLD	FORM	GRAB	GOIN
DITA	ELBE	ELKE	EASY	FADS	FOLK	FORT	GRAF	GRID
DOTE	EACH	ESKY	ELSA	FIDO	FULL	FURL	GRAM	GRIM
DOTS	ETCH	EALY	ELSE	FEED	FAME	FURS	GRAN	GRIN
DUTY	EDDA	EELS	ENSA	FEEL	FUME	FURY	GRAS	GRIP
DAUB	EDDO	EHLE	ERSE	FEES	FANG	FAST	GRAY	GRIT
DOUG	EDDY	ELLA	ERST	FEET	FANS	FISH	GRAZ	GALA
DOUR	ENDS	ELLE	ESSE	FLEA	FEND	FIST	GUAM	GALE
DRUB	EDEN	ELLS	ESSO	FLED	FENG	FUSE	GABS	GALL
DRUG	EKED	ERLE	EATS	FLEE	FENN	FUSS	GABY	GALS
DRUM	EKES	ELMO	EDTV	FLEW	FENS	FATE	GIBB	GELD
DAVE	EPEE	ELMS	EFTS	FLEX	FIND	FATS	GOBI	GELS
DAVY	EVEN	EMMA	ETTA	FOES	FINE	FETA	GOBY	GELT
DEVA	EVER	EMMY	ETTY	FRED	FINN	FETE	GYBE	GILA
DIVA	EWEN	ESMA	EHUD	FREE	FINO	FITS	GADS	GILD
DIVE	EWER	EDNA	EMUS	FRET	FINS	FITZ	GODS	GILL
DOVE	EWES	ENNA	ETUI	FUEL	FOND	FAUN	GAEL	GILT
DAWN	EXES	ERNE	EMVA	FAFF	FONT	FEUD	GEEK	GOLD
DAWS	EYED	ETNA	ENVY	FIFA	FONZ	FLUE	GHEE	GOLF
DEWY	EYES	EBON	ENYA	FIFE	FUND	FLUX	GLEE	GULF
DOWD	EDGE	EBOR	FEAR	FIFI	FUNK	FOUL	GLEN	GULL
DOWN	EDGY	EGON	FEAT	FAGS	FLOE	FOUR	GMEN	GULP
DAYS	EGGS	EGOS	FIAT	FIGO	FLOG	GOER	GAME
DAZE	EIGG	EPOS	FLAB	FIGS	FLOP	GOES	GAMP
DOZE	ERGO	EROS	FLAG	FOGG	FLOW	GREG	GEMS
DOZY	ERGS	ETON	FLAK	FEHR	FOOD	GREW	GUMP
EDAM	ECHO	EYOT	FLAN	FAIL	FOOL	GREY	GUMS
EGAD	EDIE	EPPS	FLAP	FAIR	FOOT	GWEN	GYMS
EGAN	EDIT	ESPY	FLAT	FLIP	FROG	GAFF	GANG
ELAL	ELIA	EXPO	FLAW	FLIT	FROM	FIZZ	GIFT	GENE
ELAM	EMIL	EARL	FLAX	FOIL	FOPS	FUZZ	GUFF	GENN
ELAN	EMIN	EARN	FLAY	FIJI	FARE	GEAN	GAGA	GENT
ERAS	EMIR	EARP	FOAL	FUJI	FARM	GEAR	GAGE	GINA
ESAU	EMIT	EARS	FOAM	FAKE	FARO	GHAN	GAGS	GINK
ETAL	ENID	EBRO	FRAN	FALK	FARR	GHAT	GIGI	GINO
EUAN	EPIC	ECRU	FRAU	FALL	FERN	GLAD	GIGS	GINS

GONE	GETZ	HUDD	HELM	HOPS	HIVE	IBIS	JACK	JUNG
GONG	GOTH	HYDE	HELP	HYPE	HOVE	ILIE	JOCK	JUNK
GUNK	GUTS	HEED	HILL	HARD	HAWK	IRIS	JADE	JUNO
GUNN	GAUL	HEEL	HILO	HARE	HAWN	ISIS	JEDI	JAPE
GUNS	GLUE	HEEP	HILT	HARI	HAWS	IXIA	JUDD	JAPP
GYNT	GLUG	HIED	HOLD	HARK	HEWN	INKS	JUDE	JARS
GLOW	GLUM	HOED	HOLE	HARM	HEWS	INKY	JUDI	JERK
GOOD	GLUT	HOER	HOLM	HARP	HOWE	IRKS	JUDO	JURA
GOOF	GNUS	HOES	HOLT	HART	HOWL	IDLE	JUDY	JURY
GOON	GOUT	HUED	HOLY	HERA	HWYL	IDLY	JEEP	JESS
GROG	GRUB	HUES	HULA	HERB	HAZE	ILLS	JEER	JEST
GROT	GAVE	HUEY	HULK	HERD	HAZY	ISLA	JOEL	JOSE
GROW	GIVE	HAFT	HULL	HERE	IBAN	ISLE	JOEY	JOSH
GSOH	GAWK	HEFT	HAMS	HERM	IMAM	IRMA	JEFF	JOSS
GAPE	GAWP	HIFI	HEMP	HERO	IMAN	ITMA	JAGS	JUST
GAPS	GOWN	HUFF	HEMS	HERR	IMAX	INNS	JIGS	JETS
GARB	GAYE	HAGS	HOME	HERS	IOAN	IONA	JOGS	JETT
GARP	GOYA	HIGH	HUME	HIRD	IRAN	IONS	JUGS	JOTS
GARY	GUYS	HOGG	HUMP	HIRE	IRAQ	ICON	JOHN	JUTE
GERE	GWYN	HOGS	HUMS	HORN	ITAL	IDOL	JAIL	JUTS
GERI	GAZA	HUGE	HYMN	HURD	IVAN	IGOR	JAIN	JAVA
GERM	GAZE	HUGH	HANA	HURL	INCA	IPOD	JOIN	JIVE
GERT	GOZO	HUGO	HAND	HURN	INCE	IRON	JUJU	JOVE
GIRD	HEAD	HUGS	HANG	HURT	INCH	IVOR	JAKE	JAWS
GIRL	HEAL	HAHA	HANK	HASH	ITCH	IMPI	JOKE	JEWS
GIRO	HEAP	HOHO	HANS	HASP	INDY	IMPS	JILL	JOWL
GIRT	HEAR	HAIG	HENS	HESS	IBEX	ISPY	JILT	JAYS
GORE	HEAT	HAIL	HIND	HISS	ICED	INRI	JOLT	JOYS
GORY	HOAR	HAIN	HINT	HOSE	ICES	INRO	JOLY	JAZZ
GURU	HOAX	HAIR	HONE	HOST	IDEA	IPSO	JULY	KHAN
GYRE	HEBE	HEIR	HONK	HUSH	IDES	INTO	JAMB	KNAP
GASH	HOBO	HAKA	HUNG	HUSK	IKEA	IOTA	JAMS	KPAX
GASP	HOBS	HAKE	HUNK	HUSS	IKER	IOWA	JIMI	KWAI
GCSE	HUBS	HIKE	HUNT	HATE	ILEX	INXS	JOMO	KWAN
GISH	HACK	HALE	HOOD	HATS	ITEM	JEAN	JUMP	KICK
GIST	HECK	HALF	HOOF	HITE	IVER	JOAD	JANA	KIDD
GOSH	HICK	HALL	HOOK	HITS	IVES	JOAN	JANE	KIDS
GOSS	HOCK	HALO	HOOP	HUTS	IFFY	JUAN	JINK	KUDU
GUSH	HADJ	HALS	HOOT	HUTU	INFO	JABS	JINN	KYDD
GUST	HEDY	HALT	HIPS	HAUL	IAGO	JIBE	JINX	KEEL
GATE	HIDE	HELD	HOPE	HOUR	IGGY	JIBS	JONI	KEEN
GETS	HODS	HELL	HOPI	HAVE	IAIN	JOBS	JUNE	KEEP

KIEL	KERN	LOCH	LEIS	LENI	LORE	LEWD	MAID	MIND
KIEV	KERR	LOCI	LOIN	LENO	LORI	LOWE	MAIL	MINE
KLEE	KIRI	LOCK	LOIS	LENS	LORY	LOWS	MAIM	MING
KNEE	KIRK	LOCO	LUIS	LENT	LURE	LAYS	MAIN	MINI
KNEW	KURD	LUCE	LAKE	LIND	LURK	LOYD	MEIR	MINK
KOFI	KURT	LUCK	LIKE	LINE	LYRE	LAZE	MUIR	MINT
KEGS	KISS	LUCY	LUKA	LING	LASH	LAZY	MOJO	MINX
KOHL	KATE	LADD	LUKE	LINK	LASS	LIZA	MAKE	MONA
KEIR	KATH	LADE	LALA	LINO	LAST	MAAR	MIKA	MONK
KLIM	KATY	LADS	LELY	LINT	LESS	MEAD	MIKE	MONO
KNIT	KITE	LADY	LILA	LINZ	LEST	MEAL	MALE	MONS
KRIS	KITH	LEDA	LILO	LONE	LISA	MEAN	MALI	MUNG
KEKE	KITS	LIDO	LILT	LONG	LISI	MEAT	MALL	MUNI
KIKI	KITT	LIDS	LILY	LONI	LISP	MOAN	MALT	MYNA
KOKO	KIWI	LODE	LOLA	LUNA	LIST	MOAS	MELD	MOOD
KALE	KAYE	LODZ	LOLL	LUNE	LOSE	MOAT	MELT	MOOG
KALI	KEYS	LUDO	LULL	LUNG	LOSS	MOBS	MILD	MOON
KELP	LEAD	LYDD	LULU	LUNN	LOST	MOBY	MILE	MOOR
KELT	LEAF	LEEK	LYLE	LYNN	LUSH	MACE	MILK	MOOT
KILL	LEAH	LEER	LAMA	LYNX	LUST	MACH	MILL	MAPS
KILN	LEAK	LEES	LAMB	LAOS	LATE	MACK	MILO	MOPE
KILO	LEAM	LIED	LAME	LEON	LATH	MACS	MILS	MOPS
KILT	LEAN	LIEN	LAMP	LION	LETO	MACY	MILT	MARA
KYLE	LEAP	LIES	LAMS	LOOE	LETS	MICA	MOLD	MARC
KEMP	LEAR	LEFT	LIMA	LOOK	LETT	MICE	MOLE	MARE
KANE	LEAS	LIFE	LIMB	LOOM	LOTH	MICK	MOLL	MARK
KANT	LEAT	LIFT	LIME	LOON	LOTS	MOCK	MULE	MARL
KENT	LIAM	LOFT	LIMO	LOOP	LUTE	MUCH	MULL	MARS
KIND	LIAR	LUFF	LIMP	LOOS	LUTZ	MUCK	MAMA	MART
KING	LOAD	LAGS	LOMA	LOOT	LAUD	MADE	MAME	MARX
KINK	LOAF	LEGO	LOME	LYON	LOUD	MIDI	MEMO	MARY
KNOB	LOAM	LEGS	LOMU	LAPP	LOUR	MODE	MIME	MERE
KNOT	LOAN	LOGO	LUMP	LAPS	LOUT	MODS	MIMI	MERV
KNOW	LOBE	LOGS	LYME	LIPS	LAVA	MEEK	MUMS	MIRE
KNOX	LOBO	LUGE	LANA	LOPE	LAVI	MEET	MANE	MIRO
KOOK	LOBS	LUGS	LAND	LOPS	LEVI	MIEN	MANN	MORE
KOOL	LACE	LAIC	LANE	LARA	LEVY	MIFF	MANX	MORK
KEPI	LACK	LAID	LANG	LARD	LIVE	MUFF	MANY	MORN
KEPT	LACY	LAIN	LANK	LARK	LIVY	MAGI	MENA	MURK
KIPS	LECH	LAIR	LENA	LIRA	LOVE	MEGA	MEND	MYRA
KARL	LICE	LEIA	LEND	LIRE	LAWN	MUGS	MENU	MASH
KERB	LICK	LEIF	LENG	LORD	LAWS	MAHE	MINA	MASK

MASS	NEAL	NINA	NUUK	OWES	OAST	PEEK	PILL	POOL
MAST	NEAP	NINE	NAVE	OXEN	OISE	PEEL	PILS	POOP
MESA	NEAR	NONE	NAVY	OXER	OMSK	PEEP	POLA	POOR
MESH	NEAT	NONO	NEVA	OYEZ	OSSA	PEER	POLE	PROA
MESS	NOAH	NONU	NEVE	OAFS	OUSE	PHEW	POLL	PROD
MISO	NABS	NUNN	NOVA	OFFA	OUST	PIED	POLO	PROM
MISS	NIBS	NUNS	NEWS	ORFE	OATH	PIER	POLY	PROP
MIST	NOBS	NEON	NEWT	OLGA	OATS	PIES	PULA	PROS
MOSS	NECK	NOOK	NOWT	ORGY	ONTO	PLEA	PULE	PROW
MOST	NICE	NOON	NEXT	OAHU	OPTS	PLEB	PULL	PAPA
MUSE	NICK	NOOR	NAZE	OCHE	OTTO	POEM	PULP	PEPE
MUSH	NOCK	NAPE	NAZI	OBIT	ONUS	POET	POMP	PEPS
MUSK	NIDD	NAPS	OBAN	ODIN	OPUS	PREP	POMS	PIPE
MUST	NODE	NIPS	OLAF	OHIO	OVUM	PREY	PUMA	PIPS
MATA	NODS	NOPE	OMAN	OLID	ONYX	PUFF	PUMP	POPE
MATE	NUDE	NYPD	OMAR	OLIO	ORYX	PAGE	PANE	POPP
MATS	NEED	NARK	OPAL	OMIT	OOZE	PEGG	PANG	POPS
MATT	NEEP	NARY	ORAL	OTIC	OUZO	PEGS	PANS	PUPA
METE	NOEL	NERD	ORAN	OTIS	OZZY	PIGS	PANT	PUPS
METZ	NOES	NERO	OVAL	OVID	PEAK	POGO	PENK	PARE
MITE	NAFF	NIRO	ORBS	OAKS	PEAL	PUGS	PENN	PARK
MITT	NEFF	NORA	ONCE	OIKS	PEAR	PAID	PENS	PARR
MOTE	NAGA	NORD	ORCA	OGLE	PEAS	PAIL	PENT	PART
MOTH	NAGS	NORE	ORCS	OILS	PEAT	PAIN	PERI	PERI
MUTE	NIGH	NORI	OUCH	OILY	PIAF	PAIR	PINA	PERK
MUTT	NOGO	NORM	ODDS	ONLY	PLAN	PHIL	PINE	PERM
MYTH	NAIL	NASA	ORDE	ORLA	PLAY	PLIE	PING	PERT
MAUD	NEIL	NASH	OBEY	ORLE	PRAM	PRIG	PINK	PERU
MAUI	NIKE	NESS	ODER	ORLY	PRAY	PRIM	PINS	PORE
MAUL	NIKI	NEST	ODES	OSLO	PUBS	PINT	PINT	PORK
MOUE	NELL	NOSE	OGEE	OWLS	PACE	PIKE	PONG	PORT
MOVE	NILE	NOSH	OGEN	OHMS	PACK	POKE	PONY	PURE
MEWL	NOLA	NATO	OMEN	OINK	PACT	POKY	PUNK	PURL
MEWS	NOLL	NETS	ONES	OWNS	PACY	PALE	PUNS	PURR
MOWN	NULL	NETT	OPEC	OBOE	PECK	PALI	PUNT	PYRE
MOWS	NAME	NITS	OPEL	OBOL	PICA	PALL	PUNY	PASO
MAXI	NEMO	NOTE	OPEN	OOPS	PICK	PALM	PEON	PASS
MAYA	NUMB	NOTH	ORES	OARS	PICT	PALS	PLOD	PAST
MAYO	NANA	NOTO	OVEN	OGRE	PUCE	PELE	PLOP	PESO
MOYA	NANS	NUTS	OVER	OKRA	PUCK	PELF	PLOT	PEST
MAZE	NENA	NOUN	OWED	OKRI	PADS	PELT	PLOY	PISA
NAAN	NENE	NOUS	OWEN	OURS	PODS	PILE	POOH	POSE

POSH	QUIZ	REEL	RULE	RSPB	ROVE	SOAP	SEER	SHIM
POST	RAAF	REES	RAMP	RARA	RSVP	SOAR	SEES	SHIN
POSY	READ	RHEA	RAMS	RARE	ROWS	SPAM	SHEA	SHIP
PUSH	REAL	ROEG	RIME	RORO	ROXY	SPAN	SHED	SKID
PUSS	REAM	RUED	RIMS	RORY	RAYS	SPAR	SHEM	SKIM
PATE	REAP	RUES	ROMA	RASH	RHYL	SPAS	SHEP	SKIN
PATH	REAR	RAFT	ROME	RASP	RHYS	SPAT	SHER	SKIP
PATS	RIAL	RIFE	ROMP	REST	RAZE	SPAY	SKEP	SKIS
PETA	ROAD	RIFF	ROMY	RISE	REZA	STAB	SKEW	SKIT
PETE	ROAM	RIFT	RUMP	RISK	SAAB	STAG	SLED	SLID
PETS	ROAN	RUFF	RAND	ROSA	SAAR	STAN	SLEW	SLIM
PITH	ROAR	RAGA	RANG	ROSE	SCAB	STAR	SMEE	SLIP
PITS	RYAN	RAGE	RANI	ROSS	SCAM	STAY	SMEW	SLIT
PITT	RABY	RAGI	RANK	ROSY	SCAN	STEM	SPED	SMIT
PITY	RIBS	RAGS	RANT	RUSE	SCAR	SWAB	SPEE	SNIB
POTS	ROBE	RAGU	REND	RUSH	SCAT	SWAG	SPEW	SNIP
PUTS	ROBS	RIGA	RENE	RUSK	SEAL	SWAM	SPEY	SOIL
PUTT	RUBS	RIGG	RENO	RUSS	SEAM	SWAN	STEM	SPIN
PAUL	RUBY	RIGS	RENT	RUST	SEAN	SWAP	STEN	SPIT
PIUS	RACE	RUGS	RIND	RATA	SEAR	SWAT	STEP	SPIV
PLUG	RACK	RUHR	RING	RATE	SEAS	SWAY	STET	STIG
PLUM	RACY	RAID	RINK	RATS	SEAT	SABU	STEW	STIR
PLUS	RICE	RAIL	RUNE	RETE	SHAD	SIBS	SUED	SUIR
POUR	RICH	RAIN	RUNG	RETS	SHAG	SOBS	SUES	SUIT
POUT	RICK	REID	RUNS	RITA	SHAH	SUBS	SUET	SWIG
PRUE	ROCK	REIN	RUNT	RITE	SHAM	SACK	SUEZ	SWIM
PAVE	RUCK	ROIL	RIOT	RITZ	SHAP	SECT	SAFE	SWIT
PAWL	RADA	RUIN	ROOD	ROTA	SHAW	SICK	SIFT	SEJM
PAWN	REDO	RAJA	ROOF	ROTE	SIAM	SOCA	SOFA	SAKE
PAWS	REDS	RAKE	ROOK	ROTH	SIAN	SOCK	SOFT	SAKI
PEWS	RIDD	RAKI	ROOM	ROTI	SKAT	SUCH	SUFI	SIKH
PAXO	RIDE	RALF	ROOS	ROTS	SLAB	SADE	SAGA	SALE
PAYE	RIDS	RELY	ROOT	RUTH	SLAG	SIDE	SAGE	SALK
PAYS	RODE	RILE	RAPE	RUTS	SLAM	SODA	SAGO	SALT
PUZO	RODS	RILL	RAPS	ROUE	SLAP	SODS	SAGS	SELF
QUAD	RUDD	RNLI	RAPT	ROUT	SLAT	SUDD	SEGS	SELL
QUAG	RUDE	ROLE	REPP	ROUX	SLAV	SUDS	SIGH	SILD
QUAY	RUDY	ROLF	REPS	RUUD	SLAW	SEED	SIGN	SILK
QUID	RYDE	ROLL	RIPE	RAVE	SLAY	SEEK	SOHO	SILL
QUIN	REED	ROLO	RIPS	RAVI	SNAG	SEEM	SAID	SILO
QUIP	REEF	ROLY	ROPE	REVS	SNAP	SEEN	SAIL	SILT
QUIT	REEK	RULA	ROPY	RIVE	SOAK	SEEP	SHIA	SOLD

SOLE	SLOP	SETA	SEWN	TEDS	TRIM	TONE	TORI	TIZZ
SOLO	SLOT	SETH	SEWS	TIDE	TRIO	TONG	TORN	UPAS
SULK	SLOW	SETI	SOWN	TIDY	TRIP	TONI	TORS	URAL
SAME	SMOG	SETS	SOWS	TODD	TWIG	TONK	TORT	UTAH
SAMP	SNOB	SETT	SAXE	TODO	TWIN	TONS	TORY	UNDO
SEMI	SNOG	SITE	SAXO	TEED	TWIT	TONY	TURF	URDU
SIMS	SNOW	SITH	SEXY	TEEM	TAKE	TUNA	TURK	USED
SOMA	SOOK	SITS	SAYS	TEEN	TOKE	TUNE	TURN	USER
SOME	SOON	SOTS	SKYE	TEES	TYKE	TUNS	TYRA	USES
SUMO	SOOT	SAUD	SOYA	THEA	TALC	TYNE	TYRE	UTES
SUMP	SPOT	SAUL	STYE	THEE	TALE	THOR	TYRO	UVEA
SUMS	STOA	SCUD	STYX	THEM	TALK	THOU	TASK	URGE
SYMS	STOP	SCUM	SIZE	THEN	TALL	TOOK	TESS	UNIT
SAND	STOW	SCUT	SUZI	THEO	TELL	TOOL	TEST	URIS
SANE	SWOT	SHUE	SUZY	THEY	TILE	TOOT	TOSH	UGLI
SANG	SAPS	SHUN	TEAK	TIED	TILL	TROD	TOSS	UGLY
SANK	SEPP	SHUT	TEAL	TIER	TILT	TROG	TUSH	ULNA
SEND	SIPS	SKUA	TEAM	TIES	TOLD	TRON	TUSK	URNS
SENS	SOPS	SLUB	TEAR	TOED	TOLL	TROT	TATA	UDON
SENT	SUPS	SLUG	TEAS	TOES	TULA	TROY	TATE	UPON
SIND	SARA	SLUM	TEAT	TREE	TULL	TWOS	TATI	UIST
SINE	SARD	SLUR	THAI	TREK	TAME	TAPA	TATU	UNST
SING	SARI	SMUG	THAN	TREX	TAMP	TAPE	TITI	URSA
SINK	SARK	SMUT	THAT	TREY	TEME	TAPS	TITO	USSR
SINS	SCRY	SNUB	THAW	TWEE	TEMP	TIPO	TOTE	UNTO
SONG	SERB	SNUG	TOAD	TAFF	TIME	TIPS	TOTO	ULVA
SONS	SERE	SOUK	TRAD	TAFT	TOMB	TOPE	TOTS	VEAL
SONY	SERF	SOUL	TRAM	TIFF	TOME	TOPI	TUTS	VIAL
SUNG	SIRE	SOUP	TRAP	TOFF	TOMS	TOPS	TUTU	VLAD
SUNK	SIRS	SOUR	TRAY	TOFU	TANA	TYPE	TAUT	VIBE
SCOT	SORE	SPUD	TSAR	TUFF	TANG	TYPO	THUD	VICE
SCOW	SORT	SPUN	TABS	TUFT	TANK	TARA	THUG	VEDA
SHOD	SPRY	SPUR	TOBY	TAGS	TANS	TARE	THUS	VIDA
SHOE	SURD	STUB	TUBA	TOGA	TEND	TARN	TOUR	VEER
SHOO	SURE	STUD	TUBE	TOGO	TENS	TARO	TOUT	VIED
SHOP	SURF	STUN	TUBS	TOGS	TENT	TARS	TRUE	VIES
SHOT	SURI	SWUM	TACK	TUGS	TINA	TART	TRUG	VIEW
SHOW	SASH	SAVE	TACO	TAIL	TINE	TERI	TOWN	VEGA
SKOL	SASS	SEVE	TACT	TAIT	TING	TERM	TOWS	VAIN
SLOB	SOSO	SUVA	TECK	THIN	TINS	TERN	TAXI	VEIL
SLOE	SUSS	SAWN	TICK	THIS	TINT	TIRE	TEXT	VEIN
SLOG	SATE	SAWS	TUCK	TOIL	TINY	TORE	TOYS	VOID

VALE	WEBS	WILE	WIRY	YOKO	ZIPS
VALK	WICK	WILL	WORD	YALE	ZARA
VILE	WADE	WILT	WORE	YELL	ZERO
VOLE	WADI	WILY	WORK	YELP	ZASU
VOLT	WADS	WOLD	WORM	YOLK	ZEST
VAMP	WEDS	WOLF	WORN	YULE	ZETA
VIMY	WIDE	WYLE	WASH	YAMS	ZEUS
VANE	WEED	WIMP	WASP	YOMP	ZAZU
VANS	WEEK	WOMB	WEST	YANG	ZIZI
VEND	WEEP	WAND	WISE	YANK	
VENT	WHEN	WANE	WISH	YAPS	
VINE	WHET	WANG	WISP	YIPS	
VINO	WHEY	WANT	WUSS	YARD	
VIOL	WOES	WEND	WYSS	YARE	
VARY	WREN	WENT	WATT	YARN	
VERA	WAFT	WIND	WETA	YORE	
VERB	WEFT	WINE	WETS	YORK	
VERT	WIFE	WING	WITH	YURI	
VERY	WAGE	WINK	WITS	YURT	
VASE	WAGS	WINO	WOUK	YETI	
VAST	WIGS	WINS	WAVE	YOUR	
VEST	WAIF	WONT	WAVY	YAWL	
VISA	WAIL	WHOA	WOVE	YAWN	
VOSS	WAIN	WHOM	WAXY	YAWS	
VATS	WAIT	WHOP	WAYS	YEWS	
VETO	WEIR	WOOD	XMAS	YOWL	
VETS	WHIG	WOOF	XRAY	YOYO	
VITA	WHIM	WOOL	XMEN	ZEAL	
VITO	WHIN	WOOS	XENA	ZEBU	
VOTE	WHIP	WEPT	YEAH	ZACH	
VIVA	WHIT	WIPE	YEAR	ZICO	
VOWS	WRIT	WARD	YEAS	ZOLA	
WEAK	WAKE	WARE	YUAN	ZULU	
WEAL	WOKE	WARK	YOBS	ZANY	
WEAN	WOKS	WARM	YMCA	ZENO	
WEAR	WALK	WARN	YUCK	ZINC	
WHAM	WALL	WARP	YODA	ZING	
WHAT	WALT	WARS	YVES	ZONE	
WOAD	WELD	WART	YOGA	ZION	
WRAP	WELL	WARY	YOGI	ZOOM	
WRAY	WELT	WERE	YAKS	ZOOS	
WEBB	WILD	WIRE	YOKE	ZAPS	

AQABA	ACCRA	ADEPT	ATHOS	AMITY	ANNIE	AVOWS	AESOP
AWARD	ASCOT	AGENT	AKIRA	ANJOU	ARNIE	ABORT	APSES
ABASE	ASDIC	ALERT	ANIMA	ALKYD	ANNAL	ABOUT	ASSES
ABATE	ADDED	AVERT	ANITA	ASKED	ANNUL	ADOPT	ASSET
ADAGE	AIDED	ADEUX	AVILA	ACKEE	ANNAN	AFOOT	ASSAY
AGAPE	ADDLE	APERY	ABIDE	ANKLE	ABNER	ALOFT	ARTIC
AGATE	ANDIE	AVERY	AFIRE	ARKLE	ASNER	AGONY	ATTIC
AGAVE	ANDRE	ALFIE	AGILE	ARKIN	AGNES	ALPHA	AZTEC
AMAZE	AUDIE	AWFUL	ALICE	ACKER	ANNIS	ASPIC	ACTED
APACE	ABDUL	AFFIX	ALIKE	ASKEW	AUNTS	ARPAD	APTED
AWAKE	ARDAL	AGGIE	ALINE	ASKEY	AGNEW	AMPLE	ARTIE
AWARE	ADDON	ALGAE	ALIVE	AILSA	ANNEX	APPLE	AITCH
AWASH	AIDAN	ANGIE	AMICE	ALLOA	ANNOY	APPAL	ALTAI
AMATI	ARDEN	ANGLE	ANIME	ADLIB	ARNAZ	ASPEL	ACTON
ABACK	AUDEN	ARGUE	ANISE	AILED	AGORA	ALPEN	ALTON
ALACK	AUDIO	ANGEL	ARISE	ASLEF	ALOHA	ASPEN	ANTON
AVAIL	ADDUP	ARGIL	ASIDE	ALLAH	AROMA	AMPLY	ASTON
ALARM	ADDER	ARGON	APING	ADLAI	ALOUD	APPLY	ASTRO
AGAIN	ALDER	AGGRO	AXING	ALLAN	AROAD	AORTA	ACTUP
ALAIN	AIDES	ANGER	AMISH	ALLEN	AVOID	AURIC	ACTOR
ALAMO	ANDES	AUGER	ALIBI	ALLIN	ABODE	ACRID	AFTER
ADAIR	AUDIT	AUGUR	AMICI	ASLAN	ABOVE	AIRED	ALTAR
ADAMS	ADDAX	AEGIS	ARIEL	ADLER	ADOBE	AGREE	ALTER
AMASS	AKELA	ANGUS	AXIAL	ARLES	ADORE	APRIL	ASTER
ARABS	ARECA	ARGOS	AXIOM	ATLAS	ALONE	AURAL	ASTIR
ABAFT	ARENA	ARGUS	ALIEN	AXLES	ANODE	AVRIL	ASTOR
ADAPT	AHEAD	ANGST	ALIGN	ALLOT	AROSE	AARON	ATTAR
APART	AMEND	ARGOT	ANION	AGLOW	ATONE	APRON	ALTOS
AVAST	ABELE	AUGHT	APIAN	ALLOW	AWOKE	ARRAN	AUTOS
AWAIT	ADELE	ANGRY	ARIAN	ALLAY	ADOLF	AIRER	ARTEX
ALBEE	ARETE	ASHIA	ASIAN	ALLEY	ALOOF	ACRES	ANTSY
AMBLE	ALEPH	ADHOC	AVIAN	ALLOY	ALONG	ARRAS	APTLY
ALBUM	ATEAM	ACHED	AMIGO	AIMED	AMONG	AURAS	AUTRY
AMBER	AHERN	APHID	ACIDS	ARMED	ATOLL	AYRES	ABUJA
ARBOR	ABETS	ASHEN	ADIOS	ADMAN	ACORN	ARROW	ARUBA
ABBES	AREAS	ABHOR	ALIAS	ADMEN	ADORN	ARRAY	ABUSE
ABBOT	AVENS	ASHER	AMISS	ADMIN	AMOUR	ATSEA	ACUTE
AMBIT	AVERS	ACHES	ARIAS	AMMAN	AEONS	AISLE	AMUSE
ABBEY	AXELS	APHIS	ARIES	ADMIT	ALOES	ASSAM	AZURE
ATBAY	AYERS	ASHES	ADIEU	ADMIX	ATOMS	ARSON	ADUKI

ABUTS	BLAIR	BODIE	BEFIT	BRICK	BILKO	BUNIN	BROCK
ADULT	BEADS	BUDGE	BUFFY	BRINK	BALER	BANCO	BROOK
ABUZZ	BEAKS	BADEN	BOGIE	BRISK	BALES	BANJO	BROIL
ANVIL	BEAMS	BADER	BUGLE	BRILL	BALLS	BINGO	BLOOM
ALVIN	BEANS	BIDES	BAGEL	BAIRN	BALMS	BONGO	BROOM
ASWAN	BEARS	BODES	BEGUM	BRIAN	BELLS	BONAR	BJORN
ABYSS	BEATS	BIDET	BEGAN	BLIMP	BELTS	BANDS	BLOWN
ANZAC	BLABS	BADLY	BEGIN	BRIAR	BILLS	BANGS	BROWN
ANZUS	BOARS	BIDDY	BEGUN	BAILS	BOLAS	BANKS	BLOBS
BRAVA	BOATS	BUDDY	BIGGS	BAITS	BOLES	BANNS	BLOTS
BWANA	BRADS	BREDA	BOGUS	BLIPS	BOLLS	BENDS	BLOWS
BLANC	BRAGS	BLEED	BEGAT	BLISS	BOLTS	BINDS	BOOKS
BEARD	BRASS	BLEND	BEGET	BOILS	BOLUS	BONDS	BOOMS
BLAND	BRATS	BREAD	BIGHT	BRIGS	BULBS	BONES	BOORS
BOARD	BRAYS	BREED	BIGOT	BRIMS	BULLS	BONUS	BOOTS
BRAID	BEAST	BREVE	BAGGY	BRITS	BELOW	BUNGS	BROWS
BRAND	BEAUT	BOEUF	BOGEY	BRITT	BYLAW	BUNKS	BUOYS
BEALE	BLAST	BEECH	BOGGY	BUILT	BALLY	BENET	BLOAT
BLADE	BOAST	BLEAK	BUGGY	BRINY	BALMY	BONET	BLOTT
BLAKE	BRACT	BREAK	BUGSY	BLITZ	BELAY	BANTU	BOOST
BLAME	BYATT	BREAM	BOHEA	BIJOU	BELLY	BANDY	BRONX
BLARE	BEAUX	BLEEP	BEHAN	BAKED	BILLY	BENDY	BLOWY
BLASE	BEADY	BLEAR	BAIRD	BAKER	BULKY	BENNY	BOOBY
BLAZE	BRADY	BEEFS	BLIND	BIKER	BULLY	BONEY	BOOTY
BRACE	BIBLE	BEEPS	BUILD	BYKER	BOMBE	BONNY	BOOZY
BRAKE	BABEL	BEERS	BAIZE	BAKES	BAMBI	BUNNY	BIPED
BRAVE	BEBOP	BLESS	BEIGE	BIKES	BIMBO	BLOND	BIPOD
BRAZE	BABAR	BREWS	BOISE	BALSA	BOMBS	BLOOD	BURKA
BRAGG	BABES	BLEAT	BRIBE	BELLA	BUMPS	BOOED	BURMA
BEACH	BOBBY	BRENT	BRICE	BALED	BUMPY	BROAD	BARED
BRASH	BACON	BREST	BRIDE	BELIE	BONED	BROOD	BORED
BHAJI	BACKS	BRETT	BRINE	BELLE	BINGE	BLOKE	BARGE
BLACK	BECKS	BEEFY	BSIDE	BILGE	BONCE	BOONE	BARRE
BLANK	BUCKS	BEERY	BRIEF	BULGE	BUNCE	BOOZE	BERNE
BRAWL	BACCY	BAFTA	BEING	BELCH	BANFF	BROKE	BORNE
BLAIN	BECKY	BEFOG	BOING	BALTI	BENCH	BEOFF	BURKE
BRAIN	BIDED	BIFFO	BRING	BOLAM	BUNCH	BOOTH	BYRNE
BRAWN	BODED	BYFAR	BLIGH	BOLAN	BONDI	BROTH	BERTH
BEANO	BADGE	BIFFS	BLINI	BALOO	BANAL	BJORK	BIRCH
BRAVO	BODGE	BUFFS	BLINK	BILBO	BENIN	BLOCK	BIRTH

BURGH	BOSCH	BITTY	BOXES	CLAIM	CABOT	CLEAN	CHINE
BERYL	BASAL	BOTHY	BIXBY	CHAIN	CUBIT	CREAN	CHIVE
BARON	BASIL	BUTTY	BAYED	CHAMP	CUBBY	CREDO	CLIME
BORON	BESOM	BLURB	BOYCE	CLAMP	COCOA	CHEAP	CLINE
BURIN	BOSOM	BOUND	BOYLE	CLASP	CACHE	CHEEP	CLIVE
BYRON	BASIN	BRUCE	BOYNE	CRAMP	CYCLE	CREEP	CRIME
BARDO	BISON	BRUTE	BLYTH	CHAIR	CACTI	CHEER	CHIEF
BURRO	BOSUN	BLUFF	BRYAN	CLAIR	CECIL	CLEAR	CLIFF
BARER	BASHO	BLUSH	BOYER	CHAOS	CACAO	CHEFS	CLING
BORER	BISTO	BOUGH	BUYER	CHAPS	COCKS	CHESS	CHILI
BARBS	BASER	BRUSH	BAYOU	CHARS	COCKY	CHEWS	CHICK
BARDS	BASES	BAULK	BEZEL	CHATS	CEDED	CLEFS	CHINK
BARES	BASIS	BLUTO	BIZET	CLAMS	CODED	CRESS	CLICK
BARKS	BASKS	BRUNO	BUZZY	CLANS	CADGE	CREWS	CLINK
BARNS	BESTS	BAUER	CLARA	CLAPS	CADRE	CHEAT	CRICK
BERGS	BUSES	BLUER	CHARD	CLASS	CEDAR	CHEST	CHILL
BIRDS	BUSKS	BLUES	CEASE	CLAWS	CIDER	CLEAT	CAIRN
BIROS	BUSTS	BLURS	CHAFE	COALS	CADIS	CLEFT	CAIRO
BORES	BESET	BOUTS	CHASE	COATS	CEDES	CREPT	CHICO
BORIS	BOSSY	BLUNT	CLARE	CRABS	CODAS	CREST	CHINO
BURNS	BUSBY	BLURT	CRANE	CRAGS	CODES	CHEVY	CHIMP
BURRS	BUSHY	BOULT	CRATE	CRAMS	CADET	CHEWY	CHIRP
BYRDS	BOTHA	BRUNT	CRAVE	CRAPS	CADDY	CAFES	CRIMP
BYRES	BATED	BEVEL	CRAZE	CRASS	CADIZ	CUFFS	CRISP
BERET	BATHE	BEVAN	CHAFF	CHANT	CREED	CAGED	CRIER
BORAT	BETTE	BEVIN	CLANG	CHART	CREPE	COGAN	CHINS
BURNT	BATCH	BEVVY	CRAIG	COAST	CRETE	CIGAR	CHIPS
BURST	BITCH	BOWED	CLASH	CRAFT	CREWE	CAGES	CHITS
BORAX	BOTCH	BOWIE	COACH	CHARY	CLEEF	CSGAS	CLIPS
BARMY	BUTCH	BOWEN	CRASH	CLARY	CLEGG	CAGEY	COILS
BARRY	BATIK	BOWER	COATI	CRAZY	CZECH	COHEN	COINS
BERRY	BETEL	BAWDS	CHALK	COBRA	CHECK	CHIBA	CRIBS
BIRDY	BATON	BAWLS	CLACK	CUBIC	CHEEK	CHINA	CRIES
BURLY	BATES	BEWES	CLANK	CUBED	CLEEK	CLIMB	CLIFT
BASRA	BATHS	BOWLS	CLARK	CABLE	CLERK	CHILD	CLINT
BASIC	BITES	BAWDY	CRACK	CABAL	CREAK	CRIED	CAJUN
BASED	BUTTS	BYWAY	CRANK	CABIN	CREEK	CAINE	CAKED
BASIE	BYTES	BOXED	CRAWL	CUBAN	CREEL	CHIDE	CUKOR
BASLE	BATTY	BUXOM	CHARM	CABER	CHEAM	CHILE	CAKES
BASTE	BETTY	BOXER	CHASM	CUBES	CREAM	CHIME	CELIA

CILIA	COMFY	CHOCK	COPAL	CARPS	CYSTS	CLUBS	DUANE
CILLA	CANNA	CLOAK	CAPON	CARTS	CASEY	CLUES	DWARF
CALEB	CONGA	CLOCK	CAPER	CERES	COSBY	COUPS	DEATH
CELEB	CYNIC	CLONK	COPER	CERTS	CUSHY	COUNT	DRANK
COLIC	CANED	CROAK	CUPAR	CHRIS	CITED	COURT	DRAWL
CALID	CONED	CROCK	CAPES	CORDS	CUTIE	CRUET	DRAIN
CALVE	CANOE	CROOK	COPES	CORES	CATCH	CRUST	DRAWN
CHLOE	CONTE	CLOWN	COPTS	CORKS	CUTUP	CIVIC	DRACO
COLNE	CINCH	CROON	COPIT	CORNS	CATER	CAVED	DEALS
COLIN	CONCH	CROWN	CARLA	CORPS	CATES	CAVIL	DEANS
COLON	CONTI	CHOMP	CIRCA	CORRS	CITES	CIVIL	DEARS
CELLO	CANAL	CROUP	CURIA	CURBS	COTES	CAVAN	DIALS
CALOR	CANON	CHOIR	CAROB	CURDS	CATHY	COVEN	DRABS
COLOR	CONAN	CHOPS	CARED	CURES	CATTY	CAVER	DRAGS
CALLS	CANDO	CHOWS	CORED	CURLS	CEUTA	COVER	DRAMS
CALMS	CANTO	CLODS	CURED	CYRUS	CHUBB	CAVES	DRAWS
CELLS	CONDO	CLOGS	CARNE	CARAT	CRUMB	COVES	DRAYS
CELTS	CONGO	CLOTS	CARRE	CARET	CLUED	CIVET	DEALT
COLDS	CANES	CLOYS	CARTE	COROT	COULD	COVET	DRAFT
COLTS	CANTS	COOKS	CARVE	CORFU	CAUSE	COVEY	DIARY
CULLS	CENTS	COOLS	CORFE	CAREY	CHUTE	CAWED	DEBRA
CULTS	CONES	COOPS	CURIE	CARLY	COUPE	CLWYD	DUBYA
CALYX	CANDY	COOTS	CURSE	CARRY	CRUDE	COWED	DEBAG
COLBY	CANNY	CROPS	CURVE	CARTY	CHUFF	COWER	DEBUG
COLEY	CINDY	CROSS	CORGI	CORNY	CLUNG	COWES	DUBAI
COMMA	CONWY	CROWS	CAROL	CURLY	COUCH	COWLS	DUBBO
COMIC	CHORD	CLOUT	CORAL	CURRY	COUGH	COXED	DEBAR
COMTE	CLOUD	COOPT	CYRIL	CURVY	CRUSH	COXES	DEBTS
CAMEL	CROWD	CROAT	CDROM	CASCA	CAULK	CLYDE	DOBBS
CUMIN	CHOKE	CROFT	CARON	CASTA	CHUCK	CRYER	DEBIT
CAMEO	CHORE	CHOUX	COREN	COSTA	CHUNK	CRYPT	DEBUT
COMBO	CHOSE	CRONY	CORIN	CASED	CLUCK	COYPU	DOBBY
COMPO	CLONE	CAPRA	CARGO	CASTE	CLUNK	COYLY	DOBEY
CAMPS	CLOSE	COPRA	CARLO	CISCO	CHURL	COZEN	DACHA
CAMUS	CLOVE	CUPPA	CURIO	CESAR	CRUEL	DHAKA	DECCA
COMAS	COOKE	CAPED	CARER	CASES	CHURN	DIANA	DECAD
COMBS	CROME	COPED	CORER	CASKS	CHUMP	DRAMA	DICED
COMES	CRONE	CUPID	CURER	CASTS	CLUMP	DIANE	DECAF
COMET	CROWE	COPSE	CARDS	COSTS	CHUGS	DRAKE	DUCAL
CYMRU	CLOTH	CAPRI	CARES	CUSPS	CHUMS	DRAPE	DECOR

DICER	DYERS	DEKKO	DIMES	DROID	DARES	DRUNK	DRYAD
DECKS	DWELT	DAKAR	DOMES	DROOD	DARNS	DOURO	DOYLE
DICES	DYFED	DUKAS	DUMAS	DIODE	DARTS	DAUBS	DAYAK
DOCKS	DAFOE	DUKES	DUMPS	DOONE	DIRKS	DRUBS	DAYAN
DUCKS	DEFOE	DYKES	DIMLY	DRONE	DORIS	DRUGS	DOYEN
DUCTS	DEFER	DELIA	DUMMY	DROVE	DORMS	DRUMS	DRYUP
DUCAT	DOFFS	DELLA	DUMPY	DHOBI	DURST	DAUNT	DRYER
DECAY	DAFFY	DELTA	DONNA	DHOTI	DARBY	DOUBT	DAZED
DECOY	DUFFY	DOLED	DINED	DROLL	DARCY	DAVID	DOZED
DECRY	DOGMA	DELVE	DANAE	DROOL	DERBY	DIVED	DOZEN
DICEY	DIGIN	DOLCE	DANCE	DROWN	DERRY	DEVIL	DOZER
DICKY	DOGGO	DELHI	DANTE	DROOP	DIRTY	DEVON	DAZES
DUCHY	DIGUP	DALEK	DENSE	DOORS	DOSED	DIVAN	DOZES
DUCKY	DUGUP	DELON	DONNE	DROPS	DISCO	DAVRO	DIZZY
DODGE	DEGAS	DYLAN	DUNCE	DROSS	DESKS	DIVER	ELAND
DODIE	DIGIT	DALES	DUNNE	DOPED	DISCS	DOVER	ELATE
DRDRE	DIGBY	DELLS	DENCH	DUPED	DISKS	DAVIS	ERASE
DADOS	DOGGY	DOLES	DINAH	DUPLE	DOSES	DAVOS	EVADE
DUDES	DRIED	DOLLS	DENIM	DEPTH	DUSTS	DIVAS	EMAIL
DADDY	DEICE	DOLTS	DANDO	DUPER	DISHY	DIVES	ERATO
DIDDY	DRIVE	DALAI	DINGO	DOPES	DUSKY	DOVES	EVANS
DODGY	DOING	DALIT	DINAR	DUPES	DUSTY	DAVIT	EXAMS
DWEEB	DYING	DELFT	DINER	DEPOT	DATED	DIVOT	ENACT
DREAD	DRINK	DULUX	DONOR	DIPPY	DOTED	DUVET	EWART
DREDD	DRILL	DALEY	DANES	DIPSY	DITCH	DAVEY	EXACT
DRECK	DEISM	DALLY	DENIS	DOPEY	DUTCH	DIVVY	EXALT
DWELL	DEIGN	DELAY	DENTS	DARLA	DATUM	DOWSE	EBBED
DREAM	DRIER	DOLBY	DINES	DERMA	DITTO	DOWEL	EMBED
DIEGO	DRIES	DOLLY	DINGS	DURRA	DETER	DEWAR	EMBER
DUETO	DRIPS	DEMOB	DONGS	DORIC	DATES	DAWES	ELBOW
DREAR	DEIST	DOMED	DUNES	DARED	DOTES	DAWNS	ELCID
DEEDS	DRIFT	DAMME	DYNES	DIRGE	DETOX	DOWDS	EMCEE
DEEMS	DAILY	DAMON	DONAT	DURIE	DITTY	DOWNS	EXCEL
DIETS	DAIRY	DEMON	DUNST	DORFF	DITZY	DEWEY	EXCON
DOERS	DAISY	DUMBO	DANDY	DEREK	DOTTY	DOWDY	ENDED
DREGS	DEIFY	DEMUR	DANNY	DARYL	DRUID	DOWNY	EDDIE
DRESS	DEITY	DAMES	DINGY	DURUM	DEUCE	DOWRY	ENDUE
DREYS	DOILY	DAMNS	DINKY	DARIN	DOUSE	DIXIE	EBDON
DUELS	DRILY	DEMIS	DONNY	DARIO	DRUZE	DIXON	EGDON
DUETS	DIJON	DEMOS	DOONA	DURER	DOUGH	DEXYS	ENDUP

EIDER	ETHAN	ENNUI	EXTRA	FRAIL	FREED	FLITS	FANTA
ELDER	ESHER	ENNIO	EXTOL	FRAYN	FREUD	FOILS	FONDA
ENDOW	ETHER	ERNES	EATEN	FLAIR	FLESH	FRIES	FINED
ELENA	ETHOS	ENOLA	EATON	FEARS	FRESH	FAINT	FENCE
EMEND	EDINA	ELOPE	ELTON	FEATS	FLECK	FEINT	FINCH
EWELL	ELIZA	EMOTE	ESTOP	FLAGS	FREAK	FLINT	FENDI
EYEUP	ERICA	ERODE	EATER	FLANS	FUEGO	FLIRT	FUNGI
EVENS	ERIKA	EVOKE	ENTER	FLAPS	FLEUR	FOIST	FINAL
EWERS	EVITA	ENOCH	ESTER	FLATS	FREER	FAIRY	FINER
EGEST	ELIDE	EPOCH	EDUCE	FLAWS	FEEDS	FRIZZ	FANGS
EJECT	ELISE	ECOLI	ELUDE	FLAYS	FEELS	FAKED	FENDS
ELECT	ELITE	EBOAT	ETUDE	FOALS	FLEAS	FAKER	FINDS
ERECT	EMILE	EBONY	EXUDE	FOAMS	FLEES	FAKIR	FINES
EVENT	EXILE	EPOXY	EQUAL	FRAYS	FREES	FAKES	FUNDS
EVERT	EKING	EXPEL	EQUIP	FEAST	FRETS	FILED	FANCY
EXEAT	EWING	EXPAT	EQUUS	FLAKY	FIERY	FALSE	FANNY
EXERT	EDITH	EMPTY	ERUCT	FOAMY	FIFTH	FILCH	FUNKY
ELEGY	ERICH	ERRED	ERUPT	FRANZ	FAFFS	FILTH	FUNNY
EMERY	EVIAN	EARLE	EXULT	FABLE	FIFTY	FELON	FIONA
ENEMY	EDITS	EERIE	ELVER	FIBRE	FAGIN	FALCO	FLORA
EVERY	EMIRS	EYRIE	EAVES	FAFFS	FIGHT	FALDO	FJORD
ELFIN	EMITS	EARTH	ELVES	FACED	FOGEY	FOLIO	FLOOD
EDGED	EPICS	ENROL	ELVIS	FOCAL	FOGGY	FALLS	FLOYD
EGGED	EVILS	ERROL	ENVOY	FACUP	FRIDA	FELLS	FROND
EAGLE	EXITS	ENRON	EDWIN	FACES	FRIED	FILES	FROBE
EAGRE	EDICT	ERROR	EDWYN	FICUS	FLING	FILLS	FROME
ELGIN	ELIOT	EARLS	EGYPT	FOCUS	FAITH	FILMS	FROZE
EAGER	EVICT	EARNS	FRANC	FUCHS	FLICK	FOLDS	FROTH
EDGAR	EXIST	EGRET	FRAUD	FACET	FRISK	FELIX	FLOCK
EDGER	EDIFY	EASED	FLAKE	FICHU	FRILL	FILEY	FROCK
EGGAR	EMILY	EASES	FLAME	FADED	FRIEL	FILLY	FLOWN
EIGER	ENJOY	ELSIE	FLARE	FUDGE	FRIAR	FILMY	FROWN
ELGAR	ELLIE	ENSUE	FRAME	FIDEL	FRIEL	FOLLY	FLOOR
EDGES	ELLEN	EASEL	FLASH	FODEN	FRILL	FULLY	FLOUR
EIGHT	EALES	EPSOM	FLACK	FEDUP	FEIGN	FELTZ	FLOES
ERGOT	ELLIS	EBSEN	FLANK	FADES	FRIAR	FAMED	FLOGS
ETHIC	ECLAT	ESSEN	FLASK	FADDY	FAILS	FUMED	FLOPS
ETHEL	ELMER	ESSES	FRANK	FREYA	FAIRS	FEMME	FLOSS
ETHYL	EMMET	ESSEX	FLAIL	FIELD	FLIES	FEMUR	FLOWS
EGHAM	ERNIE	ESSAY	FIEND	FUMES	FLIPS	FUMES	FOODS

FOOLS	FOSSE	FAUST	GLARE	GODOT	GRIME	GULLS	GROVE
FROGS	FUSIL	FOUNT	GLAZE	GIDDY	GRIPE	GULPS	GEOFF
FLOAT	FASTS	FRUIT	GRACE	GODLY	GUIDE	GYLES	GOOFF
FLOUT	FISTS	FLUKY	GRADE	GEENA	GUILE	GILET	GOOCH
FRONT	FUSES	FEVER	GRAPE	GRETA	GUISE	GOLLY	GHOUL
FROST	FISHY	FIVER	GRATE	GREED	GRIEF	GULLY	GROHL
FOOTY	FUSSY	FIVES	GRAVE	GEESE	GRIFF	GAMMA	GROWL
FARAD	FUSTY	FEWER	GRAZE	GLEBE	GOING	GEMMA	GLOOM
FARED	FATWA	FAWNS	GNASH	GREBE	GRIEG	GOMAD	GROOM
FIRED	FATED	FOWEY	GRAPH	GREGG	GRILL	GAMIN	GROAN
FARCE	FETID	FAXED	GNARL	GREEK	GRIMM	GUMBO	GROIN
FORCE	FATAH	FIXED	GRAIL	GLEAM	GAINS	GAMER	GROWN
FORGE	FETCH	FOXED	GRAIN	GLEAN	GRIDS	GAMES	GLOOP
FORME	FATAL	FIXER	GUANO	GLENN	GRINS	GAMPS	GROUP
FORTE	FITIN	FAXES	GRASP	GREEN	GRIPS	GAMUT	GLOSS
FURZE	FUTON	FIXES	GEARS	GRECO	GRITS	GAMEY	GLOWS
FIRTH	FITUP	FOXES	GLASS	GEEUP	GLINT	GAMMY	GOODS
FORTH	FATES	FLYBE	GNATS	GREER	GRIFT	GANJA	GOOFS
FARSI	FETES	FLYTE	GNAWS	GAELS	GRIST	GENOA	GOONS
FERAL	FATTY	FOYLE	GOADS	GLENS	GUILT	GUNGA	GROSS
FORUM	FAUNA	FLYIN	GOALS	GLESS	GAILY	GENIE	GROWS
FARGO	FLUID	FLYNN	GOATS	GREYS	GRIMY	GENRE	GHOST
FORGO	FOUND	FLYMO	GRABS	GUESS	GLITZ	GUNGE	GLOAT
FARES	FAURE	FRYUP	GRAMS	GHENT	GIJOE	GONZO	GOOUT
FARMS	FAUVE	FLYER	GRASS	GREAT	GILDA	GENUP	GROAT
FERNS	FLUKE	FOYER	GIANT	GREET	GOLDA	GONER	GROUT
FIRES	FLUME	FRYER	GRAFT	GUEST	GELID	GANGS	GLORY
FIRMS	FLUTE	FLYAT	GRANT	GWENT	GULAG	GENES	GOODY
FORDS	FLUFF	FLYBY	GRAVY	GEEKY	GALAH	GENTS	GOOEY
FORKS	FLUNG	FAZED	GABBA	GAFFE	GULCH	GENUS	GOOFY
FORMS	FLUSH	FAZES	GUBBA	GOFAR	GOLEM	GONGS	GAPED
FORTS	FLUNK	FIZZY	GOBAD	GOFER	GALOP	GENET	GAPER
FURLS	FLUMP	FUZZY	GABLE	GAFFS	GALAS	GUNGY	GAPES
FIRST	FRUMP	GHANA	GOBBI	GIFTS	GALES	GEODE	GAPPY
FERRY	FAUNS	GUAVA	GABON	GIGLI	GALLS	GLOBE	GUPPY
FORAY	FEUDS	GLAND	GABOR	GOGOL	GILDS	GLOVE	GYPSY
FORTY	FLUES	GRAND	GIBBS	GIGGS	GILES	GLOZE	GARDA
FURRY	FOULS	GUARD	GABBY	GRIND	GILLS	GNOME	GORED
FUSED	FOURS	GLACE	GUCCI	GUILD	GILTS	GOOSE	GORGE
FESTE	FAULT	GLADE	GECKO	GLIDE	GULFS	GROPE	GORSE

GARTH	GAUDI	HUBBY	HEINZ	HOMER	HYPED	HERTZ	HOVER
GIRTH	GRUEL	HACKS	HIJAB	HAMAS	HIPPO	HOSEA	HAVES
GORAN	GRUMP	HICKS	HIKED	HOMES	HYPER	HOSTA	HIVES
GOREN	GLUES	HOCKS	HOKUM	HUMPS	HOPES	HASTE	HOVIS
GARBO	GAUNT	HECHT	HIKER	HUMUS	HYPES	HESSE	HEWED
GERMS	GRUNT	HEDDA	HIKES	HYMNS	HOPIT	HASPS	HAWKE
GIRDS	GAUDY	HYDRA	HALMA	HENNA	HAPPY	HOSES	HAWSE
GIRLS	GAUZY	HEDGE	HALVA	HONDA	HOPPY	HOSTS	HYWEL
GIROS	GOUTY	HODGE	HILDA	HONED	HARED	HUSKS	HEWER
GORES	GAVEL	HADJI	HYLDA	HENCE	HEROD	HASTY	HAWES
GURUS	GAVIN	HYDRO	HOLED	HENGE	HIRED	HUSKY	HAWKS
GERRY	GIVEN	HADES	HALLE	HINGE	HERGE	HUSSY	HOWES
GORKY	GIVER	HIDES	HALVE	HUNCH	HORDE	HATED	HOWLS
GESTE	GIVES	HADOW	HULCE	HANOI	HORNE	HYTHE	HOWDY
GESSO	GOWAN	HYENA	HALAL	HENRI	HORSE	HATCH	HEXAD
GUSTO	GOWER	HEEDS	HELEN	HINDI	HARSH	HITCH	HAYLE
GASES	GOWNS	HEELS	HELLO	HANDL	HAREM	HUTCH	HOYLE
GASPS	GAWKY	HOFFA	HALER	HONDO	HERON	HOTEL	HAYEK
GUSTS	GAYLE	HAFTS	HALLS	HONOR	HURON	HITON	HAYDN
GASSY	GAZZA	HIFIS	HALTS	HANDS	HARPO	HETUP	HAYES
GUSHY	GAZED	HUFFS	HELLS	HANGS	HARES	HOTUP	HAZEL
GUSTY	GIZMO	HEFTY	HELMS	HANKS	HARKS	HATES	IVANA
GATED	GAZES	HUFFY	HELPS	HINES	HARMS	HETTY	ISAAC
GETON	HEARD	HAGUE	HILLS	HINTS	HARPS	HOTLY	IMAGE
GETUP	HOARD	HEGEL	HOLDS	HONES	HERBS	HAUSA	INANE
GOTUP	HEAVE	HOGAN	HOLES	HUNKS	HERDS	HOUND	IRATE
GATES	HEATH	HAGAR	HULLS	HUNTS	HIRES	HAUTE	IRAQI
GETBY	HEADS	HAIFA	HELOT	HINDU	HORNS	HOUSE	IDAHO
GETTY	HEALS	HAILE	HOLST	HANDY	HORUS	HOURI	IMAGO
GOTBY	HEAPS	HAIGH	HULOT	HANKY	HURLS	HAUER	IMAMS
GUTSY	HEARS	HAITI	HELIX	HENRY	HURTS	HAULS	INAPT
GOUDA	HEATS	HEIDI	HALEY	HONEY	HERAT	HOURS	ITALY
GLUED	HEART	HOICK	HILLY	HUNKY	HIRST	HAUNT	IMBUE
GOULD	HEADY	HAILS	HOLBY	HOOCH	HURST	HAVOC	INCUR
GOURD	HEALY	HAIRS	HOLLY	HOODS	HYRAX	HIVED	INCAS
GAUGE	HEAVY	HEIRS	HUMID	HOOKS	HARDY	HAVEL	INCUS
GAUZE	HOAGY	HEIST	HEMAN	HOOPS	HARPY	HOVEL	ITCHY
GOUGE	HOARY	HOIST	HEMEN	HOOTS	HARRY	HAVEN	INDIA
GRUFF	HABIT	HAIKU	HEMIN	HOOEY	HARTY	HAVER	INDIE
GOUGH	HOBBY	HAIRY	HUMAN	HOPED	HURRY	HEVER	INDRI

INDUS	ISLAY	JUDAS	JUMPS	JEWEL	KUFFS	KNOLL	KIWIS
INDEX	ISLEY	JEEPS	JAMMY	JOWLS	KEIRA	KNOWN	KEYED
IRENE	INMAN	JEERS	JEMMY	JAYNE	KLINE	KYOTO	KAYAK
ICENI	IZMIR	JOEYS	JIMMY	JOYCE	KNIFE	KNOBS	KEYIN
IDEAL	IONIC	JOELY	JUMPY	JAZZY	KEITH	KNOTS	KEYES
ILEUM	INNER	JAFFA	JENNA	KOALA	KRILL	KNOWS	KAZAN
IDEAS	INNES	JAFFE	JUNTA	KEANE	KNITS	KOOKY	KAZOO
ITEMS	IMOLA	JOFFE	JONAH	KNAVE	KRISS	KAPPA	LHASA
INEPT	INONE	JIFFY	JINGO	KEACH	KLIMT	KAPOK	LIANA
INERT	INOFF	JIHAD	JUNOR	KHADI	KOJAK	KOPEK	LLAMA
INFUN	ICONS	JOHAN	JANIS	KHAKI	KUKRI	KAPIL	LEASE
INFER	IDOLS	JOHNS	JANUS	KNACK	KYLIE	KEPIS	LEAVE
INGLE	IRONS	JAIME	JINKS	KRAAL	KULFI	KIPPS	LEACH
INGOT	IRONY	JUICE	JONES	KNAPP	KILIM	KAPUT	LEASH
ICHOR	IVORY	JAILS	JANET	KEATS	KELIS	KARMA	LOACH
IBIZA	IMPEL	JOINS	JENNY	KHANS	KELLS	KORDA	LEARN
ILIAD	INPUT	JOINT	JONNY	KNAPS	KILLS	KOREA	LLANO
ICING	IMPLY	JOIST	JOOLS	KVASS	KILNS	KORMA	LEADS
IRISH	IMRIE	JUICY	JAPAN	KRAFT	KILOS	KYRIE	LEAKS
IWISH	IMRAN	JOKED	JAPES	KRAIT	KILTS	KURSK	LEANS
IWILL	IDRIS	JOKER	JARED	KEANU	KELLY	KARAN	LEAPS
IDIOM	ISSUE	JOKES	JARRE	KEBAB	KAMEN	KAREN	LIARS
ILIUM	IBSEN	JOKEY	JUROR	KABUL	KHMER	KORAN	LOADS
INIGO	INSET	JULIA	JERKS	KICKS	KUMAR	KARNO	LOANS
ICIER	ISTLE	JOLIE	JERKY	KACEY	KENYA	KERBS	LEANT
IDIOT	INTRO	JULIE	JERRY	KEDGE	KENCO	KURDS	LEAPT
ICILY	INTER	JELLO	JESSE	KODAK	KENDO	KIROV	LEAST
INKED	INTOW	JULIO	JOSIE	KUDOS	KINDS	KERRY	LEAFY
IRKED	INURE	JULEP	JASON	KNEAD	KINGS	KASEY	LEAKY
INKIN	INUIT	JILTS	JESTS	KEELE	KINKS	KESEY	LEARY
IDLED	IRWIN	JOLTS	JESUS	KNEEL	KANDY	KATIE	LIBRA
ISLAM	IDYLL	JULES	JOSEY	KNELL	KENNY	KETCH	LIBYA
IGLOO	JEANS	JELLY	JETTY	KLEIN	KINKY	KOTCH	LABEL
IDLER	JABOT	JILLY	JOULE	KEELS	KRONA	KITES	LIBEL
IDLES	JACOB	JOLLY	JAUNT	KEENS	KNOLE	KATHY	LEBON
ISLES	JACKS	JEMMA	JOUST	KEEPS	KRONE	KITTY	LABOR
INLET	JADED	JAMIE	JIVED	KNEES	KUONI	KLUTE	LOBES
ISLET	JODIE	JUMBO	JIVER	KNELT	KIOSK	KLUTZ	LIBBY
INLAW	JUDGE	JAMBS	JIVES	KEELY	KNOCK	KOVAC	LOBBY
INLAY	JADES	JAMES	JAWED	KAFKA	KWOUK	KEVIN	LYCRA

LACED	LUFFS	LILLI	LONER	LORNA	LITHE	LEVIS	MOBIL
LUCID	LOFTY	LILTS	LUNAR	LYRIC	LITRE	LIVES	MECCA
LECCE	LOGIC	LOLLS	LANDS	LURED	LOTTE	LOVES	MOCHA
LOCKE	LOGIE	LULLS	LANES	LURID	LATCH	LOVAT	MACON
LUCRE	LEGAL	LALAW	LENDS	LARGE	LATIN	LOVEY	MACHO
LYCEE	LAGAN	LOLLY	LINES	LARUE	LETIN	LUVVY	MACRO
LOCAL	LOGAN	LAMIA	LINKS	LORNE	LETON	LOWED	MACES
LOCUM	LOGON	LYMPH	LINUS	LORRE	LUTON	LOWER	MACYS
LUCAN	LEGUP	LEMON	LONGS	LARCH	LETGO	LAWNS	MOCKS
LACES	LAGER	LIMBO	LUNGS	LURCH	LOTTO	LEWES	MACAW
LACKS	LUGER	LAMER	LANKY	LOREN	LETUP	LEWIS	MCCOY
LICKS	LAGOS	LEMUR	LENNY	LARGO	LITUP	LOWLY	MUCKY
LOCHS	LOGOS	LAMAS	LUNDY	LARKS	LATER	LOWRY	MEDEA
LOCKS	LEGIT	LAMBS	LLOYD	LORDS	LATHS	LUXOR	MEDIA
LOCUS	LIGHT	LAMPS	LOOSE	LORIS	LETTS	LEXIS	MADOC
LUCAS	LEGGY	LIMBS	LEONI	LURES	LOTUS	LEXUS	MEDIC
LICIT	LOHAN	LIMES	LAOIS	LURKS	LUTES	LAXLY	MEDOC
LACEY	LAHAR	LIMPS	LIONS	LYRES	LATEX	LAYLA	MADGE
LUCKY	LEHAR	LUMPS	LOOKS	LUREX	LAUDA	LOYAL	MIDGE
LYDIA	LAIKA	LIMIT	LOOMS	LARDY	LAURA	LAYON	MEDAL
LADLE	LAILA	LIMEY	LOONS	LARRY	LOUPE	LAYUP	MODEL
LEDGE	LAIRD	LUMPY	LOOPS	LEROY	LOUSE	LAYER	MADAM
LODGE	LAINE	LANZA	LOOTS	LORRY	LAUGH	LAYBY	MODEM
LADEN	LOIRE	LENYA	LYONS	LURGY	LOUGH	LAZED	MEDAN
LYDON	LAIRG	LINDA	LOONY	LASSE	LOUTH	LAZIO	MIDON
LIDOS	LYING	LYNDA	LOOPY	LISLE	LAUDS	LAZES	MODER
LEELA	LEIGH	LINED	LOPED	LASSO	LOUIS	MEATH	MIDAS
LIEGE	LEITH	LANCE	LAPSE	LASER	LOURS	MIAMI	MODES
LOEWE	LAIRS	LANGE	LIPPI	LOSER	LOUTS	MEALS	MODUS
LEECH	LOINS	LUNGE	LAPEL	LASTS	LOUSY	MEANS	MIDST
LIESL	LAITY	LYNNE	LEPEN	LISPS	LIVED	MEARS	MADDY
LIEIN	LIKED	LUNCH	LUPIN	LISTS	LIVID	MEATS	MADLY
LEEDS	LIKUD	LYNCH	LAPUP	LOSES	LOVED	MOANS	MIDDY
LEEKS	LIKEN	LENDL	LEPER	LISZT	LEVEE	MOATS	MUDDY
LEERS	LAKER	LYNAM	LAPIS	LOSEY	LEVEL	MEANT	MAEVE
LOESS	LAKES	LENIN	LOPES	LUSTY	LEVIN	MIAOW	MBEKI
LEERY	LIKES	LINEN	LIPPY	LATHE	LAVER	MEALY	MEETS
LIFER	LUKAS	LENTO	LAPAZ	LATKE	LEVER	MEATY	MYERS
LIFTS	LILAC	LINGO	LOPEZ	LATTE	LIVER	MRBIG	MAFIA
LOFTS	LILLE	LINER	LARVA	LETHE	LOVER	MABEL	MUFTI

MIFFS	MALLE	MAMBO	MENUS	MORAG	MISTS	MOTET	MUZAK
MUFFS	MELEE	MAMAS	MINDS	MARCH	MOSES	MATEY	MEZZO
MCFLY	MILNE	MEMOS	MINES	MARSH	MUSES	MITTY	MAZES
MIFFY	MILCH	MIMES	MINIS	MIRTH	MESSY	MAURA	MUZZY
MAGDA	MULCH	MUMPS	MINOS	MORPH	MISSY	MOULD	NYASA
MAGMA	MALFI	MAMET	MINTS	MYRRH	MISTY	MOUND	NEAVE
MAGNA	MALIK	MAMMY	MINUS	MARDI	MOSEY	MAUVE	NEAGH
MAGIC	MALIN	MOMMY	MONKS	MARGI	MUSHY	MEUSE	NEATH
MCGEE	MELON	MUMMY	MANET	MARNI	MUSKY	MOUSE	NIAMH
MAGOG	MILAN	MUMSY	MONET	MARTI	MUSTY	MOUTH	NAAFI
MOGUL	MULAN	MANGA	MANDY	MERYL	MATED	MOURN	NGAIO
MEGAN	MALMO	MANIA	MANGY	MORAL	METED	MAULS	NEARS
MAGOO	MALAR	MANNA	MANKY	MOREL	MUTED	MOULT	NABOB
MUGUP	MILER	MANOA	MANLY	MURAL	METRE	MOUNT	NOBLE
MAGUS	MOLAR	MANTA	MINDY	MARIN	MITRE	MOUSY	NOBEL
MIGHT	MYLAR	MENSA	MINGY	MORAN	MOTTE	MOVED	NOBBS
MUGGY	MALES	MONZA	MINTY	MARCO	MOTIF	MOVIE	NOBLY
MAHDI	MALLS	MANIC	MONEY	MARIO	MATCH	MAVEN	NACRE
MAHAL	MELDS	MINED	MONTY	MORAR	MITCH	MOVER	NICHE
MAHON	MELTS	MANGE	MOOED	MARES	MITZI	MAVIS	NICKI
MYHAT	MILES	MANSE	MOORE	MARKS	METAL	MEWED	NICAM
MAIDA	MILKS	MINCE	MOOSE	MARTS	MOTEL	MOWED	NACHO
MOIRA	MILLS	MONTH	MOOCH	MERES	MATZO	MOWER	NICER
MAINE	MILOS	MUNCH	MAORI	MORES	METRO	MYWAY	NECKS
MAIZE	MOLES	MYNAH	MOODS	MARAT	MOTTO	MIXED	NICKS
MOIRE	MOLLS	MENAI	MOONS	MERIT	METUP	MIXIN	NICKY
MAIDS	MULES	MINSK	MOORS	MARRY	MATER	MAXIM	NADIA
MAILS	MULLS	MINIM	MOODY	MARTY	METER	MIXIN	NUDGE
MAIMS	MYLES	MANON	MOONY	MERCY	MOTOR	MIXUP	NODAL
MAINS	MALAY	MANGO	MOPED	MERRY	MATES	MIXER	NADIR
MOIST	MELLY	MONDO	MAPLE	MORAY	MATHS	MIXES	NODES
MAINZ	MILKY	MONRO	MOPUP	MURKY	METES	MIXIT	NODUS
MAJOR	MOLLY	MUNGO	MOPES	MUSIC	METHS	MAYBE	NUDES
MEKON	MAMBA	MUNRO	MARIA	MUSED	MITES	MAYLE	NEDDY
MAKER	MAMMA	MANOR	MYRNA	MOSHE	MITTS	MAYAN	NODDY
MAKES	MOMMA	MINER	MARGE	MASAI	MOTES	MAYER	NIECE
MCKAY	MUMBA	MINOR	MARIE	MASON	MOTHS	MAYOR	NOELE
MALTA	MIMIC	MANES	MERGE	MISER	MUTES	MEYER	NEEDS
MELBA	MIMED	MANUS	MERLE	MASKS	MUTTS	MAYAS	NEEPS
MILLA	MRMOM	MENDS	MORSE	MASTS	MYTHS	MOYET	NEEDY

NIFTY	NONCE	NOSES	OMARA	OCEAN	OAKUM	OUTRE	PSALM
NIGEL	NENEH	NASTY	OSAKA	ODEON	OAKEN	OFTEL	PLAIN
NEGRO	NINTH	NOSEY	OHARE	ONEUP	OGLED	OFTEN	PRAWN
NIGER	NINON	NOTED	ORATE	OBEYS	OILED	ORTON	PIANO
NEGUS	NONES	NITRE	OSAGE	OMENS	OLLIE	OUTDO	PLATO
NIGHT	NONET	NOTCH	OVATE	OPENS	OFLAG	ONTAP	PRADO
NEGEV	NANCY	NATAL	OMAGH	OVENS	ORLON	ONTOP	PEAKS
NIGHY	NANNY	NOTON	OKAPI	OVERS	ORLOP	OTTER	PEALS
NAHUM	NINNY	NOTES	OKARO	OWENS	OXLIP	OUTER	PEARS
NEHRU	NIOBE	NATTY	OTAGO	OXERS	OGLER	OXTER	PLANS
NAIRA	NOONE	NUTTY	ONAIR	OVERT	OILER	OATES	PLAYS
NAIAD	NOOSE	NOUNS	OPALS	OVETT	OGLES	OATHS	PRAMS
NAIVE	NAOMI	NAURU	ORALS	OFFAL	OWLET	OCTET	PRAYS
NOISE	NKOMO	NIVEA	OVALS	OXFAM	OTLEY	OFUSE	PLAIT
NAISH	NOOKS	NOVAK	OPART	OFFER	OOMPH	OVULE	PLANT
NEIGH	NAPPA	NAVAL	OVARY	OFFAS	ORMER	OFWAT	PLATT
NEILL	NEPAL	NAVEL	OMBRE	ORGAN	OWNED	OTWAY	PRATT
NAIRN	NAPES	NEVIL	ORBIT	ONGAR	OUNCE	OOZED	PEAKY
NAILS	NAPPY	NOVEL	OXBOW	OLGAS	OWNUP	OUZEL	PEATY
NOISY	NIPPY	NAVAN	OHBOY	OUGHT	OWNER	OOZES	PABLO
NOKIA	NORMA	NAVIN	ONCUE	OSHEA	OLNEY	PLAZA	POBOX
NAKED	NERVE	NIVEN	OCCUR	OCHRE	OVOID	PRAIA	PACED
NIKKI	NORSE	NEVER	ONCER	OGHAM	OZONE	PLAID	PECAN
NELLE	NURSE	NAVES	OSCAR	OTHER	ODOUR	PRAED	PACER
NOLTE	NYREE	NEVIS	ORCZY	OUIJA	OBOES	PEACE	PACES
NOLAN	NORAH	NAVVY	ODDIE	OGIVE	OARED	PEAKE	PACKS
NYLON	NORTH	NAWAB	OLDIE	OLIVE	OPRAH	PEASE	PACTS
NILES	NARES	NEWEL	OGDEN	ONICE	OGRES	PHASE	PECKS
NELLY	NARKS	NEWER	OLDEN	OPINE	ORRIS	PLACE	PICKS
NAMED	NERDS	NEWTS	ODDER	OVINE	OLSEN	PLANE	PICTS
NOMAD	NERYS	NEWLY	OLDER	OXIDE	ORSON	PLATE	PUCKS
NYMPH	NORMS	NEWRY	ORDER	OWING	OASES	PRASE	PICOT
NUMAN	NARKY	NEWSY	ODDLY	ORIEL	OASIS	PRATE	PICKY
NIMMO	NERDY	NOWAY	OMEGA	ODIUM	OASTS	PRANG	PADUA
NAMES	NERVY	NIXON	OPERA	OPIUM	OUSTS	PEACH	PODIA
NIMES	NESTA	NEXUS	OREAD	ONION	ONSET	PLATH	PADME
NUMBS	NYSSA	NSYNC	OBESE	ORION	OSTIA	POACH	PADRE
NIMOY	NOSED	NOYES	OXEYE	OSIER	OPTIC	PLANK	PEDAL
NINIA	NASAL	OHARA	OBELI	OMITS	OCTAD	PRANK	PEDRO
NINJA	NESTS	OMAHA	ONEAL	OBJET	OPTED	PEARL	PADDY

PODGY	PRIDE	PALER	PINUP	POOLS	PERIL	POSIT	PLUSH
PUDGY	PRIME	POLAR	PANES	PRODS	PERON	PASTY	POUCH
PIETA	PRISE	PALES	PANGS	PROMS	PURER	PESKY	PLUCK
PLEAD	PRIZE	PALLS	PANTS	PROPS	PARAS	PUSHY	PLUTO
PSEUD	PRICK	PALMS	PENDS	PROWS	PARES	PUSSY	PLUMP
PEEVE	PHIAL	PELTS	PINES	PROST	PARIS	PATNA	PLUGS
PIECE	PRIAL	PILES	PINKS	PEONY	PARKS	PETRA	PLUMS
PAEAN	PRIAM	PILLS	PINTS	PROBY	PARTS	PITTA	POURS
PAEON	PRISM	POLES	PONDS	PROSY	PERES	PATHE	POUTS
PREEN	PRIMO	POLLS	PONGS	PROXY	PERKS	PATCH	POULT
PEEKS	PRIMP	PULLS	PUNKS	PAPUA	PERMS	PITCH	PAVED
PEELS	PRIOR	PILOT	PUNTS	PIPPA	PORES	PATTI	PAVES
PEEPS	PAILS	PALAU	PINOT	PIPED	PORTS	PETRI	PIVOT
PEERS	PAINS	PILAU	PINGU	PUPAE	PURRS	PETAL	PAWED
PIERS	PAIRS	PHLOX	PANSY	PAPAL	PYRES	PATEN	POWER
PLEAS	PLIES	PALLY	PENNY	PUPIL	PYREX	PITON	PAWNS
PLEBS	PRIES	PALSY	PINKY	POPUP	PARKY	PUTIN	POWYS
POEMS	PRIGS	POLLY	PINNY	PAPER	PARRY	PUTON	PIXIE
POETS	PAINT	PIMMS	PROUD	PIPER	PARTY	PATIO	PIXEL
PRESS	POINT	PUMAS	PHONE	PEPYS	PERCY	PUTUP	PAYEE
PREYS	PRINT	PUMPS	POOLE	PIPES	PERKY	PATER	PAYNE
PLEAT	PLINY	POMMY	PROBE	POPES	PERRY	PETER	PRYCE
PIETY	PRIVY	PANDA	PROLE	PIPIT	PORGY	PATHS	PAYIN
POESY	PUKKA	PINNA	PRONE	PAPPY	PORKY	PITTS	PAYUP
PUFFS	POKED	PINTA	PROSE	POPPY	PASHA	PUTTS	PAYER
PUFFY	PEKOE	PANIC	PROVE	PUPPY	PASTA	PETIT	PRYOR
PAGED	POKER	PUNIC	PROOF	PIQUE	POSED	PATSY	PAYTV
PAGAN	PEKES	PINED	PRONG	PARKA	PASSE	PATTY	PIZZA
PAGER	PIKES	PUNKD	POOCH	PARMA	PASTE	PETTY	QUAKE
PAGES	POKES	PENCE	PRODI	PARED	PISTE	PITHY	QUAFF
PEGGY	PALMA	PENGE	PLONK	PORED	POSSE	POTTY	QUASH
PIGGY	PILEA	PENNE	PROWL	PARSE	POSTE	PUTBY	QUACK
PYGMY	POLKA	PINCH	PROAM	PERSE	PESCI	PUTTY	QUARK
PRIMA	PALED	PUNCH	PHOTO	PUREE	PUSAN	PAULA	QUAIL
PLIED	PILED	PONTI	PROMO	PURGE	PESTO	PLUMB	QUALM
PRIED	PULSE	PANEL	PIOUS	PURSE	POSER	POUND	QUADS
PAIGE	PALIN	PENAL	PLODS	PARCH	PESOS	PAUSE	QUAYS
PAINE	PYLON	PANTO	PLOPS	PERCH	PESTS	PLUME	QUANT
POISE	POLIO	PINTO	PLOTS	PERTH	POSES	PRUDE	QUART
PRICE	POLYP	PONGO	PLOYS	PORCH	POSTS	PRUNE	QUAKY

QUEUE	ROAMS	RUDGE	REGER	ROLES	RUNUP	RIPER	RATTY
QUEEG	ROARS	RADII	ROGER	ROLLS	RANDS	ROPER	RETRY
QUELL	RYANS	RYDAL	RAGES	RULES	RANIS	ROPES	RITZY
QUEEN	REACT	RADON	REGIS	RELET	RANKS	REPOT	ROUND
QUERN	RIANT	RODIN	RIGGS	RELIT	RANTS	REPAY	REUSE
QUEER	ROAST	RADIO	RIGHT	RELAX	RENDS	REPLY	ROUGE
QUEST	READY	RODEO	ROGET	ROLEX	RENTS	RURAL	ROUSE
QUERY	REBEC	RADAR	RIGBY	RALLY	RINGS	RERAN	ROUTE
QUIRE	RABID	RIDER	RUGBY	RELAY	RINKS	RERUN	ROUGH
QUITE	REBID	RUDER	REHAB	RILEY	RUNES	RARER	ROUEN
QUIFF	ROBED	RYDER	ROHAN	RUMBA	RUNGS	RASTA	ROUES
QUICK	RABBI	RIDES	RAISA	RIMED	RUNTS	ROSIE	ROUTS
QUIRK	RUBIK	RADIX	RAINE	RAMEN	RENEW	ROSSI	ROUST
QUILL	REBEL	REDUX	RAISE	RAMON	RANDY	ROSTI	RAVED
QUINN	RABIN	REDDY	RHINE	ROMAN	RANGY	RASEN	ROVED
QUITO	ROBIN	RUDDY	REICH	RUMEN	RUNNY	RESIN	REVIE
QUIDS	REBUS	REECE	REITH	RAMBO	RHODA	RISEN	REVUE
QUINS	ROBES	REESE	REIKI	ROMEO	RHONA	ROSIN	RAVEL
QUIPS	RABAT	REEVE	REIGN	RUMER	RIOJA	RISER	REVEL
QUITS	REBUT	REEDS	RHINO	RAMPS	RHOMB	RASPS	RIVAL
QUIET	ROBOT	REEFS	RAIDS	REMUS	RHODE	RESTS	RAVEN
QUILT	RACED	REEKS	RAILS	RIMES	RHONE	RISES	RIVEN
QUOTA	RECCE	REELS	RAINS	ROMPS	RIOCH	RISKS	REVUP
QUOTE	RUCHE	RHEAS	REINS	RUMPS	RIOTS	ROSES	RAVER
QUOIN	RICCI	RHETT	ROILS	REMIT	ROODS	RUSES	RIVER
QUORN	RICKI	REEDY	RUINS	REMIX	ROOFS	RUSKS	ROVER
QUOIT	RICIN	RIFLE	RAINY	RUMMY	ROOKS	RUSTS	RAVES
QATAR	RECTO	REFER	REIFY	RUNIC	ROOMS	RESAT	ROVES
ROALD	ROCCO	RAFTS	REJIG	RANDE	ROOTS	RESET	RIVET
READE	RECAP	RIFFS	RAJAS	RANGE	ROOST	RESIT	ROWED
REAVE	RACER	RIFTS	RAKED	RENEE	ROOMY	RISKY	RAWLE
REACH	RECUR	RUFFS	RIKKI	RINSE	RSPCA	RUSTY	ROWEL
ROACH	RACES	RUFUS	RAKES	RANCH	RAPID	RATED	ROWAN
REALM	RACKS	REFIT	RELIC	RONNI	ROPED	RATEL	ROWEN
REARM	RICKS	RAGGA	RILED	RENAL	RUPEE	RATIO	ROWER
READS	ROCKS	RAGED	RULED	RONAN	REPEL	RETRO	ROWDY
REAMS	RICKY	RIGID	RALPH	RONIN	RIPEN	ROTOR	ROXIE
REAPS	ROCKY	ROGUE	RULER	RUNIN	RIPON	RATES	RHYME
REARS	REDID	REGAL	RILES	RINGO	REPRO	RITES	ROYCE
ROADS	RIDGE	REGAN	RILLS	RONDO	RIPUP	ROTAS	ROYLE

RIYAL	STARE	SLAIN	SWABS	SEDUM	SWELL	SPENT	SNIDE
ROYAL	STATE	SPAIN	SWANS	SODOM	SPERM	SWEAT	SNIPE
RAYON	STAVE	SPAWN	SWAPS	SEDAN	STEAM	SWEET	SPICE
RAZED	SUAVE	STAIN	SWATS	SUDAN	SHEEN	SWEPT	SPIKE
RAZOR	SWALE	SWAIN	SWAYS	SADKO	SKEAN	SEEDY	SPILE
RAZES	SCARF	SWANN	SCANT	SEDER	SKEIN	SOFIA	SPINE
SCAPA	STAFF	SHAKO	SHAFT	SODOR	STEIN	SAFIN	SPIRE
SKARA	SLANG	SCALP	SLANT	SIDES	STERN	SAFER	SPITE
SCALD	SLASH	SCAMP	SMALT	SADAT	SEETO	SOFAR	STILE
SHARD	SMASH	SCARP	SMART	SADHU	SHEEP	SAFES	STIPE
STAID	STASH	SCAUP	START	SADLY	SLEEP	SIFTS	SUITE
STAND	SWASH	SHARP	SCALY	SUDSY	STEEP	SOFAS	SWINE
SWARD	SWAMI	STAMP	SCARY	SHEBA	SWEEP	SIGMA	SWIPE
SCALE	SWAZI	SWAMP	SEAMY	SIENA	SHEAR	SEGUE	SKIFF
SCAPE	SHACK	STAIR	SHADY	SPEED	SHEER	SEGAL	SNIFF
SCARE	SHANK	STARR	SHAKY	SPEND	SMEAR	SIGIL	SPIFF
SHADE	SHARK	SCABS	SNAKY	STEAD	SNEER	SAGAN	STIFF
SHAKE	SKANK	SCANS	SOAPY	STEED	SPEAR	SUGAR	SLING
SHALE	SLACK	SCARS	STACY	SCENE	STEER	SAGAS	STING
SHAME	SMACK	SEALS	STAGY	SHERE	SWEAR	SAGES	SUING
SHANE	SNACK	SEAMS	SABLE	SIEGE	SEEDS	SIGHS	SWING
SHAPE	SNARK	SEARS	SABRE	SIEVE	SEEKS	SIGNS	SMITH
SHARE	SPANK	SEATS	SIBYL	SKENE	SEEMS	SIGHT	STICH
SHAVE	SPARK	SHAHS	SYBIL	STEVE	SEEPS	SAGGY	SWISH
SKATE	STACK	SLABS	SEBUM	SUEDE	SEERS	SOGGY	SCIFI
SLADE	STALK	SLAMS	SOBER	SWEDE	SHEDS	SAHIB	SHIRK
SLAKE	STANK	SLAPS	SABOT	SHEAF	SKEPS	SHIVA	SKINK
SLATE	STARK	SLATS	SACHA	SHELF	SLEDS	SHIED	SLICK
SLAVE	SWANK	SLAYS	SUCRE	STEPH	SMEWS	SKIED	SLINK
SNAKE	SHALL	SNAGS	SECCO	SLEEK	SPECS	SPIED	SMIRK
SNAPE	SHAWL	SNAPS	SACHS	SNEAK	SPEWS	SEINE	SNICK
SNARE	SMALL	SOAKS	SACKS	SPEAK	STEMS	SEIZE	SPICK
SOAVE	SNAIL	SOARS	SECTS	SPECK	STEPS	SHINE	STICK
SPACE	SNARL	SPANS	SOCKS	STEAK	STEWS	SHIRE	STINK
SPADE	SPALL	SPARS	SUCKS	SHELL	SCENT	SKIVE	SKILL
SPARE	STALL	SPATS	SIDED	SMELL	SHEET	SLICE	SKIRL
SPATE	SMARM	STABS	SADIE	SNELL	SKEET	SLIDE	SPIEL
STAGE	SPASM	STAGS	SEDGE	SPELL	SLEET	SLIME	SPILL
STAKE	SWARM	STARS	SIDHE	STEAL	SLEPT	SMILE	STILL
STALE	SHAUN	STAYS	SIDLE	STEEL	SMELT	SMITE	SWILL

SWIRL	SWIFT	SOLOS	SINAI	STOVE	SPOOR	STORY	SURER
SCION	SHINY	SULKS	SUNNI	STOWE	STOUR	SEPIA	SARIS
SPION	SLIMY	SALUT	SUNUP	SWORE	SCOTS	SAPID	SERBS
SLIGO	SPICY	SPLAT	SANER	SCOFF	SCOWS	SEPAL	SERFS
SPIRO	SPIKY	SPLIT	SENOR	SPOOF	SHOES	SUPER	SIRES
SKIMP	SPINY	SALLY	SONAR	SLOSH	SHOPS	SEPOY	SORES
SKIER	SPITZ	SALTY	SANDS	SLOTH	SHOTS	SOPPY	SORTS
SAILS	SWIZZ	SELBY	SENDS	SHOJI	SHOWS	SYRIA	SURFS
SHIES	SAKER	SILKY	SINGS	SHOCK	SLOBS	SCRUB	SPRAT
SHIMS	SIKES	SILLY	SINKS	SHOOK	SLOES	SHRUB	STRUT
SHINS	SIKHS	SPLAY	SINUS	SMOCK	SLOGS	SHRED	SCREW
SHIPS	SYKES	SULKY	SONGS	SLOPS	SLOPS	SIRED	SHREW
SKIDS	SALMA	SULLY	SINEW	SPOOK	SLOTS	STRAD	STRAW
SKIES	SALSA	SAMBA	SANDY	STOCK	SLOWS	SCREE	STREW
SKIMS	SELMA	SAMIA	SONNY	STOOK	SNOBS	SERGE	SARKY
SKINS	SOLFA	SAMOA	SUNNY	STORK	SNOWS	SERLE	SORRY
SKIPS	SALAD	SAMSA	SHONA	SCOWL	SPOTS	SERVE	SPRAY
SKITS	SOLED	SIMBA	SKODA	SEOUL	STOPS	SPREE	STRAY
SLIMS	SOLID	SUMAC	STOIC	SHOAL	STOWS	SURGE	SURLY
SLIPS	SALVE	SOMME	SCOLD	SPOIL	SWOTS	SERIF	SUSIE
SLITS	SOLVE	SIMON	SNOOD	SPOOL	SCOOT	SCRAG	SUSHI
SNIPS	SYLPH	SUMUP	STOOD	STOOL	SCOTT	SHRUG	SISAL
SOILS	SALMI	SUMER	SWORD	STORM	SCOUT	SPRIG	SASIN
SPIES	SOLTI	SAMMS	SCONE	SCORN	SHOOT	SPROG	SUSAN
SPINS	SALEM	SEMIS	SCOPE	SHORN	SHORT	SARAH	SASSY
SPIVS	SALON	SUMPS	SCORE	SHOWN	SHOUT	SERAI	SISSY
STIES	SALVO	SAMEY	SHONE	SLOAN	SMOLT	SHREK	SITKA
STIRS	SALOP	SAMMY	SHORE	SPOON	SNORT	SCRAM	SATED
SUITS	SOLAR	SANAA	SHOVE	SWOON	SNOUT	SCRUM	SITED
SWIGS	SALES	SANTA	SLOPE	SWORN	SPORT	SERUM	SATIE
SWIMS	SALTS	SENNA	SMOKE	SLOMO	SPOUT	STRUM	SITCH
SWISS	SELES	SONIA	SMOTE	SMOKO	STOAT	SERIN	SUTCH
SAINT	SELLS	SONJA	SNORE	SCOOP	STOTT	SIREN	SHTUM
SHIFT	SILAS	SONIC	SPODE	SLOOP	STOUT	SERVO	SATAN
SHIRT	SILKS	SYNOD	SPOKE	SNOOP	SIOUX	SCRAP	SATIN
SKINT	SILLS	SENSE	SPORE	STOEP	SHOWY	SCRIP	SETON
SKIRT	SILOS	SINCE	STOKE	STOMP	SMOKY	STRAP	SITIN
SPILT	SILTS	SINGE	STOLE	STOOP	SNOWY	STRIP	SETTO
STILT	SOLES	SINGH	STONE	SWOOP	SOOTY	STROP	SETUP
STINT	SOLIS	SANDI	STORE	SCOUR	STONY	SYRUP	SITUP

SATYR	SPURN	SEWER	TEAMS	TODDY	TAGUS	TWIST	TEMPO
SITAR	SCUDO	SOWER	TEARS	THEDA	TOGAS	TAJIK	TAMAR
SATES	SLUMP	SIXTH	TEATS	THETA	TIGHT	TIKKA	TAMER
SETTS	SLURP	SAXON	THATS	THEOC	TAIGA	TAKEN	TIMER
SITES	STUMP	SIXER	THAWS	TREAD	THIRD	TOKEN	TIMOR
SATAY	SCUDS	SIXES	TOADS	TREND	TRIAD	TOKYO	TAMES
SETBY	SCUTS	SIXTY	TRAMS	TWEED	TRIED	TAKER	TAMPS
SAUNA	SEUSS	SAYLE	TRAPS	TEESE	THINE	TAKES	TEMPS
SCUBA	SHUNS	STYLE	TRASS	THEME	TOILE	TYKES	TIMES
SOUSA	SHUTS	SPYRI	TRAYS	THERE	TRIBE	TOKAY	TOMBS
SQUAB	SKUAS	SAYSO	TSARS	THESE	TRICE	TILDA	TOMES
SQUIB	SLUGS	STYLO	TOAST	TEETH	TRIKE	TULSA	TEMPT
SOUND	SLUMS	SAYER	TRACT	TREVI	TRIPE	TILED	TAMMY
SQUAD	SLURS	SHYER	TRAIT	TWEAK	TRITE	TILDE	TIMMY
SQUID	SMUTS	SLYER	TOADY	THERM	TWICE	TULLE	TOMMY
SAUCE	SNUBS	STYES	TRACY	TIEIN	TWINE	TILTH	TUMMY
SAUTE	SOULS	SHYLY	TIBIA	TIEUP	THIEF	TALON	TANGA
SHUTE	SOUPS	SLYLY	TABLE	TWERP	THING	TULIP	TANYA
SOUSE	SOURS	SOYUZ	TOBIN	THEIR	TYING	TILER	TONGA
SPUME	SPUDS	SIZES	TABOO	TEEMS	THIGH	TYLER	TONIC
SCUFF	SPURS	TIARA	TABOR	TEENS	THICK	TALES	TUNIC
SCURF	STUBS	TEASE	TIBER	TIERS	THINK	TALKS	TONED
SMURF	STUDS	TIBER	TUBER	TREES	TRICK	TALUS	TUNED
SNUFF	STUNS	THANE	TIBBS	TREKS	TRIAL	TELLS	TENSE
STUFF	SHUNT	TRACE	TUBAS	TRESS	TRILL	TILES	TINGE
SLUNG	SPURT	TRADE	TUBES	TREWS	TWILL	TILLS	TONNE
STUNG	SQUAT	TWANG	TIBET	TREYS	TWIRL	TILTS	TENCH
SWUNG	STUNT	TEACH	TABBY	THEFT	TEIGN	TOLLS	TENTH
SHUSH	SAUCY	TRASH	TUBBY	TREAT	TRIER	TOLET	TANNI
SLUSH	STUDY	THALI	TACKS	TRENT	TAILS	TELEX	TONAL
SOUTH	SAVED	TRACI	TACOS	TWEET	THINS	TALLY	TENON
SAUDI	SEVEN	THANK	TICKS	TEENY	TOILS	TELLY	TANGO
SHUCK	SAVER	TRACK	TUCKS	TIFFS	TRIES	TILLY	TENKO
SKULK	SEVER	TRAIL	TACIT	TOFFS	TRIMS	TULLY	TONTO
SKUNK	SAVES	TRAWL	TACKY	TUFTS	TRIOS	TAMPA	TONUP
SLUNK	SAVOY	TRAIN	TIDAL	TAFFY	TRIPS	TAMED	TENOR
STUCK	SAVVY	TWAIN	TUDOR	TUFTY	TWIGS	TIMED	TONER
STUNK	SAWED	THABO	TIDES	TIGRE	TWINS	TIMID	TUNER
SCULL	SEWED	TRAMP	TEDDY	TEGAN	TWITS	TAMIL	TANGS
SKULL	SOWED	TEALS	TODAY	TIGER	TAINT	TIMON	TANKS

TENDS	TEPID	TARTS	TATUM	TOXIC	USING	VICKY	VOLTS
TENTS	TOPED	TERMS	TOTEM	TAXED	URIAH	VODKA	VALET
TINES	TYPED	TERNS	TATIN	TEXAN	URICH	VEDIC	VELDT
TINGS	TEPEE	TIRES	TITAN	TOXIN	UNION	VIDAL	VAMPS
TINTS	TIPPI	TORUS	TUTIN	TAXES	UNITS	VADIM	VANYA
TONES	TOPOL	TURFS	TOTUP	TAXIS	UNIFY	VIDEO	VANCE
TONGS	TIPUP	TURKS	TUTOR	TEXAS	UNITY	VADER	VENUE
TONKS	TOPUP	TURNS	TITUS	TEXTS	UHLAN	VIDOR	VINCE
TUNES	TAPER	TURPS	TOTES	TOYED	UNLET	VJDAY	VINCI
TUNIS	TAPIR	TYRES	TUTUS	THYME	UNLIT	VADUZ	VENAL
TENET	TOPER	TYROS	TATTY	TOYAH	UNMET	VNECK	VINYL
TANDY	TAPAS	TAROT	THUMB	TRYON	ULNAR	VEERS	VENOM
TANGY	TAPES	TURKU	TAUPE	TRYST	UBOAT	VIEWS	VANES
TANSY	TOPES	THREW	THULE	TIZZY	UPPED	VAGUE	VENDS
TENBY	TYPES	THROW	TRUCE	UKASE	UNPEG	VOGUE	VENTS
TINNY	TYPOS	TARDY	TRUDE	USAGE	UNPIN	VIGIL	VENUS
TUNNY	TIPSY	TARRY	TOUCH	URALS	UPPER	VEGAN	VINES
THORA	TOPSY	TERRY	TOUGH	UMBRA	UGRIC	VIGGO	VINNY
TBONE	TOPAZ	TASHA	TRUTH	UZBEK	UPSET	VAGUS	VIOLA
THOSE	TOQUE	TESLA	TRUCK	URBAN	ULTRA	VEGAS	VROOM
TROPE	TARKA	TESSA	TRUNK	UMBER	UNTIE	VOILA	VIOLS
TROVE	TERRA	TOSCA	TRURO	UNCLE	UNTIL	VOICE	VAPID
THONG	THROB	TASTE	THUMP	UNCAP	UPTON	VOILE	VIPER
THOTH	TIRED	TOSTI	TRUMP	ULCER	UTTER	VYING	VARNA
TOOTH	TERCE	TYSON	TRUER	UNCAS	UHURA	VEILS	VIRNA
TROTH	TERSE	TASSO	THUDS	UNCUT	UVULA	VEINS	VERGE
TROLL	THREE	TESCO	THUGS	UNDID	USUAL	VOIDS	VERNE
THORN	TIREE	TASKS	TOURS	UNDUE	UTURN	VEIDT	VERSE
TROON	TORME	TESTS	TOUTS	UDDER	USURP	VELMA	VERVE
TROOP	TORTE	TUSKS	TRUGS	UNDER	ULURU	VILLA	VERDI
TWOUP	TORAH	TASTY	TRUSS	UPEND	USURY	VOLGA	VIRAL
TOOLS	TORCH	TESTY	TAUNT	USEUP	UNWIN	VOLTA	VIREN
TOONS	TERRI	TETRA	TRUST	USERS	UNZIP	VALID	VERSO
TOOTS	TYROL	TOTED	TRULY	UNFED	VIALS	VALUE	VIRGO
TROGS	THRUM	TITHE	TOWED	UNFIT	VIBES	VALVE	VERBS
TROTS	TURIN	TITLE	TAWSE	URGED	VICKI	VALLI	VIRUS
TROUT	TORSO	TITCH	TOWEL	URGES	VOCAL	VOLVO	VESPA
TOPIC	TURBO	TUTSI	TOWER	USHER	VICAR	VILER	VESTA
TUPAC	TARES	TUTTI	TOWNS	UTHER	VICES	VALES	VISTA
TAPED	TARNS	TOTAL	TAWNY	UNITE	VICHY	VOLES	VISOR

VASES	WODEN	WHIFF	WILES	WHOOP	WITTY	YULAN	ZONES
VESTS	WADER	WRING	WILLS	WOODS	WOULD	YELLS	ZINGY
VISAS	WIDER	WEIGH	WILTS	WOOFS	WOUND	YELPS	ZOOMS
VISIT	WIDOR	WHICH	WOLDS	WOODY	WRUNG	YOLKS	ZLOTY
VOTED	WADES	WHISK	WALLY	WOOZY	WAUGH	YEMEN	ZAPPA
VETCH	WIDOW	WEILL	WELLY	WIPED	WAVED	YOMPS	ZEPPO
VITTI	WIELD	WHIRL	WILBY	WIPER	WOVEN	YUMMY	ZIPPY
VITAL	WHERE	WHIRR	WILLY	WIPES	WAVER	YENTL	ZORBA
VOTER	WHELK	WAIFS	WALTZ	WIRED	WAVES	YANKS	ZORRO
VOTES	WREAK	WAILS	WOMAN	WORLD	WIVES	YONKS	ZEROS
VOUCH	WRECK	WAINS	WOMEN	WARNE	WAXED	YARRA	
VAULT	WHEEL	WAITS	WYMAN	WORSE	WAXEN	YERBA	
VAUNT	WHELP	WEIRS	WIMPS	WORTH	WAXES	YORKE	
VIVID	WEEDS	WHIGS	WIMPY	WIRER	WAYNE	YARDS	
VOWED	WEEKS	WHIMS	WANDA	WARDS	WRYER	YARNS	
VOWEL	WEEPS	WHINS	WONGA	WARES	XRAYS	YPRES	
VEXED	WHETS	WHIPS	WONKA	WARMS	XEBEC	YATES	
VIXEN	WRENS	WRITS	WANED	WARNS	XYLEM	YOUNG	
VEXES	WHEAT	WAIST	WINCE	WARPS	XENON	YOUTH	
WEALD	WIEST	WHIST	WYNNE	WARTS	XHOSA	YOURS	
WEAVE	WREST	WRIST	WENCH	WIRES	XEROX	YAWED	
WHALE	WEEDY	WHIZZ	WINCH	WORDS	YEARN	YOWIE	
WHARF	WEENY	WAKEN	WANDS	WORKS	YEARS	YAWLS	
WRATH	WEEPY	WOKEN	WANES	WORMS	YEATS	YAWNS	
WHACK	WAFER	WAKES	WANTS	WORST	YEAST	YOYOS	
WRACK	WAFTS	WELLA	WENDS	WURST	YOBBO	ZCARS	
WEALS	WAGED	WILMA	WINDS	WARTY	YABBY	ZEBRA	
WEANS	WAGON	WILDE	WINES	WORDY	YUCCA	ZUBIN	
WEARS	WIGAN	WOLFE	WINGS	WORRY	YACHT	ZADIE	
WHATS	WOGAN	WOLOF	WINKS	WASTE	YUCKY	ZIGGY	
WRAPS	WAGER	WALSH	WENDY	WESER	YODEL	ZAIRE	
WYATT	WAGES	WELCH	WINDY	WISER	YIELD	ZUKOR	
WEARY	WIGHT	WELSH	WONKY	WASPS	YAHOO	ZELDA	
WEBER	WEIRD	WILCO	WOOED	WISPS	YOKED	ZELIG	
WICKS	WAITE	WYLER	WHOLE	WASPY	YOKEL	ZILCH	
WACKY	WAIVE	WALES	WHOSE	WISPY	YUKON	ZULUS	
WADED	WHILE	WALKS	WROTE	WATCH	YIKES	ZENDA	
WEDGE	WHINE	WALLS	WOOLF	WITCH	YOKES	ZONED	
WIDTH	WHITE	WELDS	WRONG	WATER	YAKUT	ZANTE	
WIDEN	WRITE	WELLS	WHORL	WATTS	YALTA	ZONAL	

ABADAN	AWAITS	ASCENT	APERCU	AFFORD	ATHINA	ABJURE
ARAFAT	ABACUS	ANCHOR	AGENDA	AEGEAN	ASHTON	ADJURE
ARARAT	ACARUS	ACCEPT	AMENDS	AFGHAN	ABHORS	ADJUST
AVATAR	ABBACY	ACCORD	ABELES	ANGLED	ADHERE	ACKACK
AMANDA	AUBADE	ACCESS	ALEVEL	ANGLEE	ASHORE	AIKIDO
AWARDS	AMBLED	ACCOST	ALEXEI	ANGLER	AGHAST	ANKLES
ABASED	AMBLER	ACCUSE	APEMEN	ANGLES	ADIDAS	ANKLET
ABASES	AMBLES	ALCOTT	APEXES	ARGUED	ANIMAL	AUKLET
ABATED	AUBREY	ACCRUE	AVENGE	ARGUER	AKIMBO	ALKALI
ABATES	ALBEIT	ALCOVE	AWEIGH	ARGUES	APIECE	ASKING
ADAGES	AMBLIN	ANDEAN	AMECHE	ANGLIA	ABIDED	ATKINS
AMAZED	ALBUMS	ABDABS	ARETHA	ANGELA	ABIDES	ANKARA
AMAZES	ALBANS	ABDUCT	AYESHA	ANGELI	ARISEN	AFLOAT
AWAKEN	ALBANY	ADDICT	ACETIC	ANGELO	ARISES	AGLEAM
AWAKES	ALBINO	ADDUCE	ALESIA	ANGELS	ASIDES	ADLIBS
AZALEA	ALBION	ADDUCT	ALEXIS	ANGOLA	ALIGHT	ALLUDE
AGATHA	ALBERT	ADDLED	AMELIA	ARGYLE	ACIDIC	AELRED
APACHE	AUBURN	ADDLES	AMELIE	ANGINA	ALIBIS	ALLIED
APATHY	ABBESS	ANDREA	AMERIE	ARGENT	ALICIA	ALLIES
ACACIA	AMBUSH	ANDREW	AGEOLD	ALGORE	AFIELD	ASLEEP
ACARID	ATBEST	AUDREY	AREOLA	ANGERS	ARIDLY	AYLMER
ADAGIO	ABBOTS	ALDRIN	AGEING	ANGORA	AVIDLY	ALLEGE
AGADIR	ABBOTT	AEDILE	AHERNE	ASGARD	AXIOMS	AFLAME
AGARIC	ARBOUR	ADDAMS	ALEPPO	AUGERS	ALIENS	APLOMB
ANAKIN	ABBEYS	ADDING	ATEMPO	AUGURS	ALIGNS	AILING
ARABIA	ALCOCK	ADDONS	AGEISM	AUGURY	AMIENS	ARLENE
ARABIC	ACCEDE	AIDING	AGEIST	ARGOSY	ARIANE	ASLANT
ARABIS	ARCADE	ARDENT	ATEASE	AUGUST	ASIANS	ABLOOM
ARALIA	ARCADY	ANDHOW	AVERSE	ASHCAN	ALISON	ALLURE
ARAMIS	AACHEN	ADDERS	ADEPTS	ASHLAR	AMIGOS	ABLEST
ALASKA	ARCHED	AIDERS	AGENTS	ASHRAM	ASIMOV	ABLUSH
ARABLE	ARCHER	ALDERS	ALERTS	APHIDS	APIARY	ALLISS
AVAILS	ARCHES	ALDISS	AVERTS	ASHLEE	AVIARY	ATLAST
ALARMS	ARCHIE	AUDITS	AVENUE	ASHLEY	AMIDST	ALLOTS
AMATOL	ARCTIC	ALDOUS	AYEAYE	ACHILL	AVIATE	ARLOTT
AMAZON	ARCHLY	ARDOUR	AFFRAY	AWHILE	ADIEUS	ABLAUT
ARAGON	ACCENT	ACETAL	AFFECT	ATHOME	AMICUS	ALLIUM
AVALON	ANCONA	APEMAN	ALFRED	ACHING	ANIMUS	ALLOUT
AGASSI	ARCANA	ARENAL	AFFAIR	ATHAND	ABJECT	ALLOWS
ADAPTS	ARCANE	ARENAS	AUFAIT	ATHENA	ADJOIN	ALLAYS
AVANTI	ASCEND	AGENCY	AFFIRM	ATHENS	ADJANI	ALLEYS

ALLOYS	AVOIDS	ALPINE	AIRBUS	AZTECA	ABUSED	BRANDO
ABLAZE	ABODES	APPEND	AIRGUN	AITKEN	ABUSER	BRANDS
ARMADA	ADOBES	AMPERE	ATRIUM	ANTHEA	ABUSES	BRANDT
ARMIES	ADORED	ASPERN	ARRIVE	ANTHEM	ACUMEN	BRANDY
ARMLET	ADORER	ASPIRE	ARROWS	ANTHER	AMULET	BEADED
ARMAGH	ADORES	APPOSE	ARRAYS	ANTLER	AMUSED	BEAKED
ARMPIT	ANODES	ACQUIT	ALSACE	ASTLEY	AMUSES	BEAKER
AIMING	APOGEE	ABROAD	AISLES	ATTLEE	ANUBIS	BEAMED
ALMOND	ATONED	ADRIAN	AMSTEL	ANTRIM	APULIA	BEAMER
ARMANI	ATONES	AERIAL	ANSWER	ARTOIS	ALUMNA	BEARER
ARMING	AVOCET	AIRBAG	AUSTEN	ASTRID	ALUMNI	BEATEN
ADMIRE	AVOWED	AIRMAN	ASSIGN	ATTAIN	AQUINO	BEATER
ASMARA	AWOKEN	AIRSAC	ABSEIL	ATTILA	ACUITY	BEAVER
ADMASS	AZORES	AIRWAY	ASSAIL	ASTHMA	ADULTS	BIASED
ALMOST	ADONIS	AEROBE	AUSSIE	AUTUMN	AOUITA	BLADES
ADMITS	ATOMIC	AFRICA	AUSTIN	ACTING	ADVICE	BLAMED
ARMFUL	APOLLO	ARRACK	ANSELM	ACTONE	ANVILS	BLAMES
ARMOUR	ATOLLS	ABRADE	ASSUME	ANTONY	ADVENT	BLARED
ANNEAL	ABOUND	ADRIEN	ABSENT	ASTANA	ADVERB	BLARES
ANNUAL	ACORNS	AGREED	ASSENT	ATTEND	ADVERT	BLAZED
ARNICA	ADORNS	AGREES	ABSORB	ATTUNE	ADVISE	BLAZER
ARNHEM	AMOUNT	AIRBED	ABSURD	ACTION	ASWELL	BLAZES
AUNTIE	ANOINT	AIRIER	ADSORB	AUTHOR	ATWELL	BOATER
ANNEKA	AROUND	AIRMEN	ASSERT	ACTORS	ATWILL	BRACED
ANNALS	ABOARD	ADRIFT	ASSORT	AFTERS	ALWAYS	BRACER
ANNULS	AMOURS	ADROIT	ASSURE	ALTARS	ANYWAY	BRACES
ARNOLD	AROUSE	AFRAID	ASSESS	ALTERS	ANYONE	BRADEN
AWNING	ABORTS	AIRILY	ASSISI	ARTERY	AMYFOX	BRAKED
ARNESS	ADOPTS	AFRAME	ASSIST	ASTERN	ANYHOW	BRAKES
AGNATE	AGOUTI	AIRING	ANSETT	ASTERS	ALYSSA	BRAVED
ANNEXE	ANONYM	APRONS	ASSETS	ATTARS	ADYTUM	BRAVER
ANNOYS	APPEAL	ARRANT	ASSAYS	ATTIRE	ASYLUM	BRAVES
ADONAI	APPEAR	AYRTON	ACTUAL	ARTIST	BRAMAH	BRAYED
AMORAL	ALPACA	ABRUPT	ALTMAN	ATTEST	BIANCA	BRAZED
ANORAK	ASPECT	AIRERS	ASTRAL	ASTUTE	BLANCH	BRAZEN
AROMAS	AMPLER	AURORA	ASTRAY	ACTIUM	BLANCO	BRAZES
ATONAL	APPLES	ACROSS	ANTICS	ACTOUT	BRACCO	BEACHY
AVOWAL	APPLET	AFRESH	ATTACH	ARTFUL	BRANCH	BEANIE
AMOEBA	AUPAIR	ARREST	ATTACK	ARTHUR	BEARDS	BEATIT
ATONCE	APPALS	ATRISK	ATTICA	AUTEUR	BOARDS	BRAZIL
ATODDS	ALPENA	AERATE	ATTICS	ACTIVE	BRAIDS	BLANKS

BEADLE	BECKET	BEDBUG	BEFOGS	BEHEAD	BUJOLD	BALING
BEAGLE	BICKER	BIERCE	BAFFIN	BEHALF	BYJOVE	BELONG
BEATLE	BUCKED	BLEACH	BOFFIN	BEHELD	BAKING	BYLINE
BRAWLS	BUCKET	BLENCH	BAFFLE	BEHOLD	BBKING	BALBOA
BRAHMA	BACALL	BREACH	BEFALL	BEHIND	BIKING	BALLOT
BRAHMS	BECALM	BREECH	BEFELL	BYHAND	BIKINI	BELLOC
BAAING	BUCKLE	BLEEDS	BEFORE	BEHEST	BAKERS	BELLOW
BEAUNE	BECAME	BLENDS	BEFITS	BEHAVE	BAKERY	BILLOW
BLAINE	BECOME	BREEDS	BEFOUL	BRIDAL	BIKERS	BILSON
BRAINE	BECKON	BRENDA	BAGMAN	BHINDI	BALKAN	BOLTON
BRAINS	BECOOL	BEEFED	BEGGAR	BLINDS	BALLAD	BALERS
BRAINY	BICEPS	BEEPED	BIGCAT	BUILDS	BALSAM	BELFRY
BRAWNY	BACKUP	BEEPER	BAGGED	BAILED	BALZAC	BOLERO
BEACON	BEDLAM	BREMEN	BAGMEN	BAILEY	BELGAE	BELTUP
BEATON	BEDECK	BREVES	BEGGED	BAITED	BILBAO	BULBUL
BRAISE	BODICE	BREVET	BIGBEN	BAIZED	BULGAR	BYLAWS
BRASSY	BADGER	BREWED	BIGGER	BLIMEY	BALDER	BOLEYN
BEASTS	BADGES	BREWER	BUGGED	BOILED	BALEEN	BELIZE
BEATTY	BEDDED	BRECHT	BUGLER	BOILER	BALLED	BEMOAN
BEAUTY	BIDDEN	BREAKS	BUGLES	BRIBED	BALLET	BOMBAY
BLASTS	BIDDER	BREEKS	BUGNER	BRIBER	BELIED	BUMBAG
BOASTS	BODGED	BEETLE	BAGNIO	BRIBES	BELIEF	BAMBER
BEARUP	BODGER	BOEING	BIGWIG	BRIDES	BELIES	BOMBED
BEATUP	BODGES	BEETON	BAGELS	BRIEFS	BELLES	BOMBER
BRAQUE	BODIES	BRECON	BOGGLE	BEINGS	BELTED	BUMPED
BRAZZI	BUDGED	BRETON	BIGAMY	BRIDGE	BELTER	BUMPER
BOBCAT	BUDGES	BLEEPS	BEGINS	BRIGGS	BILLED	BAMAKO
BABIES	BUDGET	BLEARY	BEGONE	BRINGS	BILLET	BUMBLE
BOBBED	BADEGG	BREAST	BIGEND	BLIGHT	BOLDER	BAMBOO
BOBBIE	BODEGA	BLEATS	BYGONE	BLITHE	BOLGER	BEMUSE
BOBBIN	BUDDHA	BREATH	BIGTOE	BRIGHT	BOLTED	BANJAX
BABBLE	BADDIE	BEEFUP	BIGTOP	BLINKS	BULGED	BANTAM
BOBBLE	BEDSIT	BLEWUP	BOGNOR	BRICKS	BULGES	BANYAN
BOBBLY	BODKIN	BREWUP	BOGART	BRIDLE	BULLET	BANZAI
BUBBLE	BODMIN	BYEBYE	BEGETS	BRILLO	BELUGA	BENGAL
BUBBLY	BUDGIE	BREEZE	BIGHTS	BAIRNS	BALTIC	BINBAG
BABOON	BODILY	BREEZY	BIGOTS	BRIAND	BELAIR	BINMAN
BUCHAN	BUDDLE	BIFFED	BOGOTA	BRITON	BILLIE	BONHAM
BACKED	BIDING	BUFFED	BIGGUN	BRIARS	BALDLY	BONSAI
BACKER	BODING	BUFFER	BIGSUR	BRIERS	BOLDLY	BUNYAN
BECKER	BEDAUB	BUFFET	BIGEYE	BEIRUT	BELAMI	BANDED

BANGED	BANJOS	BROKEN	BOPEEP	BURRED	BURROW	BASELY
BANGER	BANKON	BROKER	BOPPED	BEREFT	BURTON	BUSILY
BANKED	BENSON	BROLGA	BOPPER	BORAGE	BARBRA	BUSTLE
BANKER	BONBON	BOOTHS	BYPASS	BERTHA	BORERS	BESOMS
BANNED	BONMOT	BIONIC	BARMAN	BERTHS	BAREST	BASING
BANNEN	BUNION	BIOPIC	BARSAC	BIRTHS	BERATE	BASINS
BANNER	BUNTON	BIOTIC	BUREAU	BURGHS	BERETS	BOSUNS
BANTER	BINARY	BLOWIT	BURIAL	BARBIE	BURSTS	BASHON
BENDER	BANISH	BMOVIE	BURLAP	BARDIC	BARIUM	BESTOW
BENLEE	BONITO	BOOGIE	BURSAR	BARKIN	BARNUM	BISHOP
BENNET	BANGUI	BOOKIE	BYROAD	BARRIE	BARQUE	BOSTON
BINDER	BANGUP	BOOKIN	BARBED	BARRIO	BISCAY	BISTRO
BINGEN	BANJUL	BRODIE	BARBEL	BERLIN	BUSMAN	BASEST
BINGES	BANQUO	BROLIN	BARBER	BERNIE	BASICS	BASQUE
BINMEN	BENAUD	BLOCKS	BARGED	BERTIE	BISECT	BISQUE
BINNED	BENHUR	BROOKE	BARGEE	BIRDIE	BESIDE	BUSTUP
BONDED	BUNKUM	BROOKS	BARGES	BIRKIN	BASHED	BATEAU
BONIER	BONEYM	BOOTLE	BARKED	BORGIA	BASHES	BATMAN
BONNET	BAOBAB	BROILS	BARKER	BURNIE	BASKED	BETRAY
BONZER	BLOTCH	BROLLY	BARLEY	BARELY	BASKET	BITMAP
BUNGED	BROACH	BLOOMS	BARMEN	BARFLY	BASSES	BOTHAM
BUNGEE	BRONCO	BROOME	BARNES	BAROLO	BASSET	BETIDE
BUNKER	BROOCH	BROOMS	BARNET	BURBLE	BASSEY	BATHED
BUNSEN	BIONDI	BOOING	BARNEY	BURGLE	BASTED	BATHER
BUNTER	BLONDE	BROWNE	BARRED	BIREME	BASTES	BATHES
BENIGN	BLONDS	BROWNS	BARREL	BARING	BISSET	BATMEN
BANDIT	BLOODY	BOOBOO	BARREN	BARONE	BOSLEY	BATTED
BENDIX	BROADS	BIOPSY	BARRET	BARONS	BOSSES	BATTEN
BONNIE	BROODS	BLOUSE	BARTER	BARONY	BUSHED	BATTER
BUNYIP	BROODY	BLOWSY	BERBER	BERING	BUSHEL	BETHEL
BANGLE	BLOKES	BROWSE	BERGEN	BORING	BUSHES	BETTER
BUNDLE	BLOWER	BLOATS	BORDER	BARDOT	BUSIER	BITTEN
BUNGLE	BOOKED	BLOTTO	BORGES	BARLOW	BUSKED	BITTER
BENUMB	BOOKER	BOOSTS	BORNEO	BARRON	BUSKER	BOTHER
BYNAME	BOOMED	BRONTE	BURDEN	BARROW	BUSMEN	BUTLER
BANANA	BOOMER	BLOWUP	BURGER	BARTOK	BUSTED	BUTTED
BENING	BOOTED	BOOKUP	BURIED	BARTON	BUSTER	BUTTER
BINEND	BOOTEE	BROGUE	BURIES	BORROW	BYSSHE	BITCHY
BANDOG	BOOZED	BRONZE	BURNED	BORZOI	BESSIE	BATTIE
BANGON	BOOZER	BYPLAY	BURNER	BURBOT	BOSNIA	BUTTIN
BANGOR	BOOZES	BIPEDS	BURNET	BURDON	BASALT	BATTLE

BOTTLE	BOVINE	BAYOUS	CHANGE	COASTS	CUCKOO	CHEEKY
BATONS	BOVARY	BUYOUT	CHARGE	CRAFTS	CICERO	CLERKS
BETONY	BOWMAN	BAZAAR	CLAGGY	CRAFTY	CACTUS	CREAKS
BITING	BOWSAW	BUZZED	CLANGS	CLAMUP	COCKUP	CREAKY
BOTANY	BAWBEE	BUZZER	CRAGGY	CLAQUE	COCCYX	CREEKS
BUTANE	BAWLED	BUZZES	CHACHA	CABMAN	CADEAU	CREELS
BATHOS	BOWLED	BEZELS	CHALKS	COBRAS	CADGED	CREOLE
BOTTOM	BOWLER	CIARAN	CHALKY	CABLED	CADGER	CREAMS
BUTTON	BOWLES	CRAVAT	CLACKS	CABLES	CADGES	CREAMY
BHUTAN	BOWMEN	CRABBE	CLANKS	COBBER	CODGER	CLEANS
BRUTAL	BOWYER	CRABBY	CLARKE	COBWEB	CUDGEL	CUEING
BLURBS	BEWAIL	CHANCE	CRACKS	CABBIE	CODIFY	CHEAPO
BRUMBY	BOWTIE	CHANCY	CRANKS	COBAIN	CADDIE	CHEEPS
BOUNCE	BOWING	CLANCY	CRANKY	CUBOID	CADDIS	CREEPS
BOUNCY	BOWWOW	CLAUDE	CRADLE	CABALS	CADELL	CREEPY
BRUNCH	BEWARE	CEASED	CRAWLS	COBALT	CODDLE	CHEERS
BOUNDS	BOWERS	CEASES	CHARMS	COBBLE	CUDDLE	CHEERY
BOULES	BYWORD	CHAFED	CHASMS	CYBILL	CUDDLY	CHERRY
BRUGES	BOWOUT	CHAFER	CLAIMS	CABINS	CEDING	CHEVRE
BRUNEI	BYWAYS	CHAFES	CLAMMY	CUBING	CODING	CLEARS
BRUNEL	BOXCAR	CHALET	CHAINS	CABERS	CEDARS	CHEESE
BRUTES	BAXTER	CHANEL	CRANNY	COBURN	CADETS	CHEESY
BLUFFS	BEXLEY	CHANEY	CHADOR	CYBORG	CAESAR	CLEESE
BOUGHS	BOXPEW	CHAPEL	CHARON	CUBISM	CEEFAX	CREASE
BOUGHT	BOXING	CHASED	CRAYON	CUBIST	CRETAN	CHEATS
BAULKS	BUXTON	CHASER	CHAMPS	CUBITS	CLENCH	CHESTS
BAUBLE	BOXERS	CHASES	CLAMPS	COBNUT	COERCE	CHESTY
BOUCLE	BOXFUL	CLARET	CLASPS	CICADA	CREEDS	CREATE
BOURNE	BUYOFF	CLAWED	CRAMPS	CACHES	CHENEY	CRESTA
BRUTON	BLYTHE	COATED	CHAIRS	CACHET	CHEWED	CRESTS
BLURRY	BOYCIE	COAXED	CHAKRA	COCKED	CLEVER	CHEQUE
BLUESY	BAYING	COAXES	CLAIRE	COCKER	CLEVES	CHERUB
BOURSE	BEYOND	CRANES	CHAISE	CYCLED	CREWED	CLEAVE
BRUISE	BRYANT	CRATED	CHASSE	CYCLES	CREWEL	CHERYL
BHUTTO	BRYONY	CRATER	CLASSY	CYCLIC	CLERGY	COFFEE
BLURTS	BUYING	CRATES	CLAUSE	CACKLE	CRECHE	COFFER
BOUNTY	BLYTON	CRAVED	COARSE	CECILY	CHERIE	CUFFED
BRUTUS	BRYDON	CRAVEN	CHANTS	CICELY	CLERIC	COFFIN
BOVVER	BUYERS	CRAVES	CHARTS	COCKLE	CREDIT	COGNAC
BOVRIL	BOYISH	CRAZED	CHASTE	CACHOU	CHECKS	CAGIER
BEVELS	BAYEUX	CRAZES	CHATTY	COCOON	CHEEKS	CAGNEY

CYGNET	CRITIC	CALVED	COMEIN	CONNED	CHORAL	CLOTHS
CAGEIN	CHICKS	CALVES	COMFIT	CONNER	COOGAN	CHOPIN
CAGILY	CHINKS	COLDER	COMMIE	CONTEH	CROSBY	COOKIE
CAGING	CLICKS	COLEEN	COMMIT	CONVEX	CHOICE	COOLIE
COGENT	CLINKS	COLLET	CAMELS	CONVEY	CLOACA	COOLIT
CIGARS	CRICKS	CULLED	COMELY	CANDID	CROUCH	CRONIN
CYGNUS	CHILLI	CALAIS	COMPLY	CONAIR	CHORDS	CHOCKS
COHERE	CHILLS	CALVIN	CEMENT	CONFIT	CLOUDS	CHOCKY
COHORT	CHILLY	CELTIC	COMING	CONNIE	CLOUDY	CLOAKS
CAIMAN	CAIRNS	COLLIE	CAMEOS	CANALS	CROWDS	CLOCKS
CHIRAC	CLIENT	CULKIN	COMEON	CANDLE	CHOKED	CLONKS
CLIMAX	CLIPON	CALMLY	COMMON	CANTLE	CHOKER	CROAKS
CLIMBS	COINOP	COLDLY	CAMERA	CINEMA	CHOKES	CROAKY
CLINCH	CHIMPS	COLUMN	CAMETO	CANINE	CHOKEY	CROCKS
CHILDE	CHIPPY	CELINE	COMETO	CANING	CHOLER	CROOKS
CHIDED	CHIRPS	COLONS	COMETS	CANONS	CHOREA	COOLLY
CHIDES	CHIRPY	COLONY	CAMPUS	CANNON	CHORES	CLOWNS
CHILES	CRIMPS	CALLOW	CANAAN	CANNOT	CHOSEN	COOING
CHIMED	CRIPPS	CALPOL	CANCAN	CANTON	CLONED	CROONS
CHIMER	CRISPS	CELLOS	CANVAS	CANTOR	CLONES	CROWNS
CHIMES	CRISPY	CALIPH	CONFAB	CANTOS	CLOSED	CHOMPS
CHINES	CRIERS	CELERY	CONMAN	CANYON	CLOSER	CHOPPY
CHISEL	CHINTZ	CALLUP	CONRAD	CENSOR	CLOSES	CHOIRS
CHIVES	CHITTY	CALLUS	CONRAN	CONDON	CLOSET	CHOOSE
CLIMES	CAIQUE	CILIUM	CONWAY	CONDOR	CLOVEN	CHOOSY
COILED	CHINUP	COLEUS	CYNICS	CONNOR	CLOVER	CLOUTS
COINED	CLIQUE	COLOUR	CANADA	CONVOY	CLOVES	CROFTS
CRIKEY	CHIVVY	CULLUM	CANCEL	CANAPE	CLOYED	CHOPUP
CRIMEA	CAJOLE	COMBAT	CANCER	CANOPY	COOKED	CHORUS
CRIMES	CAKING	COMMAS	CANKER	CANARD	COOKER	CROCUS
CRISES	CALLAN	CYMBAL	CANNED	CANARY	COOLED	CROPUP
CHIEFS	CALLAS	COMICE	CANNES	CENTRE	COOLER	CAPLET
CLIFFS	CELLAR	COMICS	CANOES	CONTRA	COOPED	CAPPED
CLINGS	COLLAR	COMEDY	CANTED	CUNARD	COOPER	CIPHER
CLINGY	CALLBY	CAMBER	CANTER	CANUTE	CROMER	COPIED
CRINGE	CALICO	CAMDEN	CENSER	CANCUN	CRONES	COPIER
CHICHI	CELICA	CAMPED	CINDER	CANFUL	CROWED	COPIES
CLICHE	CALLED	CAMPER	CONFER	CENSUS	CHOUGH	COPPED
CLINIC	CALLER	COMBED	CONGER	CINQUE	CLOUGH	COPPER
COINIT	CALMED	COMPEL	CONKER	CONCUR	CLOCHE	CUPPED
CRISIS	CALMER	CAMEIN	CONLEY	CONSUL	CLOTHE	COPTIC

CUPTIE	CORNER	CURSOR	COSMIC	CHURCH	CRUETS	CRYOUT
CUPOLA	CORNET	CARERS	CUSPID	CLUNCH	CRUFTS	DEADEN
CAPONE	CORSET	CURARE	CASTLE	CLUTCH	CRUSTS	DEADER
CAPONS	CORTES	CURERS	COSILY	CRUNCH	CRUSTY	DEAFEN
COPING	CORTEX	CARESS	COSTLY	CRUTCH	CAUCUS	DEAFER
CAPTOR	CURBED	CARUSO	CASING	CLUEDO	CAVEAT	DEALER
CAPERS	CURFEW	CERISE	CASINO	CRUDDY	CAVIAR	DEARER
COPERS	CURLED	CHRISM	COSINE	CAUSED	CAVIES	DIADEM
CAPOTE	CURLER	CHRIST	CASTOR	CAUSES	CAVEIN	DIAPER
COPOUT	CURLEW	CORPSE	COSMOS	CHUTES	CAVELL	DRAGEE
CUPFUL	CURSED	CURTSY	CPSNOW	CLUNES	CAVILS	DRAPED
CYPRUS	CURSES	CARATS	CUSTOM	CRUDER	CAVING	DRAPER
CARNAC	CURVED	CARETS	CASTRO	CRUYFF	COVENS	DRAPES
CARNAL	CURVES	CURATE	CASQUE	CAUGHT	COVING	DRAWER
CARPAL	CARAFE	CARPUS	CUSCUS	COUGHS	CAVERN	DWARFS
CEREAL	CARDIN	CIRCUS	CATHAY	COULIS	CAVERS	DEATHS
CORRAL	CARRIE	CIRRUS	CATNAP	COUSIN	CAVORT	DRACHM
CURACY	CORGIS	CORPUS	CITIES	CAULKS	COVERS	DEAKIN
CARDED	CURRIE	CURLUP	COTTER	CHUCKS	COVERT	DEARIE
CAREEN	CURTIS	CASUAL	CUTLER	CHUKKA	CAVITY	DEADLY
CAREER	CURTIZ	COSTAR	CUTLET	CHUNKS	CIVETS	DEARLY
CARIES	CAROLE	CUSACK	CUTTER	CHUNKY	COVETS	DRAWLS
CARMEL	CAROLS	CASHED	CUTOFF	CLUCKS	COWPAT	DEARME
CARMEN	CIRCLE	CASHES	CATCHY	CLUNKS	COWLEY	DHARMA
CARNET	CURDLE	CASHEW	CATKIN	CLUNKY	COWRIE	DRAINS
CARNEY	CURTLY	CASKED	CATNIP	COUPLE	COWELL	DEACON
CARPED	CHROMA	CASKET	CITRIC	CHUMMY	CAWING	DRAGON
CARPEL	CHROME	CASPER	CATTLE	CRUMMY	COWING	DRALON
CARPET	CARING	CASTER	CUTTLE	CHURNS	COWBOY	DEARTH
CARREY	CORONA	CASTES	CITING	CLUING	COWPOX	DRAFTS
CARTED	CURING	COSHED	CITRON	COUPON	COWARD	DRAWUP
CARTEL	CYRANO	COSHES	COTTON	CRUSOE	COWERS	DIBNAH
CARTER	CARBON	COSIER	CATERS	CHUMPS	COXING	DABBED
CARVED	CARBOY	COSSET	CATGUT	CLUMPS	CAXTON	DABBER
CARVER	CARLOS	COSTED	CITRUS	CLUMPY	CAYMAN	DIBBER
CARVES	CARLOW	CUSTER	CUTOUT	CLUMSY	CRYOFF	DIBLEY
CORBEL	CARROT	CASEIN	CAUDAL	COURSE	CRYING	DUBBED
CORDEN	CARSON	CASHIN	CAUSAL	CRUISE	CEYLON	DEBAGS
CORKED	CARTON	CASSIA	COUGAR	COUNTS	COYOTE	DEBUGS
CORKER	CORDON	CASSIO	CHUBBY	COUNTY	CRYPTS	DEBBIE
CORNEA	CURIOS	CASSIS	CRUMBS	COURTS	COYPUS	DEBRIS

DOBBIN	DICTUM	DAFTER	DRIVES	DELUXE	DUNCAN	DUNLOP
DUBBIN	DACTYL	DEFIED	DUIKER	DELAYS	DANUBE	DENIRO
DUBLIN	DECAYS	DEFIES	DRINKS	DAMIAN	DENUDE	DINARS
DUBOIS	DECOYS	DEFTER	DRILLS	DEMEAN	DANCED	DINERS
DABBLE	DEDUCE	DIFFER	DEIGNS	DEMOBS	DANCER	DONORS
DIBBLE	DEDUCT	DOFFED	DEIMOS	DOMECQ	DANCES	DANESH
DUBBLE	DODDER	DUFFEL	DRIPPY	DAMIEN	DANDER	DANISH
DEBUNK	DODGED	DUFFER	DRIEST	DAMMED	DANGER	DENISE
DEBTOR	DODGEM	DEFILE	DAINTY	DAMNED	DANIEL	DYNAST
DOBSON	DODGER	DEFTLY	DEISTS	DAMPED	DANKER	DENOTE
DEBARS	DODGES	DEFAME	DRIFTS	DAMPEN	DANNER	DONATE
DOBIRD	DUDLEY	DEFEND	DEJECT	DAMPER	DENIED	DINKUM
DEBASE	DIDDLE	DEFINE	DUJOUR	DAMSEL	DENIER	DONEUP
DEBATE	DODDLE	DEFERS	DEJAVU	DIMMED	DENIES	DVORAK
DEBITS	DODOMA	DEFORM	DIKTAT	DIMMER	DENSER	DROPBY
DEBUTS	DIDCOT	DEFUSE	DAKOTA	DOMBEY	DENTED	DIODES
DACHAS	DRENCH	DUFFUP	DALLAS	DUMPED	DENVER	DOOMED
DECLAN	DREADS	DAFFYD	DOLLAR	DUMPER	DENZEL	DRONED
DECOCT	DEEMED	DAGMAR	DOLMAN	DAMAGE	DINNER	DRONES
DECADE	DEEPEN	DOGEAR	DELUDE	DIMWIT	DONKEY	DROVER
DECIDE	DEEPER	DOGTAG	DELVED	DOMAIN	DONNED	DROVES
DECODE	DIESEL	DAGGER	DELVES	DIMPLE	DUNCES	DRONGO
DECKED	DIETED	DEGREE	DILLER	DUMBLY	DUNDEE	DIOXIN
DECKER	DIETER	DIGGER	DOLMEN	DAMONE	DUNKED	DROPIN
DECREE	DREDGE	DOGGED	DULCET	DEMAND	DINGHY	DOODLE
DECTET	DEEPLY	DOGGER	DULLER	DEMONS	DANNII	DROLLY
DOCKED	DWELLS	DOGLEG	DELUGE	DOMINO	DANZIG	DROOLS
DOCKER	DREAMS	DOGEND	DELPHI	DUMONT	DENNIS	DIONNE
DOCKET	DREAMT	DUGONG	DULCIE	DAMSON	DONEIN	DROWNS
DUCKED	DREAMY	DIGEST	DALEKS	DEMURE	DONNIE	DROOPS
DACOIT	DUENNA	DIGITS	DOLENZ	DEMURS	DUNLIN	DROOPY
DECEIT	DYEING	DUGOUT	DALTON	DAMASK	DANDLE	DROWSE
DUCCIO	DIEPPE	DAHLIA	DELBOY	DEMISE	DANGLE	DROWSY
DECOKE	DREARY	DRHOOK	DOLLOP	DEMIST	DINGLE	DROGUE
DOCILE	DRESSY	DAILEY	DELIST	DEMOTE	DONALD	DEPICT
DECAMP	DIEOUT	DEICED	DELETE	DIMITY	DONIMS	DAPPER
DECANT	DREWUP	DEICER	DILATE	DIMSUM	DENIMS	DIPPED
DECENT	DEFEAT	DEICES	DILUTE	DUMDUM	DYNAMO	DIPPER
DICING	DEFRAY	DRIVEL	DULUTH	DENHAM	DINING	DOPIER
DOCTOR	DEFACE	DRIVEN	DELIUS	DENIAL	DANSON	DUPLEX
DUCATS	DEFECT	DRIVER	DOLOUR	DENTAL	DENTON	DEPTHS

DAPPLE	DORRIT	DESIST	DAVIES	DOYENS	ELBRUS	EXETER
DAPHNE	DURBIN	DISUSE	DEVOID	DRYING	ELBOWS	EYELET
DEPEND	DARKLY	DISCUS	DEVILS	DIYSOS	EMBRYO	EMERGE
DOPING	DERVLA	DISHUP	DUVALL	DRYROT	ENCODE	ENERGY
DUPING	DARING	DUSTUP	DAVINA	DRYFRY	ESCUDO	EMETIC
DEPLOY	DURING	DISOWN	DIVANS	DAYOUT	ECCLES	EYELID
DEPART	DERMOT	DETACH	DIVINE	DRYRUN	ESCHEW	EVENLY
DEPORT	DIREST	DETECT	DIVING	DAZZLE	ETCHED	EVERLY
DUPERS	DURESS	DITHER	DIVERS	DAZING	ETCHER	EXEUNT
DEPOSE	DARIUS	DOTTED	DIVERT	DOZENS	ETCHES	EYEING
DEPOTS	DERIVE	DUTIES	DEVISE	DOZING	EXCEED	EXEMPT
DEPUTE	DARRYL	DOTAGE	DIVEST	ELANDS	EUCLID	EVENSO
DEPUTY	DISBAR	DETAIL	DOVISH	ELATED	EXCELS	EVERSO
DEPAUL	DISMAL	DETAIN	DAVITS	ELATES	ENCAMP	EGESTS
DIPOUT	DISMAY	DOTIME	DEVITO	ENAMEL	EOCENE	EJECTS
DERMAL	DESICA	DATING	DEVOTE	ERASED	ESCAPE	ELECTS
DIRHAM	DOSIDO	DOTING	DIVOTS	ERASER	EXCEPT	ERECTS
DORIAN	DASHED	DOTCOM	DUVETS	ERASES	ENCORE	EVENTS
DORSAL	DASHER	DETERS	DEVOUR	EVADED	ESCORT	EXERTS
DURBAN	DASHES	DOTARD	DEVOUT	EVADES	EUCHRE	EREBUS
DURBAR	DESRES	DETEST	DEWLAP	ENABLE	ENCASE	EVENUP
DURHAM	DISHES	DATSUN	DAWNED	ELAINE	EXCESS	EYEFUL
DURIAN	DISNEY	DETOUR	DOWNED	EVADNE	EXCISE	EVELYN
DIRECT	DISPEL	DATIVE	DOWNER	ELAPSE	EXCUSE	EFFACE
DERIDE	DISTEL	DOUGAL	DOWNEY	ECARTE	EXCITE	EFFECT
DIRNDL	DOSSED	DRUIDS	DOWSED	ENACTS	ENDEAR	EIFFEL
DARCEY	DOSSES	DAUBED	DOWSER	EXACTS	EDDIED	EFFIGY
DARKEN	DUSTED	DAUBER	DOWSES	EXALTS	EDDIES	ENFOLD
DARKER	DUSTER	DEUCES	DAWDLE	EMBEDS	EDDOES	EFFORT
DARNED	DESIGN	DOUSED	DIWALI	EMBODY	ENDING	ERFURT
DARNER	DOSAGE	DOUSES	DOWELL	EMBLEM	EDDERY	EFFUSE
DARREN	DISTIL	DRUDGE	DOWELS	EMBALM	EIDERS	ELFISH
DARTED	DUSTIN	DOUCHE	DAWSON	EBBING	ELDERS	EFFETE
DARTER	DOSING	DOUGHY	DEXTER	EUBANK	ENDORA	EAGLES
DERREN	DESPOT	DRUNKS	DRYICE	ENBLOC	ENDURE	EAGLET
DIRGES	DISCOS	DOUBLE	DRYADS	EDBERG	ELDEST	EDGIER
DORMER	DESCRY	DOUBLY	DAYBED	EKBERG	ENDIVE	ENGAGE
DORSET	DESERT	DAUNTS	DRYDEN	EMBARK	ENDOWS	EDGILY
DARRIN	DESIRE	DOUBTS	DAYOFF	EMBERG	EMENDS	ENGELS
DARWIN	DESTRY	DEVICE	DAYGLO	EMBERS	ELEVEN	ENGULF
DERAIL	DISARM	DIVIDE	DRYFLY	EMBOSS	EVENED	EDGING

EGGING	ENJOYS	EGOISM	ERRAND	EXTORT	FLAKES	FACING
ENGINE	ESKIMO	EGOIST	ERRANT	ENTITY	FLAMES	FECUND
EUGENE	ELLICE	ELOISE	ERRING	ESTATE	FLARED	FACTOR
EGGNOG	ENLACE	EXODUS	ENRAPT	EATOUT	FLARES	FACETS
EDGERS	EILEEN	EVOLVE	EUROPE	EDUCED	FLAWED	FIDGET
EIGHTH	EULOGY	EPONYM	ERRORS	EDUCES	FLAXEN	FODDER
EIGHTS	ECLAIR	ESPIAL	EGRESS	ELUDED	FLAYED	FUDGED
EIGHTY	EALING	ESPACE	EGRETS	ELUDES	FOAMED	FUDGES
EGGCUP	EKLAND	EXPECT	ERRATA	ETUDES	FRAMED	FIDDLE
ECHUCA	ELLIOT	ESPIED	EARFUL	EXUDED	FRAMES	FIDDLY
ETHICS	ELLERY	ESPIES	EASIER	EXUDES	FRASER	FUDDLE
ECHOED	ENLIST	ESPRIT	EASTER	EQUALS	FRAYED	FADING
ECHOES	EAMONN	EXPELS	ENSUED	EQUINE	FRAZER	FEDORA
ETHNIC	EDMUND	EPPING	ENSUES	EQUIPS	FLANGE	FIERCE
EXHALE	EGMONT	ESPANA	ENSIGN	EQUATE	FLASHY	FLEECE
EXHUME	ERMINE	EXPAND	EASELS	EQUITY	FLANKS	FLEECY
ETHANE	ESMOND	EXPEND	EASILY	ERUPTS	FLASKS	FLETCH
EXHORT	EXMOOR	EMPLOY	EASING	EXULTS	FLAILS	FRENCH
ELIJAH	ELMORE	EMPIRE	EASTON	ENVIED	FLATLY	FRESCO
EVINCE	ENMESH	EXPERT	EUSTON	ENVIES	FLAUNT	FIELDS
EDITED	EMMETS	EXPIRE	ENSURE	EDVARD	FLACON	FIENDS
ELIDES	EMMETT	EXPIRY	ERSATZ	ELVERS	FLAGON	FLEADH
EMINEM	ENMITY	EXPORT	ESSAYS	ELVISH	FRAPPE	FREDDY
EXILED	EUNUCH	ELPASO	ENTRAP	ENVOYS	FIACRE	FEEDER
EXILES	ELNINO	EXPOSE	EXTRAS	FEALTY	FEELER
EXITED	ERNEST	EARWAX	ENTICE	EDWINA	FEASTS	FLEXED
ELISHA	EROICA	ENROBE	EITHER	EDWOOD	FABIAN	FLEXES
ELICIT	ELOPED	EDRICH	ENTREE	ELWOOD	FABLED	FLEDGE
ELIXIR	ELOPER	ENRICH	ESTEEM	EDWARD	FABLES	FLECHE
EMILIA	ELOPES	ENRICO	ESTHER	EEYORE	FIBBED	FLESHY
EMILIO	EMOTED	EARNED	ENTAIL	ECZEMA	FIBBER	FAERIE
EDIBLE	EMOTES	EARNER	EXTOLS	ENZYME	FIBRES	FLECKS
EVILLY	ERODED	EERIER	ENTOMB	FRACAS	FOBBED	FREAKS
ENIGMA	ERODES	ENRAGE	EATING	FLABBY	FOBOFF	FREAKY
EDISON	EVOKED	EARTHA	EXTANT	FLAMBE	FABRIC	FEEBLE
EDITOR	EVOKES	EARTHS	EXTEND	FIANCE	FIBULA	FEEBLY
EMIGRE	EXOCET	EARTHY	EXTENT	FIASCO	FABLON	FREELY
EDICTS	ENOUGH	EARWIG	EATERS	FRANCE	FACIAL	FLEXOR
EVICTS	EPOCHS	EUREKA	EATERY	FRANCO	FACADE	FIESTA
EXISTS	EROTIC	EERILY	ENTERS	FRANCS	FACILE	FLEETS
ENJOIN	EXOTIC	ENROLS	ENTIRE	FEARED	FICKLE	FREEZE
				FLAKED		

FRENZY	FEINTS	FELLOW	FINALS	FLOATY	FIRKIN	FETTLE
FAFFED	FEISTY	FOLIOS	FINELY	FLOUTS	FORBID	FUTILE
FIFTHS	FLINTS	FOLLOW	FONDLE	FRONTS	FIRMLY	FATIMA
FAGGED	FLINTY	FULTON	FONDLY	FROSTY	FARINA	FATHOM
FOGGED	FLIRTS	FOLKSY	FINING	FROWZY	FARING	FUTURE
FUGUES	FLIRTY	FILLUP	FINERY	FARRAH	FIRING	FETISH
FAGEND	FRIEZE	FULLUP	FINEST	FERGAL	FORINT	FITFUL
FAGGOT	FRIZZY	FAMILY	FINISH	FORFAR	FARNON	FEUDAL
FIGARO	FIJIAN	FEMALE	FINITE	FORMAL	FARROW	FRUGAL
FIGURE	FAKING	FUMBLE	FINITO	FORMAN	FORGOT	FLUIDS
FIGHTS	FAKERS	FAMINE	FANOUT	FORMAT	FURROW	FOUNDS
FAISAL	FAKERY	FOMENT	FONDUE	FORMBY	FARCRY	FAUCET
FRIDAY	FAKIRS	FUMING	FUNFUR	FARADS	FURORE	FEUDED
FLINCH	FELLAH	FAMISH	FUNGUS	FARCES	FOREST	FLUKED
FLITCH	FELLAS	FAMOUS	FUNRUN	FARMED	FIRSTS	FLUKES
FRIEDA	FILIAL	FENIAN	FLORAL	FARMER	FAROUT	FLUMES
FAILED	FOLIAR	FINGAL	FJORDS	FAROES	FORAYS	FLUTES
FAIRER	FULHAM	FINIAL	FLOODS	FERRER	FISCAL	FOULED
FOILED	FULMAR	FINLAY	FRONDS	FERRET	FASCES	FLUFFY
FRISEE	FALLEN	FINNAN	FLORES	FIRMER	FASTED	FOUGHT
FLINGS	FALTER	FUNGAL	FLORET	FORBES	FASTEN	FLUNKS
FRIDGE	FELLED	FANGED	FLOWED	FORCED	FASTER	FLUENT
FRINGE	FELLER	FANJET	FLOWER	FORCES	FESTER	FRUMPS
FAITHS	FILLED	FANNED	FOOLED	FORGED	FISHED	FRUMPY
FLIGHT	FILLER	FENCED	FOOTER	FORGER	FISHER	FLURRY
FRIGHT	FILLET	FENCER	FROZEN	FORGES	FISHES	FAULTS
FRIGID	FILMED	FENCES	FROTHY	FORGET	FOSTER	FAULTY
FLICKS	FILTER	FENDED	FLOGIT	FORKED	FUSSED	FOUNTS
FRISKS	FOLDED	FENDER	FLORID	FORMED	FASCIA	FOURTH
FRISKY	FOLDER	FENNEC	FLORIN	FORMER	FOSSIL	FRUITS
FAIRLY	FULLER	FENNEL	FOODIE	FURIES	FUSION	FRUITY
FOIBLE	FILTHY	FENNER	FROLIC	FURLED	FESCUE	FOULUP
FRIELS	FILLIN	FINDER	FLOCKS	FAROFF	FATCAT	FAVELA
FRILLS	FILLIP	FINGER	FROCKS	FORAGE	FATHEN	FIVERS
FRILLY	FULFIL	FINNED	FOOTLE	FOREGO	FATHER	FAVOUR
FEIGNS	FELINE	FINNEY	FROWNS	FIRTHS	FATTED	FOWLDS
FRIEND	FELONS	FONDER	FLOPPY	FURPHY	FATTEN	FAWKES
FRIARS	FELONY	FUNDED	FLOORS	FERGIE	FATTER	FAWNED
FRIARY	FILING	FUNKED	FLOURY	FERRIC	FETTER	FOWLER
FLIMSY	FALCON	FUNNEL	FLOSSY	FERRIS	FITTED	FOWLES
FAINTS	FALLOW	FINALE	FLOATS	FERVID	FITTER	FEWEST

FAWLTY	GRAVEN	GOBBLE	GIFTED	GOKART	GAMEST	GROCER
FAXING	GRAVER	GOBANG	GAGTAG	GALWAY	GAMETE	GROPED
FIXING	GRAVES	GIBBON	GAGGED	GELLAR	GENIAL	GROPES
FOXING	GRAZED	GIBSON	GAGGLE	GALLED	GUNMAN	GROVEL
FIXATE	GRAZES	GADDED	GIGGLE	GALLEY	GANDER	GROVES
FOYLES	GRANGE	GADGET	GIGGLY	GELLED	GANGED	GROWER
FLYTIP	GRAPHS	GEDDES	GIGOLO	GELLER	GANGER	GEORGE
FLYING	GLAMIS	GODBER	GOGGLE	GILDED	GANGES	GEORGY
FRYING	GOALIE	GODWIT	GEHRIG	GOLDEN	GANNET	GROGGY
FOYERS	GRACIE	GADFLY	GUITAR	GOLFER	GENDER	GLORIA
FLYASH	GRATIN	GIDEON	GLITCH	GULLET	GENRES	GNOMIC
FLYOUT	GRATIS	GODSON	GRINDS	GULPED	GINGER	GOOGIE
FIZZED	GLADLY	GODIVA	GAINED	GALLIC	GUNMEN	GROMIT
FIZZES	GNARLS	GREGAN	GAITER	GILLIE	GUNNED	GHOULS
FIZGIG	GRABLE	GREECE	GEIGER	GOLDIE	GUNNEL	GOODLY
FIZZLE	GRAEME	GLENDA	GLIDED	GALENA	GUNNER	GOOGLE
FAZING	GRAMMY	GREEDY	GLIDER	GALLON	GINKGO	GOOGLY
GOAWAY	GOANNA	GEEGEE	GLIDES	GALLOP	GANDHI	GROWLS
GRAHAM	GRAINS	GEEZER	GRIPED	GELDOF	GUNGHO	GLOOMY
GLANCE	GRAINY	GREBES	GRIPER	GALORE	GANGLY	GROOMS
GLANDS	GRANNY	GRETEL	GRIPES	GALOSH	GENTLE	GROANS
GRANDE	GRAPPA	GOETHE	GUIDED	GELATO	GENTLY	GROUND
GUARDS	GRASPS	GAELIC	GUIDER	GULATI	GINOLA	GROYNE
GEARED	GDANSK	GREEKS	GUIDES	GALLUP	GENOME	GNOMON
GLADES	GLASSY	GLEAMS	GUINEA	GOLIVE	GUNDOG	GLOOPY
GLARED	GRASSY	GLEANS	GRINGO	GALAXY	GANTRY	GROUPS
GLARES	GIANTS	GREENE	GEISHA	GIMLET	GENERA	GLOSSY
GLASER	GRAFTS	GREENS	GLINKA	GUMMED	GENTRY	GROUSE
GLAZED	GRANTA	GRETNA	GLIBLY	GUMMER	GONERS	GHOSTS
GNAWED	GRANTS	GEESON	GRILLE	GAMBIA	GANGUP	GIOTTO
GOADED	GLADYS	GREGOR	GRILLS	GAMBIT	GENIUS	GLOATS
GOATEE	GOBACK	GREASE	GRIMLY	GYMPIE	GENEVA	GROATS
GRACES	GABLED	GREASY	GRISLY	GAMBLE	GLOBAL	GROTTO
GRADED	GABLER	GHETTO	GOITRE	GAMELY	GROUCH	GROTTY
GRADER	GABLES	GREATS	GRILSE	GAMINE	GLOBES	GROUTS
GRADES	GIBBER	GREETS	GAIETY	GAMING	GLOVER	GROWTH
GRAPES	GIBBET	GUESTS	GLINTS	GAMINS	GLOVES	GROWUP
GRATED	GOBBET	GLENYS	GRITTY	GEMINI	GLOWED	GROOVE
GRATER	GOBLET	GUFFAW	GUILTY	GAMBOL	GLOWER	GROOVY
GRATES	GOBLIN	GAFFER	GRIEVE	GAMBON	GNOMES	GOOLWA
GRAVEL	GABBLE	GAFFES	GLITZY	GAMMON	GOOFED	GOPHER

GAPING	GASHED	GAUCHO	HOAXES	HEDGES	HIKING	HEMPEN
GAPERS	GASHES	GLUMLY	HEATHS	HEDREN	HIKERS	HUMBER
GYPSUM	GASKET	GLUING	HAAKON	HIDDEN	HOLTBY	HUMMED
GARDAI	GASMEN	GOUNOD	HEADON	HODGES	HALLEY	HUMPED
GERMAN	GASPED	GRUMPY	HEARSE	HIDEHI	HALOED	HOMAGE
GARBED	GASSED	GRUNTS	HEARST	HEDWIG	HALOES	HAMILL
GARDEN	GOSPEL	GAVEIN	HOARSE	HODDLE	HALTED	HOMELY
GARNER	GUSHED	GIVEIN	HEALTH	HUDDLE	HALTER	HOMILY
GARNET	GUSHER	GIVING	HEARTH	HIDING	HALVED	HUMBLE
GARRET	GUSHES	GIVERS	HEARTS	HUDSON	HALVES	HUMBLY
GARTER	GUSSET	GOVERN	HEARTY	HEENAN	HELLER	HOMING
GIRDER	GASLIT	GAVEUP	HIATUS	HYENAS	HELMET	HUMANE
GORGED	GOSSIP	GIVEUP	HUBCAP	HEEDED	HELPED	HUMANS
GORGES	GISELE	GEWGAW	HEBDEN	HEELED	HELPER	HOMBRE
GORGET	GASCON	GAWAIN	HEBREW	HOEING	HOLDEN	HAMISH
GURNEY	GASTON	GEYSER	HOBBES	HUFFED	HOLDER	HUMBUG
GARAGE	GOSLOW	GUYLER	HOBLEY	HEFLIN	HOLIER	HUMMUS
GURKHA	GATEAU	GLYNIS	HOBOES	HAGMAN	HOLLER	HUMOUR
GARCIA	GSTAAD	GUYANA	HOBBIT	HIGHER	HOLMES	HANGAR
GARLIC	GATSBY	GWYNNE	HUBRIS	HOGGED	HULLED	HANNAH
GERBIL	GATHER	GAYNOR	HYBRID	HOGGER	HELENA	HANNAY
GIRLIE	GUTTED	GLYCOL	HOBBLE	HUGGED	HALLOO	HENMAN
GARBLE	GUTTER	GAZEBO	HUBBLE	HUGHES	HALLOW	HINTAT
GARGLE	GETOFF	GUZZLE	HEBRON	HAGGIS	HELIOS	HANDED
GERALD	GOTCHA	GAZUMP	HOBNOB	HAGRID	HELLOS	HANDEL
GIRDLE	GOTHIC	GAZING	HOBART	HUGHIE	HILTON	HANGED
GURGLE	GUTROT	GIZMOS	HABITS	HAGGLE	HOLDON	HANGER
GERUND	GATISS	HOARDS	HUBBUB	HIGHLY	HOLLOW	HANKER
GORING	GETOUT	HEADED	HACKED	HUGELY	HILARY	HANSEL
GARCON	GRUBBY	HEADER	HACKER	HEGIRA	HELDUP	HINDER
GARSON	GOURDS	HEALED	HOCKED	HIGHUP	HELIUM	HINGED
GIRTON	GRUNDY	HEALER	HOCKEY	HAIRDO	HELMUT	HINGES
GORDON	GAUGED	HEALEY	HECTIC	HAILED	HOLDUP	HINTED
GORGON	GAUGES	HEAPED	HACKLE	HAILER	HOLEUP	HUNGER
GERARD	GLUTEN	HEATED	HECKLE	HEIFER	HAMMAM	HUNKER
GARISH	GOUGED	HEATER	HECTOR	HEINEY	HYMNAL	HUNTED
GARETH	GOUGES	HEAVED	HICKOK	HEIGHT	HAMLET	HUNTER
GYRATE	GRUDGE	HEAVEN	HECATE	HOISIN	HAMMER	HONCHO
GASBAG	GRUNGE	HEAVES	HICCUP	HEISTS	HAMPER	HONSHU
GASMAN	GRUNGY	HOAXED	HEDGED	HOISTS	HEMMED	HINGIS
GUSTAV	GAUCHE	HOAXER	HEDGER	HIJACK	HEMPEL	HANDLE

HONING	HEPTON	HAROLD	HATTER	HAWKES	INCOME	INFLOW
HANDON	HIPHOP	HERALD	HITHER	HAWSER	IDCARD	ILFORD
HANGON	HIPPOS	HURDLE	HITLER	HOWLED	INCARE	INFERS
HANSOM	HYPEUP	HURTLE	HITTER	HOWLER	INCURS	INFIRM
HANSON	HARMAN	HAREMS	HOTBED	HAWAII	INCASE	INFORM
HENDON	HERBAL	HARING	HOTKEY	HOWELL	INCISE	INFEST
HENSON	HERMAN	HERONS	HOTTER	HEWING	INCITE	INFUSE
HENDRY	HURRAH	HIRING	HATPIN	HEWSON	INDIAN	INFLUX
HUNGRY	HEREBY	HARLOT	HATTIE	HOWARD	INDABA	INGMAR
HONEST	HORNBY	HARLOW	HOTAIR	HOWERD	INDEBT	INGLES
HANGUP	HORACE	HARROW	HOTELS	HEWITT	ILDUCE	INGRES
HONOUR	HARDEN	HERZOG	HATING	HEXHAM	INDICT	INGRID
HUNGUP	HARDER	HORROR	HATBOX	HUXLEY	INDOCK	ITGIRL
HENRYV	HARKER	HARARE	HATTON	HEYDAY	INDUCE	INGEST
HOOKAH	HARLEM	HARASS	HOTDOG	HAYDEN	INDUCT	INGOTS
HOORAY	HARLEY	HERESY	HOTPOT	HAYLEY	INDEED	ISHTAR
HOODED	HARMED	HARDUP	HOTROD	HAYNES	INDEEP	INHOCK
HOOFED	HARPER	HUSSAR	HUTTON	HOYDEN	INDIES	ITHACA
HOOFER	HARVEY	HASHED	HOTTUB	HAYLIE	INDIGO	INHALE
HOOKED	HERDED	HASHES	HAUNCH	HAZIER	INDENT	ICHING
HOOKER	HERDER	HASLET	HOUNDS	HAZILY	IODINE	INHAND
HOOKEY	HEROES	HASTEN	HAULED	HAZARD	INDOOR	IDIOCY
HOOPED	HORDES	HISSED	HOUSED	IBADAN	INDIRA	IBISES
HOOPER	HORNED	HISSES	HOUSES	ISAIAH	INDIUM	IRISES
HOOTED	HORNER	HOSIER	HOURIS	IMAGES	ILDIVO	ICICLE
HOOTER	HORNET	HOSTED	HOURLY	ISABEL	ICECAP	IFIELD
HOOVER	HORSES	HOSTEL	HAUNTS	ITALIC	ICEMAN	IDIOMS
HOOVES	HORSEY	HUSHED	HOVELL	ICARUS	IMELDA	ICIEST
HOODIE	HURLED	HUSHES	HOVELS	INARUT	IBEXES	IDIOTS
HOOPLA	HURLER	HUSSEY	HAVANA	IMBIBE	ICEAGE	INJECT
HOODOO	HURLEY	HASSLE	HAVANT	IMBUED	IBERIA	INJOKE
HOOPOE	HARDIE	HUSTLE	HAVENS	IMBUES	IDEALS	INJURE
HOOKUP	HARRIS	HESTON	HAVING	INBRED	ICEBOX	INJURY
HAPPEN	HERBIE	HISLOP	HIVING	INBORN	IREFUL	INKCAP
HOPPED	HERMIA	HUSTON	HAVEON	IMBRUE	ICEAXE	INKPEN
HOPPER	HERMIT	HYSSOP	HAVERS	INCHED	INFOAL	INKIND
HYPHEN	HERNIA	HUSHUP	HOVERS	INCHES	INFACT	INKING
HIPPIE	HEROIC	HITMAN	HAWHAW	ITCHED	INFECT	IRKING
HOPKIN	HEROIN	HOTTAP	HOWDAH	ITCHES	INFILL	INKPOT
HOPING	HORRID	HATPEG	HOWZAT	ISCHIA	INFAMY	INLIEU
HYPING	HARDLY	HATRED	HAWKER	INCALF	INFANT	INLAID

IDLING	IMPISH	INVENT	JOGGER	JIMINY	JESUIT	KIBBLE
INLAND	IMPOSE	IRVINE	JUGGED	JINNAH	JUSTIN	KIBOSH
INLINE	IMPUTE	IRVING	JIGGLE	JUNEAU	JOSTLE	KIBITZ
ISLAND	INROAD	INVERT	JOGGLE	JUNTAS	JUSTLY	KICKED
IGLOOS	ISRAEL	INVEST	JUGGLE	JANICE	JOSEPH	KICKER
IDLERS	INRUSH	INVITE	JUGFUL	JENNER	JUSTSO	KICKUP
ILLUSE	INSECT	IRWELL	JOHANN	JINKED	JOSHUA	KIDMAN
INLETS	INSIDE	INWARD	JOHNNY	JUNKER	JETLAG	KIDNAP
ISLETS	INSTEP	IDYLLS	JAILED	JUNKET	JETSAM	KIDDED
INLAWS	ISSUED	IZZARD	JAILER	JANCIS	JETSET	KIDDER
INLAYS	ISSUER	JEANNE	JOINED	JENNIE	JETTED	KIDNEY
IAMBIC	ISSUES	JOANNA	JOINER	JUNKIE	JITTER	KODALY
IMMUNE	INSTIL	JOANNE	JUICER	JANGLE	JOTTED	KEEGAN
INMATE	INSOLE	JABBED	JUICES	JANGLY	JOTTER	KEENAN
IAMBUS	INSULT	JABBER	JOININ	JINGLE	JUTTED	KIERAN
IONIAN	ITSELF	JOBBER	JOINTS	JINGLY	JETSKI	KNEADS
INNEED	INSANE	JOBLOT	JOISTS	JUNGLE	JETHRO	KEELER
IGNORE	INSERT	JACKAL	JOINUP	JANINE	JAUNTS	KEELEY
IGNITE	INSURE	JACOBI	JOJOBA	JENSON	JAUNTY	KEENED
INNATE	INSIST	JACKED	JUJUBE	JONSON	JOUSTS	KEENER
ISOBAR	INSETS	JACKET	JEJUNE	JUNIOR	JOVIAL	KEEPER
ISOLDE	INSITU	JOCKEY	JEKYLL	JOPLIN	JIVING	KIEFER
IMOGEN	INTRAY	JACKIE	JOKILY	JORDAN	JIVERS	KIEREN
IRONED	INTACT	JOCUND	JOKING	JARRED	JEWELS	KEENLY
ISOBEL	INTRIM	JOCOSE	JOKERS	JERKED	JOWELL	KNEELS
ICONIC	ISTRIA	JUDDER	JULIAN	JERSEY	JAWING	KIELTY
IRONIC	INTAKE	JUDGED	JILTED	JURIES	JEWISH	KEEPUP
IROBOT	INTIME	JUDGES	JOLTED	JARVIS	JAYKAY	KAFTAN
ISOPOD	INTEND	JUDFRY	JULIET	JERKIN	JOYFUL	KIGALI
IMPACT	INTENT	JUDITH	JOLENE	JARULE	JOYOUS	KAHLUA
IMPEDE	INTONE	JAEGER	JOLSON	JEREMY	KOALAS	KAISER
IMPUGN	INTUNE	JEERED	JOLYON	JEROME	KNAVES	KEITEL
IMPAIR	INTERN	JEEVES	JALOPY	JARGON	KRAKEN	KNIFED
IMPALA	INTERS	JAFFNA	JCLOTH	JARROW	KRAMER	KNIFES
IMPALE	INTOTO	JAGUAR	JULIUS	JERBOA	KEATON	KNIVES
IMPELS	INURED	JIGSAW	JAMJAR	JURORS	KLAXON	KNIGHT
IMPEND	IGUANA	JAGGED	JAMMED	JOSIAH	KIAORA	KAKADU
IMPART	INVADE	JAGGER	JUMPED	JASPER	KRAUSE	KUKRIS
IMPORT	INVIEW	JIGGED	JUMPER	JESTED	KRANTZ	KAKAPO
IMPURE	INVAIN	JIGGER	JUMBLE	JESTER	KEBABS	KIKUYU
INPART	INVOKE	JOGGED	JEMIMA	JESSIE	KABUKI	KELLER

KELLEY	KOREAN	LUANDA	LACIER	LEERED	LILACS	LANCED
KELSEY	KIRSCH	LAAGER	LACKED	LEEVES	LILIES	LANCER
KILLED	KERNEL	LEADED	LACKEY	LIEDER	LOLLED	LANCES
KILLER	KERMIT	LEADEN	LECTER	LEESON	LULLED	LANCET
KILMER	KERALA	LEADER	LICHEN	LIELOW	LILKIM	LANDED
KILTED	KARPOV	LEAKED	LICKED	LIFFEY	LILLIE	LANGER
KILTER	KARATE	LEANED	LOCKED	LIFTED	LOLLOP	LENDER
KULCHA	KIRSTY	LEANER	LOCKER	LUFFED	LILITH	LENSES
KELPIE	KASBAH	LEAPED	LOCKET	LEFTIE	LOLITA	LINDEN
KELVIN	KISMET	LEASED	LUCIEN	LOGJAM	LPLATE	LINGER
KILROY	KISSED	LEASES	LYCEES	LEGACY	LAMMAS	LINKED
KUMMEL	KISSER	LEAVEN	LYCHEE	LAGGED	LUMBAR	LINNET
KIMCHI	KISSES	LEAVER	LACTIC	LOGGED	LAMBDA	LINTEL
KIMONO	KOSHER	LEAVES	LOCKIN	LOGGER	LIMBER	LONGED
KUMARA	KISSME	LOADED	LOCALE	LUGGED	LIMPED	LONGER
KANSAS	KOSOVO	LOADER	LOCALS	LUGGER	LIMPET	LUNGED
KENDAL	KITBAG	LOAFER	LACING	LOGGIA	LUMBER	LUNGES
KENYAN	KITSCH	LOANED	LACUNA	LEGUME	LUMLEY	LANCIA
KENNEL	KITTED	LOAVES	LUCENT	LAGUNA	LIMPID	LANDIS
KENNET	KITTEN	LOATHE	LECTOR	LEGEND	LAMELY	LENNIE
KINDER	KETTLE	LEADIN	LOCUST	LOGANS	LIMPLY	LENTIL
KINKED	KATONA	LIABLE	LOCATE	LAGOON	LAMENT	LONNIE
KINSEY	KETONE	LEANNE	LOCKUP	LEGION	LAMINA	LENSKA
KUNGFU	KATIPO	LEARNS	LUCIUS	LAGERS	LEMANS	LANKLY
KENSIT	KAUNDA	LEARNT	LYCEUM	LUGOSI	LEMOND	LONELY
KONNIE	KRUGER	LEADON	LADIDA	LEGATE	LEMONS	LINING
KINDLE	KLUDGE	LEANON	LADDER	LEGATO	LEMONY	LANDOR
KINDLY	KRUSTY	LIAISE	LADIES	LIGHTS	LOMOND	LENNON
KINGLY	KEVLAR	LEANTO	LADLED	LEGBYE	LEMMON	LENNOX
KENHOM	KOVACS	LEAGUE	LADLES	LAHORE	LOMBOK	LINDOS
KINDOF	KUWAIT	LABIAL	LEDGER	LAIRDS	LUMMOX	LINTON
KAOLIN	KEWELL	LIBRAN	LEDGES	LEIDEN	LAMARR	LONDON
KIOSKS	KOWTOW	LIBYAN	LODGED	LOITER	LEMURS	LYNDON
KNOCKS	KEYPAD	LIBIDO	LODGER	LAIDON	LAMEST	LENORA
KNOLLS	KEYNES	LIBDEM	LODGES	LAIDUP	LIMITS	LINERS
KNOTTY	KHYBER	LOBBED	LADDIE	LIKELY	LAMOUR	LONERS
KEPPEL	KRYTEN	LUBBER	LUDWIG	LIKENS	LIMEYS	LANATE
KIPPED	KAYAKS	LABELS	LADING	LIKING	LANDAU	LENGTH
KIPPER	KEYING	LIBELS	LUDLOW	LAKERS	LINEAL	LYNOTT
KARNAK	LAALAA	LABOUR	LEEWAY	LIKESO	LINEAR	LINEUP
KARVAN	LLAMAS	LACHEY	LEELEE	LILIAN	LUNACY	LINGUA

LINKUP	LURKED	LATHES	LOVAGE	LIZARD	MEDIAN	MCEWAN
LOOFAH	LARKIN	LATTER	LIVEIN	MCADAM	MEDLAR	MEEKER
LOOKAT	LORDLY	LETTER	LOVEIN	MEANER	MEDWAY	MEEKLY
LLOYDS	LARYNX	LITRES	LEVELS	MOANED	MIDDAY	MUESLI
LIONEL	LURING	LITTER	LIVELY	MOANER	MIDWAY	MEETUP
LOOKED	LARDON	LUTHER	LOVELY	MEALIE	MEDICI	MIFFED
LOOMED	LARSON	LETOFF	LEVANT	MEANIE	MEDICO	MUFFIN
LOONEY	LASCAR	LETSGO	LIVING	MEANLY	MEDICS	MUFFLE
LOOPED	LASHED	LATVIA	LOVING	MEASLY	MADDEN	MYFOOT
LOOSEN	LASHES	LETRIP	LEVERS	MIASMA	MADDER	MAGYAR
LOOSER	LASSES	LETWIN	LIVERS	MEADOW	MADMEN	MUGABE
LOOTED	LASTED	LATELY	LIVERY	MEAGRE	MADRES	MAGNET
LOOTER	LESLEY	LETFLY	LOVERS	MIAOWS	MADSEN	MUGGED
LOOKIN	LESSEE	LITTLE	LAVISH	MCBEAL	MEDLEY	MUGGER
LOOKUP	LESSEN	LATENT	LEVITY	MOBCAP	MIDDEN	MAGGIE
LIPMAN	LESSER	LITANY	LAWMAN	MOBLAW	MIDGES	MAGPIE·
LAPPED	LESTER	LOTION	LAWLEY	MRBEAN	MIDGET	MOGGIE
LAPSED	LISPED	LUTHOR	LAWMEN	MOBBED	MIDLER	MAGILL
LAPSES	LISTED	LATEST	LAWYER	MCBAIN	MIDOFF	MOGULS
LOPPED	LISTEN	LETOUT	LOWKEY	MOBILE	MODIFY	MUGGLE
LAPELS	LISTER	LITMUS	LOWING	MRBUMP	MADRID	MCGANN
LOPING	LOSSES	LATOYA	LAWSON	MACKAY	MIDAIR	MAGGOT
LUPINE	LISAHO	LAUNCH	LOWOOD	MRCHAD	MEDALS	MAGNOX
LUPINO	LASSIE	LAUDED	LOWERS	MACKEY	MEDDLE	MEGARA
LUPINS	LESLIE	LAUPER	LOWEST	MACNEE	MIDDLE	MYGIRL
LAPDOG	LUSAKA	LAUREL	LAWFUL	MICHEL	MODELS	MIGHTY
LAPTOP	LASTLY	LAUREN	LUXURY	MICKEY	MODULE	MAGNUM
LEPTON	LOSING	LOUDER	LAXITY	MOCKED	MUDDLE	MAGNUS
LEPERS	LESION	LOURED	LAYMAN	MUCKER	MADAME	MIHRAB
LIPARI	LESSON	LOUSES	LAYMEN	MUCKIN	MODEMS	MRHYDE
LAPUTA	LESSOR	LOUNGE	LAYOFF	MCCALL	MEDINA	MAHLER
LIQUID	LISBON	LAUGHS	LOYOLA	MCCANN	MODENA	MOHAIR
LIQUOR	LISSOM	LOUCHE	LAYING	MCCUNE	MADCOW	MAHOUT
LARIAT	LISTON	LOUGHS	LAYLOW	MICRON	MADDOX	MOHAWK
LARVAE	LOSERS	LAURIE	LAYERS	MOCKUP	MODERN	MAITAI
LARVAL	LUSTRE	LOUDLY	LAYOUT	MACAWS	MEDUSA	MAIDEN
LOREAL	LATHAM	LOUVRE	LAZIER	MADCAP	MODEST	MAILED
LYRICS	LETHAL	LOUISA	LIZZIE	MADMAN	MODISH	MAILER
LARDER	LYTHAM	LOUISE	LAZILY	MADMAX	MADEUP	MAIMED
LARGER	LATEEN	LEVIED	LAZULI	MADRAS	MEDIUM	MAISIE
LERNER	LATHER	LEVIES	LAZING	MEDIAL	MAENAD	MAINLY

MAJOLI	MALAGA	MENTAL	MINGLE	MARGAM	MARTIN	MARQUE
MAJORS	MALIGN	MINOAN	MANAMA	MARIAH	MARVIN	MORGUE
MAJURO	MILLIE	MONDAY	MINIMS	MARIAN	MERCIA	MURMUR
MOJAVE	MOLLIE	MENACE	MANANA	MARRAM	MERLIN	MARTYN
MAKEDO	MILDLY	MENSCH	MINING	MERMAN	MORBID	MARTYR
MIKADO	MALONE	MINACK	MANIOC	MIRIAM	MORRIS	MERVYN
MAKING	MELINA	MONACO	MANSON	MOREAU	MARKKA	MISHAP
MEKONG	MELONS	MONICA	MENTOR	MORGAN	MARBLE	MISLAY
MAKERS	MILANO	MUNICH	MINION	MORNAY	MARPLE	MISSAL
MCKERN	MOLINA	MANGEL	MINNOW	MORTAL	MERELY	MUSCAT
MAKEUP	MALLOW	MANGER	MINTON	MORTAR	MORALE	MASHED
MCLEAN	MELLOR	MANNED	MONGOL	MURRAY	MORALS	MASHES
MULLAH	MELLOW	MANNER	MONROE	MYRIAD	MURALS	MASKED
MALABO	MELTON	MANTEL	MANORS	MARACA	MYRTLE	MASSED
MALIBU	MILTON	MANUEL	MANTRA	MARCEL	MARINA	MASSES
MALICE	MOLLOY	MENDED	MANURE	MARKED	MARINE	MASSEY
MOLOCH	MALORY	MENDER	MINERS	MARKER	MERINO	MASTER
MALADY	MILERS	MENDES	MINORS	MARKET	MORONI	MESHED
MELODY	MILORD	MINCED	MINUTE	MARLEY	MARCOS	MESHES
MILADY	MOLARS	MINCER	MANFUL	MARNER	MARGOT	MESSED
MYLADY	MYLORD	MINCES	MANQUE	MARRED	MARION	MESSES
MALDEN	MOLEST	MINDED	MANTUA	MARTEN	MARLON	MISLED
MALLEE	MULISH	MINDER	MOOLAH	MARVEL	MARLOW	MISSED
MALLET	MALAWI	MINTED	MOORED	MERCER	MARMOT	MISSES
MALTED	MELVYN	MINTER	MOOTED	MERGED	MAROON	MISTER
MELDED	MAMMAL	MINUET	MOONIE	MERGER	MARRON	MOSLEY
MELTED	MUMBAI	MONIES	MYOPIA	MERGES	MARROW	MOSSES
MILDER	MIMICS	MONKEY	MYOPIC	MERSEY	MERLOT	MOSTEL
MILDEW	MEMBER	MANAGE	MOOING	MIRREN	MERTON	MUSKET
MILIEU	MUMMER	MANEGE	MAOISM	MORLEY	MIRROR	MUSSEL
MILKED	MEMOIR	MENAGE	MAOIST	MORSEL	MORMON	MUSTER
MILLED	MUMBLE	MANCHA	MAPLES	MURDER	MORROW	MISCHA
MILLER	MIMING	MANCHU	MAPPED	MURIEL	MARISA	MASHIE
MILLET	MOMENT	MONTHS	MOPPED	MIRAGE	MEREST	MASSIF
MOLTEN	MAMMON	MANTIS	MOPPET	MARSHY	MORASS	MASTIC
MULDER	MEMORY	MENHIR	MUPPET	MARTHA	MOROSE	MISFIT
MULLED	MIMOSA	MINNIE	MAPPIN	MURPHY	MERITS	MISHIT
MULLEN	MRMOTO	MANGLE	MOPING	MARCIA	MARAUD	MOSAIC
MULLER	MANIAC	MANILA	MAPUTO	MARGIN	MARCUS	MUSLIM
MULLET	MANUAL	MANOLO	MAPOUT	MARLIN	MARIUS	MUSLIN
MYLIFE	MENIAL	MANTLE	MAQUIS	MARNIE	MARKUP	MYSTIC

MASALA	MOTTLE	MOVING	NEBULA	NEGATE	NIPPED	NETTED
MOSTLY	MATING	MOVERS	NIBBLE	NIGHTS	NIPPER	NUTMEG
MUSCLE	MATINS	MOWLAM	NOBALL	NAGPUR	NAPKIN	NUTTER
MYSELF	METING	MOWGLI	NOBBLE	NAIADS	NAPALM	NOTIFY
MASONS	MUTANT	MEWING	NUBILE	NAILED	NIPPLE	NITRIC
MUSING	MUTING	MOWING	NECTAR	NAILER	NIPPON	NITWIT
MASCOT	MUTINY	MAWSON	NECKED	NOIDEA	NEPETA	NUTRIA
MOSCOW	MATRON	MOWERS	NICKED	NOISES	NORMAL	NETTLE
MUSKOX	MATZOS	MYWORD	NICKEL	NEIGHS	NORMAN	NATANT
MASERU	METEOR	MEXICO	NICKER	NOJOKE	NORWAY	NOTING
MISERE	METHOD	MAXIMS	NUCLEI	NIKITA	NARKED	NUTANT
MISERS	MOTION	MIXING	NICELY	NELLIE	NERVES	NATION
MISERY	MOTSON	MIXERS	NICOLA	NOLANS	NORDEN	NOTION
MISUSE	MUTTON	MAYDAY	NICOLE	NYLONS	NURSED	NATURE
MASQUE	MATURE	MAYHAP	NICEST	NELSON	NURSES	NOTARY
MESSUP	METERS	MAYHEM	NICETY	NUMBAT	NARNIA	NOTATE
MISCUE	MOTORS	MAYHEW	NODICE	NUMNAH	NEREID	NUTATE
MISSUS	MOTETS	MOYLES	NODDED	NOMADS	NORDIC	NOTOUT
MOSQUE	MUTATE	MAYALL	NUDGED	NUMBED	NORRIS	NATIVE
MOSTUE	MOTIVE	MAYFLY	NUDGES	NUMBER	NEROLI	NEURAL
MUSEUM	MOTOWN	MAYBUG	NODOFF	NYMPHS	NARROW	NOUGAT
MOSEYS	METHYL	MIZZEN	NODDLE	NAMELY	NORTON	NAUTCH
MUTUAL	MAUMAU	MUZZLE	NODULE	NIMBLE	NASSAU	NAUSEA
MATTED	MAUNDY	MOZART	NADINE	NIMBLY	NISSAN	NEUTER
MATTER	MOULDS	NEARBY	NODOSE	NAMING	NASEBY	NAUGHT
METIER	MOULDY	NUANCE	NUDISM	NIMROD	NASSER	NOUGHT
METRES	MOUNDS	NEARED	NUDIST	NIMBUS	NESTED	NEURON
MITHER	MAULED	NEARER	NOMORE	NOSIER	NEVADA
MITRED	MOUSER	NEATEN	NEEDED	NANSEN	NOSIER	NEVADA
MITRES	MOUTHS	NEATER	NIECES	NANTES	NESBIT	NAVIES
MITTEN	MOUTHY	NIAMEY	NEEDLE	NONAGE	NESSIE	NAVAJO
MOTHER	MOULIN	NOAKES	NEESON	NUNCIO	NESTLE	NOVELS
MOTLEY	MOURNS	NIACIN	NOFEAR	NINETY	NOSILY	NOVENA
MUTTER	MOUTON	NEAGLE	NAGGED	NONETS	NOSING	NEWHAM
MOTIFS	MOUSSE	NEARLY	NAGGER	NOOSES	NESTOR	NEWMAN
MATHIS	MOULTS	NEATLY	NUGGET	NOODLE	NOSHOW	NAWABS
MATRIX	MOUNTS	NABOBS	NOGGIN	NAPIER	NOSHUP	NEWLEY
METRIC	MUUMUU	NOBODY	NIGGLE	NAPLES	NATHAN	NEWAGE
METALS	MOVIES	NABBED	NIGGLY	NAPPED	NOTICE	NEWELS
METTLE	MOVEIN	NOBLER	NUGENT	NAPPER	NATTER	NEWTON
MOTELS	MAVENS	NOBLES	NOGOOD	NEPHEW	NETHER	NEWARK

NEWEST	OLDEST	ONFOOT	OILIER	OFSTED	OUTPUT	PLACID
NEWISH	ODDITY	OFFERS	OBLIGE	ONSPEC	OUTRUN	PRATIE
NEXTTO	ONDUTY	ONFIRE	OOLOGY	OUSTED	OCTAVE	PRAXIS
NOZZLE	ONEDAY	ONFORM	OILRIG	OYSTER	OCTAVO	PLANKS
NUZZLE	ONEWAY	OXFORD	OBLONG	OSSIFY	OTTAWA	PRANKS
ONAPAR	OPERAS	OAFISH	OGLING	ONSALE	OCULAR	PEARLS
OCASEY	OVERDO	OFFISH	OILING	ONSONG	OEUVRE	PEARLY
OKAYED	OBEYED	OFFCUT	ONLINE	ORSINI	ONVIEW	PLASMA
ONAGER	OLEVEL	ORGEAT	OXLIPS	ORSINO	ORWELL	PSALMS
ORATED	OPENED	ORGIES	OGLERS	ONSLOW	OSWALD	PLAINS
ORATES	OPENER	ORGANS	OILERS	OPSHOP	ONWARD	PRAWNS
ORANGE	ONEOFF	ONHOLD	OBLATE	OBSESS	OXYGEN	PHAROS
OXALIS	ONEDGE	OTHERS	OFLATE	OUTLAW	OOZING	PIANOS
ORACLE	ONEDIN	OVIEDO	OWLETS	OUTLAY	PEARCE	PRAISE
ORALLY	ONEGIN	OLIVER	OOMPAH	OUTRAN	PLAICE	PLAITS
ORATOR	ONEILL	OLIVES	ORMOLU	ONTICK	PLANCK	PLANTS
OPAQUE	OPENLY	OPINED	OSMOND	OPTICS	PRANCE	PEANUT
ORBITS	OTELLO	OPINES	OGMORE	OSTLER	PLAIDY	PLAGUE
ORCHID	OVERLY	OLIVIA	OLMERT	OUTLET	PRAVDA	PLAQUE
OCCULT	OCEANS	ORIGIN	OSMIUM	OUTSET	PEAHEN	PLAYUP
ONCALL	OBERON	OSIRIS	OUNCES	ORTEGA	PEAKED	PRAGUE
OCCUPY	OCELOT	OTITIS	OWNING	OUTAGE	PEALED	PIAZZA
OCCURS	OREGON	ORIOLE	OWNERS	OBTAIN	PHASED	PUBLIC
OSCARS	OLEARY	ONIONS	OFNOTE	OUTBID	PHASES	PEBBLE
OHDEAR	ODENSE	ORIANA	ORNATE	OUTDID	PLACED	PEBBLY
OLDHAM	ODESSA	ORIENT	OTOOLE	OUTFIT	PLACES	PACMAN
OLDHAT	ORELSE	ORISON	ODOURS	OUTWIT	PLANED	PACIER
OLDLAG	ODETTE	OSIERS	OBOIST	OXTAIL	PLANER	PACKED
OLDMAN	OBELUS	OSIERY	ONOATH	ONTIME	PLANES	PACKER
ORDEAL	OPENUP	ORISSA	OPORTO	OCTANE	PLANET	PACKET
OLDIES	ONETWO	OTIOSE	ORPHAN	OPTING	PLATED	PECKED
OODLES	OFFDAY	OPIATE	OSPREY	OSTEND	PLATEN	PECKER
OLDAGE	OFFPAT	ODIOUS	OPPUGN	OUTING	PLATER	PICKED
OLDVIC	OFFICE	OGILVY	OPPOSE	OPTION	PLATES	PICKET
ORDAIN	OFFKEY	OBJECT	OGRADY	OUTFOX	PLAYED	POCKET
ODDJOB	OFFSET	OAKLEY	OBRIEN	OTTERS	PLAYER	PUCKER
ODDSON	OFFALY	ORKNEY	ORRERY	OUTCRY	PRATED	PACIFY
OLDBOY	ONFILE	OILCAN	OGRESS	OBTUSE	PRATES	PECTIN
ORDERS	ONFILM	OILMAN	ONRUSH	OCTETS	PRAYED	PICNIC
ORDURE	OFFEND	ONLOAN	OSSIAN	OPTOUT	PRAYER	PICKLE
ODDEST	OFFING	OCLOCK	ONSIDE	OUTGUN	PEACHY	PACING

PACINO	PRESET	PRIMAL	PAIDUP	PILLOW	PINTER	PROBES
PECANS	PREYED	PHILBY	PAIRUP	POLYPS	PONDER	PROLES
PACERS	PLEDGE	PRINCE	PRIMUS	PALTRY	PONIES	PROPEL
PICARD	PEEWIT	PAINED	PRINZE	PALEST	PUNIER	PROPER
PACKUP	POETIC	PAIRED	PAJAMA	POLISH	PUNNED	PROTEA
PICKUP	PRECIS	POISED	PEKING	PALATE	PUNNET	PROTEM
PEDLAR	PREFIX	POISES	POKING	PELOTA	PUNTER	PROVED
PADDED	PRELIM	PRICED	PAKORA	PILATE	PONCHO	PROVEN
PADRES	PREVIN	PRICES	PELHAM	PILOTS	PUNCHY	PROVES
PUDSEY	PAELLA	PRICEY	PILLAR	POLITE	PENCIL	PROOFS
PIDGIN	PUEBLO	PRIDES	PULSAR	PILEUP	PINKIE	PLOUGH
PADDLE	PREENS	PRIMED	PALACE	PULLUP	PUNDIT	PRONGS
PEDALO	PHENOL	PRIMER	POLICE	PAMPAS	PANELS	PHOBIA
PEDALS	PYEDOG	PRIMES	POLICY	PUMICE	PENDLE	PHOBIC
PEDDLE	PHELPS	PRISED	PALLED	POMADE	PINTLE	PHONIC
PUDDLE	PIERRE	PRISES	PALLET	PAMPER	PUNILY	PROFIT
PEDANT	POETRY	PRIVET	PALMER	POMMEL	PANAMA	PROSIT
PADOUT	PLEASE	PRIZED	PELLET	POMPEY	PENANG	PEOPLE
PODIUM	PLEATS	PRIZES	PELLEW	PUMMEL	PINING	POODLE
PIEMAN	PLENTY	PLIGHT	PELMET	PUMPED	PENNON	POORLY
PREFAB	PRESTO	PAIDIN	PELTED	PAMELA	PINION	POOTLE
PREPAY	PRETTY	PHILIP	PILFER	PIMPLE	PINTOS	PROWLS
PRETAX	PLENUM	PRICKS	POLDER	PIMPLY	PANFRY	PHOTON
PREWAR	PUFFED	PHIALS	POLLED	POMELO	PANTRY	PHOTOS
PIERCE	PUFFER	PRIMLY	POLLEN	POMPOM	PENURY	PROCOL
PREACH	PUFFIN	PRISMA	PULLED	PUMPUP	PINERO	PROTON
PLEADS	PIFFLE	PRISMS	PULLET	PANDAS	PUNISH	PROMPT
PSEUDO	PAGODA	PLIANT	PULLEY	PENPAL	PENTUP	PROUST
PEEKED	PEGGED	POIROT	PALAIS	PENTAD	PENRYN	PROWSE
PEELED	PEGLEG	POISON	PALLID	PUNJAB	POOBAH	PRONTO
PEELER	PIGLET	PRISON	PELVIC	PUNKAH	PROZAC	PROPUP
PEEPED	POGUES	PLIERS	PELVIS	PANICS	PHOEBE	POPLAR
PEEPER	PAGANS	PRIORS	PULLIN	PANDER	PHONED	PAPACY
PEERED	PAGING	PRIORY	PULPIT	PANNED	PHONES	PEPPER
PEEVED	PIGEON	PRIEST	PALOMA	PANTED	PHONEY	PIPPED
PEEVES	POGROM	PRISSY	PALING	PANZER	PHOOEY	POPPED
PEEWEE	PUGDOG	PAINTS	PILING	PENNED	PLOVER	POPPER
PIECED	PAGETT	PLINTH	POLAND	PENNEY	POOLED	POPPET
PIECES	PIGSTY	POINTS	POLONY	PINCER	POORER	PUPPET
PREFER	PEGOUT	POINTY	PYLONS	PINNED	POOTER	POPOFF
PREMED	PIGOUT	PRINTS	PALLOR	PINNER	PROBED	PEPSIN

PEPTIC	PARTED	PERSON	POSTIT	PETULA	PLUMMY	QUAKER
PIPPIN	PERMED	PURDOM	PESTLE	PATENT	PLUMPS	QUAKES
POPLIN	PORKER	PARISH	POSING	PATINA	POULTS	QUAVER
PUPILS	PORTER	PERISH	PASCOE	PITONS	PRUNUS	QUAFFS
PIPING	PURDEY	PERUSE	PASSON	POTENT	PAVANE	QUAGGA
PAPHOS	PURGED	PHRASE	PASTOR	PATHOS	PAVING	QUANGO
POPTOP	PURGES	PUREST	PISTOL	PATIOS	PAVLOV	QUACKS
PAPERS	PURLER	PURISM	PISTON	PATROL	PIVOTS	QUARKS
PAPERY	PURLEY	PURIST	POSTOP	PATRON	PAWPAW	QUAILS
PIPERS	PURRED	PARITY	PASTRY	PATTON	PAWNED	QUAYLE
POPART	PURSED	PIRATE	POSERS	PETROL	PAWNEE	QUALMS
POPERY	PURSER	PURITY	PESETA	POTION	PCWREN	QUAINT
PAPISM	PURSES	PERKUP	POSITS	PYTHON	PEWTER	QUARRY
PAPIST	PURVEY	POROUS	POSEUR	PETIPA	POWDER	QUATRO
POPISH	PURIFY	PURSUE	POSSUM	PETARD	POWELL	QUARTO
PUPATE	PARKIN	PASCAL	PITMAN	PETERS	PAWING	QUARTS
PEPLUM	PERMIT	PASHAS	PITSAW	POTASH	POWWOW	QUARTZ
PIPEUP	PERRIN	PASSAT	POTMAN	PETITE	POWERS	QUENCH
POPGUN	PERSIA	POSTAL	PUTSCH	POTATO	PAXMAN	QUEBEC
PAPAYA	PERSIL	PASSBY	PATTED	PUTOUT	PIXIES	QUEUED
POPEYE	PORTIA	PASSED	PATTEN	PLURAL	PAXTON	QUEUES
PIQUED	PURLIN	PASSES	PATTER	PAUNCH	PAYDAY	QUELLS
PIQUES	PERUKE	PASTED	PETREL	POUNCE	PAYEES	QUEENS
PIQUET	PAROLE	PASTEL	PITIED	POUNDS	PAYOFF	QUEASY
PARIAH	PARTLY	PASTES	PITIES	PAUPER	PSYCHE	QUESTS
PARIAN	PERILS	PESTER	PITMEN	PAUSED	PSYCHO	QWERTY
PARKAS	PERTLY	PISCES	PITNEY	PAUSES	PHYSIC	QUINCE
PORTAL	PORTLY	PISTES	PITTED	PHUKET	PHYSIO	QUINCY
PURDAH	PURELY	POSHER	POTEEN	PLUMED	PAYOLA	QUITCH
PERABO	PURPLE	POSIES	POTTED	PLUMES	PAYING	QUIRES
PIRACY	PARANG	POSSET	POTTER	PLUSES	PLYING	QUIVER
PARADE	PARENT	POSTED	PUTTED	POURED	PRYING	QUIFFS
PARODY	PARING	POSTER	PUTTEE	POUTED	PEYTON	QUICHE
PARCEL	PORING	PUSHED	PUTTER	PRUDES	PAYERS	QUIRKE
PARGET	PYRENE	PUSHER	PUTOFF	PRUNED	PAYOUT	QUIRKS
PARKED	PARDON	PUSHES	POTAGE	PRUNES	PHYLUM	QUIRKY
PARKER	PARROT	PASSIM	PATCHY	POUFFE	PIZZAS	QUILLS
PARLEY	PARSON	PASTIS	PATOIS	PLUNGE	POZNAN	QUINOA
PARSEC	PARTON	PASTIT	POTSIE	PLUGIN	PUZZLE	QUINSY
PARSED	PERIOD	PISTIL	PUTRID	PLUCKS	QUASAR	QUILTS
PARSES	PERNOD	POSTIE	PETALS	PLUCKY	QUAKED	QUMRAN

QANTAS	REBUKE	RICHLY	RODNEY	RAFFLE	RIGOUR	ROLLUP
QUOTAS	RABBLE	RACEME	RUDDER	REFILL	REHEAR	RELIVE
QUOTED	REBELS	RACINE	RIDDLE	RIFFLE	REHEAT	RELAYS
QUOTES	RIBALD	RACING	RUDELY	RUFFLE	REHEEL	RAMSAY
QUOKKA	RIBBLE	RECANT	RUDOLF	REFINE	REHASH	REMICK
QUOITS	RUBBLE	RECENT	REDONE	REFUND	RHINAL	REMEDY
QUORUM	RIBAND	RECKON	RIDING	REFERS	RAIDED	RAMJET
REAGAN	RIBENA	RECTOR	RODENT	REFORM	RAIDER	RAMMED
RWANDA	ROBING	RECAPS	RADIOS	REFUSE	RAILED	RAMSEY
READER	ROBINS	RECIPE	REDHOT	REFUTE	RAINED	RIMMED
REAMED	RUBENS	RACERS	REDSOX	REFLUX	RAISED	RIMMER
REAMER	REBOOT	RECORD	RODEOS	RAGBAG	RAISES	ROMMEL
REAPED	RIBBON	RECURS	RIDERS	RAGDAY	RUINED	ROMNEY
REAPER	ROBROY	RACISM	RADISH	RAGLAN	RAISIN	ROMPED
REARED	ROBSON	RACIST	RUDEST	RAGMAN	REIGNS	ROMPER
ROAMED	REBORE	RECAST	RADIUM	RAGTAG	RHINOS	ROMSEY
ROAMER	REBORN	RECESS	RADIUS	REGGAE	REJECT	RAMIFY
ROARED	ROBERT	RECITE	REDGUM	RUGRAT	REJIGS	REMAIN
ROACHE	ROBUST	RECOUP	REDRUM	RIGSBY	REJOIN	ROMAJI
ROADIE	REBATE	RICTUS	REDEYE	RAGGED	RAJPUT	ROMIJN
REALLY	REBUTS	RUCKUS	REEDED	RAGMEN	RAKEIN	REMAKE
REALMS	ROBOTS	RADIAL	REEFER	REGRET	RAKING	RAMBLE
REARMS	RUBATO	RADIAN	REEKED	RIGGED	RAKISH	ROMOLA
REASON	RUBOUT	REDCAP	REELED	RIGGER	RELOAD	RUMBLE
REACTS	RIBEYE	REDCAR	REEVES	ROGUES	RELICS	RUMPLE
REALTY	RACIAL	REDIAL	REECHO	RUGGED	RELIED	REMAND
RIALTO	ROCOCO	REDMAN	REEKIE	RUGGER	RELIEF	REMIND
ROASTS	RECEDE	REDRAW	RHEIMS	REGAIN	RELIES	RIMINI
REBIDS	RACHEL	RODHAM	RHEUMY	REGALE	ROLLED	ROMANA
RABIES	RACIER	RODMAN	RUEING	REGULO	ROLLER	ROMANO
RIBBED	RACKET	REDACT	REEBOK	REGIME	RELAID	ROMANS
ROBBED	RICHER	REDUCE	RHESUS	RAGING	RELENT	ROMANY
ROBBER	RICHES	REDDEN	RUEFUL	REGENT	RILING	RAMROD
RUBBED	ROCKED	REDDER	RAFTER	REGINA	ROLAND	ROMEOS
RUBBER	ROCKER	REDEEM	REFLEX	REGION	RULING	REMARK
RUBIES	ROCKET	REDOES	REFUEL	REGARD	RELYON	ROMERO
REBUFF	RUCHED	REDSEA	RIFLED	ROGERS	RIGHTO	REMISS
RABBIS	RECIFE	RIDDEN	RIFLES	RIGHTO	RULERS	REMITS
RABBIT	RECOIL	RIDGED	RUFFED	RIGHTS	RELISH	REMOTE
ROBBIE	RICHIE	RIDGES	REFUGE	RAGOUT	RELATE	RUMOUR
RUBRIC	RECALL	RIDLEY	RAFFIA	REGIUS	RELETS	RUMPUS

REMOVE	RUNOUT	RUPERT	RESUME	RETARD	RIVERS	STANCE
RENTAL	RENEWS	REPAST	RESENT	RETIRE	ROVERS	STARCH
RUNWAY	RENOWN	REPOSE	RESINS	RETORT	RAVISH	SWATCH
RANGED	ROOBAR	RIPEST	RISING	RETURN	REVISE	SCALDS
RANGER	RHONDA	REPOTS	ROSCOE	ROTARY	RIVETS	SHANDY
RANGES	REOPEN	REPUTE	RESORT	ROTORS	RAVEUP	SHARDS
RANKED	RHODES	REPAYS	RISERS	ROTATE	REVIVE	STAGDO
RANKER	RIOTED	RAQUEL	ROSARY	RATRUN	ROWELS	STANDS
RANTED	RIOTER	REREAD	ROSERY	ROTGUT	REWIND	SCALED
RANTER	ROOFER	RAREFY	ROSTRA	ROUNDS	ROWENA	SCALES
RENDER	ROOKED	RARELY	RESIST	REUBEN	ROWING	SCARED
RENNES	ROONEY	RARING	RESETS	REUSED	REWARD	SCARES
RENNET	ROOTED	RERUNS	RESITS	REUTER	REWIRE	SEABED
RENTED	ROOKIE	RAREST	RESCUE	ROUSED	REWORD	SEALED
RINGED	ROOSTS	RARITY	RISQUE	ROUSES	REWORK	SEALER
RINGER	REPEAL	RASCAL	RATTAN	ROUTED	ROWERS	SEAMED
RINSED	REPEAT	RESEAL	RITUAL	ROUTER	RIYADH	SEAMEN
RINSES	REPLAN	ROSEAU	RATHER	ROUTES	RAYNER	SEARED
RONDEL	REPLAY	RESIDE	RATTED	ROUGHS	RHYMED	SEATED
RUNNEL	RIPSAW	RASHER	RATTER	ROURKE	RHYMES	SHADED
RUNNER	RUPIAH	RASHES	RITTER	ROUBLE	RHYTHM	SHADES
RANOFF	RAPIDS	RASPED	ROTTED	ROUSTS	ROYALE	SHAKEN
RUNOFF	RAPIER	RESTED	ROTTEN	REVEAL	ROYALS	SHAKER
RENEGE	RAPPED	RISKED	ROTTER	REVIEW	RHYTON	SHAKES
RANCID	RAPPER	ROSIER	RUTGER	REVUES	RAYGUN	SHAMED
RENNIE	RIPPED	ROSTER	RUTLES	REVVED	ROZZER	SHAMES
RENNIN	RIPPER	RUSHED	RUTTED	RAVAGE	RAZZLE	SHAPED
RENOIR	RUPEES	RUSHES	RATIFY	REVOKE	RAZING	SHAPER
RONNIE	RIPOFF	RUSSET	RETAIL	REVELS	RAZORS	SHAPES
RUNCIE	REPAID	RUSTED	RETAIN	REVILE	SCARAB	SHARED
RANKLE	REPAIR	RESIGN	RETAKE	REVOLT	SEACAT	SHARES
RONALD	ROPEIN	ROSLIN	ROTHKO	RIVALS	SEAMAN	SHAVED
RENAME	REPELS	RUSKIN	RATELS	REVAMP	SEAWAY	SHAVEN
RANDOM	RIPPLE	RUSSIA	RATTLE	RAVENS	SHAMAN	SHAVER
RANSOM	REPENT	RUSTIC	RETELL	RAVINE	STALAG	SHAVES
RONDOS	REPINE	RASHLY	RETOLD	RAVING	SWARAJ	SKATED
RUNLOW	RIPENS	RESALE	RATING	ROVING	SHABBY	SKATER
RUNYON	ROPING	RESELL	RETINA	RAVERS	SCARCE	SKATES
RANGUP	RAPTOR	RESOLD	ROTUND	REVERB	SEANCE	SLAKED
RANOUT	RIPPON	RESULT	RATION	REVERE	SEARCH	SLAKES
RINGUP	REPORT	RUSTLE	RATIOS	REVERT	SNATCH	SLATED

SLATER	SLANGY	SEASON	SUBLET	SIDNEY	SLEWED	STEINS
SLATES	SNAGGE	SHADOW	SUBSET	SODDEN	SPEWED	STERNE
SLAVED	SPARGE	SHALOM	SUBMIT	SUDDEN	STEREO	SEEYOU
SLAVER	SCATHE	SHARON	SUBTLE	SYDNEY	STEVEN	STEROL
SLAVES	SWATHE	SLALOM	SUBTLY	SEDAKA	STEWED	SHERPA
SLAYER	SHANIA	STATOR	SABENA	SUDOKU	SWEDEN	SLEEPS
SNAKED	SHARIF	SCALPS	SABINE	SADDLE	SWEDES	SLEEPY
SNAKES	STACIE	SCAMPI	SOBERS	SIDING	SEEOFF	STEEPS
SNARED	STALIN	SCAMPS	SUBORN	SIDEON	STEFFI	STEPPE
SNARES	STASIS	SCARPS	SUBURB	SADISM	SLEDGE	SWEEPS
SOAKED	STATIC	SHARPE	SABOTS	SADIST	SLEIGH	SHEARS
SOAMES	STAYIN	SNAPPY	SUBDUE	SEDATE	SEETHE	SHERRY
SOARED	SHACKS	STAMPS	SOCIAL	SODIUM	SCENIC	SIERRA
SPACED	SHANKS	SWAMPS	SUCHAS	SEESAW	SEEFIT	SMEARS
SPACEK	SHARKS	SWAMPY	SECEDE	STEFAN	SPECIE	SMEARY
SPACER	SLACKS	STAIRS	SACHET	SHELBY	STEPIN	SNEERS
SPACES	SMACKS	STARRY	SACKED	SHERBO	STEVIE	SPEARS
SPACEY	SNACKS	SPARSE	SACRED	SKETCH	SHEIKH	STEERS
SPADES	SPANKS	SCANTY	SECRET	SPEECH	SNEAKS	SWEARS
SPARED	SPARKS	SCATTY	SICKEN	SPENCE	SNEAKY	SCENTS
SPARES	STACKS	SHAFTS	SOCCER	STENCH	SPEAKS	SHEATH
SPATES	STALKS	SHANTY	SOCKED	SHEEDY	SPECKS	SHEETS
STAGED	SWANKS	SLANTS	SOCKET	SPEEDO	STEAKS	SIESTA
STAGES	SWANKY	SMARTS	SUCHET	SPEEDS	SEEMLY	SLEETY
STAKES	SHAWLS	SPARTA	SUCKED	SPEEDY	SHEILA	SLEUTH
STALER	SMALLS	STARTS	SUCKER	SPENDS	SHELLS	SMELTS
STAMEN	SNAILS	SEAMUS	SICKIE	STEADY	SMELLS	SVELTE
STAPES	SNARLS	SLAPUP	SICILY	STEEDS	SMELLY	SWEATS
STARED	STABLE	SNAPUP	SICKLE	SCENES	SPELLS	SWEATY
STARES	STALLS	STATUE	SICKLY	SEEDED	STEALS	SWEETS
STATED	STAPLE	STATUS	SUCKLE	SEEDER	STEELE	STEPUP
STATEN	SHAMMY	STAYUP	SECOND	SEEGER	STEELS	SHEAVE
STATES	SMARMY	STARVE	SECTOR	SEEKER	STEELY	SHELVE
STAVES	SPASMS	SNAZZY	SECURE	SEEMED	STELLA	SLEEVE
STAYED	SWARMS	STANZA	SEDUCE	SEEPED	SWELLS	SWERVE
STAYER	SHAYNE	SWAYZE	SADDEN	SEERED	STEAMS	SHERYL
SWAYED	SPAWNS	SUBWAY	SADDER	SHEKEL	STEAMY	SLEAZE
SCARFE	STAINS	SABLES	SADLER	SIEGES	SEEING	SLEAZY
STAFFA	SWAINS	SABRES	SEDGES	SIEVES	SHEENA	SNEEZE
STAFFS	SEACOW	SOBBED	SIDLED	SKEWED	SHEENE	SNEEZY
SHAGGY	SEADOG	SUBBED	SIDLES	SKEWER	SIENNA	SIFTED

SIFTER	SNITCH	STIVES	SKINNY	SOLIDS	SELDOM	SUNDAY
SOFTEN	STITCH	SUITED	SAIGON	SALTED	SALARY	SUNHAT
SOFTER	SWITCH	SUITES	SAILOR	SALVED	SULTRY	SUNTAN
SUFFER	SHINDY	SWIPED	SHIMON	SALVER	SPLASH	SYNTAX
SOFFIT	SAILED	SWIPES	SKIBOB	SALVES	SALUTE	SENECA
SOFTIE	SEIBER	SWIVEL	SKIDOO	SELLER	SOLUTE	SONICS
SUFFIX	SEIZED	SKIFFS	SLIPON	SELSEY	SPLITS	SYNODS
SAFELY	SEIZES	SNIFFS	SPIGOT	SILKEN	SALIVA	SANDER
SOFTLY	SHINER	SNIFFY	SUITOR	SILTED	SELWYN	SANTER
SAFARI	SHINES	SLINGS	SKIMPS	SILVER	SPLAYS	SENDER
SAFEST	SHIRES	STINGO	SKIMPY	SOLDER	SAMPAN	SENSED
SUFISM	SHIVER	STINGS	SKIPPY	SOLVED	SIMIAN	SENSES
SAFETY	SKIVED	STINGY	SLIPPY	SOLVER	SAMUEL	SINDEN
SIGNAL	SKIVER	SWINGS	SKIERS	SOLVES	SEMTEX	SINGED
SAGGED	SKIVES	SLIGHT	SAINTS	SPLEEN	SIMMER	SINGER
SIGHED	SLICED	SMITHS	SHIFTS	SULKED	SIMNEL	SINGES
SIGNED	SLICER	SMITHY	SHIFTY	SULLEN	SIMPER	SINKER
SIGNET	SLICES	SCIPIO	SHIITE	SILAGE	SOMMER	SINNED
SUGDEN	SLIDES	SPIRIT	SHINTO	SYLPHS	SUMMER	SINNER
SIGNIN	SLIVER	SHIRKS	SHINTY	SALLIS	SUMMIT	SONNET
SAGELY	SMILED	SKINKS	SHIRTS	SALVIA	SAMPLE	SUNBED
SIGNON	SMILER	SLINKS	SHIRTY	SILVIA	SIMILE	SUNDER
SIGNOR	SMILES	SLINKY	SKIRTS	SYLVIA	SIMPLE	SUNDEW
SUGARS	SMILEY	SMIRKS	STILTS	SYLVIE	SIMPLY	SUNKEN
SUGARY	SMITES	SNICKS	STINTS	SALUKI	SOMALI	SUNSET
SIGHTS	SNIPER	STICKS	SWIFTS	SOLELY	STMALO	SANCHO
SIGNUP	SNIPES	STICKY	SKIRUN	SALAMI	SIMONE	SANKIN
SCHLEP	SNIVEL	STINKO	SLIPUP	SALOME	SIMONY	SINBIN
SCHULZ	SOILED	STINKS	STIRUP	SOLEMN	SAMSON	SINKIN
SCHAMA	SOIREE	SCILLA	SKIVVY	SALINE	SIMOOM	SONNIE
SCHEMA	SPICED	SHIELD	SALAAM	SALONS	SUMMON	SUNLIT
SCHEME	SPICES	SKILLS	SALMAN	SELENA	SYMBOL	SANELY
SPHINX	SPIDER	SPILLS	SILVAS	SELINA	SOMBRE	SINGLE
SCHOOL	SPIKED	STIFLE	SULTAN	SILENT	SOMERS	SINGLY
SAHARA	SPIKES	STILLS	SYLVAN	SOLENT	SAMOSA	SENIOR
SPHERE	SPINES	SWILLS	SELECT	SOLONG	SEMITE	SENSOR
SCHISM	SPINET	SWIRLS	SILICA	SPLINE	SOMNUS	SUNGOD
SHIRAZ	SPIRES	SHIMMY	SOLACE	SPLINT	SANDAL	SANDRA
SPINAL	SPITED	STIGMA	SPLICE	SALLOW	SINBAD	SENORA
SPIRAL	SPITES	SCIONS	SALADO	SALMON	SINEAD	SENTRY
SMIRCH	STILES	SKIING	SALADS	SALOON	SUNDAE	SINTRA

SUNDRY	SMOKED	SPOOKY	SNOOTY	STREAM	SHRUGS	STRONG
SANEST	SMOKER	STOCKS	SNORTS	SURTAX	SPRIGS	STRUNG
SANITY	SMOKES	STOCKY	SNOTTY	SYRIAN	SERBIA	SYRINX
SENATE	SMOKEY	STOOKS	SNOUTS	SCRIBE	SERGIO	SARTOR
SONATA	SNORED	STORKS	SPORTS	SCRUBS	SERKIS	SERMON
SUNITA	SNORER	SCOWLS	SPORTY	SHRUBS	SORBIE	SORROW
SENDUP	SNORES	SHOALS	SPOTTY	STROBE	SORDID	SCRAPE
SENTUP	SNOWED	SHOULD	SPOUTS	SPRUCE	SORTIE	SCRAPS
SINFUL	SOONER	SLOWLY	STOATS	STRICT	SPRAIN	SCRIPT
SINEWS	SPOKEN	SPOILS	SWOTTY	STRUCK	STRAIN	SERAPE
SINEWY	SPOKES	SPOILT	SHOGUN	SHREDS	STRAIT	SERAPH
SHOFAR	SPORES	SPOOLS	SHOWUP	STRIDE	SHRIKE	STRAPS
SLOGAN	STOKED	STOLLE	SLOWUP	STRODE	STRIKE	STRIPE
SLOVAK	STOKER	STOOLS	SWOTUP	SCREED	STROKE	STRIPS
SCONCE	STOKES	STORMS	SNOOZE	SCREEN	SCROLL	STROPS
SCORCH	STOLEN	STORMY	SAPPED	SCRIED	SHRILL	SYRUPY
SCOTCH	STOLES	SCORNS	SAPPER	SCRIES	SORELY	SARTRE
SLOUCH	STONED	SHOBNA	SEPTET	SCRYER	SPRYLY	STRESS
SMOOCH	STONES	SLOANE	SIPPED	SERIES	STROLL	SUREST
STOICS	STOPES	SPOONS	SUPPED	SERVED	SURELY	SPRATS
SCOLDS	STORED	SWOONS	SUPPER	SERVER	SCRIMP	SPRITE
SHODDY	STORES	SPOTON	SAPPHO	SERVES	SCRUMP	STRATA
SNOODS	STOREY	SCOOPS	SEPTIC	SHRIEK	SCRUMS	STRATH
SWORDS	STOVES	SLOOPS	SOPHIA	SORBET	SERUMS	STRUTS
SCONES	STOWED	SLOPPY	SOPHIE	SORREL	SHRIMP	SURETY
SCORED	SCOFFS	SNOOPS	SAPELE	SORTED	STRUMS	SHROUD
SCORER	SLOUGH	SNOOPY	SEPALS	SORTER	SARONG	SIRIUS
SCORES	SPONGE	STOMPS	SUPPLE	SPREES	SERENA	SPROUT
SCOTER	SPONGY	STOOPS	SUPPLY	STREEP	SERENE	STROUD
SHORED	STODGE	SWOOPS	SUPINE	STREET	SHRANK	SHREVE
SHORES	STODGY	SCOURS	SIPHON	SURFED	SHRINE	SHRIVE
SHOVED	STOOGE	SPOORS	SUPERB	SURFER	SHRINK	SHROVE
SHOVEL	SLOTHS	SCOUSE	SEPTUM	SURGED	SHRUNK	STRIVE
SHOVES	SOOTHE	SPOUSE	STPAUL	SURGES	SIRENS	STROVE
SHOWED	SCOTIA	SWOOSH	SEPOYS	SURREY	SPRANG	SCRAWL
SHOWER	STOLID	SCOOTS	SEQUEL	SURVEY	SPRING	SCREWS
SKOMER	STOPIT	SCOUTS	SEQUIN	SCRUFF	SPRINT	SCREWY
SLOPED	SKOPJE	SHOOTS	SCREAM	SERIFS	SPRUNG	SHREWD
SLOPES	SHOCKS	SHORTS	SERIAL	SHRIFT	STRAND	SHREWS
SLOWED	SMOCKS	SHOUTS	SPREAD	STRAFE	STRINE	SPRAWL
SLOWER	SPOOKS	SMOOTH	STREAK	STRIFE	STRING	STRAWS

STREWN	SQUIBS	SPURNS	SEWAGE	TIARAS	TOASTS	TEDEUM
STREWS	STUBBS	SQUINT	SAWFIT	TOAMAN	TRACTS	TEDIUM
SPRAYS	STUBBY	STUPOR	SEWELL	TRAJAN	TRAITS	THEJAM
STRAYS	SLUICE	SCULPT	SAWING	THATCH	TEACUP	TOECAP
SASHAY	SOURCE	SLUMPS	SEWING	TRANCE	TEARUP	TREPAN
SASHES	STUCCO	SLURPS	SOWING	TEAMED	TOBIAS	THENCE
SISTER	SOUNDS	STUMPS	SEWERS	TEASED	TABLED	TIERCE
SUSSED	SQUADS	STUMPY	SOWERS	TEASEL	TABLES	TRENCH
SUSSES	STURDY	SCURRY	SOWETO	TEASER	TABLET	TRESCO
SUSSEX	SAUCER	SLURRY	SEWNUP	TEASES	TOBAGO	TREADS
SYSTEM	SAUCES	SQUARE	SEXUAL	TEASET	TEBBIT	TRENDS
SISKIN	SOURED	SQUIRE	SEXTET	THALER	TABULA	TRENDY
SESAME	SOURER	SQUIRM	SAXONS	THAMES	TUBING	TWEEDS
SUSANN	SOUSED	SQUIRT	SAXONY	THANES	TABOOS	TWEEDY
SATNAV	SOUSES	STUART	SEXTON	THANET	TOBOOT	TEEHEE
SATRAP	STUMER	SQUASH	SIXERS	THAWED	TABARD	TEEMED
SATEEN	SCUFFS	SHUFTI	SEXISM	TRACED	TABORS	TEETER
SETTEE	SNUFFS	SHUNTS	SEXIST	TRACER	TUBERS	THEBES
SETTER	STUFFS	SMUTTY	SIXGUN	TRACES	TICTAC	THEMES
SITTER	STUFFY	SPURTS	SKYLAB	TRACEY	TACKED	THESES
SUTTEE	SLUDGE	SQUATS	SKYWAY	TRADED	TICKED	TIERED
SETOFF	SLUDGY	STUNTS	STYLED	TRADER	TICKER	TEEOFF
SETTLE	SMUDGE	SHUTUP	STYLER	TRADES	TICKET	THEBFG
SATING	SNUDGE	SCURVY	STYLES	TRALEE	TUCKED	THEAGE
SITING	SPURGE	SQUAWK	SCYTHE	TRAVEL	TUCKER	TEETHE
SHTOOK	SLUSHY	SEVRES	STYMIE	TUAREG	TACTIC	THEWHO
SITCOM	SOUGHT	SOVIET	SCYLLA	TWANGY	TOCSIN	THEKID
SUTTON	SHUTIN	SAVAGE	SAYING	TRASHY	TUCKIN	THESIS
SITUPS	STUDIO	SAVILE	SHYING	TOADIE	TACKLE	THEWIZ
SATIRE	STUPID	SAVANT	SKYING	TRAGIC	TICKLE	TIEDIN
SATURN	SHUCKS	SAVING	SPYING	TRAVIS	TECHNO	TIEPIN
SATYRS	SKULKS	SAVERS	SAYERS	THANKS	TYCOON	TWEAKS
SITARS	SKUNKS	SAVORY	SHYEST	TRACKS	TEDRAY	THEFLY
SUTURE	SPUNKY	SEVERE	SLYEST	TRAILS	TIDIED	TREBLE
SATOUT	SCULLS	SEVERN	STYLUS	TRAWLS	TIDIER	THELMA
SETOUT	SCULLY	SEVERS	SUZMAN	TRAUMA	TIDIES	THERMS
SITOUT	SKULLS	SUVARI	SYZYGY	TRAINS	TIDDLY	TEEING
SEURAT	SMUGLY	SAVEUP	SIZZLE	TEAPOT	TIDILY	THEEND
SQUEAK	SNUGLY	SAVOUR	SIZING	TEAPOY	TODDLE	TOEING
SQUEAL	SOURLY	SAWRED	SIZEUP	TRAMPS	TUDORS	TWEENY
SQUABS	SQUALL	SAWYER	TEABAG	TEAURN	TODATE	THEFOG

THERON	TAILED	TWITTY	TOMLIN	TINNED	TROWEL	TAPING
TREMOR	TAIPEI	TRIPUP	TOMMIX	TINSEL	TROYES	TOPEND
TREVOR	TOILED	THIEVE	TOMTIT	TINTED	THONGS	TOPING
TWERPS	TOILER	TAKEIN	TAMEKA	TONKED	THOUGH	TYPING
THEIRS	TOILET	TAKING	TAMELY	TONNES	TROGGS	TIPTOE
THEORY	TRIBES	TOKENS	TEMPLE	TUNNEL	TROUGH	TIPTOP
THEISM	TRIKES	TAKEON	TIMELY	TENTHS	TOOTHY	TOPDOG
THEIST	TRIVET	TAKERS	TUMBLE	TANNIC	TROPHY	TYPHOO
TSETSE	TWINED	TAKETO	TUMULI	TANNIN	TROPIC	TAPERS
THEFTS	TWINES	TAKEUP	TUMULT	TENNIS	TWOBIT	TAPIRS
TREATS	THINGS	TUKTUK	TAMING	TENPIN	TROIKA	TOPERS
TREATY	THINGY	TOLEDO	TIMING	TINNIE	TOOTLE	TYPIST
TWENTY	TRIAGE	TALKED	TEMPOS	TINTIN	TROLLS	TOPGUN
TIEDUP	TWIGGY	TALKER	TOMBOY	TONSIL	THORNE	TYPHUS
TWELVE	TWINGE	TALLER	TOMTOM	TUNEIN	THORNS	TOQUES
TIEDYE	TAICHI	TELLER	TIMBRE	TANGLE	THORNY	TARMAC
TOFFEE	THIGHS	TILLED	TIMERS	TINGLE	TOOTOO	TARSAL
TUFFET	TRISHA	TILLER	TAMEST	TINGLY	THORPE	TARTAN
TUFTED	TRICIA	TILTED	TEMPTS	TINKLE	TROOPS	TARTAR
TIFFIN	TRIVIA	TOLLED	TOMATO	TENANT	TROUPE	TARZAN
TEFLON	TWILIT	TOLTEC	TINCAN	TONING	TAOISM	THREAD
TAGGED	THINKS	TALKIE	TINHAT	TUNING	TAOIST	THREAT
TIGGER	TRICKS	TALENT	TINMAN	TANGOS	TOPCAT	THROAT
TOGGED	TRICKY	TALONS	TENACE	TANNOY	TOPHAT	TORBAY
TUGGED	THINLY	TILING	TONICS	TENDON	TOPICS	TURBAN
TIGRIS	TRIALS	TALBOT	TUNICS	TINPOT	TAPPED	THROBS
TOGGLE	TRIFLE	TALLOW	TANDEM	TANTRA	TAPPER	THRICE
TAGORE	TRILLS	TULIPS	TANKER	TENORS	TAPPET	TIRADE
TIGERS	TRIPLE	TILERS	TANNED	TENURE	TEPEES	TARGET
TIGHTS	TWIRLS	TALCUM	TANNER	TUNDRA	TIPPED	TARMEY
TEHRAN	TRINNY	TALMUD	TENDED	TANITH	TIPPER	TARRED
TAHINI	TAILOR	TELLUS	TENDER	TENETS	TIPPET	TARTER
TSHIRT	TRICOT	TIMTAM	TENNER	TINCUP	TIPPEX	TERFEL
TAHITI	TRIPOD	TOMCAT	TENSED	TONGUE	TOPHER	TERMED
TAIPAN	TRIPOS	TAMPER	TENSES	THOMAS	TOPPED	THROES
TAIWAN	TRITON	TEMPED	TENTED	THORAX	TOPPER	TORIES
TRIBAL	TRIERS	TEMPEH	TINDER	TROJAN	TIPOFF	TUREEN
TRILBY	THIRST	TEMPER	TINGED	TWOWAY	TYPIFY	TURKEY
TWITCH	TAINTS	TIMBER	TINGES	TOOLED	TOPEKA	TURNED
THIRDS	THIRTY	TAMSIN	TINIER	TOOTED	TIPPLE	TURNER
TRIADS	TWISTS	TAMZIN	TINKER	TROVES	TOPPLE	TURRET

TARIFF	THROWN	TATTOO	TOWELS	URCHIN	UNITES	ULRIKA
THRIFT	THROWS	TITIPU	TOWING	UNCLOG	UNIONS	UNROLL
TARDIS	TASMAN	TUTORS	TAWDRY	UNCOOL	UNIPOD	UNRULY
TORPID	TISWAS	TUTTUT	THWART	UNCAPS	UNISON	UPROOT
TORRID	TUSCAN	TOUCAN	TOWERS	ULCERS	UNIQUE	UNRIPE
TURBID	TASSEL	TRUMAN	TAXMAN	UNCORK	UNJUST	UNREST
TURBIT	TASTED	THUMBS	TUXEDO	UNCURL	UPKEEP	UPRATE
TURGID	TASTER	TAUTEN	TAXIED	UNDEAD	UNKIND	UNSEAT
TURNIN	TASTES	TOUPEE	TAXIES	UNDIES	UNKNOT	UPSIDE
TURNIP	TESTED	TOURED	TAXMEN	UNDOES	ULLMAN	ULSTER
TURPIN	TESTER	TOURER	TEXMEX	UPDIKE	UNLOAD	UNSEEN
TARTLY	TOSSED	TOUTED	TAXING	UNDULY	UPLOAD	UNSAFE
THRALL	TOSSES	TRUCES	TEXANS	UNDONE	UNLACE	UNSAID
THRILL	TUSKER	TRUDGE	TOXINS	UDDERS	UNLOCK	UNSOLD
TURTLE	TUSSLE	TAUGHT	TOYING	UPDATE	UNLADE	URSULA
THRUMS	TISANE	TOUCHE	TRYING	URECAL	UGLIER	UNSUNG
THRONE	TISSUE	TOUCHY	TAYLOR	UPENDS	UPLIFT	URSINE
THRONG	TOSSUP	TOUGHS	TOYBOY	UNEVEN	ULLAGE	UPSHOT
TIRANA	TETRAD	TRUTHS	TOYOTA	UNEASE	UNLIKE	UNSURE
TIRING	TITIAN	TRUDIE	TRYSTS	UNEASY	UPLAND	UPSETS
TORINO	TATLER	TRUCKS	THYMUS	USEDUP	UNLESS	UNTIDY
TURING	TETHER	TRUNKS	TRYOUT	USEFUL	UMLAUT	UNTIED
TYRANT	TITFER	TAUTLY	TYZACK	UTERUS	UNMADE	UNTIES
TYRONE	TITHES	TOUSLE	UGANDA	UNFAIR	UNMASK	UTTLEY
TERROR	TITLED	TRUANT	UNABLE	UNFELT	UTMOST	UPTAKE
TORPOR	TITLES	TEUTON	USABLE	UNFOLD	UTOPIA	UNTOLD
TORSOS	TITTER	TOULON	URANUS	UNFURL	UBOATS	UPTURN
TURBOT	TOTNES	THUMPS	UPBEAT	UFFIZI	UNPACK	UTTERS
THRIPS	TOTTED	TRUMPS	UMBLES	URGENT	UNPICK	UNTRUE
TORERO	TOTTER	THURSO	UMBRIA	URGING	UNPAID	UPTOWN
TERESA	TUTTED	TRUEST	UMBELS	UNHOLY	UNPINS	UNUSED
THRASH	TETCHY	TRUISM	UNBOLT	UPHELD	UPPING	USURER
THRESH	TITCHY	TAUNTS	UNBEND	UPHILL	UMPIRE	USURPS
THRUSH	TATLIN	TRUSTS	UNBENT	UPHOLD	UPPERS	UNVEIL
THRUST	TATTIE	TRUSTY	UNBIND	USHANT	UPPISH	UNWRAP
TAROTS	TITBIT	TAURUS	URBANE	UNHOOK	UPPITY	UNWELL
TARSUS	TATTLE	TUVALU	UNBORN	UNHURT	UNPLUG	UNWIND
TORQUE	TOTALS	TAVERN	UNCIAL	USHERS	UNREAD	UNWARY
TURNUP	TOTEMS	TOWBAR	UNCLAD	UNICEF	UNREAL	UPWARD
THRIVE	TITANS	THWACK	UNCLES	UNISEX	UPROAR	UNWISE
TARAWA	TOTING	TOWNIE	UNCOIL	UNITED	UNREEL	UNZIPS

VIABLE	VOLLEY	VERGED	VETTED	WRAPUP	WREATH	WHIFFS
VECTIS	VILIFY	VERGER	VOTEIN	WEBCAM	WRESTS	WHINGE
VICTIM	VALOIS	VERGES	VOTING	WEBBED	WOEFUL	WRINGS
VOCALS	VOLUME	VERSED	VOTARY	WEBBER	WHEEZE	WEIGHS
VACANT	VALERY	VERSES	VOTERS	WOBBLE	WHEEZY	WEIGHT
VICUNA	VELCRO	VERTEX	VOTIVE	WOBBLY	WAFTED	WRIGHT
VECTOR	VALISE	VORTEX	VOULEZ	WICKED	WAFFLE	WRITHE
VICTOR	VILEST	VERIFY	VAUGHN	WICKER	WAFERS	WHISKS
VICARS	VALETS	VIRAGO	VAULTS	WICKET	WAFERY	WHISKY
VACATE	VELETA	VERMIN	VAUNTS	WEDDED	WIGWAM	WHIRLS
VACUUM	VALIUM	VIRGIL	VIVIAN	WEDGED	WAGGED	WHINNY
VIDEOS	VALOUR	VIRGIN	VIVACE	WEDGES	WAGNER	WHIPPY
VEERED	VELLUM	VERILY	VIVIEN	WIDGET	WAGGLE	WHIRRS
VIEWED	VELOUR	VIRILE	VOWELS	WIDNES	WAGGLY	WHILST
VIEWER	VAMPED	VERONA	VOWING	WIDTHS	WIGGLE	WHIMSY
VIENNA	VANDAL	VARDON	VEXING	WADDLE	WIGGLY	WAISTS
VIEIRA	VENIAL	VERNON	VIXENS	WIDELY	WOGGLE	WRISTS
VAGUER	VENICE	VERITY	VOXPOP	WADING	WAGING	WAITUP
VOGUES	VENEER	VERDUN	VOYAGE	WIDENS	WAGONS	WAKENS
VEGGIE	VENTED	VERSUS	VOYEUR	WADERS	WIGEON	WAKING
VIGILS	VENUES	VIRTUE	VIZIER	WIDEST	WAGERS	WOKING
VEGANS	VINNIE	VASSAL	WEAKEN	WIDOWS	WEIMAR	WAKEUP
VAGARY	VENDOR	VESTAL	WEAKER	WHENCE	WHITBY	WOKEUP
VIGOUR	VINERY	VESTAS	WEANED	WRENCH	WEIRDO	WALLAH
VEILED	VANISH	VISTAS	WEANER	WRETCH	WAILED	WALDEN
VEINED	VANITY	VISUAL	WEASEL	WIELDS	WAILER	WALKED
VOICED	VENETO	VESPER	WEAVED	WEEDED	WAITED	WALKEN
VOICES	VENOUS	VESSEL	WEAVER	WEEDER	WAITER	WALKER
VOIGHT	VINOUS	VESTED	WEAVES	WEEVER	WAIVED	WALLED
VAINLY	VIOLAS	VOSGES	WHALER	WEEZER	WAIVER	WALLER
VIKRAM	VIOLET	VISAGE	WHALES	WIENER	WAIVES	WALLET
VIKING	VIOLIN	VASTLY	WHARFE	WEEPIE	WHILED	WALTER
VILLAS	VOODOO	VISHNU	WHARFS	WEEVIL	WHILES	WELDED
VULCAN	VIPERS	VISION	WHATIF	WREKIN	WHINED	WELDER
VULGAR	VAPOUR	VOSTOK	WHACKS	WHELKS	WHINER	WELLER
VALLEY	VERBAL	VESTRY	WEAKLY	WREAKS	WHINES	WELLES
VALUED	VERNAL	VISORS	WHAMMY	WRECKS	WHITEN	WELTER
VALUER	VARIED	VISITS	WEAPON	WEEKLY	WHITER	WILDER
VALUES	VARIES	VATMAN	WRASSE	WHEELS	WHITES	WILIER
VALVES	VARLET	VETOED	WEALTH	WHELPS	WRITER	WILKES
VELVET	VARNEY	VETOES	WRAITH	WHERRY	WRITES	WILLEM

WILMER	WINDER	WARMED	WITHIN	YOKELS	ZEEHAN
WILTED	WINGER	WARMER	WITHIT	YOKING	ZIGZAG
WOLVES	WINKED	WARNED	WATTLE	YELLED	ZAGREB
WALKIT	WINNER	WARNER	WATSON	YELPED	ZYGOTE
WALLIS	WINTER	WARNES	WETROT	YELLOW	ZAHARA
WILKIE	WONDER	WARPED	WATERS	YOMPED	ZIMMER
WILLIE	WYNTER	WARREN	WATERY	YAMAHA	ZAMBIA
WILLIS	WINNIE	WORKED	WATUSI	YEMENI	ZOMBIE
WULLIE	WANGLE	WORKER	WOUNDS	YANKED	ZANUCK
WILDLY	WINKLE	WORSEN	WAVIER	YANKEE	ZANDER
WILILY	WANING	WORZEL	WAVING	YONDER	ZONKED
WALKON	WINONA	WORTHY	WAVERS	YENTOB	ZINNIA
WALLOP	WANTON	WARBLE	WYVERN	YEOMAN	ZONING
WALLOW	WINDOW	WARILY	WOWSER	YEOMEN	ZENITH
WALTON	WINNOW	WARMLY	WAXING	YOOTHA	ZOOMED
WELDON	WINTON	WIRING	WAYLAY	YEOVIL	ZAPPED
WILCOX	WONTON	WARHOL	WRYEST	YVONNE	ZIPPED
WILLOW	WINERY	WARCRY	WAYOUT	YAPPED	ZIPPER
WILSON	WINTRY	WARMTH	WIZARD	YIPPEE	ZAPATA
WILTON	WINDUP	WARMUP	XRATED	YUPPIE	ZEPHYR
WALESA	WOODED	WASABI	XRAYED	YORUBA	ZURICH
WALLUP	WOODEN	WASHED	XFILES	YORICK	ZEROED
WALNUT	WOOFED	WASHER	XYLENE	YORKER	ZIRCON
WALRUS	WOOFER	WASHES	XYLOSE	YARDIE	ZITHER
WILBUR	WRONGS	WASTED	XANADU	YORKIE	ZOUNDS
WILFUL	WHOLLY	WASTER	XERXES	YARROW	ZEUGMA
WOMBAT	WHORLS	WASTES	XAVIER	YESMAN	
WOMACK	WOOLLY	WESLEY	YEARLY	YASSER	
WIMSEY	WOOING	WESSEX	YEARNS	YESMEN	
WIMPLE	WHOOPI	WISHED	YEASTY	YASMIN	
WOMBLE	WHOOPS	WISHES	YABBER	YOUBET	
WYMARK	WHOOSH	WASPIE	YUCCAS	YOUTHS	
WAMPUM	WIPING	WISELY	YACHTS	YAWNED	
WENHAM	WIPERS	WESTON	YODELS	YAWING	
WANDER	WAPITI	WISDOM	YIELDS	YOYOMA	
WANKEL	WARSAW	WISEST	YVETTE	ZEALOT	
WANTED	WIRRAL	WASHUP	YAFFLE	ZSAZSA	
WENDED	WORLDS	WETTED	YOGURT	ZEBRAS	
WINCED	WARDEN	WETTER	YAHWEH	ZODIAC	
WINCES	WARDER	WITHER	YAHOOS	ZYDECO	
WINDED	WARIER	WITTER	YOICKS	ZIDANE	

ALABAMA	AMAZONS	ARCHERY	ADDENDA	ALERTLY	AUGURED
ATACAMA	ATALOSS	ALCOHOL	ALDENTE	AVENUES	ALGARVE
ARAMAIC	AMATORY	ARCHIVE	ANDANTE	AVEBURY	AUGURER
ARAPAHO	ANALOGY	ASCRIBE	ANDROID	ACETYLS	ALGESIA
ADAMANT	ANATOMY	ARCHING	ANDSOON	AFFRAYS	AUGUSTA
AJACCIO	ANAGRAM	AUCTION	ARDUOUS	AFFABLE	ANGEVIN
AFARCRY	AMASSED	ACCENTS	ANDORRA	AFFABLY	ATHEART
ANARCHY	ADAMSON	ASCENDS	ANDIRON	AFFECTS	ATHWART
AWARDED	AMASSES	ASCENTS	ADDISON	ANFIELD	ADHIBIT
ACAUDAL	ADAPTED	ANCHORS	AUDITED	AFFLECK	ACHIEVE
ABANDON	AWAITED	ANCHOVY	AUDITOR	ALFREDO	ATHLETE
ALADDIN	ADAPTOR	ALCOPOP	ANDOVER	AFFAIRE	ACHAEAN
ATANEND	ASARULE	ACCEPTS	ALDWYCH	AFFAIRS	ATHEISM
ACADEME	ATAPUSH	ACCARDO	ABELARD	AFFLICT	ATHEIST
AMATEUR	AKABUSI	ACCORDS	ACETATE	ALFALFA	ASHAMED
AMADEUS	ATATURK	ACCUSED	AVERAGE	AWFULLY	ASHANTI
AWAKENS	ANALYSE	ACCUSAL	ABEYANT	ALFONSO	ASHFORD
AZALEAS	ANALYST	ACCUSER	ACERBIC	AFFRONT	ATHLONE
ACADEMY	ASBYATT	ACCOSTS	ALEMBIC	AFFIRMS	ASHDOWN
AMALGAM	AMBLERS	ACCUSES	AMENDED	AFFORDS	AMHARIC
ABASHED	AMBIENT	ASCETIC	AHEADOF	ATFIRST	ADHERED
AGAKHAN	AMBLING	ACCRUED	AGELESS	ATFAULT	ADHERES
ARABICA	ALBUMEN	ACCRUAL	AVENGED	AFFIXED	ASHTRAY
ACARINE	ALBANIA	ACCRUES	AVENGER	AFFIXES	ACHATES
AVARICE	ALBINOS	ACCOUNT	AVENGES	AFGHANI	ALIBABA
ABASING	AMBROSE	ALCOVES	AMERICA	AFGHANS	AGITATE
ABATING	ALBERTA	ARCHWAY	ALEWIFE	ALGEBRA	ANIMATE
AMAZING	AUBERGE	ALCAZAR	ATELIER	ALGIERS	ABIGAIL
AWAKING	AUBERON	ALDGATE	AMENITY	ANGLERS	AGITATO
ATALICK	ARBORIO	AUDIBLE	ABECKET	AUGMENT	ANIMATO
ATAVISM	ARBITER	AUDIBLY	ACETONE	ANGLING	ANIMALS
ARABIAN	ARBUTUS	ABDUCTS	ANEMONE	ARGUING	AMIABLE
ACACIAS	ARCHAIC	ADDICTS	AWESOME	ANGUISH	AMIABLY
ADAGIOS	ACCLAIM	ADDEDUP	ADELPHI	ANGRIER	ARIADNE
ANANIAS	ARCLAMP	ADDRESS	AVERRED	ANGRILY	ANISEED
ALASKAN	ARCADIA	ANDRESS	ANEURIN	ANGELIC	ABILENE
ANAEMIA	ACCEDED	ANDREWS	ASEPTIC	ANGOLAN	AGILELY
ANAEMIC	ACCEDES	AUDREYS	ABETTED	ANGULAR	ALIGHTS
ALARMED	ARCADES	ADDLING	ALERTED	ANGELES	ANILINE
AGAINST	ARCHERS	ALDRICH	AVERTED	ANGELUS	ASININE
ABALONE	ANCIENT	ABDOMEN	ABETTOR	ALGERIA	ABIDING
ALAMODE	ALCHEMY	ANDAMAN	ADEPTLY	ANGERED	ARISING

ANIMISM	AILMENT	ADMIRES	AMORIST	ACQUIRE	ARRANGE
ANIMIST	ALLOFME	AMMETER	ADORNED	ASQUITH	ADRENAL
ABILITY	ALLEGRA	ARMOURY	ABOUNDS	ACQUITS	ACRONYM
ACIDIFY	ALLEGED	ADMIXED	AMOUNTS	AIRRAID	AIRINGS
ACIDITY	ALLEGRO	ADMIXES	ANOINTS	ACREAGE	AIRHOLE
AGILITY	ALLEGES	ANNEALS	AXOLOTL	AIRBASE	AUREOLE
ARIDITY	ALLTIME	ANNUALS	AMOROSO	AIRWAVE	AIRWOLF
AVIDITY	ALLYING	ALNWICK	AMOROUS	AIRMAIL	APRIORI
ABIDJAN	ATLANTA	AUNTIES	APOLOGY	AERIALS	AIRLOCK
ALIGNED	ALLENDE	ANNUITY	ANOUSKA	AIRWAYS	AIRPORT
AVIGNON	ALLENBY	ANNULAR	AROUSED	ARREARS	AGRIPPA
ARIZONA	APLENTY	ARNOLDS	AROUSAL	ABREAST	APROPOS
ADIPOSE	ALLTOLD	AINSLEY	AROUSES	ALREADY	ATROPHY
ALIMONY	ALLURED	AGNOMEN	ABORTED	AEROBIC	AIRDROP
ATISSUE	ATLARGE	AWNINGS	ADOPTED	AEROBES	AIRCREW
ALIASES	AILERON	ANNTODD	APOSTLE	AEROBUS	AEROSOL
ASIATIC	ALLURES	AINTREE	ACOLYTE	ACROBAT	ARRESTS
AMISTAD	ALLERGY	AMNESIA	ANODYNE	AURICLE	AERATED
AVIATED	ALLISON	ANNASUI	APPLAUD	AFRICAN	AERATOR
ANISTON	ALLYSON	AMNESTY	APPEASE	AUROCHS	AERATES
AVIATOR	ATLASES	ANNETTE	ATPEACE	APRICOT	AGROUND
AVIATES	ABLAUTS	ANNEXED	APPEALS	ABRADED	AIRPUMP
AZIMUTH	ASLEVEL	ANNEXES	APPEARS	ABRIDGE	ARRIVED
ADJUDGE	ALLOVER	ANNOYED	ASPHALT	ABRADES	ARRIVAL
ADJOINS	ALLOWED	AVOCADO	ALPACAS	AIRHEAD	ARRIVES
ADJUNCT	ALLAYED	ANORAKS	ASPECTS	AIRLESS	ABRAXAS
ABJURED	ARMBAND	ANOMALY	AMPLEST	AIRIEST	ARRAYED
ABJURES	AIMLESS	AVOIDED	APPLIED	ABRAHAM	ASSUAGE
ADJUSTS	ARMREST	AVOCETS	APPRISE	AIRSHIP	ABSTAIN
ADJOURN	ARMOIRE	AMONGST	APPLIES	AIRLINE	ATSPEED
ACKLAND	AAMILNE	ANOTHER	APPOINT	AIRMILE	AUSLESE
AWKWARD	AMMONIA	ACONITE	AMPLIFY	AIRSIDE	AUSTERE
ANKLETS	ARMENIA	AGONISE	AMPULLA	AIRTIME	AMSTELL
ALKALIS	ALMANAC	ANODISE	APPENDS	AIRSICK	ABSCESS
ASKANCE	ALMONER	ATOMISE	AMPHORA	ARRAIGN	ANSWERS
ALKANET	ALMONDS	ADORING	APPROVE	AIRKISS	ASSEGAI
ACKROYD	ALMONRY	ATONING	ASPIRED	AIRLIFT	ASSIGNS
AYKROYD	ARMHOLE	AVOWING	APPAREL	ACRYLIC	ABSEILS
ATLEAST	ARMLOCK	ABOLISH	ASPIRIN	ACRILAN	ASSAILS
ALLUDED	ADMIRED	ASOCIAL	AMPERES	AIRFLOW	ABSOLVE
ALLUDES	ADMIRAL	AEOLIAN	ASPIRES	AIRPLAY	ABSALOM
ALLHEAL	ADMIRER	AGONIES	AMPOULE	AURALLY	ASSUMED

ASSUMES	ANTIGEN	ASUNDER	BEANBAG	BRACING	BLASTER
ARSENIC	AITCHES	AMULETS	BLABBER	BRAKING	BLATTER
ABSENCE	ANTOINE	ACUTELY	BEATBOX	BRAVING	BOASTER
ARSENAL	ASTAIRE	AQUIFER	BRAMBLY	BRAYING	BEASTLY
ABSENTS	ASTRIDE	ACUSHLA	BEARCUB	BRAZING	BRAVURA
ASSENTS	ALTHING	ABUSIVE	BLANCHE	BEAMISH	BHAGWAN
ABSCOND	ANTHILL	ABUSING	BEARCAT	BRAZIER	BABBAGE
AUSTRIA	ATTAINS	AMUSING	BEARDED	BEATIFY	BOBTAIL
ASSURED	ARTEMIS	ALUMNAE	BOARDED	BLACKED	BOBPARR
ALSORAN	ATTIMES	ALUMNUS	BRAIDED	BLACKEN	BABYBIO
ASSURER	ATTEMPT	AQUINAS	BRANDED	BRACKEN	BOBPECK
ABSORBS	AUTOMAT	AQUEOUS	BRANDON	BLACKER	BABYGRO
ADSORBS	ANTENNA	AQUARIA	BLADDER	BLANKET	BABYING
ASSERTS	ANTONIA	AQUATIC	BLANDER	BRACKET	BOBBING
ASSORTS	ATTUNED	ABUTTED	BOARDER	BLANKLY	BABYISH
ASSURES	ANTONYM	ABUTTAL	BLANDLY	BRAWLED	BOBBIES
ASSISTS	ANTONIO	AGUTTER	BEAKERS	BRAILLE	BOBBINS
ASSAULT	ATTENDS	ASUSUAL	BEAMERS	BRAWLER	BABBITT
ASSAYED	ATTUNES	AQUIVER	BEARERS	BEADLES	BABBLED
ASSAYER	ARTWORK	AQUAVIT	BEATERS	BEAGLES	BABYLON
ASSIZES	ARTFORM	ADVANCE	BEAVERS	BEATLES	BABBLER
ACTUATE	ALTHORP	ADVERSE	BLAZERS	BRADLEY	BABBLES
ATTRACT	ACTIONS	ADVERBS	BOATERS	BRAMLEY	BOBBLES
ACTUARY	AUTHORS	ADVERTS	BRAVEST	BOATMAN	BUBBLES
ATTABOY	ANTHONY	ADVISED	BRAVELY	BOATMEN	BIBELOT
ANTACID	AUTOPSY	ADVISER	BRAVERY	BRADMAN	BUBONIC
ARTICLE	ANTIQUE	ADVISES	BHANGRA	BRAHMAN	BOBTODD
ATTACHE	ASTORIA	ATWORST	BRAGGED	BEATNIK	BOBDOLE
AUTOCUE	ALTERED	ANXIETY	BLAGGER	BLAHNIK	BOBHOPE
ATTACKS	ATTIRED	ANXIOUS	BEACHED	BLARNEY	BABOONS
ATTICUS	ASTARTE	ANYTIME	BEARHUG	BYANOSE	BABYSAT
ACTAEON	AUTARCH	ABYSMAL	BEACHAM	BEACONS	BABYSIT
ARTDECO	ATTIRES	ANYBODY	BRASHER	BEARPIT	BICYCLE
ANTWERP	ANTHRAX	ALYSSUM	BEACHES	BEATRIX	BACKEND
ANTBEAR	ASTERIX	ABYSSES	BEADING	BRAISED	BACKERS
ACTRESS	ARTISTE	ASYLUMS	BEAMING	BRASSIE	BICKERS
ANTHEMS	ARTISAN	BRANAGH	BEARING	BRANSON	BUCKETS
ANTHERS	ARTISTS	BRADAWL	BEATING	BRAISES	BECKETT
ANTLERS	ATTESTS	BRAVADO	BLAMING	BRANTUB	BACCHIC
APTNESS	ASTOUND	BLATANT	BLARING	BLASTED	BECKHAM
ARTLESS	ADULATE	BLABBED	BLAZING	BOASTED	BACCHUS
ANTIGUA	ARUNDEL	BRAMBLE	BOATING	BEASTIE	BACKING

BUCKING	BUDGIES	BREAKIN	BIGJAKE	BIGGUNS	BRINJAL
BUCOLIC	BEDFORD	BREAKUP	BIGBANG	BUGEYED	BLINKED
BUCKLED	BEDSORE	BLEAKER	BAGWASH	BAHRAIN	BRICKIE
BACKLOG	BEDROCK	BREAKER	BEGGARS	BEHEADS	BLINKER
BACILLI	BEDROLL	BLEAKLY	BIGEARS	BYHEART	BRISKER
BUCKLER	BADFORM	BEETLED	BAGLADY	BAHAMAS	BRISKET
BECCLES	BEDROOM	BEETLES	BIGEASY	BEHAVED	BRISKLY
BUCKLES	BADBOYS	BEESLEY	BUGABOO	BEHAVES	BRIDLED
BACKLOT	BEDPOST	BEERMAT	BAGHDAD	BRIGAND	BRIDLES
BECOMES	BODEREK	BRENNAN	BIGHEAD	BRIGADE	BEIGNET
BACKOFF	BUDERIM	BREMNER	BIGDEAL	BRITAIN	BRITNEY
BECKONS	BODHRAN	BRENNER	BUGBEAR	BRIOCHE	BRITONS
BACKOUT	BADLUCK	BRETONS	BUGLERS	BLINDED	BAILOUT
BACKPAY	BEDOUIN	BLEEPED	BIGGEST	BUILDUP	BLIPPED
BACARDI	BEDBUGS	BLEEPER	BAGSHOT	BLINDER	BRITPOP
BUCKRAM	BEDEVIL	BLESSED	BIGSHOT	BUILDER	BRISTLE
BACKROW	BRESCIA	BLESSES	BAGPIPE	BLINDLY	BRITTLE
BECAUSE	BLENDED	BEEFTEA	BEGUILE	BAILEES	BRISTOL
BADMASH	BREADED	BLEATED	BEGUINE	BAILEYS	BRITTEN
BODYART	BREADTH	BREATHE	BIGBITE	BOILERS	BRITTON
BEDECKS	BRENDAN	BREATHS	BIGTIME	BRIBERS	BRIXTON
BODICES	BLENDER	BREATHY	BAGGING	BRIBERY	BUILTIN
BEDHEAD	BREEDER	BEERWAH	BEGGING	BRIEFED	BUILTUP
BADGERS	BEEGEES	BOERWAR	BUGGING	BRIMFUL	BLISTER
BADNESS	BEEPERS	BEESWAX	BIGFISH	BRIEFER	BRISTOW
BADNEWS	BREWERS	BYEBYES	BAGGIER	BRIEFLY	BRISTLY
BIDDERS	BREWERY	BREEZES	BAGGINS	BRIDGED	BLITZED
BODGERS	BRENGUN	BUFFALO	BAGNIOS	BRINGUP	BLITZEN
BUDGETS	BEECHAM	BIFOCAL	BIGGINS	BRINGER	BAKLAVA
BADDEBT	BLETHYN	BUFFERS	BUGGIES	BRIDGES	BAKUNIN
BADEGGS	BEECHER	BUFFETS	BAGGILY	BRIDGET	BIKINIS
BEDSIDE	BLETHER	BIFFING	BIGGLES	BRIGHAM	BALLARD
BEDTIME	BEECHES	BUFFING	BOGGLES	BRIXHAM	BOLLARD
BEDDING	BEEHIVE	BOFFINS	BEGONIA	BLIGHTS	BALLADE
BIDDING	BEELINE	BAFFLED	BYGONES	BLIGHTY	BELTANE
BODGING	BEEFING	BAFFLER	BIGHORN	BAILIFF	BULLACE
BUDDING	BEEPING	BAFFLES	BIGFOOT	BAILING	BULWARK
BUDGING	BREWING	BEFALLS	BEGORRA	BAITING	BALKANS
BADDIEL	BLEMISH	BUFFOON	BOGARDE	BEIJING	BALLADS
BADDIES	BEEFIER	BIGBAND	BIGOTED	BOILING	BALSAMS
BEDSITS	BLERIOT	BAGGAGE	BUGATTI	BRIBING	BALLAST
BUDDIES	BREVITY	BIGGAME	BIGOTRY	BRITISH	BELFAST

BELLAMY	BULLOCK	BENEATH	BANDIES	BLONDES	BLOOPER
BULLBAR	BALLOON	BONEASH	BANDITS	BLOWDRY	BROWSED
BALLBOY	BALFOUR	BENGALI	BUNNIES	BROADLY	BRONSKI
BELLBOY	BALLOTS	BANTAMS	BENOKRI	BLOFELD	BLOSSOM
BULLDOG	BELLOWS	BANYANS	BANGKOK	BIOTECH	BLOUSON
BELIEVE	BILIOUS	BUNKBED	BUNDLED	BOOLEAN	BRONSON
BALLETS	BILLOWS	BINOCHE	BUNGLED	BOOZEUP	BROWSER
BELIEFS	BULBOUS	BONEDRY	BUNGLER	BOOTEES	BLOUSES
BILLETS	BELTOUT	BENZENE	BANGLES	BOOZERS	BROWSES
BULLETS	BALCONY	BANGERS	BUNDLES	BROKERS	BLOATED
BALDEST	BILLOWY	BANKERS	BUNGLES	BLOWFLY	BLOTTED
BOLDEST	BALDRIC	BANNERS	BENELUX	BLOGGER	BOOSTED
BALEFUL	BELARUS	BANTERS	BANALLY	BROUGHT	BLOATER
BOLOGNA	BOLEROS	BINDERS	BENTLEY	BROTHER	BLOTTER
BOLSHIE	BELUSHI	BONKERS	BONANZA	BROMIDE	BOOSTER
BOLSHOI	BELATED	BONNETS	BANANAS	BROMINE	BROGUES
BELLHOP	BALATON	BUNKERS	BONJOVI	BLOWING	BRONZED
BULLIED	BOLSTER	BENNETT	BANNOCK	BOOKING	BIPLANE
BALDING	BOLETUS	BONIEST	BONJOUR	BOOMING	BIPEDAL
BALLING	BULRUSH	BANDEAU	BANDOGS	BOOTING	BAPTISE
BELTING	BOLIVIA	BANEFUL	BONBONS	BOOZING	BOPPING
BELYING	BELOVED	BENEFIT	BUNIONS	BROKING	BAPTISM
BILLING	BOLIVAR	BANSHEE	BANKSIA	BOOKISH	BAPTIST
BOLTING	BALDWIN	BINGHAM	BONUSES	BOORISH	BEQUEST
BULGING	BELLYUP	BENCHES	BANDSAW	BIONICS	BARBARA
BULLISH	BOMBARD	BUNCHES	BENITEZ	BMOVIES	BARMAID
BELLINI	BUMMALO	BANDIED	BENGUNN	BOOKIES	BARNARD
BALLIOL	BEMOANS	BENTINE	BANQUET	BOOZILY	BERNARD
BELGIUM	BOMBAST	BENZINE	BANBURY	BLOCKED	BARRAGE
BELGIAN	BOMBERS	BONFIRE	BUNBURY	BROILED	BIRIANI
BILLION	BUMPERS	BANDING	BENLYON	BOOTLEG	BARRACK
BULLION	BOMBING	BANGING	BROCADE	BROILER	BARGAIN
BALMIER	BUMPING	BANKING	BAOBABS	BOOKLET	BURIALS
BULKIER	BAMBINO	BANNING	BUOYANT	BLOOMED	BURSARS
BULLIES	BUMPIER	BANTING	BRONCHI	BOORMAN	BYROADS
BULLITT	BUMPKIN	BENDING	BRONCOS	BLOOMER	BUREAUX
BELLJAR	BUMBLER	BINDING	BLOTCHY	BROWNED	BARBARY
BELINDA	BUMPOFF	BINNING	BROODED	BROWNIE	BARNABY
BALANCE	BEMUSED	BONDING	BLONDIE	BROSNAN	BURSARY
BELONGS	BANDAID	BUNTING	BLONDIN	BLOTOUT	BORACIC
BYLINES	BANDAGE	BENDIGO	BROADEN	BLOWOUT	BARACUS
BALONEY	BONDAGE	BENDIER	BROADER	BIOLOGY	BORSCHT

BOREDOM	BURGLES	BESEECH	BASQUES	BATSMEN	BRUISER
BORODIN	BARTLET	BUSCEMI	BISCUIT	BITUMEN	BRUISES
BURMESE	BURNLEY	BOSWELL	BETRAYS	BATHMAT	BLUESKY
BERSERK	BERGMAN	BASKETS	BITPART	BOTANIC	BLURTED
BARBELL	BIRDMAN	BASSETS	BATEAUX	BETTONG	BLUSTER
BURRELL	BYRONIC	BUSHELS	BETTANY	BETROTH	BLUETIT
BARGEIN	BURUNDI	BUSKERS	BATHBUN	BUTTONS	BLUNTLY
BURGEON	BARENTS	BUSTERS	BETWEEN	BATHTUB	BOUQUET
BARBELS	BARONET	BASSETT	BITTERN	BLUTACK	BEVVIED
BARBERS	BARCODE	BUSIEST	BATHERS	BAUHAUS	BIVALVE
BARGEES	BARNONE	BASHFUL	BATTENS	BOURBON	BAVARIA
BARKERS	BURDOCK	BASHING	BATTERS	BLUBBER	BIVOUAC
BARRELS	BARNOWL	BASKING	BETTERS	BOUNCED	BAWBEES
BARTERS	BARBOUR	BASTING	BITTERS	BOUNCER	BOWLERS
BORDERS	BARROWS	BUSKING	BOTHERS	BOUNCES	BOWYERS
BURDENS	BORROWS	BUSTING	BUTLERS	BOUNDED	BOWLINE
BURGERS	BORZOIS	BESTIAL	BUTTERS	BLUNDER	BAWLING
BURGESS	BURNOUS	BASTION	BATTERY	BOULDER	BOWLING
BURNERS	BURROWS	BOSNIAN	BUTTERY	BOUNDER	BAWDIER
BARRETT	BURNOUT	BUSHIDO	BATCHED	BRUBECK	BEWAILS
BERTHED	BAROQUE	BOSSIER	BOTCHED	BLUFFED	BAWDILY
BURGHER	BERTRAM	BUSHIER	BOTCHER	BLUEFIN	BEWITCH
BIRCHES	BIRETTA	BUSTIER	BUTCHER	BLUFFER	BOXCARS
BARLINE	BERATED	BUSBIES	BATCHES	BLUDGER	BOXKITE
BARGING	BURETTE	BASSIST	BITCHES	BLUSHED	BEXHILL
BARKING	BORSTAL	BOSSILY	BOTCHES	BRUSHED	BOXWOOD
BARRING	BURSTYN	BISHKEK	BATHING	BRUSHUP	BOXROOM
BURNING	BERATES	BUSTLED	BATTING	BLUSHER	BAYLEAF
BURRING	BARBUDA	BUSTLES	BATWING	BLUSHES	BUYTIME
BURYING	BERMUDA	BESTMAN	BETTING	BRUSHES	BEYONCE
BURNISH	BOROUGH	BUSHMAN	BATTIER	BAUXITE	BRYNNER
BURRITO	BARQUES	BUSHMEN	BUTLINS	BRUTISH	BAYONET
BARRIER	BUSTARD	BASENJI	BUTTIES	BOUVIER	BOYHOOD
BURLIER	BUSFARE	BASINET	BETWIXT	BAULKED	BOYZONE
BERRIES	BUSLANE	BESPOKE	BETOKEN	BAUBLES	BOYCOTT
BIRDIES	BASMATI	BASSOON	BATTLED	BRUMMIE	BUYAPUP
BERLIOZ	BUSPASS	BESTOWS	BOTTLED	BOUDOIR	BUZZARD
BURBLED	BESTBET	BISHOPS	BATTLER	BRUMOUS	BAZAARS
BURGLED	BESTBOY	BISTROS	BOTTLER	BRUSQUE	BUZZERS
BURSLEM	BISECTS	BUSSTOP	BATTLES	BLURRED	BUZZING
BURGLAR	BESIDES	BASCULE	BOTTLES	BRUISED	BAZOOKA
BURBLES	BESIEGE	BISMUTH	BATSMAN	BOURSIN	BUZZOFF

BEZIQUE	CRASHES	CHARLEY	CHATTEL	COCKLES	CHEDDAR
BIZARRE	CHALICE	CRAWLEY	COASTAL	COCONUT	CLEMENS
BUZZSAW	CLARICE	CHARMED	CHASTEN	COCKNEY	CLEMENT
CHARADE	CYANIDE	CLAIMED	CLACTON	CUCKOLD	CHECHEN
CRANACH	CEASING	CRAMMED	CLAPTON	CICCONE	CRECHES
CHAPATI	CHAFING	CHAPMAN	CLAYTON	CYCLONE	CHEKHOV
CHAGALL	CHARING	COALMAN	CHANTER	CACHOUS	COELIAC
CRAVATS	CHASING	COALMEN	CHAPTER	COCOONS	CHEMISE
CRABBED	CLAWING	CHARMER	CHARTER	CUCKOOS	CREVICE
CHAMBRE	COATING	CLAIMER	CHATTER	CYCLOPS	CHEWING
CHAMBER	COAXING	CRAMMER	CLATTER	COCKPIT	CREWING
CLAMBER	CRANING	CHAINED	COALTAR	COCHRAN	CHERISH
CHANCED	CRATING	CLANNAD	COASTER	CADFAEL	CAESIUM
CHANCEL	CRAVING	CHANNEL	COALTIT	CADEAUX	CLERICS
CHANCER	COAXIAL	CLAMOUR	CABBAGE	CODICIL	CREDITS
CHAUCER	CRANIAL	CHAMOIS	CABRANK	CADGERS	CHEMIST
CHANCES	CRANIUM	CRAYONS	CUBICLE	CODGERS	CHEVIOT
CLAUDIA	CLARION	CHAPPED	COBWEBS	CUDGELS	COEXIST
CHANDON	CLAVIER	CLAMPED	CABLING	CADDIED	CHECKED
CLAUDIO	CRAZIER	CLAPPED	CABBIES	CODEINE	CREAKED
CSARDAS	CHARIOT	CLASPED	COBBLED	CADGING	CHECKIN
CHALETS	CHARILY	CRAMPED	COBBLER	CODLING	CHECKUP
CHAPELS	CHARITY	CHAPPIE	COBBLES	CADDISH	CHECKER
CHASERS	CLARIFY	CRAMPON	CABINET	CADDICK	CREAMER
CRATERS	CLARITY	CLAMPER	CABOOSE	CADMIUM	CLEANED
CHATEAU	CRAZILY	CLAPPER	COBLOAF	CADDIES	CLEANSE
CHAMFER	CLACKED	COALPIT	CABARET	CEDILLA	CLEANUP
CHANGED	CLANKED	CHAIRED	CUBISTS	CODDLED	CLEANER
CHARGED	CRACKED	CHARRED	COBNUTS	CUDDLED	CHESNEY
CLANGED	CRACKLE	CHAGRIN	COCKADE	CODDLES	CREMONA
CHARGER	CRACKUP	CLASSIC	CICADAS	CUDDLES	CHEROOT
CLANGER	CRACKER	CLASSED	CACHETS	CADENZA	CHEAPIE
CHANGES	CRACKLY	CHANSON	COCTEAU	CADENCE	CHEAPEN
CHARGES	CRADLED	COARSEN	COCAINE	CADENCY	CHEAPER
CLASHED	CRAWLED	COARSER	CYCLING	CADAVER	CREEPER
COACHED	CHARLIE	CHASSIS	COCKIER	CUECARD	CHEAPLY
CRASHED	CHAPLIN	CLASSES	CYCLIST	CREMATE	CHEERED
CHATHAM	CRAWLER	CLAUSES	COCKILY	CUEBALL	CLEARED
CLAPHAM	CHABLIS	CRASSLY	CECILIA	CAESARS	CHEVRON
CRANHAM	CHARLES	CHAOTIC	COCHLEA	COERCED	CHEERIO
CLASHES	CRADLES	CHANTED	CACKLED	COERCES	CHEERUP
COACHES	CHAPLET	CHATTED	CACKLES	CREWCUT	CLEARUP

CLEARER	CUIRASS	CHICORY	CALMEST	CALTROP	COMMITS
CLEARLY	CLIPART	CHIPPED	COLBERT	CULPRIT	CAMILLA
CHELSEA	CLIMBED	CHIRPED	COLDEST	CALISTA	CAMILLE
CREASED	CRIBBED	CLIPPED	COLLECT	CELESTA	CUMULUS
CHEESES	CLIMBER	CRIMPED	CULVERT	CELESTE	CAMELOT
CREASES	COINBOX	CLIPPIE	COLOGNE	COLETTE	COMPLEX
CRESSET	CHIMERA	CRIPPLE	CULSHAW	COLLUDE	CEMENTS
CREASEY	CHINESE	CRISPIN	CALCINE	CULTURE	COMMODE
CHEATED	CHILEAN	CHIPPER	CALCITE	COLOURS	COMPOSE
CREATED	CHIMEIN	CLIPPER	COLLIDE	COLDWAR	COMPOTE
CRESTED	CRIMEAN	CRIMPER	CALLING	CSLEWIS	COMMONS
CHEETAH	CHIMERS	CRISPER	CALMING	CALYXES	CAMPOUT
CHEATER	CHISELS	CRISPLY	CALVING	COMMAND	COMBOUT
CHESTER	CHIFFON	CHIRRUP	CULLING	COMPARE	COMFORT
CREATOR	CHIEFLY	CAISSON	CALCIUM	COMRADE	COMFORT
CREATES	CRINGED	CRIMSON	CULTISM	CAMPARI	COMPOST
CAESURA	CRINGES	CLIFTON	COLLIER	CEMBALO	CUMBRIA
CHEQUER	CLICHED	CLINTON	CELSIUS	COMBATS	CAMBRIC
CHEQUES	CLICHES	CRITTER	COLLIES	COMPASS	CAMERON
CHERUBS	CUISINE	CHINTZY	COLLINS	CYMBALS	CWMBRAN
CHERVIL	CEILING	CLIQUES	CELLIST	COMPACT	CAMERAS
CLEAVER	CHIDING	CLIQUEY	CULTIST	COMPANY	COMOROS
CLEAVES	CHIMING	CHINWAG	CALCIFY	CAMPBED	COMFREY
CHEGWIN	COILING	CAJOLED	COLDITZ	CIMABUE	COMPTON
COFFERS	COINING	CAJOLES	COLUMBA	COMICAL	COMMUNE
CUFFING	CEILIDH	CALLARD	CALOMEL	COMEDIC	COMMUTE
COFFINS	CLINICS	COLLAGE	COLEMAN	COMMEND	COMPUTE
COGNATE	CRITICS	COLLATE	COLOMBO	COMPERE	COMBUST
CAGEDIN	CLICKED	CELLARS	COLUMBO	COMPETE	CANTATA
CYGNETS	CLINKED	COLLARS	CALAMUS	CAMBERS	CANDACE
CAGIEST	CRINKLE	CALGARY	COLUMNS	CAMPERS	CONCAVE
CIGGIES	CHICKEN	CALVARY	CALUMET	COMPELS	CONTAIN
COGENCY	CLINKER	CALIBRE	CALUMNY	COMMENT	CENTAVO
CAGOULE	CRICKET	COLIBRI	COLONEL	CAMOGIE	CINZANO
COHABIT	CRINKLY	CALIBAN	CILENTO	CAMPHOR	CENTAUR
CAHOOTS	CHILLED	COLOBUS	CALZONE	COMBINE	CANCANS
COHORTS	CHILLER	CALLBOX	CALLOFF	COMPILE	CANVASS
CHICANE	CHIANTI	COLICKY	CALLOUS	CAMPING	CONTACT
CLIMATE	CHIGNON	CALDERA	CALLOUT	COMBING	CONICAL
COINAGE	CLIENTS	COLLEGE	CALYPSO	CAMPION	CYNICAL
CHICAGO	CHIMNEY	COLLEEN	CALIPHS	COMFIER	CANDELA
CHICANO	CHINOOK	CALLERS	CALORIE	COMFITS	CONTEND

CONCEDE	CONFINE	CENTRIC	COOKERY	COOKSON	CAPITAL
CONVENE	CONNIVE	CENTRED	CLOGGED	CHOOSES	CAPITOL
CONCEAL	CANNING	CENTRAL	CHOUGHS	CROESUS	CAPSTAN
CONGEAL	CONNING	CONTROL	CLOTHED	CROSSES	CAPSULE
CANTEEN	CUNNING	CANTRIP	CLOCHES	CROSSLY	CAPTURE
CONCERN	CONNICK	CENTRES	CLOTHES	CROATIA	CARCASE
CONDEMN	CONFIRM	CANASTA	CROCHET	CLOTTED	CARNAGE
CANCELS	CONSIGN	CENSURE	CHOCICE	CLOUTED	CORKAGE
CANKERS	CENTIMO	CONFUSE	CHOKING	CHORTLE	CORSAGE
CANNERS	CANNIER	CONFUTE	CLONING	CROUTON	CARWASH
CANTERS	CANDIES	CONJURE	CLOSING	CROPTOP	CARPARK
CENSERS	CONSIST	CONSUME	CLOYING	CROFTER	CUREALL
CINDERS	CONVICT	CONQUER	COOKING	CHOCTAW	CURTAIL
CONFERS	CANNILY	CONCURS	COOLING	CLOSURE	CERTAIN
CONFESS	CONAKRY	CONCUSS	COOPING	CROQUET	CURTAIN
CONKERS	CONKLIN	CONSULS	CROWING	CUPCAKE	CORSAIR
CONVEYS	CANDLES	CONDUCT	CHORIZO	CAPTAIN	CARPALS
CONCEIT	CANTLES	CONDUIT	CROSIER	CAPABLE	CEREALS
CONCEPT	CINEMAS	CONSULT	COOKIES	CAPABLY	CORRALS
CONCERT	CANINES	CENTURY	CRONIES	CAPECOD	CURRANT
CONNECT	CANINGS	CHORALE	CLOAKED	COPYCAT	CURABLE
CONSENT	CANONRY	COOLANT	CLONKED	CIPHERS	CARIBOU
CONSETT	CANTONA	CROSBIE	CROAKED	COPIERS	CORNCOB
CONTENT	CONCORD	CLOBBER	CROCKED	COPPERS	CORACLE
CONTEST	CONDONE	CROWBAR	CROOKED	CYPRESS	CARACAL
CONTEXT	CONNOTE	COOLBOX	CLOCKIN	COPSHOP	CURACAO
CONVENT	CONSOLE	CHOICES	CROWLEY	CAPRICE	CARACAS
CONVERT	CONFORM	CLOUDED	CLONMEL	CAPRINE	CBRADIO
CANNERY	CANDOUR	CROWDED	CLOWNED	CAPSIZE	CARMELA
CONNERY	CONTOUR	CROYDON	CROONED	CAPTIVE	CARRERA
CONIFER	CANNONS	CHOWDER	CROWNED	COPPICE	CORTEGE
CYNTHIA	CANTONS	CHOLERA	CROONER	COPPING	CORNEAL
CONCHIE	CANTORS	CLOSEIN	CLOONEY	COPYING	CORNELL
CONCHES	CANYONS	CLOSEUP	COOLOFF	CAPTION	CARLEEN
CANDIDA	CENSORS	CHOKERS	CHOMPED	COPYIST	CARVEUP
CANTINA	CONDORS	CLOSETS	CHOPPED	CYPRIOT	CARDERS
CANDICE	CONNORS	COOKERS	CLOPPED	CAPULET	CAREENS
CANDIDE	CONVOYS	COOPERS	CROPPED	COPILOT	CAREERS
CENTILE	CONCOCT	CLOSEST	CHOPPER	COPPOLA	CARPELS
CENTIME	CONSORT	COOLEST	CROPPER	CAPTORS	CARPETS
CONCISE	CONTORT	CLOSEBY	CHOISYA	COPIOUS	CARTELS
CONFIDE	CANAPES	CLOSELY	CROSSED	CAPERED	CARTERS

CARVERS	CURLIER	CURATES	COSTNER	CITRONS	CHUCKED
CORNERS	CARRIES	CAROUSE	CASINGS	CATERED	CLUCKED
CORNETS	CURRIES	CIRCUIT	CASINOS	COTERIE	CLUNKED
CORSETS	CERTIFY	CORRUPT	CASTOFF	CATARRH	CHUCKLE
CURFEWS	COROLLA	CARAVEL	CASSOCK	CATERER	CLUNKER
CURLERS	CIRCLED	CARAVAN	CASTORS	CATESBY	CRUELLA
CURLEWS	CURDLED	CARAWAY	CUSTOMS	CATSUIT	COUPLED
CORBETT	CIRCLES	CARLYLE	CUSTODY	CUTAWAY	COUPLER
CORRECT	CURDLES	CARRYON	CESSPIT	CITIZEN	COUPLES
CURRENT	CIRCLET	CASSATA	COSTUME	CAUDATE	COUPLET
CARVERY	CARAMBA	CASSAVA	CASQUES	COURAGE	CRUELLY
CORNFED	CERAMIC	COSTARD	COTTAGE	CRUSADE	CRUELTY
CAREFUL	CARAMEL	CUSTARD	CATWALK	COUGARS	CLUBMAN
CARAFES	CARTMAN	CASCADE	CUTBACK	CLUBBED	CHURNED
CORSICA	CERUMEN	COSSACK	CATCALL	CRUMBLE	CHUNNEL
CORTINA	CHRONIC	CASUALS	CATNAPS	CLUBBER	CHUTNEY
CARDIAC	CORONER	COSTARS	CUTLASS	COURBET	COULOMB
CARRIED	CORONET	CASHBOX	CUTICLE	CRUMBLY	COUPONS
CURRIED	CORDOBA	CASHCOW	CATSCAN	COUNCIL	CLUMPED
CARBIDE	CARLOAD	CISTERN	CITADEL	CLUBCAR	CRUMPLE
CARBINE	CORRODE	CASHEWS	CATSEYE	CRUNCHY	CRUMPET
CARMINE	CARPOOL	CASKETS	CITTERN	CLUEDUP	COURSED
CORDITE	CARROLL	COSSETS	COTTERS	CRUDEST	CRUISED
CORNICE	CORNOIL	COSIEST	CUTLETS	CRUDELY	COUNSEL
CURSIVE	CARTOON	CASTILE	CUTTERS	CHUFFED	COURSER
CARDIFF	CARBONS	CASHING	CATTERY	CHUGGED	CRUISER
CARDING	CARBOYS	CASKING	CUTLERY	COUGHED	COURSES
CARLING	CARROTS	CASTING	CATCHON	CRUSHED	CRUISES
CARPING	CARTONS	COSHING	CATCHUP	CAUTHEN	CAUSTIC
CARTING	CORDONS	COSTING	CATCHER	COUGHUP	COUNTED
CARVING	CURIOUS	CUSHING	CATCHES	CRUSHER	COURTED
CORKING	CARPORT	CUSSING	CUTTING	COUCHES	COUNTON
CURBING	CARROTT	CASPIAN	CATFISH	CRUSHES	CHUNTER
CURLING	CARROTY	CUSHION	CATTIER	CRUDITE	CLUSTER
CURSING	CURSORY	CASHIER	CATKINS	CAUSING	CLUTTER
CURVING	CORPSED	CUSHIER	CATNIPS	CRUCIAL	COUNTER
CORNISH	CORPSES	CASSIUS	CATMINT	CAUTION	COUNTRY
CARSICK	CHRISSY	CASUIST	CATTILY	COURIER	COURTLY
CORDIAL	CHRISTY	CASSIDY	CATALAN	COUSINS	COUTURE
CARRION	CAROTID	CASTLED	CATFLAP	CRUCIFY	CAVEATS
CARRIER	CARLTON	CASTLES	CATHODE	CRUDITY	CAVEDIN
CARTIER	CURATOR	CASELAW	CITROEN	CAULKED	CIVVIES

CAVALRY	DRAWERS	DOABUNK	DUCHESS	DIDDLES	DEFRAYS
CIVILLY	DEAFEST	DABHAND	DECAGON	DIDEROT	DEFIANT
CAVEMAN	DEAREST	DEBACLE	DECRIED	DODGSON	DEFACED
CAVEMEN	DIALECT	DABBERS	DECEIVE	DIDDUMS	DEFACTO
COVERED	DEANERY	DIBBERS	DECLINE	DIEHARD	DEFACES
COVERUP	DRAPERY	DEBRIEF	DUCTILE	DIECAST	DEFECTS
CAVERNS	DWARFED	DABBING	DECKING	DIETARY	DEFICIT
CAVORTS	DRAGGED	DUBBING	DOCKING	DREADED	DIFFERS
COVETED	DRAUGHT	DABBLED	DUCKING	DRESDEN	DUFFERS
COWHAND	DRACHMA	DABBLER	DECRIAL	DEEPEND	DAFTEST
COWHERD	DRACHMS	DABBLES	DICTION	DEEPENS	DEFLECT
COWBELL	DEATHLY	DEBUNKS	DACOITS	DIETERS	DEFYING
COWSHED	DEALING	DEBTORS	DECEITS	DEEPEST	DOFFING
COWHIDE	DRAWING	DUBIOUS	DECRIES	DUEWEST	DEFILED
COWLING	DIARIES	DEBORAH	DECOKED	DEEPFRY	DEFILER
COWLICK	DIARIST	DEBURGH	DECOKES	DREDGED	DEFILES
COWGIRL	DUALITY	DEBASED	DECIMAL	DREDGER	DEFAMED
COWSLIP	DIALLED	DEBASES	DECAMPS	DREDGES	DEFAMES
COWPOKE	DRAWLED	DEBUSSY	DICANIO	DEESIDE	DEFINED
COWBOYS	DEADLEG	DEBATED	DECANTS	DEETIME	DEFENCE
COWERED	DIALLER	DEBITED	DECENCY	DEEMING	DEFENDS
COWARDS	DRAYMAN	DEBATER	DOCTORS	DIETING	DEFINES
COXCOMB	DRAYMEN	DEBATES	DECAPOD	DOESKIN	DEFUNCT
CAYMANS	DRAINED	DEBAUCH	DECORUM	DUELLED	DEFROCK
CRYBABY	DRAINER	DECEASE	DICKSON	DWELLER	DEFROST
COYNESS	DRAGNET	DECLARE	DECAYED	DREAMED	DEFORMS
CAYENNE	DIAMOND	DICTATE	DACTYLS	DREAMUP	DEFUSED
CRYWOLF	DRAGOON	DECLAIM	DEDUCED	DREAMER	DEFUSES
CRYPTIC	DIABOLO	DECIBEL	DIDICOI	DIEDOFF	DIFFUSE
CRYSTAL	DEACONS	DECOCTS	DEDUCES	DIEDOWN	DEFAULT
CEZANNE	DRAGONS	DECIDED	DEDUCTS	DIEDOUT	DEGRADE
DIAHANN	DEALOUT	DECODED	DUDGEON	DEEPSEA	DOGDAYS
DRABBLE	DEADPAN	DECIDER	DODGEMS	DEEPFRY	DAGGERS
DRAWBAR	DIAGRAM	DECODER	DODGERS	DRESSED	DEGREES
DIANDRA	DEADSEA	DECADES	DODDERY	DRESSUP	DIGGERS
DEADEND	DHANSAK	DECIDES	DODGING	DRESSER	DIGRESS
DEADENS	DEARSIR	DECODES	DADAISM	DRESSES	DOGSHOW
DEAFENS	DEADSET	DECREED	DADDIES	DEEPSET	DIGGING
DEALERS	DRASTIC	DECREES	DADAIST	DOEEYED	DOGGING
DIADEMS	DRAFTED	DICKENS	DIDDLED	DEFRAUD	DOGFISH
DIAPERS	DEAYTON	DOCKERS	DIDDLER	DEFLATE	DIGNIFY
DRAPERS	DRACULA	DOCKETS	DEDALUS	DEFEATS	DIGNITY

DAGWOOD	DELIBES	DAMAGES	DANVERS	DONATES	DAPPLED
DOGWOOD	DELUDED	DAMMING	DINNERS	DENEUVE	DAPPLES
DOGROSE	DELUDES	DAMNING	DONKEYS	DENTURE	DAPHNES
DOGTROT	DULLEST	DAMPING	DANKEST	DONJUAN	DEPENDS
DIGESTS	DOLEFUL	DIMMING	DENSEST	DONOVAN	DIPLOMA
DIGITAL	DELUGED	DUMPING	DENSELY	DUNAWAY	DEPLORE
DOGSTAR	DELUGES	DIMWITS	DONEFOR	DINKYDI	DIPLOCK
DUGOUTS	DELIGHT	DOMAINS	DONEGAL	DENIZEN	DEPLOYS
DAHLIAS	DELPHIC	DUMMIES	DONEGAN	DIORAMA	DEPARTS
DAHOMEY	DOLPHIN	DIMPLED	DONOHOE	DOOMBEN	DEPORTS
DOHERTY	DALLIED	DEMILLE	DENTINE	DOORDIE	DEPOSED
DRIBBLE	DELVING	DIMPLES	DANCING	DROSERA	DEPOSES
DRIBBLY	DOLTISH	DEMONIC	DENNING	DIOCESE	DEPOSIT
DEIRDRE	DULLISH	DOMINIC	DENTING	DROVERS	DIPTYCH
DWINDLE	DALZIEL	DOMINGO	DENYING	DROUGHT	DORMANT
DRIEDUP	DALLIES	DEMANDS	DONKING	DIOXIDE	DURMAST
DRIPDRY	DOLLIES	DIMMOCK	DONNING	DNOTICE	DURABLE
DRIVEIN	DELILAH	DAMSONS	DENBIGH	DRONING	DIRECTS
DRIVERS	DILEMMA	DOMJOLY	DONNISH	DOODLED	DERIDED
DEIFIED	DELIMIT	DEMERIT	DANDINI	DROOLED	DERIDES
DEICING	DOLUNCH	DEMISEC	DUNKIRK	DOODLER	DIRNDLS
DRIVING	DELANEY	DEMESNE	DINGIER	DOODLES	DARLENE
DAILIES	DELTOID	DEMPSEY	DANDIES	DROPLET	DARNELL
DAIRIES	DOLLOPS	DEMOTIC	DENTIST	DOORMAN	DORRELL
DAISIES	DALTREY	DEMOTED	DANDIFY	DOORMAT	DURRELL
DEIFIES	DELETED	DEMETER	DENSITY	DROWNED	DARKENS
DEITIES	DILATED	DEMOTES	DANGLED	DROPOFF	DARNERS
DOILIES	DILUTED	DANDARE	DANGLES	DROPOUT	DARTERS
DRINKUP	DELETES	DENTATE	DANELAW	DUOPOLY	DARKEST
DRINKER	DILATES	DENMARK	DYNAMIC	DROOPED	DERWENT
DRILLED	DILUTES	DUNDALK	DYNAMOS	DROPPED	DIRTIED
DAIMLER	DELIVER	DENIALS	DUNNOCK	DROPPER	DORMICE
DEIGNED	DELAYED	DUNNART	DENHOLM	DIOPTRE	DARLING
DRIPPED	DEMEANS	DINGBAT	DINGOES	DOORWAY	DARNING
DRIFTED	DAMPENS	DUNEDIN	DINEOUT	DEPRAVE	DARTING
DRIFTER	DAMPERS	DENUDES	DENISON	DEPICTS	DORKING
DRIZZLE	DAMSELS	DANIELA	DYNASTS	DEPLETE	DERVISH
DRIZZLY	DIMNESS	DUNGEON	DYNASTY	DEPRESS	DERRICK
DEJECTS	DAMPEST	DANSEUR	DENOTED	DIPPERS	DIRTIER
DUKEDOM	DIMMEST	DANCERS	DONATED	DOPIEST	DARBIES
DULLARD	DAMAGED	DANGERS	DINETTE	DEPRIVE	DARKMAN
DOLLARS	DEMIGOD	DANIELS	DENOTES	DIPPING	DERANGE

DURANTE	DUSTMAN	DETAINS	DIVINER	DAZZLED	EXCLAIM
DARIOFO	DUSTMEN	DITTIES	DEVIOUS	DAZZLER	ENCHANT
DOROTHY	DESMOND	DETENTE	DIVERGE	DAZZLES	ENCODED
DERIVED	DESPOND	DETTORI	DIVERSE	EMANATE	ENCODES
DERIVES	DISCORD	DUTEOUS	DIVORCE	EVANDER	ESCUDOS
DASTARD	DISPOSE	DETROIT	DIVERTS	ENAMELS	EXCRETE
DISBAND	DISROBE	DETESTS	DEVISED	ERASERS	EXCEEDS
DISCARD	DESPOIL	DETOURS	DAVISON	EGALITE	ETCHING
DESCALE	DESPOTS	DRUBBED	DEVISES	EVASIVE	ENCLOSE
DISEASE	DISHOUT	DRUIDIC	DIVESTS	EXAMINE	ESCAPED
DISTAFF	DISPORT	DAUBERS	DEVOTED	ERASING	ESCAPEE
DISDAIN	DISTORT	DRUGGED	DEVOTEE	EVADING	ESCAPES
DESPAIR	DUSTPAN	DAUPHIN	DEVOTES	ELATION	ENCORES
DISMAYS	DESIRED	DOUGHTY	DEVOURS	EVASION	ESCORTS
DESCANT	DESERVE	DAUBING	DEVIZES	ENABLED	EXCERPT
DISTANT	DESIREE	DOUSING	DOWSERS	ENABLES	ENCASED
DISABLE	DESERTS	DRUNKEN	DOWAGER	ERASMUS	EXCISED
DUSTBIN	DESIRES	DRUMKIT	DAWNING	EDASNER	EXCUSED
DISOBEY	DISARMS	DOUBLED	DOWNING	EVAPOPE	ENCASES
DESCEND	DESTROY	DRUMLIN	DOWSING	EXAMPLE	EXCISES
DISTEND	DISUSED	DOUBLES	DOWDIER	ELAPSED	EXCUSES
DISCERN	DESISTS	DOUGLAS	DOWDILY	ELAPSES	EXCITED
DISPELS	DESKTOP	DOUBLET	DAWDLED	ELASTIC	EXCITES
DUSTERS	DISTURB	DRUMMED	DAWDLER	ENACTED	EXCLUDE
DESCENT	DISPUTE	DRUMMER	DAWDLES	EXACTED	EACHWAY
DESSERT	DISCUSS	DIURNAL	DEWDROP	EXALTED	ENCRYPT
DISSECT	DRSEUSS	DRUMPAD	DRYLAND	EXACTOR	ENDGAME
DISSENT	DISGUST	DAUNTED	DAYCARE	EXACTLY	ENDEARS
DESIGNS	DISRUPT	DOUBTED	DRYCELL	ERASURE	ENDEDUP
DESPISE	DISAVOW	DOUBTER	DAYWEAR	EVACUEE	ENDLESS
DESPITE	DISOWNS	DEVIATE	DRYNESS	EMANUEL	ENDWISE
DISLIKE	DETRACT	DEVIANT	DAYTIME	EMBRACE	EDDYING
DASHING	DATABLE	DEVICES	DOYENNE	EMBLEMS	ENDEMIC
DOSSING	DETECTS	DIVIDED	DAYLONG	EBBTIDE	ENDINGS
DUSTING	DITHERS	DAVEDEE	DAYBOOK	EMBALMS	ENDMOST
DOSSIER	DITHERY	DIVIDER	DRYDOCK	EMBROIL	ENDURED
DUSTIER	DUTIFUL	DIVIDES	DAYROOM	EMBARGO	ENDORSE
DISMISS	DITCHED	DEVALUE	DAYTRIP	EMBARKS	ENDURES
DISTILS	DITCHES	DEVOLVE	DAYSTAR	EMBASSY	ELDERLY
DESTINY	DOTRICE	DIVULGE	DRYEYED	ELBOWED	ENDUSER
DESKJOB	DOTTIER	DEVELOP	DAZEDLY	EMBRYOS	ENDIVES
DISPLAY	DETAILS	DEVILRY	DIZZILY	ENCLAVE	ENDOWED

EMERALD	EXERTED	ECHOING	EPISTLE	EXPECTS	ENRAGED
ELEVATE	EVERTON	EXHALED	EPICURE	EMPRESS	ENRAGES
EVERAGE	EJECTOR	ECHELON	ENJOYED	EXPRESS	EARTHED
EYEBATH	ELECTOR	EXHALES	ECLOGUE	EMPTIED	EARTHEN
EYELASH	ERECTOR	EXHUMED	ECLAIRS	ENPRISE	EARSHOT
EYEWASH	EVENTER	EXHUMES	EELWORM	ESPYING	EARTHLY
EYEBALL	EXECUTE	ENHANCE	ELLIOTT	ELPHICK	EARNING
ELEGANT	EFFACED	ETHANOL	ECLIPSE	EMPTIES	EARRING
EMENDED	EFFACES	EPHESUS	ELLIPSE	EXPANSE	EARLIER
ELEVENS	EFFECTS	EXHAUST	ENLARGE	EXPENSE	EARWIGS
EYELETS	ENFIELD	EMIRATE	ELLISON	EXPUNGE	EARPLUG
ELEMENT	ESFAHAN	EPILATE	ENLISTS	EXPANDS	EARFLAP
EVEREST	ENFOLDS	EPITAPH	ENLIVEN	EXPENDS	ERRANDS
EVERETT	EFFENDI	EVINCED	EDMONDS	EXPLODE	EARLOBE
EMERGED	ENFORCE	EVILEYE	ENMASSE	EXPLORE	ENRIQUE
EPERGNE	EFFORTS	EMINENT	EDMOSES	EMPLOYS	ETRURIA
EMERGES	EFFUSED	EVIDENT	EXMOUTH	EXPLOIT	EARDRUM
EVESHAM	EFFUSES	EXIGENT	ENNOBLE	EUPHONY	EARDROP
EREWHON	ENGLAND	EPITHET	EUNUCHS	EMPORIA	ERRATIC
EVELINA	EDGWARE	EDIFIED	ELOPERS	EXPIRED	ERRATUM
ELEGIAC	ENGRAVE	EDIFICE	EROTICA	ESPARTO	ENROUTE
ELEGISE	EGGHEAD	EDITING	EXOTICA	EMPEROR	EUSKARA
EREMITE	ELGRECO	EXILING	EBONITE	EMPIRES	ENSLAVE
EVENING	EAGLETS	EXITING	EMOTIVE	EXPERTS	ENSNARE
EZEKIEL	EDGIEST	ELITISM	EROSIVE	EXPIRES	EUSTACE
ELEGIES	ENGAGED	EDITION	ELOPING	EXPORTS	ECSTASY
ENEMIES	ENGAGES	ELISION	EMOTING	EXPOSED	EUSEBIO
EYELIDS	ENGLISH	EDIFIES	ERODING	EXPOSES	EASTEND
ELEGIST	EGGFLIP	ELICITS	EVOKING	EMPATHY	ELSPETH
ETERNAL	ENGULFS	ELIXIRS	EGOTISM	EXPOUND	EASTERN
ELEANOR	EUGENIE	ELITIST	EMOTION	ESPOUSE	EISWEIN
EYESORE	ENGINES	EDIBLES	EROSION	EMPOWER	EPSTEIN
EVENOUT	EGGNOGS	ENIGMAS	ETONIAN	ENQUIRE	EASIEST
EXEMPTS	ENGROSS	EPISODE	EGOTIST	ESQUIRE	EASEFUL
EYEDROP	ENGARDE	EPITOME	ECOLOGY	ENQUIRY	ENSIGNS
EYEBROW	ENGORGE	EDITORS	ECONOMY	EARMARK	ENSUITE
EMERSON	EAGERLY	ERITREA	EGOTRIP	EARHART	EASTING
ELECTRA	EIGHTHS	EPIGRAM	EGOISTS	EARACHE	ENSUING
ELEKTRA	EGGCUPS	EMIGRES	EVOLVED	EARLDOM	EASYJET
EJECTED	EXHIBIT	EMITTED	EVOLVES	EARNERS	EPSILON
ELECTED	ETHICAL	EVICTED	EXPIATE	EARNEST	EASTMAN
ERECTED	ECHIDNA	EXISTED	EXPLAIN	EERIEST	ESSENCE

ESSENES	ENUMBER	FLAKING	FACULTY	FLEXING	FRIGHTS
EASEOFF	EQUABLY	FLAMING	FACTOID	FREEING	FLIGHTY
ENSURED	ECUADOR	FLARING	FACEOFF	FLEMISH	FAILING
ELSTREE	ELUSIVE	FLAYING	FACTORS	FRECKLE	FAIRING
ENSURES	ERUDITE	FOAMING	FACTORY	FRECKLY	FOILING
ESSAYED	EDUCING	FRAMING	FUCHSIA	FEEBLER	FAIRIES
ENTRAPS	ELUDING	FRAYING	FOCUSED	FREEMAN	FLICKED
ENTRANT	EXUDING	FRASIER	FOCUSES	FIENNES	FRISKED
EXTRACT	EQUALLY	FRANKIE	FACTUAL	FLEXORS	FLICKER
ESTUARY	EQUINOX	FLANKER	FIDGETS	FLEAPIT	FRICKER
EATABLE	EQUERRY	FRANKLY	FIDGETY	FLEURON	FRILLED
ENTICED	EQUATED	FLAILED	FUDGING	FREESIA	FOIBLES
ENTICES	ERUPTED	FRAILER	FADDISH	FRETSAW	FEIGNED
EXTREME	EXULTED	FLATLET	FADDIST	FRETTED	FAIENCE
ENTREES	EQUATOR	FIATLUX	FIDDLED	FLEXURE	FRIENDS
ENTREAT	EQUATES	FRAILTY	FIDELIO	FREEWAY	FLIPPED
ESTEFAN	ENVYING	FLANNEL	FIDDLER	FREEZER	FLIPPER
ENTWINE	ENVELOP	FLAUNTS	FIDDLES	FREEZES	FRISSON
ENTAILS	ENVIOUS	FLAVOUR	FADEOUT	FIFTEEN	FAINTED
ENTRIES	EDWARDS	FLAGONS	FEDERAL	FAFFING	FLIRTED
EATDIRT	ELYSIUM	FLATOUT	FEDERER	FIFTIES	FLITTED
ESTELLA	ELYSIAN	FLAPPED	FEDORAS	FLIPTOP	FLIPTOP
ESTELLE	ENZYMES	FLAPPER	FREEBIE	FOGLAMP	FAINTER
ENTOMBS	FLACCID	FRANTIC	FLEECED	FIGLEAF	FRITTER
ESTONIA	FIANCEE	FEASTED	FLEECES	FIGMENT	FAINTLY
ENTENTE	FLATCAP	FLATTIE	FIELDED	FAGGING	FAILURE
EXTENDS	FIANCES	FLATTEN	FREDDIE	FOGGIER	FAIRWAY
EXTINCT	FRANCES	FLATTOP	FIEFDOM	FIGROLL	FRIEZES
ENTROPY	FRANCIS	FLATTER	FREEDOM	FOGHORN	FAJITAS
ENTERIC	FLAGDAY	FEATURE	FIELDER	FAGGOTS	FOLIAGE
ENTERED	FLAREUP	FRAZZLE	FEEDERS	FIGURED	FELLAHS
ENTHRAL	FRAMEUP	FIBBERS	FEELERS	FIGURES	FULMARS
EXTORTS	FEARFUL	FEBRILE	FRETFUL	FIGHTER	FALLACY
ENTITLE	FLAGGED	FIBBING	FLEDGED	FRIGATE	FELUCCA
ESTATES	FLANGED	FOBBING	FREIGHT	FRIABLE	FALTERS
ENTHUSE	FRAUGHT	FABRICS	FRESHEN	FRISBEE	FELLERS
EXTRUDE	FLASHED	FIBROUS	FRESHER	FAIRDOS	FILLERS
ENTRUST	FEATHER	FABERGE	FRESHLY	FTINDEX	FILLETS
ESTEVEZ	FLASHER	FACIALS	FEEDING	FAIREST	FILTERS
EDUCATE	FLASHES	FACADES	FEELING	FAIRFAX	FOLDERS
EMULATE	FRAGILE	FACTION	FLEEING	FRIDGES	FALSEST
EQUABLE	FEARING	FICTION	FLEMING	FLIGHTS	FILBERT

FOLLETT	FAMINES	FINALLY	FOOYUNG	FORAGES	FARROWS
FULGENT	FEMORAL	FINANCE	FOPPERY	FAREHAM	FERROUS
FULLEST	FONTANA	FINDOUT	FOPPISH	FARNHAM	FURIOUS
FALSELY	FENLAND	FUNERAL	FORWARD	FURTHER	FURROWS
FALAFEL	FINLAND	FINESSE	FORBADE	FORMICA	FARMOST
FILMFUN	FANFARE	FANATIC	FORGAVE	FERRIED	FARMOUT
FILOFAX	FANMAIL	FOOTAGE	FORSAKE	FERTILE	FORKOUT
FALLGUY	FANTAIL	FROMAGE	FORSALE	FORGIVE	FURCOAT
FILCHED	FUNFAIR	FLOODED	FURNACE	FORHIRE	FORESEE
FILCHER	FINIANS	FLODDEN	FERRARI	FURTIVE	FORESTS
FILCHES	FINEART	FLORETS	FIREARM	FARMING	FORESAW
FALLING	FONDANT	FLOWERS	FOREARM	FORCING	FIRSTUP
FELLING	FANTASY	FLOWERY	FARRAGO	FORGING	FORSTER
FILLING	FINICKY	FLOGGED	FAREAST	FORMING	FIRSTLY
FILMING	FONTEYN	FLORIDA	FIREANT	FURLING	FORMULA
FOLDING	FENCERS	FLOWING	FIREBUG	FURNISH	FERRULE
FELLINI	FENDERS	FOOLING	FIREBOX	FOREIGN	FORSURE
FALKIRK	FINGERS	FOOTING	FIREDOG	FARRIER	FORTUNE
FILLIES	FUNNELS	FOOLISH	FIREDUP	FERRIER	FOREVER
FILLIPS	FANBELT	FLORINS	FARADAY	FURRIER	FARAWAY
FOLLIES	FONDEST	FROLICS	FARRELL	FERRIES	FORSYTE
FULFILS	FINAGLE	FLORIST	FERRELL	FIRKINS	FORSYTH
FALSIFY	FUNCHAL	FLOELLA	FORREAL	FORBIDS	FUSEBOX
FALSITY	FINCHES	FOOTMAN	FURSEAL	FORTIES	FISHEYE
FELDMAN	FANCIED	FOOTMEN	FORTEAN	FORTIFY	FASTENS
FALANGE	FANZINE	FROGMAN	FARCEUR	FORELEG	FESTERS
FELINES	FANNING	FROGMEN	FORBEAR	FARTLEK	FOSTERS
FILINGS	FENCING	FROWNED	FARMERS	FIREMAN	FASTEST
FULSOME	FENDING	FLOUNCE	FERRETS	FIREMEN	FISHERY
FALLOFF	FINDING	FROWNON	FORCEPS	FOREMAN	FISTFUL
FALCONS	FUNDING	FLOUNCY	FORGERS	FOREMEN	FISCHER
FELLOWS	FUNKING	FLOPPED	FORGETS	FORONCE	FESTIVE
FOLLOWS	FINNISH	FOOTPAD	FERMENT	FORMOSA	FASTING
FALLOUT	FENWICK	FLOORED	FERVENT	FORGOOD	FISHING
FELLOUT	FANCIER	FOOTROT	FIRMEST	FARGONE	FOSSICK
FULCRUM	FUNNIER	FOOTSIE	FORFEIT	FIRCONE	FASCISM
FALASHA	FANCIES	FLOTSAM	FORRENT	FORGONE	FASHION
FILMSET	FUNNILY	FROWSTY	FORREST	FURLONG	FISSION
FUMBLED	FENELLA	FLOATED	FORGERY	FORSOOK	FUSTIAN
FUMBLER	FANCLUB	FLOUTED	FIREFLY	FORLORN	FOSSILS
FEMALES	FONDLED	FROSTED	FORAGED	FURIOSO	FASCIST
FUMBLES	FONDLES	FRONTAL	FORAGER	FERVOUR	FUSSILY

FUSILLI	FLUNKEY	GRANDAD	GRAPPLE	GODUTCH	GAGGLES
FASTNET	FLUMMOX	GUARDED	GRASPER	GIDDYUP	GIGGLES
FISHNET	FLUENCY	GRANDEE	GRAMPUS	GRENADA	GOGGLES
FESTOON	FAUXPAS	GLADDEN	GRASSED	GRENADE	GAGARIN
FUSSPOT	FAULTED	GRANDER	GRAYSON	GLENCOE	GEHENNA
FISSURE	FLUSTER	GRANDLY	GLASSES	GEEZERS	GRIMACE
FATHEAD	FLUTTER	GOAHEAD	GRASSES	GLEEFUL	GUITARS
FATHERS	FAUSTUS	GLADEYE	GRAFTED	GIELGUD	GRIDDLE
FATNESS	FOURTHS	GRADERS	GRANTED	GEEWHIZ	GRINDER
FATTENS	FAVOURS	GRAVELY	GRAFTON	GOERING	GUILDER
FETTERS	FAWCETT	GRANGER	GRAFTER	GREYISH	GAITERS
FITNESS	FAWNING	GLASGOW	GHASTLY	GRECIAN	GLIDERS
FITTERS	FOXTAIL	GRAPHIC	GRANULE	GHERKIN	GRIPERS
FATTEST	FIXEDLY	GNASHED	GRAVURE	GREYLAG	GUINEAS
FITMENT	FOXHOLE	GNASHER	GRADUAL	GREMLIN	GAINFUL
FITTEST	FOXTROT	GNASHES	GIBLETS	GLEAMED	GRIFFIN
FATEFUL	FIXTURE	GRANITA	GOBLETS	GLEANED	GRIFFON
FATIGUE	FOXHUNT	GRANITE	GABRIEL	GLEANER	GOINGIN
FETCHED	FLYHALF	GEARING	GOBLINS	GREENER	GRISHAM
FETCHES	FLYPAST	GLARING	GUBBINS	GEELONG	GEISHAS
FITTING	FLYLEAF	GLAZING	GABBLED	GREGORY	GAINING
FATTIER	FLYHIGH	GNAWING	GOBBLED	GREASED	GLIDING
FATUITY	FLYSOLO	GOADING	GOBELIN	GUESSED	GRIPING
FATALLY	FLYPOST	GRADING	GABBLER	GLEASON	GUIDING
FETLOCK	FLYTRAP	GRATING	GABBLES	GREGSON	GRILLED
FATHOMS	FAYWRAY	GRAZING	GOBBLES	GREASER	GRILLES
FATUOUS	FLYOVER	GLACIAL	GIBBONS	GREASES	GLIMMER
FITZROY	FLYSWAT	GLACIER	GIBBOUS	GUESSES	GRINNED
FLUBBER	FLYAWAY	GLAZIER	GIBLUES	GREETED	GRIPPED
FOUNDED	FUZZBOX	GOAMISS	GODDARD	GREATER	GLIMPSE
FOUNDER	FIZZING	GRATIFY	GADDAFI	GREETER	GRIPPER
FOUNDRY	FIZZIER	GRAVITY	GADWALL	GREATLY	GRISSOM
FAUCETS	GRANADA	GNARLED	GODSEND	GREAVES	GRIGSON
FLUFFED	GRAHAME	GRAVLAX	GUDGEON	GRETZKY	GAINSAY
FLUSHED	GUARANI	GRAMMAR	GADGETS	GUFFAWS	GRIMSBY
FLUSHES	GRANARY	GRAMMER	GODDESS	GAFFERS	GLINTED
FEUDING	GRABBED	GRAINED	GODLESS	GOFORIT	GRISTLE
FLUKING	GEARBOX	GRAPNEL	GODLIKE	GAGGING	GLISTEN
FOULING	GLANCED	GRAINER	GADDING	GIGGING	GLITTER
FAUVISM	GLANCES	GRANOLA	GIDDIER	GIGGLED	GRIFTER
FAUVIST	GRANDMA	GLAMOUR	GODFREY	GOGGLED	GRITTER
FLUNKED	GRANDPA	GRASPED	GODETIA	GIGGLER	GRISTLY

GRIEVED	GAMBITS	GONERIL	GLOSSOP	GARRICK	GOSPORT
GRIEVES	GAMBLED	GINTRAP	GROUSES	GERBILS	GASTRIC
GRIZZLE	GAMELAN	GENESIS	GROSSLY	GERAINT	GESTURE
GRIZZLY	GYMSLIP	GENETIC	GNOSTIC	GORILLA	GETBACK
GOLIATH	GAMBLER	GANGWAY	GLOATED	GARBLED	GOTBACK
GALLANT	GAMBLES	GOODBYE	GROUTED	GARGLED	GATEAUX
GOLFBAG	GAMINES	GROWBAG	GLOTTIS	GURGLED	GOTOBED
GALICIA	GAMBOGE	GNOCCHI	GROWTHS	GERALDO	GATHERS
GOLDCUP	GUMBOIL	GROUCHO	GHOSTLY	GARBLES	GUTLESS
GALLEON	GAMBOLS	GROUCHY	GLOBULE	GARGLES	GUTTERS
GALLEYS	GUMBOOT	GEORDIE	GROOVED	GIRDLES	GOTHIKA
GOLFERS	GUMTREE	GOOLDEN	GROOVES	GURGLES	GATLING
GULLETS	GUMDROP	GOODDAY	GOODWIN	GORMLEY	GATTING
GILBERT	GUNWALE	GLOWERS	GAPYEAR	GARONNE	GETTING
GALLERY	GANDALF	GROCERS	GOPHERS	GARDNER	GSTRING
GALAHAD	GUNNERA	GROVELS	GUPPIES	GORGONS	GUTTING
GALLING	GINSENG	GROWERS	GYPSIES	GYRATED	GATWICK
GELDING	GUNDECK	GEODESY	GARLAND	GYRATES	GATELEG
GELLING	GENTEEL	GROCERY	GURNARD	GORETEX	GETLOST
GILDING	GUNNELL	GEORGIA	GARBAGE	GESTATE	GOTOPOT
GOLDING	GANDERS	GEORGIE	GERMANE	GOSPARE	GUTHRIE
GOLFING	GANGERS	GIORGIO	GERMANS	GASMASK	GOTOSEA
GULPING	GANNETS	GOODHEW	GERVAIS	GOSHAWK	GETOVER
GILLIAM	GUNNERS	GLOWING	GERMANY	GESTAPO	GATEWAY
GILLIAN	GINGERY	GOOFING	GERBERA	GASLAMP	GETAWAY
GALLICO	GINGHAM	GROPING	GARDENS	GESTALT	GOULASH
GILLIES	GUNSHIP	GROWING	GARNETS	GASKELL	GRUMBLE
GALILEE	GUNTHER	GOODIES	GARRETS	GASKETS	GOUACHE
GALILEO	GENGHIS	GLORIFY	GARTERS	GOSPELS	GOUNDER
GALUMPH	GUNSHOT	GROWLED	GIRDERS	GUSHERS	GRUYERE
GALLONS	GENTILE	GROWLER	GARMENT	GASHING	GLUEEAR
GALLOPS	GENUINE	GROOMED	GARNETT	GASPING	GLUTEUS
GALLOWS	GUNFIRE	GOODMAN	GARRETT	GASSING	GRUFFLY
GOLDWYN	GANGING	GROMMET	GARGERY	GOSLING	GRUDGED
GULFWAR	GENTIAN	GROANED	GIRAFFE	GUSHING	GRUDGES
GYMNAST	GONDOLA	GROWNUP	GARAGED	GUSTING	GAUCHOS
GEMSBOK	GINGOLD	GROUNDS	GARAGES	GASBILL	GAUGING
GUMSHOE	GONEOFF	GEOLOGY	GURKHAS	GASSIER	GOUGING
GYMSHOE	GUNROOM	GROUPIE	GARBING	GOSSIPS	GAUDIER
GUMMING	GUNBOAT	GROUPER	GORGING	GOSSIPY	GAUDILY
GIMMICK	GENERIC	GOODREM	GARNISH	GISELLE	GOURMET
GAMBIAN	GENERAL	GROUSED	GIRLISH	GASEOUS	GLUCOSE

GOUJONS	HEARING	HACKSAW	HIGHTEA	HELPFUL	HUMMING
GRUNTED	HEATING	HICCUPS	HIGHWAY	HALIFAX	HUMPING
GLUTTON	HEAVING	HYDRATE	HAIRCUT	HALOGEN	HOMOLKA
GRUNTER	HOAXING	HYDRANT	HAILERS	HILAIRE	HUMBLED
GAUGUIN	HEAVIER	HEDGING	HEIFERS	HALTING	HUMBLER
GIVEEAR	HEAVIES	HADRIAN	HEIRESS	HALVING	HUMBLES
GAVEOUT	HEAVILY	HUDDLED	HEIGHHO	HELPING	HOMINID
GIVEOUT	HEARKEN	HIDALGO	HEIGHTS	HOLDING	HOMONYM
GOVERNS	HAARLEM	HUDDLES	HAILING	HULKING	HAMMOND
GIVERNY	HEADLEY	HADDOCK	HAITIAN	HELLISH	HAMMOCK
GAVOTTE	HEADMAN	HIDEOUS	HAIRIER	HOLLIES	HEMLOCK
GAVEWAY	HEARSES	HYDROUS	HEINKEL	HOLYJOE	HUMMOCK
GIVEWAY	HEADSET	HIDEOUT	HAIRNET	HELLMAN	HUMDRUM
GAWPING	HEARSAY	HEELBAR	HAIROIL	HELDOFF	HOMERUN
GAWKILY	HEARTEN	HEEDFUL	HEINOUS	HOLDOFF	HUMERUS
GOWRONG	HEARTHS	HEEDING	HAIRPIN	HILLOCK	HAMPTON
GWYNEDD	HEALTHY	HOEDOWN	HOISTED	HOLMOAK	HAMSTER
GWYNETH	HEADWAY	HEELTAP	HIJACKS	HOLBORN	HAMBURG
GEYSERS	HEBREWS	HUFFING	HALYARD	HALLOWS	HOMBURG
GAYLORD	HOBBIES	HEFTIER	HOLLAND	HELDOUT	HONIARA
GUYROPE	HOBBITS	HOFFMAN	HALSALL	HELPOUT	HANSARD
GIZZARD	HYBRIDS	HUFFMAN	HOLDALL	HOLDOUT	HENBANE
GUZZLED	HOBBLED	HAGGARD	HALFAMO	HELIPAD	HANGARS
GAZELLE	HOBBLES	HOGGARD	HILLARY	HOLYSEE	HUNGARY
GUZZLER	HOBNOBS	HOGWASH	HALIBUT	HELSTON	HANDBAG
GUZZLES	HABITUE	HOGBACK	HELLBOY	HILLTOP	HANDCAR
GAZUMPS	HEBATES	HOGGART	HELICAL	HOLSTER	HANGDOG
GAZANIA	HABITAT	HIGHDAY	HELICON	HELOTRY	HENREID
GAZETTE	HECTARE	HOGWEED	HALFCUT	HOLYWAR	HENPECK
HOARDED	HACKERS	HYGIENE	HELLCAT	HALFWIT	HANGERS
HOARDER	HACKETT	HIGHEST	HOLYCOW	HALFWAY	HANKERS
HEAVEHO	HACKING	HIGHHAT	HOLIDAY	HALLWAY	HINDERS
HEADERS	HOCKING	HOGTIED	HOLYDAY	HALCYON	HUNKERS
HEALERS	HECKLED	HOGWILD	HALBERD	HYMNALS	HUNTERS
HEATERS	HECKLER	HOGGING	HELLENE	HOMEBOY	HANDFUL
HEAVENS	HACKLES	HUGGING	HALTERS	HAMPDEN	HANDGUN
HOAXERS	HECKLES	HAGFISH	HELMETS	HUMIDOR	HUNCHED
HEATHEN	HACKMAN	HIGGINS	HELPERS	HIMSELF	HUNCHES
HEATHER	HACKNEY	HAGGLED	HOLDERS	HAMLETS	HANDING
HEADING	HOCKNEY	HAGGLER	HOLLERS	HAMMERS	HANGING
HEALING	HICKORY	HAGGLES	HOLNESS	HAMPERS	HINTING
HEAPING	HICKSON	HOGARTH	HOLIEST	HEMLINE	HUNTING

HANDIER	HOPPING	HERMITS	HOSIERS	HUTCHES	HAWTREY
HANKIES	HOPKIRK	HEROICS	HOSTELS	HATCHET	HOWMUCH
HENGIST	HAPPIER	HURRIES	HOSTESS	HOTSHOT	HOWEVER
HANDILY	HIPPIES	HARPIST	HOSIERY	HITTITE	HEXAGON
HANDLED	HOPKINS	HARRIET	HOSPICE	HOTLINE	HEXAPOD
HINDLEG	HAPPILY	HERRIOT	HOSTILE	HOTWIRE	HAYWARD
HANDLER	HEPATIC	HORRIFY	HUSSITE	HITTING	HOYLAND
HANDLES	HEPBURN	HARIJAN	HASHING	HATPINS	HOYLAKE
HANDLEY	HARVARD	HURDLED	HISSING	HITLIST	HUYGENS
HANGMAN	HERBAGE	HURTLED	HOSTING	HITHOME	HAYWIRE
HANUMAN	HIRECAR	HURDLER	HUSHING	HOTFOOT	HAYRICK
HANDOFF	HARICOT	HERALDS	HASHISH	HOTSPUR	HAYCOCK
HANCOCK	HERSELF	HURDLES	HESSIAN	HOTSPOT	HAYDOCK
HANSOLO	HARLECH	HURTLES	HUSKIER	HAULAGE	HAYLOFT
HENCOOP	HARDENS	HARTLEY	HASKINS	HAUTBOY	HEYJUDE
HANDOUT	HARNESS	HARDMAN	HOSKINS	HOUNDED	HAZIEST
HANGOUT	HORNETS	HARTMAN	HUSKIES	HYUNDAI	HAZARDS
HUNDRED	HARDEST	HORMONE	HUSSIES	HAUTEUR	INAIDOF
HENDRIX	HARVEST	HARPOON	HASTILY	HAUGHTY	IPANEMA
HANDSUP	HERBERT	HARBOUR	HUSKILY	HAULING	IMAGERY
HANDSET	HARMFUL	HARRODS	HASSLED	HOUSING	INANELY
HANDSAW	HURTFUL	HORRORS	HUSTLED	HOUDINI	IRATELY
HONESTY	HORSHAM	HIREOUT	HUSTLER	HAULIER	IVANHOE
HONOURS	HARSHER	HARMONY	HASSLES	HAUNTED	IMAGINE
HINAULT	HARDHAT	HARDPAD	HUSTLES	HOUSTON	IRANIAN
HANOVER	HARSHLY	HORNSEA	HOSANNA	HAVEAGO	ITALIAN
HONEYED	HARRIED	HERETIC	HASSOCK	HAVENOT	ITALICS
HENTZAU	HURRIED	HORATIO	HISTORY	HIVEOFF	INANITY
HOOFERS	HEROINE	HARDTOP	HATBAND	HOVERED	ISADORA
HOOTERS	HIRCINE	HERCULE	HITACHI	HOWDAHS	INABODY
HOOGHLY	HARDING	HIRSUTE	HOTHEAD	HOWMANY	INASPOT
HOOKING	HARKING	HARDWON	HATTERS	HAWKEYE	INAPTLY
HOOTING	HARMING	HURRYUP	HITTERS	HAWKERS	IMBIBED
HOODLUM	HERDING	HORIZON	HOTSEAT	HAWSERS	IMBIBER
HIPBATH	HERRING	HUSBAND	HOTTEST	HOWLERS	IMBIBES
HOPSACK	HURLING	HOSTAGE	HATEFUL	HAWKING	INBREED
HYPEDUP	HURTING	HUSSARS	HATCHED	HOWLING	INBRIEF
HOPHEAD	HARWICH	HUSHABY	HITCHED	HAWKISH	IMBUING
HAPLESS	HEROISM	HASIDIC	HOTSHOE	HAWKINS	INBUILT
HAPPENS	HARDIER	HASBEEN	HATCHER	HGWELLS	IMBRUED
HYPHENS	HARRIER	HUSSEIN	HATCHES	HOWCOME	INBOUND
HOPEFUL	HARRIES	HASTENS	HITCHES	HAWORTH	IMBRUES

INCHECK	IBERIAN	IMHOTEP	INNARDS	IMPERIL	INSERTS
IPCRESS	ICEFLOE	INHOUSE	IONISED	IMPARTS	INSURES
INCLINE	IDEALLY	IMITATE	IONESCO	IMPORTS	INSISTS
INCHING	INERROR	ICINESS	IONISER	IMPOSED	IASKYOU
ITCHING	ICEDTEA	ILIKEIT	IGNITED	IMPASSE	INTRAIN
INCOMES	INERTIA	INITIAL	IGNITES	IMPASTO	INTEARS
INCENSE	INEPTLY	IRIDIUM	IANRUSH	IMPOSES	INTEGER
INCROWD	ICECUBE	ICICLES	IRONAGE	IMPUTED	ISTHMUS
INCISED	ICEOVER	IDIAMIN	ISOLATE	IMPETUS	INTONED
INCISOR	INFLAME	INIRONS	ISOBATH	IMPUTES	INTENSE
INCISES	INFLATE	IDIOTIC	ISOBARS	IMPOUND	INTONER
INCITED	INFECTS	INJECTS	IDOLISE	INPOWER	INTENDS
INCITER	INFIDEL	INJURED	IRONING	INQUEST	INTONES
INCITES	INFIELD	INJURES	IRONIES	INQUIRE	INTROIT
INCLUDE	INFLICT	INKWELL	IVORIES	INQUIRY	INTERIM
INDIANA	INFANTA	INKLING	IRONMAN	INROADS	INTERNS
INDIANS	INFANTS	IRKSOME	IRONORE	ISRAELI	INTRUDE
INDUCED	INFUNDS	INKATHA	ISOTOPE	INRUINS	INTOUCH
INDICES	INFANCY	IRKUTSK	IRONOUT	INSCALE	INTRUTH
INDICTS	INFRONT	ILLFAME	ISOHYET	INSPACE	INUTERO
INDUCES	INFORCE	ILLICIT	INPLACE	INSPATE	INURING
INDULGE	INFERNO	ILLNESS	IMPEACH	INSTALL	IGUANAS
INDENTS	INFORMS	ILLEGAL	IMPLANT	INSTANT	INVADED
INDOORS	INFUSED	ILLWIND	IMPACTS	INSECTS	INVADER
INDEPTH	INFESTS	ILLWILL	IMPEDED	INSIDER	INVADES
INDOUBT	INFUSES	ISLAMIC	IMPEDES	INSIDES	INVOICE
INDEXED	INGRATE	INLIMBO	IMPRESS	INSTEAD	INVEIGH
INDEXER	INGRAIN	ISLANDS	IMPIETY	ISSUERS	INVOKED
INDEXES	INGRAMS	ILLYRIA	IMPLIED	INSPECT	INVOKES
IKEBANA	INGRESS	ILLBRED	IMPAIRS	INSIGHT	INVALID
ICELAND	INGENUE	IMMENSE	IMPLIES	INSPIRE	INVOLVE
IRELAND	IGGYPOP	IMMERSE	IMPRINT	ISSUING	INVENTS
ITERATE	INGESTS	IMMORAL	INPRINT	IPSWICH	INVERSE
ICEPACK	ISHMAEL	INMATES	IMPALED	INSULIN	INVERTS
ICEFALL	INHABIT	IGNOBLE	IMPULSE	INSULAR	INVESTS
INEXACT	INHIBIT	IGNOBLY	IMPALER	INSOLES	INVITED
ICEBERG	ICHDIEN	IANBELL	IMPALES	INSULTS	INVITEE
ICEBEER	INHALED	INNINGS	IMPINGE	INSHORE	INVITRO
ICESHOW	INHALER	IANHOLM	IMPLODE	INSTORE	INVITES
ITEMISE	INHALES	IGNEOUS	IMPLORE	INSIPID	INWARDS
ICEPICK	INHUMAN	IGNORED	IMPROVE	INSURED	IDYLLIC
ICERINK	INHERIT	IGNORES	IMPIOUS	INSURER	JEANNIE

JEALOUS	JOGGERS	JAMELIA	JOSTLES	KIDNEYS	KAMPALA
JOAQUIN	JIGGING	JUMBLED	JITTERS	KIDDING	KIMONOS
JOBRAND	JOGGING	JUMBLES	JOTTERS	KADDISH	KUMQUAT
JABBERS	JIGGLED	JUMANJI	JITTERY	KIDDIES	KENDALL
JOBLESS	JOGGLED	JUMPOFF	JETTING	KNEECAP	KINGCUP
JABBING	JUGGLED	JIMEOIN	JOTTING	KNEADED	KINGDOM
JOBCLUB	JUGGLER	JOMARCH	JUTTING	KIELDER	KENNETH
JUBILEE	JUGULAR	JAMESON	JETTIES	KEEPERS	KINNEAR
JACKALS	JIGGLES	JUMBUCK	JETFOIL	KEENEST	KENNELS
JACKASS	JOGGLES	JANUARY	JOURDAN	KEEPFIT	KINDEST
JACOBIN	JUGGLES	JANKERS	JOURNAL	KHEDIVE	KENNEDY
JACKDEE	JOGTROT	JUNKETS	JOURNEY	KEELING	KINSHIP
JACKDAW	JOHNDOE	JINKING	JOUSTED	KEENING	KINKING
JACKETS	JOHNSON	JUNGIAN	JOUSTER	KEEPING	KENTISH
JOCKEYS	JEHOVAH	JENKINS	JAVELIN	KREMLIN	KINDLED
JACKING	JAILERS	JUNKIES	JAWLINE	KNEELER	KINDLES
JACKLIN	JOINERS	JANGLED	JAWBONE	KEEPMUM	KINSMAN
JOCELYN	JOINERY	JINGLED	JAYWALK	KEEPNET	KINSMEN
JOCULAR	JAILING	JANGLES	JOYLESS	KLEENEX	KENDODD
JACKMAN	JOINING	JINGLES	JOYRIDE	KEEPOFF	KENDONE
JACINTH	JAINISM	JUNGLES	JAZZAGE	KNEEPAD	KINNOCK
JACKPOT	JUICIER	JUNIORS	JEZEBEL	KNEESUP	KINGPIN
JOCASTA	JAIALAI	JUNIPER	JAZZMAN	KNESSET	KINDRED
JACKSON	JOINTED	JONSSON	JAZZMEN	KAFTANS	KINGRAT
JACKTAR	JOINTLY	JANITOR	KNAVERY	KLINGON	KINESIS
JACQUES	JUJITSU	JONQUIL	KEATING	KRISHNA	KINETIC
JACUZZI	JUKEBOX	JUPITER	KNAVISH	KNIGHTS	KINTYRE
JADEDLY	JAKARTA	JURYBOX	KRAVITZ	KNIFING	KINGZOG
JUDAEAN	JELLIED	JERICHO	KNACKER	KNITTED	KNOWALL
JUDDERS	JILTING	JERSEYS	KLAXONS	KRISTIN	KNOBBLY
JUDDERY	JOLTING	JARRING	KNAPPED	KNITTER	KNOWHOW
JUDGING	JOLLIER	JERKING	KNAPPER	KOIZUMI	KNOWING
JUDAISM	JELLIES	JERBOAS	KHAMSIN	KIKIDEE	KNOCKED
JUDELAW	JOLLITY	JESTERS	KABADDI	KILDARE	KNOCKON
JODURIE	JIMDALE	JESSICA	KOBLENZ	KULTARR	KNOCKUP
JEEPERS	JAMJARS	JASMINE	KUBRICK	KILLEEN	KNOCKER
JEERING	JIMJAMS	JUSTICE	KIBBUTZ	KILLERS	KNOWLES
JEFFREY	JUMPERS	JUSTINE	KICKERS	KILLING	KNOTTED
JUGBAND	JAMAICA	JESTING	KICKING	KELPIES	KIPPERS
JAGUARS	JAMMING	JESUITS	KICKOFF	KILLJOY	KIPLING
JIGSAWS	JUMPING	JUSTIFY	KICKOUT	KILOTON	KIPPING
JOGRANT	JUMPJET	JOSTLED	KIDNAPS	KILBURN	KURSAAL

KOREANS	KEYNOTE	LOBWORM	LECTURE	LUGGING	LPLATES
KARACHI	KEYGRIP	LIBERIA	LACQUER	LOGGINS	LSLOWRY
KERNELS	KRYPTON	LIBERAL	LADYDAY	LEGSLIP	LAMBADA
KERSHAW	LEAKAGE	LIBERTY	LADDERS	LEGALLY	LAMPARD
KARTING	LEANDER	LOBSTER	LEDGERS	LEGUMES	LOMBARD
KURDISH	LEAVEGO	LABOURS	LODGERS	LEGENDS	LIMEADE
KARELIA	LLANERO	LUCIANO	LUDDITE	LUGHOLE	LUMBAGO
KARAOKE	LEADERS	LUCIDLY	LODGING	LEGWORK	LAMBAST
KARLOFF	LEAVENS	LECTERN	LADDISH	LOGBOOK	LUMIERE
KIRSTIE	LOADERS	LACKEYS	LUDDISM	LEGROOM	LAMBETH
KERATIN	LOAFERS	LICHENS	LYDFORD	LUGWORM	LIMPETS
KIRSTEN	LEANEST	LOCKERS	LEDERER	LEGHORN	LUMBERS
KEROUAC	LOATHED	LOCKETS	LADETTE	LAGOONS	LAMBENT
KASBAHS	LEATHER	LYCHEES	LEEWARD	LEGIONS	LAMBERT
KISSING	LEASHES	LECHERY	LEEMACK	LEGSPIN	LAMBING
KESWICK	LOATHES	LUCIFER	LEECHES	LIGURIA	LEMMING
KASHMIR	LEADING	LACKING	LEETIDE	LIGHTED	LIMPING
KASTNER	LEAKING	LICKING	LEEMING	LIGHTEN	LUMPISH
KESTREL	LEANING	LOCKING	LEERING	LIGHTUP	LUMPIER
KOSOVAN	LEAPING	LUCKIER	LIEDOWN	LIGHTER	LUMUMBA
KITSCHY	LEASING	LUCKILY	LLEYTON	LIGATES	LAMENTS
KATYDID	LEAVING	LOCKJAW	LAERTES	LIGHTLY	LAMPOON
KITTENS	LOADING	LUCILLE	LIFTING	LEGPULL	LIMEPIT
KITCHEN	LOAFING	LACHLAN	LUFFING	LEHMANN	LAMPREY
KETCHUP	LOANING	LUCYLIU	LOFTIER	LEHAVRE	LUMPSUM
KUTCHER	LEAFLET	LOCALLY	LEFTIST	LOITERS	LIMITED
KETCHES	LEARNED	LUCINDA	LOFTILY	LYINGIN	LANTANA
KATRINA	LEARNER	LACONIC	LEFTOFF	LEIBNIZ	LANYARD
KITTING	LEAKOUT	LICENCE	LIFTOFF	LAIDOFF	LINEAGE
KETTLES	LIAISED	LICENSE	LEFTOUT	LEITRIM	LINKAGE
KETELBY	LIAISON	LOCKNUT	LAFORGE	LEISURE	LONGAGO
KETTLEY	LIAISES	LUCKNOW	LAGGARD	LEIPZIG	LONGBOW
KATHRYN	LEANTOS	LACTOSE	LUGGAGE	LIKEMAD	LINOCUT
KRUEGER	LEAGUES	LOCKOUT	LEGIBLE	LIKENED	LANGDON
KNUCKLE	LEBLANC	LACROIX	LEGIBLY	LIKENED	LINEDUP
KUWAITI	LIBRARY	LECARRE	LOGICAL	LOLLARD	LINSEED
KOWLOON	LUBBERS	LUCERNE	LEGLESS	LULLABY	LANTERN
KOWTOWS	LOBBING	LOCARNO	LUGGERS	LOLLING	LANCERS
KEYCARD	LIBRIUM	LOCUSTS	LIGNITE	LILLIAN	LANCETS
KEYRING	LOBBIES	LOCATED	LOGFIRE	LOLLIES	LENDERS
KEYWORD	LOBELIA	LOCATES	LAGGING	LOLLOPS	LINGERS
KEYHOLE	LEBANON	LICITLY	LOGGING	LILYPAD	LINNETS

LINTELS	LANGUOR	LURCHER	LATCHES	LOVEJOY	MOABITE
LENIENT	LEONARD	LARCHES	LATRINE	LIVINIA	MEANING
LONGEST	LEOPARD	LURCHES	LATTICE	LAVERNE	MOANING
LUNGFUL	LEOTARD	LARDING	LETTING	LIVORNO	MEATIER
LYNCHED	LOOFAHS	LURKING	LITHIUM	LEVERET	MEALIES
LYNEHAM	LIONCUB	LERWICK	LATVIAN	LOWLAND	MEASLES
LONGHOP	LIONESS	LORRIES	LETSLIP	LOWPAID	MYANMAR
LUNCHES	LOOSENS	LORDJIM	LETINON	LOWTECH	MEADOWS
LYNCHES	LOOTERS	LORELEI	LATENCY	LAWLESS	MEASURE
LANCING	LOOSEST	LARAMIE	LETDOWN	LAWYERS	MIAOWED
LANDING	LOOSELY	LORIMAR	LOTIONS	LOWLIFE	MCBRIDE
LANSING	LEONINE	LARONDE	LETUPON	LOWRISE	MOBBING
LENDING	LIONISE	LORENZO	LATERAL	LOWTIDE	MOBSTER
LINKING	LOOKING	LORETTA	LITERAL	LAWFORD	MOBRULE
LONGING	LOOMING	LDRIVER	LATERON	LAWLORD	MACRAME
LUNGING	LOOPING	LASCALA	LITURGY	LOWDOWN	MICHAEL
LANKIER	LOOTING	LESPAUL	LETSSAY	LOWERED	MECCANO
LENTILS	LEONIAN	LASCARS	LETITIA	LOWBROW	MACABRE
LINEKER	LEOPOLD	LESSENS	LETITBE	LAWSUIT	MACADAM
LONGLEG	LOOKOUT	LESSEPS	LITOTES	LEXICAL	MACHETE
LANOLIN	LOOKSEE	LISTENS	LETTUCE	LEXICON	MACBETH
LENGLEN	LEONTES	LUSTFUL	LAUNDER	LAXNESS	MACLEAN
LINEMAN	LAPLAND	LASAGNE	LOURDES	LAYBARE	MOCKERY
LINKMAN	LIPREAD	LASHING	LAUNDRY	LAYODDS	MACHINE
LINKMEN	LAPPING	LASTING	LOUREED	LOYALLY	MOCKING
LONGMAN	LAPSING	LESSING	LAURENT	LOYALTY	MUCKIER
LINFORD	LAPWING	LISPING	LOUDEST	LAYDOWN	MRCHIPS
LANCOME	LOPPING	LISTING	LOUNGED	LAYERED	MYCELLA
LONGOFF	LEPANTO	LUSTILY	LOUNGER	LAYETTE	MCCLOUD
LINCOLN	LAPDOGS	LISMORE	LOUNGES	LIZDAWN	MICROBE
LINEOUT	LEPROSY	LESSONS	LAUGHED	LAZYEYE	MACCOLL
LINDSAY	LIPSYNC	LOSEOUT	LAUGHIN	LAZIEST	MYCROFT
LUNATIC	LIQUEUR	LUSARDI	LAUDING	LOZENGE	MACAQUE
LUNETTE	LIQUEFY	LUSTRUM	LOURING	LAZENBY	MACGRAW
LYNETTE	LIQUIDS	LESOTHO	LOUTISH	LAZARUS	MYCOSIS
LANGTON	LARIATS	LISBURN	LOUVRED	LIZARDS	MACDUFF
LENGTHS	LYRICAL	LATHERS	LOUVRES	MBABANE	MCCOURT
LINCTUS	LARDERS	LETTERS	LIVEAID	MIANDAD	MIDLAND
LANGTRY	LARGEST	LITTERS	LOVABLE	MEANDER	MEDIATE
LENGTHY	LARCENY	LATHERY	LIVEDIN	MOANERS	MUDBATH
LANGUID	LARGELY	LOTTERY	LAVIGNE	MEANEST	MUDBANK
LINGUAL	LURCHED	LATCHED	LEVYING	MYALGIA	MUDLARK

MUDPACK	MAEWEST	MOHICAN	MULLETS	MIMICRY	MONKEES
MEDLARS	MEEKEST	MAHONIA	MILDEST	MEMBERS	MONKEYS
MEDICAL	MEETING	MAHJONG	MULLETT	MUMMERS	MANTEAU
MODICUM	MEERKAT	MRHAPPY	MILDEWY	MUMMERY	MINDFUL
MEDICOS	MCENROE	MAHATMA	MALIGNS	MRMAGOO	MANAGUA
MIDWEEK	MAESTRO	MAHOUTS	MALAISE	MCMAHON	MANAGED
MADKEEN	MUEZZIN	MAILBAG	MALTING	MEMPHIS	MINOGUE
MADDENS	MIFFING	MAILBOX	MELDING	MEMOIRS	MANAGER
MADNESS	MUFFINS	MAIDENS	MELTING	MUMMIES	MANAGES
MIDGETS	MUFFLED	MAILING	MILKING	MUMMIFY	MUNCHED
MADDEST	MUFFLER	MAIMING	MILLING	MUMBLED	MENTHOL
MIDWEST	MUFFLES	MAILLOT	MULLING	MUMBLES	MUNCHES
MADIGAN	MRFUNNY	MAILMAN	MILLION	MEMENTO	MONTHLY
MIDSHIP	MAFIOSI	MAILMEN	MULLION	MCMANUS	MANKIND
MADEIRA	MAFIOSO	MOIDORE	MOLLIFY	MOMENTS	MANNING
MUDDIED	MRFUSSY	MAIGRET	MILKMAN	MAMMOTH	MENDING
MIDWIFE	MAGNATE	MEISSEN	MILKMEN	MYMUSIC	MINCING
MIDRIFF	MIGRATE	MEIOSIS	MELINDA	MANDALA	MINDING
MADDING	MCGRATH	MOISTEN	MELANGE	MONTANA	MINGING
MIDWICH	MIGRANT	MAILVAN	MELANIE	MANDATE	MONKISH
MUDDIER	MAGICAL	MRJAMES	MELANIN	MANMADE	MANCINI
MIDDLEC	MOGADON	MRJINKS	MALONEY	MONTAGE	MANSION
MEDDLED	MAGNETO	MAJORCA	MOLDOVA	MUNDANE	MENTION
MUDDLED	MAGNETS	MAJESTY	MILFOIL	MANJACK	MENDIPS
MUDFLAP	MUGGERS	MIKHAIL	MALCOLM	MANIACS	MENZIES
MEDDLER	MUGSHOT	MCKENNA	MELLOWS	MANUALS	MUNTJAC
MODULAR	MCGUIRE	MALLARD	MILHOUS	MINIBAR	MONIKER
MEDDLES	MUGGING	MILLAND	MALARIA	MINIBUS	MANGLED
MIDDLES	MAGPIES	MILEAGE	MILDRED	MINICAB	MINGLED
MODULES	MOGGIES	MALLAIG	MELDRUM	MENACED	MANGLES
MODULUS	MUGGINS	MILLAIS	MCLAREN	MANACLE	MINGLES
MUDDLES	MAGNIFY	MULLAHS	MILKRUN	MONOCLE	MANILOW
MADELEY	MUGGLES	MALABAR	MELDREW	MINICAM	MONSMEG
MADEMAN	MAGENTA	MILKBAR	MELISSA	MENACES	MINIMAL
MADONNA	MAGINOT	MALACHI	MILKSOP	MANXCAT	MINIMUM
MODCONS	MAGGOTS	MELODIC	MOLESTS	MANDELA	MANXMAN
MIDIRON	MAGGOTY	MALTESE	MALMSEY	MANSELL	MENDOZA
MODISTE	MEGATON	MOLIERE	MILITIA	MANGERS	MANHOOD
MADISON	MUGWUMP	MALVERN	MOLOTOV	MANNERS	MANHOLE
MODESTY	MAGNUMS	MULLEIN	MOLLUSC	MENDERS	MENFOLK
MEDIUMS	MCGOWAN	MALLETS	MILBURN	MINCERS	MONSOON
MOESBAR	MEGRYAN	MILLERS	MAMMALS	MINDERS	MANHOUR

MANGOES	MAPLINS	MORAINE	MARJORY	MISTIME	METHANE
MENTORS	MAPBOOK	MORTISE	MARISSA	MASTIFF	MUTABLE
MINIONS	MCQUEEN	MARKING	MERITED	MASHING	MATADOR
MINNOWS	MIQUITA	MARRING	MARITAL	MASKING	MATHERS
MONGOLS	MARSALA	MERGING	MARQUEE	MASSING	MATTERS
MENSREA	MERMAID	MORNING	MARAUDS	MESHING	MITTENS
MINERVA	MARGATE	MOREISH	MARQUES	MESSING	MOTHERS
MINORCA	MURRAIN	MARTINI	MARQUIS	MISSING	MUTTERS
MENORAH	MARRANO	MERRICK	MURMURS	MESSIAH	MATCHED
MONARCH	MORTALS	MARTIAL	MERCURY	MISKICK	MITCHUM
MINERAL	MORTARS	MARXISM	MORAVIA	MISDIAL	MATCHES
MONGREL	MORDANT	MARTIAN	MARTYRS	MISSION	MATTHAU
MANTRAP	MARABOU	MERRION	MARRYAT	MESSIER	MATTHEW
MINARET	MIRACLE	MARNIER	MASCARA	MISTIER	MATTING
MINDSET	MOROCCO	MERRIER	MISLAID	MISFITS	METRICS
MINUTED	MARACAS	MURKIER	MUSTARD	MOSAICS	MATILDA
MANATEE	MARSDEN	MARGINS	MASSAGE	MYSTICS	MOTTLED
MINETTE	MIRADOR	MARRIES	MCSHANE	MESSILY	MATELOT
MINSTER	MARLENE	MARTINS	MESSAGE	MYSTIFY	MATINEE
MONITOR	MORPETH	MARXIST	MISTAKE	MYSHKIN	MUTANTS
MONSTER	MARTELL	MERRILY	MRSDALE	MOSELLE	MITFORD
MUNSTER	MARVELL	MORTIFY	MUSTANG	MUSCLES	MATLOCK
MINUTES	MORRELL	MURKILY	MISLAYS	MASONIC	MATTOCK
MANITOU	MARKERS	MORELIA	MISSALS	MASONRY	MATRONS
MANHUNT	MARKETS	MARBLED	MISCAST	MISTOOK	METEORS
MINIVER	MARVELS	MARILYN	MUSICAL	MRSPOCK	METHODS
MONEYED	MERGERS	MORELLO	MISDEED	MRSMOPP	MOTIONS
MIOCENE	MORSELS	MARBLES	MISLEAD	MASCOTS	MOTTOES
MOOCHED	MURDERS	MYRTLES	MISREAD	MISSOUT	MATURED
MOORHEN	MARCEAU	MARTLET	MISDEAL	MUSCOVY	MOTORED
MOOCHES	MIRAGES	MORALLY	MASSEUR	MISTRAL	MOTTRAM
MOORING	MRRIGHT	MARIMBA	MISHEAR	MUSKRAT	MATURES
MOORISH	MARCHED	MIRANDA	MASTERS	MISERLY	MATISSE
MOODIER	MARSHAL	MARINER	MUSSELS	MESSTIN	MUTATED
MOOMINS	MARCHER	MARINES	MUSTERS	MISCUED	MUTATES
MOONIES	MARCHES	MARLOWE	MASTERY	MISRULE	MOTIVES
MOODILY	MARSHES	MARKOFF	MYSTERY	MASQUES	MOULDED
MOONLIT	MARTHAS	MURDOCH	MESSINA	MISCUES	MAUNDER
MOPPETS	MARTINA	MARCONI	MASSIVE	MOSQUES	MOULDER
MUPPETS	MARRIED	MARMOTS	MISFIRE	MUSEUMS	MAUREEN
MAPPING	MARMITE	MARROWS	MISSILE	MOSEYED	MOUSERS
MOPPING	MARTINE	MIRRORS	MISSIVE	MISTYPE	MOUTHED

MAUGHAM	NIBLICK	NIGERIA	NONDRIP	NESTING	NATIVES
MAUGHAN	NABOKOV	NEGATED	NANETTE	NOSHING	NOUVEAU
MAURIAC	NIBBLED	NIGHTIE	NONSTOP	NASTIER	NAUGHTY
MAURICE	NOBBLED	NEGATES	NONSUCH	NESBITT	NOURISH
MAULING	NEBULAE	NIGHTLY	NINEVEH	NASTILY	NEUTRAL
MAUDLIN	NEBULAR	NOHOPER	NUNAVUT	NOSEJOB	NEUTRON
MOURNED	NIBBLES	NAIVETE	NOONDAY	NESTLED	NOVICES
MOURNER	NOBBLES	NAILERY	NOODLES	NESTLES	NAVVIES
MOULTED	NICOBAR	NAIVELY	NEPHEWS	NOSTRIL	NOVELLA
MOUNTED	NUCLEAR	NAIVETY	NIPPERS	NOSTRUM	NEVILLE
MOUNTIE	NICKELS	NEILFOX	NAPPING	NITRATE	NOVELLI
MOVABLE	NUCLEUS	NEIGHED	NIPPING	NUTCASE	NOVELLO
MOVEDIN	NECKING	NEITHER	NUPTIAL	NOTHALF	NOVELTY
MOVEOUT	NICKING	NAILING	NAPKINS	NETBALL	NAVARRE
MAWKISH	NACELLE	NOISIER	NAPPIES	NOTABLE	NOVOTNA
MAXWALL	NICOLAS	NOISILY	NAPHTHA	NOTABLY	NEWLAID
MEXICAN	NICHOLS	NOISOME	NAPSTER	NOTICED	NEWGATE
MIXEDIN	NICOSIA	NAIROBI	NEPTUNE	NOTICES	NEWWAVE
MIXEDUP	NECKTIE	NULLIFY	NIRVANA	NATTERS	NEWSBOY
MAXWELL	NODDING	NELSONS	NARRATE	NOTCHED	NOWHERE
MAXILLA	NUDGING	NILSSON	NORMANS	NOTCHES	NEWDEAL
MAXIMUM	NODULAR	NUMBATS	NURSERY	NETTING	NEWYEAR
MIXTURE	NUDISTS	NAMIBIA	NUROFEN	NOTHING	NEWNESS
MAYNARD	NODOUBT	NOMADIC	NARWHAL	NOTTING	NOWTHEN
MAYFAIR	NEEDFUL	NAMEDAY	NURDING	NITPICK	NEWLOOK
MAYPOLE	NEEDING	NUMBERS	NURSING	NUTTIER	NEWYORK
MAYORAL	NEEDIER	NYMPHET	NORWICH	NITWITS	NEWBORN
MUZZLED	NEEDILY	NUMBING	NKRUMAH	NATTILY	NEWMOON
MUZZLES	NEEDLED	NOMINEE	NORFOLK	NETTLED	NEWTOWN
MAZURKA	NEEDLES	NOMINAL	NARROWS	NATALIE	NEWPORT
NIAGARA	NIELSEN	NUMERAL	NERVOUS	NETTLES	NEWBURY
NUANCES	NOENTRY	NEMESIA	NERISSA	NOTELET	NEWQUAY
NEASDEN	NIFTIER	NAMASTE	NURTURE	NUTWOOD	NOXIOUS
NEATENS	NIGGARD	NEMESIS	NUREYEV	NUTLOAF	NUZZLED
NEAREST	NAGGERS	NANKEEN	NASTASE	NETWORK	NOZZLES
NEATEST	NUGGETS	NUNNERY	NESCAFE	NATIONS	NUZZLES
NEARING	NEGLECT	NONAGON	NOSEBAG	NITROUS	OFANAGE
NUBIANS	NAGGING	NANNIES	NESTEGG	NOTIONS	ONANDON
NABUCCO	NIGELLA	NINNIES	NASCENT	NOTEPAD	ONAGERS
NOBLEST	NIGGLED	NUNCIOS	NOSIEST	NATURAL	OTALGIA
NABBING	NIGGLES	NONPLUS	NOSWEAT	NATASHA	ORANGES
NEBBISH	NEGRONI	NINEPIN	NOSEGAY	NETSUKE	OCARINA

OFAKIND	OPERATE	OFFHAND	OAKWOOD	OPPOSES	OUTLINE
OPALINE	OVERAGE	OFFICER	OILLAMP	OURLADY	OUTLIVE
ORATING	OVERATE	OFFICES	OILCANS	OGREISH	OUTSIZE
OMARION	OVERAWE	OFFPEAK	ORLEANS	OARSMAN	OSTRICH
ORATION	OVERALL	OFFBEAM	OILSEED	OARSMEN	ONTRIAL
OVATION	OVERARM	OFFBEAT	OILWELL	OARLOCK	OBTAINS
OPACITY	OREGANO	OFFLINE	OBLIGED	OERSTED	OUTBIDS
OHANLON	OPENAIR	OFFSIDE	OBLIGES	ONSTAGE	OUTFITS
ORATORS	OPERANT	OFFENCE	OILRIGS	OSSUARY	OUTWITS
ORATORY	OVERACT	OFFENDS	OILSKIN	OSSICLE	ORTOLAN
ORATRIX	OVERBID	OFFLOAD	OBLOMOV	OBSCENE	OUTFLOW
ONASSIS	OVERDUB	OFFROAD	ORLANDO	OYSTERS	OUTPLAY
ONBOARD	OVERDID	OFFSPIN	OBLONGS	OUSTING	OPTIMAL
OSBORNE	OVERDUE	OFFERED	OBLIQUE	ONSHORE	OPTIMUM
ORBISON	OPENDAY	OFFERER	OBLOQUY	OSSEOUS	OTTOMAN
ORBITED	ONESELF	ONGOING	OILDRUM	OBSERVE	OUTINGS
ORBITAL	ONENESS	ORGANZA	OHMSLAW	OBSCURE	OUTLOUD
ORBITER	OPENERS	ORGANIC	OSMONDS	OUTLAND	OUTSOLD
ORCHARD	OVEREAT	OOHLALA	OSMOSIS	OUTWARD	OUTCOME
ORCHIDS	OVERFED	OPHELIA	OMNIBUS	OATCAKE	OUTDONE
OCCIPUT	OVERFLY	OTHELLO	OWNEDUP	OUTFACE	OUTDONE
OCCLUDE	ONETIME	OKINAWA	OWNGOAL	OUTPACE	OUTVOTE
OLDHAND	OBEYING	ORIGAMI	ODORANT	OUTRAGE	OUTLOOK
OLDMAID	OPENING	OXIDANT	ONORDER	OUTTAKE	OUTWORN
ODDBALL	OBELISK	OWINGTO	OKONEDO	OUTBACK	OUTDOOR
ORDEALS	OBESITY	ORIFICE	ONOFFER	OUTRANK	OPTIONS
OLDBEAN	OVERLAP	OXIDISE	OXONIAN	OUTFALL	OUTDOES
ODDNESS	OVERLAY	OPINING	OCONNOR	OUTLAWS	OUTPOST
ODDMENT	OVERMAN	OPINION	OLOROSO	OUTCAST	OCTUPLE
OLDSHEP	OCEANIA	OLIVIER	ODOROUS	OUTKAST	OUTSPAN
OLDTIME	OCEANIC	ORIGINS	OTOLOGY	OUTLAST	OCTOPUS
OLDNICK	OCELOTS	ORIOLES	OPOSSUM	OCTOBER	ONTARIO
OLDBILL	ONEROUS	ORINOCO	OBOISTS	OPTICAL	OUTCROP
OLDGIRL	OPENOUT	OMINOUS	OROTUND	OATMEAL	OUTGREW
ORDAINS	OVERPAY	ORISONS	ORPHANS	OUTSELL	OUTGROW
ORDINAL	OVERRAN	OMICRON	OPPRESS	ONTHEGO	OUTTRAY
OLDGOLD	OVERRUN	OMITTED	ORPHEUS	ONTHEUP	OUTSTAY
OEDIPUS	OVERSEE	OPIATES	OSPREYS	OUTWEAR	OBTRUDE
ORDERED	OVERSAW	OVIDUCT	ORPHISM	OSTLERS	OUTTURN
ORDERLY	ONESTEP	OBJECTS	ONPAPER	OUTLETS	OCTAVIA
OLDSTER	OVERTLY	OAKLAND	OPPOSED	OUTOFIT	OCTAVES
OPERAND	OVERUSE	OAKLING	OPPOSER	OCTAGON	OUTSWIM

OVULATE	PEALING	PLAGUES	PEDLARS	PREFERS	PRESSES
OPUSDEI	PLACING	PLAQUES	PADDING	PRESETS	PLECTRA
OPULENT	PLANING	PHARYNX	PUDDING	PRECEPT	PLEATED
OCULIST	PLATING	PIAZZAS	PADRINO	PREFECT	PRESTON
OBVIATE	PLAYING	PUBLISH	PODGIER	PREHEAT	PRELUDE
ORVILLE	PRAYING	PEBBLED	PADDIES	PRESENT	PRESUME
OBVIOUS	PLATINI	PABULUM	PADDLED	PRETEXT	PREQUEL
OBVERSE	PLACIDO	PEBBLES	PEDDLED	PREVENT	PIEEYED
ONWARDS	PRATIES	PUBERTY	PADDLER	PLEDGED	PREZZIE
OXYGENE	PIANIST	POCHARD	PADDLES	PLEDGES	PRETZEL
OLYMPIA	PEARLED	PACKAGE	PEDALOS	PRECISE	POFACED
OLYMPIC	PHARLAP	PICKAXE	PEDDLES	PREMISE	PUFFERS
OLYMPUS	PLAYLET	PECCARY	PUDDLES	PRESIDE	PUFFING
ODYSSEY	PLANNED	PACECAR	PEDANTS	PUERILE	PUFFIER
PLACARD	PLAINER	PICADOR	PADRONE	PEEKING	PUFFINS
PLACATE	PLANNER	PACKERS	PADDOCK	PEELING	PUGWASH
PHARAOH	PLAINLY	PACKETS	PADLOCK	PEEPING	PIGTAIL
PEASANT	PIANOLA	PICKETS	PADSTOW	PEERING	PAGEANT
PLAYACT	PLAYOFF	POCKETS	PIEBALD	PEEVING	PAGEBOY
PHALANX	PEACOCK	PUCKERS	PREPAID	PEEVISH	PAGODAS
PEATBOG	PEAFOWL	PACIEST	PEERAGE	PREMIUM	PIGSEAR
PLAYBOY	PLATOON	PICKETT	PREDATE	PREMIER	PIGLETS
PRANCED	PEASOUP	PACIFIC	PREFACE	PEEWITS	PIGMENT
PRANCER	PEACOAT	PECKHAM	PRELATE	POETICS	PIGGERY
PRANCES	PLAYPEN	PACKICE	PREPARE	PRELIMS	PEGGING
PLAUDIT	PRAIRIE	PACKING	PRESAGE	PREDICT	PIGLING
PLACEBO	PRAISED	PECKING	PREWASH	PREVIEW	PIGGISH
PEAHENS	PEARSON	PICKING	PREVAIL	PUEBLOS	PIGGIES
PLANETS	PRAISES	PECKISH	PREFABS	PRESLEY	PYGMIES
PLATERS	PLASTIC	PUCKISH	PREPAYS	PREEMPT	PIGSKIN
PLAYERS	PLANTED	PUCCINI	PRECAST	PREENED	PIGEONS
PRAYERS	PIASTRE	PICNICS	PLENARY	PFENNIG	PIGGOTT
PLATEAU	PRATTLE	PICKLED	PIERCED	PEELOFF	PIGIRON
PLAYFUL	PHANTOM	PICKLER	PIERCES	PRECOOK	PEGASUS
PLAYGOD	PHAETON	PICKLES	PREACHY	PREFORM	PAHLAVI
POACHED	PLANTER	PACKMAN	PLEADED	PREVOST	PRIMATE
PEACHUM	PLASTER	PUCKOON	PRETEND	PIERROT	PRIVATE
POACHER	PLATTER	PICCOLO	PRECEDE	PLEASED	PRIMACY
PEACHES	PRAETOR	PICKOUT	PEELERS	PRESSED	PRIMARY
POACHES	PSALTER	PICARDY	PEEPERS	PRESSON	PRIVACY
PRALINE	PLAGUED	PICASSO	PEERESS	PRESSUP	PLIABLE
PEAKING	PEANUTS	PICTURE	POETESS	PLEASES	PHILBIN

PRINCES	PALMATE	PILLORY	PENNANT	PENCILS	PHONEIN
PRIMERS	PALPATE	PILGRIM	PANACEA	PENNIES	PROTEIN
PRIVETS	PILLAGE	PALERMO	PANACHE	PINKIES	PIONEER
PAINFUL	POLEAXE	PELORUS	PANICKY	PINNIES	PLOVERS
PRITHEE	PULSATE	POLARIS	PINHEAD	PONTIUS	PROCESS
PAIRING	POLDARK	PALTROW	PANDERS	PUNDITS	PROFESS
PRIMING	POLLACK	PALFREY	PANZERS	PENALTY	PROPELS
PRISING	PILLARS	PELISSE	PINCERS	PENANCE	PROTEUS
PRIZING	PULSARS	POLITIC	PONDERS	PINENUT	PROWESS
POITIER	PILLBOX	PILOTED	PUNNETS	PANDORA	POOREST
PRICKED	POLICED	PALETTE	PUNTERS	PENFOLD	PROJECT
PRICKLE	PELICAN	PELOTON	PENDENT	PINFOLD	PROTECT
PHILKAY	PALACES	PALMTOP	PINKETT	PENROSE	PROTEST
PRICKLY	POLECAT	PILATES	PINSENT	PINHOLE	PROGENY
PHILLIP	PALADIN	PALETOT	PUNGENT	PINDOWN	PTOLEMY
PAISLEY	PALLETS	POLLTAX	PUNIEST	PONTOON	PROOFED
PLIANCY	PELLETS	POLLUTE	PINKGIN	PENNONS	PROFFER
PAIDOFF	PELMETS	PALAVER	PINCHED	PINIONS	PRONGED
PAIROFF	PILFERS	PHLOXES	PUNCHED	PANOPLY	PLOUGHS
POISONS	POLDERS	PALMYRA	PYNCHON	PENARTH	POOCHES
PRISONS	PULLETS	PALAZZO	PUNCHUP	PANCRAS	PROPHET
PAIDOUT	PULLEYS	POMPEII	PANTHER	PINETUM	PROFILE
PRIAPUS	PELAGIC	PAMPERS	PINCHES	PUNSTER	PROMISE
PRIORTO	POLYGON	PUMMELS	PUNCHES	PINGUID	PROVIDE
PRIESTS	PALLING	PUMPING	PONTIAC	PENGUIN	PHONING
PAINTED	PELTING	PIMLICO	PANTILE	PRORATA	POOLING
POINTED	POLLING	POMMIES	PENNINE	PROSAIC	PROBING
PRINTED	PULLING	PUMPKIN	PENSIVE	PROBATE	PROVING
PHILTRE	PALLIUM	PIMPLED	PONTIFF	PROFANE	PROVISO
PAINTER	PILLION	PIMPLES	PANNING	PROPANE	PEONIES
POINTER	PULPITS	PIMENTO	PANTING	POOHBAH	PHOBIAS
PRINTER	PALMIST	POMPOMS	PENDING	POORBOX	PHONICS
PLINTHS	POLEMIC	POMPOUS	PINKING	POORCOW	PROFITS
PRIMULA	PULLMAN	PANCAKE	PINNING	PLODDED	PROBITY
PDJAMES	POLYMER	PENNAME	PONTING	PRODDED	PRODIGY
PYJAMAS	POLENTA	PINNACE	PUNNING	PROUDIE	PROPJET
PAKCHOI	PALOOKA	PINNATE	PENRITH	PLODDER	PLONKER
PIKELET	PILLOCK	PUNJABI	PINKISH	PROUDLY	PROWLED
PIKEMAN	POLLOCK	PINBALL	PENSION	PROVERB	PROBLEM
POKEMON	PILLOWS	PINTAIL	PANNIER	PROCEED	PROWLER
POLLARD	PULLOUT	PINTADO	PANSIES	PHONEME	POODLES
PALEALE	PALJOEY	PENDANT	PANTIES	PROTEGE	PHOENIX

PROMOTE	PAPYRUS	PERIGEE	PERLMAN	PERFUME	PISTOLS
PROPOSE	PAPISTS	PIROGUE	PORTMAN	PERJURE	PISTONS
PROVOKE	PUPATED	PARAGON	PIRANHA	PURSUER	PASSOUT
PROLONG	PIPETTE	PYRRHIC	PARSNIP	PURSUES	PUSHROD
PRONOUN	PUPATES	PARCHED	PARTNER	PURSUIT	POSITED
PHOTONS	POPEYED	PERCHED	PARENTS	PARQUET	PESETAS
PROVOST	PAPAYAS	PARCHES	PARINGS	PERJURY	PASTURE
PROSODY	PIQUANT	PERCHES	PERGOLA	PERTWEE	POSTURE
PLOPPED	PIQUING	PORCHES	PERSONA	PERIWIG	POSEURS
PROPPED	PARTAKE	PORTHOS	PURPOSE	PARKWAY	POSSUMS
PROSPER	PERCALE	PERDITA	PARTOOK	PYREXIA	POSTWAR
PROMPTS	PERVADE	PARRIED	PARBOIL	PYREXIC	PETHATE
PROGRAM	PERTAIN	PORCINE	PERFORM	PARTYTO	PETNAME
PIOUSLY	PARIAHS	PARKING	PURLOIN	PASSATA	POTTAGE
PLOTTED	PERHAPS	PARSING	PARLOUR	PASSAGE	PATCASH
PLOTTER	PORTALS	PARTING	PARDONS	POSTAGE	PITFALL
PROCTOR	PARFAIT	PERMING	PARLOUS	POSTBAG	POTABLE
PROCURE	PARABLE	PURGING	PARROTS	POSTBOX	POTSDAM
PRODUCE	PORSCHE	PURRING	PARSONS	PASTERN	POTHERB
PROFUSE	PARODIC	PORCINI	PERIODS	PISCEAN	PITHEAD
PRODUCT	PARADED	PARTIAL	PERSONS	POSTERN	PATTERN
PEPPARD	PARADES	PERDIEM	PURPORT	PASTEUR	PETRELS
PEPTALK	PARADIS	PERMIAN	PORKPIE	PASTELS	POTTERS
POPLARS	PERIDOT	PERSIAN	PARAPET	PESTERS	PUTTEES
POPIDOL	PARADOX	PORTION	PERSPEX	POSSESS	PUTTERS
POPADUM	PORTEND	PORTICO	PORTREE	POSTERS	PATIENT
PEPPERS	PURCELL	PERKIER	PORTRAY	PASCHAL	POTTERY
POPPERS	PARCELS	PERRIER	PERUSED	PASSIVE	PUTREFY
POPPETS	PARLEYS	PARRIES	PARASOL	PASTIME	PITIFUL
PUPPETS	PARSECS	PARTIES	PERUSAL	PISCINE	PATCHED
PEPPERY	PIRAEUS	PERKINS	PHRASAL	PASSING	PITCHED
PAPRIKA	PORKERS	PERMITS	PERUSER	PASTING	PITCHIN
POPPING	PORTERS	PORKIES	PERUSES	POSTING	PATCHUP
PEPPILL	PURSERS	PERSIST	PHRASES	PUSHING	PETSHOP
POPPIES	PURVEYS	PURLIEU	PURISTS	PASSION	PITCHER
POPPINS	PARRETT	PERFIDY	PARATHA	PASTIES	PATCHES
PUPPIES	PERCENT	PERKILY	PIRATED	PUSHILY	PITCHES
PAPILLA	PERCEPT	PAROLED	PURITAN	PUSHKIN	POTSHOT
POPULAR	PERFECT	PAROLES	PIRATES	PASSKEY	PATTING
PAPOOSE	PERVERT	PERPLEX	PYRITES	POSTMAN	PITYING
POPSONG	PORTENT	PARSLEY	PERTURB	POSTMEN	POTTING
POPCORN	PARVENU	PYRAMID	PURSUED	PASTORS	PUTTING

PATRICK	PRUDENT	PHYLLIS	QUICKIE	REALISM	RUBDOWN
PATRIAL	PRUDERY	PAYLOAD	QUICKEN	REALIGN	RIBBONS
PATRIOT	POUFFES	PLYWOOD	QUICKER	ROADIES	ROBERTA
PETRIFY	PLUGGED	PAYROLL	QUICKLY	READILY	REBORED
PITHILY	PLUNGED	PIZZAZZ	QUILLER	REALITY	REBIRTH
PATELLA	PLUNGER	PUZZLED	QUIXOTE	REARMED	ROBERTO
POTOMAC	PLUNGES	PUZZLER	QUIPPED	ROADMAP	REBORES
PITTMAN	POUCHED	PUZZLES	QUIDSIN	READMIT	ROBARDS
PETUNIA	POUCHES	QUASARS	QUILTED	ROANOKE	ROBERTS
PUTTNAM	PAULINE	QUAKERS	QUITTED	REASONS	ROBESON
PATENTS	PAUSING	QUAVERS	QUIETEN	READOUT	ROBOTIC
POTENCY	POURING	QUAVERY	QUIETER	REAPPLY	RUBITIN
POTHOLE	POUTING	QUAFFED	QUILTER	REACTED	REBATES
PUTDOWN	PRUNING	QUANGOS	QUITTER	ROASTED	REBOUND
PATROLS	PRUDISH	QUASHED	QUIETUS	REACTOR	RUBYWAX
PATRONS	PLUVIAL	QUASHES	QUINTET	REALTOR	RICHARD
PITEOUS	PAUCITY	QUAKING	QUIETLY	ROCKALL	ROCKALL
POTIONS	PLUCKED	QUALIFY	QUIZZED	ROASTER	RECLAIM
PYTHONS	PLUMMER	QUALITY	QUIZZES	ROADTAX	RECYCLE
PITPONY	PLUMMET	QUACKED	QPLANES	ROADWAY	RECEDED
PUTUPON	PRUSSIA	QUAILED	QUORATE	RIBCAGE	RECEDES
PITAPAT	POUSSIN	QUARREL	QUONDAM	REBECCA	RACKETS
PETERED	POULTRY	QUANTUM	QUOTING	RUBICON	RICKETS
POTOROO	PHVALUE	QUATTRO	REALALE	ROBOCOP	ROCKERS
PITPROP	PAVLOVA	QUARTER	RYANAIR	RABIDLY	ROCKETS
PETASUS	POVERTY	QUARTET	REARDON	ROBBERS	RACIEST
PITSTOP	PIVOTED	QUEUEUP	RWANDAN	RUBBERS	RICHEST
POTLUCK	PIVOTAL	QUECHUA	READERS	ROBBERY	RICKETY
PITBULL	PAWPAWS	QUERIED	REAMERS	RUBBERY	ROCKERY
PATHWAY	POWDERS	QUEUING	REAPERS	REBUFFS	RECEIVE
PUTAWAY	POWDERY	QUERIES	REAGENT	REBUILD	RECLINE
PLUMAGE	PAWNING	QUELLED	RUAPEHU	RIBBING	ROCKING
PLUMBED	POWERED	QUEALLY	REACHED	ROBBING	RUCHING
PLUMBER	PAYSAGE	QUEENIE	ROADHOG	RUBBING	RUCTION
POUNCED	PAYBACK	QUEENLY	REACHES	RUBBISH	ROCKIER
POUNCES	PAYABLE	QUENTIN	REALISE	RABBITS	RECOILS
POUNCET	PAYMENT	QUETZAL	READING	ROBBINS	ROCKIES
PAUNCHY	PSYCHIC	QUIBBLE	REAMING	REBUILT	RECEIPT
POUNDED	PHYSICS	QUINCES	REAPING	REBUKED	RECTIFY
PLUNDER	PHYSIOS	QUIVERS	REARING	REBUKES	ROCKILY
PAUPERS	PAYDIRT	QUICHES	ROAMING	RUBELLA	RECALLS
PEUGEOT	PAYSLIP	QUININE	ROARING	ROBLOWE	RICHMAL

RICKMAN	REDEEMS	REELECT	REFUTES	RAIMENT	RELIVED
RECANTS	REDNESS	REEKING	RIGIDLY	RAIDING	RELIVES
RACCOON	REDRESS	REELING	RIGVEDA	RAILING	RELAXED
RECKONS	RODGERS	RHENIUM	RAGWEEK	RAINING	RELAXES
RECTORS	RUDDERS	REELOFF	REGRESS	RAISING	RELAYED
RECTORY	REDHEAT	REENTER	REGRETS	RUINING	RUMBABA
RECIPES	REDMEAT	REENTRY	RIGGERS	RAINIER	RAMRAID
RICARDO	REDWINE	ROEBUCK	RAGGEDY	RAISINS	RIMBAUD
RECORDS	REDDING	RAEBURN	ROGUERY	RUISLIP	RAMPAGE
RACISTS	REDOING	REFLATE	RAGTIME	RAILMAN	RUMMAGE
RECASTS	REDWING	REFRAIN	RAGGING	RAILMEN	RAMPANT
RICOTTA	RIDDING	REFRACT	RIGGING	RAINMAN	RAMPART
RECITED	REDDISH	REFOCUS	ROGUISH	REIGNED	REMNANT
RECITAL	RODDICK	REFRESH	REGAINS	RHIZOME	REMODEL
RICHTER	REDHILL	RAFTERS	REGALIA	RUINOUS	RAMADAN
RECITES	RADDLED	REFUELS	REGALED	REISSUE	RIMLESS
RECLUSE	RIDDLED	REFLECT	REGULAR	ROISTER	ROMPERS
RECOUPS	REDFLAG	REFUGEE	REGALES	RAILWAY	RAMBERT
RECOUNT	RUDOLPH	REFUGES	REGULUS	REJECTS	ROMAINE
RECRUIT	RIDDLER	RIFKIND	REGALLY	REJOICE	RAMMING
RECOVER	RIDDLES	RAFTING	REGIMEN	REJOINS	ROMPING
REDCARD	RIDINGS	RIFLING	REGIMES	RIKSDAG	RAMPION
REDHAND	RODENTS	RUFFING	REGENTS	RAKEDIN	REMAINS
RUDYARD	RADIOED	RAFFISH	REGENCY	RAKEOFF	RAMEKIN
RADIATE	REDFORD	RUFFIAN	RAGDOLL	RELEASE	RAMBLED
REDTAPE	REDMOND	RIFFLED	RAGROLL	RELOADS	RUMBLED
REDBACK	REDWOOD	RUFFLED	RAGWORM	RELIANT	RUMPLED
REDDAWN	REDNOSE	RIFFLER	REGROUP	ROLODEX	RAMBLER
REDRAWN	REDROSE	RAFFLES	REGIONS	RELIEVE	RAMBLES
REDCAPS	RUDDOCK	REFILLS	RAGWORT	ROLLERS	ROMULUS
REDRAWS	REDPOLL	RIFFLES	REGARDS	RELIGHT	RUMBLES
RADIANT	REDCOAT	RUFFLES	REGATTA	RALLIED	RUMPLES
REDRAFT	REDARMY	REFINED	RIGHTED	RELYING	ROMANIA
RUDEBOY	RIDOTTO	REFINES	RIGHTON	ROLLING	ROMANCE
REDUCED	REDRUTH	REFUNDS	RIGHTLY	RALEIGH	ROMANSH
RADICLE	REDDUST	REFEREE	RIGOURS	RALLIES	REMANDS
RADICAL	REDOUBT	REFORMS	REHEATS	ROLLMOP	REMINDS
REDUCES	REENACT	REFUSED	REHOUSE	RELENTS	ROMANOV
REDHEAD	REEDBED	REFUSAL	REIGATE	RULEOUT	ROMFORD
REDNECK	ROEDEAN	REFUSES	RAINBOW	RELAPSE	RUMPOLE
REDDEER	ROEDEER	REFUTED	RAILCAR	RELATED	RAMRODS
REDDENS	REEFERS	REFUTAL	RAIDERS	RELATES	REMORSE

REMARKS	RUNAMOK	ROOFTOP	RAPTURE	RISKING	RATPACK
REMARRY	RENAMES	ROOSTER	RUPTURE	RUSHING	RETRAIN
RAMESES	RANINTO	REPLACE	REQUEST	RUSTING	RITUALS
REMATCH	RUNINTO	RAPHAEL	REQUIRE	ROSSINI	RETRACT
REMOTER	RANSOME	REPEALS	REQUIEM	RUSSIAN	RATECAP
REMOULD	RANGOFF	REPEATS	RAREBIT	RISKIER	RETREAD
RUMOURS	RINGOFF	REPLAYS	REREDOS	ROSELLA	ROTTERS
REMOUNT	RANGOON	ROPEDIN	RAREGAS	RUSTLED	RETREAT
REMOVED	RUNCORN	RAPIDLY	RORAIMA	RESOLVE	RATAFIA
REMOVAL	RUNDOWN	REPLETE	RURALLY	ROSALIE	RITCHIE
REMOVES	RANCOUR	RIPIENO	REROUTE	ROSSLYN	RATCHET
RANSACK	RANSOMS	RAPIERS	RORQUAL	RUSTLER	RETSINA
RUNWAYS	RINGOUT	REPRESS	RESHAPE	RESULTS	ROTTING
RENDELL	RENAULT	REPLICA	RESTATE	RUSTLES	RETHINK
RANGERS	RENEWED	REPLIED	ROSEATE	RESUMED	RETRIAL
RANKERS	RENEWAL	REPRISE	RASCALS	RESUMES	RATTIER
RENDERS	RINGWAY	REPTILE	RESEALS	ROSANNA	RETAILS
RINGERS	RUNAWAY	RIPTIDE	RESTART	RESENTS	RETAINS
RUNNELS	RANTZEN	RIPPING	ROSEBUD	ROSTOVA	RATTILY
RUNNERS	RIOTACT	REPAIRS	RISIBLE	RESPOND	RETAKEN
RONDEAU	RHOMBUS	REPLIES	ROSEBAY	RESTORE	RETAKES
RENEGED	ROOIBOS	REPAINT	RESIDED	RISSOLE	RATTLED
RENEGES	REOCCUR	REPOINT	RESIDUE	RESTOCK	RITALIN
RINGGIT	RHONDDA	REPRINT	RUSHDIE	ROSTOCK	RATTLER
RANCHER	REORDER	RIPPLED	RESIDES	RESERVE	RATTLES
RANCHES	REOPENS	REPULSE	ROSBERG	ROSTRUM	RETELLS
RUNWILD	RIOTERS	RAPALLO	ROSWELL	ROSARIO	ROTUNDA
RUNTIME	ROOFERS	RIPPLES	RUSSELL	RESORTS	RETINUE
RANKING	ROOKERY	REPINED	RASHERS	RESPRAY	RETINOL
RANTING	ROOMFUL	REPENTS	ROSTERS	RATINGS	RATINGS
RENDING	RIOTING	REPINES	RUSSETS	RESISTS	RETINAS
RENTING	ROOFING	RIPCORD	RESPECT	ROSETTA	RATIONS
RINGING	ROOKING	REPROVE	ROSIEST	ROSETTE	ROTORUA
RINSING	ROOTING	REPROOF	RESTFUL	RUSHTON	RETIRED
RUNNING	RHODIUM	RAPPORT	RESIGNS	RISOTTO	RETIREE
RUNRIOT	ROOMIER	REPAPER	ROSEHIP	RESCUED	RATTRAP
RANKLED	ROOKIES	REPORTS	RESCIND	RESOUND	RETARDS
RONALDO	ROOTLET	REPOSED	RESPIRE	RESCUER	RETIRES
RANKLES	RIOLOBO	RIPOSTE	RESPITE	RESCUES	RETORTS
RINGLET	RIOTOUS	REPASTS	RESTIVE	RESTYLE	RETURNS
RENAMED	ROOTOUT	REPOSES	RASPING	RUTLAND	ROTATED
RANAMOK	ROOSTED	REPUTED	RESTING	RATRACE	ROTATOR

ROTATES	REVAMPS	ROYALLY	SCAFELL	SEABIRD	SCARILY
RATATAT	RAVENNA	ROYALTY	SHAKEUP	SEAMILE	SHADILY
RETOUCH	REVENGE	RAYMOND	SHAPEUP	SEASIDE	SHAKILY
RHUBARB	REVENUE	ROYWOOD	SEALEGS	SCALING	SMACKED
ROULADE	RAVINES	ROZZERS	SHAVERS	SCARING	SPANKED
RAUNCHY	RAVIOLI	SEAWARD	SKATERS	SEALING	SPARKED
ROUNDED	REVERED	SEAKALE	SLATERS	SEARING	STACKED
ROUNDEL	REVERIE	SEALANE	SLAVERS	SEATING	STALKED
ROUNDUP	REVERSE	SWANAGE	SLAYERS	SHADING	SWANKED
ROUNDER	REVERSI	SEAHAWK	SPACERS	SHAKING	SHACKLE
ROUNDLY	REVERES	SEAWALL	STAMENS	SHAMING	SPARKLE
REUTERS	REVERTS	SEAWASP	STAYERS	SHAPING	SLACKEN
ROULEAU	REVISED	SCARABS	STALEST	SHARING	STACKUP
ROUGHEN	REVISER	SEABASS	SHAPELY	SHAVING	SLACKER
ROUGHER	REVISES	SHAMANS	SLAVERY	SKATING	SMACKER
ROUGHIT	REVISIT	SEALANT	STATELY	SLAKING	SPANKER
ROUGHLY	RIVETED	SEASALT	SUAVELY	SLAVING	STACKER
REUNITE	RIVETER	STABBED	STARETZ	SLAYING	STALKER
ROUTINE	REVIVED	SWABBED	STAFFED	SNARING	STARKER
ROUSING	REVIVAL	SHAMBLE	SNAFFLE	SOAKING	SHANKLY
ROUTING	REVIVER	SJAMBOK	SHAFFER	SOARING	SLACKLY
REUNION	REVIVES	SOAPBOX	STAFFER	SPACING	SPARKLY
ROUBLES	ROWLAND	SCARCER	SNAGGED	SPARING	STARKLY
RAUCOUS	RAWDEAL	SEANCES	SPARGED	STAGING	SNARLED
ROUSSOS	RAWNESS	STANCES	SNAGGLE	STARING	STABLED
ROUSTED	RAWHIDE	STARCHY	SPANGLE	STATING	STALLED
REVEALS	REWRITE	SCALDED	STAGGER	STAYING	STAPLED
RIVIERA	RAWLING	SWADDLE	SWAGGER	SWAYING	SEASLUG
REVIEWS	ROWLING	SHARDIK	SPARGES	SLAVISH	SCALLOP
RAVAGED	ROWDIER	SCANDAL	SPANGLY	SPANISH	SNARLUP
RAVAGES	ROWDILY	STARDOM	SLASHED	SWAHILI	SMALLER
REVVING	ROWLOCK	STANDIN	SMASHED	SEASICK	STABLER
REVOKED	ROWBOAT	SOANDSO	STASHED	SPANIEL	STAPLER
REVOKES	REWARDS	STANDTO	SWATHED	SPATIAL	STABLES
REVILED	ROWETTA	STANDUP	SMASHUP	STADIUM	STAPLES
REVALUE	REWOUND	SLANDER	SMASHER	SEALION	SCARLET
REVOLVE	ROXANNE	SPANDAU	SLASHES	STATION	SHALLOT
REVILES	REYNARD	SPANDEX	SMASHES	SHAPIRO	STARLET
REVOLTS	RAYBANS	STANDBY	STASHES	SEAMIER	STARLIT
RIVULET	RHYTHMS	SEAWEED	SWATHES	SHADIER	SHALLOW
REVELRY	RHYMING	SCALENE	SHAKIRA	SCABIES	SWALLOW
RIVALRY	RAYALAN	SIAMESE	STAMINA	SCARIFY	STANLEY

SLAMMED	STAYPUT	SUBEDIT	SOCIETY	SHEPARD	SEEMING
SWARMED	SHARPLY	SUBZERO	SACKFUL	STEWARD	SEEPING
STARMAN	SCARRED	SUBLETS	SACKING	SEEPAGE	SPEWING
SWAGMAN	SPARRED	SUBJECT	SOCKING	SHEBANG	STEWING
SWAGMEN	STARRED	SUBTEXT	SUCKING	STEFANI	SWEDISH
SLAMMER	SEAGRAM	SUBVERT	SECTION	SEESAWS	SPECIAL
STAMMER	SHARRON	SABRINA	SUCTION	STEWART	SEEDIER
SCANNED	STAVROS	SUBLIME	SECULAR	SEEDBED	SPECIES
SPANNED	SPARROW	SUBSIDE	SICKLES	SHERBET	SEEDILY
STAINED	SWANSEA	SIBLING	SECOMBE	SEEDBOX	SPECIFY
SHAWNEE	SWANSON	SOBBING	SECONDS	STENCIL	SNEAKED
SLAINTE	SPASSKY	SUBBING	SUCROSE	SPENCER	SPECKLE
STAUNCH	STARSKY	SUBMITS	SUCCOUR	SKETCHY	SNEAKUP
SHANNEN	SLANTED	SUBSIST	SECTORS	SPEEDED	SPEAKUP
SHANNON	SLATTED	SUBSIDY	SICKPAY	SHELDON	SLEEKER
SCANNER	STARTED	SUBTLER	SECURED	SPEEDUP	SNEAKER
SHATNER	SWATTED	SUBPLOT	SECURES	SLENDER	SPEAKER
SPANNER	SEATTLE	SUBSOIL	SYCOSIS	SPENDER	SHEIKHS
STAINER	STARTLE	SUBAQUA	SUCCUMB	SEEHERE	SHELLAC
STAINES	SMARTEN	SIBERIA	SECLUDE	SHEBEEN	SHELLED
SEAFOOD	SPARTAN	SOBERUP	SIDEARM	SEEDERS	SMELLED
SEALORD	STANTON	SUBURBS	SEDUCED	SEEKERS	SPELLED
SEALOFF	STARTUP	SOBERLY	SEDUCER	SHEKELS	STEELED
SEASONS	SCATTER	SUBDUED	SIDECAR	SIEMENS	SWELLED
SHADOWS	SHATTER	SUBSUME	SEDUCES	SKEWERS	STEALTH
STATORS	SMARTER	SUBDUES	SADDENS	STEREOS	STELLAR
SEAPORT	SPATTER	SACCADE	SADNESS	STEVENS	SHELLEY
SHADOWY	STARTER	SICKBED	SADDEST	SIEVERT	STEAMED
SCALPED	SMARTLY	SACKBUT	SIDLING	SCENERY	STEMMED
SLAPPED	SWARTHY	SICKBAY	SADDLED	STENGUN	STEPMOM
SNAPPED	SCAPULA	SECEDED	SADDLER	SHERGAR	SHERMAN
STAMPED	SPATULA	SECEDES	SADDLES	STEIGER	STEAMER
SWAMPED	STATURE	SUCCEED	SODSLAW	SLEDGES	STERNUM
SWAPPED	STATUTE	SECRETE	SUDELEY	SLEIGHS	STERNER
SHARPEI	SEAGULL	SOCKEYE	SIDINGS	SLEIGHT	STEPNEY
SCALPEL	STATUES	SACHETS	SIDDONS	SEETHED	STERNLY
SHARPEN	STARVED	SECRETS	SODAPOP	STEPHEN	SWEENEY
SHAMPOO	SCARVES	SICKENS	SADISTS	SEETHES	STEROID
SCAMPER	STARVES	SOCKETS	SEDATED	STERILE	SEEKOUT
SCARPER	STANZAS	SUCCESS	SEDATES	SHERIFF	STEEPED
SHARPER	SABBATH	SUCKERS	SIDOWEN	SEEDING	STEPPED
SNAPPER	SUBWAYS	SECRECY	SMETANA	SEEKING	STEEPLE

SLEEPIN	STENTOR	SIGHTED	SHIVERY	SHIRKED	SPINOUT
STEEPEN	SWEATER	SIGMUND	SPIDERY	SMIRKED	SHINPAD
STEWPAN	SWEETER	SEGOVIA	SNIFFED	SNICKED	SHIPPED
SLEEPER	SWELTER	SCHMIDT	SKIFFLE	STICKUP	SKIMPED
STEEPER	SIESTAS	SCHOLAR	SNIFFLE	SHICKER	SKIPPED
STEPPER	SLEUTHS	SCHEMED	SKILFUL	SHIRKER	SLIPPED
SWEEPER	SWEETLY	SCHEMER	SKINFUL	SLICKER	SNIPPED
STEPPES	SHELVED	SCHEMES	STIFFEN	SNICKER	STIPPLE
STEWPOT	SWERVED	SCHLOSS	SNIFFER	STICKER	SKIDPAN
SHEPPEY	SEEOVER	SCHOOLS	STIFFLY	STINKER	SHIPPER
STEEPLY	SHEAVES	SCHERZO	STIRFRY	SNICKET	SKIPPER
SHEARED	SHELVES	SPHERES	SWIGGED	SLICKLY	SLIPPER
SMEARED	SLEEVES	SCHISMS	SHINGLE	SKIDLID	SNIPPET
SNEERED	SWERVES	SCHMUCK	STILGOE	SKILLED	STIRRED
SPEARED	SNEEZED	SPIRAEA	SMIDGEN	SPILLED	STIRRUP
STEERED	SNEEZES	SPINACH	SNIGGER	STIFLED	STIRRER
SHERRIN	SOFABED	SKIMASK	STINGER	SWILLED	SKIDROW
SWEARIN	SAFEBET	STIFADO	SWINGER	SWIRLED	SCISSOR
SHEARER	SIFTERS	SPIRALS	SHINGLY	SMILLIE	SHIFTED
STEERER	SOFTENS	SHINBET	SWITHIN	SHIPLAP	SKIRTED
SIERRAS	SUFFERS	SKIDDED	SLITHER	STILLER	STILTED
STEPSON	SOFTEST	SPINDLE	SLIGHTS	SHIELDS	SKITTLE
STETSON	SUFFICE	SWINDLE	SAILING	STIFLES	SPITTLE
SPENSER	SIFTING	SHINDIG	SEIZING	SKILLET	SHILTON
SPECTRA	SOFTIES	SWINDON	SHINING	SHIRLEY	SKIPTON
SCEPTIC	SUFFOLK	SKIDDAW	SKIVING	SEISMIC	SMITTEN
SCENTED	SOFTROE	SPINDLY	SLICING	SKIMMED	STILTON
SMELTED	SAFFRON	SPINDRY	SLIDING	SLIMMED	SHIFTER
SWEATED	SAFARIS	STIPEND	SMILING	SHIMMER	SKITTER
SCEPTRE	SOFTTOP	SLICEUP	SMITING	SKIMMER	SLIOTAR
SHEATHE	SUFFUSE	SHINERS	SNIPING	SLIMMER	SNIFTER
SHELTIE	SIGNALS	SHIVERS	SOILING	SWIMMER	SWIFTER
SPECTRE	SIGNETS	SKIVERS	SPICING	SKINNED	SHIATSU
STEPTOE	SEGMENT	SLICERS	SPIKING	SCIENCE	SHIHTZU
SWEETIE	SUGGEST	SLIVERS	SUITING	SKINNER	SAINTLY
SKELTON	SAGGING	SMILERS	SWIPING	SPINNER	SWIFTLY
SLEPTIN	SIGHING	SNIPERS	SWINISH	SPINNEY	SEIZURE
SWEETEN	SIGNING	SNIVELS	SHINIER	SPINOFF	STIMULI
SHELTER	SOGGIER	SOIREES	SLIMIER	SAILORS	SKIJUMP
SKEETER	SIGNIFY	SPIDERS	SPICIER	SLIPONS	SLIPUPS
SMELTER	SIGNORA	SPINETS	SPIRITS	SPIGOTS	SLIPWAY
SPECTOR	SUGARED	SWIVELS	SKILIFT	SUITORS	SWIZZLE

STJOHNS	SULKING	SOMEHOW	SANREMO	SYNAPSE	SNORERS
STJAMES	SELFISH	SUMMITS	SANDERS	SANDPIT	STOKERS
SOJOURN	SELKIRK	SOMALIA	SENDERS	SUNSPOT	STOREYS
SIKHISM	SALTIER	SAMPLED	SINGERS	SANGRIA	SLOWEST
STKILDA	SILLIER	SIMPLON	SINKERS	SUNTRAP	SOONEST
STKITTS	SOLDIER	SAMPLER	SINNERS	SENORAS	SHOWERY
SULTANA	SULKIER	SIMILAR	SONNETS	SYNERGY	SCOFFED
SALVAGE	SALLIES	SIMPLER	SUNBEDS	SINUSES	SCOFFER
SULTANS	SULLIES	SAMPLES	SUNDERS	SINATRA	SLOGGED
SOLUBLE	SOLOIST	SIMILES	SUNLESS	SINITTA	SHOTGUN
STLUCIA	SALSIFY	SEMINAL	SUNBELT	SANCTUM	SLOEGIN
SPLICED	SULKILY	SIMENON	SANJEEV	SENATOR	STOPGAP
SILICON	SALUKIS	SEMINAR	SANDFLY	SANCTUS	SLOGGER
SELECTS	SOLOMON	SOMEONE	SENEGAL	SONATAS	SPONGER
SPLICES	SALAMIS	SIMMONS	SANCHEZ	SENSUAL	SPONGES
SOLICIT	SILENCE	SUMMONS	SUNRISE	SANJUAN	STOOGES
SPLODGE	SPLINES	SYMBOLS	SENDING	SUNBURN	SLOSHED
SALADIN	SPLINTS	SAMURAI	SENSING	SUNSUIT	SOOTHED
SOLIDUS	SELLOFF	SAMPRAS	SINGING	STOMATA	SMOTHER
SOLIDLY	SOLDOFF	SAMISEN	SINKING	STORAGE	SOOTHER
SPLODGY	SALOONS	SIMPSON	SINNING	STOMACH	SOOTHES
SILVERA	SELLOUT	SUMATRA	SUNDIAL	SLOGANS	SCORING
SELLECK	SOLDOUT	SEMITIC	SUNNIER	SLOBBER	SHOEING
SALVERS	SPLURGE	SYMPTOM	SINCITY	SHOEBOX	SHORING
SELLERS	SALERNO	SAMBUCA	SINGLED	SHOWBIZ	SHOVING
SILVERS	SOLARIS	SAMOVAR	SANDLER	STOICAL	SHOWING
SOLDERS	SILESIA	SOMEWAY	SINGLES	SNOWCAP	SLOPING
SOLVERS	SALUTED	SAMOYED	SINGLET	SCONCES	SLOWING
SALIENT	SPLITUP	SAMRYAN	SANDMAN	SNOWCAT	SMOKING
SOLVENT	SALUTES	SANTANA	SYNONYM	SLOUCHY	SNORING
SILVERY	STLOUIS	SANTAFE	SANJOSE	SMOOCHY	SNOWING
STLEGER	SALLUST	SUNLAMP	SENDOFF	SCOLDED	STOKING
SULPHUR	SPLAYED	SANDALS	SENTOFF	SPONDEE	STONING
SALCHOW	SELTZER	SUNDAES	SUNROOF	SNOWDON	STORING
SALLIED	SAMPANS	SUNHATS	SUNROOM	SLOVENE	STOWING
SULLIED	SUMMARY	SUNTANS	SANDOWN	STONEME	STORIES
SALTIRE	SAMADHI	SANDBAG	SUNDOWN	SPOKEUP	SHOWILY
SALTING	SOMEDAY	SANICLE	SENIORS	SCORERS	SHOCKED
SALVING	SIMMERS	SINEDIE	SENSORS	SCOTERS	SMOCKED
SELLING	SIMPERS	SINCERE	SINUOUS	SHOVELS	STOCKED
SILTING	SUMMERS	SUNDECK	STNEOTS	SHOWERS	SNORKEL
SOLVING	SUMMERY	SUNBEAM	SENSORY	SMOKERS	SHOOKUP

SHOCKER	SCOUTED	SIPHONS	SURFERS	SHRILLY	STRATUM
SNOOKER	SHOUTED	SUPPORT	SURVEYS	STROMLO	SPRITES
SCOWLED	SLOTTED	STPAULS	SARGENT	SCRIMPS	STRATUS
SPOILED	SNORTED	SEQUELS	SERPENT	SCRUMPS	SHROUDS
STOLLEN	SPORTED	SEQUINS	SURFEIT	SHRIMPS	SPROUTS
SWOLLEN	SPOTTED	SEQUOIA	SERVERY	SCRUMMY	STRAUSS
SPOILER	SPOUTED	SYRIANA	SORCERY	SCRUMPY	SHRIVEL
STORMED	SWOTTED	SERRATE	SURGERY	SYRINGA	SHRIVEN
SHOWMAN	SCOTTIE	SURFACE	STRAFED	STRANGE	STRIVEN
SHOWMEN	SHORTEN	SURNAME	SARAFAN	SURANNE	SHRIVER
SNOWMAN	SCOOTER	SARCASM	STRAFES	SYRINGE	SHRIVES
SNOWMEN	SCOUTER	SCREAMS	SCRUFFY	SCRUNCH	STRIVES
SCORNED	SHOOTER	SERIALS	STRIGIL	SARONGS	STREWED
SPOONED	SHORTER	SPREADS	SCRAGGY	SHRINES	STREWTH
SWOONED	SNORTER	STREAKS	SORGHUM	SHRINKS	SARAWAK
SWORNIN	SPOTTER	STREAMS	SERRIED	SPRINGS	SCRAWLS
SPOONER	STOUTER	SURPASS	SARDINE	SPRINTS	SPRAWLS
SAOTOME	SHORTLY	SERVANT	SERVICE	STRANDS	SCRAWLY
SHOWOFF	STOUTLY	STREAKY	SERVILE	STRINGS	SCRAWNY
SLOPOUT	SHOGUNS	SCRUBUP	SURMISE	SPRINGY	SPRAYED
SNOWPEA	SNOOZED	SCRIBES	SURVIVE	STRINGY	STRAYED
SCOOPED	SNOOZER	STROBES	SCRYING	SCROOGE	SPRAYER
SHOPPED	SNOOZES	SCRUBBY	SERVING	SARPONG	SUSTAIN
SLOPPED	SAPSAGO	SARACEN	SORTING	SIRLOIN	SUSPEND
SNOOPED	SOPRANO	SIROCCO	SURFING	SERIOUS	SISTERS
STOMPED	SUPREME	SARACOX	SURGING	SERMONS	SYSTEMS
STOOPED	SUPREMO	STRUDEL	SERBIAN	SORTOUT	SUSPECT
STOPPED	SAPPERS	SERFDOM	SERPICO	SCRAPED	SISTINE
SWOOPED	SEPTETS	STRIDER	SORDINO	STRIPED	SUSSING
SCORPIO	SUPPERS	STRIDES	SURLIER	SCRAPIE	SASHIMI
SHOPPER	SAPIENT	SCREECH	SORTIES	SCRUPLE	SESSION
SNOOPER	SAPLING	SURREAL	SPRAINS	SCRAPER	SISKINS
STOPPER	SAPPING	SURGEON	STRAINS	SCRAPES	SASSILY
SHOTPUT	SIPPING	SERVEUP	STRAITS	SCRIPTS	SUSANNA
SCOURED	SOPPING	SCREEDS	STROKED	STRIPES	SYSTOLE
SCOURGE	SUPPING	SCREENS	STRIKER	SCRAPPY	SASSOON
SPORRAN	SOPHISM	SCRYERS	SHRIKES	STRAPPY	SISSONS
SCOURER	SOPPIER	SERVERS	STRIKES	STROPPY	SUSSOUT
SPONSON	SOPHIST	SHRIEKS	STROKES	SORORAL	SATIATE
SPONSOR	SOPPILY	SORBETS	SCROLLS	SCRATCH	SITUATE
SPOUSES	SAPWOOD	SORTERS	STROLLS	STRETCH	SETBACK
SCOOTED	SUPPOSE	STREETS	SURPLUS	STRITCH	SETSAIL

SITWELL	SOUNDLY	SQUALLS	SAVALAS	STYLIST	TEACHER
SETTEES	SQUIDGY	SQUALLY	SAVELOY	SKYBLUE	TEACHES
SETTERS	SHUTEYE	SHUNNED	SEVENTH	SOYINKA	TSARINA
SITTERS	SQUEEZE	SPURNED	SAVINGS	SAYINGS	TEATIME
SATIETY	SAUCERS	STUNNED	SEVENTY	SPYHOLE	TEARING
SATCHEL	STUMERS	SPUTNIK	SAVIOUR	SHYLOCK	TEASING
SATCHMO	SOUREST	STUNNER	SEVERED	SEYMOUR	THAWING
SETTING	STUDENT	SQUINTS	SEVERAL	STYPTIC	TRACING
SITTING	SQUEEZY	SPUMOUS	SAVARIN	SHYSTER	TRADING
SETTLED	STUPEFY	SHUTOUT	SAVOURS	SIZEDUP	TSARISM
SETTLER	SCUFFED	SPUNOUT	SAVOURY	SIZZLED	TOADIES
SETTLES	STUFFED	SLUMPED	SAWYERS	SOZZLED	TSARIST
SATANIC	SCUFFLE	SLURPED	SAWFISH	SIZZLER	THANKED
SATDOWN	SHUFFLE	STUMPED	SAWBILL	SIZZLES	TRACKED
SITDOWN	SNUFFLE	SCUPPER	SAWMILL	SUZANNE	TRACKER
SITCOMS	SOUFFLE	SCULPTS	SAWALHA	TUATARA	TRAILED
SETFREE	SOULFUL	SLURRED	SAWNOFF	TEACAKE	TRAWLED
SATIRES	SNUFFER	SPURRED	SAWDUST	TRAVAIL	TRAILER
SATISFY	SNUFFLY	SQUARED	SIXPACK	TEABAGS	TRAWLER
SATSUMA	SQUIFFY	SQUARES	SEXTANT	TEALADY	TRAMMEL
SAUSAGE	SMUDGED	SQUIRES	SIXTEEN	TRANCHE	TRAUMAS
SOUTANE	SMUGGLE	SQUIRMS	SEXTETS	TRAMCAR	TRAINED
SQUEAKS	SNUGGLE	SQUIRTS	SEXBOMB	TRANCES	TRAINEE
SQUEALS	STUNGUN	SQUIRMY	SAXHORN	THANDIE	TRAINER
SQUEAKY	SLUGGER	SQUASHY	SEXTONS	TWADDLE	TEAROSE
SLUBBED	SMUDGES	SQUISHY	SKYWARD	TRAPEZE	TEAROFF
SNUBBED	STUDIED	SHUNTED	SPYHARD	TEALEAF	TEAROOM
STUBBED	SOURING	SPURTED	SPYGAME	TRADEIN	TEAPOTS
STUBBLE	SOUSING	STUNTED	SKYJACK	TEASELS	THAWOUT
STUMBLE	SAURIAN	SCUTTLE	SKYLARK	TEASERS	TEACOSY
SLUMBER	SAUCIER	SHUTTLE	SHYNESS	TRACERS	TRAMPED
STUBBLY	STUDIES	SAUNTER	SLYNESS	TRADERS	TRAPPED
SOURCED	STUDIOS	SHUNTER	SAYWHEN	TRAVELS	TRAIPSE
SOUPCON	SAUCILY	SHUTTER	SCYTHES	TRAVERS	TRAMPLE
SLUICES	SHUCKED	SPUTTER	STYMIED	TRACERY	TRAPPER
SOURCES	SKULKED	STUTTER	SKYDIVE	TRAGEDY	TEATREE
SCUDDED	STUCKUP	SQUAWKS	SKYLINE	TRAFFIC	TEATRAY
SOUNDED	SCULLED	SAVEDUP	STYLISE	TEARFUL	TRANSOM
STUDDED	SQUALID	SAVAGED	STYLING	TWANGED	TRANSIT
SQUIDGE	SQUELCH	SAVAGES	STYLISH	TEARGAS	TOASTED
SHUDDER	SCULLER	SAVILLE	STYGIAN	TRACHEA	TOASTIE
SOUNDER	SQUALOR	SEVILLE	STYMIES	TEASHOP	TOASTER

TRACTOR	TEDDIES	THEBILL	TREATED	TRIREME	TRIPLET
TRAITOR	TODDIES	THEHILL	THEATRE	TOILETS	TRIPLEX
TRADUCE	TODDLED	THEFIRM	TRESTLE	TRICEPS	TRIMMED
TEACUPS	TIDDLER	TREVINO	TRENTON	TRIVETS	TRIUMPH
TRAMWAY	TODDLER	THEKISS	TREETOP	TRIDENT	TRIMMER
TOBLAME	TODDLES	THEGIFT	TREATER	TRISECT	THINNED
TOBACCO	TIDINGS	TSELIOT	TWEETER	TRITELY	TWINNED
TABLETS	TADPOLE	TREKKED	THETUBE	TRIFFID	THINNER
TABLEAU	TEDIOUS	TWEAKED	THELUMP	TAILFIN	TAILOFF
TABLING	TIDYSUM	TREKKIE	THEOVAL	TWIGGED	TRIPOLI
TUBBIER	TIDEWAY	TREKKER	TIFFANY	TYINGUP	TRICORN
TABBIES	TEENAGE	THEBLOB	TAFFETA	TRIGGER	TAILORS
TOBYJUG	THEGAME	TREBLED	TUFNELL	TWINGES	TRIPODS
TABULAR	THEMASK	TIECLIP	TOFFEES	THITHER	TRITONS
TUBULAR	TIEBACK	TOECLIP	TUFFETS	TRISHAW	TRILOGY
TABLOID	THEMALL	TREBLES	TAGGART	TAILING	TRIPPED
TABARDS	TOENAIL	TRELLIS	TAGTEAM	TOILING	TRIPPER
TABASCO	THEOAKS	THERMAE	TIGRESS	TWINING	THIMPHU
TABITHA	TOECAPS	THERMAL	TAGLINE	TBILISI	THIERRY
TIBETAN	THELADY	THEOMEN	TAGGING	TRIVIAL	TWINSET
TOCCATA	THERAPY	THERMOS	TOGGING	TUITION	THIRSTY
TUCKBOX	TREMBLE	TOEHOLD	TUGGING	TRINITY	TWINTUB
TICKERS	TREMBLY	THEROBE	TAGALOG	TRICKED	TAINTED
TICKETS	TREACLE	THEROSE	TOGGLES	TRICKLE	TWISTED
TACTFUL	TREACLY	TEEDOFF	TUGBOAT	TWINKLE	THISTLE
TACTILE	THEEDGE	THEROCK	TIGHTEN	THICKEN	TRISTAN
TACKING	TREADLE	TREFOIL	TIGHTER	THINKUP	TWISTER
TICKING	TUESDAY	TIEDOWN	TAGETES	THICKER	TWITTER
TUCKING	THERESA	TIEPOLO	TIGHTLY	THINKER	THISTLY
TACTICS	THEDEAD	TREMOLO	TOHUNGA	THICKET	TRIBUNE
TACKILY	THEJERK	TREMORS	TOHEROA	TRINKET	TRIBUTE
TACKLED	THEBELL	THEROUX	TSHIRTS	THICKLY	THIEVED
TICKLED	THEDELL	THEBODY	TRIGAMY	TRICKSY	THIEVES
TACKLER	THEREIN	THEFONZ	THIMBLE	TWINKLY	TWIZZLE
TACKLES	TEETERS	THESPIS	TWITCHY	TRIFLED	TIJUANA
TICKLES	THESEUS	THEOREM	TRIADIC	TRILLED	TAKEAIM
TICKOFF	THEREBY	THECROW	TWIDDLE	TRIPLED	TEKTITE
TYCOONS	TWELFTH	TREASON	TRINDER	TWILLED	TAKINGS
TACITUS	THEBIGE	THEISTS	THIRDLY	TWIRLED	TAKEOFF
TACITLY	TEEMING	TRESSES	TWIDDLY	TRIFLES	TAKEOUT
TIDIEST	THERING	THEYSAY	TRIBECA	TRIPLES	TILLAGE
TIDYING	THEDISH	THESTUD	TAILEND	TRIOLET	TALKBIG

TALIBAN	TEMPEST	TANGENT	TANGRAM	TROUSER	TIPTOES
TALLBOY	TIMRICE	TINIEST	TANTRUM	TROTSKY	TOPDOGS
TELECOM	TEMPING	TONNEAU	TUNISIA	TROTTED	TAPROOT
TOLUENE	TOMPION	TANNERY	TINYTIM	TWOSTEP	TOPCOAT
TALKERS	TAMPICO	TENSELY	TANKTOP	TROTTER	TOPMOST
TELLERS	TIMMINS	TANKFUL	TONGUED	TOOMUCH	TOPCOPY
TILLERS	TOMMIES	TUNEFUL	TONSURE	TOPKAPI	TOPSPIN
TALLEST	TUMMIES	TONIGHT	TONGUES	TOPSAIL	TAPERED
TALLIED	TUMBLED	TENSILE	TROJANS	TOPMAST	TYPISTS
TALKING	TIMELAG	TINMINE	TROUBLE	TOPIARY	TYPESET
TELLING	TEMPLAR	TONTINE	TOOLBAG	TOPICAL	TIPSTER
TILLING	TUMBLER	TANNING	TOOLBAR	TYPICAL	TSQUARE
TILTING	TEMPLES	TENDING	TOOLBOX	TEPIDLY	TEQUILA
TOLLING	TUMBLES	TENSING	TRODDEN	TOPGEAR	TURKANA
TALLINN	TUMULUS	TENZING	TROWELS	TAPPETS	TARTARE
TOLKIEN	TOMBOLA	TINTING	TROUGHS	TIPPERS	TERRACE
TALKIES	TOMFORD	TONKING	THOUGHT	TOPLESS	TERRAIN
TALLIES	TIMEOFF	TENNIEL	TOOTHED	TOPPERS	TORNADO
TALONED	TAMBOUR	TENSION	TROCHEE	TIPPETT	TARSALS
TALENTS	TIMEOUT	TANGIER	TWOTIME	TAPSHOE	TARTANS
TELFORD	TUMBREL	TANSIES	TOOLING	TOPLINE	TARTARS
TELLOFF	TAMARIN	TENPINS	TOOTING	TOPSIDE	THREADS
TOLDOFF	TEMPTED	TONSILS	TROPICS	TAPPING	THREATS
TILAPIA	TEMPTER	TANGLED	TROIKAS	TIPPING	TURBANS
TELSTAR	TIMOTHY	TINGLED	TOOLKIT	TOPPING	TARRANT
TOLSTOY	TEMPURA	TINKLED	TOOTLED	TIPSIER	TARBABY
TILBURY	TANKARD	TANGLES	TROLLOP	TIPPLED	THROATY
TELAVIV	TYNWALD	TINGLES	TOOTLES	TOPPLED	TIRADES
TELEXED	TINWARE	TINKLES	TROILUS	TIPPLER	TORPEDO
TELEXES	TONNAGE	TONALLY	TROLLEY	TIPPLES	TARGETS
TALLYHO	TYNDALE	TENANTS	TROUNCE	TIPPLER	TUREENS
TIMBALE	TINTACK	TENANCY	TWOFOLD	TOPPLES	TURKEYS
TIMPANI	TENABLE	TANGOED	TWOSOME	TOPONYM	TURRETS
TIMTAMS	TINTERN	TENFOLD	TOOKOFF	TOPKNOT	TORMENT
TAMMANY	TANGELO	TINFOIL	TROTOUT	TAPIOCA	TORRENT
TYMPANY	TANDEMS	TANDOOR	TROOPED	TIPTOED	TERSELY
TIMECOP	TANKERS	TENDONS	TROOPER	TYPHOID	TORPEFY
TIMIDLY	TANNERS	TENUOUS	TROUPER	TOPHOLE	TARIFFS
TEMPERA	TENDERS	TENTPEG	TROUPES	TOPSOIL	THRIFTY
TOMBELL	TENNERS	TANTRIC	TOOTSIE	TAPROOM	TORCHED
TAMPERS	TINKERS	TANCRED	THOMSON	TOPDOWN	TORCHES
TEMPERS	TUNNELS	TENDRIL	THORSON	TYPHOON	TARRIED

TERMITE	THRIVED	TATTIER	TRUCKER	THYROID	UNDATED
TERRINE	THRIVES	TITBITS	TOUSLED	TOYTOWN	UPDATED
TURBINE	THROWIN	TATTILY	TOUSLES	TRYITON	UPDATES
TARRING	THROWER	TATTLED	THURMAN	UNAWARE	USEDCAR
TERMING	TOSTADA	TATTLER	TRUEMAN	UNAIDED	UPENDED
TURNING	TUSSAUD	TITULAR	TRUANTS	UGANDAN	USELESS
TARNISH	TESTATE	TATTLES	TRUANCY	UNALIKE	UNEARTH
TURKISH	TOSCALE	TOTALLY	THUMPED	URANIUM	UTENSIL
TERMINI	TOSPARE	TOTEMIC	TRUMPED	UNASKED	UNEATEN
TORVILL	TESTACY	TITANIA	THUMPER	UNARMED	UNEQUAL
TORYISM	TUSCANY	TITANIC	TRUMPET	UPATREE	UNFOLDS
TORSION	TESTBED	TETANUS	TRUSSED	UPBRAID	UNFUNNY
TERRIER	TESSERA	TATTOOS	TRUISMS	UMBRAGE	UPFRONT
TARRIES	TASSELS	TUTORED	TRUSSES	UMBRIAN	UNFURLS
TORPIDS	TASTERS	TITMUSS	TAUNTED	UNBUILT	UNFAZED
TURNIPS	TESTERS	TSUNAMI	TRUSTED	UNBOLTS	UPGRADE
TARDILY	TUSKERS	TOUCANS	TRUSTEE	UNBENDS	UNGODLY
TERRIFY	TUSSIVE	THUMBED	TAUNTON	UNBLOCK	UNGUENT
TURNKEY	TASTING	THURBER	TAVENER	UMBERTO	URGENCY
THRILLS	TESTING	THUDDED	TAVERNA	UNBOUND	USHUAIA
TURTLES	TOSSING	TRUNDLE	TAVERNS	UNBOWED	UNHEARD
TARTLET	TASTIER	THUNDER	TOWPATH	UNCHAIN	UPHOLDS
TERENCE	TESTIFY	TAUREAN	THWACKS	UNCLASP	UNHINGE
TORONTO	TESTILY	TAUTENS	THWAITE	UNCIALS	UNHOOKS
THRONES	TUSSLED	TOUPEES	THWHITE	UNCLEAN	UNHAPPY
THRONGS	TUSSLES	TRUDEAU	TOWLINE	UNCLEAR	USHERED
TYRANTS	TUSSORE	TRUFFLE	TOWNIES	UNCTION	UNITARY
TYRANNY	TUSSOCK	TRUDGED	TOWROPE	UNCOILS	USINGUP
TURNOFF	TESTUDO	THUGGEE	TOWERED	URCHINS	UNIFIED
TORTONI	TISSUES	TRUDGES	THWARTS	UNCANNY	UTILISE
TURMOIL	TITLARK	TOUCHED	TOWARDS	UNCLOGS	UNITING
TERRORS	TOTEBAG	TOUGHIE	TAXABLE	UNCROSS	UNIFIES
TIREOUT	TATTERS	TOUGHEN	TAXICAB	UNCORKS	UTILITY
TURFOUT	TETHERS	TOUCHER	TOXTETH	UNCURLS	UNIFORM
TURNOUT	TITFERS	TOUGHER	TAXYEAR	UNCOUTH	UNICORN
TOREROS	TITTERS	TOUCHES	TAXDISC	UNCIVIL	UNKEMPT
THRUSTS	TOTTERS	TOUGHLY	TEXTILE	UNCOVER	UNKNOWN
TORTURE	TOTTERY	TOURING	TAXING	UNDRESS	UNLEASH
THROUGH	TITMICE	TOUTING	TAXFREE	UNDOING	ULLMANN
TARBUCK	TATTING	TOURISM	TEXTURE	UNDYING	UNLEARN
TARTUFO	TOTTING	TOURIST	TEXTUAL	UNDERDO	UNLOADS
TORQUAY	TUTTING	TRUCKLE	TOYSHOP	UNDERGO	UNLACED

UNLACES	UNTYING	VACATES	VULTURE	VERGING	VITRIFY
UNLOCKS	UNTWIST	VIDEOED	VAMPIRE	VARNISH	VITALLY
UNLUCKY	UNTAMED	VEDETTE	VAMPING	VERSION	VITAMIN
UNLADEN	UNTUNED	VIEWERS	VAMPISH	VERTIGO	VETERAN
UGLIEST	USTINOV	VEERING	VAMOOSE	VERNIER	VOUCHED
UPLIFTS	UTTERED	VIEWING	VINLAND	VARMINT	VAUGHAN
UNLINED	UTTERLY	VIETNAM	VANTAGE	VERDICT	VOUCHER
UPLANDS	UNTRUTH	VAGRANT	VINTAGE	VARSITY	VOUCHES
UNLATCH	UNTAXED	VAGUEST	VANDALS	VERSIFY	VOUVRAY
UNLOVED	ULULATE	VAGUELY	VANUATU	VERANDA	VAULTED
UNMANLY	UKULELE	VEHICLE	VENEERS	VARIOLA	VAUNTED
UNMASKS	USURERS	VAINEST	VINCENT	VERBOSE	VAULTER
UNMOVED	USUALLY	VEILING	VINEGAR	VIRGOAN	VIVIDLY
UNNAMED	USURPED	VOICING	VENDING	VARIOUS	VIVALDI
UNNERVE	USURPER	VIKINGS	VANILLA	VERMONT	VOYAGED
UTOPIAN	UNUSUAL	VILLAGE	VENTNOR	VERDOUX	VOYAGER
UFOLOGY	URUGUAY	VOLTAGE	VINTNER	VIRUSES	VOYAGES
UNPACKS	UNVEILS	VULGATE	VANGOGH	VERRUCA	VIYELLA
UMPTEEN	UNWRAPS	VILLAIN	VENDORS	VERDURE	WEAKENS
UMPIRED	UNWEARY	VOLCANO	VANESSA	VIRTUAL	WEASELS
UMPIRES	UNWAGED	VULCANS	VENISON	VIRTUES	WEAVERS
UNREADY	UNWINDS	VALIANT	VENTURA	VASSALS	WHALERS
UTRECHT	UPWARDS	VOLUBLE	VENTURE	VISIBLE	WEAKEST
UPRIGHT	UNWOUND	VOLUBLY	VANDYKE	VISIBLY	WHATELY
UKRAINE	ULYSSES	VILLEIN	VANDYCK	VESICLE	WHATFOR
UTRILLO	VIADUCT	VALLEYS	VIOLATE	VISCERA	WRANGLE
UPROOTS	VIBRATE	VALUERS	VIOLETS	VESPERS	WEATHER
UPRATED	VIBRATO	VOLLEYS	VIOLENT	VESSELS	WEARIED
UPRATES	VIBRANT	VELVETY	VIOLINS	VESTIGE	WEANING
UNRAVEL	VICKERY	VULPINE	VIOLIST	VISCOSE	WEARING
UPRIVER	VACCINE	VALUING	VIOLONE	VISCOUS	WEAVING
UPSTAGE	VICTIMS	VILNIUS	VAPOURS	VISIONS	WHALING
UPSTART	VACUITY	VOLUMES	VAQUERO	VISITED	WEARIER
UPSWING	VOCALLY	VALANCE	VERSACE	VISITOR	WEARIES
UPSILON	VACANCY	VALENCY	VERVAIN	VISTULA	WEARILY
UPSURGE	VACUOUS	VALLONE	VARIANT	VESTURE	WHACKED
UNSCREW	VECTORS	VOLPONE	VERDANT	VISAVIS	WEASLEY
UNSOUND	VICIOUS	VALMONT	VERBENA	VATICAN	WHATNOT
UNSTUCK	VICTORS	VALERIE	VERMEER	VOTEDIN	WEAROFF
UPTRAIN	VICTORY	VALISES	VERGERS	VETOING	WEAPONS
UPTIGHT	VICEROY	VALETED	VARIETY	VETTING	WEAROUT
UNTRIED	VACATED	VELOUTE	VARYING	VITRIOL	WRAPPED

WRAPPER	WEEPIES	WHITEST	WRITTEN	WELCOME	WINCING
WHATSIT	WEEVILS	WHINGED	WHIZZED	WALDORF	WINDING
WHARTON	WREAKED	WRIGGLE	WHIZZER	WELLOFF	WINKING
WEALTHY	WRECKED	WHINGER	WHIZZES	WALLOON	WINNING
WEBPAGE	WRECKER	WRINGER	WAKEFUL	WALLOPS	WINDIER
WEBCAST	WHEELED	WHINGES	WAKEMAN	WALLOWS	WINDILY
WEBSITE	WHEELIE	WRIGGLY	WAKENED	WALTONS	WANGLED
WEBBING	WHEELER	WEIGHED	WELLAND	WILLOWS	WANGLER
WOBBLED	WOEISME	WRITHED	WALLACE	WALKOUT	WINKLER
WOBBLES	WHETTED	WEIGHIN	WELFARE	WILLOWY	WANGLES
WEBSTER	WRESTED	WHITHER	WALLACH	WILFRED	WINKLES
WYCHELM	WREATHE	WEIGHTS	WALSALL	WILFRID	WINSLET
WICKETS	WRESTLE	WRITHES	WALMART	WINSLOW	WINSLOW
WICHITA	WHEATEN	WEIGHTY	WALLABY	WOLFRAM	WINGNUT
WACKIER	WREATHS	WAILING	WOLFCUB	WALNUTS	WINSOME
WICKLOW	WHEEZED	WAITING	WILDCAT	WALKWAY	WINDOWS
WIDMARK	WHEEZES	WAIVING	WILHELM	WALTZED	WINNOWS
WIDEBOY	WAFTING	WHILING	WALKERS	WALTZER	WINFREY
WIDGETS	WAFFLED	WHINING	WALLETS	WALTZES	WINDSOR
WADDING	WAFFLER	WHITING	WALTERS	WOMBATS	WYNETTE
WEDDING	WAFFLES	WRITING	WELDERS	WIMPISH	WINSTON
WEDGING	WAGTAIL	WAIKIKI	WILDEST	WIMPLES	WOODALL
WADDLED	WIGWAMS	WHISKED	WILIEST	WOMBLES	WOODCUT
WADDLES	WAGGING	WRINKLE	WELLFED	WEMBLEY	WOOMERA
WIDENED	WIGGING	WHICKER	WELSHED	WOMANLY	WOOFERS
WEDLOCK	WAGGISH	WHISKER	WELSHER	WANNABE	WOOLFAT
WIDOWED	WAGGLED	WHISKEY	WANTAGE	WANTAGE	WROUGHT
WIDOWER	WIGGLED	WRINKLY	WILLHAY	WINDBAG	WRONGLY
WIELDED	WAGGLES	WHIRLED	WALKING	WINEBAR	WYOMING
WHEEDLE	WIGGLES	WHITLAM	WELDING	WINEBOX	WOOLLEN
WEEKDAY	WOGGLES	WHITLOW	WILDING	WANDERS	WROCLAW
WEEKEND	WAGONER	WHITLEY	WILLING	WINDERS	WOODMAN
WHEREIN	WAGERED	WHITMAN	WILTING	WINGERS	WOOSNAM
WEEDERS	WAGEWAR	WHITNEY	WOLFISH	WINNERS	WHOOPED
WHEREAS	WEIRDER	WHIPPED	WILLIAM	WONDERS	WHOOPEE
WHEREAT	WEIRDOS	WHIMPER	WALKIES	WINEGUM	WHOOPER
WHEREBY	WEIRDLY	WHISPER	WALLIES	WINCHED	WHOPPER
WREXHAM	WRITEUP	WHIPPET	WELLIES	WYNDHAM	WOOSTER
WHETHER	WAITERS	WHIRRED	WILLIES	WENCHES	WHOEVER
WEEDING	WHINERS	WHITSUN	WALKMAN	WINCHES	WHOSWHO
WEEPING	WHITENS	WHISTLE	WOLFMAN	WANTING	WIPEOUT
WEEDIER	WRITERS	WHITTLE	WALFORD	WENDING	WARFARE

WARGAME	WARLOAN	WITCHES	YELLING	ZANIEST
WARPATH	WARTORN	WATCHET	YELPING	ZINCITE
WARRANT	WORKOUT	WETTING	YULELOG	ZINNIAS
WARBABY	WORNOUT	WETFISH	YELLOWS	ZANUSSI
WORKBAG	WORKSHY	WITTIER	YELLOWY	ZOOMING
WORLDLY	WORSTED	WITTILY	YELTSIN	ZIONISM
WARHEAD	WARATAH	WATFORD	YOMPING	ZIONIST
WARHERO	WIRETAP	WETLOOK	YANKEES	ZOOLOGY
WARDENS	WORKTOP	WITHOUT	YANKING	ZIPPERS
WARDERS	WASTAGE	WATERED	YANGTZE	ZAPPING
WARRENS	WASSAIL	WETSUIT	YAOUNDE	ZIPPING
WORKERS	WASHBAG	WOUNDED	YAPPING	ZIPPIER
WORSENS	WASHDAY	WOULDBE	YUPPIES	ZIPCODE
WARIEST	WESTEND	WAVIEST	YUPPIFY	ZERMATT
WARMEST	WISBECH	WAVELET	YARDAGE	ZESTFUL
WARTHOG	WESTERN	WAVENEY	YARDARM	ZITHERS
WAREHAM	WASHERS	WAVERED	YORKERS	ZATOPEK
WARSHIP	WASTERS	WAVERER	YORKIST	
WORSHIP	WISHFUL	WAXWING	YARDLEY	
WORRIED	WISTFUL	WEXFORD	YFRONTS	
WARLIKE	WISEGUY	WAXWORK	YARWOOD	
WARTIME	WESTHAM	WAYLAID	YEREVAN	
WARMING	WASHING	WAYWARD	YASMINE	
WARNING	WASTING	WAYLAYS	YASHMAK	
WARPING	WISHING	WAYSIDE	YTTRIUM	
WORDING	WASPISH	WAYBILL	YOUNGER	
WORKING	WASHOUT	WHYALLA	YAWNING	
WARRICK	WASTREL	WIZENED	YOWLING	
WARWICK	WASHTUB	WIZARDS	ZEALOTS	
WARRIOR	WYSIWYG	XRAYING	ZEALOUS	
WORDIER	WETLAND	XIMENES	ZEBEDEE	
WORRIER	WATTAGE	XANTHUS	ZACHARY	
WORRIES	WETNESS	XEROSIS	ZOEBALL	
WORDILY	WITHERS	XEROXED	ZIGZAGS	
WARBLED	WITLESS	YEARNED	ZHIVAGO	
WARBLER	WITNESS	YABBERS	ZWINGLI	
WARBLES	WITTERS	YOBBISH	ZAKUSKI	
WORKMAN	WETTEST	YUCATAN	ZULEIKA	
WORKMEN	WATTEAU	YIDDISH	ZILLION	
WARLORD	WATCHED	YIELDED	ZAMBEZI	
WARDOFF	WATCHER	YAFFLES	ZAMBIAN	
WARLOCK	WATCHES	YOKOONO	ZOMBIES	

ALANALDA	ABATTOIR	ACCENTED	ALDANITI	ADENITIS	ARGONAUT
ALACARTE	ALASTAIR	ASCENDED	ADDENDUM	APERITIF	ALGERIAN
AMARANTH	ADAPTING	ACCENTOR	ADDINGUP	ATELIERS	ANGERING
ATALANTA	AWAITING	ANCHORED	ANDROIDS	ABETMENT	AUGURING
ADAMBEDE	ADAPTORS	AJCRONIN	ANDROPOV	ADENOIDS	ALGERNON
ALANBALL	APARTYTO	ACCEPTED	ALDERMAN	ANEMONES	AUGUSTUS
ANARCHIC	ACANTHUS	ALCAPONE	ALDERMEN	ALEHOUSE	ANGSTROM
ATANCHOR	ACAPULCO	ALCOPOPS	ALDERNEY	ABERRANT	ASHGABAT
ARAWDEAL	ABACUSES	ACCURACY	ANDERSEN	AVERRING	ASHTANGA
ALANDALE	ADAMWEST	ACCORDED	ALDERTON	AGEGROUP	ACHIEVED
ALANDELL	ANALYSED	ACCURSED	ANDERSON	AVERSION	ACHIEVER
ABANDONS	ANALYSES	ACCURSES	ANDERTON	ABETTING	ACHIEVES
AWARDING	ANALYSIS	ASCORBIC	AUDITING	ALERTING	ATHLETES
AWAKENED	ANALYSTS	ACCURATE	ADDITION	AVERTING	ATHLETIC
ACADEMIA	ARBUCKLE	ACCESSED	AUDITION	ABETTORS	ATHEISTS
ACADEMIC	ALBACORE	ACCESSES	AUDITORS	APERTURE	ACHILLES
ARABELLA	AMBIENCE	ACCOSTED	AUDITORY	ADEQUACY	ALHAMBRA
AMATEURS	AMBRIDGE	ACCUSING	ADDITIVE	ADEQUATE	ATHENIAN
AMARETTI	AMBULANT	ACCUSTOM	ABEYANCE	ACESWILD	ABHORRED
AMARETTO	ALBANIAN	ANCESTOR	ADELAIDE	AFFIANCE	ASHCROFT
ANALECTS	AMBROSIA	ACCUSERS	ACETATES	AFFECTED	ADHERENT
ARACHNID	ARBOREAL	ANCESTRY	ADENAUER	ALFRESCO	ADHERING
ASAWHOLE	ABBESSES	ALCATRAZ	AVERAGED	AFFAIRES	ATHERTON
ANATHEMA	AMBUSHED	ASCETICS	AVERAGES	AFFLICTS	APHORISM
ATAPINCH	AMBUSHES	ACCRUALS	AVEMARIA	AFFINITY	APHORIST
AMARILLO	ASBESTOS	ACCRUING	AMENABLE	AFFRONTS	ADHESION
ALANLADD	AMBITION	ACCOUTRE	ALEMBICS	AFFIRMED	ADHESIVE
ALARMING	ATBOTTOM	ACCOUNTS	AMESBURY	AFFORDED	AGITATED
ALARMISM	ARBITERS	ABDUCTED	ALEXBEST	AFFLUENT	AGITATES
ALARMIST	ACCLAIMS	ABDUCTEE	ACERBATE	AFFIXING	ANIMATED
ANACONDA	ARCHAISM	ADDICTED	ACERBITY	AUGRATIN	ANIMATES
ABALONES	ARCADIAN	ANDYCOLE	AREACODE	ARGUABLE	ALITALIA
ANABOLIC	ARCHDUKE	ABDUCTOR	AGENCIES	ARGUABLY	AMICABLE
ANALOGUE	ACCEDING	ANDYCAPP	ABERDEEN	ANGLESEY	AMICABLY
ATAPRICE	ACCIDENT	ABDICATE	AMENDING	AUGMENTS	AGITATOR
ANAGRAMS	ACCREDIT	AUDACITY	ABERDARE	ANGLICAN	ANIMATOR
AFAIRCOP	ARCHIVES	AUDIENCE	ANECDOTE	ANGRIEST	ALICANTE
ALACRITY	ASCRIBED	ANDYGIBB	AVENGING	AGGRIEVE	ACIDBATH
ADAMSRIB	ASCRIBES	ALDRIDGE	AVENGERS	ANGELICA	ACIDDROP
ANAISNIN	AUCTIONS	ABDULLAH	ACESHIGH	ANGELICO	ANISETTE
ADAMSALE	ACCOLADE	ABDOMENS	AMETHYST	ANGELINA	ABINGDON
AMASSING	AUCKLAND	ARDENTLY	AMERICAN	ARGUMENT	ALIGHTED

ABINITIO	AILMENTS	ALMANACS	ALOPECIA	APPOINTS	ACRIDITY
ABITMUCH	ALLEGING	ALMONERS	ABOVEALL	APPLIQUE	ADRIENNE
AVIEMORE	ALLEGORY	ARMINARM	AGONISED	APPALLED	AGREEING
AVIONICS	ALLTHERE	ADMONISH	AGONISES	APPENDED	AEROFOIL
ALIGNING	ALLNIGHT	AMMONITE	ANODISED	APPENDIX	AEROFLOT
ALIENATE	ALLRIGHT	ARMORIAL	ANODISES	AMPHORAE	AERIFORM
ACIDOSIS	ALLCLEAR	ARMSRACE	ATOMISED	APPROVAL	ARROGANT
AGITPROP	ALLALONG	ADMIRALS	ATOMISER	APPROACH	ABROGATE
APIARIES	ASLONGAS	ADMIRING	ATOMISES	APPROVED	ARROGATE
AVIARIES	ALLENKEY	ADMIRERS	APOPLEXY	APPROVES	AIRSHIPS
ACIDRAIN	ATLANTIC	ADMITTED	ABOUNDED	ASPHODEL	AYRSHIRE
APIARIST	ATLANTIS	AMMETERS	ANOINTED	AMPERAGE	AIRLINER
ALISTAIR	ALLINALL	ARMATURE	ADORNING	APPARENT	AIRLINES
AVIATRIX	ALLINONE	ARMOURED	ACOUSTIC	ASPIRANT	AIRMILES
AVIATING	ATLENGTH	ARMOURER	AROUSING	ASPIRING	AIRTIGHT
AVIATION	ALLROUND	ADMIXING	ALOYSIUS	ASPIRINS	ADROITLY
AVIATORS	ALLSPICE	ANNEALED	APOSTLES	ASPERITY	AIRFIELD
ACIDTEST	ALLERGEN	ANNUALLY	ABORTING	ASPIRATE	AIRRIFLE
ASITWERE	ALLERGIC	ANNAFORD	ADOPTING	APPOSITE	ARRAIGNS
ABJECTLY	AILERONS	ABNEGATE	AGOSTINI	APPETITE	AIRLIFTS
ADJACENT	ALLURING	ANNULLED	ADOPTION	ASPHYXIA	ACRYLICS
ADJUDGED	ALLUSION	ANNALISE	ADOPTERS	APPLYING	AEROLOGY
ADJUDGES	ALLUSIVE	ANNALIST	AMORTISE	ACQUAINT	AIRPLANE
ADJOINED	ALLATSEA	ANNJONES	APOSTASY	ARQUETTE	AEROLITE
ANJELICA	ALLOTTED	ABNORMAL	APOSTATE	ACQUIRED	AURELIUS
ALJOLSON	ABLUTION	AMNESIAC	ABORTIVE	ACQUIRES	ACRIMONY
ADJUNCTS	ABLATIVE	AGNUSDEI	ADOPTIVE	AIRRAIDS	AGRIMONY
ABJURING	ALLUVIAL	AGNOSTIC	ALOEVERA	AIRWAVES	ARRANGED
ADJURING	ALLOWING	ANNOTATE	ACOLYTES	ADRIATIC	ARRANGER
ADJUSTED	ALLEYCAT	ANNOUNCE	APPLAUDS	AERIALLY	ARRANGES
ADJUSTER	ALLEYWAY	AZNAVOUR	ALPHABET	AIRMAILS	ADRENALS
ADJUTANT	ALLAYING	ANNEXING	APPEALED	AEROBICS	ACRONYMS
ADJOURNS	ARMBANDS	ANNOYING	APPEARED	ACROBATS	AGRONOMY
ALKALINE	ASMUCHAS	AROMATIC	APPEASED	AURICLES	AIRINESS
ARKANSAS	ARMYCAMP	ADORABLE	APPEASES	APRICOTS	AERONAUT
ATKINSON	ARMRESTS	ADORABLY	APPLAUSE	ATROCITY	AIRWOMAN
ARKROYAL	ARMAGNAC	AVOCADOS	APPRAISE	ABRIDGED	AIRFORCE
ALLIANCE	ALMIGHTY	ABOMASUM	ALPACINO	ABRIDGER	AIRWOMEN
ALLOALLO	ARMCHAIR	ATOMBOMB	APPLEPIE	ABRIDGES	AIRBORNE
ADLIBBED	ARMAMENT	AGOODFEW	APPLETON	AIREDALE	AIRPORTS
ALLOCATE	ARMENIAN	AVOIDING	ARPEGGIO	ABRADING	AIRSPACE
ALLUDING	ALMANACK	AGOODJOB	APPRISED	ACRIDINE	AIRSPEED

ABRUPTLY	ABSENTEE	AUTOCRAT	ALTEREGO	ABUTMENT	BRAIDING
ATROPINE	ASSENTED	ANTECEDE	ASTEROID	AQUANAUT	BRANDING
AGRARIAN	ASSENTER	ALTOCLEF	AFTERALL	AQUARIAN	BOARDERS
AIRBRICK	ABSINTHE	ARTICLES	ALTERING	AQUARIST	BLANDISH
AIRCRAFT	ABSENTLY	ATTACHED	ATTIRING	AQUARIUM	BRANDISH
AIRBRUSH	ASSONANT	ATTACHES	AFTERYOU	AQUARIUS	BRAKEPAD
AEROSTAT	ARSONIST	ATTACKED	ALTARBOY	AQUATICS	BLAKENEY
ARRESTED	ABSCONDS	ATTACKER	ANTERIOR	ABUTTING	BRACELET
ACROSTIC	ASSYRIAN	AUTODAFE	ANTEROOM	AQUATINT	BEADEVIL
APRESSKI	AUSTRIAN	ANTEDATE	ASTERISK	ADULTERY	BRAZENLY
AEROSOLS	ABSTRACT	ANTIDOTE	AFTERSUN	AYURVEDA	BEATENUP
ABRASION	ABSORBED	ACTEDOUT	ARTESIAN	ADVOCAAT	BEAUFORT
ABRASIVE	ABSORBER	ANTLERED	ARTISTES	ADVOCACY	BRADFORD
AMRITSAR	ADSORBED	ATTHEHOP	ATTESTED	ADVOCATE	BRAGGING
AIRSTRIP	ANSERMET	ARTEFACT	ATTESTER	ADVANCED	BRAGGART
AERATING	ASSERTED	ARTIFICE	ARTISTIC	ADVANCES	BEACHING
AERATION	ASSORTED	ACTOFGOD	ARTISANS	ADVISING	BIATHLON
AERATORS	ABSURDLY	AUTOGIRO	ARTISTRY	ADVISERS	BOATHOOK
AUREVOIR	ALSORANS	ANTIHERO	ALTITUDE	ADVISORY	BEANITEM
ARRIVALS	ASSURING	ATTAINED	APTITUDE	AMYACKER	BEARINGS
ARRIVING	ABSTRUSE	ANTILLES	ATTITUDE	ANYTHING	BEATINGS
AARDVARK	ASSESSED	ANTELOPE	ASTUTELY	ANYWHERE	BRASILIA
ASSUAGED	ASSESSES	AUTUMNAL	ASTOUNDS	ATYPICAL	BRAZIERS
ASSUAGES	ASSISTED	ANTIMONY	ARTFULLY	BEARABLE	BLACKCAP
ABSTAINS	ASSASSIN	ATTEMPTS	ALTRUISM	BEATABLE	BLACKCAT
ANSWERED	ASSESSOR	AUTOMATA	ALTRUIST	BRADAWLS	BLACKMAN
ASSIGNED	ALSATIAN	AUTOMATE	ACTIVELY	BRAMBLES	BLACKICE
AESTHETE	ATSOURCE	AUTOMATS	ACTIVISM	BRAMBELL	BLACKLEG
AESTIVAL	ASSAULTS	ANTENNAE	ACTIVIST	BLABBING	BLACKSEA
ABSEILED	ASSAYING	ATTENDED	ACTIVATE	BLABBERS	BLACKTIE
ABSEILER	ASSAYERS	ATTENDEE	ACTIVITY	BRADBURY	BLACKFLY
ASSAILED	ACTUATED	ANTONYMS	ADULATED	BRAEBURN	BLACKENS
AUSPICES	ACTUATES	AUTONOMY	ADULATES	BLANCHED	BLACKING
ABSOLVED	ANTEATER	ATTUNING	ADULATOR	BLANCHES	BLACKBOX
ABSOLVER	ARTMALIK	ASTONISH	ASUNCION	BRANCHED	BLACKROD
ABSOLVES	ACTUALLY	ACTINIUM	AQUEDUCT	BRANCHES	BLACKEST
ABSOLUTE	ACTUATOR	ALTHOUGH	AMUNDSEN	BRATCAMP	BRACKISH
ASSEMBLE	ATTRACTS	ARTHOUSE	ABUNDANT	BEANCURD	BLANKETS
ASSEMBLY	ARTTATUM	ANTIQUES	ABUDHABI	BOARDMAN	BRACKETS
ASSUMING	ANTIBODY	ARTERIAL	ARUMLILY	BRANDIES	BLACKOUT
ABSENCES	AUTOBAHN	ARTERIES	AQUALUNG	BRANDNEW	BLACKEYE
ABSENTED	ANTICHAY	ATTORNEY	AQUILINE	BOARDING	BOATLOAD

BEAULIEU	BUBBLIER	BECALMED	BEDIMMED	BLENHEIM	BAGPIPER
BEAGLING	BABBLING	BACKLOGS	BEDKNOBS	BEERHALL	BAGPIPES
BRAWLING	BOBOLINK	BUCKLING	BADINAGE	BEEHIVES	BEGUILED
BEAGLERS	BUBBLING	BACKLASH	BYDINTOF	BREVIARY	BEGUILES
BRAWLERS	BABBLERS	BACKLESS	BEDCOVER	BEEFIEST	BAGGIEST
BEAUMONT	BIBULOUS	BACKLIST	BEDSOCKS	BREAKOFF	BIGAMIST
BIANNUAL	BABYLOVE	BACILLUS	BEDROOMS	BREAKAGE	BIGAMOUS
BRAINIER	BOBFOSSE	BUCKLEYS	BADMOUTH	BREAKING	BEGONIAS
BRAWNIER	BABERUTH	BECOMING	BUDAPEST	BREAKERS	BEGINNER
BEATNIKS	BABUSHKA	BACKMOST	BADBREAK	BLEAKEST	BIGMONEY
BRANNING	BABYSITS	BECKONED	BYDESIGN	BREAKOUT	BIGNOISE
BRAINBOX	BABOUCHE	BACKPACK	BODYSUIT	BEETLING	BIGMOUTH
BRATPACK	BOBDYLAN	BACTRIAN	BODYSHOP	BIENNIAL	BIGAPPLE
BEANPOLE	BOBBYVEE	BACKROOM	BODYSURF	BLEEPING	BIGBREAK
BEASPORT	BOBBYPIN	BACKREST	BEDSTEAD	BLEEPERS	BEGOTTEN
BRADPITT	BACCARAT	BACKSEAT	BEDEVILS	BLEARILY	BEGRUDGE
BEATRICE	BUCHANAN	BACKSIDE	BEDIVERE	BEETROOT	BOGEYMAN
BOATRACE	BECHAMEL	BICESTER	BODYWRAP	BRESSLAW	BEHEADED
BLAIRISM	BACKACHE	BUCKSHEE	BODYWORK	BREWSTER	BEHOLDEN
BRADSHAW	BUCKAROO	BACKSLID	BODYWAVE	BLESSING	BEHOLDER
BRASSICA	BACKBEAT	BACKSPIN	BADLYOFF	BLESSYOU	BOHEMIAN
BEARSKIN	BACKBONE	BUCKSKIN	BEDAZZLE	BREATHED	BEHEMOTH
BRAISING	BACKBITE	BACKSTOP	BEEEATER	BREATHER	BEHAVING
BEAUTIES	BACKCHAT	BUCKSHOT	BEERBOHM	BREATHES	BRIGANDS
BEAUTIFY	BICYCLED	BACKWARD	BLEACHED	BRETTLEE	BRIGADES
BLASTOFF	BICYCLES	BACKWASH	BLEACHES	BLEATING	BRIBABLE
BEATTIME	BACKCOMB	BACKYARD	BREACHED	BREEZIER	BAILBOND
BLASTING	BACKDOOR	BADPATCH	BREACHES	BREEZILY	BRISBANE
BOASTING	BACKDROP	BADLANDS	BREECHES	BIFOCALS	BRINDLED
BOASTFUL	BACKDATE	BIDDABLE	BEEFCAKE	BEFUDDLE	BLINDING
BEAUVAIS	BACKDOWN	BADFAITH	BREADBIN	BEFOGGED	BUILDING
BEAUVOIR	BICKERED	BODYBLOW	BLEEDING	BEFRIEND	BUILDERS
BRANWELL	BACTERIA	BEDECKED	BLENDING	BAFFLING	BRINDISI
BOATYARD	BACHELOR	BODLEIAN	BREEDING	BAFFLERS	BRIEFING
BOBHAWKE	BACKEDUP	BADGERED	BLENDERS	BUFFOONS	BRIEFEST
BOBTAILS	BACKFLIP	BUDGETED	BREEDERS	BEFITTED	BRIDGING
BABYBOOM	BACKFILL	BUDDHISM	BAEDEKER	BIGDADDY	BRINGING
BABYDOLL	BACKFIRE	BUDDHIST	BEEFEDUP	BYGRAVES	BRINGOUT
BABYFACE	BACKHEEL	BEDLINEN	BREWEDUP	BEGGARLY	BLIGHTED
BABYFOOD	BACCHANT	BUDDLEIA	BRETHREN	BAGHEERA	BLIGHTER
BABYHOOD	BACKHAND	BODYLINE	BREZHNEV	BAGUETTE	BRIGHTEN
BIBLICAL	BACKINGS	BADBLOOD	BIERHOFF	BIGWHEEL	BRIGHTER

BLITHELY	BALLBOYS	BALUSTER	BENNEVIS	BANKROLL	BLOWFISH
BRIGHTLY	BALLCOCK	BELOSTON	BANDEAUX	BANKRUPT	BROUGHAM
BRIGHTON	BULLDOGS	BULLSEYE	BUNGEDUP	BENCROSS	BROUHAHA
BAILIFFS	BULLDOZE	BELITTLE	BENEFICE	BANKRATE	BLOWHOLE
BRICKBAT	BELIEVED	BELLTENT	BONAFIDE	BANDSMAN	BROCHURE
BRICKIES	BELIEVER	BOLSTERS	BENEFITS	BANDSMEN	BROTHERS
BRICKRED	BELIEVES	BOLIVIAN	BENIGNLY	BANISHED	BOOKINGS
BLINKING	BILLETED	BELOWPAR	BANKHEAD	BANISHES	BLOCKADE
BLINKERS	BALLETIC	BILLWARD	BONEHEAD	BANISTER	BROOKNER
BRISKEST	BULLETIN	BULAWAYO	BANSHEES	BONDSMEN	BLOCKAGE
BRIDLING	BILBERRY	BULLYOFF	BENCHLEY	BANQUETS	BLOCKING
BRISLING	BULLFROG	BULLYING	BUNGHOLE	BINDWEED	BROOKING
BRIMLESS	BALLGAME	BALLYHOO	BUNCHING	BENTWOOD	BROOKLYN
BRIMMING	BALLGIRL	BELLYFUL	BINLINER	BANDYING	BOOTLACE
BRIANMAY	BULKHEAD	BOMBARDS	BONFIRES	BUNNYHOP	BROLLIES
BRIANRIX	BOLTHOLE	BEMOANED	BUNTINGS	BUOYANCY	BLOWLAMP
BRIANENO	BELLHOPS	BOMBADIL	BUNFIGHT	BOOKABLE	BROILING
BRIDPORT	BILLINGS	BOMBHEAD	BANVILLE	BOOGALOO	BROILERS
BLIMPISH	BILLIONS	BUMPIEST	BONEIDLE	BROWBEAT	BOOKLETS
BLISSFUL	BULKIEST	BUMPINTO	BANDITRY	BOOMBOOM	BLOOMING
BRISTLED	BALLISTA	BUMPKINS	BENOJOKE	BLOTCHES	BLOOMERS
BRISTLES	BILLKERR	BUMBLING	BANKLOAN	BROACHED	BOOKMARK
BRITTANY	BALANCED	BEMUSING	BUNDLING	BROACHES	BROWNRAT
BLISTERS	BALANCES	BOMBSITE	BUNGLING	BROOCHES	BROWNIES
BLITZING	BELONGED	BAMBURGH	BENELTON	BROCCOLI	BROWNALE
BLIZZARD	BALDNESS	BANDAGED	BUNGLERS	BOOTCAMP	BROWNING
BAKELITE	BALINESE	BANDAGES	BONELESS	BOOKCASE	BROWNOWL
BAKERIES	BOLDNESS	BANJAXED	BANALITY	BOOKCLUB	BLOWOVER
BAKERLOO	BALMORAL	BENJAMIN	BINOMIAL	BRONCHUS	BLOWPIPE
BAKEWELL	BELMOPAN	BANKABLE	BONEMEAL	BROADWAY	BOOKREST
BAKEWARE	BALLOTED	BINNACLE	BENUMBED	BLONDELL	BLOSSOMS
BALLARAT	BELLOWED	BANDANNA	BONINESS	BROADENS	BLOUSONS
BOLLARDS	BILLOWED	BUNGALOW	BANKNOTE	BROODING	BROWSING
BALLADES	BILLOWEN	BUNKBEDS	BENHOGAN	BROADEST	BOOKSHOP
BALEARIC	BULLOCKS	BUNDCHEN	BENDOVER	BOOKENDS	BROWSERS
BULGARIA	BALLOONS	BANKCARD	BENTOVER	BROKEOFF	BOOBTUBE
BULWARKS	BALLPARK	BENEDICK	BONHOMIE	BOOKEDIN	BOOSTING
BULGAKOV	BALDPATE	BENEDICT	BANNOCKS	BROKENLY	BLOATERS
BALLADRY	BALDRICK	BENIDORM	BANJOIST	BLOKEISH	BLOTTERS
BELPAESE	BELGRADE	BANDERAS	BONARLAW	BOOKEDUP	BOOSTERS
BALLASTS	BULLRING	BANNERET	BANERJEE	BROKEOUT	BOOMTOWN
BELABOUR	BALLROOM	BANTERED	BANCROFT	BUOYEDUP	BOOKWORK

BOOKWORM	BORDELLO	BARNSLEY	BASILISK	BETOKENS	BLUFFERS
BIPLANES	BURGEONS	BIRDSEED	BASEMENT	BATTLING	BLUDGEON
BAPTISED	BORDERON	BIRDSONG	BASINGER	BOTTLING	BLUSHING
BAPTISES	BARBERRY	BIRDSEYE	BASENJIS	BATTLEON	BRUSHING
BAPTISMS	BURBERRY	BARATHEA	BUSHNELL	BATTLERS	BOUDICCA
BAPTISTS	BARBECUE	BARITONE	BASENESS	BOTTLERS	BOUTIQUE
BYPASSED	BORDEAUX	BERATING	BUSINESS	BOTULISM	BLUEJOHN
BYPASSES	BORNFREE	BURSTING	BUSYNESS	BETELNUT	BAULKING
BEQUEATH	BAREFOOT	BARSTOOL	BASINETS	BOTTLEUP	BLUNKETT
BEQUESTS	BIRTHDAY	BYRETURN	BESTOWAL	BOTANIST	BLUELAMP
BARNABAS	BIRKHALL	BURNTOUT	BESTOWED	BATWOMAN	BOUILLON
BOREANAZ	BOREHOLE	BERMUDAN	BASSOONS	BUTTONED	BRUMMELL
BARMAIDS	BURCHILL	BURGUNDY	BISCOTTI	BETROTHS	BLUEMOON
BARRAGES	BERTHING	BAROUCHE	BOSWORTH	BUTTONIT	BOUZOUKI
BEREAVED	BIRCHING	BOROUGHS	BESTRIDE	BUTTOCKS	BOULOGNE
BARBARIC	BIRTHING	BARNYARD	BASERATE	BATHROBE	BOUDOIRS
BOREALIS	BARCHART	BISMARCK	BESOTTED	BATHROOM	BLURRING
BARRACKS	BERNHARD	BUSTARDS	BASCULES	BUTTRESS	BRUSSELS
BARNACLE	BURGHERS	BUSTAGUT	BISCUITS	BATHTUBS	BRUISING
BARGAINS	BARBICAN	BUSHBABY	BETRAYAL	BOTSWANA	BRUISERS
BARBADOS	BERLINER	BUSYBODY	BETRAYED	BETLYNCH	BLURTING
BERGAMOT	BARRIERS	BASEBALL	BETRAYER	BITBYBIT	BLUSTERS
BARABBAS	BERGKAMP	BASSCLEF	BATHCUBE	BRUBAKER	BLUSTERY
BAREBACK	BARFLIES	BISECTED	BETJEMAN	BRUTALLY	BLURTOUT
BERIBERI	BIRDLIME	BASSDRUM	BYTHEWAY	BLUEBELL	BOUQUETS
BIRDBATH	BURBLING	BESIEGED	BATTENED	BLUBBERY	BEVELLED
BIRDCAGE	BURGLING	BESIEGER	BATTERED	BLUEBIRD	BAVARIAN
BARMCAKE	BURGLARS	BESIEGES	BETTERED	BOUNCIER	BEVERLEY
BIRDCALL	BURGLARY	BASKETRY	BOTHERED	BLUECHIP	BEVERAGE
BARNDOOR	BARTLETT	BUSHFIRE	BUTTERED	BOUNCING	BAVAROIS
BURNDOWN	BARONIAL	BESMIRCH	BATHETIC	BOUNCERS	BIVOUACS
BARGEMAN	BYRONBAY	BASSINET	BUTTEDIN	BOUNDING	BIWEEKLY
BERGERAC	BARONAGE	BASTILLE	BITTERLY	BLUNDERS	BOWBELLS
BARGEMEN	BORGNINE	BASTIONS	BITTERNS	BOULDERS	BEWIGGED
BARTERED	BARENESS	BESTIARY	BUTTERUP	BOUNDARY	BEWAILED
BARTERER	BARONESS	BOSSIEST	BATCHING	BOUNDERS	BAWDIEST
BERKELEY	BARONETS	BASSISTS	BITCHING	BLUEEYES	BEWILDER
BORDERED	BORROWED	BASILICA	BOTCHING	BRUCELEE	BOWLOVER
BURDENED	BORROWER	BASELINE	BOTCHERS	BRUNETTE	BOWSPRIT
BARGEDIN	BURROWED	BUSTLING	BUTCHERS	BLUEFLAG	BOXPLEAT
BERBERIS	BARDOLPH	BASILDON	BUTCHERY	BLUFFING	BAYWATCH
BARBELLS	BARMOUTH	BASELESS	BATTIEST	BOUFFANT	BOYRACER

BIYEARLY	CHAMFERS	CHARLTON	CLANSMAN	CABINBOY	CADENCES
BOYSCOUT	CRANFORD	CRAWLERS	CLASSACT	CABINETS	CODENAME
BAYBERRY	CRAWFORD	CHARLIZE	CLASSICO	CABOOSES	CADBURYS
BAYREUTH	CRAYFISH	CRABMEAT	CLASSICS	CABOODLE	CADAVERS
BAYONETS	CRAGGIER	CLAMMIER	CLANSMEN	CEBERANO	CADDYING
BOYCOTTS	CHANGING	CHARMING	CLASSIER	CUBEROOT	CREMATED
BOYISHLY	CHARGING	CLAIMANT	CLASSIFY	CABARETS	CREMATES
BOYSTOWN	CLANGING	CLAIMING	COARSELY	CYCLAMEN	CLEMATIS
BUZZARDS	CHARGERS	COALMINE	CLASSING	CACHALOT	CREVASSE
BUZZBOMB	CLANGOUR	CRAMMING	CHATSHOW	COCKATOO	CLENCHED
BAZOOKAS	COACHMAN	CHALMERS	COARSEST	COCACOLA	CLENCHES
BUZZWORD	COACHMEN	CHARMERS	CHASSEUR	COCKCROW	COERCING
CHATAWAY	COALHOLE	CLAYMORE	CLAPTRAP	CYCLEWAY	CRESCENT
CHARADES	CLASHING	CHAINSAW	CHARTRES	COCKEREL	COERCION
CHAPATIS	COACHING	CHARNHAM	CRAFTIER	COCKEYED	COERCIVE
CLARABOW	CRASHING	CRANNIES	CHATTELS	CYCLICAL	CLEMENCY
CIABATTA	CHALICES	CHANNELS	CHATTILY	COCKIEST	CREDENCE
CHAMBRAY	CLARINET	CHAINING	CRAFTILY	CYCLISTS	CLEVERER
CLAWBACK	CLAVICLE	CHANNING	CHANTING	CACOLOGY	CLEVERLY
CRABBIER	CHARISMA	CLANNISH	CHASTENS	CACKLING	CHEYENNE
CLAMBAKE	CHARISSE	CHAMONIX	CHATTING	CACKLERS	CHESHIRE
CRABBILY	CLARISSA	CHACONNE	COASTING	CUCUMBER	CHEMICAL
CHADBAND	CRAZIEST	CHAMORRO	CRAFTING	COCONUTS	CLERICAL
CHAPBOOK	CHARIOTS	CLAMOURS	COAUTHOR	COCKNEYS	CHEMISES
CHAMBERS	CRACKLED	CHAPPIES	CHANTERS	COCOONED	CLERIHEW
CLAMBERS	CRACKLES	CHAPPELL	CHAPTERS	CYCLONES	CREDITED
CHARCOAL	CRACKNEL	CHAMPING	CHARTERS	CYCLONIC	CREVICES
CRATCHIT	CRANKIER	CLAMPING	CHATTERS	COCKPITS	CHENILLE
CHANCELS	CRANKILY	CLAPPING	COASTERS	CICERONE	CREDIBLE
CHANCING	CLACKING	CLASPING	CHARTISM	COCKSURE	CREDIBLY
CHANCERY	CLANKING	CRAMPING	CHARTIST	CICATRIX	CREDITON
CHALDEAN	CRACKING	CRAMPONS	CHASTISE	COCKTAIL	CREDITOR
CHANDLER	CLARKSON	CHAMPION	CHASTITY	CODICILS	CHEMISTS
CLADDING	CRACKPOT	CLAYPIPE	CHASUBLE	CODIFIED	CHEVIOTS
COALDUST	CRACKERS	CHAMPERS	CABBAGES	CODIFIES	CHEEKIER
CLARENCE	CHARLOCK	COALPORT	CUBICLES	CODPIECE	CHEEKILY
COALESCE	CHARLADY	CHAIRMAN	CABLECAR	CODRIVER	CHECKING
CRATERED	CHAPLAIN	COATRACK	CABLEWAY	CADILLAC	CHEEKING
CRANEFLY	CHARLENE	CHAIRMEN	CABRIOLE	CEDILLAS	CREAKING
CRAVENLY	CHATLINE	CHAIRING	CABALLER	CODDLING	CHECKBOX
CHATEAUX	CRADLING	CHARRING	COBBLING	CUDDLING	CHECKERS
COALFACE	CRAWLING	CHATROOM	COBBLERS	CADENZAS	CHECKOUT

CREAMIER	CREATION	CHINCHIN	CHIRPING	CALIGULA	CELERITY
CREAMTEA	CREATORS	CLIPCLOP	CLIPPING	CALLIPER	CULPRITS
CREAMERY	CREATURE	CHILDREN	CRIMPING	COLLIDED	CELESTAS
CREWNECK	CHESTNUT	CHILDISH	CLIPPERS	COLLIDES	COLESLAW
CLEANSED	CREATIVE	CHINDITS	CRIMPERS	CALLIOPE	COLOSSAL
CLEANSER	CHERUBIC	CHIMEDIN	CRISPEST	COLLIERS	CALLSIGN
CLEANSES	CHERUBIM	COINEDIT	CAISSONS	COLLIERY	CALFSKIN
CLEANING	CHEQUERS	CRITERIA	CHIVVIED	CELLISTS	COLDSORE
CLEANERS	CLEAVAGE	CLIFFORD	CHIVVIES	CULTISTS	COLISEUM
CLEANEST	CLEAVING	COIFFURE	CHISWICK	CALFLOVE	COLOSSUS
CHEZNOUS	CLEAVERS	COIFFEUR	CHINWAGS	COLOMBIA	CULOTTES
CLEANCUT	CHERWELL	CLINGING	CAJOLING	COLUMBIA	CALOTYPE
CHEROKEE	CHEEZELS	CRINGING	CAJOLERS	CALAMINE	CELLULAR
CRETONNE	CAFFEINE	CHISHOLM	CAJOLERY	CALAMARI	CULTURAL
CHEROOTS	CUFFLINK	CRICHTON	CAKEHOLE	CALAMITY	CALLUSES
CREEPIER	CAFENOIR	CHISINAU	CAKEWALK	CELLMATE	COLLUDED
CREEPILY	CAGEBIRD	CLINICAL	CELLARER	COLUMBUS	COLLUDES
CHEAPENS	CAGLIARI	CRIMINAL	CELLARET	CALENDAR	COLOURED
CREEPING	CAGINGIN	CRITICAL	COLLAGEN	COLONIAL	CULTURED
CREEPERS	COGENTLY	CEILINGS	COLLARED	COLANDER	CULTURES
CHEAPEST	CAGINESS	CEILIDHS	COLLATED	COLONIES	CALCUTTA
CLEARWAY	CIGARBOX	CSIMIAMI	COLLATES	CYLINDER	CALCULUS
CHEERIER	COGITATE	CLINIQUE	CULPABLE	COLONELS	COMMANDO
CHERRIES	CAGOULES	CRITIQUE	CULPABLY	CULINARY	COMMANDS
CLEAROFF	COHERENT	CHICKPEA	CALVADOS	CALMNESS	COMPARED
CHEERILY	COHESION	CRINKLED	COLLATOR	COLDNESS	COMPARES
CHEERING	COHESIVE	CRINKLES	COLLAPSE	COLONISE	COMRADES
CHEVRONS	CHINAMAN	CHICKENS	CALLBACK	COLONIST	CAMPAIGN
CLEARING	CHICANES	CLICKING	CELIBACY	CULLODEN	CAMPANIA
CLEAREST	CHINATEA	CLINKING	CALIBRED	COLLOQUY	COMPADRE
CHEERFUL	CLIMATIC	CRICKETS	CALABASH	COLDPLAY	CAMEBACK
CLEARCUT	CHIVALRY	CHILLIER	CELIBATE	CALYPSOS	COMEBACK
CLEAROUT	CRIBBAGE	CHILLING	COLDCALL	COLOPHON	CAMPBELL
CHESSMAN	CLIMBING	CHINLESS	COLDCASE	CALORGAS	COMEDIAN
CRESSIDA	CRIBBING	CHIPMUNK	COLDCUTS	CELERIAC	COMEDIES
CHESSMEN	CRIBBINS	CHIMNEYS	CALMDOWN	CHLORIDE	COMEDOWN
CREASING	CLIMBERS	CHIPOTLE	CULDESAC	COLORADO	COMMENCE
CHEPSTOW	CHITCHAT	CHIRPIER	COLLEGES	CALORIES	COMMERCE
CREOSOTE	COINCIDE	CRIPPLED	COLLECTS	CHLORINE	COMMENDS
CHEETAHS	CLINCHED	CRISPIER	COLLETTE	COLTRANE	CAMBERED
CHEATING	CLINCHER	CHIRPILY	COLDFEET	CALTROPS	COMPERED
CREATING	CLINCHES	CHIPPING	COLIFORM	CULDROSE	COMPERES

COMPETED	COMETRUE	CONDEMNS	CONTINUE	CONCRETE	CLOSEOFF
COMPETES	COMMUNAL	CONVEYOR	CONTINUO	CONTRITE	CHOLERIC
COMMENTS	CAMPUSES	CUNJEVOI	CONFLICT	CONGREVE	CLOVELLY
CAMPFIRE	COMMUNED	CONTEMPT	CONCLUDE	CONTRIVE	CLOSERUN
CAMSHAFT	COMMUNES	CANBERRA	CANALISE	CANISTER	COOPEDUP
COMEHOME	COMMUTED	CANOEIST	CONFLATE	CONISTON	CLOGGING
COMBINED	COMMUTER	CONDENSE	CONCLAVE	CYNOSURE	CLOTHCAP
COMBINES	COMMUTES	CONTESSA	CANONLAW	CANETOAD	CLOTHIER
COMPILED	COMPUTED	CONVERSE	CANONESS	CONSTANT	CLOTHING
COMPILER	COMPUTER	CONCEPTS	CANONISE	CENOTAPH	CROCHETS
COMPILES	COMPUTES	CONCERTO	CANONIST	CONSTRUE	COOLIBAH
COMFIEST	CANTATAS	CONCERTS	CONCORDE	CONJUGAL	CHOCICES
COMEINTO	CINNABAR	CONFETTI	CANNONED	CONSULAR	COOLIDGE
CAMELEER	CANVASES	CONNECTS	CENSORED	CENSURED	CLOCKOFF
COMPLIED	CONNACHT	CONSENTS	CONDONED	CENSURES	CROAKILY
COMPLIES	CANNABIS	CONTENTS	CONDONES	CENSUSES	CLOCKING
CAMELLIA	CONTAINS	CONTESTS	CONSOLED	CONFUSED	CLONKING
COMPLAIN	CENTAVOS	CONVENTS	CONSOLES	CONFUSES	CROAKING
COMPLINE	CINNAMON	CONVERTS	CANOODLE	CONJURED	CROCKERY
COMPLETE	CENTAURS	CONCEIVE	CONNOLLY	CONJURER	CROCKETT
CAMOMILE	CENTAURY	CONSERVE	CONFORMS	CONJURES	CLOCKOUT
CEMENTED	CINEASTE	CONIFERS	CONSOMME	CONSUMED	CROMLECH
COMANCHE	CONTACTS	CINCHONA	CONFOUND	CONSUMER	CHOWMEIN
COMINGIN	CYNICISM	CANNIBAL	CONTOURS	CONSUMES	CLOWNING
COMINGTO	CANADIAN	CONVINCE	CONCOCTS	CENTUPLE	CROONING
COMMONER	CANDELAS	CENTIMES	CONSORTS	CONQUERS	CROWNING
COMPOSED	CONTENDS	CONFIDED	CONTORTS	CONQUEST	CROONERS
COMPOSER	CANKERED	CONFIDES	CANOPIED	CONVULSE	CLOWNISH
COMPOSES	CANTERED	CONFINED	CANOPIES	CONDUCTS	COOLNESS
CAMBODIA	CONCEDED	CONFINES	CONSPIRE	CONDUITS	CHOCOLAT
COMMONLY	CONCEDES	CONNIVED	CONTRACT	CONSULTS	CROUPIER
CAMBORNE	CONVENED	CONNIVER	CONTRICK	CANDYMAN	CHOMPING
COMPOUND	CONVENER	CONNIVES	CANARIES	CROMARTY	CHOPPING
COMFORTS	CONVENES	CONSIDER	CONTROLS	COOKBOOK	CLOPPING
CAMBRIAN	CONVEYED	CANDIDLY	CENTRING	CLOBBERS	CROPPING
CAMEROON	CONVERGE	CANFIELD	CONFRONT	CROTCHET	CROMPTON
COMPRESS	CONCEALS	CANTICLE	CANTRIPS	CROUCHED	CHOPPERS
COMPRISE	CONGEALS	CONFIRMS	CONTRARY	CROUCHES	CHOIRBOY
CAMISOLE	CONNELLY	CONSIGNS	CENTRISM	CHOPCHOP	CLOUSEAU
CAMPSITE	CANOEING	CANNIEST	CENTRIST	CLOUDIER	CROSSBAR
CEMETERY	CANTEENS	CONSISTS	CONGRESS	CROWDING	CHOPSUEY
COMATOSE	CONCERNS	CONVICTS	CONTRAST	CLOSETED	CLOISTER

CROSSPLY	CAPTIVES	CORLEONE	CORDLESS	CIRCUITS	CASTLOTS
CHOOSING	CAPTIONS	CARFERRY	CIRCLETS	CORRUPTS	CASEMENT
CROSSING	CYPRIOTS	CORSETRY	CORNMEAL	CARAVELS	CASHMERE
CROSSBOW	CAPSICUM	CORNETTO	CERAMICS	CARAVANS	CASEMATE
CROSSCUT	CAPTIOUS	CORRECTS	CEREMONY	CARDVOTE	COSINESS
CROATIAN	CAPULETS	CORVETTE	CHROMIUM	CORNWALL	CASANOVA
CHORTLED	CUPBOARD	CURRENTS	CORONARY	CORKWOOD	CUSTOMER
CHORTLES	CAPERING	CERBERUS	CORONERS	CAREWORN	CASSOCKS
CROWTHER	CAPERERS	CURLEDUP	CURTNESS	CARRYOFF	CESSPOOL
CLOTTING	CAPESIDE	CAREFREE	CORONETS	CARRYALL	CASTRIES
CLOUTING	CAPITALS	CARDGAME	CORUNDUM	CARRYING	CASTRATO
CROFTING	CAPSTANS	CARTHAGE	CORPORAL	CARRYCOT	COSGROVE
CROSTINI	CAPETOWN	CARPHONE	CARLOADS	CURLYTOP	COSTUMES
CROUTONS	CAPSULES	CARDIGAN	CARTONED	CARRYOUT	CASQUETS
CROFTERS	CAPTURED	CARDINAL	CORRODED	CASTAWAY	CASEWORK
CHORUSES	CAPTURES	CARNIVAL	CORRODES	CASCADED	COTTAGER
CLOSURES	COQUETTE	CORSICAN	CARBOLIC	CASCADES	COTTAGES
CROCUSES	COQAUVIN	CARBINES	CARTOONS	CASUALLY	COTTAGEY
CROMWELL	CARCASES	CARRIAGE	CARBOOTY	CASUALTY	CUTBACKS
COOKWARE	CARYATID	CARVINGS	CARPORTS	CASHBACK	CATCALLS
CHOUXBUN	CARPARKS	CORNICHE	CARAPACE	CASEBOOK	CUTHBERT
CRONYISM	CARNALLY	CARLISLE	CARCRASH	CASHBOOK	CETACEAN
CUPMATCH	CURTAILS	CORDIALE	CARESSED	CASHCROP	CUTICLES
CEPHALIC	CURTAINS	CORDIALS	CARESSES	CASHCARD	CATACOMB
CAPTAINS	CARDAMOM	CURRICLE	CHRISTEN	CASHDESK	CITADELS
COPYBOOK	CORSAIRS	CORRIDOR	CURTSIED	CASHDOWN	CITYDESK
CAPYBARA	CURRANTS	CARRIERS	CURTSIES	COSSETED	CUTADASH
CAPUCHIN	CEREBRAL	CURLIEST	CHRISSIE	CASHEDIN	CATHETER
CAPUCINE	CEREBRUM	CURLICUE	CHRISTIE	COSMETIC	CATSEYES
CAPACITY	CORACLES	CARTLOAD	CORPSING	CASTELLA	CATHEDRA
CUPIDITY	CARACALS	CERULEAN	CORETIME	COSTELLO	CITYFARM
COPPELIA	CARRERAS	CAROLLED	CAROTENE	CASSETTE	CATEGORY
COPYEDIT	CERVELAT	CAROLLER	CURATORS	CASHFLOW	CATCHIER
CAPOEIRA	CURRENCY	CORALSEA	CURATIVE	CASTINGS	CATCHALL
CAPEFEAR	CAREENED	CYRILLIC	CAROUSAL	CUSHIONS	CITYHALL
CUPOFTEA	CAREERED	CAROLINA	CIRCULAR	CASTIRON	CATCHING
CAPEHORN	CARPETED	CAROLINE	CAROUSED	CASHIERS	CATCHERS
CAPSIZAL	CARTERET	CARTLAND	CAROUSEL	CUSHIEST	CUTSHORT
CUPFINAL	CORNERED	CIRCLING	CAROUSER	CASELOAD	CUTTINGS
CAPRICES	CORSETED	CURDLING	CAROUSES	COSTLIER	CATRIONA
CAPSIZED	CARNEGIE	CARILLON	CIRCUSES	CASTLING	CATTIEST
CAPSIZES	CORDELIA	CARELESS	CORDUROY	CASHLESS	CATSKILL

CYTOLOGY	CAULDRON	CRUISING	COWPOKES	DEADLINE	DOBERMAN
CATALYST	CAUSEWAY	CRUISERS	COWHOUSE	DIALLING	DEBARRED
CUTGLASS	CAUSERIE	COUSTEAU	COWORKER	DRAWLING	DEBASING
CATULLUS	CRUDEOIL	COUNTIES	COWARDLY	DIALLERS	DEBATING
CUTENESS	CHUGGING	COURTIER	COWERING	DEADLOSS	DEBITING
CATWOMAN	CRUSHBAR	COURTNEY	COXCOMBS	DRAWLOTS	DEBUTANT
CUTNOICE	COUCHANT	COUNTING	COXSWAIN	DRAINAGE	DEBATERS
CATHODES	COUGHING	COURTING	CRYONICS	DRAINING	DECEASED
CATHOLIC	CRUSHING	CHUNTERS	CRYSTALS	DEAFNESS	DECLARED
COTTONON	CAUGHTUP	CLUSTERS	COZENAGE	DIAGNOSE	DECLARER
CUTLOOSE	CRUDITES	COUNTERS	CAZENOVE	DRABNESS	DECLARES
CATAPULT	CHURINGA	COUNTESS	DRAMATIC	DRAWNOUT	DICTATED
COTOPAXI	CRUCIFIX	COURTESY	DIAMANTE	DIAGONAL	DICTATES
CATARACT	CRUCIBLE	CAUCUSES	DEADBEAT	DRAGOMAN	DECLAIMS
CUTPRICE	CAUTIONS	CHUTZPAH	DRAWBACK	DIAMONDS	DICTATOR
CATTRALL	COURIERS	CAVEBEAR	DRAMBUIE	DRAGOONS	DECLASSE
CATERING	CAUTIOUS	CIVILIAN	DEANCAIN	DEACONRY	DECIBELS
CATERERS	CHUCKLED	CIVILLAW	DEADCALM	DIALOGUE	DECOCTED
CITATION	CHUCKLES	CIVILWAR	DEADCERT	DIASPORA	DECADENT
CUTITOUT	CHUNKIER	CAVALIER	DEADDUCK	DIATRIBE	DECIDING
CUTPURSE	CAULKING	CAVILLED	DIAZEPAM	DRAGRACE	DECODING
CATSUITS	CHUCKING	CAVILLER	DEADENED	DIAGRAMS	DECIDERS
COTSWOLD	CLUCKING	CIVILISE	DEADENER	DRAGSTER	DECODERS
CITIZENS	CLUNKING	CIVILITY	DEAFENED	DEADSHOT	DECREPIT
CRUSADED	CRUELLER	CEVENNES	DIABETES	DIASTOLE	DOCREDIT
CRUSADER	CLUBLAND	CAVINGIN	DIAMETER	DEADTIME	DECREASE
CRUSADES	COUPLING	COVENANT	DIABETIC	DRAFTING	DUCHESSE
CAUSALLY	CHURLISH	COVENTRY	DIALECTS	DEALTOUT	DECAGRAM
CHUBBIER	CLUELESS	CAVORTED	DWARFING	DIANTHUS	DECIGRAM
CRUMBLED	COUPLETS	COVERLET	DRAGGING	DEADWOOD	DECAGONS
CRUMBLES	CLUINGIN	COVERAGE	DRAUGHTS	DIALYSIS	DECKHAND
CLUBBING	CHURNING	COVERALL	DRAUGHTY	DEBACLES	DECEIVED
CLUBBERS	CHURNOUT	COVERTLY	DEADHEAD	DEBAGGED	DECEIVER
CHURCHES	CRUMPLED	COVERING	DEADHEAT	DEBUGGED	DECEIVES
CLUTCHED	CRUMPLES	CAVITIES	DEATHCAP	DABCHICK	DECLINED
CLUTCHES	CRUMPETS	CAVATINA	DRACHMAS	DEBRIEFS	DECLINES
CRUNCHED	CLUBROOM	COVETING	DEALINGS	DABBLING	DECOKING
CRUNCHER	CLUBROOT	COVETOUS	DRAWINGS	DABBLERS	DOCKLAND
CRUNCHES	CLUBSODA	COWRITER	DIARISTS	DEBILITY	DUCKLING
CRUTCHES	CLUMSIER	COWGIRLS	DRAGKING	DEBUNKED	DOCILITY
CRUNCHIE	CLUMSILY	COWSLIPS	DEADLOCK	DUBONNET	DECAMPED
COUSCOUS	COUNSELS	COWLNECK	DEADLIER	DEBONAIR	DECEMBER

DECIMALS	DIEDDOWN	DIFFERED	DEGAULLE	DULCIMER	DIMBLEBY
DOCUMENT	DEEPENED	DEFLECTS	DOGGYBAG	DULCINEA	DUMPLING
DECIMATE	DIETETIC	DEFILING	DRIBBLED	DALGLISH	DEMOLISH
DECANTED	DEEPFELT	DEFILERS	DRIBBLER	DILEMMAS	DOMINICA
DECANTER	DREYFUSS	DEFAMING	DRIBBLES	DELAMARE	DEMANDED
DECENTLY	DREDGING	DEFENCES	DWINDLED	DOLOMITE	DEMENTED
DOCTORAL	DREDGERS	DEFENDED	DWINDLES	DULLNESS	DOMINEER
DOCTORNO	DIESIRAE	DEFENDER	DRIVEWAY	DOLDRUMS	DOMINOES
DUCHOVNY	DUELLING	DEFINING	DRIVEOUT	DOLOROSO	DOMINANT
DECAPODS	DWELLING	DAFTNESS	DRIPFEED	DELIRIUM	DOMINION
DECIPHER	DWELLERS	DEFTNESS	DYINGOUT	DOLOROUS	DAMPNESS
DICAPRIO	DUELLIST	DEFINITE	DEIGHTON	DALESMAN	DEMONISE
DUCKPOND	DREAMIER	DAFFODIL	DRINKING	DALESMEN	DIMINISH
DOCTRINE	DREAMILY	DEFROSTS	DRINKERS	DELUSION	DOMINATE
DECORATE	DREAMING	DEFERRAL	DRILLING	DELUSORY	DEMURRAL
DECOROUS	DREAMERS	DEFERRED	DEIGNING	DOLITTLE	DEMERGER
DOCUSOAP	DREAMTUP	DEFORMED	DJIBOUTI	DELETING	DEMURRED
DOCKSIDE	DEEPNESS	DIFFRING	DRIPPING	DILATING	DUMFRIES
DECISION	DUENORTH	DEFUSING	DAINTIER	DILUTING	DEMURELY
DUCKSOUP	DUESOUTH	DIFFUSED	DAINTIES	DELETION	DEMERARA
DECISIVE	DEEDPOLL	DIFFUSER	DRIFTNET	DILATION	DOMESDAY
DUCKWEED	DEERPARK	DIFFUSES	DAINTILY	DILUTION	DEMISTER
DECAYING	DIETRICH	DEFAULTS	DRIFTING	DILATORY	DEMPSTER
DECRYING	DREARIER	DOGWATCH	DRIFTERS	DELATOUR	DOMESTIC
DICKYBOW	DREARILY	DEGRADED	DAIQUIRI	DELIVERS	DAMASCUS
DOCKYARD	DEEMSTER	DEGRADES	DAIRYMAN	DELIVERY	DEMOTING
DADSARMY	DRESSAGE	DOGEARED	DAIRYMEN	DELAWARE	DEMOTION
DEDUCTED	DEERSKIN	DOGMATIC	DEIFYING	DALLYING	DUMMYRUN
DIDACTIC	DRESSING	DOGSBODY	DRIZZLED	DELAYING	DONNAAIR
DEDICANT	DRESSERS	DOGGEREL	DRIZZLES	DOLLYTUB	DINGBATS
DEDUCING	DYESTUFF	DOGGEDLY	DEJECTED	DUMBBELL	DINGDONG
DEDICATE	DEFRAYAL	DAGUERRE	DRJEKYLL	DAMNABLE	DINEDOUT
DODDERER	DEFIANCE	DOGBERRY	DULLARDS	DAMNABLY	DONNELLY
DIDDLING	DEFRAUDS	DOGTIRED	DALMAHOY	DEMOBBED	DUNGEONS
DIDDLERS	DEFEATED	DOGFIGHT	DELICACY	DUMBBELL	DANSEURS
DADORAIL	DEFLATED	DOGSLIFE	DELICATE	DEMOCRAT	DANSEUSE
DIEHARDS	DEFLATES	DOGOODER	DALADIER	DAMOCLES	DANEGELD
DAEDALUS	DEFRAYED	DOGROSES	DELUDING	DOMICILE	DINGHIES
DRENCHED	DEFECTED	DOGHOUSE	DILIGENT	DAMPENED	DUNGHILL
DRENCHES	DEFACING	DOGTOOTH	DELEGATE	DIMAGGIO	DANDIEST
DREADING	DEFECTOR	DIGESTED	DELIGHTS	DAMAGING	DINGIEST
DREADFUL	DEFICITS	DIGESTIF	DOLPHINS	DEMIJOHN	DENTISTS

DANGLING	DOORSTEP	DERAILED	DISABUSE	DISCOVER	DISGUISE
DYNAMICS	DROWSIER	DARLINGS	DUSTBATH	DISPOSED	DISGUSTS
DYNAMISM	DROWSILY	DERRICKS	DUSTBOWL	DISPOSES	DISRUPTS
DYNAMITE	DOORSTOP	DERRIERE	DISOBEYS	DISROBED	DISOWNED
DINENAGE	DROPSHOT	DIRTIEST	DUSTCART	DISROBES	DASHWOOD
DANKNESS	DIONYSUS	DERELICT	DESCENDS	DISGORGE	DESLYNAM
DANDRUFF	DROPZONE	DORTMUND	DISTENDS	DISLODGE	DUTIABLE
DENDRITE	DEPRAVED	DARTMOOR	DISHEVEL	DESPOTIC	DETRACTS
DENARIUS	DEPICTED	DERANGED	DYSLEXIA	DYSTOPIA	DATABANK
DANBROWN	DEPLETED	DARINGLY	DYSLEXIC	DESPOILS	DATABASE
DYNASTIC	DEPLETES	DARKNESS	DISCERNS	DISCOUNT	DETACHED
DINOSAUR	DAPPERLY	DARROWBY	DISPENSE	DISMOUNT	DETACHES
DENOTING	DEPTFORD	DORDOGNE	DISPERSE	DISTORTS	DETECTED
DONATING	DEPRIVED	DORMOUSE	DESSERTS	DISSOLVE	DITHERED
DONATION	DEPRIVES	DARKROOM	DISKETTE	DISARRAY	DITHERER
DENOUNCE	DAPPLING	DARKSTAR	DISSECTS	DESCRIBE	DOTTEREL
DENTURES	DEPILATE	DORISDAY	DISSENTS	DISGRACE	DUTYFREE
DANNYBOY	DOPAMINE	DERISION	DISHEDUP	DISTRACT	DUTCHMAN
DANDYISH	DEPENDED	DERISORY	DESIGNED	DISTRICT	DITCHING
DANDYISM	DOPINESS	DERISIVE	DESIGNER	DESERTED	DUTCHHOE
DENIZENS	DIPLOMAS	DURATION	DISAGREE	DESERTER	DETAILED
DOOLALLY	DIPLOMAT	DERIVING	DISTINCT	DESERVED	DETAINED
DOORBELL	DEPLORED	DERBYHAT	DESPISED	DESERVES	DETAINEE
DIOCESAN	DEPLORES	DIRTYDEN	DESPISES	DISARMED	DOTTIEST
DUODENAL	DEPLOYED	DUSHANBE	DESTINED	DISCREET	DETRITUS
DROVEOUT	DEPARTED	DISPATCH	DISLIKED	DISORDER	DATELINE
DUODENUM	DEPORTED	DISTANCE	DISLIKES	DISTRAIN	DATELESS
DROPGOAL	DEPORTEE	DASTARDS	DISPIRIT	DESIRING	DETONATE
DOONICAN	DEPOSING	DISBANDS	DISCIPLE	DISTRESS	DMTHOMAS
DROPKICK	DEPOSITS	DISCARDS	DOSSIERS	DISTRUST	DUTYPAID
DOORKNOB	DIPSTICK	DESCALED	DESELECT	DISCRETE	DETERRED
DOODLING	DEPUTIES	DESCALES	DISPLACE	DESIROUS	DETHRONE
DROOLING	DEPUTISE	DISEASED	DISCLAIM	DISPROVE	DETESTED
DOODLERS	DORMANCY	DISEASES	DISALLOW	DESTROYS	DETOXIFY
DROLLERY	DARKAGES	DISMAYED	DISCLOSE	DESISTED	DRUMBEAT
DROPLETS	DIRTBIKE	DISMALLY	DESOLATE	DISASTER	DRUBBING
DOORNAIL	DIRECTED	DISRAELI	DISPLAYS	DISTURBS	DRUIDISM
DROWNING	DIRECTLY	DESPAIRS	DISINTER	DISSUADE	DIURETIC
DROOPING	DIRECTOR	DESCANTS	DISUNITY	DISPUTED	DRUGGING
DROPPING	DERIDING	DISTASTE	DISLOYAL	DISPUTES	DRUDGERY
DOORPOST	DARKENED	DISABLED	DISPOSAL	DISQUIET	DRUGGIST
DOOMSDAY	DARTFORD	DUSTBINS	DESMONDS	DISBURSE	DAUGHTER

DAUPHINE	DIVERGES	DOXOLOGY	EMBALMED	ETCETERA	EYESIGHT
DOUGHBOY	DIVERTED	DEXTROSE	EMBALMER	EXCLUDED	ELEGISTS
DOUGHNUT	DIVORCED	DAYLEWIS	EMBOLDEN	EXCLUDES	EMERITUS
DAUBINGS	DIVORCEE	DAYLIGHT	EMBROILS	EXCAVATE	EYEGLASS
DRUNKARD	DIVORCES	DRYCLEAN	EMBARKED	ENDEARED	EVERMORE
DOUBLING	DIVESTED	DRYSLOPE	EMBOSSED	ENDPAPER	EVENNESS
DOUBLOON	DEVISING	DOYENNES	EMBOSSER	ENDODERM	ETERNITY
DOUBLEUP	DIVISION	DRYINGUP	EMBOSSES	ENDYMION	EYETOOTH
DRUMMING	DAVISCUP	DAYTODAY	EMBITTER	ENDANGER	EXEMPLAR
DRUMMERS	DIVISIVE	DRYGOODS	EBBWVALE	ENDINGUP	EYEDROPS
DOURNESS	DUVETDAY	DAYBREAK	ELBOWING	ELDORADO	EXECRATE
DOUNREAY	DEVOTEES	DAYDREAM	EMBEZZLE	ENDORSED	EYEBROWS
DRUMROLL	DOVETAIL	DAYBYDAY	EXCHANGE	ENDORSER	EVENSONG
DAUNTING	DEVOTING	DAZZLING	EXCLAIMS	ENDORSES	EVENTUAL
DOUBTING	DEVOTION	DAZZLERS	ENCHANTS	ENDURING	EVENTIDE
DOUBTFUL	DEVOURED	DOZINESS	ENCODING	ENDUSERS	ELECTRIC
DEVIANCE	DEVOURER	EMANATED	ESCHEWAL	ENDOWING	EJECTING
DEVIATED	DEVOUTLY	EMANATES	EXCEEDED	ELEGANCE	ELECTING
DEVIATES	DOWNBEAT	ERASABLE	ETCHINGS	EYEPATCH	ERECTING
DIVEBOMB	DOWNCAST	EVANESCE	EXCELLED	EMERALDS	EVENTING
DOVECOTE	DEWYEYED	EVAPERON	ESCALOPE	EYECANDY	EXERTING
DIVIDEND	DOWNFALL	EXAMINED	ESCALATE	ELEVATED	EJECTION
DIVIDING	DOWAGERS	EXAMINEE	ENCUMBER	ELEVATES	ELECTION
DAVIDSON	DOWNHILL	EXAMINER	ENCROACH	EYEBALLS	ELECTRON
DIVIDERS	DOWNHOME	EXAMINES	ENCLOSED	ELEVATOR	ERECTION
DEVALUED	DOWDIEST	ENABLING	ENCLOSES	EXERCISE	EXERTION
DEVALUES	DOWNLOAD	EXAMPLES	ENCROUTE	EVERDENE	ELECTORS
DEVILLED	DAWDLING	ELAPSING	ESCAPADE	EYESDOWN	EVENTERS
DEVOLVED	DOWELROD	ELASTANE	ENCIPHER	EBENEZER	EDENTATE
DEVOLVES	DAWDLERS	ENACTING	ESCAPEES	EYELEVEL	EVENTFUL
DIVULGED	DEWINESS	EXACTING	ESCAPING	ELEMENTS	ELECTIVE
DIVULGES	DOWJONES	EXALTING	ESCAPISM	ELEVENTH	EXECUTED
DAVYLAMP	DEWPOINT	EVACUEES	ESCAPIST	EYETEETH	EXECUTES
DEVELOPS	DOWNPLAY	EVACUATE	ESCORTED	EMERGENT	EXECUTOR
DEVILISH	DOWNPIPE	EVALUATE	ENCIRCLE	EMERGING	ENERVATE
DEVONIAN	DOWNPOUR	EMBRACED	ESCARGOT	ENERGISE	EVERYDAY
DIVINELY	DOWNSIDE	EMBRACES	EXCERPTS	EYESHADE	EVERYMAN
DIVINING	DOWNSIZE	EMBLAZON	EXCUSEME	ELEPHANT	EVERYONE
DAVENTRY	DRWATSON	EMBEDDED	EXCISING	EYEPIECE	EFFICACY
DIVINERS	DOWNTURN	EMBODIED	EXCUSING	ELEGISED	EFFECTED
DIVINITY	DOWNTOWN	EMBODIES	EXCISION	ELEGISES	EFFACING
DIVERGED	DOWNWIND	EBBTIDES	EXCITING	EYELINER	ENFEEBLE

EFFIGIES	ENHANCED	EXIGUOUS	ENORMOUS	EMPATHIC	ENSNARED
ENFILADE	ENHANCES	EDIFYING	ECONOMIC	ESPOUSAL	ENSNARES
ENFOLDED	ESHANESS	ENJOYING	EGOTRIPS	EXPOUNDS	ECSTATIC
ENFORCED	ETHIOPIA	ELKHOUND	EGOISTIC	ESPOUSED	EASTCOTE
ENFORCER	ETHEREAL	EXLIBRIS	ELOQUENT	ESPOUSES	EASEDOFF
ENFORCES	ETHERNET	ECLECTIC	EVOLVING	EMPOWERS	EASTERLY
EFFUSING	EDHARRIS	ECLOGUES	EUONYMUS	EMPTYING	EASYMEAT
EFFUSION	EXHAUSTS	EULOGISE	EMPHASIS	ENQUIRED	ENSEMBLE
EFFUSIVE	EMIRATES	EULOGIST	EMPHATIC	ENQUIRER	EASEMENT
EFFLUVIA	EPITAPHS	ECLIPSED	EXPLAINS	ENQUIRES	EISENERZ
EFFLUENT	ERICBANA	ECLIPSES	ESPECIAL	ESQUIRES	ELSINORE
ENGRAVED	EVILDOER	ELLIPSES	EXPECTED	EARMARKS	EASINESS
ENGRAVER	EMINENCE	ELLIPSIS	EXPEDITE	EUROCRAT	ENSCONCE
ENGRAVES	EVIDENCE	ELLIPTIC	ESPRESSO	EARACHES	ENSHRINE
EXGRATIA	EXIGENCY	ENLARGED	EXPLICIT	ENRICHED	ENSURING
EGGHEADS	EPIDEMIC	ENLARGER	ENPOINTE	ENRICHES	EASTWICK
EAGLEEYE	EPIPHANY	ENLARGES	ESPALIER	EURYDICE	EASTWOOD
ENGAGING	EPITHETS	EELGRASS	EXPELLED	EARLGREY	EASTWARD
EDGEHILL	EDIFICES	ENLISTED	EXPANDED	ENRAGING	ESSAYING
EGGSHELL	ELICITED	ENLIVENS	EXPENSES	EARTHIER	ESSAYIST
EGGWHISK	ELIGIBLE	EDMCBAIN	EXPUNGED	EARTHILY	ENTRANCE
EGGWHITE	ERICIDLE	EMMENTAL	EXPUNGES	EARPHONE	ESTRANGE
EGGTIMER	EDITIONS	EDMONTON	EXPONENT	EARTHING	ENTRAILS
ENGULFED	ELITISTS	EMMAPEEL	EMPLOYED	EARPIECE	ENTRACTE
EGGPLANT	EPISODES	ENMESHED	EMPLOYEE	EARNINGS	ENTRANTS
EDGELESS	EPISODIC	ENMESHES	EMPLOYER	EARRINGS	EXTRACTS
EUGENICS	EPILOGUE	ENNOBLED	EXPLODED	EARLIEST	EATABLES
ENGENDER	EXITPOLL	ENNOBLES	EXPLODES	ENROLLED	ENTICING
ENGINEER	EMIGRANT	EDNADORE	EXPLORED	EARPLUGS	ENTICERS
EDGINESS	EPIGRAPH	ERNIEELS	EXPLORER	EARFLAPS	ECTODERM
ENGORGED	EMIGRATE	EINSTEIN	EXPLORES	ERRANTLY	ENTRENCH
EIGHTEEN	EMISSION	EGOMANIA	EUPHORIA	ERRANTRY	ESTEEMED
EIGHTIES	EMISSARY	EBORACUM	EUPHORIC	EERINESS	EXTREMES
EDGEWAYS	EMISSIVE	EXORCISE	EXPLOITS	EARLOBES	ENTREPOT
EXHIBITS	EPISTLES	EXORCISM	EXPORTED	EUROPEAN	ENTREATS
ECHOGRAM	EMITTING	EXORCIST	EXPORTER	EARDRUMS	ENTREATY
ETHELRED	EVICTING	ESOTERIC	EXPERTLY	EARDROPS	ENTAILED
ECHELONS	EXISTENZ	ELONGATE	EXPIRING	ETRUSCAN	ENTWINED
ETHYLENE	EXISTING	EMOTIONS	EMPERORS	EURASIAN	ENTWINES
EXHALING	EVICTION	EMOTICON	EMPORIUM	EUROSTAR	EXTOLLED
EXHUMING	EPIDURAL	EGOTISTS	EXPOSING	EARMUFFS	ENTOMBED
EPHEMERA	EPICURES	ENORMITY	EXPOSURE	ENSLAVED	ESTIMATE

ESTONIAN	ENVISION	FLAVOURS	FADDIEST	FEEBLEST	FAIRGAME
EXTENDED	EGYPTIAN	FLATPACK	FADDISTS	FREELOVE	FLINGING
ENTANGLE	FLANAGAN	FLAGPOLE	FIDDLING	FREEPORT	FAIRHEAD
EXTERNAL	FLAMBEAU	FLAPPING	FIDDLERS	FREEPOST	FRIGHTEN
EATERIES	FLAUBERT	FLAPPERS	FIDELITY	FREERIDE	FAITHFUL
EXTORTED	FIANCEES	FLATRACE	FEDERACY	FREEREIN	FAILINGS
ENTIRELY	FRANCOIS	FLAGRANT	FEDERICO	FREESIAS	FAIRISLE
ENTERING	FRANCOME	FRAGRANT	FEDERALS	FRETSAWS	FLICKING
ENTHRONE	FRASCATI	FLAGSHIP	FEDERATE	FREETIME	FRISKING
EXTERIOR	FLANDERS	FLATSPIN	FEDAYEEN	FLEETING	FLICKERS
ENTIRETY	FLAGDOWN	FEARSOME	FEEDBACK	FRETTING	FAIRLADY
ENTITLED	FLAMENCO	FEASTDAY	FLETCHER	FUELTANK	FRIENDLY
ENTHUSED	FLAMEGUN	FEASTING	FRESCOES	FREETOWN	FEIGNING
ENTHUSES	FRANFINE	FLATTENS	FIERCELY	FREQUENT	FAIRNESS
EDUCATED	FLATFOOT	FRACTION	FLEECING	FREEVOTE	FAIRPLAY
EDUCATES	FLATFISH	FLATTERS	FREEDMAN	FREEWILL	FLIPPANT
EMULATED	FLAGGING	FLATTERY	FREUDIAN	FRETWORK	FLIPPING
EMULATES	FLASHMAN	FLATTYRE	FIELDING	FREEWAYS	FAIRPORT
EDUCATOR	FLASHILY	FRACTURE	FIELDERS	FRENZIED	FLIPPERS
EMULATOR	FLASHING	FLATTEST	FIENDISH	FREEZING	FRIPPERY
ENUMBERS	FEATHERS	FLAUTIST	FREDERIC	FREEZERS	FRIESIAN
EAUDENIL	FEATHERY	FEATURED	FRENETIC	FREEZEUP	FLIPSIDE
EAUDEVIE	FLASHGUN	FEATURES	FREEFALL	FIFTIETH	FLIMSIER
EDUCIBLE	FLAMINGO	FOBWATCH	FREEFORM	FOGLAMPS	FAILSAFE
EQUALLED	FEASIBLE	FABULIST	FEELGOOD	FOGGIEST	FLINTOFF
EQUALISE	FEASIBLY	FABULATE	FRESHMAN	FOGBOUND	FEISTILY
EQUALITY	FLATIRON	FABULOUS	FRESHMEN	FIGURINE	FAINTING
EQUIPPED	FLAPJACK	FEBRUARY	FRESHAIR	FIGURING	FEINTING
EMULSIFY	FRANKLIN	FACIALLY	FREEHOLD	FIGHTOFF	FLIRTING
EMULSION	FLANKING	FOCACCIA	FREEHAND	FIGHTING	FLITTING
EQUATING	FRANKING	FACTIONS	FRESHEST	FIGHTERS	FRICTION
ERUPTING	FRAULEIN	FACTIOUS	FLESHOUT	FUGITIVE	FRITTERS
EXULTANT	FLAILING	FACELIFT	FEELINGS	FOGEYISH	FAINTEST
EXULTING	FEARLESS	FACELESS	FLEXIBLE	FOGEYISM	FAILURES
EQUATION	FLAWLESS	FECKLESS	FLEXIBLY	FRIGATES	FAIRWAYS
ERUPTION	FRAILEST	FACILITY	FREEJACK	FLINCHED	FOLDAWAY
ENVIABLE	FLATLETS	FACEMASK	FREEKICK	FLINCHES	FULLBEAM
ENVIABLY	FRAGMENT	FACTOTUM	FRECKLED	FAIRCOPY	FALLBACK
ENVELOPE	FLATMATE	FACEPACK	FRECKLES	FLINDERS	FULLBACK
ENVELOPS	FLAUNTED	FUCHSIAS	FREAKISH	FLIMFLAM	FILMBUFF
ENVIRONS	FLANNELS	FOCUSING	FREAKOUT	FLIPFLOP	FELICITY
ENVISAGE	FLATNESS	FIDGETED	FREELOAD	FOIEGRAS	FALLDOWN

FALTERED	FALSTAFF	FINENESS	FRONTAGE	FOREHEAD	FORESTRY
FILLETED	FOLKTALE	FONDNESS	FROSTILY	FARMHAND	FIRETRAP
FILTERED	FULLTIME	FUNEREAL	FLOATING	FARTHING	FIRSTOFF
FOLDEROL	FULLTOSS	FINISHED	FLOUTING	FIRMHAND	FIRSTAID
FALSETTO	FUMIGANT	FINISHES	FROSTING	FOREHAND	FORETELL
FILBERTS	FUMIGATE	FENGSHUI	FOOTWEAR	FORSHORT	FORETOLD
FILLEDUP	FAMILIAL	FINESPUN	FOOTWORK	FURTHEST	FORMULAE
FULLFACE	FAMILIAR	FANATICS	FIREAWAY	FARCICAL	FORMULAS
FELDGRAU	FAMILIES	FINETUNE	FERNANDO	FORGIVEN	FERRULES
FILIGREE	FUMBLING	FUNCTION	FORWARDS	FORGIVES	FERGUSON
FILMGOER	FEMININE	FANCYMAN	FORSAKEN	FERVIDLY	FORSWEAR
FILCHING	FEMINISE	FROMATOZ	FORSAKES	FORCIBLE	FAREWELL
FALCHION	FEMINISM	FOOTBALL	FURNACES	FORCIBLY	FIREWALL
FILCHERS	FEMINIST	FLOODLIT	FORMALIN	FARRIERS	FIREWOOD
FILLINGS	FUMAROLE	FLOODING	FARFALLE	FARRIERY	FIREWORK
FALLIBLE	FAMISHED	FLORENCE	FORMALLY	FURRIERS	FOREWARN
FOLLICLE	FUMITORY	FLOWERED	FIREARMS	FURRIERY	FOREWORD
FALKLAND	FAMOUSLY	FOOTFALL	FOREARMS	FORTIETH	FERRYMAN
FOLKLORE	FANDANCE	FROUFROU	FOREBEAR	FORTKNOX	FERRYMEN
FILAMENT	FENLANDS	FLOGGING	FIREBALL	FORELOCK	FORSYTHE
FULLMOON	FANFARES	FOOTHOLD	FIREBIRD	FORKLIFT	FERRYING
FELONIES	FANDANGO	FLOTILLA	FIRECLAY	FORELEGS	FARMYARD
FILMNOIR	FANTASIA	FLORISTS	FORECAST	FARFLUNG	FISHBOWL
FULLNESS	FANTAILS	FLOUNCED	FEROCITY	FARMLAND	FISHCAKE
FALCONER	FONTAINE	FLOUNCES	FOREDECK	FORELAND	FOSSDYKE
FALLOVER	FINEARTS	FLOUNDER	FIREDAMP	FORMLESS	FOSSEWAY
FELLOVER	FONDANTS	FROWNING	FIREDOOR	FOREMOST	FASTENED
FOLLOWED	FINGERED	FOOTNOTE	FERVENCY	FORENSIC	FASTENER
FOLLOWER	FUNAFUTI	FOOTPADS	FERRETED	FORENAME	FESTERED
FOLLOWON	FINEGAEL	FLOPPING	FERRETER	FIRMNESS	FOSTERED
FALCONRY	FINDINGS	FOOTPATH	FORGETIT	FARROWED	FASTFOOD
FALMOUTH	FANLIGHT	FLOORING	FORMERLY	FURROWED	FISHFARM
FOLLOWUP	FANCIERS	FLOURISH	FORKEEPS	FURLOUGH	FISHHAWK
FILIPINO	FANCIEST	FOOTREST	FARCEURS	FORGOING	FESTIVAL
FOLKROCK	FUNNIEST	FOOLSCAP	FORBEARS	FIRERISK	FASHIONS
FALIRAKI	FANCIFUL	FOOTSTEP	FARCEUSE	FORTRESS	FASCISTS
FILTRATE	FONDLING	FOOLSDIE	FERMENTS	FIRESIDE	FUSILIER
FALASHAS	FINALISE	FOOTSLOG	FORFEITS	FORESEES	FUSELAGE
FELDSPAR	FINALIST	FOOTSORE	FORCEFUL	FORESTER	FISHMEAL
FILMSTAR	FINALITY	FRONTMAN	FORAGING	FIRESHIP	FASTNESS
FOLKSONG	FINANCED	FRONTIER	FOREGONE	FIRESALE	FESTOONS
FULLSTOP	FINANCES	FROSTIER	FORAGERS	FORASONG	FISHPOND

FUSSPOTS	FOURSOME	GRANDEES	GLADRAGS	GREMLINS	GRIFFITH
FASTTALK	FAUSTIAN	GLADDENS	GRAFSPEE	GLEAMING	GOINGBAD
FISHTANK	FRUITBAT	GUARDING	GOATSKIN	GREENDAY	GOINGMAD
FISSURES	FAULTIER	GRANDSON	GRASSBOX	GREENMAN	GOINGOFF
FISHWIFE	FOURTEEN	GUARDDOG	GLASSEYE	GREENOCK	GOINGSON
FUSEWIRE	FOUNTAIN	GRANDCRU	GOASTRAY	GUERNICA	GOINGOUT
FATHERED	FAULTILY	GRANDEST	GRANTHAM	GREENTEA	GRIDIRON
FATTENED	FRUITFLY	GRANDEUR	GRAFTING	GUERNSEY	GRIDLOCK
FETTERED	FAULTING	GRAVELLY	GRANTING	GREENFLY	GRILLING
FITTEDIN	FRUITION	GRACEFUL	GIANTESS	GLEANING	GLIMMERS
FATHERLY	FOURTOPS	GRATEFUL	GRANULAR	GLEANERS	GRINNING
FATIGUED	FLUSTERS	GRAFFITI	GRANULES	GREENERY	GLIBNESS
FATIGUES	FLUTTERS	GRAPHICS	GRADUATE	GREENEST	GUINNESS
FETCHING	FLUTTERY	GLADHAND	GRATUITY	GREYNESS	GRIMOIRE
FITTINGS	FRUCTOSE	GNASHING	GOBACKON	GRENOBLE	GLIMPSED
FATTIEST	FRUITCUP	GNASHERS	GABRIELA	GREYSEAL	GLIMPSES
FATALISM	FRUITFUL	GOATHERD	GABRIELE	GREASIER	GRIPPING
FATALIST	FEVERFEW	GRAPHITE	GABBLING	GREASING	GRIPPERS
FATALITY	FEVERISH	GRAVITAS	GOBBLING	GUESSING	GRIMSHAW
FUTILITY	FIVESTAR	GLADIOLI	GABBLERS	GOEASYON	GLISSADE
FATHOMED	FAVOURED	GRADIENT	GOBBLEUP	GREATTIT	GAINSAID
FETLOCKS	FOXGLOVE	GRATIANO	GABORONE	GREETING	GRISSINI
FUTURAMA	FOXINESS	GLACIERS	GADWALLS	GREATAPE	GAINSAYS
FUTURISM	FOXHOUND	GLAZIERS	GODSACRE	GREATEST	GUILTILY
FATSTOCK	FIXATION	GLACIATE	GADABOUT	GREATAUK	GLINTING
FITFULLY	FIXATIVE	GRACIOUS	GADGETRY	GUFFAWED	GLISTENS
FRUGALLY	FIXTURES	GOALKICK	GODSGIFT	GIFTWRAP	GLITTERS
FOUNDING	FLYPAPER	GOALLINE	GODCHILD	GIGABYTE	GLITTERY
FOUNDERS	FLYPASTS	GRAYLING	GODZILLA	GAGGLING	GRIEVING
FLUIDITY	FLYSHEET	GOALLESS	GIDDIEST	GIGGLING	GRIEVOUS
FOUNDOUT	FLYWHEEL	GRASMERE	GADFLIES	GIGGLERS	GRIZZLED
FLUFFIER	FLYAKITE	GRANNIES	GADZOOKS	GIGANTIC	GRIZZLER
FLUSHING	FLYSPRAY	GRAINING	GODSPEED	GOGETTER	GRIZZLES
FAULKNER	FLYDRIVE	GRAINERS	GODSPELL	GUIDANCE	GUJARATI
FLUNKING	FIZZIEST	GLADNESS	GRENADES	GRIMALDI	GALLANTS
FLUELLEN	FIZBROWN	GLASNOST	GREYAREA	GRIMACED	GOLFBALL
FLUENTLY	GHANAIAN	GRAPPLED	GRENACHE	GRIMACES	GOLDBERG
FOULPLAY	GOALAREA	GRAPPLES	GRETCHEN	GRIDDLED	GOLDBLUM
FRUMPISH	GRABBING	GRASPING	GREEDIER	GRINDING	GALACTIC
FLUORIDE	GLAUCOMA	GOALPOST	GREEDILY	GUILDERS	GOLFCLUB
FLUORINE	GLANCING	GOABROAD	GRENFELL	GUIDEDOG	GOLDDISC
FOURSTAR	GUARDIAN	GLAMROCK	GHERKINS	GUILEFUL	GOLDDUST

GALLERIA	GANGEDUP	GLOXINIA	GARDENER	GATHERED	GAZUMPED
GALLEONS	GENNEDUP	GLORIANA	GARNERED	GATHERUP	HEADACHE
GOLDFISH	GINGIVAL	GLORIOUS	GARDENIA	GETAHEAD	HIAWATHA
GULLIVER	GENTILES	GROWLING	GARMENTS	GETSMART	HEADBAND
GULLIBLE	GUNFIGHT	GROWLERS	GORGEOUS	GOTOOFAR	HEADBUTT
GALLIANO	GANGLAND	GHOULISH	GIRAFFES	GATEPOST	HEADCASE
GOLDLEAF	GANGLING	GLOOMIER	GARAGING	GOTOSEED	HOARDING
GOLDMINE	GINSLING	GLOOMILY	GERSHWIN	GOTOTOWN	HOARDERS
GALLOWAY	GANGLION	GLOAMING	GIRLHOOD	GUTTURAL	HEAVENLY
GOLCONDA	GANYMEDE	GROOMING	GERMINAL	GATEWAYS	HEADGEAR
GALLOPED	GUNSMOKE	GROMMETS	GARLICKY	GRUMBLED	HEARHEAR
GALLOPER	GUNSMITH	GROUNDED	GARFIELD	GRUMBLER	HEADHUNT
GOLDRUSH	GONDOLAS	GROANING	GARRISON	GRUMBLES	HEATHENS
GALOSHES	GONCOURT	GOODNESS	GORILLAS	GRUDGING	HEATHROW
GELATINE	GUNBOATS	GROUPIES	GARYLUCY	GAUDIEST	HEATHERS
GALAXIES	GENEPOOL	GROUPING	GARBLING	GAULLIST	HEAVIEST
GYMNASTS	GANTRIES	GROSSMAN	GARGLING	GOURMAND	HYACINTH
GAMEBIRD	GENTRIFY	GLOSSIER	GURGLING	GOURMETS	HEADLOCK
GYMKHANA	GENERALS	GROUSING	GORMLESS	GLUMNESS	HEADLAMP
GIMMICKS	GANGRENE	GLOSSARY	GERONIMO	GRUMPIER	HEADLAND
GIMMICKY	GENERATE	GOODTIME	GERANIUM	GRUMPILY	HEADLINE
GAMBLING	GENEROUS	GHOSTING	GARGOYLE	GRUESOME	HEADLONG
GAMBLERS	GANGSTER	GLOATING	GARROTTE	GAULTIER	HEARMASS
GEMINIAN	GANGSHOW	GROUTING	GERTRUDE	GAUNTLET	HEADROOM
GUMBOILS	GENETICS	GOODTURN	GARISHLY	GLUTTONS	HEADREST
GUMBOOTS	GENITIVE	GLOBULAR	GYRATING	GLUTTONY	HEATRASH
GAMEPLAN	GONATIVE	GLOBULES	GYRATION	GRUNTING	HEADSHIP
GOMORRAH	GENIUSES	GROOVING	GYRATORY	GRUNTERS	HOARSELY
GIMCRACK	GINRUMMY	GOODWILL	GOSSAMER	GLUHWEIN	HEARTIER
GAMESTER	GANGWAYS	GOODWOOD	GOSTEADY	GAVEAWAY	HEARTILY
GAMESHOW	GLOBALLY	GLOWWORM	GASMETER	GIVEAWAY	HEARTENS
GEMSTONE	GIOVANNI	GOODYBAG	GOSSIPED	GIVINGIN	HEADWIND
GUMPTION	GROSCHEN	GOODYEAR	GOSLINGS	GIVINGUP	HEADWORD
GONEAWAY	GOODDEAL	GLORYBOX	GASLIGHT	GIVEODDS	HEATWAVE
GUNMAKER	GEORDIES	GOPLACES	GASOLINE	GOVERNED	HEBRIDES
GUNGADIN	GLOWERED	GOPUBLIC	GASWORKS	GOVERNOR	HOBBLING
GENIALLY	GLOVEBOX	GEPPETTO	GASCOINE	GLYCEROL	HABANERA
GENDARME	GEOMETRY	GARLANDS	GESTURED	GUYANESE	HIBERNIA
GINSBERG	GEOFFREY	GERMANIC	GESTURES	GAZPACHO	HIBISCUS
GENOCIDE	GOODFORM	GERMAINE	GETIDEAS	GAZELLES	HABITUAL
GUNMETAL	GEORGIAN	GARBANZO	GETREADY	GUZZLING	HABITUES
GINGERLY	GEORGINA	GARDENED	GOTREADY	GUZZLERS	HOBBYIST

HECTARES	HUGHORDE	HILLFORT	HOMICIDE	HANGBACK	HANDPUMP
HACIENDA	HIGHROAD	HOLDFAST	HUMIDIFY	HANDBAGS	HUNDREDS
HECKLING	HIGHRISE	HOLOGRAM	HUMIDITY	HANDBALL	HUNGRIER
HECKLERS	HIGHSEAS	HALOGENS	HAMMERED	HANDBELL	HANDRAIL
HECTORED	HIGHSPOT	HOLYHEAD	HAMPERED	HANDBILL	HUNGRILY
HUCKSTER	HIGHTECH	HELLHOLE	HEMMEDIN	HANDBOOK	HONORARY
HACKWORK	HIGHTIDE	HULAHOOP	HOMEFARM	HONECKER	HUNTRESS
HIDEAWAY	HIGHWIRE	HALFHOUR	HUMPHREY	HANDCUFF	HUNTSMAN
HYDRANTS	HAIRBALL	HALFINCH	HOMEHELP	HANDCART	HUNTSMEN
HADABALL	HAIRBAND	HELPINGS	HUMPHRYS	HANDDOWN	HONESTLY
HEDGEHOG	HAIRCUTS	HOLDINGS	HAMLISCH	HANKERED	HANDSOME
HEDGEROW	HAIRGRIP	HELSINKI	HEMMINGS	HINDERED	HANDSETS
HUDDLING	HEIGHTEN	HALFLIFE	HOMEINON	HENPECKS	HANDSAWS
HEDONISM	HAIRIEST	HELPLINE	HOMELOAN	HINGEING	HANDSEWN
HEDONIST	HAIRLINE	HELPLESS	HOMILIES	HANGERON	HONDURAS
HADWORDS	HEIRLOOM	HALFMOON	HOMELAND	HANDFULS	HONOURED
HYDROGEN	HAIRLESS	HALLMARK	HUMBLING	HANGFIRE	HINDUISM
HIDEOUTS	HAILMARY	HALFMAST	HAMILTON	HENCHMAN	HANDYMAN
HYDEPARK	HAIRPINS	HELPMATE	HOMELESS	HINDHEAD	HANDYMEN
HEEDLESS	HEINRICH	HOLINESS	HUMBLEST	HENCHMEN	HONEYBEE
HOEDOWNS	HOISTING	HOLLOWAY	HUMILITY	HENSHALL	HONEYDEW
HEFTIEST	HAILWOOD	HALLOWED	HIMALAYA	HUNCHING	HONEYPOT
HOGMANAY	HIJACKED	HOLDOVER	HOMEMADE	HENCHARD	HONEYBUN
HOGWARTS	HIJACKER	HILLOCKS	HUMANOID	HANDICAP	HOOLIGAN
HOGSBACK	HOKKAIDO	HALLOUMI	HUMANELY	HANNIBAL	HOODLUMS
HIGHBALL	HALYARDS	HELIPORT	HUMANISM	HENNIGHT	HUONPINE
HIGHBROW	HALFBACK	HILARITY	HUMANIST	HANDIEST	HOODWINK
HIGHBURY	HELDBACK	HELMSMAN	HUMANITY	HUNGJURY	HEPTAGON
HYGIENIC	HOLDBACK	HOLDSWAY	HAMMOCKS	HANUKKAH	HAPSBURG
HUGUENOT	HELLBENT	HILLSIDE	HOMEPAGE	HONGKONG	HAPPENED
HIGHFIVE	HOLOCENE	HELMSMEN	HOMERULE	HINDLEGS	HOPEFULS
HIGHGEAR	HOLYCITY	HOLISTIC	HUMORIST	HONOLULU	HAPPIEST
HOGSHEAD	HULLCITY	HALFTIME	HUMOROUS	HANDLING	HIPFLASK
HIGHJUMP	HELDDOWN	HALFTONE	HOMESICK	HANDLERS	HOPELESS
HIGHLIFE	HOLDDOWN	HALFTERM	HOMESPUN	HANDMADE	HYPINGUP
HAGGLING	HOLIDAYS	HOLSTERS	HAMSTERS	HINDMOST	HYPNOSIS
HIGHLAND	HALBERDS	HOLYWEEK	HOMETOWN	HANGNAIL	HYPNOTIC
HAGGLERS	HELMETED	HOLYWRIT	HUMOURED	HANDOVER	HEPWORTH
HEGEMONY	HOLLERED	HUMPBACK	HOMBURGS	HANGOVER	HYPERION
HIGHMASS	HELLENIC	HOMEBREW	HOMEWARD	HUNGOVER	HIPSTERS
HIGHNOON	HELVETIA	HYMNBOOK	HOMEWORK	HANDOUTS	HORNBEAM
HIGHNESS	HELLFIRE	HOMEBIRD	HENPARTY	HANDPICK	HARDBACK

HAREBELL	HERALDIC	HOSTELRY	HITOUTAT	INAWHIRL	INDUCTOR
HORNBILL	HARDLINE	HESPERUS	HAUNCHES	IMAGINED	INDICATE
HARDCOPY	HIRELING	HUSHEDUP	HOUNDING	IMAGINES	INDIGENT
HARDCORE	HURDLING	HUSHHUSH	HOUNDDOG	INAJIFFY	INDULGED
HARDCASH	HURTLING	HOSPITAL	HOUSEMAN	ITALIANS	INDULGES
HARICOTS	HERALDRY	HOSPICES	HOUSESIT	IMAGISTS	INDOLENT
HARDDISK	HURDLERS	HASTINGS	HOUSEFLY	INAFLASH	INDEMAND
HEREDITY	HARMLESS	HUSTINGS	HOUSEBOY	INACTION	INDANGER
HIREDGUN	HARTNELL	HUSKIEST	HOUSEFUL	INACTIVE	INDENTED
HIREDOUT	HARDNESS	HASSLING	HOULIHAN	INAHURRY	INDIRECT
HERNEBAY	HARANGUE	HUSTLING	HOUNSLOW	IMBIBING	INDUSTRY
HORSEMAN	HORMONAL	HUSTLERS	HAUNTING	IMBIBERS	INDETAIL
HARDENED	HORMONES	HOSANNAS	HIVEDOFF	IMBECILE	INDEXING
HARDENER	HARMONIC	HISTORIC	HAVENOTS	IMBRUING	INDEXERS
HORSEMEN	HORROCKS	HASSOCKS	HOVERFLY	INCHARGE	ICEDANCE
HERMETIC	HARPOONS	HOSEPIPE	HOVERING	INCUBATE	ITERATED
HORSEFLY	HARBOURS	HOSEREEL	HAVISHAM	INCIDENT	ITERATES
HORSEBOX	HORNPIPE	HESITANT	HOWABOUT	INCREDIT	ICEBERGS
HARVESTS	HARDROCK	HESITATE	HAWKEYED	INCREASE	INEFFECT
HARTFORD	HARDRAIN	HISSYFIT	HAWTHORN	INCLINED	IDEEFIXE
HEREFORD	HERDSMAN	HATHAWAY	HAWAIIAN	INCLINES	IDEOGRAM
HERTFORD	HARASSED	HATBANDS	HAWFINCH	INCOMING	ICESHELF
HEREGOES	HARASSES	HOTWATER	HAWKMOTH	INCOMMON	ITEMISED
HARSHEST	HERDSMEN	HOTPANTS	HOWSTHAT	INCAMERA	ITEMISES
HIROHITO	HARDSHIP	HOTHEADS	HOWITZER	INCENSED	ICEFIELD
HARRIDAN	HARDSELL	HITHERTO	HEWITSON	INCENSES	INEDIBLE
HEROINES	HARDTACK	HOTTEDUP	HUXTABLE	INCONVOY	ICESKATE
HERRINGS	HERETICS	HATCHWAY	HEXAGRAM	INCLOVER	IDEOLOGY
HORRIFIC	HERITAGE	HATCHING	HEXAGONS	INCHOATE	ICEPLANT
HORRIBLE	HERCULES	HITCHING	HAYMAKER	INCURRED	IDEALISE
HORRIBLY	HARRUMPH	HATCHERY	HAYFEVER	ISCARIOT	IDEALISM
HORRIDLY	HARDWOOD	HATCHETS	HAYRICKS	INCISING	IDEALIST
HERMIONE	HAREWOOD	HOTLINES	HAYFIELD	INCISION	ICEBOXES
HARMISON	HARDWARE	HOTELIER	HAYWORTH	INCISORS	ICEDOVER
HARRISON	HEREWITH	HOTPLATE	HAYSTACK	INCISIVE	ICELOLLY
HARRIERS	HARRYING	HOTTODDY	HAZELNUT	INCITING	INEXPERT
HARDIEST	HURRYING	HATBOXES	HAZINESS	INCLUDED	ICECREAM
HARPISTS	HUSBANDS	HOTHOUSE	INAPADDY	INCLUDES	INERTGAS
HARRIOTT	HOSTAGES	HATTRICK	ISAMBARD	INDEBTED	IDENTIFY
HARDLUCK	HISPANIC	HITITOFF	IDARESAY	INDICTED	IDENTITY
HERALDED	HASTENED	HOTSTUFF	ISABELLA	INDECENT	INEQUITY
HOROLOGY	HYSTERIA	HATSTAND	ISABELLE	INDUCING	INFLAMED

INFLATED	IRISHMAN	INNOCENT	IMPRISON	INSIDERS	INTERLAY
INFLATES	IRISHSEA	INNUENDO	INPRISON	INSPECTS	INTERNAL
INFRARED	INIMICAL	IANBEALE	IMPRINTS	ITSAGIFT	INTERVAL
INFRADIG	INITIALS	IGNOMINY	IMPELLED	INSIGNIA	INTERACT
INFECTED	INITIATE	IANSMITH	IMPELLER	INSTINCT	INTERNED
INFIDELS	INIQUITY	INNEREAR	IMPALING	INSPIRED	INTERNEE
INFRINGE	INJECTED	INNERMAN	IMPOLITE	INSPIRES	INTERNET
INFLIGHT	INJECTOR	IGNORANT	IMPINGED	INSPIRIT	INTERRED
INFLICTS	INJURIES	IGNORING	IMPINGES	INSULTED	INTARSIA
INFAMOUS	INJURING	INNATELY	IMPUNITY	INSOLENT	INTERCOM
INFANTAS	INKWELLS	INNOTIME	IMPLODED	INSULATE	INTERIOR
INFANTRY	ICKENHAM	IGNITING	IMPLODES	INSOMNIA	INTERPOL
INFINITE	INKINGIN	IGNITION	IMPLORED	INSANELY	INTEREST
INFINITY	INKINESS	INNOVATE	IMPLORES	INSANITY	INTRUDED
INFLOWER	INKSPOTS	IDOLATER	IMPROPER	INSCRIBE	INTRUDER
INFERNAL	INKERMAN	ISOLATED	IMPROVED	INSTRUCT	INTRUDES
INFORMAL	INKSTAND	ISOLATES	IMPROVER	INSERTED	INUNDATE
INFERRED	ILLFATED	ISOBATHS	IMPROVES	INSURING	INUNISON
INFORMED	INLEAGUE	IDOLATRY	IMPERIAL	INSURERS	INVADING
INFORMER	ILLTIMED	IRONCLAD	IMPARTED	INSISTED	INVADERS
INFERIOR	ILLUMINE	IRONDUKE	IMPORTED	INTRANET	INVIEWOF
INFESTED	ISLANDER	IDOMENEO	IMPORTER	INTHEBAG	INVOICED
INFUSING	IOLANTHE	ISOTHERM	IMPERILS	INTHECAN	INVOICES
INFUSION	ILLINOIS	IDOLISED	INPERSON	INTHERAW	INVEIGLE
INFUTURE	IDLENESS	IDOLISES	IMPURITY	INTHEWAY	INVOKING
INFAVOUR	ILLTREAT	ISOTOPES	IMPISHLY	INTHERED	INVOLVED
INGLETON	IGLESIAS	ISOTONIC	IMPOSING	INTHEAIR	INVOLVES
INGENUES	ILLUSION	IRONSIDE	IMPOSTOR	INTREPID	INVENTED
INGESTED	ILLUSORY	IROQUOIS	IMPETIGO	INTHEEND	INVENTOR
INHABITS	INLAYING	IRONWOOD	IMPOTENT	INTHEORY	INVERTED
INHIBITS	IMMOBILE	IRONWARE	IMPUTING	INTIFADA	INVESTED
ISHIGURO	INMYBOOK	IRONWORK	IMPOUNDS	INTEGRAL	INVASION
INHALANT	IMMODEST	ISOHYETS	IMPLYING	INTAGLIO	INVESTOR
INHALING	IMMOLATE	IMPLANTS	INQUESTS	INTEGERS	INVASIVE
INHALERS	IMMINENT	INPUBLIC	IRRIGATE	INTRIGUE	INVITING
INHUMANE	IMMUNISE	IMPACTED	INRELIEF	INTIMACY	INWARDLY
INHERENT	IMMUNITY	INPOCKET	IRRITANT	INTIMATE	JOANBAEZ
INHERITS	IMMORTAL	IMPEDING	IRRITATE	INTANDEM	JEANBOHT
IMITATED	IAMAROCK	IMPUDENT	INSTANCE	INTENDED	JEANETTE
IMITATES	IMMERSED	INPIECES	INSPADES	INTENTLY	JEALOUSY
IMITATOR	IMMERSES	IMPAIRED	INSECURE	INTONING	JEANPAUL
IAINGLEN	IMMATURE	IMPLICIT	ITSADEAL	ISTANBUL	JEANRHYS

JOANSIMS	JOINEDIN	JEOPARDY	KIBITZES	KINKAJOU	KISSABLE
JABBERED	JOINEDUP	JAPONICA	KICKBACK	KENYATTA	KASPAROV
JABBERER	JUICIEST	JAPANESE	KEDGEREE	KINGCOAL	KISSCURL
JOBSHARE	JOINTING	JERMAINE	KIDOLOGY	KINGCRAB	KISSKISS
JUBILANT	JOKINGLY	JEROBOAM	KEEPBACK	KINGDOMS	KASHMIRI
JMBARRIE	JOKINESS	JEREMIAD	KEEPCALM	KENKESEY	KESTRELS
JACKAROO	JULIANNE	JEREMIAH	KNEEDEEP	KINSHASA	KATEADIE
JACOBEAN	JULIEEGE	JURASSIC	KNEADING	KINGJOHN	KATEBUSH
JACKBOOT	JULIENNE	JERRYCAN	KEEPDARK	KINGKONG	KATTEGAT
JACOBITE	JULIETTE	JOSTLING	KNEEHIGH	KINGLEAR	KATEFORD
JACKDAWS	JOLLIEST	JUSTNESS	KEELHAUL	KINDLIER	KATYHILL
JOCKEYED	JALAPENO	JETTISON	KNEEJERK	KINDLING	KITCHENS
JACKLORD	JALFREZI	JETBLACK	KNEELING	KINDNESS	KATHLEEN
JACKPOTS	JUMPBAIL	JETPLANE	KEENNESS	KENLOACH	KITEMARK
JACKSONS	JUMPEDUP	JETFOILS	KEELOVER	KINGSLEY	KATEMOSS
JACQUARD	JAMAICAN	JAUNDICE	KEEPRANK	KINGSROW	KATARINA
JACUZZIS	JUMBLING	JOURNALS	KEEPSAKE	KINGSTON	KATOWICE
JUDICIAL	JAMBOREE	JOURNEYS	KREUTZER	KINGSIZE	KNUCKLES
JUDDERED	JIMBOWEN	JAUNTILY	KOHINOOR	KINETICS	KAVANAGH
JODHPURS	JUMBOJET	JOUSTING	KOHLRABI	KENSTOTT	KOWALSKI
JOELGREY	JUMPSUIT	JOUSTERS	KLINGONS	KENTUCKY	KOWTOWED
JOELOUIS	JIMSTARK	JOVIALLY	KNIGHTED	KLONDIKE	KAWASAKI
JOEORTON	JUNKETED	JAVELINS	KNIGHTLY	KHOMEINI	KEYLARGO
JOEBROWN	JANEEYRE	JUVENILE	KNICKERS	KNOPFLER	KAYWALSH
JEFFRIES	JUNGFRAU	JEWSHARP	KNITTING	KNOCKOFF	KEYBOARD
JIFFYBAG	JUNKFOOD	JEWELLED	KNITTERS	KNOCKING	KEYSTAGE
JIGGERED	JANEGREY	JEWELLER	KNITWEAR	KNOCKOUT	KEYSTONE
JIGGLING	JENNIFER	JAYWALKS	KELLAWAY	KNOTTING	LEASABLE
JOGALONG	JANGLING	JOYRIDER	KILLBILL	KNOTWEED	LIARDICE
JOGGLING	JINGLING	JOYSTICK	KILKENNY	KEPTBACK	LEAVENED
JUGGLING	JONGLEUR	JOYFULLY	KILOGRAM	KORFBALL	LLANELLI
JUGGLERS	JUNKMAIL	JOYOUSLY	KALAHARI	KIRIBATI	LEAVEOUT
JOHNBULL	JANSMUTS	JAZZBAND	KILLJOYS	KERCHIEF	LEADFREE
JOHNDEED	JINGOISM	KRAKATOA	KILLTIME	KERRIGAN	LEAPFROG
JOHNDORY	JINGOIST	KNAPSACK	KILOWATT	KUREISHI	LOATHING
JOHNFORD	JUNKSHOP	KHARTOUM	KAMBALDA	KARLMARX	LEATHERS
JOHNHURT	JONATHAN	KNAPWEED	KIMWILDE	KERENSKY	LEATHERY
JOHNPEEL	JUNCTION	KABBALAH	KAMIKAZE	KARENINA	LEAVINGS
JOHNSIMM	JANITORS	KABINETT	KIMNOVAK	KERBSIDE	LIARLIAR
JOHNSTON	JUNCTURE	KABIRALI	KANDAHAR	KEROSENE	LEAFLETS
JOHNTHAW	JONQUILS	KIBITZED	KENEALLY	KUROSAWA	LEARNING
JAILBIRD	JUNKYARD	KIBITZER	KANGAROO	KIRKWALL	LEARNERS

LEANNESS	LOCATION	LOGICIAN	LOMBARDY	LANDFILL	LONGSHIP
LIAISING	LECTURED	LIGNEOUS	LIMABEAN	LANGFORD	LONGSUIT
LIAISONS	LECTURER	LEGGINGS	LAMBCHOP	LONGFORD	LONESOME
LEAFSPOT	LECTURES	LEGALAID	LAMEDUCK	LUNGFISH	LANDSEND
LEADTIME	LACQUERS	LEGALESE	LUMBERED	LANDGIRL	LONGSHOT
LEAPYEAR	LACEWING	LEGALISE	LIMBERUP	LYNCHPIN	LUNATICS
LABRADOR	LUCKYBAG	LEGALITY	LUMPFISH	LONGHAND	LENGTHEN
LIBRETTO	LUCKYDIP	LIGAMENT	LEMMINGS	LUNCHING	LONGTIME
LABOHEME	LUCKYJIM	LOGBOOKS	LIMEKILN	LYNCHING	LINOTYPE
LOBELIAS	LADYBIRD	LEGBREAK	LEMONADE	LUNCHBOX	LONGTERM
LABELLED	LUDDITES	LEGIRONS	LAMENTED	LUNCHEON	LANGUAGE
LIBELLED	LODGINGS	LEGATEES	LEMONTEA	LYNCHMOB	LINGUINE
LEBANESE	LADYLIKE	LIGHTALE	LAMANCHA	LONGHORN	LANGUISH
LIBERIAN	LADYMUCK	LIGHTENS	LUMINARY	LONGHAUL	LINGUIST
LIBERACE	LODESTAR	LIGHTING	LAMENESS	LANDINGS	LONGUEUR
LIBERALS	LEEJCOBB	LEGATION	LAMINATE	LONGJUMP	LONEWOLF
LIBERATE	LAETITIA	LIGATURE	LUMINOUS	LONGLEAT	LONGWAVE
LABURNUM	LIEDOGGO	LIGHTERS	LAMPOONS	LANDLADY	LONGWAYS
LIBATION	LEEGRANT	LIGHTEST	LAMPPOST	LONELIER	LEONARDO
LOBSTERS	LEEOTWAY	LUHRMANN	LIMERICK	LONGLIFE	LEOPARDS
LABOURED	LEEHURST	LAIDBACK	LAMBSKIN	LENTLILY	LEOSAYER
LABOURER	LEEEVANS	LOITERED	LIMASSOL	LANDLINE	LOOKEDAT
LOBBYING	LIFEBOAT	LOITERER	LIMETREE	LANDLORD	LOOSENED
LOBBYIST	LEFTBACK	LYINGLOW	LIMITING	LANGLAUF	LOOSEBOX
LUCIDITY	LIFEBELT	LEIGHTON	LIMOUSIN	LINOLEUM	LOOSENUP
LACHESIS	LEFTBANK	LOISLANE	LIMEWASH	LONGLIVE	LOOPHOLE
LUCRETIA	LIFEBUOY	LEINSTER	LINNAEAN	LANDMINE	LIONISED
LECTERNS	LIFEFORM	LEISURED	LANYARDS	LINIMENT	LIONISES
LYCHGATE	LOFTIEST	LIKEABLE	LINNAEUS	LANDMARK	LEONURIS
LUCKIEST	LIFELIKE	LAKEERIE	LONGBOAT	LANDMASS	LOOKOVER
LOCKLEAR	LIFELINE	LIKEFURY	LANSBURY	LANKNESS	LOOKOUTS
LOCALISE	LIFELONG	LAKELETS	LONGBOWS	LENINISM	LEONURIS
LUCKLESS	LIFELESS	LIKENING	LINOCUTS	LININGUP	LOPEARED
LOCALITY	LEFTOVER	LIKENESS	LONSDALE	LONDONER	LIPSALVE
LICENCES	LIFEPEER	LUKEWARM	LENIENCY	LONGORIA	LAPIDARY
LICENSED	LIFERAFT	LIKEWISE	LINGERED	LUNAPARK	LIPLINER
LICENSEE	LIFESPAN	LOLLARDS	LINGERIE	LANDRAIL	LOPSIDED
LICENSES	LIFESIZE	LOLLIPOP	LANTERNS	LINESMAN	LAPWINGS
LOCHNESS	LIFETIME	LILLIPUT	LANCELOT	LONESTAR	LIPGLOSS
LACROSSE	LEFTWING	LILONGWE	LINKEDUP	LANDSEER	LIPOSOME
LACERATE	LAGGARDS	LOLLOPED	LONGFACE	LINESMEN	LIPSTICK
LOCATING	LOGCABIN	LULWORTH	LANDFALL	LANDSLIP	LIQUEURS

LORRAINE	LITTERED	LOVELIFE	LIZSMITH	MICRODOT	MEDITATE
LYREBIRD	LATTERLY	LAVALAMP	LOZENGES	MCCARTHY	MUDGUARD
LYRICISM	LITIGANT	LOVELORN	LAZINESS	MUCKRAKE	MCDOWALL
LYRICIST	LITIGATE	LOVELESS	MEATBALL	MACARONI	MEETINGS
LARGESSE	LATRINES	LOVEMEDO	MEANDERS	MACAROON	MEERKATS
LARKHALL	LATTICED	LAVENDER	MEANINGS	MACERATE	MEEKNESS
LURCHING	LITTLEMO	LEVANTER	MEATIEST	MACAULAY	MNEMONIC
LURCHERS	LETALONE	LOVINGLY	MEATLOAF	MICAWBER	MUEZZINS
LARRIKIN	LITANIES	LEVINSON	MEATLESS	MIDLANDS	MCFADDEN
LORIKEET	LATENTLY	LOVENEST	MEANNESS	MEDIATED	MUFFLING
LORDMUCK	LATENESS	LIVERIED	MCALPINE	MEDIATES	MUFFLERS
LARBOARD	LUTENIST	LEVERAGE	MEALTIME	MUDLARKS	MYFAMILY
LORDSHIP	LITTORAL	LEVERING	MEANTIME	MEDIATOR	MAGDALEN
LARKSPUR	LITERACY	LIVERISH	MEASURED	MEDICINE	MAGNATES
LAROUSSE	LITERARY	LEVERETS	MEASURES	MEDICARE	MIGRATED
LASVEGAS	LITERATE	LOVESEAT	MEACULPA	MEDICATE	MIGRATES
LESSENED	LITERATI	LOVESICK	MEANWELL	MEDIEVAL	MIGRAINE
LISTENED	LATITUDE	LAVISHLY	MIAOWING	MADDENED	MIGRANTS
LISTENER	LETTUCES	LAVATORY	MOBYDICK	MODIFIED	MEGABYTE
LISTENIN	LAUDABLE	LEVITATE	MOBILISE	MODIFIER	MAGICIAN
LISTERIA	LAUSANNE	LIVEWIRE	MOBILITY	MODIFIES	MAGICEYE
LISKEARD	LAUDANUM	LIVTYLER	MRBLOBBY	MADRIGAL	MAGNESIA
LOSEFACE	LAUNCHED	LOWLANDS	MOBSTERS	MIDWIVES	MAGNETIC
LASTGASP	LAUNCHER	LAWMAKER	MECHANIC	MIDNIGHT	MCGREGOR
LASHINGS	LAUNCHES	LOWWATER	MOCCASIN	MIDFIELD	MCGUFFIN
LISTINGS	LAUNDERS	LAWRENCE	MICHAELA	MUDDIEST	MCGUIGAN
LUSCIOUS	LAURENCE	LOWLEVEL	MACLAINE	MODELLED	MAGWITCH
LISTLESS	LAUREATE	LEWINSKY	MACHETES	MODELLER	MAGRITTE
LASTNAME	LOUNGING	LAWCOURT	MACKEREL	MADELINE	MAGELLAN
LOSLOBOS	LOUNGERS	LOWERING	MICHENER	MEDDLING	MEGALITH
LASTPOST	LAUGHTER	LEWISHAM	MICHELIN	MIDDLING	MCGOOHAN
LASTRADA	LAUGHOFF	LEWISGUN	MUCKEDIN	MUDDLING	MAGNOLIA
LUSTROUS	LAUGHING	LAWFULLY	MICHELLE	MEDDLERS	MEGASTAR
LOSTSOUL	LAUGHTON	LAWSUITS	MACYGRAY	MODULATE	MIGHTIER
LOSETIME	LOUDNESS	LEWAYRES	MACKINAW	MUDDLEUP	MIGHTILY
LETHARGY	LOVEBIRD	LOWLYING	MICHIGAN	MCDONALD	MEGATONS
LOTHARIO	LIVEITUP	LEXICONS	MACHINES	MIDSOMER	MEGAWATT
LETHALLY	LEVELLED	LUXURIES	MACHISMO	MEDIOCRE	MAGAZINE
LUTHERAN	LEVELLER	LAYABOUT	MUCKIEST	MADHOUSE	MOHICANS
LATHERED	LIVELIER	LOYALIST	MYCOLOGY	MODERATE	MAHOGANY
LETMESEE	LOVELIER	LAYINGUP	MCCALLUM	MODESTLY	MUHAMMAD
LETTERED	LEVELOFF	LAYERING	MICROBES	MADESURE	MOHAMMED

MOHARRIS	MILLIBAR	MILKYWAY	MANIFEST	MONARCHY	MOORLAND
MAHARAJA	MILLIGAN	MALAYSIA	MONKFISH	MONORAIL	MYOSOTIS
MAHARANI	MALDIVES	MAMMAMIA	MONAGHAN	MANDRAKE	MOONRISE
MAILBOAT	MILLINER	MEMSAHIB	MONOGRAM	MANDRILL	MOONSHOT
MAIDENLY	MALTINGS	MIMICKED	MONOGAMY	MINERALS	MOONUNIT
MAINLAND	MELVILLE	MIMICKER	MANAGING	MONGRELS	MOONWALK
MAINLINE	MULTIPLE	MAMELUKE	MANAGERS	MINARETS	MOPPEDUP
MAINROAD	MULTIPLY	MUMBLING	MINEHEAD	MINORITY	MEPHISTO
MAINSTAY	MILLIONS	MEMENTOS	MUNCHIES	MONTREUX	MAQUETTE
MAINSAIL	MULLIONS	MOMENTUM	MUNCHING	MANGROVE	MOQUETTE
MAILSHOT	MULTIGYM	MAMMOTHS	MINEHOST	MINISTER	MERMAIDS
MAINTAIN	MELBLANC	MEMORIAL	MANDINGO	MONASTIC	MARGARET
MOISTENS	MILKMAID	MEMORIES	MANCIPLE	MINISTRY	MARIACHI
MOISTURE	MELAMINE	MEMBRANE	MANDIBLE	MENISCUS	MARMARIS
MRJAGGER	MELSMITH	MCMURTRY	MANTILLA	MINDSEYE	MORTALLY
MAJOLICA	MALINGER	MEMORISE	MONTILLA	MINUTIAE	MARIANNE
MAJORTOM	MOLINSKY	MANDALAY	MANSIONS	MANITOBA	MYRNALOY
MAJORITY	MILANESE	MANIACAL	MENTIONS	MINSTREL	MURMANSK
MAJESTIC	MILDNESS	MANDATES	MONSIEUR	MINUTELY	MORIARTY
MAKEFAST	MOLINEUX	MANEATER	MANGLING	MINUTING	MORIBUND
MCKELLEN	MELLOWED	MANDARIN	MANTLING	MONOTONE	MARABOUT
MCKENZIE	MELLOWER	MANUALLY	MINGLING	MONOTONY	MOROCCAN
MAKINGUP	MULRONEY	MENTALLY	MINDLESS	MUNITION	MIRACLES
MAKEOVER	MALVOLIO	MONTAGUE	MONALISA	MINSTERS	MERIDIAN
MIKEREID	MALCOLMX	MUNGBEAN	MONOLITH	MONETARY	MARADONA
MAKESURE	MELTORME	MINICABS	MENELAUS	MONITORS	MEREDITH
MIKETODD	MILLPOND	MANACLED	MONUMENT	MONSTERS	MARKDOWN
MALLARDS	MALAPROP	MANACLES	MINIMISE	MUNSTERS	MARKETED
MOLECULE	MALARIAL	MONOCLED	MANTOMAN	MINUTEST	MERCEDES
MELODICA	MALTREAT	MONOCLES	MANHOLES	MINOTAUR	MURDERED
MALADIES	MILLRACE	MENACING	MANPOWER	MANFULLY	MURDERER
MELODIES	MALARKEY	MANICURE	MANDOLIN	MENSWEAR	MARBELLA
MELODEON	MALTSTER	MINIDISC	MONGOLIA	MONOXIDE	MARKEDLY
MELTDOWN	MOLASSES	MANNERED	MONROVIA	MONEYBOX	MARTELLO
MALDEMER	MOLESTED	MONTEREY	MONSOONS	MONTYDON	MARIETTE
MALVERNS	MOLESKIN	MINCEPIE	MONGOOSE	MOONBEAM	MORTGAGE
MULBERRY	MULETEER	MANNERLY	MONMOUTH	MOORCOCK	MARIGOLD
MALIGNED	MILITANT	MINNELLI	MONOPOLY	MOORGATE	MARSHGAS
MALIGNLY	MILITARY	MANTEGNA	MANORIAL	MOOCHING	MURPHIES
MOLEHILL	MILITATE	MANOFWAR	MONDRIAN	MOORHENS	MARSHTIT
MELCHIOR	MOLLUSCS	MANIFOLD	MONTREAL	MOORINGS	MARSHALL
MALVINAS	MILLWALL	MANOFGOD	MONARCHS	MOODIEST	MARSHALS

MARCHING	MARYRAND	MUSTERED	MISERERE	METAPHOR	MIXTURES
MERCHANT	MARYROSE	MESMERIC	MISTRESS	MATERIAL	MAYFLIES
MORPHINE	MARKSMAN	MASTERLY	MISTRUST	MATERNAL	MAYORESS
MARCHERS	MARKSMEN	MISDEALS	MASERATI	MOTORCAR	MAYQUEEN
MIRTHFUL	MOROSELY	MISDEALT	MRSBROWN	MOTORWAY	NEARDARK
MORPHEUS	MARASMUS	MASSEURS	MOSSSIDE	MATERIEL	NEATENED
MARGINAL	MORESQUE	MISHEARD	MESSTINS	MOTORAIL	NEAREAST
MARZIPAN	MARITIME	MUSKETRY	MUSCULAR	MATURELY	NEARMISS
MARTINET	MARKTIME	MASSEUSE	MISJUDGE	MATURING	NEARNESS
MARTINEZ	MERITING	MESSEDUP	MUSQUASH	MOTORING	NEATNESS
MORTIMER	MARATHON	MISOGAMY	MISQUOTE	MATTRESS	NEARSIDE
MARKINGS	MARAUDED	MISOGYNY	MOSQUITO	MOTORIST	NOAHSARK
MARRIAGE	MARAUDER	MASTHEAD	MOSEYING	MATURITY	NEAPTIDE
MORNINGS	MARQUEES	MISCHIEF	MESOZOIC	MUTESWAN	NOAHWYLE
MARTINIS	MURMURED	MESSHALL	METCALFE	MUTATING	NEBRASKA
MORBIDLY	MURMURER	MUSTHAVE	MUTUALLY	MUTATION	NOBLEGAS
MARCIANO	MORTUARY	MYSTICAL	MATABELE	MOTJUSTE	NOBLEMAN
MARTIANS	MARQUESS	MISSILES	MOTHBALL	MOTIVATE	NOBLEMEN
MORRISON	MARYWEBB	MISSIVES	MATADORS	MOULDING	NOBLEROT
MYRMIDON	MERRYMEN	MISTIMED	MATTERED	MOUTHING	NOBLEART
MERRIEST	MORAYEEL	MISTIMES	MUTTERED	MOUTHFUL	NOBLESSE
MURKIEST	MARRYING	MASTIFFS	MUTTERER	MEUNIERE	NIBBLING
MERCIFUL	MISMATCH	MISSIONS	MOTHERLY	MOURNING	NOBILITY
MARYKATE	MASSAGED	MESSIEST	MITIGATE	MOURNERS	NEBULOUS
MARBLING	MASSAGES	MYSTIQUE	MATCHFIT	MOURNFUL	NECKBAND
MARYLAND	MESSAGES	MISPLACE	MITCHELL	MAUSOLUS	NECKBONE
MORALISE	MISTAKEN	MUSCLEIN	MATCHING	MOUSSAKA	NICKCAVE
MORALIST	MISTAKES	MISHMASH	MATCHBOX	MOUNTIES	NACREOUS
MORALITY	MUSCADET	MESSMATE	MATAHARI	MOUNTAIN	NECKLACE
MARINADE	MUSCATEL	MISNOMER	MATTHEWS	MOULTING	NACELLES
MARINARA	MUSTANGS	MISCOUNT	METRICAL	MOUNTING	NECKLINE
MARINERS	MISCALLS	MASTODON	MYTHICAL	MOVEDOUT	NICKLAUS
MARINATE	MASCAGNI	MISSOURI	MATRICES	MOVEMENT	NICKNAME
MERINGUE	MASSACRE	MISSPELL	METALLIC	MOVINGIN	NICHOLAS
MARJORAM	MISCASTS	MISSPELT	MATELOTS	MAVERICK	NICKOWEN
MARKOWEN	MUSICIAN	MISSPENT	MUTILATE	MOWNDOWN	NICHOLLS
MARMOSET	MASACCIO	MISSREAD	MUTINEER	MIXEDBAG	NICKPARK
MAROONED	MUSICALS	MISTREAT	MUTINIES	MAXIMISE	NICKROSS
MIRRORED	MUSICBOX	MISTRIAL	MUTENESS	MIXINGIN	NECKTIES
MOREOVER	MISLEADS	MISPRINT	MUTINOUS	MIXINGUP	NICETIES
MARJORIE	MASTERED	MESSROOM	METEORIC	MAXBOYCE	NICOTINE
MERCOURI	MISTERED	MUSHROOM	MATRONLY	MIXERTAP	NOCTURNE

NECKWEAR	NUMSKULL	NARRATES	NOTELETS	NEWBROOM	ONDEMAND
NICEWORK	NAMELESS	NORMALLY	NATIONAL	NEWSROOM	ORDINEES
NEDKELLY	NOMINEES	NARRATOR	NOTIONAL	NEWLYWED	ORDINALS
NYEBEVAN	NUMBNESS	NERVEGAS	NOTTOSAY	NEXTDOOR	ORDINAND
NEEDIEST	NOMINATE	NORSEMAN	NITROGEN	NUZZLING	ORDINARY
NEEDLING	NUMINOUS	NORSEMEN	NOTARIES	NAZARENE	OLDWORLD
NEEDLESS	NUMERACY	NORTHSEA	NATURISM	NAZARETH	OMDURMAN
NOFRILLS	NUMERALS	NORTHERN	NATURIST	ORANGERY	OBDURACY
NUFFIELD	NUMERATE	NARCISSI	NOTARISE	OCARINAS	OLDFRUIT
NIFTIEST	NUMEROUS	NARROWED	NOTATALL	ONAPLATE	ORDERING
NIGGARDS	NEMESIAS	NARROWER	NOTATION	ORATORIO	OBDURATE
NOGOAREA	NAMESAKE	NARCOSIS	NOTRUMPS	ORACULAR	OLDTROUT
NEGLECTS	NOMATTER	NARCOTIC	NATIVITY	OXBRIDGE	ODDITIES
NAGSHEAD	NUNEATON	NARROWLY	NOUVELLE	ORBITING	OLDSTERS
NEGLIGEE	NINTENDO	NURTURED	NAUSEATE	OSBOURNE	OLDGUARD
NIGGLING	NANTERRE	NURTURES	NAUSEOUS	ORCHARDS	OPERAHAT
NIGERIAN	NONSENSE	NOSEBAGS	NAUTICAL	OZCLARKE	OPERANDI
NAGASAKI	NONAGONS	NOSEBAND	NAUTILUS	ORCADIAN	OPERATED
NIGHTCAP	NUNCHAKU	NOSECONE	NEUROSES	OCCIDENT	OPERATES
NIGHTJAR	NANKIPOO	NOSEDIVE	NEUROSIS	ONCREDIT	OPERATIC
NIGHTIES	NANAMOON	NESTEGGS	NEUROTIC	ONCOMING	OPERABLE
NEGATING	NINEPINS	NOSEGAYS	NEUTRALS	ONCEMORE	OVERALLS
NEGATION	NONSTICK	NASTIEST	NEUTRINO	ONCEOVER	OPERATOR
NUGATORY	NINETEEN	NESTLING	NEUTRONS	OCCUPIED	OVERACTS
NEGATIVE	NINETIES	NOSINESS	NAVYBLUE	OCCUPIER	OVERBEAR
NIGHTOWL	NONEVENT	NOSTRILS	NAVIGATE	OCCUPIES	OPENBOOK
NIHILISM	NEONATAL	NOSTROMO	NOVELLAS	OCCUPANT	OVERCOAT
NIHILIST	NEOPHYTE	NUTHATCH	NOVELESE	OCCURRED	OVERCAME
NIHILITY	NOOBJECT	NOTABENE	NOVELIST	OCCASION	OVERCOME
NUISANCE	NEOPRENE	NOTEBOOK	NOVEMBER	OCCLUDED	OVERCOOK
NAILDOWN	NOONTIDE	NOTICING	NAVARONE	OCCLUDES	OPENCAST
NOISETTE	NYPDBLUE	NOTECASE	NEWFACES	OFCOURSE	OVERCAST
NAILFILE	NOPICNIC	NATTERED	NEWHAVEN	ONCOURSE	OVERDRAW
NEIGHING	NUPTIALS	NATTERER	NEWSCAST	ORDNANCE	OVERDOES
NOISIEST	NIPPIEST	NOTLEAST	NOWADAYS	ONDAATJE	OVERDOIT
NDJAMENA	NAPOLEON	NOTIFIED	NEWDELHI	ODDBALLS	OVERDONE
NIJINSKY	NEPALESE	NOTIFIES	NOWONDER	ODDMENTS	OVERDOSE
NELLDUNN	NEPENTHE	NUTSHELL	NEWCOMER	OLDTIMER	OMELETTE
NELLGWYN	NEPOTISM	NOTCHING	NEWWORLD	ORDAINED	OPERETTA
NAMIBIAN	NEPOTIST	NOTAHOPE	NEWSPEAK	OLDFIELD	OVEREATS
NAMEDROP	NORMANDY	NUTRIENT	NEWORDER	OLDFLAME	OVERFEED
NUMBERED	NARRATED	NUTTIEST	NEWSREEL	OLDGLORY	OVERFILL

OVERFULL	OVERSEER	OLIGARCH	ORNAMENT	OUTCASTS	OUTDOORS
OVERFLOW	OVERSEES	ORIGANUM	OWNINGUP	OUTLASTS	OUTHOUSE
OPENFIRE	OVERSTEP	OLIVEOIL	OWNBRAND	OPTICIAN	OCTUPLET
OVERFISH	OVERSELL	OLIVETTI	ORNATELY	OPTEDOUT	ONTIPTOE
OVERHEAD	OVERSOLD	OLIVEOYL	OMNIVORE	ONTHEMAT	OUTBREAK
OVERHEAR	OBEISANT	ORIGINAL	OTOSCOPE	ONTHEWAY	ONTARGET
OVERHEAT	OVERSHOE	ORIFICES	ODOMETER	OUTREACH	OSTERLEY
OVERHANG	OVERSHOT	OXIDISED	ODONNELL	OUTWEIGH	OUTFRONT
OVERHAUL	OPENTOED	OXIDISES	OPOSSUMS	ONTHEAIR	OUTGROWN
ONEPIECE	OVERTAKE	OPINIONS	ORPHANED	ONTHESLY	OUTSTRIP
ONELINER	OVERTIME	OPIUMDEN	OPPONENT	OUTSELLS	OUTSTARE
ONESIDED	OVERTONE	ORIENTAL	ONPARADE	ONTHEDOT	OUTSTAYS
OPENINGS	OVERTURE	OMISSION	OPPOSING	ONTHEHOP	OUTBURST
OBELISKS	OVERTURN	OMITTING	OPPOSERS	ONTHEJOB	OCTAVIUS
OBEDIENT	OVERUSED	ODIOUSLY	OPPOSITE	ONTHENOD	OUTLYING
OVERKILL	OVERUSES	OBITUARY	ONRECORD	ONTHERUN	OPULENCE
OVERLEAF	OVERVIEW	OBJECTED	ONRELIEF	OUTOFKEY	OCULISTS
OVERLOAD	OVENWARE	OBJECTOR	ONREMAND	OCTAGONS	OBVIATED
OVERLOCK	ONEBYONE	OAKAPPLE	ONREPORT	OUTSHINE	OBVIATES
OVERLAID	OFFICIAL	OILWELLS	OGRESSES	OBTAINED	ONWHEELS
OVERLAND	OFFICERS	OBLIGING	OBSTACLE	OUTLINES	OSWESTRY
OVERLONG	OFFSHOOT	OOLOGIST	OSSICLES	OUTLIVED	OXYMORON
OVERLOOK	OFFSHORE	OBLIGATE	OBSIDIAN	OUTRIDER	OLYMPIAD
OVERLAPS	OFFWHITE	OKLAHOMA	OSSIFIED	OUTSIDER	OLYMPIAN
OVERLORD	OFFPISTE	OILFIRED	OSSIFIES	OUTRIGHT	OLYMPICS
OVERLAYS	OFFENCES	OILFIELD	ONSAFARI	OUTFIELD	ODYSSEUS
OPENMIND	OFFENDED	ONLYJUST	OBSOLETE	ORTOLANS	PLACARDS
OLEANDER	OFFENDER	OILSKINS	ONSTREAM	OUTFLANK	PLACATED
OPENNESS	OFFANDON	OILSLICK	OBSTRUCT	OUTCLASS	PLACATES
OPENPLAN	OFFLOADS	OILCLOTH	OBSERVED	OTTOMANS	PLAYALET
OVERPLAY	OFFBREAK	OILINESS	OBSERVER	OUTSMART	PHARAOHS
OVERPAID	OFFERING	ONLOOKER	OBSERVES	OPTIMISE	PLACABLE
OVERPASS	OFFPRINT	OILSTONE	ONSTRIKE	OPTIMISM	PEASANTS
OVERRIDE	OFFDRIVE	OBLATION	OBSESSED	OPTIMIST	PLAYBACK
OVERRODE	OFFSTAGE	OBLIVION	OBSESSES	OXTONGUE	PLAYBALL
OVERRULE	OFFSTUMP	ONMYCASE	OBSCURED	OPTIONAL	PLAYBILL
OVERRIPE	ORGANDIE	OHMMETER	OBSCURES	OUTMODED	PLAYBOYS
OVERRATE	ORGANISE	ORMSKIRK	OUTWARDS	OUTBOUND	PRANCING
ONEORTWO	ORGANISM	ONMYTAIL	OUTDATED	OUTDOING	PEARDROP
OVERSEAS	ORGANIST	OSNABURG	OUTLAWED	OUTGOING	PLAUDITS
OVERSTAY	OPHIDIAN	OENOLOGY	OUTRAGED	ORTHODOX	PLAYDOWN
OLEASTER	OCHREOUS	OINTMENT	OUTTAKES	OUTBOARD	PLACEMAT

PLATELET	PRAISING	PACHINKO	PREACHED	PFENNIGS	PUGILIST
PEACENIK	PRACTICE	PECULIAR	PREACHER	PIEDNOIR	PAGANINI
PLACEBOS	PEARTREE	PICKLING	PREACHES	PREENING	PAGANISM
PLACENTA	PIASTRES	POCKMARK	PIERCING	PREGNANT	PAGINATE
PEACEFUL	PRATTLED	PICKMEUP	PRESCOTT	PREMOLAR	PUGNOSED
PHASEOUT	PRATTLER	PECTORAL	PLEADING	PRETORIA	PEGBOARD
PLATEAUX	PRATTLES	PICCOLOS	PLEBEIAN	PRECOOKS	PIGSTIES
PLATEFUL	PLANTAIN	PECORINO	PRESENCE	PIECRUST	PIGSWILL
PRATFALL	PHANTOMS	PICAROON	PRETENCE	PLEURISY	PEGGYLEE
PLATFORM	PLAYTIME	PICTURED	PREBENDS	PIERROTS	PEGGYSUE
PLAYGOER	PHAETONS	PICTURES	PRETENDS	PRESSMAN	PJHARVEY
PLANGENT	PLANTING	PICKWICK	PRECEDED	PRESSMEN	PRIMATES
PLAYGIRL	PLANTERS	PODIATRY	PRECEDES	PHEASANT	PRIVATES
POACHING	PLASTERS	PEDICURE	PRECEPTS	PLEASANT	PRINCELY
POACHERS	PLATTERS	PEDIGREE	PREFECTS	PLEASING	PLIOCENE
PHARISEE	PSALTERS	PEDAGOGY	PREHEATS	PRESSING	PRINCESS
PRALINES	PSALTERY	PUDDINGS	PRESENTS	PEEPSHOW	PRIEDIEU
PLACINGS	PHANTASM	PODGIEST	PRETEXTS	PRESSBOX	PRICETAG
PLACIDLY	PRACTISE	PEDALLED	PREVENTS	PRESSUPS	PRIMEVAL
PIANISTS	PLAGUING	PEDALLER	PRESERVE	PLEASURE	PRIXFIXE
PLATINUM	PLATYPUS	PADDLING	PFEIFFER	PRESSURE	PRIGGERY
PLANKTON	PUBLICAN	PEDDLING	PEERGYNT	PRENTICE	PRIGGISH
PEARLJAM	PUBLICLY	PADDLERS	PLEDGING	PRETTIER	PHILIPPA
PLAYLIST	PUBCRAWL	PEDIMENT	PEEPHOLE	PRETTIFY	PHILIPPE
PLAYLETS	PACKAGED	PEDANTIC	PIECHART	PRESTIGE	POITIERS
PHARMACY	PACKAGES	PEDUNCLE	PLETHORA	PRETTILY	PRICKLED
PEARMAIN	PICKAXES	PEDANTRY	POETICAL	PLEATING	PRICKLES
PEATMOSS	PICADORS	PADDOCKS	PRECINCT	PRENTISS	PRICKING
PSALMIST	PICKETED	PEDESTAL	PREMISES	PLECTRUM	PHILLIPS
PLAYMATE	POCKETED	PRENATAL	PRESIDED	PRELUDES	PAINLESS
PLANNING	PUCKERED	PIEBALDS	PRESIDES	PRESUMED	PEIGNOIR
PLANNERS	POCHETTE	PLEIADES	PEELINGS	PRESUMES	PLIANTLY
PLAINEST	PACKEDUP	PREDATED	PREMIERE	PREJUDGE	POIGNANT
PLATONIC	PICKEDUP	PREDATES	PREMIERS	PREZZIES	PAIGNTON
PEACOCKS	PACIFIED	PREFACES	PREDICTS	PRETZELS	PRIMNESS
PLATOONS	PACIFIER	PRELATES	PRECIOUS	PUFFBALL	PHILOMEL
PEAGREEN	PACIFIES	PREPARED	PREVIOUS	PIFFLING	POISONED
PEABRAIN	PICKFORD	PREPARES	PREVIEWS	PIGTAILS	POISONER
PLAYROOM	PACIFISM	PRESAGES	PRECLUDE	PAGEANTS	PRISONER
PRAISEBE	PACIFIST	PREVAILS	PEERLESS	PIGMENTS	PRIORIES
PLAYSAFE	PACKHEAT	PEEKABOO	PREAMBLE	PIGLINGS	PRIMROSE
PLAYSUIT	PACKITIN	PREDATOR	PIEDMONT	PUGILISM	PRIORESS

PRIORITY	POLEMICS	POMPIDOU	PONDLILY	PROVERBS	PROMOTES
PLIMSOLL	PALLMALL	PUMPIRON	PENTLAND	PROVENCE	PROPOSED
PAINTING	PELLMELL	PUMPKINS	PENELOPE	PROCEEDS	PROPOSER
POINTING	PALIMONY	PAMPLONA	PANGLOSS	PROTEGEE	PROPOSES
PRINTING	PALOMINO	POMANDER	PENALISE	PROTEGES	PROVOKED
PRISTINE	POLYMATH	PEMBROKE	PENUMBRA	PHONETIC	PROVOKES
PAINTBOX	POLONECK	PAMAYRES	PENKNIFE	PROPERLY	PROLONGS
PAINTPOT	POLANSKI	PANDACAR	PUNINESS	PROTEINS	PHOTOFIT
PAINTERS	PALENESS	PENZANCE	PINMONEY	PHONEBOX	PROFORMA
POINTERS	POLONIUS	PANCAKES	PANGOLIN	PIONEERS	PROFOUND
PRINTERS	PULLOVER	PINNACES	PINPOINT	PROJECTS	PRONOUNS
PRINTOUT	POLARCAP	PENTACLE	PONTOONS	PROPERTY	PROPOUND
PRINTRUN	POLAROID	PINNACLE	PINBOARD	PROTECTS	PROTOCOL
PRIMULAS	PILGRIMS	PENTAGON	PANFORTE	PROTESTS	PROTOZOA
PIKELETS	PULLRANK	PENDANTS	PINGPONG	POORFOLK	PROVOSTS
PEKINESE	POLTROON	PENNANTS	PANCREAS	PROOFING	PROLOGUE
PAKISTAN	POLARISE	PANICKED	PINPRICK	PROFFERS	PROROGUE
PILLAGED	POLARITY	PINOCHET	PUNKROCK	PLOUGHED	PROSPECT
PILLAGER	POLESTAR	PINOCHLE	PANTRIES	PHOSGENE	PROMPTED
PILLAGES	PALISADE	PINECONE	PANORAMA	PROPHECY	PROMPTER
PULSATED	PILASTER	PUNGENCY	PUNISHED	PROPHESY	PROMPTLY
PULSATES	POLISHED	PANDERED	PUNISHES	PROPHETS	PLOPPING
PALPABLE	POLISHER	PINCENEZ	PUNCTUAL	PRODIGAL	PROPPING
PALPABLY	POLISHES	PONDERED	PANSTICK	PROVINCE	POOHPOOH
POLKADOT	POLLSTER	PANDEMIC	PINETREE	PROFILED	PROSPERO
PULLBACK	PALATIAL	PANCETTA	PINOTAGE	PROFILES	PROSPERS
POLICIES	POLITICO	PINAFORE	PONYTAIL	PROFITED	PROTRACT
PELICANS	POLITICS	PUNCHBAG	PENITENT	PROMISED	PROTRUDE
POLECATS	PALETTES	PENCHANT	PUNCTURE	PROMISES	PROGRAMS
PILTDOWN	PULITZER	PINCHING	PUNSTERS	PROVIDED	PROGRESS
PILFERED	POLITELY	PUNCHING	PUNITIVE	PROVIDER	POOLSIDE
PILFERER	PALATINE	PANTHEON	PENGUINS	PROVIDES	PLOTTING
PILSENER	PILOTING	PUNCHEON	PENDULUM	PROHIBIT	PLOTTERS
PULLEDIN	POLLUTED	PANTHERS	PONDWEED	PROLIFIC	PROCTORS
POLPERRO	POLLUTER	PANPIPES	PINEWOOD	PROCLAIM	PROCURED
PULLEDUP	POLLUTES	PENNINES	PROFANED	PROBLEMS	PROCURES
POLYGAMY	PELLUCID	PENLIGHT	PROBABLE	PROWLING	PRODUCED
POLYGONS	PAMPERED	PENSIONS	PROBABLY	PROWLERS	PRODUCER
POLYGLOT	PIMIENTO	PANNIERS	PROCAINE	POORNESS	PRODUCES
PWLLHELI	PUMPEDUP	PUNDITRY	PTOMAINE	PROPOSAL	PRODUCTS
PILCHARD	PAMPHLET	PANELLED	PLODDING	PROMOTED	PEPTALKS
PALMISTS	PEMMICAN	PANELPIN	PRODDING	PROMOTER	PIPEDOWN

PEPPERED	PARMESAN	PORTLAND	PERUSING	PESTERED	POTBELLY
PUPPETRY	PORTENDS	PURSLANE	PERUSERS	POSTERNS	PATTERNS
POPSICLE	PURVEYED	PARALYSE	PARASITE	POSTFREE	PATIENTS
POPULACE	PURVEYOR	PERILOUS	POROSITY	POSTHORN	PATCHING
PIPELINE	PARTERRE	PYRAMIDS	PARTTIME	PASTIMES	PITCHING
PAPILLON	PERVERSE	PARAMOUR	PURITANS	PASTICHE	PITCHERS
POPULISM	PERFECTS	PARENTAL	PORTUGAL	PASTILLE	PETTIFER
POPULIST	PERMEATE	PIRANHAS	PERTURBS	POSSIBLE	PITVIPER
POPULATE	PORTENTS	PYRENEAN	PERSUADE	POSSIBLY	PATRICIA
POPULOUS	PARVENUS	PYRENEES	PERFUMED	PASSIONS	PATRIOTS
POPINJAY	PERKEDUP	PARANOIA	PERFUMES	POSEIDON	PATELLAE
PAPOOSES	PERCEIVE	PARANOID	PERJURED	PASOLINI	POTBLACK
POPSOCKS	PURIFIED	PARSNIPS	PERJURER	PASHMINA	PETULANT
POPWORLD	PURIFIER	PARTNERS	PERJURES	POSTMARK	POTPLANT
PAPERHAT	PURIFIES	PERTNESS	PURSUANT	POSHNOSH	PITILESS
PIPERADE	PARAFFIN	PURENESS	PURSUING	PASTORAL	POTEMKIN
PAPERING	PARAGUAY	PERANNUM	PURSUERS	PASSOVER	PETUNIAS
PAPERBOY	PARAGONS	PERSONAL	PURSUITS	PUSHOVER	PATENTED
PIPETTES	PORTHOLE	PARDONED	PERUVIAN	POSTPONE	PATENTEE
PUPATING	PARCHING	PARDONER	PORTVALE	PASSPORT	PATENTLY
PUPATION	PERCHING	PERIODIC	PORTVILA	PASTRIES	PETANQUE
POPPYDAY	PORPHYRY	PARBOILS	PARAVION	PASTRAMI	PATHOGEN
PUPPYFAT	PURCHASE	PARDONME	PARTWORK	PASSRATE	POTHOLER
PIQUANCY	PARSIFAL	PERFORMS	POSITING	POTHOLES	
PARMAHAM	PARTISAN	PURLOINS	PEROXIDE	POSITION	PUTTOBED
PARLANCE	PERCIVAL	PARLOURS	PAROXYSM	POSITIVE	PUTTOSEA
PARTAKES	PORRIDGE	PORPOISE	PARRYING	PASTURES	POTBOUND
PERVADED	PARTICLE	PURPORTS	PARTYING	POSTURED	POTHOUSE
PERVADES	PORTILLO	PERSPIRE	PESHAWAR	PASQUALE	POTROAST
PORTABLE	PORTIONS	PIRIPIRI	PASSAGES	PASSWORD	PUTYOUUP
PERTAINS	PORTIERE	PARAPETS	PASSABLE	PUSSYCAT	PUTUPJOB
PARABLES	PERKIEST	PARAQUAT	PASSABLY	PITTANCE	PATERNAL
PUREBRED	PERSISTS	PORTRAIT	PISSARRO	PETNAMES	PETERKAY
PARABOLA	PURLIEUS	PERORATE	PUSHBIKE	PITFALLS	PETERMAN
PERICLES	PARAKEET	PORTRAYS	PASSBOOK	PITIABLE	PETERPAN
PORKCHOP	PARALLAX	PARISIAN	POSTCODE	PITIABLY	PETERMEN
PARODIED	PERELMAN	PARISHES	POSTCARD	PETEBEST	PATERSON
PARODIES	PARALLEL	PERISHED	PUSHCART	PATACAKE	PETERSON
PARADIGM	PORTLIER	PERISHER	PASADENA	PATIENCE	POTATOES
PARADING	PARKLAND	PERISHES	POSTDATE	POTTERED	PETITION
PARADISE	PARKLANE	PARASOLS	PASSEDBY	POTTERER	PUTATIVE
PARODIST	PAROLING	PARTSONG	PASSERBY	PATHETIC	POTAUFEU

PATHWAYS	PHYSALIS	QUICKFIX	REASSURE	RACECARD	RECESSED
PLUMBAGO	PAYMENTS	QUICKENS	REASSESS	ROCHDALE	RECESSES
PLUMBING	PAYPHONE	QUICKEST	REALTIME	RECEDING	ROCKSALT
PLUMBBOB	PHYSICAL	QUISLING	REACTANT	ROCKETED	RECUSANT
PLUMBERS	PHYSIQUE	QUIXOTIC	REACTING	ROCKETRY	RECITALS
PAUNCHES	PAYINGUP	QUIPPING	ROASTING	RACLETTE	RECITING
POUNCING	PLYMOUTH	QUIPSTER	REACTION	RECREATE	RECOUPED
POUNCETS	PIZZERIA	QUIZSHOW	REACTORS	ROCKFACE	RECOURSE
PLUMDUFF	PUZZLING	QUIETUDE	REALTORS	ROCKFALL	RECOUNTS
POUNDAGE	PUZZLERS	QUILTING	ROASTERS	ROCKFORD	RECRUITS
POUNDING	QUADBIKE	QUITTING	ROADTEST	RACEGOER	RECOVERS
PLUNDERS	QUANDARY	QUITTERS	REACTIVE	RICHHALL	RECOVERY
PRUDENCE	QUAFFING	QUIETEST	ROADUSER	RECEIVED	ROCKWELL
PRUNELLA	QUASHING	QUINTETS	REARVIEW	RECEIVER	RADIANCE
PAULETTE	QUACKING	QUIZZING	READYMIX	RECEIVES	RIDDANCE
PLUGGING	QUACKERY	QUOVADIS	RUBICUND	RECLINED	RADIATED
PLUNGING	QUAGMIRE	QUOTABLE	REBUFFED	RECLINER	RADIATES
PLUNGERS	QUARRIES	QUOTIENT	RUBAIYAT	RECLINES	REDFACED
PLUGHOLE	QUATRAIN	REAWAKEN	ROBSITCH	RECOILED	RODLAVER
PRURIENT	QUARRELS	READABLE	REBUILDS	RACHITIC	RADIATOR
PLUCKIER	QUADRANT	REAFFIRM	RUBBISHY	ROCAILLE	RADICALS
PLUCKILY	QUAYSIDE	ROADHOGS	REBUKING	ROCKIEST	RIDICULE
PLUCKING	QUANTIFY	ROADHUMP	REBELLED	RECEIPTS	REDUCING
PAULMUNI	QUARTERS	REACHING	RABELAIS	RECALLED	RIDGEWAY
PLUMMETS	QUANTITY	REACHOUT	RIBALDRY	RECKLESS	REDHEADS
PLUMPEST	QUARTETS	REALISED	ROBINDAY	RICHMOND	REDDENED
PLUMPISH	QUENCHED	REALISES	ROBINSON	RECANTED	REDEEMED
PRUFROCK	QUENCHES	REALISTS	RUBNOSES	RECENTLY	REDEEMER
PAULROSS	QUENELLE	READJUST	REBORING	RACINESS	RIDGELEY
PRUSSIAN	QUEUEDUP	REARMING	ROBUSTLY	RICHNESS	REDNECKS
PLUSSIGN	QUELLING	REARMOST	REBUTTAL	RECKONED	REDCELLS
POULTICE	QUEENMAB	READMITS	ROBOTICS	RECKONER	REDEFINE
PAVILION	QUEENBEE	REASONED	REBUTTED	RACCOONS	REDSHIFT
PAVEMENT	QUESTION	REAPPEAR	REBOUNDS	RECKONUP	REDSHANK
PEVENSEY	QUERYING	ROADRAGE	RICHARDS	RECAPPED	REDSHIRT
PIVOTING	QUETZALS	RHAPSODY	RECHARGE	RECEPTOR	REDDITCH
POWDERED	QUIBBLED	ROADSIDE	RACIALLY	ROCKPOOL	REDRIVER
POWERING	QUIBBLER	ROADSTER	RECLAIMS	RECORDED	REDLIGHT
POWERCUT	QUIBBLES	REASSIGN	RECYCLED	RECORDER	REDGIANT
POWERFUL	QUIDDITY	ROADSIGN	RECYCLES	RECURRED	REDSKINS
PAWNSHOP	QUIVERED	ROADSHOW	RICOCHET	RICKSHAW	REDOLENT
PIXELATE	QUICKSET	REASSERT	ROCKCAKE	RUCKSACK	REDALERT

RUDENESS	REFILLED	REHOUSED	RELIEVED	RAMBLERS	RINGMAIN
RADIOHAM	RIFFLING	REHOUSES	RELIEVES	REMEMBER	RUNAMILE
REDWOODS	RUFFLING	RAINBOWS	RELIEDON	ROMANIAN	RENAMING
RADIOING	REFUNDED	RAINCOAT	ROLLEDUP	ROMANLAW	RONMOODY
REDCOATS	REFINING	RAILCARD	RELIGION	REMANDED	RANDOMLY
REDEPLOY	REFINERY	REINDEER	RELEGATE	REMINDED	RUNTOYOU
REDBRICK	REFERRAL	RAINDROP	ROLLNECK	REMINDER	RANDOLPH
REDIRECT	REFORMAT	RAINDOWN	RELENTED	ROMANCED	RINGPULL
REDCROSS	REFEREED	RAIMENTS	ROLLOVER	ROMANCES	RINGROAD
RADARGUN	REFEREES	RAINFALL	ROLEPLAY	ROMANTIC	RUNARISK
RYDERCUP	REFERRED	RAILINGS	RELAPSED	RUMINANT	RINGSIDE
REDGRAVE	REFORMED	RHINITIS	RELAPSES	RUMINATE	RONETTES
RADISHES	REFORMER	RAILLERY	ROLYPOLY	REMARKED	RENOUNCE
REDESIGN	RIFFRAFF	REIGNING	RELISHED	REMARQUE	RENOVATE
REDSTART	REFUSING	RHIZOMES	RELISHES	REMITTAL	RANDWICK
REDOUBLE	REFUTING	RAILROAD	RELATING	REMITTED	RENOWNED
REDDWARF	REGICIDE	REISSUED	RELATION	REMOTELY	RENEWING
RIEVAULX	RIGADOON	REISSUES	RELATIVE	RAMBUTAN	RINGWORM
REENACTS	RIGIDITY	RAINTREE	RELAUNCH	REMOULDS	ROOTBEER
REEMERGE	RUGGEDLY	ROISTERS	RELEVANT	RUMOURED	RHOMBOID
REELECTS	REGAINED	REINVENT	RELIVING	REMOVALS	REORDERS
REEFKNOT	REGALING	REINVEST	RELAXANT	REMOVING	REOPENED
RIESLING	REGULARS	RAINWEAR	RELAXING	RANSACKS	RHODESIA
RHETORIC	REGULATE	RAILWAYS	RALLYING	RENTAMOB	REOFFEND
REEDPIPE	REGIMENT	RAINYDAY	RELAYING	RUNSAMOK	RIOTGEAR
RYEBREAD	REGINALD	REJECTED	RAMPAGED	RENTBOOK	ROOMIEST
RYEGRASS	REGIONAL	REJIGGED	RAMPAGES	RUNABOUT	ROOTLESS
RHEOSTAT	REGROUPS	REJOICED	RUMMAGED	RINGDOVE	ROOTLETS
ROENTGEN	REGROWTH	REJOICES	RUMMAGES	RENDERED	ROOMMATE
ROEBUCKS	RAGTRADE	REJOINED	RAMPARTS	RINSEOUT	ROOFRACK
RUEFULLY	REGARDED	RAKINGIN	REMNANTS	RONDEAUX	RIOBRAVO
RAFFARIN	RIGOROUS	REKINDLE	REMEDIAL	RUNNERUP	ROOSTING
REFRAINS	REGISTER	RAKISHLY	REMEDIED	RENEGADE	ROOSTERS
REFRACTS	REGISTRY	RELIANCE	REMEDIES	RENEGING	REPEALED
RIFLEMAN	RIGATONI	RELEASED	REMODELS	RANCHERO	REPEATED
REFLEXES	RIGHTING	RELEASES	RAMSGATE	RANCHERS	REPEATER
RIFLEMEN	ROGATION	RELIABLE	REMAINED	RENMINBI	REPLACED
RAFFERTY	RIGHTFUL	RELIABLY	REMAKING	RANKINGS	REPLACES
REFLECTS	REHEATED	ROLLBACK	RAMBLING	RUNCIBLE	REPLAYED
REFREEZE	REHEARSE	ROLLCALL	RAMPLING	RANKLING	REPUBLIC
REFUGEES	REHOBOAM	RELOCATE	RUMBLING	RINDLESS	RAPACITY
RUFFIANS	REHIRING	RULEDOUT	RUMPLING	RINGLETS	RAPIDITY

REPLICAS	RORQUALS	RESUMING	RETRACTS	ROULETTE	RIVETING
REPRISAL	RESEARCH	ROSEMARY	RUTABAGA	ROUGHAGE	REVIVING
REPAIRED	RESHAPES	RUSHMORE	RATHBONE	ROUGHENS	REVIVERS
REPAIRER	ROSEANNE	RESENTED	RATSBANE	ROUGHEST	REWRITES
REPTILES	RESTARTS	RESONANT	RETICULE	ROUGHCUT	ROWDIEST
REPRINTS	RESUBMIT	RASHNESS	RETICENT	REUNITED	ROWLOCKS
REPRIEVE	ROSEBERY	ROSINESS	RATECAPS	REUNITES	ROWBOATS
REPELLED	ROSEBUSH	RESONATE	ROTHESAY	ROUTINES	RAWLPLUG
REPULSED	ROSEBOWL	RESINOUS	RETRENCH	ROUSSEAU	REWARDED
REPULSES	RESTCURE	RESPONDS	RETREADS	ROUSTING	ROWDYISM
RIPPLING	RESIDUAL	RESTORED	RETREATS	REVEALED	REXSTOUT
RAPUNZEL	RUSEDSKI	RESTORER	RATIFIED	REVIEWED	ROYKEANE
REPENTED	ROSSDALE	RESTORES	RATIFIES	REVIEWER	RAYMEARS
ROPINGIN	RESIDENT	RISSOLES	RATCHETS	REVVEDUP	RHYTHMIC
RIPENING	RESIDING	RESPONSE	RATTIGAN	RAVAGING	ROYALBOX
RIPENESS	RESIDUUM	ROSARIAN	RETAILED	REVEILLE	ROYALISM
REPROACH	ROSIELEE	RESTRICT	RETAILER	REVOKING	ROYALIST
REPROVED	RESPECTS	RESERVED	RETAINED	REVELLED	REYNOLDS
REPROVES	ROSSETTI	RESERVES	RETAINER	REVELLER	RAZORCUT
REPAPERS	RESIGNED	ROSARIES	RETHINKS	REVOLTED	SOAKAWAY
RIPARIAN	RESTHOME	ROSERIES	RATTIEST	REVOLVED	SEACADET
REPARTEE	RUSHHOUR	RESTRAIN	RETRIEVE	REVOLVER	SEAFARER
REPORTED	RESCINDS	RESTROOM	RATTLING	REVOLVES	SEAWATER
REPORTER	RESPIRED	ROSARIUM	RATTLERS	RIVALLED	SEAEAGLE
REPHRASE	RESPIRES	RESISTED	RUTHLESS	REVILING	SEALABLE
RAPESEED	RESPITES	RESISTOR	ROTUNDAS	RIVULETS	SEALANTS
RIPOSTES	ROSSITER	ROSETTES	RATIONAL	REVAMPED	SEANBEAN
REPOSING	RUSSIANS	RESETTLE	RATIONED	REVENANT	SHABBIER
REPOTTED	RISKIEST	RISOTTOS	ROTARIAN	RAVENOUS	SHAMBLES
REPAYING	ROSSKEMP	RESOURCE	RETARDED	REVERSAL	SJAMBOKS
REPLYING	RESOLVED	RESOUNDS	RETIREES	REVERSED	SEATBELT
REQUESTS	RESOLVES	RASPUTIN	RETORTED	REVERSES	SHABBILY
REQUIRED	RESULTED	RESCUEME	RETURNED	REVERTED	SLAPBANG
REQUIRES	ROSALIND	RESCUING	RETIRING	REVEREND	STABBING
REQUIEMS	ROSALINE	RESCUERS	ROTATING	REVERENT	STALBANS
RAREBIRD	RUSTLING	ROSEWALL	ROTATION	REVERING	SWABBING
RAREFIED	ROSSLARE	ROSEWOOD	ROTATORS	RAVISHED	SCABBARD
RAREFIES	RUSTLERS	RESTYLED	ROTAVATE	RAVISHES	SHAGBARK
RURALISM	RESTLESS	RESTYLES	REUSABLE	REVISING	SEARCHED
RURALIST	RESOLUTE	RETRACED	ROUNDELS	REVISION	SEARCHER
REROUTED	RUSTLEUP	RETRACES	ROUNDING	REVISERS	SEARCHES
REROUTES	RESEMBLE	RITUALLY	ROUNDERS	REVISITS	SNATCHED

SNATCHES	SCAFFOLD	SLACKENS	SWARMING	SHARPISH	STARTING
STARCHED	STAFFING	SLACKING	STAMMERS	STAMPOUT	SWATTING
SWATCHES	STAFFORD	SMACKING	SEASNAIL	SEABREAM	SCATTERS
SCARCELY	STANFORD	SPANKING	SEASNAKE	STAIRWAY	SHATTERS
SEARCHME	STARFISH	SPARKING	SCANNING	SHADRACH	SLATTERN
SEASCAPE	SHANGHAI	STACKING	SPANNING	SHAMROCK	SLATTERY
SCARCITY	SPANGLES	STALKING	STAGNANT	SHAGREEN	SPATTERS
STACCATO	SNAGGING	SWANKING	STAINING	SCARRING	STARTERS
SEASCOUT	SPARGING	SLACKERS	STAUNTON	SEAFRONT	STARTURN
STANDPAT	STAGGERS	SMACKERS	SCANNERS	SPARRING	SMARTEST
SHANDIES	SWAGGERS	STALKERS	SPANNERS	STARRING	SMARTISH
SWADDLED	STARGATE	STARKERS	STAINERS	STAIRROD	STARTOUT
SWADDLES	SLAGHEAP	STARKEST	STANNARY	SEAGRASS	SCAPULAR
STANDOFF	SHASHLIK	SHARLEEN	SWANNERY	SCABROUS	SPATULAS
SCANDALS	SMASHHIT	STARLIFT	STAGNATE	SEATROUT	STATUTES
SCALDING	SEASHELL	SWANLAKE	SEASONAL	SEAGROVE	SEAQUAKE
SLAMDUNK	SCATHING	SAARLAND	SEAPOWER	SPARROWS	SEAGULLS
SPALDING	SLASHING	SEAPLANE	SEASONED	SOAPSUDS	STATUARY
STANDING	SMASHING	SNARLING	SHADOWED	STANSTED	STARVING
SLANDERS	STASHING	STABLING	STAYOVER	STARSIGN	STANWYCK
STANDARD	SWATHING	STALLING	SLAVONIC	SEALSKIN	STALWART
SLAPDASH	STANHOPE	STALLONE	SEABORNE	STARSHIP	STARWARS
SOAPDISH	SEASHORE	STAPLING	SEABOARD	SPARSELY	SEALYHAM
STARDUST	SMASHERS	STARLING	SEAHORSE	SWANSONG	SNAZZILY
STANDOUT	STAGHORN	SCALLION	SEAPORTS	SCANSION	SUBMERGE
SPACEBAR	SEACHEST	SEAFLOOR	STAMPEDE	SLAPSHOT	SUBLEASE
SPACEMAN	SHAVINGS	SMALLPOX	SNAPPIER	SNAPSHOT	SUBJECTS
SEAFEVER	SPANIELS	STALLION	SPALPEEN	SWAPSHOP	SUBVERTS
SEALEVEL	STATIONS	SCALLOPS	SCALPELS	SPARSITY	SUBSIDED
SLAVERED	SPANIARD	SMALLFRY	SNAPPILY	SCANTIER	SUBSIDES
SLAVERER	SCARIEST	STAPLERS	SCALPING	SHANTIES	SIBLINGS
SPACEMEN	SEAMIEST	SEAMLESS	SEANPENN	SMARTIES	SUBTITLE
SHAKEOFF	SHADIEST	SMALLEST	SHARPENS	STARTLED	SOBRIETY
SCAVENGE	SCABIOUS	SMALLISH	SLAPPING	STARTLES	SUBSISTS
SPACEAGE	SPACIOUS	STABLEST	SNAPPING	STARTREK	SIBILANT
SNAKEOIL	SLAPJACK	SCARLETT	STAMPING	SWASTIKA	SUBCLASS
SPARERIB	SHACKLED	SHALLOTS	SWAPPING	SCANTILY	SUBTLEST
SHAMEFUL	SHACKLES	STARLETS	SHAMPOOS	SHANTUNG	SIBILATE
SHAREOUT	SPARKLED	SHALLOWS	SCAMPERS	SLANTING	SUBTLETY
STAKEOUT	SPARKLER	SWALLOWS	SCARPERS	SMARTENS	SIBELIUS
SCARFACE	SPARKLES	SMARMILY	SNAPPERS	SMARTING	SUBTOTAL
SNAFFLES	SHANKLIN	SLAMMING	SHARPEST	SPARTANS	SUBSONIC

SUBPOENA	SICKROOM	SEESAWED	SPECKLED	STEPPING	SPECTRUM
SIBERIAN	SECURITY	SHEBANGS	SPECKLES	STEWPANS	SHELVING
SUBURBAN	SUCCUMBS	SCENARIO	SNEAKILY	SWEEPING	SWERVING
SUBTRACT	SECLUDED	SHERATON	SNEAKING	SHEEPDOG	SHERWOOD
SUBURBIA	SECLUDES	SEEDBEDS	SPEAKING	SLEEPERS	SLEAZILY
SOBERING	SIDJAMES	SKEWBALD	SNEAKERS	SWEEPERS	SNEEZING
SYBARITE	SIDEARMS	SKETCHED	SPEAKERS	SHEEPISH	SOFTBALL
SABOTAGE	SEDUCING	SKETCHES	SLEEKEST	STEEPEST	SOFTCELL
SABATINI	SEDUCERS	SPEECHES	SHEDLOAD	STEWPOTS	SOFTENED
SOBSTORY	SIDECARS	SEEDCAKE	SPELLMAN	SHEEPRUN	SOFTENER
SABOTEUR	SIDEDISH	STEMCELL	SHERLOCK	SHERRIES	SUFFERED
SUBHUMAN	SIDEDRUM	STENCILS	STEALTHY	STEERAGE	SUFFERER
SUBSUMED	SADDENED	SPEEDWAY	SEEDLING	SHEARING	SOFTENUP
SUBSUMES	SUDDENLY	STENDHAL	SHELLING	SMEARING	SUFFICED
SUBDUING	SIDEKICK	SHELDUCK	SHETLAND	SNEERING	SUFFICES
SOCRATES	SADDLING	SPEEDIER	SMELLING	SPEARING	SUFFIXES
SACKABLE	SIDELINE	STEADIED	SPELLING	STEERING	SOFTNESS
SOCIABLE	SIDELONG	STEADIER	STEALING	SWEARING	SUFFRAGE
SOCIALLY	SADDLERS	STEADIES	STERLING	SHEARERS	SAFESEAT
SACKBUTS	SADDLERY	SPEEDILY	SWELLING	STEERERS	SOFTSOAP
SECEDING	SEDULOUS	STEADILY	STEALERS	SPEARGUN	SOFTSELL
SUCCEEDS	SEDIMENT	SHEDDING	SEEDLESS	SEEDSMAN	SOFTSHOE
SECRETED	SUDANESE	SPEEDING	STEMLESS	SEEDSMEN	SUFFUSED
SECRETES	SIDMOUTH	SPENDING	STELLATE	STETSONS	SUFFUSES
SICKENED	SIDEREAL	STEADYON	STEELEYE	SPECTRAL	SOFTWOOD
SICKENER	SIDEROAD	STEPDOWN	STEAMING	SCEPTICS	SOFTWARE
SECRETLY	SIDESMAN	SKELETAL	STEMMING	SCEPTRES	SIGNALLY
SUCCINCT	SIDESMEN	SHEDEVIL	STEAMERS	SHEATHES	SAGACITY
SECTIONS	SIDESTEP	SKELETON	STEINWAY	SHELTIES	SIGNEDON
SACRISTY	SADISTIC	STEPFORD	SKEANDHU	SPECTRES	SEGMENTS
SICILIAN	SIDESLIP	SVENGALI	STEENBOK	SWEETIES	SUGGESTS
SOCALLED	SIDESHOW	SLEDGING	SKEGNESS	SWEETPEA	SOGGIEST
SUCHLIKE	SEDATELY	SEETHING	STERNEST	SHEETING	SAGAMORE
SUCKLING	SEDATING	SHEPHERD	STEROIDS	SMELTING	SIGNORAS
SYCAMORE	SEDATION	SHERIDAN	STEPONIT	SWEATING	SIGNPOST
SECONDED	SEDITION	SPECIMEN	SLEEPIER	SWEETENS	SUGARING
SECONDER	SEDATIVE	SHERIFFS	STEEPLES	SEESTARS	SIGHTSEE
SECONDLY	STDAVIDS	SPECIFIC	SHEEPDIP	SHELTERS	SIGHTING
SICKNESS	SIDEWALK	SPECIALS	SLEEPILY	SWEATERS	SCHNAPPS
SACKRACE	SIDEWIND	SEEDIEST	SLEEPING	SWELTERS	SCHMALTZ
SECURELY	SIDEWAYS	SPECIOUS	STEEPENS	SWEETEST	SCHUBERT
SECURING	STEWARDS	SNEAKIER	STEEPING	SPECTATE	SCHEDULE

SCHIFFER	SKIDDING	STICKIER	SWIMMERS	SHIFTIER	SALADOIL
SPHAGNUM	STIPENDS	STICKLER	SKIRMISH	SKITTLED	SOLIDITY
SCHILLER	SHIVERED	STICKILY	SLIMMEST	SKITTLES	SOLVENCY
STHELIER	SPIKELEE	SHIRKING	SHIPMATE	SHIITAKE	SOLDERED
SOHELPME	SEICENTO	SLINKING	STIGMATA	SHIFTILY	SELVEDGE
STHELENA	STILETTO	SMIRKING	SCIENCES	SHIFTING	SULLENLY
STHELENS	SPITEFUL	SNICKING	SKINNIER	SKIRTING	SOLVENTS
SCHOLARS	SNIFFLES	STICKING	SKINNING	SPITTING	SULPHIDE
SCHEMING	SAINFOIN	STINKING	SPINNING	SPITTOON	SELFHELP
SCHUMANN	SEINFELD	SLIPKNOT	SPINNERS	SHIFTERS	SOLIHULL
SCHEMERS	SNIFFING	SHIRKERS	SLIMNESS	SKINTEST	SULPHATE
SCHEMATA	SPIFFING	SLICKERS	SEIGNEUR	SKITTISH	SALCHOWS
SCHOOLED	STIFFENS	SNICKERS	SPINNEYS	SWIFTEST	SULLIVAN
SCHOONER	SPITFIRE	STICKERS	SCIROCCO	STIMULUS	SALTIRES
SCHOOLIE	SAILFISH	STINKERS	SLIPOVER	SKIVVIES	SILLITOE
SCHMOOZE	STINGRAY	SNICKETS	SPINOFFS	SWIMWEAR	SOLDIERS
SCHIPHOL	SHINGLES	SCILLIES	SKIMPIER	SLIPWARE	SALTIEST
SPHEROID	STINGIER	SHIELDED	STIPPLED	SHIPYARD	SILLIEST
SPHERULE	SWINGBIN	SPILLAGE	STIPPLES	SWIZZLED	SULKIEST
SCHERZOS	SLINGING	SHILLING	SLIPPAGE	SWIZZLES	SALTLAKE
SRINAGAR	STINGING	SKIPLANE	SKIMPILY	SOJOURNS	SELFLESS
SHIRALEE	SWIGGING	SLIMLINE	SKIMPOLE	SAKHALIN	SELFLOVE
SRILANKA	SWINGING	SPILLANE	SHIPPING	SUKIYAKI	SOLEMNLY
SPIRACLE	SNIGGERS	SPILLING	SKIMPING	SULTANAS	SILKMOTH
SPIRALLY	STINGERS	STIFLING	SKIPPING	SALVAGED	SOLONGAS
SUITABLE	SWINGERS	STIRLING	SLIPPING	SALVAGES	SELZNICK
SUITABLY	SKINHEAD	SWILLING	SNIPPING	SALEABLE	SALINGER
SKIPANTS	SPITHEAD	SWIRLING	SOILPIPE	SOLVABLE	SILENCED
SHINBONE	SLIGHTED	SKILLION	SKIPPERS	SYLLABLE	SILENCER
STITCHED	SLIGHTER	STILLSON	SLIPPERS	SALVADOR	SILENCES
STITCHES	SLIGHTLY	SKISLOPE	SLIPPERY	SELLAPUP	SPLINTER
SWITCHED	SLITHERS	SKINLESS	SNIPPETS	SYLLABUB	SOLENOID
SWITCHES	SLITHERY	SKILLETS	SLIPROAD	SYLLABUS	SPLENDID
SKINCARE	SMITHERS	SHIMMIED	STIRRING	SALZBURG	SILENTLY
SLIPCASE	SCIMITAR	SHIMMIES	STIRRUPS	SALICLAW	SALINITY
SUITCASE	SPINIFEX	SHIPMENT	STIRRERS	SELECTED	SELENIUM
SPICCATO	SPIRITED	SKIMMING	SPINSTER	SILICONE	SALOPIAN
SKINDEEP	SHINIEST	SLIMMING	SWIMSUIT	SPLICING	SELFPITY
SPINDLES	SLIMIEST	SWIMMING	SHIPSLOG	SELECTOR	SALARIAT
SWINDLED	SPICIEST	SHIMMERS	SLIPSHOD	SOLECISM	SALARIED
SWINDLER	SKIPJACK	SHIMMERY	SCISSORS	SILICATE	SALARIES
SWINDLES	SLINKIER	SLIMMERS	SCIATICA	SOLIDIFY	SULTRIER

SELFRULE	SEMILLON	SUNDERED	SANDSHOE	STOICISM	SPOOKIER
SALEROOM	SAMPLERS	SUNBEAMS	SANDTRAP	SPONDEES	STOCKIER
SOLARIUM	SIMPLEST	SINGEING	SANCTIFY	SHODDILY	SNORKELS
SALESMAN	SIMULATE	SANCERRE	SANCTION	SCOLDING	SPOOKILY
SALESMEN	SIMONDAY	SINNFEIN	SANITARY	SNOWDROP	SHOCKING
SPLASHED	SAMANTHA	SUNSHADE	SENATORS	STOODOUT	SMOCKING
SPLASHES	SEMANTIC	SONDHEIM	SANITISE	SHOWDOWN	STOCKING
SELFSAME	SEMINOLE	SUNSHINE	SANCTITY	SLOWDOWN	STONKING
SOLSTICE	SEMINARS	SENTINEL	SINGULAR	STOREMAN	STOCKPOT
SOLITUDE	SEMINARY	SANDIEGO	SINFULLY	SHOWERED	SHOCKERS
SPLATTER	SAMENESS	SANTIAGO	SANGUINE	STOREMEN	STOCKIST
SPLUTTER	SIMONNYE	SUNLIGHT	SUNBURNS	STONEAGE	SHOELACE
SPLITPIN	SUMTOTAL	SENSIBLE	SUNBURNT	SLOVENIA	SHOULDER
SALUTING	SUMMONED	SENSIBLY	SUNBURST	SNOWEDIN	SMOULDER
SPLITEND	SYMBOLIC	SUNDIALS	SUNSUITS	SLOVENLY	SCOTLAND
SOLUTION	SYMPOSIA	SENTIENT	SENSUOUS	SHOWEDUP	SCOWLING
SOLATOPI	SAMCOOKE	SANDIRON	SANDWICH	SLOWEDUP	SPOILING
SALUTARY	SUMMONUP	SUNVISOR	SENDWORD	SCOFFLAW	SPOTLESS
SOLITARY	SAMSPADE	SUNNIEST	SONNYBOY	SCOTFREE	SMOLLETT
SALIVATE	SOMERSET	SANSKRIT	STOWAWAY	SNOWFALL	STORMIER
SILKWOOD	SOMBRELY	SUNBLOCK	STOMACHS	SCOFFING	STORMING
SILKWORM	SOMBRERO	SINOLOGY	SLOVAKIA	SCOFFERS	SCORNING
SALLYING	SEMESTER	SINCLAIR	SPORADIC	SPONGIER	SPOONING
SPLAYING	SIMPSONS	SUNBLIND	SHOWBOAT	STODGIER	SWOONING
SULLYING	SOMETIME	SINGLETS	SHOEBILL	SHOTGUNS	SLOWNESS
SELTZERS	SYMPTOMS	SONINLAW	SNOWBALL	SLOGGING	SCORNFUL
SAMJAFFE	SEMITONE	SYNONYMS	SNOWBOOT	SHOPGIRL	SPOONFUL
SYMPATHY	SAMOVARS	SINFONIA	SLOBBERY	SHOWGIRL	SLOCOMBE
SOMEBODY	SOMEWHAT	SYNOPSES	SNOBBERY	SLOGGERS	STOPOVER
SIMMERED	SOMEWHEN	SYNAPSIS	SLOBBISH	SPONGERS	SCORPIAN
SIMPERED	SAMOYEDS	SYNOPSIS	SNOBBISH	SHOWHOME	STOPPAGE
SAMNEILL	SAMIZDAT	SYNOPTIC	STOPCOCK	SHOSHONE	SLOPPILY
SYMMETRY	SUNDANCE	SUNCREAM	SCORCHED	SOOTHING	SCOOPING
SUMMEDUP	SUNBAKED	SENTRIES	SCORCHER	SHOEHORN	SHOPPING
SYMPHONY	SUNBATHE	SUNDRIES	SCORCHES	SMOTHERS	SLOPPING
SOMEHOPE	SENNAPOD	SYNDROME	SCOTCHED	SLOTHFUL	SNOOPING
SAMEHERE	SANDBANK	SUNDRESS	SCOTCHES	SCOFIELD	STOMPING
SAMPHIRE	SONGBOOK	SENORITA	SLOUCHED	STOLIDLY	STOOPING
SOMALIAN	SONGBIRD	SONOROUS	SLOUCHER	STOCKCAR	STOPPING
SIMPLIFY	SINECURE	SINISTER	SMOOCHED	STOCKMAN	SWOOPING
SAMPLING	SANDDUNE	SONGSTER	SMOOCHES	SPOTKICK	SCORPION
SEMOLINA	SENTENCE	SINGSONG	SHOWCASE	STOCKADE	SHOPPERS

SNOOPERS	SPORTIVE	SURFACER	SERAGLIO	SPRINGER	STRESSED
STOPPARD	SLOWWORM	SURFACES	STRAGGLE	SPRINTED	STRESSES
STOPPERS	SIOUXSIE	SURNAMED	STRAGGLY	SPRINTER	SPRITZER
SCOURGED	SNOWYOWL	SURNAMES	STRUGGLE	STRANDED	STRUTTED
SHOWREEL	SNOOZING	SURTAXED	SCRAGEND	STRANGER	SURETIES
SCOURING	SNOOZERS	SARGASSO	STROHEIM	STRINGER	STRATIFY
SPORRANS	SOPRANOS	SERVANTS	SURGICAL	STRONGER	STRATEGY
SHOWROOM	SAPIENCE	SCRUBBED	SURVIVAL	SYRINGES	SCRATCHY
SCOURERS	SUPREMES	SCRABBLE	SARDINES	SCRUNCHY	STRETCHY
SCOTSMAN	SUPREMOS	SCRIBBLE	SERVICED	SERENELY	SCRUTINY
SNOWSHOE	SAPPHIRE	SCRIBBLY	SERVICES	SPRINKLE	SHROUDED
SPONSORS	SAPLINGS	SARABAND	SPRAINED	STRANGLE	SPROUTED
SCORSESE	SOPPIEST	STROBING	STRAINED	STRONGLY	SCROUNGE
SHOETREE	SUPPLIED	SPROCKET	STRAINER	SURINAME	SHRIVELS
SMOOTHED	SUPPLIER	STRACHEY	SURMISED	SARANDON	STRIVING
SMOOTHER	SUPPLIES	STRICKEN	SURMISES	STRONGON	SCREWCAP
SNOOTIER	SUPPLANT	STRICTER	SURVIVED	SORENESS	STRAWMAN
SPOTTIER	SIPHONED	STRICTLY	SURVIVES	SPRYNESS	SCRAWLED
SHORTAGE	SUPPOSED	SYRACUSE	SERVINGS	SURENESS	SHREWDER
SMOOTHIE	SUPPOSES	SHREDDED	STRAIGHT	SERENITY	SPRAWLED
SMOOTHLY	SUPPORTS	SHREDDER	SARDINIA	STRENGTH	SHREWDLY
SNOOTILY	SUPERCAR	STRADDLE	SORDIDLY	SCROOGED	STREWING
SCOOTING	SUPERMAN	STRUDELS	SORBITOL	SCROOGES	SCREWTOP
SCOUTING	SUPERTAX	STRIDENT	SURBITON	SARDONIC	SHREWISH .
SHOOTING	SUPEREGO	STRIDING	SURVIVOR	SORBONNE	SPRAYING
SHORTENS	SUPERBLY	SARSENET	SURLIEST	SURMOUNT	STRAYING
SHOUTING	SUPERIOR	SCREENED	SARAJEVO	SURROUND	SPRAYERS
SNORTING	SUPPRESS	SHRIEKED	STRIKING	SARDONYX	SPRAYGUN
SPORTING	SEPARATE	SORCERER	STROKING	SCRAPPED	SUSTAINS
SPOTTING	SUPERBUG	SURVEYED	STRIKERS	SCRAPPER	SASHCORD
SPOUTING	SEQUENCE	SCREECHY	SURPLICE	SCRIPTED	SESTERCE
SWOTTING	SEQUOIAS	SERGEANT	SCROLLED	SCRUPLES	SUSPENDS
SCOOTERS	SERVALAN	SURGEONS	STROLLED	SHRAPNEL	SISTERLY
SHOOTERS	SCREAMED	SURVEYOR	STROLLER	STRAPPED	SUSPENSE
SPOTTERS	SCREAMER	SERPENTS	SCRIMPED	STRIPPED	SUSPECTS
SCOTTISH	SERRATED	SORRENTO	SCRUMPED	STRIPPER	SESSIONS
SHOOTIST	SPREADER	SURFEITS	STRIMMER	SERAPHIC	SUSANNAH
SHORTEST	STREAKED	SCROFULA	STRUMMED	SERAPHIM	SISYPHUS
SHORTISH	STREAKER	STRAFING	STRUMPET	SCRAPING	SATIATED
STOUTEST	STREAMED	SUREFIRE	SCRAMBLE	SCRAPERS	SATIATES
SHOOTOUT	STREAMER	SHRUGGED	SERENADE	SURPRISE	SITUATED
SHORTCUT	SURFACED	SHRUGOFF	SHRUNKEN	SORORITY	SETBACKS

SOTHEBYS	SHUDDERS	SCULLERY	SHUNTING	SOYAMILK	TRACKING
SATCHELS	SHUTDOWN	SOULLESS	SHUTTING	SAYONARA	THANKYOU
SETPIECE	SAUCEPAN	SLUMMOCK	SPURTING	SLYBOOTS	TRACKERS
SITTINGS	SQUEEGEE	SLUMMING	SAUNTERS	SHYSTERS	THANKSTO
SITTIGHT	SQUEEZED	SOURMASH	SHUNTERS	STYMYING	THANKFUL
SETTLING	SQUEEZES	SOULMATE	SHUTTERS	SIZEABLE	THAILAND
SETTLEON	SOUVENIR	SQUANDER	STUTTERS	SIZZLING	TRAILING
SETTLERS	STUDENTS	SQUINTED	SQUAWKED	SIZZLERS	TRAMLINE
SETTLEUP	SCUFFLES	SHUNNING	SQUAWKER	SIZINGUP	TRAWLING
SATANISM	SHUFFLED	SPURNING	STUDYING	TEARAWAY	TRAILERS
SATANIST	SHUFFLER	STUNNING	SAVEFACE	TEADANCE	TRAWLERS
SETPOINT	SHUFFLES	STUNNERS	SAVAGELY	TEACADDY	TEACLOTH
SATURDAY	SOUFFLES	SMUGNESS	SAVAGERY	TEACAKES	TEASMADE
SATIRISE	STUFFILY	SOURNESS	SAVELOYS	TIAMARIA	TRAMMELS
SATIRIST	SCUFFING	SCULPTED	SAVANNAH	TOAFAULT	TEAMMATE
SATURATE	STUFFING	SLUMPING	SAVINGUP	TEAPARTY	TRAINEES
SETASIDE	SNUFFBOX	SLURPING	SEVERELY	THALAMUS	TRAINSET
SATSUMAS	SOULFOOD	STUMPING	SEVERING	THATCHED	TRAINING
SAUSAGES	STUDFARM	SCULPTOR	SEVERITY	THATCHER	TRAINERS
SLUGABED	SMUGGLER	SCUPPERS	SAVOURED	THATCHES	TEATOWEL
SQUEAKED	SMUGGLES	SOURPUSS	SAVOYARD	TEARDUCT	TRAVOLTA
SQUEALED	SQUIGGLE	SCURRIED	SAWBONES	TRADDLES	TRAIPSED
SQUEALER	SQUIGGLY	SCURRIES	SEWERRAT	TEARDROP	TRAIPSES
SPUMANTE	SMUDGING	SPURRIER	SEWERAGE	TRAPDOOR	TRAMPLED
STUMBLED	STURGEON	SQUIRMED	SEXUALLY	TOANDFRO	TRAMPLES
STUMBLES	SLUGGARD	SQUIRREL	SEXTANTS	TEARDOWN	TRAMPING
SQUABBLE	SLUGGISH	SQUIRTED	SAXEBLUE	TRADEGAP	TRAPPING
SNUBBING	SOUTHPAW	SQUARELY	SIXPENCE	TRADEOFF	TEASPOON
STUBBING	SOUCHONG	SLURRING	SEXTETTE	TRAVERSE	TRAPPERS
STUDBOOK	SOUTHERN	SPURRING	SIXTIETH	TRAVESTY	TRAPPIST
SLUMBERS	STUPIDLY	SQUARING	SEXTUPLE	TOADFLAX	TRANQUIL
STUBBORN	SAUCIEST	SQUARISH	SOYSAUCE	TRAFFICS	TEABREAK
SOURCING	SPURIOUS	SQUASHED	SKYJACKS	TRASHCAN	TRANSACT
SQUADCAR	STUDIOUS	SQUASHES	SKYLARKS	TRACHOMA	TRANSECT
STURDIER	SHUCKING	STUNTMAN	SOYABEAN	TEACHING	TEAMSTER
SQUADDIE	SKULKING	SCUTTLED	SKYDIVER	TEACHERS	TRANSFER
STURDILY	SKULLCAP	SCUTTLES	STYLISED	TEACHEST	THATSAID
SCUDDING	SQUELCHY	SHUTTLES	STYLISES	TSARINAS	TRANSFIX
SOUNDING	SOUVLAKI	SQUATTED	SKYLIGHT	TRADJAZZ	TRANSMIT
SOUNDBOX	SCULLING	SQUATTER	STYLISTS	TRACKWAY	TRANSOMS
SQUADRON	SCULLION	STUNTMEN	SKYBLUES	THANKING	TRANSEPT
SAUNDERS	SCULLERS	STULTIFY	SPYGLASS	THANKING	TOASTING

TRACTION	TIDEMARK	THEFIXER	THEATEAM	TRIGGERS	THINNISH
TOASTERS	TVDINNER	THESIGER	THEATRES	TAILGATE	TRIMNESS
TRACTORS	TIDINESS	THEPIANO	TREATIES	TRINIDAD	TAILORED
TRAITORS	TADPOLES	TREKKING	TRESTLES	TWILIGHT	TRIPPING
TRADUCED	TEDDYBOY	TWEAKING	TWENTIES	THICKSET	TRIPPERS
TRADUCES	TEENAGER	TREKKERS	THESTING	TRICKIER	TRIARCHY
TRAPUNTO	THEDALES	THEOLOGY	TREATING	TRICKLED	TAILSPIN
TEAMWORK	THEGAMES	THEALAMO	TWEETING	TRICKLES	TRIASSIC
TOADYISM	THEWAVES	TREBLING	TREETOPS	TWINKLED	TRISTRAM
TZATZIKI	THEMAFIA	TOECLIPS	TREATISE	TWINKLES	TRIPTYCH
TABLEMAT	THEMATIC	TREELESS	THEMUMMY	THINKBIG	THIRTEEN
TABLETOP	THESAINT	THEBLITZ	TWEEZERS	THINKFIT	THIRTIES
TABLEAUX	THEHAGUE	THERMALS	TAFFRAIL	THICKENS	THISTLES
TOBOGGAN	THEMAGUS	THEKNACK	TUGOFWAR	THINKING	TWISTIES
TUBBIEST	TREMBLED	TWEENIES	TIGERBAY	TRICKING	TAINTING
TUBELESS	TREMBLES	TEETOTAL	TIGERISH	THINKERS	TWISTING
TABULATE	THEOCRAT	THEGOLEM	TIGHTWAD	TRICKERY	TWISTERS
TABLOIDS	TREACHER	THEJOKER	TOGETHER	THICKEST	TWITTERS
TUBERCLE	TRENCHED	THEWOMEN	TIGHTENS	THICKISH	TWITTERY
TIBERIUS	TRENCHES	THELODGE	TIGHTEST	THICKETS	TWITTISH
TUBEROUS	TREADLES	TREFOILS	TAHITIAN	TRINKETS	TRIBUNAL
TOBESURE	TRENDIER	THEDOORS	TRIMARAN	THISLIFE	TRIBUTES
TABBYCAT	TREADING	THEHOURS	TRIBALLY	TRIFLING	THIEVING
TOCCATAS	THEIDIOT	TEETOTUM	TAILBACK	TRILLING	TAILWIND
TICKETED	THEODORE	THESPIAN	TWINBEDS	TRIPLANE	TRIPWIRE
TUCKEDIN	TREDEGAR	TRESPASS	THIMBLES	TRIPLING	TRICYCLE
TUCKEROO	THEDERBY	THETRIAL	TRILBIES	TWIRLING	TAJMAHAL
TACTICAL	THEBEACH	TIEBREAK	TAILCOAT	TRILLION	TAKEAWAY
TACKLING	TEETERED	THEORIES	TWITCHED	TAILLESS	TAKEABOW
TICKLING	THEYEARS	THEOREMS	TWITCHER	TRIPLETS	TAKEBACK
TACKLERS	THEBEAST	THEORISE	TWITCHES	TRIALRUN	TAKECARE
TACTLESS	THESETUP	THEORIST	THIRDMAN	TRIUMPHS	TAKEDOWN
TICKLISH	TREEFROG	THEGROUP	THIRDWAY	THIAMINE	TAKEFIVE
TICKOVER	THETFORD	THECROWD	TWIDDLED	TRIMMING	TOKUGAWA
TUCKSHOP	TREEFERN	THEGREYS	TWIDDLES	TRIMMERS	TAKEHEED
TICKTOCK	THETHIEF	THEPRIZE	THIRDAGE	TRIMMEST	TOKENISM
TACITURN	THESHEIK	TEESSIDE	TRIEDOUT	TRIANGLE	TAKENOTE
TODIEFOR	THECHAMP	THEASHES	TRIREMES	THINNING	TEKANAWA
TEDHEATH	TEETHING	THESSALY	TOILETRY	TWINNING	TAKEODDS
TODDLING	THETHING	TRESSELL	TOILETTE	THINNERS	TAKEOVER
TIDDLERS	THEBITCH	TREASURE	TRISECTS	THINNESS	TOKYOJOE
TODDLERS	THEBIRDS	TREASURY	TRIFFIDS	THINNEST	TAKEPART

TAKEROOT	TOMTHUMB	TANTALUS	TUNSTALL	TAPDANCE	TIREDOUT
TAKETHAT	TOMAHAWK	TONYBENN	TINCTURE	TOPSAILS	TURNDOWN
TAKEWING	TIMELOCK	TENACITY	TENNYSON	TYPECAST	TARGETED
TALLBOYS	TIMALLEN	TONEDEAF	TWOFACED	TAPEDECK	TURGENEV
TELECAST	TUMBLING	TYNEDALY	THORACIC	TEPIDITY	TURRETED
TALIESIN	TUMBLERS	TONEDOWN	TOOKBACK	TUPPENCE	TURMERIC
TELEGRAM	TIMELESS	TENDENCY	TROUBLED	TOPPEDUP	TURNEDIN
TOLLGATE	TEMPLATE	TENPENCE	TROUBLES	TOPHEAVY	TORMENTS
TULLIVER	TAMENESS	TENDERED	TROMBONE	TYPEFACE	TORRENTS
TELEMARK	TEMPORAL	TINKERED	THORBURN	TYPIFIED	TURNEDUP
TALENTED	TOMJONES	TENDERLY	TOOKCARE	TYPIFIES	TORCHING
TALKOVER	TOMWOLFE	TINGEING	TWOPENCE	TOPWHACK	TERMINAL
TELEPORT	TAMWORTH	TONYHART	THOUGHTS	TAPSHOES	TERMITES
TOLERANT	TOMCONTI	TINMINER	TOOKHEED	TIPSIEST	TERRINES
TOLERATE	TIMEPOOR	TANGIBLE	TROCHEES	TOPOLOGY	TURBINES
TALISMAN	TOMPRICE	TANGIBLY	TROPHIES	TIPPLING	TORRIDGE
TALLSHIP	TIMORSEA	TENNISON	TROPICAL	TOPPLING	TERRIFIC
TALKSHOW	TUMBRELS	TANGIEST	TWOPIECE	TIPPLERS	TERRIBLE
TALLTALE	TAMARIND	TANAISTE	TWOTIMER	TAPENADE	TERRIBLY
TELLTALE	TOMORROW	TINNITUS	TOOTLING	TOPONYMY	TORTILLA
TELETHON	TAMARISK	TONGKING	TOODLEOO	TOPNOTCH	TERRIERS
TELETEXT	TEMERITY	TANGLING	TROLLOPE	TYPHOONS	TERTIARY
TALLULAH	TIMOROUS	TINGLING	TROLLOPS	TAPEROFF	TARDIEST
TELEVISE	TUMOROUS	TINKLING	TROLLEYS	TAPERING	TERMINUS
TELEWORK	TOMBROWN	TUNELESS	TAORMINA	TOPBRASS	TARAKIHI
TELEXING	TIMETEAM	TINPLATE	TROUNCED	TAPESTRY	TARAKING
TALLYMAN	TOMATOES	TONALITY	TROUNCES	TIPSTERS	TURNKEYS
TALLYMEN	TEMPTING	TENEMENT	THORNTON	TAPEWORM	TYROLEAN
TALLYING	TOMHULCE	TINSMITH	TOOKOVER	TORRANCE	THRILLED
TOMBAKER	TIMCURRY	TENONSAW	TWOWOMEN	TERRACED	THRILLER
TYMPANIC	TIMBUKTU	TININESS	THOROUGH	TERRACES	TERYLENE
TOMHANKS	TOMEWELL	TANGOING	TROOPING	THREADED	TIRELESS
TYMPANUM	TIMEWARP	TENTOONE	THOMPSON	THREATEN	TARTLETS
TIMEBOMB	TIMEWORN	TANDOORI	TOOKPART	TERRAPIN	THRUMMED
TOMYCOST	TOMMYLEE	TONEPOEM	TROOPERS	TARRAGON	TIRAMISU
TIMIDITY	TOMMYROT	TENERIFE	TOOTSIES	TOREADOR	THRENODY
TAMPERED	TOMMYGUN	TENDRILS	THOUSAND	TORIAMOS	THRONGED
TEMPERED	TIMEZONE	TANGRAMS	TROUSERS	TERRAZZO	TURANDOT
TIMBERED	TANKARDS	TANTRUMS	THOMSETT	TURNBACK	TARTNESS
TIMHEALY	TINTAGEL	TONYROME	TROTTING	THROBBED	TURBOJET
TEMPESTS	TANZANIA	TUNISIAN	TROTTERS	TERABYTE	TURNOVER
TOMYFACE	TENTACLE	TUNGSTEN	TWOBYTWO	TURNCOAT	TURLOUGH

TARBOOSH	TETRARCH	TRUTHFUL	TAXBREAK	UNCARING	UPHEAVAL
TORTOISE	TITLARKS	TRUJILLO	TAXIRANK	ULCEROUS	UNHEATED
TURNPIKE	TITICACA	TOURISTS	TAXATION	UNCOUPLE	UNHEEDED
TARAREID	TATTERED	TOURISTY	TEXTURAL	UNCTUOUS	UPHOLDER
TARTRATE	TETHERED	TRUCKLES	TEXTURED	UNCOVERS	UNHINGED
THRASHED	TITTERED	TRUCKING	TEXTURES	UNDRAPED	UNHOOKED
THRASHES	TOTTERED	TRUCKERS	TAXEXILE	UNDULATE	UNHARMED
THRESHED	TOTTEDUP	TRUELIES	TAYBERRY	UNDERLAY	USHERING
THRESHER	TETCHIER	TOUSLING	TOYSTORY	UNDERPAY	UNHOUSED
THRESHES	TETCHILY	TRUELOVE	UNABATED	UNDERWAY	UPINARMS
THRUSHES	TATTIEST	TRUNNION	UNAWARES	UNDERFED	UNIVERSE
THRUSTER	TOTALLED	TAUTNESS	UPANCHOR	UNDERSEA	UTILISED
THROSTLE	TUTELAGE	TEUTONIC	UNALLIED	UNDERAGE	UTILISES
TIRESOME	TATTLING	TOULOUSE	UNAVOWED	UNDERBID	UNIONISM
TURNSOUR	TOTALITY	THUMPING	UNAFRAID	UNDERLIE	UNIONIST
THROTTLE	TOTEMISM	TRUMPING	UNAMUSED	UNDERPIN	UNIFORMS
TORTURED	TITANIUM	THUMPERS	UPBRAIDS	UNDERDOG	UNICORNS
TORTURER	TITCOMBE	TRUMPERY	UNBEATEN	UNDERTOW	UNIQUELY
TORTURES	TATTOOED	TRUMPETS	UNBIASED	UNDERARM	UBIQUITY
TURTURRO	TITMOUSE	THURSDAY	UNBUCKLE	UNDERCUT	UNICYCLE
TORTUOUS	TUTORIAL	TRUSSING	UNBIDDEN	UNDERRUN	UNIFYING
THRIVING	TUTORING	TRUSTEES	UMBRELLA	UPDATING	UNJUSTLY
THROWING	TITIVATE	TAUNTING	UXBRIDGE	USEDCARS	UNKINDLY
THROWERS	THUMBSUP	TRUSTING	UNBOLTED	UNENDING	UNLEADED
THREWOUT	TRUEBLUE	TAVERNAS	URBANELY	UPENDING	UNLOADED
THROWOUT	TRUNCATE	TAVERNER	URBANITE	UNEVENLY	UNLOCKED
TERIYAKI	TRUNDLED	TOWPATHS	URBANITY	UNEDITED	UNLACING
TARRYING	TRUNDLES	THWACKED	UNBROKEN	UNEARNED	UGLIFIED
TUSSAUDS	THUDDING	TOWNHALL	UNBLOCKS	UNEARTHS	UPLIFTED
TASMANIA	THUNDERS	THWARTED	UNBURDEN	UNERRING	UNLIKELY
TESTATOR	THUNDERY	TOWERING	UNBUTTON	UTENSILS	UGLINESS
TESTCARD	TAUTENED	TOWNSHIP	UNCHAINS	USEFULLY	UNLOOSEN
TESTCASE	TRUFFLES	TOWNSEND	UNCLASPS	UNFAIRLY	ULLAPOOL
TESSDALY	TRUFFAUT	TAWNYOWL	UNCLESAM	UNFOLDED	UNLISTED
TESSERAE	TRUEGRIT	TAXHAVEN	UNCLETOM	UNFORCED	UNLAWFUL
TASTEBUD	TRUDGING	TAXPAYER	UNCOILED	UNFURLED	UNMANNED
TASTEFUL	THUGGERY	TEXTBOOK	UPCOMING	UNFASTEN	UNMARKED
TASTIEST	THUGGISH	TAXICABS	UNCOMMON	UPGRADED	UPMARKET
TASHKENT	TOUCHPAD	TOXICITY	UNCOOKED	UPGRADES	UNMASKED
TUSSLING	TOUCHING	TOXAEMIA	UNCAPPED	UNGAINLY	UNNEEDED
TUSSOCKS	TOUGHENS	TEXTILES	UNCORKED	UNGULATE	UNNERVED
TESTTUBE	TOUGHEST	TAXONOMY	UNCURLED	URGENTLY	UNNERVES

UNOPENED	UNTIDILY	VICARAGE	VALANCES	VIOLENCE	VISCERAL
UXORIOUS	UPTODATE	VICEROYS	VALENCIA	VIOLISTS	VESTIGES
UNPLACED	UNTIMELY	VACATING	VILENESS	VAPIDITY	VESPIARY
UNPACKED	ULTIMATA	VACATION	VALERIAN	VAPORISE	VASELINE
UNPICKED	ULTIMATE	VOCATION	VALOROUS	VIPERISH	VESTMENT
UNPINNED	UNTANGLE	VICTUALS	VOLATILE	VAPOROUS	VASTNESS
UNPROVEN	UPTURNED	VIDEOING	VALETING	VIPEROUS	VISCOUNT
UMPIRING	UNTIRING	VEDETTES	VOLITION	VARIANCE	VISIONON
UPPERCUT	UTTERING	VIETCONG	VULTURES	VERBATIM	VESTRIES
URQUHART	ULTERIOR	VREELAND	VALKYRIE	VARIABLE	VISITING
UPROOTED	UNTESTED	VIENNESE	VAMPIRES	VERBALLY	VISITORS
UPRISING	UNTITLED	VAGRANCY	VAMPIRIC	VARICOSE	VESPUCCI
UPRATING	UNTRUTHS	VAGRANTS	VANDAMME	VERACITY	VESUVIUS
UNRAVELS	UNTOWARD	VAGABOND	VINDALOO	VORACITY	VITREOUS
UNSEATED	ULULATED	VIGNETTE	VENABLES	VERACRUZ	VITALITY
UNSHAKEN	ULULATES	VIGILANT	VENACAVA	VIRIDIAN	VITILEVU
UNSHAVEN	UNUSABLE	VEGEMITE	VENEERED	VARIETAL	VITAMINA
UNSTATED	UKULELES	VAGARIES	VENDETTA	VERTEBRA	VITAMINB
UNSWAYED	USURIOUS	VIGOROUS	VENGEFUL	VERIFIED	VITAMINC
UPSTAGED	USURPING	VEGETATE	VONNEGUT	VERIFIES	VITAMIND
UPSTAGES	USURPERS	VEHICLES	VINEGARY	VERYGOOD	VITAMINE
UNSTABLE	UNVEILED	VEHEMENT	VANCLEEF	VERTICAL	VITAMINK
UPSTAIRS	UNVARIED	VOICEBOX	VENALITY	VIRGINAL	VITAMINS
UNSUBTLE	UNVERSED	VILLAGER	VENOMOUS	VORTICES	VOTINGIN
UNSOCIAL	UNWIELDY	VILLAGES	VINTNERS	VERBIAGE	VOTARIES
UNSADDLE	UNWANTED	VOLCANIC	VENTOLIN	VIRGINIA	VETERANS
UNSTEADY	UNWORTHY	VALHALLA	VANBRUGH	VERSIONS	VAUXHALL
UNSEEDED	UNWASHED	VALUABLE	VENERATE	VERDICTS	VOUCHING
UNSEEMLY	UNWISELY	VULGARLY	VONBRAUN	VIROLOGY	VOUCHERS
UNSEEING	UNZIPPED	VILLAINS	VANISHED	VERALYNN	VAULTING
UNSIGNED	VLADIMIR	VILLAINY	VANISHES	VIRULENT	VAUNTING
UNSUITED	VIADUCTS	VOLTAIRE	VENETIAN	VIRILITY	VIVACITY
UPSTICKS	VIBRANCY	VELOCITY	VANITIES	VERANDAS	VIVIENNE
UNSOLVED	VIBRATED	VALIDATE	VANOUTEN	VERONICA	VIVARIUM
URSULINE	VIBRATES	VALIDITY	VENTURED	VERONESE	VAVASOUR
UNSPOKEN	VIBURNUM	VOLLEYED	VENTURES	VERWOERD	VIVAVOCE
UNSPOILT	VICELIKE	VILLEINS	VANGUARD	VERMOUTH	VEXATION
UPSTREAM	VOCALISE	VALLETTA	VANQUISH	VIRTUOSI	VOYAGING
UNSCREWS	VOCALIST	VELLEITY	VONSYDOW	VIRTUOSO	VOYAGERS
UNSETTLE	VACANTLY	VILLETTE	VINEYARD	VIRTUOUS	WEARAWAY
UPTRAINS	VICINITY	VILIFIED	VIOLATED	VERYWELL	WEARDOWN
ULTRAVOX	VICTORIA	VILIFIES	VIOLATES	VISUALLY	WEAKENED

WHATEVER	WEEKENDS	WHITEFLY	WILDCARD	WILDWEST	WOOLLIES
WEASELLY	WHENEVER	WHITEANT	WILDCATS	WALKWAYS	WOODLAND
WRANGLED	WHEREVER	WHITEHOT	WILDDUCK	WALTZING	WOOLPACK
WRANGLER	WEEDIEST	WAITEDUP	WELLDONE	WALTZERS	WHOOPING
WRANGLES	WRECKAGE	WHITEOUT	WALLEYED	WOMANISE	WHOPPING
WEATHERS	WREAKING	WRIGGLED	WILDFELL	WINNABLE	WHOPPERS
WRATHFUL	WRECKING	WRIGGLES	WILDFIRE	WANDERED	WOODSMAN
WEARIEST	WRECKERS	WRINGING	WILDFOWL	WANDERER	WOOLSACK
WHACKING	WEEKLIES	WHINGERS	WALLGAME	WINTERED	WOODSHED
WEAKLING	WHEELIES	WRINGERS	WOLFGANG	WONDERED	WOOLSHED
WEAKNESS	WHEELING	WEIGHING	WELLHEAD	WINIFRED	WOODWIND
WHATNOTS	WHEATEAR	WRITHING	WELSHMAN	WINDFALL	WOOPWOOP
WRAPOVER	WHEATLEY	WHISKIES	WALDHEIM	WINDFARM	WOODWARD
WHATOFIT	WREATHED	WRINKLED	WELSHING	WINEGUMS	WOODWORK
WEAPONRY	WREATHES	WRINKLES	WELSHERS	WINDHOEK	WOODWORM
WRAPPING	WRESTLED	WHISKING	WALLIAMS	WINCHING	WOODYATT
WRAPPERS	WRESTLER	WHISKERS	WILLIAMS	WINNIPEG	WOREAWAY
WHATSITS	WRESTLES	WHISKERY	WILDLIFE	WINNINGS	WORKADAY
WEARTHIN	WHETTING	WHIRLING	WELLMADE	WINDIEST	WORNAWAY
WHATWITH	WRESTING	WHIPLASH	WELLNIGH	WANGLING	WARDANCE
WEARYING	WOEFULLY	WHINNIED	WELLNESS	WANGLERS	WARGAMES
WOBBLIER	WHEEZING	WHINNIES	WILDNESS	WINDLASS	WARFARIN
WOBBLIES	WCFIELDS	WHIPPING	WILINESS	WINELIST	WORKABLE
WOBBLING	WAFFLING	WHIMPERS	WALKONBY	WINGLESS	WARPAINT
WICKEDLY	WAGTAILS	WHISPERS	WALKOVER	WINDMILL	WARRANTS
WYCLIFFE	WAGGLING	WHIPPETS	WALLOPED	WINNOWED	WARRANTY
WACKIEST	WIGGLING	WHIRRING	WALLOWED	WINNOWER	WORKBOOK
WIDEEYED	WAGONLIT	WAITRESS	WELCOMED	WANTONLY	WARTBURG
WEDDINGS	WAGONERS	WAINSCOT	WELCOMES	WINDPIPE	WORKCAMP
WADDLING	WAGERING	WHISTLED	WOLFPACK	WONDROUS	WORMCAST
WIDENING	WHIMBREL	WHISTLER	WELLREAD	WINGSPAN	WORLDWAR
WIDEOPEN	WHINCHAT	WHISTLES	WILDRICE	WINDSOCK	WORLDCUP
WEDGWOOD	WHIPCORD	WHITTLED	WOLFROCK	WINSTONE	WOREDOWN
WIDOWERS	WEIRDEST	WHITTLES	WILDSILK	WINDWARD	WORNDOWN
WRENCHED	WHITELAW	WHIZZKID	WILLSELF	WOODBINE	WARHEADS
WRENCHES	WHITELEY	WHIZZING	WALLSEND	WOODBURN	WORSENED
WRETCHED	WHITENED	WAKENING	WELLTODO	WOODCOCK	WORSEOFF
WRETCHES	WHITENER	WAKINGUP	WALKTALL	WOODCHIP	WARMEDUP
WHEEDLED	WRITEOFF	WALLAROO	WALRUSES	WOODCUTS	WORTHIER
WHEEDLES	WAIKERIE	WILDBOAR	WILLUNGA	WOODFORD	WORMHOLE
WIELDING	WHITELIE	WELLBRED	WILFULLY	WRONGFUL	WORTHILY
WEEKDAYS	WHITETIE	WALLBARS	WELLWORN	WOODLICE	WORTHING

WARSHIPS	WASHEDUP	WAVERERS	ZIGGURAT
WORSHIPS	WASTEFUL	WAXMATCH	ZOLABUDD
WARCHEST	WISEGUYS	WAXWORKS	ZULUDAWN
WARRIGAL	WESTLIFE	WAYFARER	ZILLIONS
WARNINGS	WASTRELS	WEYMOUTH	ZULULAND
WORKINGS	WASHROOM	WIZARDRY	ZIMBABWE
WARRIORS	WESTWOOD	XMASTREE	ZANZIBAR
WORRIERS	WESTWARD	XEROXING	ZOOLATRY
WORDIEST	WETLANDS	YEARBOOK	ZOOMLENS
WORKLOAD	WITHDRAW	YEARLING	ZOOTSUIT
WARBLING	WITHDREW	YEARNING	ZEPPELIN
WARPLANE	WETHERBY	YEARSAGO	ZIPPIEST
WARBLERS	WITHERED	YABBERED	ZAPATERO
WIRELESS	WITTERED	YACHTING	ZARAGOZA
WORDLESS	WATCHMAN	YODELLED	ZEROHOUR
WORKMATE	WATCHMEN	YODELLER	
WARINESS	WITCHELL	YIELDING	
WARMNESS	WITHHELD	YOGIBEAR	
WIRINESS	WITHHOLD	YOKOHAMA	
WARLORDS	WATCHING	YAKITORI	
WARLOCKS	WATCHDOG	YALELOCK	
WARHORSE	WATCHERS	YELLOWED	
WORDPLAY	WATCHFUL	YULETIDE	
WARDROBE	WATCHOUT	YANOMAMI	
WARDROOM	WITTIEST	YEOMANRY	
WORKROOM	WATERMAN	YARDBIRD	
WORKRATE	WATERRAT	YARMOUTH	
WORKSHOP	WATERWAY	YORKTOWN	
WEREWOLF	WATERICE	YARMULKE	
WIREWOOL	WATERBED	YASHMAKS	
WORMWOOD	WATERSKI	YOSEMITE	
WORRYING	WATERING	YETAGAIN	
WASHABLE	WATERLOO	YOUNGEST	
WASSAILS	WATERJUG	YOUNGISH	
WISEACRE	WITHTHAT	YOUTHFUL	
WESTBANK	WETNURSE	YOURSELF	
WISHBONE	WOUNDING	ZEALOTRY	
WASHDOWN	WAVEBAND	ZUCCHINI	
WESLEYAN	WAVELETS	ZODIACAL	
WISTERIA	WAVINESS	ZEDEKIAH	
WESTERLY	WAVERLEY	ZIEGFELD	
WESTERNS	WAVERING	ZOETROPE	

AVALANCHE	ANALOGOUS	ACCIDENCE	ANCESTRAL	AVERAGING
ALANARKIN	ACAROLOGY	ACCIDENTS	AUCOURANT	AMENDABLE
ALABASTER	ALANPRICE	ARCHENEMY	ACCOUTRED	AMENDMENT
ATACANTER	ACAPPELLA	ACCRETION	ACCOUTRES	ANECDOTAL
ADAMANTLY	ALANPATON	ACCREDITS	ACCOUNTED	ANECDOTES
ALANBATES	ANAEROBIC	ALCHEMIST	ALDEBURGH	ALEXHALEY
ANARCHISM	ALANSUGAR	ARCHETYPE	ADDICTIVE	AMERICANA
ANARCHIST	ADAMSMITH	ALCOHOLIC	ABDUCTING	AMERICANO
ALANCOREN	ADAPTABLE	ARCHIBALD	ABDUCTION	AMERICANS
ABANDONED	ANASTACIA	ARCHITECT	ADDICTION	AMENITIES
AWARENESS	APARTHEID	ARCTICFOX	ABDUCTORS	APERITIFS
ABASEMENT	APARTMENT	ASCRIBING	AUDACIOUS	ALEDJONES
ABATEMENT	ABATTOIRS	ARCHIVIST	ABDICATED	APENNINES
AMAZEMENT	ATASTROKE	ACCLIVITY	ABDICATES	ADENOIDAL
AWAKENING	APARTFROM	AUCTIONED	AUDIENCES	ALEHOUSES
ACADEMICS	ANASTASIA	ANCILLARY	ANDREGIDE	ALEXPARKS
ACADEMIES	AFASTBUCK	ACCOLADES	ANDREWRAY	ABERRANCE
ACADEMIST	ATANYRATE	ACCOMPANY	ADDRESSED	AYERSROCK
AGAMEMNON	ANALYSING	ASCENDANT	ADDRESSEE	AVERSIONS
ARABESQUE	AMARYLLIS	ACCENTING	ADDRESSER	ALEUTIANS
ALANFREED	ATANYCOST	ASCENDING	ADDRESSES	AVERTIBLE
ADAMFAITH	AMBLESIDE	ASCENSION	ANDYHARDY	ADEPTNESS
ANALGESIA	AMBIGUITY	ACCENTORS	ANDALUSIA	ALERTNESS
ANALGESIC	AMBIGUOUS	ACCENTUAL	ABDOMINAL	APERTURES
ABASHMENT	AUBRIETIA	ANCHORAGE	ADDINSELL	AWESTRUCK
ARACHNIDS	AMBULANCE	ANCHORITE	ADDINGTON	ACETYLENE
ARACHNOID	ALBANBERG	ANCHORING	AUDIOTAPE	AFFIANCED
APATHETIC	AUBERGINE	ANCHOVIES	ANDROMEDA	AFFIANCES
AMAZINGLY	AMBERSONS	ANCHORLEG	ANDROCLES	ALFRAMSEY
ACARICIDE	AMBERGRIS	ANCHORMAN	AUDIOBOOK	AFFECTIVE
ATAVISTIC	ARBORETUM	ACCEPTANT	ARDUOUSLY	AFFECTING
ALANKNOTT	AMBUSHING	ACCEPTING	ANDROGYNY	AFFECTION
AVAILABLE	ARBITRATE	ASCERTAIN	ANDYPANDY	AFFIDAVIT
ALARMBELL	ARBITRARY	ACCORDANT	ALDERSHOT	ALFIEBASS
ALARMISTS	ALBATROSS	ACCORDING	ADDERWORT	ALFIEMOON
ADAMOKARO	AMBITIOUS	ACCORDION	ADDITIONS	AFFLICTED
ANACONDAS	ABBEYROAD	ACCESSING	AUDITIONS	AFFILIATE
ATALOWEBB	ARCHANGEL	ACCOSTING	ADDITIVES	AWFULNESS
AMAZONIAN	ACCLAIMED	ACCESSION	ARDIZZONE	AFFRONTED
ANALOGIES	AYCKBOURN	ACCUSTOMS	ALEXANDRA	AFFIRMANT
ANATOMIST	ARCHDUCHY	ANCESTORS	ALEXANDRE	AFFIRMING
AYATOLLAH	ACCEDENCE	ACCESSORY	ALEXANDER	AFFORDING

ALFAROMEO	APHORISTS	ADJUSTERS	AIMLESSLY	ADNAUSEAM
AFFLUENCE	ADHESIVES	ADJUSTING	ARMCHAIRS	ANNOYANCE
AGGRAVATE	ANITAWARD	ADJUTANTS	ALMSHOUSE	ADORATION
ALGEBRAIC	AGITATING	ADJUTANCY	ARMAMENTS	ANOMALIES
ARGYBARGY	ANIMATING	ADJOURNED	ALMAMATER	AMORALITY
AGGREGATE	AGITATION	AWKWARDLY	ALMONDOIL	ANOMALOUS
AGGRESSOR	ANIMATION	ARKWRIGHT	AXMINSTER	AMOSBURKE
AUGMENTED	AGITATORS	ACKERBILK	ADMIRABLE	ACONCAGUA
ANGRINESS	ANIMATORS	ALLIANCES	ADMIRABLY	AGOODMANY
ANGUISHED	ANITALOOS	ALLMANNER	ADMIRALTY	AVOIDABLE
ANGLICISE	AGINCOURT	ALLSAINTS	ADMISSIVE	AVOIDANCE
ANGLICISM	ACIDDROPS	ALLABOARD	ARMISTICE	AFORESAID
AGGRIEVED	ALICEBAND	ADLIBBING	ADMISSION	ATONEMENT
ANGELCAKE	ALICEFAYE	ATLIBERTY	ADMITTING	ATONETIME
ANGELFISH	ASIDEFROM	ALLOCATED	ARMSTRONG	ALOOFNESS
ANGELEYES	ALIGHTING	ALLOCATES	ARMATURES	ALONGSIDE
ARGUMENTS	ACIDHOUSE	ALLSEATER	ADMIXTURE	ALONGWITH
ARGENTINA	ABIDINGLY	ALLEGEDLY	ANNEALING	ANOPHELES
ARGENTINE	ACIDIFIED	ALLEGORIC	ANNIEHALL	ABOMINATE
ALGONQUIN	ABILITIES	ALLIGATOR	ANNEFRANK	ATOMISERS
ARGONAUTS	ACIDIFIES	ALLTHUMBS	ANNAFRIEL	ADORINGLY
ALGERIANS	ASININITY	ALLTICKET	ANNEGREGG	ABOLISHED
ANGORACAT	AXIOMATIC	ATLEISURE	ABNEGATED	ABOLISHES
ALGORITHM	ALIGNMENT	ALLBLACKS	ABNEGATES	ABORIGINE
AUGUSTINE	ALIENATED	ALLEMANDE	ANNUITIES	AGONISING
ANGOSTURA	ALIENATOR	ALLANLAMB	ANNULMENT	ANODISING
APHRABEHN	ALIENATES	ARLINGTON	ANNULLING	ATOMISING
ADHIBITED	ABITOFADO	ALLWORTHY	ANNALISTS	ABOLITION
ACHIEVERS	AMINOACID	ALLOPATHY	ANNAPOLIS	ADORNMENT
ACHIEVING	ADIPOSITY	ALLSQUARE	ANNAPURNA	ABOUNDING
ATHLETICS	ANIMOSITY	ALLERGIES	AMNESIACS	ANOINTING
ATHEISTIC	APIARISTS	AYLESBURY	AGNOSTICS	APOLOGISE
ASHBLONDE	AMIDSHIPS	ALLOTMENT	AMNESTIES	APOLOGIES
ASHAMEDLY	ABITTHICK	ALLOTTING	AUNTSALLY	APOLOGIST
ATHENAEUM	ARISTOTLE	ALLATONCE	AGNESGREY	AMOROUSLY
ASHMOLEAN	ACIDULATE	ABLUTIONS	AUNATUREL	AMORPHOUS
APHRODITE	ACIDULOUS	ALLOUTWAR	ANNOTATED	APOCRYPHA
ABHORRENT	ADJECTIVE	ALLEVIATE	ANNOTATOR	ADOGSLIFE
ABHORRING	ABJECTION	ALLOWABLE	ANNOTATES	ACOUSTICS
ADHERENCE	ADJACENCY	ALLOWANCE	ANNOUNCED	ABOUTFACE
ADHERENTS	ADJUDGING	ALLEYWAYS	ANNOUNCER	ABOUTABOY
APHORISMS	ADJOINING	ARMADILLO	ANNOUNCES	APOSTOLIC

APOSTATES	APPARATUS	AIRPOCKET	ASSAILING	ACTUATORS
ABOUTTURN	APPETISER	AIRWORTHY	ABSOLVERS	ATTRACTED
ANONYMITY	ACQUAINTS	AEROPLANE	ABSOLVING	AUTOBAHNS
ANONYMOUS	ACQUIRING	ATROPHIED	ASSEMBLED	AUTOCLAVE
AGONYAUNT	ACQUIESCE	ATROPHIES	ASSEMBLER	AUTOCRACY
APPLAUDED	ACQUITTED	ACROPOLIS	ASSEMBLES	ANTECEDES
ALPHABETS	ACQUITTAL	AIRBRAKES	ABSENTEES	ATTACKERS
APPEALING	AERIALIST	AIRFRANCE	ASSENTERS	ATTACHING
APPEARING	AIRMAILED	AEROSPACE	ABSENTING	ATTACKING
APPEASING	ACROBATIC	AEROSTATS	ASSENTING	ARTICHOKE
APPRAISED	ATROCIOUS	ARRESTING	ASSONANCE	AUTOCROSS
APPRAISAL	ABRIDGERS	AEROSMITH	ARSONISTS	ANTEDATED
APPRAISES	ABRIDGING	ACROSTICS	ABSCONDED	ANTIDOTAL
APPIANWAY	AIREDALES	ABRASIONS	ABSCONDER	ANTEDATES
APPLEGATE	AERODROME	ABRASIVES	ABSTRACTS	ANTIDOTES
APPLEJACK	AGREEABLE	AIRSTREAM	ASSUREDLY	ATTHETIME
APPREHEND	AGREEABLY	AIRSTRIPS	ABSORBERS	ATTHEMOST
ATPRESENT	AGREEMENT	AIRBUBBLE	ABSORBENT	ACTRESSES
APPLETREE	AEROFOILS	AIRGUITAR	ASSERTIVE	ARTLESSLY
APPLEISLE	AIRYFAIRY	AARDVARKS	ABSORBING	AUTHENTIC
APPLICANT	ARROGANCE	ARRIVISTE	ADSORBING	ARTIFICER
AMPLIFIED	ASREGARDS	ARROWHEAD	ASSERTING	ARTEFACTS
AMPHIBIAN	ABROGATED	ARROWROOT	ASSORTING	ARTIFICES
AMPLIFIER	ABROGATOR	ASSUAGING	ASSERTION	AUTOFOCUS
AMPLIFIES	ABROGATES	ABSTAINED	ABSURDITY	ARTYFARTY
APPLIANCE	AIRLINERS	ABSTAINER	AUSTRALIA	AUTOGRAPH
APPOINTED	AERLINGUS	ASSOCIATE	ASSURANCE	ANTIGONUS
AMPLITUDE	AIRFIELDS	ASSIDUITY	ASSISTANT	AITCHBONE
APPALLING	ARRAIGNED	ASSIDUOUS	ASSESSING	ATTAINING
APPALOOSA	ARRAIGNER	AMSTERDAM	ASSISTING	ATTRITION
APPENDAGE	AIRLIFTED	AUSTERELY	ASSASSINS	ATTRIBUTE
APPENDING	AIRPISTOL	ANSWERING	ASSESSORS	ARTILLERY
ALPENHORN	AFRIKAANS	AUSTERITY	ASSAULTED	ANTELOPES
APPROVING	AFRIKANER	ABSCESSES	ASTRADDLE	ARTEMISIA
ALPARGATA	APRILFOOL	ASSIGNING	ASTRAKHAN	ASTHMATIC
AMPERSAND	AEROLITES	AESTHETIC	ACTUALISE	AUTOMATIC
ASPARTAME	AEROMETER	AESTHETES	ACTUATING	ATTEMPTED
APPERTAIN	ARRANGERS	ANSCHLUSS	ACTUARIAL	AUTOMATED
ASPARAGUS	ARRANGING	AESTIVATE	ACTUATION	AUTOMATON
APPORTION	ACRONYMIC	ASSAILANT	ACTUARIES	ALTIMETER
ASPERSION	AARONSROD	ABSTINENT	ACTUALITY	AUTOMATES
ASPIRANTS	AERONAUTS	ABSEILING	ARTCARNEY	ATTENUATE

ATTENDANT	ARTHRITIS	ALVINHALL	BEACHBALL	BOATLOADS
ANTANDDEC	AUTOROUTE	ADVANCING	BEACHHEAD	BEADLEDOM
ACTONBELL	ATTESTING	ADVENTIST	BEACHWEAR	BEAUMONDE
ATTENTIVE	ALTITUDES	ADVENTURE	BRASHNESS	BEAUMARIS
ATTENDING	ATTITUDES	ADVERSARY	BEACHBOYS	BRAINWAVE
ATTENTION	ASTOUNDED	ADVERSELY	BOATHOUSE	BRAINWASH
ACTONTOWN	ARTHURIAN	ADVERTISE	BEARINGUP	BRAINLESS
ANTENATAL	ALTRUISTS	ADVERBIAL	BEATIFIED	BRAINIEST
ASTROLABE	ACTIVISTS	ADVERSITY	BRAZILIAN	BRANNIGAN
ASTRONAUT	ACTIVATED	ADVISABLE	BEATIFIES	BEARNAISE
AUTHORESS	ACTIVATOR	ADVISABLY	BRAZILNUT	BRAINTREE
ANTIOCHUS	ACTIVATES	ADVISEDLY	BEATITUDE	BLASPHEME
AUTHORISE	ADULATING	ANXIETIES	BLACKJACK	BLASPHEMY
AUTHORITY	ADULATION	AUXILIARY	BLACKMARK	BEANPOLES
ASTRODOME	ACUTABOVE	ANXIOUSLY	BLACKBALL	BEAARTHUR
ANTHOLOGY	ADULATORS	ABYSMALLY	BLACKMAIL	BRASSBAND
ASTROLOGY	ADULATORY	ASYMMETRY	BLACKWALL	BEANSTALK
ASTRONOMY	ADUMBRATE	ANYAMOUNT	BLACKRAIN	BOATSWAIN
ASTROTURF	AVUNCULAR	ABYSSINIA	BLACKCAPS	BRASSIERE
ANTIPODES	AQUICKONE	BLATANTLY	BRACKNELL	BEARSKINS
AUTOPSIES	AQUEDUCTS	BRAMBLING	BLACKBEAR	BRASSERIE
AUTOPILOT	ABUNDANCE	BLANCHETT	BLACKBESS	BOATTRAIN
ANTIPHONY	AQUADROME	BLANCHING	BLACKLEGS	BEAUTIFUL
ANTIPASTO	ACUTENESS	BRANCHING	BLACKNESS	BRATWURST
ANTIPATHY	AMUSEMENT	BRANCHLET	BLACKBELT	BEAUXARTS
ANTIQUARY	ABUSIVELY	BOARDGAME	BLACKBIRD	BOBMARLEY
ANTIQUITY	ALUMINIUM	BRANDNAME	BLACKLIST	BABYBUGGY
AFTERCARE	AQUILEGIA	BOARDWALK	BLACKFLAG	BOBGELDOF
ALTERCATE	ABUTMENTS	BEARDLESS	BLACKENED	BIBLEBELT
ALTERNATE	AQUAPLANE	BLANDNESS	BLACKWOOD	BOBBEAMON
AFTERMATH	AQUARIANS	BEARDSLEY	BLACKHOLE	BABYGRAND
ALTERABLE	AQUARELLE	BLANDINGS	BLACKROBE	BOBWILLIS
ATTORNEYS	AQUARISTS	BLANDFORD	BLACKPOOL	BOBWILSON
AFTERLIFE	AMUGSGAME	BOARDROOM	BLACKFOOT	BUBBLECAR
ASTEROIDS	AQUITAINE	BLAMELESS	BLACKSPOT	BUBBLIEST
AFTERGLOW	ADULTHOOD	BRACELETS	BLACKARTS	BUBBLEGUM
AFTERWORD	ADULTERER	BRAKESHOE	BLANKETED	BOBBLEHAT
AFTERNOON	AYURVEDIC	BRASENOSE	BRACKETED	BOBSLEIGH
ARTHROPOD	AQUAVITAE	BEANFEAST	BLACKBURN	BABBLINGS
ASTERISKS	ADVOCATED	BEARFRUIT	BLACKSWAN	BABOONERY
ANTARCTIC	ADVOCATES	BRAGGARTS	BLACKEYES	BABOUCHES
ARTHRITIC	ADVANTAGE	BEAUGESTE	BEALLEARS	BOBBYBALL

BACHARACH	BUCKSFIZZ	BREECHING	BUFFETCAR	BRINGDOWN
BOCCACCIO	BACKSTOPS	BREADLINE	BUFFETING	BLIGHTERS
BUCCANEER	BACKTRACK	BRENDALEE	BEFRIENDS	BRIGHTENS
BUCHAREST	BUCKTEETH	BREADROLL	BIFURCATE	BRIGHTEST
BACKBONED	BUCKTHORN	BREWERIES	BYFORCEOF	BLIGHTING
BACKBONES	BECAUSEOF	BEEKEEPER	BEFITTING	BRIGHTMAN
BACKBITER	BECQUEREL	BEEFEATER	BUGSBUNNY	BAILIWICK
BACKBITES	BUCKWHEAT	BEECHMAST	BUGLECALL	BRICKYARD
BICYCLING	BACKWOODS	BEETHOVEN	BIGHEADED	BRICKWALL
BICYCLIST	BACKWARDS	BEEFINGUP	BIGLEAGUE	BRICKBATS
BACKCLOTH	BACKWATER	BREWINGUP	BIGBERTHA	BRISKNESS
BACKDRAFT	BACKYARDS	BLEMISHED	BAGUETTES	BRICKWORK
BACKDROPS	BEDJACKET	BLEMISHES	BIGCHEESE	BLINKERED
BACKDATED	BEDWARMER	BLEDISLOE	BAGPIPERS	BRILLIANT
BUCKETFUL	BODYBOARD	BREAKRANK	BAGPIPING	BRIDLEWAY
BICKERING	BUDABBOTT	BREAKCAMP	BEGUILING	BAINMARIE
BUCKETING	BODYCHECK	BREAKFAST	BIGDIPPER	BRIANLARA
BACTERIAL	BEDECKING	BREAKABLE	BIGAMISTS	BAIGNOIRE
BACTERIUM	BODYCLOCK	BREAKNECK	BEGINNERS	BRIMSTONE
BACKEDOFF	BODACIOUS	BLEAKNESS	BEGINNING	BRIQUETTE
BACHELORS	BUDGETARY	BREAKAGES	BAGATELLE	BLIZZARDS
BACKFILLS	BUDGETDAY	BREAKALEG	BEGRUDGED	BUJUMBURA
BACKFIRED	BADGERING	BREAKDOWN	BEGRUDGES	BAKEBLIND
BACKFIRES	BUDGETING	BREAKFREE	BEHEADING	BAKSHEESH
BACCHANTE	BEDFELLOW	BREAKITUP	BEHAVIOUR	BAKEHOUSE
BACCHANAL	BYDEFAULT	BREAKEVEN	BRIGANDRY	BALLADEER
BACCHANTS	BODYGUARD	BREAKAWAY	BRIGADIER	BALDACHIN
BACKHANDS	BYDEGREES	BEETLEOFF	BRITANNIA	BULGARIAN
BACKLIGHT	BEDRIDDEN	BEERMONEY	BRIGADOON	BALEARICS
BACKLISTS	BADTIMING	BIENNIALS	BRICABRAC	BELLAROSA
BECKONING	BADMINTON	BEEORCHID	BAILBONDS	BILLABONG
BACKPEDAL	BEDSITTER	BLEASDALE	BLINDDATE	BALLASTED
BACKSPACE	BUDDLEIAS	BEERSHEBA	BLINDNESS	BELEAGUER
BACKSTAGE	BEDCOVERS	BEEFSTEAK	BLINDSIDE	BILHARZIA
BACKSLANG	BADMOUTHS	BREWSTERS	BUILDINGS	BILLBOARD
BACKSLASH	BEDSPREAD	BLESSINGS	BLINDFOLD	BILLBIXBY
BACKSTAYS	BODYSHOCK	BREATHING	BLINDWORM	BALACLAVA
BACKSIDES	BODYSCRUB	BREATHILY	BLINDSPOT	BALLCOCKS
BECHSTEIN	BEDAZZLED	BRENTFORD	BOILEDEGG	BELLCURVE
BACKSIGHT	BEERBELLY	BEELZEBUB	BRIDEWELL	BILLCOSBY
BACKSLIDE	BLEACHING	BREEZIEST	BAILEDOUT	BULLDOZED
BACKSWING	BREACHING	BEFUDDLED	BRIEFCASE	BULLDOZER

BULLDOZES	BALDPATED	BUNGALOWS	BANDWIDTH	BLOCKHEAD
BELVEDERE	BALUSTERS	BANEBERRY	BANDWAGON	BROOKSIDE
BELIEVERS	BILLSIKES	BANKCLERK	BENNYHILL	BLOCKVOTE
BALDEAGLE	BELATEDLY	BONECHINA	BUNNYGIRL	BOOTLACES
BALLERINA	BELITTLED	BANKDRAFT	BIOHAZARD	BLOWLAMPS
BELIEVING	BELITTLES	BANNERETS	BUONASERA	BOOKMAKER
BILLETING	BOLSTERED	BANTERING	BLOWAFUSE	BROWNBEAR
BULLETINS	BILATERAL	BANDEROLE	BROWBEATS	BROWNRICE
BULLFIGHT	BELLTOWER	BUNDESTAG	BROACHING	BROWNCOAL
BALEFULLY	BULRUSHES	BENBECULA	BRONCHIAL	BLOWNAWAY
BELAFONTE	BILLWYMAN	BENEFICES	BROADBAND	BIOLOGIST
BULLFINCH	BELLYACHE	BANEFULLY	BLOODBATH	BOOKPLATE
BULLFROGS	BILLYIDOL	BENIGHTED	BLOODBANK	BIOSPHERE
BOLOGNESE	BULLYBEEF	BENCHMARK	BROADCAST	BLOWPIPES
BALLGIRLS	BILLYLIAR	BONEHEADS	BLOODFEUD	BIOGRAPHY
BILLGATES	BELLYFLOP	BENCHTEST	BROADBEAN	BOOKSTAND
BOLSHEVIK	BOLLYWOOD	BUNKHOUSE	BLOODLESS	BOOMSLANG
BALTHAZAR	BILLYJOEL	BONVIVEUR	BROADBENT	BOOKSTALL
BALMINESS	BILLYGOAT	BANDICOOT	BLOODSHED	BOOKSHELF
BULKINESS	BILLYBUDD	BANNISTER	BLOODSHOT	BLOSSOMED
BALTIMORE	BOMBARDED	BYNOMEANS	BLOODLINE	BOOKSHOPS
BELLICOSE	BOMBAZINE	BYNUMBERS	BROADSIDE	BOOKTOKEN
BILLIARDS	BEMOANING	BANANAMAN	BROADENED	BLOWTORCH
BALTICSEA	BOMBAYMIX	BONINGTON	BROADLOOM	BOOKWORMS
BALLISTIC	BYMEANSOF	BONVOYAGE	BLOODLUST	BOOBYTRAP
BALALAIKA	BOMBASTIC	BINGOHALL	BROKERAGE	BRONZEAGE
BELEMNITE	BUMPERCAR	BANDOLIER	BOOMERANG	BAPTISING
BALANCERS	BUMPEDOFF	BENJONSON	BRODERICK	BAPTISMAL
BILLNIGHY	BEMYGUEST	BANJOISTS	BROKEEVEN	BYPRODUCT
BALANCING	BUMPINESS	BONAPARTE	BLOWFLIES	BIPARTITE
BELONGING	BUMBLEBEE	BANTRYBAY	BROUGHAMS	BYPASSING
BILINGUAL	BIMONTHLY	BANKROLLS	BLOWHOLES	BEQUEATHS
BALLOTBOX	BAMBOOZLE	BANKRUPTS	BOOTHROYD	BORNAGAIN
BILLODDIE	BOMBPROOF	BANDSTAND	BROCHURES	BARBARISE
BALCONIED	BUMPSTART	BANISTERS	BROTHERLY	BARBARISM
BALLOTING	BOMBSHELL	BANISHING	BROCHETTE	BARBARIAN
BELLOWING	BOMBSQUAD	BANJULELE	BIORHYTHM	BORSALINO
BILLOWING	BUMPTIOUS	BENGURION	BOOKINGIN	BARBARITY
BALCONIES	BUNDABERG	BENTURPIN	BLOWINGUP	BARRACKED
BALLOONED	BANDAGING	BANQUETED	BOORISHLY	BARRACKER
BELCONNEN	BANDANNAS	BANQUETTE	BLOCKADED	BARNACLED
BALLPOINT	BANDALORE	BANQUETER	BLOCKADES	BARNACLES

BARGAINED	BARGINGIN	BASKETFUL	BUTCHERED	BLUEPRINT
BARGAINER	BURNISHED	BESEECHED	BATHHOUSE	BLUEPETER
BARCAROLE	BURNISHES	BESEECHES	BATTLEAXE	BRUSQUELY
BARBAROUS	BARBITONE	BASRELIEF	BATTLEDON	BLUERINSE
BARRACUDA	BARRISTER	BESIEGING	BOTTLEDUP	BLUESTEEL
BIRDBRAIN	BURTKWOUK	BUSSELTON	BETHLEHEM	BRUNSWICK
BARABRITH	BERYLREID	BASHFULLY	BOTTLEOUT	BLUESKIES
BAREBONES	BERYLLIUM	BOSPHORUS	BOTANYBAY	BLUNTNESS
BIRDBATHS	BAROMETER	BOSSINESS	BOTANICAL	BOUNTIFUL
BIRDCAGES	BAROMETRY	BASTIONED	BETENOIRE	BLUETOOTH
BIRDCALLS	BARENBOIM	BASILICAN	BOTANISTS	BOUNTEOUS
BARNDANCE	BARONETCY	BASILICON	BETROTHED	BLUSTERED
BARTENDER	BARROWBOY	BASILICAS	BETROTHAL	BLUSTERER
BARTERERS	BORROWERS	BASILSEAL	BOTTOMLEY	BLUEVINNY
BARRELFUL	BURROUGHS	BASILISKS	BOTTOMOUT	BLUEWHALE
BARBERING	BORROWING	BASILHUME	BOTTOMSUP	BLUTWURST
BARTERING	BURROWING	BASEMENTS	BATHROBES	BEVELLING
BORDERING	BARDOLINO	BASEMETAL	BATHROOMS	BEVERAGES
BURDENING	BERNSTEIN	BESTOWING	BATHSHEBA	BOWLEGGED
BARRELLED	BIRDSNEST	BISHOPRIC	BATHSALTS	BOWLERHAT
BARLEYMOW	BERKSHIRE	BASEPLATE	BOTSWANAN	BOWWINDOW
BURGEONED	BAROSCOPE	BUSDRIVER	BETTYBOOP	BAWDINESS
BARCELONA	BARNSTORM	BETRAYERS	BRUTALISE	BOWFINGER
BARGEPOLE	BIRDTABLE	BATRACHIA	BRUTALITY	BEWAILING
BARKEEPER	BARITONES	BETRAYING	BLUEBEARD	BEWILDERS
BURLESQUE	BURNTDOWN	BATTALION	BLUEBELLS	BOWERBIRD
BARPERSON	BARRYGIBB	BATHCHAIR	BLUEBLOOD	BOWESLYON
BARBECUED	BARRYMORE	BATHCUBES	BLUEBIRDS	BOWSTREET
BARBECUES	BARNYARDS	BYTHEYARD	BLUEBERRY	BEWITCHED
BAREFACED	BARRYRYAN	BUTTERCUP	BOUNDLESS	BEWITCHES
BAROGRAPH	BYSTANDER	BUTTERFAT	BLUNDERED	BOXCAMERA
BIRTHRATE	BOSSANOVA	BUTTERFLY	BOUNDERBY	BOXOFFICE
BIRTHMARK	BOSCASTLE	BATTENING	BOUNDOVER	BOXCLEVER
BIRTHSIGN	BESPATTER	BATTERING	BOULEVARD	BAXENDALE
BARTHOLDI	BASEBOARD	BETTERING	BRUNETTES	BOXINGDAY
BERNHARDT	BASICWAGE	BOTHERING	BLUEGRASS	BOXNUMBER
BIRDHOUSE	BUSHCRAFT	BUTTERING	BOURGEOIS	BRYLCREEM
BARRICADE	BISECTING	BATTERIES	BRUSHTAIL	BOYLESLAW
BARBICANS	BISECTION	BETTEROFF	BRUSHWOOD	BOYGEORGE
BARMINESS	BASICALLY	BYTHEBOOK	BRUSHWORK	BAYOFPIGS
BERLINERS	BASECAMPS	BATTERSEA	BRUTISHLY	BAYWINDOW
BURLINESS	BESIEGERS	BATTERSBY	BOUTIQUES	BAYONETED

BOYWONDER	CRACKNELL	CRAFTIEST	COCKFIGHT	CREAMWARE
BOYCOTTED	CLARKKENT	COASTLINE	COCHINEAL	CREAMIEST
BOYFRIEND	CRACKLING	COATTAILS	COCKINESS	CREAMSODA
BUZZCOCKS	CRACKSMAN	CHANTELLE	CUCUMBERS	CREAMHORN
BYZANTINE	CRACKSMEN	CHANTILLY	CACOPHONY	CREAMPUFF
BYZANTIUM	CRACKDOWN	CRAFTSMAN	COCKROACH	CHERNOBYL
BIZARRELY	CRACKPOTS	CRAFTSMEN	COCKSCOMB	CLEANSERS
CHARABANC	CRADLECAP	CHASTENED	COCKTAILS	CLEANSING
CRABAPPLE	CHAPLAINS	CRAFTWORK	COCKYSJOY	CHEONGSAM
CHAPARRAL	CHALLENGE	CHARTERED	CUDGELLED	CHEAPRATE
CHARACTER	CHARLEROI	CHATTERED	CODIFYING	CHEAPJACK
CLAMBERED	CHARLOTTE	CHATTERER	CEDARWOOD	CHEAPNESS
CRANBERRY	CHARLATAN	CHARTERIS	CEDARTREE	CREEPIEST
CHANDLERS	CLAIMABLE	CHASTISED	CADETSHIP	CHEAPSIDE
COATDRESS	CLAMMEDUP	CHASTISES	CAESAREAN	CHEAPENED
CHANDLERY	CHARMLESS	CHANTEUSE	CREMATING	CLEOPATRA
COALESCED	CLAMMIEST	COAGULATE	CREMATION	CHEEREDUP
COALESCES	COALMINER	COAGULANT	CHEVALIER	CHEERLESS
CHAMELEON	CLAIMANTS	CRAPULENT	CREVASSES	CHEERIEST
CEASELESS	CLAYMORES	CHARWOMAN	CHEWBACCA	CHEVROLET
CEASEFIRE	CHAINGANG	CHARWOMEN	CHERBOURG	CLEARANCE
CHAPERONE	CHAINMAIL	CRAZYGOLF	CLENCHING	CHERRYPIE
COALFIELD	CHAINSAWS	CABBALIST	CRESCENDO	CHESSCLUB
CHAUFFEUR	CHAROLAIS	CABLECARS	CRESCENTS	CRESTARUN
CHAFFINCH	CEANOTHUS	CABLEWAYS	CLEVELAND	CREATURES
CHAMFERED	CRAYONING	CABLEGRAM	CLEVEREST	CHESTNUTS
CRAIGCASH	CLAMOROUS	CABRIOLES	CLERGYMAN	CREDULITY
CHARGRILL	CLAMOURED	CABRIOLET	CLERGYMEN	CREDULOUS
CRASHLAND	CHAMPAGNE	CABALLERO	CREPITATE	CHEQUERED
CRASHTEST	CLAMPDOWN	CABALLERS	CHEMICALS	COFFEEBAR
COACHLOAD	CHAMPIONS	CUBANHEEL	CHERISHED	COFFEEPOT
COACHWORK	CHAIRLIFT	CABINCREW	CHERISHES	CUFFLINKS
COACHTOUR	COATSTAND	CYBERPUNK	CREDITING	CAFETIERE
COACHBOLT	CLASSMATE	CABDRIVER	CREDITORS	CAFETERIA
COACHTRIP	CLASSICAL	CUBBYHOLE	CHEMISTRY	CAGEBIRDS
CHARINESS	CLASSLESS	COCKATIEL	CHECKMATE	COGNISANT
CLARINETS	CRASSNESS	COCKAHOOP	CHECKEDIN	COGNITIVE
CRAZINESS	CLASSIEST	COCKATOOS	CHECKEDUP	COGNITION
CLARIFIED	CRABSTICK	COCODEMER	CHEEKIEST	CIGARILLO
COALITION	CLASSROOM	COCKERELL	CHECKLIST	CIGARETTE
CHARITIES	COASTLAND	COCKERELS	CLEOLAINE	COGITATED
CLARIFIES	CHARTWELL	COCKEDHAT	CREAMCAKE	COGITATES

COHERENCE	CLIPJOINT	COLLEAGUE	CALCULATE	COMPERING
CHINAWARE	CHICKWEED	COLLEGIAN	COLOURANT	COMPETING
CHICANERY	CRICKETER	CALLEDOFF	CALOUNDRA	CAMPESINO
CHINAGIRL	CHILLIEST	COLLECTED	COLOUREDS	COMPELLED
CHINACLAY	CHIPMUNKS	COLLECTOR	COLOURFUL	CAMPEDOUT
CHINAROSE	CLIENTELE	COLDFRAME	CELLULITE	COMMENTED
CHINATOWN	CHIPOLATA	COLDFRONT	COLLUDING	CAMSHAFTS
CHIVALRIC	CHICOMARX	CULMINATE	COLOURING	COMPILERS
CLIMACTIC	CRINOLINE	CULTIVATE	COLLUSION	COMBINING
CHIPBOARD	CHIROPODY	CALLIPERS	COLOURIST	COMPILING
CLIPBOARD	CRIMPLENE	CALCIFIED	CALPURNIA	COMMISSAR
CHILBLAIN	CRISPNESS	COLLIDING	CELLULOID	COMMITTED
CLIMBDOWN	CHIRPIEST	CALVINISM	CELLULOSE	COMMITTEE
COINCIDED	CLIPPINGS	COLLISION	COLWYNBAY	COMMITTAL
COINCIDES	CLIJSTERS	CALCIFIES	COMEAGAIN	CAMELHAIR
CLINCHERS	CHINSTRAP	CALVINIST	COMBATANT	COMPLIANT
CLINCHING	COINTREAU	COLUMBINE	COMMANDED	COMPLICIT
CHILDCARE	CHILTERNS	COLOMBIAN	COMMANDER	CAMELEERS
CHILDLESS	CHIHUAHUA	CALUMNIES	COMMANDOS	COMPLYING
CHILDLIKE	CHIVVYING	COLUMNIST	CAMPAIGNS	CAMELLIAS
CHILDLINE	CELLARAGE	COLONNADE	CAMPANILE	COMPLAINS
CHILDHOOD	CALLAHALT	CALENDARS	COMBATIVE	COMPLAINT
CHILDSTAR	CALLAGHAN	COLONIALS	COMBATING	COMPLETED
CHILEPINE	CALMATIVE	COLANDERS	COMPARING	COMPLETES
CRITERION	CELLARING	CYLINDERS	COMPANION	CAMEMBERT
CHISELLED	COLLARING	CELANDINE	COMPANIES	CEMENTING
CHISELLER	COLLATING	COLONISED	CAMBAZOLA	COMEOFAGE
CLIVEDUNN	COLLATION	COLONISES	COMEALONG	CAMCORDER
CLIVEOWEN	CELLARMAN	COLONISTS	COMEABOUT	COMMONERS
CHIEFTAIN	COLCANNON	CALENDULA	COMPASSES	COMPOSERS
CHIEFWHIP	COLLAPSED	CALLOSITY	COMPACTOR	COMPONENT
COIFFURED	COLLAPSES	CALLOUSLY	CAMPANULA	COMEOFFIT
COIFFEUSE	CALIBRATE	CALIPHATE	COMECLEAN	COMPOSITE
COIFFEURS	CELEBRATE	CELLPHONE	COMICALLY	COMPOSING
CLINGFILM	CELEBRANT	COLERIDGE	COMEDIANS	CAMBODIAN
CRIMINALS	CALABRESE	CALORIFIC	CAMPDAVID	COMMOTION
CHIMINGIN	CELEBRITY	COLERAINE	COMMENCED	COMMODITY
COININGIT	COLOSSEUM	COLOSSEUM	COMMENCES	COMMONLAW
CRITICISE	CALABOOSE	CALFSMEAT	COMMENDED	COMPOUNDS
CRITICISM	CELIBATES	CELESTIAL	COMPETENT	CAMEOROLE
CLINICIAN	COLDCREAM	COLDSTORE	CYMBELINE	COMMODORE
CRITIQUES	CALEDONIA	COLTSFOOT	CAMBERING	COMFORTED

COMFORTER	CONCEDING	CONSERVES	CANALISED	CINERARIA
COMPOSURE	CONVENING	CANEFRUIT	CANALISES	CENTRISTS
CAMBRIDGE	CONVEYING	CANDIDATE	CONGLETON	CONTRASTS
CAMERAMAN	CONGENIAL	CANNIBALS	CANALETTO	CONTRIVED
CAMERAMEN	CANCERIAN	CONFIDANT	CONCLAVES	CONTRIVES
COMPRISED	CANNERIES	CANDIDACY	CINEMATIC	CANISTERS
COMPRISES	CONVEXITY	CONVINCED	CANONICAL	CANESUGAR
CAMERASHY	CANCELLED	CONVINCES	CONUNDRUM	CONSTRAIN
CAMISOLES	CONCEALED	CENTIPEDE	CANONISED	CONSTABLE
CAMPSITES	CONGEALED	CANNINESS	CANONISES	CONSTRICT
COMMUTERS	CONCEALER	CONNIVERS	CANNONADE	CONSTANCE
COMPUTERS	CONCERNED	CONSIDERS	CONSONANT	CONSTANCY
COMMUNING	CONDEMNED	CONDIMENT	CONCORDAT	CENOTAPHS
COMMUTING	CANKEROUS	CONFIDENT	CANTONESE	CONSTRUED
COMPUTING	CONVEYORS	CONTINENT	CONGOLESE	CONSTRUES
COMMUNISM	CANCELOUT	CONCISELY	CANNONEER	CONSTRUCT
COMMUNION	CONFERRED	CUNNINGLY	CANNONING	CONJUGATE
COMMUNIST	CONDENSED	CONFIDING	CANYONING	CONSULATE
COMMUNITY	CONFESSED	CONFINING	CENSORING	CONJUREUP
CONNAUGHT	CONVERSED	CONNIVING	CONDONING	CONJURERS
CANTABILE	CONDENSER	CONVIVIAL	CONSOLING	CONSUMERS
CONTAGION	CONFESSOR	CONDITION	CANTORIAL	CONCUBINE
CONCAVITY	CANOEISTS	CANTICLES	CENSORIAL	CONDUCIVE
CONTAINED	CONDENSES	CONFIRMED	CANOODLED	CENSURING
CONTAINER	CONFESSES	CONSIGNED	CANOODLES	CONFUSING
CANVASSED	CONSENSUS	CONSIGNEE	CONFORMED	CONJURING
CANVASSER	CONVERSES	CUNEIFORM	CONFOUNDS	CONSUMING
CANVASSES	CONCEITED	CONCIERGE	CONTOURED	CENTURION
CONTACTED	CONCERTED	CENTIGRAM	CONCOURSE	CONFUSION
CONTACTOR	CONGESTED	CONSISTED	CONSORTIA	CONTUSION
CONSCRIPT	CONNECTED	CONVICTED	CONCOCTED	CENTURIES
CYNICALLY	CONSENTED	CONTINUED	CONTORTED	CONFUCIUS
CONSCIOUS	CONTENTED	CONFIGURE	CINEPHILE	CONCURRED
CONNEMARA	CONTESTED	CONTINUAL	CANOPENER	CONQUERED
CENTENARY	CONVERTED	CONTINUUM	CONSPIRED	CONQUEROR
CONTENDED	CONNECTOR	CONTINUES	CONSPIRES	CONCUSSED
CONTENDER	CONVECTOR	CONFLICTS	CONTRACTS	CONVULSED
CONGEREEL	CONVERTER	CONCLUDED	CONGRUENT	CONQUESTS
CONVENERS	CONCERTOS	CONCLUDES	CONGRUITY	CONDUCTED
CONVERGED	CONCEIVED	CANDLELIT	CONTRALTO	CONSULTED
CONVERGES	CONSERVED	CANDLEMAS	CENTRALLY	CONDUCTOR
CANTERING	CONCEIVES	CANALBOAT	CONFRONTS	CANAVERAL

CANDYTUFT	CROSSTALK	CUPBOARDS	CORRECTED	CARBONATE
CLOBBERED	CROSSWAYS	COPIOUSLY	CARPENTER	CORPORATE
CROTCHETS	CROISSANT	COPYRIGHT	CORVETTES	CARBONARI
CROTCHETY	CROSSBEAM	CAPARISON	CARPENTRY	CORPORALS
CROUCHING	CLOISTERS	CAPSULISE	CORRECTLY	CORMORANT
COOKCHILL	CROSSNESS	CAPTURING	CURRENTLY	CARTOUCHE
CLOUDBASE	CROWSFEET	CAPEVERDE	CORNFIELD	CORPOREAL
CLOUDLESS	CROWSNEST	COQUETTES	CAREFULLY	CARBONISE
CLOUDIEST	CROSSWIND	CARLALANE	CORNFLOUR	CORROSIVE
CLOGDANCE	CROSSFIRE	CARPACCIO	CARNFORTH	CARTONING
CLOUDOVER	CROSSBILL	CORIANDER	CARYGRANT	CORRODING
COOPERAGE	CLOISONNE	CARRADINE	CARTHORSE	CORROSION
COOPERATE	CROSSWORD	CARNATION	CIRRHOSIS	CURIOSITY
CLOSECALL	COOKSTOUR	CARNALITY	CARTILAGE	CORDONOFF
CLOSENESS	CROSSBOWS	CURTAILED	CURTILAGE	CURIOUSLY
COOPERING	CROSSOVER	CURTAINED	CARDIGANS	CARAPACES
CLOSEKNIT	CHORTLING	CURTAINUP	CARDINALS	CARDPUNCH
CLOSEDOWN	CROQUETTE	CERTAINLY	CARNIVALS	CARTRIDGE
CLOTHEARS	COOLWORLD	CERTAINTY	CARRIEDON	CORUSCATE
CLOTHIERS	CAPTAINED	CURRAWONG	CARDINDEX	CARDSHARP
CROCHETED	CAPTAINCY	CERVANTES	CURLINESS	CARLSBERG
CHOPHOUSE	CAPYBARAS	CURVATURE	CARRIAGES	CHRISTENS
COOKHOUSE	CAPUCHINS	CARDBOARD	CERTIFIED	CARLSAGAN
CHORISTER	CAPACIOUS	CAREBEARS	CERTIFIES	CHRISTINA
CLOCKEDIN	CAPACITOR	CORNBREAD	CORDIALLY	CARDSWIPE
CROOKEDLY	CUPIDSBOW	CARIBBEAN	CARNIVORE	CHRISTINE
CLOCKWISE	CAPEDUTCH	CORNCRAKE	CORTISONE	CARESSING
CLOCKGOLF	CUPBEARER	CORNDOLLY	CORRIDORS	CHRISTIAN
CLOCKWORK	CYPRESSES	CAREENAGE	CARRIESON	CHRYSALIS
CLOAKROOM	CAPTIVATE	CORRELATE	CERTITUDE	CHRISTMAS
CHOCKFULL	CAPRICCIO	CARPETBAG	CARTLOADS	CHRISNOTH
CHOPLOGIC	CAPSIZING	CARMELITE	COROLLARY	CHRISROCK
CLOWNFISH	CAPTIVITY	CAREENING	CARELABEL	CORKSCREW
CROWNWORK	CAPTIONED	CAREERING	CAROLREED	CARDTABLE
CHOCOLATE	CAPRIFORM	CARPETING	CAROLLERS	CARETAKER
CROCODILE	CAPRICORN	CORNERING	CAROLLING	CIRCULATE
CHOPPEDUP	CAPSICUMS	CAREERISM	CARILLONS	CAROUSALS
CROPPEDUP	CAPILLARY	CARPEDIEM	CARLLEWIS	CIRCULARS
CROUPIERS	CAPSLEEVE	CORSETIER	CARAMBOLA	CIRCUSBOY
CHOIRBOYS	CAPINHAND	CAREERIST	CHROMATIC	CARBUNCLE
CROSSFADE	COPINGSAW	CORNEILLE	CHRONICLE	CORPUSCLE
CROUSTADE	COPHOLDOF	CARDEALER	CARBONARA	CAROUSELS

CAROUSERS	CUSTOMERS	COTILLION	CRUDENESS	CIVILISED
CORPULENT	CUSTOMISE	CATTLEMAN	CAUTERISE	CIVILISES
CAROUSING	CUSTODIAL	CATTLEMEN	CAULFIELD	CAVENDISH
CORRUPTED	CUSTODIAN	CATALONIA	COURGETTE	COVENANTS
CIRCUITRY	CASSOCKED	CATALEPSY	COUGHDROP	COVERDALE
CORRUPTLY	CASSOULET	CATALYSTS	COUCHETTE	COVEREDUP
CARTWHEEL	CASTOROIL	CATALYTIC	CLUBHOUSE	COVERLETS
CAREYHART	COSMOLOGY	CATAMARAN	CRUCIFIED	CAVORTING
CURRYCOMB	COSTPRICE	CUTANEOUS	CRUCIFIES	COVERNOTE
CARRYCOTS	CASHPOINT	CUTANDRUN	CRUCIALLY	CAVERNOUS
CARRYOVER	CASESTUDY	COTTONBUD	CAUTIONED	COWARDICE
CARRYAWAY	COSTUMIER	CITYOFGOD	CRUCIFORM	COWESWEEK
CASTAWAYS	COTTAGERS	CATAPLEXY	CHUCKLING	COXSWAINS
CASSANDRA	CATCALLED	CATAPULTS	CHUCKITIN	DIALARIDE
CASTANETS	CATBALLOU	CATERWAUL	CRUELLEST	DRAMATISE
CASUARINA	CATHARSIS	CATARACTS	CRUMPLING	DIANARIGG
COSTARICA	CUTLASSES	CATARRHAL	CLUMSIEST	DRAMATICS
CASCADING	CATHARTIC	CITYSCAPE	COURTCARD	DRAMATIST
CESSATION	CETACEANS	CUTITFINE	COURTYARD	DIANADORS
COSTARRED	CATECHISE	CATATONIA	CRUSTACEA	DIANAROSS
CASEBOOKS	CATECHISM	CATATONIC	COUNTLESS	DIANELANE
COSSETING	CATECHIST	COTSWOLDS	COURTIERS	DUANEEDDY
COSMETICS	CATACOMBS	CUTTYSARK	COURTSHIP	DEADENING
CASTELLAN	CUTACAPER	CITIZENRY	COUNTRIES	DEAFENING
CASHEWNUT	CATACLYSM	CRUSADERS	COURTENAY	DEANERIES
CASSEROLE	COTEDAZUR	CAUSATIVE	COURTENEY	DIABETICS
CASSETTES	CATHETERS	CRUSADING	COURTROOM	DIANETICS
CASTIGATE	CATHERINE	CAUCASIAN	COUNTDOWN	DIALECTIC
CASHINGIN	CATTERIES	CAUSALITY	COURTEOUS	DIALECTAL
CASTILIAN	CATDEELEY	CHUBBIEST	CHUNTERED	DRAGGEDON
CUSHIONED	COTTERPIN	CRUMBLING	CLUSTERED	DEATHMASK
CASHIERED	CATHEDRAL	CLUBCLASS	CLUTTERED	DIAPHRAGM
CASUISTRY	CATCHABLE	CLUTCHBAG	COUNTERED	DEATHLESS
CASTLEBAR	CATCHIEST	CLUTCHING	COURTESAN	DEATHLIKE
COSTLIEST	CATCHMENT	CRUNCHING	COUTURIER	DEATHWISH
CESTLAVIE	CATCHFIRE	CHURCHILL	CAVECANEM	DEATHTRAP
CASEMAKER	CATCHWORD	CRUNCHIER	CAVALCADE	DEATHSTAR
CASEMENTS	CUTTHROAT	CHURCHMAN	CIVILIANS	DRAWINGUP
CASEMATES	CATTINESS	CHURCHMEN	CAVALIERS	DRAVIDIAN
COSMONAUT	CUTTINGIT	CAULDRONS	CAVILLING	DEADLIEST
CASSOWARY	CATSKILLS	COUPDETAT	CAVALRIES	DEADLINES
CUSTOMARY	CATALOGUE	CAUSEWAYS	CIVILLIST	DEADLYSIN

DEARMADAM	DECLAIMER	DECONTROL	DREAMTIME	DEFROSTER
DRAINPIPE	DICTATORS	DOCTORATE	DREAMBOAT	DEFERRALS
DIAGNOSED	DOCMARTIN	DOCTORING	DIEGOLUNA	DEFERMENT
DIAGNOSES	DECKCHAIR	DICHOTOMY	DREARIEST	DEFERRING
DIAGNOSIS	DECOCTING	DOCTORWHO	DEEPSPACE	DEFORMING
DEACONESS	DECOCTION	DECIPHERS	DRESSEDUP	DEFORMITY
DRAGONFLY	DOCUDRAMA	DECEPTIVE	DEEMSTERS	DEFERENCE
DIABOLISM	DECIDEDLY	DECEPTION	DRESSDOWN	DIFFUSING
DRACONIAN	DECADENCE	DOCTRINAL	DRESSCOAT	DIFFUSION
DRAGQUEEN	DECADENTS	DECORATED	DEEPSOUTH	DEFAULTED
DRAGRACER	DECIDUOUS	DECORATOR	DEFRAYALS	DEFAULTER
DIAERESIS	DICKEMERY	DECORATES	DEFRAUDED	DAFFYDUCK
DIACRITIC	DECREEING	DECISIONS	DEFRAUDER	DOGEATDOG
DRAGSTERS	DECREASED	DACHSHUND	DEFEATING	DEGRADING
DEANSHIPS	DECREASES	DICKTRACY	DEFLATING	DOGMATISM
DEADSOULS	DECAGRAMS	DECATHLON	DEFRAYING	DOGMATIST
DOARUNNER	DECIGRAMS	DECOUPAGE	DEFEATISM	DOGKENNEL
DEBAGGING	DECAGONAL	DUCKWORTH	DEFLATION	DIGRESSED
DEBUGGING	DECEIVERS	DEDUCIBLE	DEFEATIST	DIGRESSES
DABCHICKS	DECEITFUL	DODECAGON	DEFIANTLY	DIGNITARY
DUBLINERS	DECEIVING	DEDUCTIVE	DEFICIENT	DIGGINGUP
DEBRIEFED	DECLINING	DEDUCTING	DEFECTIVE	DIGNIFIED
DEBUNKING	DECLIVITY	DEDUCTION	DEFECTING	DEGENERES
DEBENTURE	DICKINSON	DEDICATED	DEFECTION	DOGCOLLAR
DUBROVNIK	DECOLLETE	DEDICATES	DEFECTORS	DIGUPDIRT
DUBIOUSLY	DECALOGUE	DODGEBALL	DUFFELBAG	DIGESTIVE
DOBERMANN	DOCKLANDS	DODGECITY	DIFFERENT	DIGESTING
DEBARMENT	DUCKLINGS	DUDERANCH	DIFFERING	DIGESTION
DEBARRING	DECALITRE	DODSWORTH	DEFLECTED	DIGITALIS
DEBITCARD	DECILITRE	DADDYCOOL	DEFLECTOR	DIGITALLY
DEBATABLE	DECUMBENT	DRENCHING	DIFFIDENT	DIGITISED
DEBUTANTE	DECAMPING	DIEADEATH	DIFFICULT	DEHYDRATE
DEBUTANTS	DOCUMENTS	DEEPENING	DEFOLIATE	DRIBBLERS
DEBAUCHED	DECOMPOSE	DIETETICS	DEFOLIANT	DRIBBLING
DEBAUCHEE	DECAMERON	DRECHSLER	DEFENDANT	DWINDLING
DEBAUCHES	DECIMATED	DIETICIAN	DEFINABLE	DRIVEHOME
DECLARANT	DECAMETRE	DWELLINGS	DEFENDERS	DOINGWELL
DECLARERS	DECIMETRE	DUELLISTS	DEFENSIVE	DYINGSWAN
DECLARING	DECIMATES	DREAMLAND	DEFENDING	DRINKABLE
DICTATING	DECANTERS	DREAMEDUP	DAFFODILS	DRINKDEEP
DICTATION	DECONGEST	DREAMLESS	DEFROCKED	DRILLHALL
DECLAIMED	DECANTING	DREAMLIKE	DEFROSTED	DAINTIEST

DRIFTWOOD	DUMPLINGS	DENTITION	DEPRIVING	DARWINIST
DAIQUIRIS	DEMIMONDE	DANDIFIES	DUPLICITY	DORMITORY
DAIRYMAID	DEMIMOORE	DANDIPRAT	DEPILATOR	DEREKBOND
DRIZZLING	DOMINICAN	DENTISTRY	DEPENDANT	DARTMOUTH
DEJECTING	DOMINEERS	DONALBAIN	DEPENDENT	DORMOBILE
DEJECTION	DEMANDING	DONALDSON	DEPENDING	DARKROOMS
DRKILDARE	DIMENSION	DONAMECHE	DIPLOMATS	DERISIBLE
DEKOONING	DOMINANCE	DININGCAR	DIPLOMACY	DIRTTRACK
DELTAWING	DOMINIONS	DININGOUT	DEPLORING	DARKWATER
DALMATIAN	DEMONISED	DONORCARD	DEPLOYING	DIRTYLOOK
DELICIOUS	DOMINATED	DYNASTIES	DEPORTEES	DIRTYWORK
DELACROIX	DOMINATES	DINOSAURS	DEPARTING	DISPARAGE
DALEEVANS	DAMPPROOF	DUNSTABLE	DEPORTING	DISPARATE
DOLGELLAU	DEMARCATE	DONATELLA	DEPARDIEU	DISTANCES
DOLEFULLY	DEMURRING	DONATELLO	DEPARTURE	DISBANDED
DILIGENCE	DAMASCENE	DENOUNCED	DEPOSITED	DISCARDED
DELEGATED	DEMYSTIFY	DENOUNCES	DEPOSITOR	DASTARDLY
DELIGHTED	DIMESTORE	DANQUAYLE	DIPHTHONG	DESCALING
DELEGATES	DAMPSQUIB	DANKWORTH	DEPUTISED	DISPARITY
DALAILAMA	DEMITASSE	DANNYKAYE	DEPUTISES	DISDAINED
DALLIANCE	DUMAURIER	DONIZETTI	DIPSWITCH	DESIARNAZ
DALGLIESH	DUNGAREES	DROMEDARY	DORSALFIN	DISFAVOUR
DOLOMITES	DINGALING	DOOLITTLE	DARTAGNAN	DESPAIRED
DELINEATE	DONCARLOS	DOODLEBUG	DARTBOARD	DISMANTLE
DELIRIOUS	DANDAILEY	DEODORANT	DIRTCHEAP	DESCARTES
DELETIONS	DONCASTER	DEODORISE	DIRECTHIT	DISTANTLY
DELIVERED	DONMCLEAN	DROPPEDIN	DIRECTIVE	DASHBOARD
DELIVERER	DANCEBAND	DROPPEDBY	DIRECTING	DISCBRAKE
DEMEANING	DANCEHALL	DROWSIEST	DIRECTION	DESKBOUND
DAMNATION	DUNCESCAP	DROPSCONE	DIRECTORS	DISOBEYED
DEMEANOUR	DENSENESS	DROPWAIST	DIRECTORY	DESECRATE
DAMNATORY	DANDELION	DOOMWATCH	DIRECTTAX	DESICCATE
DUMBARTON	DANGERMAN	DEPRAVITY	DAREDEVIL	DESICCANT
DEMOBBING	DANDENONG	DEPICTING	DARKENING	DISHCLOTH
DEMOCRATS	DANGEROUS	DEPICTION	DIRIGIBLE	DUSTCOVER
DEMOCRACY	DANSEUSES	DEPRECATE	DERIGUEUR	DISKDRIVE
DAMSELFLY	DINNERSET	DEPLETING	DARKHORSE	DUSTDEVIL
DAMPENING	DENIGRATE	DEPLETION	DIRTINESS	DISREGARD
DUMBFOUND	DANTHEVAN	DIPPEDOUT	DERRINGDO	DESPERATE
DEMAGOGUE	DINGINESS	DEPRESSED	DERRINGER	DESPERADO
DUMPINESS	DONSIEGEL	DEPRESSES	DERVISHES	DISREPAIR
DIMWITTED	DANDIFIED	DUPLICATE	DARWINISM	DISSEMBLE

DISMEMBER	DESTITUTE	DISCREDIT	DOTODEATH	DAVEALLEN
DESCENDED	DISFIGURE	DESERTERS	DITHERERS	DAVECLARK
DISTENDED	DISPLEASE	DESERTFOX	DOTTERELS	DAVIDLEAN
DISBELIEF	DISCLAIMS	DESERTING	DITHERING	DAVIDVINE
DYSLEXICS	DISALLOWS	DESERVING	DUTIFULLY	DIVIDENDS
DISPELLED	DESULTORY	DISARMING	DUTCHBARN	DAVIDSOUL
DISCERNED	DISCLOSED	DESERTION	DETAINEES	DAVIDOWEN
DESDEMONA	DISCLOSES	DISTRAINT	DOTTINESS	DAVEEVANS
DISHEDOUT	DISPLAYED	DYSTROPHY	DETRIMENT	DEVILMENT
DISTEMPER	DISEMBARK	DESERTRAT	DETAILING	DEVALAHAN
DYSPEPSIA	DISEMBODY	DISTRUSTS	DETAINING	DEVALUING
DISPENSED	DISENGAGE	DISPROVED	DETENTION	DEVOLVING
DISPERSED	DISINFECT	DISPROVES	DETONATED	DIVULGING
DISPERSAL	DISLOCATE	DESTROYED	DETONATOR	DEVELOPED
DISPENSER	DISSONANT	DESTROYER	DETONATES	DEVELOPER
DISPENSES	DISPOSEOF	DISASTERS	DUTEOUSLY	DAVENPORT
DISPERSES	DISCOVERS	DUSTSHEET	DETERGENT	DEVONPORT
DYSPEPTIC	DISHONEST	DESISTING	DETERRENT	DEVIOUSLY
DISSECTED	DISCOVERY	DUSTSTORM	DETERMINE	DIVORCEES
DISSENTED	DISCOMFIT	DISPUTANT	DETERRING	DIVERGENT
DISSENTER	DISLODGED	DISTURBED	DATESTAMP	DIVERGING
DISREPUTE	DISLODGES	DISSUADED	DETESTING	DIVERTING
DESIGNATE	DISPOSING	DISSUADES	DEUTERIUM	DIVORCING
DISAGREED	DISROBING	DISPUTING	DRUGGISTS	DIVERSION
DESIGNERS	DESPOTISM	DISCUSSED	DAUGHTERS	DIVERSIFY
DISAGREES	DYSTOPIAN	DISGUISED	DOUGHTILY	DIVERSITY
DESIGNING	DISCOUNTS	DISBURSAL	DOUGHNUTS	DOVERSOLE
DISCHARGE	DISMOUNTS	DISCUSSES	DRUNKARDS	DEVASTATE
DOSSHOUSE	DISCOLOUR	DISGUISES	DOUBLEACT	DIVISIBLE
DISSIPATE	DISHONOUR	DISGUSTED	DOUBLEBED	DIVESTING
DUSTINESS	DISCOURSE	DISRUPTED	DOUBLEDUP	DIVISIONS
DISSIDENT	DISTORTED	DISAVOWAL	DOUBLOONS	DEVOTIONS
DISHINGUP	DISSOLUTE	DISOWNING	DOUBLETOP	DEVOURING
DASHINGLY	DISSOLVED	DOTMATRIX	DRUMMAJOR	DAWNACTON
DESPISING	DISSOLVES	DETRACTED	DRUMSTICK	DOWNGRADE
DISLIKING	DISAPPEAR	DETRACTOR	DRUGSTORE	DOWDINESS
DISTILLED	DESCRIBED	DATABANKS	DAUNTLESS	DOWELLING
DISTILLER	DESIRABLE	DATABASES	DOUBTLESS	DOWNRIGHT
DISCIPLES	DESCRIBES	DETECTIVE	DOUBTFIRE	DOWNRIVER
DISMISSED	DISGRACED	DETACHING	DRURYLANE	DOWNSCALE
DISMISSAL	DISTRACTS	DETECTING	DEVIATING	DOWNSTAGE
DISMISSES	DISTRICTS	DETECTION	DEVIATION	DOWNSWING

DOWNSHIFT	EMBEDDING	ESCAPADES	ELEVATION	EXECUTION
DOWNTRAIN	EMBALMERS	EXCEPTING	ELEVATORS	EXECUTORS
DOWNTOOLS	EMBALMING	EXCEPTION	ELEVATORY	EDELWEISS
DOWNUNDER	EMBELLISH	ESCAPISTS	ELEGANTLY	EVERYTIME
DOWNWARDS	EMBROIDER	EXCORIATE	EVENBREAK	EVERYINCH
DIXIELAND	EMBROILED	ESCORTING	EXERCISED	EVERYBODY
DEXTERITY	EMBARRASS	EXCURSION	EXERCISES	EFFICIENT
DEXTEROUS	EMBERDAYS	ENCIRCLED	EVENEDOUT	EFFECTIVE
DAYSCHOOL	EMBARKING	ENCIRCLES	ELEVENSES	EFFECTING
DAYCENTRE	EMBARGOED	EXCUSABLE	ELEMENTAL	EFFECTUAL
DAYRETURN	EMBARGOES	EXCESSIVE	EVERGREEN	EXFOLIATE
DAYOFREST	EMBOSSING	EXCISEMAN	EMERGENCE	EXFOLIANT
DRYSHERRY	EMBASSIES	EXCISEMEN	EMERGENCY	EFFULGENT
DAYLIGHTS	EMBITTERS	EXCITABLE	ENERGISED	ENFOLDING
DRYCLEANS	EMBATTLED	EXCITEDLY	ENERGISES	ENFAMILLE
DAYDREAMS	ELBOWROOM	ENCOURAGE	ENERGETIC	ENFORCING
DIZZINESS	EMBRYONIC	EXCLUSIVE	EYESHADOW	EMFORSTER
ELALAMEIN	EMBEZZLED	EXCLUDING	ELEPHANTS	EFFLUVIUM
EMANATING	EMBEZZLER	EXCLUSION	ELEGISING	EFFLUENCE
EMANATION	EMBEZZLES	ENCRUSTED	ELEGIASTS	ENGRAVERS
EVABARTOK	EXCHANGED	ENCOUNTER	EVENMONEY	ENGRAVING
EVAMENDES	EXCHANGES	EXCAVATED	ETERNALLY	EDGBASTON
ENAMELLED	EUCHARIST	EXCAVATOR	EXEMPLARY	EGGBEATER
ERADICATE	EXCLAIMED	EXCAVATES	EXEMPTION	EAGLEEYED
EXAMINEES	ENCHANTED	ENDEARING	EXEMPLIFY	EGGSHELLS
EXAMINERS	ENCHANTER	ENDEAVOUR	EYEOPENER	ENGELBERT
EVASIVELY	EXCEEDING	ENDLESSLY	EXECRABLE	ENGULFING
EXAMINING	ECCLESTON	ENDOMORPH	EYEBRIGHT	ENGINEERS
EMACIATED	EXCHEQUER	ENDANGERS	EVERSINCE	ERGONOMIC
EPAULETTE	ENCHILADA	EDDINGTON	EVENTUATE	ENGROSSED
ELABORATE	EXCULPATE	ENDURABLE	EYESTRAIN	EAGERNESS
EVAPORATE	EXCALIBUR	ENDORSERS	ELECTABLE	EIGHTIETH
ENAMOURED	EXCELLENT	ENDORPHIN	ELECTRESS	EIGHTSMAN
EXACTNESS	EXCELLING	ELDERSHIP	ELECTRICS	EIGHTSMEN
ENACTMENT	EXCELSIOR	ENDORSING	ELECTRIFY	EIGHTFOLD
EVACUATED	ESCALATED	ENDURANCE	ELECTRODE	EIGHTSOME
EVALUATED	ESCALATOR	EIDERDOWN	ELECTIONS	EDGEWORTH
EVACUATES	ESCALATES	EIDERDUCK	ELECTRONS	EXHIBITED
EVALUATES	ENCOMPASS	EDDYSTONE	ELECTORAL	EXHIBITOR
EMBRACING	ECCENTRIC	ENDOWMENT	EDENTATES	ETHICALLY
EMBLAZONS	ENCLOSING	EYELASHES	EXECUTIVE	ECHOGRAMS
EMBRASURE	ENCLOSURE	ELEVATING	EXECUTING	ETHNICITY

ETHELBERT	ETIQUETTE	ECONOMICS	EUPHONIUM	EZRAPOUND
EPHEMERAL	ENJOYABLE	ECONOMIES	EXPLOSION	ENRAPTURE
ECHINACEA	ENJOYABLY	ECOLOGIST	EXPLOITED	EARLSPARK
ENHANCING	ENJOYMENT	ECONOMIST	EXPURGATE	EUROTRASH
ETHIOPIAN	ELKHOUNDS	EGONRONAY	EMPIRICAL	EARLYBATH
ETHNOLOGY	EULOGISED	EMOLUMENT	EMPIREDAY	EARLYDAYS
EXHAUSTED	EULOGISES	ELOCUTION	EXPORTERS	EARLYBIRD
ELISABETH	ENLIGHTEN	EVOLUTION	EXPERTISE	EASTBOUND
ELIZABETH	EGLANTINE	ELOQUENCE	EXPORTING	EASYCHAIR
EPILATION	ELLINGTON	EPONYMOUS	ESPERANCE	EASTENDER
ERICAJONG	ECLIPSING	ECOSYSTEM	ESPERANTO	EASTERDAY
ERICBLAIR	ELLIPSOID	ESPLANADE	EUPHRATES	EASTEREGG
EDINBURGH	ENLARGERS	EMPHASISE	ENPASSANT	EASTERNER
EPISCOPAL	ENLARGING	EXPIATION	EXPATIATE	EASYGOING
EVILDOERS	ELLISBELL	EXPLAINED	EMPATHISE	EASILYLED
EVILDOING	ENLISTING	EXPECTANT	EXPOUNDED	EASTLYNNE
ERINDOORS	ENLIVENED	EXPECTING	ESPOUSING	EASYLOVER
EPIDERMAL	EDMONDSON	EXPEDIENT	EMPOWERED	ENSEMBLES
EPIDERMIS	EMMERDALE	EXPLETIVE	ENQUIRERS	EASYMONEY
EMILEZOLA	ELMERFUDD	EUPHEMISM	EXQUISITE	ESSENTIAL
EPICENTRE	ENMESHING	EXPRESSED	ENQUIRING	EASINGOFF
EMINENTLY	ERNMALLEY	EMPRESSES	ENQUIRIES	ENSCONCED
EVIDENTLY	ENNOBLING	EXPRESSES	EARMARKED	EASYPEASY
EDITHPIAF	EDNABIRCH	EXPRESSLY	ENRICHING	EASYRIDER
ELIMINATE	ERNIEWISE	EMPTINESS	EARLEPAGE	ENSHRINED
ELICITING	EINDHOVEN	EXPELLING	EARNESTLY	EASTTIMOR
EDIBILITY	EGOMANIAC	EXPULSION	EGREGIOUS	EASYTERMS
ETIOLATED	EVOCATIVE	EXPANSIVE	EARTHWARD	ELSEWHERE
ENIGMATIC	EVOCATION	EXPENSIVE	EARTHIEST	ERSTWHILE
EPITOMISE	EXORCISED	EXPANDING	EARTHLING	ESSEXGIRL
EDITORIAL	EXORCISES	EXPUNGING	EARPHONES	ESSAYISTS
EMIGRANTS	EXONERATE	EXPANSION	EARTHWORK	ENTRANCED
EMIGRATED	ELOPEMENT	EXPONENTS	EARTHWORM	ENTRANCES
EMIGRATES	EXOFFICIO	ESPIONAGE	EARTHBORN	ESTRANGED
ERICSYKES	ELONGATED	EUPHORBIA	EARPIECES	EXTRADITE
EMISSIONS	ELONGATES	EMPLOYEES	EARLINESS	EXTRATIME
ELIOTNESS	EROTICISM	EMPLOYERS	EARWIGGED	ESTUARIES
EPISTOLIC	EMOTIONAL	EXPLORERS	EARLIERON	ENTRAPPED
EXISTENCE	EGOTISTIC	EXPLOSIVE	ENROLMENT	EXTRACTED
EPISTAXIS	EMOLLIENT	EMPLOYING	ENROLLING	EXTRACTOR
EPICUREAN	ECOMMERCE	EXPLODING	ERRONEOUS	ESTABLISH
EPICURISM	ECONOMISE	EXPLORING	EURIPIDES	EXTREMELY

ENTRECHAT	ENTRUSTED	FLATBROKE	FRACTURED	FIELDWORK
EXTREMISM	ENTRYFORM	FRANCHISE	FLATTERER	FIELDGOAL
EXTREMIST	EDUCATIVE	FRANCESCA	FRACTURES	FIELDTRIP
EXTREMITY	EDUCATING	FRANCISCO	FLAUTISTS	FREDERICK
ENTRECOTE	EMULATING	FRAUDSTER	FEATURING	FRETFULLY
ENTRENOUS	EDUCATION	FLAREPATH	FABIANISM	FLEDGLING
ENTREATED	EMULATION	FRAMETENT	FIBREFILL	FREIGHTER
EXTRICATE	EXUDATION	FLAGEOLET	FOBBEDOFF	FUELGAUGE
ENTAILING	EDUCATORS	FRATERNAL	FABRICATE	FRESHNESS
ENTWINING	EMULATORS	FRAMEWORK	FEBRILITY	FLESHPOTS
EXTRINSIC	EDUCATORY	FLAMETREE	FEBRIFUGE	FREEHOUSE
ENTWISTLE	EHUDBARAK	FEARFULLY	FABULISTS	FIERINESS
EXTOLLING	ENUNCIATE	FRANGLAIS	FIBONACCI	FLEXITIME
ESTIMABLE	ENUMERATE	FLASHCARD	FACECLOTH	FREDKARNO
ENTOMBING	EXUBERANT	FLASHBACK	FACEFACTS	FREELANCE
ESTAMINET	EDUCEMENT	FEATHERED	FACSIMILE	FREEMASON
EXTEMPORE	ELUCIDATE	FLASHBULB	FACTIONAL	FREDPERRY
ECTOMORPH	ELUSIVELY	FLASHCUBE	FICTIONAL	FREERANGE
ESTIMATED	ERUDITION	FLANIMALS	FACULTIES	FEELSMALL
ESTIMATOR	EBULLIENT	FLAKINESS	FECUNDITY	FREESHEET
ESTIMATES	EQUALLING	FOAMINESS	FACTORING	FLEESHMAN
EXTENUATE	EQUALISED	FRAGILITY	FACTORIAL	FEEDSTOCK
EATONHALL	EQUALISER	FLAPJACKS	FACTORIES	FREESTYLE
EXTENSIVE	EQUALISES	FRANKNESS	FACEPACKS	FREETRADE
EXTENDING	EQUIPMENT	FRANKFORT	FACESAVER	FLEETWOOD
EXTENSION	EQUIPPING	FRANKMUIR	FACETIOUS	FREETHROW
ENTANGLED	EQUERRIES	FRANKFURT	FACTUALLY	FREQUENTS
ELTONJOHN	EQUITABLE	FRAILNESS	FACEVALUE	FREQUENCY
EATINGOUT	EQUITABLY	FLAMMABLE	FIDUCIARY	FREEVERSE
EXTROVERT	EQUIVOCAL	FRAGMENTS	FIDGETING	FREEWHEEL
ECTOPLASM	ENVELOPED	FLATMATES	FADDINESS	FREEWILLY
EXTIRPATE	ENVELOPES	FLAUNTING	FADINGOUT	FREEWOMAN
ENTERTAIN	ENVISAGED	FLAVOURED	FEDERLINE	FREEZEDRY
EXTORTING	ENVISAGES	FLAGPOLES	FEDERATED	FIFTEENTH
EXTORTION	EAVESDROP	FRAGRANCE	FEDERATES	FUGACIOUS
ENTHRONED	ENWRAPPED	FLAGSTAFF	FREMANTLE	FOGGINESS
ENTERITIS	EDWARDFOX	FLAGSTONE	FRETBOARD	FIGURINES
ESTATECAR	EDWARDIAN	FEASTDAYS	FRENCHHEN	FIGUREOUT
ENTITLING	ETYMOLOGY	FLATTENED	FRENCHMAN	FIGHTBACK
ENTOURAGE	EGYPTIANS	FRACTIONS	FIELDFARE	FIGHTCLUB
ENTHUSING	FLATBREAD	FRACTIOUS	FIELDTEST	FUGITIVES
EXTRUSION	FRAMBOISE	FLATTERED	FIELDMICE	FRICASSEE

FAIRBANKS	FALSENESS	FANTASIST	FOOTHILLS	FOREBEARS
FLIPCHART	FALTERING	FANTAILED	FOOLHARDY	FIREBREAK
FAIRCHILD	FILLETING	FANTASTIC	FOOLISHLY	FIREBRICK
FLINCHING	FILTERING	FUNICULAR	FROLICKED	FIREBALLS
FRIEDRICE	FALSEHOOD	FINGERING	FLOTILLAS	FIRECREST
FRIEDRICH	FULLERTON	FINGERTIP	FLORISTRY	FORECLOSE
FLIPFLOPS	FALSESTEP	FINDFAULT	FROCKCOAT	FEROCIOUS
FAITHLESS	FILTERTIP	FENUGREEK	FOOTLIGHT	FIRECORAL
FRIGHTENS	FILMGOERS	FANCIABLE	FOOTLOOSE	FORECASTS
FRIGHTFUL	FULLHOUSE	FUNKINESS	FROGMARCH	FORECOURT
FAITHFULL	FULMINATE	FANLIGHTS	FLOUNDERS	FIREDRILL
FLICKERED	FILLINGUP	FUNGICIDE	FLOUNCING	FERRETERS
FRIVOLITY	FALSIFIED	FINALISED	FOOTNOTES	FORCEMEAT
FRIVOLOUS	FALSIFIER	FINALISES	FOOTPLATE	FORGETFUL
FLIPPANCY	FALSIFIES	FINALISTS	FOOTPRINT	FARSEEING
FRIARBIRD	FULFILLED	FINANCING	FOOLPROOF	FERRETING
FRIARTUCK	FOLLICLES	FINANCIAL	FOOTPATHS	FORGERIES
FAIRSFAIR	FOLKLORIC	FINANCIER	FLOORSHOW	FARMEDOUT
FLIMSIEST	FULLMARKS	FINEPRINT	FOOLSMATE	FERMENTED
FAIRTRADE	FOLKMUSIC	FINISHING	FROGSPAWN	FORFEITED
FAINTNESS	FALANGISM	FINISHOFF	FOOTSTEPS	FIREEATER
FAIRTRIAL	FALANGIST	FANATICAL	FOOLSGOLD	FERVENTLY
FLINTLOCK	FELONIOUS	FINETUNED	FOOTSTOOL	FARAFIELD
FRITTERED	FALCONERS	FUNCTIONS	FOOTSCRAY	FOREFFECT
FAIRYLAND	FOLLOWERS	FUNNYHAHA	FOODSTUFF	FOREFRONT
FAIRYCAKE	FOLLOWING	FUNNYFACE	FRONTIERS	FIREGUARD
FAIRYTALE	FULLQUOTA	FUNNYFARM	FROSTIEST	FORAGECAP
FAIRYLIKE	FULLSCALE	FANNYHILL	FRONTLINE	FOREGOING
FAIRYRING	FALDSTOOL	FUNNYGIRL	FROSTBITE	FORTHWITH
FRITZLANG	FILMSTRIP	FUNNYBONE	FOODVALUE	FARTHINGS
FRIZZANTE	FULLTIMER	FANCYWORK	FERMANAGH	FURTHERTO
FALLAPART	FULLWHACK	FANCYFREE	FIREALARM	FARMHOUSE
FELLAPART	FAMAGUSTA	FLOTATION	FORWARDED	FERDINAND
FALLACIES	FUMIGATED	FOOTBRAKE	FIRMAMENT	FORBIDDEN
FULLBOARD	FUMIGATOR	FOODCHAIN	FORMALISE	FURTIVELY
FULLBLAST	FUMIGATES	FLOWCHART	FORMATIVE	FURNISHED
FILMBUFFS	FEMINISED	FLOODGATE	FORSAKING	FURNISHES
FULLBLOWN	FEMINISTS	FLOODTIDE	FORMALISM	FORTIFIED
FOLICACID	FINLANDIA	FLOWERBED	FORMATION	FERTILISE
FULLCREAM	FANDANGLE	FLOWERING	FORMALIST	FORGIVING
FOLKDANCE	FANTASISE	FLOWERPOT	FORMALITY	FORTIFIES
FILLERCAP	FANTASIES	FOOTFAULT	FIREBRAND	FERTILITY

FOREIGNER	FIREWATER	FATALISTS	FAYWELDON	GRATIFIED
FIREIRONS	FORSYTHIA	FATHOMING	FLYWEIGHT	GRATIFIES
FORTITUDE	FORTYFIVE	FITTOBUST	FOYLESWAR	GLADIOLUS
FURNITURE	FORMYSINS	FETISHISM	FLYAGARIC	GRADIENTS
FIRELIGHT	FERRYBOAT	FETISHIST	FLYWHEELS	GLACIATED
FORTNIGHT	FARMYARDS	FATTYACID	FLYINGFOX	GLADIATOR
FORENAMES	FISHCAKES	FEUDALISM	FRYINGPAN	GLACIATES
FARANDOLE	FASTENERS	FRUGALITY	FLYPOSTER	GRATITUDE
FARROWING	FOSTERERS	FOUNDLING	FIZZINESS	GEARLEVER
FURROWING	FISHEAGLE	FOUNDRIES	FUZZINESS	GOALMOUTH
FORLORNLY	FASTENING	FOUNDERED	FIZZLEOUT	GLAMORGAN
FURIOUSLY	FESTERING	FLUFFIEST	GRADATION	GLAMOROUS
FORGOTTEN	FOSTERING	FOUGHTOFF	GRANARIES	GRAMPIANS
FIREPLACE	FISHERMAN	FLUMMOXED	GUACAMOLE	GRAPPLING
FIREPROOF	FISHERMEN	FLUMMOXES	GUARANTEE	GOALPOSTS
FIREPOWER	FISHGUARD	FLUORSPAR	GUARANTOR	GRASSLAND
FARBRIDGE	FASCINATE	FLUORESCE	GRANDMAMA	GLASSWARE
FORESTALL	FESTIVALS	FOURSIDED	GRANDPAPA	GEARSTICK
FORASTART	FTSEINDEX	FOURSOMES	GUARDRAIL	GLADSTONE
FARMSTEAD	FISHINESS	FOURSCORE	GUARDIANS	GLASSWOOL
FORESTERS	FUSSINESS	FLUCTUATE	GUARDEDLY	GIANTTOAD
FORESIGHT	FUSTINESS	FRUITCAKE	GRANDSLAM	GRADUALLY
FIRESTONE	FOSSILISE	FRUSTRATE	GLANDULAR	GRADUATED
FORESHORE	FESTIVITY	FRUITBATS	GUARDSMAN	GRADUATES
FIRESTORM	FOSSICKER	FAULTLESS	GUARDSMEN	GRANVILLE
FIRSTHAND	FASHIONED	FRUITLESS	GRANDIOSE	GEARWHEEL
FIRSTMATE	FASHIONER	FOUNTAINS	GUARDROOM	GRAVYBOAT
FIRSTNAME	FISHKNIFE	FLUSTERED	GRANDTOUR	GIBRALTAR
FIRSTRATE	FUSILLADE	FLUTTERED	GRANDSONS	GIBBERING
FIRSTLADY	FUSILIERS	FRUITERER	GRANDPRIX	GIBBERISH
FORETELLS	FESTOONED	FIVEASIDE	GRANDDUKE	GOBEGGING
FIRETHORN	FISHSLICE	FAVABEANS	GRANDJURY	GABRIELLE
FIRSTBORN	FASTTRACK	FIVEPENCE	GUARDSVAN	GOBBLEDUP
FIRSTFOOT	FISHWIVES	FAVERSHAM	GUATEMALA	GOBANANAS
FIRSTPOST	FATHERING	FIVESPICE	GRAVEYARD	GOBERSERK
FORETASTE	FATTENING	FAVOURITE	GRAVESEND	GABERDINE
FORMULAIC	FATHERTED	FAVOURING	GRACELESS	GOBETWEEN
FORMULATE	FATEFULLY	FAWNINGLY	GRAPESHOT	GODPARENT
FORTUNATE	FATIGUING	FIXEDODDS	GRAPEVINE	GODFATHER
FAREWELLS	FATTINESS	FOXGLOVES	GRACENOTE	GADABOUTS
FIREWORKS	FITTINGIN	FOXHOUNDS	GRAVITATE	GODDESSES
FOREWARNS	FITTINGLY	FOXHUNTER	GLARINGLY	GIDDINESS

GODLINESS	GREATNESS	GRIEVANCE	GALATIANS	GANGSTERS
GODALMING	GREATFIRE	GRIZZLERS	GOLDWATER	GUNRUNNER
GODFORBID	GREATTITS	GRIZZLING	GAMMARAYS	GENEVIEVE
GODMOTHER	GREETINGS	GOKARTING	GYMNASIUM	GONOWHERE
GRENADINE	GUESTBOOK	GALWAYBAY	GYMNASTIC	GOOSANDER
GRENADIER	GREATCOAT	GOLDAMEIR	GUMSHIELD	GOOLAGONG
GREYBEARD	GREATAUNT	GALLACHER	GYMKHANAS	GOOSEFAIR
GLENBOGLE	GRENVILLE	GALLAGHER	GIMMICKRY	GLOWERING
GREEDIEST	GUFFAWING	GALVANISE	GAMBOLLED	GROCERIES
GLENDOWER	GOFORWARD	GALLANTLY	GAMEPOINT	GROVELLED
GREYFRIAR	GIFTTOKEN	GALLANTRY	GUMARABIC	GROVELLER
GLEEFULLY	GOGGLEBOX	GOLDCOAST	GAMESTERS	GROTESQUE
GLENGARRY	GOGETTERS	GOLDCREST	GOMISSING	GEOMETRIC
GREYHOUND	GOGETTING	GOLDENAGE	GEMSTONES	GOOSESTEP
GLENLIVET	GRIMACING	GOLDENBOY	GENOACAKE	GEOFFHOON
GREENCARD	GUITARIST	GOLDENEYE	GUNMAKERS	GROSGRAIN
GREENLAND	GRIMALKIN	GILTEDGED	GENIALITY	GEORGEFOX
GREENDALE	GOITALONE	GALLERIED	GENDARMES	GOODGRIEF
GREENGAGE	GUILDHALL	GALLERIES	GENEALOGY	GEORGETTE
GREENBACK	GUILDFORD	GILLESPIE	GENEAUTRY	GOOFINESS
GREENPARK	GUINEVERE	GOLDENROD	GINGERALE	GROWINGUP
GREENBELT	GUILELESS	GALVESTON	GINGERNUT	GLORIFIED
GREENWING	GUIDELINE	GOLDFRAPP	GINGERTOM	GLORIFIES
GREENWICH	GUIDEBOOK	GOLDFIELD	GENUFLECT	GOODLOSER
GLEANINGS	GUINEAPIG	GOLDFINCH	GONCHAROV	GLOOMIEST
GLENNFORD	GAINFULLY	GELIGNITE	GENUINELY	GROOMSMAN
GREENWOOD	GRIFFITHS	GOLIGHTLY	GANGINGUP	GROOMSMEN
GREENROOM	GOINGBACK	GILCHRIST	GUNFIGHTS	GROUNDAGE
GREENHORN	GOINGLIVE	GALLIVANT	GENTILITY	GOODNIGHT
GLENORCHY	GOINGOVER	GALLINGLY	GENEKELLY	GROUNDHOG
GREGORIAN	GOINGAWAY	GALLICISM	GENTLEMAN	GROUNDING
GUERRILLA	GRIDIRONS	GALLIPOLI	GENTLEMEN	GROUNDNUT
GUESSABLE	GUILLEMOT	GOLFLINKS	GUNSMITHS	GROUNDSEL
GREASIEST	GRILLROOM	GOLDMEDAL	GUNPOWDER	GEOLOGIST
GREASEGUN	GLIMMERED	GOLDMINER	GONDOLIER	GROSPOINT
GREYSTOKE	GLIMPSING	GALLOPERS	GUNCOTTON	GEOGRAPHY
GUESSWORK	GAITSKELL	GALLOPING	GANGPLANK	GLOSSIEST
GREATDANE	GLISSANDO	GOLDPLATE	GENERALLY	GROSSMITH
GREATWALL	GUILTLESS	GALAPAGOS	GINORMOUS	GLOSSOVER
GREATDEAL	GLISTENED	GOLDSTEIN	GENERATED	GHOSTLIKE
GREATBEAR	GLITTERED	GOLDSMITH	GENERATOR	GHOSTTOWN
GUESTBEER	GUILTTRIP	GALLSTONE	GENERATES	GOODWIVES

GLORYDAYS	GETCARTER	GOVERNING	HUBRISTIC	HIGHLEVEL
GLORYHOLE	GATECRASH	GOVERNORS	HOBNOBBED	HAGIOLOGY
GIPPSLAND	GETACROSS	GOWALKIES	HOBGOBLIN	HIGHTABLE
GIPSYMOTH	GATHERING	GUYFAWKES	HIBERNATE	HUGGYBEAR
GYPSYMOTH	GUTTERING	GLYCERINE	HIBERNIAN	HAILATAXI
GYRFALCON	GOTOEARTH	GAZUMPING	HABITUATE	HAIRBRUSH
GARLANDED	GETBETTER	GAZASTRIP	HABITABLE	HAIRDRYER
GERMANDER	GATHERWAY	GAZETTEER	HUCKABACK	HEIDEGGER
GORBACHEV	GETAFIXON	HEADBOARD	HACKAMORE	HEIRESSES
GARGANTUA	GOTOGLORY	HEADCASES	HACKNEYED	HEIGHTENS
GARIBALDI	GETTHENOD	HEADCOUNT	HECTORING	HAIRINESS
GARDENERS	GETSHORTY	HEADDRESS	HYDRANGEA	HEIDIKLUM
GARDENING	GETSHOTOF	HOARFROST	HYDRAULIC	HOIPOLLOI
GARDENIAS	GATEHOUSE	HEADFIRST	HIDEBOUND	HAIRPIECE
GERTFROBE	GETWINDOF	HEADINESS	HEDGEHOGS	HAIRSLIDE
GIRLGUIDE	GUTSINESS	HEAVINESS	HEDGEROWS	HAIRSHIRT
GERMINATE	GETTINGON	HOARINESS	HEDONISTS	HAILSTONE
GARNISHED	GETTINGUP	HYACINTHS	HUDSONBAY	HAILSTORM
GARNISHES	GETTINGBY	HEADLIGHT	HYDROFOIL	HAIRSPRAY
GERMICIDE	GATEMONEY	HEADLINER	HYDROLOGY	HAIRSTYLE
GERALDINE	GUTENBERG	HEADLANDS	HIDEOUSLY	HIJACKERS
GERALDTON	GOTOPRESS	HEADLINES	HYDERABAD	HIJACKING
GIRANDOLE	GATESHEAD	HEADPIECE	HIDEYHOLE	HOLLANDER
GERANIUMS	GOTOSLEEP	HEATPROOF	HIERARCHY	HALFATICK
GARGOYLES	GETATABLE	HEADRESTS	HAEMATOID	HALFBOARD
GARYPRATT	GOTOWASTE	HEADSCARF	HEEDFULLY	HOLYBIBLE
GYROSCOPE	GRUMBLERS	HEADSTART	HUEYLEWIS	HALFBAKED
GARFUNKEL	GRUMBLING	HEADSTONE	HUEANDCRY	HILLBILLY
GARRULOUS	GAULEITER	HEARTLAND	HUFFINESS	HALFCROWN
GOREVIDAL	GRUFFNESS	HEARTACHE	HAGIARCHY	HOLOCAUST
GORKYPARK	GAUDINESS	HEARTLESS	HIGHALTAR	HELVETICA
GARRYOWEN	GLUTINOUS	HEARTBEAT	HIGHBALLS	HOLLERING
GESTATION	GRUELLING	HEARTFELT	HIGHCHAIR	HELVETIAN
GASSINESS	GRUMPIEST	HEARTIEST	HIGHCLASS	HELVELLYN
GUSHINESS	GAUNTLETS	HEALTHIER	HIGHCOURT	HELLEBORE
GOSSIPING	GAUNTNESS	HEALTHILY	HYGIENIST	HELPEDOUT
GASFITTER	GIVEBLOOD	HEARTENED	HIGHFLOWN	HELPFULLY
GASOMETER	GIVEBIRTH	HEARTHRUG	HIGHFLYER	HOLOGRAPH
GASHOLDER	GAVECHASE	HEARTBURN	HUGHGRANT	HOLYGRAIL
GASCOIGNE	GIVECHASE	HEAVYDUTY	HIGHJINKS	HOLOGRAMS
GASTROPOD	GIVINGOUT	HOBNAILED	HIGHLIGHT	HOLYGHOST
GASTRITIS	GOVERNESS	HEBRIDEAN	HIGHLANDS	HULAHOOPS

HALFHITCH	HIMALAYAS	HANSOMCAB	HYPNOTIST	HORSINESS
HALLIWELL	HOMEMAKER	HANGOVERS	HIPPOLYTA	HARBINGER
HILLINESS	HOMEMOVIE	HUNDREDTH	HYPERICUM	HORRIFIED
HALTINGLY	HUMANRACE	HUNGRIEST	HYPERBOLA	HERBICIDE
HELLISHLY	HUMANDHAW	HONORIFIC	HYPERBOLE	HORRIFIES
HOLEINONE	HUMANKIND	HINDRANCE	HEPATITIS	HERBIVORE
HALFLIGHT	HUMUNGOUS	HANDSTAND	HAPPYTALK	HOROLOGER
HALLMARKS	HUMANISTS	HANDSHAKE	HAPPYDAYS	HARDLINER
HELPMATES	HEMINGWAY	HINDSIGHT	HAPPYHOUR	HARDLINES
HELENHUNT	HOMEOPATH	HANDSFREE	HERBALISM	HIRELINGS
HALLOWEEN	HOMEOWNER	HANGTOUGH	HERBALIST	HERALDSUN
HALLOWING	HOMOPHONE	HANDTOWEL	HERBALTEA	HIRINGOUT
HELIPILOT	HAMPSTEAD	HONOURING	HARMATTAN	HARDNOSED
HALFPENCE	HOMESTEAD	HINDUSTAN	HEREAFTER	HARANGUED
HALFPENNY	HAMPSHIRE	HINDUKUSH	HARDBOARD	HARANGUES
HILARIOUS	HAMSTRING	HONEYBEAR	HARDBACKS	HARROGATE
HALLSTAND	HAMSTRUNG	HANDYANDY	HAREBELLS	HARMONICA
HOLYSMOKE	HOMETRUTH	HONEYCOMB	HORNBILLS	HARMONISE
HALITOSIS	HAMBURGER	HENRYFORD	HARDCOURT	HARROWING
HALFTRUTH	HUNGARIAN	HONKYTONK	HARTDAVIS	HARMONIUM
HOLYWATER	HANGABOUT	HONEYMOON	HORSEBACK	HARROVIAN
HOLLYOAKS	HANDBRAKE	HUNKYDORY	HORSEHAIR	HARMONIES
HOLLYAIRD	HANDBELLS	HONEYTRAP	HARLESDEN	HARMONIST
HOLBYCITY	HANDBILLS	HOOLIGANS	HARDENERS	HARPOONED
HOLLYWOOD	HANDBOOKS	HOOKNOSED	HORSESHOE	HARPOONER
HOLLYHOCK	HANDCUFFS	HOODWINKS	HORSEWHIP	HARBOURED
HOMEAGAIN	HANKERING	HAPHAZARD	HARDENING	HARBOURER
HOMEALONE	HINDERING	HEPTARCHY	HARPERLEE	HORNPIPES
HUMECTANT	HENPECKED	HEPTAGONS	HORSEPLAY	HIROSHIMA
HOMICIDAL	HANDEDOUT	HYPOCRITE	HARNESSED	HARASSING
HAMADRYAD	HENDERSON	HYPOCRISY	HARNESSES	HOROSCOPE
HAMMERING	HUNCHBACK	HOPSCOTCH	HARVESTED	HERETICAL
HAMPERING	HANDICAPS	HYPOCAUST	HARVESTER	HARDTIMES
HAMMERTOE	HANGINGON	HYPHENATE	HARLEQUIN	HERCULEAN
HOMEGUARD	HANGINGUP	HAPPENING	HERRFLICK	HARDWIRED
HOMEGROWN	HUNNIFORD	HAPLESSLY	HARMFULLY	HARRYWEBB
HUMPHRIES	HANDIWORK	HOPEFULLY	HARSHNESS	HARRYLIME
HEMMINGIN	HENRIETTA	HAPPINESS	HERMITAGE	HARRYHILL
HUMDINGER	HUNNICUTT	HOPPICKER	HURRICANE	HUSBANDRY
HAMFISTED	HANDLEBAR	HOPELANGE	HARRIDANS	HISTAMINE
HUMILIATE	HANGLOOSE	HYPNOTISE	HURRIEDLY	HASLEMERE
HIMALAYAN	HANGNAILS	HYPNOTISM	HARDINESS	HASTENING

HYSTERICS	HAUGHTILY	IDALUPINO	INDIANINK	IDENTICAL
HOSTESSES	HEURISTIC	INADVANCE	INDOCHINA	INERTNESS
HOSPITALS	HAUTMONDE	INANYCASE	INDICTING	IDENTIKIT
HASTINESS	HAVEABASH	IMBECILIC	INDUCTION	INFLATING
HUSKINESS	HAVEABALL	IMBECILES	INDECENCY	INFLATION
HUSHINGUP	HAVEASTAB	IMBALANCE	INDECORUM	INFECTING
HOSTILITY	HAVEITOUT	IMBROGLIO	INDICATED	INFECTION
HESELTINE	HAVINGAGO	IMBROGLIA	INDICATOR	INFRINGED
HUSHMONEY	HAVINGFUN	INCUBATED	INDICATES	INFRINGES
HISTORIAN	HIVINGOFF	INCUBATOR	INDEFAULT	INFLICTED
HISTOGRAM	HAVERSACK	INCUBATES	INDIGNANT	INFANTILE
HESITANCY	HOVERPORT	INCIDENCE	INDIGNITY	INFURIATE
HESITATED	HAVEWORDS	INCLEMENT	INDIGENCE	INFORMANT
HESITATES	HOWSAYYOU	INCREMENT	INDELIBLE	INFIRMARY
HITPARADE	HAWTHORNE	INCREASED	INDELIBLY	INFORMERS
HATHAYOGA	HAWKSMOOR	INCREASES	INDULGENT	INFERTILE
HOTHEADED	HEXAGONAL	INCOGNITO	INDULGING	INFERRING
HATCHBACK	HEXAMETER	ITCHINESS	INDOLENCE	INFORMING
HITTHEHAY	HAYMAKING	INCLINING	INDEMNIFY	INFIRMITY
HITCHHIKE	HAYMARKET	INCULCATE	INDEMNITY	INFERENCE
HITCHCOCK	HEYERDAHL	INCUMBENT	INDENTING	INFERIORS
HOTTINGUP	HEYPRESTO	INCOMMODE	INDONESIA	INFESTING
HOTTICKET	HAYSTACKS	INCOMETAX	INDENTURE	INFASHION
HOTELIERS	HAZELNUTS	INCONCERT	ICELANDIC	INFLUENZA
HOTPOTATO	HAZARDOUS	INCENTIVE	ICELANDER	INFLUENCE
HOTHOUSES	INAVACUUM	INCENSING	ITERATING	INGRAINED
HITFORSIX	INABADWAY	INCONTROL	ITERATION	INGLENOOK
HOTSPRING	IRASCIBLE	INCAPABLE	INELASTIC	INGENUITY
HETERODOX	IRASCIBLY	INCIPIENT	INELEGANT	INGENIOUS
HATSTANDS	INAUDIBLE	INCEPTION	INEFFABLE	INGENUOUS
HOUSEMAID	INAUGURAL	INCARNATE	ITEMISING	INGENERAL
HOUSEMATE	INANIMATE	INCURABLE	ICESKATED	INGESTING
HOUSECALL	IMAGINARY	INCORRECT	ICESKATER	INGESTION
HOUSEWIFE	ITALICISE	INCURRING	ICESKATES	INHABITED
HOUSEFLAG	IMAGINING	INCURSION	IFEELFINE	INHIBITED
HOUSEHOLD	INABILITY	INCURIOUS	IDEALISED	INHIBITOR
HOUSEWORK	INAPICKLE	INCESSANT	IDEALISTS	INHARNESS
HOUSEROOM	INABIGWAY	INCISIONS	ICEHOCKEY	ISHERWOOD
HOUSEBOAT	IVANLENDL	INCLUSIVE	INEBRIATE	INHERITED
HOUSECOAT	INAMORATA	INCLUDING	INEARNEST	INHERITOR
HOURGLASS	INACORNER	INCAUTION	INEBRIETY	IMITATIVE
HAUGHTIER	INARREARS	INCLUSION	INESSENCE	IMITATING

IMITATION	IMMODESTY	ILOVELUCY	IMPARTIAL	INSTILLED
IMITATORS	IMMIGRANT	INORGANIC	IMPERIOUS	INSTITUTE
IAINBANKS	IMMOLATED	IRONHORSE	IMPORTUNE	INSOLUBLE
ITINERATE	IMMOLATES	ISOTHERMS	IMPASSIVE	INSOLVENT
ITINERANT	IMMENSELY	IDOLISING	INPASSING	INSULTING
ITINERARY	IMMENSITY	IRONOXIDE	IMPOSTORS	INSOLENCE
ISINGLASS	IMMINENCE	IRONSIDES	IMPATIENS	INSULATED
IRISHMOSS	IMMUNISED	IRONSMITH	IMPATIENT	INSULATOR
IRISHSTEW	IMMUNISES	INOCULATE	INPATIENT	INSULATES
INITIALLY	IMMERSING	IRONWORKS	IMPOTENCE	INSOMNIAC
INITIATED	IMMERSION	IMPEACHED	IMPETUOUS	INSENSATE
INITIATOR	IMMUTABLE	IMPEACHES	IMPOUNDED	INSINUATE
INITIATES	IMMOVABLE	IMPLANTED	IMPRUDENT	INSINCERE
IDIOMATIC	IMNOANGEL	IMPUDENCE	INQUORATE	ITSSOEASY
IRIDOLOGY	IANBANNEN	IMPLEMENT	IRRADIATE	INSIPIDLY
INJECTING	IONIANSEA	IMPRECISE	ISRAELITE	INSCRIBED
INJECTION	INNSBRUCK	IMPRESSED	IRREGULAR	INSCRIBER
INJECTORS	INNOCENCE	IMPRESSES	IRRIGATED	INSCRIBES
INJIGTIME	INNOCENTS	IMPLICATE	IRRIGATES	INSTRUCTS
INJURIOUS	INNOCUOUS	INPRIVATE	IMRANKHAN	INSURGENT
INJUSTICE	IANMCEWAN	IMPAIRING	IRRITABLE	INSERVICE
INKBOTTLE	IANHENDRY	IMPRISONS	IRRITABLY	INSERTING
ILLIBERAL	INNKEEPER	IMPELLERS	IRRITATED	INSERTION
ILLICITLY	IANOGILVY	IMPULSIVE	IRRITATES	INSURANCE
ILLHEALTH	IANTHORPE	IMPELLING	IRRAWADDY	INSISTENT
ILLNESSES	IANHISLOP	IMPOLITIC	INSTALLED	INSISTING
ILLEGIBLE	IANBOTHAM	IMPENDING	INSTANTLY	INTRANSIT
ILLEGIBLY	IANWRIGHT	IMPINGING	ITSYBITSY	INTHEDARK
ILLOGICAL	INNERCITY	IMPROVERS	INSIDEJOB	INTHEMAIN
ILLEGALLY	IGNORAMUS	IMPROVISE	INSIDELEG	INTHEWARS
ISLAMABAD	IGNORANCE	INPROFILE	INSIDIOUS	INTHECART
ISLANDERS	INNERMOST	IMPLODING	INSIDEOUT	INTHENAVY
INLANDSEA	INNERTUBE	IMPLORING	INSTEADOF	INTHEPINK
ISLINGTON	INNOVATED	IMPROVING	INSPECTED	INTHECLUB
ISLEOFELY	INNOVATOR	IMPLOSION	INSPECTOR	INTHEKNOW
ISLEOFMAN	INNOVATES	IMPROBITY	IPSOFACTO	INTHEMOOD
ILLGOTTEN	ISOLATING	IMPROMPTU	INSOFARAS	INTHEDOCK
ILLATEASE	ISOLATION	IMPORTANT	INSTIGATE	INTHELOOP
ICLAUDIUS	ISOSCELES	IMPORTERS	INSTINCTS	INTHESOUP
ILLHUMOUR	IRONCROSS	IMPERFECT	INSPITEOF	INTHEBUFF
IMMEDIATE	IRONEDOUT	IMPARTING	INSWINGER	INTHESWIM
IMMEDIACY	ISOMETRIC	IMPORTING	INSPIRING	INTEGRATE

INTEGRITY	INTERLOCK	JOANALLEN	JOECOCKER	JAMESDEAN
INTRICATE	INTERBRED	JEANGENET	JOEPUBLIC	JAMESBOND
INTRICACY	INTERPRET	JEANMARSH	JOEBUGNER	JAMESHOGG
INTUITIVE	INTERESTS	JOANOFARC	JEFFBANKS	JAMESPOLK
INTUITION	INTERLUDE	JEALOUSLY	JEFFERSON	JIMMYMACK
INTRINSIC	INTERRUPT	JUANPERON	JOHNADAMS	JIMMYNAIL
INTRIGUED	INTESTATE	JABBERING	JOHNCANDY	JIMMYCARR
INTRIGUES	INTESTACY	JOBSEEKER	JOHNEALES	JIMMYCHOO
INTELLECT	INTESTINE	JOBCENTRE	JOHNINMAN	JIMMYHILL
INTIMATES	INTATTERS	JGBALLARD	JOHNKEATS	JANRAVENS
INTENSELY	INTRUDERS	JUBILANCE	JOHNLOCKE	JANEASHER
INTENSIVE	INTRUSIVE	JOBSWORTH	JOHNLYDON	JANHARVEY
INTENDING	INTRUDING	JACKANORY	JOHNMAJOR	JUNKBONDS
INTENTION	INTRUSION	JACKBLACK	JOHNMILLS	JUNEBROWN
INTENSIFY	INUNDATED	JACKBENNY	JOHNNYBOY	JUNKETING
INTENSITY	INUNDATES	JACKBOOTS	JOHANSSON	JUNOESQUE
INTROUBLE	IGUANODON	JACOBITES	JOHNOATES	JANEFONDA
INTOORBIT	IBUPROFEN	JACKBAUER	JOHNSTEED	JONVOIGHT
INTROVERT	INUKTITUT	JOCKEYCAP	JOHNSMITH	JINGOISTS
INTRODUCE	INVECTIVE	JOCKEYING	JOHNTYLER	JUNCTIONS
INTERFACE	INVIDIOUS	JMCOETZEE	JOHNWAYNE	JANEWYMAN
INTERLACE	INVOICING	JACKFROST	JAILBREAK	JENNYLIND
INTERVALS	INVEIGLED	JACKFRUIT	JAILHOUSE	JORDANIAN
INTERACTS	INVEIGLER	JACKKNIFE	JUICINESS	JEROBOAMS
INTERCEDE	INVEIGLES	JACKKETCH	JOININGIN	JAREDLETO
INTERFERE	INVENTIVE	JACKOAKIE	JOININGUP	JERSEYCOW
INTERVENE	INVENTING	JACARANDA	JELLYBABY	JERVISBAY
INTERNEES	INVENTION	JACKSPRAT	JELLYBEAN	JERKINESS
INTERCEPT	INVENTORS	JACKSTRAW	JELLYFISH	JARLSBERG
INTERJECT	INVENTORY	JUDICIARY	JAMBALAYA	JERUSALEM
INTERMENT	INVIOLATE	JUDICIOUS	JAMPACKED	JURYWOMAN
INTERSECT	INVERNESS	JUDYCARNE	JIMBACKUS	JURYWOMEN
INTERNING	INVERSELY	JUDIDENCH	JIMCARREY	JERRYHALL
INTERRING	INVERTING	JUDYDAVIS	JAMIEBELL	JERRYCANS
INTERLINK	INVERSION	JUDGEMENT	JAMIEFOXX	JUSTFANCY
INTERVIEW	INVISIBLE	JUDDERING	JIMHENSON	JESTINGLY
INTERCITY	INVISIBLY	JADEGREEN	JIMREEVES	JUSTIFIED
INTERALIA	INVESTING	JADEGOODY	JUMPINESS	JUSTIFIES
INTERFLUG	INVESTORS	JOEMANGEL	JUMPLEADS	JASONKING
INTERPLAY	INWRITING	JOEEBROWN	JAMBOREES	JOSEPHINE
INTERLOPE	IRWINSHAW	JOESCULLY	JAMESCAAN	JUSTRIGHT
INTERPOSE	IVYLEAGUE	JOEBLOGGS	JUMPSTART	JOSSSTICK

JOSSSTONE	KEELHAULS	KNOWINGLY	LEASEHOLD	LOCALTIME
JETLAGGED	KEEPQUIET	KNOCKBACK	LEAVECOLD	LOCALISED
JITTERBUG	KEEPSWEET	KNOCKDOWN	LEAKEDOUT	LOCALISES
JETSETTER	KEEPSAKES	KNOWLEDGE	LOATHSOME	LICENSING
JETTISONS	KEEPTRACK	KEPTCLEAR	LEAFINESS	LACHRYMAL
JETSKIING	KNEBWORTH	KIPPERTIE	LEAKINESS	LACERATED
JETPLANES	KEEPWATCH	KAPLINSKY	LIABILITY	LACERATES
JETENGINE	KOFIANNAN	KEPTQUIET	LEAFMOULD	LOCKSMITH
JETSTREAM	KEGBITTER	KEPTTRACK	LOANSHARK	LECTURERS
JAUNDICED	KAGEMUSHA	KEPTWOMAN	LEASTWISE	LECTURING
JOURNEYED	KNIGHTING	KOREANWAR	LIBRARIAN	LACQUERED
JOVIALITY	KNIGHTLEY	KIRKBRIDE	LIBRARIES	LADYBIRDS
JUVENILIA	KEITHMOON	KARABINER	LOBSCOUSE	LUDICROUS
JUVENILES	KILLARNEY	KERBDRILL	LUBRICATE	LADIESMAN
JEWELLERS	KILNERJAR	KERCHIEFS	LUBRICANT	LADYSMAID
JEWELLERY	KILOGRAMS	KERIHULME	LABELLING	LADYSMITH
JUXTAPOSE	KILOHERTZ	KARAMAZOV	LIBELLING	LODESTONE
JAYWALKED	KILOJOULE	KERBSTONE	LABALANCE	LEDASTRAY
JAYWALKER	KILOMETRE	KERFUFFLE	LIBELLOUS	LEEMAJORS
JOYCECARY	KALAMAZOO	KERRYBLUE	LIBERTINE	LEEMARVIN
JOYLESSLY	KILOWATTS	KIRBYGRIP	LIBERTIES	LEEREMICK
JOYRIDING	KIMBERLEY	KISSINGER	LIBERALLY	LIEGELORD
KOALABEAR	KUMBHMELA	KISSOGRAM	LABYRINTH	LIEINWAIT
KNAPSACKS	KAMCHATKA	KATHARINE	LABORIOUS	LEEBOWYER
KUBLAKHAN	KAMASUTRA	KATHERINE	LIBERATED	LIFEBOATS
KIBITZING	KAMPUCHEA	KETTERING	LIBERATOR	LIFEBELTS
KIBBUTZIM	KENBARLOW	KITTENISH	LIBERATES	LIFEBLOOD
KICKBOXER	KANGAROOS	KITCHENER	LABURNUMS	LIFECYCLE
KICKEDOFF	KINGCOBRA	KITTIWAKE	LABOURDAY	LEFTFIELD
KICKEDOUT	KANDINSKY	KATHMANDU	LABOURERS	LIFEFORCE
KICKPLEAT	KINGJAMES	KATEOMARA	LEBOUCHER	LIFEGUARD
KICKSTART	KINFLICKS	KIWIFRUIT	LABOURING	LUFTHANSA
KIDNAPPED	KINDLIEST	KOWTOWING	LUCRATIVE	LOFTINESS
KIDNAPPER	KINGMIDAS	KAYMELLOR	LACTATION	LEFTOVERS
KIDGLOVES	KINGMAKER	KEYHOLDER	LUCYDAVIS	LIFESAVER
KIDSSTUFF	KINGPRAWN	KEYBOARDS	LECHEROUS	LIFESTYLE
KEEPATBAY	KINGSTOWN	KEYSTONES	LUCBESSON	LIFESIZED
KEEPCLEAR	KINGSEVIL	KEYSTROKE	LICHFIELD	LUFTWAFFE
KIELCANAL	KINGSLYNN	LHASAAPSO	LYCHGATES	LOGICIANS
KEEPCOUNT	KINGSIZED	LIAMBRADY	LOCKHORNS	LOGICALLY
KNEEHIGHS	KINSWOMAN	LLANDUDNO	LOCALCALL	LEGOFLAMB
KEEPHOUSE	KINSWOMEN	LEAVENING	LOCALHERO	LEGOFPORK

LEGALISED	LIMABEANS	LONGBOATS	LOOKALIKE	LOSTCAUSE
LEGALISES	LUMBERING	LINDBERGH	LOOKAFTER	LOSECOUNT
LOGOMACHY	LAMPEDUSA	LONGCHAMP	LEOMCKERN	LASTDITCH
LIGAMENTS	LIMEGREEN	LINEDANCE	LLOYDPACK	LISTENERS
LEGENDARY	LIMEGROVE	LINGERING	LOOSELEAF	LESSENING
LOGANSRUN	LYMPHATIC	LONGEVITY	LOOSENESS	LISTENING
LEGIONARY	LIMEHOUSE	LENIENTLY	LOOSENING	LESDENNIS
LOGOPHILE	LUMPINESS	LONGFACED	LOOSEENDS	LOSEHEART
LAGERFELD	LIMEJUICE	LANDFORCE	LIONESSES	LESLIEASH
LAGERLOUT	LAMPLIGHT	LUNCHTIME	LIONHEART	LASSITUDE
LOGARITHM	LIMELIGHT	LONCHANEY	LOOKINGAT	LOSALAMOS
LEGISLATE	LEMONBALM	LUNCHHOUR	LIONISING	LISAMARIE
LOGISTICS	LAMENTING	LUNCHEONS	LYONNAISE	LASTNIGHT
LIGHTYEAR	LEMONSOLE	LENAHORNE	LOOKSHARP	LISTPRICE
LIGHTNESS	LEMONDROP	LYNDHURST	LIONTAMER	LASERBEAM
LIGHTSHIP	LUMINESCE	LONGHOUSE	LAPDANCER	LISARILEY
LIGHTNING	LAMINATED	LONGINGLY	LIPREADER	LISARINNA
LIGHTENED	LAMINGTON	LONGITUDE	LAPHROAIG	LASTRITES
LIGHTSOUT	LYMINGTON	LONGJOHNS	LAPOTAIRE	LASTTHING
LIGHTBULB	LAMINATES	LONELIEST	LOQUACITY	LUSITANIA
LOGRUNNER	LEMONCURD	LANDLORDS	LIQUEFIED	LETHARGIC
LOHENGRIN	LAMBOFGOD	LINKLATER	LIQUEFIER	LATECOMER
LPHARTLEY	LAMPOONED	LANDMINES	LIQUEFIES	LITTERBUG
LOINCLOTH	LAMPOONER	LANDMARKS	LIQUIDATE	LITTERBIN
LOITERERS	LIMNOLOGY	LENINGRAD	LIQUIDISE	LETTERBOX
LOITERING	LAMPPOSTS	LONDONERS	LIQUIDITY	LATTERDAY
LEICESTER	LIMERICKS	LANDOFNOD	LIQUORICE	LATHERING
LYINGDOWN	LYMEREGIS	LANDOWNER	LARKABOUT	LETTERING
LEITMOTIF	LAMBRUSCO	LANGOUSTE	LORNALUFT	LOTTERIES
LEISURELY	LAMBRETTA	LUNARYEAR	LYRICALLY	LETTERMAN
LIKEASHOT	LAMPSHADE	LONGRANGE	LARACROFT	LYTTELTON
LIKEASNOT	LIMESTONE	LANDROVER	LYRICISTS	LITIGANTS
LAKEHURON	LAMBSWOOL	LANDSCAPE	LURIDNESS	LITIGIOUS
LAKEPOETS	LIMITLESS	LONGSIGHT	LARCENIST	LITIGATED
LIKESTINK	LIMBURGER	LANDSLIDE	LARCENOUS	LITIGATES
LULLABIES	LIMOUSINE	LENGTHENS	LORDMAYOR	LATCHONTO
LOLLIPOPS	LENDAHAND	LENGTHIER	LORDNORTH	LETTINGGO
LILLICRAP	LENDANEAR	LENGTHILY	LERMONTOV	LITTLEAUK
LOLLOPING	LENTANEAR	LANGUEDOC	LARDYCAKE	LITTLEEVA
LILYWHITE	LANDAGENT	LANGUIDLY	LARRYPAGE	LITTLEMEN
LAMBASTED	LANZAROTE	LANGUAGES	LESDAWSON	LITTLETOE
LAMPBLACK	LANCASTER	LINGUISTS	LISABONET	LITHOLOGY

LATERALLY	LAWCENTRE	MOBILISES	MADHATTER	MAELSTROM
LITERALLY	LOWCHURCH	MACCABEES	MEDICALLY	MAGDALENA
LETUSPRAY	LOWLINESS	MECHANISE	MEDICINAL	MAGDALENE
LETITSNOW	LOWIMPACT	MECHANISM	MEDICINES	MIGRATING
LITHUANIA	LAWNMOWER	MECHANICS	MADDENING	MIGRATION
LAURADERN	LOWLOADER	MOCCASINS	MODIFYING	MIGRATORY
LAUDATORY	LOWCOMEDY	MUCKABOUT	MADEFUNOF	MEGABUCKS
LAUNCHING	LOWERCASE	MICKASTON	MADRIGALS	MEGABYTES
LAUNDRESS	LOWERDECK	MACFADYEN	MUDDINESS	MAGICIANS
LAUNDERED	LOWESTOFT	MACEDOINE	MIDWIFERY	MAGICALLY
LAUNDERER	LOWSUNDAY	MACADAMIA	MIDWICKET	MOGADISHU
LOUGEHRIG	LUXURIATE	MACEDONIA	MIDWINTER	MAGNETISE
LOUNGEBAR	LUXURIANT	MACKENZIE	MIDDLEAGE	MAGNETITE
LAUGHABLE	LUXURIOUS	MACCHIATO	MUDDLEDUP	MAGNESIUM
LAUGHABLY	LEXLUTHOR	MUCKINESS	MIDDLEEAR	MAGNETISM
LOUTISHLY	LEYLANDII	MACHINERY	MODELLERS	MAGNETRON
LAURIELEE	LAYABOUTS	MUCKINGIN	MADELEINE	MAGDEBURG
LJUBLJANA	LAYREADER	MACHINING	MODELLING	MEGAHERTZ
LOUDMOUTH	LEYDENJAR	MACHINIST	MEDALLION	MUGGINESS
LEUCOCYTE	LOYALTIES	MACMILLAN	MEDALLIST	MAGNIFIED
LOUISIANA	LOYALISTS	MACKINLAY	MIDDLEMAN	MAGNIFICO
LEVIATHAN	LAYHOLDOF	MCCULLOCH	MIDDLEMEN	MAGNIFIER
LOVEAPPLE	LAYTOREST	MCCONNELL	MIDDLINGS	MAGNIFIES
LOVECHILD	LAYERCAKE	MACINTOSH	MIDDLESEX	MAGGIEMAY
LUVVIEDOM	LAZYBONES	MACDONALD	MIDDLETON	MAGNITUDE
LIVEINSIN	LAZARENKO	MICROWAVE	MADEMONEY	MEGALITHS
LEVELLERS	LIZFRASER	MACDOWELL	MCDONALDS	MEGANGALE
LIVELIEST	LAZARETTO	MICROCHIP	MODERNISE	MAGNOLIAS
LOVELIEST	LAZYSUSAN	MICROFILM	MODERNISM	MEGAPHONE
LEVELLING	LIZHURLEY	MACROCOSM	MODERNIST	MEGASTORE
LOVEMATCH	MIAFARROW	MICROCOSM	MODERNITY	MIGHTIEST
LOVINGCUP	MEANDERED	MICROPSIA	MODERATED	MAGNUSSON
LEVANTINE	MEATEATER	MACGREGOR	MODERATOR	MEGAWATTS
LIVERPOOL	MEANGIRLS	MUCKRAKER	MODERATES	MAGAZINES
LIVERWORT	MEATINESS	MCCARTNEY	MADESENSE	MAHARAJAS
LIVERSPOT	MIAMIVICE	MACAROONS	MIDSTREAM	MAHARANIS
LIVEROUGH	MYAINFOLK	MCCASKILL	MEDITATED	MAHARISHI
LIVESTOCK	MEANSTEST	MACQUARIE	MEDITATES	MOHSSCALE
LOVESTORY	MEASURING	MEDIATING	MIDSUMMER	MAIDAVALE
LEVITICUS	MEANWHILE	MEDIATION	MEERASYAL	MAINBRACE
LAWMAKING	MOBHANDED	MADEAMOVE	MEETINGUP	MAINEROAD
LOWSEASON	MOBILISED	MEDIATORS	MNEMONICS	MAINECOON

MAINFRAME	MALIGNING	MILITANCY	MANNERISM	MANFRIDAY
MEINKAMPF	MALIGNITY	MILKTOOTH	MINCEPIES	MANDRILLS
MAINLINES	MOLEHILLS	MILITARIA	MANNERIST	MINERVOIS
MAILMERGE	MALTHOUSE	MELTWATER	MANDERLEY	MINORSUIT
MAILORDER	MULTIPACK	MOLLYMAWK	MINNESOTA	MINESHAFT
MAIDSTONE	MULTITASK	MALAYSIAN	MANGETOUT	MINISTERS
MOISTNESS	MILLIPEDE	MALAYALAM	MONTERREY	MONASTERY
MAINTAINS	MILLINERS	MAMMALIAN	MONTEZUMA	MINUSSIGN
MOISTENED	MILLICENT	MIMICKERS	MANNEQUIN	MINISKIRT
MUJAHEDIN	MILLINERY	MIMICKING	MANOEUVRE	MONKSHOOD
MAJORDOMO	MOLLIFIED	MUMMIFIED	MANSFIELD	MINTSAUCE
MAJORETTE	MOLLIFIES	MOMENTARY	MINEFIELD	MINUSCULE
MAJORSUIT	MULTIPLEX	MOMENTOUS	MINDFULLY	MONOTREME
MAJUSCULE	MULLIONED	MEMORABLE	MANIFESTO	MINSTRELS
MAKEAPILE	MILLIONTH	MEMORABLY	MONOGRAPH	MINUTEMAN
MAKEAMOVE	MULTIFORM	MEMORANDA	MONOGRAMS	MENATWORK
MAKEFUNOF	MILLIGRAM	MEMORISED	MINDGAMES	MONSTROUS
MIKEMYERS	MELGIBSON	MEMORISES	MENAGERIE	MUNITIONS
MAKEMONEY	MULTITUDE	MANHANDLE	MINGHELLA	MONITORED
MAKEMERRY	MILKMAIDS	MANGANESE	MONKHOUSE	MENATARMS
MAKEPEACE	MILOMETER	MANYATIME	MENSHEVIK	MANCUNIAN
MAKEREADY	MALINGERS	MANEATING	MENDICANT	MONEYBAGS
MIKESMITH	MELLOWING	MANDARINS	MANLINESS	MOONBEAMS
MAKESHIFT	MELBOURNE	MENDACITY	MENTIONED	MOONBOOTS
MAKESENSE	MALVOISIE	MENTALITY	MONSIGNOR	MOOREHEAD
MIKETYSON	MALTREATS	MUNDANITY	MANTICORE	MOONFACED
MAKEUSEOF	MELBROOKS	MANGALORE	MINTJULEP	MOODINESS
MAKEWAVES	MILKROUND	MANDATORY	MONOLOGUE	MOONLIGHT
MILWAUKEE	MILKSHAKE	MONSARRAT	MONOLITHS	MOOLOOLAH
MALACHITE	MILKSNAKE	MANHATTAN	MINELAYER	MOOTPOINT
MCLACHLAN	MALTSTERS	MINIATURE	MINIMALLY	MOONRAKER
MOLECULAR	MOLESTING	MONTBLANC	MONOMANIA	MOONRIVER
MOLECULES	MILESTONE	MUNGBEANS	MONUMENTS	MOONSCAPE
MALICIOUS	MILLSTONE	MINIBUSES	MINIMISED	MOONSHINE
MELODRAMA	MILKSTOUT	MONICAALI	MINIMISES	MOONSTONE
MELODIOUS	MILESAWAY	MONOCULAR	MANOMETER	MAPMAKING
MALADROIT	MILKTRAIN	MANICALLY	MANENOUGH	MAPLELEAF
MALLEABLE	MILKTEETH	MUNICIPAL	MANTOVANI	MAPPEDOUT
MILLENNIA	MULETEERS	MANICOTTI	MONGOLIAN	MOPPINGUP
MILKFLOAT	MALATHION	MINIDRESS	MONGOOSES	MARMALADE
MALIGNANT	MELATONIN	MINCEMEAT	MONOPLANE	MARRAKESH
MALAGUENA	MILITANTS	MANNERING	MENOPAUSE	MARGARITA

MARCASITE	MARYJANES	MUSICHALL	MUSCLEDIN	MATCHLESS
MARGARINE	MORALISED	MUSICIANS	MUSCLEMAN	MATCHPLAY
MORTALITY	MORALISER	MASOCHISM	MUSCLESIN	MATCHWOOD
MORTALSIN	MORALISES	MASOCHIST	MISTLETOE	MATCHBOOK
MERGANSER	MORALISTS	MUSICALLY	MASSMEDIA	METRICATE
MARYASTOR	MARINATED	MISBEHAVE	MUSKMELON	MATRICIDE
MIRABELLE	MARINATES	MUSKETEER	MESOMORPH	MATRIMONY
MORECAMBE	MERINGUES	MASTERFUL	MESSMATES	MATRIARCH
MARKCURRY	MARMOLADA	MESSENGER	MISINFORM	METRICTON
MERCENARY	MARMOREAL	MESMERISE	MUSCOVADO	MATTJAMES
MARKETDAY	MARMOSETS	MISBELIEF	MISGOVERN	METALWARE
MARKETEER	MARROWFAT	MASTERING	MUSCOVITE	MATTLUCAS
MURDERERS	MAROONING	MUSTERING	MUSSOLINI	METALLICA
MURDERESS	MIRRORING	MESMERISM	MRSNORRIS	METALWORK
MURDERINC	MORMONISM	MYSTERIES	MISSPIGGY	METALIOUS
MARKETING	MARCOPOLO	MESMERIST	MISTREATS	MUTILATED
MURDERING	MARIOPUZO	MASTERKEY	MISCREANT	MUTILATES
MARKEDMAN	MARYQUANT	MYSTERONS	MISERABLE	MATTMONRO
MARIEROSE	MARGRETHE	MISSEDOUT	MISERABLY	MUTINEERS
MORSECODE	MARESNEST	MASTERSON	MUSHROOMS	METROLAND
MARKEDOFF	MARKTWAIN	MASSEUSES	MISTRUSTS	METEORITE
MURDEROUS	MARYTUDOR	MRSBEETON	MISGUIDED	METHODISM
MORTENSEN	MARATHONS	MRSMERTON	MISJUDGED	METHODIST
MARIGOLDS	MORATORIA	MASEFIELD	MISJUDGES	METRONOME
MARSHLAND	MARAUDERS	MISSHAPEN	MASCULINE	METROPOLE
MARCHHARE	MURMURERS	MASTICATE	MRSHUDSON	MYTHOLOGY
MARCHPAST	MARAUDING	MESSINESS	MISQUOTED	METERMAID
MIRTHLESS	MURMURING	MISTINESS	MOSQUITOS	MOTORCADE
MERCHANTS	MARSUPIAL	MUSHINESS	MISSWORLD	MATERIALS
MARTINETS	MERCURIAL	MUSKINESS	METHADONE	MOTORWAYS
MERCILESS	MARQUETRY	MUSTINESS	METABOLIC	MOTORHEAD
MURKINESS	MARTYRDOM	MISDIRECT	MOTHBALLS	MOTORSHOW
MERRIMENT	MERRYXMAS	MASSIVELY	MOTOCROSS	MOTORBIKE
MARRIAGES	MISMANAGE	MESSINGUP	MATTDAMON	MATERNITY
MORTIFIED	MISHANDLE	MYSTIFIED	MUTTERERS	MOTORHOME
MORTICIAN	MESSALINA	MISTIMING	MATTERING	MOTORBOAT
MORTIFIES	MASSAGING	MYSTICISM	MOTHERING	MOTORISED
MORBIDITY	MISLAYING	MYSTIFIES	MUTTERING	MOTORISTS
MARTINMAS	MISTAKING	MESSIANIC	METHEGLIN	MOTIVATED
MARDIGRAS	MESSABOUT	MESSIEURS	MOTHEATEN	MOTIVATOR
MORRISSEY	MASSACRED	MISPLACED	MITIGATED	MOTIVATES
MARIJUANA	MASSACRES	MISPLACES	MITIGATES	MOULDINGS

MOUSEHARE	NOCONTEST	NIHILISTS	NEONLIGHT	NATHANIEL
MOUSEDEER	NICKNOLTE	NUISANCES	NEOLOGISM	NOTEBOOKS
MOUSEHOLE	NICKNAMES	NAILBRUSH	NEOLOGIST	NOTREDAME
MOUSETRAP	NICHOLSON	NOISELESS	NOPROBLEM	NATTERING
MOUTHWASH	NICARAGUA	NOISESOFF	NEPOTISTS	NOTNEARLY
MOUSINESS	NECESSARY	NEIGHBOUR	NAPPYRASH	NOTIFYING
MAURITIUS	NECESSITY	NEILINNES	NORMAJEAN	NUTSHELLS
MOUSKOURI	NICOTIANA	NEILSIMON	NARRATIVE	NUTRIMENT
MAUSOLEUM	NOCTURNAL	NEILYOUNG	NORMALISE	NOTLIKELY
MAULSTICK	NOCTURNES	NUKUALOFA	NARRATING	NUTRITION
MEURSAULT	NODDEDOFF	NAKEDNESS	NARRATION	NITPICKER
MOUSTACHE	NEDBEATTY	NOKIDDING	NORMALITY	NUTRIENTS
MOUNTAINS	NEEDINESS	NULLARBOR	NARRATORS	NETANYAHU
MOUNTETNA	NEEDSMUST	NULLIFIED	NORMANTON	NETWORKER
MOVIEGOER	NIETZSCHE	NULLIFIES	NORABATTY	NOTEPAPER
MOVEMENTS	NIFTINESS	NAMECHECK	NURSEMAID	NOTORIETY
MAVERICKS	NEFERTITI	NUMBERING	NERVELESS	NETPROFIT
MAWKISHLY	NEFARIOUS	NUMBERONE	NORWEGIAN	NATURALLY
MCWHIRTER	NOFLYZONE	NUMBERTEN	NURSERIES	NOTORIOUS
MAXFACTOR	NIGGARDLY	NUMBERTWO	NOREGRETS	NATURISTS
MAXMILLER	NOGOAREAS	NUMSKULLS	NORTHWARD	NOTPROVEN
MAXIMISED	NEGLECTED	NOMINALLY	NORTHEAST	NETSURFER
MAXIMISES	NEGLIGEES	NAMENAMES	NORTHWEST	NUTCUTLET
MAXFRISCH	NEGLIGENT	NOMINATED	NORTHPOLE	NOTGUILTY
MAYBEBABY	NIGELBENN	NOMINATOR	NORTHERLY	NEURALGIA
MAYFLOWER	NIGELREES	NOMINATES	NORTHSTAR	NAUSEATED
MAYERLING	NIGELBOND	NAMEPLATE	NARCISSUS	NAUSEATES
MEZZANINE	NEGOTIATE	NUMERICAL	NUREMBERG	NAUGHTIER
MUZZINESS	NIGHTMARE	NUMERATOR	NARROWEST	NAUGHTILY
MEZZOTINT	NIGHTSAFE	NUMEROUNO	NARROWING	NOURISHED
NYASALAND	NIGHTHAWK	NONPAREIL	NARCOTICS	NOURISHES
NOAHBEERY	NIGHTFALL	NONMEMBER	NERVOUSLY	NEUROLOGY
NEATENING	NIGHTMAIL	NUNNERIES	NURTURING	NEUTRALLY
NEAPTIDES	NIGHTJARS	NINEHOLES	NOSTALGIA	NOVOCAINE
NEARTHING	NIGHTWEAR	NINELIVES	NOSTALGIC	NAVIGABLE
NOBRAINER	NIGHTLIFE	NONSMOKER	NOSEBLEED	NAVIGATED
NEBULISER	NIGHTTIME	NONENTITY	NOSFERATU	NAVIGATOR
NECTARINE	NIGHTCLUB	NINOTCHKA	NISSENHUT	NAVIGATES
NICKBERRY	NIGHTGOWN	NANTUCKET	NASTINESS	NOVELTIES
NICKFALDO	NIGHTSPOT	NANNYGOAT	NESTLINGS	NOVELISTS
NECKLACES	NEGATIVES	NEOPHYTES	NOSMOKING	NOVELETTE
NOCOMMENT	NOHIGHWAY	NEOLITHIC	NASHVILLE	NEVERFEAR

NEVERMIND	OCCULTISM	OPENENDED	OVERSHOES	ORGANISER
NEVERMORE	OCCULTIST	OVEREXERT	OVERSHOOT	ORGANISES
NOVITIATE	OCCUPIERS	OVEREAGER	OVERTRAIN	ORGANISMS
NEWSAGENT	OCCUPYING	OMELETTES	OVERTHERE	ORGANISTS
NEWMARKET	OCCUPANTS	OPERETTAS	OVERTRICK	ONHOLIDAY
NEWCASTLE	OCCUPANCY	OVERFEEDS	OVERTAKEN	OTHERHALF
NEWMEXICO	OCCURRING	OVENGLOVE	OVERTAKES	OTHERNESS
NEWJERSEY	OCCASIONS	OVERGROWN	OVERTIRED	OTHERWISE
NEWSFLASH	OCCLUDING	OVERHEARD	OVERTURES	OLIGARCHY
NEWSGROUP	OCCLUSION	OVERHEARS	OVERTURNS	OXIDATION
NEWSHOUND	ONDRAUGHT	OVERHANGS	OVERTHROW	OVIPAROUS
NEWSNIGHT	OLDBAILEY	OPENHOUSE	OVERUSING	OLIVEDRAB
NEWCOMERS	ODDMANOUT	OVERHAULS	OVERVALUE	ORIGINATE
NEWFOREST	OLDMASTER	OBEDIENCE	OVERWHELM	ORIGINALS
NEWYORKER	OLDSCHOOL	OVERJOYED	OVERWRITE	OXIDISING
NEWSPRINT	ORDAINING	OVERLOADS	OVERWOUND	OPIUMWARS
NEWSPAPER	ORDINANCE	OVERLADEN	OFFHANDED	ORIENTATE
NEWTRICKS	ODDONEOUT	OVERLOOKS	OFFCAMERA	ORIENTEER
NEWSROUND	ODDJOBMAN	ONEANDALL	OFFTARGET	ONIONDOME
NEWSSTAND	ORDERLIES	OVERNIGHT	OFFICIATE	OMINOUSLY
NEWSSHEET	ORDERFORM	OWENNARES	OFFICIALS	OFITSKIND
NEWSTREET	OLDSTAGER	OVERPRICE	OFFICIANT	OBJECTIVE
NEWGUINEA	ODDNUMBER	OVERPRINT	OFFICIOUS	OBJECTING
NEWLYWEDS	OPERATIVE	OVENPROOF	OLFACTORY	OBJECTION
NEXTOFKIN	OPERATING	OVERPOWER	OFFSEASON	OBJECTIFY
NEXTWORLD	OPERATION	OVERREACH	OFFTHEAIR	OBJETDART
ORANGEADE	OPERATICS	OVERREACT	OFFTHEMAP	OILTANKER
ORANGEMAN	OPENABOOK	OVENREADY	OFFSHOOTS	OILPAINTS
ORANGUTAN	OPERATORS	OVERRULED	OFFTHEPEG	OOLOGISTS
ODALISQUE	OVERACTED	OVERRULES	OFFLIMITS	OBLIGATED
OFALLTIME	OVERBOARD	OPENRANGE	OFFENBACH	OBLIGATES
ORATORIOS	OVERBLOWN	OVERRATED	OFFENDERS	OILFILTER
ONASTRING	OVERCOATS	OVERRATES	OFFENSIVE	ONLOOKERS
OMBUDSMAN	OVERCOMES	OVERSTATE	OFFENDING	OBLIQUELY
OBBLIGATO	OVERCLOUD	OVERSPEND	OFFLOADED	OBLIVIOUS
OUBLIETTE	OVERCROWD	OVERSLEEP	OFFCOLOUR	ONMESSAGE
ONBALANCE	OVERDRAWN	OVERSTEER	OFFCOURSE	OMNIBUSES
OHBROTHER	OVERDRAFT	OVERSEERS	OFFSPRING	OINTMENTS
OXBOWLAKE	OVERDRESS	OVERSLEPT	OFFERTORY	ORNAMENTS
ONCEAGAIN	OVERDRIVE	OVERSIGHT	OBFUSCATE	OENOPHILE
ORCHESTRA	OVERDOING	OVERSPILL	ORGANZINE	OWNERLESS
OSCILLATE	OKEYDOKEY	OBEISANCE	ORGANISED	OWNERSHIP

OMNIVORES	OPTICALLY	OPTOMETRY	PLAYBYEAR	PRATTLING
OBNOXIOUS	ONTHEWANE	OCTENNIAL	PLAYBILLS	PLASTERED
ODOURLESS	ONTHEBALL	OPTINGOUT	PLAYDIRTY	PLASTERER
ORPHANAGE	ONTHENAIL	OUTANDOUT	PLACECARD	PRACTISED
OPPRESSED	ONTHEMEND	ORTANIQUE	PLACENAME	PRACTISES
OPPRESSOR	OUTWEIGHS	OSTEOPATH	PLANETARY	PUBLICANS
OPPRESSES	ONTHERISE	OUTWORKER	PEACEABLE	PUBLICBAR
OPPONENTS	ONTHESIDE	OUTGOINGS	PEACEPIPE	PUBLISHED
ORPINGTON	ONTHEWING	ORTHODOXY	PLACEMENT	PUBLISHER
ONPURPOSE	ONTHEROAD	OSTEOLOGY	PEACETIME	PUBLISHES
OPPORTUNE	ONTHEBONE	OUTSOURCE	PLACEKICK	PUBLICISE
OURFATHER	ONTHEDOLE	OUTDOORSY	PEACESIGN	PUBLICIST
OURSELVES	ONTHEMOVE	OUTHOUSES	PHASEDOUT	PUBLICITY
OARSWOMAN	ONTHENOSE	OUTSPREAD	PLAYEDOUT	PUBCRAWLS
OARSWOMEN	ONTHEHOOF	OUTSPOKEN	PRAYERRUG	PUBESCENT
ONSTANDBY	ONTHEHORN	OPTOPHONE	PLAYFALSE	PACKAGING
ONSLAUGHT	ONTHETOWN	ONTIPTOES	PLAYFULLY	PECCARIES
OBSTACLES	ONTHEHOUR	OCTOPUSES	PLATFORMS	PICKALOCK
OBSCENELY	ONTHESPOT	OCTOPUSSY	PLAYGROUP	PACKDRILL
OBSCENITY	ONTHETROT	OUTBREAKS	PLAYHOUSE	POCKETFUL
OBSTETRIC	OUTOFDATE	OUTERMOST	PLATITUDE	PICKETING
OSSIFYING	OUTOFWORK	OUTSTRIPS	PRANKSTER	POCKETING
OASTHOUSE	OUTOFFORM	OCTOTHORP	PEARLISED	PUCKERING
OBSTINATE	OUTOFTRUE	OUTSTAYED	PEARLBUCK	PACKEDOUT
OBSTINACY	OUTOFSTEP	OUTNUMBER	PTARMIGAN	PICKEDOUT
OBSEQUIES	OUTOFTUNE	OBTRUSIVE	PEARMAINS	PACIFIERS
OBSERVANT	OUTOFSYNC	OUTBURSTS	PSALMISTS	PACIFYING
OBSTRUCTS	OCTAGONAL	OUTHWAITE	PRAGMATIC	PACIFISTS
OBSERVERS	OUTSIDEOF	OVULATION	PLAYMATES	PACKHORSE
OESTROGEN	OUTRIDERS	OPULENTLY	PLAINJANE	PACKINGUP
OBSERVING	OUTSIDERS	OLUCKYMAN	PLAINNESS	PICNICKED
OBSESSIVE	OUTRIGGER	OSULLIVAN	PLAINTIVE	PICNICKER
OBSESSING	OSTRICHES	OBVIATING	PLAINTIFF	PECKINPAH
OBSESSION	ONTHINICE	OBVIOUSLY	PLAINSONG	PACEMAKER
OBSCURELY	OBTAINING	OXYGENATE	PIANOROLL	POCKMARKS
OBSCURING	OUTWITTED	ONYOUROWN	PEASOUPER	PECUNIARY
OBSCURITY	OUTFITTER	PHALANGER	PLAUSIBLE	PECTORALS
OUTWARDLY	OUTSKIRTS	PLACATING	PLAUSIBLY	PICTORIAL
OSTRACISE	OUTPLAYED	PHALAROPE	PRACTICAL	PACHYDERM
OSTRACISM	OUTSMARTS	PLAYALONG	PLASTICKY	PEDAGOGIC
OUTLASTED	OPTIMISED	PLACATORY	PRATTLERS	PEDAGOGUE
OPTICIANS	OPTIMISTS	PEASANTRY	PLAYTHING	PODGINESS

PUDGINESS	PRESERVES	PREJUDGED	POIGNANCY	POLICEMAN
PEDALLERS	PEERGROUP	PREJUDGES	POISONERS	POLICEMEN
PEDALLING	PRESHRUNK	PREJUDICE	PRISONERS	PILFERAGE
PEDOMETER	PREDICATE	PRESUMING	POISONING	PILFERERS
PEDESTALS	PRECINCTS	PRECURSOR	POISONIVY	PULVERISE
PREVALENT	PRESIDENT	PUFFADDER	POISONOUS	PILFERING
PREDATING	PRECISELY	PUFFINESS	PHILOLOGY	POLYESTER
PREPARING	PEEVISHLY	PYGMALION	POISONPEN	POLYGRAPH
PREDATION	POETICISE	PUGNACITY	PRIMROSES	POLYGONAL
PREPACKED	PRECIPICE	PIGFARMER	PRIESTESS	POLYGLOTS
PREVAILED	PRESIDING	PAGEANTRY	PRIESTLEY	PILCHARDS
PREDATORS	PRESIDIUM	PIGHEADED	PLIMSOLLS	PALPITATE
PREDATORY	PRECISION	PEGGEDOUT	PRIESTLEY	POLLINATE
POETASTER	PUERILITY	PUGILISTS	PUISSANCE	PULLINGIN
PREMATURE	PREMIERES	PAGINATED	PAINTBALL	PULLINGUP
PRESBYOPE	PREDICTED	PAGINATES	PRINTABLE	PALLIASSE
PRESBYTER	PREDICTOR	POGOSTICK	POINTEDLY	PALMISTRY
PREACHERS	PLENITUDE	PAGETHREE	POINTLESS	POLEMICAL
PRESCIENT	PREFIGURE	PIGGYBACK	PAINTSHOP	PALOMINOS
PRESCRIBE	PRECLUDED	PIGGYBANK	PAINTINGS	POLYMATHS
PREACHING	PRECLUDES	PHILANDER	PAINTWORK	POLONECKS
PREACHIFY	PNEUMONIA	PRIMAVERA	POINTDUTY	POLONAISE
PRESCHOOL	PNEUMATIC	PRIVATEER	PRIVYSEAL	POLYNESIA
PREOCCUPY	PREGNANCY	PHILATELY	POKEFUNAT	PALANQUIN
PSEUDONYM	PTEROSAUR	PRIVATELY	PEKINGMAN	PULMONARY
PLEBEIANS	PREMOLARS	PRIVATISE	POKERFACE	PULLOVERS
PRETENDED	PHENOMENA	PRIVATION	POKERDICE	PILLORIED
PRETENDER	PRECOCITY	PRIMARILY	PIKESTAFF	PALERIDER
PIECEMEAL	PRECOOKED	PRISCILLA	PAKISTANI	POLARBEAR
PRECEDENT	PHEROMONE	PRINCIPLE	PILLARBOX	POLARISED
PRESELECT	PIEDPIPER	PRINCIPAL	POLYANDRY	POLARISES
PRECEDING	PRESSGANG	PRINCETON	PILLAGERS	POLARSTAR
PIECEWORK	PRESSEDON	PHILDAVIS	PILLAGING	PALISADES
PREFERRED	PLEASENCE	PRICETAGS	PULSATING	POLLSTERS
PRESEASON	PHEASANTS	PRICELESS	PALLADIUM	PALESTINE
PREHEATED	PRESSURED	PRIMETIME	PELMANISM	POLISHING
PRESENTED	PRESSURES	PRICELIST	PALLADIAN	POLOSHIRT
PREVENTED	PLEASESIR	PAINFULLY	POLKADOTS	PALATABLE
PRESENTER	PRESSSTUD	PRIVILEGE	PALMBEACH	POLITICAL
PRESENTLY	PRETTIEST	PRIMITIVE	PHLEBITIS	POLYTHENE
PRESERVED	PLENTIFUL	PHILLIPPE	POLICEBOX	PILOTBIRD
PRESERVER	PLENTEOUS	PRISMATIC	POLICECAR	PILOTFISH

POLITESSE	PANTHEISM	PENNYLANE	PROPHETIC	PROSPERED
POLITBURO	PANTHEIST	PENNYWISE	POORHOUSE	PROCREATE
PULLULATE	PUNCHBOWL	PANTYHOSE	PROVINCES	PROTRACTS
POLLUTANT	PANKHURST	PENNYPOST	PROFITEER	PROTRUDED
POLLUTERS	PENTHOUSE	PROPAGATE	PROMINENT	PROTRUDES
POLLUTING	PENNILESS	PROBATION	PROVIDENT	PROPRIETY
POLLUTION	PENSIVELY	PROFANITY	PROFILING	PLOWRIGHT
POLEVAULT	PENCILLED	PROACTIVE	PROFITING	PROGRAMME
POLLYANNA	PENSIONER	PROSCRIBE	PROMISING	PROSTRATE
POMPADOUR	PANELGAME	PHONECARD	PROVIDING	PRODUCERS
PAMPERING	PANELLING	PROMENADE	PROVISION	PROFUSELY
PUMMELLED	PENALTIES	PROVENCAL	PRODIGIES	PROCURING
PIMPERNEL	PANELLIST	PROCEEDED	PROHIBITS	PRODUCING
PAMFERRIS	PENALISED	PROVENDER	PROXIMITY	PROFUSION
PEMBERTON	PENALISES	PROTEGEES	PSORIASIS	PROPYLENE
PAMPHLETS	PHNOMPENH	PHONETICS	PROCLAIMS	PIPEDREAM
PUMPINGUP	PANAMAHAT	PROPELLED	PROGNOSIS	PUPPETEER
POMANDERS	PENANDINK	PROPELLER	PHOTOCALL	PEPPERING
POMPOSITY	PENINSULA	PHONEBOOK	PROPOSALS	POPRECORD
POMPOUSLY	PENKNIVES	PIONEERED	PROBOSCIS	PEPPERONI
PANHANDLE	PENHOLDER	PROCESSED	PROPOSERS	PEPPERPOT
PENTANGLE	PANTOMIME	PROFESSED	PROPONENT	POPULARLY
PINNACLES	PENFRIEND	PROCESSOR	PROLONGED	POPULISTS
PANTALOON	PENDRAGON	PROFESSOR	PROMOTING	POPULATED
PINEAPPLE	PANORAMIC	PROCESSES	PROPOSING	POPULATES
PENTAGRAM	PENURIOUS	PROFESSES	PROVOKING	PIPINGHOT
PINOCCHIO	PUNISHING	PROJECTED	PROMOTION	PIPEORGAN
PANICKING	PINTSIZED	PROTECTED	PROKOFIEV	PIPSQUEAK
PANICROOM	PENETRATE	PROTESTED	PRONOUNCE	PAPAROACH
PANDERING	PUNCTUATE	PROJECTOR	PROPOUNDS	PAPERBACK
PONDERING	PINSTRIPE	PROTECTOR	PHOTOCOPY	PAPERCLIP
PENDENNIS	PANATELLA	PROTESTER	PHONOGRAM	PAPERWORK
PONDEROSA	PENITENCE	PROCEDURE	PROCONSUL	PAPERMOON
PONDEROUS	PENITENTS	PROSECUTE	PHOTOSTAT	PAPEROVER
PENTECOST	PANETTONE	PHONEYWAR	PROROGUED	PAPARAZZI
PINKERTON	PINOTNOIR	PROSELYTE	PROROGUES	PAPARAZZO
PINKFLOYD	PUNCTURED	PROOFREAD	PROTOTYPE	PUPPYLOVE
PINAFORES	PUNCTURES	PROFFERED	PHOSPHATE	POPPYCOCK
PANEGYRIC	PINNUMBER	PYONGYANG	PROSPECTS	PERMANENT
PUNCHBALL	PENPUSHER	PLOUGHING	PROPPEDUP	PERCAPITA
PINCHBECK	PENDULOUS	PLOUGHMAN	PROMPTERS	PERVASIVE
PUNCHLINE	PENDULUMS	PLOUGHMEN	PROMPTING	PURGATIVE

PARTAKING	PURCHASED	PORTOFINO	PARTYLINE	PASTTENSE
PERVADING	PURCHASER	PERSONIFY	PERRYCOMO	POSITIONS
PERVASION	PURCHASES	PARBOILED	PARTYGOER	POSTULATE
PERTAINED	PARTISANS	PERFORMED	PISTACHIO	POSTULANT
PERFAVORE	PERKINESS	PERFORMER	PUSHCHAIR	POSTWOMAN
PURGATORY	PERTINENT	PURLOINED	POSTCARDS	POSTWOMEN
PARNASSUS	PORRINGER	PERSONNEL	PASODOBLE	PUSSYCATS
PARKBENCH	PARTITION	PARTOWNER	POSTDATED	PUSSYFOOT
PAROCHIAL	PERDITION	PORPOISES	POSTDATES	PUTPAIDTO
PARACHUTE	PARTICLES	PURPORTED	PASDEDEUX	PUTACROSS
PARODYING	PARTIALLY	PERIPHERY	PASSENGER	POTTERERS
PARODISTS	PERSIMMON	PERSPIRED	PASSERINE	PUTREFIED
PORTERAGE	PERPIGNAN	PORTPIRIE	PESTERING	POTTERING
PORCELAIN	PARSIMONY	PERSPIRES	POSTERIOR	POTTERIES
PERMEABLE	PARKINSON	PARTRIDGE	POSTERITY	PUTREFIES
PORTENDED	PERMITTED	PORTRAITS	PASTERNAK	PATTERSON
PERSEVERE	PERSISTED	PERORATED	PASSEDOUT	PATIENTLY
PORBEAGLE	PARAKEETS	PERORATES	POSSESSED	PITIFULLY
PURVEYING	PORTLIEST	PORTRAYED	POSSESSOR	POTOFGOLD
PARCELLED	PARALYSED	PARKROYAL	POSSESSES	PATAGONIA
PURVEYORS	PARALYSES	PORTRAYAL	PASSERSBY	PITCHEDIN
PERFECTED	PARALYSIS	PERISHERS	POSTHASTE	PATCHEDUP
PERMEATED	PORTLOUIS	PERISHING	POSTHOUSE	PATCHTEST
PERVERTED	PERPLEXED	PORTSALUT	PUSHINESS	PATCHWORK
PARGETTER	PERPLEXES	PERISCOPE	PESTILENT	PITCHFORK
PERMEATES	PARAMEDIC	PARASITIC	PASSIVELY	PATCHOULI
PERFECTLY	PYRAMIDAL	PARASITES	PASSINGBY	PITUITARY
PERSECUTE	PYROMANIA	PIRATICAL	PESTICIDE	PETTINESS
PERPETUAL	PARAMETER	PARTTIMER	PASSIVISM	PITHINESS
PERCEIVED	PERIMETER	PERTURBED	PESSIMISM	PUTTINGBY
PERCEIVES	PARAMOURS	PERSUADED	POSTILION	PETRIFIED
PURIFYING	PARAMOUNT	PERSUADES	PASSIVIST	PATRICIDE
PORTFOLIO	PARENTAGE	PERJURERS	PESSIMIST	PETHIDINE
PARAGRAPH	PARENTING	PERFUMERY	PASSIVITY	PETRIDISH
PEREGRINE	PERENNIAL	PORCUPINE	PASTILLES	PATRICIAN
PARCHMENT	PERINATAL	PERJURING	PISCIVORE	PETRIFIES
PORTHOLES	PARSONAGE	PURSUANCE	POSTNATAL	PETTICOAT
PERCHANCE	PERCOLATE	PERTUSSIS	PASTORALE	PATRIMONY
PARTHENON	PERFORATE	PIROUETTE	POSTPONED	PATRIARCH
PORPHYRIA	PERSONAGE	PARQUETRY	POSTPONES	PATRIOTIC
PERCHERON	PURPOSELY	PARTYWALL	PASSPORTS	PETULANCE
PARKHURST	PARDONING	PERCYSHAW	PUSHSTART	POTENTATE

PATENTEES	PRUDISHLY	QUADRILLE	REANIMATE	RACIALIST
PATENTING	PRURIENCE	QUARRYMAN	READINESS	RECLAIMED
POTENTIAL	PAULJONES	QUARRYMEN	REALISING	RECLAIMER
PATRONAGE	PLUCKIEST	QUADRANTS	REALISTIC	RICOCHETS
PETROLCAN	PLUMMETED	QUADRUPED	REALITYTV	RECYCLING
PATROLCAR	PLUTONIUM	QUADRUPLE	READJUSTS	RECHERCHE
PETROLEUM	PLUTOCRAT	QUADRATIC	REARLIGHT	RACKETEER
POTHOLERS	PLUMPNESS	QUANTOCKS	ROADMETAL	ROCKETING
PATRONISE	PAULSHANE	QUARTERED	ROADMOVIE	RICHELIEU
POTHOLING	PAULSIMON	QUARTERLY	RYANONEAL	ROCKETMAN
PATROLLED	PAULSCOTT	QUENCHING	REASONING	RECREATED
POTBOILER	POULTERER	QUEUINGUP	REAPPEARS	ROCHESTER
PATROLMAN	PAULYOUNG	QUEENMARY	REAPPOINT	RECREATES
PATROLMEN	PAVILIONS	QUEENANNE	REARRANGE	RACEGOERS
PATCOOMBS	PAVEMENTS	QUESTIONS	RHAPSODIC	RECOGNISE
PATIODOOR	PAVAROTTI	QUERULOUS	ROADSTEAD	RACEHORSE
PUTTOROUT	POWDERING	QUIBBLERS	ROADSTERS	RECEIVERS
PATHOLOGY	POWDERKEG	QUIBBLING	REASSURED	RECLINERS
POTPOURRI	POWERPACK	QUIDDITCH	REASSURES	RECTIFIED
PETERFALK	POWERLESS	QUITEABIT	ROADTRAIN	RECEIVING
PETERWEIR	POWERPLAY	QUITEAFEW	ROASTBEEF	RECLINING
PETEREGAN	POWERBOAT	QUIVERING	REALTHING	RECOILING
PETERSHAM	PAWNSHOPS	QUITEALOT	ROADTORIO	RECTIFIER
PATERNITY	PIXILATED	QUICKSAND	ROADTESTS	RECTIFIES
PETERSNOW	PAYPACKET	QUICKFIRE	ROASTDUCK	RECTITUDE
PETERCOOK	PAYMASTER	QUICKLIME	ROADWORKS	RECOLLECT
POTASSIUM	PAYDEARLY	QUICKENED	READYMADE	RECALLING
PETITFOUR	PSYCHEDUP	QUICKENUP	ROBBERIES	RECOMMEND
PETITIONS	PSYCHOSIS	QUICKSTEP	REBBETZIN	RECUMBENT
PETRUSHKA	PHYSICIAN	QUIPSTERS	REBUFFING	ROCKMELON
PETRUCHIO	PHYSICIST	QUIESCENT	REBELYELL	RACINGCAR
PETTYCASH	PAYINGOUT	QUIZZICAL	REBELLING	RECONVENE
PLURALISM	PIZZERIAS	QUOTATION	REBELLION	RACONTEUR
PLURALIST	PIZZICATO	QUOTIDIAN	ROBINHOOD	RECONNECT
PLUMBLINE	QUAFFABLE	READALOUD	ROBINCOOK	RECONCILE
POUNDCAKE	QUALIFIED	ROADBLOCK	ROBERTSON	RECONDITE
PAULDACRE	QUALIFIER	ROALDDAHL	ROBOTWARS	RECANTING
PLUNDERED	QUALIFIES	READDRESS	REBUTTING	RECKONERS
PLUNDERER	QUALITIES	REARGUARD	REBOUNDED	RECKONING
PRUDENTLY	QUASIMODO	RYANGIGGS	RECHARGED	RECROSSED
PLUSFOURS	QUARRYING	REACHABLE	RECTANGLE	RECIPIENT
PAULHOGAN	QUATRAINS	ROADHOUSE	RECHARGES	RECEPTIVE

RECAPPING	REDDEVILS	RHEOSTATS	RAGROLLED	RAINWATER
RECEPTION	REDPEPPER	REEDUCATE	REGROUPED	REJECTING
RICEPAPER	REDRESSED	REFRAINED	REGARDING	REJECTION
RECAPTURE	REDRESSES	REFRACTED	REGISSEUR	REJIGGING
RECORDERS	REDCENTRE	REFRACTOR	REGISTERS	REJOINDER
RECURRENT	REDSETTER	REFECTION	REGISTRAR	REJOICING
RECORDING	RODOFIRON	REFECTORY	RIGHTHAND	REJOINING
RECURRING	REDSHANKS	REFRESHED	RIGHTBACK	RAJASTHAN
RECORDIST	RODLIDDLE	REFRESHER	RIGHTNESS	RIKMAYALL
RICKSHAWS	RUDDINESS	REFRESHES	RIGHTWING	REKINDLED
RUCKSACKS	RUDDIGORE	REFLEXIVE	RIGHTEOUS	REKINDLES
RICKSTEIN	RADCLIFFE	REFUELLED	RIGHTAWAY	ROKERPARK
RECESSIVE	REDOLENCE	REFLECTED	RUGBYBALL	RELEASING
ROCKSLIDE	REDPLANET	REFLECTOR	REHEATING	RELUCTANT
RECESSION	RUDIMENTS	REFULGENT	REHEARSED	RELOCATED
ROCKSOLID	REDUNDANT	REFILLING	REHEARSAL	RELOCATES
RACETRACK	REDENSIGN	REFUNDING	REHEARSES	RELIEVING
RECLUSIVE	RADIOGAGA	REFORMERS	REHYDRATE	RELIEFMAP
RECOUPING	RADIODAYS	REFERRING	REHOUSING	RELIGIOUS
RECOUNTED	RADIOHEAD	REFORMING	RUINATION	RELEGATED
RECRUITED	RADIOLOGY	REFURBISH	REIMBURSE	RELEGATES
RECOVERED	RADIOGRAM	REFURNISH	RAINCOATS	RELYINGON
REDHANDED	REDEPLOYS	REFORMISM	RAINCHECK	ROLLINGUP
RADIATING	REDSQUARE	REFORMIST	RAINCLOUD	ROLEMODEL
REDRAWING	REDBREAST	REFERENDA	RAINDROPS	RELENTING
RADIATION	REDIRECTS	REFERENCE	REITERATE	RULINGOUT
REDSALMON	RIDERLESS	REFUSENIK	RAISECAIN	RULEOFLAW
RADIATORS	REDDRAGON	REGVARNEY	RAISEHELL	RELAPSING
REDCARPET	RADARTRAP	RIGMAROLE	RAINEDOFF	RELIQUARY
RADIANTLY	REDGROUSE	REGRETFUL	REINFORCE	RELISHING
RADICCHIO	REDESIGNS	REGRESSED	RAINGAUGE	RELETTING
REDUCTION	REDSTARTS	REGRESSES	REICHSTAG	RELATIONS
RIDICULED	REDMULLET	REGRETTED	RAINMAKER	RELATIVES
RIDICULES	REDDUSTER	ROGUISHLY	RHINOLOGY	RELEVANCE
RADICALLY	REDEVELOP	REGAINING	RUINOUSLY	RELAYRACE
RIDGEBACK	REEXAMINE	REGULARLY	RAINPROOF	RAMRAIDER
REDBERETS	REENACTED	REGULATED	REINSTATE	RAMPAGING
REDEEMERS	REELECTED	RIGOLETTO	REISSUING	RUMMAGING
RIDGETENT	REECHOING	REGULATOR	RAINSTORM	RAMPANTLY
RIDGETILE	REEDINESS	REGULATES	ROISTERED	REMEDYING
REDDENING	RHEUMATIC	REGIMENTS	ROISTERER	REMAINDER
REDEEMING	RHEOMETER	ROGANJOSH	REINVESTS	REMAINING

RAMILLIES	RENOUNCES	REPAIRMAN	RESTARTED	RESURRECT
REMEMBERS	RENOVATED	REPAIRMEN	ROSEBYRNE	RESERVING
REMINDERS	RENOVATES	REPRINTED	RASPBERRY	RESTRAINS
REMANDING	RENEWABLE	REPRIEVED	ROSACEOUS	RESERVIST
REMINDING	RUNNYMEDE	REPRIEVES	RESIDENCE	RESTRAINT
ROMANCING	ROOTCANAL	REPELLENT	RESIDENTS	RESERVOIR
ROMANTICS	ROOTCAUSE	REPULSIVE	RESIDENCY	ROSEROYCE
RUMINANTS	REORDERED	REPELLING	RESPECTED	RESISTANT
ROMANROAD	ROOSEVELT	REPULSING	RESGESTAE	RESISTING
ROMANNOSE	REOPENING	REPULSION	RESTFULLY	RESISTORS
REMINISCE	ROOKERIES	REPENTANT	RESIGNING	RESETTING
RUMINATED	ROOTEDOUT	REPENTING	RUSTICATE	RESITTING
REMINGTON	ROOMINESS	REPROBATE	RESCINDED	RESOURCES
RUMINATES	ROOMMATES	REPROVING	RUSTINESS	RESOUNDED
REMARRIED	RIOTOUSLY	REPROGRAM	RESPIRING	RESHUFFLE
REMARKING	RIOGRANDE	REPRODUCE	RUSTICITY	ROSEWATER
REMARRIES	RIOTSQUAD	REPAPERED	RESULTANT	RESTYLING
REMBRANDT	REPEATERS	REPORTAGE	RUSTLEDUP	RETRACING
RUMPSTEAK	REPEALING	REPARABLE	RESILIENT	RITUALISM
REMISSION	REPEATING	REPORTERS	RESOLVING	RITUALIST
REMITTING	REPLACING	REPORTING	RESULTING	RETRACTED
RUMBUTTER	REPLAYING	REPERTORY	RESEMBLED	RETICULUM
RINGABELL	REPLANNED	REPOSSESS	RESEMBLES	RETICULAR
RANSACKED	REPUBLISH	REPUTABLE	ROSENBERG	RETICULES
RUNABOUTS	REPUBLICS	REPUTEDLY	RESENTFUL	RETICENCE
RENDERING	REPACKAGE	REPOTTING	ROSENTHAL	ROTTERDAM
RINSEDOUT	REPECHAGE	RAPTUROUS	RESENTING	RUTHENIUM
RUNNERSUP	RAPACIOUS	REPAYABLE	RESONANCE	RUTHELLIS
RINGFENCE	REPUDIATE	REPAYMENT	ROSINANTE	ROTTENROW
RENEGADES	REPRESENT	ROQUEFORT	RISINGSUN	RETREATED
RANCHEROS	REPLENISH	REQUESTED	RESONATED	RATIFYING
RANGINESS	REPLETION	REQUISITE	RESONATOR	RATTINESS
RENDITION	RIPPEDOFF	REQUIRING	RESONATES	RETAILERS
RINTINTIN	REPRESSED	RAREEARTH	RESPONDED	RETAINERS
RONHOWARD	REPRESSES	RAREFYING	RESTORERS	RETAILING
RANDOMISE	REPUGNANT	RERELEASE	RESTORING	RETAINING
RANCOROUS	REPRIMAND	RARASKIRT	ROSCOMMON	RETRIEVED
RINGOUZEL	REPLICATE	RAROTONGA	ROSSONWYE	RETRIEVAL
RINGROUND	REPRISALS	RURITANIA	RUSTPROOF	RETRIEVER
RUNAROUND	REPAIRERS	REROUTING	RESURFACE	RETRIEVES
RENASCENT	REPAIRING	RUSSABBOT	RESTRICTS	RETALIATE
RENOUNCED	REPTILIAN	RASPATORY	RESURGENT	RETELLING

RUTHMADOC	RIVALLING	RAZORWIRE	STATELESS	SEASHANTY
RETENTIVE	REVULSION	RAZORBILL	STATEMENT	SLAPHAPPY
RETENTION	REVAMPING	SCAMANDER	SCAVENGED	SPAGHETTI
ROTUNDITY	RAVINGMAD	SEAFARERS	SCAVENGER	STAGHOUND
RATIONALE	RIVERBANK	STARANISE	SCAVENGES	SEANHAYES
RETHOUGHT	RIVERSIDE	SEAFARING	SPACESHIP	SWAZILAND
RATIONING	REVERSING	SHAMANISM	SNAKEBITE	SCALINESS
RETROUSSE	REVERTING	SCAPAFLOW	SPARETIME	SHADINESS
RATPOISON	REVERSION	SHARAPOVA	STATESIDE	STAGINESS
RATEPAYER	REVERENCE	SHARANSKY	SLAVERING	STAYINGON
RETARDING	REVERENDS	SEANASTIN	SPARERIBS	SPARINGLY
RETORTING	RIVERBOAT	STARBOARD	SNAKESKIN	SLAVISHLY
RETURNING	RAVISHING	SHABBIEST	SHAKEALEG	STABILISE
ROTAVATED	REVISITED	SHAMBOLIC	STATESMAN	SCARIFIER
ROTAVATOR	REVETMENT	SCABBARDS	STATESMEN	STALINIST
ROTAVATES	ROWDINESS	STARBURST	SEALEDOFF	STABILITY
ROUNDEDUP	REWRITING	SEARCHERS	SPADEWORK	STATIONED
ROUNDHEAD	REWRITTEN	SEARCHFEE	STATEROOM	STATIONER
ROUNDNESS	REWARDING	SEARCHING	SHAKEDOWN	STATISTIC
ROUNDELAY	REWORDING	SNATCHING	STAGEDOOR	SHARKTALE
ROUNDSMAN	ROXIEHART	STARCHING	SCAPEGOAT	STACKABLE
ROUNDSMEN	ROXYMUSIC	STANCHION	SHAREDOUT	STACKEDUP
ROUNDTRIP	ROYWALKER	STARCHIER	STAYEDPUT	SLACKNESS
ROUGHCAST	ROYCASTLE	SEASCAPES	SNAREDRUM	SPARKLERS
ROUGHIDEA	RHYMESTER	STANDBAIL	SCARECROW	STARKNESS
ROUGHNECK	RAYLIOTTA	STANDEASY	SPACESUIT	SHACKLING
ROUGHHEWN	RHYSJONES	STANDREWS	SPARETYRE	SPARKLING
ROUGHNESS	REYKJAVIK	STANDPIPE	SNAKEEYES	SHARKSKIN
ROUGHSHOD	ROYALGALA	SWADDLING	SEAOFLOVE	SPARKPLUG
ROUGHENED	ROYALMAIL	STANDDOWN	STAFFROOM	SLACKENED
ROUTINELY	ROYALMILE	SLANDERED	STARFRUIT	SMALLTALK
REUNITING	ROYALTIES	SLANDERER	SEAOFAZOV	SNAILMAIL
ROUTLEDGE	ROYALBLUE	STANDARDS	SHANGHAIS	SMALLBEER
RAUCOUSLY	ROYCLARKE	STAGEHAND	SHANGRILA	STAPLEGUN
REVEALING	ROYALISTS	SHAREWARE	SPANGLISH	STARLIGHT
REVIEWERS	RAYROMANO	STAGENAME	STAGGERED	SMALLTIME
REVIEWING	ROYROGERS	STALEMATE	SWAGGERED	STABLELAD
REVELLERS	RAYBOLGER	SPACEWALK	SWAGGERER	SEAPLANES
REVOLVERS	ROYSROLLS	STATEFAIR	SLAUGHTER	STARLINGS
REVELLING	RAYBROOKS	SHAMELESS	STARGAZER	SIANLLOYD
REVOLTING	RAYSTUBBS	SHAPELESS	SEASHELLS	SMALLTOWN
REVOLVING	RAZORBACK	STALENESS	SEACHANGE	SCALLIONS

STALLIONS	STAIRWELL	SUBLIMELY	SICKENING	SEDITIOUS
SCALLOPED	SEAURCHIN	SUBDIVIDE	SECRETION	SEDATIVES
SMALLARMS	STAIRLIFT	SUBSIDISE	SOCIETIES	SADDUCEES
SCARLATTI	STAIRRODS	SUBSIDING	SACREBLEU	SIDEWALKS
SWALLOWED	STAUSTELL	SUBTITLES	SUCCESSOR	SODAWATER
SCALLYWAG	STARSHINE	SUBMITTED	SUCCESSES	SKEDADDLE
SHALLOWER	SLAPSTICK	SUBSISTED	SACCHARIN	SHEDATEAR
SPASMODIC	SOAPSTONE	SOBRIQUET	SACRILEGE	SEESAWING
STAMMERED	SWANSDOWN	SUBALTERN	SACRIFICE	SCENARIOS
STAMMERER	SNAPSHOTS	SIBILANCE	SECTIONAL	SUEBARKER
SHAUNTAIT	SMARTCARD	SIBILATES	SACRISTAN	SUELAWLEY
STAINLESS	SPARTACUS	SUBCLAUSE	SICKLEAVE	SKEWBALDS
STAGNIGHT	SMARTNESS	SUBPOENAS	SYCAMORES	SEEDBOXES
STAUNCHED	STARTLING	STBERNARD	SECONDARY	SPEECHDAY
SEAANCHOR	SWARTHIER	SUBTRACTS	SECONDERS	STEPCHILD
STAUNCHES	SMARTALEC	SOBEREDUP	SUCCOTASH	SKETCHING
STAUNCHLY	SMARTENED	SUBARCTIC	SOCIOLOGY	SPEECHIFY
STAGNANCY	SCATTERED	SYBARITIC	SYCOPHANT	SEEDCAKES
STAGNATED	SHATTERED	SYBARITES	SECURICOR	SKETCHMAP
STAGNATES	SPATTERED	SEBASTIAN	SECESSION	SUEZCANAL
SHADOWBOX	SLATTERNS	SUBSTRATA	SECATEURS	SKETCHOUT
SOAPOPERA	STARTOVER	SABOTAGED	SUCCUMBED	STEADFAST
SEASONING	SEAQUAKES	SABOTAGES	SUCCULENT	STEADICAM
SHADOWING	STATUTORY	SUBATOMIC	SECLUDING	SPEEDWELL
SEAHORSES	STATUSQUO	SUBSTANCE	SECLUSION	SPEEDIEST
SEAWORTHY	STATUETTE	SABOTEURS	SIDEBOARD	STEADIEST
STAMPEDED	SEALYHAMS	SUBJUGATE	SODABREAD	STEADYING
SNAPPEDUP	SUBMARINE	SUBJUDICE	SIDEBURNS	SPEEDBOAT
STAMPEDES	SUBFAMILY	SUBSUMING	SEDUCTIVE	SPEEDTRAP
SHARPNESS	SUBSCRIBE	SACRAMENT	SEDUCTION	SPEEDBUMP
SNAPPIEST	SUBSCRIPT	SOCIALISE	SADDENING	STEVENAGE
SEALPOINT	SEBACEOUS	SOCIALITE	SEDGEMOOR	STEVEPENK
SHARPENED	SUBEDITED	SOCIALISM	SIDEISSUE	SHEREKHAN
SHARPENER	SUBEDITOR	SECTARIAN	SYDLITTLE	STEVEBIKO
SHAMPOOED	SUBDEACON	SOCIALIST	SADDLEBAG	STEVEDORE
STARPUPIL	SUBMERGED	SACKCLOTH	SIDELIGHT	SKELETONS
SCAMPERED	SUBMERGES	SECRETARY	SIDELINES	STEVECRAM
SCARPERED	SUBLEASED	SACREDCOW	SEDENTARY	STEVENSON
STAGPARTY	SUBLEASES	SUCCEEDED	SIDESTEPS	STEVEOWEN
STAMPDUTY	SUBJECTED	STCLEMENT	SIDESWIPE	SHELFMARK
STAIRCASE	SUBVERTED	SECRETIVE	SIDESALAD	SHEFFIELD
SEABREEZE	SUBLIMATE	SECRETING	SIDETRACK	SIEGFRIED

SHELFLIFE	STEGOSAUR	SOFTFRUIT	SIGHTREAD	SKINDIVER
SHELFROOM	SHEEPWASH	SAFEGUARD	SIGHTSEER	SPINDRYER
STEPHANIE	SLEEPWALK	SAFEHOUSE	SIGHTLESS	SWIPECARD
SHEPHERDS	SLEEPLESS	SUFFICING	SIGHTSEES	SWINEHERD
SEEDINESS	STEEPNESS	SAFFLOWER	SIGOURNEY	SPINELESS
SPECIMENS	SLEEPIEST	SUFFOCATE	SCHMALTZY	SHIVERING
SEEMINGLY	SHEEPSKIN	SOFTPEDAL	SCHNAUZER	SNIVELLED
SPECIFIED	STEEPENED	SUFFRAGAN	SCHEDULED	SWIVELLED
STERILISE	SHEEPFOLD	SAFETYNET	SCHEDULES	SNIVELLER
SPECIFIES	SHEEPDOGS	SAFETYPIN	SCHNEIDER	SHIRELLES
STERILITY	SLEEPSUIT	SOFTTOUCH	SCHOFIELD	SPIDERMAN
SPECIALLY	SLEEPOVER	SUFFUSING	SCHWIMMER	STILETTOS
SPEAKEASY	SPEARHEAD	SUFFUSION	SCHNITZEL	SLIDERULE
SHEIKHDOM	SHEERNESS	SIGNALBOX	SCHILLING	STIFFNESS
SLEEKNESS	SPEARMINT	SIGNALLED	SCHOLARLY	STIRFRIED
SNEAKIEST	STEERSMAN	SIGNALLER	SCHEMATIC	SKINFLINT
SPECKLING	STEERSMEN	SIGNALMAN	SCHOOLBAG	SKILFULLY
STEELBAND	SWEARWORD	SIGNALMEN	SCHOOLBOY	STIFFENED
STEELYARD	SWEATBAND	SIGNATORY	SCHOONERS	STIFFENER
SHEDLOADS	SWEETTALK	SIGNATURE	SCHOOLING	SLINGBACK
SMELLIEST	SHEDTEARS	SUGABABES	SCHNOZZLE	STINGIEST
SPELLBIND	SPECTACLE	SAGEBRUSH	SPHERICAL	SLINGSHOT
SHELLFIRE	SCEPTICAL	SAGACIOUS	SPHEROIDS	SWINGEING
SHELLFISH	SHEETBEND	SAGEDERBY	SCHMUTTER	SWINGDOOR
SEEDLINGS	SWEETNESS	SEGREGATE	SPINAYARN	SWINGBOAT
SHETLANDS	SWEETPEAS	SEGMENTED	SRILANKAN	SNIGGERED
SWELLINGS	SWEETMEAT	SUGGESTED	SPIRALLED	STINGAREE
STEELWOOL	SWEATSHOP	SAGEGREEN	SPIRACLES	SNIGGERER
STEELDRUM	SWEETENED	SOGGINESS	SAILALONG	SKINHEADS
SMELLARAT	SWEETENER	SIGNINGON	SPINALTAP	SLIGHTEST
SHEILASIM	SWEETCORN	SIGNIFIED	SAILBOARD	SLIGHTING
STELLATED	SHELTERED	SIGNIFIES	SPITBLOOD	SLITHERED
SHELLSUIT	SWELTERED	STGEORGES	SWINBURNE	SCIMITARS
STEAMBATH	SPECTATED	SIGNORINA	STIRCRAZY	SLIMINESS
STEAMEDUP	SPECTATOR	SUGARCANE	STITCHING	SPICINESS
STEAMSHIP	SPECTATES	SUGARBEET	SWITCHING	SPIRITOUS
STEAMBOAT	SPECULATE	SUGARLOAF	SHIPCANAL	SPITITOUT
STEAMIRON	SPELUNKER	SUGARSOAP	SAILCLOTH	SPIRITUAL
STEINBECK	SKEWWHIFF	SUGARCOAT	SUITCASES	STICKLERS
STERNNESS	SOFTENING	SUGARCUBE	SWINDLERS	SLINKIEST
STEINBOCK	SUFFERING	SUGARRUSH	SWINDLING	STICKIEST
SEEINGRED	SOFTFOCUS	SUGARLUMP	SPINDRIFT	STINKBOMB

STINKHORN	SCINTILLA	SOLDIERON	SUMMARISE	SOMETHING
STICKATIT	SAINTHOOD	SOLDIERLY	SUMMATION	SOMETIMES
SPIELBERG	SAINTJOHN	SOLILOQUY	SIMPATICO	SEMITONES
STILLNESS	SAINTLUKE	SOLEMNISE	SUMMARIES	SUMPTUOUS
STILLLIFE	STIMULATE	SOLEMNIFY	SUMMARILY	SAMETOYOU
SHIELDING	STIPULATE	SOLEMNITY	SEMIBREVE	SOMEWHERE
SPILLIKIN	STIMULANT	SALEMSLOT	SEMICOLON	SUNBATHED
SHILLINGS	SKISUNDAY	SALAMANCA	SAMMENDES	SUNBATHER
SPILLOVER	SPIRULINA	SALTMARSH	SIMMERING	SUNBATHES
SHIMMYING	SKIJUMPER	SILENCERS	SIMPERING	SENSATION
SHIMMERED	SHIPWRECK	SPLINTERS	SOMMELIER	SANMARINO
SHIPMATES	SWIZZLING	SPLENDENT	SYMMETRIC	SUNTANNED
SKINNYDIP	SELFAWARE	SILENCING	SEMIFINAL	SINGAPORE
SKINNIEST	SULTANATE	SOLENOIDS	SYMPHONIC	SINGALONG
SCIENTIST	SALVAGING	SPLENDOUR	SUMMINGUP	SENNAPODS
SPINNAKER	SALVATION	SPLENETIC	SYMBIOSIS	SANTACRUZ
SKINNYRIB	SYLLABLES	SELLOTAPE	SYMBIOTIC	SANDBLAST
SPINNERET	SELFBUILD	SALOONCAR	SIMULCAST	SANDBANKS
SEIGNEURS	SILICAGEL	SYLLOGISM	SEMBLANCE	SONGBIRDS
SAILORING	SELECTIVE	SALTPETRE	SIMPLYRED	SONGCYCLE
SLIVOVITZ	SELECTING	SULTRIEST	SIMILARLY	SUNSCREEN
SPIROGYRA	SELECTION	SALESLADY	SIMULATED	SONICBOOM
SAILPLANE	SALACIOUS	SPLASHING	SIMPLETON	SENTENCED
SLIPPEDUP	SELECTORS	SALESGIRL	SIMULATOR	SENTENCES
SKIMPIEST	SOLICITED	SALTSPOON	SIMULATES	SONNETEER
STIPPLING	SOLICITOR	SELLSHORT	SIMONWARD	SENSELESS
SKIPPERED	SALADDAYS	SPLASHOUT	SEMANTICS	SINCERELY
SPITROAST	SOLIDGOLD	SALISBURY	SOMNOLENT	SUNDERING
STIRREDUP	SELFDOUBT	SPLATTERS	SYMBOLISE	SINCERITY
SHIPSHAPE	SOLDERING	SPLITPEAS	SUMMONING	SANHEDRIN
SLIMSHADY	SYLVESTER	SPLUTTERS	SYMBOLISM	SANDERSON
SPINSTERS	SALTFLATS	SOLITAIRE	SYMPOSIUM	SONOFAGUN
SWIMSUITS	SULPHIDES	SPLITTING	SEMIOTICS	SANGFROID
SWISSROLL	SYLPHLIKE	SPLITENDS	SEMIOLOGY	SYNAGOGUE
SAINTMARK	SULPHATES	SOLUTIONS	SUMMONSES	SANDHURST
SAINTPAUL	SELFIMAGE	SOLOWHIST	SOMEPLACE	SYNTHESIS
SAINTSDAY	SALTINESS	SELFWORTH	SEMAPHORE	SYNTHETIC
SHIFTLESS	SILKINESS	SILKWORMS	SEMIRAMIS	SYNDICATE
SWIFTNESS	SILLINESS	SALTWATER	SOMBREROS	SENTINELS
SHIFTIEST	SULKINESS	SALLYPORT	SAMARITAN	SENTIMENT
SKINTIGHT	SELFISHLY	SALLYLUNN	SAMBROWNE	SINKINGIN
SKITTLING	SOLDIERED	SAMEAGAIN	SEMESTERS	SENDINGUP

SENSITISE	SCOTCHEGG	SPONGIEST	STOPPAGES	SOPPINESS
SENSITIVE	SPOTCHECK	STODGIEST	SLOPPYJOE	SOPHISTER
SONSINLAW	SLOUCHERS	SNOWGOOSE	SNOOPDOGG	SOPHISTRY
SUNKISSED	SCORCHING	SHOWGIRLS	SCORPIONS	SUPOLLARD
SINGLETON	SCOTCHING	SMOTHERED	STOURHEAD	SUPPLIANT
SUNFLOWER	SLOUCHING	SHOWINESS	SNOWSCAPE	SUPPLIERS
SYNCOPATE	SMOOCHING	SOOTINESS	SCOTSPINE	SEPULCHRE
SANTORINI	STOICALLY	SHOWINGUP	SHOESHINE	SUPPLYING
SENIORITY	SHOWCARDS	STOCKYARD	SNOWSTORM	SUPPLANTS
SUNDOWNER	SWORDTAIL	STOCKTAKE	SNOWSHOES	STPANCRAS
SUNBONNET	SWORDFISH	STOCKADES	SPONSORED	SIPHONING
SANDPAPER	SNOWDRIFT	STOCKWELL	SHORTHAND	SUPPOSING
SANDPIPER	SWORDPLAY	SPOOKIEST	SHORTCAKE	SOPHOCLES
SENTRYBOX	SWORDSMAN	STOCKIEST	SHORTWAVE	SOPHOMORE
SANDRADEE	SWORDSMEN	STOCKPILE	SHORTFALL	SUPPORTED
SANDSNAKE	SNOWDONIA	STOCKLIST	SHORTHAUL	SUPPORTER
SONGSTERS	SNOWDROPS	STOCKINGS	SPORTSCAR	SEPARABLE
SENESCENT	SCORECARD	STOCKINET	SWOTTEDUP	SUPERSEDE
SANDSTONE	STORECARD	STOCKHOLM	SUPERHERO	SUPERHERO
SANDSTORM	STONEWARE	STOCKROOM	SOPORIFIC	SOPORIFIC
SANSSERIF	STONEWALL	STOCKPORT	SMOOTHEST	SUPERBIKE
SINUSITIS	SCORELESS	SNOOKERED	SNOOTIEST	SUPERFINE
SANCTUARY	SMOKELESS	STONKERED	SPOTTIEST	SUPERVISE
SUNSTROKE	STONECHAT	STOCKISTS	SHORTTIME	SUPERMINI
SANCTIONS	SCORELINE	STOCKCUBE	SMOOTHING	SUPERGIRL
SANITISED	SHORELINE	STOOLBALL	SHOWTRIAL	SUPERGLUE
SENSUALLY	STOVEPIPE	SHOELACES	SHORTLIST	SUPERNOVA
SUNBURNED	SHOWERING	SHOULDERS	SPORTSMAN	SUPERIORS
SANDWEDGE	SHOVELLED	SMOULDERS	SPORTSMEN	SUPERGRAN
SUNNYDALE	SHOVELLER	SPOTLIGHT	SHORTENED	SEPARATED
SONNYBONO	SPOKESMAN	STORMIEST	SHORTFUSE	SUPERSTAR
SANDYLYLE	SPOKESMEN	SHOEMAKER	SHORTCUTS	SEPARATES
STOWAWAYS	SHOWEDOFF	SLOWMARCH	SNOWWHITE	SEQUENCES
STOMACHIC	STOREROOM	SPOONFEED	STOPWATCH	SEQUESTER
STOMACHED	STONECROP	SPOONBILL	STORYLINE	SEQUINNED
SNOWBOARD	SLOPEARMS	SCOUNDREL	STORYBOOK	SCREAMERS
SCOOBYDOO	SNOWFLAKE	SPOONFULS	SFORZANDO	SPREADERS
SNOWBALLS	SHOPFLOOR	STORNOWAY	SAPODILLA	STREAKERS
SNOWBOOTS	SHOPFRONT	SHOLOKHOV	SUPREMACY	STREAMERS
SCORBUTIC	SHOTGLASS	SHOWPIECE	SEPTEMBER	SURFACERS
SNOWBOUND	SNODGRASS	SCOOPNECK	SUPREMELY	SERIALISE
SLOWCOACH	SPONGEBAG	STOPPRESS	SAPPHIRES	SCREAMING

SERRATING	SERGEANTS	SCRAMBLED	SURMOUNTS	SCREWEDUP
SPREADING	SURVEYORS	SCRAMBLER	SURROUNDS	SHREWDEST
STREAKING	SORTEDOUT	SCRAMBLES	SERIOUSLY	SCRAWLING
STREAMING	SURFEITED	STROMBOLI	SCRAPYARD	SPRAWLING
SURFACING	SCRUFFILY	SHRINKAGE	STRAPHANG	STRAWPOLL
SURNAMING	SHRUGGING	STRONGARM	SCRAPHEAP	SCREWWORM
SERRATION	STRUGGLED	STRANRAER	STRAPLESS	STRAWDOGS
STREAMLET	STRAGGLER	STRINGBAG	STRIPPERS	SPRAYGUNS
SERIALMOM	STRUGGLES	SPRINGBOK	STRAPLINE	SUSTAINED
SPREADOUT	SPRIGHTLY	STRONGBOX	SCRAPPING	SASSAFRAS
SURPASSED	SURCHARGE	SERENADED	SCRIPTING	SASSENACH
SURPASSES	STREISAND	SERENADER	STRAPPING	SISTERACT
SARCASTIC	STRAINERS	SERENADES	STRIPLING	SUSPENDED
SCRUBLAND	SURLINESS	SPRINGERS	STRIPPING	SUSPENDER
SURFBOARD	SURCINGLE	SPRINTERS	SOREPOINT	SUSSEDOUT
SHRUBBERY	SERVICING	STRANGERS	SCRAPPILY	SUSPECTED
SCRUBBING	SPRAINING	STRANGEST	SCRAPBOOK	SUSPICION
SCRIBBLED	STRAINING	STRINGENT	SCRIPTURE	SESSIONAL
SCRIBBLER	SURMISING	STRONGEST	SURPRISED	SUSANHILL
SCRIBBLES	SURVIVING	STRANGELY	SURPRISES	SASQUATCH
SPROCKETS	SARDINIAN	SCRUNCHIE	STRESSFUL	SATIATING
STRICTEST	SORTITION	SHRINKING	SPRITZERS	SATIATION
STRICTURE	SERVILITY	SPRINGING	STRATEGIC	SITUATION
STRUCTURE	SURVIVORS	SPRINTING	STRATAGEM	SETFIRETO
SHREDDERS	SERVIETTE	STRONTIUM	SCRATCHED	SETTINGUP
SHREDDING	SERVITUDE	SPRINGIER	STRETCHED	SETTLEDUP
SHREDDIES	STRIKEOUT	SPRINKLED	STRETCHER	SETALIGHT
STRADDLED	STRIKEPAY	STRANGLED	SCRATCHES	SATELLITE
STRADDLES	SCROLLBAR	SPRINKLER	STRETCHES	SATINWOOD
STRIDENCY	SURPLICES	STRANGLER	STRUTTING	SATANISTS
STREETCAR	STROLLERS	SPRINKLES	SURETHING	SATINETTE
SURRENDER	SCROLLING	STRANGLES	SEROTONIN	SOTTOVOCE
SORCERERS	STROLLING	STRONGMAN	STRATFORD	SETSQUARE
SORCERESS	SCRIMMAGE	SIRENSONG	SCRUTATOR	SATIRICAL
SCREECHED	SCRUMMAGE	STRENUOUS	SCROUNGED	SATURNINE
SCREECHER	SCRUMHALF	STRENGTHS	SCROUNGER	SATIRISED
SCREECHES	STROMNESS	SURFNTURF	SCROUNGES	SATIRISES
SERVETIME	STRUMPETS	SURROGATE	SHROUDING	SATIRISTS
SCREENING	SCRIMSHAW	SURROGACY	SPROUTING	SATURATED
SHRIEKING	SCRIMPING	SORROWFUL	SHRIVELUP	SATURATES
SURVEYING	SCRUMPING	SERMONISE	SCRIVENER	SATISFIED
SURGERIES	STRUMMING	SARTORIAL	SCREWBALL	SATISFIES

SQUEALERS	SOUTHPARK	SCUTTLING	STYROFOAM	TRAIPSING
SQUEAKING	SOUTHWARK	SQUATTING	TEARAWAYS	TRAMPLING
SQUEALING	SOUTHPAWS	SAUNTERED	TEARAPART	TRAPPINGS
SQUEAMISH	SOUTHEAST	SHUTTERED	TEAGARDEN	TEASPOONS
SCUDAMORE	SOUTHSEAS	STUTTERED	TRAFALGAR	TRAPPISTS
STUMBLING	SOUTHWEST	STUTTERER	THATCHERS	TRANSLATE
SQUABBLED	SLUSHPILE	SHUBUNKIN	THATCHING	TRANSVAAL
SQUABBLES	SOUTHPOLE	SQUAWKERS	TEARDROPS	TRANSACTS
SLUMBERED	SOUTHDOWN	SQUAWKING	TRADENAME	TRANSCEND
SLUMBERER	SOUGHTOUT	SAVILEROW	TRADEMARK	TEAMSTERS
SOURCREAM	SOUTHPORT	SEVENOAKS	TRADEWIND	TRANSFERS
SOUNDWAVE	SOUTHERLY	SEVENTEEN	TSAREVICH	TEARSHEET
SOUNDLESS	SLUSHFUND	SEVENSEAS	TRAPEZIUM	TRANSIENT
SOUNDNESS	SAUCINESS	SAVERNAKE	TRAGEDIAN	THATSTHAT
STURDIEST	STUPIDITY	SOVEREIGN	TRAGEDIES	THATSLIFE
SOUNDBITE	SAUVIGNON	SEVERANCE	TEASELLED	TRANSPIRE
SQUADDIES	SOUBIROUS	SAVOURING	TRAVELLED	TRANSMITS
SQUADRONS	STUCKATIT	SAVOURIES	TRAVELLER	TRANSPOSE
SHUDDERED	SKULLCAPS	SEXUALITY	TRADESMAN	TOADSTOOL
SOURDOUGH	SQUELCHED	SIXDAYWAR	TRADESMEN	TRANSFORM
SAUCEPANS	SQUELCHES	SIXPENCES	TRAPEZOID	TRANSPORT
STUPEFIED	SOULMUSIC	SIXTEENTH	TOADEGREE	TRANSEPTS
SQUEEZING	SQUANDERS	SAXIFRAGE	TRAVERSED	TRANSFUSE
SOUVENIRS	SQUINTING	SIXTHFORM	TRAVERSES	TRANSMUTE
STUPEFIES	SCULPTING	SEXENNIAL	TEAKETTLE	TOASTRACK
SAUTERNES	STUDPOKER	SAXROHMER	TEALEAVES	TRACTABLE
SAUCEBOAT	SCULPTORS	SEXAPPEAL	TEARFULLY	TRATTORIA
SOUWESTER	SCUPPERED	SAXOPHONE	TEACHESTS	TRADUCING
STUFFSACK	SCULPTURE	SEXTUPLET	TOANICETY	TRACYSHAW
SHUFFLERS	SQUIRRELS	SEXSYMBOL	TEASINGLY	TABLELAND
STUFFIEST	SCURRYING	SKYJACKED	TRADITION	TABLEWARE
SHUFFLING	SQUIRMING	SKYJACKER	THANKLESS	TABLEWINE
SOULFULLY	SQUIRTING	SKYWALKER	TRACKSHOE	TOBLERONE
SNUGGLEUP	SQUARELEG	SPYMASTER	TRACKDOWN	TOBOGGANS
SMUGGLERS	SQUAREPEG	STYLELESS	THACKERAY	TUBBINESS
SMUGGLING	SOUBRETTE	SAYCHEESE	TRACKSUIT	TABULATED
SQUIGGLES	SOURSWEET	STYLISHLY	TRAILBIKE	TABULATOR
STURGEONS	SPUNSUGAR	SKYDIVING	TRAMLINES	TABULATES
SLUGGARDS	SQUASHING	STYLISING	TRAILARMS	TABBOULEH
SOUTHWARD	SOUPSPOON	STYLISTIC	TRAUMATIC	TOBERMORY
SOUTHGATE	STUTTGART	SKYROCKET	TRAINLOAD	TABHUNTER
SOUTHBANK	SQUATTERS	SAYNOMORE	TEAFORTWO	TABBYCATS

TICTACTOE	THEREFORE	TREBUCHET	THINKTANK	TAKEGUARD
TACTFULLY	THEMESONG	THEOUTLAW	THICKNESS	TAKINGOFF
TACKINESS	TREMELOES	TREMULOUS	TRICKIEST	TAKEOVERS
TUCKINGIN	THEREUPON	TAEKWONDO	TRICKLING	TAKEPLACE
TACTICIAN	THEOFFICE	TIGRESSES	TWINKLING	TAKESHAPE
TECHNICAL	THEXFILES	TIGERBALM	THICKENED	TAKESIDES
TECHNIQUE	TREEHOUSE	TIGERSEYE	THICKENER	TAKESTOCK
TECTONICS	THEMIKADO	TIGERLILY	TRICKSTER	TAKETURNS
TEDDANSON	THERIVALS	TIGERMOTH	TRINKETRY	TALKATHON
TADCASTER	THETINMAN	TIGHTWADS	THINKOVER	TALKATIVE
TODDCARTY	THEPLAGUE	TIGHTHEAD	TAILLIGHT	TOLLBOOTH
TEDWILLIS	THEPLAYER	TIGHTNESS	TRIPLANES	TULSEHILL
TIDALWAVE	THERMALLY	TIGHTENED	TRIUMPHED	TELEGRAPH
TIDEMARKS	TEEINGOFF	TIGHTKNIT	TRIUMPHAL	TELEGRAMS
TEDROGERS	THEHOBBIT	TIGHTROPE	TRIMMINGS	TELEGENIC
TEDIOUSLY	TREVOREVE	TIGHTSPOT	TRIENNIAL	TOLLGATES
TUDORROSE	THELODGER	TAHITIANS	TRIANGLES	TALKINGTO
TEDHUGHES	THELONIUS	TRIMARANS	TRILOBITE	TELLINGLY
TODAYWEEK	THEROOKIE	TAIWANESE	TAILORING	TALLORDER
TEDDYBEAR	THESPIANS	TRIBALISM	TRILOGIES	TULIPWOOD
THEDABARA	THEBRIDGE	TRIBALIST	TRICOLOUR	TELEPHONE
THEWARDEN	THEYREOFF	TWITCHING	THINONTOP	TELEPHOTO
TEENAGERS	THEORISED	THIRDRATE	TAILPLANE	TELEPHONY
THERAPIST	THEORISER	TWIDDLING	TWINPEAKS	TELEPATHY
THEJACKET	THEORISES	TOILETBAG	TAILPIECE	TOLERABLE
THESAURUS	THEORISTS	TAILENDER	THIRSTIER	TOLERABLY
THEMATRIX	THEORETIC	TRITENESS	THIRSTILY	TALKRADIO
THECASTLE	TSETSEFLY	TUILERIES	TRIPTYCHS	TOLERANCE
THEMASTER	THEOSOPHY	TRIBESMAN	THIRTIETH	TOLERATED
TREBBIANO	TREASURED	TRIBESMEN	TRIATHLON	TOLERATES
TREMBLING	TREASURER	TAILEDOFF	TWITTERED	TALISMANS
THEOCRATS	TREASURES	TRIHEDRON	TWITTERER	TELESALES
TRENCHANT	THESTRAND	TRISECTED	TRIBUNALS	TELESCOPE
THEOCRACY	TREATABLE	TRIMESTER	TRIBUTARY	TALLSTORY
TREACHERY	TWENTIETH	THINGUMMY	THISWAYUP	TELLTALES
THEOCCULT	THEOTHERS	TRIGGERED	TRICYCLES	TOLDTALES
TRENDIEST	TREATMENT	TAILGATER	TAKEAPART	TOLPUDDLE
TREADMILL	TWENTYONE	THIGHBONE	TAKEASEAT	TELLURIAN
THEMEPARK	TWEETYPIE	THIGHBOOT	TAKEAHIKE	TELEVISED
THESEDAYS	TREATISES	TRINITIES	TAKEARISK	TELEVISES
TEETERING	THEKUMARS	TRIVIALLY	TAKEAFTER	TIMPANIST
THEDEVILS	THEHUNGER	THINKBACK	TAKECOVER	TIMMARLOW

TOMSAWYER	TENTACLES	TOOTHACHE	TYRABANKS	TORTOISES
TEMPERATE	TONYBLAIR	TOOTHLESS	TURNCOATS	TURNPIKES
TEMPELHOF	TENACIOUS	TOOTHPICK	TIREDNESS	TURNROUND
TAMPERING	TINDERBOX	TOOTHSOME	TERSENESS	TURKSHEAD
TEMPERING	TENSENESS	TOOLMAKER	TARGETING	THRESHERS
TIMHENMAN	TENDEREST	THORNDIKE	TORTELIER	TURNSTILE
TIMEFRAME	TANGERINE	TROUNCING	TORPEDOED	THRASHING
TOMSHARPE	TENDERISE	TOOWOOMBA	THREESOME	THRESHING
TOMAHAWKS	TENDERING	TROOPSHIP	TORPEDOES	THRUSTING
TOMLINSON	TINKERING	TAOISEACH	TURFEDOUT	THROSTLES
TAMILNADU	TANNERIES	TROUSSEAU	TURNEDOUT	THRESHOLD
TUMBLEDRY	TUNNELLED	THOUSANDS	TORMENTED	TURNSTONE
TIMELIMIT	TUNNELLER	TROUSERED	TORMENTOR	TAROTCARD
TOMCLANCY	TENNESSEE	TWOSTROKE	THRIFTILY	TURNTABLE
TIMELAPSE	TUNEFULLY	TAPDANCER	TYREGAUGE	THROTTLED
TEMPLETON	TONYHAWKS	TOPIARIST	TORCHSONG	THROTTLES
TEMPLATES	TINMINING	TOPICALLY	TURNHOUSE	TORTURERS
TOMOLIVER	TENSILITY	TYPICALLY	TERMINATE	TURBULENT
TEMPORARY	TINLIZZIE	TYPECASTS	TERMINALS	TURQUOISE
TEMPORISE	TINPLATED	TIPPERARY	TARDINESS	TORTURING
TOMBOYISH	TONYLEWIS	TIPPEDOFF	TURNINGIN	TORTUROUS
TIMEPIECE	TENEMENTS	TOPSECRET	TURNINGUP	THROWBACK
TOMCRUISE	TYNEMOUTH	TYPIFYING	TARNISHED	THROWNOUT
TAMARILLO	TUNINGPEG	TOPPINGUP	TARNISHES	THREWAWAY
TOMARNOLD	TONSORIAL	TOPFLIGHT	TERRIFIED	THROWAWAY
TOMORROWS	TENUOUSLY	TIPANDRUN	TERRIFIES	TESTAMENT
TIMESCALE	TINOPENER	TIPTOEING	TORPIDITY	TOSCANINI
TIMESHARE	TENAPENNY	TOPDRAWER	TURGIDITY	TASMANIAN
TIMESHEET	TUNBRIDGE	TOPSTITCH	TERRITORY	TESTATORS
TOMBSTONE	TUNESMITH	TIPSYCAKE	TURPITUDE	TESTATRIX
TEMPTFATE	TONYSCOTT	TERMAGANT	THRILLERS	TESTCASES
TIMETABLE	TINCTURES	THREATENS	THRILLING	TESTDRIVE
TEMPTRESS	TENDULKAR	TERRACING	THRUMMING	TASTELESS
TIMETRIAL	TWOHANDER	THREADING	TYRANNISE	TASSELLED
TIMOTHYMO	THORAHIRD	TERRARIUM	THRONGING	TASKFORCE
TIMBURTON	TROJANWAR	TERRAPINS	TARANTINO	TESTINESS
TIMEWATCH	TROUBLING	THROATILY	TYRANNOUS	TESTIFIED
TEMAZEPAM	TROMBONES	TARPAULIN	TARANTULA	TESTIFIES
TINAARENA	TOOKCOVER	TOREADORS	TERRORISE	TESTIMONY
TANTALISE	TWOREELER	TORNADOES	TERRORISM	TESTMATCH
TENTATIVE	TWOSEATER	TURNABOUT	TERRORIST	TESTPILOT
TANZANIAN	THOUGHTUP	THROBBING	TURBOPROP	TESTTUBES

TETRARCHY	TOUCHTYPE	UNASTUBBS	UNDECIDED	UNDERFUND
TETEATETE	TRUNKCALL	UNALTERED	UNDRESSED	UNDESIRED
TETRALOGY	TRUCKLOAD	UNBRANDED	UNDRESSES	UNDAUNTED
TITHEBARN	TRUNKROAD	UPBRAIDED	UNDEFINED	UNDOUBTED
TOTTENHAM	TRUCKSTOP	UNBUCKLED	UNDILUTED	UNDIVIDED
TETHERING	TOURNEDOS	UNBUCKLES	UNDULATED	USELESSLY
TITTERING	TRUNNIONS	UMBRELLAS	UNDULATES	UNELECTED
TOTTERING	TRUENORTH	UNBRIDLED	UNDAMAGED	UNETHICAL
TITLEROLE	TAUTOLOGY	UNBEKNOWN	UNDERHAND	UNEXPIRED
TOTHEBONE	TRUMPCARD	UMBILICAL	UNDERPAID	UNEXPOSED
TOTHECORE	TRUMPETED	UMBILICUS	UNDERRATE	UNEARTHED
TOTHEFORE	TRUMPETER	UNBOLTING	UNDERTAKE	UNEARTHLY
TETCHIEST	TRUSTFUND	UNBALANCE	UNDEROATH	USEBYDATE
TATTINESS	TRUCULENT	UNBENDING	UNDERSAIL	UNFOCUSED
TOTTINGUP	TOWNCLERK	URBANISED	UNDERPASS	UNFEELING
TITILLATE	THWACKING	URBANMYTH	UNDERSEAL	UNFAILING
TOTALLING	TOWNCRIER	UNBLOCKED	UNDERSELL	UNFOLDING
TOTEMPOLE	TOWNHOUSE	UNBURDENS	UNDERWEAR	UNFANCIED
TATTOOING	TOWELLING	UNBUTTONS	UNDERFELT	UNFURLING
TATTOOIST	THWARTING	UNBOUNDED	UNDERWENT	UNFASTENS
TITFORTAT	TOWERHILL	UNCHANGED	UNDERFIRE	UNFOUNDED
TITIVATED	TOWNSCAPE	UNCEASING	UNDERLINE	UNGUARDED
TITIVATES	TOWNSHEND	UNCLAIMED	UNDERMINE	UPGRADING
THUMBTACK	TOWNSFOLK	UNCHAINED	UNDERSIDE	UNGULATES
THUMBNAIL	TEXTBOOKS	UNCLASPED	UNDERLING	UNHEALTHY
TRUEBLISS	TAXIDERMY	UNCHARTED	UNDERBIDS	UNHEEDING
TRUNCHEON	TAXRETURN	UNCHECKED	UNDERPINS	UPHOLDERS
TJUNCTION	TAXIMETER	UNCLEBUCK	UNDERPLAY	UNHELPFUL
TRUNCATED	TOXOPHILY	UNCOILING	UNDERSOLD	UPHOLDING
TRUNCATES	TEXTUALLY	UNCLIPPED	UNDERWOOD	UPHOLSTER
TRUNDLING	THYLACINE	UNCANNILY	UNDERDONE	UNHOOKING
THUNDERED	TAYLFORTH	UNCLOGGED	UNDERGONE	UNHAPPIER
THUNDERER	TRYINGOUT	UNCLOTHED	UNDERTONE	UNHAPPILY
TAUTENING	UNABASHED	UNCROWNED	UNDERCOOK	UNHURRIED
TOUCHBASE	ULANBATOR	UNCERTAIN	UNDERTOOK	USHERETTE
TOUGHNESS	UNASHAMED	UNCORKING	UNDERDOGS	UNITARIAN
TOUCHLINE	UNANIMITY	UNCURLING	UNDERGOES	URIGELLER
TOUGHENED	UNALIGNED	UNCOUPLED	UNDERCOAT	UNIVERSAL
TOUCHWOOD	UNANIMOUS	UNCOUPLES	UNDERFOOT	URIAHHEEP
TOUCHTONE	UNALLOYED	UPCOUNTRY	UNDERGRAD	UTILISING
TOUCHDOWN	UNADORNED	UNCOVERED	UNDERARMS	UTILITIES
TRUTHDRUG	UNADOPTED	UPDRAUGHT	UNDERUSED	UNINJURED

UNIONJACK	UNRUFFLED	UTTOXETER	VIEWPOINT	VELAZQUEZ
UNIONFLAG	UNREFINED	ULULATING	VIENTIANE	VANUALEVU
UNIONISED	UKRAINIAN	ULULATION	VAGABONDS	VANDALISE
UNIONISTS	UNRELATED	UNUSUALLY	VAGUENESS	VANDALISM
UNIFORMED	UPROOTING	URUGUAYAN	VIGNETTES	VANPATTEN
UNIFORMLY	UNRESTING	UNVEILING	VIGILANCE	VENEERING
UNIMPEDED	UNSCATHED	UNVARYING	VIGILANTE	VANDELLAS
UNINSURED	UNSPARING	UNVISITED	VEGETABLE	VENGEANCE
UNITTRUST	UPSTAGING	UNWRAPPED	VEGETATED	VENDETTAS
UNINVITED	UNSECURED	UNWRITTEN	VEGETATES	VENTILATE
UNICYCLES	UPSADAISY	UNWILLING	VEHICULAR	VINDICATE
UNLEASHED	UNSCENTED	UNWELCOME	VEHEMENCE	VSNAIPAUL
UNLEASHES	UNSIGHTLY	UNWINDING	VOICEMAIL	VINDIESEL
UNLOADING	UNSKILFUL	UNWORLDLY	VOICEOVER	VANCOUVER
UNLEARNED	UNSMILING	UNWORRIED	VAINGLORY	VENERABLE
UNLOCKING	UNSKILLED	UNWITTING	VILLAGERS	VENTRICLE
UNLUCKIER	UNSELFISH	UNZIPPING	VULCANISE	VENERATED
UNLUCKILY	URSAMAJOR	VIABILITY	VULCANITE	VENERATES
UPLIFTING	URSAMINOR	VIBRATING	VALUATION	VENUSBERG
UGLIFRUIT	UNSCREWED	VIBRATION	VULGARIAN	VANISHING
UPLIGHTER	UPSETTING	VIBRANTLY	VULGARITY	VENETIANS
UNLIMITED	UNSETTLED	VICREEVES	VALUABLES	VINGTETUN
ULLSWATER	UNSETTLES	VACCINATE	VOLCANOES	VENTURING
UNMINDFUL	UNSAVOURY	VICTIMISE	VALIANTLY	VINEYARDS
UNMARRIED	UNTRAINED	VACILLATE	VELODROME	VENEZUELA
UNMERITED	URTICARIA	VOCALISED	VALIDATED	VIOLATING
UNMUSICAL	UPTHEANTE	VOCALISES	VALIDATES	VIOLATION
UNMASKING	UPTHEPOLE	VOCALISTS	VOLTEFACE	VIOLENTLY
UNNERVING	UNTREATED	VICENNIAL	VELVETEEN	VIOLINIST
UNNOTICED	UNTAINTED	VACANCIES	VALUELESS	VAPORISED
UNNATURAL	ULTIMATUM	VICTORIAN	VOLLEYING	VAPORISER
UFOLOGIST	UNTENABLE	VICTORIES	VOLDEMORT	VAPORISES
UNOPPOSED	UNTANGLED	VICIOUSLY	VILIFYING	VAPORETTO
UNPLANNED	UNTANGLES	VICARAGES	VALKILMER	VERBALISE
UNPACKING	UNTRODDEN	VICARIOUS	VOLUMISER	VERSATILE
UMPTEENTH	UNTYPICAL	VACATIONS	VOLTMETER	VARIATION
UPPOMPEII	UTTERANCE	VICEVERSA	VOLUNTARY	VARICELLA
UNPINNING	UTTERMOST	VIDELICET	VOLUNTEER	VERACIOUS
UNPOPULAR	UPTOSPEED	VADEMECUM	VALENTINA	VORACIOUS
UPPERCASE	UPTOSNUFF	VIDEOGAME	VALENTINE	VIRIDIANA
UPPERMOST	UNTUTORED	VIDEOTAPE	VALENTINO	VERADRAKE
UNPLUGGED	UNTOUCHED	VIDEOPLUS	VOLAUVENT	VARIETIES

VORDERMAN	WHALEBONE	WAGESLAVE	WHISPERED	WILTSHIRE
VERTEBRAE	WRANGLERS	WEHRMACHT	WHIPPERIN	WILLSMITH
VERTEBRAL	WRANGLING	WHITBREAD	WHISPERER	WILDTHING
VERIFYING	WEATHERED	WEIRDNESS	WHIPROUND	WELLVILLE
VIRGINALS	WEARINESS	WHITEFANG	WHIPSNADE	WILLYOUNG
VARNISHED	WEARISOME	WHITEWASH	WHIMSICAL	WIMBLEDON
VARNISHES	WEAKKNEED	WHITEHALL	WHINSTONE	WOMANKIND
VERMICIDE	WEAKLINGS	WHITEBAIT	WAISTBAND	WOMENSLIB
VERMILION	WRAPPEDUP	WHITEHART	WRISTBAND	WOMANHOOD
VERMIFORM	WYATTEARP	WHITELADY	WHISTLERS	WOMENFOLK
VERDIGRIS	WEALTHIER	WHITEHEAD	WAISTLINE	WOMANISER
VERMIFUGE	WEALTHTAX	WHITEBEAM	WHISTLING	WONNACOTT
VERYLIGHT	WEBMASTER	WHITENERS	WHITTLING	WINCANTON
VIRULENCE	WOBBEGONG	WHITENESS	WHITTAKER	WINDBREAK
VERONIQUE	WOBBLIEST	WHITEHEAT	WAISTCOAT	WINGCHAIR
VERBOSELY	WEBFOOTED	WHITEMEAT	WHIZZBANG	WINDCHILL
VERBOSITY	WACKINESS	WHITELIME	WAKEFIELD	WINNEBAGO
VARIOUSLY	WIDEAWAKE	WHITENING	WOKINGHAM	WUNDERBAR
VERHOEVEN	WIDEANGLE	WHITEFISH	WALLABIES	WANDERERS
VERITABLE	WEDNESDAY	WHITECITY	WALKABOUT	WONDERFUL
VIRTUALLY	WIDTHWAYS	WHITEFLAG	WELLBEING	WANDERING
VISUALISE	WODEHOUSE	WHITEGOLD	WALLCHART	WINTERING
VISIGOTHS	WIESBADEN	WHITEROSE	WILLESDEN	WONDERING
VESTIGIAL	WRENCHING	WHILEAWAY	WOLVERINE	WENCESLAS
VESTIBULE	WHEEDLING	WHITFIELD	WALKEDOUT	WANDEROFF
VESTMENTS	WEEKENDER	WHINGEING	WILDGEESE	WINEGLASS
VISIONARY	WOEBETIDE	WRIGGLING	WELSHHARP	WINDGAUGE
VISCOSITY	WHEREFORE	WEIGHTING	WOLFHOUND	WINTHEDAY
VISCOUNTS	WOEBEGONE	WEIGHTIER	WILLINGLY	WINDHOVER
VITABRITS	WHEREUPON	WHICHEVER	WILKINSON	WINDINESS
VITRIFIED	WHEYFACED	WRINKLING	WELLKNOWN	WANAMAKER
VITRIFIES	WEEDINESS	WRINKLIER	WALKONAIR	WINEMAKER
VITRIOLIC	WHEELBASE	WRINKLIES	WALLOPING	WINDMILLS
VOTARISTS	WHETSTONE	WHISKYMAC	WALLOWING	WINDOWBOX
VOUCHSAFE	WHEATEARS	WHISKERED	WELCOMING	WINNOWERS
VIVACIOUS	WHEATGERM	WHISKAWAY	WELLOILED	WINNOWING
VIVIDNESS	WRESTLERS	WHIRLIGIG	WOLFPACKS	WINDOWTAX
VOXPOPULI	WRESTLING	WHIRLWIND	WILDPALMS	WINDSCALE
VEXATIOUS	WAFERTHIN	WHIRLPOOL	WALLPAPER	WINDSWEPT
VOYEURISM	WAGNERIAN	WRITLARGE	WILLPOWER	WENTWORTH
WYANDOTTE	WAGONLOAD	WHINNYING	WOLFSBANE	WINDYCITY
WEAKENING	WAGONETTE	WHIMPERED	WELLSPENT	WOODBLOCK

WOODCHUCK	WORDINESS	WITHAWILL	WAXWORKER	ZEEBRUGGE
WHOLESALE	WARMINGUP	WITHCHILD	WAYWARDLY	ZOELUCKER
WHOLEMEAL	WORRISOME	WITHDRAWN	WAYFARERS	ZIGZAGGED
WHOLEFOOD	WURLITZER	WITHDRAWS	WAYFARING	ZIGGURATS
WHOLESOME	WARPLANES	WITHERING	WAYLAYING	ZUIDERZEE
WOODGREEN	WARCLOUDS	WITTERING	WAYZGOOSE	ZEITGEIST
WRONGDOER	WORKOFART	WUTHERING	XYLOGRAPH	ZELLWEGER
WRONGFOOT	WARMONGER	WITNESSED	XYLOPHONE	ZIMMERMAN
WOODHOUSE	WORKPLACE	WITNESSES	XANTHIPPE	ZINFANDEL
WOOZINESS	WARDROBES	WATCHABLE	XENOPHILE	ZOOLANDER
WOODLANDS	WARCRIMES	WITHHOLDS	XENOPHOBE	ZOOKEEPER
WOODLOUSE	WARGRAVES	WATCHWORD	YEARBOOKS	ZOOPHOBIA
WOODNYMPH	WORKSPACE	WITCHETTY	YEARLINGS	ZOOLOGIST
WHOOPITUP	WORKSHEET	WITCHHUNT	YEARROUND	ZEPHANIAH
WOODSTAIN	WORDSMITH	WATCHOVER	YABBERING	ZEPPELINS
WOODSHEDS	WORRYGUTS	WITTINESS	YACHTCLUB	ZAPATEADO
WOODSTOCK	WASSAILED	WITTICISM	YACHTSMAN	ZIRCONIUM
WOODSCREW	WASSAILER	WATERLAND	YACHTSMEN	ZESTFULLY
WHODUNNIT	WISEACRES	WATERGATE	YODELLERS	ZETAJONES
WOOLWORTH	WASHBOARD	WATERMARK	YODELLING	
WARGAMING	WISEBLOOD	WATERFALL	YAKETYYAK	
WARRANTED	WASHBASIN	WATERMAIN	YELLOWFIN	
WARRANTEE	WESTBOUND	WATERSHED	YELLOWING	
WARRANTOR	WISECRACK	WATERBIRD	YELLOWSEA	
WORKBENCH	WASTELAND	WATERLINE	YOMKIPPUR	
WIREBRUSH	WASTEPIPE	WATERPIPE	YUPPIEFLU	
WORLDFAIR	WASTETIME	WATERSIDE	YARDBIRDS	
WORLDSEND	WESTERNER	WATERMILL	YARDOFALE	
WORLDWIDE	WASHEDOUT	WATERLILY	YORKSHIRE	
WORLDVIEW	WASTEAWAY	WATERFORD	YARDSTICK	
WORKETHIC	WISTFULLY	WATERHOLE	YOSSARIAN	
WORSENING	WASHINGUP	WATERVOLE	YESTERDAY	
WORKEDOUT	WASPISHLY	WATERFOWL	YOUNAMEIT	
WORMEATEN	WESTMEATH	WATERDOWN	YOUNGADAM	
WORCESTER	WISCONSIN	WATERPOLO	YOUNGSTER	
WARMFRONT	WESTPOINT	WATERCURE	YOUNGTURK	
WORKFORCE	WESCRAVEN	WATERJUMP	YOUNGGUNS	
WORTHLESS	WASHSTAND	WATERPUMP	YOUTHCLUB	
WORTHIEST	WASPSNEST	WATERBUTT	ZEALOUSLY	
WORKHORSE	WESTWORLD	WITHSTAND	ZACHARIAS	
WAREHOUSE	WASTWATER	WITHSTOOD	ZACHBRAFF	
WORKHOUSE	WITHABANG	WAXJACKET	ZUCCHETTO	

PART TWO

Even-letter Intersections

BABA	ZARA	CAFE	JAKE	RAVE	HANG	RAGI	TASK	YAWL
BAJA	BARB	CAGE	JANE	RAZE	LANG	RAKI	VALK	BALM
BALA	DAUB	CAKE	JAPE	SADE	PANG	RANI	WALK	BARM
BANA	GARB	CAME	KALE	SAFE	RANG	RAVI	WARK	BAUM
BARA	JAMB	CANE	KANE	SAGE	SANG	SAKI	YANK	CALM
DADA	LAMB	CAPE	KATE	SAKE	TANG	SARI	BAAL	FARM
DANA	SAAB	CARE	KAYE	SALE	WANG	TATI	BAIL	HARM
DARA	LAIC	CASE	LACE	SAME	YANG	TAXI	BALL	MAIM
DATA	MARC	CATE	LADE	SANE	BACH	WADI	BAWL	PALM
GAGA	TALC	CAVE	LAKE	SATE	BASH	HADJ	CALL	WARM
GAIA	BALD	DACE	LAME	SAVE	BATH	BACK	CARL	BANN
GALA	BAND	DALE	LANE	SAXE	CASH	BANK	CAUL	BARN
GAZA	BARD	DAME	LATE	TAKE	DASH	BARK	DAHL	CAAN
HAHA	BAWD	DANE	LAZE	TALE	EACH	BASK	DAIL	CAEN
HAKA	CARD	DARE	MACE	TAME	GASH	CASK	EARL	CAIN
HANA	HAND	DATE	MADE	TAPE	HASH	DANK	FAIL	DAMN
JANA	HARD	DAVE	MAHE	TARE	KATH	DARK	FALL	DARN
JAVA	LADD	DAZE	MAKE	TATE	LASH	FALK	GAEL	DAWN
LALA	LAID	EASE	MALE	VALE	LATH	GAWK	GAIL	EARN
LAMA	LAND	FACE	MAME	VANE	MACH	HACK	GALL	FAUN
LANA	LARD	FADE	MANE	VASE	MASH	HANK	GAUL	FAWN
LARA	LAUD	FAKE	MARE	WADE	NASH	HARK	HAIL	GAIN
LAVA	MAID	FAME	MATE	WAGE	OATH	HAWK	HALL	HAIN
MAMA	MAUD	FARE	MAZE	WAKE	PATH	JACK	HAUL	HAWN
MARA	PAID	FATE	NAME	WANE	RASH	LACK	JAIL	IAIN
MATA	RAID	FAYE	NAPE	WARE	SASH	LANK	KARL	JAIN
MAYA	RAND	FAZE	NAVE	WAVE	WASH	LARK	MAIL	LAIN
NAGA	SAID	GAGE	NAZE	YALE	ZACH	MACK	MALL	LAWN
NANA	SAND	GALE	PACE	YARE	BALI	MARK	MARL	MAIN
NASA	SARD	GAME	PAGE	CALF	BARI	MASK	MAUL	MANN
PAPA	SAUD	GAPE	PALE	FAFF	CADI	NARK	NAIL	NAAN
RADA	WAND	GATE	PANE	GAFF	DALI	PACK	PAIL	PAIN
RAGA	WARD	GAVE	PARE	HALF	DANI	PARK	PALL	PAWN
RAJA	YARD	GAYE	PATE	NAFF	HARI	RACK	PAUL	RAIN
RARA	BABE	GAZE	PAVE	RAAF	KALI	RANK	PAWL	SAWN
RATA	BADE	HAKE	PAYE	RALF	LAVI	SACK	RAIL	TARN
SAGA	BAKE	HALE	RACE	TAFF	MAGI	SALK	SAIL	VAIN
SARA	BALE	HARE	RAGE	WAIF	MALI	SANK	SAUL	WAIN
TANA	BANE	HATE	RAKE	BANG	MAUI	SARK	TAIL	WARN
TAPA	BARE	HAVE	RAPE	FANG	MAXI	TACK	TALL	YARN
TARA	BASE	HAZE	RARE	GANG	NAZI	TALK	WAIL	YAWN
TATA	CADE	JADE	RATE	HAIG	PALI	TANK	WALL	BAIO

CAPO	PAIR	HANS	SAGS	MAST	HAZY	ACDC	ADEN	HERB
CATO	PARR	HATS	SAPS	MATT	KATY	ACED	EDEN	KERB
DADO	SAAR	HAWS	SASS	OAST	LACY	ACID	ODIN	SERB
FARO	BABS	JABS	SAWS	PACT	LADY	ICED	UDON	VERB
HALO	BAGS	JAGS	SAYS	PANT	LAZY	SCUD	EDDO	WEBB
IAGO	BANS	JAMS	TABS	PART	MACY	ACHE	ADUR	BEAD
MAYO	BAPS	JARS	TAGS	PAST	MANY	ACME	ODER	BEND
NATO	BARS	JAWS	TANS	RAFT	MARY	ACNE	ADDS	DEAD
PASO	BASS	JAYS	TAPS	RANT	NARY	ACRE	IDES	DEED
PAXO	BATS	LADS	TARS	RAPT	NAVY	GCSE	ODDS	FEED
SAGO	BAYS	LAGS	VANS	SALT	PACY	OCHE	ODES	FEND
SAXO	CABS	LAMS	VATS	TACT	RABY	ACOL	ADIT	FEUD
TACO	CADS	LAOS	WADS	TAFT	RACY	SCAM	EDIT	GELD
TARO	CAMS	LAPS	WAGS	TAIT	VARY	SCUM	EDTV	HEAD
CAMP	CANS	LASS	WARS	TART	WARY	ICON	ADDY	HEED
CAPP	CAPS	LAWS	WAYS	TAUT	WAVY	SCAN	DDAY	HELD
CARP	CARS	LAYS	YAKS	VAST	WAXY	ECHO	EDDY	HERD
DAMP	CASS	MACS	YAMS	WAFT	ZANY	ACER	EDGY	LEAD
EARP	CATS	MAPS	YAPS	WAIT	BAEZ	SCAR	IDLY	LEND
GAMP	CAWS	MARS	YAWS	WALT	JAZZ	ACAS	BELA	LEWD
GARP	DABS	MASS	ZAPS	WANT	ABBA	ACES	BETA	MEAD
GASP	DADS	MATS	BAHT	WART	ABTA	ACTS	DEVA	MELD
GAWP	DAIS	NABS	BAIT	WATT	ABED	ICES	FETA	MEND
HARP	DAKS	NAGS	BART	BAKU	ABBE	SCAT	HERA	NEED
HASP	DAMS	NANS	BAST	OAHU	ABLE	SCOT	LEDA	NERD
JAPP	DAPS	NAPS	BATT	RAGU	OBOE	SCUT	LEIA	READ
LAMP	DAWS	OAFS	CANT	SABU	ABEL	ECRU	LENA	REED
LAPP	DAYS	OAKS	CART	TATU	OBOL	CCTV	MEGA	REID
RAMP	EARS	OARS	CAST	ZASU	EBON	SCOW	MENA	REND
RASP	EATS	OATS	DAFT	ZAZU	EBRO	ACHY	MESA	SEED
SAMP	FADS	PADS	DART	CALX	IBAN	SCRY	NENA	SEND
TAMP	FAGS	PALS	EAST	MANX	OBAN	EDDA	NEVA	TEED
VAMP	FANS	PANS	FACT	MARX	EBOR	EDNA	PETA	TEND
WARP	FATS	PASS	FAST	BABY	IBIS	EBBS	REZA	VEND
WASP	GABS	PATS	GAIT	CARY	ADIE	IDEA	SETA	WEED
BARR	GADS	PAWS	HAFT	CAVY	ABET	EDGE	VEDA	WELD
CARR	GAGS	PAYS	HALT	DALY	ABUT	EDIE	VEGA	WEND
FAIR	GALS	RAGS	HART	DAVY	OBIT	IDLE	VERA	BEDE
FARR	GAPS	RAMS	KANT	EALY	IBEX	IDLE	WETA	BETE
HAIR	HAGS	RAPS	LAST	EASY	ABLY	IDOL	XENA	CEDE
LAIR	HALS	RATS	MALT	GABY	OBEY	ADAM	ZETA	CERE
MAAR	HAMS	RAYS	MART	GARY	SCAB	EDAM	BEEB	CETE

DENE	CEDI	DELL	BEEN	ZERO	PEER	LETS	CENT	TEAT
FETE	DELI	FEEL	BEHN	BEEP	REAR	MESS	CERT	TENT
GENE	DEMI	FELL	BENN	DEEP	SEAR	MEWS	DEBT	TEST
GERE	DENI	HEAL	DEAN	DEPP	SEER	NESS	DEFT	TEXT
HEBE	DESI	HEEL	DERN	HEAP	TEAR	NETS	DENT	VENT
HERE	GERI	HELL	FENN	HEEP	VEER	NEWS	FEAT	VERT
KEKE	JEDI	KEEL	FERN	HELP	WEAR	PEAS	FEET	VEST
MERE	KEPI	MEAL	GEAN	HEMP	WEIR	PEGS	FELT	WEFT
METE	LENI	MEWL	GENN	JEEP	YEAR	PENS	GELT	WELT
NENE	LEVI	NEAL	HEWN	KEEP	BEDS	PEPS	GENT	WENT
NEVE	PERI	NEIL	JEAN	KELP	BEES	PETS	GERT	WEPT
PEKE	SEMI	NELL	KEEN	KEMP	BEGS	PEWS	HEAT	WEST
PELE	SETI	PEAL	KERN	LEAP	BELS	REDS	HEFT	ZEST
PEPE	TERI	PEEL	LEAN	NEAP	BESS	REES	JEST	BEAU
PETE	YETI	REAL	LEON	NEEP	BETS	REPS	JETT	MENU
RENE	BEAK	REEL	MEAN	PEEP	BEYS	RETS	KELT	PERU
RETE	BECK	SEAL	NEON	REAP	CEPS	REVS	KENT	ZEBU
SERE	DECK	SELL	PENN	REPP	DEBS	SEAS	KEPT	DERV
SEVE	DEEK	TEAL	PEON	SEEP	DEES	SEES	LEAT	MERV
TEME	DESK	TELL	REIN	SEPP	DENS	SEGS	LEFT	BEVY
WERE	GEEK	VEAL	SEAN	TEMP	EELS	SENS	LENT	DEFY
BEEF	HECK	VEIL	SEEN	WEEP	FEES	SETS	LEST	DENY
DEAF	JERK	WEAL	SEWN	YELP	FENS	SEWS	LETT	DEWY
JEFF	LEAK	WELL	TEEN	BEAR	GELS	TEAS	MEAT	HEDY
LEAF	LEEK	YELL	TERN	BEER	GEMS	TEDS	MEET	LELY
LEIF	MEEK	ZEAL	VEIN	BEHR	GETS	TEES	MELT	LEVY
NEFF	NECK	BEAM	WEAN	DEAR	HEMS	TENS	NEAT	RELY
PELF	PEAK	DEEM	AERO	DEER	HENS	TESS	NEST	SEXY
REEF	PECK	GERM	DECO	FEAR	HERS	VETS	NETT	VERY
SELF	PEEK	HELM	DEMO	FEHR	HESS	WEBS	NEWT	BENZ
SERF	PENK	HERM	HERO	GEAR	HEWS	WEDS	NEXT	GETZ
BERG	PERK	LEAM	LEGO	HEAR	JESS	WETS	PEAT	METZ
DERG	REEK	PERM	LENO	HEIR	JETS	YEAS	PELT	OFFA
FENG	SEEK	REAM	LETO	HERR	JEWS	YEWS	PENT	AFRO
LENG	TEAK	SEAM	MEMO	JEER	KEGS	ZEUS	PERT	AFAR
PEGG	TECK	SEEM	NEMO	KEIR	KEYS	BEAT	PEST	EFTS
BETH	WEAK	SEJM	NERO	KERR	LEAS	BEET	RENT	IFFY
LEAH	WEEK	TEAM	PESO	LEAR	LEES	BELT	REST	AGRA
LECH	BELL	TEEM	REDO	LEER	LEGS	BENT	SEAT	AGED
MESH	CEIL	TERM	RENO	MEIR	LEIS	BERT	SECT	EGAD
SETH	CELL	AEON	VETO	NEAR	LENS	BEST	SENT	AGUE
YEAH	DEAL	BEAN	ZENO	PEAR	LESS	CELT	SETT	OGEE

OGLE	DHAL	RHYS	PICA	BIDE	NIKE	TIFF	BILK	RILL
OGRE	PHIL	THIS	PINA	BIKE	NILE	BING	DICK	SILL
AGOG	RHYL	THUS	PISA	BILE	NINE	DING	DINK	TILL
UGLI	AHEM	CHAT	RIGA	BISE	OISE	EIGG	DIRK	VIAL
AGIN	CHUM	CHIT	RITA	BITE	PIKE	KING	DISK	VIOL
EGAN	SHAM	GHAT	TINA	CIRE	PILE	LING	GINK	WILL
EGON	SHEM	SHOT	VIDA	CITE	PINE	MING	HICK	FILM
OGEN	SHIM	SHUT	VISA	DICE	PIPE	PING	JINK	FIRM
AGAR	THEM	THAT	VITA	DIME	RICE	RIGG	KICK	LIAM
IGOR	WHAM	WHAT	VIVA	DINE	RIDE	RING	KINK	SIAM
AGAS	WHIM	WHET	GIBB	DIRE	RIFE	SING	KIRK	DION
AGES	WHOM	WHIT	LIMB	DIVE	RILE	TING	LICK	FINN
EGGS	CHAN	THOU	DISC	EIRE	RIME	WING	LINK	JINN
EGOS	CHIN	CHAV	ZINC	FIFE	RIPE	ZING	MICK	KILN
IGGY	GHAN	CHEW	AIRD	FILE	RISE	DISH	MILK	LIEN
UGLY	KHAN	CHOW	BIND	FINE	RITE	FISH	MINK	LION
RHEA	SHIN	DHOW	BIRD	FIRE	RIVE	GISH	NICK	MIEN
SHEA	SHUN	PHEW	DIED	FIVE	SIDE	HIGH	OINK	SIAN
SHIA	THAN	SHAW	FIND	GIVE	SINE	KITH	PICK	SIGN
THEA	THEN	SHOW	GILD	HIDE	SIRE	NIGH	PINK	ZION
WHOA	THIN	THAW	GIRD	HIKE	SITE	PITH	RICK	BIKO
AHAB	WHEN	AHOY	HIED	HIRE	SIZE	RICH	RINK	BIRO
CHUB	WHIN	CHAY	HIND	HITE	TIDE	SIGH	RISK	CIAO
CHIC	CHOO	THEY	HIRD	HIVE	TILE	SIKH	SICK	DIDO
CHAD	OHIO	WHEY	KIDD	JIBE	TIME	SITH	SILK	DINO
EHUD	SHOO	CHEZ	KIND	JIVE	TINE	WISH	SINK	FIDO
SHAD	THEO	AIDA	LIED	KITE	TIRE	WITH	TICK	FIGO
SHED	CHAP	DINA	LIND	LICE	VIBE	FIFI	WICK	FILO
SHOD	CHIP	DITA	MILD	LIFE	VICE	FIJI	WINK	FINO
THUD	CHOP	DIVA	MIND	LIKE	VILE	GIGI	BILL	GINO
EHLE	SHAP	FIFA	NIDD	LIME	VINE	HIFI	DIAL	GIRO
GHEE	SHEP	GILA	PIED	LINE	WIDE	JIMI	DILL	HILO
SHOE	SHIP	GINA	RIDD	LIRE	WIFE	KIKI	FILL	KILO
SHUE	SHOP	LILA	RIND	LIVE	WILE	KIRI	GILL	LIDO
THEE	WHIP	LIMA	SILD	MICE	WINE	KIWI	GIRL	LILO
CHEF	WHOP	LIRA	SIND	MIKE	WIPE	LISI	HILL	LIMO
CHUG	CHAR	LISA	TIED	MILE	WIRE	MIDI	JILL	LINO
SHAG	CHER	LIZA	VIED	MIME	WISE	MIMI	KIEL	MILO
THUG	SHER	MICA	WILD	MINE	BIFF	MINI	KILL	MIRO
WHIG	THOR	MIKA	WIND	MIRE	MIFF	NIKI	MILL	MISO
SHAH	CHAS	MINA	AIDE	MITE	PIAF	TITI	PILL	NIRO
THAI	OHMS	NINA	AIRE	NICE	RIFF	ZIZI	RIAL	SILO

TIPO	KIDS	DIET	PITY	OLGA	PLIE	OLIO	SLOW	IMPS
TITO	KIPS	DINT	TIDY	PLEA	SLOE	BLIP	ALEX	XMAS
VINO	KISS	DIRT	TINY	ULNA	CLEF	CLAP	FLAX	EMIT
VITO	KITS	FIAT	VIMY	ULVA	OLAF	CLIP	FLEX	OMIT
WINO	LIDS	FIST	WILY	BLAB	ALIG	CLOP	FLUX	SMIT
ZICO	LIES	GIFT	WIRY	BLOB	BLAG	FLAP	ILEX	SMUT
LIMP	LIPS	GILT	DIAZ	BLUB	BLOG	FLIP	ALLY	SMEW
LISP	MILS	GIRT	FITZ	CLUB	CLOG	FLOP	CLAY	AMEX
WIMP	MISS	GIST	FIZZ	FLAB	FLAG	PLOP	CLOY	IMAX
WISP	NIBS	HILT	LINZ	GLIB	FLOG	SLAP	FLAY	AMOY
BIER	NIPS	HINT	RITZ	PLEB	GLUG	SLIP	PLAY	EMMY
DIOR	NITS	JILT	TIZZ	SLAB	PLUG	SLOP	PLOY	ANKA
LIAR	OIKS	KILT	AJAR	SLOB	SLAG	BLUR	SLAY	ANNA
PIER	OILS	KITT	AJAX	SLUB	SLOG	SLUR	EMMA	ANYA
TIER	PIES	LIFT	IKEA	ALEC	SLUG	ALAS	EMVA	ENNA
AIDS	PIGS	LILT	OKRA	BLOC	ALPH	ALES	YMCA	ENSA
AILS	PILS	LINT	SKUA	ALED	BLAH	ALMS	AMID	ENYA
AIMS	PINS	LIST	EKED	BLED	FLAK	ALPS	SMEE	INCA
AIRS	PIPS	MILT	SKID	CLAD	ELAL	ELLS	SMOG	KNOB
BIAS	PITS	MINT	SKYE	CLOD	ALUM	ELMS	SMUG	SNIB
BIBS	PIUS	MIST	OKRI	FLED	CLAM	ILLS	AMAH	SNOB
BIDS	RIBS	MITT	SKOL	GLAD	ELAM	PLUS	IMPI	SNUB
BINS	RIDS	PICT	SKIM	OLID	GLAM	BLOT	AMOK	ENID
BITS	RIGS	PINT	AKIN	PLOD	GLUM	CLOT	OMSK	ANNE
DIBS	RIMS	PITT	SKIN	SLED	KLIM	FLAT	EMIL	ANTE
DIES	RIPS	RIFT	SKEP	SLID	PLUM	FLIT	IMAM	INCE
DIGS	SIBS	RIOT	SKIP	VLAD	SLAM	GLUT	AMEN	KNEE
DIMS	SIMS	SIFT	IKER	ALEE	SLIM	PLOT	AMIN	ONCE
DIPS	SINS	SILT	EKES	ALOE	SLUM	SLAT	EMIN	SNAG
DISS	SIPS	TILT	SKIS	BLUE	ALAN	SLIT	GMEN	SNOG
FIBS	SIRS	TINT	SKAT	CLUE	ALUN	SLOT	IMAN	SNUG
FIGS	SITS	UIST	SKIT	ELBE	CLAN	BLEU	OMAN	ANKH
FINS	TIES	WILT	SKEW	ELKE	ELAN	SLAV	OMEN	INCH
FIRS	TINS	KIEV	ALBA	ELLE	FLAN	BLEW	XMEN	ANDI
FITS	TIPS	VIEW	ALDA	ELSE	GLEN	BLOW	AMBO	ANTI
GIGS	VIES	JINX	ALGA	FLEE	PLAN	CLAW	AMMO	INRI
GINS	WIGS	MINX	ALMA	FLOE	ALDO	FLAW	EMIR	RNLI
HIPS	WINS	AIRY	ELBA	FLUE	ALSO	FLEW	OMAR	ANIL
HISS	WITS	CITY	ELIA	GLEE	ALTO	FLOW	AMIS	ANON
HITS	YIPS	LILY	ELLA	GLUE	CLEO	GLOW	AMOS	ANNO
JIBS	ZIPS	LIVY	ELSA	ILIE	CLIO	SLAW	AMPS	INFO
JIGS	AINT	OILY	FLEA	KLEE	ELMO	SLEW	EMUS	INRO

INTO	IOWA	HOED	DOSE	POLE	BORG	TOPI	COOL	WORM
ONTO	LOLA	HOLD	DOTE	POPE	DONG	TORI	COWL	ZOOM
UNDO	LOMA	HOOD	DOVE	PORE	DOUG	YOGI	DOLL	BONN
UNTO	MONA	JOAD	DOZE	POSE	FOGG	BOOK	FOAL	BOON
KNAP	MOYA	LOAD	FORE	ROBE	GONG	COCK	FOIL	BORN
SNAP	NOLA	LORD	GONE	RODE	HOGG	CONK	FOOL	COIN
SNIP	NORA	LOUD	GORE	ROLE	LONG	COOK	FOUL	CORN
ANTS	NOVA	LOYD	HOLE	ROME	MOOG	CORK	FOWL	DOIN
ENDS	POLA	MOLD	HOME	ROPE	PONG	DOCK	GOAL	DOWN
GNUS	ROMA	MOOD	HONE	ROSE	ROEG	FOLK	HOWL	GOIN
INKS	ROSA	NORD	HOPE	ROTE	SONG	FORK	JOEL	GOON
INNS	ROTA	POND	HOSE	ROUE	TONG	HOCK	JOWL	GOWN
INXS	SOCA	ROAD	HOVE	ROVE	BOSH	HONK	KOHL	HORN
ONES	SODA	ROOD	HOWE	SOLE	BOTH	HOOK	KOOL	IOAN
ONUS	SOFA	SOLD	JOKE	SOME	COBH	JOCK	LOLL	JOAN
GNAT	SOMA	TOAD	JOSE	SORE	COSH	KOOK	MOLL	JOHN
KNIT	SOYA	TODD	JOVE	TOKE	DOSH	LOCK	NOEL	JOIN
KNOT	TOGA	TOED	LOBE	TOME	FOCH	LOOK	NOLL	LOAN
UNIT	YODA	TOLD	LODE	TONE	GOSH	MOCK	POLL	LOIN
UNST	YOGA	VOID	LOME	TOPE	GOTH	MONK	POOL	LOON
ANEW	ZOLA	WOAD	LONE	TORE	JOSH	MORK	ROIL	MOAN
GNAW	BOMB	WOLD	LOOE	TOTE	LOCH	NOCK	ROLL	MOON
KNEW	BOOB	WOOD	LOPE	VOLE	LOTH	NOOK	SOIL	MORN
KNOW	COBB	WORD	LORE	VOTE	MOTH	PORK	SOUL	MOWN
SNOW	COMB	BODE	LOSE	WOKE	NOAH	ROCK	TOIL	NOON
KNOX	TOMB	BOLE	LOVE	WORE	NOSH	ROOK	TOLL	NOUN
ONYX	WOMB	BONE	LOWE	WOVE	NOTH	SOAK	TOOL	ROAN
ANDY	BOLD	BORE	MODE	YOKE	POOH	SOCK	WOOL	SOON
ENVY	BOND	CODE	MOLE	YORE	POSH	SOOK	YOWL	SOWN
INDY	BOYD	COKE	MOPE	ZONE	ROTH	SOUK	BOOM	TORN
INKY	COED	COLE	MORE	COIF	TOSH	TONK	CORM	TOWN
ONLY	COLD	COME	MOTE	DOFF	AOKI	TOOK	DOOM	WORN
ANTZ	CORD	CONE	MOUE	GOLF	GOBI	WORK	DORM	BONO
COCA	DODD	COPE	MOVE	GOOF	HOPI	WOUK	FOAM	BOYO
CODA	DOWD	CORE	NODE	HOOF	JONI	YOLK	FORM	COCO
COLA	FOLD	COTE	NONE	LOAF	KOFI	YORK	HOLM	COMO
COMA	FOND	COVE	NOPE	ROLF	LOCI	BOIL	LOAM	DODO
DOHA	FOOD	DOGE	NORE	ROOF	LONI	BOLL	LOOM	DOJO
DORA	FORD	DOLE	NOSE	TOFF	LORI	BOWL	NORM	GOGO
GOYA	GOAD	DOME	NOTE	WOLF	NORI	COAL	POEM	GOZO
IONA	GOLD	DONE	OOZE	WOOF	ROTI	COIL	ROAM	HOBO
IOTA	GOOD	DOPE	POKE	BONG	TONI	COLL	ROOM	HOHO

JOMO	FOUR	GOES	ROWS	HOLT	FOXY	IPSO	TRAD	DRUM
KOKO	GOER	GOSS	SOBS	HOOT	GOBY	SPAR	TROD	FROM
LOBO	HOAR	HOBS	SODS	HOST	GORY	SPUR	ARNE	GRAM
LOCO	HOER	HODS	SONS	JOLT	HOLY	APES	BRAE	GRIM
LOGO	HOUR	HOES	SOPS	LOFT	JOEY	EPOS	BREE	PRAM
MOJO	LOUR	HOGS	SOTS	LOOT	JOLY	EPPS	BRIE	PRIM
MONO	MOOR	HOPS	SOWS	LOST	LORY	OPTS	CREE	PROM
NOGO	NOOR	IONS	TOES	LOUT	MOBY	OPUS	ERIE	TRAM
NONO	POOR	JOBS	TOGS	MOAT	POKY	SPAS	ERLE	TRIM
NOTO	POUR	JOGS	TOMS	MOOT	POLY	UPAS	ERNE	ARAN
POGO	ROAR	JOSS	TONS	MOST	PONY	SPAT	ERSE	ARUN
POLO	SOAR	JOTS	TOPS	NOWT	POSY	SPIT	FREE	BRAN
ROLO	SOUR	JOYS	TORS	POET	ROLY	SPOT	ORDE	BREN
RORO	TOUR	LOBS	TOSS	PORT	ROMY	SPIV	ORFE	BRIN
SOHO	YOUR	LOGS	TOTS	POST	ROPY	SPEW	ORLE	BRON
SOLO	BOAS	LOIS	TOWS	POUT	RORY	APEX	PRUE	BRYN
SOSO	BOBS	LOOS	TOYS	ROOT	ROSY	KPAX	TREE	CRAN
TODO	BODS	LOPS	VOSS	ROUT	ROXY	SPAY	TRUE	ERIN
TOGO	BOGS	LOSS	VOWS	SOFT	SONY	SPEY	URGE	FRAN
TOTO	BOOS	LOTS	WOES	SOOT	TOBY	SPRY	GRAF	GRAN
YOKO	BOPS	LOWS	WOKS	SORT	TONY	AQUA	BRAG	GRIN
YOYO	BOSS	MOAS	WOOS	TOOT	TORY	AREA	BRIG	IRAN
BOOP	BOWS	MOBS	YOBS	TORT	FONZ	ARIA	CRAG	IRON
COOP	BOYS	MODS	ZOOS	TOUT	LODZ	IRMA	DRAG	ORAN
COUP	COBS	MONS	BOAT	VOLT	APIA	ORCA	DRUG	TRON
HOOP	COGS	MOPS	BOHT	WONT	EPIC	ORLA	FROG	WREN
LOOP	COLS	MOSS	BOLT	LOMU	OPEC	PROA	GREG	ARGO
POMP	CONS	MOWS	BOOT	NONU	APED	URSA	GROG	ARLO
POOP	COOS	NOBS	BOTT	TOFU	IPOD	ARAB	PRIG	ARNO
POPP	COPS	NODS	BOUT	COAX	SPED	CRAB	TROG	ARVO
ROMP	COTS	NOES	COAT	FOXX	SPUD	CRIB	TRUG	BRIO
SOAP	COWS	NOUS	COLT	HOAX	APSE	DRAB	ARCH	BRNO
SOUP	DOES	OOPS	COOT	ROUX	EPEE	DRUB	ERIK	DRNO
YOMP	DOGS	PODS	COPT	BODY	SPEE	GRAB	TREK	ERGO
BOAR	DONS	POMS	COST	BONY	OPAL	GRUB	ARAL	TRIO
BOER	DORS	POPS	DOLT	BOXY	OPEL	ERIC	ORAL	CROP
BOOR	DOSS	POTS	DONT	CODY	SPAM	ARID	URAL	DRIP
COIR	DOTS	ROBS	FONT	CONY	OPEN	BRAD	ARUM	DROP
CORR	FOBS	RODS	FOOT	COPY	SPAN	BRED	BRAM	GRIP
DOER	FOES	ROOS	FORT	COSY	SPIN	FRED	BRIM	PREP
DOOR	FOPS	ROSS	GOAT	DORY	SPUN	GRID	CRAM	PROP
DOUR	GODS	ROTS	GOUT	DOZY	UPON	PROD	DRAM	TRAP

TRIP	DREW	RSVP	OTIS	RUUD	YULE	SUFI	FULL	JUMP
WRAP	GREW	TSAR	UTES	SUDD	BUFF	SURI	FURL	LUMP
IRAQ	GROW	USER	STET	SUED	BUMF	SUZI	GULL	PULP
BRER	PROW	USSR	STEW	SURD	CUFF	YURI	HULL	PUMP
ARCS	CRUX	ASKS	STOW	BUDE	DUFF	BUCK	HURL	QUIP
ARES	ORYX	ASPS	STYX	BUTE	GUFF	BULK	LULL	RUMP
ARMS	TREX	ISIS	ETTY	CUBE	GULF	BUNK	MULL	SUMP
ARTS	ARMY	USES	STAY	CURE	HUFF	BUSK	NULL	BURR
BRAS	ARTY	ESAU	AURA	CUTE	LUFF	DUCK	PULL	MUIR
BROS	BRAY	ESKY	BUPA	DUCE	MUFF	DUNK	PURL	PURR
ERAS	DRAY	ESPY	CUBA	DUDE	PUFF	DUSK	TULL	RUHR
ERGS	DREY	ISPY	DUMA	DUKE	RUFF	FUNK	GUAM	SUIR
EROS	FRAY	ETNA	HULA	DUNE	SURF	GUNK	BURN	AUKS
ERRS	GRAY	ETTA	JURA	DUPE	TUFF	HULK	DUNN	BUDS
GRAS	GREY	ITMA	LUKA	FUME	TURF	HUNK	EUAN	BUGS
IRIS	ORGY	STOA	LUNA	FUSE	BUNG	HUSK	GUNN	BUNS
IRKS	ORLY	STAB	PULA	HUGE	DUNG	JUNK	HURN	BUTS
KRIS	PRAY	STUB	PUMA	HUME	HUNG	LUCK	JUAN	BUYS
ORBS	PREY	OTIC	PUPA	JUDE	JUNG	LURK	LUNN	CUBS
ORCS	TRAY	STUD	RULA	JUNE	LUNG	MUCK	NUNN	CUES
ORES	TREY	STYE	SUVA	JUTE	MUNG	MURK	QUIN	CUPS
PROS	TROY	STAG	TUBA	LUCE	QUAG	MUSK	RUIN	CURS
URIS	WRAY	STIG	TULA	LUGE	RUNG	NUUK	TURN	CUSS
URNS	XRAY	ETCH	TUNA	LUKE	SUNG	PUCK	YUAN	CUTS
BRAT	CRUZ	ITCH	BULB	LUNE	BUSH	PUNK	AUTO	DUBS
BRIT	GRAZ	UTAH	CURB	LURE	CUSH	RUCK	CUJO	DUDS
BRUT	ASDA	ETUI	DUMB	LUTE	GUSH	RUSK	EURO	DUES
DRAT	ASIA	ETAL	NUMB	MULE	HUGH	SUCK	HUGO	DUOS
ERST	ESMA	ITAL	AULD	MUSE	HUSH	SULK	JUDO	FURS
FRET	ISLA	ATOM	BUDD	NUDE	LUSH	SUNK	JUNO	FUSS
GRIT	OSSA	ITEM	CUED	MUCH	MUSH	TUCK	LUDO	GUMS
GROT	RSPB	STEM	CURD	OUSE	MUSH	TURK	OUZO	GUNS
TROT	USED	ETON	FUND	PUCE	OUCH	TUSK	PUZO	GUTS
WRIT	ASHE	STAN	HUDD	PULE	PUSH	YUCK	SUMO	GUYS
FRAU	ESSE	STEN	HUED	PURE	RUSH	BULL	BUMP	HUBS
URDU	ISLE	STUN	HURD	RUDE	RUTH	BURL	BURP	HUES
BREW	GSOH	OTTO	JUDD	RULE	SUCH	CULL	CULP	HUGS
BROW	ASTI	ATOP	KURD	RUNE	TUSH	CURL	CUSP	HUMS
CRAW	ASBO	STEP	QUAD	RUSE	AUDI	DUAL	DUMP	HUSS
CREW	ESSO	STOP	QUID	SURE	FUJI	DUEL	GULP	HUTS
CROW	OSLO	STAR	RUDD	TUBE	JUDI	DULL	GUMP	JUGS
DRAW	ASAP	STIR	RUED	TUNE	MUNI	FUEL	HUMP	JUTS

LUGS	JUST	LUTZ	KWAN	BYRE	CYST
LUIS	KURT	QUIZ	OWEN	BYTE	EYOT
MUGS	LUST	SUEZ	SWAN	DYCE	GYNT
MUMS	MUST	UVEA	TWIN	DYKE	LYNX
NUNS	MUTT	AVID	SWAP	DYNE	OYEZ
NUTS	OUST	OVID	EWER	EYRE	EZRA
OURS	PUNT	EVIE	AWES	GYBE	AZOV
PUBS	PUTT	EVIL	AWLS	GYRE	OZZY
PUGS	QUIT	OVAL	EWES	HYDE	AZIZ
PUNS	RUNT	OVUM	OWES	HYPE	
PUPS	RUST	AVON	OWLS	KYLE	
PUSS	SUET	EVAN	OWNS	LYLE	
PUTS	SUIT	EVEN	TWOS	LYME	
RUBS	TUFT	IVAN	SWAT	LYRE	
RUES	YURT	OVEN	SWIT	PYRE	
RUGS	GURU	AVER	SWOT	RYDE	
RUNS	HUTU	EVER	TWIT	TYKE	
RUSS	JUJU	IVER	AWAY	TYNE	
RUTS	KUDU	IVOR	AWRY	TYPE	
SUBS	LULU	OVER	SWAY	TYRE	
SUDS	TUTU	AVIS	IXIA	WYLE	
SUES	ZULU	IVES	AXED	BYNG	
SUMS	BUOY	YVES	AXLE	MYTH	
SUPS	BURY	AVIV	AXEL	DYCK	
SUSS	BUSY	AVOW	AXIL	EYAM	
TUBS	DUFY	SWAB	EXAM	CYAN	
TUGS	DULY	AWED	OXEN	DYAN	
TUNS	DURY	OWED	EXPO	HYMN	
TUTS	DUTY	TWEE	OXER	LYNN	
WUSS	FURY	SWAG	AXES	LYON	
AUNT	HUEY	SWIG	AXIS	RYAN	
BURT	JUDY	TWIG	EXES	TYPO	
BUST	JULY	KWAI	EXIT	TYRO	
BUTT	JURY	AWOL	MYNA	DYER	
CULT	LUCY	HWYL	MYRA	AYES	
CURT	PUNY	SWAM	TYRA	BYES	
DUCT	QUAY	SWIM	BYRD	DYES	
DUET	RUBY	SWUM	DYED	EYAS	
DUST	RUDY	EWAN	EYED	EYES	
GUST	SUZY	EWEN	KYDD	GYMS	
HUNT	BUZZ	GWEN	LYDD	SYMS	
HURT	FUZZ	GWYN	NYPD	WYSS	

BABAR	NAIAD	SAMBA	DANDY	BABES	CAREY	FARED	JAMES
BANAL	NASAL	TABBY	FADDY	BADEN	CASED	FARES	JANET
BASAL	NATAL	YABBY	FALDO	BADER	CASES	FATED	JAPES
CABAL	NAVAL	BACCY	GARDA	BAGEL	CASEY	FATES	JARED
CACAO	NAVAN	BANCO	GAUDI	BAKED	CATER	FAXED	JAWED
CANAL	NAWAB	BATCH	GAUDY	BAKER	CATES	FAXES	KACEY
CARAT	PAEAN	CASCA	HANDL	BAKES	CAVED	FAZED	KAMEN
CAVAN	PAGAN	CATCH	HANDS	BALED	CAVER	FAZES	KAREN
DAKAR	PALAU	DANCE	HANDY	BALER	CAVES	GALES	KASEY
DALAI	PAPAL	DARCY	HARDY	BALES	CAWED	GAMER	LABEL
DANAE	PARAS	FALCO	HAYDN	BARED	DALEK	GAMES	LACED
DAYAK	QATAR	FANCY	KANDY	BARER	DALES	GAMEY	LACES
DAYAN	RABAT	FARCE	LANDS	BARES	DALEY	GAPED	LACEY
FARAD	RADAR	HATCH	LARDY	BASED	DAMES	GAPER	LADEN
FATAH	RAJAS	LANCE	LAUDA	BASER	DANES	GAPES	LAGER
FATAL	SADAT	LARCH	LAUDS	BASES	DARED	GASES	LAKER
GALAH	SAGAN	LATCH	MADDY	BATED	DARES	GATED	LAKES
GALAS	SAGAS	MARCH	MAGDA	BATES	DATED	GATES	LAMER
HAGAR	SALAD	MARCO	MAHDI	BAUER	DATES	GAVEL	LANES
HALAL	SANAA	MATCH	MAIDA	BAYED	DAVEY	GAZED	LAPEL
HAMAS	SARAH	NANCY	MAIDS	CABER	DAWES	GAZES	LASER
JAPAN	SATAN	PARCH	MANDY	CADET	DAZED	HADES	LATER
KARAN	SATAY	PATCH	MARDI	CAFES	DAZES	HALER	LATEX
KAYAK	TAMAR	RANCH	PADDY	CAGED	EAGER	HALEY	LAVER
KAZAN	TAPAS	SAUCE	PANDA	CAGES	EALES	HARED	LAYER
LAGAN	BAMBI	SAUCY	RAIDS	CAGEY	EASED	HAREM	LAZED
LAHAR	BARBS	VANCE	RANDE	CAKED	EASEL	HARES	LAZES
LALAW	DARBY	WATCH	RANDS	CAKES	EASES	HATED	MABEL
LAMAS	DAUBS	BANDS	RANDY	CALEB	EATEN	HATES	MACES
LAPAZ	GABBA	BANDY	SANDI	CAMEL	EATER	HAUER	MAKER
MACAW	GABBY	BARDO	SANDS	CAMEO	EAVES	HAVEL	MAKES
MADAM	GARBO	BARDS	SANDY	CANED	FACED	HAVEN	MALES
MAHAL	JAMBS	BAWDS	SAUDI	CANES	FACES	HAVER	MAMET
MALAR	LAMBS	BAWDY	TANDY	CAPED	FACET	HAVES	MANES
MALAY	LAYBY	CADDY	TARDY	CAPER	FADED	HAWES	MANET
MAMAS	MAMBA	CANDO	WANDA	CAPES	FADES	HAYEK	MARES
MARAT	MAMBO	CANDY	WANDS	CARED	FAKED	HAYES	MATED
MASAI	MAYBE	CARDS	WARDS	CARER	FAKER	HAZEL	MATER
MAYAN	RABBI	DADDY	YARDS	CARES	FAKES	JADED	MATES
MAYAS	RAMBO	DANDO	BABEL	CARET	FAMED	JADES	MATEY

MAVEN	RAKED	TARES	TAFFY	CACHE	JAMIE	SAHIB	MANKY
MAYER	RAKES	TAXED	WAIFS	CATHY	JANIS	SAMIA	MARKS
MAZES	RAMEN	TAXES	BADGE	DACHA	KAPIL	SAPID	MASKS
NAKED	RARER	VADER	BAGGY	KATHY	KATIE	SARIS	NARKS
NAMED	RASEN	VALES	BANGS	LATHE	LAMIA	SASIN	NARKY
NAMES	RATED	VALET	BARGE	LATHS	LAOIS	SATIE	PACKS
NAPES	RATEL	VANES	CADGE	MACHO	LAPIS	SATIN	PARKA
NARES	RATES	VASES	CARGO	MATHS	LATIN	TACIT	PARKS
NAVEL	RAVED	WADED	FANGS	NACHO	LAZIO	TAJIK	PARKY
NAVES	RAVEL	WADER	FARGO	OATHS	MAFIA	TAMIL	RACKS
OAKEN	RAVEN	WADES	GANGS	PASHA	MAGIC	TAPIR	RANKS
OARED	RAVER	WAFER	GAUGE	PATHE	MALIK	TATIN	SACKS
OASES	RAVES	WAGED	HAIGH	PATHS	MALIN	TAXIS	SADKO
OATES	RAZED	WAGER	HANGS	SACHA	MANIA	VADIM	SARKY
PACED	RAZES	WAGES	LANGE	SACHS	MANIC	VALID	TACKS
PACER	SAFER	WAKEN	LARGE	SADHU	MARIA	VAPID	TACKY
PACES	SAFES	WAKES	LARGO	TASHA	MARIE	ZADIE	TALKS
PAGED	SAGES	WALES	LAUGH	YACHT	MARIN	BANJO	TANKS
PAGER	SAKER	WANED	MADGE	BASIC	MARIO	GANJA	TARKA
PAGES	SALEM	WANES	MANGA	BASIE	MAVIS	HADJI	TASKS
PALED	SALES	WARES	MANGE	BASIL	MAXIM	BACKS	WACKY
PALER	SAMEY	WATER	MANGO	BASIN	NADIA	BANKS	WALKS
PALES	SANER	WAVED	MANGY	BASIS	NADIR	BARKS	YANKS
PANEL	SATED	WAVER	MARGE	BATIK	NAVIN	BASKS	BADLY
PANES	SATES	WAVES	MARGI	CABIN	OASIS	CASKS	BAILS
PAPER	SAVED	WAXED	PAIGE	CADIS	PALIN	GAWKY	BALLS
PARED	SAVER	WAXEN	PANGS	CADIZ	PANIC	HACKS	BALLY
PARES	SAVES	WAXES	RAGGA	CALID	PARIS	HAIKU	BASLE
PATEN	SAWED	YATES	RANGE	CAVIL	PATIO	HANKS	BAULK
PATER	SAYER	YAWED	RANGY	DALIT	PAYIN	HANKY	BAWLS
PAVED	TAKEN	BANFF	SAGGY	DARIN	RABID	HARKS	CABLE
PAVES	TAKER	DAFFY	TAIGA	DARIO	RABIN	HAWKE	CALLS
PAWED	TAKES	FAFFS	TANGA	DAVID	RADII	HAWKS	CARLA
PAYEE	TALES	GAFFE	TANGO	DAVIS	RADIO	JACKS	CARLO
PAYER	TAMED	GAFFS	TANGS	DAVIT	RADIX	KAFKA	CARLY
RACED	TAMER	HAIFA	TANGY	FAGIN	RANIS	LACKS	CAULK
RACER	TAMES	JAFFA	WAUGH	FAKIR	RAPID	LAIKA	DAILY
RACES	TAPED	JAFFE	BASHO	GAMIN	RATIO	LANKY	DALLY
RAGED	TAPER	MALFI	BATHE	GAVIN	SADIE	LARKS	DARLA
RAGES	TAPES	NAAFI	BATHS	HABIT	SAFIN	LATKE	EAGLE

EARLE	SABLE	SAMMY	PAYNE	GALOP	WAGON	DAIRY	LAPSE
EARLS	SADLY	TAMMY	RAINE	HADOW	YAHOO	DAVRO	LASSE
EARLY	SAILS	WARMS	RAINS	HANOI	CAMPS	EAGRE	LASSO
FABLE	SALLY	BANNS	RAINY	HAVOC	CARPS	FAIRS	MANSE
FAILS	SAYLE	BARNS	SAINT	JABOT	GAMPS	FAIRY	MARSH
FALLS	TABLE	CAINE	SAUNA	JACOB	GAPPY	FAURE	NAISH
FAULT	TAILS	CANNA	TAINT	JASON	GASPS	HAIRS	PALSY
GABLE	TALLY	CANNY	TANNI	KAPOK	HAPPY	HAIRY	PANSY
GAELS	VALLI	CARNE	TARNS	KAZOO	HARPO	HARRY	PARSE
GAILY	VAULT	DAMNS	TAUNT	LABOR	HARPS	JARRE	PASSE
GALLS	WAILS	DANNY	TAWNY	LAGOS	HARPY	LAIRD	PATSY
GAYLE	WALLS	DARNS	VARNA	LAYON	HASPS	LAIRG	PAUSE
HAILE	WALLY	DAUNT	VAUNT	MACON	KAPPA	LAIRS	RAISA
HAILS	YAWLS	DAWNS	WAINS	MADOC	LAMPS	LARRY	RAISE
HALLE	BALMS	EARNS	WARNE	MAGOG	NAPPA	LAURA	SALSA
HALLS	BALMY	FAINT	WARNS	MAGOO	NAPPY	MACRO	SAMSA
HAULS	BARMY	FANNY	WAYNE	MAHON	PAPPY	MAORI	SASSY
HAYLE	CALMS	FAUNA	YARNS	MAJOR	RALPH	MARRY	SAYSO
JAILS	DAMME	FAUNS	YAWNS	MANOA	RAMPS	MAURA	TANSY
LADLE	FARMS	FAWNS	AARON	MANON	RASPS	NACRE	TASSO
LAILA	GAMMA	GAINS	BACON	MANOR	TAMPA	NAIRA	TAWSE
LAXLY	GAMMY	GAUNT	BALOO	MASON	TAMPS	NAIRN	WAIST
LAYLA	HALMA	HAUNT	BARON	MAYOR	TAUPE	NAURU	WALSH
MADLY	HARMS	JAUNT	BATON	NABOB	VAMPS	PADRE	BAFTA
MAILS	JAIME	JAYNE	BAYOU	PAEON	WARPS	PAIRS	BAITS
MALLE	JAMMY	KARNO	CABOT	RADON	WASPS	PARRY	BALTI
MALLS	KARMA	LAINE	CALOR	RAMON	WASPY	SABRE	BANTU
MANLY	MAGMA	LAWNS	CANOE	RAYON	ZAPPA	TARRY	BASTE
MAPLE	MAIMS	MAGNA	CANON	RAZOR	BAIRD	YARRA	BATTY
MAULS	MALMO	MAINE	CAPON	SABOT	BAIRN	ZAIRE	CACTI
MAYLE	MAMMA	MAINS	CAROB	SALON	BARRE	BALSA	CANTO
NAILS	MAMMY	MAINZ	CAROL	SALOP	BARRY	CAUSE	CANTS
PABLO	NAOMI	MANNA	CARON	SAMOA	BASRA	DAISY	CARTE
PAILS	PADME	MARNI	DADOS	SAVOY	CADRE	FALSE	CARTS
PALLS	PALMA	NANNY	DAFOE	SAXON	CAIRN	FARSI	CARTY
PALLY	PALMS	PAINE	DAMON	TABOO	CAIRO	FAUST	CASTA
PAULA	PARMA	PAINS	DAVOS	TABOR	CAPRA	GASSY	CASTE
RAILS	SALMA	PAINT	EATON	TACOS	CAPRI	HARSH	CASTS
RALLY	SALMI	PATNA	GABON	TALON	CARRE	HAUSA	CATTY
RAWLE	SAMMS	PAWNS	GABOR	TAROT	CARRY	HAWSE	DANTE

DARTS	RASTA	SALUT	UBOAT	SCRAG	SCENT	EDGAR	EDINA
EARTH	RATTY	TAGUS	ABACK	SCRAM	SCONE	IDEAL	ADDON
FACTS	SALTS	TALUS	ABIDE	SCRAP	ACTON	IDEAS	ADHOC
FAITH	SALTY	TATUM	ABODE	SCABS	ACTOR	ADOBE	ADIOS
FANTA	SANTA	VADUZ	ABBES	SCUBA	ICHOR	EDICT	CDROM
FASTS	SAUTE	VAGUE	ABBEY	ACIDS	MCCOY	EDUCE	IDIOM
FATTY	TARTS	VAGUS	ABNER	SCUDO	SCION	ADDED	IDIOT
GARTH	TASTE	VALUE	EBBED	SCUDS	SCOOP	ADDER	ODEON
HAFTS	TASTY	YAKUT	EBSEN	ACHED	SCOOT	ADIEU	ADAPT
HAITI	TATTY	CALVE	IBSEN	ACHES	SCAPA	ADLER	ADEPT
HALTS	WAFTS	CARVE	OBJET	ACKEE	SCAPE	ADMEN	ADOPT
HARTY	WAITE	FAUVE	OBOES	ACKER	SCOPE	EDGED	ADORE
HASTE	WAITS	HALVA	ABAFT	ACRES	ACCRA	EDGER	ADORN
HASTY	WALTZ	HALVE	ABUJA	ACTED	ACORN	EDGES	EDITH
HAUTE	WANTS	LARVA	MBEKI	ICIER	OCHRE	IDLED	EDITS
LAITY	WARTS	MAEVE	ABELE	MCGEE	SCARE	IDLER	ADDUP
LASTS	WARTY	MAUVE	OBELI	OCTET	SCARF	IDLES	ADEUX
LATTE	WASTE	NAIVE	EBONY	SCREE	SCARP	ODDER	ODIUM
MALTA	WATTS	NAVVY	TBONE	SCREW	SCARS	UDDER	ODOUR
MANTA	YALTA	SALVE	ABBOT	SCIFI	SCARY	EDIFY	EDWYN
MARTI	ZANTE	SALVO	ABHOR	SCOFF	SCORE	ADAGE	BEGAN
MARTS	CAJUN	SAVVY	EBDON	SCUFF	SCORN	IDAHO	BEGAT
MARTY	CAMUS	VALVE	ABORT	ACRID	SCURF	ADAIR	BEHAN
MASTS	DATUM	WAIVE	ABASE	SCRIP	ZCARS	ADLIB	BELAY
NASTY	FACUP	FATWA	ABUSE	ECOLI	ACUTE	ADMIN	BEVAN
NATTY	GAMUT	CALYX	ABYSS	ICILY	SCOTS	ADMIT	CEDAR
OASTS	HAGUE	DARYL	OBESE	MCFLY	SCOTT	ADMIX	CESAR
PACTS	JANUS	MACYS	ABATE	SCALD	SCUTS	EDDIE	DEBAG
PANTO	KABUL	SATYR	ABETS	SCALE	ACTUP	EDWIN	DEBAR
PANTS	KAPUT	TANYA	ABUTS	SCALP	OCCUR	IDRIS	DECAD
PARTS	LAPUP	VANYA	ABDUL	SCALY	SCAUP	ODDIE	DECAF
PARTY	LARUE	BAIZE	ABOUT	SCOLD	SCOUR	ADUKI	DECAY
PASTA	LAYUP	GAUZE	ABOVE	SCULL	SCOUT	ADDLE	DEGAS
PASTE	MAGUS	GAUZY	OBEYS	SCAMP	SCRUB	ADELE	DELAY
PASTY	MANUS	GAZZA	ABUZZ	SCRUM	SCRUM	ADOLF	DEWAR
PATTI	NAHUM	JAZZY	IBIZA	ICENI	SCOWL	ADULT	FERAL
PATTY	OAKUM	LANZA	ECLAT	ICING	SCOWS	IDOLS	HEMAN
PAYTV	PADUA	MAIZE	MCKAY	ICONS	ADDAX	IDYLL	HERAT
RAFTS	PAPUA	MATZO	OCEAN	SCANT	ADLAI	ODDLY	HEXAD
RANTS	PAYUP	EBOAT	OCTAD	SCENE	ADMAN	ADAMS	KEBAB

LEGAL	TENBY	WENCH	TEDDY	JEWEL	SEWED	SERGE	LEXIS
LEHAR	VERBS	BEADS	TENDS	KESEY	SEWER	TEIGN	MEDIA
MEDAL	YERBA	BEADY	VEIDT	KEYED	TELEX	VERGE	MEDIC
MEDAN	BEACH	BENDS	VELDT	KEYES	TENET	WEDGE	MERIT
MEGAN	BEECH	BENDY	VENDS	LEPEN	TEPEE	WEIGH	NEVIL
MENAI	BELCH	DEEDS	VERDI	LEPER	VEXED	DELHI	NEVIS
METAL	BENCH	FEEDS	WEEDS	LEVEE	VEXES	HECHT	PERIL
NEPAL	DECCA	FENDI	WEEDY	LEVEL	WEBER	LETHE	PETIT
PECAN	DEICE	FENDS	WELDS	LEVER	WESER	METHS	REBID
PEDAL	DENCH	FEUDS	WENDS	LEWES	XEBEC	AEGIS	REDID
PENAL	DEUCE	GEODE	WENDY	MEDEA	YEMEN	BEFIT	REFIT
PETAL	FENCE	HEADS	ZELDA	MELEE	BEEFS	BEGIN	REGIS
RECAP	FETCH	HEADY	ZENDA	MERES	BEEFY	BELIE	REJIG
REGAL	HENCE	HEDDA	BEGET	METED	BEOFF	BENIN	RELIC
REGAN	KEACH	HEEDS	BENET	METER	DEIFY	BEVIN	RELIT
REHAB	KENCO	HEIDI	BERET	METES	DELFT	CECIL	REMIT
RELAX	KETCH	HERDS	BESET	MEWED	GEOFF	CELIA	REMIX
RELAY	LEACH	KENDO	BETEL	MEYER	LEAFY	DEBIT	RESIN
RENAL	LECCE	LEADS	BEVEL	NEGEV	REEFS	DELIA	RESIT
REPAY	LEECH	LEEDS	BEWES	NENEH	REIFY	DEMIS	REVIE
RERAN	MECCA	LENDL	BEZEL	NEVER	SERFS	DENIM	SEMIS
RESAT	MERCY	LENDS	CEDED	NEWEL	BEIGE	DENIS	SEPIA
SEDAN	PEACE	MELDS	CEDES	NEWER	BERGS	DEVIL	SERIF
SEGAL	PEACH	MENDS	CELEB	PEKES	DEIGN	EERIE	SERIN
SEPAL	PENCE	NEDDY	CERES	PERES	FEIGN	FELIX	TEPID
SERAI	PERCH	NEEDS	DEFER	PETER	HEDGE	FETID	VEDIC
TEGAN	PERCY	NEEDY	DEREK	REBEC	HENGE	GELID	ZELIG
TEXAN	PESCI	NERDS	DETER	REBEL	HERGE	GENIE	BEAKS
TEXAS	REACH	NERDY	DEWEY	REFER	KEDGE	HELIX	BECKS
VEGAN	REACT	PENDS	FETES	REGER	LEDGE	HEMIN	BECKY
VEGAS	RECCE	READE	FEVER	RELET	LEGGY	KELIS	DECKS
VENAL	REECE	READS	FEWER	RENEE	LEIGH	KEPIS	DEKKO
DERBY	REICH	READY	GENES	RENEW	LETGO	KEVIN	DESKS
GETBY	SECCO	REDDY	GENET	REPEL	MERGE	KEYIN	GECKO
HERBS	TEACH	REEDS	HEGEL	RESET	NEAGH	LEGIT	GEEKY
KERBS	TENCH	REEDY	HELEN	REVEL	NEIGH	LENIN	JERKS
MELBA	TERCE	RENDS	HEMEN	SEDER	PEGGY	LETIN	JERKY
SELBY	TESCO	SEEDS	HEVER	SELES	PENGE	LEVIN	LEAKS
SERBS	VETCH	SEEDY	HEWED	SEVEN	REIGN	LEVIS	LEAKY
SETBY	WELCH	SENDS	HEWER	SEVER	SEDGE	LEWIS	LEEKS

NECKS	MEALS	SEAMY	TERNS	SETON	HEARD	TETRA	WELSH
PEAKE	MEALY	SEEMS	VEINS	TENON	HEARS	VEERS	YEAST
PEAKS	MELLY	SELMA	VERNE	TENOR	HEART	WEARS	BEATS
PEAKY	MERLE	TEAMS	WEANS	VENOM	HEIRS	WEARY	BELTS
PECKS	NEILL	TEEMS	WEENY	XENON	HENRI	WEIRD	BERTH
PEEKS	NELLE	TERMS	AESOP	XEROX	HENRY	WEIRS	BESTS
PERKS	NELLY	VELMA	BEBOP	ZEROS	JEERS	YEARN	BETTE
PERKY	NEWLY	AEONS	BEFOG	BEEPS	JERRY	YEARS	BETTY
PESKY	PEALS	BEANO	BELOW	HEAPS	KEIRA	ZEBRA	CELTS
REEKS	PEELS	BEANS	BESOM	HELPS	KERRY	BEAST	CENTS
REIKI	REALM	BEING	DECOR	JEEPS	LEARN	CEASE	CERTS
SEEKS	REELS	BENNY	DECOY	KEEPS	LEARY	DEISM	CEUTA
TENKO	REPLY	BERNE	DEFOE	LEAPS	LEERS	DEIST	DEATH
WEEKS	SEALS	DEANS	DELON	LEAPT	LEERY	DENSE	DEBTS
BEALE	SELLS	FEINT	DEMOB	NEEPS	MEARS	FEAST	DEITY
BELLA	SERLE	FERNS	DEMON	PEEPS	MERRY	GEESE	DELTA
BELLE	TEALS	GEENA	DEMOS	REAPS	METRE	GESSO	DENTS
BELLS	TELLS	HEINZ	DEPOT	SEEPS	METRO	HEIST	DEPTH
BELLY	TELLY	HENNA	DETOX	TEMPO	NEARS	HESSE	FEATS
CELLO	TESLA	JEANS	DEVON	TEMPS	NEGRO	JESSE	FELTZ
CELLS	VEILS	JENNA	FELON	TEMPT	NEHRU	LEASE	FESTE
DEALS	WEALD	JENNY	GENOA	VESPA	NEWRY	LEASH	GENTS
DEALT	WEALS	KEANE	GETON	WEEPS	PEARL	LEAST	GESTE
DELLA	WEILL	KEANU	HELOT	WEEPY	PEARS	MENSA	GETTY
DELLS	WELLA	KEENS	HEROD	YELPS	PEDRO	MESSY	HEATH
FEELS	WELLS	KENNY	HERON	ZEPPO	PEERS	MEUSE	HEATS
FELLS	WELLY	LEANS	LEBON	BEARD	PERRY	NEWSY	HEFTY
HEALS	YELLS	LEANT	LEMON	BEARS	PETRA	PEASE	HERTZ
HEALY	BEAMS	LENNY	LEROY	BEERS	PETRI	PERSE	HETTY
HEELS	DEEMS	LEONI	LETON	BEERY	REARM	REESE	JESTS
HELLO	DERMA	MEANS	MEDOC	BERRY	REARS	REUSE	JETTY
HELLS	FEMME	MEANT	MEKON	DEARS	REPRO	SENSE	KEATS
JELLO	GEMMA	PENNE	MELON	DEBRA	RETRO	SEUSS	KEITH
JELLY	GERMS	PENNY	MEMOS	DECRY	RETRY	TEASE	LEITH
KEELE	HELMS	PEONY	PEKOE	DERRY	SEARS	TEESE	LENTO
KEELS	JEMMA	REINS	PERON	FEARS	SEERS	TENSE	LETTS
KEELY	JEMMY	SEINE	PESOS	FERRY	TEARS	TERSE	MEATH
KELLS	PERMS	SENNA	REPOT	GEARS	TERRA	TESSA	MEATS
KELLY	REAMS	TEENS	SENOR	GENRE	TERRI	VERSE	MEATY
LEELA	SEAMS	TEENY	SEPOY	GERRY	TERRY	VERSO	MEETS

MELTS	FEMUR	REAVE	AGAIN	SHOCK	THEFT	CHOMP	THING
NEATH	GEEUP	REEVE	AGGIE	SHUCK	WHIFF	CHUMP	THINK
NESTA	GENUP	SERVE	NGAIO	THICK	CHUGS	CHUMS	THINS
NESTS	GENUS	SERVO	UGRIC	WHACK	THIGH	RHOMB	THONG
NEWTS	GETUP	VERVE	AGILE	WHICH	THUGS	RHYME	WHINE
PEATY	HETUP	WEAVE	AGENT	CHIDE	WHIGS	SHAME	WHINS
PELTS	JESUS	BERYL	AGONY	KHADI	SHAHS	SHIMS	CHAOS
PERTH	LEGUP	DEXYS	AGLOW	RHODA	CHAIN	THAME	CHLOE
PESTO	LEMUR	KENYA	EGDON	RHODE	CHAIR	THEME	OHBOY
PESTS	LETUP	LENYA	IGLOO	SHADE	CHOIR	THUMB	PHLOX
PETTY	LEXUS	MERYL	AGAPE	SHADY	CHRIS	THUMP	SHOOK
RECTO	MENUS	NERYS	EGYPT	SHEDS	THEIR	THYME	SHOOT
REITH	METUP	PEPYS	AGGRO	THEDA	BHAJI	WHIMS	THEOC
RENTS	NEGUS	MEZZO	AGORA	THUDS	SHOJI	CHANT	THROB
RESTS	NEXUS	SEIZE	EGEST	CHEEK	CHOKE	CHINA	THROW
SEATS	REBUS	OFFAL	AGATE	CHEEP	DHAKA	CHINE	WHOOP
SECTS	REBUT	OFFAS	AGAVE	CHEER	KHAKI	CHINK	CHAPS
SEETO	RECUR	OFLAG	OGIVE	CHIEF	SHAKE	CHINO	CHIPS
SETTO	REDUX	OFWAT	AHEAD	KHMER	SHAKO	CHINS	CHOPS
SETTS	REMUS	AFTER	CHEAM	SHEEN	SHAKY	CHUNK	SHAPE
TEATS	RERUN	OFFER	CHEAP	SHEEP	CHALK	GHANA	SHIPS
TEETH	REVUE	OFTEL	CHEAT	SHEER	CHILD	GHENT	SHOPS
TENTH	REVUP	OFTEN	PHIAL	SHEET	CHILE	KHANS	WHIPS
TENTS	SEBUM	AFFIX	RHEAS	SHIED	CHILI	PHONE	AHERN
TESTS	SEDUM	AFOOT	SHEAF	SHIES	CHILL	RHINE	CHARD
TESTY	SEGUE	AFIRE	SHEAR	SHOES	SHALE	RHINO	CHARM
TEXTS	SEOUL	OFUSE	SHOAL	SHRED	SHALL	RHONA	CHARS
VENTS	SERUM	EGGAR	UHLAN	SHREK	SHELF	RHONE	CHART
VESTA	SETUP	EGHAM	WHEAT	SHREW	SHELL	SHANE	CHARY
VESTS	VENUE	OGHAM	CHIBA	SHYER	SHYLY	SHANK	CHIRP
YEATS	VENUS	AGNES	CHUBB	THIEF	THALI	SHINE	CHORD
YENTL	BEVVY	AGNEW	DHOBI	THREE	THULE	SHINS	CHORE
BEAUT	DELVE	AGREE	SHEBA	THREW	WHALE	SHINY	CHURL
BEAUX	HEAVE	EGGED	THABO	WHEEL	WHELK	SHONA	CHURN
BEGUM	HEAVY	EGRET	CHECK	CHAFE	WHELP	SHONE	OHARA
BEGUN	LEAVE	OGDEN	CHICK	CHAFF	WHILE	SHUNS	OHARE
DEBUG	NEAVE	OGLED	CHICO	CHEFS	WHOLE	SHUNT	SHARD
DEBUT	NERVE	OGLER	CHOCK	CHUFF	CHAMP	THANE	SHARE
DEMUR	NERVY	OGLES	CHUCK	SHAFT	CHIME	THANK	SHARK
FEDUP	PEEVE	OGRES	SHACK	SHIFT	CHIMP	THINE	SHARP

SHERE	SHUTE	MIDAS	FILCH	MINDS	FILES	LINES	RIMED
SHIRE	SHUTS	MILAN	FINCH	MINDY	FILEY	LIVED	RIMES
SHIRK	THATS	NICAM	HITCH	TILDA	FINED	LIVER	RIPEN
SHIRT	THETA	PILAU	MILCH	TILDE	FINER	LIVES	RIPER
SHORE	THOTH	RIVAL	MINCE	WILDE	FINES	MILER	RISEN
SHORN	WHATS	RIYAL	MITCH	WINDS	FIRED	MILES	RISER
SHORT	WHETS	SILAS	NIECE	WINDY	FIRES	MIMED	RISES
THERE	WHITE	SINAI	PIECE	AIDED	FIVER	MIMES	RITES
THERM	CHOUX	SISAL	PINCH	AIDES	FIVES	MINED	RIVEN
THIRD	GHOUL	SITAR	PITCH	AILED	FIXED	MINER	RIVER
THORA	SHAUN	TIDAL	RICCI	AIMED	FIXER	MINES	RIVET
THORN	SHOUT	TITAN	RIOCH	AIRED	FIXES	MISER	SIDED
UHURA	SHRUB	VICAR	SINCE	AIRER	GILES	MITES	SIDES
WHARF	SHRUG	VIDAL	SITCH	BIDED	GILET	MIXED	SIKES
WHERE	SHTUM	VIRAL	TITCH	BIDES	GIVEN	MIXER	SINEW
WHIRL	THRUM	VISAS	VINCE	BIDET	GIVER	MIXES	SIRED
WHIRR	CHEVY	VITAL	VINCI	BIKER	GIVES	NICER	SIREN
WHORL	CHIVE	WIGAN	WILCO	BIKES	HIDES	NIGEL	SIRES
CHASE	SHAVE	BILBO	WINCE	BIPED	HIKED	NIGER	SITED
CHASM	SHIVA	BIMBO	WINCH	BITES	HIKER	NILES	SITES
CHESS	SHOVE	BIXBY	WITCH	BIZET	HIKES	NIMES	SIXER
CHEST	CHEWS	DIGBY	ZILCH	CIDER	HINES	NIVEA	SIXES
CHOSE	CHEWY	GIBBS	BIDDY	CITED	HIRED	NIVEN	SIZES
GHOST	CHOWS	LIBBY	BINDS	CITES	HIRES	OILED	TIBER
LHASA	SHAWL	LIMBO	BIRDS	CIVET	HIVED	OILER	TIBET
PHASE	SHOWN	LIMBS	BIRDY	DICED	HIVES	PIKES	TIDES
SHUSH	SHOWS	NIOBE	CINDY	DICER	JIVED	PILEA	TIGER
THESE	SHOWY	RIGBY	DIDDY	DICES	JIVER	PILED	TILED
THOSE	THAWS	SIMBA	DIODE	DICEY	JIVES	PILES	TILER
WHISK	WHIZZ	TIBBS	FINDS	DIMES	KITES	PINED	TILES
WHIST	AIDAN	WILBY	GIDDY	DINED	LIBEL	PINES	TIMED
WHOSE	CIGAR	AITCH	GILDA	DINER	LIFER	PIPED	TIMER
XHOSA	DINAH	BIRCH	GILDS	DINES	LIKED	PIPER	TIMES
CHATS	DINAR	BITCH	GIRDS	DIVED	LIKEN	PIPES	TINES
CHITS	DIVAN	CINCH	HILDA	DIVER	LIKES	PIXEL	TIRED
CHUTE	DIVAS	CIRCA	HINDI	DIVES	LIMES	RIDER	TIREE
DHOTI	FINAL	CISCO	HINDU	EIDER	LIMEY	RIDES	TIRES
PHOTO	HIJAB	DISCO	KINDS	EIGER	LINED	RILED	VIBES
RHETT	JIHAD	DISCS	LINDA	FIDEL	LINEN	RILES	VICES
SHOTS	LILAC	DITCH	MIDDY	FILED	LINER	RILEY	VIDEO

VILER	MIDGE	WIGHT	HICKS	DIMLY	NIMMO	MILOS	LITRE
VINES	MINGY	CILIA	JINKS	FIELD	PIMMS	MINOR	MITRE
VIPER	PIGGY	CIVIC	KICKS	FILLS	SIGMA	MINOS	NITRE
VIREN	PINGU	CIVIL	KINKS	FILLY	TIMMY	NIMOY	PIERS
VIXEN	RIDGE	DIGIN	KINKY	GIGLI	WILMA	NINON	TIARA
WIDEN	RIGGS	DIGIT	LICKS	GILLS	DIANA	NIXON	TIERS
WIDER	RINGO	DIXIE	LINKS	GIRLS	DIANE	PICOT	TIGRE
WILES	RINGS	FITIN	MILKS	HILLS	FIEND	PILOT	AILSA
WINES	SIEGE	HIFIS	MILKY	HILLY	FIONA	PINOT	DIPSY
WIPED	SINGE	KILIM	NICKI	JILLY	GIANT	PITON	FIRST
WIPER	SINGH	KIWIS	NICKS	KILLS	KILNS	PIVOT	HIRST
WIPES	SINGS	LICIT	NICKY	LILLE	LIANA	RIPON	KIOSK
WIRED	TINGE	LIEIN	NIKKI	LILLI	LIONS	SILOS	LIESL
WIRER	TINGS	LIMIT	PICKS	LISLE	MILNE	SIMON	MIDST
WIRES	VIGGO	LIVID	PICKY	MILLA	NINNY	TIMON	MINSK
WISER	VIRGO	MIMIC	PINKS	MILLS	PIANO	TIMOR	MISSY
WIVES	WINGS	MINIM	PINKY	PILLS	PINNA	VIDOR	RINSE
YIKES	ZIGGY	MINIS	RICKI	RIFLE	PINNY	VISOR	SISSY
BIFFO	ZINGY	MIXIN	RICKS	RILLS	RIANT	WIDOR	TIPSY
BIFFS	BIGHT	MIXIT	RICKY	SIDLE	SIENA	WIDOW	WIEST
JIFFY	DISHY	NINIA	RIKKI	SILLS	SIGNS	DIPPY	BIRTH
MIFFS	EIGHT	PIPIT	RINKS	SILLY	TINNY	HIPPO	BISTO
MIFFY	FICHU	PIXIE	RISKS	TILLS	VINNY	KIPPS	BITTY
RIFFS	FIGHT	RICIN	RISKY	TILLY	VIRNA	LIMPS	DIETS
TIFFS	FISHY	RIGID	SILKS	TITLE	BIGOT	LIPPI	DIRTY
BIGGS	LIGHT	SIGIL	SILKY	VIALS	BIJOU	LIPPY	DITTO
BILGE	LITHE	SITIN	SINKS	VILLA	BIPOD	LISPS	DITTY
BINGE	MIGHT	TIBIA	SITKA	VIOLA	BIROS	NIPPY	FIFTH
BINGO	NICHE	TIEIN	TICKS	VIOLS	BISON	PIPPA	FIFTY
DIEGO	NIGHT	TIMID	TIKKA	WIELD	DIJON	TIPPI	FILTH
DINGO	NIGHY	VIGIL	VICKI	WILLS	DIVOT	WIMPS	FIRTH
DINGS	PITHY	VISIT	VICKY	WILLY	DIXON	WIMPY	FISTS
DINGY	RIGHT	VIVID	WICKS	YIELD	GIJOE	WISPS	GIFTS
DIRGE	SIDHE	NINJA	WINKS	FILMS	GIROS	WISPY	GILTS
GIGGS	SIGHS	RIOJA	AISLE	FILMY	HITON	ZIPPY	GIRTH
HINGE	SIGHT	BILKO	BIBLE	FIRMS	KILOS	DIARY	HINTS
JINGO	SIKHS	DICKY	BILLS	GIZMO	KIROV	FIBRE	JILTS
KINGS	TIGHT	DINKY	BILLY	JIMMY	LIDOS	FIERY	KILTS
LIEGE	TITHE	DIRKS	CILLA	MIAMI	MIAOW	LIARS	KITTY
LINGO	VICHY	DISKS	DIALS	NIAMH	MIDON	LIBRA	LIFTS

LILTS	MINUS	SKIFF	CLEAR	FLOCK	FLEET	ALFIE	CLIME
LISTS	MIXUP	SKEIN	CLEAT	GLACE	FLIES	ALLIN	CLUMP
MINTS	PINUP	AKELA	CLOAK	PLACE	FLOES	ALVIN	FLAME
MINTY	PIOUS	SKILL	ELGAR	PLUCK	FLUES	BLAIN	FLUME
MIRTH	PIQUE	SKULK	FLEAS	SLACK	FLYER	BLAIR	FLUMP
MISTS	RIPUP	SKULL	FLOAT	SLICE	GLUED	CLAIM	FLYMO
MISTY	SINUS	NKOMO	FLYAT	SLICK	GLUES	CLAIR	KLIMT
MITTS	SIOUX	SKIMP	GLEAM	BLADE	OLDEN	ELCID	LLAMA
MITTY	SITUP	SKIMS	GLEAN	CLODS	OLDER	ELFIN	PLUMB
NIFTY	TIEUP	EKING	GLOAT	CLYDE	OLNEY	ELGIN	PLUME
NINTH	TIPUP	SKANK	ILIAD	ELIDE	OLSEN	ELLIE	PLUMP
PICTS	TITUS	SKENE	OLGAS	ELUDE	PLIED	ELLIS	PLUMS
PIETA	VIRUS	SKINK	PLEAD	GLADE	PLIES	ELSIE	SLAMS
PIETY	DIVVY	SKINS	PLEAS	GLIDE	SLEEK	ELVIS	SLIME
PINTA	SIEVE	SKINT	PLEAT	SLADE	SLEEP	FLAIL	SLIMS
PINTO	VIEWS	SKUNK	SLOAN	SLADE	SLEET	FLAIR	SLIMY
PINTS	LIBYA	OKAPI	ULNAR	SLEDS	SLOES	FLUID	SLOMO
PISTE	SIBYL	SKEPS	ALIBI	SLIDE	SLYER	FLYIN	SLUMP
PITTA	VINYL	SKIPS	BLABS	ALBEE	ULCER	KLEIN	SLUMS
PITTS	DITZY	AKIRA	BLOBS	ALDER	ALOFT	OLDIE	ALINE
RIFTS	DIZZY	OKARO	CLUBS	ALIEN	BLUFF	OLLIE	ALONE
RIOTS	FIZZY	SKARA	FLYBE	ALLEN	CLEFS	PLAID	ALONG
SIFTS	LISZT	SKIRL	FLYBY	ALLEY	CLEFT	PLAIN	BLANC
SILTS	MITZI	SKIRT	GLEBE	ALOES	CLIFF	PLAIT	BLAND
SIXTH	PIZZA	UKASE	GLOBE	ALPEN	CLIFT	SLAIN	BLANK
SIXTY	RITZY	SKATE	PLEBS	ALTER	FLUFF	ALIKE	BLEND
TILTH	TIZZY	SKITS	SLABS	BLEED	ALIGN	BLAKE	BLIND
TILTS	VJDAY	SKIVE	SLOBS	BLEEP	BLIGH	BLOKE	BLINI
TINTS	EJECT	ALGAE	ALACK	BLUER	CLEGG	FLAKE	BLINK
VISTA	BJORK	ALIAS	ALICE	BLUES	CLOGS	FLAKY	BLOND
VITTI	BJORN	ALLAH	BLACK	CLEEF	ELEGY	FLUKE	BLUNT
WIDTH	FJORD	ALLAN	BLOCK	CLEEK	FLAGS	FLUKY	CLANG
WILTS	SKEAN	ALLAY	CLACK	CLUED	FLOGS	SLAKE	CLANK
WITTY	SKUAS	ALTAI	CLICK	CLUES	PLUGS	SLYLY	CLANS
DIGUP	SKIDS	ALTAR	CLOCK	ELDER	SLIGO	ALAMO	CLINE
FICUS	SKODA	BLEAK	CLUCK	ELLEN	SLOGS	BLAME	CLING
FITUP	SKEET	BLEAR	ELECT	ELMER	SLUGS	BLIMP	CLINK
LIKUD	SKIED	BLEAT	FLACK	ELVER	ALOHA	CLAMP	CLINT
LINUS	SKIER	BLOAT	FLECK	ELVES	ALPHA	CLAMS	CLONE
LITUP	SKIES	CLEAN	FLICK	FLEES	ALAIN	CLIMB	CLONK

CLUNG	ELTON	BLASE	PLATO	LLOYD	IMOLA	AMAZE	INSET
CLUNK	FLOOD	BLAST	PLATT	PLAYS	IMPLY	ANNAL	INTER
ELAND	FLOOR	BLESS	PLOTS	PLOYS	SMALL	ANNAN	KNEEL
ELENA	GLOOM	BLISS	PLUTO	SLAYS	SMALT	ANZAC	KNEES
FLANK	GLOOP	BLUSH	SLATE	BLAZE	SMELL	INCAS	ONCER
FLANS	SLOOP	CLASH	SLATS	ELIZA	SMELT	INLAW	ONSET
FLING	ALEPH	CLASP	SLITS	GLAZE	SMILE	INLAY	SNEER
FLINT	BLIPS	CLASS	SLOTH	GLOZE	SMOLT	INMAN	UNDER
FLUNG	CLAPS	CLOSE	SLOTS	PLAZA	IMAMS	KNEAD	UNFED
FLUNK	CLIPS	ELISE	ZLOTY	AMMAN	AMEND	ONEAL	UNLET
FLYNN	ELOPE	FLASH	ALBUM	IMRAN	AMONG	ONGAR	UNMET
GLAND	FLAPS	FLASK	ALOUD	SMEAR	EMEND	ONTAP	UNPEG
GLENN	FLIPS	FLESH	CLOUD	AMICE	OMENS	SNEAK	INOFF
GLENS	FLOPS	FLOSS	CLOUT	AMICI	EMERY	UNCAP	KNIFE
GLINT	PLOPS	FLUSH	FLEUR	SMACK	EMIRS	UNCAS	SNIFF
KLINE	SLAPS	GLASS	FLOUR	SMOCK	OMARA	KNOBS	SNUFF
LLANO	SLEPT	GLESS	FLOUT	AMBER	OMBRE	SNOBS	UNIFY
PLANE	SLIPS	GLOSS	ILEUM	EMBED	SMARM	SNUBS	INIGO
PLANK	SLOPE	PLUSH	ILIUM	EMBER	SMART	ENACT	SNAGS
PLANS	SLOPS	SLASH	ALIVE	EMCEE	SMIRK	ENOCH	ANDIE
PLANT	ALARM	SLOSH	CLIVE	EMMET	SMURF	KNACK	ANGIE
PLINY	ALERT	SLUSH	CLOVE	IMPEL	UMBRA	KNOCK	ANNIE
PLONK	BLARE	BLITZ	GLOVE	UMBER	AMASS	ONICE	ANNIS
SLANG	BLURB	BLOTS	OLIVE	AMIGO	AMISH	SNACK	ANVIL
SLANT	BLURS	BLOTT	SLAVE	IMAGE	AMISS	SNICK	ENNIO
SLING	BLURT	BLUTO	BLOWN	IMAGO	AMUSE	VNECK	INDIA
SLINK	CLARA	BLYTH	BLOWS	OMAGH	SMASH	ANODE	INDIE
SLUNG	CLARE	CLOTH	BLOWY	OMEGA	AMATI	SNIDE	INKIN
SLUNK	CLARK	CLOTS	CLAWS	OMAHA	AMITY	ANDES	INUIT
ALLOA	CLARY	ELATE	CLOWN	AMBIT	EMITS	ANGEL	ONAIR
ALLOT	CLERK	ELITE	FLAWS	EMAIL	EMOTE	ANGER	SNAIL
ALLOW	FLARE	FLATS	FLOWN	IMRIE	EMPTY	ANNEX	UNDID
ALLOY	FLIRT	FLITS	FLOWS	SMOKE	OMITS	ENDED	UNFIT
ALOOF	FLORA	FLUTE	GLOWS	SMOKO	SMITE	ENTER	UNLIT
ALTON	GLARE	FLYTE	SLOWS	SMOKY	SMITH	INDEX	UNPIN
ALTOS	GLORY	GLITZ	ALKYD	AMBLE	SMOTE	INFER	UNTIE
BLOOD	SLURP	KLUTE	CLOYS	AMPLE	SMUTS	INKED	UNTIL
BLOOM	SLURS	KLUTZ	CLWYD	AMPLY	AMOUR	INLET	UNWIN
ELBOW	ULTRA	PLATE	FLAYS	EMILE	IMBUE	INNER	UNZIP
ELIOT	ULURU	PLATH	FLOYD	EMILY	SMEWS	INNES	SNAKE

SNAKY	SNIPS	UNCUT	MOLAR	COMBO	ROYCE	TOADS	CORED
ANGLE	ANDRE	UNDUE	MORAG	COMBS	TORCH	TOADY	COREN
ANKLE	ANGRY	KNAVE	MORAL	COSBY	TOSCA	TODDY	CORER
ENOLA	ENTRY	GNAWS	MORAN	DOBBS	TOUCH	VOIDS	CORES
INGLE	GNARL	KNOWN	MORAR	DOBBY	VOICE	WOLDS	COTES
KNELL	INDRI	KNOWS	MORAY	DOLBY	VOUCH	WOODS	COVEN
KNELT	INERT	SNOWS	NODAL	DOUBT	BONDI	WOODY	COVER
KNOLE	INTRO	SNOWY	NOLAN	GOBBI	BONDS	WORDS	COVES
KNOLL	INURE	BOLAM	NOMAD	GOTBY	COLDS	WORDY	COVET
SNELL	SNARE	BOLAN	NORAH	HOBBY	CONDO	BODED	COVEY
UNCLE	SNARK	BOLAS	NOVAK	HOLBY	CORDS	BODES	COWED
ANIMA	SNARL	BONAR	NOWAY	LOBBY	DOWDS	BOGEY	COWER
ANIME	SNORE	BORAT	POLAR	NOBBS	DOWDY	BOHEA	COWES
ENEMY	SNORT	BORAX	ROHAN	TOMBS	FOLDS	BOLES	COXED
GNOME	ANGST	CODAS	ROMAN	YOBBO	FONDA	BONED	COXES
INANE	ANISE	COGAN	RONAN	ZORBA	FOODS	BONES	COZEN
INONE	ANTSY	COMAS	ROTAS	BONCE	FORDS	BONET	DOBEY
ANION	GNASH	CONAN	ROWAN	BOSCH	GOADS	BONEY	DOLED
ANJOU	ANITA	COPAL	ROYAL	BOTCH	GOLDA	BOOED	DOLES
ANNOY	GNATS	CORAL	SOFAR	BOYCE	GOODS	BORED	DOMED
ANTON	KNITS	DONAT	SOFAS	COACH	GOODY	BORER	DOMES
ENDOW	KNOTS	FOCAL	SOLAR	CONCH	GOUDA	BORES	DOPED
ENJOY	UNITE	FORAY	SONAR	COUCH	HOLDS	BOWED	DOPES
ENROL	UNITS	GOBAD	TODAY	DOLCE	HONDA	BOWEN	DOPEY
ENRON	UNITY	GOFAR	TOGAS	FORCE	HONDO	BOWER	DOSED
ENVOY	ANGUS	GOMAD	TOKAY	GOOCH	HOODS	BOXED	DOSES
INGOT	ANNUL	GORAN	TONAL	HOICK	HORDE	BOXER	DOTED
INTOW	ANZUS	GOWAN	TOPAZ	HOOCH	HOWDY	BOXES	DOTES
ONION	ENDUE	HOGAN	TORAH	JOYCE	KORDA	BOYER	DOVER
ONTOP	ENDUP	JOHAN	TOTAL	KOTCH	LOADS	CODED	DOVES
SNOOD	ENNUI	JONAH	TOYAH	LOACH	LORDS	CODES	DOWEL
SNOOP	ENSUE	KODAK	VOCAL	MOOCH	MONDO	COHEN	DOYEN
UNION	INCUR	KOJAK	WOGAN	NONCE	MOODS	COLEY	DOZED
INAPT	INCUS	KORAN	WOMAN	NOTCH	MOODY	COMES	DOZEN
INEPT	INDUS	KOVAC	ZONAL	POACH	NODDY	COMET	DOZER
KNAPP	INFUN	LOCAL	BOBBY	POOCH	PONDS	CONED	DOZES
KNAPS	INPUT	LOGAN	BOMBE	PORCH	ROADS	CONES	FODEN
SNAPE	ONCUE	LOHAN	BOMBS	POUCH	RONDO	COPED	FOGEY
SNAPS	ONEUP	LOVAT	BOOBY	ROACH	ROODS	COPER	FOWEY
SNIPE	SNOUT	LOYAL	COLBY	ROCCO	ROWDY	COPES	FOXED

FOXES	LOSER	NOTES	SORES	DORFF	PORGY	MOTIF	MONKS
FOYER	LOSES	NOVEL	SOWED	GOOFF	ROUGE	MOVIE	NOOKS
GOFER	LOSEY	NOYES	SOWER	GOOFS	ROUGH	NOKIA	POLKA
GOLEM	LOVED	OOZED	TOKEN	GOOFY	SOGGY	PODIA	PORKY
GONER	LOVER	OOZES	TOLET	HOFFA	SONGS	POLIO	PORKY
GOOEY	LOVES	POKED	TOMES	JOFFE	TONGA	POSIT	ROCKS
GORED	LOVEY	POKER	TONED	ROOFS	TONGS	ROBIN	ROCKY
GOREN	LOWED	POKES	TONER	SOLFA	TOUGH	RODIN	ROOKS
GORES	LOWER	POLES	TONES	TOFFS	VOLGA	RONIN	SOAKS
GOWER	MODEL	POPES	TOPED	WOLFE	WONGA	ROSIE	SOCKS
HOLED	MODEM	PORED	TOPER	WOOFS	BOTHA	ROSIN	TONKS
HOLES	MODER	PORES	TOPES	BODGE	BOTHY	ROXIE	VODKA
HOMER	MODES	POSED	TOTED	BOGGY	LOCHS	SOFIA	WONKA
HOMES	MOLES	POSER	TOTEM	BONGO	MOCHA	SOLID	WONKY
HONED	MONET	POSES	TOTES	BOUGH	MOSHE	SOLIS	WORKS
HONES	MONEY	POWER	TOWED	CONGA	MOTHS	SONIA	YOLKS
HONEY	MOOED	ROBED	TOWEL	CONGO	BODIE	SONIC	YONKS
HOOEY	MOPED	ROBES	TOWER	CORGI	BOGIE	TOBIN	YORKE
HOPED	MOPES	RODEO	TOYED	COUGH	BORIS	TONIC	BOILS
HOPES	MOREL	ROGER	VOLES	DODGE	BOWIE	TOPIC	BOLLS
HOSEA	MORES	ROGET	VOTED	DODGY	COLIC	TOXIC	BOULT
HOSES	MOSES	ROLES	VOTER	DOGGO	COLIN	TOXIN	BOWLS
HOTEL	MOSEY	ROLEX	VOTES	DOGGY	COMIC	YOWIE	BOYLE
HOVEL	MOTEL	ROMEO	VOWED	DONGS	COPIT	SONJA	COALS
HOVER	MOTES	ROPED	VOWEL	DOUGH	CORIN	BOOKS	COILS
HOWES	MOTET	ROPER	WODEN	FOGGY	DODIE	COCKS	COOLS
JOKED	MOVED	ROPES	WOKEN	FORGE	DORIC	COCKY	COULD
JOKER	MOVER	ROSES	WOMEN	FORGO	DORIS	COOKE	COWLS
JOKES	MOVES	ROUEN	WOOED	GONGS	FOLIO	COOKS	COYLY
JOKEY	MOWED	ROUES	WOVEN	GORGE	HOPIT	CORKS	DOILY
JONES	MOWER	ROVED	YODEL	GOUGE	HOVIS	DOCKS	DOLLS
JOSEY	MOYET	ROVER	YOKED	GOUGH	IONIC	FORKS	DOLLY
KOPEK	NOBEL	ROVES	YOKEL	HOAGY	JODIE	GORKY	DOYLE
KOREA	NODES	ROWED	YOKES	HODGE	JOLIE	HOCKS	FOALS
LOBES	NONES	ROWEL	ZONED	LODGE	JOSIE	HOOKS	FOILS
LONER	NONET	ROWEN	ZONES	LONGS	LOGIC	KOOKY	FOLLY
LOPED	NOSED	ROWER	COMFY	LOUGH	LOGIE	LOCKE	FOOLS
LOPES	NOSES	SOBER	CORFE	PODGY	LORIS	LOCKS	FOULS
LOPEZ	NOSEY	SOLED	CORFU	PONGO	LOUIS	LOOKS	FOYLE
LOREN	NOTED	SOLES	DOFFS	PONGS	MOBIL	MOCKS	GOALS
							GODLY

GOLLY	WORLD	DONNY	YOUNG	SOAPY	ZORRO	SOUSA	LOTTE
GOULD	WOULD	DOONA	BORON	SOPPY	BOAST	SOUSE	LOTTO
HOLLY	BOOMS	DOONE	BOSOM	SOUPS	BOISE	TOAST	LOUTH
HOTLY	COMMA	DOWNS	COCOA	YOMPS	BOOST	TOPSY	LOUTS
HOWLS	DOGMA	DOWNY	COLON	BOARD	BOSSY	TORSO	MOATS
HOYLE	DORMS	FOUND	COLOR	BOARS	COAST	WORSE	MONTH
JOELY	FOAMS	FOUNT	COROT	BOORS	COPSE	WORST	MONTY
JOLLY	FOAMY	GOING	DONOR	COBRA	DOUSE	AORTA	MOTTE
JOOLS	FORME	GOONS	GODOT	COPRA	DOWSE	BOATS	MOTTO
JOULE	FORMS	GOWNS	GOGOL	CORRS	FOIST	BOLTS	MOUTH
JOWLS	KORMA	HORNE	HONOR	COURT	FOSSE	BOOTH	NOLTE
KOALA	LOOMS	HORNS	LOGON	DOERS	GOOSE	BOOTS	NORTH
LOLLS	MOMMA	HOUND	LOGOS	DOORS	GORSE	BOOTY	POETS
LOLLY	MOMMY	JOHNS	MOTOR	DOURO	HOIST	BOUTS	PONTI
LOWLY	NORMA	JOINS	NOTON	DOWRY	HOLST	COATI	PORTS
MOLLS	NORMS	JOINT	POBOX	FOURS	HORSE	COATS	POSTE
MOLLY	POEMS	JONNY	ROBOT	GOURD	HOUSE	COLTS	POSTS
MOULD	POMMY	LOANS	ROTOR	HOARD	JOIST	COMTE	POTTY
MOULT	ROAMS	LOINS	SODOM	HOARY	JOUST	CONTE	POUTS
NOBLE	ROOMS	LOONS	SODOR	HOURI	LOESS	CONTI	ROOTS
NOBLY	ROOMY	LOONY	SOLOS	HOURS	LOOSE	COOTS	ROSTI
NOELE	SOMME	LORNA	TOPOL	LOIRE	LOUSE	COPTS	ROUTE
POLLS	TOMMY	LORNE	WOLOF	LORRE	LOUSY	COSTA	ROUTS
POLLY	TORME	MOANS	YOYOS	LORRY	MOIST	COSTS	SOLTI
POOLE	WORMS	MOONS	COMPO	LOURS	MOOSE	DOLTS	SOOTY
POOLS	ZOOMS	MOONY	COOPS	LOWRY	MORSE	DOTTY	SORTS
POULT	BOING	MOUND	COOPT	MOIRA	MOUSE	FOOTY	SOUTH
ROALD	BONNY	MOUNT	CORPS	MOIRE	MOUSY	FORTE	TONTO
ROILS	BOONE	NOONE	COUPE	MONRO	NOISE	FORTH	TOOTH
ROLLS	BORNE	NOUNS	COUPS	MOORE	NOISY	FORTS	TOOTS
ROYLE	BOUND	POINT	COYPU	MOORS	NOOSE	FORTY	TORTE
SOILS	BOYNE	POUND	HOOPS	MOURN	NORSE	GOATS	TOSTI
SOULS	COINS	RONNI	HOPPY	POURS	POESY	GOUTY	TOUTS
TOILE	COLNE	ROUND	LOOPS	ROARS	POISE	HOOTS	VOLTA
TOILS	CORNS	SONNY	LOOPY	SOARS	POSSE	HOSTA	VOLTS
TOLLS	CORNY	SOUND	LOUPE	SORRY	ROAST	HOSTS	WORTH
TOOLS	COUNT	TONNE	MORPH	SOURS	ROOST	JOLTS	YOUTH
VOILA	DOING	TOONS	OOMPH	TOURS	ROSSI	LOFTS	BOEUF
VOILE	DONNA	TOWNS	POPPY	WORRY	ROUSE	LOFTY	BOGUS
WOOLF	DONNE	WOUND	ROMPS	YOURS	ROUST	LOOTS	BOLUS

BONUS	APPAL	SPOIL	SPARE	ARRAN	CRABS	TRUCK	DRIED
BOSUN	OPRAH	SPRIG	SPARK	ARRAS	CRIBS	URICH	DRIER
FOCUS	SPEAK	SPIKE	SPARS	ARRAY	DRABS	WRACK	DRIES
FORUM	SPEAR	SPIKY	SPERM	BREAD	DRUBS	WRECK	DRYER
GOOUT	SPLAT	SPOKE	SPIRE	BREAK	FROBE	BRADS	ERNES
GOTUP	SPLAY	APPLE	SPIRO	BREAM	GRABS	BRADY	ERRED
HOKUM	SPRAT	APPLY	SPORE	BRIAN	GREBE	BREDA	FREED
HORUS	SPRAY	APTLY	SPORT	BRIAR	PROBE	BRIDE	FREER
HOTUP	APACE	OPALS	SPURN	BROAD	PROBY	CREDO	FREES
LOCUM	EPICS	SPALL	SPURS	BRYAN	TRIBE	CRUDE	FRIED
LOCUS	EPOCH	SPELL	SPURT	CREAK	ARECA	DREDD	FRIEL
LOTUS	SPACE	SPILE	SPYRI	CREAM	BRACE	ERODE	FRIES
MODUS	SPECK	SPILL	SPASM	CREAN	BRACT	FRIDA	FRYER
MOGUL	SPECS	SPILT	SPATE	CROAK	BRICE	GRADE	GREED
MOPUP	SPICE	SPUME	SPATS	CROAT	BRICK	GRIDS	GREEK
NODUS	SPICK	APING	SPITE	DREAD	BROCK	PRADO	GREEN
POPUP	SPICY	OPENS	SPITZ	DREAM	BRUCE	PRIDE	GREER
ROGUE	SPOCK	OPINE	SPOTS	DREAR	CRACK	PRODI	GREET
SOYUZ	SPADE	SPANK	OPIUM	DRYAD	CRICK	PRODS	GRIEF
TONUP	SPODE	SPANS	SPOUT	FREAK	CROCK	PRUDE	GRIEG
TOPUP	SPUDS	SPEND	SPIVS	FRIAR	DRACO	TRADE	GRUEL
TOQUE	APSES	SPENT	SPAWN	GREAT	DRECK	TRUDE	IRKED
TORUS	APTED	SPINE	SPEWS	GROAN	ERECT	ARDEN	ORDER
TOTUP	OPTED	SPINS	EPOXY	GROAT	ERICA	ARIEL	ORIEL
VOGUE	SPEED	SPINY	EQUAL	KRAAL	ERICH	ARIES	ORMER
SOAVE	SPIED	UPEND	SQUAB	OREAD	ERUCT	ARLES	PRAED
SOLVE	SPIEL	APRON	SQUAD	ORGAN	FROCK	ARMED	PREEN
VOLVO	SPIES	EPSOM	SQUAT	PRIAL	GRACE	ARTEX	PRIED
CONWY	SPREE	SPION	AQABA	PRIAM	GRECO	BREED	PRIES
LOEWE	UPPED	SPOOF	EQUIP	PROAM	PRICE	BRIEF	TREES
JOEYS	UPPER	SPOOK	SQUIB	TREAD	PRICK	CREED	TRIED
POLYP	UPSET	SPOOL	SQUID	TREAT	PRYCE	CREEK	TRIER
POWYS	YPRES	SPOON	EQUUS	TRIAD	TRACE	CREEL	TRIES
TOKYO	SPIFF	SPOOR	ARDAL	TRIAL	TRACI	CREEP	TRUER
BOOZE	APHID	SPROG	AREAS	URBAN	TRACK	CRIED	URGED
BOOZY	APHIS	UPTON	ARIAN	URIAH	TRACT	CRIER	URGES
GONZO	APRIL	APART	ARIAS	WREAK	TRACY	CRIES	WRYER
MONZA	OPTIC	APERY	ARNAZ	ARABS	TRICE	CRUEL	CRAFT
WOOZY	SPAIN	OPART	AROAD	ARUBA	TRICK	CRUET	CROFT
APIAN	SPLIT	OPERA	ARPAD	BRIBE	TRUCE	CRYER	DRAFT

DRIFT	ORBIT	GRAMS	GRANT	MRMOM	BRASS	BRATS	BREVE
GRAFT	ORRIS	GRIME	GRIND	ORION	BREST	BRETT	CRAVE
GRIFF	PRAIA	GRIMM	GRINS	ORLON	BRISK	BRITS	DRIVE
GRIFT	TRAIL	GRIMY	GRUNT	ORLOP	BRUSH	BRITT	DROVE
GRUFF	TRAIN	GRUMP	IRENE	ORSON	CRASH	BROTH	GRAVE
KRAFT	TRAIT	PRAMS	IRONS	ORTON	CRASS	BRUTE	GRAVY
BRAGG	BRAKE	PRIMA	IRONY	PRIOR	CRESS	CRATE	GROVE
BRAGS	BROKE	PRIME	KRONA	PROOF	CREST	CRETE	PRIVY
BRIGS	DRAKE	PRIMO	KRONE	PRYOR	CRISP	ERATO	PROVE
CRAGS	ERIKA	PRIMP	PRANG	TRIOS	CROSS	FRETS	TREVI
DRAGS	TREKS	PROMO	PRANK	TROON	CRUSH	FROTH	TROVE
DREGS	TRIKE	PROMS	PRINT	TROOP	CRUST	GRATE	BRAWL
DRUGS	ARKLE	TRAMP	PRONE	TRYON	DRESS	GRETA	BRAWN
FROGS	BRILL	TRAMS	PRONG	VROOM	DROSS	GRITS	BREWS
GREGG	DRILL	TRIMS	PRUNE	CRAPS	ERASE	IRATE	BROWN
PRIGS	DRILY	TRUMP	TREND	CREPE	FRESH	ORATE	BROWS
TROGS	DROLL	ARENA	TRENT	CREPT	FRISK	PRATE	CRAWL
TRUGS	FRILL	BRAND	TRUNK	CROPS	FROST	PRATT	CREWE
GROHL	GRILL	BRENT	WRENS	CRYPT	GRASP	TRITE	CREWS
ARGIL	KRILL	BRINE	WRING	DRAPE	GRASS	TROTH	CROWD
ARKIN	ORALS	BRING	WRONG	DRIPS	GRIST	TROTS	CROWE
ARNIE	PROLE	BRINK	WRUNG	DROPS	GROSS	TRUTH	CROWN
ARTIC	TRILL	BRINY	ARBOR	ERUPT	IRISH	WRATH	CROWS
ARTIE	TROLL	BRONX	ARGON	GRAPE	KRISS	WRITE	DRAWL
BRAID	TRULY	BRUNO	ARGOS	GRAPH	PRASE	WRITS	DRAWN
BRAIN	URALS	BRUNT	ARGOT	GRIPE	PRESS	WROTE	DRAWS
BROIL	AROMA	CRANE	ARROW	GRIPS	PRISE	ARGUE	DROWN
CRAIG	BRIMS	CRANK	ARSON	GROPE	PRISM	ARGUS	FROWN
DRAIN	CRAMP	CRONE	BROOD	PROPS	PROSE	CROUP	GROWL
DROID	CRAMS	CRONY	BROOK	TRAPS	PROST	DRYUP	GROWN
DRUID	CRIME	DRANK	BROOM	TRIPE	PROSY	FRAUD	GROWS
ERNIE	CRIMP	DRINK	CROOK	TRIPS	TRASH	FREUD	PRAWN
FRAIL	CROME	DRONE	CROON	TROPE	TRASS	FRYUP	PROWL
FRUIT	CRUMB	DRUNK	DROOD	WRAPS	TRESS	GROUP	PROWS
GRAIL	DRAMA	FRANC	DROOL	IRAQI	TRUSS	GROUT	TRAWL
GRAIN	DRAMS	FRANK	DROOP	DRDRE	TRUST	PROUD	TREWS
GROIN	DRUMS	FRANZ	ERGOT	TRURO	TRYST	TROUT	PROXY
IRWIN	FRAME	FROND	ERROL	ARISE	WREST	BRAVA	BRAYS
KRAIT	FROME	FRONT	ERROR	AROSE	WRIST	BRAVE	DRAYS
MRBIG	FRUMP	GRAND	GROOM	BRASH	ARETE	BRAVO	DREYS

FRAYN	ASNER	ATBAY	UTHER	STING	STEVE	BUSBY	FUNDS
FRAYS	ASPEL	ATEAM	UTTER	STINK	STOVE	CUBBY	GUIDE
FREYA	ASPEN	ATLAS	STAFF	STINT	STEWS	CURBS	KURDS
GREYS	ASSES	ATTAR	STIFF	STONE	STOWE	DUBBO	LUNDY
PRAYS	ASSET	ETHAN	STUFF	STONY	STOWS	DUMBO	MUDDY
PREYS	ASTER	OTWAY	OTAGO	STUNG	ETHYL	GUBBA	OUTDO
TRAYS	ESHER	STEAD	STAGE	STUNK	STAYS	GUMBO	QUADS
TREYS	ESSEN	STEAK	STAGS	STUNS	AURAL	HUBBY	QUIDS
XRAYS	ESSEX	STEAL	STAGY	STUNT	AURAS	JUMBO	RUDDY
BRAZE	ESTER	STEAM	ITCHY	ATHOS	CUBAN	MUMBA	SUEDE
CRAZE	ISLES	STOAT	ATTIC	ETHOS	CUPAR	NUMBS	AUDEN
CRAZY	ISLET	STRAD	ETHIC	STOOD	DUBAI	PUTBY	AUGER
DRUZE	ISLEY	STRAP	STAID	STOOK	DUCAL	RUGBY	BUSES
FRIZZ	OSHEA	STRAW	STAIN	STOOL	DUCAT	RUMBA	BUYER
FROZE	OSIER	STRAY	STAIR	STOOP	DUKAS	TUBBY	CUBED
GRAZE	USHER	STABS	STEIN	STROP	DUMAS	TURBO	CUBES
ORCZY	OSAGE	STUBS	STOIC	STEPH	GULAG	BUNCE	CURED
PRIZE	USAGE	STACK	STRIP	STEPS	HUMAN	BUNCH	CURER
ASIAN	ASDIC	STACY	STAKE	STIPE	JUDAS	BUTCH	CURES
ASLAN	ASHIA	STICH	STOKE	STOPS	KUMAR	DUNCE	DUDES
ASSAM	ASPIC	STICK	ATOLL	STARE	LUCAN	DUTCH	DUKES
ASSAY	ASTIR	STOCK	ITALY	STARK	LUCAS	GUCCI	DUNES
ASWAN	OSTIA	STUCK	STALE	STARR	LUKAS	GULCH	DUPED
CSGAS	OSAKA	ETUDE	STALK	STARS	LUNAR	HULCE	DUPER
ESSAY	ISTLE	STUDS	STALL	START	MULAN	HUNCH	DUPES
ISAAC	PSALM	STUDY	STILE	STERN	MURAL	HUTCH	DURER
ISLAM	NSYNC	ATSEA	STILL	STIRS	MUZAK	JUICE	DUVET
ISLAY	USING	ETHEL	STILT	STORE	NUMAN	JUICY	FUMED
OSCAR	ASCOT	ETHER	STOLE	STORK	PUMAS	LUNCH	FUMES
USUAL	ASTON	OTHER	STYLE	STORM	PUPAE	LURCH	FUSED
RSPCA	ASTOR	OTLEY	STYLO	STORY	PUSAN	MULCH	FUSES
ASIDE	ESTOP	OTTER	ATOMS	UTURN	RURAL	MUNCH	JULEP
BSIDE	ASTRO	STEED	ITEMS	STASH	SUDAN	OUNCE	JULES
ASHEN	TSARS	STEEL	STAMP	STATE	SUGAR	PUNCH	LUGER
ASHER	USERS	STEEP	STEMS	STOTT	SUMAC	QUACK	LURED
ASHES	USURP	STEER	STOMP	STOUR	SUSAN	QUICK	LURES
ASKED	USURY	STIES	STUMP	STOUT	TUBAS	SUTCH	LUREX
ASKEW	ISSUE	STOEP	ATONE	STRUM	TUPAC	YUCCA	LUTES
ASKEY	PSEUD	STREW	STAND	STRUT	YULAN	BUDDY	MULES
ASLEF	USEUP	STYES	STANK	STAVE	BULBS	CURDS	MUSED

MUSES	PUFFS	SUSHI	ZUBIN	BULLY	GUANO	LUMPY	HUSSY
MUTED	PUFFY	AUDIE	OUIJA	BURLY	KUONI	MUMPS	KURSK
MUTES	QUAFF	AUDIO	BUCKS	CULLS	QUANT	PUMPS	MUMSY
NUDES	QUIFF	AUDIT	BULKY	CURLS	QUINN	PUPPY	NURSE
OUTER	RUFFS	AURIC	BUNKS	CURLY	QUINS	QUIPS	PULSE
OUZEL	SURFS	BUNIN	BURKA	DUELS	RUINS	RUMPS	PURSE
PUREE	TURFS	BURIN	BURKE	DUPLE	RUNNY	SUMPS	PUSSY
PURER	BUDGE	CUBIC	BUSKS	FUELS	SUING	TURPS	QUASH
QUEEG	BUGGY	CUBIT	DUCKS	FULLY	SUNNI	AUTRY	QUEST
QUEEN	BULGE	CUMIN	DUCKY	FURLS	SUNNY	BURRO	SUDSY
QUEER	BUNGS	CUPID	DUSKY	GUILD	TUNNY	BURRS	TULSA
QUIET	BURGH	CURIA	FUNKY	GUILE	TURNS	CURRY	TUTSI
RUDER	FUDGE	CURIE	HUNKS	GUILT	AUTOS	DURRA	WURST
RULED	FUEGO	CURIO	HUNKY	GULLS	BUXOM	FURRY	AUNTS
RULER	FUNGI	CUTIE	HUSKS	GULLY	CUKOR	GUARD	BUSTS
RULES	GUNGA	DURIE	HUSKY	HULLS	FUTON	HURRY	BUTTS
RUMEN	GUNGE	FUSIL	LUCKY	HURLS	HULOT	KUKRI	BUTTY
RUMER	GUNGY	HUMID	LURKS	LULLS	HURON	LUCRE	CULTS
RUNES	JUDGE	JULIA	MUCKY	MULLS	JUNOR	MUNRO	DUCTS
RUPEE	LUNGE	JULIE	MURKY	PULLS	JUROR	OUTRE	DUETO
RUSES	LUNGS	JULIO	MUSKY	QUALM	KUDOS	PURRS	DUETS
SUMER	LURGY	LUCID	PUCKS	QUELL	LUTON	QUARK	DUSTS
SUPER	MUGGY	LUPIN	PUKKA	QUILL	LUXOR	QUART	DUSTY
SURER	MUNGO	LURID	PUNKD	QUILT	PUTON	QUERN	FUSTY
TUBER	NUDGE	MUSIC	PUNKS	SULLY	TUDOR	QUERY	GUSTO
TUBES	PUDGY	PUNIC	QUAKE	SURLY	TUTOR	QUIRE	GUSTS
TUNED	PURGE	PUPIL	QUAKY	TULLE	YUKON	QUIRK	GUSTY
TUNER	RUDGE	PUTIN	RUSKS	TULLY	ZUKOR	QUORN	HUNTS
TUNES	RUNGS	QUAIL	SUCKS	BURMA	BUMPS	SUCRE	HURTS
BUFFS	SURGE	QUOIN	SULKS	DUMMY	BUMPY	BUGSY	JUNTA
BUFFY	AUGHT	QUOIT	SULKY	MUMMY	CUPPA	BURST	LUSTY
CUFFS	BUSHY	RUBIK	TUCKS	RUMMY	CUSPS	CURSE	MUFTI
DUFFY	CUSHY	RUNIC	TURKS	TUMMY	DUMPS	DUNST	MUSTY
GULFS	DUCHY	RUNIN	TURKU	YUMMY	DUMPY	DURST	MUTTS
HUFFS	FUCHS	SUSIE	TUSKS	BUNNY	GULPS	FUSSY	NUTTY
HUFFY	GUSHY	TULIP	YUCKY	BURNS	GUPPY	GUESS	OUSTS
KUFFS	MUSHY	TUNIC	BUGLE	BURNT	HUMPS	GUEST	PUNTS
KULFI	OUGHT	TUNIS	BUILD	DUANE	JUMPS	GUISE	PUTTS
LUFFS	PUSHY	TURIN	BUILT	DUNNE	JUMPY	GUTSY	PUTTY
MUFFS	RUCHE	TUTIN	BULLS	FUNNY	LUMPS	HURST	QUITE

QUITO	MUZZY	SWABS	SWUNG	EXPAT	HYLDA	CYCLE	WYATT
QUITS	AVIAN	TWICE	TWANG	OXFAM	LYNDA	PYGMY	CYRUS
QUOTA	EVIAN	SWEDE	TWINE	EXACT	AYRES	BYRNE	EYEUP
QUOTE	EVICT	DWEEB	TWINS	EXUDE	BYKER	DYING	SYRUP
RUNTS	EVADE	OWLET	SWOON	OXIDE	BYRES	HYENA	CZECH
RUSTS	AVAIL	OWNED	SWOOP	AXLES	BYTES	HYMNS	AZTEC
RUSTY	AVOID	OWNER	SWAPS	EXCEL	DYFED	LYING	UZBEK
SUITE	AVRIL	SWEEP	SWEPT	EXPEL	DYKES	LYNNE	IZMIR
SUITS	OVOID	SWEET	SWIPE	OXTER	DYNES	LYONS	OZONE
TUFTS	EVOKE	TWEED	AWARD	OXLIP	GYLES	MYRNA	AZURE
TUFTY	AVILA	TWEET	AWARE	AXELS	HYPED	RYANS	
TUTTI	EVILS	SWIFT	DWARF	EXALT	HYPER	TYING	
AUGUR	OVALS	SWIGS	EWART	EXILE	HYPES	VYING	
CUTUP	OVULE	TWIGS	EWERS	EXULT	HYWEL	WYNNE	
DUGUP	UVULA	AWAIT	SWARD	EXAMS	LYCEE	BYRON	
DULUX	AVENS	SWAIN	SWARM	AXING	LYRES	LYDON	
DURUM	EVANS	TWAIN	SWIRL	AXIOM	MYLES	NYLON	
FUGUE	EVENS	AWAKE	SWORD	EXCON	NYREE	PYLON	
GURUS	EVENT	AWOKE	SWORE	EXTOL	PYRES	SYNOD	
HUMUS	IVANA	DWELL	SWORN	OXBOW	PYREX	TYPOS	
MUGUP	OVENS	DWELT	TWERP	EXERT	RYDER	TYROL	
PUTUP	OVINE	EWELL	TWIRL	EXTRA	SYKES	TYROS	
QUEUE	AVERS	IWILL	AWASH	OXERS	TYKES	TYSON	
RUFUS	AVERT	SWALE	IWISH	EXIST	TYLER	LYMPH	
RUNUP	AVERY	SWELL	SWASH	EXITS	TYPED	NYMPH	
SUMUP	EVERT	SWILL	SWISH	OXEYE	TYPES	SYLPH	
SUNUP	EVERY	TWILL	SWISS	BYFAR	TYRES	AYERS	
TUTUS	IVORY	SWAMI	TWIST	BYLAW	WYLER	CYMRU	
ZULUS	OVARY	SWAMP	SWATS	BYWAY	XYLEM	DYERS	
CURVE	OVERS	SWIMS	SWOTS	DYLAN	HYTHE	HYDRA	
CURVY	OVERT	BWANA	TWITS	HYRAX	MYTHS	HYDRO	
GUAVA	AVAST	EWING	AWFUL	LYNAM	CYNIC	LYCRA	
LUVVY	KVASS	GWENT	KWOUK	MYHAT	CYRIL	MYERS	
SUAVE	EVITA	OWENS	OWNUP	MYLAR	EYRIE	MYRRH	
BUOYS	OVATE	OWING	TWOUP	MYNAH	KYLIE	GYPSY	
DUBYA	OVETT	SWANK	SWAYS	MYWAY	KYRIE	NYASA	
QUAYS	AVOWS	SWANN	SWAZI	RYDAL	LYDIA	NYSSA	
BUZZY	SWEAR	SWANS	SWIZZ	WYMAN	LYRIC	BYATT	
FURZE	SWEAT	SWINE	AXIAL	LYNCH	SYBIL	CYSTS	
FUZZY	TWEAK	SWING	EXEAT	BYRDS	SYRIA	KYOTO	

BANANA	SALAMI	VAGARY	DAUBER	DANCES	YARDIE	SADDER
CANADA	WASABI	BALBOA	JABBER	FARCES	BANDOG	SANDER
HAVANA	DAMASK	BARBRA	YABBER	FASCES	LAPDOG	WANDER
MALAGA	BACALL	GAMBIA	IAMBUS	JANCIS	GANDHI	WARDER
MANAMA	MAYALL	LAMBDA	RABBIS	LANCES	GARDAI	ZANDER
MANANA	NAPALM	ZAMBIA	GAMBIT	MARCOS	CAUDAL	CADDIS
MARACA	SALAAM	BAOBAB	RABBIT	MARCUS	HANDEL	LANDIS
MASALA	CANAAN	IAMBIC	TALBOT	SAUCES	SANDAL	PANDAS
PAJAMA	GAWAIN	BARBED	HATBOX	FATCAT	VANDAL	TARDIS
PANAMA	BAMAKO	DABBED	CARBOY	FAUCET	RANDOM	BANDIT
PAPAYA	KAKAPO	DAUBED	FASCIA	LANCET	TANDEM	BARDOT
SAHARA	MALABO	DAYBED	GARCIA	MASCOT	CAMDEN	LANDAU
TARAWA	NAVAJO	GARBED	LANCIA	MANCHU	CARDIN	MADDOX
YAMAHA	SALADO	JABBED	MANCHA	MADCOW	GARDEN	BALDLY
ZAHARA	BAZAAR	NABBED	MARCIA	CATCHY	HANDON	HARDLY
ZAPATA	LAMARR	BABBLE	DANCED	DARCEY	HARDEN	MAYDAY
CANARD	CABALS	BARBIE	LANCED	FARCRY	HAYDEN	PAYDAY
HAZARD	CALAIS	BAUBLE	RANCID	PATCHY	LAIDON	RAGDAY
MARAUD	CANALS	BAWBEE	GAUCHE	WARCRY	LARDON	TAWDRY
TABARD	CARATS	CABBIE	PASCOE	SANDRA	MADDEN	CAMERA
CANAPE	FARADS	DABBLE	TAICHI	BARDIC	MAIDEN	FAVELA
CARAFE	HARASS	GABBLE	CANCEL	BANDED	MALDEN	GALENA
DAMAGE	KAYAKS	GAMBLE	MARCEL	CANDID	PAIDIN	PAMELA
FACADE	MACAWS	GARBLE	PARCEL	CARDED	PARDON	SABENA
GARAGE	NAIADS	MARBLE	PASCAL	GADDED	SADDEN	TAMEKA
HARARE	NAWABS	RABBLE	RASCAL	HANDED	VARDON	WALESA
KARATE	PAGANS	RAMBLE	TALCUM	LANDED	WALDEN	FAGEND
LANATE	PALAIS	WARBLE	CANCAN	LAUDED	WARDEN	GAMETE
MADAME	SALADS	GASBAG	CANCUN	PADDED	HARDUP	MANEGE
MANAGE	BASALT	MAYBUG	FALCON	RAIDED	LAIDUP	RACEME
PALACE	HAVANT	RAGBAG	GARCON	BADDIE	PAIDUP	SAPELE
PALATE	NATANT	KASBAH	GASCON	CADDIE	BALDER	BADEGG
PARADE	SAVANT	BARBEL	GAUCHO	CANDLE	DANDER	DANESH
PAVANE	VACANT	GAMBOL	SANCHO	DANDLE	GANDER	GARETH
RAVAGE	KAKADU	CARBON	MADCAP	DAWDLE	HARDER	CADELL
SAVAGE	XANADU	GAMBON	CANCER	HANDLE	LADDER	CAVELL
VACATE	CANARY	BAMBOO	DANCER	HARDIE	LANDOR	BALEEN
PARANG	GALAXY	BAMBER	LANCER	LADDIE	LARDER	CAGEIN
HAWAII	MALADY	BARBER	LASCAR	PADDLE	MADDER	CAMEIN
MALAWI	PAPACY	CAMBER	SAUCER	SADDLE	PANDER	CAREEN
SAFARI	SALARY	DABBER	CAUCUS	WADDLE	RAIDER	CASEIN

CAVEIN	HAREMS	PATENT	CANFUL	WANGLE	TANGOS	LATHER
CAVERN	HAVENS	RAREST	EARFUL	BANGUI	CATGUT	RASHER
GAVEIN	HAVERS	SAFEST	LAWFUL	MANGEL	CAUGHT	RATHER
HAVEON	LABELS	SANEST	MANFUL	MARGAM	FAGGOT	WASHER
LATEEN	LAGERS	TALENT	BAFFIN	BANGON	GADGET	BASHES
RAKEIN	LAKERS	TAMEST	GAFFER	HANGON	MAGGOT	BATHES
SATEEN	LAPELS	BATEAU	GAFFES	JARGON	MARGOT	BATHOS
TAKEIN	LAYERS	CADEAU	SAWFIT	MARGIN	NAUGHT	CACHES
TAKEON	MAKERS	GATEAU	BARFLY	RAYGUN	PARGET	CASHES
TAVERN	MAVENS	MASERU	GADFLY	SAIGON	TARGET	DACHAS
CAMETO	PACERS	BAYEUX	MAYFLY	VAUGHN	TAUGHT	DASHES
GAZEBO	PANELS	BAKERY	PANFRY	DAYGLO	GANGLY	GASHES
MAKEDO	PAPERS	BARELY	BAGGED	BANGUP	JANGLY	HASHES
TAKETO	PAYEES	BASELY	BANGED	GANGUP	WAGGLY	LASHES
GAVEUP	PAYERS	EATERY	BARGED	HANGUP	BASHED	LATHES
MADEUP	RACERS	FAKERY	CADGED	RANGUP	BATHED	MASHES
MAKEUP	RATELS	GAIETY	FAGGED	BADGER	CASHED	MATHIS
RAVEUP	RAVENS	GAMELY	FANGED	BANGER	DASHED	PAPHOS
SAVEUP	RAVERS	LAMELY	GAGGED	BANGOR	GASHED	PASHAS
TAKEUP	SAVERS	LATELY	GANGED	CADGER	HASHED	PATHOS
WAKEUP	SAYERS	NAMELY	GAUGED	DAGGER	LASHED	RASHES
CAREER	TAKERS	NASEBY	HANGED	DANGER	MASHED	SASHES
BAGELS	TAPERS	PAPERY	JAGGED	GANGER	WASHED	WASHES
BAKERS	VALETS	RAREFY	LAGGED	HANGAR	DAPHNE	YACHTS
BALERS	WADERS	RARELY	NAGGED	HANGER	MASHIE	CACHET
CABERS	WAFERS	SAFELY	RAGGED	JAEGER	RACHEL	SACHET
CADETS	WAGERS	SAFETY	RANGED	JAGGER	WARHOL	CACHOU
CAMELS	WAKENS	SAGELY	SAGGED	LAAGER	FATHOM	CASHEW
CAMEOS	WATERS	SANELY	TAGGED	LANGER	LATHAM	HAWHAW
CAPERS	WAVERS	TAMELY	WAGGED	LARGER	MAYHEM	MAYHEW
CARERS	BAREST	VALERY	BANGLE	MANGER	AACHEN	CATHAY
CARESS	BASEST	WAFERY	BARGEE	NAGGER	BASHON	LACHEY
CARETS	CAVEAT	WATERY	DANGLE	RANGER	CASHIN	RASHLY
CATERS	GAMEST	JAFFNA	GAGGLE	BADGES	FATHEN	SASHAY
CAVERS	LAMENT	RAFFIA	GARGLE	BARGES	NATHAN	DAVINA
DALEKS	LAMEST	DAFFYD	HAGGLE	CADGES	MAYHAP	FARINA
EASELS	LATENT	FAFFED	JANGLE	GANGES	WASHUP	FATIMA
EATERS	LATEST	BAFFLE	MAGGIE	GAUGES	BATHER	LADIDA
FACETS	PAGETT	RAFFLE	MANGLE	HAGGIS	DASHER	LAMINA
FAKERS	PALEST	WAFFLE	TANGLE	LAUGHS	FATHER	MANILA
GAPERS	PARENT	YAFFLE	WAGGLE	RANGES	GATHER	MARINA

MARISA	DAZING	SAYING	RACISM	DAVITS	WARILY	HAAKON
PATINA	EALING	TAKING	RADIUM	FAKIRS	BANJUL	LARKIN
SALIVA	EASING	TAMING	SADISM	GAMINS	JAMJAR	NAPKIN
MANIAC	EATING	TAPING	TAOISM	GATISS	BANJOS	PARKIN
MANIOC	FACING	TAXING	VALIUM	HABITS	FANJET	SANKIN
TAXIED	FADING	WADING	DAMIAN	LADIES	RAMJET	WALKEN
VARIED	FAKING	WAGING	DAMIEN	MARIUS	BANJAX	WALKON
CANINE	FARING	WAKING	FABIAN	MATINS	MARKKA	BACKUP
DATIVE	FAXING	WANING	MALIGN	MAXIMS	BACKED	MARKUP
FACILE	FAZING	WAVING	MARIAN	NAVIES	BANKED	PACKUP
FAMINE	GAMING	WAXING	MARION	PANICS	BARKED	BACKER
GAMINE	GAPING	YAWING	NATION	PATIOS	BASKED	BANKER
JANICE	GAZING	BANISH	PARIAN	RABIES	CASKED	BARKER
JANINE	HARING	CALIPH	RADIAN	RADIOS	HACKED	CANKER
MALICE	HATING	DANISH	RATION	RADIUS	JACKED	DANKER
MARINE	HAVING	FAMISH	CALICO	RAPIDS	LACKED	DARKER
NADINE	JAWING	GARISH	CASINO	RATIOS	MARKED	HACKER
NATIVE	LACING	HAMISH	KATIPO	TAPIRS	MASKED	HANKER
RACINE	LADING	LAVISH	PACINO	TAXIES	NARKED	HARKER
RAVINE	LAYING	MARIAH	CAGIER	VARIES	PACKED	HAWKER
SABINE	LAZING	OAFISH	CAVIAR	LARIAT	PARKED	MARKER
SALINE	MAKING	PARIAH	EASIER	MAOIST	RANKED	PACKER
SATIRE	MATING	PARISH	HAZIER	PAPIST	SACKED	PARKER
SAVILE	NAMING	RADISH	LACIER	RACIST	TACKED	RANKER
VALISE	PACING	RAKISH	LAZIER	SADIST	TALKED	TALKER
TARIFF	PAGING	RAVISH	NAPIER	TAOIST	WALKED	TANKER
BAAING	PALING	TANITH	PACIER	VARIES	YANKED	WALKER
BAKING	PARING	VANISH	RACIER	CAGILY	CACKLE	FAWKES
BALING	PAVING	TAHINI	RAPIER	CAVITY	HACKLE	HAWKES
BARING	PAWING	TAHITI	WARIER	EASILY	JACKIE	PARKAS
BASING	PAYING	WAPITI	WAVIER	FAMILY	RANKLE	BASKET
BAYING	RACING	DANIEL	XAVIER	HAZILY	TACKLE	CASKET
CAGING	RAGING	FACIAL	BABIES	LAXITY	TALKIE	GASKET
CAKING	RAKING	HAMILL	BASICS	LAZILY	YANKEE	JACKET
CANING	RARING	LABIAL	BASINS	PACIFY	JACKAL	MARKET
CARING	RATING	MAGILL	CABINS	PARITY	WANKEL	PACKET
CASING	RAVING	RACIAL	CARIES	RAMIFY	BALKAN	RACKET
CAVING	RAZING	RADIAL	CAVIES	RARITY	BANKON	WALKIT
CAWING	SATING	BARIUM	CAVILS	RATIFY	BARKIN	DARKLY
DARING	SAVING	MAOISM	DARIUS	SANITY	CATKIN	JAYKAY
DATING	SAWING	PAPISM	DAVIES	VANITY	DARKEN	LACKEY

LANKLY	FALLEN	MAPLES	HARLEY	MADMAN	MAENAD	CANNES
MACKAY	GALLON	NAPLES	HAYLEY	MADMEN	MANNED	DAUNTS
MACKEY	KAOLIN	SABLES	LAWLEY	MAMMON	PAINED	FAINTS
DAHLIA	MARLIN	SALLIS	MARLEY	PACMAN	PANNED	HAUNTS
KAHLUA	MARLON	TABLES	OAKLEY	PAXMAN	PAWNED	HAYNES
LAALAA	RAGLAN	VAULTS	PARLEY	RAGMAN	RAINED	JAUNTS
PAELLA	TATLIN	WALLIS	VALLEY	RAGMEN	TANNED	MAGNUS
GAELIC	HALLOO	BALLET	WAYLAY	SALMAN	WARNED	PAINTS
GALLIC	CALLUP	BALLOT	TARMAC	SALMON	YAWNED	SAINTS
GARLIC	GALLOP	CAPLET	CALMED	TASMAN	MACNEE	TAINTS
BAILED	GALLUP	EAGLET	DAMMED	TAXMAN	MARNIE	TAUNTS
BALLAD	WALLOP	GASLIT	FARMED	TAXMEN	PAWNEE	VAUNTS
BALLED	WALLUP	HAMLET	HARMED	VATMAN	HANNAH	WARNES
BAWLED	CALLER	HARLOT	JAMMED	YASMIN	HAUNCH	BARNET
CABLED	GABLER	HASLET	MAIMED	WARMUP	LAUNCH	CANNOT
CALLED	HAILER	MALLET	RAMMED	CALMER	PAUNCH	CARNET
FABLED	JAILER	PALLET	TALMUD	DAGMAR	DANNII	GANNET
FAILED	MAHLER	TABLET	WARMED	FARMER	KARNAK	GARNET
GABLED	MAILER	VARLET	WARMTH	HAMMER	CARNAL	MAGNET
GALLED	NAILER	WALLET	CARMEL	PALMER	BARNUM	WALNUT
HAILED	PALLOR	PAVLOV	MAMMAL	WARMER	MAGNUM	SATNAV
HAULED	SADLER	BARLOW	HAMMAM	LAMMAS	BANNEN	MAGNOX
JAILED	SAILOR	CALLOW	BAGMAN	MARMOT	CANNON	BARNEY
LADLED	TAILOR	CARLOW	BAGMEN	MAUMAU	FARNON	CAGNEY
MAILED	TALLER	FALLOW	BARMAN	MADMAX	TANNIN	CARNEY
MAULED	TATLER	HALLOW	BARMEN	CALMLY	BAGNIO	DAINTY
NAILED	TAYLOR	HARLOW	BATMAN	TARMEY	CATNAP	HANNAY
PALLED	WAILER	LAYLOW	BATMEN	WARMLY	CATNIP	JAUNTY
PALLID	WALLER	MALLOW	CABMAN	KAUNDA	BANNER	MAINLY
RAILED	BAULKS	MARLOW	CAIMAN	NARNIA	DANNER	MAUNDY
SAILED	CABLES	SALLOW	CARMEN	CARNAC	DARNER	TANNOY
TABLED	CALLAS	TALLOW	CAYMAN	TANNIC	EARNER	VAINLY
TAILED	CALLUS	WALLOW	GAMMON	BANNED	GARNER	VARNEY
WAILED	CARLOS	BAILEY	GASMAN	CANNED	GAYNOR	DAKOTA
WALLED	CAULKS	BARLEY	GASMEN	DAMNED	MANNER	KATONA
HAYLIE	DALLAS	CALLBY	HAGMAN	DARNED	MARNER	LATOYA
MALLEE	EAGLES	DAILEY	HARMAN	DAWNED	RAYNER	PAGODA
WALLAH	FABLES	FAULTY	LAWMAN	EARNED	TANNER	PAKORA
HARLEM	FAULTS	FAWLTY	LAWMEN	FANNED	WAGNER	PALOMA
CALLAN	GABLES	GALLEY	LAYMAN	FAWNED	WARNER	PAYOLA
FABLON	LADLES	HALLEY	LAYMEN	GAINED	BARNES	SAMOSA

HALOED	CAPONS	SAVORY	HARPER	CARRIE	JARROW	LARSON
HAROLD	CAROLS	SAXONY	JASPER	FAERIE	MARROW	LAWSON
BARONE	FAMOUS	CAMPED	LAUPER	LAURIE	NARROW	MADSEN
CAJOLE	FAROES	CAPPED	NAGPUR	FARRAH	YARROW	MANSON
CAPONE	HALOES	CARPED	NAPPER	BARREL	MATRIX	MAWSON
CAPOTE	MAJORS	DAMPED	PAMPER	DARRYL	CARREY	NANSEN
CAROLE	MANORS	GASPED	PAUPER	LAUREL	FAIRLY	PARSON
DAMONE	MASONS	LAPPED	RAPPER	PATROL	CASSIA	PASSON
GALORE	NABOBS	MAPPED	SAPPER	MARRAM	NAUSEA	RAISIN
LAHORE	PATOIS	NAPPED	TAMPER	BARREN	BARSAC	SAMSON
MALONE	RAZORS	RAPPED	TAPPER	BARRON	PARSEC	TAMSIN
PAROLE	SABOTS	RASPED	CAMPUS	DARREN	CAUSED	WATSON
SALOME	SALONS	SAPPED	CARPUS	DARRIN	GASSED	CASSIO
TAGORE	SAXONS	TAPPED	PAMPAS	LAUREN	LAPSED	CAESAR
DAYOFF	TABOOS	VAMPED	CARPET	MARRON	MASSED	HAWSER
FAROFF	TABORS	WARPED	RAJPUT	MATRON	PARSED	KAISER
LAYOFF	TALONS	YAPPED	TAPPET	PATRON	PASSED	NASSER
PAYOFF	TAROTS	ZAPPED	KARPOV	RATRUN	PAUSED	YASSER
RANOFF	VALOIS	DAPPLE	PAWPAW	WARREN	RAISED	BASSES
SARONG	WAGONS	MAGPIE	BARQUE	BARRIO	HASSLE	CASSIS
GALOSH	YAHOOS	MARPLE	BASQUE	HAIRDO	LASSIE	CAUSES
JACOBI	CAVORT	SAMPLE	CAIQUE	PAIRUP	MAISIE	KANSAS
MAJOLI	DACOIT	WASPIE	CASQUE	SATRAP	MASSIF	LAPSES
BABOON	DAYOUT	HATPEG	MANQUE	FAIRER	CAUSAL	LASSES
EAMONN	EATOUT	TAIPEI	MARQUE	BAIRNS	DAMSEL	MASSES
LAGOON	FANOUT	CALPOL	MASQUE	CAIRNS	FAISAL	PARSES
MAROON	FAROUT	CARPAL	BANQUO	HARRIS	HANSEL	PASSES
SALOON	LAYOUT	CARPEL	ZAGREB	LAIRDS	TARSAL	PAUSES
BAROLO	MAHOUT	WAMPUM	FABRIC	MADRAS	TASSEL	RAISES
MANOLO	MAPOUT	DAMPEN	BARRED	MADRES	VASSAL	TARSUS
FAVOUR	PADOUT	HAPPEN	HAGRID	PADRES	BALSAM	WAISTS
LABOUR	PAYOUT	HATPIN	HATRED	SABRES	HANSOM	BASSET
LAMOUR	RAGOUT	MAPPIN	JARRED	TAURUS	PASSIM	PASSAT
SAVOUR	RANOUT	SAMPAN	MADRID	WALRUS	RANSOM	NASSAU
VALOUR	SATOUT	TAIPAN	MARRED	BARRET	CARSON	WARSAW
VAPOUR	WAYOUT	SAPPHO	PAIRED	CARROT	DAMSON	BASSEY
BARONS	BARONY	CAMPER	RAMROD	GARRET	DANSON	GATSBY
BATONS	CANOPY	CASPER	SACRED	PARROT	DATSUN	MARSHY
BAYOUS	JALOPY	DAMPER	SAWRED	BARROW	DAWSON	MASSEY
CANOES	MALORY	DAPPER	TARRED	FARROW	GARSON	PASSBY
CANONS	PARODY	HAMPER	BARRIE	HARROW	HANSON	RAMSAY

RAMSEY	RATTLE	TATTOO	WALTER	WATUSI	WAIVES	ABBESS
EARTHA	SARTRE	LAPTOP	WASTER	ZANUCK	HARVEY	ABBEYS
MANTRA	TATTIE	WAITUP	BASTES	CASUAL	EARWIG	OBSESS
MANTUA	TATTLE	BANTER	CACTUS	MANUAL	YAHWEH	ABJECT
MARTHA	WATTLE	BARTER	CANTOS	MANUEL	DARWIN	ABLEST
TANTRA	GAGTAG	BATTER	CASTES	RAQUEL	TAIWAN	ABSENT
BALTIC	RAGTAG	BAXTER	EARTHS	SAMUEL	EARWAX	OBJECT
LACTIC	NAUTCH	CANTER	FAITHS	VACUUM	GALWAY	OBLIGE
MASTIC	MAITAI	CANTOR	MANTIS	SATURN	BANYAN	BBKING
TACTIC	BARTOK	CAPTOR	NANTES	CARUSO	CANYON	EBBING
BAITED	CARTEL	CARTER	PASTES	MAJURO	LAWYER	OBRIEN
BASTED	DACTYL	CASTER	PASTIS	MAPUTO	MAGYAR	OBOIST
BATTED	MANTEL	CASTOR	QANTAS	GAZUMP	SAWYER	ABELES
CANTED	PASTEL	DAFTER	TASTES	JAGUAR	SATYRS	OBELUS
CARTED	BANTAM	DARTER	WASTES	VAGUER	LARYNX	ABSORB
DARTED	BARTON	EASTER	PASTIT	VALUER	BALZAC	ABROAD
FASTED	BATTEN	FACTOR	EARTHY	MAQUIS	BAIZED	OBLONG
FATTED	CANTON	FALTER	GANTRY	VALUES	DAZZLE	ABLOOM
HALTED	CARTON	FASTER	LASTLY	LATVIA	RAZZLE	ABBOTS
LASTED	CAXTON	FATTER	PALTRY	SALVIA	DANZIG	ABHORS
MALTED	DALTON	GAITER	PANTRY	CALVED	BANZAI	ABBOTT
MATTED	EASTON	GARTER	PARTLY	CARVED	TAMZIN	IBERIA
PANTED	FASTEN	HALTER	PASTRY	HALVED	TARZAN	OBERON
PARTED	FATTEN	HATTER	TARTLY	SALVED	PANZER	ABORTS
PASTED	GASTON	LATTER	TAUTLY	WAIVED	MATZOS	ABASED
PATTED	HASTEN	MARTYR	VASTLY	LARVAE	ABOARD	ABUSED
RANTED	HATTON	MASTER	LACUNA	LARVAL	ABLAZE	ABUSER
RATTED	KAFTAN	MATTER	LAGUNA	MARVEL	ABRADE	ABASES
SALTED	MARTEN	NATTER	LAPUTA	CALVIN	OBLATE	ABUSES
TASTED	MARTIN	PASTOR	TABULA	KARVAN	OBTAIN	IBISES
WAFTED	MARTYN	PATTER	VALUED	MARVIN	ABDABS	ABATED
WAITED	PARTON	RAFTER	CANUTE	CARVER	UBOATS	ABATES
WANTED	PATTEN	RANTER	DANUBE	SALVER	ABLAUT	ABOUND
WASTED	PATTON	RAPTOR	JARULE	WAIVER	ABBACY	ABSURD
BATTIE	PAXTON	RATTER	MANURE	CALVES	ABACUS	ABJURE
BATTLE	RATTAN	SANTER	MATURE	CANVAS	ABIDED	OBTUSE
CANTLE	TARTAN	SARTOR	NATURE	CARVES	ABADAN	ABLUSH
CASTLE	TAUTEN	TARTAR	SALUTE	HALVES	IBADAN	ABDUCT
CATTLE	WALTON	TARTER	KABUKI	JARVIS	ABIDES	ABRUPT
HATTIE	WANTON	TASTER	LAZULI	SALVES	ABODES	IBEXES
MANTLE	CASTRO	WAITER	SALUKI	VALVES	ABSEIL	OBEYED

SCHAMA	SCRIED	ACTONE	SCOTER	UDDERS	IDIOTS	AERATE
ICEAGE	ACTIVE	JCLOTH	SCATTY	ADVENT	ODIOUS	BECAME
ICEAXE	SCRIBE	OCLOCK	ECHUCA	ADVERT	ADROIT	BEHAVE
OCTANE	ACHING	SCHOOL	ACCUSE	ODDEST	IDIOCY	BERATE
OCTAVE	ACTING	SCROLL	MCCUNE	EDDERY	ADAPTS	BEWARE
SCRAPE	ICHING	ACROSS	SCOUSE	ADAGIO	ADEPTS	DEBASE
ACKACK	ACHILL	ACTORS	SCRUFF	ADAGES	ADOPTS	DEBATE
MCCALL	ACTIUM	ECHOES	ACTUAL	EDWINA	ADORED	DECADE
SCRAWL	SCHISM	SCIONS	SCRUMP	EDDIED	ADORER	DEFACE
MCBAIN	ACTION	SCOOPS	OCCURS	ADMIRE	ADORES	DEFAME
MCCANN	SCRIMP	SCOOTS	SCOURS	ADVICE	ADORNS	FEMALE
MCGANN	SCRIES	ACCOST	SCOUTS	ADVISE	ODESSA	HECATE
OCTAVO	SCRIPT	ACTOUT	SCRUBS	ADDING	EDISON	LEGATE
ECLAIR	ACUITY	SCIPIO	SCRUMS	EDGING	ODDSON	MENACE
OCEANS	SCILLA	SCARAB	ACQUIT	IDLING	EDITED	MENAGE
SCRAPS	SCYLLA	ACARID	OCCULT	EDRICH	ODETTE	NEGATE
ICEBOX	SCALED	SCARED	OCCUPY	ADRIAN	ADYTUM	NEWAGE
ACACIA	SCHLEP	SCORED	SCHULZ	ADRIEN	EDITOR	REBATE
ICICLE	OCULAR	ACCRUE	MCEWAN	EDGIER	EDMUND	REGALE
ICECAP	ECCLES	ECARTE	SCOWLS	ADLIBS	ADDUCE	RELATE
ACIDIC	SCALDS	SCARCE	SCRYER	ADMITS	ADJURE	REMAKE
MCADAM	SCALES	SCARFE	EDVARD	EDDIES	ODOURS	RENAME
ECZEMA	SCALPS	SCORCH	EDWARD	ADDICT	ADDUCT	RESALE
SCHEMA	SCOLDS	PCWREN	IDCARD	ADRIFT	ADJUST	RETAKE
SCREED	SCULLS	SCORER	ADJANI	EDGILY	KERALA	SEDATE
ACCEDE	OCELOT	ACARUS	ADDAMS	ODDITY	MEGARA	SENATE
SCHEME	SCULPT	ACORNS	ADMASS	ODDJOB	NEVADA	SERAPE
MCBEAL	SCULLY	ICARUS	IDEALS	ADDLED	SEDAKA	SESAME
SCREAM	SCAMPI	SCARES	EDIBLE	ADDLES	BEDAUB	SEWAGE
MCKERN	ACUMEN	SCARPS	ADOBES	ADULTS	BENAUD	TENACE
MCLEAN	ICEMAN	SCORES	EDUCED	IDYLLS	DEMAND	BEHALF
SCREEN	SCAMPS	SCORNS	EDICTS	ODENSE	GERALD	PENANG
ACCESS	ICONIC	SCURRY	EDUCES	ADONAI	GERARD	DETACH
OCTETS	SCENIC	SCURVY	ADIDAS	GDANSK	HERALD	REHASH
SCREWS	SCONCE	OCASEY	ADVERB	ADONIS	PETARD	SERAPH
ACCENT	SCENES	SCOTIA	ADHERE	ADSORB	REGARD	BELAMI
ACCEPT	SCENTS	ACETIC	EDBERG	EDWOOD	RELAID	NEWARK
ICIEST	SCONES	SCATHE	ADDERS	ADJOIN	REMAND	REMARK
SCREWY	SCANTY	SCYTHE	ADIEUS	ADDONS	REPAID	BEFALL
SCOFFS	ACCORD	SCOTCH	EDGERS	EDDOES	RETARD	BEWAIL
SCUFFS	ECHOED	ACETAL	IDLERS	IDIOMS	REWARD	DEPAUL

DERAIL	REDACT	REDCAP	FEUDAL	HENDRY	TEDEUM	DESERT
DETAIL	REPAST	TEACUP	KENDAL	HEYDAY	AEGEAN	DETECT
RECALL	TENANT	DEICER	SELDOM	GENERA	DEMEAN	DETEST
RETAIL	DEJAVU	FENCER	DEADEN	GENEVA	SEVERN	FEWEST
BECALM	LEGACY	MERCER	HEADON	HELENA	VENETO	MEREST
DETAIN	JERBOA	REDCAR	HEBDEN	NEPETA	METEOR	NEWEST
REGAIN	SERBIA	DEICES	HENDON	PESETA	REHEAR	RECENT
REMAIN	SEABED	DEUCES	LEADEN	SELENA	VENEER	REGENT
RETAIN	WEBBED	FENCES	LEADIN	SENECA	BEGETS	REHEAT
GELATO	DEBBIE	REACTS	LEADON	SERENA	BERETS	REJECT
LEGATO	FEEBLE	SEACAT	LEIDEN	TERESA	BEVELS	RELENT
PEDALO	HERBIE	SEACOW	REDDEN	VELETA	BEZELS	REPEAT
PERABO	LEGBYE	BEACHY	TENDON	REVERB	DEFERS	REPENT
DECAMP	PEBBLE	DESCRY	VERDUN	BEHEAD	DETERS	RESENT
REVAMP	BEDBUG	PEACHY	WELDON	BEHELD	JEWELS	REVERT
BELAIR	TEABAG	TETCHY	HELDUP	DEFEND	LEPERS	SELECT
REPAIR	REEBOK	BEADED	SENDUP	DEPEND	LEVELS	CELERY
CEDARS	GERBIL	BEDDED	BENDER	LEGEND	LEVERS	HEREBY
DEBAGS	HERBAL	FENDED	DEADER	NEREID	METERS	HERESY
DEBARS	VERBAL	FEUDED	FEEDER	REREAD	NEWELS	JEREMY
DECAYS	REUBEN	HEADED	FENDER	DELETE	PETERS	MERELY
DELAYS	BERBER	HEEDED	GENDER	RECEDE	REBELS	REMEDY
KEBABS	MEMBER	HERDED	HEADER	REDEYE	RECESS	BEEFED
LEMANS	SEIBER	LEADED	HERDER	RENEGE	REFERS	TERFEL
MEDALS	WEBBER	MELDED	LEADER	REVERE	RELETS	DEAFEN
METALS	NESBIT	MENDED	LENDER	SECEDE	RENEWS	BEEFUP
PECANS	TEBBIT	NEEDED	MENDER	SERENE	REPELS	DEAFER
PEDALS	DELBOY	REEDED	READER	SEVERE	RESETS	HEIFER
PETALS	FEEBLY	SEEDED	REDDER	YEMENI	REVELS	REEFER
RECAPS	PEBBLY	TENDED	RENDER	BEDECK	SEVERS	SEEFIT
RELAYS	MERCIA	WEDDED	SEEDER	BEFELL	SEWERS	CEEFAX
REPAYS	DEICED	WEEDED	SENDER	CEREAL	TENETS	BELFRY
SEPALS	FENCED	WELDED	TENDER	KEWELL	TEPEES	LETFLY
TEXANS	FESCUE	WENDED	VENDOR	REHEEL	BEHEST	ZEUGMA
VEGANS	RESCUE	BEADLE	WEEDER	REPEAL	BEREFT	BEGGED
DECANT	PENCIL	MEDDLE	WELDER	RESEAL	CEMENT	HEDGED
DEPART	WEBCAM	NEEDLE	GEDDES	RESELL	DECEIT	MERGED
LEVANT	BEACON	PEDDLE	MENDES	RETELL	DECENT	PEGGED
PEDANT	DEACON	PENDLE	MEADOW	REVEAL	DEFEAT	VERGED
RECANT	REECHO	GELDOF	BENDIX	SEWELL	DEFECT	WEDGED
RECAST	VELCRO	SEADOG	DEADLY	REDEEM	DEJECT	BEAGLE

BELGAE	LETHAL	BESIDE	SEEING	METIER	VERITY	BENLEE
FERGIE	METHYL	BETIDE	SEWING	SENIOR	BEAKED	LEELEE
GEEGEE	DENHAM	CELINE	TEEING	BEFITS	DECKED	LESLIE
LEAGUE	HEXHAM	CERISE	VEXING	BEGINS	JERKED	MEALIE
MEAGRE	KENHOM	DECIDE	FETISH	BELIES	LEAKED	NELLIE
NEAGLE	NEWHAM	DEFILE	JEWISH	DEBITS	NECKED	JETLAG
REGGAE	PELHAM	DEFINE	NEWISH	DEFIES	PEAKED	PEGLEG
VEGGIE	WENHAM	DEMISE	PERISH	DELIUS	PECKED	FELLAH
LENGTH	PEAHEN	DENISE	RELISH	DENIES	PEEKED	HEALTH
BENGAL	ZEEHAN	DERIDE	ZENITH	DENIMS	REEKED	WEALTH
FERGAL	JETHRO	DERIVE	GEMINI	DEVILS	HECKLE	BEDLAM
REDGUM	TECHNO	DESIRE	MEDICI	GENIUS	REEKIE	PEPLUM
BERGEN	BENHUR	DEVICE	REMICK	HELIOS	BECKON	VELLUM
KEEGAN	MENHIR	DEVISE	AERIAL	LEVIES	DEAKIN	BERLIN
REAGAN	NETHER	FELINE	DENIAL	MEDICS	JERKIN	CEYLON
SERGIO	TETHER	PETITE	GENIAL	MERITS	RECKON	DECLAN
BEGGAR	ZEPHYR	RECIFE	MEDIAL	PERILS	WEAKEN	HEFLIN
GEIGER	MESHES	RECIPE	MENIAL	REBIDS	PERKUP	MERLIN
HEDGER	REDHOT	RECITE	REDIAL	REGIUS	BEAKER	REPLAN
LEDGER	NEPHEW	REFINE	REFILL	REJIGS	BECKER	TEFLON
MERGER	CELICA	REGIME	SERIAL	RELICS	DECKER	DEWLAP
SEEGER	DESICA	RELIVE	VENIAL	RELIES	MEEKER	CELLAR
VERGER	HEGIRA	REPINE	HELIUM	REMISS	PECKER	DEALER
DEIGNS	JEMIMA	RESIDE	MEDIUM	REMITS	SEEKER	FEELER
FEIGNS	MEDINA	RETIRE	SEXISM	RESINS	WEAKER	FELLER
HEDGES	MELINA	REVILE	TEDIUM	RESITS	SERKIS	GELLAR
LEDGES	PETIPA	REVISE	BENIGN	SERIES	BECKET	GELLER
MERGES	REGINA	REVIVE	DESIGN	SERIFS	MEEKLY	HEALER
NEIGHS	RETINA	REWIRE	FENIAN	DELIST	WEAKLY	HELLER
REIGNS	SELINA	SEMITE	LEGION	DEMIST	WEEKLY	KEELER
SEDGES	BEHIND	VENICE	LESION	DEPICT	BELLOC	KELLER
VERGES	BELIED	BELIEF	MEDIAN	DESIST	FELLED	KEVLAR
WEDGES	DEFIED	RELIEF	REGION	HEWITT	GELLED	MEDLAR
WEIGHS	DENIED	BENING	RESIGN	RESIST	HEALED	MELLOR
HEIGHT	LEVIED	BERING	DENIRO	SEXIST	HEELED	PEDLAR
WEIGHT	PERIOD	CEDING	DEVITO	REVIEW	PEALED	PEELER
GEWGAW	RELIED	HEWING	MEDICO	CECILY	PEELED	SEALER
MESHED	REMIND	KEYING	MERINO	EERILY	REELED	SELLER
METHOD	REWIND	METING	MEXICO	LEVITY	SEALED	TELLER
TEEHEE	AEDILE	MEWING	DENIER	VERIFY	VEILED	WELLER
BETHEL	BELIZE	PEKING	EERIER	VERILY	YELLED	BELLES

CELLOS	GERMAN	LEANNE	FEDORA	SETOFF	DEVOUT	DEEPER
FELLAS	HENMAN	LENNIE	LENORA	TEEOFF	GETOUT	HELPER
HELLOS	HERMAN	MEANIE	PELOTA	BELONG	LETOUT	KEEPER
REALMS	LEMMON	RENNIE	SENORA	MEKONG	PEGOUT	PEEPER
TELLUS	MERMAN	SEANCE	VERONA	NEROLI	REBOOT	PEPPER
WELLES	NEWMAN	FENNEL	HEROIC	REWORK	REPORT	REAPER
MERLOT	REDMAN	KENNEL	BEHOLD	BECOOL	RESORT	TEMPER
PELLET	SEAMAN	KERNEL	BEYOND	BEFOUL	RETORT	VESPER
ZEALOT	SEAMEN	VERNAL	DEVOID	RECOIL	REVOLT	TEMPOS
BELLOW	SERMON	HEENAN	LEMOND	DEFORM	SETOUT	TEMPTS
FELLOW	VERMIN	KEENAN	RECORD	REFORM	BETONY	DESPOT
MELLOW	YEOMAN	LEANON	RELOAD	BEMOAN	FELONY	TEAPOT
PELLEW	YEOMEN	LENNON	RESOLD	HEROIN	LEMONY	DEEPLY
YELLOW	YESMAN	PENNON	RETOLD	REBORN	MELODY	TEAPOY
REFLEX	YESMEN	RENNIN	REWORD	REJOIN	MEMORY	FERRIC
REFLUX	BEAMER	VERNON	SECOND	RENOWN	BEEPED	METRIC
BEXLEY	REAMER	LEANTO	VETOED	RECOUP	HEAPED	AELRED
DEPLOY	WEIMAR	SEWNUP	ZEROED	DETOUR	HELPED	FEARED
FEALTY	DEIMOS	FENNER	AEROBE	DEVOUR	KEYPAD	GEARED
HEALEY	SEAMUS	JENNER	BECOME	MEMOIR	LEAPED	JEERED
KEELEY	DERMOT	KEENER	BEFORE	RENOIR	PEEPED	LEERED
KELLEY	HELMET	LEANER	BEGONE	VELOUR	REAPED	NEARED
LESLEY	HELMUT	LERNER	DECODE	BEFOGS	SEEPED	PEERED
MEDLEY	HERMIT	MEANER	DECOKE	BESOMS	TEMPED	REARED
NEWLEY	KERMIT	TENNER	DEMOTE	DECOYS	YELPED	SEARED
REALLY	PELMET	WEANER	DENOTE	DEMOBS	KELPIE	SEERED
REALTY	PERMIT	BEINGS	DEPOSE	DEMONS	PEOPLE	TETRAD
REPLAY	TEXMEX	DENNIS	DEVOTE	DEPOTS	TEMPLE	VEERED
WESLEY	SEEMLY	FEINTS	EEYORE	FELONS	WEEPIE	DEARIE
HERMIA	HERNIA	KEYNES	GENOME	HEROES	TEMPEH	DEARME
BEAMED	FENNEC	RENNES	JEROME	HERONS	DELPHI	DECREE
DEEMED	KEENED	TENNIS	KETONE	LEMONS	HEMPEL	DEGREE
HEMMED	LEANED	BENNET	REBORE	MELONS	KEPPEL	GEORGE
PERMED	PENNED	KENNET	REDONE	REDOES	PENPAL	HEARSE
REAMED	PERNOD	PEANUT	REMOTE	REPOTS	DEEPEN	PEARCE
SEAMED	VEINED	RENNET	REMOVE	SEPOYS	HEMPEN	GEHRIG
SEEMED	WEANED	LENNOX	REPOSE	TENORS	REOPEN	DEARTH
TEAMED	BEANIE	HEINEY	REVOKE	VENOUS	TENPIN	HEARTH
TEEMED	BERNIE	KEENLY	GETOFF	VETOES	WEAPON	SEARCH
TERMED	JEANNE	MEANLY	LETOFF	DECOCT	KEEPUP	NEURAL
DERMAL	JENNIE	PENNEY	SEEOFF	DEPORT	BEEPER	PETREL

PETROL	REDRAW	LESSON	MEASLY	SEETHE	FETTER	GENTLY
REDRUM	BETRAY	NEESON	MERSEY	SETTEE	HEATER	GENTRY
DERREN	DEARLY	NELSON	SELSEY	SETTLE	HECTOR	NEATLY
HEBRON	DEFRAY	PEPSIN	YEASTY	TEETHE	JESTER	PERTLY
HEDREN	GEORGY	PERSON	BERTHA	DENTAL	LECTER	SENTRY
NEURON	HEARTY	REASON	YENTOB	KEITEL	LECTOR	VESTRY
PENRYN	NEARBY	SEASON	CELTIC	LENTIL	LESTER	BELUGA
PERRIN	NEARLY	LETSGO	HECTIC	MENTAL	LETTER	MEDUSA
TEHRAN	PEARLY	MESSUP	PEPTIC	RENTAL	MENTOR	NEBULA
WEIRDO	TEDRAY	CENSER	SEPTIC	VESTAL	NEATER	PETULA
BEARUP	YEARLY	CENSOR	BELTED	SEPTUM	NECTAR	BENUMB
LETRIP	GEISHA	DENSER	DENTED	BEATEN	NESTOR	FECUND
TEARUP	LENSKA	GEYSER	HEATED	BEATON	NEUTER	GERUND
BEARER	PERSIA	LESSER	JESTED	BEETON	PESTER	REFUND
DEARER	REDSEA	LESSOR	JETTED	DENTON	PEWTER	BEAUNE
FERRER	CEASED	SENSOR	MELTED	HEPTON	RECTOR	BEMUSE
NEARER	LEASED	TEASER	NESTED	HESTON	REUTER	DEDUCE
TERROR	MESSED	BEASTS	NETTED	KEATON	SECTOR	DEFUSE
BEARDS	REUSED	CEASES	PELTED	LEPTON	SETTER	DELUDE
DEBRIS	SENSED	CENSUS	PENTAD	MELTON	TEETER	DELUGE
DESRES	TEASED	DEISTS	RENTED	MERTON	TESTER	DELUXE
FERRIS	TENSED	FEASTS	RESTED	NEATEN	VECTOR	DEMURE
GENRES	VERSED	HEISTS	SEATED	NEWTON	WELTER	DENUDE
HEARTS	BESSIE	LEASES	TENTED	PECTIN	WETTER	DEPUTE
LEARNS	JESSIE	LENSES	TESTED	PEYTON	BERTHS	JEJUNE
METRES	LESSEE	MESSES	VENTED	SEXTON	DEATHS	LEGUME
PEARLS	NESSIE	SENSES	VESTED	TEUTON	DEPTHS	PERUKE
REARMS	MENSCH	TEASES	VETTED	WESTON	HEATHS	PERUSE
SEVRES	JETSKI	TENSES	WETTED	NEXTTO	TENTHS	REBUKE
YEARNS	PERSIL	VERSES	BEATLE	BEATUP	VECTIS	REDUCE
ZEBRAS	TEASEL	VERSUS	BEETLE	BELTUP	VESTAS	REFUGE
BEIRUT	VESSEL	BEDSIT	BERTIE	MEETUP	BEATIT	REFUSE
FERRET	WEASEL	JETSET	CENTRE	PENTUP	DECTET	REFUTE
HEARST	JETSAM	KENSIT	FETTLE	SENTUP	SEPTET	REPUTE
LEARNT	BENSON	TEASET	GENTLE	BEATER	SEXTET	RESUME
REGRET	GEESON	SEESAW	KETTLE	BELTER	BESTOW	SECURE
SECRET	HENSON	REDSOX	LEFTIE	BETTER	SEMTEX	SEDUCE
SEURAT	HEWSON	WESSEX	METTLE	DEBTOR	VERTEX	TENURE
WETROT	JENSON	FEISTY	NESTLE	DEFTER	BEATTY	REBUFF
HENRYV	LEESON	JERSEY	NETTLE	DEXTER	DEFTLY	DEBUNK
HEBREW	LESSEN	KELSEY	PESTLE	FESTER	DESTRY	REFUEL

```
SEQUEL  LEAVER  AFFAIR  EGRESS  SHOALS  OHDEAR  SHEIKH
SEXUAL  SERVER  OFFALY  EGRETS  THWART  CHEEKS  SHRIEK
RETURN  WEAVER  OFFCUT  OGLERS  PHOBIA  CHEEPS  SHRINK
SEQUIN  WEEVER  OFFDAY  OGRESS  SHOBNA  CHEERS  SHRILL
TEAURN  DELVES  AFIELD  IGNITE  PHOBIC  CHIEFS  THRILL
REGULO  HEAVES  IFIELD  AGEING  THEBFG  SHEETS  CHRISM
DEBUGS  JEEVES  OFFEND  EGGING  KHYBER  SHREDS  THEISM
DEBUTS  LEAVES  EFFETE  OGLING  THEBES  SHREWS  SHRIMP
DEMURS  LEEVES  AFRESH  AGEISM  CHUBBY  WHEELS  CHAINS
LEMURS  NERVES  AFTERS  EGOISM  SHABBY  SHYEST  CHAIRS
REBUTS  PEEVES  OFFERS  UGLIER  CHACHA  THREAT  CHOIRS
RECURS  PELVIS  AFFECT  AGEIST  CHICHI  CHEEKY  RHEIMS
RERUNS  REEVES  EFFECT  EGOIST  CHECKS  CHEERY  THEIRS
REVUES  SERVES  AFGHAN  OGILVY  CHICKS  CHEESY  THRIPS
SERUMS  WEAVES  AFRICA  AGENDA  CHOCKS  SHEEDY  CHRIST
VENUES  VELVET  OFFICE  UGANDA  CHUCKS  WHEEZY  SHRIFT
DEDUCT  PEEWEE  OFFING  EGGNOG  SHACKS  CHAFED  THEIST
JESUIT  HEDWIG  OFFISH  AGENTS  SHOCKS  THEFOG  THRIFT
RESULT  LETWIN  UFFIZI  AGENCY  SHUCKS  SHUFTI  THEJAM
BEAUTY  SELWYN  AFFIRM  AGEOLD  WHACKS  CHAFER  CHAKRA
DEPUTY  PEEWIT  EFFIGY  IGNORE  CHOCKY  SHOFAR  CHUKKA
PENURY  LEEWAY  OFFKEY  OGMORE  CHIDED  CHAFES  CHOKED
DERVLA  MEDWAY  XFILES  IGLOOS  SHADED  SHAFTS  THEKID
PELVIC  SEAWAY  AFFORD  EGMONT  CHADOR  SHIFTS  SHEKEL
DELVED  XERXES  OFNOTE  AGARIC  CHIDES  THEFTS  SHAKEN
FERVID  JEKYLL  AFLOAT  AGASSI  RHODES  WHIFFS  CHOKER
HEAVED  KENYAN  EFFORT  EGESTS  SHADES  SHIFTY  SHAKER
PEEVED  RELYON  OFFPAT  AGATHA  SHADOW  THEFLY  CHOKES
REVVED  SEEYOU  AFFRAY  AGOUTI  SHODDY  SHOGUN  SHAKES
SERVED  SEIZED  OFFSET  PHRASE  SHEENA  THIGHS  PHUKET
WEAVED  HERZOG  OFSTED  SHEAVE  SHIELD  SHAGGY  CHOKEY
OEUVRE  DENZEL  EFFUSE  THEAGE  SHREWD  SHEILA  THELMA
WEEVIL  DENZIL  IGUANA  SHEATH  THEEND  CHAISE  WHILED
YEOVIL  GEEZER  AGNATE  THRASH  THREAD  CHOICE  CHILDE
HEAVEN  WEEZER  AGHAST  SHRANK  CHEESE  SHIITE  SHELVE
KELVIN  SEIZES  OGRADY  THWACK  PHOEBE  SHRIKE  CHILLI
LEAVEN  AFRAID  EGGCUP  THRALL  SHEENE  SHRINE  PHYLUM
MELVYN  AFLAME  AGADIR  CHEAPO  SHREVE  SHRIVE  SHALOM
MERVYN  AFRAME  AGREED  CHEATS  THIEVE  THRICE  PHILIP
BEAVER  EFFACE  AGLEAM  PHIALS  WHEEZE  THRIVE  CHOLER
DENVER  OFLATE  AGREES  SHEARS  THRESH  SHYING  THALER
```

WHALER	RHONDA	SHINDY	SHARED	WHORLS	SHUTUP	TIRANA
CHALKS	SHANIA	SHINTY	SHORED	THIRST	WHITER	LIZARD
CHILES	PHONIC	THINGY	AHERNE	THORAX	CHUTES	PICARD
CHILLS	PHONED	THINLY	CHARGE	CHERRY	PHOTOS	RIBALD
PHELPS	WHINED	WHINNY	CHERIE	CHIRPY	WHITES	RIBAND
SHELLS	CHANCE	CHINTZ	SHARPE	SHERRY	CHATTY	WIZARD
WHALES	CHANGE	CHROMA	THORNE	SHIRTY	CHITTY	DILATE
WHELKS	THENCE	SHROUD	THORPE	THIRTY	WHITBY	FINALE
WHELPS	WHENCE	CHOOSE	WHARFE	THORNY	SHOULD	FIXATE
WHILES	WHINGE	CHROME	SHARIF	WHERRY	CHOUGH	MIRAGE
CHALET	BHINDI	SHROVE	CHURCH	SHIRAZ	THOUGH	PILATE
WHILST	CHANEL	THRONE	CHERYL	PHYSIC	THRUSH	PIRATE
CHALKY	PHENOL	THRONG	CHORAL	CHASED	SHRUNK	SILAGE
CHILLY	RHINAL	WHOOSH	SHERYL	PHASED	GHOULS	TIRADE
PHILBY	SHINTO	WHOOPI	CHARON	CHASSE	SHOUTS	TISANE
SHELBY	CHINUP	SHTOOK	SHARON	CHASTE	SHRUBS	VISAGE
WHOLLY	SHINER	THROWN	THERON	CHISEL	SHRUGS	VIVACE
CHIMED	WHINER	SHOOTS	SHERBO	CHOSEN	THRUMS	ZIDANE
RHYMED	CHANTS	THROBS	THURSO	PHYSIO	THRUST	RIYADH
SHAMED	CHINES	THROES	CHARMS	CHASER	RHEUMY	DIWALI
SHAMAN	CHINKS	THROWS	CHARTS	CHASES	SHAVED	KIGALI
SHIMON	CHUNKS	WHOOPS	CHIRPS	CHASMS	SHOVED	LIPARI
CHIMER	PHONES	THROAT	CHORDS	CHESTS	CHEVRE	HIJACK
CHAMPS	RHINOS	CHOOSY	CHORES	GHOSTS	SHOVEL	MINACK
CHIMES	SHANKS	PHOOEY	CHORUS	PHASES	SHAVEN	DISARM
CHIMPS	SHINES	THEORY	CHURNS	RHESUS	SHAVER	FIGARO
CHOMPS	SHUNTS	SHAPED	PHAROS	THESES	SHIVER	LISAHO
CHUMPS	THANES	CHAPEL	SHARDS	THESIS	CHIVES	MIKADO
RHYMES	THANKS	CHOPIN	SHARES	WHISKS	SHAVES	MILANO
SHAMES	THINGS	CHOPUP	SHARKS	CHESTY	SHOVES	VIRAGO
THAMES	THINKS	SHAPER	SHIRES	WHISKY	CHIVVY	MIDAIR
THEMES	THONGS	SHAPES	SHIRKS	WHATIF	CHEWED	CIGARS
THOMAS	WHINES	CHIPPY	SHIRTS	THATCH	SHOWED	DINARS
THUMBS	THANET	CHOPPY	SHORES	RHYTHM	THAWED	DIVANS
THUMPS	CHANCY	WHIPPY	SHORTS	BHUTAN	THEWHO	FINALS
THYMUS	CHANEY	CHEQUE	THERMS	PHOTON	SHOWUP	LILACS
CHUMMY	CHENEY	CHOREA	THIRDS	RHYTON	SHOWER	RIVALS
SHAMMY	CHUNKY	DHARMA	THORNS	SHUTIN	SHAWLS	SITARS
SHIMMY	PHONEY	SHERPA	WHARFS	WHITEN	THEWIZ	TITANS
WHAMMY	SHANDY	CHERUB	WHIRLS	BHUTTO	SHAYNE	VICARS
WHIMSY	SHANTY	CHIRAC	WHIRRS	GHETTO	CICADA	BIGAMY

BINARY	WINCED	KINDOF	SINEAD	LIVERS	LIVERY	TINGLE
HILARY	CIRCLE	DIADEM	BIGEYE	MILERS	MISERY	WIGGLE
LITANY	FIACRE	LIBDEM	BIREME	MINERS	NICELY	FIZGIG
MILADY	MISCUE	WISDOM	GISELE	MISERS	NICETY	FINGAL
PIRACY	KIMCHI	BIDDEN	MISERE	MIXERS	NINETY	VIRGIL
AIRBED	FISCAL	HIDDEN	RIBEYE	OILERS	SINEWY	AIRGUN
FIBBED	SITCOM	LINDEN	HIDEHI	PIPERS	TIMELY	BIGGUN
RIBBED	NIACIN	MIDDEN	LINEAL	RIDERS	VINERY	BINGEN
SINBAD	OILCAN	RIDDEN	EILEEN	RIPENS	WIDELY	PIDGIN
DIBBLE	TINCAN	SINDEN	GIDEON	RISERS	WINERY	SIXGUN
KIBBLE	ZIRCON	TIEDIN	GIVEIN	RIVERS	WISELY	VIRGIN
LIABLE	HICCUP	TIEDUP	LIVEIN	RIVETS	BIFFED	RINGUP
NIBBLE	TINCUP	WINDUP	PIGEON	SINEWS	MIFFED	BIGGER
NIMBLE	MINCER	BIDDER	SIDEON	SIRENS	PIFFLE	DIGGER
RIBBLE	PINCER	BINDER	WIGEON	SIXERS	RIFFLE	FINGER
TIMBRE	CIRCUS	CINDER	CICERO	TIGERS	EIFFEL	GINGER
VIABLE	DISCOS	FINDER	LIKESO	TILERS	FITFUL	JIGGER
AIRBAG	DISCUS	GIRDER	PINERO	TIMERS	SINFUL	LINGER
BINBAG	MINCES	HINDER	GIVEUP	VIDEOS	WILFUL	RIGGER
KITBAG	NIECES	KIDDER	LINEUP	VIPERS	TIFFIN	RINGER
BIGBEN	PIECES	KINDER	PILEUP	VIXENS	DIFFER	SINGER
GIBBON	PISCES	LIEDER	PIPEUP	WIDENS	KIEFER	TIGGER
LISBON	WINCES	MILDER	SIZEUP	WIPERS	PILFER	WINGER
RIBBON	BIGCAT	MINDER	LINEAR	BISECT	TITFER	BINGES
SINBIN	DIDCOT	TINDER	AIDERS	DIGEST	MISFIT	DIRGES
BILBAO	WILCOX	WILDER	AIRERS	DIRECT	LIFFEY	HINGES
DIBBER	BISCAY	WINDER	BICEPS	DIREST	LINGUA	HINGIS
DISBAR	BITCHY	DIODES	BIKERS	DIVERT	HINGED	MIDGES
FIBBER	TITCHY	LINDOS	BIPEDS	DIVEST	JIGGED	RIDGES
GIBBER	GILDED	MILDEW	CIVETS	FINEST	RIDGED	SIEGES
LIMBER	KIDDED	WINDOW	DINERS	NICEST	RIGGED	SINGES
TIMBER	MINDED	FIDDLY	DIVERS	RIPEST	RINGED	TINGES
WILBUR	WINDED	KINDLY	EIDERS	SILENT	SINGED	FIDGET
AIRBUS	BIRDIE	MIDDAY	FIVERS	VILEST	TINGED	MIDGET
NIMBUS	DIDDLE	MILDLY	GIVERS	WIDEST	DINGLE	WIDGET
GIBBET	FIDDLE	TIDDLY	HIKERS	WISEST	GIGGLE	DINGHY
TITBIT	GIRDLE	WILDLY	JIVERS	CICELY	JIGGLE	GIGGLY
NIMBLY	KINDLE	CINEMA	LIBELS	FINELY	JINGLE	JINGLY
MISCHA	MIDDLE	RIBENA	LIKENS	FINERY	MINGLE	KINGLY
MINCED	RIDDLE	BIGEND	LIMEYS	LIKELY	NIGGLE	NIGGLY
PIECED	TIEDYE	BINEND	LINERS	LIVELY	SINGLE	SINGLY

TINGLY	MISHIT	LINING	AIRIER	PICKLE	RIFLED	BILLOW
WIGGLY	TINHAT	LIVING	OILIER	PINKIE	SIDLED	LIELOW
FISHED	WITHIT	MIMING	TIDIER	SICKIE	TILLED	PILLOW
SIGHED	VISHNU	MINING	TINIER	SICKLE	TITLED	WILLOW
WISHED	EIGHTY	MIXING	VIZIER	TICKLE	BILLIE	DIBLEY
RICHIE	HIGHLY	OILING	WILIER	TINKLE	GILLIE	FINLAY
EIGHTH	MIGHTY	PILING	CITIES	WILKIE	GIRLIE	KIELTY
MICHEL	RICHLY	PINING	DIGITS	WINKLE	LILLIE	MISLAY
DIRHAM	NIKITA	PIPING	LILIES	HICKOK	MILLIE	RIDLEY
LICHEN	SILICA	RIDING	LIMITS	NICKEL	WILLIE	DIMMED
SIPHON	VIEIRA	RILING	MIMICS	DINKUM	WILLEM	FILMED
WITHIN	PITIED	RISING	MINIMS	LILKIM	FILLIN	RIMMED
RIGHTO	TIDIED	SIDING	PITIES	AITKEN	VIOLIN	DISMAL
BISHOP	DIVIDE	SITING	PIXIES	BIRKIN	RIALTO	AIRMAN
DISHUP	DIVINE	SIZING	SIRIUS	FIRKIN	FILLIP	AIRMEN
HIGHUP	FINITE	TILING	TIDIES	SICKEN	FILLUP	BINMAN
HIPHOP	LIAISE	TIMING	VIGILS	SILKEN	HISLOP	BINMEN
MISHAP	SIMILE	TIRING	VISITS	SINKIN	DILLER	HITMAN
CIPHER	VIRILE	VIKING	MILIEU	SISKIN	FILLER	KIDMAN
DITHER	AIDING	WIPING	TITIPU	GINKGO	HITLER	LIPMAN
EITHER	AILING	WIRING	AIRILY	KICKUP	KILLER	OILMAN
FISHER	AIMING	FINISH	DIMITY	LINKUP	MIDLER	PIEMAN
HIGHER	AIRING	LILITH	JIMINY	PICKUP	MILLER	PITMAN
HITHER	BIDING	BIKINI	SICILY	BICKER	PILLAR	PITMEN
MITHER	BIKING	RIMINI	TIDILY	KICKER	TILLER	TINMAN
RICHER	BITING	FILIAL	VILIFY	NICKER	AISLES	BITMAP
WITHER	CITING	FINIAL	WILILY	SINKER	FIELDS	DIMMER
ZITHER	DICING	CILIUM	KIBITZ	TICKER	RIFLES	FIRMER
BIGHTS	DINING	MIRIAM	JINKED	TINKER	SIDLES	KILMER
DISHES	DIVING	FIJIAN	KICKED	WICKER	TITLES	RIMMER
EIGHTS	FILING	LILIAN	KINKED	WILKES	VILLAS	SIMMER
FIGHTS	FINING	MINION	LICKED	PICKET	VIOLAS	WILMER
FISHES	FIRING	PINION	LINKED	TICKET	WIELDS	ZIMMER
LIGHTS	FIXING	SIMIAN	MILKED	WICKET	WILLIS	GIZMOS
NIGHTS	GIVING	TITIAN	NICKED	MICKEY	YIELDS	LITMUS
RICHES	HIDING	VISION	PICKED	SICKLY	BILLET	KISMET
RIGHTS	HIKING	VIVIAN	RISKED	BILLED	FILLET	DISMAY
SIGHTS	HIRING	VIVIEN	TICKED	FILLED	GIMLET	FIRMLY
TIGHTS	HIVING	AIKIDO	WICKED	KILLED	MILLET	NIAMEY
TITHES	JIVING	FINITO	WINKED	MILLED	PIGLET	BIANCA
WISHES	LIKING	LIBIDO	FICKLE	MISLED	VIOLET	SIENNA

VIENNA	WINNOW	DIPPED	PIMPLY	HISSED	DIETED	TINTIN
ZINNIA	DISNEY	KIPPED	SIMPLY	KISSED	FITTED	WILTON
BIONIC	FINNEY	LIMPED	BISQUE	MISSED	GIFTED	WINTON
PICNIC	KIDNEY	LIMPID	CINQUE	RINSED	HINTED	BISTRO
BINNED	PITNEY	LISPED	RISQUE	KISSME	JILTED	GIOTTO
FINNED	SIDNEY	NIPPED	SIERRA	TISSUE	KILTED	BIGTOP
PINNED	GINOLA	PIPPED	MIHRAB	KIRSCH	KITTED	TIPTOP
SIGNED	KIAORA	RIPPED	CITRIC	KITSCH	LIFTED	BITTER
SINNED	MIMOSA	SIPPED	NITRIC	DIESEL	LISTED	DIETER
TINNED	NICOLA	TIPPED	MITRED	MISSAL	MINTED	FILTER
DIONNE	WINONA	ZIPPED	NIMROD	TINSEL	PITTED	FITTER
FIANCE	MILORD	DIEPPE	TIERED	DIMSUM	RIOTED	HITTER
MINNIE	NICOLE	DIMPLE	BIERCE	LISSOM	SIFTED	JITTER
TINNIE	SIMONE	HIPPIE	FIERCE	BILSON	SILTED	KILTER
VINNIE	MIDOFF	NIPPLE	PIERCE	GIBSON	TILTED	LISTER
WINNIE	RIPOFF	PIMPLE	PIERRE	NISSAN	TINTED	LITTER
DIBNAH	TIPOFF	RIPPLE	TIERCE	NISSEN	WILTED	MINTER
JINNAH	KIBOSH	SIMPLE	OILRIG	WILSON	BIGTOE	MISTER
BIONDI	SIMOOM	TIPPLE	WIRRAL	FIASCO	LITTLE	PINTER
DIRNDL	DISOWN	WIMPLE	VIKRAM	BIGSUR	PINTLE	RIOTER
LIONEL	MINOAN	YIPPEE	CIARAN	KISSER	TIPTOE	RITTER
SIGNAL	GIGOLO	DISPEL	CITRON	DIYSOS	VIRTUE	SIFTER
SIMNEL	KIMONO	NIPPON	KIERAN	FIRSTS	DISTEL	SISTER
FINNAN	RIGOUR	PIPPIN	KIEREN	HISSES	DISTIL	SITTER
SIGNIN	VIGOUR	RIPPON	LIBRAN	KIOSKS	LINTEL	TITTER
SIGNON	BIGOTS	TIEPIN	MICRON	KISSES	PISTIL	VICTOR
KIDNAP	DIVOTS	DIAPER	MIRREN	MISSES	PISTOL	WINTER
SIGNUP	MIAOWS	DIPPER	MIRROR	MISSUS	DICTUM	WITTER
DINNER	MINORS	KIPPER	CIRRUS	RINSES	TIMTAM	BIRTHS
PINNER	PILOTS	NIPPER	CITRUS	BISSET	VICTIM	FIFTHS
SIGNOR	PITONS	RIPPER	FIBRES	JIGSAW	BITTEN	FIRTHS
SINNER	PIVOTS	SIMPER	LITRES	PITSAW	GIRTON	HIATUS
WIENER	VINOUS	TIPPER	MITRES	RIPSAW	HILTON	PINTOS
WINNER	VISORS	ZIPPER	TIARAS	KINSEY	KITTEN	PISTES
FIENDS	WIDOWS	HIPPOS	TIGRIS	KIRSTY	LINTON	RICTUS
GIANTS	DIEOUT	LIMPET	KILROY	PIGSTY	LISTEN	VISTAS
PIANOS	DIPOUT	TINPOT	FIESTA	RIGSBY	LISTON	WIDTHS
WIDNES	PIGOUT	TIPPET	MIASMA	WIMSEY	MILTON	DIKTAT
LINNET	SITOUT	TIPPEX	SIESTA	SINTRA	MINTON	HINTAT
SIGNET	SIMONY	BIOPSY	AIRSAC	BIOTIC	MITTEN	FILTHY
MINNOW	BIOPIC	LIMPLY	BIASED	TICTAC	PISTON	WINTRY

FIBULA	EJECTS	OLDAGE	CLICHE	FLEECE	SLIGHT	BLOKES
VICUNA	FJORDS	PLEASE	CLOCHE	SLEEVE	CLAGGY	FLAKES
LIQUID	EKLAND	SLEAZE	FLECHE	CLUEDO	OLDHAM	FLUKES
PIQUED	SKIBOB	SLOANE	GLYCOL	ALDERS	OLDHAT	SLAKES
DILUTE	SKIDOO	ULLAGE	FLACON	ALIENS	ULRIKA	OLDLAG
DISUSE	EKBERG	BLEACH	SLICER	ALLEYS	ALLIED	SLALOM
FIGURE	SKIERS	FLEADH	BLOCKS	ALTERS	ALPINE	ALUMNA
MINUTE	SKIFFS	FLYASH	CLACKS	BLEEDS	BLAINE	BLAMED
MISUSE	SKIING	ALKALI	CLICKS	BLEEPS	CLAIRE	PLUMED
RITUAL	SKYING	ELPASO	CLOCKS	ELDERS	ELAINE	FLAMBE
VISUAL	SKYLAB	ALBANS	CLUCKS	ELVERS	ELLICE	ALUMNI
LIQUOR	SKILLS	ALLAYS	ELECTS	FLEETS	ELOISE	ALTMAN
PIQUES	SKULKS	ALTARS	FLECKS	PLIERS	PLAICE	OLDMAN
SITUPS	SKULLS	ALWAYS	FLICKS	SLEEPS	SLUICE	ULLMAN
MINUET	AKIMBO	BLEATS	FLOCKS	ULCERS	CLUING	CLAMUP
PIQUET	SKOMER	BLOATS	PLACES	ALBEIT	FLYING	BLAMES
KIKUYU	SKIMPS	CLEANS	PLUCKS	ALBERT	GLUING	CLAMPS
SILVIA	SKIMPY	CLEARS	SLACKS	CLIENT	PLYING	CLIMBS
SILVER	SKINKS	CLOAKS	SLICES	ELDEST	ELFISH	CLIMES
SIEVES	SKUNKS	FLOATS	ELICIT	FLUENT	ELVISH	CLUMPS
SILVAS	SKINNY	GLEAMS	PLUCKY	OLDEST	SLEIGH	FLAMES
VIEWED	SKOPJE	GLEANS	ELUDED	OLMERT	ALLIUM	FLUMES
BIGWIG	SKIPPY	GLOATS	GLIDED	SLYEST	ALBION	GLAMIS
WIGWAM	SKIRUN	PLEADS	FLEDGE	BLUESY	ALBINO	LLAMAS
VIEWER	SKIRTS	PLEATS	KLUDGE	ELLERY	ELNINO	PLUMES
TISWAS	SKATED	PLIANT	PLEDGE	FLEECY	ILDIVO	PLUMPS
DIMWIT	SKETCH	ALBANY	SLEDGE	SLEEPY	ALDISS	SLUMPS
NITWIT	SKATER	BLEARY	SLUDGE	SLEETY	ALLIES	CLIMAX
AIRWAY	SKATES	FLOATY	GLIDER	BLUFFS	ALLISS	BLIMEY
MIDWAY	SKIVED	OLEARY	BLADES	CLIFFS	CLAIMS	CLAMMY
DIOXIN	SKIVER	SLEAZY	ELIDES	FLUFFY	FLAILS	CLUMPY
LIBYAN	SKIVES	GLOBAL	ELUDES	PLAGUE	FLUIDS	CLUMSY
PIAZZA	SKIVVY	ALIBIS	GLADES	FLAGON	OLDIES	FLIMSY
FIZZED	SKEWED	GLOBES	GLADYS	PLUGIN	PLAINS	GLUMLY
FIZZLE	SKEWER	FLABBY	GLIDES	SLOGAN	PLAITS	PLUMMY
LIZZIE	SKYWAY	GLIBLY	SLIDES	ALIGNS	ELLIOT	GLENDA
SIZZLE	OKAYED	OLDBOY	GLADLY	ALIGHT	PLAIDY	GLINKA
ZIGZAG	ALPACA	ALICIA	SLUDGY	BLIGHT	ELIJAH	CLINIC
MIZZEN	CLOACA	PLACED	ALPENA	FLIGHT	FLAKED	CLONED
FIZZES	ALSACE	PLACID	ALLEGE	FLOGIT	FLUKED	PLANED
PIZZAS	CLEAVE	SLICED	CLEESE	PLIGHT	SLAKED	BLONDE

FLANGE	SLINKS	ELOPES	ALYSSA	FLUTES	CLOVES	IMPALE
GLANCE	PLANET	SLOPES	ELISHA	PLATES	GLOVES	EMBARK
PLUNGE	CLANCY	FLOPPY	PLASMA	SLATES	OLIVES	EMBALM
BLANCH	CLINGY	SLIPPY	CLOSED	SLOTHS	SLAVES	IMPAIR
BLENCH	CLUNKY	SLOPPY	ALISON	FLATLY	CLAWED	SMEARS
CLENCH	FLINTY	CLAQUE	CLOSER	GLITZY	FLAWED	IMPACT
CLINCH	PLENTY	CLIQUE	GLASER	ALLUDE	FLOWED	IMPART
CLUNCH	SLANGY	PLAQUE	BLASTS	ALLURE	GLOWED	UMLAUT
FLINCH	SLINKY	GLORIA	CLASPS	BLOUSE	SLEWED	SMEARY
PLINTH	ALMOND	CLERIC	CLOSES	CLAUDE	SLOWED	AMECHE
PLANCK	ELWOOD	ALFRED	FLASKS	CLAUSE	BLEWUP	AMICUS
PLENUM	ILFORD	BLARED	PLUSES	ILDUCE	BLOWUP	SMACKS
BLANCO	ALCOVE	FLARED	CLOSET	ILLUSE	SLOWUP	SMOCKS
PLANER	ALGORE	FLORID	CLASSY	CLOUGH	BLOWER	SMUDGE
BLANKS	ELMORE	GLARED	FLASHY	PLOUGH	FLOWER	AMIDST
BLENDS	ALCOCK	CLARKE	FLESHY	SLEUTH	GLOWER	AMOEBA
BLINDS	ALDOUS	FLORAL	FLOSSY	SLOUCH	SLOWER	IMPEND
BLINKS	ALLOTS	PLURAL	GLASSY	SLOUGH	CLOWNS	AMPERE
BLONDS	ALLOWS	ALDRIN	GLOSSY	ALBUMS	BLOWIT	IMPEDE
CLANGS	ALLOYS	FLORIN	SLUSHY	CLOUDS	BLOWSY	EMBERG
CLANKS	BLOOMS	ALARMS	ELATED	CLOUTS	SLOWLY	AMIENS
CLINGS	ELBOWS	ALERTS	PLATED	FLOUTS	FLEXED	EMBEDS
CLINKS	FLOODS	BLARES	SLATED	FLAUNT	ALEXEI	EMBERS
CLONES	FLOORS	BLURBS	BLITHE	CLOUDY	FLAXEN	EMMETS
CLONKS	SLOOPS	BLURTS	BLYTHE	FLOURY	KLAXON	IMPELS
CLUNES	ALCOTT	CLERKS	CLOTHE	OLIVIA	ELIXIR	UMBELS
CLUNKS	ALLOUT	ELBRUS	BLOTCH	OLDVIC	FLEXOR	EMMETT
ELANDS	ALMOST	FLARES	CLUTCH	SLAVED	ALEXIS	AMYFOX
FLANKS	FLYOUT	FLIRTS	FLETCH	SLOVAK	FLEXES	EMIGRE
FLINGS	BLOODY	FLORES	FLITCH	ALEVEL	CLOYED	IMOGEN
FLINTS	GLOOMY	GLARES	GLITCH	OLEVEL	FLAYED	AMIGOS
FLUNKS	GLOOPY	SLURPS	BLYTON	CLOVEN	PLAYED	IMAGES
GLANDS	ELOPED	CLARET	GLUTEN	ELEVEN	PLAYUP	SMUGLY
GLENYS	SLOPED	FLORET	PLATEN	CLEVER	PLAYER	EMPIRE
GLINTS	ELAPSE	BLURRY	BLOTTO	CLOVER	SLAYER	IMBIBE
GLYNIS	CLIPON	CLERGY	FLYTIP	GLOVER	LLOYDS	UMPIRE
PLANES	SLIPON	FLIRTY	PLATER	OLIVER	BLAZED	IMPISH
PLANKS	ALEPPO	FLURRY	SLATER	PLOVER	GLAZED	SMOKED
PLANTS	SLAPUP	SLURRY	ULSTER	SLAVER	BLAZER	SMOKER
SLANTS	SLIPUP	ALASKA	CLOTHS	SLIVER	BLAZES	SMOKES
SLINGS	ELOPER	ALESIA	ELATES	CLEVES	IMPALA	SMOKEY

AMELIA	SMARMY	INMATE	KNOCKS	SNEERS	ENVIED	ENVIES
EMILIA	AMUSED	INNATE	SNACKS	UNLESS	INKIND	INDIES
IMELDA	AMUSES	INSANE	SNICKS	ANSETT	UNBIND	SNAILS
AMBLED	EMETIC	INTAKE	ONEDGE	INDEBT	UNKIND	UNDIES
SMILED	EMOTED	INVADE	SNUDGE	INDENT	UNTIED	UNPINS
AMELIE	AMATOL	ONSALE	ONEDIN	INFECT	UNWIND	UNTIES
EMBLEM	AMSTEL	UNEASE	ANODES	INFEST	ENDIVE	UNZIPS
AMBLIN	EMOTES	UNLACE	ONEDAY	INGEST	ENGINE	ANOINT
EMILIO	SMITES	UNLADE	ANGELA	INJECT	ENTICE	ENLIST
AMBLER	SMITHS	UNMADE	ANNEKA	INSECT	ENTIRE	INDICT
AMPLER	SMITHY	UNSAFE	INDEED	INSERT	INCISE	INSIST
SMILER	SMUTTY	INCALF	INNEED	INTENT	INCITE	INLIEU
AMBLES	IMBUED	ONOATH	INTEND	INVENT	INLINE	INSITU
SMALLS	IMMUNE	UNMASK	UNBEND	INVERT	INSIDE	INVIEW
SMELLS	IMPURE	UNPACK	UNDEAD	INVEST	INTIME	ONVIEW
SMELTS	IMPUTE	ENTAIL	UNREAD	UNBENT	INVITE	ENMITY
SMILES	AMBUSH	ONCALL	ANNEXE	UNFELT	ONFILE	ENTITY
UMBLES	IMPUGN	INVAIN	SNEEZE	UNREST	ONFIRE	UNTIDY
AMULET	AMOURS	ENCAMP	ENMESH	UNSEAT	ONLINE	SNAKED
EMPLOY	IMBUES	UNFAIR	ANGELI	SNEEZY	ONSIDE	ANAKIN
SMELLY	AMOUNT	ANNALS	ANNEAL	KNIFED	ONTIME	SNAKES
SMILEY	BMOVIE	INLAWS	UNREAL	KNIFES	UNLIKE	ANGLIA
AMANDA	AMAZED	INLAYS	UNREEL	SNIFFS	UNRIPE	ENBLOC
EMINEM	AMAZON	KNEADS	UNVEIL	SNUFFS	UNWISE	ANGLED
AMENDS	AMAZES	SNEAKS	UNWELL	SNIFFY	ENDING	UNCLAD
EMENDS	ANKARA	UNCAPS	ANSELM	ENIGMA	INKING	ANGLEE
IMPOSE	INDABA	ENRAPT	ANDEAN	SNAGGE	ENRICH	UNCLOG
SMOOCH	INHAND	INFACT	INTERN	ONEGIN	ONTICK	UNPLUG
SMOOTH	INLAID	INFANT	UNSEEN	ONAGER	UNPICK	ANGLER
EMBOSS	INLAND	INPART	ANGELO	KNIGHT	INFILL	ANTLER
IMPORT	INWARD	INTACT	INDEEP	SNUGLY	ONEILL	ANGLES
EMBODY	ONWARD	INFAMY	ENDEAR	ANTHEA	UNCIAL	ANKLES
UMBRIA	UNPAID	SNEAKY	ANGELS	INCHED	INDIUM	INGLES
AMERIE	UNSAID	UNEASY	ANGERS	ANTHEM	INFIRM	KNOLLS
EMERGE	ENCASE	UNWARY	ENGELS	ANCHOR	ONFILM	UNCLES
IMBRUE	ENGAGE	ENABLE	ENTERS	ANTHER	ENSIGN	ANKLET
SMIRCH	ENLACE	UNABLE	INFERS	INCHES	INDIAN	INFLOW
AMORAL	ENRAGE	ANUBIS	INLETS	ANDHOW	ENRICO	ONSLOW
EMBRYO	INCARE	UNICEF	INSETS	ANYHOW	INDIGO	INFLUX
SMARTS	INCASE	INKCAP	INTERS	ANGINA	ANTICS	GNOMIC
SMIRKS	INHALE	ENACTS	KNEELS	INDIRA	ANVILS	ANIMAL

ENAMEL	INFORM	ENTREE	ENOUGH	DOSAGE	LOGANS	HOBBLE
GNOMON	ONFORM	UNTRUE	INRUSH	DOTAGE	MOLARS	HOMBRE
INGMAR	ENJOIN	ANORAK	ONRUSH	FORAGE	MORALS	NOBBLE
ANIMUS	INBORN	ANTRIM	ANNUAL	HOMAGE	MORASS	ROBBIE
GNOMES	ONLOAN	INTRIM	UNCURL	HORACE	NOLANS	ROUBLE
ANONYM	UNBORN	ENTRAP	UNFURL	LOCALE	NOMADS	SOMBRE
UNKNOT	INTOTO	UNWRAP	ANNULS	LOCATE	ROMANS	SORBIE
ANCONA	INDOOR	SNORER	ENSUES	LOVAGE	ROYALS	WOBBLE
ANGOLA	ANNOYS	GNARLS	INCURS	MOJAVE	TOTALS	WOMBLE
ANGORA	ENDOWS	INGRES	SNOUTS	MORALE	VOCALS	ZOMBIE
ENDORA	ENJOYS	SNARES	INDUCT	NONAGE	BOGART	POOBAH
ENTOMB	ENROLS	SNARLS	INSULT	NOTATE	COBALT	LOMBOK
ENFOLD	ENVOYS	SNORES	UNHURT	POMADE	GOKART	CORBEL
INROAD	INGOTS	SNORTS	UNJUST	POTAGE	HOBART	BOBBIN
ONHOLD	ONIONS	INARUT	INJURY	ROTATE	MOZART	BONBON
UNFOLD	SNOODS	ANDREW	ONDUTY	ROYALE	POPART	DOBBIN
UNLOAD	SNOOPS	ENERGY	UNDULY	SOLACE	BOTANY	BOOBOO
UNSOLD	UNDOES	INTRAY	UNRULY	TODATE	BOVARY	BOMBER
UNTOLD	UNIONS	UNUSED	SNIVEL	VOYAGE	KODALY	COBBER
ANYONE	ONFOOT	UNISON	UNEVEN	GOBANG	NOTARY	GODBER
ENCODE	UNBOLT	UNISEX	KNAVES	POTASH	ROMANY	JOBBER
ENCORE	ANTONY	UNITED	KNIVES	ROMAJI	ROSARY	ROBBER
ENROBE	SNOOPY	SNATCH	GNAWED	SOMALI	ROTARY	ROOBAR
INCOME	SNOOTY	SNITCH	SNOWED	GOBACK	VOTARY	TOWBAR
INJOKE	UNHOLY	INSTIL	ANSWER	MOHAWK	BOBBED	DOUBTS
INSOLE	ONSPEC	ONETWO	ANYWAY	WOMACK	BOMBED	FORBES
INTONE	UNIPOD	INSTEP	ONEWAY	NOBALL	COMBED	HOBBES
INVOKE	INKPEN	UNITES	ENZYME	COBAIN	FOBBED	COMBAT
SNOOZE	SNAPUP	KNOTTY	SNAZZY	DOMAIN	FORBID	GOBBET
UNDONE	ONAPAR	SNOTTY	ROMANA	JOHANN	HOTBED	HOBBIT
ONEOFF	SNIPER	ENSUED	SONATA	MONACO	LOBBED	SORBET
ONSONG	SNIPES	ENDURE	MOSAIC	POTATO	MOBBED	WOMBAT
INDOCK	INKPOT	ENSURE	COWARD	ROMANO	MORBID	YOUBET
INHOCK	SNAPPY	INDUCE	DONALD	TOBAGO	ROBBED	BOBBLY
UNCORK	UNIQUE	INFUSE	DOTARD	TOMATO	SOBBED	BOMBAY
UNHOOK	ANDREA	INJURE	HOWARD	CONAIR	BOBBIE	COWBOY
UNLOCK	INBRED	INSURE	POLAND	HOTAIR	BOBBLE	DOMBEY
INFOAL	INGRID	INTUNE	ROLAND	MOHAIR	COBBLE	DOUBLY
UNCOIL	INURED	UNSURE	RONALD	FORAYS	DOUBLE	TOMBOY
UNCOOL	SNARED	ENGULF	BORAGE	KOVACS	FOIBLE	TORBAY
UNROLL	SNORED	UNSUNG	DONATE	LOCALS	GOBBLE	TOYBOY

WOBBLY	DOODLE	HOLDER	COMEIN	DOZENS	COVERT	GOLFER
GOTCHA	FONDLE	LOADER	COMEON	FOYERS	FOMENT	HOOFER
FORCED	FONDUE	LOUDER	DONEIN	GONERS	FOREST	LOAFER
VOICED	FOODIE	POLDER	GOVERN	HOTELS	HONEST	ROOFER
BOUCLE	GOLDIE	PONDER	KOREAN	HOVELS	LOWEST	WOOFER
BOYCIE	HODDLE	POWDER	LOVEIN	HOVERS	MODEST	COMFIT
DOUCHE	HOODIE	SOLDER	MODERN	JOKERS	MOLEST	CONFIT
LOUCHE	NODDLE	WONDER	MOVEIN	LONERS	MOMENT	SOFFIT
ROACHE	NOODLE	YONDER	POTEEN	LOSERS	POTENT	BORGIA
ROSCOE	POODLE	HORDES	ROPEIN	LOVERS	ROBERT	LOGGIA
TOUCHE	ROADIE	RONDOS	SOLEMN	LOWERS	RODENT	BODGED
DOTCOM	TOADIE	BOLDLY	VOTEIN	MODELS	SOLENT	DODGED
TOUCAN	TODDLE	COLDLY	BOLERO	MODEMS	MOREAU	DOGGED
HONCHO	HOTDOG	FONDLY	COMETO	MOSEYS	ROSEAU	FOGGED
PONCHO	TOPDOG	GOODLY	FOREGO	MOTELS	COMEDY	FORGED
MOBCAP	HOWDAH	LORDLY	POMELO	MOTETS	COMELY	GORGED
TOECAP	RONDEL	LOUDLY	ROMERO	MOVERS	HOMELY	GOUGED
BOXCAR	CONDON	MONDAY	SOWETO	MOWERS	LONELY	HOGGED
CONCUR	CORDEN	BODEGA	TOLEDO	NONETS	LOVELY	JOGGED
SOCCER	CORDON	MODENA	TORERO	NOVELS	POPERY	LODGED
FORCES	GOLDEN	NOVENA	BOPEEP	POSERS	ROSERY	LOGGED
VOICES	GORDON	ROWENA	DONEUP	POWERS	SOLELY	LONGED
YOICKS	HOLDEN	TOPEKA	HOLEUP	RODEOS	SORELY	TOGGED
BOBCAT	HOLDON	DOGEND	WOKEUP	ROGERS	DOLENZ	BOGGLE
TOMCAT	HOYDEN	HOWERD	DOMECQ	ROMEOS	CONFAB	BOOGIE
TOPCAT	JORDAN	TOPEND	DOGEAR	ROVERS	DOFFED	GOGGLE
MOSCOW	LONDON	COHERE	NOFEAR	ROWELS	GOOFED	GOOGIE
COCCYX	NORDEN	EOCENE	POSEUR	ROWERS	HOOFED	GOOGLE
TOUCHY	SODDEN	JOLENE	VOYEUR	SOBERS	WOOFED	JOGGLE
NOIDEA	WOODEN	POPEYE	BORERS	SOMERS	COFFEE	MOGGIE
NORDIC	HOODOO	JOSEPH	BOWERS	SOWERS	POUFFE	MORGUE
BONDED	VOODOO	COWELL	BOXERS	TOKENS	TOFFEE	TOGGLE
FOLDED	HOLDUP	DOWELL	COLEUS	TOPERS	LOOFAH	TONGUE
GOADED	BOLDER	HOVELL	COMETS	TOTEMS	BOXFUL	WOGGLE
HOODED	BORDER	HOWELL	COPERS	TOWELS	JOYFUL	MOWGLI
LOADED	COLDER	JOWELL	COVENS	TOWERS	WOEFUL	DOUGAL
NODDED	CONDOR	LOREAL	COVERS	VOTERS	BOFFIN	MONGOL
SORDID	DODDER	POWELL	COVETS	VOWELS	COFFIN	DODGEM
WOODED	FODDER	BONEYM	COWERS	YODELS	COFFER	COOGAN
CODDLE	FOLDER	BOLEYN	DOWELS	YOKELS	CONFER	GORGON
DODDLE	FONDER	COLEEN	DOYENS	COGENT	FORFAR	MORGAN

NOGGIN	DOUGHY	NODICE	POKING	TORINO	COCKED	LOCKER
POPGUN	GOOGLY	NOTICE	PORING	BONIER	COOKED	PORKER
TOPGUN	JOSHUA	NOVICE	POSING	COPIER	CORKED	ROCKER
BODGER	SOPHIA	POLICE	ROBING	COSIER	DOCKED	WORKER
BOLGER	GOTHIC	POLITE	ROPING	DOPIER	FORKED	YORKER
CODGER	COSHED	VOTIVE	ROVING	FOLIAR	HOCKED	NOAKES
CONGER	SOPHIE	BODING	ROWING	HOLIER	HOOKED	DOCKET
COUGAR	BONHAM	BOEING	SOWING	HOSIER	LOCKED	LOCKET
DODGER	BOTHAM	BOOING	TOEING	NOSIER	LOOKED	LOOKAT
DOGGER	RODHAM	BORING	TONING	ROSIER	MOCKED	POCKET
FORGER	ROTHKO	BOWING	TOPING	BODIES	ROCKED	ROCKET
HOGGER	NOSHUP	BOXING	TOTING	COMICS	ROOKED	SOCKET
JOGGER	BOTHER	CODING	TOWING	COPIES	SOAKED	DONKEY
LODGER	GOPHER	COMING	TOYING	FOLIOS	SOCKED	FOLKSY
LOGGER	KOSHER	COOING	VOTING	MONIES	TONKED	HOCKEY
LONGER	MOTHER	COPING	VOWING	MOTIFS	WORKED	HOOKEY
BODGES	POSHER	COVING	WOKING	MOVIES	ZONKED	HOTKEY
BORGES	TOPHER	COWING	WOOING	PONIES	BOOKIE	JOCKEY
BOUGHS	COSHES	COXING	YOKING	POSIES	COCKLE	LOWKEY
CORGIS	TOPHAT	DOPING	ZONING	POSITS	COOKIE	MONKEY
COUGHS	NOSHOW	DOSING	BOYISH	ROBINS	ROOKIE	GOOLWA
DODGES	AOUITA	DOTING	DOVISH	SOLIDS	YORKIE	BOILED
FORGES	GODIVA	DOZING	JOSIAH	SONICS	HOOKAH	BOWLED
GORGES	LOLITA	FOXING	MODISH	TOBIAS	BODKIN	COILED
GOUGES	LOUISA	GORING	POLISH	TONICS	BOOKIN	COOLED
HODGES	MOLINA	HOEING	POPISH	TOPICS	HOPKIN	FOILED
LODGES	MONICA	HOMING	YORICK	TORIES	LOCKIN	FOOLED
LOUGHS	ZODIAC	HONING	JOVIAL	TOXINS	LOOKIN	FOULED
ROUGHS	COPIED	HOPING	SOCIAL	FORINT	BOOKUP	HOWLED
TOUGHS	DOBIRD	JOKING	PODIUM	SOVIET	COCKUP	LOLLED
VOSGES	BODICE	LOPING	SODIUM	BODILY	HOOKUP	POLLED
BOUGHT	BOVINE	LOSING	DORIAN	CODIFY	LOCKUP	POOLED
FORGET	COMICE	LOVING	IONIAN	COSILY	LOOKUP	ROLLED
FORGOT	COSINE	LOWING	LOTION	HOMILY	MOCKUP	SOILED
FOUGHT	DOCILE	MOOING	MOTION	JOKILY	BOOKER	TOILED
GORGET	DOTIME	MOPING	NOTION	MODIFY	COCKER	TOLLED
NOUGAT	GOLIVE	MOVING	POTION	NOSILY	CONKER	TOOLED
NOUGHT	IODINE	MOWING	ROMIJN	NOTIFY	COOKER	COLLIE
ROTGUT	LOUISE	NOSING	BONITO	POLICY	CORKER	COOLIE
SOUGHT	MOBILE	NOTING	DOMINO	LOGJAM	DOCKER	GOALIE
VOIGHT	MOTIVE	OOZING	DOSIDO	BOOKED	HOOKER	MOLLIE

DOGLEG	WORLDS	DOLMAN	JOANNE	COBNUT	MOTOWN	TOUPEE
MOOLAH	COLLET	DOLMEN	KONNIE	COINIT	KOSOVO	OOMPAH
MOWLAM	COOLIT	FORMAN	LONNIE	CORNET	ROCOCO	COMPEL
GOBLIN	GOBLET	MORMON	LOUNGE	HORNET	COLOUR	GOSPEL
JOPLIN	JOBLOT	NORMAN	MOONIE	SONNET	DOLOUR	POMPOM
MOULIN	TOILET	POTMAN	POUNCE	BOUNCY	HONOUR	COUPON
POLLEN	FOLLOW	RODMAN	RONNIE	BOUNTY	COLONS	VOXPOP
POPLIN	GOSLOW	TOAMAN	SONNIE	COUNTY	DONORS	BOPPER
ROLLON	HOLLOW	BOOMER	TOWNIE	DOWNEY	HOBOES	COOPER
ROSLIN	MOBLAW	DORMER	JOININ	HORNBY	JOYOUS	COPPER
TOMLIN	BOSLEY	FORMER	POZNAN	JOHNNY	MOTORS	HOOPER
TOULON	CONLEY	ROAMER	BORNEO	LOONEY	POROUS	HOPPER
DOLLOP	COOLLY	SOMMER	COINOP	MORNAY	ROBOTS	POPPER
FOULUP	COWLEY	COMMAS	JOINUP	POINTY	ROTORS	ROMPER
LOLLOP	HOBLEY	COSMOS	BOGNOR	RODNEY	BOWOUT	TOPPER
ROLLUP	MOLLOY	HOLMES	CONNER	ROMNEY	COHORT	TORPOR
BOILER	MORLEY	SOAMES	CONNOR	ROONEY	COPOUT	CORPUS
BOWLER	MOSLEY	BONMOT	CORNER	BOGOTA	NOTOUT	COYPUS
COLLAR	MOTLEY	COMMIT	DOWNER	CORONA	TOBOOT	COWPAT
COOLER	MOULDY	FORMAT	HORNER	DODOMA	COLONY	HOTPOT
DOLLAR	VOLLEY	TOMMIX	JOINER	JOJOBA	NOBODY	MOPPET
FOWLER	WOOLLY	FORMBY	MOANER	LOYOLA	OOLOGY	POPPET
HOLLER	VOULEZ	BOSNIA	SOONER	ROMOLA	POLONY	BOXPEW
HOWLER	COSMIC	CORNEA	BOUNDS	TOYOTA	HOOPLA	COWPOX
NOBLER	BOOMED	GOANNA	COUNTS	YOYOMA	BOPPED	COMPLY
POPLAR	DOOMED	JOANNA	FOUNDS	LOMOND	COOPED	POMPEY
ROLLER	FOAMED	HOBNOB	FOUNTS	LOWOOD	COPPED	MOSQUE
TOILER	FORMED	COGNAC	HOUNDS	NOGOOD	HOOPED	TORQUE
BOULES	LOOMED	COINED	JOINTS	COYOTE	HOPPED	CONRAD
BOWLES	ROAMED	CONNED	MOUNDS	JOCOSE	LOOPED	HORRID
COULIS	ZOOMED	DONNED	MOUNTS	MOROSE	LOPPED	HOTROD
FOWLDS	COMMIE	DOWNED	POINTS	NODOSE	MOPPED	LOURED
FOWLES	FORMAL	GOUNOD	POUNDS	NOJOKE	POPPED	MOORED
FOYLES	NORMAL	HORNED	ROUNDS	NOMORE	ROMPED	POURED
KOALAS	POMMEL	JOINED	SOMNUS	FOBOFF	TOPPED	ROARED
MOULDS	ROMMEL	LOANED	SOUNDS	NODOFF	TORPID	SOARED
MOULTS	BODMIN	MOANED	TONNES	POPOFF	YOMPED	SOURED
MOYLES	BOWMAN	BONNIE	TOTNES	SOLONG	CORPSE	TORRID
NOBLES	BOWMEN	BOUNCE	WOUNDS	MOLOCH	COUPLE	TOURED
OODLES	COMMON	CONNIE	ZOUNDS	MORONI	HOOPOE	BOURNE
POULTS	CONMAN	DONNIE	BONNET	COCOON	TOPPLE	BOURSE

COARSE	HOUSED	HORSES	JOLTED	TOMTOM	YOUTHS	WOLVES
COERCE	POISED	HOUSES	JOTTED	BOLTON	POSTIT	CONVEX
COURSE	ROUSED	JOISTS	LOOTED	BOSTON	TOMTIT	CONVEY
COWRIE	SOUSED	JOUSTS	MOOTED	COTTON	KOWTOW	CONVOY
HOARSE	TOSSED	LOSSES	POSTED	MOLTEN	CORTEX	COBWEB
MONROE	MOUSSE	LOUSES	POTTED	MOUTON	VORTEX	GODWIT
ROURKE	POTSIE	MOSSES	POUTED	NORTON	COSTLY	BOWWOW
SOIREE	TOUSLE	NOISES	ROOTED	ROTTEN	HOLTBY	POWWOW
SOURCE	BONSAI	NOOSES	ROTTED	SOFTEN	MOSTLY	CONWAY
FOURTH	CONSUL	POISES	ROUTED	WONTON	MOUTHY	GOAWAY
BOVRIL	DORSAL	ROASTS	SORTED	TOOTOO	POETRY	NORWAY
CORRAL	FOSSIL	ROOSTS	TOOTED	HOTTAP	PORTLY	COAXED
SORREL	MORSEL	ROUSES	TOTTED	POPTOP	SOFTLY	HOAXED
POGROM	TONSIL	ROUSTS	TOUTED	POSTOP	TOOTHY	HOAXER
CONRAN	POSSUM	SOUSES	BOOTEE	BOATER	WORTHY	COAXES
HORROR	COUSIN	TOASTS	BOOTLE	COSTAR	YORUBA	HOAXES
POORER	DOBSON	TORSOS	BOTTLE	COTTER	JOCUND	JOLYON
SOURER	GODSON	TOSSES	BOWTIE	DOCTOR	ROTUND	BOWYER
TOURER	HOISIN	CORSET	FOOTLE	FOOTER	MODULE	POLYPS
BOARDS	JOLSON	COSSET	GOATEE	FOSTER	NODULE	BOOZED
COBRAS	JONSON	DORSET	GOETHE	HOOTER	SOLUTE	NOZZLE
COURTS	LOOSEN	POSSET	GOITRE	HOTTER	VOLUME	BORZOI
GOURDS	MOTSON	HONSHU	JOSTLE	JOTTER	COBURN	WORZEL
HOARDS	POISON	BOWSAW	LOATHE	LOITER	COLUMN	BONZER
HOURIS	ROBSON	HORSEY	MOSTUE	LOOTER	BOSUNS	BOOZER
MORRIS	TOCSIN	ROMSEY	MOTTLE	MORTAR	MOGULS	ROZZER
MOURNS	WORSEN	CONTRA	POOTLE	POOTER	POGUES	BOOZES
NORRIS	GOSSIP	PORTIA	POSTIE	PORTER	ROGUES	HOWZAT
DORRIT	TOSSUP	ROSTRA	SOFTIE	POSTER	TOQUES	UPLAND
POIROT	DOWSER	YOOTHA	SOOTHE	POTTER	VOGUES	UPWARD
BORROW	LOOSER	HOTTUB	SORTIE	ROSTER	LOCUST	LPLATE
MORROW	MOUSER	COPTIC	TOOTLE	ROTTER	ROBUST	OPIATE
SORROW	WOWSER	POETIC	DOGTAG	ROUTER	YOGURT	UPDATE
HOORAY	BOASTS	TOLTEC	CONTEH	SOFTER	SOLVED	UPRATE
HOURLY	BOOSTS	BOLTED	VOSTOK	SORTER	LOUVRE	UPTAKE
POORLY	BOSSES	BOOTED	HOSTEL	TOTTER	BOVVER	SPRANG
ROBROY	COASTS	COATED	MORTAL	BOOTHS	HOOVER	SPLASH
SOURLY	DOSSES	COSTED	MOSTEL	CORTES	SOLVER	SPRAWL
DOSSED	DOUSES	DOTTED	PORTAL	MONTHS	HOOVES	SPRAIN
DOUSED	DOWSES	HOOTED	POSTAL	MOUTHS	LOAVES	APPALS
DOWSED	HOISTS	HOSTED	BOTTOM	ROUTES	SOLVES	SPEAKS

SPEARS	SPRITE	OPENER	SPURNS	EQUITY	TREADS	TRICIA
SPLAYS	UPDIKE	OPINES	SPURTS	ARCANA	TREATS	BRACED
SPRATS	UPSIDE	SPANKS	SPIRIT	ARMADA	TRIADS	PRICED
SPRAYS	EPPING	SPENDS	APERCU	ERRATA	TRIALS	TRACED
APIARY	OPTING	SPINES	SPORTY	ORIANA	WREAKS	CRECHE
SPACED	SPRING	UPENDS	SPASMS	BRIAND	ARRANT	GRACIE
SPICED	SPYING	SPINET	SPITED	ERRAND	BREAST	ORACLE
APACHE	UPPING	CPSNOW	SPOTON	ARCADE	BRYANT	PROCOL
SPECIE	UPPISH	OPENLY	SPATES	ARCANE	DREAMT	URECAL
SPACEK	UPHILL	SPONGY	SPITES	ARIANE	ERRANT	DRACHM
SPACER	OPTION	SPUNKY	APATHY	CREASE	TRUANT	BRECON
EPOCHS	APHIDS	APLOMB	SPOTTY	CREATE	ARCADY	BRACCO
SPACES	OPTICS	UPHOLD	SPOUSE	GREASE	CREAKY	BRACER
SPECKS	SPLITS	UPLOAD	SPRUCE	ORNATE	CREAMY	GROCER
SPICES	SPOILS	APPOSE	SPRUNG	TRIAGE	CROAKY	TRACER
SPACEY	SPRIGS	OPPOSE	OPPUGN	URBANE	DREAMY	BRACES
SPIDER	SPLINT	UPTOWN	UPTURN	ARMAGH	DREARY	BRICKS
SPADES	SPOILT	UPROAR	SPOUTS	BREACH	FREAKY	CRACKS
APPEND	SPRINT	APRONS	SPEWED	BREATH	FRIARY	CRICKS
SPREAD	UPLIFT	SPOOKS	SPAWNS	BROACH	GREASY	CROCKS
UPHELD	SPHINX	SPOOLS	APEXES	PREACH	TREATY	CROCUS
APIECE	UPPITY	SPOONS	SPRYLY	WREATH	ERSATZ	ERECTS
SPHERE	SPIKED	SPOORS	EQUATE	ARMANI	ARABIA	FRACAS
SPEECH	SPOKEN	OPTOUT	SQUARE	ARRACK	ARABIC	FROCKS
APPEAL	SPIKES	SPROUT	SQUASH	ORDAIN	BRIBED	GRACES
SPLEEN	SPOKES	UPROOT	SQUAWK	ARRAYS	PROBED	PRECIS
SPEEDO	APULIA	SPOOKY	SQUALL	BREAKS	ARABLE	PRICES
UPKEEP	APOLLO	OPAQUE	EQUALS	BRIARS	CRABBE	PRICKS
APPEAR	APPLES	SPARTA	SQUABS	BROADS	GRABLE	TRACES
SPEEDS	SPELLS	SPARED	SQUADS	CREAKS	TREBLE	TRACKS
SPREES	SPILLS	SPARGE	SQUATS	CREAMS	TRIBAL	TRACTS
UPPERS	APPLET	SPARSE	SQUEAK	CROAKS	BRIBER	TRICKS
UPSETS	APEMAN	SPURGE	SQUEAL	DREADS	ARABIS	TRUCES
UPBEAT	APEMEN	SPIRAL	EQUINE	DREAMS	BRIBES	TRUCKS
SPEEDY	OPENED	OPORTO	SQUIRE	DRYADS	EREBUS	WRECKS
APOGEE	OPINED	OPERAS	SQUIRM	FREAKS	GREBES	BRECHT
SPIGOT	SPENCE	SPARES	AQUINO	FRIARS	PROBES	TRICOT
OPSHOP	SPONGE	SPARKS	EQUIPS	GREATS	TRIBES	PRICEY
UPSHOT	SPINAL	SPIRES	SQUIBS	GROANS	IROBOT	TRACEY
SPLICE	EPONYM	SPORES	SQUINT	GROATS	CRABBY	TRICKY
SPLINE	OPENUP	SPORTS	SQUIRT	ORGANS	GRUBBY	ERODED

GRADED	BREECH	TRIFLE	MRCHAD	BRAINS	TROLLS	GRANTA
TRADED	IRWELL	ARMFUL	ORCHID	BROILS	ARMLET	IRONIC
BRIDGE	ORDEAL	ARTFUL	ARCHIE	DRAINS	BROLLY	DRONED
BRIDLE	ORWELL	IREFUL	ARNHEM	DRUIDS	DROLLY	IRONED
BRODIE	MRBEAN	PREFER	GRAHAM	FRUITS	FRILLY	PRUNED
CRADLE	ARNESS	CRAFTS	ORPHAN	GRAINS	ORALLY	BRONTE
DREDGE	BREEDS	CROFTS	URCHIN	ORBITS	TRILBY	BRONZE
DRUDGE	BREEKS	CRUFTS	ARCHER	ORGIES	CRIMEA	CRINGE
FRIDGE	BRIEFS	DRAFTS	ARTHUR	TRAILS	FRAMED	FRANCE
GRUDGE	BRIERS	DRIFTS	ARCHES	TRAINS	PREMED	FRINGE
TRUDGE	CREEDS	GRAFTS	BRAHMS	TRAITS	PRIMED	GRANDE
TRUDIE	CREEKS	ARAFAT	ARCHLY	ARTIST	BRAMAH	GRANGE
BRIDAL	CREELS	PROFIT	ARNICA	BRAINY	PRIMAL	GRUNGE
BRADEN	CREEPS	PREFIX	EROICA	FRUITY	BREMEN	ORANGE
BRYDON	CRIERS	CRAFTY	TROIKA	GRAINY	TRUMAN	PRANCE
DRYDEN	CRUETS	DRYFLY	ARRIVE	TRAJAN	CROMER	PRINCE
CRUDER	FRIELS	DRYFRY	BRAINE	TROJAN	KRAMER	PRINZE
GRADER	GREEKS	TRAGIC	BRAISE	BRAKED	PRIMER	TRANCE
TRADER	GREENS	FRIGID	BRUISE	BROKEN	TREMOR	BRANCH
BRIDES	GREETS	BROGUE	CRUISE	KRAKEN	ARAMIS	BRUNCH
ERODES	ORDERS	DRAGEE	DRYICE	WREKIN	AROMAS	CRUNCH
GRADES	PREENS	DROGUE	ERMINE	BROKER	CRAMPS	DRENCH
PRIDES	TRIERS	PRAGUE	IRVINE	BRAKES	CRIMES	FRENCH
PRUDES	ARDENT	FRUGAL	PRAISE	TRIKES	CRIMPS	TRENCH
TRADES	ARGENT	ARAGON	URSINE	CRIKEY	CRUMBS	WRENCH
CREDIT	ARREST	DRAGON	ARMING	ARALIA	FRAMES	BRUNEI
ARIDLY	DRIEST	GREGAN	CRYING	BROLGA	FRUMPS	ARENAL
CRUDDY	ERNEST	OREGON	DRYING	FROLIC	PRIMES	BRUNEL
FREDDY	ORGEAT	ORIGIN	ERRING	GRILLE	PRIMUS	CRONIN
FRIDAY	ORIENT	GREGOR	FRYING	GRILSE	TRAMPS	BRANDO
FRIEDA	PRIEST	KRUGER	IRKING	ORELSE	TRUMPS	BRONCO
ORTEGA	TRUEST	BRIGGS	IRVING	TRALEE	GROMIT	DRONGO
FRIEND	URGENT	BRUGES	PRYING	PRELIM	PROMPT	FRANCO
ARLENE	WRYEST	TROGGS	TRYING	BROLIN	BRUMBY	GRINGO
BREEZE	ARTERY	BRIGHT	URGING	DRALON	CRUMMY	PRONTO
FREEZE	BREEZY	FRIGHT	WRAITH	BRILLO	FRUMPY	ARENAS
FRIEZE	CREEPY	WRIGHT	ORSINI	DRILLS	GRAMMY	BRANDS
GRAEME	FREELY	CRAGGY	TRUISM	FRILLS	GRIMLY	BRINGS
GREECE	GREEDY	GROGGY	ORSINO	GRILLS	GRUMPY	CRANES
GREENE	ORRERY	BRAHMA	ARMIES	PROLES	PRIMLY	CRANKS
GRIEVE	PREFAB	ARCHED	BRAIDS	TRILLS	BRENDA	CRONES

DRINKS	MRMOTO	TRIPUP	CRESTS	PRATIE	KRAUSE	TROVES
DRONES	ARBOUR	WRAPUP	CRISES	WRITHE	ORDURE	BREVET
DRUNKS	ARDOUR	DRAPER	CRISIS	CRUTCH	TROUPE	CRAVAT
FRANCS	ARMOUR	GRIPER	CRISPS	WRETCH	CROUCH	PRIVET
FRONDS	ARROWS	PROPER	CRUSTS	BRUTAL	GROUCH	TRIVET
FRONTS	ARTOIS	CRIPPS	ERASES	GRETEL	TROUGH	BREWED
GRANTS	BROODS	CRYPTS	FRISKS	PROTEM	MRBUMP	CREWED
GRINDS	BROOKS	DRAPES	GRASPS	BRETON	ARGUER	CROWED
GRUNTS	BROOMS	ERUPTS	IRISES	BRITON	ARGUES	BROWNE
PRANKS	CROOKS	GRAPES	PRISES	BRUTON	GROUPS	BROWSE
PRINTS	CROONS	GRAPHS	PRISMS	CRETAN	GROUTS	DROWSE
PRONGS	DROOLS	GRIPES	TRUSTS	GRATIN	ERFURT	PROWSE
PRUNES	DROOPS	GROPES	TRYSTS	KRYTEN	PROUST	GROWTH
PRUNUS	ERRORS	TRIPOS	WRESTS	PROTON	PRAVDA	CREWEL
TRENDS	GROOMS	ARMPIT	WRISTS	TRITON	TRIVIA	TROWEL
TRUNKS	PRIORS	DRIPPY	PRESET	GROTTO	BRAVED	BREWUP
URANUS	PROOFS	DROPBY	PROSIT	CRATER	CRAVED	DRAWUP
WRINGS	TROOPS	PREPAY	BRASSY	GRATER	PROVED	DREWUP
WRONGS	ARLOTT	TROPHY	CRISPY	ORATOR	DRIVEL	GROWUP
BRANDT	CRYOUT	BRAQUE	CROSBY	WRITER	GRAVEL	BREWER
BRANDY	TRYOUT	DRYRUN	CRUSTY	BRUTES	GROVEL	DRAWER
CRANKY	ORMOLU	ARARAT	DRESSY	BRUTUS	TRAVEL	GROWER
CRANNY	ARGOSY	DRYROT	FRISKY	CRATES	CRAVEN	PREWAR
FRENZY	BROODY	CRESTA	FROSTY	GRATES	DRIVEN	BRAWLS
GRANNY	BRYONY	ORISSA	GRASSY	GRATIS	GRAVEN	BROWNS
GRUNDY	DROOPY	PRISMA	GRISLY	ORATES	PREVIN	CRAWLS
GRUNGY	GROOVY	TRISHA	KRUSTY	PRATES	PROVEN	CROWDS
ORKNEY	PRIORY	ERASED	PRISSY	TRUTHS	BRAVER	CROWNS
TRENDY	GRAPPA	PRISED	TRASHY	WRITES	DRIVER	DRAWLS
TRINNY	TROPIC	CRUSOE	TRUSTY	PRETAX	DROVER	DROWNS
KRANTZ	DRAPED	FRISEE	ARETHA	FROTHY	GRAVER	FROWNS
AREOLA	GRIPED	WRASSE	GRETNA	GRITTY	TREVOR	GROWLS
ARNOLD	GROPED	ARISEN	PROTEA	GROTTY	BRAVES	PRAWNS
BROOKE	TRIPOD	ORISON	ARCTIC	PRETTY	BREVES	PROWLS
BROOME	FRAPPE	PRISON	CRITIC	TRAUMA	CRAVES	TRAWLS
CREOLE	TRIPLE	FRESCO	EROTIC	URSULA	DRIVES	BRAWNY
GROOVE	PROPEL	PRESTO	CRATED	ARGUED	DROVES	DROWSY
ORIOLE	DROPIN	TRESCO	GRATED	AROUND	GRAVES	FROWZY
CRYOFF	TREPAN	ERASER	ORATED	GROUND	GROVES	PRAXIS
BROOCH	CROPUP	FRASER	PRATED	AROUSE	PROVES	BRAYED
DRHOOK	PROPUP	ARISES	XRATED	GROUSE	TRAVIS	FRAYED

PRAYED	ASLANT	ASSIGN	ISSUER	STODGE	ETCHER	STALER
PREYED	USHANT	OSSIAN	ISSUES	STUDIO	ETCHES	STYLER
XRAYED	USABLE	ESKIMO	ZSAZSA	ATODDS	ITCHES	ATOLLS
ARGYLE	ISABEL	ESPIES	ITHACA	ETUDES	ATHINA	STALKS
GROYNE	ISOBEL	ASSIST	OTTAWA	STODGY	ATTICA	STALLS
MRHYDE	ISOBAR	TSHIRT	STRATA	ATHENA	ATTILA	STILES
CRUYFF	PSYCHE	OSSIFY	ATHAND	ATTEND	ATTIRE	STILLS
CRAYON	ASHCAN	ASHLEE	STRAND	STEELE	STRIDE	STILTS
PRAYER	PSYCHO	ISOLDE	ATEASE	ITSELF	STRIFE	STOLES
TROYES	USEDUP	ASYLUM	ETHANE	STREAK	STRIKE	STYLES
PROZAC	ASIDES	ASHLAR	STRAFE	ATWELL	STRINE	STYLUS
BRAZED	ASCEND	OSTLER	ATTACH	STREAM	STRIPE	UTTLEY
CRAZED	OSTEND	PSALMS	STRATH	STREWN	STRIVE	ATOMIC
GRAZED	ASWELL	ASHLEY	ATTACK	STREEP	STRING	STYMIE
PRIZED	ESTEEM	ASTLEY	STPAUL	ATHENS	ATRISK	STAMEN
BRAZZI	ASPERN	ASIMOV	ATTAIN	OTHERS	ATWILL	ATEMPO
BRAZIL	ASTERN	ESMOND	STRAIN	OTTERS	ITGIRL	STUMER
BRAZEN	ASLEEP	OSMOND	STMALO	STEEDS	ATRIUM	STAMPS
FROZEN	ASSESS	ASHORE	ATTARS	STEELS	ATKINS	STOMPS
FRAZER	ASSETS	ASSORT	STEAKS	STEEPS	ATTICS	STUMPS
BRAZES	ASTERS	ESCORT	STEALS	STEERS	ETHICS	STUMPY
CRAZES	ISLETS	ISOPOD	STEAMS	STRESS	STAINS	STANZA
GRAZES	OSIERS	ISTRIA	STOATS	STREWS	STAIRS	ETHNIC
PRIZES	USHERS	ASTRID	STRAPS	UTTERS	STEINS	ATONED
FRIZZY	ASCENT	ASTRAL	STRAWS	ATBEST	STOICS	STONED
ASMARA	ASPECT	ASHRAM	STRAYS	ATTEST	STRIPS	ATONCE
ASTANA	ASSENT	USURER	ATLAST	STREET	STRICT	STANCE
ESPANA	ASSERT	OSIRIS	STRAIT	STEELY	STOKED	STENCH
ASGARD	OSIERY	USURPS	STUART	STAFFA	STOKER	ATONAL
GSTAAD	USEFUL	ESPRIT	STEADY	STIFLE	STAKES	STINGO
ISLAND	ASTHMA	ASTRAY	STEAMY	STEFFI	STOKES	STINKO
OSWALD	ISCHIA	OSPREY	STABLE	STEFAN	STELLA	ATONES
ESCAPE	ESTHER	TSETSE	STUBBS	STAFFS	ITALIC	STANDS
ESPACE	ESCHEW	ASHTON	STUBBY	STUFFS	STOLID	STINGS
ESTATE	ESPIED	ISHTAR	STACIE	STUFFY	STYLED	STINKS
ASSAIL	ASPIRE	ISSUED	STUCCO	STIGMA	ATTLEE	STINTS
ISRAEL	ASKING	ASSUME	STACKS	STAGED	STOLLE	STONES
ASIANS	ISAIAH	ASSURE	STICKS	STAGDO	STALAG	STUNTS
ASSAYS	ASSISI	ASTUTE	STOCKS	STAGES	STALIN	STINGY
ESSAYS	ESPIAL	ESCUDO	STICKY	ETCHED	STOLEN	STROUD
OSCARS	OSMIUM	PSEUDO	STOCKY	ITCHED	OTELLO	ATHOME

OTIOSE	STURDY	GULATI	RUMBLE	QUACKS	CUDDLY	RUFFED
OTOOLE	STASIS	SUVARI	TUMBLE	YUCCAS	PURDEY	SURFED
STOOGE	STATIC	CUSACK	BUMBAG	DULCET	SUNDAY	MUFFLE
STROBE	STATED	EUBANK	HUMBUG	MUSCAT	SUNDRY	RUFFLE
STRODE	STATUE	DUVALL	MUMBAI	OUTCRY	EUREKA	CUPFUL
STROKE	STITCH	SUSANN	BULBUL	PUNCHY	SUPERB	DUFFEL
STROVE	STATEN	RUBATO	DUBBIN	BUDDHA	EUGENE	FULFIL
STRONG	STATOR	AUPAIR	DURBAN	TUNDRA	MUSEUM	JUGFUL
STROLL	OTITIS	DUCATS	DURBIN	FUNDED	TUNEIN	RUEFUL
STOOKS	STATES	HUMANS	TURBAN	GUIDED	TUREEN	MUFFIN
STOOLS	STATUS	MURALS	PUEBLO	OUTDID	TUXEDO	PUFFIN
STOOPS	ATTUNE	SUGARS	DURBAR	BUDDLE	AUTEUR	DUFFUP
STROPS	STRUNG	AUFAIT	HUMBER	BUNDLE	AUGERS	BUFFER
UTMOST	STRUCK	KUWAIT	LUBBER	CUDDLE	BUYERS	DUFFER
UTOPIA	STRUMS	MUTANT	LUMBAR	CURDLE	CURERS	FUNFUR
STUPID	STRUTS	NUTANT	LUMBER	DUNDEE	DUPERS	PUFFER
STAPLE	STEVIE	TUVALU	NUMBER	FUDDLE	DURESS	SUFFER
STEPPE	STEVEN	CURACY	RUBBER	HUDDLE	DUVETS	SURFER
STEPIN	STAVES	LUNACY	BURBOT	HURDLE	QUEENS	QUAFFS
STEPUP	STIVES	QUEASY	NUMBAT	MUDDLE	RUBENS	QUIFFS
STUPOR	STOVES	SUGARY	TURBIT	PUDDLE	RULERS	BUFFET
STAPES	STEWED	HUBBUB	TURBOT	SUBDUE	RUPEES	OUTFIT
STOPES	STOWED	QUEBEC	BUBBLY	SUNDAE	TUBERS	TUFFET
STOPIT	STAYED	CURBED	DUMBLY	GUNDOG	LUCENT	CURFEW
STARED	STAYIN	DUBBED	HUMBLY	PUGDOG	NUGENT	GUFFAW
STORED	STAYUP	NUMBED	KULCHA	PURDAH	PUREST	OUTFOX
STARVE	STAYER	OUTBID	DULCIE	DUMDUM	RUDEST	SUFFIX
STERNE	GUYANA	RUBBED	MUSCLE	PURDOM	RUPERT	JUDFRY
STARCH	KUMARA	SUBBED	QUICHE	BURDEN	SUREST	QUAGGA
STEROL	LUSAKA	SUNBED	RUNCIE	BURDON	BUREAU	BUDGED
STEREO	CUNARD	TURBID	DUNCAN	SUDDEN	JUNEAU	BUGGED
STIRUP	AUBADE	BUBBLE	TUSCAN	SUGDEN	HUGELY	BULGED
STARES	BUTANE	BUMBLE	VULCAN	GUIDER	PURELY	BUNGED
STARTS	CURARE	BURBLE	DUCCIO	JUDDER	RUDELY	FUDGED
STORES	CURATE	DUBBLE	NUNCIO	MULDER	SURELY	HUGGED
STORKS	HUMANE	FUMBLE	HUBCAP	MURDER	SURETY	JUDGED
STORMS	MUGABE	HUBBLE	JUICER	RUDDER	BUFFED	JUGGED
UTERUS	MUTATE	HUMBLE	CUSCUS	SUNDER	CUFFED	LUGGED
STARRY	NUTATE	JUMBLE	DUNCES	GUIDES	HUFFED	LUNGED
STOREY	OUTAGE	MUMBLE	JUICES	PUNDIT	LUFFED	MUGGED
STORMY	PUPATE	RUBBLE	OUNCES	SUNDEW	PUFFED	NUDGED

PURGED	BUSHED	LURING	QUAILS	BUSKER	DUNLOP	PURLEY
RUGGED	GUSHED	MUSING	QUOITS	DUIKER	FULLUP	GUMMED
SUNGOD	HUSHED	MUTING	RUBIES	HUNKER	PULLUP	HUMMED
SURGED	PUSHED	OUTING	TULIPS	JUNKER	BUGLER	NUTMEG
TUGGED	RUCHED	RUEING	TUNICS	MUCKER	BUTLER	KUMMEL
TURGID	RUSHED	RULING	CUBIST	PUCKER	CURLER	PUMMEL
BUDGIE	EUCHRE	TUBING	JULIET	QUAKER	CUTLER	BUSMAN
BUNGEE	HUGHIE	TUNING	NUDIST	SUCKER	DULLER	BUSMEN
BUNGLE	BUSHEL	TURING	PURIST	TUCKER	FULLER	GUNMAN
BURGLE	DURHAM	JUDITH	QUAINT	TUSKER	GUYLER	GUNMEN
GURGLE	FULHAM	MULISH	BUSILY	QUAKES	HURLER	SUMMON
JUGGLE	BUCHAN	MUNICH	MUTINY	RUCKUS	MULLER	SUZMAN
JUNGLE	HUSHUP	PUNISH	NUDITY	BUCKET	PURLER	FULMAR
MUGGLE	AUTHOR	RUPIAH	PUNILY	JUNKET	BUGLES	GUMMER
CUDGEL	GUSHER	ZURICH	PURIFY	MUSKET	BUILDS	MUMMER
FUNGAL	LUTHER	BURIAL	PURITY	MUSKOX	QUALMS	MURMUR
OUTGUN	LUTHOR	MURIEL	PUNJAB	TURKEY	QUELLS	SUMMER
GUNGHO	PUSHER	CUBISM	GURKHA	PUBLIC	QUILLS	HUMMUS
HUNGUP	BUSHES	NUDISM	QUOKKA	CULLED	QUILTS	SUBMIT
BULGAR	GUSHES	PURISM	BUCKED	CURLED	RUTLES	SUMMIT
BURGER	HUGHES	SUFISM	BUSKED	EUCLID	AUKLET	MUUMUU
HUNGER	HUSHES	BUNION	DUCKED	FURLED	BULLET	LUMMOX
LUGGER	PUSHES	DURIAN	DUNKED	HULLED	CUTLET	DUENNA
MUGGER	RUSHES	FUSION	FUNKED	HURLED	GULLET	GUINEA
RUGGER	SUCHAS	JULIAN	LURKED	LULLED	MULLET	LUANDA
RUTGER	SUCHET	LUCIEN	QUAKED	MULLED	OUTLET	QUINOA
VULGAR	SUNHAT	LUPINO	SUCKED	PULLED	PULLET	BURNED
BUDGES	SUNITA	BUSIER	SULKED	WULLIE	SUBLET	GUNNED
BULGES	BURIED	JUNIOR	TUCKED	MULLAH	SUNLIT	PUNNED
BURGHS	FUTILE	PUNIER	BUCKLE	NUCLEI	CURLEW	RUINED
FUDGES	LUPINE	AUDITS	JUNKIE	CULLUM	LUDLOW	TURNED
FUNGUS	NUBILE	BURIES	SUCKLE	MUSLIM	OUTLAW	BURNIE
JUDGES	PUMICE	CUBITS	PUNKAH	DUBLIN	RUNLOW	NUANCE
LUNGES	SUPINE	CURIOS	BUNKUM	DUNLIN	DUPLEX	QUINCE
NUDGES	BUYING	DUTIES	CULKIN	MULLEN	DUDLEY	NUMNAH
PURGES	CUBING	FURIES	MUCKIN	MUSLIN	GUILTY	QUENCH
SURGES	CUEING	JULIUS	RUSKIN	PULLIN	HURLEY	FUNNEL
BUDGET	CURING	JURIES	SUNKEN	PURLIN	HUXLEY	GUNNEL
NUGGET	DUPING	LUCIUS	TUCKIN	SULLEN	LUMLEY	RUNNEL
KUNGFU	DURING	LUPINS	CUCKOO	BURLAP	OUTLAY	TUNNEL
HUNGRY	FUMING	PUPILS	BUNKER	CURLUP	PULLEY	TURNIN

QUANGO	SUDOKU	OUTRUN	QUASAR	SUTTEE	CURTIS	SUBWAY
TURNIP	EULOGY	QUMRAN	BURSTS	TURTLE	JUNTAS	QUAYLE
TURNUP	BUMPED	QUARTO	CURSES	QUITCH	QUOTAS	BUNYAN
BUGNER	CUPPED	GUARDS	GUESTS	TUKTUK	QUOTES	RUNYON
BURNER	CUSPID	HUBRIS	NURSES	CUSTOM	SUITES	BUNYIP
GUNNER	DUMPED	KUKRIS	PURSES	AUSTEN	TUTTUT	BUZZED
RUNNER	GULPED	QUARKS	QUESTS	AUSTIN	GUSTAV	GUZZLE
TURNER	HUMPED	QUARTS	SUSSES	BUNTON	SURTAX	MUZZLE
BURNET	JUMPED	QUIRES	GUSSET	BURTON	CURTLY	NUZZLE
PUNNET	PUMPED	QUIRKS	OUTSET	BUTTIN	CURTSY	PUZZLE
GURNEY	SUPPED	GUTROT	RUSSET	BUTTON	JUSTLY	BUZZER
QUINCY	PURPLE	RUGRAT	SUBSET	BUXTON	SUBTLY	BUZZES
QUINSY	RUMPLE	TURRET	SUNSET	DUSTIN	SULTRY	AVIATE
AURORA	SUPPLE	BURROW	SUSSEX	EUSTON	CURTIZ	AVIARY
CUPOLA	YUPPIE	FURROW	HUSSEY	FULTON	SUBURB	EVICTS
BUJOLD	TURPIN	AUBREY	PUDSEY	HUSTON	QUEUED	AVOCET
CUBOID	PUMPUP	AUDREY	RUSTIC	HUTTON	FUTURE	EVADED
EUROPE	BUMPER	MURRAY	BUSTED	JUSTIN	JUJUBE	EVADNE
FURORE	DUMPER	QUARRY	BUTTED	MUTTON	SUTURE	EVADES
BUYOFF	JUMPER	QUIRKY	DUSTED	SULTAN	DULUTH	AVIDLY
CUTOFF	SUPPER	SURREY	GUTTED	SUNTAN	EUNUCH	OVIEDO
PUTOFF	RUMPUS	QUARTZ	HUNTED	SUTTON	TUMULI	AVAILS
RUDOLF	MUPPET	RUSSIA	JUTTED	JUSTSO	MUTUAL	AVOIDS
RUNOFF	OUTPUT	CURSED	OUSTED	QUATRO	AUBURN	EVOKED
DUGONG	PULPIT	FUSSED	PUTTED	BUSTUP	AUTUMN	EVOKES
LUGOSI	PUPPET	NURSED	QUOTED	DUSTUP	AUGURS	EVOLVE
SUBORN	FURPHY	PURSED	RUSTED	BUNTER	FUGUES	SVELTE
DUJOUR	MURPHY	SUSSED	RUTTED	BUSTER	QUEUES	AVALON
HUMOUR	SUPPLY	AUSSIE	SUITED	BUTTER	AUGUST	EVELYN
RUMOUR	NUTRIA	PURSUE	TUFTED	CUSTER	TUMULT	EVILLY
DUBOIS	RUBRIC	TUSSLE	TUTTED	CUTTER	AUGURY	EVENED
JURORS	BURRED	PUTSCH	AUNTIE	DUSTER	LUXURY	AVENGE
TUDORS	PURRED	MUESLI	BUSTLE	GUITAR	CURVED	AVENUE
TUTORS	PUTRID	MUSSEL	CUPTIE	GUTTER	QUAVER	EVINCE
BUYOUT	CURRIE	BUNSEN	CUTTLE	HUNTER	QUIVER	YVONNE
CUTOUT	QUIRKE	HUDSON	HURTLE	MUSTER	CURVES	AVANTI
DUGOUT	TUAREG	BURSAR	HUSTLE	MUTTER	PURVEY	EVENSO
DUMONT	HURRAH	CURSOR	LUSTRE	NUTTER	SURVEY	EVENUP
PUTOUT	QUORUM	HUSSAR	PUTTEE	PUNTER	LUDWIG	EVENTS
RUBOUT	FUNRUN	PULSAR	RUSTLE	PUTTER	OUTWIT	EVENLY
RUNOUT	OUTRAN	PURSER	SUBTLE	SUITOR	RUNWAY	AVERSE

DVORAK	SWAMPY	EXTANT	EXETER	DYEING	MYOPIC
EVERSO	RWANDA	EXACTS	EXCUSE	EYEING	GYMPIE
OVERDO	TWINED	EXOCET	EXHUME	HYPING	NYMPHS
AVERTS	GWYNNE	EXUDED	EXEUNT	TYPING	SYLPHS
EVERLY	TWINGE	EXODUS	BYHAND	CYBILL	HYBRID
OVERLY	SWANKS	EXUDES	AYEAYE	MYGIRL	CYPRUS
YVETTE	SWINGS	EXCEED	BYNAME	SYRIAN	AYESHA
AVATAR	TWINES	EXPEND	GYRATE	CYNICS	BYSSHE
AVOWED	SWANKY	EXTEND	TYZACK	LYRICS	GYPSUM
AVOWAL	TWANGY	EXCELS	WYMARK	TYPIST	HYSSOP
SWEARS	TWENTY	EXCESS	CYRANO	SYRINX	MYSTIC
SWEATS	SWOOSH	EXPELS	DYNAMO	TYPIFY	MYRTLE
TWEAKS	SWOONS	EXCEPT	BYLAWS	CYCLIC	SYSTEM
SWEATY	SWOOPS	EXPECT	BYPASS	CYCLED	AYRTON
TWOBIT	SWIPED	EXPERT	BYWAYS	EYELID	OYSTER
SWEDEN	SWIPES	EXTENT	DYNAST	CYCLES	WYNTER
SWEDES	SWERVE	OXYGEN	TYRANT	EYELET	SYNTAX
OWLETS	SWARAJ	EXCISE	MYLADY	BYPLAY	SYRUPY
OWNERS	AWARDS	EXCITE	BYEBYE	AYLMER	SYLVIA
SWEEPS	DWARFS	EXPIRE	CYMBAL	HYMNAL	SYLVIE
SWEETS	SWARMS	OXLIPS	SYMBOL	CYGNUS	SYLVAN
TWEEDS	SWIRLS	EXPIRY	PYEDOG	HYENAS	SYZYGY
TWEEDY	SWORDS	EXILED	LYNDON	CYGNET	IZZARD
TWEENY	TWERPS	EXALTS	PYRENE	SYDNEY	AZTECA
SWIFTS	TWIRLS	EXILES	XYLENE	BYROAD	AZALEA
TWIGGY	QWERTY	EXULTS	MYSELF	BYWORD	AZORES
AWHILE	TWISTS	OXALIS	LYCEUM	MYLORD	
AWNING	SWATHE	EXEMPT	WYVERN	MYWORD	
OWNING	SWATCH	OXFORD	ZYDECO	BYGONE	
AWEIGH	SWITCH	EXPOSE	HYPEUP	BYJOVE	
AWAITS	TWITCH	EXMOOR	LYCEES	TYRONE	
SWAINS	SWOTUP	AXIOMS	EYEFUL	XYLOSE	
AWAKEN	SWOTTY	EXTOLS	LYCHEE	ZYGOTE	
AWOKEN	TWITTY	EXHORT	LYTHAM	CYBORG	
AWAKES	SWIVEL	EXPORT	HYPHEN	TYCOON	
TWELVE	TWOWAY	EXTORT	PYTHON	NYLONS	
DWELLS	SWAYED	EXERTS	TYPHOO	PYLONS	
SWELLS	SWAYZE	EXTRAS	TYPHUS	SYNODS	
SWILLS	EXPAND	EXISTS	MYRIAD	LYNOTT	
TWILIT	EXHALE	EXOTIC	BYLINE	MYFOOT	
SWAMPS	OXTAIL	EXITED	MYLIFE	MYOPIA	

BAHAMAS	FALAFEL	SALAMIS	MANAGUA	CABBAGE	RAMBERT
BANANAS	GARAGED	SATANIC	PALAZZO	GAMBOGE	YABBERS
CARACAL	GARAGES	SAVARIN	GAMBIAN	GARBAGE	LAMBAST
CARACAS	MANAGED	TAMARIN	ZAMBIAN	KASBAHS	BABBITT
CARAVAN	MANAGER	KARAOKE	BAOBABS	CAMBRIC	GAMBITS
CARAWAY	MANAGES	BANALLY	TARBABY	PARBOIL	LAMBETH
CATALAN	MANATEE	CAPABLE	WARBABY	BARBELL	MACBETH
FARADAY	PALACES	CAPABLY	PAYBACK	BARBELS	RABBITS
FARAWAY	PALAVER	DATABLE	SAMBUCA	FANBELT	SABBATH
GALAHAD	PANACEA	EATABLE	TARBUCK	GAMBOLS	BARBOUR
JAIALAI	PARADED	FATALLY	BARBUDA	GASBILL	HARBOUR
MACADAM	PARADES	MANACLE	CARBIDE	IANBELL	TAMBOUR
MALABAR	PARAPET	PARABLE	LAMBADA	SAWBILL	BADBOYS
MARACAS	RAVAGED	PAYABLE	BABBLED	WAYBILL	CARBOYS
PAPAYAS	RAVAGES	RAPALLO	BABBLER	BAMBINO	ZAMBEZI
RAMADAN	SARACEN	TAXABLE	BABBLES	CARBINE	MARCEAU
RATATAT	SAVAGED	MAHATMA	BAUBLES	CARBONS	PANCRAS
RAYALAN	SAVAGES	LASAGNE	BAWBEES	DABBING	PASCHAL
SARAFAN	VACATED	BALATON	CABBIES	DAUBING	HANCOCK
SARAWAK	VACATES	MARABOU	DABBLED	GARBING	HAYCOCK
SAVALAS	FALANGE	MATADOR	DABBLER	HATBAND	BARCODE
WARATAH	EARACHE	PARADOX	DABBLES	JABBING	CASCADE
CARAMBA	FALASHA	PARAGON	DARBIES	JAWBONE	SACCADE
BALANCE	KARACHI	PARASOL	GABBLED	LAMBENT	BATCHED
JAMAICA	MALACHI	RANAMOK	GABBLER	LAMBING	BATCHES
TABASCO	NATASHA	SARACOX	GABBLES	NABBING	CATCHER
VACANCY	PANACHE	TAGALOG	GAMBLED	RAYBANS	CATCHES
VALANCE	PARATHA	BAZAARS	GAMBLER	DAYBOOK	FANCIED
BACARDI	SAMADHI	CATARRH	GAMBLES	MAPBOOK	FANCIER
HAZARDS	SAWALHA	CAVALRY	GARBLED	BANBURY	FANCIES
KABADDI	BAVARIA	MACABRE	GARBLES	BARBARA	HATCHED
MARAUDS	FANATIC	NAVARRE	HASBEEN	BARBARY	HATCHER
TABARDS	GAGARIN	DADAISM	MARBLED	BARBERS	HATCHES
CABARET	GAZANIA	DADAIST	MARBLES	CAMBERS	HATCHET
CADAVER	LARAMIE	MALAISE	RAMBLED	DABBERS	LARCHES
CANAPES	MALARIA	CANASTA	RAMBLER	DAUBERS	LATCHED
CARAFES	NATALIE	JAKARTA	RAMBLES	HALBERD	LATCHES
CARAMEL	PALADIN	NAMASTE	TABBIES	HAMBURG	MARCHED
CARAVEL	PARADIS	BARACUS	WARBLED	JABBERS	MARCHER
DAMAGED	RATAFIA	CALAMUS	WARBLER	LAMBERT	MARCHES
DAMAGES	SAFARIS	LAZARUS	WARBLES	LAYBARE	MATCHED
FACADES	SALADIN	MACAQUE	BABBAGE	RAEBURN	MATCHES

PARCHED	GAUCHOS	SANDBAG	SADDLES	HANDING	LADDISH
PARCHES	HALCYON	SANDMAN	SANDLER	HARDENS	MADDEST
PATCHED	PAKCHOI	BADDEBT	WADDLED	HARDING	SADDEST
PATCHES	RACCOON	CADDICK	WADDLES	LANDING	SAWDUST
RANCHER	SALCHOW	CANDACE	YARDLEY	LARDING	TAXDISC
RANCHES	DANCERS	CANDICE	CARDIFF	LAUDING	BANDITS
RATCHET	DAYCARE	HADDOCK	DANDIFY	MADDENS	CAUDATE
SANCHEZ	LANCERS	HAYDOCK	GADDAFI	MADDING	MANDATE
SATCHEL	LASCARS	PADDOCK	HANDOFF	MAIDENS	CANDOUR
SAUCIER	MASCARA	VANDYCK	LAIDOFF	PADDING	EARDRUM
TANCRED	SAUCERS	CANDIDA	MACDUFF	PARDONS	HANDFUL
WATCHED	CARCASE	CANDIDE	PAIDOFF	RAIDING	HANDGUN
WATCHER	FASCISM	BADDIEL	WARDOFF	SADDENS	HANDOUT
WATCHES	FASCIST	BADDIES	BANDAGE	SARDINE	HANDSUP
WATCHET	PATCASH	BANDIED	BANDOGS	WADDING	PAIDOUT
CALCIFY	SARCASM	BANDIES	LAPDOGS	WARDENS	LAYDOWN
BACCHIC	CALCITE	BAWDIER	YARDAGE	EARDROP	SANDOWN
OATCAKE	FAUCETS	CADDIED	BALDRIC	HARDTOP	SATDOWN
PANCAKE	FAWCETT	CADDIES	BALDWIN	HARDWON	CAMERAS
BASCULE	LANCETS	CANDIES	BANDAID	TANDOOR	CASELAW
CANCELS	MASCOTS	CANDLES	MAUDLIN	CALDERA	CAVEMAN
CATCALL	PAUCITY	DADDIES	SANDPIT	CARDERS	DANELAW
LASCALA	BACCHUS	DANDIES	VANDYKE	DANDARE	FAREHAM
MACCOLL	CALCIUM	DAWDLED	BAWDILY	EATDIRT	GAMELAN
MALCOLM	CATCHUP	DAWDLER	CANDELA	GANDERS	GATEWAY
PARCELS	FANCLUB	DAWDLES	GANDALF	LADDERS	GAVEWAY
RASCALS	FARCEUR	GARDNER	GAUDILY	LARDERS	LATERAL
SAUCILY	PATCHUP	GAUDIER	HANDILY	PANDERS	MADEMAN
LANCOME	RANCOUR	HANDIER	MANDALA	PANDORA	NAMEDAY
SATCHOM	RAUCOUS	HANDLED	MANDELA	PAYDIRT	PACECAR
BALCONY	SANCTUM	HANDLER	RAGDOLL	RAIDERS	RAREGAS
CALCINE	SANCTUS	HANDLES	SANDALS	SANDERS	RATECAP
CANCANS	BANDEAU	HANDLEY	SANDFLY	WALDORF	WAGEWAR
DANCING	BANDSAW	HANDSET	TARDILY	WANDERS	WAKEMAN
FALCONS	CARDIAC	HARDIER	VANDALS	WARDERS	WAREHAM
LANCING	HANDBAG	PADDIES	TANDEMS	YARDARM	CATESBY
LARCENY	HANDCAR	PADDLED	BALDING	BALDEST	LAZENBY
MANCINI	HANDSAW	PADDLER	BANDING	CADDISH	CADENCE
MARCONI	HARDHAT	PADDLES	CARDING	FADDISH	CADENCY
NASCENT	HARDMAN	RADDLED	DANDINI	FADDIST	FAIENCE
VACCINE	HARDPAD	SADDLED	GADDING	HARDEST	LATENCY
CATCHON	RAWDEAL	SADDLER	GARDENS	KADDISH	VALENCY

CAPERED	GAZELLE	BALEFUL	WATFORD	WANGLES	CADGERS
CATERED	JADEDLY	BANEFUL	CATFISH	RANGOFF	CALGARY
CATERER	NACELLE	BATEAUX	HAGFISH	BAGGAGE	DAGGERS
CAVEMEN	PALEALE	CADEAUX	RAFFISH	VANGOGH	DANGERS
DAVEDEE	PATELLA	CAREFUL	SAWFISH	BARGAIN	GANGERS
GATELEG	PALERMO	EASEFUL	TAFFETA	BARGEIN	GARGERY
LAYERED	CAREENS	FADEOUT	BALFOUR	GAUGUIN	HAGGARD
MADELEY	CAVERNS	FATEFUL	HALFCUT	LANGUID	HANGARS
RAMESES	CAYENNE	GASEOUS	GANGWAY	LAUGHIN	HANGERS
SAFEBET	LAVERNE	GATEAUX	HANGMAN	SANGRIA	LAGGARD
TAGETES	PAGEANT	GAVEOUT	MACGRAW	BAGGILY	LANGTRY
TAPERED	RAVENNA	HATEFUL	MAUGHAM	LARGELY	MANGERS
TAVENER	SALERNO	SAVEDUP	MAUGHAN	TANGELO	NAGGERS
VALETED	TAVERNA	TAKEOUT	TANGRAM	WARGAME	RANGERS
WAGERED	TAVERNS	WAKEFUL	VAUGHAN	BAGGING	TAGGART
WAKENED	CAMELOT	CADENZA	RAGGEDY	BAGGINS	LARGEST
WATERED	CAMERON	CATFLAP	BAGGIER	BANGING	WAGGISH
WAVELET	CAPECOD	EARFLAP	BANGLES	BARGING	FAGGOTS
WAVENEY	HAVENOT	HALFWAY	BARGEES	CADGING	GADGETS
WAVERED	JAMESON	BAFFLED	DANGLED	FAGGING	HAUGHTY
WAVERER	LATERON	BAFFLER	DANGLES	FARGONE	MAGGOTS
EASEOFF	MATELOT	BAFFLES	GAGGLES	GAGGING	MAGGOTY
FACEOFF	PAGEBOY	CADFAEL	GARGLED	GANGING	MARGATE
RAKEOFF	PALETOT	PALFREY	GARGLES	GAUGING	NAUGHTY
TAKEOFF	SAVELOY	RAFFLES	HAGGLED	HANGING	TARGETS
BADEGGS	CAREERS	TAXFREE	HAGGLER	LAGGING	HANGOUT
FABERGE	MADEIRA	WAFFLED	HAGGLES	MARGINS	YANGTZE
HAVEAGO	FAREAST	WAFFLER	JANGLED	NAGGING	BAGHDAD
RALEIGH	VANESSA	WAFFLES	JANGLES	RAGGING	BATHMAT
CAGEDIN	BARENTS	YAFFLES	LAUGHED	SAGGING	EACHWAY
CAVEDIN	CAVEATS	HALFWIT	MAIGRET	SARGENT	FATHEAD
JAMELIA	GAZETTE	MAYFAIR	MANGLED	TAGGING	LACHLAN
JAVELIN	LADETTE	PARFAIT	MANGLES	TANGENT	PATHWAY
KARELIA	LAMENTS	HALFAMO	MANGOES	WAGGING	WARHEAD
RAKEDIN	LAYETTE	FAFFING	TANGIER	BANGKOK	WASHBAG
RAMEKIN	MAGENTA	SAFFRON	TANGLED	HANGDOG	WASHDAY
RAREBIT	MAJESTY	BADFORM	TANGLES	LANGDON	YASHMAK
TAKEAIM	NANETTE	FANFARE	TANGOED	LANGTON	CATHODE
VALERIE	PALETTE	GAFFERS	WAGGLED	LANGUOR	RAWHIDE
BASENJI	PARENTS	LAWFORD	WAGGLES	RANGOON	CASHIER
DAZEDLY	PATENTS	WALFORD	WANGLED	BADGERS	DAPHNES
EAGERLY	TALENTS	WARFARE	WANGLER	BANGERS	RAPHAEL

NAPHTHA	CACHOUS	CANINGS	VALIANT	SAVIOUR	BACKOFF
KASHMIR	MANHOUR	CASINGS	VARIANT	TACITUS	MARKOFF
IANHOLM	WASHOUT	PARINGS	CAPITOL	VARIOUS	PACKAGE
MANHOLE	WASHTUB	RATINGS	CARIBOU	MARILYN	BANKSIA
FATHOMS	CASHEWS	SAVINGS	CASINOS	SANJUAN	JACKLIN
SASHIMI	KATHRYN	SAYINGS	DAVISON	MANJACK	TALKBIG
BASHING	CALIBAN	TAKINGS	HARICOT	PALJOEY	WAIKIKI
BATHING	CAPITAL	CALIPHS	JANITOR	SANJEEV	GASKELL
CASHING	FAJITAS	PARIAHS	MADISON	MAHJONG	GAWKILY
DABHAND	HABITAT	TABITHA	MAGINOT	JAMJARS	JACKALS
DASHING	HALIFAX	GALICIA	MANILOW	MARJORY	TACKILY
GASHING	HARIJAN	HASIDIC	MANITOU	SANJOSE	BACKEND
HASHING	MADIGAN	NAMIBIA	CALIBRE	BACKPAY	BACKING
LASHING	MAGICAL	PACIFIC	RAPIERS	DARKMAN	BALKANS
MACHINE	MARITAL	PANICKY	CAGIEST	HACKMAN	BANKING
MANHUNT	RADICAL	BACILLI	EASIEST	HACKSAW	BARKING
MASHING	TALIBAN	CAMILLA	HAZIEST	JACKDAW	BASKING
WASHING	TAXICAB	CAMILLE	LAZIEST	JACKMAN	CASKING
CASHBOX	VATICAN	DANIELA	MAFIOSI	JACKTAR	CATKINS
CASHCOW	MARIMBA	DANIELS	MAFIOSO	PACKMAN	DARKENS
FASHION	MANIACS	FACIALS	MARISSA	PARKWAY	HACKING
MANHOOD	TAPIOCA	MAXILLA	MATISSE	WALKMAN	HARKING
BATHERS	MATILDA	PAPILLA	PACIEST	WALKWAY	HASKINS
EARHART	BASINET	RABIDLY	RACIEST	PACKICE	HAWKING
FATHERS	CABINET	RADICLE	WARIEST	CACKLED	HAWKINS
GATHERS	CANINES	RAPIDLY	WAVIEST	CACKLES	JACKING
LATHERS	FAMINES	RAVIOLI	ZANIEST	HACKLES	LACKING
LATHERY	GALILEE	SANICLE	CALISTA	HACKNEY	MANKIND
MATHERS	GALILEO	SAVILLE	JACINTH	HANKIES	MARKING
RASHERS	GAMINES	TACITLY	LARIATS	JACKDEE	MASKING
SAXHORN	MARINER	VANILLA	PAPISTS	LANKIER	NAPKINS
WARHERO	MARINES	VARIOLA	RACISTS	MADKEEN	PACKING
WASHERS	MATINEE	AAMILNE	RADIATE	NANKEEN	PARKING
ZACHARY	NATIVES	LAVIGNE	RANINTO	RANKLED	RANKING
HASHISH	RADIOED	MALIGNS	SADISTS	RANKLES	SACKING
CACHETS	RAVINES	NATIONS	SATIATE	TACKLED	TACKING
MACHETE	SAMISEN	PATIENT	SATIETY	TACKLER	TALKING
SACHETS	SATIRES	RADIANT	VARIETY	TACKLES	WALKING
BASHFUL	VALISES	RATIONS	FATIGUE	TALKIES	YANKING
BATHBUN	DARIOFO	SALIENT	HABITUE	WACKIER	BACKLOG
BATHTUB	SATISFY	SAPIENT	HALIBUT	WALKIES	BACKLOT
BAUHAUS	TARIFFS	TAXING	MAXIMUM	YANKEES	BACKROW

IASKYOU	DAHLIAS	SALLIES	LAPLAND	LAWLORD	BALMIER
JACKPOT	HALLWAY	TALLIED	MAILING	MALLARD	DAIMLER
JACKSON	MACLEAN	TALLIES	MAPLINS	NAILERY	MALMSEY
TANKTOP	MAILBAG	VAULTED	MARLENE	SAILORS	BARMAID
BACKERS	MAILMAN	VAULTER	MAULING	TAILORS	FANMAIL
BANKERS	MAILVAN	WALLIES	NAILING	WARLORD	CARMELA
BARKERS	PAYLOAD	BAILIFF	OAKLAND	BALLAST	MAMMALS
CANKERS	RAILCAR	CALLOFF	OAKLING	HAPLESS	SAWMILL
FALKIRK	RAILMAN	FALLOFF	PALLING	LAWLESS	CALMING
HACKERS	RAILWAY	HAYLOFT	PAULINE	SALLUST	CARMINE
HANKERS	TABLEAU	KARLOFF	RAILING	TALLEST	CATMINT
HAWKERS	WARLOAN	TAILOFF	RAWLING	BALLETS	CAYMANS
JANKERS	EARLOBE	HAULAGE	SAILING	BALLOTS	DAMMING
MARKERS	WALLABY	TALLYHO	SAPLING	EAGLETS	FARMING
PACKERS	BADLUCK	MALLAIG	TABLING	HAMLETS	GARMENT
RANKERS	FALLACY	TABLOID	TAGLINE	MALLETS	HAMMOND
TALKERS	GALLICO	TAILFIN	TAILEND	PALLETS	HARMING
TANKARD	HARLECH	WAYLAID	TAILING	TABLETS	HARMONY
TANKERS	MATLOCK	WARLIKE	TALLINN	WALLETS	JAMMING
WALKERS	OARLOCK	CARLYLE	VALLONE	BAILOUT	JASMINE
DANKEST	PADLOCK	GASLAMP	WAILING	CALLOUS	MAIMING
DARKEST	WALLACE	BAILING	BALLBOY	CALLOUT	PAYMENT
HAWKISH	WALLACH	BALLING	BALLIOL	FALLGUY	RAIMENT
JACKASS	WARLOCK	BARLINE	BALLOON	FALLOUT	RAMMING
MAWKISH	BAGLADY	BAWLING	CALLBOX	PALLIUM	RAYMOND
BASKETS	BALLADE	CABLING	CARLTON	PARLOUR	TAMMANY
CASKETS	BALLADS	CALLING	EARLDOM	PARLOUS	VALMONT
GASKETS	BAILEES	CARLING	GALLEON	BAKLAVA	VARMINT
HACKETT	BAULKED	DARLENE	MAILBOX	PAHLAVI	WARMING
JACKETS	CARLEEN	DARLING	MAILLOT	PAVLOVA	YASMINE
MARKETS	CAULKED	DAYLONG	TALLBOY	GALLOWS	PALMTOP
PACKETS	DAILIES	FAILING	WALLOON	HALLOWS	EARMARK
RACKETS	DALLIED	FALLING	GALLOPS	MARLOWE	FARMERS
BACKOUT	DALLIES	GALLANT	WALLOPS	WALLOWS	HAMMERS
SACKBUT	EARLIER	GALLING	BALLARD	BAILEYS	PALMYRA
SACKFUL	FAULTED	GALLONS	CALLARD	GALLEYS	WALMART
TANKFUL	HAULIER	GARLAND	CALLERS	PARLEYS	BADMASH
WALKOUT	MAILMEN	GATLING	FAILURE	VALLEYS	CALMEST
HAWKEYE	RAILMEN	HAILING	GALLERY	WAYLAYS	FARMOST
LACKEYS	RALLIED	HAULING	GAYLORD	OATMEAL	GASMASK
BAYLEAF	RALLIES	JAILING	HAILERS	HAMMOCK	PALMIST
CARLOAD	SALLIED	JAWLINE	JAILERS	MANMADE	WARMEST

BASMATI	BARNONE	SADNESS	JACOBIN	HAPPIER	LAMPOON
MAMMOTH	CANNING	TARNISH	LACONIC	LAMPREY	RAMPION
MARMITE	CANNONS	VAINEST	LANOLIN	MAGPIES	BAGPIPE
MARMOTS	DAMNING	VARNISH	MAHONIA	NAPPIES	CAMPARI
PALMATE	DARNING	GANNETS	MASONIC	SAMPLED	CAMPERS
CADMIUM	DAWNING	GARNETS	PARODIC	SAMPLER	CARPARK
FARMOUT	EARNING	GARNETT	BAZOOKA	SAMPLES	CARPORT
HARMFUL	FANNING	MAGNATE	PALOOKA	RAMPAGE	DAMPERS
FARNHAM	FAWNING	MAGNETO	CAGOULE	DAUPHIN	HAMPERS
GAINSAY	GAINING	MAGNETS	PANOPLY	CARPALS	LAMPARD
RAINMAN	MANNING	WALNUTS	BABOONS	CARPELS	PAMPERS
BARNABY	PANNING	GAINFUL	GARONNE	HAPPILY	PAUPERS
WANNABE	PAWNING	PAINFUL	LAGOONS	KAMPALA	RAMPART
BANNOCK	RAINING	BADNEWS	MADONNA	MAYPOLE	RAPPORT
CANNIER	TANNING	BARNOWL	SALOONS	TADPOLE	SAPPERS
DAUNTED	WARNING	MAYORAL	NABOKOV	WALPOLE	TAMPERS
FAINTED	YAWNING	PAGODAS	CANONRY	CAMPING	VAMPIRE
FAINTER	BAGNIOS	SAMOVAR	FAVOURS	CARPING	DAMPEST
HAUNTED	RAINBOW	MAJORCA	LABOURS	DAMPENS	HARPIST
LAUNDER	TAUNTON	LARONDE	MASONRY	DAMPING	VAMPISH
MARNIER	CATNAPS	LAYODDS	SAVOURS	GASPING	WASPISH
MAUNDER	CATNIPS	BALONEY	SAVOURY	GAWPING	CARPETS
NANNIES	BANNERS	BARONET	VAPOURS	HAPPENS	PALPATE
PAINTED	BARNARD	BAYONET	CABOOSE	HATPINS	TAPPETS
PAINTER	CANNERS	CAJOLED	CAROUSE	LAPPING	WARPATH
PANNIER	CANNERY	CAJOLES	PAPOOSE	MAPPING	CAMPOUT
RAINIER	DARNERS	CALOMEL	VAMOOSE	NAPPING	EARPLUG
SAUNTER	EARNERS	DAHOMEY	CAHOOTS	RAMPANT	PAWPAWS
TAINTED	LAUNDRY	HALOGEN	CAVORTS	RASPING	BANQUET
TAUNTED	MANNERS	HANOVER	DACOITS	SAMPANS	BARQUES
VAUNTED	MAYNARD	MALONEY	GAVOTTE	SAPPING	BASQUES
MAGNIFY	TANNERS	PAROLED	HAWORTH	SARPONG	CASQUES
SAWNOFF	TANNERY	PAROLES	MAHOUTS	TAPPING	JACQUES
CARNAGE	BADNESS	SAMOYED	BAROQUE	VAMPING	LACQUER
PAUNCHY	EARNEST	TALONED	CASPIAN	WARPING	MARQUEE
RAUNCHY	FATNESS	WAGONER	SAMPRAS	YAPPING	MARQUES
CANNILY	GARNISH	ZATOPEK	RATPACK	ZAPPING	MASQUES
DARNELL	HARNESS	LAFORGE	TAMPICO	CAMPHOR	PARQUET
FAINTLY	JAINISM	SARONGS	CAMPBED	CAMPION	MARQUIS
SAINTLY	LAXNESS	CALORIE	DAPPLED	CARPOOL	FAIRFAX
MAGNUMS	MADNESS	CAMOGIE	DAPPLES	HAMPTON	FAIRWAY
BANNING	RAWNESS	CAROTID	HAMPDEN	HARPOON	HADRIAN

MARRYAT	BARRAGE	PATRIOT	MARSDEN	GASSING	CAPSIZE
MAURIAC	FARRAGO	TAPROOM	MARSHES	LANSING	CARTMAN
PATRIAL	BAHRAIN	TAPROOT	NAPSTER	LAPSING	EASTMAN
SAMRYAN	HAIROIL	WARRIOR	OARSMEN	MASSING	FACTUAL
SAURIAN	HAIRPIN	CARRERA	PAISLEY	PARSING	HAITIAN
TAUREAN	LACROIX	FAIREST	PANSIES	PARSONS	HARTMAN
NAIROBI	RAMRAID	IANRUSH	PARSLEY	PASSING	MANTEAU
BARRACK	PAPRIKA	BARRETT	PASSKEY	PAUSING	MANTRAP
CAPRICE	BARRELS	CARROTS	TANSIES	RAISING	MARTHAS
FABRICS	CARROLL	CARROTT	FALSIFY	RAISINS	MARTIAL
GARRICK	FARRELL	CARROTY	SALSIFY	BAGSHOT	MARTIAN
HAYRICK	PATROLS	GARRETS	MASSAGE	BASSOON	MATTHAU
MAURICE	PAYROLL	GARRETT	PASSAGE	CAISSON	PARTIAL
PATRICK	RAGROLL	NARRATE	PAYSAGE	EARSHOT	RATTRAP
RATRACE	MACRAME	PARRETT	SAPSAGO	MANSION	TAGTEAM
WARRICK	SANREMO	PARROTS	SAUSAGE	PADSTOW	WATTEAU
HARRODS	BARRING	HAIRCUT	CATSUIT	PASSION	LATTICE
RAMRODS	CABRANK	BARROWS	CAUSTIC	SASSOON	MATTOCK
BARRIER	CAPRINE	FARROWS	LAWSUIT	TAPSHOE	TACTICS
CARRIED	EARRING	MARROWS	PARSNIP	CAESARS	BARTLET
CARRIER	FAIRING	NARROWS	PAYSLIP	CAESURA	BATTIER
CARRIES	JARRING	BATSMAN	WARSHIP	HANSARD	BATTLED
DAIRIES	KATRINA	CAPSTAN	WASSAIL	HAWSERS	BATTLER
FAIRIES	LATRINE	CATSCAN	CAPSULE	MAESTRO	BATTLES
FARRIER	LAURENT	DAYSTAR	DAMSELS	BASSIST	CANTEEN
GABRIEL	MARRANO	MARSHAL	FALSELY	FALSEST	CANTLES
HAARLEM	MARRING	OARSMAN	HALSALL	BASSETS	CARTIER
HAIRIER	MATRONS	CARSICK	HANSOLO	BASSETT	CASTLED
HAIRNET	PADRINO	CASSOCK	HARSHLY	CASSATA	CASTLES
HARRIED	PADRONE	HASSOCK	MANSELL	FALSITY	CATTIER
HARRIER	PAIRING	PARSECS	MARSALA	PASSATA	CAUTHEN
HARRIES	PATRONS	RANSACK	SASSILY	VARSITY	DALTREY
HARRIET	SABRINA	CASSIDY	TARSALS	CAESIUM	EARTHED
LAERTES	TARRANT	WAYSIDE	TASSELS	CASSIUS	EARTHEN
MARRIED	TARRING	BANSHEE	VASSALS	DANSEUR	FARTLEK
MARRIES	VAGRANT	BATSMEN	WALSALL	FAUSTUS	FASTNET
MAUREEN	WARRANT	DAISIES	BALSAMS	MASSEUR	FATTIER
PARRIED	WARRENS	GASSIER	RANSOME	PASSOUT	HARTLEY
PARRIES	CARRION	HAMSTER	RANSOMS	CASSAVA	HAWTREY
TARRIED	CARRYON	HARSHER	SATSUMA	MASSIVE	KASTNER
TARRIES	DAYROOM	HASSLED	CAUSING	PASSIVE	MARTLET
PAIROFF	FAIRDOS	HASSLES	DAMSONS	CATSEYE	MATTHEW

NASTIER	DACTYLS	MARTINA	CASTORS	NASTASE	VANUATU
PANTHER	EARTHLY	MARTINE	CATTERY	CANTATA	FATUOUS
PANTIES	HASTILY	MARTINI	DARTERS	PARTYTO	PABULUM
PARTIES	MARTELL	MARTINS	DASTARD	HAUTEUR	VACUOUS
PARTNER	NASTILY	MATTING	EASTERN	PASTEUR	JACUZZI
PASTIES	NATTILY	PANTING	FACTORS	TACTFUL	LATVIAN
RANTZEN	PANTILE	PARTING	FACTORY	TANTRUM	NAVVIES
RATTIER	PASTELS	PASTING	FALTERS	XANTHUS	SALVAGE
RATTLED	RATTILY	PATTING	GAITERS	CAPTIVE	MARVELL
RATTLER	TACTILE	RAFTING	GARTERS	HANUMAN	MARVELS
RATTLES	TATTILY	RANTING	HALTERS	NATURAL	NAIVELY
SALTIER	BANTAMS	SALTING	HATTERS	SAMURAI	CALVING
TARTLET	DAYTIME	SANTANA	LANTERN	TABULAR	CARVING
TASTIER	PASTIME	TARTANS	MARTYRS	NABUCCO	HALVING
TATTIER	RAGTIME	TASTING	MASTERS	YAOUNDE	PARVENU
TATTLED	SAOTOME	TATTING	MASTERY	CALUMET	SALVING
TATTLER	WARTIME	TAUTENS	MATTERS	CAPULET	WAIVING
TATTLES	BAITING	WAFTING	NATTERS	MATURED	CALVARY
WALTZED	BANTING	WAITING	PASTERN	MATURES	CARVERS
WALTZER	BASTING	WALTONS	PASTORS	SALUTED	CARVERY
WALTZES	BATTENS	WANTING	PASTURE	SALUTES	DANVERS
WASTREL	BATTING	WASTING	PATTERN	BAKUNIN	HARVARD
CASTOFF	CANTINA	BASTION	RAFTERS	SALUKIS	MALVERN
MASTIFF	CANTONA	CALTROP	RAPTURE	MAZURKA	SALVERS
SANTAFE	CANTONS	CAPTION	SALTIRE	ZAKUSKI	CANVASS
TARTUFO	CARTING	CARTOON	TARTARE	CASUALS	FAUVISM
VANTAGE	CARTONS	CAUTION	TARTARS	MANUALS	FAUVIST
WANTAGE	CASTING	FACTION	TASTERS	VAGUELY	HARVEST
WASTAGE	DARTING	HAUTBOY	TATTERS	CALUMNY	NAIVETE
WATTAGE	EASTEND	PALTROW	WAITERS	VALUING	NAIVETY
CANTRIP	EASTING	PARTOOK	WALTERS	GALUMPH	CARVEUP
CAPTAIN	FASTENS	TATTOOS	WARTORN	GAZUMPS	DAYWEAR
DAYTRIP	FASTING	WARTHOG	WASTERS	JAGUARS	FAYWRAY
FACTOID	FATTENS	BANTERS	BAPTISE	JANUARY	NARWHAL
FANTAIL	GATTING	BARTERS	BAPTISM	VALUERS	GATWICK
GASTRIC	HALTING	BATTERS	BAPTIST	VAQUERO	HARWICH
TANTRIC	HASTENS	BATTERY	DAFTEST	CASUIST	WARWICK
WAGTAIL	KAFTANS	CANTERS	FANTASY	VAGUEST	RAGWEEK
PARTAKE	KARTING	CANTORS	FASTEST	ZANUSSI	SAYWHEN
CARTELS	LANTANA	CAPTORS	FATTEST	FACULTY	EARWIGS
CASTILE	LASTING	CAPTURE	LACTOSE	FATUITY	CATWALK
CATTILY	MALTING	CARTERS	MALTESE	VACUITY	GADWALL

JAYWALK	LAWYERS	ABRIDGE	OBEYING	ACCEDES	SCALING
MAXWALL	SAWYERS	OBOISTS	ACHAEAN	SCHEMED	SCALLOP
MAXWELL	BABYISH	OBVIATE	SCRATCH	SCHEMER	OCULIST
BATWING	CALYPSO	OBLIQUE	ACCARDO	SCHEMES	SCHLOSS
LAPWING	PAPYRUS	OBVIOUS	ACHATES	ACREAGE	ACOLYTE
WAXWING	LAZYEYE	ABALONE	MCLAREN	SCREAMS	OCELOTS
DAGWOOD	JAZZMAN	ABILENE	OCTAVES	MCKENNA	SCULPTS
OAKWOOD	DALZIEL	ABELARD	SCRAPED	SCREENS	MCCLOUD
SAPWOOD	DAZZLED	ABOLISH	SCRAPER	ECHELON	SCHMUCK
YARWOOD	DAZZLER	OBELISK	SCRAPES	ACCENTS	SCHMIDT
HAYWARD	DAZZLES	TBILISI	SCRAGGY	ACCEPTS	SCAMPER
HAYWIRE	JAZZMEN	ABILITY	OCEANIA	SCHERZO	SCANDAL
RAGWORM	JAZZAGE	ABANDON	OCEANIC	SCOFFED	SCANNED
RAGWORT	CALZONE	EBONITE	OCTAVIA	SCOFFER	SCANNER
WAXWORK	FANZINE	ABSORBS	SCRAPIE	SCUFFED	SCENTED
WAYWARD	PANZERS	ABDOMEN	SCRAWLS	ICEFALL	SCONCES
BAGWASH	ABRAHAM	OBLONGS	SCRAWLY	SCAFELL	ECONOMY
CARWASH	ABRAXAS	OBLOMOV	SCRAWNY	SCUFFLE	MCENROE
MAEWEST	ABRADED	OBLOQUY	ACTAEON	ICEFLOE	OCONNOR
FAUXPAS	ABRADES	ABSOLVE	ECUADOR	MCSHANE	SCENERY
MANXCAT	CBRADIO	IBERIAN	MCMAHON	ACRILAN	ICINESS
MANXMAN	OBTAINS	OBTRUDE	OCTAGON	SCRIBES	ACONITE
MARXISM	ABSALOM	ABORTED	SCRAPPY	SCHISMS	ACROBAT
MARXIST	ABLAUTS	ABYSMAL	ECLAIRS	ACTIONS	MCGOWAN
BAUXITE	MBABANE	ABASHED	MCMANUS	ECHIDNA	SCHOLAR
BABYSAT	ABECKET	ABYSSES	ICEBEER	SCRIMPS	ACCORDS
GAPYEAR	ABSCOND	ABASING	SCABIES	ECLIPSE	ICEOVER
LADYDAY	OBSCENE	ABUSING	ICEBERG	SCRIPTS	OCTOBER
TAXYEAR	OBSCURE	OBESITY	ACACIAS	OCCIPUT	SCOOPED
CALYXES	ABSCESS	ABUSIVE	ICECUBE	ACHIEVE	SCOOTED
EASYJET	ABIDJAN	ABUTTAL	ICICLES	OCCLUDE	SCOOTER
BABYBIO	ABIDING	EBBTIDE	ICEDTEA	SCALDED	SCROOGE
BABYSIT	ABSENCE	ABETTED	ICHDIEN	SCALPED	SCHOOLS
KATYDID	ABSEILS	ABUTTED	SCUDDED	SCALPEL	SCROLLS
BABYING	ABREAST	ABSTAIN	ACIDIFY	SCOLDED	ACCOUNT
BANYANS	OBVERSE	ABATING	ACADEME	SCULLED	ECHOING
CANYONS	ABSENTS	ABETTOR	ACADEMY	SCULLER	MCCOURT
VARYING	OBJECTS	ABOUNDS	ACIDITY	ECOLOGY	ACCOSTS
BABYLON	OBSERVE	ABJURED	SCIENCE	ACCLAIM	ECLOGUE
BABYGRO	ABIGAIL	ABJURES	SCREECH	ACKLAND	OCTOPUS
HALYARD	OBLIGED	ABDUCTS	SCREEDS	ICELAND	ACRONYM
LANYARD	OBLIGES	ABEYANT	ACCEDED	SCALENE	ICEPACK

ICEPICK	ACAUDAL	ADHERES	ADORNED	DEFACED	DEBACLE
SCUPPER	ACCUSAL	ADVERSE	ADORING	DEFACES	DEFAULT
SCEPTIC	SCRUBBY	ADVERTS	ODORANT	DEFAMED	DETAILS
SCAPULA	SCRUNCH	ADDEDUP	ADDRESS	DEFAMES	LEGALLY
SCEPTRE	ACCUSED	EDIFICE	ODOROUS	DELANEY	RECALLS
ACCRUAL	ACCUSER	EDIFIED	EDASNER	DELAYED	REGALLY
SCARABS	ACCUSES	EDIFIES	ODYSSEY	FEMALES	RENAULT
MCBRIDE	MCQUEEN	ADAGIOS	EDITING	HEBATES	RETAILS
ACCRUED	SCOURED	ADMIRAL	EDITION	LEGATEE	TENABLE
ACCRUES	SCOURER	ADMIRED	EDITORS	LEGATES	REDARMY
SCARCER	SCOUTED	ADMIRER	ADJUNCT	MENACED	CEZANNE
SCARLET	SCOUTER	ADMIRES	ADJUDGE	MENACES	DETAINS
SCARPER	SCRUFFY	ADMIXED	ADJUSTS	NEGATED	GERAINT
SCARRED	SCOURGE	ADMIXES	EDGWARE	NEGATES	REGAINS
SCARVES	OCTUPLE	ADVISED	EDDYING	REBATES	REMAINS
SCORNED	SCRUPLE	ADVISER	GETAWAY	REGALED	REPAINT
SCARIFY	SCRUMMY	ADVISES	DEBAUCH	REGALES	RETAINS
ACERBIC	SCRUMPS	LDRIVER	PENANCE	RELATED	AERATOR
SCORPIO	SCRUMPY	ADHIBIT	REMATCH	RELATES	DECAGON
SCARILY	ACQUIRE	ADDISON	TENANCY	RELAXED	DECAPOD
ACARINE	ACTUARY	EDGIEST	DEMANDS	RELAXES	HEXAGON
ICERINK	MCGUIRE	ADDICTS	GERALDO	RELAYED	HEXAPOD
OCARINA	ACQUITS	ADELPHI	HERALDS	RENAMED	LEBANON
SCARING	ACTUATE	IDYLLIC	REGARDS	RENAMES	MEGATON
SCORING	SCRUBUP	ADDLING	REMANDS	REPAPER	PEDALOS
SCORERS	SCOWLED	IDOLISE	RETARDS	RETAKEN	SENATOR
ACTRESS	ACRYLIC	ADULATE	REWARDS	RETAKES	DECAMPS
MCGRATH	SCRYING	ADAMANT	VERANDA	SEDATED	REVAMPS
ACKROYD	SCRYERS	ODDMENT	AERATED	SEDATES	LECARRE
ACUSHLA	ADVANCE	ADAMSON	AERATES	DERANGE	LEHAVRE
ICESHOW	EDWARDS	ODDNESS	BEHAVED	MELANGE	REMARRY
SCISSOR	PDJAMES	ADSORBS	BEHAVES	CERAMIC	REPAIRS
SCATTER	IDIAMIN	EDMONDS	BELATED	HEPATIC	BECAUSE
SCYTHES	IDEALLY	EDMOSES	BERATED	KERATIN	RELAPSE
SCOTTIE	EDIBLES	IDIOTIC	BERATES	MELANIE	DECANTS
ACETYLS	ODDBALL	ADJOINS	DEBASED	MELANIN	DEFACTO
ACUTELY	EDUCING	ADJOURN	DEBASES	PELAGIC	DEPARTS
SCUTTLE	EDUCATE	ADAPTED	DEBATED	REGALIA	LEPANTO
ACETONE	ADRENAL	ADOPTED	DEBATER	TELAVIV	PEDANTS
SCOTERS	ADVERBS	ADEPTLY	DEBATES	REMARKS	PENALTY
ECSTASY	ADDENDA	ADAPTOR	DECADES	BEFALLS	PENARTH
ACETATE	ADHERED	ADIPOSE	DECAYED	BEWAILS	RECANTS

RECASTS	NESBITT	MECCANO	REDDEER	RENDING	MENDOZA
REGATTA	BEACHAM	PERCENT	REEDBED	SEEDING	FEDERAL
REPASTS	BEECHAM	RESCIND	SEEDBED	SENDING	GENERAL
TENANTS	PEACOAT	HENCOOP	SEEDIER	TENDING	PESETAS
BELARUS	REDCOAT	REACTOR	TEDDIES	TENDONS	RENEWAL
DEDALUS	PEACOCK	PERCEPT	WEEDIER	VENDING	SENEGAL
DEVALUE	BEACHED	REDCAPS	HELDOFF	VERDANT	SEVERAL
PEGASUS	BEACHES	TEACUPS	SENDOFF	WEDDING	VETERAN
PETASUS	BECCLES	FENCERS	TEEDOFF	WEEDING	YEREVAN
REVALUE	BEECHER	KEYCARD	BENDIGO	WELDING	KETELBY
TETANUS	BEECHES	MERCURY	HENDRIX	WENDING	BESEECH
JERBOAS	BENCHES	PECCARY	READMIT	DEWDROP	DECENCY
SERBIAN	FETCHED	REDCARD	TENDRIL	SEEDBOX	DEFENCE
GETBACK	FETCHES	TEACOSY	KENDALL	MENDIPS	REBECCA
REDBACK	KETCHES	WEBCAST	NEEDILY	FEEDERS	REGENCY
SETBACK	LEECHES	KETCHUP	READILY	FENDERS	TERENCE
FEEBLER	PEACHES	PEACHUM	RENDELL	HEADERS	BEHEADS
PEBBLED	PERCHED	REOCCUR	SEEDILY	LEADERS	DEFENDS
PEBBLES	PERCHES	DEADPAN	BEADING	LENDERS	DEPENDS
WEMBLEY	REACHED	FELDMAN	BEDDING	MENDERS	LEGENDS
BEDBUGS	REACHES	HEADMAN	BENDING	READERS	DELETED
DENBIGH	REACTED	HEADWAY	DEADEND	RENDERS	DELETES
HERBAGE	RESCUED	NEWDEAL	DEADENS	SEEDERS	DEMETER
TEABAGS	RESCUER	VERDICT	FEEDING	SENDERS	FEDERER
LEIBNIZ	RESCUES	KENDODD	FENDING	TENDERS	JEZEBEL
CEMBALO	TEACHER	BEADLES	FEUDING	VENDORS	LEDERER
GERBILS	TEACHES	BENDIER	GELDING	VERDURE	LEVERET
NETBALL	WENCHES	DEADLEG	HEADING	WEEDERS	PETERED
SEXBOMB	NESCAFE	DEADSEA	HEEDING	WELDERS	RECEDED
HENBANE	TEACAKE	DEADSET	HERDING	GEODESY	RECEDES
VERBENA	DESCALE	HEADLEY	KENDONE	REDDISH	REFEREE
WEBBING	HERCULE	HEADSET	LEADING	REDDUST	RENEGED
GERBERA	PENCILS	MEDDLED	LENDING	PERDITA	RENEGES
HEPBURN	PERCALE	MEDDLER	MELDING	HEEDFUL	RENEWED
HERBERT	WELCOME	MEDDLES	MENDING	HELDOUT	REVERED
MEMBERS	BEACONS	MELDREW	NEEDING	MELDRUM	REVERES
NEWBORN	DEACONS	NEEDIER	PENDANT	NEEDFUL	SECEDED
NEWBURY	DEICING	NEEDLED	PENDENT	READOUT	SECEDES
SEABIRD	DESCANT	NEEDLES	PENDING	VERDOUX	SEVERED
NEBBISH	DESCEND	PEDDLED	READING	LETDOWN	TELEXED
SEABASS	DESCENT	PEDDLES	REDDENS	MEADOWS	TELEXES
VERBOSE	FENCING	PERDIEM	REDDING	REDDAWN	ZEBEDEE

REVENGE	DETECTS	BEDFORD	VERGING	MEDICAL	MERITED
BEDEVIL	DETENTE	HEIFERS	WEDGING	MEXICAN	PERIGEE
BENEFIT	DETESTS	PERFORM	PEUGEOT	PELICAN	RECIPES
DEMERIT	MEMENTO	REDFORD	BEGGARS	RECITAL	RECITED
GENERIC	REGENTS	REEFERS	LEDGERS	RETINAS	RECITES
GENESIS	REHEATS	TELFORD	MERGERS	REVIVAL	REFINED
GENETIC	REJECTS	WELFARE	VERGERS	SEMINAL	REFINES
HERETIC	RELENTS	WEXFORD	HENGIST	SEMINAR	REGIMEN
NEMESIA	REPEATS	BELFAST	HEIGHTS	LETITBE	REGIMES
NEMESIS	REPENTS	DEAFEST	NEWGATE	BEWITCH	RELIVED
REVERIE	RESENTS	SELFISH	REIGATE	BELINDA	RELIVES
BEDECKS	REVERTS	WETFISH	WEIGHTS	MELINDA	REPINED
CEREALS	SELECTS	PEAFOWL	WEIGHTY	PERIODS	REPINES
FENELLA	SEVENTH	BELGIAN	BELGIUM	REMINDS	RESIDED
REPEALS	SEVENTY	BERGMAN	BEDHEAD	BENITEZ	RESIDES
RESEALS	VEDETTE	SEAGRAM	REDHEAD	BESIDES	RETIRED
RETELLS	BENELUX	BEAGLES	REDHEAT	DEBITED	RETIREE
REVEALS	REVENUE	BEEGEES	METHODS	DECIBEL	RETIRES
REDEEMS	DECEIVE	BEIGNET	BEXHILL	DECIDED	REVILED
DEMEANS	DENEUVE	DEIGNED	DENHOLM	DECIDER	REVILES
DEMESNE	DESERVE	FEIGNED	KEYHOLE	DECIDES	REVISED
GEHENNA	RECEIVE	LEAGUES	REDHILL	DEFILED	REVISER
DEVELOP	RESERVE	LENGLEN	MESHING	DEFILER	REVISES
REREDOS	REDFLAG	NEIGHED	METHANE	DEFILES	REVIVED
TELECOM	PERFECT	REIGNED	PEAHENS	DEFINED	REVIVER
RECEIPT	PERFIDY	WEIGHED	REDHAND	DEFINES	REVIVES
METEORS	BEEFIER	HEIGHHO	RETHINK	DELIBES	BELIEFS
REVELRY	BEEFTEA	LENGTHS	PERHAPS	DELIVER	BESIEGE
VENEERS	DEIFIED	LENGTHY	RESHAPE	DEMISEC	DELIGHT
DECEASE	DEIFIES	GENGHIS	LECHERY	DENIZEN	JERICHO
RELEASE	JEFFREY	KEYGRIP	LEGHORN	DERIDED	RELIGHT
REVERSE	LEAFLET	PENGUIN	SEEHERE	DERIDES	CECILIA
REVERSI	SETFREE	WEIGHIN	TETHERS	DERIVED	DEFICIT
BENEATH	JETFOIL	BENGALI	PETHATE	DERIVES	DELIMIT
CELESTA	MENFOLK	PERGOLA	BEEHIVE	DESIRED	LETITIA
CELESTE	PENFOLD	SEAGULL	NEPHEWS	DESIREE	PERIWIG
CEMENTS	TENFOLD	BEGGING	SEAHAWK	DESIRES	REVISIT
DECEITS	PERFUME	BENGUNN	DECIMAL	DEVICES	SEMITIC
DEFEATS	BEEFING	HEDGING	DELILAH	DEVISED	AERIALS
DEFECTS	DEAFENS	MERGING	HELICAL	DEVISES	CEDILLA
DEJECTS	SEAFOOD	PEGGING	HELIPAD	DEVIZES	DEMILLE
DESERTS	SERFDOM	REAGENT	LEXICAL	FELINES	DENIALS

LEGIBLE	RESIDUE	MEEKEST	SEALEGS	HELLBOY	MELLOWS
LEGIBLY	RETINUE	PECKISH	FELLAHS	NEILFOX	YELLOWS
NEVILLE	SERIOUS	WEAKEST	HEALTHY	NEWLOOK	YELLOWY
REFILLS	TEDIOUS	BECKETT	WEALTHY	REALTOR	DEPLOYS
SERIALS	BELIEVE	LEAKOUT	DECLAIM	SEALION	REPLAYS
SEVILLE	RELIEVE	SEEKOUT	NEWLAID	WETLOOK	PERMIAN
TEPIDLY	REVIEWS	AEOLIAN	RECLAIM	CELLARS	REDMEAT
VEHICLE	HEYJUDE	BELLJAR	REALALE	DEALERS	LEEMACK
VESICLE	BEIJING	HEELBAR	BELLAMY	DECLARE	BERMUDA
MEDIUMS	PERJURE	HEELTAP	BEELINE	DEPLORE	SEAMIER
DEFIANT	PERJURY	HELLCAT	BELLINI	FEELERS	VERMEER
DESIGNS	BECKHAM	HELLMAN	CEILING	FELLERS	MERMAID
DEVIANT	PECKHAM	PERLMAN	DEALING	HEALERS	SEAMILE
LEGIONS	WEEKDAY	TEALEAF	DECLINE	MEDLARS	BEAMING
LENIENT	HECKLED	DEFLECT	FEELING	PEDLARS	DEEMING
REGIONS	HECKLER	FETLOCK	FELLING	PEELERS	DESMOND
RELIANT	HECKLES	HEMLOCK	FELLINI	SEALORD	FERMENT
RESIGNS	PERKIER	NEGLECT	FENLAND	SELLERS	GERMANE
DEMIGOD	LEAKAGE	REELECT	GEELONG	TELLERS	GERMANS
DENISON	NECKTIE	REFLECT	GELLING	CELLIST	GERMANY
HELICON	PERKILY	REPLACE	HEALING	GETLOST	LEEMING
LETINON	SEAKALE	REPLICA	HELLENE	HELLISH	LEHMANN
LEXICON	BECKONS	SELLECK	HEMLINE	LEGLESS	LEMMING
MEDICOS	DECKING	WEDLOCK	KEELING	REALISE	PERMING
PERIDOT	JENKINS	CEILIDH	LEBLANC	REALISM	REAMING
RETINOL	JERKING	SECLUDE	PEALING	REALIST	REDMOND
VENISON	LEAKING	TEALADY	PEELING	RECLUSE	SEEING
DEVILRY	NECKING	JELLIED	RECLINE	DEFLATE	SEGMENT
SENIORS	PEAKING	JELLIES	REELING	DEPLETE	SERMONS
EERIEST	PECKING	MEALIES	SEALANE	PELLETS	TEEMING
MELISSA	PEEKING	REPLIED	SEALANT	REALITY	TERMING
NERISSA	PERKINS	REPLIES	SEALING	REFLATE	TERMINI
PELISSE	RECKONS	WELLFED	SELLING	REPLETE	VERMONT
DEPICTS	REEKING	WELLIES	TELLING	ZEALOTS	NEWMOON
DESISTS	SEEKING	PEELOFF	VEILING	BELLYUP	BEAMERS
DEVIATE	WEAKENS	REELOFF	WELLAND	DEALOUT	DENMARK
MEDIATE	WEEKEND	SEALOFF	WETLAND	FELLOUT	REAMERS
REBIRTH	DESKJOB	SELLOFF	YELLING	JEALOUS	BEAMISH
RESISTS	DESKTOP	TELLOFF	BELLBOY	SELLOUT	HELMETS
BEZIQUE	BEAKERS	WELLOFF	BELLHOP	ZEALOUS	HERMITS
DEVIOUS	SEEKERS	GEOLOGY	BENLYON	BELLOWS	PELMETS
OEDIPUS	SELKIRK	REALIGN	BERLIOZ	FELLOWS	PERMITS

TERMITE	KEENEST	DENOTES	REMOUNT	PERPLEX	JEEPERS
ZERMATT	LEANEST	DEPOSED	REPOINT	TEMPLES	KEEPERS
SEYMOUR	MEANEST	DEPOSES	RESOUND	TEMPTED	LEOPARD
BEANBAG	NEWNESS	DEVOTED	REWOUND	TEMPTER	NEWPORT
LEONIAN	REDNESS	DEVOTEE	VETOING	WEEPIES	PEEPERS
REDNECK	REDNOSE	DEVOTES	AEROSOL	KEEPOFF	PEPPARD
REENACT	WETNESS	GETOVER	PELOTON	SEEPAGE	PEPPERS
KENNEDY	BENNETT	REBORED	RECOUPS	WEBPAGE	PEPPERY
HEINKEL	KENNETH	REBORES	BEGORRA	DELPHIC	REAPERS
LEANDER	KEYNOTE	RECOVER	BENOKRI	DESPAIR	RESPIRE
LEONTES	PEANUTS	REMODEL	DETOURS	DESPOIL	SEAPORT
MEANDER	REUNITE	REMOTER	DEVOURS	KEEPFIT	TEMPERA
PENNIES	HEINOUS	REMOVED	HELOTRY	LEIPZIG	TEMPERS
PEONIES	DEBORAH	REMOVES	MEMOIRS	MEMPHIS	TEMPURA
REENTER	FEDORAS	REPOSED	HEROISM	BESPOKE	VESPERS
SEANCES	FEMORAL	REPOSES	REHOUSE	LEGPULL	BEDPOST
TENNIEL	JEHOVAH	REVOKED	REMORSE	LEOPOLD	DEEPEST
VERNIER	KEROUAC	REVOKES	DECOCTS	PEPPILL	DESPISE
TEENAGE	MENORAH	SEEOVER	DEPORTS	REAPPLY	TEMPEST
JEANNIE	REMOVAL	XEROXED	REPORTS	REDPOLL	DESPITE
KENNELS	SENORAS	BELONGS	REROUTE	BEEPING	DESPOTS
KERNELS	REDOUBT	LESOTHO	RESORTS	DEEPEND	RESPITE
PENNAME	SECOMBE	AEROBIC	RETORTS	DEEPENS	TEAPOTS
PETNAME	BEYONCE	BEDOUIN	REVOLTS	DESPOND	HELPFUL
DENNING	HEROICS	BEGONIA	VELOUTE	HEAPING	HELPOUT
KEENING	REJOICE	DEMONIC	AEROBUS	HELPING	KEEPMUM
LEANING	RETOUCH	DEMOTIC	DECORUM	KEEPING	LESPAUL
LEONINE	RECORDS	DEPOSIT	PELORUS	LEAPING	NEWQUAY
MEANING	RELOADS	MEIOSIS	REFOCUS	PEEPING	BEARCAT
PENNANT	SECONDS	MELODIC	DEVOLVE	REAPING	BEERMAT
PENNINE	AEROBES	SEGOVIA	RESOLVE	REOPENS	BEERWAH
PENNONS	BECOMES	XEROSIS	REVOLVE	RESPOND	DECRIAL
REMNANT	BELOVED	RECOILS	RESPRAY	SEEPING	HEARSAY
WEANING	BETOKEN	REMOULD	TEMPLAR	SERPENT	MEERKAT
LEANTOS	DECODED	DEFORMS	HENPECK	TEMPING	MEGRYAN
REUNION	DECODER	REFORMS	RESPECT	TENPINS	RETREAD
BERNARD	DECODES	BEMOANS	SERPICO	WEAPONS	RETREAT
DEANERY	DECOKED	HEROINE	DEEPSEA	WEEPING	RETRIAL
LEONARD	DECOKES	REBOUND	DEEPSET	YELPING	TEARGAS
REENTRY	DEMOTED	RECOUNT	DEMPSEY	BEEPERS	BEDROCK
REYNARD	DEMOTES	REDOING	KEEPNET	DEEPFRY	DEFROCK
TENNERS	DENOTED	REJOINS	KELPIES	HELPERS	DERRICK

DETRACT	WEAROFF	HERRIOT	TEARFUL	CESSPIT	SESSION
MERRICK	PEERAGE	LEGROOM	WEAROUT	LEGSLIP	TEASHOP
METRICS	HEARTHS	MERRION	DEPRAVE	LEGSPIN	TENSION
REFRACT	BEARPIT	PEARSON	DEPRIVE	LETSLIP	VERSION
RETRACE	DEARSIR	REARDON	REPROVE	MESSTIN	LESSEPS
RETRACT	DETROIT	REPROOF	HEBREWS	SEISMIC	BEDSORE
SECRECY	GEORDIE	TEAROOM	REDRAWN	SETSAIL	BERSERK
TERRACE	GEORGIA	WEIRDOS	REDRAWS	WETSUIT	CENSERS
VERRUCA	GEORGIE	BEARERS	BETRAYS	NETSUKE	CENSORS
DEGRADE	HENREID	DEIRDRE	DEFRAYS	BEASTLY	CENSURE
BEARDED	RECRUIT	FERRARI	BEESWAX	DENSELY	DESSERT
BERRIES	REFRAIN	TERRORS	GEISHAS	HERSELF	GEYSERS
DEBRIEF	RETRAIN	DEAREST	HESSIAN	MESSILY	LEISURE
DECREED	TERRAIN	DEFROST	KERSHAW	SEASALT	MEASURE
DECREES	BEDROLL	DEPRESS	LETSSAY	TEASELS	SENSORS
DECRIED	FEBRILE	HEIRESS	MESSIAH	TENSELY	SENSORY
DECRIES	FERRELL	LEPROSY	PERSIAN	TENSILE	TEASERS
DEGREES	FERRULE	NEAREST	SENSUAL	TERSELY	TESSERA
FERRIED	MERRILY	PEERESS	TELSTAR	VESSELS	DENSEST
FERRIER	PETRELS	PENROSE	JESSICA	WEASELS	PERSIST
FERRIES	WEARILY	REDRESS	SEASICK	CEASING	BEDSITS
HEARKEN	WEIRDLY	REDROSE	VERSACE	LEASING	DENSITY
HEARSES	BEARING	REFRESH	BEDSIDE	LESSENS	WEBSITE
HEARTEN	FEARING	REGRESS	DEESIDE	LESSING	CELSIUS
LEARNED	GEARING	REPRESS	SEASIDE	LESSONS	PEASOUP
LEARNER	HEARING	REPRISE	BEESLEY	MESSINA	REISSUE
MERRIER	HERRING	TEAROSE	FEASTED	MESSING	SEASLUG
PEARLED	JEERING	BETROTH	LEASHES	NELSONS	PENSIVE
PERRIER	KEYRING	FERRETS	MEASLES	PEASANT	SEESAWS
REARMED	LEERING	PENRITH	MEISSEN	PERSONA	JERSEYS
REORDER	NEARING	REDRUTH	MENSREA	PERSONS	BERTRAM
SERRIED	NEGRONI	REGRETS	MESSIER	REASONS	BESTIAL
TERRIER	PEERING	REWRITE	NEASDEN	RETSINA	BESTMAN
WEARIED	REARING	SECRETE	OERSTED	SEASONS	CENTRAL
WEARIER	REPRINT	SECRETS	PERSPEX	SENSING	GENTIAN
WEARIES	SEARING	SERRATE	WEASLEY	TEASING	HENTZAU
WEIRDER	TEARING	BEARCUB	WEBSTER	TENSING	NEUTRAL
YEARNED	TERRINE	BEARHUG	WELSHED	GEMSBOK	TEATRAY
PETRIFY	VEERING	DEFRAUD	WELSHER	HELSTON	TEXTUAL
REDRAFT	WEARING	FEARFUL	VERSIFY	NEWSBOY	WESTHAM
TEAROFF	BEDROOM	FERROUS	MESSAGE	PENSION	LETTUCE
TERRIFY	GEARBOX	REGROUP	BEASTIE	PETSHOP	RESTOCK

TESTACY	LEFTOFF	GETTING	FESTERS	LEFTOUT	REFUTES
LEETIDE	RECTIFY	HEATING	FETTERS	RESTFUL	REPUTED
TESTUDO	SENTOFF	JESTING	GESTURE	ZESTFUL	REQUIEM
BEATLES	TESTIFY	JETTING	HEATERS	CENTAVO	RESUMED
BEETLED	NESTEGG	KEATING	HECTARE	FESTIVE	RESUMES
BEETLES	VERTIGO	LETTING	JESTERS	RESTIVE	SECURED
BENTLEY	VESTIGE	MEETING	LECTERN	BESTOWS	SECURES
BERTHED	BEATNIK	MELTING	LECTURE	NEWTOWN	SEDUCED
BESTBET	BEATRIX	NEATENS	LEOTARD	NEBULAE	SEDUCER
CENTRED	CENTRIC	NEPTUNE	LETTERS	NEBULAR	SEDUCES
CENTRES	CERTAIN	NESTING	MENTORS	PERUSAL	REBUFFS
DEITIES	DELTOID	NETTING	PERTURB	REFUSAL	DEBURGH
FEATHER	LEITRIM	PELTING	PESTERS	REFUTAL	BELUSHI
GENTEEL	PERTAIN	RENTING	RECTORS	REGULAR	PETUNIA
HEATHEN	YELTSIN	RESTING	RECTORY	SECULAR	SEQUOIA
HEATHER	CENTILE	SEATING	RESTART	DEFUNCT	DEBUNKS
HEFTIER	DEATHLY	SETTING	RESTORE	FELUCCA	BEGUILE
JETTIES	FERTILE	SEXTANT	REUTERS	REFUNDS	REBUILD
KESTREL	GENTILE	SEXTONS	SECTORS	BEMUSED	REBUILT
KETTLES	GESTALT	TESTING	SETTERS	CERUMEN	REFUELS
KETTLEY	LENTILS	VETTING	TEETERS	DEDUCED	SEQUELS
LEATHER	PEPTALK	WESTEND	TESTERS	DEDUCES	TEQUILA
MEATIER	REPTILE	WETTING	TEXTURE	DEFUSED	BEGUINE
NEITHER	RESTYLE	BEATBOX	VECTORS	DEFUSES	GENUINE
NESTLED	SEATTLE	BESTBOY	VENTURA	DELUDED	RETURNS
NESTLES	TESTILY	DESTROY	VENTURE	DELUDES	SEQUINS
NETTLED	TEXTILE	FESTOON	VESTURE	DELUGED	LETUPON
NETTLES	BEDTIME	MENTHOL	WESTERN	DELUGES	REQUIRE
PERTWEE	CENTIME	MENTION	DENTIST	DENUDES	BEQUEST
SEETHED	CENTIMO	NEUTRON	KENTISH	LEGUMES	DEBUSSY
SEETHES	DEETIME	PEATBOG	LEFTIST	PERUSED	REPULSE
SELTZER	TEATIME	SECTION	NEATEST	PERUSER	REQUEST
SETTEES	BEATING	VENTNOR	WETTEST	PERUSES	DEDUCTS
SETTLED	BELTANE	GESTAPO	DENTATE	REBUKED	JESUITS
SETTLER	BELTING	REDTAPE	GESTATE	REBUKES	RESULTS
SETTLES	BENTINE	BEATERS	RESTATE	REDUCED	REGULUS
TEATREE	BETTANY	BETTERS	SEPTETS	REDUCES	TENUOUS
TENTPEG	BETTING	CENTURY	SEXTETS	REFUGEE	SERVICE
TESTBED	BETTONG	DEBTORS	TEKTITE	REFUGES	PERVADE
WEATHER	DENTINE	DENTURE	TESTATE	REFUSED	BEVVIED
BEATIFY	DENTING	DETTORI	BELTOUT	REFUSES	HEAVIER
CERTIFY	DESTINY	FEATURE	CENTAUR	REFUTED	HEAVIES

LEAVEGO	LEEWARD	AFRICAN	AGILITY	THEBODY	CHIDING
HEAVEHO	LEGWORK	AFFIXED	EGALITE	SHEBEEN	SHADING
GERVAIS	NETWORK	AFFIXES	UGANDAN	THEBIGE	THEDISH
VERVAIN	SEAWARD	OFFICER	AGONIES	CHABLIS	RHODIUM
HEAVILY	SEAWASP	OFFICES	EGGNOGS	THEBELL	KHEDIVE
SERVILE	PEEWITS	AFFIRMS	AGONISE	THEBILL	SHADOWS
WEEVILS	NEWWAVE	OFAKIND	AGNOMEN	SHEBANG	SHADOWY
DELVING	BETWIXT	OFFLOAD	IGNORED	THEBLOB	CHEETAH
FERVENT	NEWYEAR	AFFLECK	IGNORES	RHUBARB	SHIELDS
HEAVENS	RECYCLE	AFFLICT	IGNOBLE	CHOCTAW	THREADS
HEAVING	BELYING	UFOLOGY	IGNOBLY	CHOCICE	CHEERED
LEAVENS	DEFYING	OFFLINE	AGROUND	CHECHEN	CHEESES
LEAVING	DENYING	OFANAGE	AGUTTER	CHECKED	THIEVED
PEEVING	LEVYING	PFENNIG	EGOTRIP	CHECKER	THIEVES
REVVING	RELYING	AFFORDS	EGOTISM	CHICKEN	WHEELED
SERVANT	DEAYTON	EFFORTS	EGOTIST	CHUCKED	WHEELER
SERVING	NEWYORK	YFRONTS	AGITATE	SHICKER	WHEEZED
WEAVING	MENZIES	OFFPEAK	AGITATO	SHOCKED	WHEEZES
BEAVERS	BENZENE	OFFROAD	IGGYPOP	SHOCKER	WHOEVER
PERVERT	BENZINE	AFFRONT	PHRASAL	SHUCKED	THEEDGE
SERVERS	SEIZING	AFARCRY	CHEAPEN	THICKEN	CHEERIO
SERVERY	TENZING	AFFRAYS	CHEAPER	THICKER	PHOENIX
WEAVERS	GEEZERS	OFFSIDE	CHEATED	THICKET	WHEELIE
DERVISH	SEIZURE	OFFSPIN	CHEATER	WHACKED	CHIEFLY
PEEVISH	EFFACED	EFFUSED	PHRASES	WHICKER	WHEEDLE
VELVETY	EFFACES	EFFUSES	SHEARED	CHICAGO	SHOEING
FERVOUR	AFFABLE	IGUANAS	SHEARER	CHECKIN	PHAETON
NERVOUS	AFFABLY	EGGCUPS	SHEAVES	CHUCKLE	SHOEBOX
SERVEUP	AFFAIRE	HGWELLS	WHEATEN	SHACKLE	THIERRY
FENWICK	AFFAIRS	OGREISH	SHEATHE	THICKLY	THREATS
KESWICK	OFFBEAM	IGNEOUS	CHEAPIE	CHICANE	CHEERUP
LERWICK	OFFBEAT	EGGFLIP	THWACKS	CHICANO	CHUFFED
BETWEEN	OFFENCE	EGGHEAD	CHEAPLY	THECROW	SHAFFER
SEAWEED	EFFENDI	IGNITED	WHYALLA	CHICORY	SHIFTED
GEEWHIZ	OFFENDS	IGNITES	AHEADOF	CHECKUP	SHIFTER
SEAWALL	OFFERED	AGRIPPA	THEATRE	CHEDDAR	SHUFFLE
DERWENT	OFFERER	AGAINST	SHIATSU	THEDEAD	CHAFING
REDWINE	AFFECTS	UGLIEST	CHIANTI	SHADIER	THEFONZ
REDWING	EFFECTS	EGOISTS	THWAITE	SHUDDER	CHIFFON
REDWOOD	AFGHANI	AGAKHAN	THWARTS	THUDDED	THEFIRM
EELWORM	AFGHANS	AGILELY	PHVALUE	SHADILY	BHAGWAN
KEYWORD	OFFHAND	AGELESS	PHOBIAS	THEDELL	CHUGGED

THUGGEE	SHAKEUP	CHIMEIN	THINNED	THRONGS	WHEREAS
THEGIFT	CHILEAN	KHAMSIN	THINNER	THROUGH	WHEREAT
CHAGRIN	PHILKAY	SHAMBLE	THUNDER	CHAOTIC	CHERUBS
CHEGWIN	SHELLAC	THEMALL	WHINGED	CHRONIC	THEREBY
CHAGALL	CHALICE	THIMBLE	WHINGER	THROWIN	THEROBE
THEGAME	SHYLOCK	CHIMING	WHINGES	THEOAKS	WHEREBY
SHOGUNS	THELADY	RHYMING	PHONEIN	THROATY	THEROCK
CHIGNON	CHELSEA	SHAMANS	SHINDIG	SHOOKUP	CHARADE
THEHILL	CHILLED	SHAMING	THANDIE	CHAPMAN	CHARGED
THWHITE	CHILLER	SHAMPOO	SHANKLY	SHIPLAP	CHARGER
SHIHTZU	SHELLED	THOMSON	SHINGLE	CHAPLET	CHARGES
CHAINED	SHELLEY	CHAMBRE	SHINGLY	CHAPPED	CHARLES
CHAIRED	SHELTER	CHIMERA	PHONEME	CHAPTER	CHARLEY
CHOICES	SHELVED	CHIMERS	PHONING	CHIPPED	CHARMED
SHRIKES	SHELVES	CHEMISE	SHINING	CHIPPER	CHARMER
SHRINES	PHILBIN	CHEMIST	WHINING	CHOPPED	CHARRED
SHRIVEL	PHILLIP	THEMASK	CHANDON	CHOPPER	CHARTER
SHRIVEN	PHYLLIS	RHOMBUS	CHANSON	SHEPPEY	CHIRPED
SHRIVER	SHELTIE	CHINWAG	CHINOOK	SHIPPED	CHURNED
SHRIVES	THELUMP	DHANSAK	OHANLON	SHIPPER	SHARPEI
THRIVED	PHALANX	SHINPAD	PHANTOM	SHOPPED	SHARPEN
THRIVES	WHALING	PHONICS	SHANNON	SHOPPER	SHARPER
SHEIKHS	WHILING	RHONDDA	BHANGRA	WHIPPED	SHERBET
SHRIEKS	SHALLOT	CHANCED	SHINERS	WHIPPET	SHIRKED
SHRINKS	SHALLOW	CHANCEL	WHINERS	WHOPPER	SHIRKER
SHRILLY	SHELDON	CHANCER	CHINESE	CHAPLIN	SHIRLEY
THRILLS	SHILTON	CHANCES	SHYNESS	CHAPPIE	SHORTEN
SHRIMPS	CHOLERA	CHANGED	RHENIUM	CHAPELS	SHORTER
CHRISSY	PHILTRE	CHANGES	THINKUP	SHAPELY	THURBER
CHRISTY	WHALERS	CHANNEL	CHINTZY	SHAPING	WHIRLED
THEISTS	CHALETS	CHANTED	THEOVAL	SHAPIRO	WHIRRED
THRIFTY	CHAMBER	CHANTER	SHROUDS	SHEPARD	SHERIFF
CHOISYA	CHAMFER	CHUNNEL	CHOOSES	CHAPATI	CHARLIE
THEJERK	CHIMNEY	CHUNTER	PHLOXES	SHAPEUP	CHERVIL
SHAKILY	CHOMPED	SHANNEN	SHOOTER	CHEQUER	GHERKIN
SHEKELS	SHIMMER	SHINBET	THEOMEN	CHEQUES	SHARDIK
CHOKING	THUMBED	SHINIER	THEOREM	PHARLAP	SHERRIN
SHAKING	THUMPED	SHUNNED	THRONES	SHERGAR	THEREIN
CHEKHOV	THUMPER	SHUNTED	THROWER	SHERMAN	THYROID
CHOKERS	WHIMPER	SHUNTER	WHOOPED	THERMAE	WHEREIN
SHAKIRA	THIMPHU	THANKED	WHOOPEE	THERMAL	CHARILY
THEKISS	CHAMOIS	THINKER	WHOOPER	THURMAN	CHORALE

CHORTLE	THISTLY	CHAUCER	DILATED	DIABOLO	FISCHER
SHARPLY	WHISTLE	SHOUTED	DILATES	PIEBALD	HITCHED
SHORTLY	CHASING	CHOUGHS	MINARET	PINBALL	HITCHES
THIRDLY	PHYSIOS	THOUGHT	MIRAGES	PITBULL	KITCHEN
CHARING	CHASERS	THRUSTS	PILATES	TIMBALE	MISCUED
PHARYNX	THESEUS	ZHIVAGO	PIRATED	BIGBAND	MISCUES
SHARING	THESTUD	SHOVELS	PIRATES	BIGBANG	PINCHED
SHORING	CHATEAU	SHAVING	TIRADES	DISBAND	PINCHES
THERING	CHATHAM	SHOVING	GIRAFFE	FIBBING	PITCHED
CHARIOT	WHITLAM	CHEVIOT	HIDALGO	GIBBONS	PITCHER
CHEROOT	WHITMAN	CHEVRON	HITACHI	RIBBING	PITCHES
PHARAOH	THETUBE	SHAVERS	PIRANHA	RIBBONS	WINCHED
SHARRON	CHATTED	SHIVERS	DICANIO	DIBBERS	WINCHES
THERMOS	CHATTEL	SHIVERY	RITALIN	FIBBERS	WITCHES
THORSON	CHATTER	SHOWMAN	TILAPIA	FILBERT	RIBCAGE
WHARTON	CHUTNEY	CHOWDER	TITANIA	GILBERT	BISCUIT
THERAPY	SHATNER	SHAWNEE	TITANIC	KILBURN	CIRCUIT
CHERISH	SHATTER	SHOWMEN	VISAVIS	LISBURN	PITCHIN
THERESA	SHUTTER	SHOWOFF	VITAMIN	MILBURN	RITCHIE
THEROSE	THITHER	SHOWBIZ	HIJACKS	TILBURY	TIECLIP
CHARITY	WHETHER	SHOWILY	DISABLE	AIRBASE	LINCOLN
THIRSTY	WHETTED	CHEWING	FINAGLE	BIGBITE	PICCOLO
CHIRRUP	WHITHER	SHOWING	FINALLY	HIPBATH	SITCOMS
THEROUX	WHITLEY	THAWING	HINAULT	KIBBUTZ	CICCONE
CHORIZO	WHITNEY	SHOWERS	MIRACLE	TITBITS	FIRCONE
OHMSLAW	WHATSIT	SHOWERY	VITALLY	GIBBOUS	HIRCINE
PHYSICS	SHUTTLE	THAWOUT	DISARMS	RIMBAUD	MINCING
CHASTEN	WHATELY	THEYSAY	DISAVOW	PISCEAN	MIOCENE
CHESNEY	WHITTLE	WHIZZED	MIRADOR	ZIPCODE	OILCANS
CHESTER	RHYTHMS	WHIZZER	PICADOR	AIRCREW	PISCINE
SHYSTER	PHOTONS	WHIZZES	BIZARRE	AITCHES	VINCENT
WHISKED	WHITENS	RHIZOME	HILAIRE	BIRCHES	WINCING
WHISKER	WHITING	CICADAS	RIVALRY	BITCHES	HICCUPS
WHISKEY	WHATFOR	PITAPAT	SINATRA	CIRCLED	DISCARD
WHISPER	WHATNOT	FINANCE	PICASSO	CIRCLES	DISCERN
WHOSWHO	WHITLOW	LIZARDS	CIMABUE	CIRCLET	DISCORD
CHASSIS	WHITEST	MIRANDA	PIRAEUS	DITCHED	MINCERS
THESPIS	SHOTGUN	PICARDY	BIVALVE	DITCHES	PINCERS
CHISELS	SHOTPUT	RICARDO	TIEBACK	FILCHED	RIPCORD
GHASTLY	SHUTOUT	VIVALDI	WISBECH	FILCHER	SINCERE
GHOSTLY	WHITSUN	WIZARDS	NIBBLED	FILCHES	VISCERA
THISTLE	SHUTEYE	CITADEL	NIBBLES	FINCHES	DIECAST

DIOCESE	DISDAIN	BIPEDAL	KINETIC	CILENTO	TIFFANY
DISCUSS	JIMDALE	CINEMAS	LIBERIA	DIGESTS	AIRFLOW
MISCAST	WINDILY	FIREMAN	LIMEPIT	DINETTE	BIGFOOT
VISCOSE	DIADEMS	GIVEEAR	LIVEAID	DIRECTS	FIEFDOM
SINCITY	DIDDUMS	GIVEWAY	LIVEDIN	DIVERTS	DIFFERS
ZINCITE	BIDDING	HIRECAR	MIXEDIN	DIVESTS	LINFORD
LINCTUS	BINDING	LIBERAL	NIGERIA	LIBERTY	MISFIRE
MITCHUM	FINDING	LIKEMAD	NINEPIN	MINETTE	MITFORD
VISCOUS	GILDING	LINEMAN	SIBERIA	PIMENTO	PILFERS
BIGDEAL	KIDDING	LITERAL	SILESIA	PIPETTE	TITFERS
BIRDMAN	MINDING	MINERAL	SINEDIE	DINEOUT	BIGFISH
LINDSAY	RIDDING	PIKEMAN	FIREFLY	FIREBUG	DIFFUSE
MISDEAL	SIDDONS	SIDECAR	FIXEDLY	FIREDUP	MISFITS
MISDIAL	WILDING	TIBETAN	GISELLE	GIVEOUT	BINGHAM
WILDCAT	WINDING	TIDEWAY	MISERLY	HIDEOUS	DIAGRAM
WINDBAG	AIRDROP	TIMELAG	NIGELLA	HIDEOUT	DINGBAT
VIADUCT	WINDSOR	VINEGAR	VIYELLA	HIREOUT	GINGHAM
BIRDIES	BIDDERS	WINEBAR	DILEMMA	LINEDUP	KINGRAT
DIDDLED	BINDERS	WIRETAP	FIREANT	LINEOUT	LINGUAL
DIDDLER	CINDERS	LICENCE	GIVERNY	MIXEDUP	RINGWAY
DIDDLES	GIRDERS	SILENCE	PIGEONS	PINENUT	VIRGOAN
FIDDLED	HINDERS	LIMEADE	AILERON	PINETUM	BIGGLES
FIDDLER	KILDARE	FIREMEN	BIBELOT	PITEOUS	CIGGIES
FIDDLES	MINDERS	LIKENED	DIDEROT	SIZEDUP	DINGIER
GIDDIER	WINDERS	LINEKER	FIREBOX	TIMEOUT	DINGOES
GIRDLES	KINDEST	NINEVEH	FIREDOG	TIREOUT	GIGGLED
HINDLEG	MILDEST	PIEEYED	SIMENON	WINEGUM	GIGGLER
KIDDIES	WILDEST	PIKELET	TIMECOP	WIPEOUT	GIGGLES
KINDLED	YIDDISH	RIVETED	VICEROY	WISEGUY	JIGGLED
KINDLES	DIEDOUT	RIVETER	WIDEBOY	MINERVA	JIGGLES
KINDRED	FINDOUT	VIDEOED	WINEBOX	RIFFLED	JINGLED
MIDDLEC	GIDDYUP	WIDENED	BIGEARS	RIFFLER	JINGLES
MIDDLES	MINDFUL	WIZENED	FINEART	RIFFLES	MINGLED
MILDRED	OILDRUM	XIMENES	FIREARM	WILFRED	MINGLES
MINDSET	DIEDOWN	HIVEOFF	SIDEARM	WINFREY	NIGGLED
MISDEED	LIEDOWN	TIMEOFF	BIGEASY	MILFOIL	NIGGLES
RIDDLED	LIZDAWN	DIVERGE	DISEASE	TINFOIL	PIGGIES
RIDDLER	MILDEWY	LINEAGE	DIVERSE	WILFRID	RINGLET
RIDDLES	PINDOWN	MILEAGE	FINESSE	PINFOLD	SINGLED
TIDDLER	SITDOWN	FIDELIO	LICENSE	PITFALL	SINGLES
WINDIER	TIEDOWN	JIMEOIN	BIRETTA	BIFFING	SINGLET
DIEDOFF	WINDOWS	KINESIS	BISECTS	MIFFING	TINGLED

TINGLES	KINGCUP	SIPHONS	AIRINGS	BIGJAKE	RISKING
WIGGLED	RINGOUT	WISHING	FILINGS	JIMJAMS	SICKENS
WIGGLES	WINGNUT	RIGHTON	RIDINGS	LINKMAN	SINKING
RINGOFF	AIRHEAD	BISHOPS	SIDINGS	MILKBAR	SISKINS
KINGPIN	BIGHEAD	BIGHORN	TIDINGS	MILKMAN	TICKING
PILGRIM	HIGHDAY	CIPHERS	VIKINGS	RICKMAN	WINKING
PINGUID	HIGHHAT	DIEHARD	BIKINIS	SICKBAY	DICKSON
RINGGIT	HIGHWAY	DITHERS	LIVINIA	SICKPAY	HICKSON
GINGOLD	MISHEAR	DITHERY	MILITIA	MISKICK	MILKSOP
BIGGAME	PINHEAD	FISHERY	FINICKY	DINKYDI	WICKLOW
BIGGINS	PITHEAD	RICHARD	CIVILLY	LINKMEN	BICKERS
BIGGUNS	RICHMAL	WITHERS	LICITLY	MILKMEN	HICKORY
DIGGING	BISHKEK	ZITHERS	RIGIDLY	PICKLED	KICKERS
GIGGING	FIGHTER	HIGHEST	RISIBLE	PICKLER	SINKERS
HIGGINS	FISHNET	RICHEST	TIMIDLY	PICKLES	TICKERS
JIGGING	HIGHTEA	SIKHISM	VISIBLE	PINKIES	TINKERS
MINGING	LIGHTED	WICHITA	VISIBLY	RISKIER	VICKERY
RIGGING	LIGHTEN	DISHOUT	VIVIDLY	SICKBED	AIRKISS
RINGING	LIGHTER	LIGHTUP	BIRIANI	SICKLES	PINKISH
SINGING	MICHAEL	LITHIUM	FINIANS	TICKLED	PICKETS
WIGGING	RICHTER	MILHOUS	MINIONS	TICKLES	PICKETT
KINGDOM	RIGHTED	WISHFUL	PINIONS	TINKLED	PINKETT
KINGZOG	SIGHTED	WITHOUT	RIPIENO	TINKLES	RICKETS
DIGGERS	TIGHTEN	FISHEYE	VISIONS	WINKLER	RICKETY
FINGERS	TIGHTER	DIGITAL	DIDICOI	WINKLES	TICKETS
GINGERY	EIGHTHS	MINIBAR	LIAISON	KICKOFF	WICKETS
LINGERS	MIKHAIL	MINICAB	MIDIRON	TICKOFF	KICKOUT
NIAGARA	NIGHTIE	MINICAM	PIGIRON	LINKAGE	MILKRUN
NIGGARD	AIRHOLE	MINIMAL	SILICON	PINKGIN	PICKOUT
PIGGERY	LIGHTLY	SIMILAR	VISITOR	NICKELS	PICKAXE
RIGGERS	NICHOLS	CITIZEN	MIMICRY	DICKENS	FIGLEAF
RINGERS	NIGHTLY	DIVIDED	RIVIERA	FIRKINS	GILLIAM
SINGERS	PINHOLE	DIVIDER	AIRIEST	JINKING	GILLIAN
WINGERS	PITHILY	DIVIDES	TIDIEST	KICKING	LILLIAN
BIGGEST	RIGHTLY	DIVINER	TINIEST	KINKING	MISLEAD
DISGUST	TIGHTLY	KIKIDEE	WILIEST	LICKING	WILLHAY
PIGGISH	WILHELM	LIAISED	SINITTA	LINKING	WILLIAM
FIDGETS	HITHOME	LIAISES	BILIOUS	MILKING	RIOLOBO
FIDGETY	DIAHANN	LIMITED	MINIBUS	NICKING	AIRLOCK
MIDGETS	FISHING	MINIVER	MINIMUM	PICKING	DIALECT
PIGGOTT	LICHENS	SIMILES	PITIFUL	PINKING	DIPLOCK
WIDGETS	SIGHING	VISITED	VICIOUS	RIFKIND	HILLOCK

NIBLICK	SIBLING	WILLOWY	PINNIES	PIVOTAL	TIPPLER
PILLOCK	SIDLING	MISLAYS	PIONEER	DIVORCE	TIPPLES
PIMLICO	TILLING	DIMMOCK	DIGNIFY	MINORCA	WIMPLES
DIALLED	VINLAND	GIMMICK	SIGNIFY	SIROCCO	ZIPPIER
DIALLER	VIOLENT	TITMICE	DIRNDLS	BIGOTED	DISPELS
FIELDED	VIOLINS	FILMSET	PIANOLA	DISOBEY	TIEPOLO
FIELDER	VIOLONE	AIRMAIL	SIGNALS	LITOTES	AIRPUMP
FILLIES	WILLING	AIRMILE	BINNING	MIAOWED	DIPPING
GIBLUES	BILLION	AILMENT	PINNING	PILOTED	KIPPING
GILLIES	HILLTOP	DIAMOND	SIGNING	PIVOTED	LIMPING
KIELDER	KILLJOY	DIMMING	SINNING	SIDOWEN	LISPING
KILLEEN	MILLION	FIGMENT	WINNING	WIDOWED	NIPPING
NIELSEN	PILLBOX	FILMING	KIDNAPS	WIDOWER	PITPONY
SILLIER	PILLION	FITMENT	DIANDRA	BINOCHE	RIPPING
WIELDED	ZILLION	PIGMENT	DINNERS	TIMOTHY	SIPPING
WILLIES	FILLIPS	SIEMENS	SIGNORA	NICOSIA	TIMPANI
YIELDED	FILLERS	SIGMUND	SINNERS	DISOWNS	TIPPING
AIRLIFT	HILLARY	SIMMONS	WINNERS	LIVORNO	ZIPPING
BIOLOGY	KILLERS	TIMMINS	DIMNESS	KILOTON	PITPROP
PILLAGE	MILLERS	TINMINE	FINNISH	KIMONOS	SIMPLON
TILLAGE	PILLARS	LISMORE	FITNESS	BIGOTRY	SIMPSON
VILLAGE	PILLORY	SIMMERS	LIONESS	RIGOURS	AIRPORT
MILLAIS	TILLERS	WIDMARK	LIONISE	RICOTTA	BITPART
MISLAID	TITLARK	DIMMEST	PIANIST	RIDOTTO	DIAPERS
SIRLOIN	AIMLESS	DISMISS	WITNESS	RIPOSTE	DIOPTRE
VILLAIN	AIRLESS	FIRMEST	ZIONISM	RISOTTO	DIPPERS
VILLEIN	GIRLISH	SIAMESE	ZIONIST	LINOCUT	DISPORT
DISLIKE	HITLIST	TITMUSS	DIGNITY	MINOGUE	KIPPERS
DIPLOMA	RIMLESS	BISMUTH	LIGNITE	PIROGUE	NIPPERS
OILLAMP	VIOLIST	FILMFUN	LINNETS	AIRPLAY	SIMPERS
AIRLINE	WITLESS	DISMAYS	PINNATE	DISPLAY	TIPPERS
BILLING	BILLETS	KINNEAR	SIGNETS	NITPICK	ZIPPERS
BIPLANE	FILLETS	MIANDAD	LIONCUB	SIXPACK	DISPOSE
FILLING	GIBLETS	ZINNIAS	VILNIUS	DIMPLED	WIMPISH
FINLAND	PIGLETS	BIONICS	MINNOWS	DIMPLES	DISPUTE
KILLING	VIOLATE	KINNOCK	WINNOWS	HIPPIES	LIMPETS
KIPLING	VIOLETS	PICNICS	KIDNEYS	PIMPLED	TIPPETT
MIDLAND	GIELGUD	PINNACE	BIFOCAL	PIMPLES	DIURNAL
MILLAND	BILLOWS	FIANCEE	BIVOUAC	RIPPLED	LIPREAD
MILLING	BILLOWY	FIANCES	FILOFAX	RIPPLES	MISREAD
PIGLING	PILLOWS	FIENNES	NICOBAR	SIMPLER	SIERRAS
RIFLING	WILLOWS	NINNIES	NICOLAS	TIPPLED	DISROBE

MICROBE	LINSEED	MISSIVE	VICTIMS	JITTERY	PIQUING
TIMRICE	MINSTER	JIGSAWS	DIETING	KINTYRE	TIJUANA
CITROEN	OILSEED	GINTRAP	DISTANT	LITTERS	MIQUITA
DIARIES	TIPSIER	MISTRAL	DISTEND	MIXTURE	SITUATE
PIERCED	TIPSTER	PITTMAN	FITTING	PICTURE	LIQUEUR
PIERCES	TISSUES	VIETNAM	HINTING	RIOTERS	SINUOUS
MIDRIFF	WINSLET	VIRTUAL	HITTING	SIFTERS	RIGVEDA
VITRIFY	KITSCHY	BIOTECH	JILTING	SISTERS	CIVVIES
OILRIGS	AIRSHIP	DIPTYCH	KITTENS	SITTERS	NIRVANA
AIRRAID	KINSHIP	RIOTACT	KITTING	TINTERN	SIEVERT
GIORGIO	KIRSTIE	TINTACK	LIFTING	TITTERS	SILVERA
FIGROLL	MIDSHIP	PINTADO	LISTENS	VICTORS	SILVERS
MISRULE	OILSKIN	RIPTIDE	LISTING	VICTORY	SILVERY
DIORAMA	PIGSKIN	AINTREE	MITTENS	WINTERS	MIDWICH
CITRONS	FIRSTLY	DIRTIED	PISTONS	WITTERS	MIDWEEK
MIGRANT	HIMSELF	DIRTIER	RIOTING	FITTEST	MIDWIFE
VIBRANT	MISSALS	DITTIES	SIFTING	DICTATE	EISWEIN
PIERROT	MISSILE	FIFTEEN	SILTING	HITTITE	AIRWOLF
VITRIOL	RISSOLE	FIFTIES	SISTINE	FIATLUX	OILWELL
DISRUPT	TIPSILY	MISTIER	SITTING	FISTFUL	SITWELL
LIBRARY	WINSOME	NIFTIER	TILTING	RIOTOUS	WIGWAMS
MIRRORS	DISSENT	SIXTEEN	TINTING	WISTFUL	VIEWING
DIARIST	GINSENG	TIPTOED	WILTING	TITULAR	TINWARE
DIGRESS	HISSING	TIPTOES	BISTROS	LIQUIDS	VIEWERS
TIGRESS	KISSING	VINTNER	DICTION	BITUMEN	MIDWEST
MIGRATE	LIPSYNC	VIRTUES	FICTION	DILUTED	DIMWITS
NITRATE	MISSING	WITTIER	MISTOOK	DILUTES	NITWITS
VIBRATE	PINSENT	DISTAFF	MISTYPE	DISUSED	AIRWAVE
VIBRATO	RINSING	LIFTOFF	BITTERN	FIGURED	AIRWAYS
FIBROUS	SISSONS	VINTAGE	BITTERS	FIGURES	DIOXIDE
LIBRIUM	BIGSHOT	PIGTAIL	CISTERN	MINUTED	LILYPAD
NITROUS	FISSION	PINTAIL	CITTERN	MINUTES	TINYTIM
KINSMAN	MISSION	MISTAKE	DIETARY	RIVULET	BICYCLE
PIGSEAR	NILSSON	DISTILS	DIETERS	SINUSES	PITYING
RIKSDAG	PITSTOP	LINTELS	DISTORT	VIRUSES	TIDYING
SIESTAS	WINSLOW	PISTOLS	DISTURB	LIQUEFY	TIDYSUM
AIRSICK	WINSTON	VISTULA	FILTERS	DIVULGE	PIAZZAS
DISSECT	FISSURE	WITTILY	FITTERS	LITURGY	FIZZIER
AIRSIDE	PIASTRE	AIRTIME	FIXTURE	LIGURIA	SIZZLED
AINSLEY	HIRSUTE	BIGTIME	HISTORY	PIOUSLY	SIZZLER
KINSMEN	FIRSTUP	MISTIME	HITTERS	RITUALS	SIZZLES
KIRSTEN	MISSOUT	TIMTAMS	JITTERS	PIQUANT	ZIGZAGS

DIZZILY	SKIPPED	ALFALFA	CLUCKED	ILLEGAL	FLAGDAY
CINZANO	SKIPPER	ALBANIA	ELECTED	ALLENBY	ALIGNED
FIZZING	SKIPTON	ALKALIS	FLICKED	FLUENCY	BLAGGER
FITZROY	SKIRTED	FLEAPIT	FLICKER	ALLENDE	BLOGGER
GIZZARD	SKITTER	BLEAKLY	GLACIER	ALREADY	CLOGGED
PIZZAZZ	SKETCHY	CLEARLY	PLUCKED	ALLEGED	ELEGIES
EJECTED	SKITTLE	PLIABLE	SLACKEN	ALLEGES	FLAGGED
AJACCIO	SKATING	ELEANOR	SLACKER	ALTERED	FLOGGED
EJECTOR	SKATERS	GLEASON	SLICKER	BLEEPED	PLAGUED
SJAMBOK	NKRUMAH	CLEANSE	CLOCKIN	BLEEPER	PLAGUES
UKRAINE	SKIVING	CLEANUP	FLACCID	FLEECED	PLUGGED
IKEBANA	SKIVERS	CLEARUP	SLACKLY	FLEECES	SLOGGED
AKABUSI	SKEWERS	ALGARVE	SLICKLY	KLEENEX	SLOGGER
SKYBLUE	SKYWARD	CLUBCAR	PLACING	SLEEKER	SLUGGER
SKIDDAW	ALCAZAR	CLUBMAN	SLICING	SLEEPER	OLDGOLD
SKIDPAN	ALMANAC	OLDBEAN	CLACTON	SLEEVES	ELEGANT
SKIDDED	ALPACAS	ALIBABA	ELECTOR	ALLERGY	FLAGONS
SKIDLID	FLYAWAY	BLABBED	ELECTRA	ALGERIA	SLOGANS
SKIDROW	PLIANCY	BLABBER	PLACARD	ALGESIA	OLDGIRL
SKYDIVE	ALIASES	BLUBBER	PLECTRA	BLUEFIN	ELEGISE
SKEETER	ALKANET	CLOBBER	SLICERS	BLUETIT	ELEGIST
SKIFFLE	ALLAYED	CLUBBED	GLUCOSE	SLEEPIN	ALDGATE
SKYJACK	BLEAKER	CLUBBER	ELICITS	SLOEGIN	ALIGHTS
SKIJUMP	BLEATED	FLUBBER	PLACATE	BLUESKY	BLIGHTS
SKILLED	BLOATED	ILLBRED	SLICEUP	ELDERLY	BLIGHTY
SKILLET	BLOATER	SLOBBER	BLADDER	FLOELLA	FLIGHTS
SKULKED	CLEANED	SLUBBED	BLUDGER	FLEEING	FLIGHTY
SKILIFT	CLEANER	GLOBULE	FLEDGED	ALGEBRA	SLIGHTS
UKULELE	CLEARED	OLDBILL	FLODDEN	ALLEGRA	ALLHEAL
SKYLINE	CLEARER	ALABAMA	GLADDEN	ALLEGRO	ELPHICK
SKELTON	CLEAVER	GLACIAL	PLEDGED	ALBERTA	FLYHIGH
SKYLARK	CLEAVES	PLACEBO	PLEDGES	ALDENTE	BLAHNIK
SKILFUL	CLOAKED	PLACIDO	PLODDED	CLIENTS	FLYHALF
SKIMMED	FLOATED	BLACKED	PLODDER	CLUEDUP	ALCHEMY
SKIMMER	GLEAMED	BLACKEN	SLEDGES	GLEEFUL	ALTHING
SKIMPED	GLEANED	BLACKER	ALADDIN	BLUFFED	OLDHAND
SKIMASK	GLEANER	BLOCKED	ELUDING	BLUFFER	ALTHORP
OKONEDO	GLOATED	CLACKED	GLIDING	FLUFFED	CLAIMED
SKINNED	PLEADED	CLICHED	SLIDING	BLOFELD	CLAIMER
SKINNER	PLEASED	CLICHES	GLIDERS	ILLFAME	FLAILED
SKINFUL	PLEASES	CLICKED	GLADEYE	CLIFTON	PLAINER
OKINAWA	PLEATED	CLOCHES	GLUEEAR	ELEGIAC	SLUICES

SLEIGHS	OLYMPIC	FLANNEL	ALMONER	CLIPART	BLASTER
SLEIGHT	ALIMONY	FLUNKED	BLOOMED	ELOPERS	BLESSED
ILLICIT	BLAMING	FLUNKEY	BLOOMER	FLYPAST	BLESSES
PLAINLY	CLEMENS	GLANCED	BLOOPER	FLYPOST	BLISTER
ALBINOS	CLEMENT	GLANCES	CLOONEY	ELSPETH	BLUSHED
ALLISON	ELEMENT	GLINTED	ELBOWED	SLOPOUT	BLUSHER
ELLISON	FLAMING	PLANNED	FLOODED	CLIQUES	BLUSHES
ALGIERS	FLEMING	PLANNER	FLOORED	CLIQUEY	BLUSTER
ELLIPSE	ULLMANN	PLANTED	FLYOVER	PLAQUES	CLASHED
ELLIOTT	FLUMMOX	PLANTER	ALLOFME	ALDRICH	CLASHES
SLAINTE	BLEMISH	PLONKER	ALCOHOL	CLARICE	CLASPED
ILIKEIT	FLEMISH	PLUNDER	ALCOPOP	CLERICS	CLASSED
FLAKING	GLIMPSE	PLUNGED	ALMONRY	ELGRECO	CLASSES
FLUKING	CLIMATE	PLUNGER	ALFONSO	ALFREDO	CLUSTER
SLAKING	ALUMNUS	PLUNGES	CLAPHAM	FLORIDA	FLASHED
ELEKTRA	CLAMOUR	SLANDER	SLIPWAY	ALARMED	FLASHER
FLYLEAF	GLAMOUR	SLANTED	BLIPPED	ALERTED	FLASHES
ULULATE	OLYMPUS	SLENDER	CLAPPED	BLARNEY	FLUSHED
ALUMNAE	CLANNAD	BLANCHE	CLAPPER	BLURRED	FLUSHES
ALAMODE	CLINICS	PLINTHS	CLIPPED	BLURTED	FLUSTER
CLAMBER	OLDNICK	BLONDIE	CLIPPER	FLIRTED	GLASSES
CLAMPED	BLANDER	BLONDIN	CLOPPED	SLURPED	GLISTEN
CLAMPER	BLANKET	BLANDLY	ELAPSED	SLURRED	OLDSHEP
CLIMBED	BLENDED	BLANKLY	ELAPSES	CLARIFY	OLDSTER
CLIMBER	BLENDER	BLINDLY	FLAPPED	GLORIFY	PLASTER
CLUMPED	BLINDED	BLUNTLY	FLAPPER	ALERTLY	SLASHED
GLIMMER	BLINDER	CLONING	FLIPPED	BLARING	SLASHES
PLUMBED	BLINKED	PLANING	FLIPPER	FLARING	SLOSHED
PLUMBER	BLINKER	CLINTON	FLOPPED	FLORINS	ULYSSES
PLUMMER	BLONDES	GLENCOE	PLOPPED	GLARING	CLASSIC
PLUMMET	BLUNDER	KLINGON	SLAPPED	BLERIOT	CLOSEIN
SLAMMED	CLANGED	LLANERO	SLIPPED	CLARION	ELASTIC
SLAMMER	CLANGER	PLENARY	SLIPPER	FLORIST	PLASTIC
SLIMIER	CLANKED	ILLNESS	SLOPPED	OLOROSO	CLOSELY
SLIMMED	CLINKED	SLYNESS	CLIPPIE	CLARITY	FLYSOLO
SLIMMER	CLINKER	PLANETS	SLEPTIN	FLORETS	CLOSING
SLUMBER	CLONKED	ALSORAN	ELOPING	FLAREUP	BLOSSOM
SLUMPED	CLONMEL	SLIOTAR	SLIPONS	ALASKAN	ELISION
PLUMAGE	CLUNKED	ALMONDS	SLOPING	ELYSIAN	GLASGOW
ALEMBIC	CLUNKER	ALCOVES	CLAPTON	FLYSWAT	GLOSSOP
OLDMAID	FLANGED	ALLOVER	FLIPTOP	CLOSEBY	CLOSURE
OLYMPIA	FLANKER	ALLOWED	SLIPUPS	BLASTED	CLOSEST

CLOSETS	PLATINI	SLAVERY	PLAYBOY	IMMENSE	EMULATE
ALYSSUM	ELATION	SLIVERS	PLAYGOD	IMMERSE	EMPLOYS
CLOSEUP	FLATTOP	SLAVISH	PLAYERS	AMNESTY	AMENDED
ELYSIUM	GLUTTON	ELEVATE	SLAYERS	UMBERTO	EMANUEL
ELUSIVE	PLATOON	FLAVOUR	PLAYFUL	IMPETUS	EMENDED
FLATCAP	PLATERS	ALDWYCH	GLAZIER	EMIGRES	EMINENT
FLOTSAM	SLATERS	ALNWICK	BLAZING	SMUGGLE	AMONGST
FLYTRAP	ELITISM	CLOWNED	GLAZING	IMAGINE	AMENITY
PLATEAU	ELITIST	ALEWIFE	BLAZERS	IMAGERY	EMANATE
BLUTACK	BLOTOUT	BLOWFLY	IMPALED	AMPHORA	OMINOUS
BLATTER	FLATOUT	ILLWILL	IMPALER	EMPIRES	IMMORAL
BLETHER	GLUTEUS	BLOWING	IMPALES	IMBIBED	EMPOWER
BLITZED	BLETHYN	CLAWING	SMEARED	IMBIBER	IMHOTEP
BLITZEN	FLOUNCE	FLOWING	EMBARGO	IMBIBES	IMPOSED
BLOTTED	FLOUNCY	GLOWING	EMPATHY	UMPIRED	IMPOSES
BLOTTER	ALBUMEN	ILLWIND	AMHARIC	UMPIRES	SMOOCHY
CLATTER	ALLUDED	SLOWING	EMBARKS	IMPINGE	AMMONIA
CLOTHED	ALLUDES	PLYWOOD	AMIABLE	AMBIENT	EMPORIA
CLOTHES	ALLURED	BLOWDRY	AMIABLY	IMPIETY	AMPOULE
CLOTTED	ALLURES	FLOWERS	EMBALMS	IMPIOUS	IMPOUND
CLUTTER	BLOUSES	FLOWERY	IMPAIRS	OMNIBUS	IMPORTS
ELSTREE	CLAUSES	GLOWERS	EMBASSY	SMOKING	UMBRIAN
FLATLET	CLOUDED	SLOWEST	IMPASSE	SMOKERS	AMERICA
FLATTEN	CLOUTED	BLOWOUT	IMPACTS	AMALGAM	EMBRACE
FLATTER	FLOUTED	FLEXING	IMPARTS	IMPLODE	EMERGED
FLITTED	PLOUGHS	KLAXONS	IMPASTO	IMPLIED	EMERGES
FLUTTER	SLEUTHS	ELIXIRS	SMACKED	IMPLIES	IMBRUED
GLITTER	SLOUCHY	FLEXORS	SMACKER	SMALLER	IMBRUES
PLATTER	CLAUDIA	FLEXURE	SMOCKED	SMELLED	SMARTEN
PLOTTED	CLAUDIO	PLAYACT	OMICRON	SMELTED	SMARTER
PLOTTER	PLAUDIT	PLAYLET	SMIDGEN	SMELTER	SMIRKED
SLATTED	BLOUSON	PLAYPEN	SMUDGED	AMPLIFY	UMBRAGE
SLITHER	FLEURON	PLAYOFF	SMUDGES	SMILLIE	EMBROIL
SLOTTED	FLAUNTS	ILLYRIA	AMADEUS	EMBLEMS	EMERALD
BLOTCHY	PLUVIAL	ALLYING	IMPEACH	AMBLING	SMARTLY
FLATTIE	CLAVIER	CLOYING	AMMETER	IMPLANT	IMPRINT
GLOTTIS	OLIVIER	FLAYING	AMPERES	SMILING	EMBRYOS
ALLTOLD	ELEVENS	PLAYING	IMPEDED	AMBLERS	EMERSON
ALLTIME	SLAVING	SLAYING	IMPEDES	IMPLORE	OMARION
OLDTIME	SLOVENE	ALLYSON	AMNESIA	SMILERS	AMBROSE
BLATANT	PLOVERS	CLAYTON	IMPERIL	AMPLEST	AMORIST
PLATING	SLAVERS	LLEYTON	EMPEROR	AMULETS	AMOROSO

EMPRESS	ENGARDE	UNCANNY	ENTERED	INJECTS	INCHING
IMPRESS	INNARDS	UNHAPPY	INDEXED	INSECTS	ANCHORS
EMIRATE	INWARDS	ENMASSE	INDEXER	INSERTS	ANTHERS
AMOROUS	ONWARDS	ANDANTE	INDEXES	INVENTS	INSHORE
IMPROVE	ENCASED	INFANTA	INTEGER	INVERTS	ONSHORE
AMISTAD	ENCASES	INFANTS	KNEELER	INVESTS	ENTHUSE
AMASSED	ENGAGED	UNEARTH	SNEERED	ANGELUS	ONTHEUP
AMASSES	ENGAGES	ANNASUI	SNEEZED	ENDEDUP	ANCHOVY
SMASHED	ENRAGED	SNEAKUP	SNEEZES	INGENUE	INLIMBO
SMASHER	ENRAGES	ANTBEAR	INVEIGH	KNEESUP	UNWINDS
SMASHES	INHALED	ANYBODY	UNDERGO	UNNERVE	ANTIGEN
AMUSING	INHALER	INABODY	ANAEMIA	ONOFFER	ENDIVES
SMASHUP	INHALES	ENABLED	ANAEMIC	SNIFFED	ENGINES
EMITTED	INMATES	ENABLES	ANGELIC	SNIFFER	ENLIVEN
EMPTIED	INVADED	SNUBBED	ANGEVIN	SNIFTER	ENTICED
EMPTIES	INVADER	KNOBBLY	ENDEMIC	SNUFFER	ENTICES
OMITTED	INVADES	ENACTED	ENTERIC	UNIFIED	INCISED
SMITTEN	KNEADED	KNACKER	INHERIT	UNIFIES	INCISES
SMOTHER	ONPAPER	KNOCKED	INTERIM	SNAFFLE	INCITED
UMPTEEN	SNEAKED	KNOCKER	ANNEALS	SNIFFLE	INCITER
AMSTELL	SNEAKER	SNICKED	UNVEILS	SNUFFLE	INCITES
EMOTING	UNDATED	SNICKER	ANTENNA	SNUFFLY	INDICES
SMETANA	UNEATEN	SNICKET	INFERNO	KNIFING	INFIDEL
SMITING	UNFAZED	UNSCREW	INTERNS	UNIFORM	INSIDER
EMOTION	UNLACED	GNOCCHI	ENVELOP	ANAGRAM	INSIDES
AMATORY	UNLACES	INSCALE	UNKEMPT	ENIGMAS	INVITED
IMITATE	UNLADEN	KNUCKLE	ENDEARS	SNAGGED	INVITEE
AMATEUR	UNNAMED	KNOCKON	INTEARS	SNIGGER	INVITES
EMOTIVE	UNRAVEL	UNICORN	UNHEARD	SNAGGLE	UNAIDED
IMPUTED	UNTAMED	KNOCKUP	UNLEARN	SNUGGLE	UNLINED
IMPUTES	UNTAXED	ANODYNE	UNWEARY	ENDGAME	ENDINGS
AMPULLA	UNWAGED	ANODISE	INCENSE	ONAGERS	INNINGS
IMBUING	ENLARGE	KNEECAP	INTENSE	KNIGHTS	UNHINGE
IMPULSE	INKATHA	KNEEPAD	INVERSE	ANTHRAX	INSIGHT
AMOUNTS	ANTACID	INTENDS	UNLEASH	ENTHRAL	INHIBIT
BMOVIES	INHABIT	UNBENDS	ANNETTE	INCHECK	INSIPID
AMAZING	INVALID	UNDERDO	ENTENTE	ONTHEGO	UNCIVIL
AMAZONS	ONTARIO	UNREADY	INDENTS	UNCHAIN	ANFIELD
ANDAMAN	UNMASKS	ANGELES	INDEPTH	ANTHILL	ENFIELD
ENHANCE	UNPACKS	ANGERED	INFECTS	ANTHEMS	ENTITLE
INFANCY	ENTAILS	ANNEXED	INFESTS	ANTHONY	INFIELD
UNLATCH	UNMANLY	ANNEXES	INGESTS	ENCHANT	UNCIALS

ANCIENT	INFLATE	INTONED	INSPACE	INIRONS	DNOTICE
ENSIGNS	ENCLAVE	INTONER	INSPECT	INPRINT	UNSTUCK
INDIANA	ENSLAVE	INTONES	KNAPPED	INURING	ANNTODD
INDIANS	ENEMIES	INVOKED	KNAPPER	SNARING	ANOTHER
ANDIRON	ENUMBER	INVOKES	SNAPPED	SNORING	KNITTED
INAIDOF	ANIMALS	SNOOKER	SNAPPER	INERROR	KNITTER
INCISOR	ANOMALY	SNOOPED	SNIPPED	ENCRYPT	KNOTTED
INVITRO	ENAMELS	SNOOPER	SNIPPET	ENTRAPS	ONSTAGE
ANOINTS	ANEMONE	SNOOZED	INAPTLY	ENTROPY	INSTALL
ANXIETY	ANIMISM	SNOOZER	INEPTLY	UNWRAPS	ANATOMY
ENLISTS	ANIMIST	SNOOZES	SNIPING	SNORERS	ANYTIME
INDICTS	ENDMOST	UNBOWED	INSPIRE	ANDRESS	ONETIME
INSISTS	ANIMATE	UNCOVER	SNIPERS	ENGROSS	INSTANT
ANTIGUA	ANIMATO	UNLOVED	INSPATE	ENPRISE	UNITING
ANTIQUE	ANANIAS	UNMOVED	UNEQUAL	ENTRUST	UNCTION
ANXIOUS	INANELY	ENGORGE	ENTREAT	INGRESS	INSTORE
ENRIQUE	ONANDON	ANTONIA	ONTRIAL	UNCROSS	INUTERO
ENVIOUS	ENSNARE	ANTONIO	INTRUDE	UNDRESS	UNITARY
UNCLEAN	ONENESS	UNCORKS	ANGRIER	INGRATE	ANGULAR
UNCLEAR	INANITY	UNHOOKS	ENTREES	INTRUTH	ANNULAR
INFLICT	UNKNOWN	UNLOCKS	ENTRIES	UNTRUTH	INHUMAN
INPLACE	ANGOLAN	ENNOBLE	INBREED	ONEROUS	INSULAR
UNBLOCK	ENTOMBS	UNCOILS	INBRIEF	SNARLUP	INFUNDS
INCLUDE	INDOUBT	UNGODLY	ONORDER	ENGRAVE	ENDURED
ANALOGY	ENFORCE	INFORMS	ANDREWS	INCROWD	ENDURES
UNCLOGS	INFORCE	ANTOINE	SNARLED	ENDUSER	
UNALIKE	INTOUCH	INBOUND	SNORKEL	UNUSUAL	ENSURED
INFLAME	INVOICE	ONGOING	SNORTED	ANISEED	ENSURES
ANGLING	ENFOLDS	UNBOUND	SNORTER	GNASHED	INDUCED
ANILINE	INROADS	UNDOING	UNARMED	GNASHER	INDUCES
ENGLAND	UNFOLDS	UNSOUND	UNTRIED	GNASHES	INFUSED
INCLINE	UNLOADS	UNWOUND	ANARCHY	KNESSET	INFUSES
INKLING	ANDOVER	ANDORRA	ANDROID	ONESTEP	INJURED
ANGLERS	ANNOYED	INDOORS	INERTIA	UNASKED	INJURES
ANTLERS	ENCODED	ONBOARD	INGRAIN	GNOSTIC	INSURED
ANALYSE	ENCODES	ENDORSE	INTRAIN	ONASSIS	INSURER
ANALYST	ENCORES	INHOUSE	INTROIT	ONESELF	INSURES
ENCLOSE	ENDOWED	ENROUTE	ANORAKS	ANDSOON	UNTUNED
ENDLESS	ENJOYED	UNBOLTS	ANGRILY	ANISTON	ENGULFS
ENGLISH	INCOMES	UNCOUTH	INGRAMS	INASPOT	INDULGE
UNCLASP	INPOWER	INVOLVE	ENTRANT	INITIAL	ANEURIN
ANKLETS	INSOLES	ANTONYM	INFRONT	INSTEAD	INSULIN

ANOUSKA	INEXACT	SOLARIS	ROEBUCK	ROBBING	POACHES
UNLUCKY	ENZYMES	SOMALIA	FORBADE	ROBBINS	POOCHES
ANNUALS	ENVYING	CORACLE	FORBIDS	SOBBING	PORCHES
INBUILT	UNDYING	LOCALLY	BOBBIES	LOGBOOK	POUCHED
UNBUILT	UNTYING	LOVABLE	BOBBLES	LOWBROW	POUCHES
UNCURLS	SONATAS	LOYALLY	COBBLED	BOMBARD	TORCHED
UNFURLS	JOMARCH	MORALLY	COBBLER	BOMBERS	TORCHES
ENSUING	MONARCH	MOVABLE	COBBLES	COLBERT	TOUCHED
INRUINS	MOSAICS	NOTABLE	DOUBLED	HOLBORN	TOUCHER
UNFUNNY	ROMANCE	NOTABLY	DOUBLES	HOMBURG	TOUCHES
UNGUENT	TOBACCO	POTABLE	DOUBLET	LOMBARD	VOUCHED
ENQUIRE	BOGARDE	ROYALLY	DOUBTED	ROBBERS	VOUCHER
ENQUIRY	COWARDS	TONALLY	DOUBTER	ROBBERY	VOUCHES
INQUIRE	ROBARDS	TOTALLY	FOIBLES	ROSBERG	CONCEIT
INQUIRY	RONALDO	VOCALLY	GOBBLED	BOMBAST	CONCHIE
ANGUISH	TOWARDS	WOMANLY	GOBBLES	COMBUST	TOECLIP
INQUEST	DONATED	RORAIMA	HOBBIES	YOBBISH	TOSCALE
ANNUITY	DONATES	COCAINE	HOBBLED	COMBATS	COXCOMB
ENSUITE	DOWAGER	DOMAINS	HOBBLES	CORBETT	HOWCOME
INSULTS	FORAGED	HOSANNA	LOBBIES	HOBBITS	FORCING
SNIVELS	FORAGER	LOCARNO	NOBBLED	MOABITE	MODCONS
KNAVERY	FORAGES	MORAINE	NOBBLES	SORBETS	PORCINE
KNAVISH	LOCATED	ROMAINE	ROUBLES	WOMBATS	PORCINI
SNOWCAP	LOCATES	ROSANNA	WOBBLED	COMBOUT	TOUCANS
SNOWCAT	POFACED	ROXANNE	WOBBLES	COWBOYS	VOICING
SNOWMAN	ROTATED	MOGADON	WOMBLES	CONCEAL	VOLCANO
KNOWLES	ROTATES	NONAGON	ZOMBIES	TOPCOAT	CONCEPT
SNOWMEN	SOFABED	ROMANOV	COWBELL	CONCOCT	FORCEPS
SNOWPEA	VOYAGED	ROTATOR	TOMBELL	CONCEDE	TOECAPS
INKWELL	VOYAGER	SODAPOP	TOMBOLA	BOTCHED	TOPCOPY
KNOWALL	VOYAGES	CONAKRY	ZOEBALL	BOTCHER	BOXCARS
ENTWINE	GOUACHE	ROMANSH	BOBBING	BOTCHES	CONCERN
GNAWING	BORACIC	HOGARTH	BOBBINS	COACHED	CONCERT
KNOWING	BOTANIC	JOCASTA	BOMBING	COACHES	CONCORD
SNOWING	COHABIT	LOYALTY	BONBONS	CONCHES	CONCURS
KNOWHOW	HORATIO	ROYALTY	COMBINE	COUCHES	POPCORN
SNOWDON	MORAVIA	POPADUM	COMBING	MOOCHED	SORCERY
ANSWERS	NOMADIC	BONANZA	DOABUNK	MOOCHES	CONCISE
ANTWERP	POLARIS	FORBEAR	FOBBING	NOTCHED	CONCUSS
UNAWARE	ROMANIA	ROWBOAT	FOGBANK	NOTCHES	BOYCOTT
ENDWISE	ROSALIE	GOTBACK	LOBBING	POACHED	TOCCATA
UNTWIST	ROSARIO	HOGBACK	MOBBING	POACHER	JOBCLUB

CONCAVE	TOPDOGS	POWDERS	COWERED	DOYENNE	HOMERUN
COLDWAR	HOWDAHS	POWDERY	DOEEYED	GOVERNS	HOPEFUL
CORDIAL	BOUDOIR	SOLDERS	FORELEG	KOREANS	LOSEOUT
GOODDAY	CONDUIT	WONDERS	FOREMEN	SOMEONE	MOVEOUT
GOODMAN	GOODWIN	BOLDEST	FORESEE	BOLEROS	ROSEBUD
ROADMAP	LORDJIM	COLDEST	FOREVER	BOREDOM	SOBERUP
ROADTAX	NONDRIP	FONDEST	GORETEX	DONEFOR	POLEAXE
ROADWAY	BOBDOLE	GODDESS	HONEYED	HOMEBOY	JOCELYN
ROEDEAN	DOWDILY	LOUDEST	HOVERED	LOVEJOY	LORENZO
RONDEAU	GONDOLA	COLDITZ	HOWEVER	NOSEJOB	GOLFBAG
WOODMAN	HOLDALL	CORDITE	LORELEI	POKEMON	HOFFMAN
CORDOBA	MOODILY	GOLDCUP	LOWERED	ROBESON	WOLFMAN
CONDUCT	ROWDILY	HOLDOUT	MONEYED	SOMEHOW	WOLFRAM
RODDICK	WOODALL	HOODLUM	MOSEYED	TOHEROA	CONFIDE
CODDLED	WORDILY	SOLDOUT	NOTELET	TOREROS	COMFIER
CODDLES	CONDEMN	WOODCUT	POPEYED	BONEDRY	COMFREY
DOODLED	BONDING	MOLDOVA	POWERED	FOREARM	GODFREY
DOODLER	CONDONE	HOEDOWN	TOWERED	POSEURS	POUFFES
DOODLES	CORDONS	LOWDOWN	GONEOFF	BONEASH	TOFFEES
DOWDIER	FOLDING	TOPDOWN	FOREIGN	MOREISH	LOOFAHS
FONDLED	FONDANT	DOGDAYS	LOZENGE	COLETTE	FORFEIT
FONDLES	GOADING	GOLDWYN	COMEDIC	DOHERTY	NORFOLK
GOODHEW	GOLDING	GOODBYE	COTERIE	FORESTS	SOUFFLE
GOODIES	HOLDING	COLEMAN	GOBELIN	HONESTY	BOFFINS
GOODREM	HOUDINI	DONEGAL	GODETIA	LORETTA	COFFINS
MOODIER	LOADING	DONEGAN	GONERIL	MODESTY	CONFINE
NOODLES	MORDANT	FOREMAN	LOBELIA	MOLESTS	DOFFING
POODLES	NODDING	FORESAW	MORELIA	MOMENTS	GOLFING
ROADIES	SORDINO	NOSEBAG	MOVEDIN	NOVELTY	GOOFING
ROEDEER	WORDING	NOSEGAY	POLEMIC	POLENTA	LOAFING
ROWDIER	ROADHOG	NOTEPAD	ROPEDIN	POVERTY	ROOFING
SOLDIER	BORDERS	POLECAT	ROSEHIP	ROBERTA	HOTFOOT
TOADIES	CONDORS	ROSEBAY	TOTEMIC	ROBERTO	ROOFTOP
TODDIES	DODDERY	SOMEDAY	VOTEDIN	ROBERTS	BONFIRE
TODDLED	FOLDERS	SOMEWAY	MORELLO	RODENTS	COFFERS
TODDLER	GODDARD	TOTEBAG	MOSELLE	ROSEATE	COMFORT
TODDLES	HOLDERS	COGENCY	NOVELLA	ROSETTA	CONFERS
WORDIER	LOADERS	IONESCO	NOVELLI	ROSETTE	CONFIRM
HOLDOFF	MOIDORE	POTENCY	NOVELLO	ROWETTA	CONFORM
SOLDOFF	POLDARK	BODEREK	ROSELLA	BOLETUS	GOLFERS
TOLDOFF	POLDERS	COVERED	SOBERLY	COVERUP	HOOFERS
BONDAGE	PONDERS	COVETED	CODEINE	DOLEFUL	LOAFERS

LOGFIRE	ROUGHLY	COCHRAN	CONIFER	COSIEST	PORKPIE
ROMFORD	TOUGHLY	GOAHEAD	IONISED	DOPIEST	COCKILY
ROOFERS	DODGEMS	HOPHEAD	IONISER	HOLIEST	ROCKALL
TOMFORD	BODGING	HOTHEAD	MONIKER	NOSIEST	ROCKILY
WOOFERS	DODGING	POOHBAH	MOTIVES	ROSIEST	BOOKING
CONFESS	DOGGING	COWHIDE	NOMINEE	GOLIATH	COOKING
CONFUSE	FORGING	COCHLEA	NOTICED	MODISTE	CORKING
DOGFISH	FORGONE	GOTHIKA	NOTICES	SOCIETY	DOCKING
WOLFISH	GORGING	FOXHOLE	NOVICES	COPIOUS	DONKING
COMFITS	GORGONS	NOTHALF	POLICED	MODICUM	DORKING
CONFUTE	GOUGING	POTHOLE	POSITED	NOXIOUS	HOCKING
WOLFCUB	HOGGING	TOEHOLD	DOMINGO	SOLIDUS	HOOKING
CONGEAL	JOGGING	TOPHOLE	FOLIAGE	DONJUAN	HOPKINS
DOUGLAS	LODGING	COSHING	TONIGHT	DOMJOLY	HOSKINS
LONGMAN	LOGGING	COWHAND	BOLIVIA	GOUJONS	LOCKING
TOPGEAR	LOGGINS	FOXHUNT	CODICIL	CONJURE	LOOKING
BOGGLES	LONGING	NOSHING	DOMINIC	BONJOUR	MOCKING
COUGHED	TOGGING	NOTHING	HOMINID	BONJOVI	ROCKING
FOGGIER	DODGSON	BOYHOOD	POLITIC	LOCKJAW	ROOKING
GOGGLED	FORGOOD	BOBHOPE	SOLICIT	WORKBAG	SOAKING
GOGGLES	LONGBOW	BOTHERS	COLICKY	WORKMAN	SOCKING
JOGGLED	LONGHOP	COWHERD	SOYINKA	COCKADE	TONKING
JOGGLES	BODGERS	FOGHORN	GORILLA	BOOKIES	WORKING
LONGLEG	CODGERS	FORHIRE	SOLIDLY	BOOKLET	COOKSON
MOGGIES	COUGARS	GOPHERS	WOEISME	COCKIER	TOPKNOT
MONGREL	COWGIRL	MOTHERS	LOTIONS	COCKLES	WORKTOP
PODGIER	DODGERS	NOWHERE	MOTIONS	COCKNEY	TOPKAPI
ROUGHEN	FORGERS	POCHARD	NOTIONS	COOKIES	BONKERS
ROUGHER	FORGERY	POTHERB	POTIONS	HOCKNEY	CONKERS
SOGGIER	HOGGARD	SOPHISM	COPILOT	LOOKSEE	COOKERS
TOGGLES	HOGGART	SOPHIST	HORIZON	MONKEES	COOKERY
TONGUED	JOGGERS	GOSHAWK	MONITOR	PORKIES	DOCKERS
TONGUES	LODGERS	BOLIVAR	POPIDOL	ROCKIER	HOPKIRK
TOUGHEN	RODGERS	COMICAL	ROOIBOS	ROCKIES	LOCKERS
TOUGHER	LONGEST	CONICAL	COLIBRI	ROOKIES	MOCKERY
WOGGLES	DOUGHTY	HOLIDAY	COPIERS	TOLKIEN	PORKERS
LONGOFF	FORGETS	LOGICAL	HONIARA	WORKMEN	ROCKERS
LONGAGO	COUGHUP	LORIMAR	HOSIERS	TOOKOFF	ROCKERY
ROUGHIT	SORGHUM	MOHICAN	HOSIERY	CORKAGE	ROOKERY
TOUGHIE	FORGAVE	NOMINAL	MOLIERE	WORKSHY	WORKERS
HOOGHLY	FORGIVE	TOPICAL	TOPIARY	COCKPIT	YORKERS
MONGOLS	BODHRAN	BODICES	BONIEST	CONKLIN	BOOKISH

MONKISH	DOILIES	HOTLINE	JOYLESS	ZOOMING	POUNCET
YORKIST	DOLLIES	HOWLING	MOLLUSC	WOOMERA	POUNDED
BOXKITE	FOLLIES	HOYLAND	NOBLEST	FORMOSA	ROUNDED
DOCKETS	GOOLDEN	KOBLENZ	TOPLESS	GOAMISS	ROUNDEL
LOCKETS	HOLLIES	LOLLING	COLLATE	TOPMAST	ROUNDER
POCKETS	JOLLIER	LOWLAND	FOLLETT	TOPMOST	SOUNDED
ROCKETS	LOLLIES	POLLING	GOBLETS	COMMITS	SOUNDER
SOCKETS	MOULDED	POOLING	JOLLITY	COMMUTE	TOWNIES
FORKOUT	MOULDER	ROLLING	POLLUTE	ROOMFUL	WOUNDED
LOCKNUT	MOULTED	ROWLAND	TOILETS	BOSNIAN	YOUNGER
LOCKOUT	WOOLLEN	ROWLING	SOULFUL	CORNEAL	COINAGE
LOOKOUT	COOLOFF	SOILING	FOLLOWS	NOONDAY	TONNAGE
WORKOUT	LOWLIFE	TOILING	ROBLOWE	TONNEAU	CORNOIL
DONKEYS	MOLLIFY	TOLLING	VOLLEYS	HOBNOBS	COUNCIL
JOCKEYS	COLLAGE	TOOLING	HOLMOAK	CONNECT	GOINGIN
MONKEYS	COLLEGE	TOPLINE	DORMICE	CONNICK	MOONLIT
SOCKEYE	ZOOLOGY	TOWLINE	FORMICA	CORNICE	MOUNTIE
BOOLEAN	COALPIT	YOWLING	HOWMUCH	TORNADO	TOENAIL
COALMAN	COALTIT	COOLBOX	TOOMUCH	BOUNCED	ROANOKE
COALTAR	TOOLKIT	KOWLOON	COMMODE	BOUNCER	CORNELL
COBLOAF	GODLIKE	ROLLMOP	DOOMBEN	BOUNCES	JOINTLY
COELIAC	HOYLAKE	TOOLBOX	GORMLEY	BOUNDED	ROUNDLY
POLLTAX	OOHLALA	DOLLOPS	POMMIES	BOUNDER	SOUNDLY
ROULEAU	WORLDLY	LOLLOPS	ROOMIER	CORNFED	COINING
TOOLBAG	COULOMB	BOILERS	TOMMIES	COUNSEL	CONNING
TOOLBAR	FOGLAMP	BOLLARD	FORMULA	COUNTED	DONNING
WOOLFAT	TOBLAME	BOWLERS	BOOMING	COUNTER	DOWNING
WOULDBE	BOILING	COLLARS	COMMAND	FOUNDED	JOINING
COLLECT	BOWLINE	DOLLARS	COMMEND	FOUNDER	LOANING
COWLICK	BOWLING	FORLORN	COMMENT	GOUNDER	MOANING
POLLACK	CODLING	HOLLERS	COMMONS	HORNSEA	MORNING
POLLOCK	COILING	HOWLERS	COMMUNE	HOUNDED	COINBOX
POTLUCK	COLLINS	LOLLARD	DORMANT	JOINTED	CORNCOB
ROWLOCK	COOLANT	POLLARD	FOAMING	LOUNGED	COUNTON
COLLIDE	COOLING	POPLARS	FORMING	LOUNGER	JOHNDOE
COLLUDE	COWLING	POULTRY	HORMONE	LOUNGES	JOHNSON
ROULADE	FOILING	ROLLERS	HOWMANY	MOONIES	CONNERY
BOULDER	FOOLING	COOLEST	LOOMING	MOUNTED	CONNORS
COALMEN	FOULING	FOOLISH	MOOMINS	POINTED	CORNERS
COLLEEN	GOBLINS	GODLESS	NORMANS	POINTER	COUNTRY
COLLIER	GOSLING	GOULASH	ROAMING	POUNCED	FOUNDRY
COLLIES	HOLLAND	JOBLESS	TORMENT	POUNCES	JOINERS

JOINERY	MONOCLE	TORPEFY	TOPPERS	COURIER	SOURING
MOANERS	BOLOGNA	DOLPHIN	TOSPARE	COURSED	TORRENT
NOENTRY	COCOONS	LOWPAID	COMPASS	COURSER	TOURING
CORNISH	COLOGNE	POMPEII	COMPOSE	COURSES	BOURBON
COYNESS	NOVOTNA	COWPOKE	COMPOST	COURTED	BOXROOM
DONNISH	YOKOONO	COMPELS	FOPPISH	GOURMET	POORBOX
HOLNESS	COMOROS	COMPILE	COMPETE	HOARDED	POORCOW
SOANDSO	DONOHOE	COPPOLA	COMPOTE	HOARDER	CORRUPT
SOONEST	GOTOPOT	GOSPELS	COMPUTE	JOURNEY	TOWROPE
BONNETS	MOLOTOV	SOPPILY	MOPPETS	LORRIES	HORRORS
COBNUTS	POTOROO	POMPOMS	MORPETH	LOURDES	BOORISH
COGNATE	ROBOCOP	BOPPING	POPPETS	LOUREED	DOGROSE
CONNOTE	SOLOMON	COMPANY	TOWPATH	MOORHEN	FORREST
CORNETS	COLOURS	COOPING	NONPLUS	MOURNED	LOWRISE
HORNETS	HONOURS	COPPING	POMPOUS	MOURNER	MOORISH
SONNETS	SOJOURN	COUPONS	RORQUAL	SOIREES	NOURISH
ROUNDUP	SOLOIST	HOPPING	TORQUAY	SOURCED	POOREST
WORNOUT	COHORTS	LOOPING	BOUQUET	SOURCES	SOUREST
CONNIVE	TORONTO	LOPPING	CONQUER	WORRIED	TOURISM
DONOVAN	COCONUT	MOPPING	MOSQUES	WORRIER	TOURIST
KOSOVAN	COLOBUS	POPPING	JOAQUIN	WORRIES	BORROWS
POTOMAC	ROTORUA	POPPINS	JONQUIL	HORRIFY	BORSTAL
SORORAL	HOMONYM	ROMPING	BOERWAR	COURAGE	COASTAL
COLOMBO	TOPONYM	SOPPING	BOORMAN	FOURTHS	DOGSTAR
NODOUBT	BOBPECK	TOPPING	DOORMAN	BOURSIN	HORSHAM
FORONCE	COMPACT	VOLPONE	DOORMAT	DOORDIE	HOTSEAT
MOROCCO	COPPICE	YOMPING	DOORWAY	CORRALS	MOESBAR
COLONEL	HOSPICE	COMPTON	FORREAL	COURTLY	POTSDAM
CORONER	TORPEDO	SOAPBOX	JOURDAN	DORRELL	SODSLAW
CORONET	TORPIDS	SOUPCON	JOURNAL	MOBRULE	WOOSNAM
GOTOBED	COMPLEX	TOMPION	CORRECT	MORRELL	CORSICA
GOTOSEA	CORPSED	BOBPARR	DOTRICE	FORRENT	COSSACK
MOTORED	CORPSES	COMPARE	COMRADE	GOERING	FOSSICK
NOHOPER	COUPLED	COMPERE	CORRODE	GOWRONG	HOPSACK
ROLODEX	COUPLER	COMPORT	JOYRIDE	JOBRAND	NONSUCH
BOROUGH	COUPLES	COOPERS	BOARDED	JOGRANT	TOPSIDE
DOROTHY	COUPLET	COPPERS	BOARDER	LOURING	BOASTED
BORODIN	POPPIES	FOPPERY	COARSEN	MOORING	BOASTER
GOFORIT	SOPPIER	GOSPARE	COARSER	POURING	BOLSTER
ROBOTIC	TOPPLED	GOSPORT	COERCED	ROARING	BOOSTED
HOMOLKA	TOPPLES	POPPERS	COERCES	SOARING	BOOSTER
COROLLA	TOUPEES	ROMPERS	COURBET	SOPRANO	BOSSIER

COASTER	CONSOLE	TOYSHOP	BOTTLER	FOXTAIL	TOOTING
COWSHED	CONSULS	GOSSIPS	BOTTLES	NOSTRIL	TORTONI
DOSSIER	CONSULT	GOSSIPY	COSTNER	TOOTSIE	TOTTING
FORSTER	FORSALE	CONSORT	DOTTIER	HOSTELS	TOUTING
HOISTED	FOSSILS	DOWSERS	FOOTMEN	HOSTILE	CONTROL
HOLSTER	LOOSELY	FORSURE	FORTIES	LOFTILY	DOGTROT
JOUSTED	MORSELS	MOUSERS	HOGTIED	MONTHLY	FOOTROT
JOUSTER	NOISILY	TONSURE	JOSTLED	MORTALS	FOXTROT
LOBSTER	TONSILS	CONSIST	JOSTLES	PORTALS	JOGTROT
MOBSTER	CONSUME	LOOSEST	LOATHED	COSTUME	PONTOON
MOISTEN	NOISOME	POSSESS	LOATHES	BOATING	PORTHOS
MONSMEG	POSSUMS	CONSETT	LOFTIER	BOLTING	PORTION
MONSTER	CONSENT	CORSETS	MOTTLED	BOOTING	POSTBOX
NOISIER	COUSINS	COSSETS	MOTTOES	COATING	SOFTROE
ROASTED	DOSSING	FORSYTE	MOUTHED	CONTEND	SOFTTOP
ROASTER	DOUSING	FORSYTH	NOWTHEN	CONTENT	BOATERS
ROISTER	DOWSING	HOTSPUR	POITIER	CORTINA	CONTORT
ROOSTED	GODSEND	ROSSLYN	PORTREE	COSTING	COSTARD
ROOSTER	HOUSING	BOATMAN	POSTMEN	FONTANA	COSTARS
ROUSTED	LOOSENS	COCTEAU	ROOTLET	FOOTING	COTTERS
TOASTED	POISONS	FOOTMAN	SOFTIES	FORTUNE	COUTURE
TOASTER	POPSONG	FOOTPAD	SOOTHED	HOOTING	DOCTORS
TOUSLED	ROSSINI	FORTEAN	SOOTHER	HOSTING	FOSTERS
TOUSLES	ROUSING	MOTTRAM	SOOTHES	JOLTING	HOOTERS
WOOSTER	SOUSING	PONTIAC	SORTIES	JOTTING	JOTTERS
WORSTED	TOSSING	PORTMAN	TOOTHED	LOOTING	LOITERS
CONSIGN	WORSENS	PORTRAY	TOOTLED	MONTANA	LOOTERS
CORSAGE	BOLSHOI	POSTBAG	TOOTLES	NOTTING	LOTTERY
BORSCHT	COPSHOP	POSTMAN	FORTIFY	PONTING	MORTARS
PORSCHE	DOGSHOW	POSTWAR	MORTIFY	PORTEND	PORTERS
BOLSHIE	FORSOOK	CONTACT	PONTIFF	PORTENT	POSTERN
CORSAIR	HOTSHOE	LOWTECH	CORTEGE	POSTING	POSTERS
COWSLIP	HOTSHOT	POETICS	COTTAGE	POTTING	POSTURE
DOESKIN	HOTSPOT	PORTICO	FOOTAGE	POUTING	POTTERS
POUSSIN	HOUSTON	ROSTOCK	HOSTAGE	ROOTING	POTTERY
TOASTIE	JONSSON	BOBTODD	MONTAGE	ROTTING	ROSTERS
TOPSAIL	MONSOON	LOWTIDE	POSTAGE	ROUTINE	ROTTERS
TOPSOIL	NONSTOP	TOSTADA	POTTAGE	ROUTING	SORTERS
TOPSPIN	POTSHOT	BOATMEN	VOLTAGE	SOFTENS	TORTURE
WORSHIP	ROUSSOS	BOOTEES	BOBTAIL	SORTING	TOTTERS
FORSAKE	TOLSTOY	BOOTLEG	CONTAIN	SOUTANE	TOTTERY
BOSSILY	TORSION	BOTTLED	FOOTSIE	TONTINE	CONTEST

DOLTISH	LOCUSTS	COPYING	SPECKLE	EPSILON	SPINDLE
HOSTESS	MODULUS	FOOYUNG	SPACING	UPSILON	SPINDLY
HOTTEST	ROMULUS	HOLYCOW	SPICING	APRIORI	IPANEMA
LOUTISH	NOUVEAU	HOLYJOE	SPECTOR	SPLINTS	OPENING
MORTISE	VOUVRAY	POLYGON	EPICURE	SPRINTS	OPINING
POETESS	CONVICT	BODYART	SPACERS	UPLIFTS	OPINION
SOFTEST	BOUVIER	BOWYERS	SPECTRA	OPTIMUM	SPONSON
TOXTETH	LOUVRED	COPYIST	SPECTRE	SPLITUP	SPONSOR
CONTOUR	LOUVRES	TORYISM	OPACITY	SPIKING	OPENERS
NOSTRUM	TORVILL	TOBYJUG	SPIDERS	SPOKEUP	SPINDRY
PONTIUS	CONVENE	NOZZLES	SPIDERY	APPLIED	APTNESS
ROOTOUT	CONVENT	SOZZLED	APPENDS	APPLIES	SPANISH
ROSTRUM	SOLVENT	BORZOIS	SPREADS	SPELLED	SPINETS
SORTOUT	SOLVING	BOOZILY	SPEEDED	SPILLED	OPENOUT
ROSTOVA	CONVERT	KOIZUMI	SPHERES	APOLOGY	SPINOUT
KOWTOWS	SOLVERS	BOOZING	OPHELIA	OPALINE	SPUNOUT
TOYTOWN	CONVEYS	BOYZONE	APPEALS	OPULENT	UPHOLDS
CONTEXT	CONVOYS	BOOZERS	APPEARS	EPILATE	OPPOSED
FONTEYN	NOSWEAT	ROZZERS	APPEASE	APPLAUD	OPPOSER
JOCULAR	COBWEBS	BOOZEUP	APLENTY	SPUMOUS	OPPOSES
MODULAR	NORWICH	UPLANDS	EPHESUS	OPENDAY	SPOONED
NODULAR	HOGWEED	UPWARDS	SPEEDUP	SPANDAU	SPOONER
POPULAR	BOSWELL	APPAREL	EPIGRAM	SPINACH	SPLODGE
COLUMBA	HOGWILD	LPLATES	SPYGAME	SPANDEX	SPLODGY
COLUMBO	ROSWELL	OPIATES	SPIGOTS	SPANIEL	APPOINT
DOLUNCH	BOXWOOD	QPLANES	SPYHOLE	SPANKED	APROPOS
GODUTCH	DOGWOOD	SPEAKER	SPYHARD	SPANKER	SPROUTS
ROTUNDA	ROYWOOD	SPEARED	OPTICAL	SPANNED	UPROOTS
BONUSES	FORWARD	SPLAYED	OPTIMAL	SPANNER	SPARTAN
FOCUSED	HOTWIRE	SPRAYED	SPLICED	SPENCER	SPORRAN
FOCUSES	LOBWORM	SPRAYER	SPLICES	SPENDER	UPGRADE
MODULES	HOGWASH	UPDATED	SPLINES	SPENSER	SPARGED
VOLUMES	COAXIAL	UPDATES	SPOILED	SPINNER	SPARGES
TOHUNGA	COAXING	UPRATED	SPOILER	SPINNEY	SPARKED
JODURIE	HOAXING	UPRATES	SPRITES	SPONDEE	SPARRED
SOLUBLE	HOAXERS	SPRAWLS	UPRIVER	SPONGER	SPIRAEA
VOLUBLE	COEXIST	SPRAINS	SPRINGS	SPONGES	SPORTED
VOLUBLY	COPYCAT	SPEAKUP	SPRINGY	UPENDED	SPURNED
COLUMNS	HOLYDAY	SPECIAL	UPRIGHT	SPINOFF	SPURRED
TOLUENE	HOLYWAR	SPECIES	UPTIGHT	OPENAIR	SPURTED
ROGUERY	HOLYSEE	SPICIER	OPTIONS	SPANGLE	UPBRAID
ROGUISH	POLYMER	SPECIFY	APRICOT	SPANGLY	UPTRAIN

SPARKLE	UPSWING	ARCADES	FRIABLE	CRUCIAL	PRECOOK
SPARKLY	EQUATED	ARRAYED	GREATLY	GRECIAN	PROCTOR
SPIRALS	EQUATES	BREADED	TREACLE	WROCLAW	TRACTOR
EPERGNE	SQUARED	BREAKER	TREACLY	BROCADE	PRECEPT
OPERAND	SQUARES	BROADEN	TREADLE	PRECEDE	TRICEPS
OPERANT	SQUASHY	BROADER	ARIADNE	BRACKEN	GROCERS
SPARING	AQUARIA	CREAKED	ORDAINS	BRACKET	GROCERY
UPFRONT	AQUATIC	CREAMER	CREATOR	CRACKED	PROCURE
SPARROW	AQUAVIT	CREASED	MRMAGOO	CRACKER	TRACERS
APPRISE	SQUALID	CREASES	TREASON	CRECHES	TRACERY
IPCRESS	SQUAWKS	CREASEY	MRHAPPY	CRICKET	TRICORN
OPPRESS	EQUABLE	CREATED	BREADTH	CROCHET	PRECAST
OPERATE	EQUABLY	CREATES	TRUANTS	CROCKED	PRECISE
SPIRITS	EQUALLY	CROAKED	BREAKUP	ERECTED	PROCESS
APPROVE	SQUALLS	DREADED	DREAMUP	FRICKER	TRICKSY
EPISODE	SQUALLY	DREAMED	ERRATUM	PRICKED	CRACKUP
OPUSDEI	EQUATOR	DREAMER	PRIAPUS	PROCEED	BRADMAN
SPASSKY	SQUALOR	GREASED	ORGANZA	TRACHEA	GRADUAL
APOSTLE	SQUELCH	GREASER	ARABIAN	TRACKED	TRUDEAU
EPISTLE	SQUEAKS	GREASES	ARABICA	TRACKER	ARTDECO
OPOSSUM	SQUEAKY	GREATER	BRUBECK	TRICKED	DRYDOCK
SPATIAL	SQUEALS	GREAVES	TRIBECA	TROCHEE	PREDICT
EPITHET	EQUERRY	GROANED	CRABBED	TRUCKER	PRODUCE
SPATTER	AQUEOUS	MRJAMES	CRIBBED	WRECKED	PRODUCT
SPOTTED	SQUEEZE	TREATED	DRUBBED	WRECKER	TRADUCE
SPOTTER	SQUEEZY	TREATER	GRABBED	CRUCIFY	BRADLEY
SPUTTER	AQUINAS	WREAKED	PROBLEM	BRICKIE	BRIDGED
UPATREE	AQUIFER	ARRAIGN	TREBLED	CRACKLE	BRIDGES
UPSTAGE	AQUIVER	ARRANGE	TREBLES	CRACKLY	BRIDGET
EPSTEIN	SQUIRES	BREATHE	TREBLES	DRACULA	BRIDLED
SPUTNIK	SQUIFFY	BREATHS	DRABBLE	DRYCELL	BRIDLES
SPATULA	SQUIDGE	BREATHY	DRIBBLE	FRECKLE	CRADLED
SPITTLE	SQUIDGY	PREACHY	DRIBBLY	FRECKLY	CRADLES
EPITOME	SQUISHY	WREATHE	ARMBAND	PRICKLE	DREDGED
EPITAPH	SQUIRMS	WREATHS	BRIBING	PRICKLY	DREDGER
UPSTART	SQUIRMY	ARCADIA	PROBING	TRICKLE	DREDGES
SPOUSES	EQUINOX	BREAKIN	TRIBUNE	TRUCKLE	FRIDGES
SPOUTED	SQUINTS	CROATIA	BRIBERS	DRACHMA	GRUDGED
SPLURGE	SQUIRTS	ERRATIC	BRIBERY	DRACHMS	GRUDGES
UPSURGE	TRUANCY	ORGANIC	PROBATE	BRACING	PRODDED
IPSWICH	ERRANDS	TRIADIC	PROBITY	TRACING	TRODDEN
SPEWING	ORLANDO	BROADLY	TRIBUTE	ERECTOR	TRUDGED

TRUDGES	GREETER	TRIFLES	GRIGSON	FRAILER	GRILLED
PRODIGY	GRIEVED	GRIFFIN	GREGORY	GRAINED	GRILLES
FREDDIE	GRIEVES	TRAFFIC	FRIGATE	GRAINER	TRILLED
TRADEIN	KRUEGER	TREFOIL	FRIGHTS	ORBITED	TROLLEY
CRUDELY	ORDERED	TRIFFID	ARCHWAY	ORBITER	TRILOGY
GRIDDLE	PREENED	GRUFFLY	BRAHMAN	PRAISED	TRELLIS
MRSDALE	ARMENIA	PROFILE	PREHEAT	PRAISES	ARCLAMP
ERODING	ARSENIC	TRUFFLE	ORCHIDS	TRAILED	PRELIMS
GRADING	ARTEMIS	PROFANE	ARCHAIC	TRAILER	DRYLAND
PRUDENT	FREEBIE	GRAFTON	ARMHOLE	TRAINED	IRELAND
TRADING	FREESIA	GRIFFON	GRAHAME	TRAINEE	PRALINE
TRIDENT	BRIEFLY	ARTFORM	ARCHING	TRAINER	PROLONG
GRADERS	CRUELLA	PREFERS	ORPHANS	FREIGHT	TROLLOP
PRUDERY	CRUELLY	PREFORM	URCHINS	MRRIGHT	ARTLESS
TRADERS	ORDEALS	PROFESS	MRCHIPS	DRUIDIC	PRELATE
CRUDEST	ORDERLY	PROFUSE	ARCHERS	PRAIRIE	CRIMEAN
PRUDISH	FREEING	PROFITS	ARCHERY	MRJINKS	DRUMPAD
ARIDITY	ORLEANS	BRIGHAM	ORCHARD	ARTICLE	GRAMMAR
CREDITS	FREEDOM	FROGMAN	ORPHISM	BRAILLE	TRAMCAR
CRUDITE	PRAETOR	PROGRAM	ORPHEUS	ORVILLE	TRAMWAY
CRUDITY	TREETOP	URUGUAY	ARCHIVE	TRUISMS	GRIMSBY
ERUDITE	PREEMPT	BRIGADE	ARRIVAL	ORBISON	GRIMACE
PREDATE	ARREARS	TRAGEDY	ARTISAN	TRAITOR	PRIMACY
IRIDIUM	DRSEUSS	BRAGGED	ORBITAL	TRYITON	BROMIDE
BRADAWL	ARRESTS	BROGUES	ORDINAL	TRAIPSE	BRAMLEY
ARSENAL	CRUELTY	DRAGGED	TROIKAS	ARTISTE	BREMNER
FREEMAN	PRIESTS	DRAGNET	ARBITER	ARTISTS	CRAMMED
FREEWAY	CROESUS	DRUGGED	ARRIVED	FRAILTY	CRAMMER
TRUEMAN	DRIEDUP	FROGMEN	ARRIVES	TROILUS	CRAMPED
URGENCY	PREFABS	TRIGGER	BRAIDED	PROJECT	CRIMPED
FRIENDS	ORIFICE	FRAGILE	BRAISED	TROJANS	CRIMPER
BREEDER	PREFACE	WRIGGLE	BRAISES	TREKKED	CRUMPET
BREEZES	PREFECT	WRIGGLY	BROILED	TREKKER	DRUMMED
BRIEFED	CROFTER	ORIGAMI	BROILER	TREKKIE	DRUMMER
BRIEFER	DRAFTED	TRIGAMY	BRUISED	BRAKING	GRAMMER
CREEPER	DRIFTED	BRIGAND	BRUISER	BROKING	GROMMET
DRYEYED	DRIFTER	DRAGONS	BRUISES	BROKERS	PREMIER
FREEZER	GRAFTED	OREGANO	CRUISED	ARMLOCK	TRAMMEL
FREEZES	GRAFTER	ORIGINS	CRUISER	FROLICS	TRAMPED
FRIEZES	GRIFTER	PROGENY	CRUISES	PRELUDE	TRIMMED
GREENER	PROFFER	DRAGOON	DRAINED	DRILLED	TRIMMER
GREETED	TRIFLED	GREGSON	DRAINER	FRILLED	TRUMPED

TRUMPET	BRENNAN	TRANCES	TRINITY	GRIPPER	BROSNAN
FROMAGE	BRINJAL	TRINDER	BRANTUB	PROPHET	CRYSTAL
ARAMAIC	CRANHAM	TRINKET	BRENGUN	PROPJET	GRISHAM
BRUMMIE	CRANIAL	WRINGER	BRINGUP	PROPPED	TRISHAW
DRUMKIT	FRONTAL	BRANAGH	CRANIUM	TRAPPED	TRISTAN
DRUMLIN	GRANDAD	IRONAGE	DRINKUP	TRAPPER	TRISECT
GREMLIN	IRANIAN	BRONCHI	IRONOUT	TRIPLED	CRUSADE
KREMLIN	IRONMAN	CRUNCHY	PRONOUN	TRIPLES	PRESIDE
BRAMBLE	CRANACH	TRANCHE	URANIUM	TRIPLET	PROSODY
BRAMBLY	ORINOCO	FRANCIS	ORTOLAN	TRIPLEX	BRASHER
CRUMBLE	GRANADA	FRANKIE	ARNOLDS	TRIPPED	BRISKER
CRUMBLY	GRENADA	FRANTIC	BROODED	TRIPPER	BRISKET
CRUMPLE	GRENADE	TRANSIT	CROOKED	WRAPPED	BRUSHED
GRUMBLE	ARUNDEL	BRONSKI	CROONED	WRAPPER	BRUSHES
PRIMULA	BRANDED	CRINKLE	CROONER	DROPOFF	CRASHED
TRAMPLE	BRENNER	CRINKLY	DROOLED	ARAPAHO	CRASHES
TREMBLE	BRINGER	FRANKLY	DROOPED	CRYPTIC	CRESSET
TREMBLY	BRONZED	GRANDLY	GROOMED	GRAPHIC	CRESTED
TREMOLO	BRYNNER	GRANOLA	GROOVED	PREPAID	CRISPER
BROMINE	CRINGED	GRANULE	GROOVES	CRIPPLE	CROSIER
CREMONA	CRINGES	TRUNDLE	ORIOLES	GRAPPLE	CROSSED
FRAMING	CRONIES	WRANGLE	PROOFED	PROPELS	CROSSES
PRIMING	DRINKER	WRINKLE	TRIOLET	TRIPOLI	CRUSHED
CRAMPON	DRUNKEN	WRINKLY	TROOPED	GRIPING	CRUSHER
CRIMSON	FRANCES	WRONGLY	TROOPER	GROPING	CRUSHES
MRSMOPP	GRANDEE	GRANDMA	BRIOCHE	PROPANE	DRESDEN
PRIMARY	GRANDER	CRANING	ARBORIO	CROPTOP	DRESSED
PRIMERS	GRANGER	DRONING	ARMOIRE	KRYPTON	DRESSER
TREMORS	GRANTED	IRONING	ARMOURY	DRAPERS	DRESSES
PREMISE	GRINDER	PRUNING	PRIORTO	DRAPERY	FRASIER
PROMISE	GRINNED	BRANDON	MRSPOCK	DRIPDRY	FRESHEN
CREMATE	GRUNTED	BRANSON	TROPICS	GRIPERS	FRESHER
EREMITE	GRUNTER	BRONCOS	TRIPODS	PREPARE	FRISBEE
PRIMATE	IRONIES	BRONSON	CROPPED	PROPOSE	FRISKED
PROMOTE	ORANGES	TRANSOM	CROPPER	DROPOUT	FROSTED
PROMPTS	PRANCED	TRENTON	DRIPPED	PREPAYS	GRASPED
BRIMFUL	PRANCER	GRANDPA	DROPLET	TRAPEZE	GRASPER
BRUMOUS	PRANCES	GRANARY	DROPPED	CROQUET	GRASSED
FRAMEUP	PRINCES	IRONORE	DROPPER	PREQUEL	GRASSES
GRAMPUS	PRINTED	DRYNESS	ERUPTED	TRIREME	PRESLEY
PREMIUM	PRINTER	GRANITA	GRAPNEL	ARMREST	PRESSED
BRENDAN	PRONGED	GRANITE	GRIPPED	PRORATA	PRESSES

PROSPER	PRESSON	TRITELY	GROUCHO	PROVERB	CREWING
TRESSES	PRESTON	BRETONS	GROUCHY	TRAVERS	CROWING
TRUSSED	DROSERA	BRITONS	TROUGHS	BRAVEST	DRAWING
TRUSSES	ERASERS	CRATING	WROUGHT	PREVOST	GROWING
TRUSTED	ERASURE	GRATING	GROUPIE	PROVISO	EREWHON
TRUSTEE	PRESETS	ORATING	PROUDIE	PROVOST	FROWNON
WRESTED	BRUSHUP	OROTUND	PROUDLY	BREVITY	ARTWORK
PRESAGE	BRUSQUE	PRETEND	TROUBLE	CRAVATS	BREWERS
BRASSIE	DRESSUP	TRITONS	ARGUING	GRAVITY	BREWERY
BRESCIA	ERASMUS	WRITING	MRFUNNY	KRAVITZ	DRAWERS
CRISPIN	PRESSUP	BRITPOP	CROUTON	PRIVATE	GROWERS
CROSBIE	EROSIVE	BRITTON	TRIUMPH	PRIVETS	PREWASH
DRASTIC	FRETSAW	ORATION	IRKUTSK	TRIVETS	PROWESS
KRISTIN	CRITICS	CRATERS	MRFUSSY	CROWBAR	FROWSTY
PROSAIC	EROTICA	ORATORS	ARBUTUS	DRAWBAR	CREWCUT
PRUSSIA	PROTECT	ORATORY	ARDUOUS	GROWBAG	GROWNUP
BRISKLY	BRITNEY	WRITERS	GRAVLAX	BRAWLED	BRIXHAM
BRISTLE	BRITTEN	BRITISH	TRIVIAL	BRAWLER	WREXHAM
BRISTLY	BROTHER	BRUTISH	CREVICE	BROWNED	BRIXTON
CRASSLY	CRITTER	PROTEST	PRIVACY	BROWSED	DRAYMAN
CRISPLY	ERITREA	FRETFUL	BRAVADO	BROWSER	GREYLAG
CROSSLY	FRETTED	PROTEUS	PROVIDE	BROWSES	DRAYMEN
FRESHLY	FRITTER	TROTOUT	PREVIEW	CRAWLED	BRAYING
GRISTLE	GRITTER	WRITEUP	DRIVEIN	CRAWLER	CRAYONS
GRISTLY	PRATIES	PRETEXT	PREVAIL	CRAWLEY	FRAYING
GROSSLY	PRETZEL	AROUSAL	TRAVAIL	CROWDED	PRAYING
TRESTLE	PRITHEE	TRAUMAS	PROVOKE	CROWLEY	XRAYING
WRESTLE	TROTTED	TROUNCE	BRAVELY	CROWNED	CROYDON
IRKSOME	TROTTER	GROUNDS	GRAVELY	DRAWLED	GRAYSON
PRESUME	WRITHED	AROUSED	GROVELS	DROWNED	GRUYERE
ARISING	WRITHES	AROUSES	TRAVELS	FROWNED	PRAYERS
ERASING	WRITTEN	GROUPER	BRAVING	GROWLED	GREYISH
KRISHNA	GRATIFY	GROUSED	CRAVING	GROWLER	BRAZIER
ORISONS	PROTEGE	GROUSES	DRIVING	PROWLED	CRAZIER
PRESENT	BRITAIN	GROUTED	PREVENT	PROWLER	PREZZIE
PRISING	ORATRIX	TROUPER	PROVING	TRAWLED	CRAZILY
PRISONS	PROTEIN	TROUPES	TREVINO	TRAWLER	DRIZZLE
BRISTOL	GRETZKY	TROUSER	BRAVERY	GROWTHS	DRIZZLY
BRISTOW	TROTSKY	BROUGHT	BRAVURA	BROWNIE	FRAZZLE
EROSION	BRITTLE	DRAUGHT	DRIVERS	CRYWOLF	GRIZZLE
FRISSON	IRATELY	DROUGHT	DROVERS	TROWELS	GRIZZLY
GRISSOM	PRATTLE	FRAUGHT	GRAVURE	BREWING	ARIZONA

BRAZING	ESTELLA	CSARDAS	STRANGE	STEEPEN	ATTIMES
GRAZING	ESTELLE	ASCRIBE	ATTACHE	STEEPER	ATTIRED
PRIZING	ASCENTS	OSTRICH	ATTACKS	STEERED	ATTIRES
ESFAHAN	ASPECTS	ASTRIDE	ATFAULT	STEERER	STAINED
ASKANCE	ASSENTS	USURPED	STPAULS	STLEGER	STAINER
ISLANDS	ASSERTS	USURPER	ATTAINS	STREWED	STAINES
ASHAMED	OSSEOUS	ASARULE	STRAINS	UTTERED	STEIGER
ASSAYED	ASHFORD	GSTRING	ATTABOY	UTRECHT	STRIDER
ASSAYER	ISOHYET	TSARINA	ETHANOL	STREAKS	STRIDES
ESCAPED	ASPHALT	USURERS	STRAPPY	STREAKY	STRIKER
ESCAPEE	ISTHMUS	TSARISM	STRAUSS	OTHELLO	STRIKES
ESCAPES	ASPIRED	TSARIST	ATLANTA	STEEPLE	STRIPED
ESSAYED	ASPIRES	OSPREYS	STEALTH	STEEPLY	STRIPES
ESTATES	ASSIZES	ASUSUAL	STRAITS	UTTERLY	STRIVEN
ASIATIC	ASPIRIN	ASHTRAY	STRATUM	STREAMS	STRIVES
ISLAMIC	OSSICLE	ISOTOPE	STRATUS	ATTEMPT	STRINGS
ASSAILS	ASSIGNS	ASSUMED	STABBED	ATHEART	STRINGY
ASSAULT	USTINOV	ASSUMES	STABLED	ATHEISM	STRIGIL
ISRAELI	ASSISTS	ASSURED	STABLER	ATHEIST	UTRILLO
USUALLY	TSHIRTS	ASSURER	STABLES	ATLEAST	ATFIRST
ASTAIRE	PSALTER	ASSURES	STUBBED	ATTESTS	STKITTS
ASHANTI	ASYLUMS	ASSUAGE	STUBBLE	STNEOTS	ATTICUS
ASTARTE	TSELIOT	USHUAIA	STUBBLY	STREETS	STOKING
ESPARTO	OSTLERS	ISSUING	STACKED	STREWTH	STOKERS
ISOBARS	USELESS	ESCUDOS	STACKER	STIFADO	ITALIAN
ISOBATH	ISOLATE	ESQUIRE	STICKER	STAFFED	STELLAR
ASOCIAL	ISHMAEL	ESTUARY	STOCKED	STAFFER	ATALICK
PSYCHIC	ASUNDER	ISSUERS	ATACAMA	STIFFEN	ITALICS
USEDCAR	TSUNAMI	OSSUARY	STACKUP	STIFLED	ATELIER
ISADORA	ASININE	TSQUARE	STICKUP	STIFLES	STALKED
ASHDOWN	USINGUP	ASQUITH	STUCKUP	STUFFED	STALKER
ASSEGAI	OSMONDS	ESPYING	STUDDED	STIFFLY	STALLED
ESTEFAN	ASTORIA	ASBYATT	STUDIED	STEFANI	STILLER
ESSENCE	ESTONIA	STRANDS	STUDIES	STYGIAN	STILTED
ASCENDS	OSMOSIS	ATLASES	STUDENT	STAGGER	STOLLEN
ASLEVEL	ASTOUND	STEAMED	STUDIOS	STAGING	OTOLOGY
ESSENES	OSBORNE	STEAMER	STADIUM	ETCHING	OTALGIA
ESTEVEZ	LSLOWRY	STJAMES	ATPEACE	ITCHING	PTOLEMY
USHERED	ESPOUSE	STRAFED	STRETCH	ETHICAL	ATHLONE
ASCETIC	ASSORTS	STRAFES	ATTENDS	STOICAL	STYLING
ASTERIX	ESCORTS	STRAYED	STEELED	STRITCH	STILGOE
CSLEWIS	ASEPTIC	ATLARGE	STEEPED	STKILDA	STILTON

ATALOSS	STANTON	ATTRACT	STETSON	JUMANJI	HUMBLES
STALEST	STENTOR	STARKER	ATATURK	AURALLY	JUMBLED
STYLISE	STANDTO	STARLET	STATORS	CURABLE	JUMBLES
STYLISH	STANDUP	STARRED	STATURE	DURABLE	MUMBLED
STYLIST	STENGUN	STARTED	STATUTE	MUTABLE	MUMBLES
UTILISE	STUNGUN	STARTER	STAUNCH	QUEALLY	RUMBLED
ATHLETE	OTTOMAN	STARVED	ATTUNED	RURALLY	RUMBLES
UTILITY	STOOGES	STARVES	ATTUNES	SURANNE	TUBBIER
STOMACH	STOOPED	STERNER	STOUTER	SUSANNA	TUMBLED
STAMMER	STROBES	STIRRED	STRUDEL	SUZANNE	TUMBLER
STAMPED	STROKED	STIRRER	ETRURIA	BUGABOO	TUMBLES
STEMMED	STROKES	STORIES	STLUCIA	CURATOR	TUMBREL
STOMPED	ATROPHY	STORMED	STOUTLY	RUNAMOK	LUMBAGO
STUMPED	STLOUIS	STORAGE	STEVENS	SUMATRA	CUMBRIA
STYMIED	STROLLS	STARCHY	STAVROS	JUDAISM	GUMBOIL
STYMIES	STROMLO	STARLIT	ATAVISM	BUGATTI	CUEBALL
STIMULI	STJOHNS	STEROID	STEWPAN	DURANTE	QUIBBLE
STUMBLE	STROPPY	STARSKY	STEWING	KUWAITI	SUNBELT
STAMENS	ATWORST	STARKLY	STOWING	MUTANTS	CURBING
STAMINA	STOPGAP	STARTLE	STEWPOT	BUYAPUP	DUBBING
STUMERS	UTOPIAN	STERILE	ATHWART	NUNAVUT	GUBBINS
ATOMISE	ATSPEED	STERNLY	STEWARD	SUBAQUA	HUSBAND
ITEMISE	STAPLED	STARING	STEWART	BUGBEAR	JUGBAND
STOMATA	STAPLER	STORING	STAYING	GUNBOAT	MUDBANK
ETONIAN	STAPLES	STARDOM	STAYERS	SUNBEAM	NUMBING
STANZAS	STEPHEN	STEREOS	STAYPUT	TUGBOAT	RUBBING
STANDBY	STEPNEY	STIRFRY	CURACAO	RUMBABA	SUBBING
FTINDEX	STEPPED	ITERATE	CUTAWAY	CUTBACK	TURBANS
STANCES	STEPPER	STARETZ	DUNAWAY	JUMBUCK	TURBINE
STANLEY	STEPPES	STARTUP	JUDAEAN	OUTBACK	GUMBOOT
STINGER	STOPPED	STERNUM	PUTAWAY	OUTBIDS	PUEBLOS
STINKER	STOPPER	STIRRUP	RUNAWAY	SUNBEDS	BUNBURY
STUNNED	STUPEFY	YTTRIUM	YUCATAN	BUBBLES	LUBBERS
STUNNER	STYPTIC	STOREYS	AUTARCH	BUMBLER	LUMBERS
STUNTED	STIPPLE	STASHED	LUSARDI	BURBLED	NUMBERS
STANDIN	STIPEND	STASHES	CURATES	BURBLES	RUBBERS
STENCIL	STEPMOM	ATISSUE	MUTATED	BUSBIES	RUBBERY
UTENSIL	STEPSON	STATUES	MUTATES	FUMBLED	SUNBURN
STONEME	STEPTOE	STUTTER	PUPATED	FUMBLER	RUBBISH
ATANEND	ATAPUSH	STATELY	PUPATES	FUMBLES	MUDBATH
ATONING	ETERNAL	STATING	SUGARED	HUMBLED	NUMBATS
STONING	STARMAN	STATION	LUNATIC	HUMBLER	BULBOUS

FUNCHAL	QUECHUA	OUTDOOR	JUKEBOX	BUFFOON	HUYGENS
FURCOAT	SUCCOUR	JUDDERS	RUDEBOY	OUTFLOW	JUDGING
BUNCHES	MUSCOVY	JUDDERY	YULELOG	BUFFERS	LUGGING
BUTCHER	SUNDIAL	MURDERS	DUEEAST	BUSFARE	LUNGING
HUNCHED	BURDOCK	RUDDERS	BURETTE	DUFFERS	MUGGING
HUNCHES	GUNDECK	SUNDERS	LUNETTE	GUNFIRE	MUGGINS
HUTCHES	MURDOCH	KURDISH	PUBERTY	PUFFERS	NUDGING
JUICIER	RUDDOCK	LUDDISM	BUREAUX	SUFFERS	PUNGENT
KUTCHER	SUNDECK	LUDDITE	DUTEOUS	SURFERS	PURGING
LUNCHES	BUDDIES	PUNDITS	HUMERUS	SUFFUSE	SURGING
LURCHED	BUNDLED	HUMDRUM	QUIETUS	BUFFETS	TUGGING
LURCHER	BUNDLES	PUTDOWN	RULEOUT	OUTFITS	BURGEON
LURCHES	CUDDLED	RUBDOWN	TUNEFUL	TUFFETS	DUDGEON
MUNCHED	CUDDLES	RUNDOWN	GULFWAR	TURFOUT	DUNGEON
MUNCHES	CURDLED	SUNDOWN	HUFFMAN	CURFEWS	GUDGEON
MUSCLES	CURDLES	FUNERAL	MUDFLAP	GUFFAWS	OUTGROW
PUNCHED	HUDDLED	JUDELAW	RUFFIAN	BURGLAR	SURGEON
PUNCHES	HUDDLES	NUMERAL	OUTFACE	JUNGIAN	BURGERS
QUACKED	HUNDRED	BUGEYED	SUFFICE	BUDGIES	HUNGARY
QUICHES	HURDLED	NUREYEV	SURFACE	BUGGIES	LUGGERS
QUICKEN	HURDLER	QUIETEN	MUFFLED	BUNGLED	MUGGERS
QUICKER	HURDLES	QUIETER	MUFFLER	BUNGLER	SURGERY
SUCCEED	MUDDIED	SUDELEY	MUFFLES	BUNGLES	BURGESS
QUICKIE	MUDDIER	AUBERGE	PUFFIER	BURGHER	SUGGEST
CUPCAKE	MUDDLED	BUDERIM	QUAFFED	BURGLED	BUDGETS
PURCELL	MUDDLES	DUNEDIN	RUFFLED	BURGLES	NUGGETS
QUICKLY	OUTDOES	EUGENIE	RUFFLES	GURGLED	VULGATE
BUSCEMI	PUDDLES	EUSEBIO	FUNFAIR	GURGLES	LUNGFUL
OUTCOME	SUBDUED	QUEENIE	SURFEIT	JUGGLED	BUSHMAN
SUCCUMB	SUBDUES	SUBEDIT	BUFFALO	JUGGLER	HUSHABY
PUCCINI	SUNDAES	ZULEIKA	FULFILS	JUGGLES	BUSHIDO
TUSCANY	QUIDSIN	AUREOLE	OUTFALL	JUNGLES	BUSHIER
VULCANS	DUNDALK	CUREALL	SUFFOLK	MUGGLES	BUSHMEN
NUNCIOS	BUDDING	QUEENLY	BUFFING	OUTGREW	CUSHIER
OUTCROP	BURDENS	QUIETLY	CUFFING	LUGGAGE	FUCHSIA
CUECARD	FUNDING	RUBELLA	HUFFING	CUDGELS	GUTHRIE
RUNCORN	GUIDING	MUSEUMS	LUFFING	BUDGING	PUSHKIN
NUTCASE	MUNDANE	LUCERNE	MUFFINS	BUGGING	RUSHDIE
OUTCAST	NURDING	TUREENS	PUFFING	BULGING	BUSHELS
SUCCESS	OUTDONE	AUBERON	PUFFINS	FUDGING	LUGHOLE
FULCRUM	PUDDING	DUKEDOM	RUFFING	FULGENT	PUSHILY
PUNCHUP	GUMDROP	FUSEBOX	SURFING	HUGGING	CUSHING

EUPHONY	BUSIEST	SULKING	SULLIED	SUNLESS	DURMAST
GUSHING	FURIOSO	TUCKING	SULLIES	BULLETS	SURMISE
HUSHING	JUJITSU	TURKANA	SURLIER	BULLITT	SUBMITS
PUSHING	PUNIEST	CUCKOOS	NULLIFY	CUTLETS	SUMMITS
RUCHING	CUBISTS	LUCKNOW	QUALIFY	DUALITY	GUINEAS
RUSHING	NUDISTS	PUCKOON	MULLAHS	GULLETS	QUONDAM
CUSHION	PURISTS	TUCKBOX	BUILTIN	MULLETS	DUNNOCK
PUSHROD	RUNINTO	BUNKERS	MULLEIN	MULLETT	FURNACE
RUSHTON	CURIOUS	BUSKERS	PURLOIN	OUTLETS	BUNNIES
AUTHORS	DUBIOUS	DUNKIRK	SUBLIME	PULLETS	BURNLEY
GUSHERS	DUTIFUL	EUSKARA	SUNLAMP	QUALITY	FUNNIER
DUCHESS	FURIOUS	HUNKERS	BUSLANE	SUBLETS	NUANCES
SUNHATS	PUNJABI	PUCKERS	BUTLINS	BUILDUP	QUINCES
MUSICAL	SUBJECT	QUAKERS	CULLING	BUILTUP	QUINTET
PURITAN	BUCKRAM	SUCKERS	CURLING	NUCLEUS	SUNNIER
LUCINDA	GURKHAS	TUSKERS	FURLING	OUTLOUD	TURNKEY
AUDITED	MUSKRAT	OUTKAST	FURLONG	PULLOUT	TURNOFF
JUBILEE	BUCKLED	PUCKISH	HURLING	OUTLIVE	QUENTIN
JUNIPER	BUCKLER	TURKISH	MULLING	CURLEWS	FUNNELS
JUPITER	BUCKLES	BUCKETS	OUTLAND	OUTLAWS	FUNNILY
LUCIFER	BULKIER	JUNKETS	OUTLINE	PULLEYS	GUNNELL
QUAILED	BUNKBED	TURKEYS	PULLING	HUMMOCK	RUNNELS
OUTINGS	HUSKIER	BULLBAR	RUTLAND	DUMMIES	TUFNELL
RUBITIN	HUSKIES	NUCLEAR	BULLDOG	MUMMIES	TUNNELS
TUNISIA	JUNKIES	NUTLOAF	BULLION	TUMMIES	SURNAME
AUDIBLE	LUCKIER	PULLMAN	MULLION	MUMMIFY	BURNING
AUDIBLY	MUCKIER	LULLABY	OUTLOOK	RUMMAGE	CUNNING
AURICLE	MURKIER	BULLACE	BUGLERS	TURMOIL	PUNNING
BURIALS	SULKIER	BULLOCK	BUTLERS	BUMMALO	QUININE
CUBICLE	CUCKOLD	OURLADY	CURLERS	PUMMELS	RUINING
CUTICLE	HUSKILY	BUILDER	CUTLERY	AUGMENT	RUNNING
FUSILLI	LUCKILY	BULLIED	DULLARD	GUMMING	TURNING
LUCIDLY	MURKILY	BULLIES	MUDLARK	HUMMING	QUANGOS
LUCILLE	SULKILY	BURLIER	AUSLESE	SUMMONS	TURNIPS
BUNIONS	BUCKING	CURLIER	BULLISH	FULMARS	BURNERS
LUCIANO	BUSKING	DUELLED	CUTLASS	MUMMERS	DUNNART
NUBIANS	DUCKING	GUILDER	DULLEST	MUMMERY	GUNNERA
AUDITOR	FUNKING	PURLIEU	DULLISH	MURMURS	GUNNERS
HUMIDOR	HULKING	QUELLED	FULLEST	SUMMARY	GURNARD
RUBICON	LURKING	QUILLER	GUTLESS	SUMMERS	NUNNERY
JUNIORS	QUAKING	QUILTED	OUTLAST	SUMMERY	RUNNERS
LUMIERE	SUCKING	QUILTER	PUBLISH	BURMESE	BURNISH

FURNISH	DUMPING	MURRAIN	HUSSIES	QUASARS	QUITTER
PUNNETS	GULPING	BURRELL	MUNSTER	TUSSORE	RUSTLED
BURNOUS	HUMPING	DURRELL	PUNSTER	SUBSIST	RUSTLER
BURNOUT	JUMPING	PUERILE	PURSUED	HUSSITE	RUSTLES
QUANTUM	PUMPING	SUPREME	PURSUER	PULSATE	SUBTLER
RUINOUS	SUPPING	SUPREMO	PURSUES	RUSSETS	TURTLES
TURNOUT	SUSPEND	BURRING	QUASHED	SUSSOUT	JUSTIFY
AUTOMAT	VULPINE	CURRANT	QUASHES	TUSSAUD	AUSTRIA
NUROFEN	SUBPLOT	CURRENT	TUSSLED	CURSIVE	CURTAIL
TUTORED	BUMPERS	GUARANI	TUSSLES	TUSSIVE	CURTAIN
AUROCHS	JUMPERS	OUTRANK	GUNSHIP	BURSTYN	DUSTBIN
BUBONIC	PURPORT	PURRING	HUSSEIN	OUTSIZE	SUSTAIN
BUCOLIC	SUPPERS	GUNROOM	OUTSWIM	DUSTMAN	OUTTAKE
OUTOFIT	SUPPORT	RUNRIOT	PURSUIT	DUSTPAN	DUCTILE
RUDOLPH	BUSPASS	SUNROOF	RUISLIP	FUSTIAN	LUSTILY
RUMOURS	LUMPISH	SUNROOM	SUBSOIL	MUNTJAC	BUYTIME
AUTOPSY	OUTPOST	GUYROPE	SUNSUIT	NUPTIAL	CUSTOMS
DUGOUTS	PURPOSE	BULRUSH	FUSSILY	OUTTRAY	RUNTIME
AUTOCUE	SUPPOSE	CUIRASS	MUSSELS	PUTTNAM	BUNTING
OUTPLAY	SURPASS	SUCROSE	OUTSELL	QUETZAL	BUSTING
MUDPACK	MUPPETS	SUNRISE	OUTSOLD	SUNTRAP	BUTTONS
OUTPACE	PULPITS	BURRITO	RUSSELL	EUSTACE	CUTTING
SUSPECT	PUPPETS	QUORATE	FULSOME	JUSTICE	DUSTING
BUMPIER	LUMPSUM	TURRETS	SUBSUME	CUSTODY	GUSTING
GUPPIES	SULPHUR	HURRYUP	CUISINE	AUNTIES	GUTTING
JUMPJET	SURPLUS	BURROWS	CURSING	BUSTIER	HUNTING
LUMPIER	KUMQUAT	FURROWS	CUSSING	BUSTLED	HURTING
PUPPIES	SURREAL	AUDREYS	NURSING	BUSTLES	JUSTINE
QUIPPED	KUBRICK	CULSHAW	SUSSING	BUTTIES	JUTTING
RUMPLED	CURRIED	FURSEAL	BUSSTOP	DUSTIER	MUSTANG
RUMPLES	CURRIES	KURSAAL	FUSSPOT	DUSTMEN	OUSTING
YUPPIES	FURRIER	OUTSPAN	GUMSHOE	FURTHER	PUTTING
BUMPOFF	GUARDED	OUTSTAY	GUNSHOT	GUMTREE	QUOTING
JUMPOFF	HURRIED	RUSSIAN	MUGSHOT	GUNTHER	RUSTING
YUPPIFY	HURRIES	TUESDAY	SUNSPOT	HURTLED	SUITING
RUAPEHU	QUARREL	TUSSOCK	BURSARS	HURTLES	SULTANA
BUMPKIN	QUARTER	OUTSIDE	BURSARY	HUSTLED	SULTANS
CULPRIT	QUARTET	SUBSIDE	CURSORY	HUSTLER	SUNTANS
PUMPKIN	QUERIED	SUBSIDY	HUSSARS	HUSTLES	TUTTING
DUOPOLY	QUERIES	BURSLEM	NURSERY	NUTTIER	AUCTION
RUMPOLE	PUTREFY	GUESSED	PULSARS	PUTTEES	RUCTION
BUMPING	OUTRAGE	GUESSES	PURSERS	QUITTED	SUCTION

TUITION	PUTUPON	MUZZLES	EVENING	SWEATER	RWANDAN
AUSTERE	AUGUSTA	NUZZLED	IVANHOE	TWEAKED	GWYNEDD
BUSTARD	CUMULUS	NUZZLES	EVENOUT	SWEARIN	SWANKED
BUSTERS	QUEUEUP	PUZZLED	EVAPOPE	CWMBRAN	SWANSEA
BUTTERS	TUMULUS	PUZZLER	OVEREAT	SWABBED	SWINGER
BUTTERY	SUAVELY	PUZZLES	OVERLAP	SWADDLE	TWANGED
CULTURE	CURVING	QUIZZED	OVERLAY	TWADDLE	TWINGES
CUSTARD	CULVERT	QUIZZES	OVERMAN	TWIDDLE	TWINNED
CUTTERS	QUAVERS	BUZZOFF	OVERPAY	TWIDDLY	TWINSET
DUSTERS	QUAVERY	MUEZZIN	OVERRAN	SWEDISH	SWANAGE
GUITARS	QUIVERS	BUZZING	OVERSAW	SWEENEY	DWINDLE
GUTTERS	SUBVERT	FUZZBOX	AVARICE	SWEEPER	SWINDLE
HUNTERS	OUTVOTE	BUZZARD	OVERACT	SWEETEN	TWINKLE
KULTARR	SURVIVE	BUZZERS	AVERRED	SWEETER	TWINKLY
MUSTARD	PURVEYS	SUBZERO	AVERTED	TWEETER	ZWINGLI
MUSTERS	SURVEYS	AVIATED	IVORIES	SWEETIE	TWINING
MUTTERS	OUTWEAR	AVIATES	OVERFED	SWEETLY	SWANSON
NURTURE	GUNWALE	AVIATOR	OVERSEE	OWNEDUP	SWINDON
OUTTURN	RUNWILD	AVEBURY	AVERAGE	SWIFTER	SWINISH
PUNTERS	MUGWUMP	AVOCADO	EVERAGE	SWIFTLY	GWYNETH
PUTTERS	NUTWOOD	EVACUEE	OVERAGE	TWOFOLD	OWINGTO
QUATTRO	BULWARK	EVICTED	OVERBID	OWNGOAL	TWINTUB
RUPTURE	LUGWORM	AVOCETS	OVERDID	SWAGMAN	SWOONED
SUITORS	OUTWARD	OVIDUCT	OVERALL	SWAGGER	SWOOPED
TUATARA	OUTWORN	EVADING	OVERFLY	SWAGMEN	SWAPPED
VULTURE	DUEWEST	EVIDENT	OVERTLY	SWIGGED	SWIPING
CULTISM	PUGWASH	AVIDITY	EVERTON	TWIGGED	AWARDED
CULTIST	OUTWITS	AVIGNON	OVERARM	SWAHILI	DWARFED
HURTFUL	RUNWAYS	AVOIDED	EVEREST	AWAITED	SWARMED
LUSTFUL	SUBWAYS	EVOKING	OVERUSE	AWNINGS	SWERVED
LUSTRUM	QUIXOTE	EVOLVED	EVERETT	AWAKENS	SWERVES
FURTIVE	RUBYWAX	EVOLVES	OVERATE	AWAKING	SWIRLED
SUBTEXT	LUCYLIU	EVELINA	OVERDUB	DWELLER	TWIRLED
JUGULAR	BUOYANT	OVULATE	OVERDUE	SWELLED	SWARTHY
TUBULAR	BURYING	EVILEYE	OVERRUN	SWELTER	SWORNIN
LUMUMBA	JURYBOX	AVENGED	OVERAWE	SWILLED	TWISTED
SUBURBS	RUDYARD	AVENGER	EVESHAM	SWOLLEN	TWISTER
BURUNDI	BUZZSAW	AVENGES	EVASION	TWILLED	TWOSTEP
AUGURED	GUZZLED	AVENUES	EVASIVE	SWALLOW	AWESOME
AUGURER	GUZZLER	EVANDER	OVATION	TWELFTH	TWOSOME
EUNUCHS	GUZZLES	EVENTER	AVOWING	SWAMPED	SWATHED
QUEUING	MUZZLED	EVINCED	SWEATED	SWIMMER	SWATHES

SWATTED	EXCLUDE	DYNASTS	TYPISTS	GYMSLIP
SWOTTED	EXPLODE	DYNASTY	WYSIWYG	GYMSHOE
TWITTER	EXALTED	TYRANTS	EYELIDS	EYESORE
TWITCHY	EXULTED	BYEBYES	MYALGIA	MYSTICS
SWITHIN	EXCLAIM	CYMBALS	CYCLING	MYRTLES
TWOTIME	EXPLAIN	EYEBALL	CYCLONE	MYSTIFY
AWFULLY	EXPLOIT	SYMBOLS	CYCLOPS	CYNTHIA
SWIVELS	EXILING	EYEBROW	CYCLIST	SYSTOLE
AWKWARD	EXPLORE	EYEBATH	EYELASH	SYSTEMS
SWAYING	AXOLOTL	LYNCHED	EYELETS	MYSTERY
SWIZZLE	EXAMPLE	LYNCHES	PYGMIES	OYSTERS
TWIZZLE	EXAMINE	PYNCHON	WYOMING	MYMUSIC
EXPANDS	EXEMPTS	WYNDHAM	HYUNDAI	TYNWALD
EXHALED	OXONIAN	TYNDALE	MYANMAR	EYEWASH
EXHALES	EXPOSED	EYEDROP	CYANIDE	EZEKIEL
EXHAUST	EXPOSES	LYNEHAM	LYINGIN	AZALEAS
EXPANSE	EXPOUND	TYPESET	RYANAIR	AZIMUTH
EXACTED	EXMOUTH	SYNERGY	HYMNALS	
EXACTLY	EXPORTS	PYREXIA	BYANOSE	
EXACTOR	EXTORTS	PYREXIC	GYMNAST	
EXECUTE	EXTRACT	MYCELLA	CYGNETS	
EXUDING	EXTRUDE	BYHEART	TYINGUP	
OXIDANT	EXERTED	LYNETTE	BYROADS	
OXIDISE	EXTREME	WYNETTE	BYGONES	
EXCEEDS	EXPRESS	HYPEDUP	BYRONIC	
EXPENDS	EXCRETE	LYDFORD	MYCOSIS	
EXTENDS	EXISTED	LYCHEES	SYCOSIS	
EXCERPT	EXOTICA	MYSHKIN	TYCOONS	
EXPENSE	EXITING	TYPHOID	SYNONYM	
EXPECTS	EXCUSED	WYCHELM	NYMPHET	
EXPERTS	EXCUSES	HYPHENS	TYMPANY	
EXIGENT	EXHUMED	PYTHONS	SYMPTOM	
OXYGENE	EXHUMES	TYPHOON	HYBRIDS	
EXTINCT	EXPUNGE	CYNICAL	MYCROFT	
EXCISED	PYJAMAS	LYRICAL	PYRRHIC	
EXCISES	GYRATED	TYPICAL	HYDRANT	
EXCITED	GYRATES	BYLINES	CYPRIOT	
EXCITES	DYNAMIC	PYRITES	CYPRESS	
EXPIRED	PYRAMID	SYRINGA	HYDRATE	
EXPIRES	TYRANNY	SYRINGE	HYDROUS	
EXHIBIT	DYNAMOS	HYGIENE	AYKROYD	
EXPIATE	SYNAPSE	SYRIANA	GYPSIES	

MAHARAJA	CARAVELS	HAWAIIAN	MACARONI	DABBLERS	HALBERDS
SARABAND	MANAGERS	PARAVION	IAMAROCK	GABBLERS	BARBERRY
CARAPACE	PARAPETS	TAXATION	SALADOIL	GAMBLERS	BAYBERRY
DATABASE	PARAKEET	VACATION	MACAROON	RAMBLERS	TAYBERRY
PATACAKE	SAVAGELY	CAVALIER	NANAMOON	WARBLERS	RAMBUTAN
CALABASH	SAVAGERY	DALADIER	PARAMOUR	CABBAGES	VANBRUGH
KAVANAGH	PARAFFIN	CANARIES	VAVASOUR	LAMBCHOP	HARBOURS
CALAMARI	HARANGUE	FANATICS	BAVAROIS	BABBLING	HATBOXES
KALAHARI	RADARGUN	GALAXIES	MATADORS	DABBLING	MAXBOYCE
KAWASAKI	BARATHEA	MALADIES	PARAGONS	GABBLING	CARCRASH
MAHARANI	MARATHON	SALARIES	PARASOLS	GAMBLING	CATCHALL
MATAHARI	EARACHES	VAGARIES	GADABOUT	GARBLING	MARCIANO
NAGASAKI	FALASHAS	FATALIST	LAYABOUT	MARBLING	BACCHANT
DATABANK	CAVATINA	SALARIAT	MARABOUT	RAMBLING	BARCHART
HADABALL	KATARINA	SATANIST	LAVATORY	WARBLING	MATCHBOX
LAVALAMP	SALARIED	BANALITY	OAKAPPLE	CAMBRIAN	FARCICAL
CARACALS	TAMARIND	CALAMITY	MALAPROP	PARBOILS	CASCADED
CARAVANS	CALAMINE	CAPACITY	PAMAYRES	LAMBSKIN	WATCHDOG
CATARACT	CANALISE	FATALITY	MALAYSIA	KAMBALDA	CASCADES
BARABBAS	MAGAZINE	RAPACITY	HARASSED	MARBELLA	VANCLEEF
LAMANCHA	PALATINE	SAGACITY	TANAISTE	CARBOLIC	RANCHERO
BALANCED	PARADISE	MALARKEY	HARASSES	KABBALAH	CATCHERS
JAMAICAN	PARASITE	MANACLED	SAMANTHA	BARBELLS	FANCIERS
MASACCIO	DAMAGING	PARALLEL	GALACTIC	GARBANZO	HATCHETS
BALANCES	GARAGING	CABALLER	VACANTLY	CARBINES	MARCHERS
DAMASCUS	MANAGING	EATABLES	CATAPULT	DAUBINGS	PANCREAS
VALANCES	PARADING	MANACLES	PARAQUAT	HATBANDS	RANCHERS
MARAUDED	RAVAGING	PARABLES	PARAGUAY	SAWBONES	RATCHETS
SARANDON	TARAKING	PARALLAX	PARALYSE	BADBLOOD	SATCHELS
MARAUDER	VACATING	MACAULAY	CATALYST	TARBOOSH	WATCHERS
HABANERA	PAGANINI	MARASMUS	LARBOARD	DANBROWN	FANCIEST
PASADENA	SABATINI	SAVANNAH	IANBEALE	CARBOOTY	SAUCIEST
TARAREID	TARAKIHI	CASANOVA	BARBECUE	CANBERRA	WARCHEST
JAPANESE	TAMARISK	MARADONA	BARBICAN	BARBARIC	HATCHERY
MATABELE	MALARIAL	PARABOLA	TABBYCAT	CAMBERED	FANCIFUL
NAZARENE	PALATIAL	PARANOIA	CAMBODIA	JABBERED	WATCHFUL
NAZARETH	FATALISM	ZARAGOZA	BARBADOS	YABBERED	MATCHFIT
JALAPENO	PAGANISM	CATACOMB	DAYBYDAY	CAMBORNE	MASCAGNI
SARAJEVO	PARADIGM	PARANOID	BADBREAK	JAMBOREE	GASCOINE
ZAPATERO	SATANISM	VAGABOND	DAYBREAK	BAMBURGH	BATCHING
CABARETS	BAVARIAN	NAVARONE	TAXBREAK	JABBERER	CATCHING
CADAVERS	CANADIAN	SAGAMORE	BABBLERS	CADBURYS	HATCHING

MARCHING	HATCHWAY	HARDNESS	MAGDALEN	LANDLORD	TAKECARE
MATCHING	BALDPATE	PADDLERS	MANDOLIN	CARDVOTE	TAPENADE
PARCHING	CARDGAME	SADDLERS	LANDSLIP	HANDSOME	MASERATI
PATCHING	HANDMADE	BAWDIEST	CANDELAS	HARDCORE	BAREBACK
WATCHING	HARDWARE	DANDIEST	DAEDALUS	WARDROBE	CAKEWALK
DABCHICK	MANDRAKE	FADDIEST	MANDALAY	TANDOORI	CAMEBACK
FALCHION	HARDCASH	GAUDIEST	PANDEMIC	HANDBOOK	FACEMASK
SANCTION	AARDVARK	HANDIEST	VANDAMME	HARDROCK	FACEPACK
CATCHIER	HARDBACK	HARDIEST	CARDAMOM	WARDROOM	TAKEBACK
SANCTIFY	HARDTACK	TARDIEST	BANDSMAN	HANDDOWN	BASEBALL
SANCTITY	LAIDBACK	SADDLERY	BANDSMEN	EARDROPS	GATEWAYS
PANCAKES	LANDMARK	BANDAGED	CANDYMAN	HARDCOPY	RABELAIS
BASCULES	SANDBANK	CARDIGAN	HANDYMAN	PANDERED	RATECAPS
CALCULUS	HANDBALL	BANDAGES	HANDYMEN	WANDERED	MAKEFAST
CATCALLS	HANDRAIL	SANDSHOE	MALDEMER	MANDARIN	TAKEPART
LANCELOT	LANDFALL	HARDSHIP	RANDOMLY	SANDIRON	WATERBED
MALCOLMX	LANDRAIL	KANDAHAR	BANDANNA	SANDTRAP	SALEABLE
FANCYMAN	HARDRAIN	YARDBIRD	GARDENIA	WANDERER	TAKEABOW
WATCHMAN	HANDBAGS	HARDLINE	SARDINIA	BANDERAS	PAPERBOY
WATCHMEN	HANDSAWS	LANDLINE	SARDONIC	FADDISTS	VALENCIA
FALCONER	LANDMASS	LANDMINE	GARDENED	MANDATES	CADENCES
FALCONRY	HANDCART	BANDYING	HARDENED	BANDITRY	KATEADIE
SAMCOOKE	BANDEAUX	CADDYING	MADDENED	SANDDUNE	CALENDAR
RACCOONS	LANDLADY	DAWDLING	PARDONED	DANDRUFF	LAVENDER
SALCHOWS	LAUDABLE	HANDLING	SADDENED	HANDCUFF	TAKEODDS
BANCROFT	MANDIBLE	PADDLING	FANDANCE	HARDLUCK	DANEGELD
WATCHOUT	HANDICAP	SADDLING	PARDONME	HANDPUMP	RAPESEED
MANCIPLE	PANDACAR	WADDLING	TAPDANCE	EARDRUMS	TAKEHEED
SAUCEPAN	PADDOCKS	DANDYISH	WARDANCE	HANDFULS	SAMEHERE
SANCERRE	CANDIDLY	SANDWICH	CARDINAL	HANDOUTS	TAPEDECK
BACCARAT	LANDSEND	BALDRICK	EAUDENIL	EAUDEVIE	BAKEWELL
NARCISSI	HANDBELL	HANDPICK	LAUDANUM	HANDOVER	FAREWELL
CARCASES	HARDSELL	HARDDISK	FANDANGO	MALDIVES	HAREBELL
CAUCUSES	DAYDREAM	RANDWICK	MANDINGO	RACECARD	CAMELEER
FASCISTS	WALDHEIM	HANDBILL	GARDENER	WAVEBAND	CAPEFEAR
NARCOSIS	HANDSEWN	LANDFILL	HARDENER	BAKEWARE	CAVEBEAR
CALCUTTA	SANDIEGO	LANDGIRL	PARDONER	BASERATE	BARENESS
PANCETTA	LANDSEER	MANDRILL	LANDINGS	CASEMATE	BASELESS
NARCOTIC	BALDNESS	DANDYISM	SARDINES	LACERATE	BASENESS
FARCEUSE	DAWDLERS	BAEDEKER	SARDONYX	MACERATE	CAPERERS
FARCEURS	HANDLERS	BARDOLPH	MAIDENLY	NAMESAKE	CARELESS
LAWCOURT	HANDSETS	RANDOLPH	HARDWOOD	SAVEFACE	CATERERS

DATELESS	WAKENING	KATEFORD	TALENTED	MAYFLIES	GANGLING
FACELESS	WATERING	CAKEHOLE	PATENTEE	CALFSKIN	GARGLING
LAKELETS	WAVERING	CAZENOVE	PARENTAL	FARFALLE	HAGGLING
LAMENESS	MAVERICK	TAKENOTE	GAMESTER	LAWFULLY	JANGLING
LATENESS	MATERIAL	EASEDOFF	MANEATER	MANFULLY	LAUGHING
NAMELESS	MATERIEL	TAPEROFF	PALETTES	HALFINCH	MANGLING
PALENESS	VALERIAN	CASEBOOK	DAVENTRY	HAWFINCH	TANGLING
SAMENESS	BAKERIES	CASEWORK	LATENTLY	CALFLOVE	TANGOING
TAMENESS	EATERIES	YALELOCK	PATENTLY	HALFTONE	WAGGLING
WAVELETS	JAVELINS	SALEROOM	TAPESTRY	HALFMOON	WANGLING
WAVERERS	RAREFIES	TAPEWORM	MADESURE	HALFHOUR	DALGLISH
BASEMENT	FACELIFT	CAMEROON	MAKESURE	PANFORTE	LANGUISH
CASEMENT	BANERJEE	CAPEHORN	MAMELUKE	RAFFARIN	GANGLION
EASEMENT	WATERJUG	CAPETOWN	BABERUTH	WARFARIN	BARGAINS
PAVEMENT	BASENJIS	CAREWORN	KATEBUSH	WAYFARER	PANGOLIN
SAFESEAT	CAMELLIA	TAKEDOWN	LAMEDUCK	FANFARES	BARGEMAN
PAPERHAT	LABELLED	CAFENOIR	MAKEOVER	CARFERRY	BARGEMEN
TAKETHAT	PANELLED	RACEGOER	TAKEOVER	RAFFERTY	WARGAMES
GAMESHOW	PATELLAE	HAVENOTS	GAVEAWAY	FARFLUNG	MARGINAL
KARENINA	SAXEBLUE	KATEMOSS	TAKEAWAY	HAYFEVER	LANGFORD
CAGEBIRD	GAMEPLAN	MATELOTS	WATERWAY	GANGLAND	MANGROVE
GAMEBIRD	MAGELLAN	RAVENOUS	JANEEYRE	VANGUARD	LAUGHOFF
RAREBIRD	BAKERLOO	SAVELOYS	CADENZAS	LANGUAGE	PANGLOSS
RAREFIED	WATERLOO	BAREFOOT	HALFBACK	LANGLAUF	BADGERED
BAKELITE	GAZELLES	GATEPOST	TAFFRAIL	HANGBACK	HANGERON
BASELINE	NACELLES	TAKEROOT	EARFLAPS	HANGNAIL	KANGAROO
CAPESIDE	WAVERLEY	CATEGORY	HALFMAST	GANGWAYS	LAGGARDS
DATELINE	DALESMAN	PANELPIN	DAFFODIL	TANGRAMS	MARGARET
MADELINE	DALESMEN	BALEARIC	CANFIELD	TANGIBLE	LARGESSE
TAKEFIVE	SALESMAN	CAREERED	GARFIELD	TANGIBLY	SARGASSO
TAXEXILE	SALESMEN	CAREFREE	HAYFIELD	BARGEDIN	TARGETED
VASELINE	WATERMAN	LAKEERIE	JALFREZI	GANGEDUP	LAUGHTON
WATERICE	CAREENED	NAMEDROP	HALFTERM	GANGRENE	PAIGNTON
CAPERING	MATERNAL	WATERRAT	BAFFLERS	HAGGLERS	CAUGHTUP
CATERING	PATERNAL	JANEGREY	CAFFEINE	WANGLERS	DAUGHTER
LACEWING	TAVERNER	CARESSED	HALFLIFE	BAGGIEST	GANGSTER
LAYERING	PAGEANTS	WATERSKI	HALFTIME	TANGIEST	LAUGHTER
PAPERING	TAVERNAS	PATERSON	BAFFLING	GANGSHOW	GADGETRY
TAKEWING	HAZELNUT	CARESSES	WAFFLING	HANGFIRE	HANGOVER
TAPERING	CANETOAD	MAJESTIC	BADFAITH	SANGUINE	GARGOYLE
VALETING	CASELOAD	LAMENTED	BARFLIES	DANGLING	CASHCARD
WAGERING	HAREWOOD	PATENTED	GADFLIES	GAGGLING	CASHBACK

PATHWAYS	GATHERED	BASILDON	BASILICA	HACIENDA	TACITURN
WARHEADS	LATHERED	SAMIZDAT	PACIFIED	MALIGNED	FATIGUES
YASHMAKS	WARHORSE	BALINESE	RATIFIED	RATIONED	HABITUES
WASHABLE	CASHCROP	MAGICEYE	MARITIME	MARIANNE	SAMJAFFE
CATHEDRA	GATHERUP	BASINETS	MAXIMISE	PATIENCE	BANJOIST
CASHEDIN	FATHERLY	CABINETS	SANITISE	RADIANCE	MARJORIE
WASHEDUP	MACHISMO	CAGINESS	SATIRISE	SAPIENCE	MARJORAM
CATHODES	LACHESIS	EASINESS	RADIOING	VARIANCE	BANJAXED
BAGHEERA	BATHETIC	HAZINESS	BASILISK	NATIONAL	BACKHAND
CASHMERE	PATHETIC	LAZINESS	FAMILIAL	RATIONAL	BACKWARD
CASHDESK	RACHITIC	MARINERS	PACIFISM	PATIENTS	BACKYARD
KATHLEEN	CATHETER	RACINESS	MAGICIAN	MALIGNLY	BANKCARD
CASHIERS	MACHETES	WARINESS	NAMIBIAN	MANITOBA	FALKLAND
CASHLESS	BATHCUBE	WAVINESS	PARISIAN	MANIFOLD	PARKLAND
RASHNESS	MADHOUSE	KABINETT	PAVILION	MARIGOLD	BACKDATE
TASHKENT	BATHTUBS	MANIFEST	TAHITIAN	BARITONE	BANKRATE
PATHOGEN	TAXHAVEN	CAGINGIN	FAMILIAR	CAMISOLE	PARKLANE
PASHMINA	HATHAWAY	CAVINGIN	PACIFIER	VARICOSE	SACKRACE
YACHTING	MARINARA	RAKINGIN	CAVITIES	YAKITORI	BACKLASH
KASHMIRI	BADINAGE	LAYINGUP	FAMILIES	HARICOTS	BACKWASH
VALHALLA	KAMIKAZE	MAKINGUP	PACIFIES	JANITORS	BACKPACK
CATHOLIC	LAMINATE	PAYINGUP	RATIFIES	PALIMONY	LARKHALL
SAKHALIN	MARINADE	SAVINGUP	VANITIES	CALIBRED	WALKTALL
BACHELOR	MARINATE	WAKINGUP	PACIFIST	DAVIDSON	JACKDAWS
MANHOLES	NAVIGATE	BASINGER	SATIRIST	TALIESIN	WALKWAYS
CACHALOT	PAGINATE	MALINGER	FACILITY	SADISTIC	BANKABLE
CASHFLOW	PALISADE	SALINGER	NATIVITY	RADIATED	SACKABLE
FATHOMED	SALIVATE	DARINGLY	RAPIDITY	SATIATED	BACKACHE
PACHINKO	VALIDATE	BANISHED	SALINITY	MARIETTE	BACKEDUP
LASHINGS	FALIRAKI	FAMISHED	VALIDITY	VARIETAL	PACKEDUP
MACHINES	KABIRALI	RAVISHED	VAPIDITY	HAMILTON	MARKEDLY
DASHWOOD	TAXIRANK	VANISHED	PANICKED	PAKISTAN	BANKHEAD
SASHCORD	CAPITALS	HAVISHAM	CADILLAC	BANISTER	BACKHEEL
BATHROBE	RADICALS	RADIOHAM	CAVILLED	CANISTER	BACKLESS
RATHBONE	TAXICABS	BANISHES	CARILLON	RADIATOR	CACKLERS
CASHBOOK	LAPIDARY	PARISHES	PAPILLON	RADIATES	DANKNESS
BATHROOM	SANITARY	RADISHES	CAVILLER	SATIATES	DARKNESS
WASHROOM	VARIABLE	RAVISHES	BACILLUS	CALIGULA	LANKNESS
CASHDOWN	CABINBOY	VANISHES	SALICLAW	FATIGUED	TACKLERS
WASHDOWN	MARIACHI	GARISHLY	FACIALLY	LATITUDE	BACKBEAT
FASHIONS	MANIACAL	LAVISHLY	RACIALLY	MANICURE	BACKREST
FATHERED	DAVISCUP	RAKISHLY	TALISMAN	HABITUAL	BACKSEAT

PACKHEAT	BACKMOST	KARLMARX	RAWLPLUG	BALLARAT	TASMANIA
WACKIEST	JACKBOOT	TABLEAUX	TALLULAH	EARLGREY	HARMONIC
PACKAGED	BACKSPIN	HAILMARY	TALLYMAN	BALLISTA	GARMENTS
DARKAGES	NANKIPOO	FALLIBLE	TALLYMEN	CARLISLE	PAYMENTS
PACKAGES	LARKSPUR	EARLOBES	TABLEMAT	HAMLISCH	RAIMENTS
BACKCHAT	CANKERED	CABLECAR	PARLANCE	BALLASTS	CALMDOWN
TALKSHOW	HANKERED	WARLOCKS	FAULKNER	CALLUSES	HAMMERED
BACKBITE	VALKYRIE	GARLICKY	BADLANDS	VALLETTA	BALMORAL
BACKFIRE	WAIKERIE	BALLADES	DARLINGS	BALLETIC	EARMARKS
BACKSIDE	MACKEREL	BALLADRY	FAILINGS	BALLOTED	MARMARIS
MARKTIME	JACKAROO	WALLSEND	GALLANTS	PAULETTE	HARMISON
CACKLING	BACKDROP	EAGLEEYE	GARLANDS	RACLETTE	PARMESAN
RANKLING	TANKARDS	TAILLESS	RAILINGS	TABLETOP	PALMISTS
TACKLING	MARKETED	EARLIEST	SAPLINGS	HALLOUMI	MARMOSET
BACKFILL	PACKITIN	RAILLERY	BAILBOND	PAULMUNI	WAXMATCH
BACKLIST	BACKSTOP	BAILIFFS	HAILWOOD	PARLOURS	GASMETER
BACKSLID	DARKSTAR	DAYLIGHT	RAILROAD	FALLOVER	MAMMOTHS
BACKFLIP	BASKETRY	FANLIGHT	CALLIOPE	HALLOWED	BADMOUTH
MARKSMAN	SACKBUTS	GASLIGHT	BADLYOFF	WALLOWED	BARMOUTH
MARKSMEN	BANKRUPT	BALLYHOO	BALLCOCK	DAYLEWIS	FALMOUTH
DARKENED	TALKOVER	TALLSHIP	BALLROOM	CABLEWAY	YARMOUTH
BACKINGS	WALKOVER	MAILSHOT	FALLDOWN	GALLOWAY	BARNYARD
MARKINGS	MARKOWEN	JAILBIRD	NAILDOWN	WALLEYED	GAINSAID
RANKINGS	HAWKEYED	TAILWIND	BALLBOYS	FARMHAND	MAINLAND
MACKINAW	RAILCARD	MACLAINE	BALLOONS	FARMLAND	MAINSAIL
WALKONBY	BALLGAME	NAILFILE	GALLEONS	FARMYARD	RAINFALL
BACKCOMB	FAILSAFE	BAULKING	PAULROSS	BARMCAKE	MAINTAIN
JACKLORD	TAILGATE	CAULKING	TALLBOYS	RAYMEARS	GAINSAYS
BACKBONE	TALLTALE	DALLYING	MAILBOAT	HAMMOCKS	DAMNABLE
BANKNOTE	WALLGAME	FAULTING	TAILCOAT	WARMEDUP	CANNIBAL
HAWKMOTH	CAGLIARI	RALLYING	GALLOPED	CALMNESS	HANNIBAL
HACKWORK	BALLPARK	SALLYING	WALLOPED	HARMLESS	BARNABAS
BANKROLL	CALLBACK	TALLYING	TAILSPIN	WARMNESS	CANNABIS
BACKROOM	FALLBACK	VAULTING	CALLIPER	EARMUFFS	PAINTBOX
DARKROOM	HALLMARK	SAILFISH	GALLOPER	TAJMAHAL	DAMNABLY
BACKDOWN	TAILBACK	BALLGIRL	GALLERIA	PARMAHAM	DANNYBOY
BANKLOAN	PALLMALL	CALLSIGN	TAILORED	DALMAHOY	BARNACLE
MARKDOWN	GALLIANO	FAULTIER	CAULDRON	BARMAIDS	BANNOCKS
BACKDOOR	CARLOADS	GAULTIER	WALLAROO	HAYMAKER	WAINSCOT
BACKLOGS	RAILWAYS	TABLOIDS	FAILURES	LAWMAKER	RAINYDAY
JACKPOTS	WALLBARS	GAULLIST	MALLARDS	YARMULKE	RAINWEAR
JACKSONS	WALLIAMS	FAULTILY	WARLORDS	MAMMAMIA	LAUNDERS

PAINLESS	RAINCOAT	MANOFGOD	CACOLOGY	TADPOLES	DAIQUIRI
PAINTERS	PAINTPOT	CALORGAS	TAXONOMY	PAMPHLET	HAIRBAND
PANNIERS	GARNERED	GALOSHES	FAVOURED	CAMPANIA	SAARLAND
SAUNDERS	MANNERED	CAPOEIRA	LABOURED	DAMPENED	CARRIAGE
SAUNTERS	RAINTREE	CAROLINA	SAVOURED	HAPPENED	FAIRGAME
CANNIEST	RAINDROP	JAPONICA	LABOURER	PAMPLONA	LAUREATE
FAINTEST	BANNERET	MAJOLICA	CAROUSED	CARPHONE	MARRIAGE
CARNEGIE	MANNERLY	CANOPIED	LAROUSSE	EARPHONE	CARRYALL
LAUNCHED	MAGNESIA	PARODIED	CAROUSAL	PAYPHONE	HAIRBALL
PAWNSHOP	MAGNETIC	CAMOMILE	CAROUSEL	HARPOONS	FAIRWAYS
LAUNCHER	MAGNATES	CANONISE	CAROUSER	LAMPOONS	FAIRLADY
HAUNCHES	MAINSTAY	CAROLINE	CABOOSES	LAMPPOST	PATRICIA
LAUNCHES	CARNIVAL	GASOLINE	CAROUSES	BAGPIPER	BARRACKS
PAUNCHES	PANORAMA	JACOBITE	PAPOOSES	BAGPIPES	CAPRICES
JAUNDICE	SAYONARA	KATOWICE	FAMOUSLY	PANPIPES	HAYRICKS
MAINLINE	SAVOYARD	VAPORISE	CAVORTED	VAMPIRIC	MATRICES
DAUNTING	BARONAGE	CAJOLING	MAJORTOM	HAMPERED	CARRYCOT
FAINTING	SABOTAGE	CANOEING	VANOUTEN	PAMPERED	HARRIDAN
HAUNTING	YANOMAMI	PAROLING	MANOFWAR	TAMPERED	LABRADOR
PAINTING	DADORAIL	PASOLINI	CALOTYPE	CARPARKS	GABRIELA
TAINTING	SAMOVARS	BARONIAL	PAROXYSM	CARPORTS	FAIRHEAD
TAUNTING	MAHOGANY	MANORIAL	WARPLANE	RAMPARTS	GABRIELE
VAUNTING	BABOUCHE	SALOPIAN	PALPABLE	VAMPIRES	BARRIERS
SAMNEILL	BAROUCHE	PALOMINO	PALPABLY	KASPAROV	CARRIERS
DAINTIER	RAZORCUT	CALORIES	GAZPACHO	DAPPERLY	FAIRNESS
DAINTIES	CABOODLE	CANOPIES	EARPIECE	CAMPUSES	FARRIERS
DAINTILY	CANOODLE	PARODIES	CAMPBELL	HARPISTS	HAIRLESS
JAUNTILY	CAROTENE	CANOEIST	DAMPNESS	CARPETED	HARRIERS
MAGNOLIA	LABOHEME	CANONIST	SAMPLERS	BADPATCH	HAIRIEST
IAINGLEN	JACOBEAN	PARODIST	HAPPIEST	RASPUTIN	FARRIERY
GAUNTLET	NAPOLEON	MAJORITY	RAMPAGED	EARPLUGS	MADRIGAL
BARNSLEY	SABOTEUR	BAZOOKAS	RAMPAGES	MANPOWER	WARRIGAL
CARNALLY	BARONESS	CAROLLED	CAMPFIRE	TAXPAYER	TARRAGON
CANNONED	BARONETS	CAROLLER	CAMPSITE	JACQUARD	BARRAGES
EARNINGS	BAYONETS	CAGOULES	DAUPHINE	PASQUALE	TAORMINA
WARNINGS	CAJOLERS	DAMOCLES	SAMPHIRE	MAYQUEEN	HAIRLINE
MAINROAD	CANONESS	WAGONLIT	SAPPHIRE	BANQUETS	CARRYING
TAWNYOWL	HALOGENS	CANONLAW	DAPPLING	CASQUETS	HARRYING
RAINDOWN	MAYORESS	MAROONED	RAMPLING	LACQUERS	MARRYING
SAINFOIN	SAMOYEDS	GABORONE	SAMPLING	MARQUEES	PARRYING
BARNDOOR	WAGONERS	VALOROUS	CAMPAIGN	MARQUESS	TARRYING
RAINBOWS	CAJOLERY	VAPOROUS	WARPAINT	VANQUISH	HAIRPINS

LARRIKIN	DARROWBY	BASSCLEF	CARTLAND	WAITRESS	WAGTAILS
FAIRPLAY	NARROWLY	CAPSULES	EASTWARD	WALTZERS	EARTHILY
HARRUMPH	HATSTAND	MAUSOLUS	CARTHAGE	WASTRELS	PARTAKES
DAIRYMAN	NAUSEATE	CAUSALLY	LASTNAME	BARTLETT	CASTELLA
DAIRYMEN	PASSRATE	SATSUMAS	RAGTRADE	BATTIEST	MANTILLA
LAURENCE	RAMSGATE	LAUSANNE	SALTLAKE	CATTIEST	BASTILLE
LAWRENCE	RATSBANE	BASSINET	TARTRATE	FATTIEST	PASTILLE
EARRINGS	SAMSPADE	SARSENET	PASTRAMI	MALTREAT	MARTELLO
LATRINES	FALSTAFF	PASSWORD	FASTTALK	NASTIEST	NAUTILUS
VAGRANTS	HAYSTACK	FATSTOCK	CATTRALL	RATTIEST	TANTALUS
WARRANTS	MARSHALL	PASSBOOK	CASTRATO	SALTIEST	MANTOMAN
MATRONLY	CAPSTANS	BARSTOOL	SANTIAGO	TASTIEST	PASTIMES
VAGRANCY	MARSHALS	BASSOONS	LASTGASP	TATTIEST	BATTENED
WARRANTY	CAMSHAFT	CAISSONS	MARTIANS	FAITHFUL	CARTONED
CATRIONA	PASSABLE	MANSIONS	TASTEBUD	TASTEFUL	FASTENED
CABRIOLE	PASSABLY	NAUSEOUS	LATTICED	WASTEFUL	FATTENED
CARRYOFF	MASSACRE	PASSIONS	CANTICLE	MASTIFFS	HASTENED
NACREOUS	CAPSICUM	TAPSHOES	PARTICLE	MANTEGNA	TAUTENED
PATRIOTS	CASSOCKS	PASSPORT	PASTICHE	RATTIGAN	FASTENER
WARRIORS	HASSOCKS	CAUSERIE	NAUTICAL	KATTEGAT	CASTINGS
CARRYOUT	RANSACKS	BASSDRUM	TACTICAL	PARTTIME	HASTINGS
FAIRPORT	PASSEDBY	SANSKRIT	MASTODON	BATTLING	MALTINGS
HARRIOTT	NAGSHEAD	DADSARMY	WAITEDUP	CASTLING	MARTINIS
FAIRCOPY	BANSHEES	PASSERBY	DAYTODAY	EARTHING	MARTINET
HAIRGRIP	HAMSTERS	BASSISTS	MASTHEAD	FARTHING	WANTONLY
CARRERAS	HARSHEST	CASSETTE	HARTNELL	MANTLING	MARTINEZ
FAIRISLE	PARSIFAL	FALSETTO	BATTLEON	PARTYING	CARTLOAD
LACROSSE	MASSAGED	MARSHTIT	PANTHEON	RATTLING	DARTFORD
GARRISON	MARSHGAS	DANSEUSE	BATTLERS	TATTLING	EASTWOOD
HARRISON	MASSAGES	MASSEUSE	CANTEENS	WALTZING	FASTFOOD
WALRUSES	PASSAGES	HAPSBURG	DAFTNESS	PARTWITH	HARTFORD
SACRISTY	SAUSAGES	DANSEURS	FASTNESS	EASTWICK	TATTOOED
NARRATED	HASSLING	JANSMUTS	MATTHEWS	HATTRICK	EASTCOTE
GARROTTE	IANSMITH	MASSEURS	MATTRESS	BACTRIAN	PARTSONG
MAGRITTE	PANSTICK	LANSBURY	PANTHERS	EARTHIER	PARTWORK
NARRATOR	CATSKILL	PASSOVER	PARTNERS	CANTRIPS	HAWTHORN
NARRATES	FAUSTIAN	CAUSEWAY	RATTLERS	CAPTAINS	DARTMOOR
BAYREUTH	CATSUITS	CATSEYES	TACTLESS	CASTRIES	BASTIONS
HAIRCUTS	LAWSUITS	CAPSIZED	TARTLETS	FANTAILS	CALTROPS
FARROWED	PARSNIPS	CAPSIZAL	TARTNESS	GANTRIES	CAPTIONS
NARROWED	WARSHIPS	CAPSIZES	TAUTNESS	PANTRIES	CAPTIOUS
NARROWER	WASSAILS	LASTRADA	VASTNESS	PASTRIES	CARTOONS

CASTLOTS	CANTATAS	MALVOLIO	LANYARDS	ABDICATE	ABETMENT
CAUTIONS	WARTBURG	CARVINGS	MACYGRAY	OBLIGATE	ABUTMENT
CAUTIOUS	TANTRUMS	MALVINAS	CALYPSOS	OBEISANT	ABETTING
FACTIONS	CAPTIVES	PARVENUS	CARYATID	ABRIDGED	ABUTTING
FACTIOUS	CASTAWAY	MALVERNS	LADYMUCK	ABRIDGER	ABSTAINS
LASTPOST	FABULATE	CANVASES	GARYLUCY	ABRIDGES	ABATTOIR
BACTERIA	SATURATE	HARVESTS	JAZZBAND	OBLIGING	ABETTORS
BANTERED	TABULATE	KAYWALSH	ZANZIBAR	OBLIVION	ABSTRUSE
BARTERED	SALUTARY	GADWALLS	DAZZLERS	OBSIDIAN	ABITMUCH
BATTERED	VALUABLE	JAYWALKS	DAZZLING	OBVIATED	OBSTRUCT
CANTERED	SATURDAY	BATWOMAN	TANZANIA	ABSINTHE	ODURATE
CAPTURED	CAPULETS	CATWOMAN	GADZOOKS	OBVIATES	OBDURACY
FALTERED	MATURELY	LAPWINGS	MARZIPAN	ABALONES	ABOUNDED
MASTERED	BABUSHKA	HAYWORTH	SALZBURG	OBELISKS	ABSURDLY
MATTERED	CAPUCHIN	TAMWORTH	ABLATIVE	ABOMASUM	ABJURING
NATTERED	CAPUCINE	GASWORKS	ABRASIVE	ABUNDANT	ABLUTION
TATTERED	MATURING	HADWORDS	ABRADING	ABINGDON	ABDULLAH
NANTERRE	SALUTING	WAXWORKS	ABRASION	ABANDONS	ABDUCTED
PARTERRE	NATURISM	BAYWATCH	OBLATION	ABINITIO	ABDUCTEE
PASTORAL	FABULIST	MAGWITCH	OBTAINED	EBENEZER	ABDUCTOR
CASTIRON	NATURIST	VAUXHALL	ABSCONDS	ABROGATE	ABRUPTLY
BARTERER	MATURITY	CAPYBARA	OBSCURED	ABSORBED	ABOVEALL
NATTERER	HANUKKAH	MARYLAND	OBSCURES	ABSORBER	EBBWVALE
CAPTURES	CATULLUS	MARYRAND	ABACUSES	OBSOLETE	ABEYANCE
DASTARDS	CASUALLY	BABYFACE	ABUDHABI	ABDOMENS	SCRABBLE
LANTERNS	CASUALTY	MARYKATE	OBEDIENT	ABNORMAL	SCRAMBLE
PASTURES	MANUALLY	DAVYLAMP	ABNEGATE	ABHORRED	SCRATCHY
PATTERNS	LABURNUM	MARYWEBB	ABSENCES	ABSOLUTE	MCFADDEN
SALTIRES	FABULOUS	GANYMEDE	ABSEILED	ABSOLVED	SCRAGEND
CARTERET	GAZUMPED	EASYMEAT	ABSEILER	ABSOLVER	SCRAPERS
EASTERLY	DAGUERRE	LADYBIRD	OBSESSED	ABSOLVES	SCIATICA
LATTERLY	BAGUETTE	LADYLIKE	ABBESSES	UBIQUITY	SCRAPING
MASTERLY	MAQUETTE	KATYHILL	OBSESSES	ABERDARE	OCCASION
FANTASIA	BALUSTER	BABYSITS	ABSENTED	ABERRANT	OCTAVIUS
BAPTISED	RAPUNZEL	NAVYBLUE	OBJECTED	EBORACUM	SCRAWLED
PARTISAN	JACUZZIS	BABYFOOD	ABSENTEE	ABERDEEN	MCCALLUM
BAPTISES	SALVADOR	BABYHOOD	OBJECTOR	ABORTIVE	OCTAGONS
BAPTISMS	CALVADOS	BABYLOVE	ABJECTLY	ABORTING	SCRAPPED
BAPTISTS	SALVAGED	MARYROSE	ABSENTLY	ABSTRACT	SCRAPPER
LAETITIA	LASVEGAS	BABYDOLL	OBSERVED	OBITUARY	MCCARTHY
FACTOTUM	SALVAGES	BABYBOOM	OBSERVER	OBSTACLE	SCABBARD
MALTSTER	BANVILLE	HALYARDS	OBSERVES	EBBTIDES	SCABIOUS

SCABROUS	SCUFFING	SCILLIES	ACROSTIC	SCISSORS	ACOUSTIC
ICEBERGS	SCUFFLES	ICELOLLY	ACCOSTED	SCOTLAND	ACTUATED
ICEBOXES	SCOFFLAW	SCALLOPS	ACCOUTRE	SCATTERS	ACCUSTOM
ICECREAM	SCAFFOLD	OCULISTS	SCROFULA	SCOTCHED	ACTUATOR
ACIDBATH	ACTIVATE	SCULPTED	ECLOGUES	SCOTCHES	ACTUATES
ACIDRAIN	SCRIBBLE	SCULPTOR	ACRONYMS	SCATHING	MCMURTRY
ACIDTEST	SCRIBBLY	ACOLYTES	ICEPLANT	SCOTTISH	SCAVENGE
SCUDDING	ACCIDENT	SCAMPERS	SCUPPERS	SCUTTLED	SCOWLING
ACADEMIA	OCCIDENT	SCHMALTZ	SCEPTICS	SCUTTLES	ACRYLICS
ACADEMIC	ACTIVELY	SCHMOOZE	ACAPULCO	SCOTSMAN	ADVANCED
ICEDANCE	SCHIFFER	SCIMITAR	SCAPULAR	SCOTFREE	ADVANCES
ACIDDROP	SCHIPHOL	SCANDALS	SCEPTRES	ECSTATIC	NDJAMENA
ACIDOSIS	ACRIDINE	SCANNERS	ACERBATE	ACETATES	ADJACENT
ICEDOVER	ACTINIUM	ACANTHUS	SCARFACE	ACCURATE	IDEALISE
SCHEMATA	ACTIVISM	SCANNING	ACCRUALS	SCHUMANN	IDEALISM
SCREWCAP	ACTIVIST	SCANSION	SCIROCCO	OCCUPANT	IDEALIST
SCIENCES	ACRIDITY	SCANTIER	ACCREDIT	ACCURACY	EDNADORE
SCREECHY	ACTIVITY	SCANTILY	SCORSESE	SCRUBBED	EDHARRIS
SCHEMERS	SCHILLER	ECONOMIC	SCARPERS	SCRUNCHY	ODDBALLS
ICKENHAM	ACHILLES	SCHNAPPS	SCARIEST	ACCUSERS	EDMCBAIN
ACCEDING	WCFIELDS	SCENARIO	SCARLETT	SCOURERS	EDUCIBLE
SCHEMING	ACRIMONY	MCDONALD	SCARCELY	SCHUBERT	EDUCATED
MCKELLEN	SCRIMPED	ACCOLADE	SCORNFUL	MCGUFFIN	EDUCATOR
SCREAMED	ECLIPSED	MCDOWALL	MCGREGOR	SCOURGED	EDUCATES
SCREAMER	ECLIPSES	ACROBATS	SCORCHED	MCGUIGAN	ADRENALS
SCREENED	SCRIPTED	SCHOLARS	SCORCHER	OCCUPIED	EDGEWAYS
ECHELONS	ACHIEVED	ACCORDED	SCORCHES	ACCUSING	ADDENDUM
ACTEDOUT	ACHIEVER	ECTODERM	SCURRIED	SCOURING	EDGELESS
ACCESSED	ACHIEVES	SCOOTERS	ACCRUING	SCOUTING	IDLENESS
ACCESSES	OCCLUDED	ACTOFGOD	SCARRING	OCCUPIER	ADHERENT
ECLECTIC	OCCLUDES	SCROOGED	SCORNING	OCCUPIES	ADHESIVE
ACCENTED	SCALPELS	SCROOGES	SCORPIAN	ACQUAINT	IDEEFIXE
ACCEPTED	SCULLERS	MCGOOHAN	SCORPION	SCRUTINY	ADHERING
SCREWTOP	SCULLERY	SCOOPING	SCURRIES	SCRUPLES	EDGEHILL
ACCENTOR	MCALPINE	SCOOTING	ACERBITY	OCTUPLET	ADHESION
SCHEDULE	SCALDING	SCHOOLED	SCARCITY	ACTUALLY	EDIFICES
MCKENZIE	SCALPING	SCROLLED	OCARINAS	SCRUMPED	EDIFYING
SCHERZOS	SCOLDING	SCHOOLIE	OCHREOUS	ACQUIRED	ADMIRALS
ICEFIELD	SCULLING	SCROUNGE	ICESKATE	OCCURRED	ADLIBBED
SCOFIELD	SCALLION	SCHOONER	ICESHELF	ACQUIRES	ADMIRERS
SCOFFERS	SCULLION	ACCOUNTS	ACESWILD	ACCURSED	ADVISERS
SCOFFING	ACCLAIMS	ECHOGRAM	ACESHIGH	ACCURSES	EDGINESS

ADDINGUP	IDEOGRAM	VERANDAS	RELAXING	PERANNUM	MELBLANC
ADDITIVE	ADJOURNS	HERALDRY	RELAYING	RETAINER	KEYBOARD
ADMIRING	ODIOUSLY	GETAHEAD	REMAKING	LETALONE	PEGBOARD
ADMIXING	EDMONTON	LEBANESE	RENAMING	BELABOUR	SEABOARD
ADVISING	ADROITLY	LEGALESE	REPAYING	DELATOUR	MEMBRANE
ADDITION	ADOPTERS	NEPALESE	SEDATING	AERATORS	VERBIAGE
ODDITIES	ADOPTIVE	CETACEAN	MEGALITH	DECAGONS	JETBLACK
ADRIENNE	ADAPTING	FEDAYEEN	GERANIUM	DECAPODS	PEABRAIN
ADVISORY	ADOPTING	DEBATERS	AERATION	HEXAGONS	SETBACKS
ADRIATIC	ADOPTION	LEGATEES	LEGATION	MEGATONS	LEGBREAK
ADDICTED	ADAPTORS	REPAPERS	NEGATION	SENATORS	TEABREAK
ADMITTED	ADEQUATE	DECADENT	RELATION	PEDAGOGY	SEABREAM
ADULTERY	ADEQUACY	REDALERT	SEDATION	DECAMPED	FEEBLEST
ADELAIDE	ADORABLE	SEDATELY	VEXATION	RECAPPED	DERBYHAT
IDOLISED	ADORABLY	DEBAGGED	CERAMICS	REVAMPED	KERBSIDE
IDOLISES	ADORNING	DERANGED	DENARIUS	PETANQUE	REDBRICK
ADULATED	IDARESAY	SERAPHIC	LEGALITY	REMARQUE	VERBALLY
ADULATOR	ODYSSEUS	DETACHED	TENACITY	DEBARRED	PEMBROKE
IDOLATER	EDITIONS	SERAPHIM	VENALITY	REPAIRED	NEWBROOM
ADULATES	ADJUTANT	METAPHOR	VERACITY	DECAGRAM	SEABORNE
IDOLATRY	ADJUNCTS	DETACHES	REMARKED	HEXAGRAM	BERBERIS
ADAMSALE	ADJUDGED	GELATINE	METALLIC	REPAIRER	CERBERUS
ADAMBEDE	ADJUDGES	LEGALISE	BEWAILED	LEWAYRES	VERBATIM
ADAMWEST	ADJURING	MELAMINE	DERAILED	VERACRUZ	HENCHARD
IDOMENEO	ADJUSTED	NEGATIVE	DETAILED	RELAPSED	REDCOATS
ODDMENTS	ADJUSTER	PENALISE	PEDALLED	RELAPSES	MERCHANT
ADAMSRIB	TEKANAWA	RELATIVE	RECALLED	PEDANTIC	PENCHANT
ODOMETER	VENACAVA	SEDATIVE	RETAILED	SEMANTIC	REACTANT
EDENTATE	LEGALAID	SETASIDE	DEGAULLE	DECANTED	PEACOCKS
ODONNELL	DELAMARE	AERATING	SERAGLIO	DEPARTED	MERCEDES
ADENOIDS	DELAWARE	BEHAVING	PEDALLER	RECANTED	SEACADET
IDENTIFY	SEPARATE	BERATING	RETAILER	REPARTEE	TEACADDY
IDENTITY	YETAGAIN	DEBASING	DEBACLES	DECANTER	RESCUEME
ADENITIS	MEGAWATT	DEBATING	DEFAULTS	LEVANTER	RESCUERS
ADENAUER	RELAXANT	DECAYING	VENABLES	MEGASTAR	TEACHERS
ADVOCATE	HERALDIC	DEFACING	BECALMED	PEDANTRY	SEACHEST
ADVOCAAT	DEMANDED	DEFAMING	DETAINED	DEVALUED	TEACHEST
ADVOCACY	HERALDED	DELAYING	REGAINED	DEVALUES	MERCIFUL
ADSORBED	REGARDED	MENACING	REMAINED	MEGABYTE	PEACEFUL
ADMONISH	REMANDED	NEGATING	RETAINED	TERABYTE	DESCRIBE
ADJOINED	RETARDED	REGALING	DETAINEE	VERALYNN	PERCEIVE
IDEOLOGY	REWARDED	RELATING	RELAUNCH	BEDAZZLE	REACTIVE

KERCHIEF	SEEDCAKE	HERDSMAN	LEVERAGE	TELETHON	TEMERITY
BEACHING	REDDWARF	HERDSMEN	RELEGATE	CELERIAC	BEDECKED
FETCHING	FEEDBACK	SEEDSMAN	RENEGADE	JEREMIAD	PETERKAY
PERCHING	HELDBACK	SEEDSMEN	SERENADE	REMEDIED	BEVELLED
REACHING	DEADCALM	READYMIX	SEWERAGE	BENEFICE	JEWELLED
REACTING	HEADLAMP	DEADENED	VEGETATE	REDEFINE	LEVELLED
RESCUING	READABLE	REDDENED	VENERATE	TELEVISE	REBELLED
TEACHING	TEDDYBOY	TEADANCE	TELEMARK	TENERIFE	REPEALED
REACTION	HEADACHE	DEADENER	CEBERANO	VEGEMITE	REPELLED
MELCHIOR	VERDICTS	PENDANTS	FEDERALS	DELETING	REVEALED
TETCHIER	DEADHEAD	WEDDINGS	GENERALS	LEVERING	REVELLED
TETCHILY	HEADGEAR	TENDENCY	LEEVANS	RECEDING	REVEILLE
TEACAKES	HEEDLESS	DEADWOOD	MENELAUS	RENEGING	JEWELLER
MEACULPA	MEDDLERS	HEADWORD	VETERANS	RENEWING	LEVELLER
DESCALED	NEEDLESS	SENDWORD	RELEVANT	REVERING	REVELLER
METCALFE	SEEDBEDS	HEADLONG	REVENANT	SECEDING	BEVERLEY
DESCALES	SEEDLESS	DEADLOCK	TELECAST	SEVERING	KENEALLY
HERCULES	DEADBEAT	HEADLOCK	FEDERACY	TELEXING	REDEPLOY
REDCELLS	DEADCERT	DEEDPOLL	RESEMBLE	FEVERISH	REDEEMED
BENCHLEY	DEADHEAT	HEADROOM	DECEMBER	HEREWITH	PERELMAN
WELCOMED	HEADREST	HELDDOWN	REMEMBER	JEREMIAH	PETERMAN
HENCHMAN	NEEDIEST	DEADLOSS	DEFENCES	MEREDITH	PETERMEN
HENCHMEN	SEEDIEST	FELDSPAR	BEHEADED	ZEDEKIAH	REDEEMER
NEWCOMER	WEEDIEST	RENDERED	DEFENDED	BENEDICK	DEMEANED
WELCOMES	HEADSHIP	TENDERED	DEPENDED	REMEDIAL	CEVENNES
PEACENIK	DEADSHOT	GENDARME	DEFENDER	SELENIUM	BETELNUT
SEICENTO	HEADWIND	LEADFREE	REFEREED	DELETION	HEREFORD
DESCANTS	DEADLINE	FELDGRAU	REVEREND	REDESIGN	PENELOPE
DESCENDS	DEADTIME	TENDERLY	LEVERETS	VENETIAN	LEVELOFF
RESCINDS	DENDRITE	VENDETTA	REFEREES	FEDERICO	WEREWOLF
DEACONRY	HEADLINE	REDDITCH	DESELECT	BEDEVILS	BEHEMOTH
TEACLOTH	LEADTIME	DEADDUCK	PETEBEST	BENEFITS	TELEWORK
BENCROSS	REEDPIPE	HEADBUTT	REVERENT	GENETICS	GENEPOOL
REACTORS	MEDDLING	HEADHUNT	TELETEXT	HERETICS	DEVELOPS
REDCROSS	NEEDLING	READJUST	TENEMENT	NEMESIAS	GENEROUS
REACHOUT	PEDDLING	BEADEVIL	VEHEMENT	REMEDIES	HEREGOES
MERCOURI	SEEDLING	BENDOVER	CEMETERY	BENEDICT	TELEPORT
PERCIVAL	DEADLIER	DEMERARA	SERENELY	DERELICT	CEREMONY
BEDCOVER	READMITS	BEVERAGE	SEVERELY	CELERITY	HEGEMONY
HEADBAND	TENDRILS	DELEGATE	FEVERFEW	HEREDITY	PETERPAN
HEADLAND	NEWDELHI	FEDERATE	SEAEAGLE	SERENITY	RECEIPTS
HEADCASE	PENDULUM	GENERATE	DEMERGER	SEVERITY	METEORIC

DEFERRED	BENELTON	PERFUMES	KEDGEREE	DECIMALS	BESIEGED
DETERRED	BEEEATER	DEAFENED	HEDGEROW	PELICANS	BEWIGGED
REFERRED	DEFECTOR	REEFKNOT	BEGGARLY	RECITALS	REJIGGED
VENEERED	DESERTER	SELFLOVE	PEGGYSUE	SEMINARS	MERINGUE
REHEARSE	RECEPTOR	SEAFLOOR	FERGUSON	DEDICANT	LEWISGUN
RESEARCH	REPEATER	SEAFRONT	DEIGHTON	HESITANT	BESIEGER
CEREBRAL	SELECTOR	LEAFSPOT	HEIGHTEN	CELIBACY	BESIEGES
DEFERRAL	SEMESTER	SEAFARER	LEIGHTON	DELICACY	PERISHED
REFERRAL	CELESTAS	PERFORMS	REPHRASE	SEMINARY	RELISHED
CEREBRUM	MEMENTOS	GEOFFREY	TEDHEATH	RELIABLE	LEWISHAM
TELEGRAM	VEDETTES	SELFRULE	REDHEADS	RELIABLY	DECIPHER
SEWERRAT	DECENTLY	SEAFEVER	BENHOGAN	MEDIOCRE	PERISHER
DECEASED	RECENTLY	BELGRADE	CEPHALIC	MENISCUS	DELIGHTS
RECESSED	BEREAVED	REDGRAVE	LETHALLY	PERIODIC	PERISHES
RELEASED	DECEIVED	BERGKAMP	BECHAMEL	REMINDED	RELISHES
REVERSED	DESERVED	EELGRASS	MECHANIC	REKINDLE	VERIFIED
REVERSAL	RECEIVED	SEAGRASS	RETHINKS	RELIEDON	DECISIVE
PETERSON	RESERVED	LEEGRANT	DETHRONE	BEWILDER	DEFINITE
RECESSES	DECEIVER	REDGIANT	RESHAPES	REMINDER	DERISIVE
RELEASES	RECEIVER	SERGEANT	TETHERED	BEDIVERE	FEMININE
REVERSES	DECEIVES	PEAGREEN	RECHARGE	PEKINESE	FEMINISE
KERENSKY	DESERVES	SEIGNEUR	SEAHORSE	BERIBERI	GENITIVE
PEVENSEY	RECEIVES	BEAGLERS	LEEHURST	DECIBELS	MEDICINE
CEMENTED	RESERVES	VENGEFUL	LETHARGY	DECIDERS	REGICIDE
DEFEATED	BEEFCAKE	HEDGEHOG	WETHERBY	DEFILERS	DEBITING
DEFECTED	SELFSAME	FENGSHUI	MEPHISTO	DELIVERS	DECIDING
DEJECTED	REDFACED	LENGTHEN	NEWHAVEN	DENIZENS	DEFILING
DEMENTED	NEWFACES	BEAGLING	BEEHIVES	DEWINESS	DEFINING
DESERTED	PERFECTS	DEIGNING	PESHAWAR	EERINESS	DERIDING
DETECTED	BEEFEDUP	FEIGNING	REGINALD	GETIDEAS	DERIVING
DETESTED	REOFFEND	NEIGHING	CELIBATE	RETIREES	DESIRING
REHEATED	SELFHELP	REIGNING	DECIMATE	REVISERS	DEVISING
REJECTED	DEAFNESS	WEIGHING	DEDICATE	REVIVERS	MERITING
RELENTED	LEAFLETS	PENGUINS	DELICATE	PEDIMENT	RECITING
REPEATED	SELFLESS	PEGGYLEE	DEPILATE	PENITENT	REFINING
REPENTED	BEEFIEST	SEAGULLS	HERITAGE	REDIRECT	REHIRING
RESENTED	DEIFYING	BERGAMOT	HESITATE	REGIMENT	RELIVING
REVERTED	REAFFIRM	LEGGINGS	LEVITATE	RESIDENT	RESIDING
SELECTED	JEFFRIES	WEDGWOOD	MEDICARE	RETICENT	RETIRING
NEPENTHE	JETFOILS	SEAGROVE	MEDICATE	SEDIMENT	REVILING
RESETTLE	SELFPITY	PEIGNOIR	MEDITATE	DELIVERY	REVISING
PEDESTAL	PERFUMED	BERGERAC	TERIYAKI	REFINERY	REVIVING

DEVILISH	DEMIJOHN	BENJAMIN	PELLUCID	DEALINGS	MELLOWED
DELIRIUM	DESIROUS	BETJEMAN	REPLACED	DECLINES	NEWLYWED
FEMINISM	LEGIRONS	LEEJCOBB	DEFLECTS	FEELINGS	YELLOWED
LENINISM	LEXICONS	PERJURED	FETLOCKS	FENLANDS	NELLGWYN
DECISION	PERILOUS	PERJURER	NEGLECTS	PEELINGS	MELLOWER
DERISION	RESINOUS	PERJURES	REELECTS	RECLINES	KELLAWAY
GEMINIAN	HELIPORT	DECKHAND	REFLECTS	SEALANTS	REFLEXES
MERIDIAN	DERISORY	NECKBAND	REPLACES	WETLANDS	DEPLOYED
PETITION	PEDIGREE	NECKLACE	REPLICAS	FEELGOOD	REPLAYED
RELIGION	DECIGRAM	WEEKDAYS	SECLUDED	HELLHOLE	WESLEYAN
REVISION	HEWITSON	PEEKABOO	CEILIDHS	WELLDONE	PERMEATE
SEDITION	LEVINSON	PERKEDUP	SECLUDES	WELLWORN	TEAMMATE
DEFICITS	GENIUSES	NECKWEAR	WELLHEAD	WELLTODO	PEMMICAN
REVISITS	LEWINSKY	FECKLESS	WELLREAD	BELLHOPS	BERMUDAN
VERIFIES	BEFITTED	HECKLERS	PELLMELL	REALTORS	HEMMEDIN
FEMINIST	DEPICTED	MEEKNESS	WELLNESS	DEALTOUT	SEAMLESS
DEBILITY	DESISTED	RECKLESS	BELLTENT	SELLAPUP	SEAMIEST
FELICITY	DEVIATED	WEAKNESS	HELLBENT	DECLARED	GERMAINE
TEPIDITY	MEDIATED	PERKIEST	BELLYFUL	DEPLORED	JERMAINE
DEVILLED	REMITTED	NECKLINE	NEGLIGEE	WELLBRED	MERMAIDS
REFILLED	RESISTED	PENKNIFE	PENLIGHT	KEYLARGO	HELMSMAN
SEMILLON	BELITTLE	HECKLING	REDLIGHT	CELLARER	HELMSMEN
CEDILLAS	REMITTAL	WEAKLING	SEALYHAM	DECLARER	GERMANIC
PERICLES	DEMISTER	NECKTIES	HELLFIRE	DECLARES	RENMINBI
VEHICLES	MEDIATOR	WEEKLIES	MEALTIME	DEPLORES	GERMINAL
AERIALLY	REGISTER	BERKELEY	REALTIME	CELLARET	TERMINAL
GENIALLY	RESISTOR	NEDKELLY	REPLYING	REALISED	DESMONDS
BEDIMMED	DEVIATES	BECKONED	WELLNIGH	DECLASSE	FERMENTS
DESIGNED	MEDIATES	RECKONED	DECLAIMS	CELLISTS	HEMMINGS
RESIGNED	REGISTRY	WEAKENED	RECLAIMS	REALISES	LEMMINGS
DEFIANCE	PEDICURE	RECKONUP	VELLEITY	REALISTS	SEGMENTS
DEVIANCE	RETICULE	RECKONER	SEALSKIN	DEFLATED	TERMINUS
RELIANCE	RESIDUAL	WEEKENDS	CELLULAR	DEPLETED	YEOMANRY
REGIONAL	RESIDUUM	NECKBONE	HELLENIC	DEFLATES	HERMIONE
BEGINNER	BELIEVED	BEDKNOBS	DECLINED	DEPLETES	TEAMWORK
DESIGNER	RELIEVED	KENKESEY	RECLINED	ZEALOTRY	BELMOPAN
BENIGNLY	MEDIEVAL	CELLMATE	BETLYNCH	NELLDUNN	MESMERIC
LENIENCY	BELIEVER	TELLTALE	DESLYNAM	JEALOUSY	REEMERGE
SEMINOLE	BELIEVES	WELLMADE	BEDLINEN	SEALEVEL	BESMIRCH
SEMITONE	RELIEVES	KENLOACH	BERLINER	FELLOVER	LETMESEE
AERIFORM	REVIEWED	KEELHAUL	RECLINER	KEELOVER	HERMETIC
BENIDORM	REVIEWER	SEALABLE	CEILINGS	BELLOWED	HELMETED

DEEMSTER	WETNURSE	DECODERS	FELONIES	REHOUSED	NEOPRENE
TEAMSTER	LEONARDO	DEVOTEES	MELODIES	REHOUSES	SETPIECE
TERMITES	LEONURIS	RECOVERS	MEMORIES	TENONSAW	LEAPYEAR
GEOMETRY	TENNISON	REMODELS	HEDONIST	LEMONTEA	REAPPEAR
VERMOUTH	TENNYSON	REDOLENT	NEPOTIST	BESOTTED	DEEPNESS
WEYMOUTH	REUNITED	RECOVERY	DETOXIFY	DECOCTED	HELPLESS
BERNHARD	JEANETTE	REMOTELY	FEROCITY	DEPORTED	DEEPFELT
JEANPAUL	NEONATAL	BEFOGGED	VELOCITY	REPORTED	PEEPSHOW
DEANCAIN	BEANITEM	BELONGED	RECOILED	REPOTTED	HELPLINE
HERNEBAY	LEINSTER	MELODICA	REMOULDS	REROUTED	NEAPTIDE
REDNECKS	REUNITES	SEMOLINA	AEROFLOT	RETORTED	TEMPTING
REENACTS	BEANCURD	SENORITA	DEFORMED	REVOLTED	DESPAIRS
GENNEDUP	BENNEVIS	VERONICA	REFORMED	DEPORTEE	DESPOILS
SEINFELD	DECORATE	AEROLITE	REFORMER	BEGOTTEN	DEWPOINT
MEUNIERE	DESOLATE	DEMONISE	REFORMAT	BELOSTON	SETPOINT
MEANWELL	DETONATE	GENOCIDE	BEMOANED	REPORTER	ZEPPELIN
SEANBEAN	LEMONADE	MEMORISE	REJOINED	REROUTES	DEEPENED
SEANPENN	PERORATE	PEROXIDE	RENOWNED	AEROSTAT	REOPENED
REINDEER	RELOCATE	BECOMING	DENOUNCE	DEVOUTLY	RESPONSE
KEENNESS	RENOVATE	DECODING	RENOUNCE	RESOLUTE	TENPENCE
LEANNESS	RESONATE	DECOKING	HEROINES	DEVOLVED	HELPINGS
MEANDERS	CENOTAPH	DEMOTING	REBOUNDS	RESOLVED	RESPONDS
MEANNESS	DEBONAIR	DENOTING	RECOUNTS	REVOLVED	SERPENTS
REINVENT	REMOVALS	DEPOSING	RESOUNDS	REVOLVER	WEAPONRY
REINVEST	AERONAUT	DEVOTING	MESOZOIC	DEVOLVES	PEEPHOLE
JENNIFER	RESONANT	REBORING	BENOJOKE	RESOLVES	PEPPERED
TEENAGER	DEMOBBED	REMOVING	AEROFOIL	REVOLVES	RESPIRED
HENNIGHT	REDOUBLE	REPOSING	JEROBOAM	LEEOTWAY	TEMPERED
JEANRHYS	REJOICED	REVOKING	REHOBOAM	HELPMATE	LEAPFROG
MEANTIME	REJOICES	XEROXING	ZEROHOUR	JETPLANE	TEMPORAL
FEINTING	RECORDED	DEMOLISH	AEROSOLS	KEEPSAKE	HESPERUS
HEINRICH	SECONDED	MEMORIAL	DECOROUS	SEAPLANE	LEOPARDS
REYNOLDS	BEHOLDEN	HEDONISM	VENOMOUS	TEMPLATE	RESPIRES
PETNAMES	BEHOLDER	NEPOTISM	AEROLOGY	KEEPBACK	SEAPORTS
FERNANDO	NEWORDER	DEMOTION	OENOLOGY	KEEPDARK	HENPARTY
MEANINGS	RECORDER	DEVONIAN	RECOUPED	KEEPRANK	JEOPARDY
PENNANTS	SECONDER	DEVOTION	BELOWPAR	KEEPCALM	TEAPARTY
PENNINES	SECONDLY	GERONIMO	DEVOURED	VESPIARY	DESPISED
REMNANTS	KEROSENE	PECORINO	RECOURSE	VESPUCCI	DESPISES
BEANPOLE	VERONESE	AEROBICS	RESOURCE	HENPECKS	TEMPESTS
JEANBOHT	MELODEON	BEGONIAS	DEVOURER	RESPECTS	DESPOTIC
SENNAPOD	BETOKENS	DEPOSITS	DEMOCRAT	BELPAESE	GEPPETTO

DEMPSTER	HEARHEAR	MERRYMEN	DEPRIVES	REASSESS	CENSURED
RESPITES	DEBRIEFS	RETRENCH	REPROVES	WELSHERS	LEISURED
SEAPOWER	FEARLESS	BEARINGS	REGROWTH	MESSIEST	MEASURED
NEOPHYTE	HEARTENS	HERRINGS	TEARAWAY	REASSERT	TESSERAE
SEAQUAKE	LEARNERS	REPRINTS	WEARAWAY	MESSAGES	CENSURES
DECREASE	NEARNESS	TERRINES	BETRAYED	MEMSAHIB	DESSERTS
RECREATE	PEERLESS	FEARSOME	DEFRAYED	PERSPIRE	MEASURES
REPROACH	REORDERS	YEARBOOK	BETRAYAL	TEESSIDE	CENSUSES
DEERPARK	TERRIERS	BEERBOHM	DEFRAYAL	FEASTING	PERSISTS
NEARDARK	MERRIEST	HEIRLOOM	BETRAYER	WELSHING	REISSUED
BEERHALL	WEARIEST	TEARDOWN	PEERGYNT	MELSMITH	REASSURE
PEARMAIN	WEIRDEST	WEARDOWN	TERRAZZO	REASSIGN	REISSUES
YEARSAGO	TERRIFIC	BEDROOMS	KEYSTAGE	MESSTINS	SEESAWED
HEARMASS	KERRIGAN	REARMOST	MESSMATE	REDSKINS	GERSHWIN
MEERKATS	SEARCHED	TERRAPIN	PERSUADE	REDSHIFT	LEOSAYER
RETREADS	SEARCHME	DECREPIT	SEASCAPE	REDSHIRT	PENTLAND
RETREATS	WEARTHIN	PEARTREE	SEASNAKE	FEISTILY	TESTCARD
NEAREAST	SEARCHER	TETRARCH	TEASMADE	WEASELLY	WESTWARD
FEBRUARY	SEARCHES	PEARDROP	REDSHANK	WELSHMAN	HEATWAVE
GETREADY	GEORGINA	TEARDROP	HENSHALL	LESSENED	TESTCASE
BEARABLE	NEARSIDE	NEBRASKA	MESSHALL	REASONED	HEATRASH
TERRIBLE	DECRYING	REPRISAL	SEASNAIL	SEASONED	KEPTBACK
TERRIBLY	FERRYING	DEFROSTS	JEWSHARP	HELSINKI	LEFTBACK
RETRACED	LEARNING	NEUROSES	SEESTARS	PERSONAL	LEFTBANK
TERRACED	REARMING	NEUROSIS	GETSMART	SEASONAL	WESTBANK
METRICAL	WEARYING	NEUROTIC	NEWSCAST	PEASANTS	MEATBALL
JERRYCAN	YEARLING	FERRETED	REDSTART	GEMSTONE	RESTRAIN
DERRICKS	YEARNING	SECRETED	TESSDALY	KEYSTONE	NEUTRALS
DETRACTS	GEORGIAN	SERRATED	FEASIBLE	SEASHORE	BESTIARY
REFRACTS	HEARTIER	FERRETER	LEASABLE	CESSPOOL	TERTIARY
RETRACES	GEORDIES	BETROTHS	REUSABLE	MESSROOM	VERTEBRA
RETRACTS	NEARMISS	DETRITUS	SENSIBLE	NEWSROOM	BEATABLE
TERRACES	RECRUITS	REWRITES	FEASIBLY	TEASPOON	PENTACLE
DEGRADED	REFRAINS	SECRETES	SENSIBLY	PENSIONS	TENTACLE
BEGRUDGE	REARVIEW	SECRETLY	BEDSOCKS	SENSUOUS	VERTICAL
DEGRADES	HEARTILY	DEFRAUDS	MESSEDUP	SESSIONS	DEATHCAP
HEBRIDES	PEARLJAM	REGROUPS	FEASTDAY	VERSIONS	LETTUCES
BEFRIEND	BEARSKIN	TEARDUCT	BEDSTEAD	BEASPORT	KENTUCKY
DERRIERE	DEERSKIN	DEPRAVED	NEWSPEAK	KENSTOTT	AESTHETE
REFREEZE	FERRULES	DEPRIVED	NEWSREEL	REXSTOUT	SETTLEON
REPRIEVE	FERRYMAN	REPROVED	SEASHELL	SEASCOUT	SETTLEUP
RETRIEVE	FERRYMEN	REDRIVER	MENSWEAR	CENSORED	DEFTNESS

FEATHERS	CENTRIST	BEETROOT	TESTATOR	REDUCING	REBUTTED
HEATHENS	RESTRICT	SEATROUT	GERTRUDE	REFUSING	RESULTED
HEATHERS	GENTRIFY	CENTUPLE	RESTCURE	REFUTING	REBUTTAL
KESTRELS	LENTLILY	SEXTUPLE	TESTTUBE	RESUMING	SERVICED
LEATHERS	RESTYLED	BETTERED	CENTAURS	SECURING	SERVICES
MEATLESS	VENTOLIN	FEATURED	CENTAURY	SEDUCING	PERVADED
NEATNESS	GENTILES	FESTERED	AESTIVAL	DELUSION	SELVEDGE
PERTNESS	PEPTALKS	FETTERED	FESTIVAL	PERUVIAN	REVVEDUP
RESTLESS	REPTILES	GESTURED	BENTOVER	PECULIAR	PERVADES
SELTZERS	RESTYLES	HECTORED	LEFTOVER	BEAUTIES	FERVIDLY
SETTLERS	TEXTILES	LECTURED	CENTAVOS	DEPUTIES	HEAVIEST
WEATHERS	MENTALLY	LETTERED	BESTOWED	PETUNIAS	NERVEGAS
HEFTIEST	RENTAMOB	PESTERED	BESTOWAL	SEQUOIAS	MELVILLE
MEATIEST	CENTIMES	RESTORED	TEATOWEL	VESUVIUS	SERVALAN
SEATBELT	TEUTONIC	TEETERED	REGULATE	BEAULIEU	CERVELAT
SENTIENT	DESTINED	TEXTURED	BEQUEATH	BEAUTIFY	LEAVENED
VESTMENT	NEATENED	VENTURED	BEAUVAIS	SECURITY	LEAVINGS
FEATHERY	SENTENCE	MELTORME	REGULARS	DEBUNKED	SERVANTS
LEATHERY	SENTINEL	SESTERCE	DEBUTANT	REPUBLIC	SERVINGS
PETTIFER	BEATENUP	PECTORAL	PETULANT	BEGUILED	FERVENCY
HEPTAGON	BEATINGS	TEXTURAL	RECUSANT	BEGUILES	HEAVENLY
PENTAGON	MEETINGS	LECTURER	PENUMBRA	REBUILDS	LEAVEOUT
NESTEGGS	SEXTANTS	RESTORER	BENUMBED	SEXUALLY	PERVERSE
VESTIGES	BENTWOOD	DENTURES	PEDUNCLE	RESUBMIT	HELVETIA
BEATRICE	DEPTFORD	FEATURES	REFUNDED	RETURNED	VERWOERD
BEATTIME	HERTFORD	GESTURES	BEFUDDLE	SEQUENCE	REAWAKEN
BESTRIDE	WESTWOOD	HECTARES	CERULEAN	BEAUVOIR	REDWOODS
WESTLIFE	DEXTROSE	LECTERNS	PERUSERS	NEBULOUS	NEWWORLD
BEETLING	RESTHOME	LECTURES	REFUGEES	SEDULOUS	HEPWORTH
BERTHING	TENTOONE	PERTURBS	REQUIEMS	BEAUFORT	SEAWATER
CENTRING	MEATLOAF	RESTARTS	SEDUCERS	BEAUMONT	TERYLENE
LEFTWING	RENTBOOK	RESTORES	DEMURELY	DELUSORY	VERYWELL
NESTLING	TEXTBOOK	TEXTURES	SECURELY	DEMURRED	RECYCLED
SEETHING	RESTROOM	VENTURES	REBUFFED	RECURRED	RECYCLES
SETTLING	MELTDOWN	WESTERNS	DEBUGGED	REQUIRED	VERYGOOD
TEETHING	NEXTDOOR	HEATHROW	DEPUTISE	DEMURRAL	KENYATTA
CENTRISM	DESTROYS	WESTERLY	BEMUSING	REQUIRES	DEWYEYED
NEUTRINO	FESTOONS	JETTISON	DEDUCING	REPULSED	SELZNICK
BEATNIKS	MENTIONS	DENTISTS	DEFUSING	BEQUESTS	PENZANCE
PERTAINS	NEUTRONS	SEXTETTE	DELUDING	REPULSES	OFFANDON
SENTRIES	PEATMOSS	TEETOTAL	PERUSING	REQUESTS	EFFACING
VESTRIES	SECTIONS	TEETOTUM	REBUKING	DEDUCTED	AFFAIRES

OFFBREAK	IGLESIAS	CHEAPEST	CHACONNE	SHREWISH	THEIDIOT
OFFDRIVE	OGRESSES	THRASHED	CHICANES	SHOEBILL	SHRIEKED
AFTERALL	AGEGROUP	SHEATHES	THECROWD	CHEEKIER	THRILLED
OFFENCES	EGGHEADS	THEASHES	CHECKOUT	CHEERIER	THRILLER
OFFENDED	UGLINESS	THRASHES	CHICKPEA	WHEELIES	CHAIRMAN
OFFENDER	UGLIFIED	THIAMINE	THICKSET	CHEEKILY	CHAIRMEN
OFFERING	IGNITING	CHEATING	CHADBAND	CHEERILY	CHRISSIE
AFTERSUN	IGNITION	SHEARING	SHADRACH	WHEEDLED	CHAINSAW
AFFECTED	AGRIMONY	THWACKED	SHUDDERS	WHEEDLES	CHRISTIE
EFFECTED	EGOISTIC	WHEATLEY	SHADIEST	SHOEHORN	CHRISTEN
AFTERYOU	EGOMANIA	SHRAPNEL	SHEDDING	PHAETONS	THEJOKER
EFFICACY	AGENCIES	THEATRES	THUDDING	THREWOUT	THEKNACK
AFAIRCOP	AGONISED	THWARTED	SHODDILY	THRENODY	SHAKEOFF
OFFICERS	AGONISES	THEBEACH	THEDALES	SHOETREE	CHALICES
PFEIFFER	IGNORANT	THEBEAST	SHEDLOAD	SHEEPRUN	THELODGE
AFFIXING	AGOODFEW	CHUBBIER	THEDOORS	THREATEN	CHALDEAN
OFFICIAL	IGNORING	SHABBIER	THEDERBY	SHIFTERS	CHALMERS
EFFIGIES	IGNOMINY	SHABBILY	RHODESIA	SHIFTING	SHELTERS
AFFINITY	AGOODJOB	THEBLITZ	SHEDEVIL	SHIFTIER	CHILLING
AFFIRMED	AGRONOMY	SHEBANGS	SHADOWED	SHIFTILY	SHELLING
AFFIANCE	AGNOSTIC	THEBIRDS	SHOELACE	SHUFFLED	SHELVING
OFFLOADS	EGGPLANT	THEBITCH	CHEETAHS	SHUFFLER	SHILLING
AFFLICTS	EGYPTIAN	THECHAMP	SHIELDED	SHUFFLES	CHILDISH
AFFLUENT	AGGRIEVE	CHECKBOX	SHREDDED	THEFIXER	CHILLIER
EFFLUENT	EGGSHELL	CHOCICES	THREADED	SHAGBARK	PHILLIPS
EFFLUVIA	AGOSTINI	CHECKERS	SHEEPDOG	SHAGREEN	SHELTIES
PFENNIGS	EGOTRIPS	CHICKENS	SHEEPDIP	THEGREYS	PHILOMEL
AFFORDED	EGGTIMER	SHOCKERS	SHREDDER	THUGGERY	THALAMUS
OFCOURSE	AGITPROP	THICKENS	SHREWDER	CHUGGING	SHALLOTS
OFFPRINT	EGOTISTS	THICKETS	SHREWDLY	THUGGISH	SHALLOWS
OFFPISTE	AGITATED	THICKEST	CHEEZELS	THEGOLEM	PHILIPPA
AFFRONTS	AGITATOR	CHECKING	CHEERFUL	THEGAMES	PHILIPPE
OFFSTAGE	AGITATES	CHUCKING	THRESHED	THEGROUP	CHOLERIC
OFFSHORE	AGNUSDEI	SHOCKING	THRESHER	THEHAGUE	CHILDREN
OFFSHOOT	EGGWHITE	SHUCKING	THRESHES	THEHOURS	SHELDUCK
OFFSTUMP	EGGWHISK	WHACKING	CHEEKING	THAILAND	CHEMICAL
EFFUSIVE	THEALAMO	THICKISH	CHEERING	SHIITAKE	CHIMEDIN
EFFUSING	PHEASANT	CHUCKLED	SHEETING	CHOIRBOY	CHAMBERS
EFFUSION	THEATEAM	SHACKLED	THIEVING	SHRIVELS	CHAMFERS
OFFWHITE	WHEATEAR	CHUCKLES	WHEELING	CHAINING	CHAMPERS
AGRARIAN	CHEAPENS	SHACKLES	WHEEZING	CHAIRING	CHIMNEYS
AGREEING	SHEARERS	CHOCOLAT	SHEEPISH	THRIVING	SHIMMERS

THUMPERS	THINNESS	THANKYOU	CHOPPING	CHARNHAM	CHORUSES
WHIMPERS	THUNDERS	THROBBED	SHIPPING	CHURCHES	CHARLTON
THOMSETT	WHINGERS	SHROUDED	SHOPPING	CHARLIZE	SHERATON
SHIMMERY	SHINIEST	SHOOTERS	WHIPPING	CHARGING	THORNTON
THEMAFIA	THINNEST	THEOREMS	WHOPPING	CHARMING	THOROUGH
SHAMEFUL	CHANCERY	THROWERS	SHOPGIRL	CHARRING	THORBURN
THEMAGUS	THUNDERY	THRONGED	CHAPPIES	CHIRPING	WHEREVER
SHIMMIED	THANKFUL	CHLORIDE	SHIPSLOG	CHURNING	THIRDWAY
CHAMPING	THINKFIT	CHLORINE	WHIPCORD	SHIRKING	THESSALY
CHOMPING	SHANGHAI	THEORISE	CHAPBOOK	WHIRLING	CHASUBLE
THUMPING	CHINCHIN	CHOOSING	RHAPSODY	WHIRRING	PHYSICAL
KHOMEINI	WHINCHAT	SHOOTING	CHIPOTLE	CHURLISH	PHOSGENE
CHAMPION	WHINNIED	THROWING	CHAPATIS	SHARPISH	THESHEIK
SHIMMIES	CHANCING	WHOOPING	CHEPSTOW	SHORTISH	CHASSEUR
SHAMBLES	CHANGING	CHROMIUM	CHIPMUNK	CHARTISM	CHASTENS
THIMBLES	CHANNING	THEORIES	CHOPSUEY	CHIRPIER	SHYSTERS
THEMUMMY	CHANTING	SHOOTIST	CHEQUERS	CHERRIES	WHISKERS
CHAMONIX	SHUNNING	THEORIST	SHORTAGE	GHERKINS	WHISPERS
RHOMBOID	SHUNTING	THEODORE	THIRDAGE	SHERRIES	WHISKERY
SHAMROCK	THANKING	SHOOTOUT	THERMALS	THIRTIES	THESIGER
SHAMPOOS	THINKING	THROWOUT	CHARLADY	CHARTIST	CHASTISE
WHIMBREL	THINNING	THEOLOGY	PHARMACY	CHIRPILY	CHESHIRE
CHAMORRO	THINNISH	THEOCRAT	CHERUBIC	CHEROKEE	THISLIFE
CHAMBRAY	GHANAIAN	THROSTLE	CHERUBIM	CHORTLED	GHOSTING
THOMPSON	CHUNKIER	THROTTLE	THORACIC	SHIRALEE	THESTING
THUMBSUP	CHINDITS	RHEOSTAT	SHORTCUT	CHORTLES	WHISKING
CHEMISES	SHANDIES	SHIPYARD	SHERIDAN	THIRDMAN	CHISWICK
CHEMISTS	SHANTIES	SHIPMATE	CHARADES	CHURINGA	THESPIAN
THEMATIC	WHINNIES	WHIPLASH	THURSDAY	SHERWOOD	WHISKIES
OHMMETER	CHENILLE	CHAPLAIN	CHARLENE	CHARLOCK	THESAINT
PHANTASM	SHANKLIN	THEPIANO	CHERWELL	SHERLOCK	CHASTITY
CHINWAGS	CHANDLER	SHEPHERD	SHARLEEN	CHARCOAL	WHISTLED
THINKBIG	SHINGLES	CHAPPELL	THIRTEEN	KHARTOUM	SHASHLIK
PHONEBOX	CHINAMAN	CHAPTERS	CHARGERS	CHARIOTS	WHISTLER
CHANCELS	SHINBONE	CHOPPERS	CHARMERS	CHEROOTS	PHYSALIS
CHANNELS	PHANTOMS	SHOPPERS	CHARTERS	PHARAOHS	THISTLES
CHANTERS	THANKSTO	WHIPPETS	SHARPENS	CHURNOUT	WHISTLES
CHINLESS	CHINATEA	WHOPPERS	SHIRKERS	SHAREOUT	CHESSMAN
CHUNTERS	PHONETIC	SHIPMENT	SHORTENS	CHARTRES	CHESSMEN
SHUNTERS	RHINITIS	CHOPCHOP	SHARPEST	CHARISMA	CHESTNUT
THINKERS	SHANTUNG	THEPRIZE	SHORTEST	CHARISSE	CHISINAU
THINNERS	WHENEVER	CHIPPING	SHERIFFS	PHARISEE	SHOSHONE

CHISHOLM	SHUTDOWN	WHIZZING	FINALITY	TIMBUKTU	MISCALLS
PHASEOUT	WHATNOTS	WHIZZKID	HILARITY	PIEBALDS	PICCOLOS
PHYSIQUE	WHITEOUT	RHIZOMES	VITALITY	DISBANDS	TITCOMBE
THESETUP	CHUTZPAH	CHEZNOUS	VIVACITY	FIZBROWN	PINCENEZ
SHETLAND	RHETORIC	HIMALAYA	HIJACKED	TIMBERED	CINCHONA
THATSAID	WHITETIE	VICARAGE	HIJACKER	AIRBORNE	DISCLOSE
WHITEANT	SHOTGUNS	MICAWBER	DISABLED	DISBURSE	OILCLOTH
CHATEAUX	WHATEVER	CIGARBOX	RIVALLED	LIMBERUP	DISCIPLE
CHATTELS	CHATAWAY	FINANCED	TIMALLEN	FILBERTS	MINCEPIE
CHATTERS	THOUSAND	FINANCES	MIRACLES	BILBERRY	VISCERAL
SHATTERS	CHOUXBUN	RIBALDRY	DISALLOW	CIABATTA	DISCARDS
SHUTTERS	SHOULDER	WIZARDRY	DISARMED	DIABETIC	DISCERNS
PHOTOFIT	SHRUGGED	MILANESE	PINAFORE	DIABETES	TIMCURRY
WHATOFIT	THOUGHTS	LIMABEAN	VIVAVOCE	AIRBRUSH	DIOCESAN
WHITEFLY	THRUSHES	CITADELS	RIGATONI	JIMBOWEN	CIRCUSES
THATCHED	SHOUTING	MINARETS	PICAROON	PILCHARD	MISCASTS
THATCHER	GHOULISH	FILAMENT	RIGADOON	GIMCRACK	BISCOTTI
THATCHES	SHRUNKEN	LIGAMENT	BIGAMOUS	DISCLAIM	TINCTURE
CHITCHAT	THRUMMED	GIRAFFES	PICADORS	SINCLAIR	DISCOUNT
WHITEHOT	SHRUGOFF	DIMAGGIO	DILATORY	AIRCRAFT	MISCOUNT
CHATSHOW	THRUSTER	PIRANHAS	BIGAPPLE	PIECHART	PIECRUST
CHATLINE	CHIVVIED	VITAMINA	DISAGREE	DISCRETE	VISCOUNT
THETHIEF	CHIVVIES	VITAMINB	DICAPRIO	MITCHELL	DISCOVER
CHATTING	CHIVALRY	VITAMINC	CICATRIX	WITCHELL	WILDCARD
SHUTTING	SHAVINGS	VITAMIND	DISARRAY	CIRCLETS	WINDWARD
THETHING	CHEVIOTS	FINALISE	LIMASSOL	FILCHERS	BIRDCAGE
WHETTING	CHEVRONS	FIXATIVE	DIDACTIC	KITCHENS	BIRDBATH
WHATWITH	SHIVERED	VITAMINE	GIGANTIC	PITCHERS	BIRDCALL
THETRIAL	SHOWCASE	DILATING	DISASTER	DISCREET	WINDFALL
WHATSITS	SHOWEDUP	VITAMINK	PILASTER	MISCHIEF	WINDFARM
CHATTILY	SHOWREEL	TITANIUM	DISABUSE	BIRCHING	MISDEALS
WHITTLED	CHOWMEIN	VIVARIUM	LIGATURE	BITCHING	WILDCATS
WHITELIE	SHOWGIRL	CITATION	GIGABYTE	CIRCLING	WINDLASS
SHUTTLES	THEWOMEN	DILATION	PINBOARD	DITCHING	MISDEALT
WHITTLES	SHOWHOME	FIXATION	RIOBRAVO	FILCHING	BIDDABLE
WHITELAW	SHOWROOM	LIBATION	ZIMBABWE	HITCHING	VIADUCTS
WHITELEY	SHOWDOWN	RIPARIAN	BITBYBIT	PINCHING	BIGDADDY
RHYTHMIC	SHOWBOAT	LITANIES	BIGBREAK	PITCHING	BINDWEED
WHITENED	SHOWERED	VITAMINS	TIEBREAK	WINCHING	BIRDSEED
WHITENER	THEWAVES	BIGAMIST	DIMBLEBY	BISCUITS	HINDHEAD
THETFORD	THEYEARS	FINALIST	NIBBLING	CIRCUITS	BIRDSEYE
CHATROOM	CHEYENNE	TIRAMISU	AIRBRICK	CIRCULAR	MINDSEYE

WILDFELL	AIREDALE	LIFEPEER	SIDEKICK	PIPEDOWN	DIRECTLY
DIDDLERS	DINENAGE	FINENESS	LIBERIAN	TIMEWORN	SILENTLY
FIDDLERS	FIRESALE	LIFELESS	LIMEKILN	FIREDOOR	FINETUNE
HINDLEGS	LIBERACE	LIKENESS	NIGERIAN	TIMEPOOR	SINECURE
KINDNESS	LIBERATE	PIKELETS	SIBERIAN	AILERONS	HIDEOUTS
MILDNESS	LITERATE	RIPENESS	LIVELIER	VICEROYS	WINEGUMS
MINDLESS	PIPERADE	TIMELESS	KINETICS	VIPEROUS	WISEGUYS
RINDLESS	PIXELATE	TIRELESS	NICETIES	DINEDOUT	LIFEBUOY
TIDDLERS	LIMEWASH	VILENESS	NINEPINS	HIREDOUT	LIKEFURY
WILDNESS	LITERATI	WIRELESS	NINETIES	LIFEBOAT	FIREAWAY
GIDDIEST	KITEMARK	LIFEBELT	SIBELIUS	MINEHOST	GIVEAWAY
WILDWEST	SIDEWALK	EISENERZ	TIBERIUS	TIREDOUT	HIDEAWAY
WINDIEST	TIDEMARK	DIVERGED	WINELIST	FINESPUN	WIDEEYED
LIEDOGGO	FINEGAEL	HIREDGUN	FIDELITY	LIFESPAN	RIFFRAFF
BIRDLIME	FIREBALL	DIVERGES	BIWEEKLY	WIDEOPEN	HIPFLASK
WILDFIRE	FIREWALL	FIRESHIP	LIBELLED	LIMETREE	JIFFYBAG
WILDLIFE	FIREDAMP	SIDESHOW	SIDESLIP	PINETREE	AIRFIELD
WILDRICE	TIMEWARP	FIREBIRD	FIRECLAY	SIDEDRUM	MIDFIELD
WINDPIPE	LIBERALS	LIVERIED	LINESMAN	FIRETRAP	OILFIELD
DIDDLING	MINERALS	SIDEWIND	LINESMEN	FINEARTS	DIFFRING
FIDDLING	SIDECARS	FIRESIDE	SIDESMAN	FIREARMS	PIFFLING
KINDLING	SIDEWAYS	LIFELIKE	SIDESMEN	SIDEARMS	RIFFLING
MIDDLING	LIFERAFT	LIFELINE	DILEMMAS	BIYEARLY	PITFALLS
WILDSILK	LITERACY	LIFESIZE	HIBERNIA	DISEASED	FITFULLY
WINDMILL	LITERARY	LIFETIME	DIVEBOMB	LICENSED	SINFULLY
HINDUISM	VINEGARY	LIKEWISE	TIMEBOMB	CINEASTE	WILFULLY
KINDLIER	LIKEABLE	LIVEWIRE	FIREWOOD	LICENSEE	SINFONIA
VINDALOO	SIZEABLE	PIPELINE	MIKETODD	DISEASES	DIFFERED
RIDDANCE	MIXEDBAG	SIDELINE	PINEWOOD	LICENSES	OILFIRED
FINDINGS	TIGERBAY	VICELIKE	SIDEROAD	BISECTED	PILFERED
BIRDSONG	SILENCED	HIRELING	CICERONE	DIGESTED	AIRFORCE
WINDHOEK	WISEACRE	LIKENING	PINECONE	DIRECTED	PILFERER
WINDSOCK	SILENCER	RIPENING	TIMEZONE	DIVERTED	DIFFUSED
WILDFOWL	LICENCES	RIVETING	TIRESOME	DIVESTED	DIFFUSER
DIEDDOWN	SILENCES	VIDEOING	HIVEDOFF	DIGESTIF	DIFFUSES
PIEDNOIR	GIVEODDS	WIDENING	LIFELONG	LIVEITUP	DISGRACE
WILDBOAR	MIKEREID	LIVERISH	SIDELONG	MIXERTAP	RINGMAIN
HINDMOST	MINEHEAD	SIDEDISH	FIREWORK	SIDESTEP	DIAGRAMS
PIEDMONT	MISERERE	TIGERISH	NICEWORK	BICESTER	DINGBATS
HINDERED	SIDEREAL	VIPERISH	TIMELOCK	DIRECTOR	ZIEGFELD
WILDDUCK	TIMETEAM	FIRERISK	WIREWOOL	FIVESTAR	KINGLEAR
VINEYARD	NINETEEN	LIMERICK	LIFEFORM	PIPETTES	GIGGLERS

RINGLETS	KINGCRAB	TIGHTENS	RICHARDS	MIXINGIN	LIAISONS
SINGLETS	FINGERED	LIGHTEST	HIGHBROW	GIVINGUP	VISITORS
WINGLESS	JIGGERED	TIGHTEST	WITHDRAW	LININGUP	WINIFRED
DINGIEST	LINGERED	RIGHTFUL	WITHDREW	MIXINGUP	FILIGREE
DISGUISE	DISGORGE	MICHIGAN	SIGHTSEE	SIZINGUP	NIJINSKY
KINGSIZE	LINGERIE	WITHTHAT	HIGHJUMP	FINISHED	DISINTER
LINGUINE	NIGGARDS	FISHWIFE	HIGHBURY	FINISHES	MINISTER
RINGSIDE	ZIGGURAT	HIGHFIVE	DISHEVEL	MINIDISC	SINISTER
GIGGLING	KINGSROW	HIGHLIFE	TIGHTWAD	VILIFIED	MINISTRY
HINGEING	GINGERLY	HIGHRISE	TITICACA	CIVILISE	RIDICULE
JIGGLING	DISGUSTS	HIGHTIDE	LITIGATE	DIVISIVE	CIVILWAR
JINGLING	FIDGETED	HIGHWIRE	MILITATE	MINIMISE	KIBITZED
MINGLING	KINGSTON	FIGHTING	MITIGATE	DIVIDING	KIBITZER
NIGGLING	RINGPULL	LIGHTING	SIBILATE	DIVINING	KIBITZES
SINGEING	GINGIVAL	RIGHTING	SILICATE	LIAISING	MISJUDGE
TINGEING	RIDGEWAY	SIGHTING	TITIVATE	LIMITING	SIDJAMES
TINGLING	HIGHLAND	MIGHTIER	KIRIBATI	VISITING	LISKEARD
WIGGLING	MISHEARD	EIGHTIES	MINICABS	DIMINISH	MILKMAID
JINGOISM	FISHCAKE	NIGHTIES	LITIGANT	PIRIPIRI	NICKCAVE
DINGHIES	LIGHTALE	MIGHTILY	MILITANT	NIHILISM	NICKNAME
PILGRIMS	MISHMASH	NIGHTJAR	SIBILANT	CIVILIAN	KICKBACK
JINGOIST	FISHHAWK	MICHELLE	VIGILANT	DIVISION	NICKPARK
LINGUIST	FISHTANK	MICHELIN	MILITARY	SICILIAN	BIRKHALL
SINGULAR	HIGHBALL	NICHOLAS	PITIABLE	VIRIDIAN	KIRKWALL
KINGSLEY	RICHHALL	NICHOLLS	PITIABLY	FILIPINO	NICKLAUS
RIDGELEY	FISHFARM	SIPHONED	HIBISCUS	VILIFIES	DICKYBOW
VIRGINIA	HIGHMASS	MICHENER	DIVIDEND	NIHILIST	LINKEDUP
DIAGONAL	TIMHEALY	FISHPOND	AIRINESS	CIVILITY	PICKEDUP
VIRGINAL	NIGHTCAP	HIGHROAD	CITIZENS	DIVINITY	WICKEDLY
RINGGOAL	DISHEDUP	RICHMOND	DIVIDERS	NIHILITY	PICKMEUP
DIAGNOSE	MICHAELA	WITHHOLD	DIVINERS	RIGIDITY	SICKNESS
RINGDOVE	WITHHELD	WISHBONE	OILINESS	TIMIDITY	RISKIEST
DINGDONG	HIGHTECH	FIGHTOFF	PITILESS	VICINITY	RICKSHAW
KINGKONG	FISHMEAL	FISHBOWL	TIDINESS	VIRILITY	PICKLING
PINGPONG	EIGHTEEN	NIGHTOWL	TININESS	MIMICKED	TICKLING
SINGSONG	HIGHGEAR	HIGHNOON	WILINESS	MIMICKER	TINKLING
KINGCOAL	FIGHTERS	HIGHSPOT	WIRINESS	CIVILLAW	TICKLISH
RINGWORM	HIGHNESS	DITHERED	DILIGENT	VIVIENNE	PICKWICK
KINGJOHN	HIGHSEAS	WITHERED	LINIMENT	VISIONON	KINKAJOU
KINGDOMS	LIGHTENS	HITHERTO	VITILEVU	PIMIENTO	SICKENED
LIPGLOSS	LIGHTERS	DITHERER	DIVINELY	SILICONE	SICKENER
WINGSPAN	RICHNESS	DIEHARDS	GIVINGIN	HITITOFF	KILKENNY

PICKFORD	DIALLING	VILLETTE	FIANCEES	WIDOWERS	MISPRINT
SILKWOOD	FIELDING	VIOLATES	GIANTESS	LILONGWE	PINPOINT
SILKMOTH	WIELDING	BILLOWED	LINNAEUS	PINOCHLE	SIMPLIFY
TICKTOCK	YIELDING	BILLOWEN	PIONEERS	PINOCHET	HISPANIC
SICKROOM	KILLBILL	DISLOYAL	MIDNIGHT	RICOCHET	DISPENSE
SILKWORM	VILLAINS	FIRMHAND	DIANTHUS	NICOTINE	SIXPENCE
NICKROSS	VILLEINS	GIMMICKS	BIGNOISE	MIAOWING	DISPROVE
BICKERED	VILLAINY	GIMMICKY	FIENDISH	PILOTING	SIMPSONS
TINKERED	DISLIKED	FIRMNESS	BIENNIAL	PIVOTING	SIMPERED
PICKETED	DISLIKES	AIRMAILS	MINNELLI	BINOMIAL	DISPERSE
TICKETED	RIFLEMAN	AIRMILES	SIGNALLY	HIROHITO	AIRPORTS
DISKETTE	RIFLEMEN	DISMALLY	CINNAMON	MINORITY	DISPIRIT
TICKOVER	DIPLOMAS	DIAMANTE	MISNOMER	DISOWNED	DISPOSED
NICKOWEN	DIPLOMAT	TINMINER	WINNINGS	SIMONNYE	DISPOSAL
MILKYWAY	WILLUNGA	AILMENTS	LIGNEOUS	LIPOSOME	DISPOSES
PICKAXES	VIOLENCE	DIAMONDS	SIGNPOST	RIGOROUS	DISPUTED
BILLWARD	AIRLINER	PIGMENTS	WINNIPEG	TIMOROUS	DISPATCH
MILLRACE	BINLINER	BIGMONEY	SIGNORAS	VIGOROUS	DISPUTES
MILLWALL	LIPLINER	PINMONEY	LIONISED	KIDOLOGY	DISQUIET
MISLEADS	MILLINER	FILMGOER	DIONYSUS	SINOLOGY	MISQUOTE
WILLIAMS	AIRLINES	FILMNOIR	LIONISES	VIROLOGY	DISROBED
MILLIBAR	BILLINGS	TIAMARIA	PIANISTS	KILOGRAM	DISROBES
BIBLICAL	BIPLANES	SIMMERED	VIGNETTE	TIMORSEA	MICROBES
DIALECTS	FILLINGS	BISMARCK	TINNITUS	LIMOUSIN	MICRODOT
HILLOCKS	MIDLANDS	MISMATCH	BIANNUAL	RIPOSTES	DISRAELI
DISLODGE	PIGLINGS	DIAMETER	KIMNOVAK	RISOTTOS	FIERCELY
FILLEDUP	SIBLINGS	FILMSTAR	WINNOWED	HITOUTAT	AIRRIFLE
WILLSELF	GIRLHOOD	TITMOUSE	WINNOWER	LINOCUTS	NITROGEN
BILLKERR	MILLPOND	FILMBUFF	PINOTAGE	LINOTYPE	LIARDICE
DIALLERS	BILLIONS	BIGMOUTH	DINOSAUR	MISOGYNY	MIGRAINE
FIELDERS	KILLJOYS	SIDMOUTH	MINOTAUR	AIRPLANE	PIERCING
SILLIEST	MILLIONS	DISMOUNT	BIFOCALS	DISPLACE	LIARLIAR
AIRLIFTS	ZILLIONS	DISMAYED	BIVOUACS	MISPLACE	AIRRAIDS
PILLAGED	HILLFORT	WINNABLE	KILOWATT	TINPLATE	GINRUMMY
DIALOGUE	LILLIPUT	CINNABAR	MISOGAMY	DISPLAYS	MIGRANTS
MILLIGAN	TITLARKS	BINNACLE	DIVORCED	TIPPLERS	VIBRANCY
PILLAGER	DIALYSIS	PINNACLE	DIVORCEE	NIPPIEST	BIERHOFF
VILLAGER	VIOLISTS	PINNACES	DIVORCES	SIMPLEST	PIERROTS
PILLAGES	BILLETED	SIGNEDON	DISORDER	ZIPPIEST	VITREOUS
VILLAGES	FILLETED	VIENNESE	SIMONDAY	RIPPLING	DISRUPTS
HILLSIDE	VIOLATED	LINNAEAN	LINOLEUM	TIPPLING	MIRRORED
KILLTIME	SILLITOE	SINNFEIN	DISOBEYS	PINPRICK	DIARISTS

DIURETIC	PILSENER	DIATRIBE	BITTERNS	OILWELLS	SKIMPILY
MIGRATED	DISSENTS	DIRTBIKE	DISTORTS	AIRWOMAN	SKIMPOLE
VIBRATED	DIASPORA	BIRTHING	DISTURBS	AIRWOMEN	SKINCARE
LIBRETTO	DIASTOLE	DIETRICH	FIXTURES	HIAWATHA	SKINHEAD
MIGRATES	OILSTONE	MISTRIAL	MIXTURES	AIRWAVES	SKINDEEP
VIBRATES	WINSTONE	PIGTAILS	PICTURES	MIDWIVES	SKINLESS
KINSHASA	FIRSTOFF	DISTRICT	BITTERLY	CITYHALL	SKINTEST
FIRSTAID	MISSIONS	MISTAKEN	SISTERLY	CITYFARM	SKINNING
AIRSPACE	RINSEOUT	MISTAKES	DISTASTE	CITYDESK	SKINNIER
DISSUADE	DIESIRAE	BIATHLON	DIETETIC	SISYPHUS	SKIPLANE
JIMSTARK	MINSTREL	LIVTYLER	DICTATED	BICYCLED	SKIPJACK
KISSABLE	PISSARRO	MISTIMED	DICTATOR	BICYCLES	SKIPPERS
DISSECTS	AIRSTRIP	MISTIMES	DICTATES	SIZZLERS	SKIPPING
AIRSPEED	FISSURES	LISTENED	DISTRUST	FIZZIEST	SKIPANTS
MISSREAD	PIASTRES	DISTANCE	MISTRUST	SIZZLING	SKIRTING
GINSBERG	MISSOURI	PITTANCE	SIMULATE	DIAZEPAM	SKIRMISH
MISSPELL	KISSCURL	LISTENIN	RIVULETS	PIZZERIA	SKISLOPE
EINSTEIN	MISSIVES	NINTENDO	MINUTEST	PJHARVEY	SKETCHED
HIPSTERS	FILTRATE	LISTENER	VIRULENT	DJIBOUTI	SKETCHES
MINSTERS	DISTRAIN	DISTENDS	MINUTELY	EJECTING	SKITTISH
TIPSTERS	VICTUALS	FITTINGS	DIVULGED	EJECTION	SKITTLED
MISSPELT	DISTRACT	LISTINGS	DIVULGES	SJAMBOKS	SKITTLES
MISSPENT	DIRTYDEN	SITTINGS	FIGURINE	AJCRONIN	SKIVVIES
TIPSIEST	FITTEDIN	DISTINCT	MINUTIAE	SKEANDHU	SKEWBALD
HISSYFIT	BIRTHDAY	VIETCONG	DILUTING	OKLAHOMA	CLEAVAGE
GINSLING	FIFTIETH	VIRTUOSI	FIGURING	SKYBLUES	ALMANACK
RIESLING	SIXTIETH	PILTDOWN	MINUTING	SKIDDING	ALMANACS
LIZSMITH	LITTLEMO	VIRTUOSO	DILUTION	SKYDIVER	PLEASANT
TINSMITH	RIOTGEAR	VIRTUOUS	DISUNITY	SKEGNESS	ALHAMBRA
DIPSTICK	DISTRESS	LISTERIA	RITUALLY	SKYJACKS	ALTARBOY
LIPSTICK	LISTLESS	VICTORIA	VISUALLY	SKULLCAP	CLEANCUT
OILSLICK	MISTRESS	WISTERIA	VIBURNUM	SKILLETS	CLEARCUT
PIGSWILL	VINTNERS	HISTORIC	PIQUANCY	SKYLIGHT	OLEANDER
AIRSHIPS	DIRTIEST	FILTERED	BIBULOUS	SKULKING	BLOATERS
KISSKISS	MISTREAT	LITTERED	SIOUXSIE	SKILLION	CLEANERS
OILSKINS	NIFTIEST	MISTERED	SITUATED	UKULELES	CLEAVERS
PIGSTIES	OINTMENT	PICTURED	LIQUEURS	SKYLARKS	GLEANERS
DISSOLVE	WITTIEST	TITTERED	GIOVANNI	SKELETAL	BLEAKEST
LIPSALVE	MIRTHFUL	WINTERED	PITVIPER	SKELETON	CLEANEST
MISSILES	TINTAGEL	WITTERED	RIEVAULX	SKIMMING	CLEAREST
RISSOLES	AIRTIGHT	LITTORAL	BIGWHEEL	SKIMPING	BLEACHED
MIDSOMER	SITTIGHT	GIFTWRAP	KIMWILDE	SKIMPIER	BLEACHES

ALKALINE	SLOBBERY	SLACKING	ALLEYCAT	FLUFFIER	ALLINALL
FLYAKITE	BLABBING	ELECTION	ALOEVERA	CLIFFORD	CLAIMANT
ALLAYING	CLUBBING	PLUCKIER	BLUEBELL	ILLFATED	PLEIADES
BLEATING	SLOBBISH	ALACRITY	ALTEREGO	OLDFRUIT	PLAINEST
CLEANING	PLEBEIAN	PLUCKILY	BLEEPERS	OLDGUARD	CLUINGIN
CLEARING	GLOBULAR	BLACKLEG	CLUELESS	SLUGGARD	ALMIGHTY
CLEAVING	GLOBULES	SLOCOMBE	SLEEPERS	FLAGRANT	CLAIMING
FLOATING	GLOBALLY	BLACKMAN	SLEEKEST	SLUGABED	FLAILING
GLEAMING	CLUBSODA	PLACEMAT	ALLERGIC	ELIGIBLE	BLAIRISM
GLEANING	CLUBROOM	PLACENTA	ALLERGEN	SLAGHEAP	FLUIDITY
GLOAMING	SLYBOOTS	ALICANTE	BLUECHIP	SLOGGERS	ALLIANCE
GLOATING	CLUBROOT	PLACINGS	BLUEBIRD	FLAGSHIP	ALLINONE
PLEADING	BLOCKADE	CLOCKOFF	ALLEGING	ALIGNING	ELSINORE
PLEASING	BLOCKAGE	ELECTORS	ALTERING	CLOGGING	ILLINOIS
PLEATING	GLACIATE	BLACKOUT	BLEEDING	FLAGGING	ELLIPSES
ALDANITI	PLACABLE	CLOCKOUT	BLEEPING	FLOGGING	ELLIPSIS
ALBANIAN	PLACEBOS	ELECTRIC	FLEECING	PLAGUING	ELLIPTIC
ALSATIAN	BLACKBOX	BLACKROD	FLEETING	PLUGGING	CLOISTER
ALPACINO	BLACKCAP	ALACARTE	SLEEPING	SLOGGING	ALTITUDE
BLEARILY	BLACKCAT	GLYCEROL	ALGERIAN	SLUGGISH	BLOKEISH
SLEAZILY	PLACIDLY	PLECTRUM	SLEEPIER	ELEGANCE	BLAKENEY
ALBACORE	BLACKEYE	ELECTRON	ULTERIOR	FLAGPOLE	ULULATED
ALCAPONE	ALLCLEAR	PLACARDS	SLEEPILY	PLUGHOLE	ULULATES
CLEAROFF	BLACKENS	BLACKSEA	ALLENKEY	FLAGDOWN	CLAMBAKE
ALLALONG	FLICKERS	ELICITED	BLUEFLAG	OLDGLORY	PLUMBAGO
ULLAPOOL	GLACIERS	PLACATED	FLUELLEN	OLIGARCH	PLUMBBOB
CLEAROUT	SLACKENS	BLACKTIE	ALDERMAN	ELEGISED	CLAMBERS
ALCATRAZ	SLACKERS	PLACATES	ALDERMEN	ELEGISTS	CLIMBERS
ALLATSEA	SLICKERS	GLADHAND	ALGERNON	ALIGHTED	GLIMMERS
CLEANSED	BLACKEST	GLADRAGS	ALDERNEY	BLIGHTED	GLUMNESS
CLEANSER	BLACKFLY	BLUDGEON	BLUEJOHN	BLIGHTED	PLUMBERS
CLEANSES	BLACKICE	GLADDENS	BLUEMOON	SLIGHTED	PLUMMETS
OLEASTER	ELECTIVE	GLADNESS	ULCEROUS	BLIGHTER	SLIMMERS
PLIANTLY	BLACKING	FLYDRIVE	ALLEGORY	SLIGHTER	SLIMNESS
PLEASURE	BLOCKING	CLADDING	ALDERTON	SLIGHTLY	SLUMBERS
CLEARWAY	CLACKING	PLEDGING	FLUENTLY	ALPHABET	PLUMPEST
CLUBLAND	CLICKING	PLODDING	ALLEYWAY	GLUHWEIN	SLIMIEST
BLABBERS	CLOCKING	SLEDGING	BLUEEYES	ELKHOUND	SLIMMEST
CLOBBERS	CLUCKING	VLADIMIR	OLDFLAME	ALEHOUSE	FLAMBEAU
CLUBBERS	ELECTING	GLADIOLI	OLDFIELD	ALTHOUGH	FLAMEGUN
GLIBNESS	FLICKING	ALIENATE	BLUFFERS	ULTIMATA	OLYMPIAD
BLUBBERY	PLUCKING	BLUELAMP	BLUFFING	ULTIMATE	SLIMLINE

CLAMPING	BLENDERS	SLANTING	SLAPJACK	BLURRING	CLASHING
CLIMBING	BLINKERS	SLINGING	ELEPHANT	BLURTING	CLASPING
PLUMBING	BLUNDERS	SLINKING	FLIPPANT	FLIRTING	CLASSING
SLAMMING	FLANDERS	BLANDISH	ALOPECIA	SLURPING	FLASHING
SLIMMING	FLANNELS	CLANNISH	CLIPPERS	SLURRING	FLUSHING
SLUMMING	FLINDERS	SLINKIER	FLAPPERS	ALARMISM	SLASHING
SLUMPING	PLANNERS	ALANALDA	FLIPPERS	ALTRUISM	PLUSSIGN
BLIMPISH	PLANTERS	LLANELLI	SLIPPERS	ALARMIST	CLASSICO
PLUMPISH	PLUNDERS	CLANSMAN	SLIPPERY	ALTRUIST	CLASSIER
OLYMPIAN	PLUNGERS	CLANSMEN	SLIPSHOD	CLARENCE	GLOSSIER
CLAMMIER	SLANDERS	FLINTOFF	SLAPSHOT	FLORENCE	CLASSICS
CLUMSIER	BLUNKETT	CLANGOUR	FLIPSIDE	CLARINET	CLASSIFY
FLIMSIER	PLANGENT	KLINGONS	CLAPPING	GLORIOUS	FLASHILY
ALEMBICS	FLANAGAN	CLINIQUE	CLIPPING	BLURTOUT	FLASHMAN
OLYMPICS	ALLNIGHT	PLANKTON	CLOPPING	CLARISSA	BLASTOFF
CLUMSILY	BLANCHED	ALLOCATE	ELAPSING	CLARKSON	CLOSEOFF
FLIMFLAM	CLENCHED	ELDORADO	FLAPPING	ALFRESCO	BLOSSOMS
FLAMENCO	CLINCHED	ALSORANS	FLIPPING	FLORISTS	FLESHOUT
FLAMINGO	FLINCHED	PLIOCENE	FLOPPING	ALLROUND	GLASNOST
ELEMENTS	CLINCHER	ALMONERS	PLOPPING	ULTRAVOX	CLOSERUN
CLEMENCY	BLANCHES	BLOOMERS	SLAPPING	ELASTANE	CLOSURES
GLAMROCK	CLENCHES	FLUORIDE	SLIPPING	GLISSADE	FLYSPRAY
SLUMMOCK	CLINCHES	FLUORINE	SLOPPING	ALASTAIR	CLOSETED
PLIMSOLL	FLINCHES	ALLOWING	SLOPPILY	ALISTAIR	BLESSYOU
GLIMPSED	KLONDIKE	BLOOMING	CLIPCLOP	CLASSACT	FLATMATE
GLIMPSES	BLENDING	ELBOWING	FLIPFLOP	GLOSSARY	FLATRACE
CLIMATIC	BLINDING	FLOODING	SLIPKNOT	GLASSEYE	FLATPACK
CLEMATIS	BLINKING	FLOORING	SLIPROAD	BLISTERS	PLATEAUX
PLUMDUFF	CLANGING	GLOOMIER	FLYPAPER	BLUSTERS	CLOTHCAP
PLYMOUTH	CLANKING	GLOOMILY	CLAPTRAP	CLUSTERS	ALLTHERE
SLAMDUNK	CLINGING	ALTOCLEF	FLYPASTS	FLUSTERS	SLATTERN
CLAMOURS	CLINKING	ALLOALLO	SLIPOVER	GLISTENS	BLOTTERS
ALANLADD	CLONKING	FLOODLIT	ELOQUENT	OLDSTERS	FLATLETS
ALANDALE	CLUNKING	ALCOPOPS	GLORIABOW	PLASTERS	FLATNESS
ELONGATE	FLANKING	ALJOLSON	CLARABOW	FLYSHEET	FLATTENS
ALANBALL	FLINGING	ALLOTTED	GLORYBOX	BLUSTERY	FLATTERS
PLANTAIN	FLUNKING	SLIPCASE	CLERICAL	BLISSFUL	FLUTTERS
CLINICAL	GLANCING	SLIPPAGE	ALDRIDGE	FLASHGUN	GLITTERS
ALANDELL	GLINTING	SLIPWARE	ALLRIGHT	ALLSPICE	PLATTERS
BLONDELL	PLANNING	SLAPBANG	CLERIHEW	BLASTING	PLOTTERS
BLENHEIM	PLANTING	SLAPDASH	ALARMING	BLESSING	SLITHERS
BLANKETS	PLUNGING	FLAPJACK	ALERTING	BLUSHING	FLATTEST

ILLTREAT	FLAUBERT	CLAWBACK	EMMAPEEL	IMAGISTS	AMENDING
BLITHELY	CLOUSEAU	BLOWLAMP	EMPATHIC	DMTHOMAS	EMINENCE
FLATTERY	PLOUGHED	SLOWEDUP	IMPALING	AMPHORAE	AMUNDSEN
FLUTTERY	SLOUCHED	FLYWHEEL	SMEARING	EMPHASIS	EMANATED
GLITTERY	SLOUCHER	FLAWLESS	EMBARKED	EMPHATIC	EMANATES
SLATTERY	ALLUSIVE	SLOWNESS	AMYACKER	IMBIBERS	IMMOLATE
SLITHERY	ILLUMINE	BLOWPIPE	EMBALMED	IMMINENT	EMBOLDEN
PLATEFUL	ALLUDING	CLOWNING	EMBALMER	IMPINGED	EMPOWERS
SLOTHFUL	ALLURING	BLOWFISH	IMPAIRED	IMPINGES	IMMODEST
CLUTCHED	CLOUTING	CLOWNISH	JMBARRIE	IMPISHLY	IMPOTENT
FLETCHER	FLOUTING	BLOWHOLE	IMPACTED	IMBIBING	SMOOCHED
BLOTCHES	FLOURISH	GLOWWORM	IMPARTED	UMPIRING	SMOOTHED
CLUTCHES	ALLUVIAL	SLOWWORM	IMMATURE	AMBITION	SMOOTHIE
BLITZING	ALLUSION	SLOWDOWN	AMICABLE	AMBIENCE	SMOOTHER
CLOTHING	ILLUSION	FLOWERED	AMICABLY	OMNIVORE	SMOOCHES
CLOTTING	CLOUDIER	GLOWERED	SMACKERS	AMRITSAR	SMOOTHLY
FLITTING	PLAUDITS	OLDWORLD	SMACKING	EMBITTER	EMBODIED
PLOTTING	FLAUTIST	BLOWOVER	SMOCKING	IMPLICIT	AMMONITE
FLATFISH	PLEURISY	FLEXIBLE	SMUDGING	IMPLODED	IMMOBILE
CLOTHIER	GLAUCOMA	FLEXIBLY	AMPERAGE	IMPLODES	IMPOLITE
ALITALIA	BLOUSONS	ALEXBEST	EMBEDDED	SMALLEST	IMPOSING
FLOTILLA	ILLUSORY	GLOXINIA	AMMETERS	SMOLLETT	EMPORIUM
PLATELET	FLAUNTED	PLAYMATE	AMNESIAC	SMALLFRY	EMBODIES
ILLTIMED	GLOVEBOX	PLAYSAFE	IMBECILE	IMPLYING	IMPOUNDS
OLDTIMER	CLAVICLE	PLAYBACK	IMPEDING	SMELLING	EMBOSSED
PLATONIC	SLOVAKIA	PLAYBALL	IMPERIAL	SMELTING	EMBOSSER
PLATINUM	CLOVELLY	PLAYLETS	IMPETIGO	SMALLISH	EMBOSSES
PLETHORA	SLOVENIA	CLAYPIPE	IMPERILS	EMULSION	IMPORTED
PLATFORM	SLAVONIC	PLAYTIME	IMPELLED	EMULSIFY	IMMORTAL
GLUTTONS	ELEVENTH	PLAYBILL	IMPELLER	IMPLANTS	IMPORTER
PLATOONS	SLOVENLY	PLAYGIRL	EMPERORS	SMALLPOX	IMPOSTOR
FLATFOOT	OLIVEOIL	ALOYSIUS	IMMERSED	IMPLORED	EMBRACED
OLDTROUT	OLIVEOYL	PLAYLIST	IMMERSES	IMPLORES	AMERICAN
GLUTTONY	SLAVERED	PLAYALET	EMMENTAL	EMULATED	EMBRACES
FLATSPIN	CLEVERER	CLAYMORE	EMBEZZLE	OMELETTE	AMBRIDGE
PLATYPUS	SLAVERER	PLAYROOM	EMIGRATE	EMULATOR	SMARTENS
FLATIRON	CLEVERLY	PLAYDOWN	EMIGRANT	EMULATES	EMERGENT
ELITISTS	ELEVATED	PLAYGOER	SMUGNESS	EMPLOYED	SMARTEST
FLATTYRE	OLIVETTI	PLAYBOYS	SMUGGLER	EMPLOYEE	AMORTISE
FLOUNCED	ELEVATOR	PLAYSUIT	SMUGGLES	EMPLOYER	EMERGING
FLOUNCES	ELEVATES	BLIZZARD	IMAGINED	EMBLAZON	IMBRUING
FLOUNDER	FLAVOURS	GLAZIERS	IMAGINES	AMENABLE	SMARTING

SMIRKING	AMBULANT	INLAYING	SNICKERS	KNEEDEEP	INTERNEE
SMARTISH	SMOULDER	INVADING	SNICKETS	INNEREAR	INFERNAL
EMBROILS	IMPUDENT	KNEADING	UNSCREWS	INDEXERS	INTERNAL
SMARTIES	AMBUSHED	SNEAKING	INACTIVE	INTEGERS	INTERNET
SMARMILY	AMBUSHES	UNCARING	INSCRIBE	INDECENT	ONRECORD
UMBRELLA	IMMUNISE	UNLACING	ENACTING	INHERENT	ANTELOPE
AMARILLO	IMPUTING	INVASION	KNOCKING	INTEREST	ENVELOPE
EMERALDS	IMMUNITY	SNEAKIER	SNICKING	UNDERFED	ONCEMORE
AMARANTH	IMPUNITY	INHABITS	INACTION	INLEAGUE	ANTEROOM
IMPRINTS	IMPURITY	ANNALIST	KNUCKLES	INVEIGLE	ENVELOPS
IMPROPER	OMDURMAN	INSANITY	ANACONDA	ENMESHED	ONREPORT
AMBROSIA	ONPARADE	SNEAKILY	ENSCONCE	ENMESHES	INTERPOL
IMPRISON	ONSAFARI	UNMARKED	ANECDOTE	ANGELICA	UNDERPIN
AMARETTI	INHALANT	UNMASKED	KNOCKOFF	ANGELINA	UNDERPAY
AMARETTO	ENHANCED	UNPACKED	KNOCKOUT	ANJELICA	ENDEARED
EMERITUS	ENHANCES	ENTAILED	UNICORNS	INRELIEF	INFERRED
EMIRATES	UNSADDLE	INTAGLIO	INEDIBLE	ONRELIEF	INTERRED
IMPROVED	INTANDEM	UNHARMED	ANODISED	ANGERING	INTEGRAL
IMPROVER	INWARDLY	UNEARNED	ANODISES	ANNEXING	UNDERRUN
IMPROVES	INCAMERA	UNMANNED	UNEDITED	ENTERING	UNDERSEA
EMISSARY	INHALERS	UNGAINLY	INDEMAND	INDEXING	INCENSED
SMASHERS	INVADERS	ANNAFORD	ONDEMAND	KNEELING	UNVERSED
SMASHHIT	SNEAKERS	INFAVOUR	ONREMAND	SNEERING	ANDERSEN
EMISSIVE	UNRAVELS	INFAMOUS	ANTEDATE	SNEEZING	ANDERSON
AMASSING	INNATELY	UNCAPPED	UNDERAGE	UNSEEING	INPERSON
SMASHING	INSANELY	UNFAIRLY	INDETAIL	KNEEHIGH	INCENSES
EMISSION	UNLAWFUL	INTARSIA	UNDERARM	ANGELICO	INDEBTED
OMISSION	ENLARGED	UNWANTED	INTERACT	ANTERIOR	INDENTED
XMASTREE	ENTANGLE	ONDAATJE	UNDERBID	INFERIOR	INFECTED
AMESBURY	UNTANGLE	UNFASTEN	ENFEEBLE	INTERIOR	INFESTED
EMOTICON	ENDANGER	INFANTAS	ENSEMBLE	INHERITS	INGESTED
SMITHERS	ENLARGER	UNEARTHS	INTERCOM	ANNEALED	INJECTED
SMOTHERS	INDANGER	INFANTRY	UNDERCUT	UNVEILED	INSERTED
EMITTING	ENLARGES	SNOBBERY	INTENDED	UNDERLIE	INVENTED
EMPTYING	ONTARGET	ENABLING	UNHEEDED	INTERLAY	INVERTED
OMITTING	UNWASHED	SNUBBING	UNLEADED	UNDERLAY	INVESTED
EMOTIONS	UNVARIED	SNOBBISH	UNNEEDED	INKERMAN	UNHEATED
IMITATED	ANNALISE	ANABOLIC	UNSEEDED	INNERMAN	UNSEATED
IMITATOR	INVASIVE	ONEBYONE	UNDERDOG	ANSERMET	UNTESTED
IMITATES	ENGAGING	UNABATED	ENGENDER	UNSEEMLY	UNSETTLE
AMATEURS	ENRAGING	UNICYCLE	ANTECEDE	INTERNED	ANDERTON
AMETHYST	INHALING	KNICKERS	KNEEJERK	ANTENNAE	UNBEATEN

ANCESTOR	ONTHEMAT	UNTIMELY	ONTIPTOE	ANIMATED	SNOOTIER
ANTEATER	ONTHENOD	UNWISELY	ANTIQUES	ANIMATOR	UNIONIST
INJECTOR	ENCHANTS	UNHINGED	INVIEWOF	ANIMATES	SNOOTILY
INVENTOR	ENTHRONE	INKINGIN	INAJIFFY	INUNDATE	UNCOOKED
INVESTOR	INTHEORY	ENDINGUP	ANNJONES	UNENDING	UNCORKED
UNDERTOW	ANCHORED	ENRICHED	SNAKEOIL	ENSNARED	UNHOOKED
ANCESTRY	INTHERED	ENCIPHER	UNPLACED	ENSNARES	UNLOCKED
INTENTLY	INCHARGE	ENRICHES	ANGLICAN	INUNISON	ONLOOKER
INSECURE	ONTHERUN	ANTICHAY	ANALECTS	UNTOWARD	INPOCKET
INGENUES	INTHERAW	INCISIVE	INFLICTS	ANNOTATE	ENNOBLED
UNNERVED	INAHURRY	INFINITE	UNBLOCKS	INNOVATE	ENROLLED
INTERVAL	ENTHUSED	ENTICING	INCLUDED	ENTOMBED	UNCOILED
ONCEOVER	ENTHUSES	INCISING	INCLUDES	ENFORCED	ENNOBLES
UNNERVES	ONTHESLY	INCITING	ANALOGUE	INVOICED	INFORMED
UNDERWAY	UNSHAVEN	INVITING	INFLIGHT	UNFORCED	INFORMAL
UNAFRAID	INTHEWAY	UNTIRING	UNALLIED	ENFORCER	INCOMMON
INAFLASH	ONTHEWAY	ENVISION	INFLAMED	ENFORCES	UNCOMMON
SNUFFBOX	INTIFADA	INCISION	INCLINED	INVOICES	INFORMER
INEFFECT	ENFILADE	INHIBITS	ONELINER	ENFOLDED	INSOMNIA
SNIFFING	ENVISAGE	INFINITY	INCLINES	UNFOLDED	ANNOUNCE
UNIFYING	INDICATE	UNTIDILY	ANTLERED	UNLOADED	ENPOINTE
SNAFFLES	INTIMATE	UNPICKED	ANALYSED	ENDODERM	UNCOUPLE
SNIFFLES	INTIMACY	ENTITLED	ENCLOSED	SNOOPERS	ONCOURSE
UNIFORMS	ENVIABLE	UNTITLED	UNCLESAM	SNOOZERS	ENDORSED
ANAGRAMS	ENVIABLY	ANTILLES	ANALYSES	UNCOVERS	UNHOUSED
SNIGGERS	ENCIRCLE	UNWIELDY	ANALYSIS	INDOLENT	UNLOOSEN
SNAGGING	INPIECES	INSIGNIA	ANALYSTS	INNOCENT	ENDORSER
KNIGHTED	UNBIDDEN	UNPINNED	ENCLOSES	INSOLENT	ENDORSES
KNIGHTLY	UNKINDLY	UNSIGNED	UNCLASPS	ENGORGED	UNBOLTED
INCHOATE	ANTIHERO	ANAISNIN	ANGLESEY	INNOTIME	ONEORTWO
INTHEAIR	ENGINEER	ANTIDOTE	INFLATED	ANNOYING	UNWORTHY
ONTHEAIR	ENLIVENS	ENVIRONS	UNCLETOM	ENCODING	INVOLVED
INTHEBAG	ENTICERS	INCISORS	INGLETON	ENDOWING	UNSOLVED
INTHECAN	INFIDELS	ANTIBODY	INFLATES	ENJOYING	INVOLVES
ONTHEDOT	INKINESS	ANTIMONY	ENSLAVED	INCOMING	INCONVOY
INTHEEND	INSIDERS	UNZIPPED	INCLOVER	INTONING	ANTONYMS
ONWHEELS	INCIDENT	UNBIASED	INFLOWER	INVOKING	ONAPLATE
ONTHEHOP	INDIGENT	ANOINTED	INIMICAL	ONCOMING	KNAPSACK
ENSHRINE	INDIRECT	ENLISTED	ENUMBERS	SNOOPING	INSPECTS
UNCHAINS	ENTIRELY	INDICTED	MNEMONIC	SNOOZING	INSPADES
ONTHEJOB	ENTIRETY	INSISTED	ANEMONES	UNSOCIAL	INAPADDY
UNSHAKEN	UNLIKELY	UNLISTED	UNAMUSED	UNIONISM	KNAPWEED

ONEPIECE	ENORMITY	KNOTTING	INDUCTOR	ROMANCES	ROTARIAN
SNAPPERS	UNBROKEN	INSTANCE	INDUSTRY	MONARCHY	ROTATION
SNIPPETS	ENTRANCE	INSTINCT	UNJUSTLY	COLANDER	SOMALIAN
SNAPSHOT	INFRINGE	UNCTUOUS	INFUTURE	POMANDER	VOCATION
SNAPPING	ENTRENCH	UNSTATED	UNEVENLY	COWARDLY	NOTARIES
SNIPPING	ENTRANTS	INSTRUCT	UNIVERSE	NOTABENE	ROSARIES
SNAPPIER	INTRANET	INCUBATE	UNAVOWED	MORAYEEL	VOTARIES
UNSPOILT	ENORMOUS	INHUMANE	SNOWBALL	SOYABEAN	BOTANIST
SNAPPILY	INTREPID	INSULATE	SNOWFALL	DOWAGERS	LOYALIST
UNSPOKEN	UNDRAPED	UNDULATE	SNOWEDIN	FORAGERS	MORALIST
KNOPFLER	ENTREPOT	UNGULATE	ANYWHERE	VOYAGERS	ROYALIST
UNOPENED	ANDROPOV	ENCUMBER	SNOWSHOE	POTAUFEU	VOCALIST
ENDPAPER	INFRARED	UNBURDEN	INAWHIRL	JONATHAN	LOCALITY
INSPIRED	INPRISON	ENDUSERS	INKWELLS	MONAGHAN	MORALITY
INSPIRES	UNTRUTHS	INSURERS	ENTWINED	MONALISA	POLARITY
INSPIRIT	ENCROUTE	ENGULFED	ENTWINES	ROSALIND	TONALITY
UNIQUELY	ENGRAVED	INDULGED	SNOWYOWL	BONAFIDE	TOTALITY
INEQUITY	UNPROVEN	INDULGES	SNOWBOOT	DOPAMINE	VORACITY
INIQUITY	ENGRAVER	ENDURING	ANSWERED	GONATIVE	GOBACKON
ENERVATE	ENGRAVES	ENSURING	SNOWDROP	LOCALISE	SOCALLED
INCREASE	INKSTAND	INDUCING	UNAWARES	MORALISE	TOTALLED
ENCROACH	UNUSABLE	INFUSING	UNSWAYED	NOTARISE	ROCAILLE
ENTREATS	ONESIDED	INJURING	INEXPERT	POLARISE	CORACLES
ENTREATY	GNASHERS	INSURING	ONMYCASE	ROSALINE	BONARLAW
ENTRACTE	GNASHING	INFUSION	ONMYTAIL	VOCALISE	ROMANLAW
INTRUDED	INKSPOTS	INJURIES	ANDYCAPP	VOLATILE	TOXAEMIA
INFRADIG	ANGSTROM	UNBUCKLE	ANDYGIBB	WOMANISE	MOHAMMED
INTRUDER	ANISETTE	INPUBLIC	ENDYMION	DONATING	HOSANNAS
INTRUDES	INITIATE	ANNULLED	ANDYCOLE	FORAGING	COCACOLA
INCREDIT	INITIALS	UNCURLED	INMYBOOK	LOCATING	POLAROID
ONCREDIT	UNSTEADY	UNFURLED	ONLYJUST	ROTATING	COMATOSE
SNORKELS	UNSTABLE	ANNUALLY	SNAZZILY	VOYAGING	NOTAHOPE
ANGRIEST	ANATHEMA	INNUENDO	ROTAVATE	SOYAMILK	FORASONG
INTRIGUE	KNOTWEED	ENQUIRED	TOMAHAWK	ROSARIUM	JOGALONG
INERTGAS	ONSTREAM	INCURRED	NOTATALL	ROYALISM	SOLATOPI
ANARCHIC	KNITWEAR	ENQUIRER	NOWADAYS	SOLARIUM	NONAGONS
ENERGISE	KNITTERS	ENQUIRES	ROYALBOX	DONATION	POTATOES
SNARLING	SNATCHED	INQUESTS	FOCACCIA	LOCATION	ROTATORS
SNORTING	SNATCHES	INSULTED	ROMANCED	NOTATION	TOMATOES
UNERRING	ONSTRIKE	UNSUITED	COMANCHE	ROGATION	HOWABOUT
ANDROIDS	ANYTHING	UNSUBTLE	POLARCAP	ROMANIAN	MOHARRIS
ENTRAILS	KNITTING	UNBUTTON	MONARCHS	ROSARIAN	CORALSEA

KOWALSKI	SORBONNE	TOECLIPS	GOODYEAR	PONDLILY	GOODTURN
POLANSKI	COMBINES	COACHMAN	BOLDNESS	CORDELIA	WOODBURN
MOLASSES	GOABROAD	COACHMEN	COLDNESS	GOLDBLUM	ROADHUMP
MONASTIC	DOUBLOON	COXCOMBS	CORDLESS	BOBDYLAN	COLDCUTS
ROMANTIC	JOEBROWN	GOLCONDA	DOODLERS	BORDELLO	DOLDRUMS
IOLANTHE	TOMBROWN	VOLCANIC	FONDNESS	GONDOLAS	HOODLUMS
NOMATTER	LOGBOOKS	TOMCONTI	GOODNESS	TOADFLAX	WOODCUTS
ZOLABUDD	BOBBYPIN	SOUCHONG	LOUDNESS	COLDPLAY	GOLDDUST
COQAUVIN	BOMBARDS	TOUCHPAD	SOLDIERS	WORDPLAY	HOLDOVER
GOEASYON	HOMBURGS	CONCEPTS	TODDLERS	BONDSMEN	HOEDOWNS
POTBLACK	DOGBERRY	CONCORDE	WORDLESS	WOODSMAN	FOLDAWAY
VONBRAUN	LOMBARDY	CONCERTO	COLDFEET	CONDEMNS	HOLDSWAY
FORBEARS	SORBITOL	SORCERER	DOWDIEST	CONDONED	FOREHAND
ROWBOATS	FOGBOUND	CONCERNS	MOODIEST	CONDENSE	FORELAND
TOPBRASS	POTBOUND	CONCERTS	ROADTEST	LONDONER	HOMELAND
ROEBUCKS	BOOBTUBE	MOCCASIN	ROWDIEST	CONDONES	HOMEWARD
BOMBADIL	BOBBYVEE	BOYCOTTS	WORDIEST	FONDANTS	NOSEBAND
MORBIDLY	CONCLAVE	TOCCATAS	DORDOGNE	HOLDINGS	CODENAME
BOMBHEAD	CONCEALS	CONCLUDE	WOODSHED	GOODWOOD	COVERAGE
SOMBRERO	COUCHANT	GONCOURT	LORDSHIP	WOODFORD	COZENAGE
DOUBLEUP	FORCIBLE	WOODLAND	WOODCHIP	COLDSORE	FORENAME
GOBBLEUP	LOGCABIN	WOODWARD	ROADSHOW	WOODCOCK	HOMEMADE
COBBLERS	VOICEBOX	COLDCASE	GOLDDISC	WOODWORK	HOMEPAGE
NOOBJECT	FORCIBLY	CORDIALE	WOODWIND	GOODFORM	LOSEFACE
SOMBRELY	CONCOCTS	ROADRAGE	GOLDMINE	WOODWORM	MODERATE
DOUBTFUL	CONCEDED	HOLDBACK	GOODTIME	HOLDDOWN	NOTECASE
BOMBSITE	CONCEDES	COLDCALL	ROADSIDE	ROADHOGS	TOLERATE
COBBLING	CONCRETE	CORDIALS	WOODBINE	WONDROUS	COMEBACK
DOUBLING	BOTCHERS	HOLDFAST	WOODLICE	BORDERED	COVERALL
DOUBTING	POACHERS	WOODYATT	CODDLING	PONDERED	DOVETAIL
GOBBLING	VOUCHERS	BORDEAUX	DOODLING	POWDERED	ROSEWALL
HOBBLING	FORCEFUL	RONDEAUX	FONDLING	SOLDERED	HOMEFARM
LOBBYING	GODCHILD	GOODYBAG	TODDLING	WONDERED	FOREWARN
WOBBLING	CONCEIVE	BOUDICCA	GOLDFISH	FOLDEROL	NOSEBAGS
WOBBLIER	BOTCHING	CONDUCTS	HOODWINK	BORDERON	NOSEGAYS
WOBBLIES	COACHING	SORDIDLY	GOODWILL	DODDERER	POLECATS
HOBBYIST	MOOCHING	PONDWEED	ROWDYISM	HONDURAS	COVENANT
LOBBYIST	NOTCHING	GOLDLEAF	TOADYISM	CORDUROY	FORECAST
TOMBAKER	POACHING	GOLDBERG	MONDRIAN	ROADUSER	TOLERANT
BOWBELLS	TORCHING	GOODDEAL	ROADSIGN	ROADSTER	MONETARY
POTBELLY	TOUCHING	SONDHEIM	BOUDOIRS	GOLDRUSH	ROSEMARY
COMBINED	VOUCHING	TOODLEOO	CONDUITS	LORDMUCK	HONEYBEE

HONEYBUN	LOVEBIRD	MODELLER	MOVEDOUT	WOLFPACK	CONGREVE
NOVEMBER	COHESIVE	YODELLER	SOMEBODY	GOLFBALL	LONGTERM
MONEYBOX	CORETIME	BOREALIS	SOHELPME	KORFBALL	JONGLEUR
POWERCUT	HOSEPIPE	NOVELLAS	HOMESPUN	BOUFFANT	LONGUEUR
BONEIDLE	LOSETIME	COVERLET	HONEYPOT	CONFIDED	CONGRESS
POSEIDON	LOVELIFE	COLESLAW	MORESQUE	CONFIDES	MONGRELS
TOREADOR	NOSEDIVE	ROLEPLAY	DOGEARED	COIFFEUR	ROUGHENS
HONEYDEW	SOMETIME	BOGEYMAN	DOWELROD	COMFIEST	TOUGHENS
DOMESDAY	YOSEMITE	DOBERMAN	LOPEARED	DOGFIGHT	FOGGIEST
BONEHEAD	COVERING	GOVERNED	COMETRUE	FORFEITS	LONGLEAT
FOREHEAD	COVETING	ROSEANNE	FOIEGRAS	CONFLICT	PODGIEST
NOVELESE	COWERING	HOMEINON	FOREARMS	GOLFCLUB	ROUGHEST
TONEDEAF	HOVERING	COMEINTO	HOMEBREW	SOUFFLES	SOGGIEST
FOREDECK	LOWERING	GOVERNOR	FORENSIC	JOYFULLY	TOUGHEST
BONEMEAL	MOSEYING	DOYENNES	SOMERSET	WOEFULLY	LONGSHIP
FORETELL	POWERING	SOLEMNLY	DOMESTIC	CONFINED	LONGSHOT
HOSEREEL	SOBERING	BOREANAZ	MOLESTED	CONFINES	SONGBIRD
TOMEWELL	TOWERING	FORETOLD	MOMENTUM	WOLFROCK	BORGNINE
LOVEMEDO	FOGEYISH	FOREWORD	FORESTER	CONFRONT	LONGLIFE
HOMEHELP	HOMESICK	ROSEWOOD	GOGETTER	BONFIRES	LONGLIVE
FOREBEAR	LOVESICK	SOLENOID	LODESTAR	COMFORTS	LONGTIME
BONELESS	MOLEHILL	BOREHOLE	LONESTAR	CONFIRMS	COUGHING
FORELEGS	FOGEYISM	COMEHOME	POLESTAR	CONFORMS	FORGOING
FORESEES	SOLECISM	DOVECOTE	RONETTES	CONFUSED	JOGGLING
HOMELESS	TOKENISM	FOREGONE	ROSETTES	BOBFOSSE	TONGKING
HOPELESS	TOTEMISM	LONESOME	COGENTLY	CONFUSES	MONGOLIA
LOVELESS	BOHEMIAN	NOSECONE	COVENTRY	CONFETTI	BOOGALOO
NOTELETS	COHESION	SOMEHOPE	COVERTLY	CONFOUND	LODGINGS
SORENESS	COMEDIAN	LONEWOLF	FORESTRY	COIFFURE	DOUGHNUT
COHERENT	HOTELIER	FORELOCK	HONESTLY	TOAFAULT	LONGFORD
LOVENEST	LONELIER	HOMEWORK	MODESTLY	LONGHAND	COSGROVE
LOVESEAT	LOVELIER	NOTEBOOK	HOMERULE	LONGFACE	FOXGLOVE
MOVEMENT	COMEDIES	ROSEBOWL	MOLECULE	LONGWAVE	MONGOOSE
NONEVENT	LOBELIAS	TONEPOEM	TOBESURE	ROUGHAGE	HONGKONG
ROSEBERY	POLEMICS	COMEDOWN	ROSEBUSH	LONGHAUL	SONGBOOK
POWERFUL	ROSERIES	HOMELOAN	HOPEFULS	CONGEALS	LONGHORN
HOVERFLY	NOVELIST	HOMETOWN	MOREOVER	LONGWAYS	GORGEOUS
LOZENGES	MOLESKIN	LOVELORN	GONEAWAY	POIGNANT	LONGBOWS
SOMEWHEN	POTEMKIN	TONEDOWN	WOREAWAY	DOGGYBAG	LONGBOAT
TOGETHER	HONECKER	WOREDOWN	CONFLATE	DOUGHBOY	LONGORIA
SOMEWHAT	MODELLED	COVETOUS	WOLFGANG	ROUGHCUT	DOGGEREL
HOMEBIRD	YODELLED	FOREMOST	ROOFRACK	DOGGEDLY	COWGIRLS

SONGSTER	ZODIACAL	BOLIVIAN	SOLITUDE	BOOKREST	COALFACE
FORGETIT	DORISDAY	DOMINION	SOLIHULL	COCKIEST	SOULMATE
LONGJUMP	ROBINDAY	LOGICIAN	HOWITZER	ROCKIEST	TOLLGATE
LONGSUIT	COLISEUM	POSITION	CONJUGAL	BOOKSHOP	KOHLRABI
FORGIVEN	DOMINEER	VOLITION	DOWJONES	PORKCHOP	ROLLBACK
FORGIVES	YOGIBEAR	POLITICO	TOMJONES	WORKSHOP	WOOLPACK
ROCHDALE	BONINESS	MODIFIER	CONJURED	DOCKSIDE	WOOLSACK
NOAHSARK	CONIFERS	CODICILS	CONJURER	MONKFISH	ROLLCALL
MOTHBALL	COSINESS	CODIFIES	CONJURES	HOKKAIDO	NOBLEART
HOTHEADS	DOPINESS	HOMILIES	MOTJUSTE	COCKPITS	NOTLEAST
TOPHEAVY	DOZINESS	MODIFIES	DOCKLAND	FORKLIFT	COOLIBAH
SOTHEBYS	FOXINESS	NOTIFIES	DOCKYARD	BOOKCLUB	LOSLOBOS
LOCHNESS	HOLINESS	POLICIES	BOOKCASE	LOOKINTO	FOLLICLE
TOMHULCE	JOKINESS	POLITICS	COOKWARE	BOOKENDS	FOOLSCAP
POTHOLER	NOMINEES	DOCILITY	FOLKTALE	BOOKINGS	WORLDCUP
POTHOLES	NOSINESS	MOBILITY	ROCKCAKE	WORKINGS	COLLECTS
BONHOMIE	ROSINESS	NOBILITY	ROCKFACE	CORKWOOD	GOPLACES
TOMHANKS	LORIKEET	SOLIDIFY	ROYKEANE	ROCKFORD	ROWLOCKS
POOHPOOH	MOLINEUX	SOLIDITY	TOOKCARE	WORKLOAD	COLLIDED
POSHNOSH	POLITELY	TOXICITY	WORKMATE	FOLKLORE	COLLUDED
BOTHERED	TODIEFOR	POPINJAY	WORKRATE	FOLKSONG	COOLIDGE
LOTHARIO	COMINGIN	ROSIELEE	BOOKMARK	BOOKWORK	FOOLSDIE
MOTHERLY	MOVINGIN	BOUILLON	POCKMARK	COOKBOOK	ROLLEDUP
ROTHESAY	ROPINGIN	GORILLAS	TOOKBACK	FOLKROCK	COLLIDES
POCHETTE	VOTINGIN	SONINLAW	COCKTAIL	WORKBOOK	COLLUDES
FOXHOUND	COMINGTO	JOVIALLY	ROCKFALL	ROCKPOOL	COWLNECK
COWHOUSE	JOKINGLY	SOCIALLY	WORKCAMP	BOOKWORM	ROLLNECK
DOGHOUSE	LOVINGLY	TORIAMOS	ROCKSALT	WORKROOM	BOULDERS
HOTHOUSE	POLISHED	NOPICNIC	TOOKPART	YORKTOWN	COLLIERS
POTHOUSE	POLISHER	NOTIONAL	BOOKABLE	COCKEREL	COOLNESS
JODHPURS	POLISHES	COLIFORM	WORKABLE	COCKCROW	GOALLESS
BOBHAWKE	BOYISHLY	KOHINOOR	BOOKEDIN	POCKETED	SOULLESS
NOAHWYLE	DOMINICA	DOMINOES	BOOKEDUP	ROCKETED	JOLLIEST
COGITATE	CODIFIED	MONITORS	LOOKEDAT	COCKATOO	COLLIERY
DOMINATE	MODIFIED	MORIARTY	POLKADOT	ROCKETRY	BOULOGNE
MOTIVATE	NOTIFIED	ROBINSON	WORKADAY	COCKSURE	COLLAGEN
NOMINATE	DOMICILE	MOLINSKY	TOOKHEED	LOOKOUTS	HOOLIGAN
HOLIDAYS	HOMICIDE	HOLISTIC	ROCKWELL	LOOKOVER	COLLEGES
MOHICANS	MOBILISE	DOLITTLE	LOCKLEAR	TOOKOVER	NOBLEGAS
DOMINANT	POSITIVE	CONISTON	BOOKLETS	SOAKAWAY	WOOLSHED
SOLITARY	NOTICING	PODIATRY	COCKNEYS	COCKEYED	HOULIHAN
SOCIABLE	POSITING	MORIBUND	FORKEEPS	JOCKEYED	COALMINE

GOALLINE	TOILETTE	COMMANDS	CONNACHT	FOUNDING	JOHNSTON
POOLSIDE	COLLATOR	COMMENDS	HOUNDDOG	HOUNDING	CORNETTO
POULTICE	POLLSTER	COMMENTS	JOINEDIN	JOINTING	JOHNBULL
SOILPIPE	POLLUTER	COMMUNES	JOINEDUP	LOUNGING	DOWNTURN
LOWLYING	COLLATES	HORMONES	COINEDIT	MOUNTING	JOHNHURT
MOULDING	POLLUTES	TORMENTS	JOHNDEED	POINTING	CONNIVED
MOULTING	TOILETRY	COMMONLY	TOWNSEND	POUNCING	CONNIVER
GOALKICK	ZOOLATRY	DORMANCY	CORNMEAL	POUNDING	CONNIVES
BODLEIAN	TOULOUSE	HOGMANAY	JOHNPEEL	ROUNDING	WORNAWAY
WOOLLIES	JOELOUIS	NORMANDY	HORNBEAM	SOUNDING	YOKOHAMA
DOOLALLY	COALDUST	WORMWOOD	MOONBEAM	WOUNDING	COTOPAXI
FOULPLAY	LOWLEVEL	WORMHOLE	BOUNCERS	YOUNGISH	MONORAIL
NOBLEMAN	BOWLOVER	BOOMBOOM	BOUNDERS	DOWNHILL	MOTORAIL
NOBLEMEN	RODLAVER	BOOMTOWN	COUNSELS	HORNBILL	COLORADO
FOGLAMPS	ROLLOVER	RONMOODY	COUNTERS	JOHNSIMM	CORONARY
GOSLINGS	FOLLOWED	COMMERCE	COUNTESS	BOUNCIER	HONORARY
HOTLINES	FOLLOWON	TOMMYROT	FOUNDERS	COUNTIES	MONOGAMY
LOWLANDS	FOLLOWUP	FORMERLY	LOUNGERS	JOANSIMS	COLOMBIA
SOULFOOD	FOLLOWER	COSMETIC	POINTERS	MOUNTIES	MOROCCAN
COALHOLE	WORLDWAR	DOGMATIC	POUNCETS	HOUNSLOW	MOTORCAR
CORLEONE	HOLLOWAY	COMMUTED	ROUNDELS	CONNELLY	DOGOODER
COALPORT	VOLLEYED	COMMUTER	ROUNDERS	CONNOLLY	NOWONDER
GOALPOST	ROOMMATE	COMMUTES	DOWNBEAT	DONNELLY	GOTOSEED
LOLLOPED	WORMCAST	DORMOUSE	YOUNGEST	DOWNPLAY	HOLOCENE
COLLAPSE	DOOMSDAY	MONMOUTH	DOUNREAY	GOINGMAD	POLONECK
LOLLIPOP	FORMLESS	POUNDAGE	TOANDFRO	MORNINGS	COLONELS
COLLOQUY	GORMLESS	MOONWALK	ROENTGEN	MOONUNIT	CORONERS
GOALAREA	ZOOMLENS	CORNWALL	VONNEGUT	DOWNLOAD	CORONETS
COLLARED	ROOMIEST	DOWNFALL	TOWNSHIP	JOHNFORD	MOROSELY
HOLLERED	TOMMYGUN	TOWNHALL	MOONSHOT	DOWNHOME	GOTOOFAR
BOLLARDS	FORMULAE	FOUNTAIN	JOHNTHAW	GOINGOFF	TOBOGGAN
LOLLARDS	TOMMYLEE	MOUNTAIN	DOWNWIND	DOWNTOWN	BOROUGHS
NOBLEROT	FORMALIN	DONNAAIR	COINCIDE	MOWNDOWN	SOLONGAS
JOELGREY	FORMULAS	DOWNCAST	DOWNPIPE	WORNDOWN	COLOPHON
COALESCE	FORMALLY	BOUNDARY	DOWNSIDE	DOWNPOUR	COLONISE
NOBLESSE	NORMALLY	JOANBAEZ	DOWNSIZE	FOUNDOUT	DOLOMITE
MOLLUSCS	COMMUNED	GOINGBAD	HORNPIPE	GOINGOUT	MONOXIDE
DOLLYTUB	COMMENCE	SOUNDBOX	MOONRISE	JOHNDORY	MOTORING
COLLATED	COMMUNAL	SONNYBOY	NOONTIDE	CORNERED	MONOLITH
POLLUTED	HORMONAL	CORNICHE	BOUNCING	BORNFREE	BOBOLINK
COLLETTE	COMMANDO	DOONICAN	BOUNDING	GOINGSON	COLONIAL
ROULETTE	COMMONER	CONNECTS	COUNTING	TOPNOTCH	COLONIES

POLONIUS	COOPEDUP	COMPUTED	DOURNESS	CORRUPTS	MONSIEUR
ROBOTICS	MOPPEDUP	HOSPITAL	GOURMETS	MORRISON	BOLSTERS
COLONIST	TOPPEDUP	COMPUTER	HOARDERS	DOGROSES	BOOSTERS
MOTORIST	POMPIDOU	COMPETES	JOURNEYS	TOURISTS	COASTERS
OOLOGIST	POPPYDAY	COMPUTES	MOORHENS	TOURISTY	DOSSIERS
POROSITY	CODPIECE	TOWPATHS	MOURNERS	DOORSTEP	HOLSTERS
SORORITY	COMPLETE	COMPOUND	POORNESS	DOORSTOP	JOUSTERS
COWORKER	COMPRESS	SOAPSUDS	SOURNESS	COWRITER	LOBSTERS
MONOCLED	COUPLETS	PORPHYRY	WORRIERS	FOURSTAR	MOBSTERS
MONOCLES	MORPHEUS	RORQUALS	COARSEST	SOCRATES	MOISTENS
COCOONED	BOXPLEAT	BOUQUETS	COARSELY	SOURPUSS	MONSTERS
MONOTONE	SOPPIEST	CONQUERS	COURTESY	MONROVIA	ROASTERS
GOTOTOWN	COMPLIED	CONQUEST	HOARSELY	CODRIVER	ROISTERS
DOLOROSO	COMPLINE	MOSQUITO	SOBRIETY	BORROWED	ROOSTERS
DOLOROUS	COMPRISE	JONQUILS	HORRIFIC	BORROWER	TOASTERS
SONOROUS	MORPHINE	GOURMAND	MOURNFUL	BOTSWANA	BOSSIEST
DOXOLOGY	PORPOISE	MOORLAND	COERCIVE	MOUSSAKA	NOISIEST
HOROLOGY	TOMPRICE	MOORGATE	LORRAINE	JOBSHARE	COUSTEAU
MONOPOLY	CORPSING	SOURMASH	BOARDING	LOISLANE	ROUSSEAU
MONOTONY	COUPLING	DOORNAIL	COERCING	LONSDALE	BOASTFUL
TOPOLOGY	TOPPLING	JOURNALS	COURTING	ROSSDALE	HOUSEFUL
NOGOAREA	SOAPDISH	POTROAST	HOARDING	ROSSLARE	HORSEFLY
COLOURED	COMPLIES	GOTREADY	MOURNING	HOGSBACK	HOUSEFLY
HONOURED	DOLPHINS	HORRIBLE	SOURCING	COXSWAIN	CONSIGNS
GOMORRAH	COWPOKES	HORRIBLY	WORRYING	CONSTANT	HOWSTHAT
HOLOGRAM	COPPELIA	BOYRACER	COERCION	POSSIBLE	CONSPIRE
MONOGRAM	COMPILED	CORRECTS	COURTIER	HORSEBOX	DOGSLIFE
SOJOURNS	COMPILER	HORROCKS	NOFRILLS	LOOSEBOX	MOSSSIDE
TOMORROW	COMPILES	CORRODED	BOARDMAN	HOUSEBOY	SOLSTICE
COLOSSAL	HOTPANTS	PORRIDGE	NOTRUMPS	POSSIBLY	BOASTING
COLOSSUS	LOOPHOLE	TORRIDGE	DOORKNOB	GODSACRE	BOOSTING
JOYOUSLY	WOOPWOOP	CORRIDOR	TORRANCE	POPSICLE	COASTING
JOEORTON	COMPARED	JOYRIDER	SORRENTO	CORSICAN	HOISTING
COCONUTS	COMPERED	COMRADES	MOORINGS	POPSOCKS	JOUSTING
HONOLULU	CORPORAL	CORRODES	SOPRANOS	LOPSIDED	ROASTING
MOTORWAY	POLPERRO	DOCREDIT	TORRENTS	CONSIDER	ROOSTING
TOPONYMY	COMPARES	HORRIDLY	COURTNEY	VONSYDOW	ROUSTING
HOTPLATE	COMPERES	YOURSELF	FOURSOME	GODSPEED	TOASTING
COMPLAIN	COMPOSED	DOORBELL	MOORCOCK	HOGSHEAD	TOUSLING
POTPLANT	COMPOSER	FOURTEEN	POORFOLK	GODSPELL	JOYSTICK
HOSPICES	COMPOSES	BOARDERS	FOURTOPS	ROSSKEMP	NONSTICK
COMPADRE	COMPETED	COURIERS	DOORPOST	FORSWEAR	CORSAIRS

COWSLIPS	GOASTRAY	POETICAL	TORTOISE	FOOTHOLD	CONTESSA
TOPSAILS	CONSISTS	CONTACTS	VOLTAIRE	SOFTWOOD	NORTHSEA
WORSHIPS	HOUSESIT	VORTICES	BOTTLING	BOLTHOLE	CONTESTS
GODSGIFT	CORSETED	MONTYDON	JOSTLING	FOOTNOTE	NOTTOSAY
FORSAKEN	COSSETED	HOTTEDUP	LOATHING	FOOTSORE	FOOTSTEP
FORSAKES	FORSYTHE	TOTTEDUP	MOUTHING	PORTHOLE	TOMTHUMB
CONSOLED	NOISETTE	HOTTODDY	SOOTHING	POSTCODE	DORTMUND
CONSULAR	ROBSITCH	GOATHERD	TOOTLING	POSTPONE	CONTOURS
CONSOLES	ROSSETTI	PORTIERE	WORTHING	ZOETROPE	ZOOTSUIT
CONSULTS	ROSSITER	FORTIETH	CONTRICK	DOGTOOTH	KOWTOWED
CONSUMED	CORSETRY	MONTREAL	COSTLIER	BOATHOOK	TOKUGAWA
CONSOMME	MOISTURE	SOFTCELL	PORTLIER	FOOTWORK	MODULATE
HORSEMAN	SOYSAUCE	SOFTSELL	WORTHIER	LOSTSOUL	POPULACE
HORSEMEN	HOTSTUFF	NORTHERN	BOBTAILS	POLTROON	POPULATE
HOUSEMAN	FOSSEWAY	SOUTHERN	CONTAINS	POSTHORN	COLUMBIA
NORSEMAN	FOSSDYKE	BOTTLEUP	NOSTRILS	NOSTROMO	COLUMBUS
NORSEMEN	BOATYARD	FOOTWEAR	TOOTSIES	SOFTSOAP	CORUNDUM
CONSUMER	PORTLAND	ROOTBEER	WORTHILY	CONTROLS	ROTUNDAS
GOSSAMER	POSTCARD	BOTTLERS	GOATSKIN	PONTOONS	DOCUMENT
CONSUMES	BOATRACE	FORTRESS	MONTILLA	PORTIONS	MONUMENT
LOOSENED	BOOTLACE	POITIERS	TORTILLA	TORTUOUS	COAUTHOR
POISONED	COLTRANE	ROOTLESS	FOOTSLOG	SOUTHPAW	FOCUSING
WORSENED	MORTGAGE	ROOTLETS	COSTELLO	BOUTIQUE	BOTULISM
NONSENSE	PORTVALE	SOFTNESS	PORTILLO	DOGTIRED	POPULISM
LOOSENUP	POSTDATE	DOTTIEST	HOSTELRY	FOSTERED	SOLUTION
POISONER	SOFTWARE	FOOTREST	MORTALLY	LOITERED	POPULIST
CONSENTS	FOOTPATH	LOFTIEST	MORTIMER	POSTURED	GOPUBLIC
COTSWOLD	COATRACK	MONTREUX	COSTUMES	POTTERED	DOCUSOAP
WORSEOFF	POSTMARK	MOUTHFUL	CONTEMPT	TORTURED	POPULOUS
BOYSTOWN	FOOTBALL	YOUTHFUL	SOFTENED	TOTTERED	COQUETTE
COUSCOUS	FOOTFALL	MONTAGUE	CONTINUE	NOCTURNE	MOQUETTE
MONSOONS	SOFTBALL	PORTUGAL	COTTONON	POSTFREE	ROBUSTLY
BOYSCOUT	BOOTCAMP	COTTAGER	CONTINUO	DOCTORAL	SOUVLAKI
FORSHORT	FOOTPADS	COTTAGES	SOFTENUP	DOTTEREL	SOLVABLE
DOGSBODY	PORTRAYS	HOSTAGES	SOFTENER	DOCTORNO	CONVICTS
SOBSTORY	CONTRACT	COTTAGEY	CONTENDS	LOITERER	CONVULSE
TOYSTORY	CONTRAST	SOFTSHOE	CONTENTS	POTTERER	NOUVELLE
GOSSIPED	PORTRAIT	PORTVILA	PORTENDS	TORTURER	CONVENED
CONSERVE	CONTRARY	CONTRITE	PORTENTS	CONTORTS	CONVINCE
CONSTRUE	GOSTEADY	CONTRIVE	ROUTINES	POSTERNS	CONVENER
CONSORTS	MORTUARY	DOCTRINE	FORTKNOX	TORTURES	SOUVENIR
BOWSPRIT	PORTABLE	FONTAINE	BOATLOAD	MONTEREY	CONVENES

CONVENTS	BODYWRAP	SPECTRUM	SPLITPIN	UPENDING	APPRAISE
SOLVENTS	HOLYWRIT	EPICURES	SPRINTED	SPONGIER	SPORTIVE
SOLVENCY	BODYSURF	SPECTRES	UPLIFTED	OPENPLAN	SPARGING
CONVERGE	BODYSUIT	EPIDEMIC	SPLINTER	SPANGLES	SPARKING
CONVERSE	GODZILLA	EPIDURAL	SPRINTER	SPINDLES	SPARRING
CONVERTS	BOUZOUKI	UPPERCUT	APTITUDE	OPENINGS	SPORTING
CORVETTE	SPEAKERS	APPENDED	SPRITZER	OPENTOED	SPURNING
CONVEYED	SPRAYERS	SPLENDID	SPIKELEE	OPENBOOK	SPURRING
CONVEYOR	APPARENT	SPREADER	SPILLAGE	OPINIONS	SPURTING
TOPWHACK	SPEARGUN	APPENDIX	SPILLANE	SPONSORS	SPURRIER
TOMWOLFE	SPRAYGUN	EPHEMERA	SPALPEEN	UPINARMS	UPBRAIDS
POPWORLD	SPLASHED	SPEECHES	EPILOGUE	SPINSTER	UPTRAINS
BOSWORTH	SPLASHES	APPETITE	APPLYING	UPTODATE	SPARSITY
FORWARDS	SPEAKING	SPEEDING	SPALDING	UPHOLDER	SPARKLED
HOGWARTS	SPEARING	SPEEDIER	SPELLING	OPPOSERS	SPARKLER
DOGWATCH	SPLAYING	SPEEDILY	SPILLING	OPPONENT	SPARKLES
FOBWATCH	SPRAYING	APPEALED	SPELLMAN	SPOONFUL	SPIRALLY
HOTWATER	UPDATING	SPHEROID	OPULENCE	APPOSITE	OPERANDI
LOWWATER	UPRATING	OPTEDOUT	APPLEPIE	OPPOSITE	SPARROWS
BODYWAVE	APIARIES	APPEARED	APPLIQUE	OPPOSING	SPURIOUS
TOMYFACE	APIARIST	APPEASED	APPLETON	SPOONING	SPARERIB
POLYMATH	UPMARKET	APRESSKI	APPLAUSE	UPCOMING	APPRISED
PONYTAIL	APPALLED	APPEASES	APPLAUDS	APHORISM	OPERETTA
TONYHART	SPRAWLED	SPHERULE	SPUMANTE	SPOOKIER	OPERATIC
POLYGAMY	SPRAINED	UPHEAVAL	SPANIARD	APHORIST	OPERATED
COPYEDIT	SPHAGNUM	SPEEDWAY	OPENCAST	SPOOKILY	SPIRITED
HOLYHEAD	SPLATTER	SPIFFING	OPENNESS	SPROCKET	APERITIF
HOLYWEEK	SPACEAGE	EPIGRAPH	SPANIELS	APPOINTS	OPERATOR
TONYBENN	SPECTATE	SPYGLASS	SPANNERS	SPROUTED	OPERATES
BODYSHOP	SPICCATO	SPLITEND	SPINNERS	UPROOTED	APERTURE
BODYLINE	SPECIALS	SPRINGER	SPINNEYS	EPIPHANY	APPROVED
MOBYDICK	SPACEBAR	OPTIMISE	SPONDEES	APOPLEXY	APPROVAL
HOLYCITY	SPICIEST	SPLICING	SPONGERS	APPROACH	APPROVES
TOKYOJOE	SPECIFIC	SPOILING	SPINOFFS	SPARTANS	APARTYTO
POLYGLOT	SPECKLED	UPRISING	SPINIFEX	SPORRANS	APOSTATE
BODYBLOW	SPECKLES	OPTIMISM	UPANCHOR	OPERABLE	APOSTASY
TONYROME	SPACEMAN	OPHIDIAN	OPENMIND	SPIRACLE	EPISODIC
BODYWORK	SPACEMEN	OPTICIAN	OPENFIRE	SPORADIC	EPISODES
COPYBOOK	SPECIMEN	OPTIMIST	SPANKING	UPGRADED	APOSTLES
POLYGONS	SPACIOUS	SPRINKLE	SPANNING	UPGRADES	EPISTLES
TOMYCOST	SPECIOUS	OPTIONAL	SPENDING	SPARSELY	OPOSSUMS
ROLYPOLY	SPECTRAL	APRICOTS	SPINNING	OPERAHAT	UPSTICKS

SPITHEAD	EQUALITY	DREADFUL	CREAMIER	DRUBBING	PRACTICE
UPSTREAM	SQUAWKED	ARRANGED	DREAMIER	GRABBING	PRACTISE
EPITHETS	SQUAWKER	TRIANGLE	DREARIER	TREBLING	PROCAINE
SPATTERS	EQUALLED	ARRANGER	GREASIER	CRABBIER	CRACKING
SPOTLESS	SQUADRON	MRJAGGER	TREATIES	CRIBBINS	ERECTING
SPOTTERS	SQUATTED	ARRAIGNS	ORGANIST	CRABBILY	PRICKING
SPITEFUL	SQUATTER	ARRANGES	CROAKILY	BRUBAKER	TRACKING
UPSTAGED	AQUALUNG	BREACHED	DREAMILY	ARABELLA	TRICKING
UPSTAGES	SQUELCHY	BREATHED	DREARILY	DRIBBLED	TRUCKING
SPITFIRE	SQUEEGEE	BROACHED	URBANITY	DRIBBLER	WRECKING
SPITTING	SQUEAKED	PREACHED	TREADLES	DRIBBLES	BRACKISH
SPOTTING	SQUEALED	WREATHED	BRIANMAY	TRIBALLY	ERECTION
SPOTKICK	SQUEALER	BREATHER	ARMAGNAC	TRIBUNAL	FRACTION
SPOTTIER	AQUEDUCT	PREACHER	ORDAINED	ARMBANDS	FRICTION
UPSTAIRS	SQUEEZED	TREACHER	AREACODE	PREBENDS	TRACTION
SPATULAS	SQUEEZES	BREACHES	BREAKOFF	MRSBROWN	TRICKIER
SPITTOON	SQUIGGLE	BREATHES	CREATORS	TRIBUTES	BRICKIES
EPITAPHS	SQUIGGLY	BROACHES	BREAKOUT	ERICBANA	CRACKLED
OPIUMDEN	AQUILINE	PREACHES	FREAKOUT	WRECKAGE	FRECKLED
SPOUTING	SQUIRMED	WREATHES	TRIALRUN	PROCLAIM	PRICKLED
UPTURNED	EQUIPPED	CREATIVE	BRIANRIX	ARMCHAIR	TRICKLED
SPLUTTER	SQUIRREL	ORGANISE	TRIASSIC	CRUCIBLE	BRUCELEE
SPRYNESS	SQUINTED	TREATISE	DRWATSON	BRICKBAT	ORACULAR
AQUANAUT	SQUIRTED	URBANITE	ARKANSAS	TRICYCLE	CRACKLES
SQUABBLE	BREAKAGE	BREAKING	CREAMTEA	PRECEDED	FRECKLES
SQUADCAR	GREATAPE	CREAKING	DREAMTUP	ERICIDLE	PRICKLES
SQUADDIE	GREATAUK	CREASING	GREATTIT	PRECEDES	TRICKLES
SQUANDER	PREAMBLE	CREATING	ERRANTLY	DRYCLEAN	TRUCKLES
SQUARELY	BREADBIN	CROAKING	ERRANTRY	BRACKETS	BRACELET
SQUASHED	TRIARCHY	DREADING	ARMATURE	CRACKERS	DRACHMAS
SQUASHES	ORGANDIE	DREAMING	CREATURE	CRICKETS	ARACHNID
EQUALISE	BRIANENO	GREASING	TREASURE	CROCHETS	CRACKNEL
EQUATING	BREAKERS	GROANING	TREASURY	PROCEEDS	PRECINCT
SQUARING	BROADENS	TREADING	BROADWAY	TRACKERS	TRACHOMA
SQUARISH	DREAMERS	TREATING	CRIBBAGE	TROCHEES	FRUCTOSE
AQUARIUM	ARMAMENT	WREAKING	BRIBABLE	TRUCKERS	BROCCOLI
AQUARIAN	BROADEST	FREAKISH	PROBABLE	WRECKERS	GRACIOUS
EQUATION	GREATEST	ORGANISM	PROBABLY	CROCKETT	PRECIOUS
AQUARIUS	ORNAMENT	ARCADIAN	DRABNESS	CROCKERY	PRECOOKS
AQUATICS	CREAMERY	CREATION	PROBLEMS	CROCKERY	PROCTORS
AQUARIST	ORNATELY	CROATIAN	CRABMEAT	GRACEFUL	TRACTORS
AQUATINT	URBANELY	ORCADIAN	CRIBBING	CRUCIFIX	PRECEPTS

CRACKPOT	TRADEOFF	GREETING	ORIENTAL	PROGRESS	ARTISANS
BRICKRED	GRIDLOCK	GRIEVING	ARDENTLY	TRIGGERS	ORDINALS
PROCURED	CRUDEOIL	ORDERING	URGENTLY	FRAGMENT	IRRITANT
PROCURES	BRIDPORT	PREENING	BRAEBURN	PRIGGERY	ORDINARY
CROCUSES	FREDERIC	FREEKICK	DRJEKYLL	BRAGGING	FRUITBAT
PRICETAG	GRIDIRON	ARTERIAL	TRUFFAUT	DRAGGING	BRAINBOX
CRICHTON	CREDITED	FREEWILL	ORIFICES	DRAGKING	FRUITCUP
BROCHURE	PREDATED	ARMENIAN	PREFACES	DRUGGING	PRAISEBE
FRACTURE	CREDITON	ARTESIAN	PREFECTS	PRIGGISH	ARBITERS
PRECLUDE	CREDITOR	FRIESIAN	CROFTERS	CRAGGIER	BROILERS
TRACKWAY	PREDATOR	BREEZIER	DRIFTERS	DRUGGIST	BRUISERS
GRADUATE	CRUDITES	CREEPIER	PROFFERS	WRIGGLED	CRUISERS
TRADJAZZ	PREDATES	GREEDIER	CRAFTING	WRIGGLES	ERNIEELS
CREDIBLE	BRADBURY	ARTERIES	CROFTING	FRUGALLY	GRAINERS
CREDIBLY	BRADAWLS	FREESIAS	DRAFTING	DRAGOMAN	ORDINEES
PRODUCED	FREEHAND	TRUELIES	DRIFTING	ORIGINAL	TRAILERS
TRADUCED	VREELAND	PRIEDIEU	GRAFTING	ORIGANUM	TRAINEES
PRODUCER	FREEJACK	BREEZILY	TRIFLING	BRIGANDS	TRAINERS
PREDICTS	FREEFALL	CREEPILY	GRIFFITH	DRAGOONS	FRAILEST
PRODUCES	FREEWAYS	GREEDILY	GRAFFITI	DRYGOODS	FRUITFUL
PRODUCTS	ARTEFACT	TRUEBLUE	CRAFTIER	BRIGHTEN	FRUITFLY
TRADUCES	FRIENDLY	CRUELLER	TRAFFICS	BRIGHTON	DRYINGUP
DREDGERS	GREENDAY	FREEDMAN	TREFOILS	FRIGHTEN	ARTIFICE
GRADIENT	FREEREIN	GREENMAN	TRIFFIDS	BRIGHTER	ARRIVING
DRUDGERY	TREEFERN	FREEHOLD	CRAFTILY	DRAGSTER	BRAIDING
PRODIGAL	FREEZEUP	FREELOAD	PROFILED	FRIGATES	BRAISING
TRADEGAP	BREEDERS	FREELOVE	PROFILES	BRIGHTLY	BROILING
TREDEGAR	CREEPERS	FREEVOTE	TRUFFLES	PREHEATS	BRUISING
BRADSHAW	FREEZERS	GRUESOME	ARTFULLY	PROHIBIT	CRUISING
BRIDGING	TREELESS	TRUELOVE	PROFANED	ORTHODOX	DRAINING
BRIDLING	BRIEFEST	GREENOCK	DRIFTNET	ARCHAISM	GRAINING
CRADLING	GREENEST	FREEFORM	PRUFROCK	ORPHANED	ORBITING
DREDGING	GREENERY	FREETOWN	GRAFSPEE	ORCHARDS	PRAISING
GRUDGING	GREENFLY	GRIEVOUS	PROFORMA	ARCHDUKE	TRAILING
PRODDING	ARPEGGIO	TREETOPS	PROFITED	ARTHOUSE	TRAINING
TRUDGING	BREECHES	FREEPORT	PROFOUND	ARCHIVES	DRUIDISM
BRADPITT	FREERIDE	FREEPOST	DRAGRACE	ORDINAND	FRUITION
GRIDDLED	FREETIME	TRIEDOUT	PROGRAMS	DRAINAGE	BRAINIER
TRADDLES	BREEDING	TREEFROG	BRAGGART	IRRIGATE	ARTICLES
CREDENCE	BRIEFING	TRUEGRIT	FRAGRANT	IRRITATE	TRAITORS
PRUDENCE	CREEPING	GREENTEA	PREGNANT	ARMINARM	TRAIPSED
BRADFORD	FREEZING	ARRESTED	BRIGADES	ARRIVALS	TRAIPSES

TRAINSET	DRUMMERS	TREMBLES	PRINCESS	PRANCING	PRINTRUN
ARTISTIC	GROMMETS	CRIMINAL	PRINTERS	PRINTING	GRANDSON
ARTISTES	PREMIERS	PRIMROSE	TRINKETS	WRINGING	FRENETIC
ARTISTRY	PRIMNESS	TROMBONE	WRINGERS	BRANDISH	BRUNETTE
PROJECTS	TRAMMELS	DRUMROLL	GRANDEST	BRINDISI	PRENATAL
PREJUDGE	TRIMMERS	CRAMPONS	TRANSECT	CRONYISM	IRONDUKE
TRUJILLO	TRIMNESS	TRIMARAN	TRANSEPT	TRUNNION	TRANQUIL
TREKKERS	TRUMPETS	CROMARTY	ORANGERY	CRANKIER	PRONOUNS
TREKKING	DRUMBEAT	PROMISED	PRINCELY	FRONTIER	ARROGATE
BROKENLY	TRIMMEST	PREMISES	WRONGFUL	TRENDIER	ORTOLANS
BROKEOFF	TRUMPERY	PROMISES	TRANSFER	BRANDIES	ARGONAUT
BROKEOUT	GRIMSHAW	AROMATIC	TRANSFIX	CRANNIES	ARROGANT
BRAKEPAD	GRIMOIRE	DRAMATIC	CRANEFLY	GRANNIES	ARBOREAL
KRAKATOA	TRAMLINE	CREMATED	SRINAGAR	PRENTISS	CROONERS
MRBLOBBY	BRIMMING	PROMOTED	BRANCHED	CRANKILY	PRIORESS
PRELUDES	CRAMMING	PROMPTED	CRUNCHED	PRUNELLA	TROOPERS
TROLLEYS	CRAMPING	CROMPTON	DRENCHED	BRINDLED	BROOCHES
DROLLERY	CRIMPING	PROMOTER	TRENCHED	CRINKLED	BROODING
PROLIFIC	DRUMMING	PROMPTER	WRENCHED	IRONCLAD	BROOKING
PROLOGUE	TRAMPING	CREMATES	CRUNCHIE	TRUNDLED	CROONING
DRILLING	TRIMMING	PRIMATES	GRANTHAM	WRANGLED	DROOLING
GRILLING	TRUMPING	PROMOTES	CRUNCHER	WRINKLED	DROOPING
TRILLING	FRUMPISH	PROMPTLY	BRANCHES	FRANKLIN	GROOMING
TRILLION	GRUMPIER	FROMATOZ	BRONCHUS	GRANULAR	GROOVING
BROLLIES	GREMLINS	DRAMBUIE	CRUNCHES	WRANGLER	PROOFING
TRILBIES	ARUMLILY	PRIMEVAL	DRENCHES	CRINKLES	TROOPING
SRILANKA	GRUMPILY	DRUNKARD	TRENCHES	GRANULES	ARMORIAL
PRALINES	CRUMBLED	FRONTAGE	WRENCHES	TRUNDLES	CRYONICS
PROLONGS	CRUMPLED	IRONWARE	FRENZIED	WRANGLES	PRIORIES
TROLLOPE	GRUMBLED	TRUNCATE	FRANFINE	WRINKLES	ARSONIST
TROLLOPS	TRAMPLED	TRANSACT	IRONSIDE	FRONTMAN	PRIORITY
PRELATES	TREMBLED	GRENOBLE	PRENTICE	TRANSMIT	BROOKLYN
GRIMACED	GRIMALDI	GRENACHE	BRANDING	ORDNANCE	BROOKNER
GRIMACES	ARTMALIK	GRANDCRU	BRANNING	BRANDNEW	CREOSOTE
PREMIERE	GRUMBLER	TRINIDAD	BRINGING	CRANFORD	ARMOURED
CROMLECH	PREMOLAR	GRENADES	CRINGING	IRONWOOD	ARMOURER
BRAMBELL	BRAMBLES	BRANWELL	DRINKING	FRANCOME	TRIPLANE
BRUMMELL	CRUMBLES	GRENFELL	FRANKING	IRONWORK	TROPICAL
CROMWELL	CRUMPLES	GRANDEUR	GRANTING	FRANCOIS	DRIPFEED
BRIMLESS	GRUMBLES	DRINKERS	GRINDING	TRANSOMS	DROPLETS
CRIMPERS	PRIMULAS	GRANDEES	GRINNING	BRINGOUT	GRIPPERS
CRUMPETS	TRAMPLES	GRUNTERS	GRUNTING	PRINTOUT	PROPHETS

TRAPPERS	TRIPTYCH	GROSCHEN	PRISONER	PRETTIFY	GROUTING
TRIPLETS	FREQUENT	BRASSICA	PRESENTS	PRETTILY	FREUDIAN
TRIPPERS	IROQUOIS	CRESSIDA	DRYSLOPE	PRATTLED	CROUPIER
WRAPPERS	PRURIENT	PRESTIGE	FRESCOES	BRETTLEE	GROUPIES
FRIPPERY	PROROGUE	PRISTINE	PRESCOTT	PRATTLER	ARBUCKLE
PROPHECY	TRIREMES	BRISLING	CROSSPLY	PRATTLES	TROUBLED
PROPHESY	ARMRESTS	BRUSHING	PRESERVE	BRUTALLY	TROUBLES
DROPSHOT	ARKROYAL	CRASHING	TRISTRAM	CRETONNE	CROUTONS
GRAPHITE	ARMSRACE	CROSSING	IRISHSEA	PRETENCE	TRIUMPHS
TRIPWIRE	BRISBANE	CRUSHING	PRESSURE	PRETENDS	FROUFROU
CROPPING	DRESSAGE	DRESSING	PRESSUPS	WRITEOFF	ARQUETTE
DRIPPING	FRASCATI	FRISKING	BRATPACK	FRETWORK	KREUTZER
DROPPING	FRESHAIR	FROSTING	PRATFALL	CRITIQUE	BREVIARY
ERUPTING	CRYSTALS	GRASPING	GRATIANO	CRITERIA	CREVICES
GRIPPING	TRESPASS	PRESSING	BRATCAMP	PRETORIA	PROVIDED
PROPPING	ERASABLE	TRUSSING	FRETSAWS	CRATERED	PROVIDER
TRAPPING	CROSSBAR	TRUSTING	PROTRACT	BRETHREN	PROVIDES
TRIPLING	CRUSHBAR	WRESTING	BRITTANY	ORATORIO	PREVIEWS
TRIPPING	CROSSBOW	CROSTINI	CRITICAL	PROTESTS	PREVAILS
WRAPPING	GRASSBOX	GRISSINI	PROTOCOL	ARTTATUM	PROVOKED
DROPKICK	PRESSBOX	ORMSKIRK	PROTECTS	PROTRUDE	PROVOKES
ERUPTION	TRASHCAN	PRUSSIAN	BROTHERS	PRETEXTS	TRAVOLTA
GRAPHICS	TRISECTS	CRISPIER	FRITTERS	PROTOZOA	GRAVELLY
TROPHIES	CROSSCUT	FROSTIER	PRETZELS	BROUHAHA	PROVENCE
TRAPPIST	CRUSADED	FROSTILY	TROTTERS	URQUHART	PROVINCE
CRIPPLED	PRESIDED	BRASILIA	GRATEFUL	ARGUABLE	PREVENTS
GRAPPLED	CRUSADER	BRISTLED	TRUTHFUL	ARGUABLY	CRAVENLY
GRAPPLES	CRUSADES	WRESTLED	WRATHFUL	TROUNCED	PREVIOUS
TRAPUNTO	PRESIDES	WRESTLER	PROTEGEE	TROUNCES	DRIVEOUT
DROPZONE	GRASMERE	BRISTLES	PROTEGES	GROUNDED	DROVEOUT
DROPGOAL	TRESSELL	TRESTLES	WRETCHED	FRAULEIN	TRAVERSE
TRAPDOOR	PROSPERO	WRESTLES	GRETCHEN	TROUSERS	PROVERBS
PREPARED	BRUSSELS	BRESSLAW	CRUTCHES	ARGUMENT	CREVASSE
PREPARES	DRESSERS	PRESUMED	WRETCHES	CROUCHED	PROVOSTS
PROPERLY	PROSPERS	FRESHMAN	CRATCHIT	BROUGHAM	TRAVESTY
PROPERTY	TRUSTEES	FRESHMEN	CROTCHET	CROUCHES	GRAVITAS
PROPOSED	BRISKEST	GROSSMAN	FRETTING	DRAUGHTS	PRIVATES
PROPOSAL	CRESCENT	IRISHMAN	TROTTING	DRAUGHTY	DRIVEWAY
PROPOSER	CRISPEST	PRESSMAN	WRITHING	URSULINE	BROWNALE
PROPOSES	FRESHEST	PRESSMEN	PRETTIER	AROUSING	DRAWBACK
PROPOUND	PROSPECT	PRESUMES	PROTEINS	GROUPING	BREWEDUP
WRAPOVER	PRESAGES	PRESENCE	GRATUITY	GROUSING	CREWNECK

ARAWDEAL	PREZZIES	OSTERLEY	OSBOURNE	ATTACHES	STOCKPOT
BRAWLERS	DRIZZLED	ESTEEMED	ESPOUSED	STRACHEY	STUDFARM
BROWSERS	GRIZZLED	ASTEROID	ESPOUSAL	STEADIED	STUDYING
CRAWLERS	GRIZZLER	ASSESSED	ESPOUSES	STEALING	STODGIER
GROWLERS	DRIZZLES	ASSESSOR	ASSORTED	STEAMING	STUDENTS
PROWLERS	GRIZZLES	ASSESSES	ESCORTED	STRAFING	STUDBOOK
TRAWLERS	BREZHNEV	ASSENTED	ASCRIBED	STRAYING	STUDIOUS
BROWBEAT	BRAZENLY	ASSERTED	ASCRIBES	STEADIER	STEERAGE
CROWTHER	ESCALATE	ASSENTER	USURPERS	STDAVIDS	STEENBOK
BRAWLING	ESCAPADE	ASBESTOS	USURPING	STEADIES	STRETCHY
BROWNING	ISTANBUL	OSWESTRY	ESTRANGE	ITSAGIFT	ATTENDED
BROWSING	ISLANDER	USEFULLY	TSARINAS	STEADILY	ATTENDEE
CRAWLING	ASSAYERS	ASHGABAT	USURIOUS	STRATIFY	ETCETERA
CROWDING	ESCAPEES	ASPHODEL	ESPRESSO	ATTACKED	STHELENA
CROWNING	ESHANESS	ISOHYETS	TSARISTS	ATTACKER	STEELEYE
DRAWLING	ESCARGOT	ESCHEWAL	ASITWERE	STRAWMAN	ETHEREAL
DROWNING	ASSAYING	ASPHYXIA	ISOTHERM	ATTAINED	STEEPENS
FROWNING	ESCAPING	ASPIRATE	ASHTANGA	STRAINED	STEERERS
GROWLING	ESSAYING	ESTIMATE	ISOTONIC	STRAINER	STHELENS
PROWLING	ESCAPISM	ASPIRANT	ISOTOPES	STRAPPED	STEEPEST
TRAWLING	ESPALIER	OSSIFIED	ESOTERIC	ATLANTIC	ATLENGTH
BRAWNIER	ESCAPIST	ASPIRING	ASTUTELY	ATLANTIS	STRENGTH
DROWSIER	ESSAYIST	ASPIRINS	ASSUAGED	STEALTHY	STEEPING
BROWNIES	ISCARIOT	OSSIFIES	ASSUAGES	STEADYON	STEERING
DROWSILY	ASSAILED	OSSICLES	ASMUCHAS	STABLEST	STREWING
DRAWINGS	ASSAULTS	ASSIGNED	ASSUMING	STABBING	UTTERING
CRAWFORD	ESCALOPE	ASSISTED	ASSURING	STABLING	ATHENIAN
BROWNOWL	ASSASSIN	ISHIGURO	ESQUIRES	STUBBING	STHELIER
DRAWLOTS	OSNABURG	PSALTERS	ASAWHOLE	STUBBORN	STREAKED
DRAWNOUT	ISABELLA	PSALTERY	ASSYRIAN	STOCKADE	STREAKER
BROWNRAT	ISABELLE	PSALMIST	STRANDED	STACCATO	STEEPLES
BREWSTER	ISOBATHS	ISOLATED	STRADDLE	STOCKCAR	STREAMED
PRIXFIXE	ASHCROFT	ISOLATES	ITSADEAL	STICKERS	STREAMER
ARMYCAMP	USEDCARS	ISAMBARD	STEALERS	STACKING	ETHERNET
GREYSEAL	ASSEMBLE	CSIMIAMI	STEAMERS	STICKING	ATTEMPTS
GREYNESS	ASSEMBLY	ASUNCION	STRATEGY	STOCKING	ETHELRED
GRAYLING	ASCENDED	ASSONANT	STRAGGLE	STICKIER	STRESSED
CRAYFISH	USHERING	ASCORBIC	STRANGLE	STOCKIER	ATHEISTS
GREYAREA	ASTERISK	ASLONGAS	STRANGER	STOCKIST	STRESSES
DREYFUSS	ESPECIAL	ASTONISH	STRAIGHT	STICKILY	ATTESTED
BRAZIERS	ASCETICS	ESTONIAN	STRAGGLY	STICKLER	ATHERTON
CRAZIEST	ASPERITY	ASTOUNDS	ATTACHED	STOCKMAN	ATTESTER

STIFFENS	STALKERS	STUNNERS	STOPPERS	STARTLED	SUDANESE
STAFFING	STALKING	STENDHAL	ATAPRICE	STARTLES	BUDAPEST
STIFLING	STALLING	ATANCHOR	STAPLING	STOREMAN	HUMANELY
STUFFING	STALLION	STANDING	STEPPING	STOREMEN	CURATIVE
STUFFILY	STULTIFY	STINGING	STOPPING	STARTOUT	PUTATIVE
STAFFORD	ATALANTA	STINKING	STIPPLED	STARTREK	RUNAMILE
STIGMATA	STALLONE	STONKING	STIPPLES	ITERATED	MUTATING
STAGNATE	STYLISED	STUNNING	ATAPINCH	ITERATES	PUPATING
STAGNANT	UTILISED	STINGIER	STIPENDS	STARTURN	SUGARING
STAGGERS	STILLSON	STENCILS	STEPONIT	STIRRUPS	RUNARISK
STAGHORN	STYLISES	UTENSILS	STEPFORD	STARDUST	HUMANISM
ATTHEHOP	STYLISTS	STUNTMAN	STOPCOCK	STASHING	RURALISM
ETCHINGS	UTILISES	STUNTMEN	STEPDOWN	OTOSCOPE	DURATION
STAINERS	ATHLETIC	STANFORD	STOPOVER	STATUARY	EURASIAN
STRIKERS	STILETTO	STANHOPE	STARGATE	STUTTERS	MUTATION
STRIDENT	ATHLETES	STANDOFF	STARWARS	STITCHED	PUPATION
STRINGER	STOMACHS	STANDOUT	ATTRACTS	STITCHES	LUNATICS
ATTIRING	STAMPEDE	STANDPAT	STURGEON	STATIONS	HUMANIST
STAINING	STEMCELL	STINGRAY	STARKERS	STETSONS	RURALIST
STRIDING	STAMMERS	STANSTED	STARLETS	STATUTES	AUDACITY
STRIKING	STEMLESS	STANWYCK	STARTERS	ETRUSCAN	HUMANITY
STRIVING	PTOMAINE	OTTOMANS	STIRRERS	STRUDELS	MUHAMMAD
STOICISM	STAMPING	STROHEIM	STARKEST	STOUTEST	SUSANNAH
STRICKEN	STEMMING	STRONGON	STERNEST	STRUGGLE	HUMANOID
STRIMMER	STOMPING	STRONGER	STARCHED	ATTUNING	FUMAROLE
ETHIOPIA	STUMPING	STRONGLY	STARSHIP	STRUMMED	HULAHOOP
STRIPPED	STYMYING	ATROPINE	STARLING	STRUMPET	CURATORS
STRIPPER	STUMBLED	STOOPING	STARRING	STRUTTED	RUNABOUT
STAIRROD	STIMULUS	STROBING	STARTING	STAUNTON	NUGATORY
ATKINSON	STUMBLES	STROKING	STARVING	STEWPANS	JURASSIC
STRICTER	ATOMBOMB	ATROCITY	STERLING	STEWPOTS	FUNAFUTI
STRICTLY	STAMPOUT	STROLLED	STIRLING	STEWARDS	RUBAIYAT
ATTITUDE	ATOMISED	STROLLER	STIRRING	STOWAWAY	CUPBOARD
STAIRWAY	ITEMISED	ATTORNEY	STORMING	ETHYLENE	OUTBOARD
STEINWAY	ATOMISER	STOODOUT	STARFISH	STAYOVER	GUNBOATS
STAKEOUT	ATOMISES	ATSOURCE	STARSIGN	RUTABAGA	SUNBEAMS
STELLATE	ITEMISES	ATBOTTOM	STORMIER	CUTADASH	CUTBACKS
ITALIANS	STANDARD	STOPPARD	STURDIER	GUJARATI	OUTBREAK
STALBANS	STONEAGE	STOPPAGE	STEROIDS	LUNAPARK	DUMBBELL
STALWART	STANNARY	ATYPICAL	STARLIFT	BULAWAYO	NUMBNESS
STOLIDLY	STINGERS	STUPIDLY	ETERNITY	TURANDOT	TUMBLERS
ATELIERS	STINKERS	STAPLERS	STURDILY	GUYANESE	TUMBRELS

HUMBLEST	PUNCHBAG	SUNDIALS	TUTELAGE	QUIETUDE	BURGHERS
TUBBIEST	LUNCHBOX	QUADRANT	LUKEWARM	MUTESWAN	JUGGLERS
SUNBLIND	MUSCADET	GUIDEDOG	NUMERALS	SUFFRAGE	QUAGMIRE
BUBBLING	SUNCREAM	BUDDLEIA	NUMERACY	OUTFLANK	BUNGLING
BUMBLING	LUNCHEON	MUDDLEUP	QUEENBEE	PUFFBALL	BURGLING
BURBLING	MUSCLEIN	HUNDREDS	SUPERBUG	RUFFIANS	GURGLING
FUMBLING	PUNCHEON	HURDLERS	SUPERBLY	SUFFICED	JUGGLING
HUMBLING	BUTCHERS	SUNDRESS	TUBERCLE	SURFACED	OUTGOING
JUMBLING	LURCHERS	MUDDIEST	SUPERCAR	SURFACER	LUNGFISH
MUMBLING	QUICKENS	BUNDCHEN	DUVETDAY	SUFFICES	DUNGHILL
RUMBLING	SUCCEEDS	QUADBIKE	FUNEREAL	SURFACES	HUNGRIER
TUMBLING	JUICIEST	BUNDLING	SUPEREGO	NUFFIELD	HUNGRILY
BUBBLIER	QUICKEST	CUDDLING	MULETEER	OUTFIELD	BULGAKOV
GUMBOILS	BUTCHERY	CURDLING	CUTENESS	MUFFLERS	BUNGALOW
JUMBOJET	QUACKERY	HUDDLING	MUTENESS	BUNFIGHT	TURGENEV
TURBOJET	QUICKFIX	HURDLING	PURENESS	GUNFIGHT	BURGUNDY
SUNBAKED	DUTCHHOE	MUDDLING	RUDENESS	MUFFLING	PUNGENCY
QUIBBLED	BUNCHING	OUTDOING	SURENESS	QUAFFING	BUNGHOLE
QUIBBLER	HUNCHING	SUBDUING	TUBELESS	RUFFLING	OUTGROWN
QUIBBLES	LUNCHING	BUDDHISM	TUNELESS	CUFFLINK	BURGEONS
HUSBANDS	LURCHING	SUNDRIES	QUIETEST	DUMFRIES	DUNGEONS
TURBINES	MUNCHING	BUDDHIST	FUSEWIRE	SURFEITS	SURGEONS
SUNBLOCK	PUNCHING	QUIDDITY	JUVENILE	RUEFULLY	BULGARIA
GUMBOOTS	QUACKING	BURDENED	SUREFIRE	CUPFINAL	JUNGFRAU
LUMBERED	ZUCCHINI	GUIDANCE	YULETIDE	BUFFOONS	VULGARLY
NUMBERED	BURCHILL	SUNDANCE	SUPERIOR	OUTFRONT	SUGGESTS
SUNBURNS	FUNCTION	DUODENAL	AURELIUS	SUFFERED	BUDGETED
OUTBURST	JUNCTION	DUODENUM	EUGENICS	SUFFERER	TUNGSTEN
SUNBURNT	MUNCHIES	PUDDINGS	SURETIES	SUFFUSED	HUNGJURY
SUNBURST	MUSCULAR	SUDDENLY	LUTENIST	SUFFUSES	HUNGOVER
BURBERRY	DUTCHMAN	CULDROSE	QUEENMAB	GUFFAWED	PUSHCART
MULBERRY	DULCIMER	OUTDOORS	SUPERMAN	SUFFIXES	BUSHBABY
RUBBISHY	SUCCUMBS	JUDDERED	AUREVOIR	MUDGUARD	HUSHEDUP
SUNBATHE	DULCINEA	MURDERED	NUMEROUS	BURGLARS	BUSHNELL
SURBITON	SUCCINCT	SUNDERED	TUBEROUS	CUTGLASS	RUTHLESS
OUTBOUND	LUSCIOUS	MURDERER	CUBEROOT	BURGLARY	CUSHIEST
PURCHASE	OUTCASTS	CULDESAC	RULEDOUT	SURGICAL	CUTHBERT
PUBCRAWL	QUICKSET	OUTDATED	PUREBRED	GUNGADIN	BUSHFIRE
OUTCLASS	MUSCATEL	LUDDITES	KUREISHI	BUNGEDUP	PUSHBIKE
SUBCLASS	JUNCTURE	PUNDITRY	RUSEDSKI	RUGGEDLY	SUCHLIKE
NUNCHAKU	PUNCTURE	FUSELAGE	NUNEATON	MUNGBEAN	FUCHSIAS
RUNCIBLE	PUNCTUAL	NUMERATE	SUPERTAX	BUNGLERS	SUBHUMAN

DUSHANBE	AUDITION	BULKHEAD	PULLEDIN	FULLSTOP	HUONPINE
BUCHANAN	MUNITION	DUCKWEED	CURLEDUP	FURLOUGH	TURNPIKE
RUSHMORE	MUSICIAN	BUCKLEYS	PULLEDUP	TURLOUGH	QUANTIFY
MUSHROOM	TUNISIAN	BUNKBEDS	BULLSEYE	OUTLIVED	QUANTITY
RUSHHOUR	FUSILIER	LUCKLESS	FULLBEAM	SULLIVAN	QUENELLE
CUSHIONS	PURIFIER	BULKIEST	BUILDERS	GULLIVER	SURNAMED
EUPHORIA	MUTINIES	HUSKIEST	DULLNESS	PULLOVER	EUONYMUS
EUPHORIC	PURIFIES	LUCKIEST	FULLNESS	TULLIVER	SURNAMES
HUGHORDE	PUGILIST	MUCKIEST	GUILDERS	OUTLAWED	BURNDOWN
LUTHERAN	CUPIDITY	MURKIEST	PURLIEUS	OUTMODED	TURNDOWN
DUCHESSE	FUTILITY	SULKIEST	CURLIEST	SUMMEDUP	TURNSOUR
NUTHATCH	HUMIDIFY	BUCKSHEE	SURLIEST	RUMMAGED	BURNTOUT
OUTHOUSE	HUMIDITY	JUNKSHOP	GUILEFUL	RUMMAGES	TURNCOAT
HUSHHUSH	HUMILITY	TUCKSHOP	SUNLIGHT	GUNMAKER	DUENORTH
PUSHOVER	LUCIDITY	BUCKSHOT	FULLTIME	SUMMONED	RUNNERUP
DUCHOVNY	AURICLES	BUCKLING	BUILDING	MURMANSK	PUGNOSED
FUMIGATE	CUBICLES	DUCKLING	BULLRING	SUMMONUP	RUBNOSES
MUTILATE	CUTICLES	SUCKLING	BULLYING	AUGMENTS	TURNOVER
RUMINATE	AUDIENCE	LUCKYJIM	DUELLING	TURMERIC	AUTOMATA
SURINAME	JULIANNE	BUCKSKIN	OUTLYING	MURMURED	KUROSAWA
SUKIYAKI	JULIENNE	DUCKPOND	QUELLING	SUBMERGE	AUTODAFE
MUSICALS	AUDITORS	JUNKFOOD	QUILTING	DUMMYRUN	AUTOMATE
PURITANS	LUMINOUS	PUNKROCK	SULLYING	MURMURER	AUTOBAHN
FUMIGANT	MUTINOUS	DUCKSOUP	PURLOINS	SURMISED	AUTOMATS
JUBILANT	NUMINOUS	PUCKERED	DUELLIST	SURMISES	EUROPEAN
RUMINANT	CUTITOUT	BUCKAROO	GUILTILY	CUPMATCH	EULOGISE
CULINARY	AUDITORY	TUCKEROO	HULLCITY	GUNMETAL	TUTORING
LUMINARY	FUMITORY	JUNKETED	OUTLINES	SURMOUNT	TUTORIAL
DUTIABLE	JULIETTE	HUCKSTER	SULLENLY	TURNBACK	AUTOGIRO
MUSICBOX	RUBICUND	MUSKETRY	BULLDOZE	QUANDARY	EULOGIST
JULIEEGE	PULITZER	FULLFACE	CUTLOOSE	FURNACES	HUMORIST
MUTINEER	SUBJECTS	SUBLEASE	BULLYOFF	TURNEDIN	OUTOFKEY
BUSINESS	CUNJEVOI	FUELTANK	FULLMOON	TURNEDUP	DUBONNET
PUNINESS	AUCKLAND	FULLBACK	BULLDOGS	GUINNESS	HUMOROUS
PUNISHED	JUNKYARD	PULLBACK	FULLTOSS	QUINTETS	TUMOROUS
PUNISHES	MUCKRAKE	PULLRANK	MULLIONS	TURNKEYS	AUTONOMY
PURIFIED	RUCKSACK	GULLIBLE	BULLFROG	FUNNIEST	HUMOURED
FUGITIVE	JUNKMAIL	CURLICUE	DULLARDS	SUNNIEST	RUMOURED
PUNITIVE	LUCKYBAG	PUBLICAN	MUDLARKS	QUENCHED	AUTOCRAT
AUDITING	MUCKEDIN	BULLOCKS	OUTLASTS	BUNNYHOP	EUROCRAT
JUDICIAL	TUCKEDIN	PUBLICLY	BULLETIN	QUENCHES	CUPOFTEA
PUGILISM	LUCKYDIP	CULLODEN	CURLYTOP	CUTNOICE	EUROSTAR

CULOTTES	SUPPOSED	OUTSTAYS	SUITCASE	OUTTAKES	CUCUMBER
TUGOFWAR	SUPPOSES	RUSSIANS	DUSTBATH	HUNTSMAN	QUEUEDUP
SULPHATE	QUIPSTER	OUTSMART	QUATRAIN	HUNTSMEN	AUGURING
HUMPBACK	PUPPETRY	PURSUANT	NUPTIALS	CUSTOMER	FUTURISM
JUMPBAIL	JUMPSUIT	TUSSOCKS	QUETZALS	BUTTONED	LUXURIES
SUPPLANT	MUSQUASH	PUSSYCAT	DUSTCART	BUNTINGS	PUTUPJOB
CULPABLE	OUTREACH	SUBSIDED	SUBTRACT	CUTTINGS	MUTUALLY
CULPABLY	LUHRMANN	OUTSIDER	PUTTOBED	HUSTINGS	AUTUMNAL
AUSPICES	CURRICLE	SUBSIDES	HUXTABLE	MUSTANGS	HUGUENOT
SUSPECTS	GUARDDOG	NUTSHELL	QUOTABLE	SULTANAS	AUGUSTUS
JUMPEDUP	OUTRIDER	MUNSTERS	SUITABLE	BUTTONIT	QUOVADIS
PUMPEDUP	FURRIERS	PUNSTERS	SUITABLY	DUSTBOWL	QUIVERED
SUBPOENA	QUARRELS	PURSUERS	BUTTOCKS	AUCTIONS	SUBVERTS
SUPPRESS	QUARTERS	OUTSHINE	BUTTEDIN	LUSTROUS	SUNVISOR
BUMPIEST	QUARTETS	SUNSHINE	RUSTLEUP	MULTIPLE	SURVIVED
PUPPYFAT	NUTRIENT	BURSTING	BUTTRESS	MULTIPLY	SURVIVAL
SUPPLIED	FURRIERY	GUESSING	CURTNESS	BUTTERED	SURVIVOR
CUTPRICE	OUTRAGED	PURSUING	HUNTRESS	CULTURED	SURVIVES
SULPHIDE	OUTRIGHT	QUASHING	HUSTLERS	MUSTERED	PURVEYED
SURPLICE	GUERNICA	QUISLING	JUSTNESS	MUTTERED	SURVEYED
SURPRISE	GUARDING	TUSSLING	QUITTERS	NURTURED	PURVEYOR
DUMPLING	HURRYING	GUNSMITH	RUSTLERS	CULTURAL	SURVEYOR
QUIPPING	QUERYING	QUESTION	FURTHEST	GUTTURAL	OUTWEIGH
RUMPLING	GUARDIAN	PURSUITS	NUTTIEST	TURTURRO	LULWORTH
LUMPFISH	QUARRIES	SUNSUITS	QUOTIENT	BUTTERUP	BULWARKS
GUMPTION	SUPREMES	OUTSELLS	SUBTLEST	MUTTERER	OUTWARDS
SUPPLIER	SUPREMOS	SUBSUMED	SUBTLETY	BUSTARDS	QUIXOTIC
BUMPKINS	CURRANTS	RUNSAMOK	MULTIGYM	CULTURES	DUTYPAID
CULPRITS	CURRENTS	SUBSUMES	BUSTAGUT	NURTURES	BUOYEDUP
MURPHIES	CURRENCY	SUBSONIC	CURTSIED	VULTURES	BUSYNESS
PUMPKINS	MULRONEY	NUISANCE	BUSTLING	PUTTOSEA	EURYDICE
SUPPLIES	GUERNSEY	GUNSMOKE	HURTLING	CULTISTS	QUAYSIDE
SUSPENSE	LUCRETIA	FUSSPOTS	HUSTLING	SUBTITLE	BUOYANCY
TUPPENCE	TURRETED	CUTSHORT	QUITTING	SUBTOTAL	BUSYBODY
BUMPINTO	AUGRATIN	OUTSTRIP	RUSTLING	SUMTOTAL	DUTYFREE
SUSPENDS	SURROUND	SUBSISTS	AUSTRIAN	SURTAXED	PUTYOUUP
CUTPURSE	BURROWED	PULSATED	SULTRIER	RUNTOYOU	GUZZLERS
PUMPIRON	FURROWED	PULSATES	CURTAILS	FUTURAMA	PUZZLERS
HUMPHRYS	OUTSTARE	DUESOUTH	CURTAINS	ZULULAND	QUIZSHOW
PURPORTS	PURSLANE	NUMSKULL	CURTSIES	ZULUDAWN	GUZZLING
SUPPORTS	SUNSHADE	TUSSAUDS	DUSTBINS	SUBURBIA	NUZZLING
HUMPHREY	TUNSTALL	MUSTHAVE	SUSTAINS	SUBURBAN	PUZZLING

QUIZZING	OVERTAKE	EVERMORE	SWEETPEA	TWOPENCE	EXCELLED
MUEZZINS	OVERHANG	EVERYONE	TWOFACED	AWARDING	EXPELLED
BUZZBOMB	OVERHAUL	OVERCOME	SWIFTEST	DWARFING	EXTERNAL
BUZZWORD	OVEREATS	OVERDONE	SWAGGERS	SWARMING	EXCERPTS
BUZZARDS	OVERLAPS	OVERDOSE	SWIGGING	SWERVING	EXPENSES
AVIATING	OVERLAYS	OVERRODE	OWNINGUP	SWIRLING	EXPECTED
AVIATION	OVERPASS	OVERTONE	AWAITING	TWIRLING	EXPERTLY
AVIARIES	OVERCAST	OVERLONG	AWAKENED	TWISTERS	EXIGENCY
AVIATORS	OVERACTS	OVERCOOK	PWLLHELI	SWASTIKA	EXIGUOUS
AVIATRIX	EVERYDAY	OVERLOCK	DWELLERS	TWISTING	EXCHANGE
EVACUATE	OVERFEED	OVERLOOK	SWELTERS	TWISTIES	EXCISING
AVOCADOS	OVERHEAD	OVERDOES	TWILIGHT	TWITTERS	EXCITING
EVACUEES	EVERDENE	OVERCOAT	DWELLING	TWITTERY	EXPIRING
EVICTING	OVERLEAF	OVERDOIT	SWELLING	SWITCHED	EXCISION
EVICTION	OVERSELL	OVERDRAW	SWILLING	TWITCHED	EXHIBITS
EVIDENCE	OVERBEAR	OVERUSED	SWALLOWS	TWITCHER	EXLIBRIS
AVIEMORE	OVERHEAR	OVERUSES	SWIMWEAR	SWATCHES	EXULTANT
AVOIDING	OVERSEER	OVERSTEP	SWIMMERS	SWITCHES	EXPLICIT
TVDINNER	OVERSEAS	OVERSTAY	SWIMMING	TWITCHES	EXCLUDED
EVALUATE	OVERSEES	OVERRULE	SWIMSUIT	SWATHING	EXPLODED
EVOLVING	OVERHEAT	OVERTURE	SWANLAKE	SWATTING	EXCLUDES
EVILDOER	AVERAGED	OVERFULL	SWINGBIN	SWOTTING	EXPLODES
AVEMARIA	AVERAGES	OVERTURN	SWINGERS	TWITTISH	EXALTING
OVENWARE	OVERSHOE	SWEATERS	TWINBEDS	TWOTIMER	EXULTING
SVENGALI	OVERSHOT	SWEARING	SWANNERY	TWOWOMEN	EXCLAIMS
AVENGERS	OVERRIDE	SWEATING	SWANKING	SWIZZLED	EXPLAINS
EVENNESS	OVERRIPE	TWEAKING	SWINGING	SWIZZLES	EXPLOITS
EVENTERS	OVERTIME	OWNBRAND	TWINNING	EXCAVATE	EXPLORED
EVENTFUL	AVERRING	SWABBING	TWENTIES	EXPANDED	EXPLORER
EVENTIDE	AVERTING	TWOBYTWO	DWINDLED	EXHALING	EXPLORES
AVENGING	OVERFISH	SWADDLED	SWINDLED	EXHAUSTS	EXEMPLAR
EVENTING	OVERFILL	TWIDDLED	TWINKLED	EXECRATE	EXAMPLES
EVENSONG	OVERKILL	SWADDLES	SWINDLER	EXACTING	EXAMINED
EVANESCE	AVERSION	TWIDDLES	DWINDLES	EXECUTED	EXAMINEE
EVENTUAL	OVERVIEW	SWEEPERS	SWINDLES	EXECUTOR	EXAMINER
AVIONICS	OVERALLS	SWEETENS	TWINKLES	EXECUTES	EXAMINES
EVAPERON	OVERFLOW	TWEEZERS	SWANSONG	OXIDISED	OXYMORON
OVERLAID	OVERPLAY	SWEETEST	SWOONING	OXIDISES	EXPONENT
OVERLAND	EVERYMAN	SWEEPING	SWOOPING	EXCEEDED	OXTONGUE
OVERPAID	OVERLOAD	TWEETING	TWOPIECE	EXTENDED	EXPOSING
OVERCAME	OVERLORD	SWEETIES	SWAPSHOP	EXPEDITE	EXTOLLED
OVERRATE	OVERSOLD	TWEENIES	SWAPPING	EXTERIOR	EXPOUNDS

EXPORTED	EYEBROWS	CYCLICAL	EYESHADE
EXTORTED	NYEBEVAN	WYCLIFFE	EYESIGHT
EXPORTER	LYNCHING	CYCLAMEN	AYRSHIRE
EXPOSURE	LYNCHMOB	CYCLONIC	EYESDOWN
EXTRACTS	HYACINTH	EYELINER	MYOSOTIS
OXBRIDGE	EYECANDY	CYCLONES	DYESTUFF
UXBRIDGE	LYNCHPIN	CYCLISTS	MYSTICAL
EXERCISE	NYPDBLUE	EYELEVEL	EYETEETH
EXORCISE	SYNDROME	CYCLEWAY	EYETOOTH
EXERTING	EYEDROPS	DYSLEXIA	DYSTOPIA
EXORCISM	TYPEFACE	DYSLEXIC	MYSTIQUE
EXERTION	HYDEPARK	MYRMIDON	HYSTERIA
EXORCIST	TYPECAST	SYMMETRY	AZNAVOUR
EXTREMES	TYNEDALY	LYINGLOW	OZCLARKE
UXORIOUS	RYDERCUP	MYRNALOY	TZATZIKI
EXGRATIA	PYRENEAN	HYMNBOOK	
EXISTENZ	PYRENEES	DYINGOUT	
EXISTING	LYREBIRD	GYMNASTS	
EXITPOLL	BYDESIGN	HYPNOSIS	
EXCUSEME	HYPERION	HYPNOTIC	
EXPUNGED	BYRETURN	BYRONBAY	
EXPUNGES	EYEGLASS	TYROLEAN	
EXCUSING	RYEGRASS	CYTOLOGY	
EXHUMING	LYCHGATE	MYCOLOGY	
DYNAMITE	MYTHICAL	SYNOPSES	
SYBARITE	TYPHOONS	SYNOPSIS	
GYRATING	BYTHEWAY	SYNOPTIC	
DYNAMISM	CYLINDER	CYNOSURE	
GYRATION	HYPINGUP	SYNONYMS	
DYNAMICS	SYRINGES	EYEPIECE	
PYRAMIDS	TYPIFIED	TYMPANIC	
MYFAMILY	CYNICISM	TYMPANUM	
SYCAMORE	LYRICISM	SYMPTOMS	
GYRATORY	TYPIFIES	SYMPHONY	
BYPASSED	LYRICIST	SYMPOSIA	
BYPASSES	CYRILLIC	EYEPATCH	
SYNAPSIS	HYGIENIC	SYMPATHY	
DYNASTIC	BYDINTOF	AYURVEDA	
SYRACUSE	GYMKHANA	HYDROGEN	
RYEBREAD	SYLLABUB	HYDRANTS	
SYMBOLIC	SYLLABLE	CYPRIOTS	
EYEBALLS	SYLLABUS	BYGRAVES	

BANANAMAN	CATALEPSY	PAPAROACH	BARBICANS	LAMBSWOOL
CATAMARAN	CANALETTO	VAGABONDS	TABBYCATS	CAMBAZOLA
MAHARAJAS	LAZARETTO	CATALONIA	CAMBODIAN	BACCHANAL
MALAYALAM	PARAKEETS	CATATONIA	LAMBRETTA	SACCHARIN
PANAMAHAT	HARANGUED	CATATONIC	LAMBOFGOD	KAMCHATKA
LABALANCE	HARANGUES	PATAGONIA	PARBOILED	CATCHABLE
SALAMANCA	FALANGISM	MACAROONS	BABBLINGS	FANCIABLE
JACARANDA	FALANGIST	PARAMOUNT	CAMBRIDGE	WATCHABLE
CARAPACES	MARATHONS	PARAMOURS	FARBRIDGE	BACCHANTE
DATABASES	MALATHION	CALABOOSE	GAMBOLLED	BACCHANTS
WANAMAKER	MALACHITE	GADABOUTS	RAYBOLGER	SAUCEBOAT
MACADAMIA	PARACHUTE	LAYABOUTS	CATBALLOU	HATCHBACK
MAHARANIS	FANATICAL	PAVAROTTI	CABBALIST	MACCABEES
BALALAIKA	SAMARITAN	CATALOGUE	JAMBALAYA	DANCEBAND
DATABANKS	CANALISED	PALANQUIN	HARBINGER	MATCHBOOK
PALATABLE	CANALISES	CATARRHAL	IANBANNEN	CASCADING
GALAPAGOS	KARABINER	HAMADRYAD	CARBUNCLE	RANCHEROS
KALAMAZOO	MAGAZINES	CAVALRIES	CARBONARA	SAYCHEESE
KARAMAZOV	PARASITES	LARACROFT	CARBONARI	PATCHEDUP
CATARACTS	MAHARISHI	MALADROIT	CARBONISE	CALCIFIED
PAPARAZZI	PARASITIC	PARAGRAPH	CARBONATE	CALCIFIES
PAPARAZZO	FARAFIELD	CALABRESE	RAYBROOKS	FANCYFREE
CANALBOAT	TAMARILLO	BARABRITH	BAMBOOZLE	CATCHFIRE
CARAMBOLA	GALATIANS	MALAYSIAN	SAMBROWNE	DANCEHALL
CAVALCADE	VACATIONS	HARASSING	BARBARIAN	MARCHHARE
VACANCIES	CAPACITOR	RADARTRAP	HAMBURGER	WARCRIMES
BALANCING	CAPARISON	RAJASTHAN	JAMBOREES	RADCLIFFE
DAMASCENE	CAVALIERS	GAZASTRIP	BARBERING	DABCHICKS
BALANCERS	FATALISTS	TARANTULA	CAMBERING	GASCOIGNE
FARANDOLE	SATANISTS	TARANTINO	JABBERING	SANCTIONS
MARAUDING	CAPACIOUS	MALAGUENA	YABBERING	CATCHIEST
MARAUDERS	RAPACIOUS	KAMASUTRA	BARBARISE	MACCHIATO
HAZARDOUS	SAGACIOUS	CATAPULTS	BARBARISM	CANCELLED
SALADDAYS	SALACIOUS	FAMAGUSTA	BARBARITY	CATCALLED
CANAVERAL	RARASKIRT	PARALYSED	BARBAROUS	PARCELLED
ZAPATEADO	DALAILAMA	PARALYSES	LAMBASTED	BARCELONA
PARAMETER	CABALLERO	CATALYTIC	IANBOTHAM	MASCULINE
PARAMEDIC	CABALLERS	PARALYSIS	BARBITONE	MATCHLESS
LAZARENKO	CATACLYSM	CATALYSTS	LAMBRUSCO	CALCULATE
BAGATELLE	BALACLAVA	MAYBEBABY	HARBOURED	CANCELOUT
PANATELLA	CATAPLEXY	BARBECUED	HARBOURER	CATCHMENT
FAVABEANS	CATACOMBS	BARBECUES	TABBOULEH	PARCHMENT

MANCUNIAN	CARDEALER	YARDBIRDS	GARDENERS	MACDOWELL
BALCONIED	SANDPAPER	CABDRIVER	HARDENERS	CARDSWIPE
BALCONIES	SANDRADEE	DANDAILEY	BAWDINESS	HANDIWORK
DAYCENTRE	AARDVARKS	HARDLINER	FADDINESS	CAMERAMAN
FALCONERS	HARDBACKS	HARDLINES	GAUDINESS	BAREFACED
LAWCENTRE	LANDMARKS	HARDTIMES	HARDINESS	CAMERAMEN
LARCENIST	SANDBANKS	HARDWIRED	TARDINESS	CARELABEL
SAUCINESS	BALDEAGLE	LANDMINES	LANDFORCE	CARETAKER
FASCINATE	CARDTABLE	SANDPIPER	LANDLORDS	CASEMAKER
VACCINATE	PAYDEARLY	HANDBILLS	HANDTOWEL	CASEMATES
LARCENOUS	BANDWAGON	MANDRILLS	HARDNOSED	CAVECANEM
PATCOOMBS	MAGDEBURG	BANDWIDTH	LANDROVER	FACESAVER
WARCLOUDS	SADDUCEES	VANDELLAS	WARDROBES	LACERATED
WATCHOVER	BALDACHIN	LANDSLIDE	HANDBOOKS	LACERATES
PATCHOULI	LARDYCAKE	BANDOLIER	CARDBOARD	MAKEWAVES
LATCHONTO	BANDICOOT	SANDYLYLE	HARDBOARD	NAMENAMES
MATCHPLAY	DADDYCOOL	BARDOLINO	HARDCOURT	PACEMAKER
MARCOPOLO	HANDICAPS	MAGDALENA	DANDIPRAT	RATEPAYER
SAUCEPANS	LANDSCAPE	MAGDALENE	MANDERLEY	CAMERASHY
MARCHPAST	CANDIDACY	DANDELION	WANDEROFF	FACEPACKS
CANCERIAN	CANDIDATE	BANDALORE	HANDBRAKE	LATERALLY
CAMCORDER	HANDEDOUT	SANDBLAST	BANDEROLE	BASECAMPS
BARCAROLE	PASDEDEUX	VANDALISE	MANDARINS	FACEFACTS
RANCOROUS	CANDLEMAS	VANDALISM	PANDERING	RAREEARTH
CAUCASIAN	HANDLEBAR	RANDOMISE	WANDERING	FACEVALUE
LANCASTER	SADDLEBAG	BANDANNAS	SANDERSON	LASERBEAM
TADCASTER	CATDEELEY	GARDENIAS	WANDERERS	PAPERBACK
SARCASTIC	SANDWEDGE	SARDINIAN	YARDSTICK	BARENBOIM
MARCASITE	CANDLELIT	CARDINDEX	CANDYTUFT	HAVEABALL
NARCISSUS	HANDBELLS	LAPDANCER	BANDSTAND	JAMESBOND
NARCOTICS	DAYDREAMS	TAPDANCER	HANDSTAND	CAMEMBERT
PATCHTEST	DANDIFIED	KANDINSKY	MAIDSTONE	WATERBIRD
VANCOUVER	DANDIFIES	SANDSNAKE	SANDSTONE	HAVEABASH
RAUCOUSLY	HANDSFREE	CARDINALS	FALDSTOOL	WATERBUTT
SANCTUARY	YARDOFALE	FANDANGLE	LAUDATORY	JAMESCAAN
MATCHWOOD	LANDOFNOD	MACDONALD	MANDATORY	PAPERCLIP
CATCHWORD	MARDIGRAS	DANDENONG	SANDSTORM	LAYERCAKE
FANCYWORK	BANDAGING	GARDENING	CARDPUNCH	WATERCURE
PATCHWORK	CARDIGANS	HARDENING	HANDCUFFS	JAMESDEAN
WATCHWORD	LANDAGENT	MADDENING	SANDHURST	BAXENDALE
HANDYANDY	HANDSHAKE	PARDONING	MAIDAVALE	CALENDULA
BALDPATED	CARDSHARP	SADDENING	LANDOWNER	GABERDINE

EAVESDROP	CAREYHART	CAREENAGE	TAKEAPART	CANESUGAR
CALENDARS	CATECHISE	SAVERNAKE	BALEARICS	CAPEDUTCH
CAVENDISH	CATECHISM	CAREENING	RACETRACK	KAGEMUSHA
WATERDOWN	CATECHIST	PAGEANTRY	JADEGREEN	BALEFULLY
BASEMETAL	GAVECHASE	EAGERNESS	SAGEGREEN	BANEFULLY
SAGEDERBY	CAGEBIRDS	MARESNEST	CANEFRUIT	CAREFULLY
MAKEPEACE	PALERIDER	NAKEDNESS	CAMEOROLE	FATEFULLY
CAPEVERDE	TAKESIDES	HAZELNUTS	CAREERING	TAKETURNS
MAKEREADY	MAVERICKS	MATERNITY	CAREERISM	LAKEHURON
CAFETERIA	MASEFIELD	PATERNITY	CAREERIST	MADEFUNOF
DAREDEVIL	MATERIALS	CAVERNOUS	GATECRASH	MAKEFUNOF
FAREWELLS	WAKEFIELD	HAVEWORDS	SAGEBRUSH	SAFEGUARD
HAREBELLS	CAFETIERE	JADEGOODY	TAKEARISK	TAKEGUARD
MADELEINE	FACETIOUS	JANEFONDA	FAVERSHAM	WATERVOLE
BANEBERRY	WATERJUMP	BAREBONES	HAVEASTAB	DALEEVANS
CAMELEERS	CAMELLIAS	GATEMONEY	TAKEASEAT	DAVEEVANS
CAREBEARS	TAKEPLACE	LATECOMER	HAVERSACK	TAKEOVERS
MAKEMERRY	SALESLADY	MADEMONEY	WATERSIDE	PAPERWORK
MADESENSE	DAVEALLEN	MAKEMONEY	JANEASHER	CATERWAUL
MAKESENSE	WATERLILY	PAPEROVER	WATERSHED	JANEWYMAN
BASEMENTS	BAKEBLIND	TAKECOVER	CADETSHIP	YAKETYYAK
CASEMENTS	LABELLING	MANENOUGH	CARESSING	SAFETYNET
PAVEMENTS	MAYERLING	CALEDONIA	MAKEUSEOF	PANEGYRIC
VADEMECUM	PANELLING	MACEDONIA	SALEMSLOT	SAFETYPIN
TAKEAFTER	WATERLAND	CASEBOOKS	TAKESTOCK	RAREFYING
LAGERFELD	WATERLINE	GAMEPOINT	CASESTUDY	HALFBAKED
WATERFALL	DAVECLARK	MACEDOINE	GAZETTEER	MAXFACTOR
WATERFORD	PANELLIST	SAMETOYOU	PATENTEES	DAFFYDUCK
WATERFOWL	BASEPLATE	BASEBOARD	PARENTAGE	MACFADYEN
SAMEAGAIN	FACECLOTH	RACEGOERS	WAFERTHIN	DAFFODILS
PANELGAME	JAREDLETO	BAKEHOUSE	DATESTAMP	HALFPENCE
SALESGIRL	NAMEPLATE	GATEHOUSE	LAMENTING	HALFPENNY
WATERGATE	SATELLITE	RACEHORSE	MANEATING	MANFRIDAY
GATESHEAD	LAGERLOUT	SAFEHOUSE	PALESTINE	HALFHITCH
NAMECHECK	WAGESLAVE	WAREHOUSE	PANETTONE	MAXFRISCH
PAGETHREE	WATERMAIN	LAKEPOETS	PARENTING	HALFLIGHT
MAKESHIFT	WATERMILL	JAMESPOLK	PATENTING	CALFSMEAT
JAMESHOGG	PAPERMOON	MAKEAPILE	VALENTINA	GARFUNKEL
CAMELHAIR	KATEOMARA	WATERPOLO	VALENTINE	MAYFLOWER
TAKEAHIKE	WATERMARK	WATERPUMP	VALENTINO	SAFFLOWER
WATERHOLE	MADEAMOVE	WATERPIPE	GAMESTERS	HALFBOARD
TAKESHAPE	MAKEAMOVE	DAVENPORT	HAVEITOUT	PAMFERRIS

WAYFARING	DANGEROUS	BATHROBES	NAVIGATES	PAYINGOUT
WAYFARERS	HAUGHTIER	FASHIONED	PAGINATED	RADIOHEAD
HALFTRUTH	NAUGHTIER	FASHIONER	PAGINATES	BASILHUME
HALFCROWN	PARGETTER	LAPHROAIG	PALISADES	BANISHING
HAMFISTED	HAUGHTILY	BATHROOMS	VALIDATED	CAPINHAND
HALFATICK	NAUGHTILY	CASHPOINT	VALIDATES	RAVISHING
GASFITTER	TARGETING	DASHBOARD	BASICALLY	VANISHING
LANGUAGES	DAUGHTERS	WASHBOARD	HABITABLE	CALIPHATE
WARGRAVES	GANGSTERS	BATHHOUSE	MAGICALLY	BASILICAN
HANGNAILS	MANGETOUT	GATHERWAY	MANICALLY	BASILICAS
LAUGHABLE	LANGOUSTE	ZACHARIAS	NAVIGABLE	SATIRICAL
LAUGHABLY	HANGOVERS	BACHARACH	RADICALLY	MAXIMISED
HANGABOUT	GARGOYLES	FATHERTED	NAVIGATOR	MAXIMISES
MAGGIEMAY	KATHMANDU	JANHARVEY	CARIBBEAN	SANITISED
MARGRETHE	WASHBASIN	ZACHBRAFF	JAMIEBELL	SATIRISED
LANGUEDOC	BATHSALTS	CATHARSIS	SALISBURY	SATIRISES
MACGREGOR	YACHTCLUB	CATHARTIC	CABINCREW	BASILISKS
BARGAINED	CATHEDRAL	CATHERINE	RADICCHIO	MAGICIANS
BARGAINER	SANHEDRIN	FATHERING	PATIODOOR	PAVILIONS
LANGUIDLY	PACHYDERM	GATHERING	RADIODAYS	TAHITIANS
DALGLIESH	WASHEDOUT	KATHARINE	TAOISEACH	BASILICON
GANGPLANK	CASHIERED	KATHERINE	TAXIMETER	PACIFIERS
MANGALORE	BATHSHEBA	LATHERING	VARICELLA	PACIFISTS
WARGAMING	BATHCHAIR	YACHTSMAN	TAXIDERMY	SATIRISTS
BARGINGIN	DACHSHUND	YACHTSMEN	SAVILEROW	MALICIOUS
HANGINGON	NASHVILLE	IANHISLOP	MANIFESTO	PANICKING
MANGANESE	GASHOLDER	MANHATTAN	SATINETTE	DAVIDLEAN
RANGINGUP	PATHOLOGY	MADHATTER	SATISFIED	RAMILLIES
GANGINGUP	LAYHOLDOF	WASHSTAND	SATISFIES	HAGIOLOGY
GARGANTUA	BACHELORS	CATHETERS	JAMIEFOXX	RADIOLOGY
HANGINGUP	FATHOMING	BATHCUBES	RACINGCAR	CARILLONS
HANGTOUGH	NATHANIEL	BASHFULLY	RADIOGRAM	CAVILLING
BAIGNOIRE	TABHUNTER	CASHEWNUT	RAVINGMAD	CAPILLARY
HANGLOOSE	CASHINGIN	LACHRYMAL	EASINGOFF	RACIALIST
BARGEPOLE	DASHINGLY	HATHAYOGA	TAKINGOFF	VACILLATE
DANGERMAN	MANHANDLE	HAPHAZARD	HAVINGAGO	TALISMANS
SANGFROID	PANHANDLE	GARIBALDI	RADIOGAGA	TAMILNADU
BADGERING	MACHINING	LAMINATED	LAMINGTON	PATIENTLY
MARGARINE	IANHENDRY	LAMINATES	MALINGERS	RADIANTLY
TANGERINE	MACHINERY	MARINATED	EATINGOUT	RATIONALE
KANGAROOS	MACHINIST	MARINATES	FADINGOUT	VALIANTLY
MARGARITA	WASHINGUP	NAVIGATED	HAVINGFUN	MALIGNANT

MALIGNING	BANJULELE	HACKAMORE	TALKATHON	GALLAGHER
RATIONING	BACKHANDS	MACKINLAY	BACKSTOPS	DAYLIGHTS
FABIANISM	BACKWARDS	JACKKNIFE	BASKETFUL	FANLIGHTS
MALIGNITY	BACKYARDS	MACKENZIE	TALKATIVE	CALLAHALT
MARIGOLDS	BACKDATED	WALKONAIR	BACKSTAYS	PAULSHANE
BARITONES	BACKWATER	DARKENING	MARKCURRY	WALLCHART
CAMISOLES	DARKWATER	PARKINSON	PANKHURST	TAILPIECE
DAVIDOWEN	JACKBAUER	JACKANORY	PARKHURST	GAULEITER
HALITOSIS	JACKOAKIE	TACKINESS	BANKRUPTS	TAILLIGHT
MANICOTTI	TALKRADIO	WACKINESS	MARKTWAIN	BALLGIRLS
MARIOPUZO	LARKABOUT	TALKINGTO	BACKSWING	CAULFIELD
SAXIFRAGE	WALKABOUT	PACKINGUP	CARLSAGAN	PAULSIMON
HAGIARCHY	MARKEDMAN	PARKROYAL	DALLIANCE	MAPLELEAF
PANICROOM	BACKEDOFF	TASKFORCE	TAILGATER	CARLALANE
MARIEROSE	MARKEDOFF	BACKWOODS	WALLPAPER	SAILALONG
CALIBRATE	PACKEDOUT	TAEKWONDO	HALLMARKS	SAILPLANE
BASILSEAL	WALKEDOUT	BACKBONED	MALLEABLE	SALLYLUNN
LADIESMAN	BACKPEDAL	BACKBONES	PAULDACRE	TABLELAND
DAVIDSOUL	JACKKETCH	BANKROLLS	PALLIASSE	TAILPLANE
VARIETIES	PARKBENCH	DARKROOMS	WALLABIES	FAULTLESS
PAKISTANI	BARKEEPER	DARKHORSE	CARLSBERG	SAILCLOTH
RADIATING	HACKNEYED	PACKHORSE	EARLYBIRD	HASLEMERE
SATIATING	JACKBENNY	DANKWORTH	JARLSBERG	GARLANDED
RADIATION	PACKAGING	JACKBOOTS	EARLYBATH	TAILENDER
SATIATION	BACKBITER	JACKSPRAT	FALLACIES	KAPLINSKY
VARIATION	BACKBITES	BACKSPACE	GALLACHER	GALLANTLY
BANISTERS	BACKFIRED	BACKTRACK	CABLECARS	GALLINGLY
CANISTERS	BACKFIRES	BACKDRAFT	GALLICISM	GALLANTRY
RADIATORS	BACKSIDES	BANKDRAFT	PAULSCOTT	EARLINESS
MACINTOSH	BACKLIGHT	JACKFRUIT	PALLADIAN	MANLINESS
VARIOUSLY	BACKSIGHT	PACKDRILL	BALLADEER	PAULHOGAN
FATIGUING	BACKFILLS	HANKERING	CALLEDOFF	BAILBONDS
MARIJUANA	BACKLISTS	BACKDROPS	TAILEDOFF	BALLOONED
HABITUATE	JACKBLACK	JACKFROST	BAILEDOUT	PAULJONES
DAVIDVINE	BACKSLIDE	CANKEROUS	PALLADIUM	BALLCOCKS
BASICWAGE	VALKILMER	MAWKISHLY	EARLYDAYS	BALLPOINT
SATINWOOD	BACKSLANG	JACKSTRAW	EAGLEEYED	PAULYOUNG
EASILYLED	BANKCLERK	MARKETDAY	MAILMERGE	SAILBOARD
PACIFYING	BACKSLASH	MARKETEER	CARLLEWIS	JAILHOUSE
RATIFYING	BACKCLOTH	RACKETEER	EARLIERON	RAYLIOTTA
WAXJACKET	SACKCLOTH	BACKSTAGE	CABLEGRAM	TAYLFORTH
BANJOISTS	HAWKSMOOR	MARKETING	CALLAGHAN	EARLEPAGE

GALLIPOLI	TABLEWARE	DALMATIAN	SAINTLUKE	VARNISHES
GALLOPING	CABLEWAYS	FARMSTEAD	VAINGLORY	EARNESTLY
WALLOPING	WAYLAYING	HARMATTAN	DAUNTLESS	MAGNUSSON
CALLIPERS	BARLEYMOW	HAEMATOID	CARNALITY	PAINTSHOP
EARLSPARK	FARMYARDS	CALMATIVE	GAUNTLETS	MAGNESIUM
FALLAPART	FARMEDOUT	BADMOUTHS	RAINCLOUD	PARNASSUS
GALLOPERS	IANMCEWAN	HARMFULLY	SAINTMARK	MAGNITUDE
SALLYPORT	PALMBEACH	BARNDANCE	SAYNOMORE	CARNATION
HARLEQUIN	HAYMAKING	BARNYARDS	CANNONADE	DAMNATION
JAILBREAK	LAWMAKING	RAINMAKER	CANNONEER	MAGNETRON
GALLERIED	MAPMAKING	RAINWATER	FAWNINGLY	BARNSTORM
GALLERIES	MACMILLAN	RAINGAUGE	CANNONING	DAMNATORY
MAILORDER	MAMMALIAN	BAINMARIE	CANNINESS	RAINSTORM
TALLORDER	MARMALADE	IAINBANKS	FAINTNESS	MAGNETISE
BALLERINA	MARMOLADA	MAINTAINS	GAUNTNESS	MAGNETISM
CAULDRONS	MAXMILLER	CANNIBALS	LAWNMOWER	MAGNETITE
SAILORING	KAYMELLOR	PAINTBALL	CARNFORTH	GAINFULLY
TAILORING	CARMELITE	BARNACLED	RAINCOATS	PAINFULLY
NAILBRUSH	TASMANIAN	BARNACLES	SAINTPAUL	CARNIVALS
BALLASTED	HARMONICA	DAWNACTON	MANNEQUIN	CARNIVORE
HARLESDEN	HARMONIES	MAINECOON	MAINEROAD	PAINTWORK
BALLISTIC	SAMMENDES	RAINEDOFF	WAGNERIAN	SABOTAGED
HAPLESSLY	WARMONGER	LAUNDERED	MAINBRACE	SABOTAGES
CALLOSITY	BADMINTON	LAUNDERER	CANNERIES	PANORAMIC
MAULSTICK	BALMINESS	SAUNTERED	TANNERIES	LAPOTAIRE
BALLOTING	BARMINESS	MAGNIFICO	MAINFRAME	RAZORBACK
GALLSTONE	HARMONISE	MAGNIFIED	MANNERING	RAZORBILL
HAILSTONE	HARMONIST	MAGNIFIER	RAINPROOF	BABOUCHES
HALLSTAND	HARMONIUM	MAGNIFIES	RAINDROPS	BAROSCOPE
BALLOTBOX	WARMINGUP	NANNYGOAT	LAUNDRESS	TAROTCARD
MAELSTROM	FARMHOUSE	RAINCHECK	MANNERISM	CANOODLED
HAILSTORM	MARMOREAL	FANNYHILL	MANNERIST	CANOODLES
TALLSTORY	EARMARKED	LAUNCHING	BANNERETS	MAJORDOMO
HAILATAXI	HAYMARKET	SAINTHOOD	SAINTSDAY	BARONETCY
CALLOUSLY	HAMMERING	PAWNSHOPS	BANNISTER	BAROMETER
GALLIVANT	SANMARINO	JAUNDICED	GARNISHED	BAYONETED
BAILIWICK	WARMFRONT	MAINLINES	GARNISHES	CANOPENER
HALLOWEEN	HAMMERTOE	PAINTINGS	HARNESSED	GASOMETER
HALLIWELL	GAMMARAYS	DAINTIEST	HARNESSES	MANOMETER
HALLOWING	PAYMASTER	SAINTJOHN	TARNISHED	BAROMETRY
TABLEWINE	PALMISTRY	DANNYKAYE	TARNISHES	SABOTEURS
WALLOWING	MARMOSETS	MAGNOLIAS	VARNISHED	MAJORETTE

VAPORETTO	FAVOURITE	CARPENTRY	PATRIARCH	PATROLMAN
WAGONETTE	MAJORSUIT	HAPPINESS	CARRIAGES	HAIRSLIDE
PAROCHIAL	CAROUSALS	WASPSNEST	LAYREADER	BARRELLED
EATONHALL	CAROUSELS	EARPHONES	MARRIAGES	BASRELIEF
CACOPHONY	CAROUSING	HARPOONED	FAIRBANKS	PATROLLED
SAXOPHONE	AARONSROD	HARPOONER	SACREBLEU	PATROLMEN
MASOCHISM	CAROUSERS	LAMPOONED	PATRICIAN	RAGROLLED
MASOCHIST	CAVORTING	LAMPOONER	BARRACUDA	SACRILEGE
CANONICAL	RACONTEUR	LAMPPOSTS	BARRICADE	FAIRYLIKE
CANONISED	MANOEUVRE	BAGPIPING	MATRICIDE	HARRYLIME
CANONISES	RAZORWIRE	BAGPIPERS	PATRICIDE	FAIRYLAND
JACOBITES	PARODYING	DAMPSQUIB	BARRACKED	BARRELFUL
VAPORISED	WARPLANES	HARPERLEE	BARRACKER	GARRULOUS
VAPORISER	CAMPDAVID	CALPURNIA	BATRACHIA	DAIRYMAID
VAPORISES	JAMPACKED	HAMPERING	CAPRICCIO	MATRIMONY
CALORIFIC	KAMPUCHEA	PAMPERING	FAIRYCAKE	PATRIMONY
SAPODILLA	PAYPACKET	TAMPERING	CAPRICORN	RAYROMANO
PALOMINOS	CARPACCIO	BARPERSON	MACROCOSM	SACRAMENT
CANOEISTS	CARPEDIEM	DAMPPROOF	CARRYCOTS	BARRYMORE
PARODISTS	LAMPEDUSA	NAPPYRASH	FABRICATE	WARRANTED
LABORIOUS	CAMPEDOUT	WASPISHLY	CARRADINE	WARRANTEE
IANOGILVY	MAPPEDOUT	CAMPESINO	HARRIDANS	PATRONAGE
JASONKING	HAPPYDAYS	CARPETBAG	SACREDCOW	WARRANTOR
WAGONLOAD	EARPIECES	HAMPSTEAD	LAURADERN	HAIRINESS
CAROLLING	RASPBERRY	VANPATTEN	LAURIELEE	PATRONISE
CAROLLERS	RAMPAGING	HAPPYTALK	GABRIELLE	CABRIOLES
SALOONCAR	LAMPSHADE	CARPETING	CARRIEDON	CABRIOLET
MAROONING	HAMPSHIRE	RASPATORY	CARRIESON	CARRYOVER
BABOONERY	HAPPYHOUR	PALPITATE	SACRIFICE	GARRYOWEN
CALOUNDRA	CAMPSITES	TARPAULIN	FAIRSFAIR	PATRIOTIC
RAROTONGA	SAPPHIRES	SASQUATCH	CAPRIFORM	HAIRSPRAY
PASODOBLE	LAMPLIGHT	MACQUARIE	BARRYGIBB	LARRYPAGE
BAYOFPIGS	CAMPAIGNS	DANQUAYLE	MADRIGALS	BARRYRYAN
LABOURDAY	RATPOISON	BANQUETED	HARROGATE	FAIRTRIAL
CAROLREED	LAMPBLACK	BANQUETER	SAXROHMER	FAIRTRADE
SAVOURIES	PAMPHLETS	LACQUERED	FAIRCHILD	HAIRDRYER
FAVOURING	CARPENTER	MARQUETRY	HARRYHILL	FAIRYRING
LABOURING	CAMPANILE	PARQUETRY	HAIRSHIRT	HAIRBRUSH
SAVOURING	CAMPANULA	BANQUETTE	HAIRPIECE	SACRISTAN
BAROGRAPH	RAMPANTLY	DAIQUIRIS	RAMRAIDER	BARRISTER
LABOURERS	DAMPENING	CARRYAWAY	MARRAKESH	FAIRYTALE
DAYOFREST	HAPPENING	MATRIARCH	PATROLCAR	HAIRSTYLE

NARRATING	FALSEHOOD	PASSIVELY	PARTYGOER	BATTENING
NARRATION	WASSAILED	PASSIVISM	CASTIGATE	CARTONING
DAYRETURN	WASSAILER	PASSIVIST	CARTWHEEL	FASTENING
NARRATORS	CATSKILLS	PASSIVITY	LASTTHING	FATTENING
TAXRETURN	MANSFIELD	CASSOWARY	PANTYHOSE	HASTENING
MAURITIUS	TASSELLED	CAUSEWAYS	CAPTAINCY	TAUTENING
NARRATIVE	DAMSELFLY	CAPSIZING	LASTDITCH	FASTENERS
HARROVIAN	MARSHLAND	BALTHAZAR	CAPTAINED	CANTONESE
JANRAVENS	WAISTLINE	WASTEAWAY	FANTAILED	CATTINESS
MARROWFAT	CAPSULISE	MATTJAMES	LASTRITES	FATTINESS
HARRYWEBB	CAUSALITY	SALTWATER	PARTTIMER	HASTINESS
FARROWING	MAUSOLEUM	WASTWATER	CARTRIDGE	NASTINESS
HARROWING	HANSOMCAB	FATTYACID	FARTHINGS	RATTINESS
NARROWING	FACSIMILE	HARTDAVIS	PARTRIDGE	SALTINESS
BARROWBOY	PARSIMONY	FACTUALLY	LASTNIGHT	TATTINESS
NARROWEST	PASSINGBY	PARTIALLY	GASTRITIS	CASTANETS
HATSTANDS	SASSENACH	MATTDAMON	EASTTIMOR	MARTINETS
NAUSEATED	PASSENGER	SALTMARSH	XANTHIPPE	FACTIONAL
NAUSEATES	PARSONAGE	CANTABILE	EARTHIEST	BARTHOLDI
HAYSTACKS	CASSANDRA	EARTHBORN	GAITSKELL	CARTLOADS
CAMSHAFTS	FALSENESS	TACTICIAN	PARTAKING	HAUTMONDE
WAISTBAND	GASSINESS	BALTICSEA	CASTELLAN	BASTIONED
WAISTCOAT	HARSHNESS	CANTICLES	CASTILIAN	CAPTIONED
CASSOCKED	OARSWOMAN	NANTUCKET	PASTILLES	CAUTIONED
MASSACRED	OARSWOMEN	PARTICLES	CARTILAGE	EASTBOUND
MASSACRES	PASSPORTS	MANTICORE	TAUTOLOGY	HAWTHORNE
RANSACKED	MARSUPIAL	MASTICATE	EARTHLING	TATTOOING
RAISECAIN	CAESAREAN	SANTACRUZ	PARTYLINE	GASTROPOD
CAPSICUMS	PASSERSBY	CASTLEBAR	WASTELAND	IANTHORPE
PASSEDOUT	CASSEROLE	CATTLEMAN	BATTALION	DARTBOARD
MASSMEDIA	HAMSTRING	DANTHEVAN	PANTALOON	MATTMONRO
SANSSERIF	HAMSTRUNG	CATTLEMEN	FAITHLESS	CARTHORSE
FARSEEING	PASSERINE	BATTLEDON	TANTALISE	MALTHOUSE
BAKSHEESH	FALSESTEP	PARTHENON	TASTELESS	OASTHOUSE
CAPSLEEVE	LASSITUDE	SALTPETRE	SALTFLATS	TATTOOIST
SASSAFRAS	CASSETTES	PANTHEISM	PANTOMIME	DARTMOUTH
FALSIFIED	CAUSATIVE	PANTHEIST	BADTIMING	SALTSPOON
FALSIFIER	RAYSTUBBS	PASTTENSE	BALTIMORE	WASTEPIPE
FALSIFIES	CASSOULET	MALTREATS	MARTINMAS	BACTERIAL
MASSAGING	DANSEUSES	BATTLEAXE	BARTENDER	CANTORIAL
RAISEHELL	MASSEUSES	FAITHFULL	EASTENDER	EASTERDAY
DAYSCHOOL	MASSIVELY	DARTAGNAN	HALTINGLY	FACTORIAL

LATTERDAY	FANTASIST	BALUSTERS	CARYGRANT	OBSERVERS
PASTERNAK	WASTETIME	SALVAGING	GARYPRATT	OBEISANCE
SARTORIAL	LACTATION	SAUVIGNON	MARYASTOR	ABDICATED
BATTERSBY	PARTITION	MALVOISIE	MANYATIME	ABDICATES
FASTTRACK	MALTSTERS	CALVINISM	LAZYSUSAN	OBLIGATED
BATTERIES	MATTLUCAS	CALVINIST	BABYBUGGY	OBLIGATES
BATTERSEA	CARTOUCHE	GALVANISE	MARYQUANT	ABRIDGING
CATTERIES	TACTFULLY	CANVASSED	MARYTUDOR	ABRIDGERS
EASTERNER	MANTOVANI	CANVASSER	TANZANIAN	OBLIVIOUS
FACTORIES	CAPTIVATE	CANVASSES	WAYZGOOSE	OBVIATING
MASTERKEY	CAPTIVITY	HARVESTED	LANZAROTE	OBLIQUELY
SAUTERNES	PARTOWNER	HARVESTER	ABRASIVES	OBVIOUSLY
EASTEREGG	PARTYWALL	GALVESTON	ABRASIONS	OBBLIGATO
CASTOROIL	EARTHWARD	SALVATION	OBTAINING	EBULLIENT
DASTARDLY	EARTHWORK	EARWIGGED	ABSCONDED	ABOLISHED
PASTORALE	EARTHWORM	IANWRIGHT	ABSCONDER	ABOLISHES
BANTERING	CASTAWAYS	JAYWALKED	OBSCENELY	ABILITIES
BARTERING	BANTRYBAY	JAYWALKER	OBSCENITY	ABOLITION
BATTERING	EASTLYNNE	FAYWELDON	OBSCURELY	ABOMINATE
CANTERING	SATURATED	BAYWINDOW	OBSCURING	ABUNDANCE
CAPTURING	SATURATES	DARWINISM	OBSCURITY	ABANDONED
FACTORING	TABULATED	DARWINIST	ABSCESSES	ABROGATED
FALTERING	TABULATES	TAIWANESE	OBEDIENCE	ABROGATES
MASTERING	NATURALLY	WAXWORKER	ABIDINGLY	ABROGATOR
MATTERING	TABULATOR	WAYWARDLY	ABNEGATED	ABSORBENT
NATTERING	VALUABLES	GALWAYBAY	ABNEGATES	ABSORBING
SANTORINI	MAJUSCULE	CAPYBARAS	OBJETDART	ABSORBERS
MARTYRDOM	CAPUCHINS	MARYJANES	ABSEILING	ABDOMINAL
MASTERSON	FABULISTS	EASYTERMS	ABBEYROAD	OBNOXIOUS
PATTERSON	NATURISTS	EASYPEASY	OBSESSING	ABHORRENT
BARTERERS	VALUELESS	EASYCHAIR	OBSESSION	ABHORRING
CAUTERISE	VANUALEVU	LADYBIRDS	OBSESSIVE	ABSOLVING
LAYTOREST	CALUMNIES	EASYRIDER	ABSENTEES	ABSOLVERS
BACTERIUM	LABURNUMS	LABYRINTH	OBJECTIFY	IBUPROFEN
MASTERFUL	SATURNINE	LADYSMAID	ABSENTING	ABERRANCE
RAPTUROUS	VAGUENESS	LADYSMITH	OBJECTING	ABORIGINE
BAPTISMAL	GAZUMPING	CANYONING	ABJECTION	OBTRUSIVE
FANTASIES	CASUARINA	EASYLOVER	OBJECTION	ABYSMALLY
FANTASTIC	CASUISTRY	EASYMONEY	OBJECTIVE	ABYSSINIA
BAPTISING	BAGUETTES	LAZYBONES	OBSEQUIES	ABASEMENT
PARTISANS	FACULTIES	EASYGOING	OBSERVANT	ABASHMENT
FANTASISE	VALUATION	BABYGRAND	OBSERVING	ABUSIVELY

ABSTRACTS	ACIDIFIED	SCRIBBLER	ECONOMIST	ACAPPELLA
OBSTACLES	ACIDIFIES	SCRIBBLES	SCENARIOS	SCAPAFLOW
ABUTMENTS	ACIDULATE	ACCIDENCE	SCHNITZEL	SCAPEGOAT
ABITOFADO	ACIDULOUS	SCRIVENER	SCHNAUZER	SCEPTICAL
ABITTHICK	ACADEMICS	ACCIDENTS	SCHNOZZLE	SCARLATTI
ABSTAINED	ACADEMIES	ACTIVISTS	MCDONALDS	ACARICIDE
ABSTAINER	SCUDAMORE	SCHILLING	ACCOLADES	SCARECROW
ABATEMENT	ACADEMIST	SCRIMMAGE	ACROBATIC	SCORECARD
OBSTINACY	ACIDHOUSE	SCRIMPING	SCHOLARLY	ACCREDITS
ABSTINENT	ACIDDROPS	SCRIMSHAW	ACTONBELL	SCARPERED
OBSTINATE	SCHEMATIC	ECLIPSING	ACCORDANT	SCARIFIER
ABATTOIRS	ACKERBILK	SCRIPTING	ACCORDING	SCORCHING
OBSTETRIC	SCREWBALL	SCRIPTURE	ACCORDION	SCORPIONS
OBSTRUCTS	SCREECHED	ACHIEVING	OCTOTHORP	ACAROLOGY
ABOUTABOY	SCREECHER	ACHIEVERS	SCHOFIELD	SCORELINE
OBFUSCATE	SCREECHES	OCCLUDING	SCHOOLBAG	SCORELESS
ABOUNDING	ACCEDENCE	ECOLOGIST	SCROLLBAR	ACTRESSES
ABSURDITY	SCREWEDUP	ACCLAIMED	SCHOOLING	ACCRETION
ABOUTFACE	SCREAMING	SCALLIONS	SCROLLING	SCORBUTIC
ABLUTIONS	SCREAMERS	ICELANDER	SCHOOLBOY	SCURRYING
ABDUCTING	OCTENNIAL	ICELANDIC	ECTOPLASM	ICESKATED
ABDUCTION	SCREENING	SCALINESS	SCOOPNECK	ICESKATER
ABDUCTORS	ACCESSING	SCALLOPED	ACCOUNTED	ICESKATES
ABOUTTURN	ACCESSION	ECCLESTON	SCROUNGED	ECOSYSTEM
SCRAMBLED	ACCESSORY	OCCLUSION	SCROUNGER	ACUTABOVE
SCRAMBLER	ACCENTUAL	SCULPTING	SCROUNGES	SCATTERED
SCRAMBLES	ECCENTRIC	SCULPTORS	MCCONNELL	SCOTCHEGG
SCRAPBOOK	ACCENTING	SCULPTURE	SCHOONERS	SCOTCHING
SCRATCHED	ACCEPTANT	ACCLIVITY	ACROPOLIS	ACETYLENE
SCRATCHES	ACCEPTING	SCALLYWAG	ECTOMORPH	SCUTTLING
ICLAUDIUS	ACCENTORS	ECOMMERCE	ACCOMPANY	ACUTENESS
MCLACHLAN	SCIENTIST	SCAMPERED	ECHOGRAMS	SCOTSPINE
SCRAPHEAP	SCHEDULED	SCHMALTZY	ACROSTICS	OCCUPANCY
OCCASIONS	SCHEDULES	SCAMANDER	ACCOUTRED	SCRUTATOR
MCCASKILL	SCREWWORM	SCHMUTTER	ACCOUTRES	OCCUPANTS
SCRAWLING	ICEHOCKEY	SCIMITARS	ACCOSTING	SCRUBBING
OCTAGONAL	MCWHIRTER	ACONCAGUA	ACTONTOWN	SCRUNCHIE
SCRAPPILY	ACTIVATED	SCHNEIDER	OCTOPUSES	SCOUNDREL
SCRAPPING	ACTIVATES	SCINTILLA	OCTOPUSSY	ACQUIESCE
MCCARTNEY	ECHINACEA	ECONOMICS	ACRONYMIC	SCRUFFILY
SCRAPYARD	ACTIVATOR	ECONOMIES	SCOOBYDOO	SCRUMHALF
SCABBARDS	SCRIBBLED	ECONOMISE	SCUPPERED	OCCUPIERS

ACQUAINTS	ADVERBIAL	ADULATORS	SEPARATED	DETACHING
MCCULLOCH	ADHERENCE	ADULATORY	SEPARATES	MEGAPHONE
SCRUBLAND	ADHERENTS	ADAMFAITH	DEBATABLE	DECATHLON
ACTUALISE	ADHESIVES	ADAMOKARO	GETATABLE	SEMAPHORE
ACTUALITY	EDGEWORTH	ADAMSMITH	REPARABLE	LEGALISED
SCRUMMAGE	ADVERSELY	ADAMANTLY	REPAYABLE	LEGALISES
SCRUMPING	ADVERSARY	ODDMANOUT	SEPARABLE	NEGATIVES
ACTUARIAL	ADVERSITY	ADUMBRATE	MENATARMS	PENALISED
ACTUARIES	ADVENTURE	EDENTATES	MEGAWATTS	PENALISES
ACQUIRING	ADVENTIST	ADENOIDAL	DEBAUCHED	RELATIVES
OCCURRING	ADVERTISE	IDENTICAL	DEBAUCHEE	SEDATIVES
ACQUITTAL	ADJECTIVE	IDENTIKIT	DEBAUCHES	MEGALITHS
ACOUSTICS	ADDERWORT	ODDNUMBER	RENASCENT	SETALIGHT
ACQUITTED	ADOGSLIFE	EDINBURGH	SEAANCHOR	HEPATITIS
ACCUSTOMS	ADMIRABLE	ADVOCATED	DEMARCATE	GERANIUMS
ACTUATING	ADMIRABLY	ADVOCATES	DEPARDIEU	RELATIONS
ACTUATION	ADVISABLE	IDIOMATIC	CELANDINE	GETAFIXON
ACTUATORS	ADVISABLY	ADSORBING	DEMANDING	DECALITRE
OCCULTISM	ADMIRALTY	EDMONDSON	GERALDINE	RETALIATE
OCCULTIST	ADLIBBING	ODDONEOUT	PENANDINK	BEHAVIOUR
OCCUPYING	ADVISEDLY	ADJOINING	REGARDING	METALIOUS
SCAVENGED	ADDINGTON	ADJOURNED	REMANDING	NEFARIOUS
SCAVENGER	EDDINGTON	ADAPTABLE	RETARDING	TENACIOUS
SCAVENGES	ADDITIVES	ADEPTNESS	REWARDING	VERACIOUS
SCHWIMMER	ADHIBITED	ADIPOSITY	GERALDTON	VEXATIOUS
ADVANCING	ADDITIONS	ADORNMENT	HERALDSUN	REPACKAGE
EDWARDIAN	ADDINSELL	ADORINGLY	TEMAZEPAM	REMARKING
EDWARDFOX	ADMISSION	ADDRESSED	DECADENCE	METALLICA
ADJACENCY	ADMISSIVE	ADDRESSEE	HEXAMETER	DEFAULTED
EDNABIRCH	ADMITTING	ADDRESSER	REPAPERED	DEFAULTER
IDEALISED	ADDICTION	ADDRESSES	MENAGERIE	BEWAILING
IDEALISTS	ADMIXTURE	ADORATION	BELATEDLY	DETAILING
ADNAUSEAM	ADDICTIVE	EDITHPIAF	CETACEANS	PEDALLING
ADVANTAGE	ODDJOBMAN	EDITORIAL	TENAPENNY	RECALLING
EDIBILITY	ADULTERER	ADJUTANCY	DECAMERON	RETAILING
EDGBASTON	EDELWEISS	ADJUTANTS	DECAMETRE	MEDALLION
EDUCEMENT	ADULTHOOD	ADJUDGING	SECATEURS	PEDALLERS
EDUCATING	IDALUPINO	ODOURLESS	DECADENTS	RETAILERS
EDUCATION	IDOLISING	ADJUSTING	MEGAHERTZ	MEDALLIST
EDUCATORS	ODALISQUE	ADJUSTERS	SEBACEOUS	DEBARMENT
EDUCATORY	ADULATING	EDDYSTONE	MEGANGALE	REPAYMENT
EDUCATIVE	ADULATION	DEVALAHAN	DEBAGGING	DETAINEES

REMAINDER	DEPARTING	MELBOURNE	PECCARIES	DESDEMONA
DETAINING	LEVANTINE	HERBIVORE	REDCARPET	NEEDSMUST
REGAINING	RECANTING	LEEBOWYER	PERCYSHAW	LENDANEAR
REMAINING	DECANTERS	PERCHANCE	REICHSTAG	LEYDENJAR
RETAINING	DEPARTURE	WESCRAVEN	WENCESLAS	LESDENNIS
RETAINERS	MEGASTORE	SEACHANGE	LEICESTER	PENDENNIS
DECAGONAL	RECAPTURE	PEACEABLE	PEACESIGN	DEADENING
HEXAGONAL	DEVASTATE	REACHABLE	NEWCASTLE	FERDINAND
ZETAJONES	BEAARTHUR	MERCHANTS	PEACETIME	REDDENING
MELATONIN	MEGABUCKS	BEACHBALL	BENCHTEST	TEDDANSON
METABOLIC	DEVALUING	BEACHBOYS	BEDCOVERS	HEADINESS
PEDAGOGIC	CEDARWOOD	LEUCOCYTE	BEACHWEAR	NEEDINESS
LENAHORNE	MENATWORK	PERCHERON	HEADLANDS	READINESS
BELAFONTE	METALWARE	TEACHESTS	HEADCASES	REEDINESS
DECALOGUE	METALWORK	BEACHHEAD	SEEDCAKES	SEEDINESS
DEMAGOGUE	MEGABYTES	DESCRIBED	PENDRAGON	WEEDINESS
PEDAGOGUE	NETANYAHU	DESCRIBES	REDDRAGON	SENDINGUP
SEXAPPEAL	BEDAZZLED	PERCEIVED	TEDDYBEAR	SEEDBOXES
DECAMPING	SEMBLANCE	PERCEIVES	MENDICANT	DEADSOULS
RECAPPING	KEYBOARDS	KERCHIEFS	HEADSCARF	HEADCOUNT
REVAMPING	REMBRANDT	TETCHIEST	MENDACITY	HEADBOARD
VELAZQUEZ	NEDBEATTY	HERCULEAN	REEDUCATE	GENDARMES
REPAIRMAN	HERBICIDE	PENCILLED	BEADLEDOM	DEODORANT
RELAYRACE	BENBECULA	DESCALING	HEADRESTS	RENDERING
REMARRIED	REDBREAST	MERCILESS	HEIDEGGER	TENDERING
REMARRIES	SEABREEZE	PERCOLATE	VERDIGRIS	HENDERSON
REPAIRMEN	HERBALTEA	WELCOMING	LENDAHAND	DEODORISE
DELACROIX	HERBALISM	BENCHMARK	HEADPIECE	HEADDRESS
VERADRAKE	HERBALIST	NEWCOMERS	DEADLINES	READDRESS
DECAGRAMS	VERBALISE	BEECHMAST	HEADLINER	TENDEREST
DEBARRING	MELBROOKS	BELCONNEN	HEADLINES	TENDERISE
REPAIRING	KERBDRILL	DESCENDED	SEEDLINGS	REDDUSTER
REPAIRERS	KENBARLOW	RESCINDED	HEADLIGHT	VENDETTAS
GETACROSS	PEMBERTON	MERCENARY	DEADLIEST	FEEDSTOCK
RELAPSING	REDBERETS	REDCENTRE	HEADFIRST	HEADSTONE
BECAUSEOF	VERBOSELY	DEACONESS	HEIDIKLUM	PERDITION
LEDASTRAY	VERBOSITY	REECHOING	TENDULKAR	RENDITION
SEBASTIAN	GETBETTER	PEACEPIPE	PENDULUMS	HEADSTART
SEMANTICS	KEGBITTER	PERCAPITA	FEUDALISM	HEEDFULLY
CEDARTREE	REBBETZIN	MERCURIAL	PENDULOUS	READJUSTS
PENALTIES	KERBSTONE	DESCARTES	READALOUD	REDDEVILS
DECANTING	ZEEBRUGGE	GETCARTER	READYMADE	LESDAWSON

DEADLYSIN	DEPENDING	REPELLENT	CELEBRATE	DEFECTION
RELEVANCE	DEFENDERS	REPELLING	CELEBRITY	DEJECTION
SEVERANCE	LEGENDARY	RETELLING	DESECRATE	DESERTFOX
BEVERAGES	PETEREGAN	REVEALING	METEORITE	DESERTION
DELEGATED	DEFERENCE	REVELLING	PENETRATE	DETECTION
DELEGATES	REFERENCE	REBELLION	PETERSHAM	DETENTION
FEDERATED	REVERENCE	JEWELLERS	SEVENSEAS	RECEPTION
FEDERATES	VEHEMENCE	JEWELLERY	REDENSIGN	REFECTION
GENERATED	REFERENDA	LEVELLERS	RELEASING	REJECTION
GENERATES	REVERENDS	REVELLERS	REVERSING	RETENTION
RELEGATED	DEGENERES	REDEPLOYS	PETERSNOW	SELECTION
RELEGATES	TELEGENIC	METERMAID	RECESSION	DEBENTURE
RENEGADES	GENEKELLY	DEFERMENT	REVERSION	DEFECTORS
SERENADED	REDEVELOP	DETERMINE	SECESSION	DESERTERS
SERENADER	RERELEASE	NEVERMIND	NECESSARY	REFECTORY
SERENADES	TENEMENTS	REDEEMING	NECESSITY	REPEATERS
TELESALES	NEVERFEAR	REVETMENT	DEFENSIVE	REPERTORY
VEGETATED	HEREAFTER	NEVERMORE	RECESSIVE	SEDENTARY
VEGETATES	PETERFALK	REDEEMERS	CELESTIAL	SELECTORS
VENERATED	BELEAGUER	PERENNIAL	DESERTRAT	SEMESTERS
VENERATES	DETERGENT	SEXENNIAL	SEVENTEEN	DEFEATISM
TELEPATHY	JETENGINE	DEMEANING	PEDESTALS	DEFEATIST
GENERALLY	REPECHAGE	BELEMNITE	CEMENTING	NEFERTITI
RENEWABLE	HELENHUNT	DEMEANOUR	DEFEATING	TETEATETE
VEGETABLE	TELEPHONE	DEVELOPED	DEFECTING	DECEITFUL
VENERABLE	TELEPHONY	DEVELOPER	DEJECTING	RESENTFUL
GENERATOR	TELEPHOTO	SEVENOAKS	DESERTING	DECEPTIVE
RESEMBLED	HERETICAL	HETERODOX	DETECTING	DEFECTIVE
RESEMBLES	BENEFICES	BETENOIRE	DETESTING	DETECTIVE
DEREKBOND	TELEVISED	REHEARSAL	HESELTINE	RECEPTIVE
REMEMBERS	TELEVISES	REHEARSED	REHEATING	RETENTIVE
BESEECHED	DELETIONS	REHEARSES	REJECTING	SELECTIVE
BESEECHES	REDESIGNS	DEFERRALS	RELENTING	VENEZUELA
SENESCENT	VENETIANS	TELEGRAMS	RELETTING	GENEAUTRY
PETERCOOK	GENEVIEVE	CELEBRANT	REPEATING	RESERVOIR
TELESCOPE	BEDECKING	DEFERRING	REPENTANT	DECEIVING
HEYERDAHL	GENEALOGY	DETERRENT	REPENTING	DESERVING
BEHEADING	BEVELLING	DETERRING	RESENTING	RECEIVING
DEFENDANT	FEDERLINE	PEREGRINE	RESETTING	RESERVING
DEFENDING	LEVELLING	REFERRING	REVERTING	DECEIVERS
DEPENDANT	REBELLING	VENEERING	SELECTING	RECEIVERS
DEPENDENT	REPEALING	TELEGRAPH	DECEPTION	RESERVIST

PETERWEIR	HEDGEHOGS	HESITANCY	RELIEFMAP	REFILLING
REBELYELL	LENGTHILY	CELIBATES	PETITFOUR	SERIALMOM
REMEDYING	LENGTHENS	DECIMATED	HEMINGWAY	AERIALIST
BEEFEATER	NEWGUINEA	DECIMATES	LENINGRAD	SERIALISE
JEFFBANKS	SEDGEMOOR	DEDICATED	PEKINGMAN	GENIALITY
PERFECTED	MERGANSER	DEDICATES	MERINGUES	LEGISLATE
PERFECTLY	REDGROUSE	HESITATED	SEEINGRED	DEVILMENT
KERFUFFLE	TEAGARDEN	HESITATES	TEEINGOFF	DEFIANTLY
GEOFFHOON	BENGURION	MEDITATED	BESIEGING	LENIENTLY
PENFRIEND	HEDGEROWS	MEDITATES	REJIGGING	BEGINNING
BEDFELLOW	RESGESTAE	SEMIRAMIS	REMINGTON	DESIGNING
SELFIMAGE	WEIGHTIER	DEFINABLE	BESIEGERS	RESIGNING
PERFUMERY	HEIGHTENS	DESIRABLE	BENIGHTED	BEGINNERS
DEAFENING	WEIGHTING	MEDICALLY	DELIGHTED	DESIGNERS
LEAFINESS	METHADONE	VERITABLE	PERISHING	LEGIONARY
BEEFINGUP	PETHIDINE	DEPILATOR	RELISHING	DESIGNATE
SELFDOUBT	METHODISM	DEMITASSE	DECIPHERS	GELIGNITE
WEBFOOTED	METHODIST	BEWITCHED	PERIPHERY	DEMIMONDE
LEAFMOULD	BETHLEHEM	BEWITCHES	PERISHERS	SEMITONES
SELFWORTH	VERHOEVEN	DESICCANT	FETISHISM	SEMICOLON
PERFORMED	RESHUFFLE	PERISCOPE	FETISHIST	DEMIMOORE
PERFORMER	TEDHUGHES	DEBITCARD	MEDICINAL	DESIARNAZ
SEAFARING	METHEGLIN	DESICCATE	SEMIFINAL	DECIGRAMS
JEFFERSON	TECHNICAL	REKINDLED	REMINISCE	DENIGRATE
SEAFARERS	TECHNIQUE	REKINDLES	FEMINISED	SENIORITY
NEWFOREST	KEYHOLDER	REMINDING	MEDICINES	SEMIBREVE
PERFORATE	PENHOLDER	BEWILDERS	REVISITED	PENINSULA
SETFIRETO	ZEPHANIAH	REMINDERS	DERISIBLE	LETITSNOW
TEAFORTWO	MECHANICS	PENITENCE	DECISIONS	REMISSION
SELFISHLY	REDHANDED	RESIDENCE	DEFICIENT	REGISSEUR
BEEFSTEAK	MECHANISE	RESIDENCY	PETITIONS	LEVIATHAN
SELFBUILD	MECHANISM	RETICENCE	RECIPIENT	REGISTRAR
PERFAVORE	RECHARGED	DELIVERED	RESILIENT	SEMIOTICS
SELFAWARE	RECHARGES	DELIVERER	HELIPILOT	BELITTLED
VENGEANCE	SEAHORSES	PERIMETER	DECILITRE	BELITTLES
GEOGRAPHY	RECHERCHE	DECIDEDLY	FEMINISTS	BEFITTING
SERGEANTS	LETHARGIC	DECIMETRE	DELICIOUS	DEPICTING
MELGIBSON	TETHERING	DELINEATE	DELIRIOUS	DESISTING
NEIGHBOUR	LECHEROUS	PENITENTS	LEVITICUS	DEVIATING
PEGGEDOUT	BECHSTEIN	REDIRECTS	RELIGIOUS	MEDIATING
SEIGNEURS	RETHOUGHT	REGIMENTS	SEDITIOUS	REMITTING
LENGTHIER	PERINATAL	RESIDENTS	SEMIOLOGY	RESISTANT

RESISTING	RECKONING	HEALTHILY	REALISTIC	FERMANAGH
RESITTING	WEAKENING	SEALYHAMS	HELLISHLY	HEMMINGIN
DEPICTION	RECKONERS	CELLPHONE	REALISING	SEEMINGLY
DEVIATION	JERKINESS	REALTHING	SECLUSION	TERMINALS
MEDIATION	LEAKINESS	SELLSHORT	RECLUSIVE	PERMANENT
MEDIATORS	PERKINESS	DECLAIMED	NEOLITHIC	LERMONTOV
REGISTERS	DESKBOUND	DECLAIMER	DEFLATING	PELMANISM
RESISTORS	TEAKETTLE	RECLAIMED	DEPLETING	SERMONISE
RETICULAR	TEALEAVES	RECLAIMER	DEFLATION	GERMINATE
VEHICULAR	TELLTALES	WELLOILED	DEPLETION	TERMINATE
RETICULES	BELLYACHE	WELLVILLE	LEXLUTHOR	NEWMARKET
DEVIOUSLY	KEELHAULS	NEILSIMON	REPLETION	LEEMARVIN
SERIOUSLY	JELLYBEAN	CELLULOID	SELLOTAPE	MESMERISE
TEDIOUSLY	JELLYBABY	CELLULOSE	REALITYTV	MESMERISM
KERIHULME	HELLEBORE	CELLULITE	JEALOUSLY	MESMERIST
RELIQUARY	DEFLECTED	FEELSMALL	ZEALOUSLY	WEBMASTER
DECIDUOUS	NEGLECTED	NEILINNES	BELLCURVE	PERMITTED
DERIGUEUR	REELECTED	REPLANNED	DECLIVITY	HERMITAGE
RETICULUM	REFLECTED	LEYLANDII	NEWLYWEDS	GEOMETRIC
BELIEVING	REPLACING	TELLINGLY	YELLOWSEA	DEEMSTERS
RELIEVING	DEFLECTOR	DECLINING	YELLOWFIN	TEAMSTERS
BELIEVERS	REFLECTOR	RECLINING	BELLOWING	REIMBURSE
REVIEWING	BELLICOSE	BERLINERS	MELLOWING	NEWMEXICO
REVIEWERS	REPLICATE	RECLINERS	YELLOWING	BERNHARDT
VERIFYING	SEALEDOFF	REPLENISH	REFLEXIVE	SEANHAYES
BEDJACKET	SECLUDING	AERLINGUS	DEPLOYING	MEINKAMPF
BENJONSON	ZELLWEGER	WELLKNOWN	REPLAYING	JEANMARSH
NEWJERSEY	WELLBEING	BELLTOWER	PERMEATED	REENACTED
PERJURING	BEALLEARS	NEILYOUNG	PERMEATES	JEANGENET
PERJURERS	LESLIEASH	SEALPOINT	PERMEABLE	MEANDERED
NECKLACES	BEELZEBUB	WELLSPENT	GERMICIDE	BEANFEAST
REYKJAVIK	BELLYFLOP	FELLAPART	VERMICIDE	REINVESTS
LEAKEDOUT	JELLYFISH	CELLARMAN	VERMIFUGE	TEENAGERS
BEEKEEPER	JETLAGGED	TELLURIAN	VERMIFORM	BENNYHILL
DECKCHAIR	NEGLIGEES	CELLARMEN	TERMAGANT	MEANWHILE
BERKSHIRE	NEGLIGENT	CELLARAGE	LEEMAJORS	DEANSHIPS
PENKNIVES	GEOLOGIST	CELLARING	LEOMCKERN	NEONLIGHT
WEAKLINGS	NEOLOGISM	DECLARANT	REDMULLET	MEANGIRLS
PECKINPAH	NEOLOGIST	DECLARING	VERMILION	JENNYLIND
WEAKKNEED	WEALTHTAX	DEPLORING	FERMENTED	PENNYLANE
WEEKENDER	HEALTHIER	DECLARERS	GERMANDER	PENNILESS
BECKONING	WEALTHIER	BELLAROSA	SEGMENTED	REANIMATE

REINFORCE	GENOACAKE	SEAOFLOVE	DEPORTEES	REOPENING
BEANPOLES	RECONCILE	DEFORMING	REPORTAGE	NETPROFIT
SENNAPODS	REJOICING	RECOMMEND	DECOCTING	KEEPCOUNT
PENNYPOST	LEMONCURD	REFORMING	DEPORTING	REAPPOINT
DEANERIES	RECORDING	REFORMERS	REPORTING	KEEPHOUSE
WEDNESDAY	REWORDING	REFORMISM	REPOTTING	DEEPSOUTH
TENNESSEE	LEMONDROP	REFORMIST	REROUTING	DEEPSPACE
SEANASTIN	RECORDERS	AEROSMITH	RETORTING	REDPEPPER
BERNSTEIN	SECONDARY	DEFORMITY	REVOLTING	KEEPTRACK
BEANSTALK	SECONDERS	RECONNECT	DECOCTION	DESPERADO
REUNITING	RECORDIST	DENOUNCED	DECONTROL	PEPPERING
MEANSTEST	RECONDITE	DENOUNCES	REPORTERS	PEPPERONI
REINSTATE	REDOLENCE	REBOUNDED	AEROSTATS	RESPIRING
CEANOTHUS	AEROMETER	RECOUNTED	DEVOLVING	TEMPERING
PENNYWISE	PEDOMETER	REJOINDER	RECONVENE	PEPPERPOT
RESONANCE	RECOVERED	RENOUNCED	RESOLVING	TEMPORARY
MEMORANDA	BELONGING	RENOUNCES	REVOLVING	TEMPORISE
DECORATED	DECONGEST	RESOUNDED	REVOLVERS	TEMPTRESS
DECORATES	XENOPHOBE	BEMOANING	KEEPWATCH	DESPERATE
DETONATED	OENOPHILE	DEKOONING	HELPMATES	TEMPERATE
DETONATES	XENOPHILE	REJOINING	JETPLANES	PENPUSHER
PERORATED	AEROLITES	RECOGNISE	KEEPSAKES	DESPISING
PERORATES	DEMONISED	SEROTONIN	REDPLANET	KEEPATBAY
RELOCATED	DEPOSITED	AEROFOILS	SEAPLANES	PERPETUAL
RELOCATES	MEMORISED	JEROBOAMS	TEMPLATES	BESPATTER
RENOVATED	MEMORISES	MESOMORPH	HENPECKED	DESPOTISM
RENOVATES	DEFOLIANT	AEROSPACE	RESPECTED	KEEPQUIET
RESONATED	DEVOTIONS	DECOUPAGE	HELPEDOUT	HELPFULLY
RESONATES	DEPOSITOR	RECOUPING	PERPLEXED	KEEPSWEET
CENOTAPHS	DEFOLIATE	DEVONPORT	PERPLEXES	NEOPHYTES
MEMORABLE	HEDONISTS	LEGOFPORK	TEMPLETON	SEAQUAKES
MEMORABLY	NEGOTIATE	DECOMPOSE	REAPPEARS	BECQUEREL
DECORATOR	NEPOTISTS	DEMOCRACY	HEYPRESTO	DEARMADAM
DETONATOR	FELONIOUS	RESOURCES	TEMPTFATE	DECREASED
RESONATOR	FEROCIOUS	AERODROME	PERPIGNAN	DECREASES
SEAOFAZOV	MELODIOUS	MELODRAMA	DESPAIRED	RECREATED
MENOPAUSE	VERONIQUE	VELODROME	NEAPTIDES	RECREATES
AERONAUTS	RECOLLECT	DEVOURING	KEEPCLEAR	RETREATED
LEMONBALM	LEGOFLAMB	DEMOCRATS	ZEPPELINS	REARRANGE
DEMOBBING	AEROPLANE	LEMONSOLE	TEMPELHOF	HEARTACHE
LEBOUCHER	RECOILING	REHOUSING	RESPONDED	WEHRMACHT
BEEORCHID	DECOLLETE	REPOSSESS	DEEPENING	MEURSAULT

PEARMAINS	GEORGEFOX	MERRIMENT	REPRISALS	REDSHANKS
BEARNAISE	GEORGETTE	REPRIMAND	WEARISOME	SENSUALLY
FERRYBOAT	HENRIETTA	DERRINGDO	REPRESENT	REDSTARTS
HEARTBEAT	PETRIFIED	DERRINGER	BETROTHAL	SEASHANTY
PEARLBUCK	PETRIFIES	REPRINTED	GEARSTICK	MESSABOUT
HEARTBURN	TERRIFIED	METRONOME	BETROTHED	PERSECUTE
REPROBATE	TERRIFIES	WEARINESS	REGRETTED	FEASTDAYS
KERRYBLUE	FEBRIFUGE	WEIRDNESS	REWRITTEN	MENSHEVIK
DEFROCKED	HEARTFELT	BEARINGUP	FERRETING	SEASHELLS
DETRACTED	HENRYFORD	BEERMONEY	REWRITING	MESSIEURS
REFRACTED	REPROGRAM	YEARBOOKS	SECRETING	CEASEFIRE
RETRACTED	TEDROGERS	YEARROUND	SERRATING	NEWSAGENT
PETRUCHIO	SEGREGATE	METROPOLE	SECRETION	NEWSSHEET
PERRYCOMO	BEERSHEBA	TERRAPINS	SERRATION	LEASEHOLD
JERRYCANS	GEARWHEEL	TEARAPART	FERRETERS	WELSHHARP
RETRACING	SEARCHFEE	TETRARCHY	SECRETARY	PERSPIRED
TERRACING	TEARSHEET	BEARFRUIT	TERRITORY	PERSPIRES
DETRACTOR	JERRYHALL	TEARDROPS	REGRETFUL	NEWSNIGHT
METRICTON	NEARTHING	TERRORISE	SECRETIVE	JETSKIING
REFRACTOR	SEARCHING	TERRORISM	DEFRAUDED	TEASELLED
DEPRECATE	SEARCHERS	TERRORIST	DEFRAUDER	MESSALINA
METRICATE	HEARTHRUG	PEERGROUP	REGROUPED	REDSALMON
HEBRIDEAN	PEARLISED	TERRARIUM	FEARFULLY	CEASELESS
REPRODUCE	RECRUITED	MEERASYAL	TEARFULLY	NEWSFLASH
BEDRIDDEN	REFRAINED	BEARDSLEY	REARGUARD	SENSELESS
BEGRUDGED	YEARLINGS	DEFROSTED	RETROUSSE	TENSILITY
BEGRUDGES	REARLIGHT	DEFROSTER	DEPRIVING	PERSIMMON
DEGRADING	HEARTIEST	DEPRESSED	REPROVING	SEXSYMBOL
PETRIDISH	BEARSKINS	DEPRESSES	DEPRAVITY	PESSIMISM
RETRIEVAL	PETROLCAN	HEIRESSES	REDRAWING	PESSIMIST
BEFRIENDS	HERRFLICK	RECROSSED	TEARAWAYS	MESSENGER
DEBRIEFED	NEUROLOGY	REDRESSED	MERRYXMAS	PERSONNEL
GEARLEVER	TETRALOGY	REDRESSES	DEFRAYALS	PERSONIFY
HEARTENED	NEURALGIA	REFRESHED	BETRAYING	PERSONAGE
REORDERED	HEARTLAND	REFRESHER	DEFRAYING	TEASINGLY
REPRIEVED	METROLAND	REFRESHES	BETRAYERS	LESSENING
REPRIEVES	BEARDLESS	REGRESSED	MESSMATES	REASONING
RETRIEVED	HEARTLESS	REGRESSES	NEWSPAPER	SEASONING
RETRIEVER	FEBRILITY	REPRESSED	PERSUADED	PEASANTRY
RETRIEVES	PETROLEUM	REPRESSES	PERSUADES	DENSENESS
BEERBELLY	LEEREMICK	HEURISTIC	SEASCAPES	MESSINESS
DECREEING	DETRIMENT	PETRUSHKA	MESSIANIC	TENSENESS

TERSENESS	LEASTWISE	NEXTOFKIN	NEATENING	FEATURING
MESSINGUP	JERSEYCOW	CENTIGRAM	PERTINENT	FESTERING
SESSIONAL	TESTMATCH	PENTAGRAM	GETTINGON	HECTORING
GEMSTONES	MEATEATER	VESTIGIAL	CENTENARY	KETTERING
KEYSTONES	MELTWATER	HEPTAGONS	MEATINESS	LECTURING
PENSIONER	TESTCASES	PERTAINED	PETTINESS	LETTERING
NEWSHOUND	CESTLAVIE	NESTLINGS	TESTINESS	NECTARINE
NEWSROUND	CENTRALLY	NEWTRICKS	GETTINGUP	PESTERING
TEASPOONS	NEUTRALLY	CERTAINLY	MEETINGUP	RESTORING
GETSHOTOF	TEXTUALLY	LEFTFIELD	SETTINGUP	TEETERING
GETSHORTY	RESTRAINS	VENTRICLE	KEPTWOMAN	VENTURING
BEDSPREAD	RESTRAINT	TESTPILOT	SECTIONAL	CENTURION
CENSORIAL	VERTEBRAE	CENTRISTS	BEETHOVEN	HEATPROOF
JETSTREAM	VERTEBRAL	CERTAINTY	DESTROYED	LETTERBOX
NETSURFER	VESTIBULE	RESTRICTS	DESTROYER	LECTURERS
NEWSTREET	BETTYBOOP	KEPTCLEAR	FESTOONED	RESTORERS
KEYSTROKE	PETTICOAT	REPTILIAN	MENTIONED	DEXTERITY
LEISURELY	PESTICIDE	DEATHLIKE	OESTROGEN	REITERATE
CENSORING	TENTACLES	PESTILENT	LEITMOTIF	DEUTERIUM
CENSURING	PENTECOST	RESTYLING	TEXTBOOKS	DEXTEROUS
MEASURING	PETTYCASH	DEATHLESS	NEXTWORLD	TESTDRIVE
NEWSPRINT	GENTLEMAN	FERTILISE	WESTWORLD	DEATHSTAR
NEWSGROUP	AESTHETES	FERTILITY	WESTBOUND	PERTUSSIS
PERSISTED	FEATHERED	GENTILITY	WESTPOINT	JETTISONS
BEDSITTER	GENTLEMEN	MENTALITY	PENTHOUSE	DENTISTRY
JETSETTER	WEATHERED	VENTILATE	WENTWORTH	DEATHTRAP
REDSETTER	BEETLEOFF	SEPTEMBER	CENTIPEDE	BEATITUDE
VERSATILE	AESTHETIC	SENTIMENT	SEXTUPLET	CERTITUDE
NEWSSTAND	GETTHENOD	TESTAMENT	LETTERMAN	RECTITUDE
CESSATION	ZEITGEIST	TESTIMONY	SECTARIAN	TESTATRIX
SENSATION	VESTMENTS	KEITHMOON	YESTERDAY	DENTITION
SENSITISE	WESTMEATH	DEATHMASK	GERTFROBE	GESTATION
SENSITIVE	SETTLEDUP	LENTANEAR	KEPTTRACK	TESTATORS
PEASOUPER	BEATIFIED	GETTINGBY	CENTURIES	DESTITUTE
REASSURED	BEATIFIES	TECTONICS	PERTURBED	TENTATIVE
REASSURES	CERTIFIED	SENTENCED	RESTARTED	KEPTQUIET
REISSUING	CERTIFIES	SENTENCES	WESTERNER	TESTTUBES
REDSQUARE	RECTIFIED	LETTINGGO	BETTEROFF	RESTFULLY
SETSQUARE	RECTIFIER	JESTINGLY	HEPTARCHY	ZESTFULLY
PENSIVELY	RECTIFIES	PENTANGLE	BENTURPIN	FESTIVALS
PERSEVERE	TESTIFIED	RECTANGLE	PECTORALS	LEFTOVERS
SEESAWING	TESTIFIES	SENTINELS	BETTERING	AESTIVATE

FESTIVITY	BEAUTIFUL	LEAVECOLD	MEZZANINE	OFFLIMITS
BESTOWING	PENURIOUS	SERVICING	MEZZOTINT	OFALLTIME
DELTAWING	DEBUNKING	PERVADING	OFFCOLOUR	EFFLUVIUM
DEATHWISH	GENUFLECT	BELVEDERE	OFFCAMERA	AFFORDING
SENTRYBOX	REPUBLICS	HEAVYDUTY	OFFCOURSE	SFORZANDO
PETULANCE	REFUELLED	SERVIETTE	OFFENBACH	AFFRONTED
JERUSALEM	BEGUILING	NERVELESS	AFTERCARE	AFORESAID
REGULATED	REPUBLISH	SERVILITY	OFFENDING	OFFSEASON
REGULATES	SEXUALITY	HELVELLYN	OFFENDERS	AFASTBUCK
BEQUEATHS	SEQUENCES	CERVANTES	IFEELFINE	OFFSHOOTS
BEAUMARIS	SEQUINNED	FERVENTLY	AFTERGLOW	OFFSPRING
REGULARLY	GENUINELY	LEAVENING	AFTERLIFE	OFFTHEMAP
REPUTABLE	REPUGNANT	HEAVINESS	AFTERMATH	OFFTHEPEG
REGULATOR	RETURNING	PERVERTED	AFTERNOON	OFFTHEAIR
BEAUXARTS	REFURNISH	REGVARNEY	OFFENSIVE	OFITSKIND
DEBUTANTE	BEAUMONDE	JERVISBAY	EFFECTUAL	OFFTARGET
DEBUTANTS	LETUSPRAY	DERVISHES	AFFECTING	EFFULGENT
DECUMBENT	RESURRECT	PEEVISHLY	EFFECTING	JGBALLARD
RECUMBENT	FENUGREEK	PERVASION	AFFECTION	IGUANODON
VENUSBERG	DEMURRING	PERVASIVE	OFFERTORY	EGLANTINE
REFURBISH	RECURRENT	HELVETIAN	AFFECTIVE	EGGBEATER
SEAURCHIN	RECURRING	HELVETICA	EFFECTIVE	AGREEABLE
SEPULCHRE	REQUIRING	SERVITUDE	AFTERWORD	AGREEABLY
BEFUDDLED	REQUESTED	VELVETEEN	OFFHANDED	AGNESGREY
REDUNDANT	SEQUESTER	SERVETIME	AFRIKANER	EGREGIOUS
REFUNDING	REPULSING	NERVOUSLY	AFFIDAVIT	AGREEMENT
FECUNDITY	REPULSION	TEDWILLIS	AFRIKAANS	UGLIFRUIT
REFUSENIK	REVULSION	GETWINDOF	OFFICIALS	AGAMEMNON
REPUTEDLY	REQUISITE	BEDWARMER	EFFICIENT	EGOMANIAC
BEAUGESTE	REPULSIVE	NETWORKER	OFFICIANT	AGONYAUNT
RESURFACE	DEDUCTING	SEAWORTHY	AFFILIATE	EGONRONAY
REBUFFING	REBUTTING	REEXAMINE	OFFICIATE	AGINCOURT
DEBUGGING	RELUCTANT	VERYLIGHT	OFFICIOUS	AGONISING
REFULGENT	RESULTANT	RECYCLING	AFFIRMANT	IGNORANCE
RESURGENT	RESULTING	BERYLLIUM	AFFIRMING	IGNORAMUS
DEPUTISED	DEDUCTION	RELYINGON	AFFIANCED	AGOODMANY
DEPUTISES	REDUCTION	NEWYORKER	AFFIANCES	AGNOSTICS
NEBULISER	SEDUCTION	BERYLREID	OFFLOADED	EGYPTIANS
DEDUCIBLE	DESULTORY	DEHYDRATE	AFFLICTED	AGGRIEVED
SECURICOR	DEDUCTIVE	REHYDRATE	AFFLUENCE	AGGREGATE
PECUNIARY	SEDUCTIVE	DEMYSTIFY	EFFLUENCE	AGGRESSOR
REPUDIATE	TENUOUSLY	BEMYGUEST	UFOLOGIST	AGGRAVATE

EGGSHELLS	WHODUNNIT	SHIFTLESS	SHELLFISH	RHYMESTER
EGOTISTIC	SHADINESS	THIGHBONE	CHILDHOOD	THEMASTER
AGITATING	SHEDLOADS	THIGHBOOT	SHILLINGS	THEMESONG
AGITATION	SHEDATEAR	CHIHUAHUA	PHILLIPPE	CHEMISTRY
AGITATORS	THEDEVILS	THEHOBBIT	CHILLIEST	THUMBTACK
PHEASANTS	SHADOWING	THEHUNGER	SHOLOKHOV	THEMATRIX
CHEAPENED	SHADOWBOX	SHEILASIM	SHELFLIFE	SHIMMYING
WHEATEARS	THREWAWAY	CHOIRBOYS	PHILOLOGY	THINKBACK
WHEATGERM	SHOELACES	SHRIVELUP	CHILBLAIN	PHONEBOOK
THRASHING	SHOEMAKER	CHAINGANG	CHILDLIKE	CHINACLAY
CHEAPJACK	SHEETBEND	SHEIKHDOM	CHILDLINE	PHONECARD
THWACKING	WHEELBASE	SHRINKAGE	CHILDLESS	CHUNTERED
CHEAPNESS	SHREDDIES	SHRIEKING	WHOLEMEAL	THUNDERED
CHEAPRATE	SHEEPDOGS	SHRINKING	SHELFMARK	THUNDERER
CHEAPSIDE	SHIELDING	CHAIRLIFT	PHALANGER	CHANTELLE
THWARTING	SHREDDING	THRILLING	PHILANDER	WHINGEING
THEBRIDGE	THREADING	THRILLERS	THELONIUS	CHANTEUSE
CHUBBIEST	SHREDDERS	CHAINMAIL	SHALLOWER	PHONOGRAM
SHABBIEST	SHREWDEST	CHRISNOTH	CHILEPINE	CHINAGIRL
SHUBUNKIN	CHEEREDUP	CHRISROCK	SHELFROOM	SHANGHAIS
THACKERAY	SHEEPFOLD	CHAINSAWS	PHALAROPE	CHANTILLY
THICKENED	THRESHOLD	CHRISTIAN	CHILDSTAR	RHINOLOGY
THICKENER	SHOESHINE	CHRISTMAS	SHELLSUIT	CHANDLERS
WHICHEVER	THRESHING	THRIFTILY	WHOLESALE	CHANDLERY
CHECKEDIN	THRESHERS	CHRISTENS	WHOLESOME	THANKLESS
CHECKEDUP	PHLEBITIS	CHRISTINA	PHILATELY	PHENOMENA
CHOCKFULL	CHEEKIEST	CHRISTINE	CHAMPAGNE	THINONTOP
CHUCKITIN	CHEERIEST	THEJACKET	CHEMICALS	THINKOVER
CHUCKLING	WHEEDLING	SHAKEALEG	CHAMFERED	SHANGRILA
SHACKLING	CHEERLESS	SHAKEDOWN	SHIMMERED	CHINAROSE
CHECKLIST	SHEERNESS	THEKUMARS	WHIMPERED	CHINSTRAP
CHOCOLATE	SHEEPSKIN	WHILEAWAY	WHIMSICAL	PHONETICS
CHICOMARX	THREESOME	PHILDAVIS	CHAMPIONS	THINKTANK
CHECKMATE	CHIEFTAIN	WHALEBONE	THEMIKADO	WHINSTONE
CHICANERY	THREATENS	THYLACINE	CHAMELEON	CHINATOWN
THICKNESS	CHIEFWHIP	CHILDCARE	SHAMELESS	THINGUMMY
THECASTLE	SHEEPWASH	THELODGER	CHIMINGIN	CHINAWARE
CHICKWEED	CHAFFINCH	SHELTERED	THUMBNAIL	PHONEYWAR
EHUDBARAK	SHEFFIELD	CHALLENGE	SHAMANISM	WHINNYING
THEDABARA	SHIFTIEST	CHILTERNS	SHAMPOOED	THROWAWAY
SHUDDERED	SHUFFLING	WHOLEFOOD	SHAMBOLIC	CHROMATIC
SHEDTEARS	SHUFFLERS	SHELLFIRE	THEMEPARK	THROWBACK

THROBBING	CHIPBOARD	PHEROMONE	PHASEDOUT	WHITFIELD
THEOCCULT	CHOPHOUSE	SHARANSKY	THESEDAYS	WHITELADY
SHROUDING	CHAPARRAL	CHARINESS	CHASTENED	THATSLIFE
RHEOMETER	SHIPWRECK	SHARPNESS	WHISKERED	WHITELIME
THEORETIC	CHAPERONE	SHORTNESS	WHISPERED	WHITTLING
THEOFFICE	SHOPFRONT	CHARWOMAN	WHISPERER	SHOTGLASS
CHEONGSAM	CHIPMUNKS	CHARWOMEN	PHOSPHATE	WHITEMEAT
THRONGING	CHEQUERED	THEROOKIE	CHASTISED	THETINMAN
THEOTHERS	CHARLATAN	CHERBOURG	CHASTISES	WHITENING
THEORISED	THERMALLY	CHARLOTTE	THESPIANS	WHITENERS
THEORISER	CHARABANC	CHERNOBYL	CHISELLED	WHITENESS
THEORISES	CHARACTER	CHIROPODY	CHISELLER	WHITBREAD
CHRONICLE	SHORTCAKE	WHIRLPOOL	GHOSTLIKE	WHITEROSE
THEORISTS	SHORTCUTS	THERAPIST	WHISTLING	PHOTOSTAT
WHOOPITUP	THORNDIKE	SHARAPOVA	WHISTLERS	THATSTHAT
THROWNOUT	SHAREDOUT	CHARGRILL	CHESTNUTS	WHETSTONE
THEOSOPHY	CHARTERED	THIRDRATE	RHYSJONES	WHITEWASH
PHNOMPENH	SHARPENED	CHERISHED	THESTRAND	THOUSANDS
THEOCRACY	SHARPENER	CHERISHES	GHOSTTOWN	RHEUMATIC
THEOCRATS	SHORTENED	CHORISTER	THESAURUS	SHRUBBERY
THEOUTLAW	CHARTERIS	SHARKSKIN	WHISKYMAC	SHOULDERS
THROSTLES	CHARLEROI	CHARITIES	SHETLANDS	CHAUFFEUR
THROTTLED	SHORTFALL	OHBROTHER	WHITTAKER	SHRUGGING
THROTTLES	THEREFORE	THIRSTIER	WHITEBEAM	THOUGHTUP
THROATILY	WHEREFORE	SHARKTALE	WHITEBAIT	THRUMMING
RHEOSTATS	SHORTFUSE	THIRSTILY	PHOTOCALL	SHAUNTAIT
SHIPCANAL	CHURCHMAN	SHORTTIME	PHOTOCOPY	THRUSTING
SHIPMATES	CHURCHMEN	SHORTTERM	WHITECITY	CHEVALIER
THEPLAYER	CHURCHILL	THEREUPON	CHATTERED	SHOVELLED
CHAPLAINS	SHORTHAND	WHEREUPON	CHATTERER	SHOVELLER
THEPLAGUE	THORAHIRD	THERIVALS	SHATTERED	CHIVALRIC
SHEPHERDS	SHORTHAUL	CHARTWELL	SHUTTERED	CHEVROLET
WHIPPERIN	WHIRLIGIG	WHIRLWIND	WHITEFLAG	SHIVERING
CHOPPEDUP	CHIRPIEST	SHAREWARE	WHITEFANG	CHIVVYING
SHIPSHAPE	THIRTIETH	SHORTWAVE	WHITEFISH	CHEWBACCA
SHOPFLOOR	SHEREKHAN	CHERRYPIE	WHITEGOLD	SHOWCARDS
SHAPELESS	SHIRELLES	WHISKAWAY	WHITEHEAD	SHOWEDOFF
CHIPOLATA	CHAROLAIS	LHASAAPSO	WHITEHEAT	SHOWPIECE
WHIPSNADE	CHORTLING	THISWAYUP	WHITEHALL	SHOWGIRLS
CHOPLOGIC	SHORELINE	PHYSICIAN	THATCHING	SHOWINESS
RHAPSODIC	CHARMLESS	PHYSICIST	THATCHERS	SHOWINGUP
WHIPROUND	SHORTLIST	CHESSCLUB	WHITEHART	SHOWTRIAL

THEWARDEN	DISAPPEAR	PITCHFORK	BIRDCALLS	SIXDAYWAR
SHOWERING	DISAGREED	HITCHHIKE	BIRDTABLE	MILESAWAY
THEXFILES	DISAGREES	WITCHHUNT	FINDFAULT	SIDESALAD
WHEYFACED	BIZARRELY	DIACRITIC	WILDPALMS	LINEDANCE
CHRYSALIS	TINAARENA	CIRCUITRY	WINDSCALE	TIMEWATCH
THEYREOFF	VITABRITS	CIRCULARS	VINDICATE	VINEYARDS
WHIZZBANG	DISASTERS	CIRCULATE	WINDYCITY	AIREDALES
HIMALAYAN	BIPARTITE	DISCOLOUR	MIDDLEEAR	FIREEATER
HIMALAYAS	TIDALWAVE	MINCEMEAT	MIDDLEMAN	FIREWATER
VICARAGES	AIRBRAKES	PIECEMEAL	MIDDLEMEN	LIBERATED
LISAMARIE	AIRBUBBLE	DISCOMFIT	MIDDLESEX	LIBERATES
NICARAGUA	JIMBACKUS	WISCONSIN	VINDIESEL	LIFESAVER
FINANCIAL	WIMBLEDON	WINCANTON	LINDBERGH	MINELAYER
FINANCIER	KIRBYGRIP	ZIRCONIUM	MIDDLEAGE	RICEPAPER
FINANCING	MISBEHAVE	DISCLOSED	MIDDLETON	WINEMAKER
GIRANDOLE	DISBELIEF	DISCLOSES	WILDGEESE	CINEMATIC
TIPANDRUN	MISBELIEF	DISCIPLES	WINDCHILL	CINERARIA
BILATERAL	DIABOLISM	MINCEPIES	WILDTHING	SIDEWALKS
MIRABELLE	LIABILITY	DISCARDED	DISDAINED	TIDEMARKS
LIMABEANS	VIABILITY	DISCERNED	PIEDPIPER	FIREBALLS
CIGARETTE	DISBANDED	JIMCARREY	MIDDLINGS	LIBERALLY
DIEADEATH	DISBURSAL	DISCBRAKE	HINDSIGHT	LITERALLY
LIGAMENTS	KIMBERLEY	SINCERELY	WINDMILLS	MISERABLE
PIRATICAL	LIMBURGER	GILCHRIST	KINDLIEST	MISERABLY
FINALISED	BIGBERTHA	SINCERITY	HINDUKUSH	TIMETABLE
FINALISES	GIBBERING	DISCUSSED	BIRDSNEST	LIBERATOR
LISARILEY	TIMBURTON	DISCUSSES	GIDDINESS	TIMELAPSE
CIGARILLO	GIBBERISH	CIRCUSBOY	WINDINESS	RIVERBOAT
LISARINNA	DIABETICS	VISCOSITY	EINDHOVEN	DISEMBODY
BIGAMISTS	KIBBUTZIM	TINCTURES	WINDHOVER	TIGERBALM
FINALISTS	PILCHARDS	DISCOURSE	BIRDHOUSE	NIGELBENN
HILARIOUS	DISCHARGE	DISCOUNTS	BIGDIPPER	NIGELBOND
VICARIOUS	DISCLAIMS	VISCOUNTS	WINDBREAK	RIVERBANK
VIVACIOUS	PINCHBECK	DISCOVERS	MISDIRECT	DISEMBARK
HIJACKING	AITCHBONE	DISCOVERY	BIRDBRAIN	WISEACRES
HIJACKERS	HITCHCOCK	PISCIVORE	HINDERING	TIMESCALE
RIVALLING	KITCHENER	PIECEWORK	TINDERBOX	SILENCING
DISALLOWS	DISCREDIT	HINDRANCE	HINDUSTAN	SILENCERS
DISARMING	PITCHEDIN	BIRDCAGES	MINDFULLY	EIDERDUCK
DISAVOWAL	MISCREANT	MINDGAMES	WINDOWTAX	EIDERDOWN
LISABONET	BIGCHEESE	WINDGAUGE	WINDOWBOX	FIVEPENCE
PINAFORES	WITCHETTY	BIRDBATHS	WINDSWEPT	DIAERESIS

VICEVERSA	WIDEANGLE	DIVERSION	SIDESWIPE	AIRGUITAR
LIFEBELTS	TIREDNESS	LIKEASHOT	LIVERWORT	KINGMIDAS
DISENGAGE	HIBERNATE	LIKEASNOT	LIFECYCLE	DISGUISED
VIDEOGAME	FIRECORAL	LIVERSPOT	MIKETYSON	DISGUISES
DIVERGENT	LIFEFORCE	DIVERSITY	MIKEMYERS	KINGSIZED
DIVERGING	FIXEDODDS	SIDEISSUE	AIRFRANCE	MISGUIDED
TIMESHEET	FIREPOWER	TIGERSEYE	LIZFRASER	JINGOISTS
MINESHAFT	NINEHOLES	DIRECTTAX	DIFFICULT	LINGUISTS
CINEPHILE	LIVEROUGH	LIVESTOCK	DIFFIDENT	DIEGOLUNA
HIDEYHOLE	FIREWORKS	LIBERTIES	AIRFIELDS	DINGALING
FIRETHORN	HIDEBOUND	PIKESTAFF	DISFIGURE	KINGSLYNN
TIMESHARE	SIDEBOARD	DIRECTHIT	KINFLICKS	SINGALONG
GIVECHASE	LIMEHOUSE	LIFESTYLE	OILFILTER	LIEGELORD
TIMEPIECE	LIFEBOATS	BISECTING	ZINFANDEL	VIRGINALS
LIFESIZED	FIVESPICE	DIGESTING	TITFORTAT	DINGINESS
NINELIVES	PINEAPPLE	DIRECTING	PIGFARMER	DIGGINGUP
SIDELINES	LIVERPOOL	DIVERTING	PILFERAGE	DIAGNOSED
VIDELICET	VIDEOPLUS	DIVESTING	HITFORSIX	DIAGNOSES
HIRELINGS	FIREBREAK	FIRESTONE	DIFFERENT	KIDGLOVES
FIRELIGHT	PIPEDREAM	LIBERTINE	DIFFERING	DIAGNOSIS
LIMELIGHT	PIPEORGAN	LIKESTINK	PILFERING	RINGROUND
SIDELIGHT	TIMETRIAL	LIMESTONE	MIAFARROW	KINGCOBRA
TIMELIMIT	FIREBRICK	MILESTONE	PILFERERS	SINGAPORE
LIMERICKS	SIDETRACK	BISECTION	DIFFUSING	SIEGFRIED
MINEFIELD	WISECRACK	DIGESTION	DIFFUSION	FINGERTIP
LIVELIEST	LIMEGREEN	DIRECTION	DISFAVOUR	GINGERALE
GIVEBIRTH	NIGELREES	SIDESTEPS	RIOGRANDE	NIGGARDLY
FIREPLACE	FIREDRILL	VIDEOTAPE	DISGRACED	FINGERING
TIGERLILY	TIMEFRAME	DIMESTORE	KINGJAMES	LINGERING
LIBELLING	FINEPRINT	DIRECTORS	KINGMAKER	GINGERTOM
GIVEBLOOD	FIREBRAND	DIRECTORY	BIOGRAPHY	ZIGGURATS
LIFEBLOOD	FIREIRONS	FIRESTORM	PIGGYBACK	GINGERNUT
WISEBLOOD	FIREPROOF	DIGESTIVE	RIDGEBACK	KINGPRAWN
FIREALARM	FIRECREST	DIRECTIVE	RINGABELL	DISGUSTED
RIDERLESS	WIREBRUSH	LIMEJUICE	PIGGYBANK	RIDGETILE
WINEGLASS	LIMEGROVE	FINETUNED	RINGFENCE	FIDGETING
LIBELLOUS	FIVEASIDE	HIDEOUSLY	KINGSEVIL	RIDGETENT
MIKESMITH	RIVERSIDE	SIDEBURNS	MINGHELLA	KINGSTOWN
TIGERMOTH	DIVERSIFY	FIREGUARD	SINGLETON	RINGOUZEL
HIBERNIAN	LICENSING	LIFEGUARD	VINGTETUN	MISGOVERN
VICENNIAL	SIRENSONG	MINERVOIS	WINGCHAIR	RIGHTAWAY
LIVEINSIN	DIMENSION	WIDEAWAKE	BINGOHALL	HIGHLANDS

BIGHEADED	NICHOLSON	NIGHTSPOT	PIPINGHOT	MISJUDGES
FISHCAKES	HIGHCLASS	TIGHTSPOT	DININGOUT	MILKMAIDS
PIGHEADED	SIGHTLESS	LIGHTSOUT	GIVINGOUT	NICKFALDO
LITHUANIA	DISHCLOTH	DICHOTOMY	HIRINGOUT	LINKLATER
FISHEAGLE	HIGHFLOWN	NIGHTTIME	RISINGSUN	NICKNAMES
HIGHBALLS	NIGHTMAIL	WITHSTAND	FINISHOFF	KICKEDOFF
HIGHTABLE	NIGHTMARE	WITHSTOOD	FINISHING	KICKEDOUT
FIGHTBACK	TIMHENMAN	FISHGUARD	CIVILISED	PICKEDOUT
RIGHTBACK	FISHKNIFE	NIGHTWEAR	CIVILISES	NICKBERRY
LIGHTBULB	MISHANDLE	TIGHTWADS	DIGITISED	MILKTEETH
WITHABANG	LIGHTNING	WITHAWILL	MINIMISED	SICKLEAVE
TITHEBARN	SIPHONING	RIGHTWING	MINIMISES	MILKSHAKE
FIGHTCLUB	JIMHENSON	LIGHTYEAR	DIRIGIBLE	RICKSHAWS
NIGHTCLUB	DISHONEST	BIOHAZARD	DIVISIBLE	KICKPLEAT
DISHEDOUT	FISHINESS	MILITANCY	CIVILIANS	MILKFLOAT
HIGHLEVEL	LIGHTNESS	SIBILANCE	DIVISIONS	PICKALOCK
LIGHTENED	PITHINESS	VIGILANCE	VIRIDIANA	PINKFLOYD
TIGHTENED	RIGHTNESS	LITIGATED	NIHILISTS	DICKEMERY
RIGHTEOUS	TIGHTNESS	LITIGATES	LITIGIOUS	SINKINGIN
EIGHTFOLD	DISHINGUP	MITIGATED	MIMICKING	MILKSNAKE
NIGHTFALL	DISHONOUR	MITIGATES	MIMICKERS	SICKENING
NIGHTGOWN	WITHHOLDS	PIXILATED	MINISKIRT	DICKINSON
TIGHTHEAD	HIGHCOURT	SIBILATES	DIXIELAND	WILKINSON
HIGHCHAIR	BISHOPRIC	SILICAGEL	CIVILLIST	SILKINESS
WITHCHILD	FISHERMAN	TITIVATED	LIMITLESS	KICKBOXER
DIPHTHONG	SIGHTREAD	TITIVATES	TITILLATE	SILKWORMS
RIGHTHAND	FISHERMEN	DIGITALIS	VISIONARY	MILKROUND
NIGHTHAWK	LIZHURLEY	MILITARIA	VIVIDNESS	MILKTOOTH
FISHWIVES	BILHARZIA	DIGITALLY	VISIGOTHS	NICKNOLTE
HIGHLIGHT	DITHERING	MINIMALLY	KIWIFRUIT	DICKTRACY
HIGHJINKS	WITHERING	SIMILARLY	MINIDRESS	KIRKBRIDE
LICHFIELD	TIGHTROPE	LITIGANTS	MINIATURE	MILKTRAIN
MIGHTIEST	DITHERERS	MILITANTS	MINISTERS	BICKERING
EIGHTIETH	WITHDRAWN	VIGILANTE	MINIBUSES	TINKERING
NIGHTJARS	WITHDRAWS	DILIGENCE	RIDICULED	PINKERTON
TIGHTKNIT	EIGHTSMAN	DIVIDENDS	RIDICULES	DISKDRIVE
HIGHALTAR	EIGHTSMEN	CITIZENRY	PITIFULLY	MICKASTON
FISHSLICE	SIGHTSEER	DISINFECT	VICIOUSLY	RICKSTEIN
HIGHFLYER	SIGHTSEES	MISINFORM	LIEINWAIT	PICKETING
RICHELIEU	NIGHTSAFE	BILINGUAL	VILIFYING	KICKSTART
NIGHTLIFE	LIGHTSHIP	DININGCAR	KIBITZING	MILKSTOUT
LITHOLOGY	EIGHTSOME	HIVINGOFF	MISJUDGED	KIELCANAL

BILLIARDS	HILLINESS	DISMANTLE	DINNERSET	SIGOURNEY
BILLGATES	SILLINESS	TINMINING	DIANARIGG	KILOGRAMS
BIGLEAGUE	VIOLINIST	FILMGOERS	PIANOROLL	MINORSUIT
BILLYBUDD	FILLINGUP	ZIMMERMAN	SIGNORINA	LIMOUSINE
BIBLEBELT	BILLCOSBY	LIAMBRADY	DIANAROSS	BIMONTHLY
BILLABONG	WILLPOWER	RIGMAROLE	LIONESSES	SIMONWARD
DIALECTAL	WILLYOUNG	SIMMERING	WITNESSED	DISPLAYED
LILLICRAP	BILLBOARD	TIMMARLOW	WITNESSES	MISPLACED
DIALECTIC	MILLIONTH	DISMISSAL	LIONISING	MISPLACES
MILLICENT	MILLIPEDE	DISMISSED	MINNESOTA	TINPLATED
DISLOCATE	FILLERCAP	DISMISSES	GIANTTOAD	AIRPOCKET
DISLODGED	DIALARIDE	FILMSTRIP	DIANETICS	NITPICKER
DISLODGES	KILLARNEY	FILMBUFFS	VIGNETTES	RIPPEDOFF
BILLODDIE	PILLORIED	DISMOUNTS	DIGNITARY	TIPPEDOFF
AIRLIFTED	TITLEROLE	MIAMIVICE	SIGNATORY	DIPPEDOUT
FIELDFARE	PILLARBOX	RIKMAYALL	SIGNATURE	SIMPLETON
BILLYGOAT	WILLESDEN	LIONTAMER	WINNOWING	DISPLEASE
FIELDGOAL	GILLESPIE	WINNEBAGO	WINNOWERS	OILPAINTS
MILLIGRAM	AIMLESSLY	PICNICKED	FIBONACCI	DISPELLED
PILLAGING	FIELDTRIP	PICNICKER	DINOSAURS	GIPPSLAND
PILLAGERS	BILLETING	PINNACLES	KILOWATTS	HIPPOLYTA
VILLAGERS	FILLETING	DIANADORS	PILOTBIRD	DISPENSED
BIOLOGIST	MILLSTONE	PIONEERED	DIVORCEES	DISPENSER
BILLBIXBY	VIOLATING	LIONHEART	PINOCCHIO	DISPENSES
BILLSIKES	VIOLATION	DIGNIFIED	NINOTCHKA	SIXPENCES
BILLNIGHY	FIELDTEST	SIGNIFIED	DIVORCING	TIMPANIST
HILLBILLY	GIRLGUIDE	SIGNIFIES	DISOBEYED	DISPROVED
BILLYIDOL	BILLOWING	BIENNIALS	MILOMETER	DISPROVES
BILLYJOEL	FIELDWORK	VIENTIANE	TINOPENER	DISPERSAL
DISLIKING	BILLWYMAN	SIGNALMAN	KILOMETRE	HITPARADE
BILLYLIAR	MISLAYING	SIGNALLED	KILOHERTZ	DISPERSED
DIPLOMACY	TINLIZZIE	SIGNALLER	PIROUETTE	DISPERSES
FIELDMICE	JIMMYCHOO	SIGNALMEN	RIGOLETTO	PIMPERNEL
DIPLOMATS	GIMMICKRY	LIMNOLOGY	PILOTFISH	DIAPHRAGM
WILLSMITH	JIMMYCARR	DIANELANE	HIROSHIMA	DISPARAGE
FINLANDIA	JIMMYHILL	SIGNALBOX	TIMOTHYMO	KIPPERTIE
MILLENNIA	AIRMAILED	SIANLLOYD	RICOCHETS	SIMPERING
VIOLENTLY	JIMMYMACK	PINNUMBER	NICOTIANA	TIPPERARY
WILLINGLY	DISMEMBER	SIGNINGON	GINORMOUS	DISPARATE
AIRLINERS	FIRMAMENT	KIDNAPPED	PINOTNOIR	DISPARITY
MILLINERS	MISMANAGE	KIDNAPPER	DISOWNING	DISPOSING
MILLINERY	JIMMYNAIL	KILNERJAR	KILOJOULE	AIRPISTOL

DISPOSEOF	MISSHAPEN	VIRTUALLY	DISTANTLY	DIRTYWORK
SIMPATICO	WIESBADEN	DISTRAINT	FITTINGLY	WIDTHWAYS
DISPUTANT	FIRSTBORN	DISTRACTS	LISTENING	SIMULATED
DISPUTING	DISSECTED	FITTOBUST	LISTENERS	SIMULATES
SIMPLYRED	TIPSYCAKE	DIETICIAN	DIRTINESS	SIMULATOR
MISQUOTED	DISSIDENT	PISTACHIO	KITTENISH	MINUSCULE
LIPREADER	MISSEDOUT	TICTACTOE	MISTINESS	SIMULCAST
DISROBING	RINSEDOUT	WITTICISM	NIFTINESS	BIFURCATE
MICROCHIP	FIRSTFOOT	GILTEDGED	WITTINESS	DIGUPDIRT
MICROCOSM	KISSOGRAM	HITTHEHAY	FICTIONAL	LIQUIDISE
JIMREEVES	FIRSTHAND	WINTHEDAY	GIFTTOKEN	LIQUIDATE
VICREEVES	BIOSPHERE	LITTLEMEN	RIOTSQUAD	LIQUIDITY
VITRIFIED	DIPSWITCH	TIPTOEING	HISTORIAN	MINUTEMAN
VITRIFIES	MISSPIGGY	LITTLETOE	PICTORIAL	VIRULENCE
FIBREFILL	FIRSTLADY	MISTLETOE	VICTORIAN	FIGUREOUT
MICROFILM	DISSOLVED	FIFTEENTH	DIRTTRACK	LIQUEFIED
DISREGARD	DISSOLVES	MISTREATS	LISTPRICE	LIQUEFIER
GIBRALTAR	DISSOLUTE	OINTMENTS	SISTERACT	LIQUEFIES
VIBRANTLY	MIDSUMMER	SIXTEENTH	DISTORTED	DIVULGING
FIERINESS	DISSEMBLE	LITTLEAUK	DISTURBED	FIGURINES
CIRRHOSIS	FIRSTMATE	LITTLEEVA	VICTORIES	SINUSITIS
VITRIOLIC	GIPSYMOTH	SIXTHFORM	FILTERTIP	FIDUCIARY
DISRUPTED	DISSENTED	HISTOGRAM	LITTERBIN	RITUALISM
DISREPAIR	DISSENTER	DIRTCHEAP	FILTERING	RITUALIST
MICROPSIA	KISSINGER	WILTSHIRE	TITTERING	VISUALISE
DISREPUTE	FIRSTNAME	PINTSIZED	WINTERING	LIQUORICE
LIBRARIAN	DISSONANT	DISTRICTS	WITTERING	MINUSSIGN
LIBRARIES	NISSENHUT	MISTAKING	BIRTHRATE	SITUATION
HIERARCHY	KINSWOMAN	DISTILLED	JITTERBUG	PITUITARY
MIRRORING	KINSWOMEN	DISTILLER	LITTERBUG	MIDWICKET
DIGRESSED	MISSWORLD	DIRTYLOOK	BIRTHSIGN	MIDWIFERY
DIGRESSES	FIRSTPOST	MIRTHLESS	NIETZSCHE	MIDWINTER
TIGRESSES	DISSIPATE	DISTEMPER	DIETETICS	VIEWPOINT
MIGRATING	AIRSTREAM	HISTAMINE	DICTATING	AIRWORTHY
VIBRATING	MIDSTREAM	MISTIMING	DICTATION	DIMWITTED
MIGRATION	MINSTRELS	BIRTHMARK	DICTATORS	MILWAUKEE
VIBRATION	AIRSTRIPS	VICTIMISE	MINTJULEP	AIRYFAIRY
MIGRATORY	PINSTRIPE	DISTANCES	RIOTOUSLY	CITYSCAPE
MICROWAVE	FIRSTRATE	DISTENDED	WISTFULLY	CITYOFGOD
BIORHYTHM	KIDSSTUFF	OILTANKER	DISTRUSTS	LILYWHITE
DISSUADED	PIPSQUEAK	FITTINGIN	MISTRUSTS	BICYCLING
DISSUADES	MINTSAUCE	RINTINTIN	KITTIWAKE	BICYCLIST

PIZZICATO	PLEASESIR	SLACKENED	OLUCKYMAN	ALGEBRAIC
FIZZLEOUT	ILLATEASE	CLOCKEDIN	GLADIATOR	BLUEPRINT
ZIGZAGGED	ALPARGATA	BLACKFLAG	FLEDGLING	BLUEGRASS
DIZZINESS	BLEACHING	BLACKFOOT	ALEDJONES	ELDERSHIP
FIZZINESS	GLEANINGS	ALICEFAYE	GLADIOLUS	SLEEPSUIT
PIZZERIAS	ALLANLAMB	CLOCKGOLF	SLIDERULE	ALDERSHOT
LJUBLJANA	BLEAKNESS	BLOCKHEAD	BLEDISLOE	BLUESTEEL
TJUNCTION	ALLATONCE	BLACKHOLE	GLADSTONE	CLIENTELE
UKRAINIAN	ALFAROMEO	ELECTIONS	ALLEMANDE	ALDEBURGH
SKEDADDLE	ALLABOARD	PLUCKIEST	ALIENATED	GLEEFULLY
SKYDIVING	CLOAKROOM	BLACKJACK	ALIENATES	SLEEPWALK
SKYJACKED	ALBATROSS	PLACEKICK	ALTERABLE	FLEETWOOD
SKYJACKER	CLEANSING	BLACKLEGS	ILLEGALLY	ALLEYWAYS
SKIJUMPER	CLEANSERS	BLACKLIST	ALIENATOR	FLUFFIEST
SKULLCAPS	OLFACTORY	BLACKMAIL	ALTERCATE	CLOGDANCE
SKELETONS	ALLBLACKS	PLACEMENT	BLUEPETER	SLUGGARDS
SKILFULLY	CLOBBERED	BLACKMARK	ALLEGEDLY	ELEGIASTS
SKIMPIEST	OLDBAILEY	PLACENAME	BLUEBELLS	ALIGNMENT
SKINHEADS	PLEBEIANS	BLACKNESS	BLUEBEARD	ELEGANTLY
SKINDIVER	CLUBCLASS	SLACKNESS	BLUEBERRY	FLAGEOLET
SKINTIGHT	CLUBHOUSE	ELECTORAL	ELMERFUDD	FLAGPOLES
SKINNIEST	ELABORATE	BLACKPOOL	ALLERGIES	OLIGARCHY
SKINFLINT	ALABASTER	BLACKROBE	FLEESHMAN	ELEGISING
SKINNYDIP	BLOCKADED	ELECTRICS	BLUEWHALE	ILLGOTTEN
SKINNYRIB	BLOCKADES	ELECTRODE	ALPENHORN	FLAGSTAFF
SKIPPERED	GLACIATED	ELECTRIFY	ELSEWHERE	ALIGHTING
SKYROCKET	GLACIATES	BLACKRAIN	BLUEBIRDS	BLIGHTING
SKISUNDAY	ELECTABLE	ELECTRONS	ILLEGIBLE	FLAGSTONE
SKETCHMAP	BLACKARTS	GLYCERINE	ILLEGIBLY	SLIGHTING
SKETCHING	BLACKBEAR	ELECTRESS	ALGERIANS	BLIGHTERS
SKETCHOUT	BLACKBALL	BLACKSWAN	BLUEVINNY	SLIGHTEST
SKITTLING	BLACKBELT	BLACKSPOT	BLUERINSE	ILLHEALTH
SKEWBALDS	ALICEBAND	ELICITING	SLEEPIEST	ALPHABETS
SKEWWHIFF	BLACKBIRD	PLACATING	ALLEVIATE	ALCHEMIST
SKYWALKER	BLACKBURN	ELOCUTION	BLUESKIES	ILLHUMOUR
OKEYDOKEY	BLACKBESS	PLACATORY	BLUEBLOOD	ELKHOUNDS
CLEARANCE	BLACKCAPS	FLUCTUATE	SLEEPLESS	ALEHOUSES
ALMAMATER	PLACECARD	BLOCKVOTE	SLEEKNESS	CLAIMABLE
FLYAGARIC	ELUCIDATE	BLACKWALL	ALTERNATE	ALLIGATOR
ALBANBERG	BLACKENED	BLACKWOOD	SLEEPOVER	CLAIMANTS
BLEASDALE	BLACKEYES	CLOCKWORK	ALLEGORIC	ULTIMATUM
PLEASENCE	FLICKERED	CLOCKWISE	BLUETOOTH	ELLISBELL

ALFIEBASS	SLIMINESS	GLENLIVET	ILLOGICAL	GLORYHOLE
ILLIBERAL	ELIMINATE	BLANDINGS	ALGORITHM	ALARMISTS
ALTIMETER	ALUMINIUM	SLINKIEST	GLOOMIEST	ALTRUISTS
ELLINGTON	FLUMMOXED	PLENTIFUL	ELTONJOHN	CLARKKENT
FLYINGFOX	FLUMMOXES	FLINTLOCK	BLOODLINE	PLURALISM
ALVINHALL	PLIMSOLLS	FLANIMALS	BLOODLESS	PLURALIST
ILLICITLY	GLAMORGAN	BLANDNESS	BLOODLUST	ALFRAMSEY
PLAINJANE	CLAMOROUS	BLINDNESS	ALLOTMENT	GLARINGLY
ALFIEMOON	GLAMOROUS	BLUNTNESS	ALOOFNESS	ALERTNESS
ALLIANCES	BLEMISHED	ALANKNOTT	ELIOTNESS	CLARINETS
PLAINNESS	BLEMISHES	ALANCOREN	ALCOHOLIC	FLAREPATH
CLOISONNE	OLDMASTER	GLENDOWER	ALGONQUIN	FLORISTRY
ELLIPSOID	GLIMPSING	GLENBOGLE	ELBOWROOM	CLERGYMAN
PLAINSONG	FLAMETREE	ALANPRICE	FLUORSPAR	CLERGYMEN
PLAINTIFF	CLAMOURED	ALANFREED	BLOODSHED	GLISSANDO
CLOISTERS	ALANBATES	GLENORCHY	BLOODSHOT	ALLSEATER
PLAINTIVE	ELONGATED	ALANARKIN	FLOORSHOW	OLDSTAGER
ALTITUDES	ELONGATES	ALONGSIDE	ALLOUTWAR	ULLSWATER
CLIJSTERS	ALANPATON	BLINDSIDE	FLOODTIDE	FLASHBACK
FLAKINESS	ULANBATOR	ILLNESSES	ALLOTTING	FLASHBULB
ELALAMEIN	GLENGARRY	BLINDSPOT	FLIPPANCY	ELISABETH
ULULATING	SLINGBACK	SLINGSHOT	FLAPJACKS	FLASHCUBE
ULULATION	CLINICIAN	PLENITUDE	SLOPEARMS	CLOSECALL
FLAMMABLE	BLINDDATE	PLANETARY	SLAPHAPPY	FLASHCARD
CLIMACTIC	BLANKETED	ALANSUGAR	ELEPHANTS	CLOSEDOWN
CLAMPDOWN	BLINKERED	GLANDULAR	SLIPPEDUP	BLUSTERED
CLIMBDOWN	BLUNDERED	LLANDUDNO	FLIPCHART	BLUSTERER
CLAMBERED	PLUNDERED	BLINDWORM	CLIPPINGS	CLUSTERED
GLIMMERED	PLUNDERER	ALONGWITH	FLIPFLOPS	FLUSTERED
PLUMMETED	SLANDERED	ALLOWANCE	ELOPEMENT	GLISTENED
SLUMBERED	SLANDERER	ALLOCATED	CLIPJOINT	PLASTERED
SLUMBERER	PLENTEOUS	ALLOCATES	CLIPBOARD	PLASTERER
CLAMMEDUP	BLINDFOLD	ALLOPATHY	FLYPOSTER	SLUSHFUND
SLIMSHADY	CLINGFILM	ALLOWABLE	SLAPSTICK	BLASPHEME
CLAMMIEST	BLANDFORD	CLEOLAINE	SLOPPYJOE	BLASPHEMY
CLUMSIEST	GLENNFORD	CLEOPATRA	ELOQUENCE	OLDSCHOOL
FLIMSIEST	BLANCHING	BLOODBANK	ALARMBELL	CLASSICAL
PLUMBLINE	CLENCHING	BLOODBATH	GLORYDAYS	BLESSINGS
BLAMELESS	CLINCHING	ALMONDOIL	CLARIFIED	PLASTICKY
ELEMENTAL	FLINCHING	FLUORESCE	CLARIFIES	CLASSIEST
ALLMANNER	CLINCHERS	BLOODFEUD	GLORIFIED	GLOSSIEST
PLUMPNESS	BLANCHETT	FLOODGATE	GLORIFIES	ALLSAINTS

CLOSEKNIT	FLOUNCING	BLOWINGUP	EMBASSIES	IMAGINARY
CLASSLESS	FLOUNDERS	BLOWTORCH	IMPASSIVE	AMPHIBIAN
CLASSMATE	PLOUGHMAN	SLOWCOACH	IMPARTIAL	EMPHASISE
CLOSENESS	PLOUGHMEN	BLOWHOLES	EMBATTLED	EMPIREDAY
BLOSSOMED	SLAUGHTER	FLOWERBED	IMPARTING	IMMINENCE
GLOSSOVER	PLOUGHING	ALLWORTHY	EMACIATED	IMPINGING
PLUSFOURS	SLOUCHING	FLOWERING	AMIDSHIPS	EMPIRICAL
ALMSHOUSE	SLOUCHERS	GLOWERING	IMPEACHED	UMBILICAL
SLUSHPILE	PLAUSIBLE	FLOWERPOT	IMPEACHES	AMBITIOUS
FLESHPOTS	PLAUSIBLY	ALEXHALEY	EMMERDALE	UMBILICUS
CLASSROOM	ALEUTIANS	ALEXPARKS	EMBEDDING	OMNIVORES
ALLSQUARE	CLOUDIEST	ALEXANDER	IMPENDING	IMMIGRANT
ELUSIVELY	FLAUTISTS	ALEXANDRA	EMBERDAYS	EMBITTERS
GLASSWOOL	CLOUDLESS	ALEXANDRE	IMPERFECT	OMNIBUSES
GLASSWARE	CLOUDOVER	FLEXITIME	AMBERGRIS	AMBIGUITY
FLATMATES	FLAUNTING	PLAYMATES	AMNESIACS	AMBIGUOUS
PLUTOCRAT	OLIVEDRAB	PLAYFALSE	IMMEDIACY	SMOKELESS
ALLTICKET	CLIVEDUNN	PLAYEDOUT	IMBECILES	SMELLARAT
CLUTTERED	ILOVELUCY	PLAYTHING	IMBECILIC	SMALLARMS
FLATTENED	CLEVELAND	PLAYBILLS	IMMEDIATE	SMALLBEER
FLATTERED	ELEVENSES	PLAYDIRTY	IMPERIOUS	IMPLICATE
FLATTERER	CLIVEOWEN	PLAYALONG	IMPELLING	IMPLODING
FLUTTERED	SLAVERING	CLAYMORES	IMPELLERS	AMPLIFIED
GLITTERED	CLEVEREST	PLAYHOUSE	EMBELLISH	AMPLIFIER
SLITHERED	SLAVISHLY	LLOYDPACK	IMMENSELY	AMPLIFIES
SLATTERNS	ELEVATING	PLAYGROUP	AMBERSONS	EMOLLIENT
CLOTHEARS	ELEVATION	PLAYFULLY	AMPERSAND	SMELLIEST
CLUTCHBAG	ELEVATORS	PLAYBYEAR	IMMERSING	EMOLUMENT
CLUTCHING	ELEVATORY	BLIZZARDS	IMMERSION	IMPLEMENT
CLOTHIERS	FLAVOURED	ELIZABETH	IMMENSITY	IMPLANTED
FLOTILLAS	SLIVOVITZ	IMBALANCE	AMNESTIES	IMPLORING
BLATANTLY	BLOWNAWAY	EMBARGOED	IMPETUOUS	AMBLESIDE
GLUTINOUS	SLOWMARCH	EMBARGOES	EMBEZZLED	IMPLOSION
PLUTONIUM	BLOWLAMPS	EMPATHISE	EMBEZZLER	AMPLITUDE
PLATFORMS	FLYWHEELS	IMPATIENS	EMBEZZLES	OMELETTES
FLATBREAD	BLOWAFUSE	IMPATIENT	EMIGRATED	SMALLTALK
FLATBROKE	CLOWNFISH	IMRANKHAN	EMIGRATES	SMALLTIME
PLATITUDE	FLOWCHART	EMBARKING	EMIGRANTS	EMULATING
FLOTATION	BLOWPIPES	EMBALMING	AMUGSGAME	EMULATION
ALLTHUMBS	FLYWEIGHT	EMBALMERS	SMUGGLING	EMULATORS
BLUTWURST	PLOWRIGHT	IMPAIRING	SMUGGLERS	SMALLTOWN
CLOUDBASE	BLOWFLIES	EMBARRASS	IMAGINING	EMPLOYEES

EMPLOYING	EMERGENCY	IMPULSIVE	UNMARRIED	SNODGRASS
EMPLOYERS	SMARTENED	AMAZEMENT	ENPASSANT	ANODISING
EMILEZOLA	IMBROGLIO	AMAZONIAN	INPASSING	ANTENATAL
EMBLAZONS	IMBRUGLIA	AMAZINGLY	UNEARTHED	ANTEDATED
AMINOACID	AMORPHOUS	ONBALANCE	INFANTILE	ANTEDATES
AMENDABLE	EMBROIDER	UNBALANCE	UNEARTHLY	UNRELATED
AMENDMENT	EMBROILED	UNDAMAGED	UNFASTENS	INTERALIA
EMINENTLY	UMBRELLAS	INCAPABLE	INCAUTION	INDEFAULT
AMENITIES	AMARYLLIS	UNFANCIED	ENRAPTURE	UNTENABLE
EMANATING	AMORALITY	ANTARCTIC	INTATTERS	UNDERARMS
EMANATION	IMPROMPTU	ENHANCING	UNNATURAL	INTERACTS
OMINOUSLY	SMARTNESS	ANTANDDEC	ANDALUSIA	UNDERBIDS
IMMOLATED	EMBRYONIC	INLANDSEA	ANNAPURNA	ENSEMBLES
IMMOLATES	EMPRESSES	ONEANDALL	UNVARYING	INTERBRED
IMMOVABLE	IMPRESSED	ENTANGLED	INABADWAY	ENGELBERT
IMPOTENCE	IMPRESSES	UNTANGLED	INABIGWAY	UNDERCOAT
EMPOWERED	IMPRISONS	UNTANGLES	INEBRIATE	INTERCEDE
IMMODESTY	EMBRASURE	ENLARGING	INEBRIETY	ANGELCAKE
SMOOCHING	AMOROUSLY	ENDANGERS	INABILITY	UNWELCOME
SMOOTHING	IMPROVING	ENLARGERS	KNEBWORTH	UNDERCOOK
SMOOTHEST	IMPROVERS	INFASHION	UNABASHED	INTERCEPT
IMPOLITIC	IMPROVISE	INHABITED	INKBOTTLE	INNERCITY
IMNOANGEL	EMISSIONS	ENFAMILLE	KNOCKBACK	INTERCITY
IMPOUNDED	AMUSEMENT	INPATIENT	UNICYCLES	UNDERDOGS
EMFORSTER	AMOSBURKE	SNEAKIEST	KNOCKDOWN	INTENDING
EMBOSSING	SMOTHERED	ANNALISTS	UNSCREWED	UNBENDING
JMCOETZEE	UMPTEENTH	UNMASKING	INSCRIBED	UNDERDONE
IMPORTANT	EMPTINESS	UNPACKING	INSCRIBER	UNHEEDING
IMPORTING	EMOTIONAL	ENTAILING	INSCRIBES	INGENERAL
IMPORTUNE	AMSTERDAM	UNFAILING	ANSCHLUSS	INDECENCY
IMPORTERS	IMITATING	UNDAUNTED	INOCULATE	INFERENCE
IMPOSTORS	IMITATION	UNTAINTED	ENACTMENT	ANGELEYES
SMARTALEC	IMITATORS	UNCANNILY	ANACONDAS	ANTECEDES
IMPROBITY	IMITATIVE	INEARNEST	ENSCONCED	INTERESTS
AMERICANA	AMBULANCE	INHARNESS	UNSCENTED	INTERFACE
AMERICANO	IMMUTABLE	INCARNATE	ANECDOTAL	UNDERFELT
AMERICANS	SMOULDERS	ANNAPOLIS	ANECDOTES	UNDERFUND
EMBRACING	IMPUDENCE	ANYAMOUNT	INACORNER	UNDERFOOT
SMARTCARD	AMBUSHING	UNSAVOURY	UNSCATHED	INTERFERE
IMPRECISE	IMMUNISED	UNHAPPIER	INADVANCE	UNDERFIRE
IMPRUDENT	IMMUNISES	UNHAPPILY	UNADOPTED	ANGELFISH
EMERGENCE	OMBUDSMAN	ANNAFRIEL	UNADORNED	UNSELFISH

INTERFLUG	INVERNESS	INVERSION	INVENTIVE	ONTHEMEND
UNDERGRAD	INDEMNITY	INSENSATE	UNDERUSED	INTHEMOOD
INVEIGLED	UNBEKNOWN	INTENSITY	UNSECURED	ONTHEMOVE
INVEIGLER	ANTELOPES	INTENSIVE	INGENUITY	ONTHINICE
INVEIGLES	ENVELOPED	ANCESTRAL	INGENUOUS	ENCHANTED
UNDERGOES	ENVELOPES	INNERTUBE	INSERVICE	ENCHANTER
ONCEAGAIN	ANAEROBIC	INTESTACY	INTERVIEW	UNCHANGED
UNDERGONE	UNDEROATH	UNSETTLED	INTERVALS	ONTHENAIL
ENMESHING	INDECORUM	UNSETTLES	INTERVENE	ONTHENOSE
UNDERHAND	INTERPLAY	ENTERTAIN	UNNERVING	INTHENAVY
INHERITED	UNDERPLAY	UNCERTAIN	ENDEAVOUR	ENTHRONED
UNDECIDED	INTERPRET	UNDERTAKE	UNDERWEAR	INTHEPINK
UNDEFINED	UNDERPAID	INFERTILE	UNDERWENT	ANCHORMAN
UNDESIRED	UNDERPINS	INDENTING	UNDERWOOD	ONTHEROAD
UNMERITED	INTERPOSE	INFECTING	INEFFABLE	ANCHORLEG
UNREFINED	UNDERPASS	INFESTING	UNIFORMED	UNCHARTED
KNEEHIGHS	UNHELPFUL	INGESTING	UNIFORMLY	ANCHORAGE
ENTERITIS	UNLEARNED	INJECTING	ENIGMATIC	ANCHORING
INDELIBLE	ANNEGREGG	INSERTING	SNIGGERED	ONTHERISE
INDELIBLY	ANNEFRANK	INTESTINE	SNIGGERER	ANCHORITE
INHERITOR	ENDEARING	INVENTING	SNUGGLEUP	ONTHESIDE
INFERIORS	INFERRING	INVERTING	KNIGHTLEY	INTHESWIM
INGENIOUS	INTERRING	INVESTING	KNIGHTING	ENTHUSING
INTERJECT	INTERRUPT	UNDERTONE	INTHEBUFF	ONTHESPOT
INTELLECT	INTEGRATE	UNRESTING	ONTHEBALL	INTHESOUP
INTERLACE	INTEGRITY	INCEPTION	ONTHEBONE	ONTHETROT
INTERLOCK	UNDERRATE	INFECTION	UNCHECKED	ONTHETOWN
INTERLUDE	UNDERSEAL	INGESTION	INTHECART	ANCHOVIES
UNHEALTHY	INTERSECT	INJECTION	INTHECLUB	ONTHEWANE
ANNEALING	UNDERSIDE	INSERTION	INTHEDOCK	ONTHEWING
INTERLINK	UNLEASHED	INTENTION	ONTHEDOLE	INTHEWARS
UNDERLINE	UNLEASHES	INVENTION	INTHEDARK	ENVISAGED
UNDERLING	INTENSIFY	UNDERTOOK	ONTHEHOOF	ENVISAGES
UNFEELING	ONMESSAGE	ANCESTORS	ONTHEHORN	INDICATED
UNVEILING	UNDERSAIL	INDENTURE	ONTHEHOUR	INDICATES
INTERLOPE	INTENSELY	INJECTORS	ENSHRINED	INTIMATES
INTERMENT	INVERSELY	INVENTORS	UNCHAINED	ANTIPATHY
UNDERMINE	UNDERSELL	INVENTORY	INTHEKNOW	INDICATOR
INNERMOST	UNDERSOLD	INVESTORS	ENCHILADA	ANTIPASTO
INTERNEES	INCENSING	INTESTATE	ANTHOLOGY	ENCIRCLED
INDEMNIFY	INCESSANT	INCENTIVE	INTHELOOP	ENCIRCLES
INTERNING	UNCEASING	INVECTIVE	INTHEMAIN	INSINCERE

ANTIOCHUS	UNZIPPING	UNPLANNED	ANGORACAT	UNWORLDLY
UNWINDING	ANXIETIES	INCLINING	INSOFARAS	ENNOBLING
UNMINDFUL	ONTIPTOES	INGLENOOK	ANNOYANCE	ENROLLING
INCIDENCE	INJIGTIME	UNALLOYED	ANNOTATED	UNCOILING
INDIGENCE	ANOINTING	UNCLIPPED	ANNOTATES	INCOMMODE
ENLIVENED	ENLISTING	UNCLASPED	INNOVATED	ENDOWMENT
INSIDELEG	INDICTING	INELASTIC	INNOVATES	ENJOYMENT
INSIDEJOB	INSISTENT	ENDLESSLY	ENJOYABLE	ENROLMENT
ENGINEERS	INSISTING	ANALYSING	ENJOYABLY	INFORMANT
INSIDEOUT	UNWITTING	ENCLOSING	ANNOTATOR	INFORMING
ENLIGHTEN	UNDILUTED	INCLUSION	INNOVATOR	INFORMERS
ANNIEHALL	ANXIOUSLY	ENCLOSURE	UNDOUBTED	INSOMNIAC
UNSIGHTLY	ANTIQUARY	INCLUSIVE	ENTOMBING	ANNOUNCED
ANTIPHONY	ANTIQUITY	UNCLOTHED	UNTOUCHED	ANNOUNCER
ENRICHING	INSINUATE	INFLATING	ENFORCING	ANNOUNCES
INHIBITED	SNAKEBITE	INFLATION	INVOICING	ENCOUNTER
UNDIVIDED	INNKEEPER	ONSLAUGHT	INCONCERT	UNBOUNDED
UNLIMITED	SNAKEEYES	UNIMPEDED	SNOOPDOGG	UNFOUNDED
UNVISITED	INUKTITUT	ANOMALIES	ONIONDOME	INCOGNITO
INSIPIDLY	UNSKILLED	ENAMELLED	ENFOLDING	ENDOMORPH
INVISIBLE	UNSKILFUL	UNSMILING	UNFOLDING	UNCOUPLED
INVISIBLY	SNAKESKIN	ANOMALOUS	UNLOADING	UNCOUPLES
INCIPIENT	UNCLEBUCK	MNEMONICS	INCOMETAX	ENDORPHIN
INCISIONS	INFLICTED	ENUMERATE	INDOLENCE	ENCOMPASS
INHIBITOR	UNBLOCKED	INAMORATA	INNOCENCE	INCORRECT
INSIDIOUS	UNELECTED	ANIMOSITY	INSOLENCE	UNWORRIED
INVIDIOUS	ANGLICISE	ANIMATING	SNOOKERED	ENCOURAGE
ENTITLING	ANGLICISM	ANIMATION	UNCOVERED	ENTOURAGE
UNWILLING	INCLUDING	ANIMATORS	INDONESIA	INTOORBIT
ANCILLARY	INFLUENCE	ENAMOURED	INNOCENTS	ONYOUROWN
INVIOLATE	UNALTERED	INUNDATED	UNIONFLAG	ENDORSING
SNAILMAIL	ANALGESIA	INUNDATES	INDOCHINA	ENDORSERS
INFIRMARY	ANALGESIC	INANYCASE	ONHOLIDAY	UNBOLTING
INFIRMITY	INFLUENZA	UNINVITED	UNIONISED	INCONTROL
INDIANINK	ANALOGIES	ENUNCIATE	UNNOTICED	ANGOSTURA
INDIGNANT	UNALIGNED	ANONYMITY	SNOOTIEST	UNPOPULAR
UNPINNING	UNCLOGGED	INANIMATE	UNIONISTS	UNFOCUSED
INDIGNITY	UNPLUGGED	UNANIMITY	UNIONJACK	INSOLUBLE
ANTIDOTAL	INELEGANT	ANONYMOUS	UNCORKING	INNOCUOUS
ANTIDOTES	ANALOGOUS	UNANIMOUS	UNHOOKING	INSOLVENT
ANTIPODES	UNCLAIMED	UNINJURED	UNLOCKING	KNAPSACKS
ANTIGONUS	INCLEMENT	UNINSURED	ONLOOKERS	INSPECTED

INAPICKLE	ENTRANCED	INSTEADOF	INJURIOUS	SNOWDONIA
INSPECTOR	ENTRANCES	INSTIGATE	UNBUCKLED	SNOWBOUND
ANOPHELES	INFRINGED	SNATCHING	UNBUCKLES	SNOWBOARD
SNAPPEDUP	INFRINGES	UNETHICAL	UNLUCKIER	SNOWGOOSE
SNAPSHOTS	UNBRANDED	INSTALLED	UNLUCKILY	SNOWBOOTS
SNAPPIEST	INTRANSIT	INSTILLED	ANNULLING	SNOWDRIFT
UNOPPOSED	INTRINSIC	ANITALOOS	UNCURLING	ANSWERING
INSPIRING	ANGRINESS	ANATOMIST	UNFURLING	SNOWDROPS
UNSPARING	INERTNESS	ONSTANDBY	ANNULMENT	ENTWISTLE
INSPITEOF	ENTRENOUS	INSTANTLY	UNTUTORED	SNOWSTORM
ENTREATED	ENTRAPPED	INSTINCTS	PNEUMONIA	UNEXPIRED
INCREASED	ENWRAPPED	UNITARIAN	ONPURPOSE	UNEXPOSED
INCREASES	UNWRAPPED	UNITTRUST	ENQUIRIES	ANDYHARDY
UNTREATED	ENCRUSTED	INSTITUTE	UNGUARDED	ANDYPANDY
INORGANIC	ENGROSSED	INSTRUCTS	UNHURRIED	UNTYPICAL
ENTRECHAT	ENTRUSTED	ANITAWARD	ENQUIRING	GOBANANAS
INTRICACY	UNDRESSED	ENDURANCE	INCURRING	ROTAVATED
ANDROCLES	UNDRESSES	INSURANCE	ENQUIRERS	ROTAVATES
ENTRECOTE	INTRUSION	INCUBATED	INQUORATE	SODAWATER
INTRICATE	INTRUSIVE	INCUBATES	ANGUISHED	TOMAHAWKS
INTRODUCE	UNWRITTEN	INSULATED	INCURSION	LOSALAMOS
UNBRIDLED	INWRITING	INSULATES	INJUSTICE	ROTAVATOR
UNTRODDEN	ONDRAUGHT	UNDULATED	ANNUITIES	BONAPARTE
INTRUDING	INTROUBLE	UNDULATES	INSULTING	NORABATTY
INTRUDERS	ENGRAVING	UNGULATES	UNBUTTONS	POLARBEAR
SNAREDRUM	ENGRAVERS	PNEUMATIC	INDUCTION	DONALBAIN
ENERGETIC	INTROVERT	ENDURABLE	INTUITION	ROYALBLUE
INARREARS	INPRIVATE	INCURABLE	INTUITIVE	LOCALCALL
INPROFILE	ANDREWRAY	INCUBATOR	INAUGURAL	ROMANCING
ENTRYFORM	UNCROWNED	INSULATOR	INAVACUUM	COWARDICE
ANDREGIDE	UNASHAMED	INCUMBENT	SNIVELLED	DONALDSON
INTRIGUED	ANASTACIA	INCULCATE	SNIVELLER	COLANDERS
INTRIGUES	ANASTASIA	UNBURDENS	UNIVERSAL	POMANDERS
ANDROGYNY	UNUSUALLY	UNRUFFLED	SNOWBALLS	FORAGECAP
ANARCHISM	INESSENCE	ENGULFING	SNOWSCAPE	DONAMECHE
ANARCHIST	INNSBRUCK	INDULGENT	KNOWLEDGE	DONATELLA
ENERGISED	ONASTRING	INDULGING	SNOWSHOES	DONATELLO
ENERGISES	UNASTUBBS	INSURGENT	SNOWWHITE	ROSACEOUS
INGRAINED	INITIATED	UNMUSICAL	SNOWFLAKE	ROYALGALA
UNTRAINED	INITIATES	INAUDIBLE	INSWINGER	WOMANHOOD
ANDROMEDA	INITIALLY	INFURIATE	KNOWINGLY	LOCALHERO
INCREMENT	INITIATOR	INCURIOUS	ENTWINING	BOTANICAL

LOCALISED	MONASTERY	COMBATIVE	CONCERNED	GOLDMEDAL
LOCALISES	VOLAUVENT	BOMBAYMIX	CONCERTED	ROADMETAL
MORALISED	TODAYWEEK	TOMBOYISH	CONCURRED	SOLDIERED
MORALISER	BOTANYBAY	BOMBAZINE	CONCERTOS	SOLDIERLY
MORALISES	PORBEAGLE	TOMCLANCY	DONCARLOS	SOLDIERON
POLARISED	BOBBEAMON	CONCEALED	SORCERERS	ROADTESTS
POLARISES	BOBBYBALL	CONCEALER	SORCERESS	DOODLEBUG
VOCALISED	GORBACHEV	CONCLAVES	CONCUSSED	TOADEGREE
VOCALISES	HOLBYCITY	LONCHANEY	DONCASTER	WOODCHUCK
WOMANISER	FORBIDDEN	ROYCLARKE	WORCESTER	WOODSHEDS
LOGARITHM	FOBBEDOFF	GONCHAROV	VOUCHSAFE	FOODCHAIN
MOGADISHU	MORBIDITY	COACHBOLT	BOSCASTLE	GOLDFINCH
BOTANISTS	BOBBLEHAT	CONCUBINE	CONCISELY	GOLDMINER
LOYALISTS	DOUBLEACT	TOUCHBASE	ROYCASTLE	GOODWIVES
MORALISTS	DOUBLEBED	CONCOCTED	MOCCASINS	GOODNIGHT
ROYALISTS	DOUBLETOP	JOECOCKER	TORCHSONG	HOODWINKS
VOCALISTS	SOMBREROS	BOCCACCIO	BOYCOTTED	GOLDFIELD
VOTARISTS	SOUBRETTE	JOYCECARY	COACHTRIP	ROADBLOCK
BODACIOUS	DOUBLEDUP	CONCEDING	TOUCHTONE	WOODBLOCK
VORACIOUS	GOBBLEDUP	TOUCHDOWN	TOUCHTYPE	GONDOLIER
ROGANJOSH	DOUBTFIRE	BOXCLEVER	COACHTOUR	GOLDPLATE
GOWALKIES	JOEBUGNER	CONCIERGE	LOWCHURCH	CONDEMNED
WOMANKIND	WOBBEGONG	COUCHETTE	CONCLUDED	GOLDAMEIR
TOTALLING	WOEBEGONE	CONCEITED	CONCLUDES	CONDIMENT
ROYALMAIL	BOMBSHELL	CONCEIVED	CONCOURSE	VOLDEMORT
ROYALMILE	POTBOILER	CONCEIVES	TOMCRUISE	GOLDSMITH
GODALMING	WOBBLIEST	COACHLOAD	CONCAVITY	WORDSMITH
TOMARNOLD	DOUBTLESS	DOGCOLLAR	TOUCHWOOD	JORDANIAN
ROMANNOSE	COMBINING	PORCELAIN	COACHWORK	CONDENSED
MORATORIA	JOEBLOGGS	TOUCHLINE	WOODLANDS	CONDENSER
ROMANROAD	DOUBLOONS	FORCEMEAT	GOLDWATER	CONDENSES
SODABREAD	BOMBSQUAD	LOWCOMEDY	TOLDTALES	CORDONOFF
POLARSTAR	BOMBARDED	VOICEMAIL	TOPDRAWER	GOLDENAGE
JOHANSSON	ROBBERIES	ROSCOMMON	CORDIALLY	CONDONING
LOGANSRUN	BOMBPROOF	BOXCAMERA	LORDMAYOR	GOLDENBOY
POTASSIUM	SOUBIROUS	VOLCANOES	TODDCARTY	GOLDENROD
ROMANTICS	BOMBASTIC	TOSCANINI	FOODVALUE	LONDONERS
LOYALTIES	BOOBYTRAP	COLCANNON	CONDUCTED	DOWDINESS
ROYALTIES	WOEBETIDE	JOBCENTRE	WOODSCREW	MOODINESS
LOCALTIME	COMBATANT	VOICEOVER	CONDUCTOR	ROWDINESS
GOKARTING	COMBATING	PORCUPINE	CONDUCIVE	WORDINESS
FORASTART	TOMBSTONE	CONCORDAT	NODDEDOFF	GOLDENEYE

GOODLOSER	FORENAMES	FOREFFECT	COVERLETS	GOBERSERK
ROADMOVIE	HOMEMAKER	POKERFACE	DOBERMANN	HOMESTEAD
ROADTORIO	MODERATED	COMEOFAGE	HONEYMOON	HONEYTRAP
ROADWORKS	MODERATES	COMEOFFIT	TOBERMORY	POTENTIAL
GOLDCOAST	NOTEPAPER	WOMENFOLK	KOREANWAR	ROSENTHAL
ROADHOUSE	ROSEWATER	FOREIGNER	SOLEMNIFY	NOVELTIES
WOODHOUSE	TOLERATED	COMEAGAIN	GOVERNING	LOWESTOFT
WOODLOUSE	TOLERATES	HOMEAGAIN	HOLEINONE	FORESTALL
LORDNORTH	HOPELANGE	LOHENGRIN	GOVERNORS	GOGETTING
LOUDMOUTH	POLEVAULT	GOBEGGING	GOVERNESS	LODESTONE
COLDCREAM	TOLERABLE	LOVECHILD	MODERNISE	MOLESTING
VORDERMAN	TOLERABLY	TOWERHILL	MODERNISM	DOGEATDOG
GOODGRIEF	COLERAINE	BONECHINA	MODERNIST	ROBERTSON
POWDERKEG	FOREWARNS	JOSEPHINE	SOLEMNISE	FORESTERS
WOODGREEN	DODECAGON	SOMETHING	COVERNOTE	GOGETTERS
ROADTRAIN	MODERATOR	FORESHORE	MODERNITY	LOVESTORY
COLDFRAME	COVENANTS	SOMEWHERE	SOLEMNITY	MOMENTARY
BORDERING	FORECASTS	GOREVIDAL	ROSEROYCE	NONENTITY
COLDFRONT	FORETASTE	POLEMICAL	SOLENOIDS	POTENTATE
PONDERING	COTEDAZUR	SOMETIMES	ROLEMODEL	MOMENTOUS
POWDERING	HONEYBEAR	COLERIDGE	HOMEMOVIE	MOLECULAR
SOLDERING	POWERBOAT	FORESIGHT	NOTEBOOKS	POKEFUNAT
WONDERING	MONEYBAGS	MOLEHILLS	FOREGOING	MOLECULES
GOLDFRAPP	BOWERBIRD	COMEDIANS	LOSECOUNT	DOLEFULLY
GOLDCREST	ROSENBERG	HOTELIERS	SOREPOINT	HOPEFULLY
PONDEROSA	COMEABOUT	LONELIEST	FORECOURT	HOMEGUARD
PONDEROUS	HONEYCOMB	LOVELIEST	WODEHOUSE	COWESWEEK
WONDERFUL	LOWERCASE	NOVELISTS	POWERPLAY	GOBETWEEN
GODDESSES	LOWERDECK	COMECLEAN	POWERPACK	HOMEOWNER
ROADSTEAD	POKERDICE	SOMEPLACE	LOVEAPPLE	ROSEBYRNE
WOODSTOCK	COVERDALE	NOSEBLEED	TOTEMPOLE	WOLFPACKS
FOODSTUFF	TOREADORS	COMEALONG	HOVERPORT	WOLFSBANE
GOLDSTEIN	COHERENCE	DOWELLING	ROKERPARK	CONFUCIUS
WOODSTAIN	BONEHEADS	HOMEALONE	HOMEOPATH	CONFIDANT
CONDITION	SOVEREIGN	MODELLING	FOREFRONT	CONFIDENT
TOADSTOOL	FORETELLS	TOWELLING	VOYEURISM	CONFIDING
COLDSTORE	FOREBEARS	YODELLING	HOMETRUTH	COFFEEBAR
ROADSTERS	LOSEHEART	BOWESLYON	NOREGRETS	COFFEEPOT
WOODNYMPH	MOVEMENTS	MODELLERS	HOMEGROWN	COIFFEURS
MORECAMBE	NOVELETTE	YODELLERS	JOEBROWN	COIFFEUSE
LOVEMATCH	COVEREDUP	FORECLOSE	WOMENSLIB	CONFIGURE
TOLERANCE	SOBEREDUP	POWERLESS	DOVERSOLE	FORFEITED

TOPFLIGHT	LONGSIGHT	TOTHEBONE	NOKIDDING	IONIANSEA
GOLFLINKS	NOTGUILTY	SOPHOCLES	POLICECAR	MONITORED
BOYFRIEND	DOLGELLAU	TOTHECORE	POLICEMAN	SOLILOQUY
CONFLICTS	MONGOLIAN	NOAHBEERY	POLICEMEN	LOWIMPACT
BOWFINGER	COAGULANT	TOTHEFORE	POLICEBOX	TOPIARIST
CONFINING	BOBGELDOF	POTHOLING	POLICEDOG	GOMISSING
GOOFINESS	CONGOLESE	COPHOLDOF	DOMINEERS	LOGISTICS
WOLFHOUND	COAGULATE	POTHOLERS	POLITESSE	SOCIETIES
CONFRONTS	CONGENIAL	SOPHOMORE	DONIZETTI	COPIOUSLY
COMFORTED	ROUGHNECK	COCHINEAL	BOXINGDAY	CODIFYING
COMFORTER	LONGINGLY	FOXHUNTER	COPINGSAW	MODIFYING
CONFERRED	FOGGINESS	MOBHANDED	WOKINGHAM	NOTIFYING
CONFIRMED	PODGINESS	BOTHERING	MOVIEGOER	CONJUGATE
CONFORMED	ROUGHNESS	MOTHERING	SOLIDGOLD	CONJURING
GODFORBID	SOGGINESS	ROCHESTER	BONINGTON	CONJURERS
NOSFERATU	TOUGHNESS	SOPHISTER	LOVINGCUP	CONJUREUP
CONFESSED	DOUGHNUTS	SOPHISTRY	NOHIGHWAY	FOLKDANCE
CONFESSES	FOXGLOVES	FOXHOUNDS	GOLIGHTLY	DOCKLANDS
CONFUSING	MONGOOSES	HOTHOUSES	POLISHING	BOOKMAKER
CONFESSOR	BOYGEORGE	RONHOWARD	ROBINHOOD	POCKMARKS
CONFUSION	LONGJOHNS	DOMINANCE	ROXIEHART	COCKTAILS
GODFATHER	LONGHOUSE	COGITATED	DOMINICAN	CORKSCREW
CONFOUNDS	LONGBOATS	COGITATES	HOMICIDAL	COCKSCOMB
COIFFURED	CONGEREEL	DOMINATED	POLITICAL	COCKEDHAT
POIGNANCY	FORGERIES	DOMINATES	MOBILISED	POLKADOTS
CONGEALED	CONGESTED	MOTIVATED	MOBILISES	WORKEDOUT
LONGFACED	ROUGHSHOD	MOTIVATES	SOLICITED	WORKBENCH
LONGRANGE	LONGITUDE	NOMINATED	DOMINIONS	ZOOKEEPER
HOBGOBLIN	FORGOTTEN	NOMINATES	LOGICIANS	ROCKMELON
DODGEBALL	FOUGHTOFF	FOLICACID	LOUISIANA	LOOKAFTER
ROUGHCAST	DOUGHTILY	COMICALLY	POSITIONS	WORKOFART
DODGECITY	SONGSTERS	LOGICALLY	SOLICITOR	WORKSHEET
COUGHDROP	FORGETFUL	MONICAALI	NOVITIATE	BOOKSHELF
ROUGHENED	SOUGHTOUT	NOMINALLY	SOCIOLOGY	COOKCHILL
TOUGHENED	CONGRUENT	TOPICALLY	COTILLION	COCKAHOOP
CONGLETON	CONGRUITY	MOTIVATOR	SOCIALISE	MONKSHOOD
GOGGLEBOX	FORGIVING	NOMINATOR	SOCIALISM	BOOKSHOPS
LOUGEHRIG	LONGEVITY	SOLITAIRE	SOCIALIST	LOOKSHARP
LONGCHAMP	SONGCYCLE	ROSINANTE	JOVIALITY	YORKSHIRE
ROUGHHEWN	HOTHEADED	SONICBOOM	SOCIALITE	COCKFIGHT
SONGBIRDS	MOTHEATEN	POLITBURO	KOFIANNAN	WORKPLACE
ROUGHIDEA	MOTHBALLS	ROBINCOOK	CORIANDER	ROCKSLIDE

LOOKALIKE	LOWLOADER	COOLWORLD	FOLLOWERS	MORMONISM
BOOKPLATE	TOLLGATES	GOALMOUTH	VOLLEYING	ROOMINESS
LOCKSMITH	TOOLMAKER	GOALPOSTS	NOFLYZONE	COMMUNITY
LOOKINGAT	POLLYANNA	TOLLBOOTH	DOOMWATCH	COSMONAUT
DOGKENNEL	HOLLYAIRD	WOOLWORTH	ROOMMATES	BOBMARLEY
BOOKINGIN	COLLEAGUE	COLLAPSED	WORMEATEN	DOCMARTIN
COCKINESS	KOALABEAR	COLLAPSES	DORMOBILE	BOOMERANG
COCKROACH	COLLECTED	LOLLOPING	COMMODORE	CORMORANT
WORKFORCE	FOLLICLES	LOLLIPOPS	COMMODITY	COMMISSAR
BOOKTOKEN	ZOELUCKER	BOWLERHAT	NORMAJEAN	FORMYSINS
HOOKNOSED	COLLECTOR	FORLORNLY	NOSMOKING	COMMITTAL
TOOKCOVER	BOILEDEGG	COLLARING	DONMCLEAN	COSMETICS
FOLKLORIC	ROALDDAHL	HOLLERING	SOMMELIER	COMMITTED
ROCKSOLID	RODLIDDLE	TOBLERONE	COSMOLOGY	COMMITTEE
BOOKWORMS	COLLIDING	FOOLPROOF	FORMULAIC	GODMOTHER
LOCKHORNS	COLLUDING	BOYLESLAW	BOOMSLANG	DOTMATRIX
COOKHOUSE	POULTERER	FOYLESWAR	FORMALISE	COMMUTING
MONKHOUSE	MOLLIFIED	COALESCED	FORMALISM	COMMOTION
WORKHORSE	MOLLIFIES	COALESCES	FORMALIST	FORMATION
WORKHOUSE	WORLDFAIR	FOOLISHLY	NORMALISE	COMMUTERS
WORKSPACE	COLLEGIAN	JOYLESSLY	FORMALITY	DORMITORY
GORKYPARK	BOWLEGGED	WORLDSEND	FORMULATE	DOGMATISM
YOMKIPPUR	FOOLSGOLD	COLLISION	NORMALITY	DOGMATIST
ROOKERIES	GOOLAGONG	COLLUSION	NONMEMBER	FORMATIVE
COCKERELL	HOOLIGANS	TOILETBAG	COMMONLAW	GOINGAWAY
COCKERELS	ZOOLOGIST	DOOLITTLE	COMMANDED	YOUNGADAM
COCKYSJOY	HOLLYHOCK	COLLATING	COMMANDER	DOWNWARDS
ROCKETMAN	COALMINER	POLLUTANT	COMMENCED	JOHNCANDY
COCKATIEL	MOULDINGS	POLLUTING	COMMENCES	JOHNEALES
WORKETHIC	COALFIELD	COALITION	COMMENDED	JOHNOATES
BOOKSTALL	NOTLIKELY	COLLATION	COMMENTED	MOONFACED
BOOKSTAND	FOOLSMATE	POLLUTION	JOEMANGEL	MOONRAKER
HONKYTONK	MOLLYMAWK	POLLSTERS	TORMENTED	NOTNEARLY
POCKETING	HOLLANDER	POLLUTERS	COMMUNING	FOUNTAINS
ROCKETING	ZOOLANDER	SOULMUSIC	COMMANDOS	JOHNWAYNE
COCKATOOS	TOMLINSON	SOULFULLY	COMMUNION	MOUNTAINS
COOKSTOUR	GODLINESS	WORLDVIEW	NORMANTON	JOHNMAJOR
POCKETFUL	LOWLINESS	BOULEVARD	TORMENTOR	GOINGBACK
FOLKMUSIC	POLLINATE	WORLDWIDE	COMMONERS	HOBNOBBED
JOCKEYCAP	ROLLINGUP	FOLLOWING	COMMUNISM	SONNYBONO
JOCKEYING	MOOLOOLAH	BOLLYWOOD	COMMUNIST	SOUNDBITE
FOOLHARDY	HOLLYOAKS	HOLLYWOOD	FOAMINESS	CONNECTED

POUNDCAKE	JOHNMILLS	ROUNDSMEN	TOXOPHILY	MOTOCROSS
DOWNSCALE	BOUNTIFUL	YOUNGSTER	MOTORHOME	COLOURFUL
CONNECTOR	JOANALLEN	COGNISANT	HOMOPHONE	TOMORROWS
MOONSCAPE	LORNALUFT	JOHNSTEED	GONOWHERE	MOTORSHOW
TOWNSCAPE	FOUNDLING	SONNETEER	POLOSHIRT	COLOSSEUM
TOANICETY	SOMNOLENT	DOWNSTAGE	SOLOWHIST	POGOSTICK
WONNACOTT	TOWNCLERK	ROUNDTRIP	COLONISED	NOCONTEST
TORNADOES	BOUNDLESS	MOONSTONE	COLONISES	MONOCULAR
JOHNADAMS	COUNTLESS	COGNITION	DOLOMITES	GOFORWARD
POINTDUTY	POINTLESS	YOUNGTURK	MOTORISED	ROBOTWARS
COUNTDOWN	SOUNDLESS	COGNITIVE	TOMOLIVER	MOTORWAYS
LOUNGEBAR	LOINCLOTH	CONNAUGHT	MONOLITHS	COMPLAINS
ROUNDELAY	CORNFLOUR	CONNIVING	HONORIFIC	COMPLAINT
BOUNDERBY	GOINGLIVE	CONNIVERS	SOPORIFIC	JOEPUBLIC
COUNTERED	BOXNUMBER	DOINGWELL	COLONIALS	POPPYCOCK
FOUNDERED	YOUNAMEIT	DOWNSWING	RODOFIRON	HOPPICKER
POINTEDLY	CONNEMARA	SOUNDWAVE	COLONISTS	COMPACTOR
MOONBEAMS	JOHNSMITH	JOHNTYLER	MOTORISTS	TORPEDOED
MOUNTETNA	JOHNINMAN	JOHNLYDON	NOTORIETY	TORPEDOES
JOHNKEATS	DOWNUNDER	JOHNNYBOY	OOLOGISTS	TOLPUDDLE
BOUNTEOUS	COININGIT	LOGOMACHY	NOTORIOUS	TORPIDITY
ROUNDEDUP	JOININGIN	MONOMANIA	GOTOSLEEP	POMPADOUR
TOWNSFOLK	ROUNDNESS	NOVOCAINE	MONOPLANE	COUPDETAT
JOANOFARC	SOUNDNESS	HOLOCAUST	COROLLARY	COMPLETED
BORNAGAIN	JOININGUP	POLONAISE	GOTOGLORY	COMPLETES
YOUNGGUNS	BOUNDOVER	GOTOEARTH	NOCOMMENT	COMPRISED
ROUNDHEAD	GOINGOVER	GOTOWASTE	COLONNADE	COMPRISES
DOWNSHIFT	JOHNLOCKE	SONOFAGUN	BOLOGNESE	PORPOISES
MOONSHINE	CORNDOLLY	COLOMBIAN	HOROLOGER	COMPLICIT
TOWNSHEND	DOWNTOOLS	MOTORBOAT	MONOLOGUE	COMPLIANT
LOANSHARK	TOWNHOUSE	MOTORBIKE	NOGOAREAS	COMPELLED
COINCIDED	MOONBOOTS	MOTORCADE	COLOUREDS	COMPILING
COINCIDES	COINTREAU	HOROSCOPE	HOLOGRAMS	CORPULENT
DOWNRIVER	CORNBREAD	DONORCARD	MONOGRAMS	HOIPOLLOI
HOBNAILED	DOWNGRADE	COCODEMER	MONOTREME	COMPILERS
HORNPIPES	COUNTRIES	POLONECKS	COLOURANT	COMPANIES
MOONRIVER	FOUNDRIES	DOTODEATH	COLOURING	COMPONENT
DOWNRIGHT	TOWNCRIER	BOXOFFICE	HONOURING	COMPANION
MOONLIGHT	DOWNTRAIN	POTOFGOLD	HOLOGRAPH	SOPPINESS
CORNEILLE	CORNCRAKE	TOBOGGANS	MONOGRAPH	MOPPINGUP
CORNFIELD	CORNERING	MOTORHEAD	COLOURIST	TOPPINGUP
HORNBILLS	ROUNDSMAN	LOGOPHILE	GOTOPRESS	NOTPROVEN

ZOOPHOBIA	FOURSCORE	COURTSHIP	CONSIGNED	POISONOUS
BOSPHORUS	POPRECORD	BOORISHLY	CONSIGNEE	BOSSANOVA
VOXPOPULI	NOTREDAME	WORRISOME	MONSIGNOR	POISONIVY
SOUPSPOON	CORRODING	CORROSION	HORSEHAIR	ROSSONWYE
SOAPOPERA	JOYRIDING	CORROSIVE	HOUSEHOLD	HOPSCOTCH
CORPOREAL	CORRIDORS	SOURSWEET	MOUSEHOLE	COTSWOLDS
COOPERAGE	COURTENAY	BOARDWALK	MOUSEHARE	NONSMOKER
NONPAREIL	COURTESAN	BORROWING	TOPSTITCH	ROYSROLLS
CORPORALS	COURTENEY	BORROWERS	CONSPIRED	MOUSKOURI
COMPARING	JOURNEYED	SORROWFUL	CONSPIRES	DOSSHOUSE
COMPERING	BOURGEOIS	COURTYARD	CONSCIOUS	LOBSCOUSE
COOPERING	TOURNEDOS	BOTSWANAN	FORSAKING	DODSWORTH
GODPARENT	COURGETTE	CONSTANCE	LOOSELEAF	JOBSWORTH
COOPERATE	COURTEOUS	CONSTANCY	CONSULTED	HORSEPLAY
CORPORATE	HORRIFIED	MOUSTACHE	DORSALFIN	GOSSIPING
COMPASSES	HORRIFIES	CONSTABLE	BORSALINO	MONSARRAT
CORPUSCLE	BOARDGAME	COXSWAINS	COASTLAND	TONSORIAL
COMPOSING	ROYROGERS	LOWSEASON	COASTLINE	YOSSARIAN
COMPOSERS	WORRYGUTS	TOMSHARPE	CONSOLING	CONSTRICT
COMPOSURE	MOOREHEAD	HOUSEBOAT	FOSSILISE	CONSTRUCT
COMPOSITE	FOURSIDED	HORSEBACK	NOISELESS	TOASTRACK
POMPOSITY	NOBRAINER	ROASTBEEF	CONSULATE	BOWSTREET
HOSPITALS	COURTIERS	HOUSECOAT	HOUSEMAID	CONSERVED
COMPETENT	HOURGLASS	MORSECODE	CONSUMING	CONSERVES
COMPETING	CORRELATE	FOSSICKER	CONSUMERS	CONSTRUED
COMPUTING	DOARUNNER	TOPSECRET	HOUSEMATE	CONSTRUES
SOAPSTONE	LOGRUNNER	HOUSECALL	LOWSUNDAY	CONSORTIA
COMPUTERS	PORRINGER	MOHSSCALE	SONSINLAW	CONSTRAIN
HOTPOTATO	HOARINESS	ROASTDUCK	CONSENTED	HOTSPRING
COMPOUNDS	FOURSOMES	MOUSEDEER	GOOSANDER	HOUSEROOM
POMPOUSLY	SOURDOUGH	CONSIDERS	POISONPEN	CONSCRIPT
POTPOURRI	POORHOUSE	LOOSEENDS	CONSONANT	MONSTROUS
PORPHYRIA	CORRUPTED	BOLSTERED	LOOSENING	CONSISTED
COMPLYING	CORRUPTLY	DONSIEGEL	POISONING	GOOSESTEP
CONQUERED	SOBRIQUET	JOBSEEKER	WORSENING	POSSESSED
CONQUEROR	SOURCREAM	MOISTENED	POISONERS	POSSESSES
CONQUESTS	BOARDROOM	ROISTERED	BOSSINESS	NOISESOFF
MOSQUITOS	COURTROOM	ROISTERER	HORSINESS	HORSESHOE
NOPROBLEM	HOARFROST	BOBSLEIGH	LOOSENESS	POSSESSOR
CORRECTED	MORRISSEY	BOLSHEVIK	MOISTNESS	MOUSETRAP
CORRECTLY	NOURISHED	HOUSEFLAG	MOUSINESS	JOSSSTICK
COURTCARD	NOURISHES	GOOSEFAIR	CONSENSUS	CORSETIER

FORSYTHIA	VOLTMETER	FOOTPLATE	POSTHOUSE	TORTUROUS
COSSETING	ROUTLEDGE	HOSTILITY	SOFTFOCUS	BOOTHROYD
JOSSSTONE	NORTHERLY	MORTALITY	TOOTHPICK	NORTHSTAR
JOESCULLY	SOUTHERLY	POSTULATE	NORTHPOLE	SOUTHSEAS
ROOSEVELT	NORTHEAST	BOTTOMLEY	SOUTHPOLE	CONTESTED
TOMSAWYER	SOUTHEAST	COSTUMIER	SOUTHPARK	HOSTESSES
HOUSEWIFE	BOTTLEDUP	BOTTOMOUT	SOUTHPORT	POETASTER
HORSEWHIP	BOTTLEOUT	BOTTOMSUP	SOUTHPAWS	LOUTISHLY
HOUSEWORK	VOLTEFACE	CONTINUAL	BOUTIQUES	LOATHSOME
HOWSAYYOU	FORTIFIED	TOTTENHAM	NOCTURNAL	TOOTHSOME
PORTRAYAL	FORTIFIES	CONTENDED	ROTTERDAM	CORTISONE
POSTNATAL	MORTIFIED	CONTENDER	COSTARICA	CONTUSION
ROOTCANAL	MORTIFIES	CONTENTED	COSTPRICE	FORTITUDE
POSTCARDS	PORTOFINO	CONTINUED	CONTORTED	COATSTAND
BOOTLACES	COLTSFOOT	CONTINUES	COSTARRED	FOOTSTOOL
PORTRAYED	FORTYFIVE	MORTENSEN	COUTURIER	SORTITION
POSTDATED	CONTAGION	PORTENDED	LOTTERIES	FOOTSTEPS
POSTDATES	COTTAGERS	ROUTINELY	MONTERREY	CONTOURED
FOOTPATHS	SOUTHGATE	CONTINENT	NOCTURNES	SOTTOVOCE
TOOTHACHE	DOCTRINAL	SOFTENING	POTTERIES	BOATSWAIN
COATTAILS	CONTAINED	ROTTENROW	PORTERAGE	KOWTOWING
FOOTFAULT	CONTAINER	DOTTINESS	DOCTORWHO	NORTHWARD
LOSTCAUSE	CONTRIVED	LOFTINESS	BOATTRAIN	SOUTHWARD
ROOTCAUSE	CONTRIVES	SOOTINESS	COTTERPIN	SOUTHWARK
CONTRACTS	TORTOISES	FORTUNATE	SOFTFRUIT	MOUTHWASH
CONTRALTO	FOOTLIGHT	CONTINUUM	FOOTBRAKE	NORTHWEST
CONTRASTS	FORTNIGHT	COTTONBUD	DOTTERELS	SOUTHWEST
PORTRAITS	PORTPIRIE	HOTTINGUP	DOCTORING	FORTHWITH
POSTHASTE	FOOTHILLS	TOTTINGUP	FOOTPRINT	MONTEZUMA
PORTSALUT	COSTLIEST	POSTWOMAN	FOSTERING	POPULATED
SOUTHBANK	PORTLIEST	SOFTTOUCH	LOITERING	POPULATES
FOOTSCRAY	WORTHIEST	BOATLOADS	POTTERING	POPULARLY
MORTICIAN	TORTELIER	FOOTNOTES	TORTURING	COLUMBINE
CONTACTED	MORTALSIN	PORTHOLES	TOTTERING	CORUSCATE
HOTTICKET	NOSTALGIA	POSTPONED	POSTERIOR	LOQUACITY
CONTACTOR	NOSTALGIC	POSTPONES	FOSTERERS	ROTUNDITY
POETICISE	GOITALONE	POSTWOMEN	LOITERERS	CONUNDRUM
YOUTHCLUB	MONTBLANC	PORTFOLIO	POTTERERS	DOCUMENTS
ROOTEDOUT	POSTULANT	PORTLOUIS	TORTURERS	MONUMENTS
SORTEDOUT	POSTILION	MOOTPOINT	COATDRESS	ROQUEFORT
SOUTHDOWN	TOOTHLESS	BOATHOUSE	DOCTORATE	VOLUMISER
SOFTPEDAL	WORTHLESS	FOOTLOOSE	POSTERITY	SOLUTIONS

POPULISTS	TONYHAWKS	SPECTACLE	SPEEDTRAP	APPLEJACK
COLUMNIST	TONYSCOTT	SPECTATOR	APPERTAIN	SPELUNKER
DOCUDRAMA	BODYSCRUB	SPECIFIED	UPSETTING	OPULENTLY
ROGUISHLY	POLYNESIA	SPECIFIES	SPEEDWELL	SPILLOVER
COQUETTES	TONYLEWIS	SPECKLING	SPAGHETTI	APPLETREE
VOLUNTEER	BODYCHECK	SPECULATE	UPTHEANTE	EPILATION
VOLUNTARY	BODYSHOCK	SPECIMENS	UPTHEPOLE	APPLAUDED
CONVICTED	POLYTHENE	EPICENTRE	OPTICALLY	SPYMASTER
CONVECTOR	HOLYGHOST	SPICINESS	SPLITENDS	SPINNAKER
JONVOIGHT	COPYRIGHT	EPICUREAN	APRILFOOL	OPENRANGE
CONVULSED	HOLYBIBLE	EPICURISM	SPRINGIER	OPENABOOK
CONVINCED	BODYCLOCK	SPACESHIP	SPRINGING	SPONGEBAG
CONVINCES	TONYBLAIR	SPACESUIT	SPRINGBOK	SPINNERET
CONVENING	POLYGLOTS	SPACEWALK	SPRINGERS	APENNINES
CONVENERS	HOLYSMOKE	APOCRYPHA	OPTINGOUT	SPONGIEST
SOUVENIRS	POLYANDRY	EPIDERMAL	UPLIGHTER	SPINALTAP
CONVERGED	POLYGONAL	SPIDERMAN	SPRIGHTLY	SPANGLISH
CONVERGES	BODYBOARD	EPIDERMIS	OPTIMISED	SPINELESS
CONVERSED	HOLYGRAIL	SPADEWORK	OPTICIANS	EPONYMOUS
CONVERSES	POLYGRAPH	SPEEDBOAT	OPTIMISTS	OPENENDED
CONVERTED	POLYESTER	SPEEDBUMP	SPRINKLED	SPONSORED
CONVERTER	ROXYMUSIC	SPIELBERG	SPRINKLER	OPENHOUSE
WOLVERINE	BODYGUARD	UPPERCASE	SPRINKLES	SPINDRYER
CORVETTES	WOOZINESS	APPENDAGE	APPIANWAY	SPINDRIFT
CONVIVIAL	UPSADAISY	APPENDING	SPLITPEAS	SPINSTERS
BONVIVEUR	APPARATUS	SPLENDENT	SPLITTING	SPUNSUGAR
CONVEXITY	SPEAKEASY	SPREADING	SPRINTING	SPINAYARN
BONVOYAGE	SPRAYGUNS	SPREADERS	UPLIFTING	IPSOFACTO
CONVEYING	SPEARHEAD	SPLENDOUR	SPLINTERS	SPOONBILL
CONVEYORS	SPLASHING	SPREADOUT	SPRINTERS	UPHOLDING
NORWEGIAN	SPLASHOUT	EPHEMERAL	SPRITZERS	UPHOLDERS
ROYWALKER	APIARISTS	SPLENETIC	SPOKESMAN	OPTOMETRY
BOBWILLIS	APPALLING	SPEECHDAY	SPOKESMEN	OPPONENTS
BOBWILSON	SPRAWLING	SPEECHIFY	APPLIANCE	SPOONFEED
COLWYNBAY	SPEARMINT	SPHERICAL	SPELLBIND	SPOONFULS
BOYWONDER	SPRAINING	APPETISER	APPLICANT	OPTOPHONE
BOWWINDOW	APPALOOSA	SPEEDIEST	APOLOGIES	APHORISMS
TOOWOOMBA	LPHARTLEY	APPEALING	APOLOGISE	SPOOKIEST
FORWARDED	SPLATTERS	UPPERMOST	APOLOGIST	APHORISTS
SOUWESTER	SPECTATED	SPHEROIDS	APPLEGATE	SPROCKETS
HOLYWATER	SPECTATES	APPEARING	SPILLIKIN	APPOINTED
POLYMATHS	SPECIALLY	APPEASING	APPLEISLE	UPTOSNUFF

UPCOUNTRY	OPERATORS	AQUAPLANE	GREATCOAT	GREASIEST
UPTOSPEED	SPARETYRE	EQUALLING	CREAMCAKE	IRRADIATE
UPPOMPEII	SPIRITOUS	AQUADROME	BREAKCAMP	ORGANISTS
UPHOLSTER	OPERATIVE	SQUADRONS	BROADCAST	BREAKITUP
OPPORTUNE	APERTURES	SQUATTING	GREATDEAL	ORTANIQUE
SPROUTING	UPDRAUGHT	SQUATTERS	GREATDANE	DREAMLIKE
UPROOTING	APPROVING	SQUELCHED	BREAKDOWN	BREADLINE
APPORTION	APOSTATES	SQUELCHES	BREAKEVEN	DREAMLAND
SPARTACUS	EPISTAXIS	SQUEAKING	BROADENED	BROADLOOM
APHRABEHN	EPISCOPAL	SQUEALING	ARMAMENTS	BRIANLARA
SPIRACLES	APOSTOLIC	SQUEALERS	ORNAMENTS	DREAMLESS
UPGRADING	EPISTOLIC	SQUEAMISH	DREAMEDUP	TREADMILL
APHRODITE	SPASMODIC	EQUERRIES	GREASEGUN	TREATMENT
APARTFROM	SPATTERED	AQUEDUCTS	BREAKFREE	URBANMYTH
SPIROGYRA	APATHETIC	SQUEEZING	GREATFIRE	BREAKNECK
APARTHEID	UPSTAGING	EQUITABLE	BREAKFAST	ORDAINING
APPREHEND	SPOTCHECK	EQUITABLY	ARRAIGNED	GREATNESS
APPRAISAL	SPOTLIGHT	AQUITAINE	ARRAIGNER	CREAMPUFF
APPRAISED	SPOTTIEST	AQUILEGIA	TRIANGLES	BREADROLL
APPRAISES	SPITBLOOD	SQUIGGLES	ARRANGING	BREAKRANK
UPBRAIDED	EPITOMISE	AQUICKONE	ARRANGERS	BROADSIDE
SPIRALLED	SPITROAST	EQUIPMENT	URIAHHEEP	CREAMSODA
SPARKLING	SPITITOUT	SQUIRMING	PREACHIFY	FRIARTUCK
SPIRULINA	EPAULETTE	EQUIVOCAL	BREATHILY	DREAMTIME
SPARKLERS	SPLUTTERS	EQUIPPING	BREACHING	GREATTITS
APARTMENT	OPIUMWARS	SQUIRRELS	BREATHING	PROACTIVE
SPARINGLY	SQUABBLED	SQUINTING	BROACHING	ARMATURES
SPARKPLUG	SQUABBLES	SQUIRTING	PREACHING	CREATURES
SPARERIBS	SQUADDIES	BREAKAWAY	TRIATHLON	TREASURED
SPORTSCAR	SQUANDERS	IRRAWADDY	CREAMHORN	TREASURER
SPORTSMAN	SQUARELEG	BREAKAGES	PREACHERS	TREASURES
OPPRESSED	SQUAREPEG	BREAKALEG	TREACHERY	GREATWALL
OPPRESSES	AQUARELLE	BREAKABLE	ORGANISED	CREAMWARE
SPORTSMEN	SQUASHING	TREATABLE	ORGANISER	ORGANZINE
OPPRESSOR	AQUAVITAE	GREATAUNT	ORGANISES	TREBUCHET
OPERETTAS	EQUALISED	URSAMAJOR	TREATISES	MRSBEETON
SPIRITUAL	EQUALISER	BROADBEAN	URBANISED	TREBBIANO
OPERATICS	EQUALISES	DREAMBOAT	ARMADILLO	DRIBBLING
APERITIFS	AQUARIANS	GREATBEAR	ORGANISMS	DRIBBLERS
SPARETIME	AQUARISTS	BROADBAND	URSAMINOR	TRIBALISM
OPERATING	SQUAWKING	BROADBENT	CREAMIEST	TRIBALIST
OPERATION	SQUAWKERS	FRIARBIRD	DREARIEST	TRIBUNALS

CRABAPPLE	CRACKLING	PRECLUDES	PREDATORY	GREENROOM
TRIBESMAN	TRICKLING	BRICKWALL	BRIDEWELL	ORIENTEER
TRIBESMEN	TRUCULENT	BRICKWORK	TRADEWIND	PRIESTLEY
PROBOSCIS	GRACELESS	ERICSYKES	FREELANCE	FREESTYLE
ARABESQUE	PRICELESS	BRICKYARD	GRIEVANCE	ARGENTINA
CRABSTICK	PRICELIST	GRADUATED	FREERANGE	ARGENTINE
PROBATION	BRACELETS	GRADUATES	FREEMASON	ARRESTING
TRIBUTARY	TRICOLOUR	GRADUALLY	ARTEFACTS	PRIESTESS
CRUCIALLY	DRACONIAN	FREDKARNO	GREENBACK	ORIENTATE
TRACTABLE	ARACHNIDS	PREDICTED	GREENBELT	IRREGULAR
PROCLAIMS	ARACHNOID	PRODUCING	GREENCARD	GREENWICH
ARMCHAIRS	BRACKNELL	TRADUCING	BRIEFCASE	GREENWING
BRICABRAC	CRACKNELL	PREDICTOR	GREENDALE	GREENWOOD
BRICKBATS	GRACENOTE	PRODUCERS	FREEZEDRY	PROFFERED
FROCKCOAT	PRECINCTS	ERADICATE	FREEVERSE	PREFIGURE
TRICYCLES	PROCONSUL	PREDICATE	ORDERFORM	GRIFFITHS
PRECOCITY	PRECOOKED	BRIDLEWAY	GREENGAGE	CRAFTIEST
CROCODILE	PRECIPICE	CRADLECAP	FREESHEET	TRAFALGAR
PRECEDENT	CRACKPOTS	FREDPERRY	FREEWHEEL	PROFILING
PRECEDING	ARTCARNEY	GRADIENTS	BREECHING	GRUFFNESS
PROCEDURE	GROCERIES	PRODIGIES	FREETHROW	PROFANITY
CRACKDOWN	PROCURING	IRIDOLOGY	GREENHORN	PREFERRED
TRACKDOWN	PRECURSOR	CREDULITY	GREETINGS	CRAFTSMAN
BRACKETED	CRACKSMAN	CREDULOUS	ARTEMISIA	CRAFTSMEN
CRICKETER	TRACYSHAW	TRADEMARK	FREEWILLY	PROFESSED
CROCHETED	CRACKSMEN	PRUDENTLY	BREEZIEST	PROFESSES
PROCEEDED	DRECHSLER	TRADENAME	CREEPIEST	PROFUSELY
DRYCLEANS	FRICASSEE	CRUDENESS	GREEDIEST	PROFESSOR
BROCHETTE	PROCESSED	BRODERICK	ORDERLIES	PROFUSION
PROCREATE	PROCESSES	FREDERICK	GREENLAND	PROFITEER
CRUCIFIED	TRICKSTER	GRIDIRONS	GRUELLING	PROFITING
CRUCIFIES	TRACKSUIT	TRADESMAN	CRUELLEST	DRIFTWOOD
CRUCIFORM	PRECISELY	TRADESMEN	TRUEBLISS	CRAFTWORK
PRACTICAL	PRECISION	PRUDISHLY	TRIENNIAL	URUGUAYAN
PRACTISED	PROCESSOR	CREDITING	FREEWOMAN	FRAGRANCE
PRACTISES	TRACKSHOE	PREDATING	FREEHOUSE	FROGMARCH
FRACTIONS	TRUCKSTOP	ERUDITION	TREEHOUSE	PREGNANCY
TRICKIEST	PRICETAGS	GRADATION	TRUENORTH	DRAGRACER
FRACTIOUS	BROCHURES	PREDATION	GREENPARK	PRAGMATIC
ERICAJONG	FRACTURED	TRADITION	FRIEDRICE	PROGRAMME
TRUCKLOAD	FRACTURES	CREDITORS	FRIEDRICH	BRAGGARTS
ERICBLAIR	PRECLUDED	PREDATORS	FREETRADE	TRAGEDIAN

BRIGADIER	ARCHDUCHY	BRAINWAVE	TREMBLING	DRINKDEEP
TRAGEDIES	ARCHIVIST	ARDIZZONE	GRUMBLERS	GRENADIER
BRIGADOON	ORDINANCE	PROJECTED	PREMOLARS	WRONGDOER
TRIGGERED	IRRIGATED	PROJECTOR	TREMULOUS	GRANDDUKE
DRAGGEDON	IRRIGATES	PREJUDICE	PROMENADE	GRENADINE
FRAGMENTS	IRRITATED	PREJUDGED	CRIMINALS	IRONEDOUT
DRUGGISTS	IRRITATES	PREJUDGES	FREMANTLE	BRINGDOWN
URIGELLER	URTICARIA	TROJANWAR	PROMINENT	ORANGEMAN
WRIGGLING	IRRITABLE	BROKEEVEN	PRIMROSES	FRANCESCA
FRAGILITY	IRRITABLY	PROKOFIEV	TROMBONES	ORANGEADE
FRUGALITY	TRAILARMS	BROKERAGE	FRAMBOISE	BRONZEAGE
DRAGONFLY	TRAILBIKE	BRAKESHOE	PRIMARILY	PRINCETON
ORIGINALS	FRUITBATS	TRILOBITE	TRIMARANS	CRANBERRY
BRIGANDRY	FRUITCAKE	FROLICKED	MRSMERTON	TRINKETRY
ORIGINATE	CRAIGCASH	TRILOGIES	TRIMESTER	TRANSEPTS
PROGNOSIS	DRKILDARE	DRILLHALL	PROMISING	WRONGFOOT
FROGSPAWN	FRUITERER	BRILLIANT	DRAMATICS	BRENTFORD
GREGORIAN	FRYINGPAN	SRILANKAN	DRUMSTICK	FRANKFORT
BRIGHTMAN	ARLINGTON	PROLONGED	PRIMETIME	FRANKFURT
BRIGHTENS	ORPINGTON	BRYLCREEM	BRIMSTONE	TRANSFERS
FRIGHTENS	TRYINGOUT	GRILLROOM	CREMATING	TRANSFORM
DRAGSTERS	FREIGHTER	ARTLESSLY	FRAMETENT	TRANSFUSE
DRUGSTORE	ARTICHOKE	DRUMMAJOR	PROMOTING	BRONCHIAL
BRIGHTEST	ARTIFICER	GRIMACING	PROMPTING	FRENCHMAN
FRIGHTFUL	ARTIFICES	TRUMPCARD	CREMATION	BRANCHLET
DRAGQUEEN	BRAINIEST	DROMEDARY	PROMOTION	CRUNCHIER
PREHEATED	ARRIVISTE	PREMIERES	PREMATURE	FRENCHHEN
ARCHIBALD	TRAINLOAD	TRUMPETED	PROMPTERS	BRANCHING
PROHIBITS	ARTILLERY	TRUMPETER	DRAMATISE	CRUNCHING
MRSHUDSON	BRAINLESS	TRAMLINES	DRAMATIST	DRENCHING
TRIHEDRON	FRUITLESS	TRIMMINGS	PRIMITIVE	TRENCHANT
ORTHODOXY	FRAILNESS	GRAMPIANS	PRIMAVERA	WRENCHING
ARTHRITIC	DRAINPIPE	GRUMPIEST	FRAMEWORK	TRUNCHEON
ARTHRITIS	ARBITRARY	ERNMALLEY	DRUNKARDS	FRANCHISE
ARCHANGEL	ARBITRATE	TREMELOES	BRENDALEE	BRANNIGAN
ORPHANAGE	IRWINSHAW	GRIMALKIN	TRUNCATED	PRINCIPAL
ARCHENEMY	CROISSANT	BRAMBLING	TRUNCATES	FRANCISCO
ARTHROPOD	TRAIPSING	CRIMPLENE	DRINKABLE	IRONSIDES
ARTHURIAN	ARMISTICE	CRUMBLING	PRINTABLE	GRANVILLE
ORCHESTRA	BRAINTREE	CRUMPLING	TRANSACTS	GRENVILLE
ARCHITECT	BRAINWASH	GRUMBLING	TRUNKCALL	PRINCIPLE
ARCHETYPE	ERNIEWISE	TRAMPLING	TRANSCEND	TRANSIENT

TRUNNIONS	TRANSVAAL	PROPOSERS	CROSSFADE	FRUSTRATE
FRONTIERS	BRUNSWICK	CREPITATE	TRUSTFUND	PROSTRATE
GRANDIOSE	IRONOXIDE	PROPOUNDS	CROSSFIRE	IRISHSTEW
TRENDIEST	ARROGANCE	GRAPEVINE	PRESSGANG	PRESSSTUD
GRANDJURY	ARGONAUTS	TRIPTYCHS	PRESCHOOL	BRUSHTAIL
WRINKLIER	PREOCCUPY	TRAPEZOID	IRASCIBLE	CROSSTALK
WRINKLIES	CROOKEDLY	TRAPEZIUM	IRASCIBLY	CRASHTEST
FRANGLAIS	ARBORETUM	FREQUENCY	PRISCILLA	PRESSURED
CRINOLINE	ERRONEOUS	BRIQUETTE	PRESCIENT	PRESSURES
FRONTLINE	ARROWHEAD	CROQUETTE	BRASSIERE	BRUSQUELY
TRUNDLING	ARSONISTS	FREQUENTS	FROSTIEST	CROSSWIND
WRANGLING	ERGONOMIC	PRURIENCE	PRESELECT	BRUSHWOOD
WRINKLING	PROOFREAD	PROROGUED	CRASHLAND	BRUSHWORK
WRANGLERS	ARROWROOT	PROROGUES	GRASSLAND	CROSSWORD
TRANSLATE	GROOMSMAN	DRURYLANE	WRESTLING	CROSSWAYS
FRANKMUIR	BROOKSIDE	CRUSTACEA	WRESTLERS	PRESBYTER
GRANDMAMA	GROOMSMEN	PRISMATIC	PROSELYTE	PRESBYOPE
IRONSMITH	TROOPSHIP	PRESEASON	PRESUMING	WRITLARGE
TRANSMITS	TRIPLANES	CRESTARUN	IRISHMOSS	PROTRACTS
TRANSMUTE	DROPWAIST	CROSSBEAM	GROSSMITH	PROTECTED
BRANDNAME	PREPACKED	CROSSBILL	PRESENTED	ARCTICFOX
FRANKNESS	DROPSCONE	BRASSBAND	PRESENTER	PROTECTOR
IRONWORKS	DROPPEDBY	WRISTBAND	PRESENTLY	CRITICISE
ERINDOORS	DROPPEDIN	FROSTBITE	PRISONERS	CRITICISM
IRONHORSE	PROPHETIC	CROSSBOWS	BRASENOSE	EROTICISM
GRANDPRIX	CROPPEDUP	DRESSCOAT	BRASHNESS	TRUTHDRUG
GRANDPAPA	PROPPEDUP	TRISECTED	BRISKNESS	FRITTERED
TRANSPIRE	WRAPPEDUP	PROSECUTE	CRASSNESS	BROTHERLY
TRANSPORT	PROPAGATE	CRUSADING	CRISPNESS	GRATIFIED
TRANSPOSE	TRAPPINGS	PRESIDENT	CROSSNESS	GRATIFIES
TRUNKROAD	PROPRIETY	PRESIDING	FRESHNESS	PROTEGEES
GRANARIES	TRAPPISTS	CRUSADERS	CROSSOVER	ERSTWHILE
MRSNORRIS	PROPELLED	PRESIDIUM	ARISTOTLE	CROTCHETS
IRONCROSS	PROPELLER	DRESSDOWN	GROSPOINT	CROTCHETY
GRANDSLAM	CRAPULENT	CRESCENDO	PRESCRIBE	PRETTIEST
PRANKSTER	GRAPPLING	PROSPERED	PROSCRIBE	FRITZLANG
GRANDSONS	PROPYLENE	BRASSERIE	PRESERVED	PRATTLING
BRUNETTES	PROPONENT	PRESSEDON	PRESERVER	PRATTLERS
TRINITIES	PREPARING	DRYSHERRY	PRESERVES	BRUTALISE
GRANDTOUR	PROPOSALS	CRESCENTS	GROSGRAIN	BRUTALITY
ORANGUTAN	PROPOSING	PROSPECTS	ARMSTRONG	PRETENDED
PRONOUNCE	GRAPESHOT	DRESSEDUP	PRESHRUNK	PRETENDER

BRITANNIA	DRIVEHOME	PROXIMITY	ESPERANCE	OSSIFYING
TRITENESS	PREVAILED	ARGYBARGY	ASREGARDS	OSULLIVAN
TRATTORIA	PROVOKING	ARTYFARTY	ESPERANTO	PSALMISTS
FRETBOARD	GROVELLED	GREYBEARD	ASSEMBLED	ESPLANADE
CRITIQUES	GROVELLER	CRAYONING	ASSEMBLER	USELESSLY
FRATERNAL	TRAVELLED	GREYHOUND	ASSEMBLES	ISOLATING
CRITERION	TRAVELLER	GREYFRIAR	ASCENDANT	ISOLATION
ORATORIOS	PRIVILEGE	PRAYERRUG	ASCENDING	ASYMMETRY
PROTESTED	PREVALENT	GREYSTOKE	USHERETTE	ASHMOLEAN
PROTESTER	FRIVOLITY	FRIZZANTE	ISLEOFMAN	ISOMETRIC
BRUTISHLY	FRIVOLOUS	CRAZYGOLF	ISLEOFELY	ISINGLASS
GROTESQUE	PROVENCAL	BRAZILIAN	ESSEXGIRL	ASININITY
GRATITUDE	PREVENTED	DRIZZLING	ASTERISKS	ASSONANCE
PROTOTYPE	PROVENDER	GRIZZLING	OSTEOLOGY	ASSOCIATE
PROTRUDED	PROVINCES	GRIZZLERS	ASTEROIDS	ASTOUNDED
PROTRUDES	TRAVERSED	BRAZILNUT	OSTEOPATH	ESPOUSING
FRETFULLY	TRAVERSES	CRAZINESS	ASSESSING	ASSORTING
BRATWURST	TREVOREVE	ISLAMABAD	ASCENSION	ESCORTING
TRAUMATIC	PRIVYSEAL	ESCALATED	ASPERSION	PSORIASIS
TROUNCING	CREVASSES	ESCALATES	ASSESSORS	ASCRIBING
GROUNDSEL	GRAVESEND	ESCAPADES	ESSENTIAL	OSTRICHES
GROUNDAGE	PROVISION	ESCALATOR	ASCERTAIN	OSTRACISE
GROUNDING	PRIVATEER	ASPARAGUS	ASSENTING	OSTRACISM
GROUNDHOG	PRIVATELY	ISLANDERS	ASSERTING	ASTRADDLE
GROUNDNUT	PRIVATION	ESTATECAR	ASSERTION	ASTRODOME
TROUSERED	PRIVATISE	ASHAMEDLY	ASSENTERS	ASTRAKHAN
ARGUMENTS	GRAVITATE	ESTAMINET	ASSERTIVE	ASTROLABE
BROUGHAMS	GRAVEYARD	ESCAPISTS	ISHERWOOD	ASTROLOGY
CROUCHING	BROWNBEAR	ESSAYISTS	ASTHMATIC	ESTRANGED
CROUPIERS	BROWNCOAL	ASSAULTED	ESTIMATED	ASTRONOMY
TROUBLING	BROWBEATS	ASSAILANT	ESTIMATES	ASTRONAUT
TRIUMPHAL	CROWSFEET	ASSAILING	ESTIMABLE	ASTROTURF
TRIUMPHED	ARKWRIGHT	ESTABLISH	ESTIMATOR	TSAREVICH
TROUSSEAU	DROWSIEST	ISRAELITE	ASPIRANTS	ISOSCELES
FRAUDSTER	CROWSNEST	VSNAIPAUL	ISLINGTON	TSETSEFLY
CROUSTADE	BREWINGUP	ASSASSINS	OSCILLATE	ISOTHERMS
ARDUOUSLY	DRAWINGUP	ASPARTAME	ESPIONAGE	ASSURANCE
TRIVIALLY	GROWINGUP	USEBYDATE	ASSIGNING	ASSUREDLY
GRAVYBOAT	BROWNRICE	ASHBLONDE	ASSISTANT	ASSUAGING
DRAVIDIAN	BREWERIES	PSYCHEDUP	ASSISTING	PSEUDONYM
PROVIDENT	BREWSTERS	PSYCHOSIS	ASSIDUITY	ESTUARIES
PROVIDING	CROWNWORK	ASIDEFROM	ASSIDUOUS	STRATAGEM

STEAMBOAT	STACKEDUP	STGEORGES	STRIKEPAY	ETYMOLOGY
STEAMBATH	STOCKHOLM	STEERSMAN	STRIDENCY	STIMULANT
STPANCRAS	STOCKINET	STEERSMEN	ATLIBERTY	STUMBLING
STRADDLED	STOCKINGS	ATHEISTIC	STRIKEOUT	STIMULATE
STRADDLES	STICKIEST	STREISAND	STRINGBAG	ATOMISING
STRAWDOGS	STOCKIEST	ATLEISURE	STRINGENT	ITEMISING
STRATEGIC	STOCKISTS	STRESSFUL	STAIRLIFT	ATOMISERS
STEAMEDUP	STICKLERS	STREETCAR	STRIPLING	STANDARDS
STRATFORD	STOCKLIST	ATTESTING	STAINLESS	STINGAREE
STEADFAST	ATACANTER	ATTENTION	ETHIOPIAN	STANDBAIL
STRAGGLER	STOCKPILE	ATTENTIVE	STRIPPING	STINKBOMB
STRANGLED	STOCKPORT	ATTENUATE	STRIPPERS	STONECHAT
STRANGLER	STOCKROOM	STRENUOUS	STAIRRODS	STONECROP
STRANGLES	STOCKTAKE	STEELWOOL	STRICTURE	ATANYCOST
STRANGELY	STOCKWELL	OTHERWISE	STRICTEST	ETHNICITY
STRANGERS	STOCKYARD	STEELYARD	ATTITUDES	STANDDOWN
STRANGEST	STODGIEST	STIFFENED	STAIRWELL	STONKERED
ATTACHING	STUDPOKER	STIFFENER	STELLATED	STANDEASY
STRAPHANG	UTTERANCE	STUFFIEST	ITALICISE	STANCHION
STEADICAM	ATHENAEUM	STIFFNESS	STALLIONS	STINKHORN
STEAMIRON	STEELBAND	STAFFROOM	STILLLIFE	STINGIEST
STEADIEST	ETHELBERT	STUFFSACK	STYLELESS	ETHNOLOGY
ATTACKING	STRETCHED	STAGNANCY	STCLEMENT	ATONEMENT
ATTACKERS	STRETCHER	STAGNATED	STALEMATE	STANDPIPE
STRAPLINE	STRETCHES	STAGNATES	STALENESS	ITINERANT
STRAPLESS	ATTENDANT	STAGPARTY	STALINIST	ITINERARY
ATTAINING	ATTENDING	STAGEDOOR	STILLNESS	ATANYRATE
STRAINING	STEELDRUM	STAGGERED	STYLISTIC	ITINERATE
STRAINERS	STEEPENED	STAGEHAND	STYLISHLY	STANDREWS
STRAWPOLL	STRENGTHS	STAGNIGHT	STYLISING	ATONETIME
STRAPPING	OTHERHALF	STAGENAME	UTILISING	STONEWALL
STRANRAER	STREAKING	STAGINESS	ATHLETICS	STONEWARE
STEAMSHIP	STREAKERS	STAGHOUND	UTILITIES	ETIOLATED
STEADYING	STREAMLET	STEGOSAUR	STILETTOS	STOOLBALL
STABLELAD	STREAMING	ATTHEMOST	ATALOWEBB	STROMBOLI
STABILISE	STREAMERS	ITCHINESS	STOMACHED	UTTOXETER
STABILITY	UTTERMOST	ATTHETIME	STOMACHIC	STRONGMAN
STOCKADES	FTSEINDEX	ETHICALLY	STAMPDUTY	STRONGBOX
STICKATIT	STBERNARD	STOICALLY	STAMMERED	STRONGARM
STUCKATIT	OTHERNESS	STEINBECK	STAMMERER	STRONGEST
STACKABLE	STEEPNESS	STEINBOCK	STAMPEDED	ATROPHIED
STOCKCUBE	ATTEMPTED	STAIRCASE	STAMPEDES	ATROPHIES

ATROCIOUS	STORNOWAY	STRUTTING	HUMANRACE	PURCHASED
STROLLING	STARTOVER	STRUCTURE	DUMAURIER	PURCHASER
STROLLERS	STARBOARD	STEVEBIKO	PUTACROSS	PURCHASES
STROMNESS	STIRFRIED	STEVECRAM	SUGARRUSH	SURCHARGE
ATTORNEYS	STARFRUIT	STEVEDORE	SUGARSOAP	PUBCRAWLS
STRONTIUM	STOREROOM	STEVENAGE	SUBALTERN	SUBCLAUSE
STOPWATCH	STIRCRAZY	STEVENSON	AUNATUREL	HUNCHBACK
STOPPAGES	ATPRESENT	STEVEOWEN	LUNARYEAR	PUNCHBALL
STEPHANIE	PTEROSAUR	STEVEPENK	CUPBOARDS	DUTCHBARN
STUPIDITY	ITERATING	STOVEPIPE	CUPBEARER	PUNCHBOWL
STAPLEGUN	ATTRITION	ATAVISTIC	RUGBYBALL	MUSCLEMAN
STUPEFIED	ITERATION	STOWAWAYS	BUBBLECAR	BUTCHERED
STUPEFIES	STARPUPIL	STAYEDPUT	BUMBLEBEE	QUICKENED
STEPCHILD	STARBURST	ITSYBITSY	OUTBREAKS	SUCCEEDED
STIPPLING	ITSSOEASY	STAYINGON	TUMBLEDRY	MUSCLEDIN
STIPULATE	ATASTROKE	CUTACAPER	BUBBLEGUM	MUSCLESIN
STOPPRESS	STUTTERED	SUGABABES	CUBBYHOLE	LUNCHEONS
ETIQUETTE	STUTTERER	GUMARABIC	TUNBRIDGE	ZUCCHETTO
STARGAZER	STATUETTE	SUGARBEET	BUBBLIEST	QUICKENUP
ETERNALLY	STATEFAIR	BUDABBOTT	QUIBBLING	QUICKFIRE
STORYBOOK	STUTTGART	SUGARCOAT	TURBULENT	LUNCHHOUR
ATTRIBUTE	STITCHING	SUGARCUBE	QUIBBLERS	FUNCTIONS
ATTRACTED	STATELESS	SUBARCTIC	KUMBHMELA	JUNCTIONS
STORECARD	STATEMENT	SUGARCANE	SUNBONNET	QUICKLIME
STURGEONS	STATIONED	HUMANDHAW	HUSBANDRY	PUNCHLINE
STIRREDUP	STATIONER	HUEANDCRY	TUBBINESS	SUCCULENT
STYROFOAM	STATEROOM	CUTANDRUN	DUMBFOUND	SUCCUMBED
STARCHIER	STATESMAN	OUTANDOUT	TURBOPROP	GUACAMOLE
STARCHING	STATESIDE	MUJAHEDIN	NUMBERTEN	BUCCANEER
STARSHINE	STATESMEN	CUTANEOUS	SUEBARKER	SURCINGLE
PTARMIGAN	STATISTIC	CUBANHEEL	SUNBURNED	JUICINESS
STARLINGS	STATUSQUO	SUSANHILL	LUMBERING	VULCANISE
STARLIGHT	STATUTORY	HUMANISTS	NUMBERING	VULCANITE
STORMIEST	STAUNCHED	AUDACIOUS	NUMBERONE	DUNCESCAP
STURDIEST	STAUNCHES	FUGACIOUS	DUMBARTON	QUICKSTEP
STARTLING	STAUNCHLY	HUMANKIND	OUTBURSTS	SUCCESSES
STORYLINE	STRUGGLED	SUGARLOAF	NUMBERTWO	QUICKSAND
STERILISE	STRUGGLES	SUGARLUMP	LUCBESSON	SUCCESSOR
STERILITY	STOURHEAD	SUBATOMIC	RUMBUTTER	NUTCUTLET
STARANISE	STRUMMING	RUNAROUND	SUNBATHED	LUNCHTIME
STARKNESS	STRUMPETS	HULAHOOPS	SUNBATHER	GUNCOTTON
STERNNESS	STAUSTELL	RUNABOUTS	SUNBATHES	SUCCOTASH

PUNCTURED	GUTENBERG	SURFEITED	PURGATIVE	LUMINESCE
PUNCTURES	NUREMBERG	CUFFLINKS	EUPHRATES	MUTINEERS
PUNCTUATE	PUBESCENT	DUFFELBAG	RUTHMADOC	RUDIMENTS
MUSCOVADO	QUIESCENT	FULFILLED	OUTHWAITE	CUTITFINE
MUSCOVITE	MULETEERS	SUBFAMILY	PUSHCHAIR	TUNINGPEG
QUADRATIC	RULEOFLAW	HUFFINESS	RUTHELLIS	RULINGOUT
SUBDEACON	SUPERFINE	PUFFINESS	EUPHEMISM	MUSICHALL
QUADRANTS	CUNEIFORM	SUNFLOWER	AUTHENTIC	PUNISHING
GUIDEBOOK	SUPERGRAN	SURFBOARD	GUSHINESS	MUNICIPAL
BUNDABERG	AUBERGINE	SUFFERING	MUSHINESS	EURIPIDES
BUDDLEIAS	SUPERGIRL	SUFFUSING	PUSHINESS	FUGITIVES
HUNDREDTH	SUPERGLUE	SUFFUSION	EUPHONIUM	AUDITIONS
MUDDLEDUP	SURETHING	BUFFETCAR	HUSHINGUP	MUNITIONS
RUDDIGORE	SUPERHERO	OURFATHER	RUTHENIUM	MUSICIANS
QUIDDITCH	NUMERICAL	OUTFITTER	CUSHIONED	AUXILIARY
BUSDRIVER	JUVENILES	BUFFETING	HUSHMONEY	FUSILIERS
QUADRILLE	SUBEDITED	SURFNTURF	MUSHROOMS	JUDICIARY
GUIDELINE	JUVENILIA	GUYFAWKES	BUSHCRAFT	HUMILIATE
HUMDINGER	SUBEDITOR	GUFFAWING	EUPHORBIA	PUGILISTS
BURDENING	SUPERIORS	HUGGYBEAR	HUGHGRANT	JUDICIOUS
MUDDINESS	SUPERMINI	FUNGICIDE	WUTHERING	FUSILLADE
RUDDINESS	QUEENMARY	TURGIDITY	AUTHORESS	AUDIENCES
MUNDANITY	OUTERMOST	MUNGBEANS	AUTHORISE	LURIDNESS
OUTDOORSY	TUNESMITH	OUTGOINGS	BUCHAREST	LUDICROUS
WUNDERBAR	SUPERNOVA	HUNGRIEST	EUCHARIST	CUPIDSBOW
ZUIDERZEE	NUMEROUNO	CUDGELLED	AUTHORITY	CURIOSITY
JUDDERING	JUNEBROWN	BUNGALOWS	PUSHSTART	AUDIOTAPE
MURDERINC	SUPERSTAR	JUDGEMENT	OUTHOUSES	FUNICULAR
MURDERING	SUPERSEDE	MUGGINESS	JUBILANCE	CURIOUSLY
SUNDERING	HUMECTANT	PUDGINESS	FUMIGATED	DUBIOUSLY
MURDERERS	DUTEOUSLY	BURGEONED	FUMIGATES	DUTIFULLY
MURDERESS	TUNEFULLY	BULGARIAN	MUTILATED	FURIOUSLY
MURDEROUS	SUPERVISE	HUNGARIAN	MUTILATES	TULIPWOOD
BUNDESTAG	SUFFRAGAN	VULGARIAN	RUMINATED	PURIFYING
QUADRUPED	QUAFFABLE	DUNGAREES	RUMINATES	SUBJECTED
QUADRUPLE	SUFFICING	SURGERIES	LUSITANIA	SUBJUDICE
SUBDIVIDE	SURFACING	VULGARITY	RURITANIA	SUBJUGATE
SUNDOWNER	SURFACERS	SUGGESTED	MUSICALLY	MUCKRAKER
DUDERANCH	SUFFOCATE	BUDGETDAY	FUMIGATOR	RUCKSACKS
QUEENANNE	PUFFADDER	BUDGETING	RUMINANTS	HUCKABACK
NUMERATOR	TURFEDOUT	BUDGETARY	AUDIOBOOK	MUCKABOUT
SUPERBIKE	GUNFIGHTS	PURGATORY	JUDIDENCH	HUNKYDORY

MUSKMELON	NULLIFIED	PUBLISHER	DUANEEDDY	EULOGISED
BUCKTEETH	NULLIFIES	PUBLISHES	JUANPERON	EULOGISES
BUCKSFIZZ	QUALIFIED	BURLESQUE	FUNNYFACE	AUTOPILOT
BUCKWHEAT	QUALIFIER	QUALITIES	FUNNYFARM	SUPOLLARD
TURKSHEAD	QUALIFIES	WURLITZER	HUNNIFORD	AUTOCLAVE
BUCKTHORN	GUILDFORD	GUILTTRIP	BUNNYGIRL	AUTOROUTE
DUCKLINGS	FULLWHACK	BULLETINS	FUNNYGIRL	AUTOFOCUS
MUCKINGIN	GUILDHALL	FULLQUOTA	FUNNYHAHA	AUTOCRACY
TUCKINGIN	BULLFINCH	PULLOVERS	QUENCHING	AUCOURANT
BULKINESS	FULLTIMER	SUELAWLEY	TURNPIKES	AUTOGRAPH
FUNKINESS	PURLOINED	MUMMIFIED	TUNNELLED	AUTOCROSS
HUSKINESS	BUILDINGS	RUMMAGING	TUNNELLER	EUROTRASH
MUCKINESS	BULLFIGHT	GUNMAKERS	RUNNYMEDE	TUDORROSE
MURKINESS	DUELLISTS	PUMMELLED	OUTNUMBER	AUTOPSIES
MUSKINESS	KUBLAKHAN	AUGMENTED	SURNAMING	OUTOFSTEP
SULKINESS	FULLBLAST	SUMMONSES	TURNINGIN	OUTOFSYNC
JUNKBONDS	GUILELESS	SUMMONING	CUNNINGLY	JUNOESQUE
BUNKHOUSE	GUILTLESS	PULMONARY	TURNINGUP	OUTOFTUNE
DUCKWORTH	PULLULATE	CULMINATE	QUANTOCKS	OUTOFTRUE
PUCKERING	FULLBLOWN	FULMINATE	TURNROUND	OUTOFWORK
SUNKISSED	SUBLIMELY	SUMMINGUP	TURNHOUSE	OUTPLAYED
MUSKETEER	SUBLIMATE	SUBMERGED	TURNCOATS	SULPHATES
BUCKETING	PULLINGIN	SUBMERGES	NUNNERIES	SUPPLANTS
JUNKETING	DUBLINERS	SUMMARIES	RUNNERSUP	SUSPECTED
BUCKETFUL	BURLINESS	SUMMARILY	BURNISHED	SUSPICION
SUBLEASED	CURLINESS	MURMURING	BURNISHES	BUMPEDOFF
SUBLEASES	SURLINESS	SUBMARINE	FURNISHED	SUBPOENAS
FUELGAUGE	PULLINGUP	MURMURERS	FURNISHES	JUMPLEADS
FULLMARKS	BULLDOZED	SUMMARISE	BUONASERA	YUPPIEFLU
BULLYBEEF	BULLDOZER	SURMISING	TURNSTILE	SULPHIDES
LULLABIES	BULLDOZES	SUBMITTED	TURNSTONE	SURPLICES
PUBLICBAR	MULLIONED	SUMMATION	RUINATION	SURPRISED
BUGLECALL	FULLBOARD	SURMOUNTS	FURNITURE	SURPRISES
FULLSCALE	FULLHOUSE	GUINEAPIG	RUINOUSLY	DUMPLINGS
PUBLICANS	FULLCREAM	TURNTABLE	GUINEVERE	SUPPLIANT
PUBLICISE	TUILERIES	FUNNYBONE	AUTOMATED	SUPPLIERS
PUBLICIST	BULLFROGS	TURNABOUT	AUTOMATES	PUTPAIDTO
DUPLICATE	FULLERTON	HUNNICUTT	AUTOMATIC	BUMPTIOUS
DUPLICITY	NULLARBOR	PUGNACITY	AUTOBAHNS	PUPPYLOVE
PUBLICITY	CUTLASSES	SUNNYDALE	AUTOMATON	SUSPENDED
GUILLEMOT	OUTLASTED	TURNEDOUT	OUTOFDATE	SUSPENDER
OUBLIETTE	PUBLISHED	BURNTDOWN	OUTOFFORM	BUMPINESS

DUMPINESS	QUERULOUS	SUSSEDOUT	LUFTHANSA	BUTTERING
JUMPINESS	SUPREMACY	NUTSHELLS	SUBTRACTS	GUTTERING
LUMPINESS	SUPREMELY	PUSSYFOOT	RUSTICATE	MUSTERING
PUMPINGUP	NUTRIMENT	TULSEHILL	RUSTICITY	MUTTERING
BUMPERCAR	GUARANTEE	GUNSMITHS	CUSTODIAL	NURTURING
HUMPHRIES	GUNRUNNER	GUMSHIELD	CUSTODIAN	RUSTPROOF
PURPORTED	SURRENDER	QUESTIONS	QUOTIDIAN	MUTTERERS
SUPPORTED	CURRENTLY	OUTSKIRTS	DUSTDEVIL	GUITARIST
SUPPORTER	GUARANTOR	OURSELVES	FURTHERTO	AUSTERITY
SURPASSED	GUARDRAIL	MUSSOLINI	RUSTLEDUP	BUTTERCUP
SURPASSES	GUARDROOM	BUSSELTON	JUSTIFIED	PUTTOROUT
PURPOSELY	GUARDSMAN	QUASIMODO	JUSTIFIES	CUTTYSARK
SUPPOSING	GUARDSVAN	NURSEMAID	MULTIFORM	MULTITUDE
RUMPSTEAK	BULRUSHES	SUBSUMING	DUSTSHEET	SUBTITLES
TURPITUDE	GUARDSMEN	HUDSONBAY	CURTAILED	QUOTATION
PUPPETEER	HUBRISTIC	NUISANCES	CURTAINED	DUSTSTORM
BUMPSTART	NUTRITION	FUSSINESS	SUSTAINED	MULTITASK
JUMPSTART	LUCRATIVE	GUTSINESS	JUSTRIGHT	FURTIVELY
QUIPSTERS	SURROUNDS	OUTSPOKEN	SULTRIEST	CULTIVATE
SUMPTUOUS	BURROUGHS	OUTSPREAD	CURTAINUP	BURTKWOUK
GUNPOWDER	DUBROVNIK	SUBSCRIBE	CURTILAGE	BUJUMBURA
SUPPLYING	BURROWING	NURSERIES	GUATEMALA	CUCUMBERS
TURQUOISE	CURRAWONG	SUNSCREEN	CUSTOMARY	HUMUNGOUS
CURRYCOMB	FURROWING	SUNSTROKE	CUSTOMERS	LUXURIANT
HURRICANE	QUARRYMAN	OUTSTRIPS	CUSTOMISE	LUXURIATE
LUBRICANT	QUARRYMEN	SUBSCRIPT	PUTTINGBY	LUXURIOUS
LUBRICATE	QUARRYING	SUBSTRATA	SUNTANNED	NUKUALOFA
OUTRIDERS	PUISSANCE	SUBSISTED	CUTTINGIT	QUEUINGUP
QUARTERED	PURSUANCE	PULSATING	DUSTINESS	AUGUSTINE
AUBRIETIA	SUBSTANCE	OUTSOURCE	FUSTINESS	LUVVIEDOM
GUARDEDLY	OUTSTAYED	NUMSKULLS	MUSTINESS	SUBVERTED
HURRIEDLY	DUNSTABLE	BUGSBUNNY	RUSTINESS	QUIVERING
QUARTERLY	GUESSABLE	GUESSWORK	SULTANATE	PULVERISE
NUTRIENTS	OUTSMARTS	JUSTFANCY	AUCTIONED	CURVATURE
PUTREFIED	GUESTBEER	QUITEAFEW	DUSTCOVER	SURVIVING
PUTREFIES	GUESTBOOK	SUITCASES	MULTIPACK	SURVIVORS
SURROGACY	RUSSABBOT	LUFTWAFFE	MULTIPLEX	PURVEYING
OUTRIGGER	PUSSYCATS	AUSTRALIA	JUXTAPOSE	SURVEYING
SURROGATE	SUBSIDING	QUITEABIT	BUTTERFAT	PURVEYORS
GUERRILLA	OUTSIDEOF	AUNTSALLY	CUTTHROAT	SURVEYORS
GUARDIANS	OUTSIDERS	QUATRAINS	AUSTERELY	OUTWEIGHS
PUERILITY	SUBSIDISE	QUITEALOT	BUTTERFLY	OUTWORKER

OUTWARDLY	OVEREAGER	OVERCOATS	SWAGGERER	AWKWARDLY
OUTWITTED	OVERLADEN	OVERSPILL	TWOHANDER	SWAZILAND
JUDYDAVIS	OVERRATED	OVERSPEND	AWAKENING	SWIZZLING
LUCYDAVIS	OVERRATES	OVERPRICE	SWELTERED	EXCAVATED
JUDYCARNE	OVERTAKEN	OVERTRICK	DWELLINGS	EXCAVATES
HUEYLEWIS	OVERTAKES	EVERGREEN	SWELLINGS	EXCAVATOR
JURYWOMAN	OVERHANGS	OVERDRAFT	SWALLOWED	EXPANDING
JURYWOMEN	OVERHAULS	OVERTRAIN	SWIMSUITS	EXPATIATE
SUEZCANAL	OVERVALUE	OVERPRINT	OWENNARES	EXCALIBUR
QUIZZICAL	EVERYBODY	OVERDRESS	SWINGBOAT	EXHAUSTED
FUZZINESS	OVERACTED	OVERWRITE	SWINGDOOR	EXPANSION
MUZZINESS	OVERREACH	OVERDRIVE	SWANSDOWN	EXPANSIVE
BUZZCOCKS	OVERREACT	OVERCROWD	TWINPEAKS	EXUBERANT
EVABARTOK	OVERFEEDS	OVERDRAWN	SWINGEING	EXECRABLE
EVACUATED	OVERHEARD	OVERGROWN	SWINEHERD	EXACTNESS
EVACUATES	OVERHEARS	OVERUSING	TWENTIETH	EXECUTING
EVOCATION	OVERSEERS	OVERSTEER	DWINDLING	EXECUTION
EVOCATIVE	AVERAGING	EVERYTIME	SWINDLING	EXECUTORS
EVIDENTLY	OVERSHOES	OVERSTATE	TWINKLING	EXECUTIVE
AVOIDANCE	OVERWHELM	OVERRULED	SWINDLERS	OXIDISING
AVAILABLE	OVERSHOOT	OVERRULES	SWINBURNE	EXUDATION
AVOIDABLE	OVERTHROW	OVERTURES	TWENTYONE	OXIDATION
EVALUATED	OVERTHERE	OVERTURNS	SWIPECARD	EXCEEDING
EVALUATES	EVERSINCE	OVEREXERT	TWOREELER	EXTENDING
IVYLEAGUE	EVERYINCH	EVASIVELY	SWORDFISH	EXPEDIENT
AVALANCHE	OVERTIRED	SWEATBAND	SWARTHIER	EXCELLENT
EVILDOING	OVERNIGHT	SWEATSHOP	AWARENESS	EXCELLING
EVILDOERS	OVERSIGHT	SWEARWORD	SWORDPLAY	EXPELLING
EVOLUTION	AVERTIBLE	SWADDLING	SWORDSMAN	EXTEMPORE
OVULATION	AVERSIONS	TWIDDLING	SWORDSMEN	EXCELSIOR
EVAMENDES	OVERSLEEP	SWEETCORN	SWORDTAIL	EXTENSION
EVENEDOUT	OVERSLEPT	SWEETENED	TWOSEATER	EXCESSIVE
IVANLENDL	OVERCLOUD	SWEETENER	AWESTRUCK	EXPENSIVE
OVENREADY	OVERBLOWN	OWNERLESS	TWOSTROKE	EXTENSIVE
OVENGLOVE	OVERLOADS	SWEETMEAT	SWISSROLL	EXCEPTING
EVENMONEY	OVERCOMES	SWEETNESS	TWITTERED	EXPECTANT
EVENBREAK	OVERJOYED	SWEETPEAS	TWITTERER	EXPECTING
OVENPROOF	OVERPOWER	OWNERSHIP	SWOTTEDUP	EXCEPTION
AVUNCULAR	OVERLOOKS	SWEETTALK	SWITCHING	EXPERTISE
EVENTUATE	OVERDOING	TWEETYPIE	TWITCHING	EXTENUATE
EVAPORATE	OVERWOUND	SWIFTNESS	AWFULNESS	EXOFFICIO
OVIPAROUS	OVERBOARD	SWAGGERED	SWIVELLED	OXYGENATE

EXCHANGED	EXPORTERS	SYMBOLISE	DYSLEXICS	GYPSYMOTH
EXCHANGES	EXTRACTED	SYMBOLISM	PYGMALION	EYESTRAIN
EXCHEQUER	EXTRACTOR	SYMBIOSIS	SYMMETRIC	MYSTICISM
EXCITABLE	EXTRICATE	SYMBIOTIC	LYONNAISE	SYNTHESIS
EXCISEMAN	EXTRADITE	HYACINTHS	LYINGDOWN	SYNTHETIC
EXCISEMEN	EXERCISED	SYNCOPATE	RYANGIGGS	WYATTEARP
EXCITEDLY	EXERCISES	SYNDICATE	RYANONEAL	MYSTIFIED
EXHIBITED	EXORCISED	LYNDHURST	WYANDOTTE	MYSTIFIES
EXHIBITOR	EXORCISES	HYDERABAD	DYINGSWAN	AYATOLLAH
EXTIRPATE	EXTREMELY	TYREGAUGE	GYMNASTIC	LYTTELTON
AXMINSTER	EXTREMISM	BYDEFAULT	GYMNASIUM	BYSTANDER
EXPIATION	EXTREMIST	TYPECASTS	HYPNOTISE	DYSTROPHY
EXCLUDING	EXTREMITY	HYPERBOLA	HYPNOTISM	DYSTOPIAN
EXPLODING	EXTRINSIC	HYPERBOLE	HYPNOTIST	HYSTERICS
EXCLAIMED	EXPRESSED	AYLESBURY	PYONGYANG	MYSTERIES
EXPLAINED	EXPRESSES	LYMEREGIS	PYROMANIA	MYSTERONS
EXPLOITED	EXPRESSLY	HYPERICUM	HYPOCAUST	BYNUMBERS
EXPLORING	EXTRUSION	BYMEANSOF	BYFORCEOF	SYLVESTER
EXPLORERS	EXTRATIME	TYNEMOUTH	GYROSCOPE	EZRAPOUND
EXCLUSION	EXTROVERT	CYBERPUNK	EYEOPENER	
EXPLOSION	EXISTENCE	BYDEGREES	BYNOMEANS	
EXCLUSIVE	EXCUSABLE	GYRFALCON	SYCOPHANT	
EXPLOSIVE	EXPUNGING	LYCHGATES	XYLOPHONE	
EXPLETIVE	EXPURGATE	BYTHEBOOK	XYLOGRAPH	
EXEMPLIFY	EXCULPATE	MYTHOLOGY	HYPOCRISY	
EXEMPLARY	EXCURSION	HYPHENATE	HYPOCRITE	
EXAMINEES	EXPULSION	BYTHEYARD	LYMPHATIC	
EXAMINING	EXQUISITE	CYNICALLY	SYLPHLIKE	
EXAMINERS	TYRABANKS	LYRICALLY	SYMPHONIC	
EXEMPTION	PYRAMIDAL	TYPICALLY	DYSPEPSIA	
EXONERATE	SYBARITES	CYLINDERS	DYSPEPTIC	
AXIOMATIC	SYBARITIC	MYAINFOLK	SYMPOSIUM	
EXPONENTS	TYRANNISE	LYMINGTON	BYPRODUCT	
EXFOLIANT	TYRANNOUS	LYRICISTS	AYURVEDIC	
EXCORIATE	SYCAMORES	HYGIENIST	HYDROFOIL	
EXFOLIATE	SYNAGOGUE	TYPIFYING	HYDROLOGY	
OXBOWLAKE	BYPASSING	GYMKHANAS	HYDRANGEA	
EXTOLLING	DYNASTIES	AYCKBOURN	AYERSROCK	
EXPOUNDED	BYZANTINE	SYLLABLES	CYPRESSES	
EXPORTING	BYZANTIUM	SYLLOGISM	HYDRAULIC	
EXTORTING	EYEBRIGHT	EYELASHES	EYESHADOW	
EXTORTION	CYMBELINE	SYDLITTLE	NYASALAND	

PENGUIN PUZZLES

SUMMER HOLIDAY SUDOKU

So you've mastered the crossword puzzle, now for a different kind of brain strain. Sudoku are number puzzles requiring a logical, systematic approach. The basic rule is this: every row, column and 3x3 box must contain the numbers 1 to 9. Have a go!

			6			2		
	6					5	9	
2	4		3			6		
			9	3				5
5		6	8		1	3		9
4				6	7			
		4			9		3	8
	8	1					7	
		2			3			

Puzzle No. 1 – Classic

Finished? Want the answer or fancy more? Look out for *Penguin Holiday Sudoku*, with over 365 scorching puzzles from classic sudoku through to the infamous and deadly killer sudoku.

www.penguin.com

PENGUIN PUZZLES

THE PENGUIN BOOK OF KAKURO

Discover Japan's best-kept secret! Kakuro is similar to sudoku in that it is a box containing blocks of squares which are to be filled with the numbers 1 to 9. But beware, there's an added element of difficulty, the totals for each block are shown in the circles to the left of horizontal blocks and above vertical blocks. Your challenge is to solve the puzzle by filling in each block using the numbers 1 to 9, ensuring that the squares within add up to the totals shown. Have a go!

Puzzle No. 40

Finished? Want the answer or fancy more? Look out for *The Penguin Book of Kakuro*, with 100 brain boggling puzzles. Entertaining and highly addictive.

PENGUIN POCKET REFERENCE

PORTABLE　　　**DESIRABLE**　　　**INDISPENSABLE**

Penguin Pocket Babies' Names

Penguin Pocket Book of Facts

Penguin Pocket Crossword Finisher

Penguin Pocket Dictionary of Quotations

Penguin Pocket English Dictionary

Penguin Pocket Famous People

Penguin Pocket French Dictionary

Penguin Pocket German Dictionary

Penguin Pocket Italian Dictionary

Penguin Pocket Jokes

Penguin Pocket Kings and Queens

Penguin Pocket On This Day

Penguin Pocket Rhyming Dictionary

Penguin Pocket Roget's Thesaurus

Penguin Pocket School Dictionary

Penguin Pocket Spanish Dictionary

Penguin Pocket Spelling Dictionary

Penguin Pocket Thesaurus

Penguin Pocket Writer's Handbook

Our Penguin Pockets are part of the extensive Penguin Reference Library – a resource that draws on over 70 years of experience bringing reliable, useful and clear information to millions of readers around the world. We want to make knowledge everybody's property.

PENGUIN POCKET REFERENCE

THE PENGUIN POCKET ENGLISH DICTIONARY

This pocket edition of the bestselling *Penguin English Dictionary* is the perfect reference book for everyday use. Compiled by Britain's foremost lexicographers, up to date and easy to use, it is the ideal portable companion for quick reference.

– Includes a wealth of words, phrases and clear definitions, with more information than other comparable dictionaries

– Covers standard and formal English, as well as specialist terms, slang and jargon

– Provides invaluable guidance on correct usage, commonly confused words and grammar and spelling

PENGUIN POCKET REFERENCE

THE PENGUIN POCKET DICTIONARY OF BABIES' NAMES
DAVID PICKERING

The Penguin Pocket Dictionary of Babies' Names is essential reading
for all expectant parents wishing to choose the perfect name for their
child. It gives the meanings and stories behind thousands of names
from all parts of the world – ranging from the most well-known choices
to more unusual names.

– Gives variations and shortened forms for each name

– Highlights names popularized by books, films and celebrities

– Lists the most popular girls' and boys' names from 1700 to the
present

– Shows how tastes for names have changed in the twenty-first century

He just wanted a decent book to read ...

Not too much to ask, is it? It was in 1935 when Allen Lane, Managing Director of Bodley Head Publishers, stood on a platform at Exeter railway station looking for something good to read on his journey back to London. His choice was limited to popular magazines and poor-quality paperbacks – the same choice faced every day by the vast majority of readers, few of whom could afford hardbacks. Lane's disappointment and subsequent anger at the range of books generally available led him to found a company – and change the world.

'We believed in the existence in this country of a vast reading public for intelligent books at a low price, and staked everything on it'
Sir Allen Lane, 1902–1970, founder of Penguin Books

The quality paperback had arrived – and not just in bookshops. Lane was adamant that his Penguins should appear in chain stores and tobacconists, and should cost no more than a packet of cigarettes.

Reading habits (and cigarette prices) have changed since 1935, but Penguin still believes in publishing the best books for everybody to enjoy. We still believe that good design costs no more than bad design, and we still believe that quality books published passionately and responsibly make the world a better place.

So wherever you see the little bird – whether it's on a piece of prize-winning literary fiction or a celebrity autobiography, political tour de force or historical masterpiece, a serial-killer thriller, reference book, world classic or a piece of pure escapism – you can bet that it represents the very best that the genre has to offer.

Whatever you like to read – trust Penguin.